DATE DUE

DOCUMENTS ON
INTERNATIONAL AFFAIRS
1961

DOCUMENTS ON INTERNATIONAL AFFAIRS

1961

SELECTED AND EDITED

BY

D. C. WATT

WITH THE ASSISTANCE OF

JOHN MAJOR

RICHARD GOTT

GEORGE SCHÖPFLIN

Issued under the auspices of the
Royal Institute of International Affairs

OXFORD UNIVERSITY PRESS

LONDON   NEW YORK   TORONTO

1965

Oxford University Press, Amen House, London E.C.4

GLASGOW   NEW YORK   TORONTO   MELBOURNE   WELLINGTON
BOMBAY   CALCUTTA   MADRAS   KARACHI   LAHORE   DACCA
CAPE TOWN   SALISBURY   NAIROBI   IBADAN   ACCRA
KUALA LUMPUR   HONG KONG

PRINTED IN GREAT BRITAIN

PREFACE

LIKE its predecessor, this volume of *Documents on International Affairs* has been edited in conjunction with the *Survey of International Affairs*, and has been edited by the team responsible for the writing of the *Survey*. The documents here printed have been arranged in sections corresponding with the arrangement of chapters in the accompanying volume of the *Survey*.

This has led to two departures from the editorial practice of the previous volumes. Firstly, the headings and description of the documents have been greatly simplified. Secondly, documents are printed in the section to which the bulk of their contents are relevant. Where a document, as for example, a press conference by President Kennedy on President de Gaulle, or a speech by Mr. Khrushchev, covers topics dealt with in more than one section to this volume, this appears in the chronological list of documents at the end of the volume.

The editor would like to thank all those who have assisted in the production of this volume.

September 1964   D. C. WATT

CONTENTS

B. THE ATLANTIC ALLIANCE AND WESTERN EUROPEAN UNITY

C. THE SOVIET BLOC

D. EAST-WEST RELATIONS

F. SOUTH-EAST ASIA

II. THE 'THIRD WORLD' OF THE 'UNCOMMITTED NATIONS'

A. THE NEUTRALIST MOVEMENT

B. THE EMERGENCE OF AFRICAN RIVALRIES

B. THE KUWAIT INCIDENT

C. FRANCE IN THE WESTERN MEDITERRANEAN

(a) Algeria

(b) Tunisia and Bizerta

CONTENTS

D. LATIN AMERICA

SOURCE ABBREVIATIONS

Cmnd.	Command Papers (London, H.M.S.O.)
Congo 1961	*Congo 1961 — Les dossiers du C.R.I.S.P.* (Brussels, Centre de Recherche et d'Information Socio-Polotiques, 1962)
Documents	*Documents on International Affairs* (Oxford University Press for the Royal Institute of International Affairs)
D.S.B.	*Department of State Bulletin* (Washington, D.C., U.S.A., G.P.O.)
G.A.O.R.	United Nations, *General Assembly Official Records*
H.C. Deb.	House of Commons Debates (Hansard)
H.L. Deb.	House of Lords Debates (Hansard)
H.N.A.	Hsinhua News Agency
La Documentation Française	Articles et Documents (Ministère des Affaires Etrangères, Paris)
Public Papers, 1961	*Public Papers of the Presidents of the United States, 1961* (Washington, 1962)
S.C.O.R.	United Nations, *Security Council Official Records*
Survey	*Survey of International Affairs* (Oxford University Press for the Royal Institute of International Affairs)
S.W.B.	*Summary of World Broadcasts* (Monitoring Service of the British Broadcasting Corporation)

I. THE POWER BLOCS, INTER-BLOC AND INTRA-BLOC TENSIONS

A. THE ADVENT OF THE NEW PRESIDENTIAL RÉGIME IN THE UNITED STATES

(a) General Statements of United States Foreign Policy

1. Inaugural address of President Kennedy, 20 January 1961[1]

. . . We observe today not a victory of party but a celebration of freedom—symbolizing an end as well as a beginning—signifying renewal as well as change. For I have sworn before you and Almighty God the same solemn oath our forebears prescribed nearly a century and three quarters ago.

The world is very different now. For man holds in his mortal hands the power to abolish all forms of human poverty and all forms of human life. And yet the same revolutionary beliefs for which our forebears fought are still at issue around the globe—the belief that the rights of man come not from the generosity of the state but from the hand of God.

We dare not forget today that we are the heirs of that first revolution. Let the word go forth from this time and place, to friend and foe alike, that the torch has been passed to a new generation of Americans—born in this century, tempered by war, disciplined by a hard and bitter peace, proud of our ancient heritage—and unwilling to witness or permit the slow undoing of those human rights to which this Nation has always been committed, and to which we are committed today at home and around the world.

Let every nation know, whether it wishes us well or ill, that we shall pay any price, bear any burden, meet any hardship, support any friend, oppose any foe to assure the survival and the success of liberty.

This much we pledge—and more.

To those old allies whose cultural and spiritual origins we share, we pledge the loyalty of faithful friends. United, there is little we cannot do in a host of cooperative ventures. Divided, there is little we can do—for we dare not meet a powerful challenge at odds and split asunder.

To those new states whom we welcome to the ranks of the free, we pledge our word that one form of colonial control shall not have passed away merely to be replaced by a far more iron tyranny. We shall not always expect to find them supporting our view. But we shall always hope to find them strongly supporting their own freedom—and to remember that, in the past, those who foolishly sought power by riding the back of the tiger ended up inside.

To those people in the huts and villages of half the globe struggling to break the bonds of mass misery, we pledge our best efforts to help them help themselves, for whatever period is required—not because the Communists may be

[1] *Public Papers*, 1961, pp. 1–3

doing it, not because we seek their votes, but because it is right. If a free society cannot help the many who are poor, it cannot save the few who are rich.

To our sister republics south of our border, we offer a special pledge—to convert our good words into good deeds—in a new alliance for progress—to assist free men and free governments in casting off the chains of poverty. But this peaceful revolution of hope cannot become the prey of hostile powers. Let all our neighbors know that we shall join with them to oppose aggression or subversion anywhere in the Americas. And let every other power know that this hemisphere intends to remain the master of its own house.

To that world assembly of sovereign states, the United Nations, our last and best hope in an age where the instruments of war have far outpaced the instruments of peace, we renew our pledge of support—to prevent it from becoming merely a forum for invective—to strengthen its shield of the new and the weak—and to enlarge the area in which its writ may run.

Finally, to those nations who would make themselves our adversary, we offer not a pledge but a request: that both sides begin anew the quest for peace, before the dark powers of destruction unleashed by science engulf all humanity in planned or accidental self-destruction.

We dare not tempt them with weakness. For only when our arms are sufficient beyond doubt can we be certain beyond doubt that they will never be employed.

But neither can two great and powerful groups of nations take comfort from our present course—both sides overburdened by the cost of modern weapons, both rightly alarmed by the steady spread of the deadly atom, yet both racing to alter that uncertain balance of terror that stays the hand of mankind's final war.

So let us begin anew—remembering on both sides that civility is not a sign of weakness, and sincerity is always subject to proof. Let us never negotiate out of fear. But let us never fear to negotiate.

Let both sides explore what problems unite us instead of belaboring those problems which divide us.

Let both sides, for the first time, formulate serious and precise proposals for the inspection and control of arms—and bring the absolute power to destroy other nations under the absolute control of all nations.

Let both sides seek to invoke the wonders of science instead of its terrors. Together let us explore the stars, conquer the deserts, eradicate disease, tap the ocean depths, and encourage the arts and commerce.

Let both sides unite to heed in all corners of the earth the command of Isaiah —to 'undo the heavy burdens . . . [and] let the oppressed go free'.

And if a beachhead of cooperation may push back the jungle of suspicion, let both sides join in creating a new endeavor, not a new balance of power, but a new world of law, where the strong are just and the weak secure and the peace preserved.

All this will not be finished in the first one hundred days. Nor will it be finished in the first one thousand days, nor in the life of this administration, nor even perhaps in our lifetime on this planet. But let us begin.

In your hands, my fellow citizens, more than mine, will rest the final success or failure of our course. Since this country was founded, each generation of

Americans has been summoned to give testimony to its national loyalty. The graves of young Americans who answered the call to service surround the globe.

Now the trumpet summons us again—not as a call to bear arms, though arms we need—not as a call to battle, though embattled we are—but a call to bear the burden of a long twilight struggle, year in and year out, 'rejoicing in hope, patient in tribulation'—a struggle against the common enemies of man: tyranny, poverty, disease, and war itself.

Can we forge against these enemies a grand and global alliance, North and South, East and West, that can assure a more fruitful life for all mankind? Will you join in that historic effort?

In the long history of the world, only a few generations have been granted the role of defending freedom in its hour of maximum danger. I do not shrink from this responsibility—I welcome it. I do not believe that any of us would exchange places with any other people or any other generation. The energy, the faith, the devotion which we bring to this endeavor will light our country and all who serve it—and the glow from that fire can truly light the world.

And so, my fellow Americans: ask not what your country can do for you—ask what you can do for your country.

My fellow citizens of the world: ask not what America will do for you, but what together we can do for the freedom of man.

Finally, whether you are citizens of America or citizens of the world, ask of us here the same high standards of strength and sacrifice which we ask of you. With a good conscience our only sure reward, with history the final judge of our deeds, let us go forth to lead the land we love, asking His blessing and His help, but knowing that here on earth God's work must truly be our own.

2. Annual message of President Kennedy to the United States Congress on the State of the Union, 30 January 1961[1] (extracts)

. . . No man entering upon this office, regardless of his party, regardless of his previous service in Washington, could fail to be staggered upon learning—even in this brief 10-day period—the harsh enormity of the trials through which we must pass in the next 4 years. Each day the crises multiply. Each day their solution grows more difficult. Each day we draw nearer the hour of maximum danger, as weapons spread and hostile forces grow stronger. I feel I must inform the Congress that our analyses over the last 10 days make it clear that—in each of the principal areas of crisis—the tide of events has been running out and time has not been our friend.

In Asia, the relentless pressures of the Chinese Communists menace the security of the entire area—from the borders of India and south Viet-Nam to the jungles of Laos, struggling to protect its newly won independence. We seek in Laos what we seek in all Asia, and, indeed, in all of the world—freedom for the people and independence for the government. And this Nation shall persevere in our pursuit of these objectives.

In Africa, the Congo has been brutally torn by civil strife, political unrest, and public disorder. We shall continue to support the heroic efforts of the United

[1] *Public Papers*, 1961, pp. 22–27.

Nations to restore peace and order—efforts which are now endangered by mounting tensions, unsolved problems, and decreasing support from many member states.

In Latin America, Communist agents seeking to exploit that region's peaceful revolution of hope have established a base on Cuba, only 90 miles from our shores. Our objection with Cuba is not over the people's drive for a better life. Our objection is to their domination by foreign and domestic tyrannies. Cuban social and economic reform should be encouraged. Questions of economic and trade policy can always be negotiated. But Communist domination in this hemisphere can never be negotiated.

We are pledged to work with our sister Republics to free the Americas of all such foreign domination and all tyranny, working toward the goal of a free hemisphere of free governments, extending from Cape Horn to the Arctic Circle.

In Europe our alliances are unfulfilled and in some disarray. The unity of NATO has been weakened by economic rivalry and partially eroded by national interest. It has not yet fully mobilized its resources nor fully achieved a common outlook. Yet no Atlantic power can meet on its own the mutual problems now facing us in defense, foreign aid, monetary reserves, and a host of other areas; and our close ties with those whose hopes and interests we share are among this nation's most powerful assets.

Our greatest challenge is still the world that lies beyond the cold war—but the first great obstacle is still our relations with the Soviet Union and Communist China. We must never be lulled into believing that either power has yielded its ambitions for world domination—ambitions which they forcefully restated only a short time ago. On the contrary, our task is to convince them that aggression and subversion will not be profitable routes to pursue these ends. Open and peaceful competition—for prestige, for markets, for scientific achievement, even for men's minds—is something else again. For if freedom and communism were to compete for man's allegiance in a world at peace, I would look to the future with ever-increasing confidence.

To meet this array of challenges—to fulfill the role we cannot avoid on the world scene—we must re-examine and revise our whole arsenal of tools: military, economic, and political.

One must not overshadow the other. On the Presidential coat of arms, the American eagle holds in his right talon the olive branch, while in his left he holds a bundle of arrows. We intend to give equal attention to both.

First, we must strengthen our military tools. We are moving into a period of uncertain risk and great commitment in which both the military and diplomatic possibilities require a free-world force so powerful as to make any aggression clearly futile. Yet in the past, lack of a consistent, coherent military strategy, the absence of basic assumptions about our national requirements, and the faulty estimates and duplication arising from interservice rivalries have all made it difficult to assess accurately how adequate—or inadequate—our defenses really are.

I have, therefore, instructed the Secretary of Defense to reappraise our entire defense strategy—our ability to fulfill our commitments—the effectiveness, vulnerability, and dispersal of our strategic bases, forces, and warning systems—the efficiency and economy of our operation and organization—the elimination of obsolete bases and installations—and the adequacy, modernization, and mobility of our present conventional and nuclear forces and weapons systems in the light of present and future dangers. I have asked for preliminary conclusions by the end of February—and I then shall recommend whatever legislative, budgetary, or executive action is needed in the light of these conclusions.

In the meantime, I have asked the Defense Secretary to initiate immediately three new steps most clearly needed now:

(a) First, I have directed prompt attention to increase our airlift capacity. Obtaining additional air transport mobility—and obtaining it now—will better assure the ability of our conventional forces to respond, with discrimination and speed, to any problem at any spot on the globe at any moment's notice. In particular it will enable us to meet any deliberate effort to avoid or divert our forces by starting limited wars in widely scattered parts of the world.

(b) I have directed prompt action to step up our Polaris submarine program. Using unobligated shipbuilding funds now (to let contracts originally scheduled for the next fiscal year) will build and place on station—at least 9 months earlier than planned—substantially more units of a crucial deterrent—a fleet that will never attack first, but possess sufficient powers of retaliation, concealed beneath the seas, to discourage any aggressor from launching an attack upon our security.

(c) I have directed prompt action to accelerate our entire missile program. Until the Secretary of Defense's reappraisal is completed, the emphasis here will be largely on improved organization and decision-making—on cutting down the wasteful duplications and the time/lag that have handicapped our whole family of missiles. If we are to keep the peace, we need an invulnerable missile force powerful enough to deter any aggressor from even threatening an attack that he would know could not destroy enough of our force to prevent his own destruction. For as I said upon taking the oath of office: 'Only when our arms are sufficient beyond doubt can we be certain beyond doubt that they will never be employed.'

Secondly, we must improve our economic tools. Our role is essential and unavoidable in the construction of a sound and expanding economy for the entire non-Communist world, helping other nations build the strength to meet their own problems, to satisfy their own aspirations—to surmount their own dangers. The problems in achieving this goal are towering and unprecedented—the response must be towering and unprecedented as well, much as lend-lease and the Marshall plan were in earlier years, which brought such fruitful results.

(a) I intend to ask the Congress for authority to establish a new and more effective program for assisting the economic, educational, and social development of other countries and continents. That program must stimulate and take more effectively into account the contributions of our allies, and provide central policy direction for all our own programs that now so often overlap, conflict, or diffuse our energies and resources. Such a program, compared to past programs, will require

—more flexibility for short-run emergencies

—more commitment to long-term development

—new attention to education at all levels

—greater emphasis on the recipient nation's role, their effort, their purpose, with greater social justice for their people, broader distribution and participation by their people, and more efficient public administration and more efficient tax systems of their own

—and orderly planning for national and regional development instead of a piecemeal approach.

(b) I hope the Senate will take early action approving the convention establishing the Organization for Economic Cooperation and Development.[1] This will be an important instrument in sharing with our allies this development effort—working toward the time when each nation will contribute in proportion to its ability to pay. For, while we are prepared to assume our full share of these huge burdens, we cannot and must not be expected to bear them alone.

(c) To our sister Republics to the south, we have pledged a new alliance for progress—*alianza para progreso*. Our goal is a free and prosperous Latin America, realizing for all its states and all its citizens a degree of economic and social progress that matches their historic contributions of culture, intellect, and liberty. To start this Nation's role at this time in that alliance of neighbors, I am recommending the following:

—That the Congress appropriate in full the $500 million fund pledged by the Act of Bogotá,[2] to be used not as an instrument of the cold war, but as a first step in the sound development of the Americas.

—That a new Inter-Departmental Task Force be established under the leadership of the Department of State, to coordinate at the highest level all policies and programs of concern to the Americas.

—That our delegates to the OAS, working with those of other members, strengthen that body as an instrument to preserve the peace and to prevent foreign domination anywhere in the hemisphere.

—That, in cooperation with other nations, we launch a new hemispheric attack on illiteracy and inadequate educational opportunities to all levels; and, finally,

—That a food-for-peace mission be sent immediately to Latin America to explore ways in which our vast food abundance can be used to help end hunger and malnutrition in certain areas of suffering in our own hemisphere.

(d) This administration is expanding its food-for-peace program in every possible way. The product of our abundance must be used more effectively to relieve hunger and help economic growth in all corners of the globe. And I have asked the director of this program to recommend additional ways in which these surpluses can advance the interests of world peace—including the establishment of world food reserves.

(e) An even more valuable national asset is our reservoir of dedicated men and women—not only on our college campuses but in every age group—who

[1] Signed in Paris, 14 December 1960. *Documents*, 1960, pp. 174–9.
[2] Proclaimed in Bogotá, Columbia, 13 September 1960. *Documents*, 1960, pp. 607–12.

have indicated their desire to contribute their skills, their efforts, and a part of their lives to the fight for world order. We can mobilize this talent through the formation of a National Peace Corps, enlisting the services of all those with the desire and capacity to help foreign lands meet their urgent needs for trained personnel.

(f) Finally, while our attention is centred on the development of the non-Communist world, we must never forget our hopes for the ultimate freedom and welfare of the Eastern European peoples. In order to be prepared to help re-establish historic ties of friendship, I am asking the Congress for increased discretion to use economic tools in this area whenever this is found to be clearly in the national interest. This will require amendment of the Mutual Defense Assistance Control Act[1] along the lines I proposed as a member of the Senate, and upon which the Senate voted last summer. Meanwhile, I hope to explore with the Polish Government the possibility of using our frozen Polish funds on projects of peace that will demonstrate our abiding friendship for and interest in the people of Poland.

Third, we must sharpen our political and diplomatic tools—the means of co-operation and agreement on which an enforceable world order must ultimately rest.

(a) I have already taken steps to coordinate and expand our disarmament effort—to increase our programs of research and study—and to make arms control a central goal of our national policy under my direction. The deadly arms race, and the huge resources it absorbs, have too long overshadowed all else we must do. We must prevent that arms race from spreading to new nations, to new nuclear powers, and to the reaches of outer space. We must make certain that our negotiators are better informed and better prepared—to formulate workable proposals of our own and to make sound judgments about the proposals of others.

I have asked the other governments concerned to agree to a reasonable delay in the talks on a nuclear test ban—and it is our intention to resume negotiations prepared to reach a final agreement with any nation that is equally willing to agree to an effective and enforceable treaty.

(b) We must increase our support of the United Nations as an instrument to end the cold war instead of an arena in which to fight it. In recognition of its increasing importance and the doubling of its membership

—we are enlarging and strengthening our own mission to the U.N.

—we shall help insure that it is properly financed.

—we shall work to see that the integrity of the office of the Secretary-General is maintained.

—And I would address a special plea to the smaller nations of the world—to join with us in strengthening this Organization, which is far more essential to their security than it is to ours—the only body in the world where no nation need be powerful to be secure, where every nation has an equal voice, and where any nation can exert influence not according to the strength of its armies but according to the strength of its ideas. It deserves the support of all.

[1] The Battle Act, passed in 1951 to restrict governmental assistance to countries exporting strategic goods to the Communist bloc; partial text in *Documents*, 1951, pp. 52–55.

(c) Finally, this administration intends to explore promptly all possible areas of cooperation with the Soviet Union and other nations 'To invoke the wonders of science instead of its terrors'. Specifically, I now invite all nations—including the Soviet Union—to join with us in developing a weather prediction program, in a new communications satellite program, and in preparation for probing the distant planets of Mars and Venus, probes which may someday unlock the deepest secrets of the universe.

Today this country is ahead in the science and technology of space, while the Soviet Union is ahead in the capacity to lift large vehicles into orbit. Both nations would help themselves as well as other nations by removing these endeavors from the bitter and wasteful competition of the cold war. The United States would be willing to join with the Soviet Union and the scientists of all nations in a greater effort to make the fruits of this new knowledge available to all—and, beyond that, in an effort to extend farm technology to hungry nations —to wipe out disease—to increase the exchanges of scientists and their knowledge —and to make our own laboratories available to technicians of other lands who lack the facilities to pursue their own work. Where nature makes natural allies of us all, we can demonstrate that beneficial relations are possible even with those with whom we must deeply disagree—and this must someday be the basis of world peace and law. . . .

3. Special message of President Kennedy to the United States Congress on the Peace Corps, 1 March 1961[1] (extracts)

I recommend to the Congress the establishment of a permanent Peace Corps —a pool of trained American men and women sent overseas by the U.S. Government or through private organizations and institutions to help foreign countries meet their urgent needs for skilled manpower.

I have today signed an Executive Order establishing a Peace Corps on a temporary pilot basis.

The temporary Peace Corps will be a source of information and experience to aid us in formulating more effective plans for a permanent organization. In addition, by starting the Peace Corps now we will be able to begin training young men and women for overseas duty this summer with the objective of placing them in overseas positions by late fall. This temporary Peace Corps is being established under existing authority in the Mutual Security Act and will be located in the Department of State. Its initial expenses will be paid from appropriations currently available for our foreign aid program.

Throughout the world the people of the newly developing nations are struggling for economic and social progress which reflects their deepest desires. Our own freedom, and the future of freedom around the world, depend, in a very real sense, on their ability to build growing and independent nations where men can live in dignity, liberated from the bonds of hunger, ignorance and poverty.

One of the greatest obstacles to the achievement of this goal is the lack of trained men and women with the skill to teach the young and assist in the operation of development projects—men and women with the capacity to cope with

[1] *Public Papers*, 1961, pp. 143–6.

the demands of swiftly evolving economies, and with the dedication to put that capacity to work in the villages, the mountains, the towns and the factories of dozens of struggling nations.

The vast task of economic development urgently requires skilled people to do the work of the society—to help teach in the schools, construct development projects, demonstrate modern methods of sanitation in the villages, and perform a hundred other tasks calling for training and advanced knowledge.

To meet this urgent need for skilled manpower we are proposing the establishment of a Peace Corps—an organization which wil recruit and train American volunteers, sending them abroad to work with the people of other nations.

This organization will differ from existing assistance programs in that its members will supplement technical advisers by offering the specific skills needed by developing nations if they are to put technical advice to work. They will help provide the skilled manpower necessary to carry out the development projects planned by the host governments, acting at a working level and serving at great personal sacrifice. There is little doubt that the number of those who wish to serve will be far greater than our capacity to absorb them.

The Peace Corps or some similar approach has been strongly advocated by Senator Humphrey, Representative Reuss and others in the Congress. It has received strong support from universities, voluntary agencies, student groups, labor unions and business and professional organizations.

Last session, the Congress authorized a study of these possibilities. Preliminary reports of this study show that the Peace Corps is feasible, needed, and wanted by many foreign countries.

Most heartening of all, the initial reaction to this proposal has been an enthusiastic response by student groups, professional organizations and private citizens everywhere—a convincing demonstration that we have in this country an immense reservoir of dedicated men and women willing to devote their energies and time and toil to the cause of world peace and human progress.

Among the specific programs to which Peace Corps members can contribute are: teaching in primary and secondary schools, especially as part of national English language teaching programs; participation in the worldwide program of malaria eradication; instruction and operation of public health and sanitation projects; aiding in village development through school construction and other programs; increasing rural agricultural productivity by assisting local farmers to use modern implements and techniques. The initial emphasis of these programs will be on teaching. Thus the Peace Corps members will be an effective means of implementing the development programs of the host countries—programs which our technical assistance operations have helped to formulate.

The Peace Corps will not be limited to the young, or to college graduates. All Americans who are qualified will be welcome to join this effort. But undoubtedly the Corps will be made up primarily of young people as they complete their formal education.

Because one of the greatest resources of a free society is the strength and diversity of its private organizations and institutions much of the Peace Corps program will be carried out by these groups, financially assisted by the Federal Government.

Peace Corps personnel will be made available to developing nations in the following ways:

1. Through private voluntary agencies carrying on international assistance programs.
2. Through overseas programs of colleges and universities.
3. Through assistance programs of international agencies.
4. Through assistance programs of the United States government.
5. Through new programs which the Peace Corps itself directly administers.

In the majority of cases the Peace Corps will assume the entire responsibility for recruitment, training and the development of overseas projects. In other cases it will make available a pool of trained applicants to private groups who are carrying out projects approved by the Peace Corps.

In the case of Peace Corps programs conducted through voluntary agencies and universities, these private institutions will have the option of using the national recruitment system—the central pool of trained man power—or developing recruitment systems of their own.

In all cases men and women recruited as a result of Federal assistance will be members of the Peace Corps and enrolled in the central organization. All private recruitment and training programs will adhere to Peace Corps standards as a condition of Federal assistance.

In all instances the men and women of the Peace Corps will go only to those countries where their services and skills are genuinely needed and desired. U.S. Operations Missions, supplemented where necessary by special Peace Corps teams, will consult with leaders in foreign countries in order to determine where Peace Corpsmen are needed, the types of job they can best fill, and the number of people who can be usefully employed. The Peace Corps will not supply personnel for marginal undertakings without a sound economic or social justification. In furnishing assistance through the Peace Corps careful regard will be given to the particular country's developmental priorities.

Membership in the Peace Corps will be open to all Americans, and applications will be available shortly. Where application is made directly to the Peace Corps—the vast majority of cases—they will be carefully screened to make sure that those who are selected can contribute to Peace Corps programs, and have the personal qualities which will enable them to represent the United States abroad with honor and dignity. In those cases where application is made directly to a private group, the same basic standards will be maintained. Each new recruit will receive a training and orientation period varying from six weeks to six months. This training will include courses in the culture and language of the country to which they are being sent and specialized training designed to increase the work skills of recruits. In some cases training will be conducted by participant agencies and universities in approved training programs. Other training programs will be conducted by the Peace Corps staff.

Length of service in the Corps will vary depending on the kind of project and the country, generally ranging from two to three years. Peace Corps members will often serve under conditions of physical hardship, living under primitive conditions among the people of developing nations. For every Peace Corps member service will mean a great financial sacrifice. They will receive no salary. Instead they will be given an allowance which will only be sufficient to meet their basic needs and maintain health. It is essential that Peace Corpsmen and women live simply and unostentatiously among the people they have come to assist. At the conclusion of their tours, members of the Peace Corps will receive a small sum in the form of severance pay based on length of service abroad, to assist them during their first weeks back in the United States. Service with the Peace Corps will not exempt volunteers from Selective Service.

The United States will assume responsibility for supplying medical services to Peace Corps members and ensuring supplies and drugs necessary to good health.

I have asked the temporary Peace Corps to begin plans and make arrangements for pilot programs. A minimum of several hundred volunteers could be selected, trained and at work abroad by the end of this calendar year. It is hoped that within a few years several thousand Peace Corps members will be working in foreign lands.

It is important to remember that this program must, in its early stages, be experimental in nature. This is a new dimension in our overseas program and only the most careful planning and negotiation can ensure its success.

The benefits of the Peace Corps will not be limited to the countries in which it serves. Our own young men and women will be enriched by the experience of living and working in foreign lands. They will have acquired new skills and experience which will aid them in their future careers and add to our own country's supply of trained personnel and teachers. They will return better able to assume the responsibilities of American citizenship and with greater understanding of our global responsibilities.

Although this is an American Peace Corps, the problem of world development is not just an American problem. Let us hope that other nations will mobilize the spirit and energies and skill of their people in some form of Peace Corps—making our own effort only one step in a major international effort to increase the welfare of all men and improve understanding among nations.

4. Address by the Secretary of State, Mr. Rusk, to the American Historical Association, 30 December 1961[1] (extracts)

. . . The community of historians and a Secretary of State are linked by a common task—that of finding and articulating the scarlet threads of meaning and direction in the flow of tumultuous events. Their approach may differ both in time and in purpose because of their differing responsibilities. What to the historian becomes a swirling blizzard of papers is for a Secretary of State an unrelenting parade of precise day-to-day business. The historian has a slight advantage in that he knows a bit more about how the story came out; a Secretary has the stimulation which comes from a commitment, as the President's adviser, to try to shape the story toward a tolerable conclusion.

Both historian and Secretary must wrestle with the problem of complexity, each in his own way. At no point in our history has this been more exigent than

---

[1] *D.S.B.*, 15 January 1962, pp. 83–88.

now, and it would be naive to hope that we are moving toward simplicity. It was not until 1823 that John Quincy Adams established our tenth diplomatic mission abroad, not until a century later that Charles Evans Hughes established our fiftieth, and only 40 years later that Christian Herter established our hundredth. Before World War II less than 10 capitals disposed of the foreign relations of the vast continent of Africa; today the number is over 30. With 104 members in the United Nations and approximately 100 items on the agenda of the recent General Assembly, some 10,000 primary votes were cast in which the United States had a larger or lesser interest. Our missions in a number of capitals exchange some 10,000 telegrams with the Department in the course of a year. How grateful we become to those capitals which are never responsible for a telephone call past midnight! When Thomas Jefferson or John Marshall bade Godspeed to an American ambassador departing for his post, they knew that it might be months before they would hear from him again. How tempting it now is to say to his modern colleague, 'If I don't hear from you for the first year, you would please me very much.'

There is a widespread illusion that modern communications have degraded the role of the ambassador—that cable, telephone, and radio have made him merely the messenger boy of impulses from his capital. The trouble with this notion is that it overlooks the breathtaking acceleration of the flow of events, brought about largely by these same communications and the latest modes of travel and transport. The man on the spot is more just exactly that than ever before, and every week brings instances of the critical responsibility of the ambassador abroad.

This question of pace is perhaps more difficult for a Secretary than for the historian, who can make certain choices. For a Secretary lives with the spurs of time upon him. His is not the luxury of a leisurely conclusion but the pressures of inescapable decisions, [for he knows that both action and inaction are decisions where the United States is concerned. He is conscious of the decisions made, but he is haunted by the limitless possibilities of the decisions which are taken by not being made—the decisions which tantalize and often escape the view of the historian.

It occurred to me that it would be appropriate for me to comment on the larger issues of contemporary history . . . and to relate these to my daily tasks.

First is this searching question: Does our comfortable democracy have the nerve and will to protect its essential interests and the frontiers of freedom in the face of potential enemies who command nuclear weapons and the capacity to deliver them against our homeland?

This is not a rhetorical issue, and we must clearly understand its grim reality. There are several paths to nuclear war. It could happen if one side or the other deliberately sets out to provoke one. I am inclined to believe that the irrationality of such a course makes it relatively unlikely. Another would be a situation in which two sides confront each other, each utterly convinced that under no circumstances would the other resort to nuclear war, each therefore tempted to press its demands across the threshold of disaster. A third path lies in simple confusion about essential interests, misapprehensions about the tolerable limits of conduct.

We confront a direct challenge, in Berlin, to the vital interests of the United States and the West. The challenge takes the form of the assertion that our presence there, on the basis of well-established rights, and access to Berlin from the West, can be radically altered or extinguished by the unilateral act of the other side and that this act would require us to petition the authorities in East Germany for the privilege of maintaining the freedom of West Berlin.

Before the President spoke to the American people on July 25th,[1] he and other Western leaders decided that vital interests and commitments in West Berlin, crucial to our own security, must be defended at whatever cost. That decision remains the basis on which we intend to explore the possibilities of a peaceful resolution of the Berlin crisis. If peace depends on clarity, the other side must not be allowed any dangerous illusion.

This clarity is the basis of an assurance to our own and other peoples that the possibilities of patient diplomacy will be exhausted to insure that vital interests are protected and that the other side will not be permitted to make a fatal mistake. We regard it as essential that our negotiators—wherever they may sit—work with measured confidence, knowing that behind them there exist well-balanced, flexible, and highly mobile military strength and a government and people prepared to use that strength if vital interests are threatened.

Since George Washington first enjoined the American people to recognize a connection between the maintenance of adequate military strength and the maintenance of the peace, our history has underlined that the danger of war is greatest when potential enemies are in doubt about the capacity of nations to defend their vital interests, about their will to defend them, or about how they define those vital interests. All three of those conditions for a peaceful resolution of differences are heightened in a world where the use of nuclear weapons may quickly come into play once conflict begins at any level.

I believe the American people, and other free peoples with whom we are allied, have long memories and understand that unlimited appetite grows in the act of devouring and, as President Kennedy has put it, '. . . if there is one path above all others to war, it is the path of weakness and disunity.' I believe free peoples understood him when he said,

> We do not want to fight, but we have fought before. And others in earlier times have made the same dangerous mistake of assuming that the West was too selfish and too soft and too divided to resist invasions of freedom in other lands.

The answer to . . . [this] first question is and must be 'Yes', because the other answer would make war inevitable.

A second question . . . which . . . confronts us is this: Do the United States, its allies, and other non-Communist nations have the capacity to deal with the techniques of Communist power now being applied to Asia, the Middle East, Africa, and Latin America?

In the 2 years preceding this administration's assumption of responsibility four significant holes had been punched in the truce lines which had emerged

[1] For extracts from President Kennedy's radio and television address to the American people of 25 July 1961, see below, Part I, Section D (a), pp. 332–9.

after the Second World War: Pathet Lao forces in Laos had moved out of the two northern provinces which had been identified by the Geneva Agreement of 1954;[1] the authorites in Hanoi, building on foundations which they had maintain in the south since 1954, systematically expanded the guerrilla forces in South Viet-Nam from something like 2,000 in 1959 to more than 16,000 at present, in a purposeful and organized act of international aggression; in the Congo, amidst the confusion which followed the end of colonialism, the Communists were rigorously seeking to establish a central African base; in Cuba a Communist regime was installed, having seized and successfully subverted what appeared to be a broad-based national movement to escape an intolerable dictatorship. These limited breakthroughs carried with them serious threats to the security of southeast Asia, to Africa, and to Latin America.

It has been a first charge on our energies to find ways to deal with these problems. I shall not detail here the policies we have adopted in each case, for they are undoubtedly familiar to you. In different ways, however, they all pose for us the test of learning to deal with what is called, in the inverted language of communism, 'wars of national liberation'. Behind this concept is the notion that the safest way to extend Communist power and influence in the contemporary world is to exploit the inevitable turbulence which accompanies the revolutionary movement toward modernization, by building a political base rooted in local frustrations, painful memories, and unfulfilled aspirations, and by mounting, on that base, insurrectional activity aided from outside the country. The objective is, of course, not national liberation but entrapment within the Communist bloc. This method, from the Communist point of view, is designed to bypass American nuclear strength, to bypass the conventional strength that we have helped build with our allies, and to tear down institutions not under their own control.

Over the past year we have given increased attention to this form of mixed political and military aggression, and in South Viet-Nam we—and the whole world community—are up against a formidable problem: mounting from outside an independent nation of a guerrilla war with men trained, infiltered, supplied, and directed from day to day across international boundaries. The free world must recognize this familiar form of aggression and act accordingly.

I cannot report to you that we have fully solved these problems which were waiting for us in January of this year. I do believe that we have made some headway, but they remain on the list of unfinished business. We can draw confidence from the long list of failures in other and somewhat similar Communist efforts to expand their empire. And we can be encouraged to note that the large numbers of new nations which have become independent since World War II have shown a stubborn resistance to the imposition of Communist rule.

But the points of crisis which dominate the headlines do not reflect adequately all that is going forward in the underdeveloped areas in the southern half of the world.

Our objective in these regions of revolution is simple. We wish to see emerge

[1] The reference is to the group of agreements reached at the Conference on the future of Indo-China held at Geneva, 26 April–21 July 1954 and the final declaration on Indo-China with which the Conference was wound up. *Documents*, 1954, Part III, Section A, *passim*.

out of the powerful ferment of modernization a community of independent nations. We wish them to modernize, not in our image but in the image they themselves formulate out of their own unique histories, cultures, and aspirations. We are confident that if, in this crucial transitional process, they maintain their independence, they will fashion societies which, in one way or another, will move in the direction of consent.

Democracy is not an absolute; and the conditions for democracy are complex. It requires not merely a literate population but a sense of national direction and of consensus, a linkage of urban and rural peoples, the existence of rules and institutions of law, a civil service and armed forces dedicated to nationhood and not to faction. And in the end political freedom requires a citizenry which assumes substantial individual responsibility for the fate of the community.

All this takes time. Our first objective, therefore, is to help preserve the independence of the modernization process, meanwhile working to help build the conditions which will make consent increasingly a reality and to encourage those who would remain steadfast to their own version of the democratic objective.

How should we assess our chances? What are the possibilities of seeing emerge in the southern half of the world an environment of independent and increasingly democratic states which would permit our own society to maintain and develop its humane and open character?

The task ahead is long, but I am basically optimistic. The impulse of these peoples and governments to remain independent is strong. I sense that there is a new generation emerging, dedicated to modernizing their societies with vigor and imagination. I sense that the word is spreading that the pragmatic and apparently diffuse methods of free men are more effective than the illusory efficiency of totalitarianism.

The issue is not yet fully decided. There are certain to be frustations and setbacks; but I would doubt that the Communist leadership, assessing recent developments and trends, believes with confidence that communism is the wave of the future in the underdeveloped areas of the free world. It is our assessment that the wave of the future will lie with those who struggle for their independence, face their problems pragmatically, and maintain loyalty to the longrun goal of political and social democracy.

It is in this sober but confident spirit that we are going forward with the Alliance for Progress, with our programs of long-term economic development elsewhere, and with other measures of authentic partnership with the new nations who are entering the world community.

. . . [There is] . . . a third question, which I might phrase as follows: Can a free-world system, based on a loose alliance of sovereign nations, stand up against the outward thrust of a highly centralized Communist bloc? Can an international democracy of nations deal with disciplined and purposeful totalitarian adversaries?

No Secretary of State can be unmindful of the complexities of alliance policy in a period when our allies number more than 40. The problem of clarifying a national policy within our own Federal Government is, in all conscience, complex enough; and to achieve common action within a large alliance is, as you well know, major business.

Nevertheless, having seen that business at close range, I can again report to you a mood of temperate optimism. Over the past year our Western allies have been subjected to an ugly threat: the threat of being held in nuclear hostage by the intermediate-range ballistic missiles which the Soviet Union now commands. They have stood firm against that threat, and I have no doubt but that the Soviet Union will find, in the response of the West, that this form of black-mail is counter-productive.

More than that, there is a wholesome ferment in Europe and throughout the Atlantic community, generating a debate which historians may well rank with the American constitutional debate of the 1780's. This ferment centers on the emergence and articulation of a new vision: the vision of a Europe moving toward unity and establishing, as it does so, a transatlantic partnership in all the affairs with which great powers must be concerned in the 1960's—the problems of defense in a nuclear age, the problems of sustained assistance to the underdeveloped areas, the problems of trade, the problems of using our international monetary reserves with economy and wisdom in the mutual support of each other's currencies, and problems of economic growth itself. This ferment has not yet yielded a resolution of all the complicated matters involved. But beneath the surface our alliance arrangements are moving into a new and rather grand phase.

In 1947 the American Government decided that it would link the recovery of Europe to efforts at European unification. We chose quite consciously not to play a balance-of-power game with the nations of Europe but to build toward a strong partnership in the affairs of the West. At that moment we joined forces with those Europeans who drew from the lessons of the Second World War, and indeed from the longer history of Europe, the conclusion that the great European center of Western culture and strength could play its proper part on the world scene only if it transcended its national divisions and moved toward unity. The extraordinary resurgence in Europe of the 1950's now provides the base for a major move forward, and I am confident that we shall see the 'grand design' unfold in coming months and years.

Our relations with the countries of Western Europe have, of course, been complicated from time to time since the Second World War by problems arising from the end of the colonial era. During the past year we have confronted several problems where there have been divergencies, in emphasis at least, with some of our European partners. These inevitable difficulties should not, however, obscure the larger pattern which is emerging—a pattern of constructive association among the whole of the northern half of the world, from Tokyo to Bonn, and with the new nations to the south—an association based on principles of partnership among equals, a shared interest in the economic development of the emerging nations, and, in the end, a shared commitment to the objectives of the United Nations Charter.

A fourth question . . . is, in effect, whether we are wholly on the defensive. Must we look to a future in which we can, at best, hold the frontiers of freedom? Must we abandon hope that the principles of independence and democracy might emerge within what is now the Communist bloc?

It would not be prudent to close one's eyes to the capacity of totalitarian methods to maintain a surface of unity and order. It is infinitely harder, for example, for opposition to make itself felt in a police state than in an open society. Nor should we underestimate the capacity of a totalitarian system to produce striking results by mobilizing men and resources around high-priority objectives. But it is inaccurate to believe that history has stopped within the Communist world or that the currents of history are moving automatically to its advantage.

In Europe we have had, in the postwar years, a fundamental test of Western and Communist concepts as they apply to economic, social, and political life. No one can question, I believe, the outcome of that test thus far. It is Western, and not Eastern, Europe that constitutes the more vital center.

Despite a Communist monopoly of education and propaganda, the peoples of Eastern Europe remain loyal to their culture and to their nationhood. In every field—from natural and social science to painting and music—they find ways to express their traditional association with Western civilization. And in time, as Communists know perhaps better than others, these tests of historical vitality count.

In free Asia there has been another test; and there, too, free men are doing vastly better than even the greatest optimists would have predicted only a few years ago. The economic progress of the new Japan—democratic and working in cooperation with other free nations—is one of the splendid achievements of the postwar era. In the Indian Peninsula, in southeast Asia, in Hong Kong, on Formosa, and now in Korea, there is a resilience, a will to get on with the job, the emergence of a new, modern generation of men and women which promise well for the future. Meanwhile, in the areas controlled by communism the techniques of totalitarianism, applied in regions where three-fourths of the people live in the countryside, have been unable to deal with hunger and apathy. Every day it becomes clear that the Communist methods for modernizing an under-developed area are old-fashioned, reactionary, and restrictive, quite aside from their simple inhumanity. And this, too, will count.

Finally, it is becoming clear that the same powerful forces which are diffusing power and influence within the free world—forces which our own political history and instinctive methods teach us how to weave together in new patterns of interdependence—are operating within the Communist world itself. We should take no cheap comfort from the deep schisms within the Communist bloc. On the other hand, we should be aware that the concept of independent nationhood, of national interest, and of national culture are day to day asserting themselves strongly. And if we are wise, we can patiently find ways to pick up strands of overlapping national interest between Communist nations and the free world, moving toward a cushioning of the raw clash of power.

From Berlin to Laos, from the question of arms control and disarmament to the exchange of persons, we are prepared to look at each proposal and possibility on its merits and to look systematically toward a world which would permit us all to live easier on a planet shadowed by nuclear weapons. And we are prepared to do so not defensively, out of fear, but out of an inner confidence that, if we use time well, time is on the side of the forces making for independent nationhood, dignified interdependence, and human freedom. . . .

(b) The United States and Cuba

1. President Kennedy's press conference of 12 April 1961[1] (extracts)

. . . Q. Mr. President, has a decision been reached on how far this country will be willing to go in helping an anti-Castro uprising or invasion of Cuba? What could you say with respect to recent developments as far as the anti-Castro movements in Cuba are concerned?

THE PRESIDENT: First, I want to say that there will not be, under any conditions, an intervention in Cuba by the United States Armed Forces. This Government will do everything it possibly can, and I think it can meet its responsibilities, to make sure that there are no Americans involved in any actions inside Cuba.

Secondly, the Justice Department's recent indictment of Mr. Masferrer,[2] of Florida, on the grounds that he was plotting an invasion of Cuba, from Florida, in order to establish a Batista-like regime should indicate the feelings of this country towards those who wish to re-establish that kind of an administration inside Cuba.

Third, we do not intend to take any action with respect to the property or other economic interests which American citizens formerly held in Cuba, other than formal and normal negotiations with a free and independent Cuba.

The basic issue in Cuba is not one between the United States and Cuba. It is between the Cubans themselves. I intend to see that we adhere to that principle and as I understand it this administration's attitude is so understood and shared by the anti-Castro exiles from Cuba in this country. . . .

. . . Q. Mr. President, your white paper[3] last week, referred in very diplomatic language to the takeover by communism in Cuba. Is it your view that Fidel Castro is personally a Communist?

THE PRESIDENT: Well, he has indicated his admiration on many occasions for the Communist revolution; he has appointed a great many Communists to high positions. A great many of those, I think, in the white paper—well, rather, the state paper—he indicated that two-thirds of those who had been members of his first government had fled Cuba, people who had a strong feeling for the revolution but who did not propose to see it come under the domination of the Communists.

So I would not want to characterize Mr. Castro except to say that by his own words he has indicated his hostility to democratic rule in this hemisphere, to democratic liberal leaders in many of the countries of the hemisphere who are attempting to improve the life of their people, and has associated himself most intimately with the Sino-Soviet bloc, and has indicated his desire to spread the influence of that bloc throughout this hemisphere. . . .

. . . Q. At the beginning of the news conference, sir, you told us what the United States cannot do in Cuba. Last night in the broadcast you said, "I think Latin America is in a more critical period in its relations with us. Therefore, if we don't move now, Mr. Castro may become a much greater danger than he is

---

[1] *Public Papers*, 1961, pp. 258–9, 264–5.

[2] Rolando Masferrer, right-wing Cuban exile leader. His indictment by the U.S. Department of Justice was announced on 9 April. *Survey*, 1961, p. 21, n. 6.

[3] 'Cuba' (Department of State Publication 7171, Inter-American Series 66, April 1961).

to us today.' Can you explore, sir, what we can or are doing in the line of that now?

THE PRESIDENT: Well, I think that we attempted to indicate some of the areas where I hoped we could take affirmative action, in the speech I made to the ambassadors in March.[1] Mr. Dillon is in Rio at the meeting of the Inter-American Bank.[2] And we are, in the months of April and May and June, going to attempt in other ways to implement the concept behind *alianza para progresso*. I hope that the Congress will appropriate as quickly as possible the $500 million suggested by the Act of Bogotá.[3] That would be at least an important start. We will have other proposals to make, but I think that it's important that we seize the initiative and do not permit those who are not friends of freedom to become the spokesmen for the material aspirations of the people of Latin America. So that I hope we identify ourselves with both the social, political or the social and the material aspirations of the people of Latin America.

Q. Mr. President, in that same question, you said that—you pointed out that this Government has indicted a pro-Batista Cuban. But I am not clear from your answer, sir, whether this Government will oppose any attempt to mount an offensive against Castro from this country. Could you clarify that?

THE PRESIDENT: If your phrase 'to mount an offensive' is as I understand it, I would be opposed to mounting an offensive.

Q. Are we barred by our own neutrality acts or by the OAS treaty from giving any aid or arms to anti-Castro elements in the country?

THE PRESIDENT: Well, there are, of course, as I stated—there is a revolutionary committee here which is, of course, extremely anxious to see a change in government in that country. I am sure that they have—that they are very interested in associating with all those who feel the same way. Mr. Castro enjoyed some support here in the United States and received some assistance when he was attempting to carry out his revolution. In fact, some Americans were involved in the military actions with him. That latter is what we are particularly anxious to—— . . .

2. The Chairman of the Council of Ministers of the Soviet Union, Mr. Khrushchev to President Kennedy, 18 April 1961[4]

I address this message to you at an alarming hour which is fraught with danger against universal peace. An armed aggression has been started against Cuba. It is an open secret that the armed bands which have invaded that country have been prepared, equipped, and armed in the United States. The planes which bomb Cuban towns belong to the United States of America, the bombs which they drop have been put at their disposal by the American Government.

All this arouses in the Soviet Union, the Soviet Government, and the Soviet people an understandable feeling of indignation. Only recently, exchanging

---

[1] The reference is to President Kennedy's speech of 13 March 1961 to members of the United States Congress and to the Diplomatic Corps of the Latin American Republics.
[2] The second meeting of the Inter-American Development Bank was held at Rio de Janeiro, 11–14 April 1961. Douglas Dillon, Secretary of the Treasury, headed the United States delegation.
[3] *Documents*, 1960, pp. 607–12.   [4] *D.S.B.*, 8 May 1961, p. 662.

views through our representatives, we talked with you about the mutual wish of the parties to exert joint efforts directed toward the improvement of relations between our countries and the prevention of a danger of war. Your statement a few days ago to the effect that the United States of America would not participate in military actions against Cuba created an impression that the leading authorities of the United States are aware of the consequences which aggression against Cuba could have for the whole world and the United States of America itself.

How are we to understand what is really being done by the United States now that the attack on Cuba has become a fact?

It is yet not too late to prevent the irreparable. The Government of the U.S. can still prevent the flames of war kindled by the interventionists on Cuba from spreading into a conflagration which it will be impossible to cope with. I earnestly appeal to you, Mr. President, to call a halt to the aggression against the Republic of Cuba. The military techniques and the world political situation now are such that any so-called 'small war' can produce a chain reaction in all parts of the world.

As for the U.S.S.R., there must be no mistake about our position. We will extend to the Cuban people and its Government all the necessary aid for the repulse of the armed attack on Cuba. We are sincerely interested in the relaxation of international tension, but if others go in for its aggravation, then we will answer them in full measure. In general it is impossible to carry on affairs in such a way that in one area the situation is settled and the fire is put out, and in another area a new fire is lit.

I hope that the U.S. Government will take into consideration these reasons, dictated only by concern that steps should not be permitted which might lead the world to a catastrophe of war.

3. Statement by the Soviet Government, 18 April 1961[1]

The Government of the Republic of Cuba has announced that in the morning of 15 April airplanes of the U.S. B–26 bomber type subjected separate districts of the capital of Cuba—Havana—and a number of other inhabited localities to barbarous bombing. There were many killed and injured among the inhabitants of the capital.

Following the bombing, early in the morning of 17 April armed forces of the interventionists landed at various places on the Cuban coast. The landing took place under the cover of U.S. aircraft and warships.

Cuban Government troops and the People's Militia are engaged in fighting the invading gangs.

In connection with the invasion of Cuba the Government of the Soviet Union states:

The attack on Cuba is an open challenge to all freedom-loving peoples, a dangerous provocation against peace in the area of the Caribbean Sea, against universal peace. There can be no justification of this criminal invasion. The organizers of the aggression against Cuba are encroaching on the inalienable

<hr>

[1] *D.S.B.*, 8 May 1961, pp. 662–3.

right of the Cuban people to live freely and independently. They are trampling underfoot the elementary norms of international relations, the principles of peaceful coexistence of states.

The Cuban nation has not threatened and is not threatening anyone. Having overthrown the tyranny of the bloody despot Batista, lackey of the big U.S. monopolies, the Cuban nation has embarked upon the pursuit of an independent policy, of raising its economy, and improving its life. It demands to be left in peace, to be left to build its life in conformity with its national ideals.

Can small Cuba with its population of 6 million threaten anyone—and such a big state as the United States at that? Of course not. Yet since the first days of the victory of the national revolution in Cuba the United States became the center where the counter-revolutionary elements thrown out from Cuba gathered, where they were formed into gangs and armed for struggle against the popular government of Fidel Castro. Recent events show that the present U.S. Government, which declared itself heir to Roosevelt's policy, is in essence pursuing the reactionary imperialist policy of Dulles and Eisenhower so condemned by the nations.

The U.S. Government declared through President Kennedy that the basic controversial question on Cuba is not a matter of a quarrel between the United States and Cuba but concerns the Cubans alone. The President said that he advocated a free and independent Cuba. In fact, however, everything was done on the territory of the United States and the countries dependent on it to prepare an aggressive attack on Cuba. But for the open aggressive policy of the United States towards Cuba would the counterrevolutionary gangs of the hirelings of U.S. capital have been able to create the so-called Cuban Government on U.S. territory? What territory served as a starting point for the piratical attack on Cuba?

It was the territory of the United States and that of the neighboring countries which are under its control. Whose are the arms with which the counter-revolutionary gangs are equipped? They are U.S. arms. With whose funds have they been supported and are they being maintained? With funds appropriated by the United States.

It is clear from this that it is precisely the United States which is the inspirer and organizer of the present bandit-like attack on Cuba. Why did the United States organize this criminal attack on the Cuban Republic? Because, after the overthrow of the tyranny of Batista, the Cuban people were finished with the plunder and exploitation of their homeland by foreign monopolies. These monopolies do not wish to concede anything to the people of Cuba, the peoples of Latin America. They fear that Cuba, building its independent life, will become an example for other countries of Latin America. With the hands of base mercenaries they want to take from the Cuban people their right to determine their own fate, as they did with Guatemala.

But every nation has the right to live as it wishes, and no one, no state has the right to impose its own way of life on other nations. The Cuban nation has passed through a long, harsh, and difficult school of struggle for its freedom and independence against foreign oppressors and their accomplices, and it will not be brought to its knees, will not permit the yoke of foreign enslavers to be placed upon its shoulders. All progressive mankind, all upright people are on the side of Cuba.

The Government of the Soviet Union states that the Soviet Union, as other peace-loving countries, will not abandon the Cuban people in their trouble nor will it refuse it all necessary aid and support in the just struggle for the freedom and independence of Cuba.

The Soviet Government, at this crucial moment, for the sake of preserving universal peace, appeals to the Government of the United States to take measures to stop the agression against Cuba and intervention in Cuba's affairs. Protection of and aid to the counterrevolutionary bands must be stopped immediately.

The Soviet Government hopes that it will be understood in the United States that aggression goes against the interests of the American people and is capable of jeopardizing the peaceful life of the population of the United States itself.

The Soviet Government demands urgent study by the U.N. General Assembly of the question of aggressive actions of the United States, which has prepared and unleashed armed intervention against Cuba.

The Government of the U.S.S.R. appeals to the governments of all member states of the United Nations to take all necessary measures for the immediate cessation of aggressive actions against Cuba, the continuation of which may give rise to the most serious consequences for universal peace.

In this hour, when the sovereignty and independence of Cuba, a sovereign member of the United Nations, are in danger, the duty of all countries members of the United Nations is to render it all necessary aid and support.

The Soviet Government reserves the right, if armed intervention in the affairs of the Cuban people is not stopped, to take all measures with other countries to render the necessary assistance to the Republic of Cuba.

4. President Kennedy to Mr. Khrushchev, 18 April 1961[1]

MR. CHAIRMAN: You are under a serious misapprehension in regard to events in Cuba. For months there has been evident and growing resistance to the Castro dictatorship. More than 100,000 refugees have recently fled from Cuba into neighboring countries. Their urgent hope is naturally to assist their fellow Cubans in their struggle for freedom. Many of these refugees fought alongside Dr. Castro against the Batista dictatorship; among them are prominent leaders of his own original movement and government.

These are unmistakable signs that Cubans find intolerable the denial of democratic liberties and the subversion of the 26th of July Movement by an alien-dominated regime. It cannot be surprising that, as resistance within Cuba grows, refugees have been using whatever means are available to return and support their countrymen in the continuing struggle for freedom. Where people are denied the right of choice, recourse to such struggle is the only means of achieving their liberties.

I have seriously stated, and I repeat now, that the United States intends no military intervention in Cuba. In the event of any military intervention by outside force we will immediately honor our obligations under the inter-American

[1] *D.S.B.*, 8 May 1961, pp. 661–2.

system to protect this hemisphere against external aggression. While refraining from military intervention in Cuba, the people of the United States do not conceal their admiration for Cuban patriots who wish to see a democratic system in an independent Cuba. The United States government can take no action to stifle the spirit of liberty.

I have taken careful note of your statement that the events in Cuba might affect peace in all parts of the world. I trust that this does not mean that the Soviet government, using the situation in Cuba as a pretext, is planning to inflame other areas of the world. I would like to think that your government has too great a sense of responsibility to embark upon any enterprise so dangerous to general peace.

I agree with you as to the desirability of steps to improve the international atmosphere. I continue to hope that you will cooperate in opportunities now available to this end. A prompt cease-fire and peaceful settlement of the dangerous situation in Laos, cooperation with the United Nations in the Congo and a speedy conclusion of an acceptable treaty for the banning of nuclear tests would be constructive steps in this direction. The regime in Cuba could make a similar contribution by permitting the Cuban people freely to determine their own future by democratic processes and freely to cooperate with their Latin American neighbors.

I believe, Mr. Chairman, that you should recognize that free peoples in all parts of the world do not accept the claim of historical inevitability for Communist revolution. What your government believes is its own business; what it does in the world is the world's business. The great revolution in the history of man, past, present and future, is the revolution of those determined to be free.

5. Address by President Kennedy to the American Society of Newspaper Editors, 20 April 1961[1]

The President of a great democracy such as ours, and the editors of great newspapers such as yours, owe a common obligation to the people: an obligation to present the facts, to present them with candor, and to present them in perspective. It is with that obligation in mind that I have decided in the last 24 hours to discuss briefly at this time the recent events in Cuba.

On that unhappy island, as in so many other arenas of the contest for freedom, the news has grown worse instead of better. I have emphasized before that this was a struggle of Cuban patriots against a Cuban dictator. While we could not be expected to hide our sympathies, we made it repeatedly clear that the armed forces of this country would not intervene in any way.

Any unilateral American intervention, in the absence of an external attack upon ourselves or an ally, would have been contrary to our traditions and to our international obligations. But let the record show that our restraint is not inexhaustible. Should it ever appear that the inter-American doctrine of non-interference merely conceals or excuses a policy of nonaction—if the nations of this Hemisphere should fail to meet their commitments against outside Communist penetration—then I want it clearly understood that this Government

1 *Public Papers*, 1961, pp. 304–6.

will not hesitate in meeting its primary obligations which are to the security of our Nation!

Should that time ever come, we do not intend to be lectured on 'intervention' by those whose character was stamped for all time on the bloody streets of Budapest! Nor would we expect or accept the same outcome which this small band of gallant Cuban refugees must have known that they were chancing, determined as they were against heavy odds to pursue their courageous attempts to regain their Island's freedom.

But Cuba is not an island unto itself; and our concern is not ended by mere expressions of nonintervention or regret. This is not the first time in either ancient or recent history that a small band of freedom fighters has engaged the armor of totalitarianism.

It is not the first time that Communist tanks have rolled over gallant men and women fighting to redeem the independence of their homeland. Nor is it by any means the final episode in the eternal struggle of liberty against tyranny, anywhere on the face of the globe, including Cuba itself.

Mr. Castro has said that these were mercenaries. According to press reports, the final message to be relayed from the refugee forces on the beach came from the rebel commander when asked if he wished to be evacuated. His answer was: 'I will never leave this country.' That is not the reply of a mercenary. He has gone now to join in the mountains countless other guerrilla fighters, who are equally determined that the dedication of those who gave their lives shall not be forgotten, and that Cuba must not be abandoned to the Communists. And we do not intend to abandon it either!

The Cuban people have not yet spoken their final piece. And I have no doubt that they and their Revolutionary Council, led by Dr. Cardona[1]—and members of the families of the Revolutionary Council, I am informed by the Doctor yesterday, are involved themselves in the Islands—will continue to speak up for a free and independent Cuba.

Meanwhile we will not accept Mr. Castro's attempts to blame this nation for the hatred which his onetime supporters now regard his repression. But there are from this sobering episode useful lessons for us all to learn. Some may be still obscure, and await further information. Some are clear today.

First, it is clear that the forces of communism are not to be underestimated, in Cuba or anywhere else in the world. The advantages of a police state—its use of mass terror and arrests to prevent the spread of free dissent—cannot be overlooked by those who expect the fall of every fanatic tyrant. If the self-discipline of the free cannot match the iron discipline of the mailed fist—in economic, political, scientific and all the other kinds of struggles as well as the military—then the peril to freedom will continue to rise.

Secondly, it is clear that this Nation, in concert with all the free nations of this hemisphere, must take an ever closer and more realistic look at the menace of external Communist intervention and domination in Cuba. The American people are not complacent about Iron Curtain tanks and planes less than 90 miles from their shore. But a nation of Cuba's size is less a threat to our survival than it is a base for subverting the survival of other free nations throughout

---

[1] Dr. José Miró Cardona, President of the Cuban Revolutionary Council.

the hemisphere. It is not primarily our interest or our security but theirs which is now, today, in the greater peril. It is for their sake as well as our own that we must show our will.

The evidence is clear—and the hour is late. We and our Latin friends will have to face the fact that we cannot postpone any longer the real issue of survival of freedom in this hemisphere itself. On that issue, unlike perhaps some others, there can be no middle ground. Together we must build a hemisphere where freedom can flourish; and where any free nation under outside attack of any kind can be assured that all of our resources stand ready to respond to any request for assistance.

Third, and finally, it is clearer than ever that we face a relentless struggle in every corner of the globe that goes far beyond the clash of armies or even nuclear armaments. The armies are there, and in large number. The nuclear armaments are there. But they serve primarily as the shield behind which subversion, infiltration, and a host of other tactics steadily advance, picking off vulnerable areas one by one in situations which do not permit our own armed intervention.

Power is the hallmark of this offensive—power and discipline and deceit. The legitimate discontent of yearning people is exploited. The legitimate trappings of self-determination are employed. But once in power, all talk of discontent disappears, and the promise of a revolution of hope is betrayed, as in Cuba, into a reign of terror. Those who on instruction staged automatic 'riots' in the streets of free nations over the efforts of a small group of young Cubans to regain their freedom should recall the long roll call of refugees who cannot now go back—to Hungary, to North Korea, to North Viet-Nam, to East Germany, or to Poland, or to any of the other lands from which a steady stream of refugees pours forth, in eloquent testimony to the cruel oppression now holding sway in their homeland.

We dare not fail to see the insidious nature of this new and deeper struggle. We dare not fail to grasp the new concepts, the new tools, the new sense of urgency we will need to combat it—whether in Cuba or South Viet-Nam. And we dare not fail to realize that this struggle is taking place every day, without fanfare, in thousands of villages and markets—day and night—and in classrooms all over the globe.

The message of Cuba, of Laos, of the rising din of Communist voices in Asia and Latin America—these messages are all the same. The complacent, the self-indulgent, the soft societies are about to be swept away with the debris of history. Only the strong, only the industrious, only the determined, only the courageous, only the visionary who determine the real nature of our struggle can possibly survive.

No greater task faces this country or this administration. No other challenge is more deserving of our every effort and energy. Too long we have fixed our eyes on traditional military needs, on armies prepared to cross borders, on missiles poised for flight. Now it should be clear that this is no longer enough—that our security may be lost piece by piece, country by country, without the firing of a single missile or the crossing of a single border.

We intend to profit from this lesson. We intend to reexamine and reorient our forces of all kinds—our tactics and our institutions here in this community. We intend to intensify our efforts for a struggle in many ways more difficult than war, where disappointment will often accompany us.

For I am convinced that we in this country and in the free world possess the necessary resource, and the skill, and the added strength that comes from a belief in the freedom of man. And I am equally convinced that history will record the fact that this bitter struggle reached its climax in the late 1950's and the early 1960's. Let me then make clear as the President of the United States that I am determined upon our system's survival and success, regardless of the cost and regardless of the peril!

6. Resolution of the First Committee of the United Nations General Assembly, adopted 21 April 1961[1]

The General Assembly,

Having heard the statements made by the Minister for External Relations of Cuba, the representative of the United States of America and other representatives,

Deeply concerned over the situation described therein, the continuation of which is likely to endanger peace,

Considering that it is a permanent aim of the United Nations to develop friendly relations based on respect for the principle of equal rights and self-determination of peoples,

Firmly believing that the principle of non-intervention in the internal affairs of any State imposes an obligation on Members of the United Nations to refrain from encouraging or promoting civil strife in other States,

Mindful that it is the duty of all States, under Article 33 of the Charter of the United Nations, to seek the pacific settlement of disputes by the means enumerated therein,

1. *Makes an urgent appeal* to all States to ensure that their territories and resources are not used to promote a civil war in Cuba;

2. *Urges* them to put an immediate end to any activity that might result in further bloodshed;

3. *Requests* them to co-operate, in keeping with the spirit of the Charter of the United Nations, in the search for a peaceful solution to the present situation.[2]

7. Resolution of the First Committee of the United Nations General Assembly, adopted 21 April 1961[3]

The General Assembly,

Having heard the statements made by the Minister for External Relations of Cuba, the representative of the United States of America and other representatives,

---

[1] *G.A.O.R.*, Fifteenth Session, Annexes, Agenda item 90, p. 7. Document A/C.1/L275; introduced by Mexico on 18 April.

[2] The voting on the Mexican draft resolution was as follows:
The first, second, third and fifth preambular paragraphs were adopted without objection. The fourth preambular paragraph was adopted by a roll-call vote of 86 to none with 11 abstentions. Operative paragraph 1 was adopted by a roll-call vote of 47 to 7, with 44 abstentions. Operative paragraph 2 was adopted by a roll-call vote of 45 to none with 53 abstentions. Operative paragraph 3 was adopted without objection. The draft resolution as a whole was adopted by a roll-call vote of 42 to 31, with 25 abstentions.

[3] ibid., Fifteenth Session, Annexes, Agenda item 90, p. 7. Document A/C.1/L.276; introduced by Argentina, Colombia, Chile, Honduras, Panama, Uruguay, and Venezuela on 19 April.

Deeply concerned over the situation disclosed therein, which is disturbing the[1] American continent[1] and the continuation of which could endanger[1] peace,

Recalling the last two paragraphs of the Security Council resolution of 19 July 1960[2] and the peaceful means of settlement established at the Seventh Meeting of Consultation of Foreign Ministers of the American Republics,

Considering that the States Members of the United Nations are under an obligation to settle their disputes by negotiation and other peaceful means in such a manner that international peace and security, and justice, are not endangered,

1. *Exhorts* those[1] Member States which[1] belong to the Organization of American States[1] to lend their assistance with a view to achieving a settlement by peaceful means in accordance with the Purposes and Principles of the Charter of the United Nations[1] and of the Charter of the Organization of American States;[1, 3]

2. *Exhorts* all Member States to abstain from any action which may aggravate existing tensions.[1, 4]

[1] At the 1159th meeting held on 20/21 April 1961, amendments were submitted to the seven-Power draft resolution by the Sudan (A/C.1/L.278) as follows:
1. In the second preambular paragraph:
(*a*) Delete the words 'the American continent' and substitute the words 'world public opinion';
(*b*) At the end of the second line, insert the word 'world' between the words 'endanger' and 'peace'.
2. In operative paragraph 1:
(*a*) In the first line, replace the word 'those' by the word 'all';
(*b*) Delete the words 'which belong to the Organization of American States';
(*c*) Delete the words 'and of the charter of the Organization of American States'.
3. Replace operative paragraph 2 by the following:
'*Exhorts* all Member States to take such action as is open to them to remove existing tension.' The amendments by the Sudan (A/C.1/L.278, paras. 1 and 3) to the second preambular paragraph and to operative paragraph 2 of the seven-Power draft resolution (A/C.1/L.276) were accepted by the sponsors of the draft resolution. The representative of Saudi Arabia orally proposed an amendment to the text of operative paragraph 2, as put forward by the Sudan and accepted by the sponsors, whereby the word 'peaceful' would be inserted between the words 'such' and 'action'.
At the 1161st meeting, held on 21 April 1961, the sponsors of the seven-Power draft resolution (A/C.1/L.276) accepted the Saudi Arabian oral amendment. At the same meeting, the Committee, began to vote on the draft resolutions and amendments before it, as follows:
(*a*) The Sudanese amendments (A/C.1/L.278, para. 2) to operative paragraph 1 of the seven-Power draft resolution (A/C.1/L.276) were rejected by a roll-call vote of 43 to 31, with 23 abstentions.
[2] *Documents*, 1960, Section 10, No. 12, pp. 571–2.
[3] At the 1159th meeting the following amendment was also submitted by the Nigerian representative:
1. At the end of operative paragraph 1, add the following: 'and to report to the United Nations General Assembly at its sixteenth session the measures they have taken to achieve settlement by peaceful means';
2. Between operative paragraphs 1 and 2, insert operative paragraphs 1, 2 and 3 of the draft resolution submitted by Mexico (A/C.1/L.279).
At the 1160th meeting, held on 21 April 1961, Nigeria withdrew its amendments (A/C.1/L.279). At the 1161st meeting, held the same day, having reintroduced the first of the Nigerian amendments (A/C.1/L.279, para. 1), to the seven-Power draft resolution at the previous meeting, the representative of Cyprus orally submitted a revised text reading as follows: 'and to report to the United Nations, as soon as possible, within the present year, the measures they have taken to achieve settlement by peaceful means'. This revised text was also accepted by the sponsors of the draft resolution.
[4] The voting on the seven-Power draft resolution (A/C.1/L.276), incorporating the amendments accepted by the sponsors to the second preambular paragraph and to operative paragraphs 1 and 2, was as follows:

8. General Assembly resolution, adopted 21 April 1961[1]

The General Assembly,

Having heard the statements made by the Minister for External Relations of Cuba, the representative of the United States of America and other representatives,

Deeply concerned over the situation disclosed therein, which is disturbing world public opinion and the continuation of which could endanger world peace,

Recalling the last two paragraphs of the Security Council resolution of 19 July 1960[2] and the peaceful means of settlement established at the Seventh Meeting of Consultation of Foreign Ministers of the American Republics,

Considering that the States Members of the United Nations are under an obligation to settle their disputes by negotiation and other peaceful means in such a manner that international peace and security, and justice, are not endangered,

Exhorts all Member States to take such peaceful action as is open to them to remove existing tension.[3]

9. Mr. Khrushchev to President Kennedy, 22 April 1961[4]

MR. PRESIDENT: I received your reply of 18 April.[5] You write that the United States does not intend to carry out a military intervention in Cuba. However, numerous facts known to the entire world, and certainly known better by the Government of the United States of America than anybody else—present a different story. However much the opposite is assured, it is now indisputably ascertained that the preparations for the intervention, the financing of armament, and the transfer of hired gangs which have invaded the territory of Cuba were indeed carried out by the United States.

The armed forces of the United States of America have directly participated in implementing the piratic assault on Cuba. American bombers and fighter planes supported the operation of the hirelings who have entered Cuban territory and participated in the military acts against the armed forces of the lawful government and people of Cuba.

Such are the facts. They illustrate the direct participation of the United States of America in the armed aggression against Cuba.

The first preambular paragraph was adopted without objection. The second preambular paragraph was adopted without objection. The third preambular paragraph was adopted by a roll-call vote of 55 to 14, with 29 abstentions. The fourth preambular paragraph was adopted without objection.

Operative paragraph 2 was adopted by a roll-call vote of 56 to 28, with 14 abstentions. Operative paragraph 2 was adopted without objection.

The draft resolution as a whole was adopted by a roll-call vote of 61 to 27 with 10 abstentions.

[1] *G.A.O.R.*, Fifteenth Session, Annexes, Agenda item 90, p. 111. Resolution 1616(XV).
[2] See p. 27, n. 2.
[3] The Mexican draft resolution (see above) failed to obtain the two-thirds majority necessary for its adoption by the General Assembly.
[4] *D.S.B.*, 8 May 1961, pp. 664–7.   [5] This section, document 4, p. 22, above.

In your message you took the stand of justification and even eulogy of the assault on Cuba, this crime which has shocked the whole world.

The organization of military aggression against Cuba—only because the way of life chosen by its people does not correspond to the tastes of the leading circles in the United States and the North American monopolies acting in Latin America you seek to justify by reasoning about the devotion of the U.S. Government to the ideals of 'freedom'. I take the liberty to ask: What freedom do you mean?

The freedom to strangle the Cuban people with the bony hand of starvation by means of economic blockade? Is this freedom? The freedom to send military planes over the territory of Cuba, to expose to barbaric bombardment peaceful Cuban cities, to set fire to sugar cane plantations? Is this freedom?

History knows numerous examples when, under the excuse of the defense of freedom, bloody reprisals were carried out against the people, colonial wars were waged, and one country after the other was taken by the throat.

Apparently, in the case given, you mean the aspiration of the U.S. Government to reestablish in Cuba this kind of 'freedom' under which the country would dance to the tune of a stronger neighbor, and the foreign monopolies again could plunder the national riches of Cuba and make profit out of the blood and sweat of the Cuban people. But the Cuban people made their revolution against exactly this kind of 'freedom', driving out Batista who, perhaps, faithfully served the interests of his foreign masters but who was a foreign element in the body of the Cuban nation.

Thus you, Mr. President, express solicitude about a band of enemies chased out by their nation, who have found refuge under the wing of those who try to hold Cuba under the muzzle of the arms of their cruisers and minesweepers. But why are you not moved by the destiny of the 6-million-strong Cuban nation? Why do you not wish to reckon with its inalienable right to freedom and independent life, with its right to arrange its internal affairs as it thinks fit? Where is the code of international law, or, finally, of human morality, with the aid of which such a position could be justified? In short, they do not exist.

The Cuban people have expressed their will once again with a degree of clarity which could not leave a single doubt even with those who prefer to close their eyes to reality. They have shown that they not only know their interests best, but know also how to defend them. Cuba today is, of course, not the Cuba which you identified with the band of traitors who fought against their own nation. This is the Cuba of workers, peasants, and intelligentsia. This is a nation which has rallied closely round its revolutionary government headed by the national hero, Fidel Castro. And this nation, judging by all things, has met the interventionists in a worthy manner. Surely this is true evidence of the real will of the people of Cuba. I think this is convincing. And if this is so, then surely the time is ripe to draw sober conclusions from it.

As for the Soviet Union, I have said many times and I affirm again: Our Government does not seek any advantages or privileges in Cuba. We have no bases in Cuba and do not intend to establish any. This is well known to you, and to your generals and admirals. If, despite this, they still insist on scaring people with inventions about 'Soviet bases' in Cuba, they do it for the benefit of simpletons. However, the number of such simpletons is ever diminishing, including, I hope, in the United States.

I would like to take this opportunity, Mr. President, to express my opinion as to your declarations, and the declarations of some other U.S. statesmen, that rockets and other armaments might be placed on Cuban territory and used against the United States.

From this a conclusion is drawn as if the United States had a right to attack Cuba—either directly or through the enemies of the Cuban people whom you arm with your weapons, train on your territory, maintain with the money of U.S. taxpapers, transport by the transport units of your armed forces, at the same time striving to mask the fact that they are fighting the Cuban people and its legal government.

You also refer to some duty of the United States 'to defend the Western Hemisphere against external aggression'. But what kind of duty can it be in this case? No one has a duty to defend rebels against the legal government in a sovereign state, which Cuba is.

Mr. President, you are taking a very dangerous path. Think about it. You speak about your rights and obligations. Certainly, everyone can have pretensions to these rights or those rights, but then you must also permit other states to base their acts in analogous instances on the same kind of reasons and considerations.

You declare that Cuba is allegedly able to use its territory for acts against the United States. This is your assumption, and it is not based on any facts. We, however, on our side, are able now to refer to concrete facts and not to assumptions: In some countries bordering directly on the Soviet Union by land and by sea there are now governments which conduct a far from wise policy, governments which have concluded military agreements with the United States and have put their territory at its disposal to accommodate American military bases there.

In addition, your military people openly declare that these bases are directed toward the Soviet Union. Even so, this is clear to all: If you consider yourself to be in the right to implement such measures against Cuba which have lately been taken by the United States of America, you must admit that other countries, also, do not have lesser reason to act in a similar manner in relation to states on whose territories preparations are actually being made which represent a threat against the security of the Soviet Union. If you do not wish to sin against elementary logic, you evidently must admit such a right to other states. We, on our side, do not adhere to such views.

We consider that the reasonings voiced on this subject in the United States are not only a highly free interpretation of international law, but, speaking frankly, a blunt preaching of perfidious policy.

Certainly, a strong state always can, if it wishes, find an excuse to attack a weaker country and then justify the attack, alleging that this country was a potential threat. But is this the morality of the 20th century? This is the morality of colonizers and brigands who were conducting precisely this policy some time ago. Now, in the second half of the 20th century, it is impossible to follow the piratic morality of colonizers anymore. All of us are now witnesses to the fact of how the colonial system falls to the ground and fades away. The Soviet Union, for its part, does its best to contribute to this, and we are proud of it.

Or let us consider U.S. activities in regard to China. In reference to what legal norms can one justify these activities? It is known to all that Taiwan is an integral part of China. This has also been recognized by the U.S. Government, whose signature was put on the Cairo Declaration of 1943. However, later on the United States seized Taiwan or, actually, entered on the path of robbery. The Chinese People's Republic declared its natural aspiration to reunite the territory of Taiwan with the rest of the Chinese territory. But what was the United States reaction to this? It declared that armed force would be used to prevent the reunion of this seized Chinese territory with the rest of China. It threatens war in case China takes steps aiming at the reunification of Taiwan. And this from a country which has officially recognized Taiwan as belonging to China! Is this not perfidy in international policy?

If such methods prevailed in relations between states then there would be no room for law, and instead of it lawlessness and arbitrariness would take its place.

Thus, Mr. President, your sympathies are one thing, and actions against the security and independence of other nations, undertaken on the strength of those sympathies, is quite another matter. Naturally you can express your sympathies toward the imperialist and colonialist countries and this does not astonish anyone. You, for instance, cast your vote with them in the United Nations. This is a question of your morality. But what was done against Cuba—this is not morality. This is warlike action.

I wish to stress that if the United Nations is destined to attain true strength and fulfill the functions for which it was created—at the present time this Organization, unfortunately, represents an organism that is contaminated with the germs of colonialism and imperialism—then the United Nations must resolutely condemn the warlike actions against Cuba.

The question here is not only one of condemning the United States. It is important that the condemnation of aggression should become a precedent, a lesson which should also be learned by other countries with a view to stopping the repetition of aggression. Because if one starts to approve, or even to condone, the morality of aggressors, this can be taken as a guide by other states, and this will inevitably lead to war conflicts, any one of which may suddenly lead to World War III.

The statement which you made in your last speech to the press representatives[1] must greatly alarm the whole world, for, in essence, you speak openly about some right of yours to use military force when you consider it necessary, and to suppress other nations each time you yourself decide that the expression of will by those nations represents 'communism'. What right do you have, or what right has anyone, to deprive a nation of the possibility of deciding according to its own desire to choose its own social system?

Have you ever thought that other countries could present you with similar demands, and could say that you, in the United States, have a system which gives rise to wars, pursues imperialistic policies, policies of threats and attacks on other states? There are all grounds for such accusations. And if we assume

[1] On 20 April 1961. See this section, document No. 5, pp. 23–26 above.

the premises which you yourself proclaim now, then, obviously, we can require the change of the system in the United States.

We, as you know, are not embarking on this road. We support peaceful coexistence among all states and noninterference in the internal affairs of other countries.

You hint at Budapest, but we can tell you straight, without hints, that it is you, the United States, which crushed the independence of Guatemala by sending your hirelings there, as you are trying to do in the case of Cuba as well. It is the United States, indeed, and not any other country which has so far been mercilessly exploiting and keeping in economic dependence the Latin American countries and many other countries of the world. Everyone is aware of that. And according to your logic, Mr. President, obviously, actions could also be organized against your country from without, which would put an end once and for all to this imperialist policy, the policy of threats, and the policy of reprisals against freedom-loving peoples.

As to your anxiety about emigrants, expelled by the Cuban people, I would say the following in this connection:

You, of course, know that in many countries there are emigrants who are not satisfied with the regime prevailing in those countries from which they fled. If such abnormal practices are introduced in the relations between states as for such emigrants to be armed and used against the countries from which they have fled, then we can surely say that this will inevitably lead to conflicts and wars. And, therefore, one should refrain from such unwise activities because this is a slippery and dangerous road which might lead to world war.

In your answer you considered it to be appropriate to touch on problems not related to the theme of my message—among them, in your interpretation, the problem of the historical inevitability of the Communist revolution.

I am only able to evaluate it as a tendency to divert from the main question—the question of the aggression against Cuba. Under suitable conditions we are also ready to exchange views on the question regarding the ways and means for the development of human society, although such a question is not being solved by disputes between groups or individual persons, regardless of the high position they may occupy in the state. The fact of whose system will turn out to be the better will be solved by the peoples.

You, Mr. President, have spoken frequently and much about your wish to see Cuba liberated. But all acts of the United States in regard to this small country contradict this. I do not even mention the last armed assault on Cuba, which was organized with the aim of changing its inner structure by force.

It was no one but the United States, indeed, which thrust on Cuba the cabalistic condition of the Havana agreement almost 60 years ago and created on its territory its Guantanamo military base. But the United States of America is the most powerful country in the Western Hemisphere, and no one in this hemisphere is able to threaten you with military invasion. It follows, therefore, that if you continue to maintain your military base on the territory of Cuba against the clearly expressed wish of the Cuban people and government, this base serves not for defense from aggression by any foreign powers, but has the aim of suppressing the will of the Latin American peoples. It has been created for the implementation of gendarmery functions and for keeping the Latin American peoples in political and economic dependence.

The Government of the United States is now thundering against Cuba. But this only shows one thing—your lack of confidence in your own system, in the policy carried out by the United States. And this is understandable since this is a policy of exploitation, the policy of enslaving underdeveloped countries. You have no faith in your system, and this is why you are afraid that the example of Cuba might infect other countries.

But aggressive, bandit acts cannot save your system. In the historical process of developing mankind, every nation has been, and will be, deciding its own destiny on its own. As for the U.S.S.R., the peoples of our country solved this problem over 43 years ago definitely and irrevocably.

We are a socialist state and our social system is the most just of all that have existed to date because by us he who labors is also the master of all means of production. This is indeed an infectious example, and the sooner the necessity for transition to such a system is understood, the sooner all mankind will have a truly just community. At the same time, also, wars will be ended once and or all.

You did not like it, Mr. President, when I said in my previous message that there could be no firm peace in the entire world if the flame of war was raging anywhere. But this is precisely so. Peace is indivisible—whether anyone likes it or not. And I can only affirm what I said: Things cannot be done in such a way that in one region the situation is made easier and the conflagration dampened, and in another one a new conflagration is started.

The Soviet Government has always consequently defended the freedom and independence of all nations. It is obvious, then, that we cannot recognize any U.S. rights to decide the fate of other countries, including the Latin American countries. We regard any interference by one government in the affairs of another—and armed interference, especially—as a breach of all international laws, and of the principles of peaceful coexistence which the Soviet Union has been unfailingly advocating since the first days of its establishment. If it is a duty of all states and their leaders, in our times more than ever before, to refrain from acts which might threaten universal peace, it concerns even more the leaders of great powers. This is my appeal to you, Mr. President.

The Soviet Government's position in international affairs remains unchanged. We wish to build up our relations with the United States in such a manner that the Soviet Union and the United States, as the two most powerful states in the world, would stop sabre-rattling and bringing forward their military or economic advantage, because this will not result in improvement of the international situation, but in its deterioration. We sincerely wish to reach an agreement with you and other countries of the world on disarmament, as well as other problems the solution of which would facilitate peaceful coexistence, recognition of the people's right to the social and political system which they themselves have established in their countries, and would also facilitate true respect for the people's will and noninterference in their internal affairs.

Only under such conditions is it actually possible to speak about coexistence, as coexistence is only possible if states with different social systems submit to international law, and recognize as their highest aim the insuring of peace in the entire world. Only under such circumstances will peace rest on a sound basis.[1]

10. Speech by the Prime Minister of Cuba, Dr. Castro, Havana, 2 December 1961[2] (extracts)

. . . When we arrived in the Sierra Maestra, nevertheless, it was evident that there were certain aspects of the struggle which we proposed to carry out which had not been organised. That is to say, we had not even made a geographic study of the Sierra Maestra. We had not even previously formed an organisation there. A struggle could not have been begun in worse circumstances. Perhaps it is a good thing that these things be emphasised so that they can serve as an example to other exploited people. We did not know even one peasant in Sierra Maestra, and the only ideas that we had about the Sierra Maestra were those that we had studied in geography books. I am sure that if I ask anybody here what they learned in geography books on the Sierra Maestra, they would not know even one river of it. It is possible that they know that El Cauto has its origins somewhere in the Sierra Maestra, also the Contramestre and the Yara. What we knew about the Yara was the song "On the Rio Yara", that was all.

What I mean to say is that conditions were very difficult. Nevertheless, it is very true that where favourable objective conditions exist a revolution can be carried out, and only on the basis of objective conditions is it possible in an historic moment to make a revolution. It was more fully demonstrated because the other circumstances, the subjective ones, did not exist. We launched ourselves into that fight basing our beliefs on a series of suppositions, suppositions that were real . . . The theatre for the struggle was the mountains. Then began our task of organising the guerrilla movement, of giving it experience, acquiring experience and at the same time winning over the peasant masses for the revolution. It was perfectly logical that, under those objective conditions which existed in the Sierra Maestra, the revolutionary work was carried out to the extent that it could count with the almost unanimous support of the peasants of the Sierra Maestra. That is to say, already we could count on that social force, although with few arms, and a whole series of circumstances. The fight continued to develop and did develop throughout the entire country. The guerrilla struggle extended throughout the nation, first on the second front of Las Villas, and later on the second front of Oriente. The tactics which we used had triumphed. That is to say, events had demonstrated that under certain conditions the tactics were correct. Putschist-type tactics began to be abandoned, as well as organisation of forces in an attempt to gain power in a frontal fight, at great disadvantage, against the armed forces.

The tactics which we espoused wore away the forces of tyranny. In addition, it can be said that we have, because of this, a tremendous faith in guerilla warfare. We believe that in guerrilla war, under the conditions in our country which are similar to the conditions of many countries of Latin America—and do not think

[1] President Kennedy did not reply to this communication. For the statement of the United States Department of State on this message see *D.S.B.*, 8 May 1961, pp. 663–4.
[2] *S.W.B.*, Appendix to Monitoring Report, Second Series, No. 814, 7 December 1961.

because of this that we are promoting [Castro chuckles, and laughter and applause are heard]. You didn't let me finish [laughter]. That is what we seriously believe because we have every right to believe it, because we have had that experience. Naturally we know that when this belief reaches other people who are equally oppressed by imperialism, by the cliques at the service of imperialism and by the military castes, and who are equally exploited by the large landed estates in other countries where what happened in Cuba is also happening and where the peasants are hungry, exploited, landless, without schools, without doctors, without credit, without help of any kind; when these people are convinced of those things of which we were convinced and above all by things which have already happened, I am sure that there will be no force—be it imperialist, reactionary, military caste or the NATO army—which can in reality hold back the revolutionary movement. . . .

. . . What is it that makes it possible for a revolutionary movement to avoid what is happening in Santo Domingo and to prevent what reaction and imperialism have always attempted to do in every part of America? It is a revolutionary consciousness which has developed in the people and active participation by the masses. What was it that caused the manoeuvres of the American Embassy and reaction to disappear like a sugarplum in a schoolyard? Simply the general strike! It was not necessary to fire even one more shot. That was the right time to issue the call for a general strike. . . .

. . . We are sure that if a handful of any men who launch themselves into battle in countries where the objective conditions are found to be what we have in Cuba—and I do not refer to any country in particular [laughter and applause] —and this revolutionary movement, this group, fulfils the rules which should be fulfilled by a guerrilla, we are completely certain it would be the spark that would light the flame. . . .

. . . Undoubtedly we made a call at a premature moment, but what did this mean? It means that the subjective conditions predominated and the objective conditions were not known. Our revolution has many examples of everything. We did not want those conditions to exist. We wanted, with the simple call, to go on general strike and overthrow the tyranny. That is what we wished. But as it happened we converted our wishes into reality only in our imagination. What is it that a revolutionary has to do? He has to interpret reality. We did not interpret that reality and we made a mistake. The result was that there was no strike, because the conditions were not completely ripe, due to the tactics we used. Fundamentally, conditions were not ripe. The military forces of the revolution were less than 200 men. When we issued our call the second time, we already had entire provinces isolated. Complete units of the enemy were destroyed. The enemy was really broken up. On the other occasion the enemy had always done what he wanted, crossed any territory he wanted, and had always dominated the situation in the country. When the moment when the call is made is right, then the strategy and the conquest by the revolutionary power is carried out with the masses. That is what simply made the difference between a truly revolutionary movement and a coup d'etat.

What one factor had mobilised the masses? The guerrilla warfare was converted into the factor that mobilised the masses. The fight intensified. Repression intensified. The contradictions of the regime intensified and the people by themselves seized power. Power is taken with the masses. That was the first fundamental characteristic. Power can be liquidated, as can the military apparatus, the machinery that had maintained the regime. That is to say, a series of revolutionary laws could be and were implemented, but the seizure of power is for the masses.

The second factor is the liquidation of the apparatus of the military machine which maintained the regime of privilege. What is it that reaction and imperialism wish to accomplish? What do they try to preserve in any crisis? The history of Latin America is full of examples. What they try to preserve at all costs is the military apparatus, the military machine of the system. . . .

We, with the revolution itself, are every day more revolutionary. Was there a time when we were not revolutionary? There was a time when I had nothing of the revolutionary. Ah, but was it because I was a reactionary, a thief, corrupt? No, none of these! . . .

. . . I was a political illiterate when I ended college, and even when I was a student. Should I be ashamed to admit it? No! On the contrary, I feel very proud of knowing that I was a college student and knew nothing of politics or revolution. Nevertheless, today I know something about it, and that demonstrates that I have advanced somewhat [applause]. . . .

. . . Which is the most revolutionary class? The worker class, without any doubt! Why? Because its social condition makes it revolutionary. What are the reactionary classes? [Few indistinct words.] Their social condition makes them that way. Their mentality and their thinking become reactionary. But within the revolution there are many cases of revolutionary companeros from castes which are not workers' castes. What has happened in some countries with the presence of many nuclei of the middle class in the worker movement? They have tainted the workers' mind with the mind of the petty bourgeoisie and the middle class. That has happened. We have to fight so that will not happen. We have to fight and tremendously insist on revolutionary education. Why? So that the presence of many of those elements will not instill ideas that belong to a vacillating social class, which does not understand discipline, which despairs and has a whole series of vices.

We have to put special emphasis on educating the worker class, on continuing the political development of the most advanced nuclei of the worker class, and on raising to the highest possible level of political education the nuclei of the worker class. We must forge the revolutionary consciousness of the peasants of the sectors of the middle class that are with the revolution, of the students and of all the revolutionary sectors of the country. We must widen as much as possible the basis of the revolutionary movement.

What has made us revolutionaries? That which has made us revolutionaries is, first of all, the vocation to be revolutionaries, because when one comes from a social class that has not a revolutionary tendency, one is most probably not a revolutionary; secondly, the sense of inborn honour, that is to say that when people believe in something, they believe in it; when they believe in something else, they believe in that and they do it honourably, and when they believe they have found a truth they cling to it. . . .

. . . I always clung, as many have done, to things I discovered. In the university we began to have the first contacts with the Communist Manifesto, with the works of Marx, Engels, Lenin and the like. That was part of the process, I can honourably confess, because many of the things that we have done in the revolution are not things we have invented, not in the least. When we left the university, in my particular case, I was in reality greatly influenced. I am not going to say I was a Marxist-Leninist. Not in the least. It was possible that I had two million prejudices of a petty bourgeois and a series of ideas which I am very happy I do not have today. But fundamentally, if I had not had these prejudices I would not have been in a position to make a contribution to the revolution such as we have done. . . .

. . . I am a convinced revolutionary. Yes, I am a convinced revolutionary. . . .

. . . I consider myself more revolutionary than I was on 1st January. What was I on 1st January? I believe that I was revolutionary on 1st January! [Voice answers: 'Yes'.] That is to say, all the ideas that I have today I had on 1st January. Very well, I am at this moment a man who can call himself completely revolutionary. . . .

. . . Do I have any doubts on Marxism? I understand that some interpretations are mistaken and that it must be revised. I have not the slightest doubt [prolonged applause]. It occurs to me that, on the contrary, while we are taught more by life and while we know more about what imperialism is, not just words but the flesh and the blood of our people—while we have to confront imperialism more and more, while we know more and more what imperialist policy is in the entire world, in South Vietnam, in the Congo, in Algeria, in Korea and in all parts of the world; while we become more aware and see the bloody claws of imperialism, of miserable exploitation, of the abuses it commits in the world and the crimes it commits against humanity—more and more we become sentimentally and emotionally Marxist first of all; and we see more and discover all the truths contained in the doctrine of Marxism. . . .

. . . I have talked at some length on this subject, but it is simply to arrive at the following conclusion: When the revolution arrived in power it had two paths. It could remain on the existing social regime or go forward. It could remain within the capitalist system, within the imperialist orbit, within the criminal policy of imperialism in America, Asia and Africa, within the policy which associated with Franco in Spain, Adenauer, Chiang Kai-shek, all the military dictatorships and the colonialists of Algeria; or simply within the policy which would place our country where it should be, and that is at the side of the exploited countries, at the side of the oppressed people, at the side of the colonised people. Our country, seeing things with clarity, had never accepted being at the side of France against the Algerians, nor at the side of Franco against the Spaniards, nor at the side of Chiang Kai-shek against the great Chinese people, nor at the side of the imperialists against the South Vietnamese who struggle there for their independence, nor at the side of Portugal against the Angolans, nor at the side of Romula Betancourt against the Communist Party and the Leftist Revolutionary movement, nor at the side of the Somozas, nor at the side of all those regimes.

In spite of the fact that here the imperialist literature attempted to show differently, the great reality is that the policy of imperialism is exactly the same in Spain, in Nicaragua, in Cuba under Prio or under Batista, in Venezuela under Perez Jimenez or under Betancourt, in Peru under Odria or under Prado. From the point of view of the march of history in the world—from the point of view of the great effort being made by all the people to free themselves from hunger, poverty, exploitation, colonialism, discrimination, as the people of Asia, Africa and Latin America are fighting—we could never with a clear conscience be at the side of imperialism. It is possible that many people, stuffed with selected magazines, Yankee films, 'Life' magazine, UP and AP wires, which have told so many lies, may have come to believe that the policy of the United States was a proper, noble, and humanitarian policy as they have tried to make them believe. . . .

. . . The anti-imperialist and socialist revolution had to be made. The anti-imperialist and socialist revolution could only be one—just one revolution, because there is only one revolution. That is the great dialectical truth of humanity: Imperialism against imperialism is socialism. The result is the triumph of socialism, the surpassing of the stage of capitalism and imperialism, the establishment of the era of socialism and later of the era of communism [applause]. Let no one be frightened [pause]. Let no one be frightened, there will be no communism—in case there is some anti-communist out there—for at least 30 years [laughter]. So let us, including our enemies, learn to understand what Marxism is like in two words [Castro chuckles]. One cannot skip over the historic stage. Perhaps the historic stage which some underdeveloped nations can skip is the construction of capitalism. That is, they can begin the development of the economy of a nation, through planning and through socialism. What cannot be skipped is socialism. . . .

So it is that we are in the phase of the construction of socialism. Which socialism do you wish to apply? The utopian socialism? We must simply apply scientific socialism. That is why with all frankness I began by saying that we believed in Marxism, that we believe that it is the most proper theory, the most scientific, the only true theory, the only true revolutionary theory. Yes, I say it here with full satisfaction [applause] and with full confidence, I am a Marxist-Leninist [pounds the table] until the last day of my life [tumult and applause]. . . .

. . . [Socialism does not abuse its power; it struggles to overcome extremism and sectarianism.] It replaces the Government of oppression by a class, by an exploiting class over the working classes, with a workers' democracy, which is also in Marxist terminology the dictatorship of the proletariat [sustained applause]. However, because it is called a dictatorship of the proletariat, this does not mean that it is torture, murder or crime. No. That would be the dictatorship of the bourgeoisie, which meant torture, murder, robbery and arbitrary injustice. The government of the proletariat simply means that the class takes power to develop an historic cycle. It exercises this power over the rest of the classes against which it must struggle, during the entire phase of socialism.

. . . The criteria of selection for membership of the United Party of the Socialist Revolution will be strict. It is better to select before admission than to have to expel after admission. . . . [Membership open to all real revolutionaries willing to fulfil the norms and fully accept the Party's programme. No special privileges because of long membership of Socialist Party, of 26th July Movement or of the Revolutionary Directorate.] The party has not as yet been officially established as a party. The first congress has not yet been convened. It will be done. When? It is not pressing. It will be done. The important thing is that extraordinary progress is being made in integration and in union, and that this vanguard revolutionary organisation exists in fact, and that hundreds of schools are operating, and that more than 10,000 citizens are receiving revolutionary instruction. [The masses must be educated, not indoctrinated. That word to be eliminated. No one can be indoctrinated with Marxism, or against it. The function of the United Party of the Socialist Revolution is to organise and lead through the mass organisations, through its nuclei, and at the same time organise the people.] I believe that the ideal system, the most perfect one, yet found by man to govern a nation—a system which does not aspire to be eternal, but simply transitory, as transitory as the phases which it is called upon to encompass in the history of a nation, and the phases which it is called upon to achieve—is the system of government based on one revolutionary party, democratically organised and through collective direction; that is, the party must exercise executive functions. . . . I believe in collective leadership.

(c) United States Defence Policy

1. Special message of President Kennedy to the United States Congress on the Defence Budget, 28 March 1961[1]

In my role as Commander-in-Chief of the American Armed Forces, and with my concern over the security of this nation now and in the future, no single question of policy has concerned me more since entering upon these responsibilities than the adequacy of our present and planned military forces to accomplish our major national security objectives.

In January, while ordering certain immediately needed changes, I instructed the Secretary of Defense to reappraise our entire defense strategy, capacity, commitments and needs in the light of present and future dangers. The Secretary of State and others have been consulted in this reappraisal, and I have myself carefully reviewed their reports and advice.

Such a review is obviously a tremendous task and it still continues. But circumstances do not permit a postponement of all further action during the many additional months that a full reappraisal will require. Consequently we are now able to present the most urgent and obvious recommendations for inclusion in the fiscal 1962 Budget.

Meaningful defense budget decisions, however, are not possible without preliminary decisions on defense policy, reflecting both current strategic assumptions and certain fundamental principles. These basic policies or principles, as stated below, will constitute the essential guidelines and standards to be followed by all civilian and military personnel who work on behalf of our nation's security. The Budget which follows, if enacted by the Congress under its solemn duty 'to provide for the common defense', is designed to implement these assumptions

[1] *Public Papers*, 1961, pp. 229–40.

as we now see them, and to chart a fresh, clear course for our security in a time of rising dangers and persistent hope.

I. BASIC DEFENSE POLICIES

1. The primary purpose of our arms is peace, not war—to make certain that they will never have to be used—to deter all wars, general or limited, nuclear or conventional, large or small—to convince all potential aggressors that any attack would be futile—to provide backing for diplomatic settlement of disputes —to insure the adequacy of our bargaining power for an end to the arms race. The basic problems facing the world today are not susceptible to a military solution. Neither our strategy nor our psychology as a nation—and certainly not our economy—must become dependent upon the permanent maintenance of a large military establishment. Our military posture must be sufficiently flexible and under control to be consistent with our efforts to explore all possibilities and to take every step to lessen tensions, to obtain peaceful solutions and to secure arms limitations. Diplomacy and defense are no longer distinct alternatives, one to be used where the other fails—both must complement each other.

Disarmament, so difficult and so urgent, has been much discussed since 1945, but progress has not been made. Recrimination in such matters is seldom useful, and we for our part are determined to try again. In so doing, we note that, in the public position of both sides in recent years, the determination to be strong has been coupled with announced willingness to negotiate. For our part, we know there can be dialectical truth in such a position, and we shall do all we can to prove it in action. This budget is wholly consistent with our earnest desire for serious conversation with the other side on disarmament. If genuine progress is made, then as tension is reduced, so will be our arms.

2. Our arms will never be used to strike the first blow in any attack. This is not a confession of weakness but a statement of strength. It is our national tradition. We must offset whatever advantage this may appear to hand an aggressor by so increasing the capability of our forces to respond swiftly and effectively to any aggressive move as to convince any would-be aggressor that such a movement would be too futile and costly to undertake. In the area of general war, this doctrine means that such capability must rest with that portion of our forces which would survive the initial attack. We are not creating forces for a first strike against any other nation. We shall never threaten, provoke or initiate aggression—but if aggression should come, our response will be swift and effective.

3. Our arms must be adequate to meet our commitments and ensure our security, without being bound by arbitrary budget ceilings. This nation can afford to be strong—it cannot afford to be weak. We shall do what is needed to make and to keep us strong. We must, of course, take advantage of every opportunity to reduce military outlays as a result of scientific or managerial progress, new strategic concepts, a more efficient, manageable and thus more effective defense establishment, or international agreements for the control and limitation of arms. But we must not shrink from additional costs where they are

necessary. The additional $650 million in expenditures for fiscal 1962 which I am recommending today, while relatively small, are too urgent to be governed by a budget largely decided before our defense review had been completed. Indeed, in the long run the net effect of all the changes I am recommending will be to provide a more economical budget. But I cannot promise that in later years we need not be prepared to spend still more for what is indispensable. Much depends on the course followed by other nations. As a proportion of gross national product, as a share of our total Budget, and in comparison with our national effort in earlier times of war, this increase in Defense expenditure is still substantially below what our citizens have been willing and are now able to support as insurance on their security—insurance we hope is never needed—but insurance we must nevertheless purchase.

4. Our arms must be subject to ultimate civilian control and command at all times, in war as well as peace. The basic decisions on our participation in any conflict and our response to any threat—including all decisions relating to the use of nuclear weapons, or the escalation of a small war into a large one—will be made by the regularly constituted civilian authorities. This requires effective and protected organization, procedures, facilities and communication in the event of attack directed toward this objective, as well as defensive measures designed to insure thoughtful and selective decisions by the civilian authorities. This message and budget also reflect that basic principle. The Secretary of Defense and I have had the earnest counsel of our senior military advisers and many others—and in fact they support the great majority of the decisions reflected in this Budget. But I have not delegated to anyone else the responsibilities for decision which are imposed upon me by the Constitution.

5. Our strategic arms and defenses must be adequate to deter any deliberate nuclear attack on the United States or our allies—by making clear to any potential aggressor that sufficient retaliatory forces will be able to survive a first strike and penetrate his defenses in order to inflict unacceptable losses upon him. As I indicated in an address to the Senate some 31 months ago, this deterrence does not depend upon a simple comparison of missiles on hand before an attack. It has been publicly acknowledged for several years that this nation has not led the world in missile strength. Moreover, we will not strike first in any conflict. But what we have and must continue to have is the ability to survive a first blow and respond with devastating power. This deterrent power depends not only on the number of our missiles and bombers, but on their state of readiness, their ability to survive attack, and the flexibility and sureness with which we can control them to achieve our national purpose and strategic objectives.

6. The strength and deployment of our forces in combination with those of our allies should be sufficiently powerful and mobile to prevent the steady erosion of the Free World through limited wars; and it is this role that should constitute the primary mission of our overseas forces. Non-nuclear wars, and sub-limited or guerrilla warfare, have since 1945 constituted the most active and constant threat to Free World security. Those units of our forces which are stationed overseas, or designed to fight overseas, can be most usefully oriented toward deterring or confining those conflicts which do not justify and must not lead to a general nuclear attack. In the event of a major aggression that could not be

repulsed by conventional forces, we must be prepared to take whatever action with whatever weapons are appropriate. But our objective now is to increase our ability to confine our response to non-nuclear weapons, and to lessen the incentive for any limited aggression by making clear what our response will accomplish. In most areas of the world, the main burden of local defense against overt attack, subversion and guerrilla warfare must rest on local populations and forces. But given the great likelihood and seriousness of this threat, we must be prepared to make a substantial contribution in the form of strong, highly mobile forces trained in this type of warfare, some of which must be deployed in forward areas, with a substantial airlift and sealift capacity and prestocked overseas bases.

7. Our defense posture must be both flexible and determined. Any potential aggressor contemplating an attack on any part of the Free World with any kind of weapons, conventional or nuclear, must know that our response will be suitable, selective, swift and effective. While he may be uncertain of its exact nature and location, there must be no uncertainty about our determination and capacity to take whatever steps are necessary to meet our obligations. We must be able to make deliberate choices in weapons and strategy, shift the tempo of our production and alter the direction of our forces to meet rapidly changing conditions or objectives at very short notice and under any circumstances. Our weapon systems must be usable in a manner permitting deliberation and discrimination as to timing, scope and targets in response to civilian authority; and our defenses must be secure against prolonged re-attack as well as a surprise first-strike. To purchase productive capacity and to initiate development programs that may never need to be used—as this Budget proposes—adopts an insurance policy of buying alternative future options.

8. Our defense posture must be designed to reduce the danger of irrational or unpremeditated general war—the danger of an unnecessary escalation of a small war into a large one, or of miscalculation or misinterpretation of an incident or enemy intention. Our diplomatic efforts to reach agreements on the prevention of surprise attack, an end to the spread of nuclear weapons—indeed all our efforts to end the arms race—are aimed at this objective. We shall strive for improved communication among all nations, to make clear our own intentions and resolution, and to prevent any nation from underestimating the response of any other, as has too often happened in the past. In addition our own military activities must be safeguarded against the possibility of inadvertent triggering incidents. But even more importantly, we must make certain that our retaliatory power does not rest on decisions made in ambiguous circumstances, or permit a catastrophic mistake.

It would not be appropriate at this time or in this message to either boast of our strength or dwell upon our needs and dangers. It is sufficient to say that the budgetary recommendations which follow, together with other policy, organizational and related changes and studies now underway administratively, are designed to provide for an increased strength, flexibility and control in our defense establishment in accordance with the above policies.

II. Strengthening and Protecting our Strategic Deterrent and Defenses

A. *Improving our missile deterrent.* As a power which will never strike first, our hopes for anything close to an absolute deterrent must rest on weapons which come from hidden, moving, or invulnerable bases which will not be wiped out by a surprise attack. A retaliatory capacity based on adequate numbers of these weapons would deter any aggressor from launching or even threatening an attack—an attack he knew could not find or destroy enough of our force to prevent his own destruction.

1. *Polaris*—the ability of the nuclear-powered Polaris submarine to operate deep below the surface of the seas for long periods and to launch its ballistic, solid fuel nuclear-armed missiles while submerged gives this weapons system a very high degree of mobility and concealment, making it virtually immune to ballistic missile attack.

In the light of the high degree of success attained to date in its development, production and operation, I strongly recommend that the Polaris program be greatly expanded and accelerated. I have earlier directed the Department of Defense, as stated in my State of the Union Message,[1] to increase the fiscal year 1961 program from 5 submarine starts to 10, and to accelerate the delivery of these and other Polaris submarines still under construction. This action will provide 5 more operational submarines about nine months earlier than previously planned.

For fiscal year 1962, I recommend the construction of 10 more Polaris submarines, making a total of 29, plus one additional tender. These 10 submarines, together with the 10 programmed for fiscal year 1961, are scheduled to be delivered at the rate of one a month or twelve a year, beginning in June 1963, compared with the previous rate of 5 a year. Under this schedule, a force of 29 Polaris submarines can be completed and at sea two months before the present program which called for 19 boats, and two years earlier than would be possible under the old 5-a-year rate. These 29 submarines, each with a full complement of missiles, will be a formidable deterrent force. The sooner they are on station, the safer we will be. And our emphasis upon a weapon distinguished primarily for its invulnerability is another demonstration of the fact that our posture as a nation is defensive and not aggressive.

I also recommend that the development of the long-range Polaris A-3 be accelerated in order to become available a year earlier at an eventual savings in the procurement of the A-2 system.

This longer range missile with improved penetration capability will greatly enhance the operational flexibility of the Polaris force and reduce its exposure to shore-based anti-submarine warfare measures. Finally, we must increase the allowance of Polaris missiles for practice firing to provide systematic 'proving ground' data for determining and improving operational reliability.

The increases in this program, including $15 million in new obligational authority for additional crews, constitute the bulk of the budget increases—$1.34 billion in new obligational authority on a full funded basis, over a 4 year

[1] Of 30 January 1961. See above, pp. 3–8.

period though only $270 million in expenditures in fiscal 1962. I consider this a wise investment in our future.

2. *Minuteman*—another strategic missile system which will play a major role in our deterrent force, with a high degree of survivability under ballistic missile attack, is the solid fuel Minuteman. This system is planned to be deployed in well-dispersed, hardened sites and, eventually, in a mobile mode on railroad cars. On the basis of the success of tests conducted to date and the importance of this system to our over-all strategy, I recommend the following steps:

(1) Certain design changes to improve the reliability, guidance accuracy, range and re-entry of this missile should be incorporated earlier than previously planned, by additional funding for research and development.

(2) A more generous allotment of missiles for practice firing should, as in the case of the Polaris, be provided to furnish more operational data sooner.

(3) The three mobile Minuteman squadrons funded in the January budget should be deferred for the time being and replaced by three more fixed-base squadrons (thus increasing the total number of missiles added by some two-thirds). Development work on the mobile version will continue.

(4) Minuteman capacity production should be doubled to enable us to move to still higher levels of strength more swiftly should future conditions warrant doubling our production. There are great uncertainties as to the future capabilities of others; as to the ultimate outcome of struggles now going on in many of the world's trouble spots; and as to future technological breakthroughs either by us or any other nation. In view of these major uncertainties, it is essential that, here again, we adopt an insurance philosophy and hedge our risks by buying options on alternative courses of action. We can reduce lead-time by providing, *now*, additional standby production capacity that may never need to be used, or used only in part, and by constructing additional bases which events may prove could safely have been postponed to the next fiscal year. But that option is well worth the added cost.

Together, these recommendations for Minuteman will require the addition of $96 million in new obligational authority to the January budget estimate.

3. *Skybolt*—another type of missile less likely to be completely eliminated by enemy attack is the air-to-ground missile carried by a plane that can be off the ground before an attack commences. Skybolt is a long-range (1000 mile) air-launched, solid-fuel nuclear-warhead ballistic missile designed to be carried by the B-52 and the British V bombers. Its successful development and production may extend the useful life of our bombers into the missile age—and its range is far superior to the present Hound Dog missiles.

I recommend that an additional $50 million in new obligational authority be added to the 1962 budget to enable this program to go forward at an orderly rate.

B. *Protecting our bomber deterrent.* The considerably more rapid growth projected for our ballistic missile force does not eliminate the need for manned bombers—although no funds were included in the January budget for the further procurement of B-52 heavy bombers and B-58 medium bombers, and I do not propose any. Our existing bomber forces constitute our chief hope for deterring attack during this period prior to the completion of our missile expansion.

However, only those planes that would not be destroyed on the ground in the event of a surprise attack striking their base can be considered sufficiently invulnerable to deter an aggressor.

I therefore recommend the following steps to protect our bomber deterrent:

1. *Airborne alert capacity.* That portion of our force which is constantly in the air is clearly the least vulnerable portion. I am asking for the funds to continue the present level of indoctrination training flights, and to complete the stand-by capacity and materials needed to place one-eighth of our entire heavy bomber force on airborne alert at any time. I also strongly urge the re-enactment of Section 512(b) of the Department of Defense Appropriation Act for 1961, which authorizes the Secretary of Defense, if the President determines it is necessary, to provide for the cost of a full airborne alert as a deficiency expense approved by the Congress.

2. *Increased ground alert force and bomb alarms.* Strategic bombers standing by on a ground alert of 15 minutes can also have a high degree of survivability provided adequate and timely warning is available. I therefore recommended that the proportion of our B-52 and B-47 forces on ground alert should be increased until about half of our total force is on alert. In addition, bomb alarm detectors and bomb alarm signals should be installed at key warning and communication points and all SAC bases, to make certain that a dependable notification of any surprise attack cannot be eliminated. $45 million in new obligational authority will pay for all of these measures.

C. *Improving our continental defense and warning systems.* Because of the speed and destructiveness of the intercontinental ballistic missile and the secrecy with which it can be launched, timely warning of any potential attack is of crucial importance not only for preserving our population but also for preserving a sufficient portion of our military forces—thus deterring such an attack before it is launched. For any attacker knows that every additional minute gained means that a larger part of our retaliatory force can be launched before it can be destroyed on the ground. We must assure ourselves, therefore, that every feasible action is being taken to provide such warning.

To supplement the Ballistic Missile Early Warning System (BMEWS), on which construction is now proceeding as fast as is practical, the satellite-borne Midas system, now under development, is designed to provide about 30 minutes of warning by detecting missiles immediately after launching. Together with BMEWS, Midas would greatly increase the assurance and reliability of timely warning. I recommend that an additional $60 million in new obligational authority be added to the 1962 budget to accelerate completion of the development phase of the Midas program, with the goal of achieving an operational system at an earlier date.

For the next several years at least, however, we shall have to continue to provide a defense against manned bomber attack. Such an attack is most likely to coincide with, or follow, a ballistic missile attack seeking to incapacitate our anti-bomber defense system. Measures must therefore be taken to enhance the ability of the air defense system to cope with a combined attack. I recommend $23 million in new obligational authority be added to the 1962 budget for this purpose.

D. *Improving the command and control of our strategic deterrent.* The basic policies stated at the beginning of this message lay new emphasis on improved command and control—more flexible, more selective, more deliberate, better protected and under ultimate civilian authority at all times. This requires not only the development and installation of new equipment and facilities, but, even more importantly, increased attention to all organizational and procedural arrangements for the President and others. The invulnerable and continuous command posts and communications centers provided in these recommendations (requiring an additional $16 million in new obligational authority) are only the beginning of a major but absolutely vital effort to achieve a truly unified, nationwide, indestructible system to insure high-level command, communication and control and a properly authorized response under any conditions.

E. There are a number of other space and research programs related to our strategic and continental air defense forces which I find require additional support. These include missile defense and penetration aids, Dynasoar, Advent, Defender, Discoverer and certain other programs. An additional $226 million in new obligational authority is requested to finance them.

III. STRENGTHENING OUR ABILITY TO DETER OR CONFINE LIMITED WARS

The Free World's security can be endangered not only by a nuclear attack, but also by being slowly nibbled away at the periphery, regardless of our strategic power, by forces of subversion, infiltration, intimidation, indirect or non-overt aggression, internal revolution, diplomatic blackmail, guerrilla warfare or a series of limited wars.

In this area of local wars, we must inevitably count on the cooperative efforts of other peoples and nations who share our concern. Indeed, their interests are more often directly engaged in such conflicts. The self-reliant are also those whom it is easiest to help—and for these reasons we must continue and reshape the Military Assistance Program which I have discussed earlier in my special message on foreign aid.

But to meet our own extensive commitments and needed improvements in conventional forces, I recommend the following:

A. *Strengthened capacity to meet limited and guerrilla warfare*—limited military adventures and threats to the security of the Free World that are not large enough to justify the label of 'limited war'. We need a great ability to deal with guerrilla forces, insurrections, and subversion. Much of our effort to create guerrilla and anti-guerrilla capabilities has in the past been aimed at general war. We must be ready now to deal with any size of force, including small externally supported bands of men; and we must help train local forces to be equally effective.

B. *Expanded research on non-nuclear weapons.* A few selected high priority areas—strategic systems, air defense and space—have received the overwhelming proportion of our defense research effort. Yet, technology promises great improvements in non-nuclear armaments as well; and it is important that we be in the forefront of these developments. What is needed are entirely new types of non-nuclear weapons and equipment—with increased fire-power, and more suited to the kind of tasks our limited war forces will most likely be required to perform. I include here anti-submarine warfare as well as land and air operations. I recommend, therefore, an additional $122 million in new obligational authority to speed up current limited warfare research and development programs and to provide for the initiation of entirely new programs.

C. *Increased flexibility of conventional forces.* Our capacity to move forces in sizable numbers on short notice and to be able to support them in one or more crisis areas could avoid the need for a much larger commitment later. Following my earlier direction, the Secretary of Defense has taken steps both to accelerate and increase the production of airlift aircraft. A total of 129 new, longer range, modern airlift aircraft will be procured through fiscal year 1962, compared with the 50 previously programmed. An additional $172 million new obligational authority will be required in the 1962 budget to finance this expanded program.

These additional aircraft will help to meet our airlift requirements until the new specially designed, long-range, jet powered C-141 transport becomes available. A contractor for this program has been selected and active development work will soon be started. Adequate funds are already included in the January budget to finance this program through the coming fiscal year.

I am also recommending in this message $40 million in new obligational authority for the construction of an additional amphibious transport of a new type, increasing both the speed and the capability of Marine Corps sealift capacity; and $84 million in new obligational authority for an increase in the Navy's ship rehabilitation and modernization program, making possible an increase in the number of ship overhauls (as well as a higher level of naval aircraft maintenance).

But additional transport is not enough for quick flexibility. I am recommending $230 million in new obligational authority for increased procurement of such items as helicopters, rifles, modern non-nuclear weapons, electronics and communications equipment, improved ammunition for artillery and infantry weapons, and torpedoes. Some important new advances in ammunition and bombs can make a sizeable qualitative jump in our limited war capabilities.

D. *Increased non-nuclear capacities of fighter aircraft.* Manned aircraft will be needed even during the 1965–75 missile era for various limited war missions. Target recognition, destruction of all types of targets when extreme accuracy is required, and the control of air space over enemy territory will all continue to be tasks best performed by manned aircraft.

Expected phase-out of Navy and Air Force fighters by 1965, together with reduced numbers and increasing obsolescence of the remaining aircraft, make necessary the development of an advanced tactical fighter emphasizing non-nuclear capabilities. I am requesting $45 million in new obligational authority for this purpose.

Meanwhile, I am recommending $25 million in new obligational authority for the modification of the F-105 tactical fighter to improve its capability to handle conventionally armed ordnance items, and to increase its suitability for airstrips of all types of areas.

E. *Increased personnel, training and readiness for conventional forces.* I am recommending $39 million in new obligational authority for increases in Army personnel strength to expand guerrilla warfare units and round out other existing units, and an increase in the Marine Corps to bring it up closer to authorized strength levels. (In addition, personnel is being added to the Navy for Polaris crews, and to the Air Force for the ground alert expansion.) The sum of these personnel additions is 13,000 men. I am also recommending $25 million additional in new obligational authority for pay of retired personnel of the military forces.

But more personnel alone is not enough. I am recommending an additional $65 million in new obligational authority for increased readiness training of Army and Air Force units. These funds will provide for additional field training and mobility exercises for the Army and test exercises for the composite air strike forces and MATS unit. We recognize the role of exercises and deployments in demonstrating to our friends and opponents our ability to deploy forces rapidly in a crisis.

IV. SAVINGS MADE POSSIBLE BY PROGRESS

The elimination of waste, duplication and outmoded or unjustifiable expenditure items from the Defense Budget is a long and arduous undertaking, resisted by special arguments and interests from economic, military, technical and other special groups. There are hundreds of ways, most of them with some merit, for spending billions of dollars on defense; and it is understandable that every critic of this Budget will have a strong preference for economy on some expenditures other than those that affect his branch of the service, or his plant, or his community.

But hard decisions must be made. Unneeded facilities or projects must be phased out. The defense establishment must be lean and fit, efficient and effective, always adjusting to new opportunities and advances, and planning for the future. The national interest must be weighed against special or local interests; and it is the national interest that calls upon us to cut our losses and cut back those programs in which a very dim promise no longer justifies a very large cost.

Specifically:

1. Our decision to acquire a very substantial increase in second-generation solid-fuel missiles of increased invulnerability (Polaris and Minuteman) enables us to eliminate safely the last two squadrons of Titan originally contemplated. These would not have become operational until 1964, and at a cost of $270 million—a cost several times that of the Minuteman missiles we are purchasing for the same period and could increase with our stand-by facility. $100 million in the 1962 budget can be saved by this adjustment.

2. The phase-out of a number of B-47 medium bomber wings already planned will be accelerated to provide promptly the trained crews required for the expanded ground alert program. (Fiscal 1962 savings: $35 million.)

3. Additional personnel will also be made available by the immediate phase-out of the subsonic Snark airbreathing long-range missile, which is now considered obsolete and of marginal military value in view of ICBM developments,

the Snark's low reliability and penetrability, the lack of positive control over its launchings, and the location of the entire wing at an unprotected site. (Fiscal 1962 savings: $7 million.)

4. The acquired missile capability programmed by this message also makes unnecessary and economically unjustifiable the development of the B-70 Mach 3 manned bomber as a full weapons system at this time. The B-70 would not become available in operational numbers until well beyond 1965. By that time we expect to have a large number of intercontinental ballistic missiles, fully tested and in place, as well as a substantial manned bomber force mostly equipped with air-to-ground missiles. In view of the extremely high cost of the B-70 system, its lesser survivability as a ground-based system and its greater vulnerability as a ground-based system and its greater vulnerability in the air compared to missiles, its capabilities as a second strike system do not appear to have sufficient advantages over a much less expensive missile, or even a B-52 or successor bomber equipped with Skybolt, to justify a request in fiscal 1962 for $358 million.

We recognize, however, that there are still uncertainties with respect to the operational characteristics of our planned missile force. We also recognize that there are certain advantages inherent in a controlled force of manned bombers. To preserve the option of developing this manned bomber weapon system, if we should later determine such a system is required, I recommend that the B-70 program be carried forward essentially to explore the problems of flying at three times the speed of sound with an airframe potentially useful as a bomber, with the development of a small number of prototype aircraft and related bomb-navigation systems. We should also explore the possibility of developing a manned bomber system specifically designed to operate in an environment in which both sides have large ICBM forces.

Even on this more limited basis, the B-70 project will cost $1.3 billion before it is completed in 1967. Approximately $800 million has already been provided, $220 million is now requested for 1962—$138 million less than the amount included in the January budget—and the balance will be required in subsequent years. The total development program which I am recommending will cost $1.4 billion less than that previously planned.

5. Nearly fifteen years and about $1 billion have been devoted to the attempted development of a nuclear-powered aircraft; but the possibility of achieving a militarily useful aircraft in the foreseeable future is still very remote. The January budget already recommended a severe curtailment of this project, cutting the level of effort in half by limiting the scope to only one of the two different engines under development, although not indicating which one. We believe the time has come to reach a clean-cut decision in this matter. Transferring the entire subject matter to the Atomic Energy Commission budget where it belongs, as a non-defense research item, we propose to terminate development effort on both approaches on the nuclear powerplant, comprising reactor and engine, and on the airframe; but to carry forward scientific research and development in the fields of high temperature materials and high performance reactors, which is related to AEC's broad objectives in atomic reactor development including some work at the present plants, making use of their scientific teams.

This will save an additional $35 million in the Defense budget for fiscal 1962 below the figure previously reduced in January, and will avoid a future expenditure of at least $1 billion, which would have been necessary to achieve first experimental flight.

6. The January budget did not include funds for the continued development of the Navy's 'Missileer' fleet defense aircraft, but funds were included for the continued development of the Eagle missile—designed for use by the Missileer—in the hope that it could be adapted for use by some other aircraft. I am now advised that no such alternative use is in prospect; and I have directed the cancellation of that project, with a saving estimated at almost $57 million in 1961 and 1962.

7. The plan to install Polaris missiles on the Cruiser Long Beach has been cancelled. For effectiveness in a nuclear war, the money would be better spent on the far less vulnerable Polaris submarines. In a limited war, the cruiser's utility would be reduced by the presence of the missiles. (Savings in fiscal 1962: $58 million.)

8. Finally, technological progress causes obsolescence not only in military hardware but also in the facilities constructed for their deployment. We must continually review our nearly 7,000 military installations in the light of our needs now and in the event of emergency. Those bases and installations which are no longer required must be inactivated, and disposed of where feasible, and I have so directed the Secretary of Defense. He has already taken steps to have 73 domestic and foreign installations discontinued as excess to our needs now and at any time in the future; and studies are continuing now to identify additional facilities which are surplus to our requirements.

I am well aware that in many cases these actions will cause hardships to the communities and individuals involved. We cannot permit these actions to be deferred; but the Government will make every practicable effort to alleviate these hardships, and I have directed the Secretary of Defense to take every possible step to ease the difficulties for those displaced. But it is difficult, with so many defense and other budgetary demands, to justify support of military installations, with high operating and payroll costs and property values, which are no longer required for the defense of the nation. The closing of excess installations overseas will in many cases help alleviate our balance of payments deficit.

No net savings are expected to be realized in 1962 from these inactivations because of the added costs involved in closing, and no reduction in the 1962 budget are proposed on that account. Substantial savings, approximately $220 million per year, will be realized, however, in subsequent years.

(I am also proposing that $320 million of the obligational authority required be provided by transfer from the current balances of working capital funds in the Defense Department.)

CONCLUSION

Our military position today is strong. But positive action must be taken now if we are to have the kind of forces we will need for our security in the future. Our preparation against danger is our hope of safety. The changes in the

Defense program which I have recommended will greatly enhance the security of this Nation in the perilous years which lie ahead. It is not pleasant to request additional funds at this time for national security. Our interest, as I have emphasized, lies in peaceful solutions, in reducing tension, in settling disputes at the conference table and not on the battlefield. I am hopeful that these policies will help secure these ends. I commend them to the Congress and to the Nation.

2. President Kennedy's special message to the United States Congress on urgent national needs, 25 May 1961[1] (extracts)

The Constitution imposes upon me the obligation to 'from time to time give to the Congress information of the State of the Union'. While this has traditionally been interpreted as an annual affair, this tradition has been broken in extraordinary times.

These are extraordinary times. And we face an extraordinary challenge. Our strength as well as our convictions have imposed upon this nation the role of leader in freedom's cause.

No role in history could be more difficult or more important. We stand for freedom. That is our conviction for ourselves—that is our only commitment to others. No friend, no neutral and no adversary should think otherwise. We are not against any man— or any nation—or any system—except as it is hostile to freedom. Nor am I here to present a new military doctrine, bearing any one name or aimed at any one area. I am here to promote the freedom doctrine.

I

The great battleground for the defense and expansion of freedom today is the whole southern half of the globe—Asia, Latin America, Africa and the Middle East—the lands of the rising peoples. Their revolution is the greatest in human history. They seek an end to injustice, tyranny, and exploitation. More than an end, they seek a beginning.

And theirs is a revolution which we would support regardless of the Cold War, and regardless of which political or economic route they should choose to freedom.

For the adversaries of freedom did not create the revolution; nor did they create the conditions which compel it. But they are seeking to ride the crest of its wave—to capture it for themselves.

Yet their aggression is more often concealed than open. They have fired no missiles; and their troops are seldom seen. They send arms, agitators, aid, technicians and propaganda to every troubled area. But where fighting is required, it is usually done by others—by guerrillas striking at night, by assassins striking alone—assassins who have taken the lives of four thousand civil officers in the last twelve months in Vietnam alone— by subversives and saboteurs and insurrectionists, who in some cases control whole areas inside of independent nations.[2]

---

[1] *Public Papers*, 1961, pp. 397–406.
[2] At this point the following paragraph, which appears in the text as signed and transmitted to the Senate and House of Representatives, was omitted in the reading of the message:
They possess a powerful intercontinental striking force, large forces for conventional war,

With these formidable weapons, the adversaries of freedom plan to consolidate their territory—to exploit, to control, and finally to destroy the hopes of the worlds' newest nations; and they have ambition to do it before the end of this decade. It is a contest of will and purpose as well as force and violence—a battle for minds and souls as well as lives and territory. And in that contest, we cannot stand aside.

We stand, as we have always stood from our earliest beginnings, for the independence and equality of all nations. This nation was born of revolution and raised in freedom. And we do not intend to leave an open road for despotism.

There is no single simple policy which meets this challenge. Experience has taught us that no one nation has the power or the wisdom to solve all the problems of the world or manage its revolutionary tides—that extending our commitments does not always increase our security—that any initiative carries with it the risk of a temporary defeat—that nuclear weapons cannot prevent subversion—that no free people can be kept free without will and energy of their own—and that no two nations or situations are exactly alike.

Yet their is much we can do—and must do. The proposals I bring before you are numerous and varied. They arise from the host of special opportunities and dangers which have become increasingly clear in recent months. Taken together I believe that they can mark another step forward in our effort as a people. I am here to ask the help of this Congress and the nation in approving these necessary measures. . . .

III.[1] ECONOMIC AND SOCIAL PROGRESS ABROAD

I stress the strength of our economy because it is essential to the strength of our nation. And what is true in our case is true in the case of other countries. Their strength in the struggle for freedom depends on the strength of their economic and their social progess.

We would be badly mistaken to consider their problems in military terms alone. For no amount of arms and armies can help stabilize those governments which are unable or unwilling to achieve social and economic reform and development. Military pacts cannot help nations whose social injustice and economic chaos invite insurgency and penetration and subversion. The most skillful counter-guerrilla efforts cannot succeed where the local population is too caught up in its own misery to be concerned about the advance of communism.

But for those who share this view, we stand ready now, as we have in the past, to provide generously of our skills, and our capital, and our food to assist the peoples of the less-developed nations to reach their goals in freedom—to help them before they are engulfed in crisis.

This is also our great opportunity in 1961. If we grasp it, then subversion to

---

a well-trained underground in nearly every country, the power to conscript talent and manpower for any purpose, the capacity for quick decisions, a closed society without dissent or free information, and long experience in the techniques of violence and subversion. They make the most of their scientific successes, their economic progress and their pose as a foe of colonialism and friend of popular revolution. They prey on unstable or unpopular governments, unsealed, or unknown boundaries, unfilled hopes, convulsive change, massive poverty, illiteracy, unrest and frustration.

[1] Section II, 'Economic and Social Progress at Home', has been omitted.

prevent its success is exposed as an unjustifiable attempt to keep these nations from either being free or equal. But if we do not persue it, and if they do not pursue it, the bankruptcy of unstable governments, one by one, and of unfilled hopes will surely lead to a series of totalitarian receiverships.

Earlier in the year, I outlined to the Congress a new program for aiding emerging nations; and it is my intention to transmit shortly draft legislation to implement this program, to establish a new Act for International Development, and to add to the figures previously requested, in view of the swift pace of critical events, an additional 250 million dollars for a Presidential Contingency Fund, to be used only upon a Presidential determination in each case, with regular and complete reports to the Congress in each case, when there is a sudden and extra-ordinary drain upon our regular funds which we cannot foresee—as illustrated by recent events in Southeast Asia—and it makes necessary the use of this emergency reserve. The total amount requested—now raised to 2.65 billion dollars—is both minimal and crucial. I do not see how anyone who is concerned —as we all are—about the growing threats to freedom around the globe—and who is asking what more we can do as a people—can weaken or oppose the single most important program available for building the frontiers of freedom.

IV

All that I have said makes it clear that we are engaged in a world-wide struggle in which we bear a heavy burden to preserve and promote the ideals that we share with all mankind, or have alien ideals forced upon them. That struggle has high-lighted the role of our Information Agency. It is essential that the funds pre-viously requested for this effort be not only approved in full, but increased by 2 million, 400 thousand dollars, to a total of 121 million dollars.

This new request is for additional radio and television to Latin America and Southeast Asia. These tools are particularly effective and essential in the cities and villages of those great continents as a means of reaching millions of uncertain peoples to tell them of our interest in their fight for freedom. In Latin America, we are proposing to increase our Spanish and Portuguese broadcasts to a total of 154 hours a week, compared to 42 hours today, none of which is in Portuguese, the language of about one-third of the people of South America. The Soviets, Red Chinese and satellites already broadcast into Latin America more than 134 hours a week in Spanish and Portuguese. Communist China alone does more public information broadcasting in our own hemisphere than we do. Moreover, powerful progaganda broadcasts from Havana now are heard throughout Latin America, encouraging new revolutions in several countries.

Similarly, in Laos, Vietnam, Cambodia, and Thailand, we must communicate our determination and support to those upon whom our hopes for resisting the communist tide in that continent ultimately depend. Our interest is in the truth.

V. OUR PARTNERSHIP FOR SELF-DEFENSE

But while we talk of sharing and building and the competition of ideas, others talk of arms and threaten war. So we have learned to keep our defences strong—

and to cooperate with others in a partnership of self-defense. The events of recent weeks have caused us to look anew at these efforts.

The centre of freedom's defense is our network of world alliances, extending from NATO, recommended by a Democratic President and approved by a Republican Congress, to SEATO, recommended by a Republican President and approved by a Democratic Congress. These alliances were constructed in the 1940's and 1950's—it is our task and responsibility in the 1960's to strengthen them.

To meet the changing conditions of power—and power relationships have changed—we have endorsed an increased emphasis on NATO's conventional strength. At the same time we are affirming our conviction that the NATO nuclear deterrent must also be kept strong. I have made clear our intention to commit to the NATO command, for this purpose, the 5 Polaris submarines originally suggested by President Eisenhower, with the possibility, if needed, of more to come.

Second, a major part of our partnership for self-defense is the Military Assistance Program. The main burden of local defense against local attack, subversion, insurrection or guerrilla warfare must of necessity rest with local forces. Where these forces have the necessary will and capacity to cope with such threats, our intervention is rarely necessary or helpful. Where the will is present and only capacity is lacking, our Military Assistance Program can be of help.

But this program, like economic assistance, needs a new emphasis. It cannot be extended without regard to the social, political and military reforms essential to internal respect and stability. The equipment and training provided must be tailored to legitimate local needs and to our own foreign and military policies, not to our supply of military stocks or a local leader's desire for military display. And military assistance can, in addition to its military purposes, make a contribution to economic progress, as do our own Army Engineers.

In an earlier message, I requested 1.6 billion dollars for Military Assistance, stating that this would maintain existing force levels, but that I could not foresee how much more might be required. It is now clear that this is not enough. The present crisis in Southeast Asia, on which the Vice President has made a valuable report—the rising threat of communism in Latin America—the increased arms traffic in Africa—and all the new pressures on every nation found on the map by tracing your fingers along the borders of the Communist bloc in Asia and the Middle East—all make clear the dimension of our needs.

I therefore request the Congress to provide a total of 1.885 billion dollars for Military Assistance in the coming fiscal year—an amount less than that requested a year ago—but a minimum which must be assured if we are to help those nations make secure their independence. This must be prudently and wisely spent—and that will be our common endeavor. Military and economic assistance has been a heavy burden on our citizens for a long time, and I recognize the strong pressures against it; but this battle is far from over, it is reaching a crucial stage, and I believe we should participate in it. We cannot merely state our opposition to totalitarian advance without paying the price of helping those now under the greatest pressure.

VI. Our own Military and Intelligence Shield

In line with these developments, I have directed a further reinforcement of our own capacity to deter or resist non-nuclear aggression. In the conventional field, with one exception, I find no present need for large new levies of men. What is needed is rather a change of position to give us still further increases in flexibility.

Therefore, I am directing the Secretary of Defense to undertake a reorganization and modernization of the Army's divisional structure, to increase its non-nuclear firepower, to improve its tactical mobility in any environment, to insure its flexibility to meet any direct or indirect threat, to facilitate its coordination with our major allies, and to provide more modern mechanized divisions in Europe and bring their equipment up to date, and new airborne brigades in both the Pacific and Europe.

And secondly, I am asking the Congress for an additional 100 million dollars to begin the procurement task necessary to re-equip this new Army structure with the most modern material. New helicopters, new armored personnel carriers, and new howitzers, for example, must be obtained now.

Third, I am directing the Secretary of Defense to expand rapidly and substantially, in cooperation with our Allies, the orientation of existing forces for the conduct of non-nuclear war, para-military operations and sub-limited or unconventional wars.

In addition, our special forces and unconventional warfare units will be increased and reoriented. Throughout the services new emphasis must be placed on the special skills and languages which are required to work with local populations.

Fourth, the Army is developing plans to make possible a much more rapid deployment of a major portion of its highly trained reserve forces. When these plans are completed and the reserve is strengthened, two combat-equipped divisions, plus their supporting forces, a total of 89,000 men, could be ready in an emergency for operations with but 3 weeks' notice—2 more divisions with but 5 weeks' notice—and six additional divisions and their supporting forces, making a total of 10 divisions, could be deployable with less than 8 weeks' notice. In short, these new plans will allow us to almost double the combat power of the Army in less than two months, compared to the nearly nine months heretofore required.

Fifth, to enhance the already formidable ability of the Marine Corps to respond to limited war emergencies, I am asking the Congress for 60 million dollars to increase the Marine Corps strength to 190,000 men. This will increase the initial impact and staying power of our three Marine divisions and three air wings, and provide a trained nucleus for further expansion, if necessary for self-defense.

Finally, to cite one other area of activities that are both legitimate and necessary as a means of self-defense in an age of hidden perils, our whole intelligence effort must be reviewed, and its coordination with other elements of policy assured. The Congress and the American people are entitled to know that we will institute whatever new organization, policies, and control are necessary.

VII. Civil Defense

One major element of the national security program which this nation has never squarely faced up to is civil defense. This problem arises not from present trends but from national inaction in which most of us have participated. In the past decade we have intermittently considered a variety of programs, but we have never adopted a consistent policy. Public considerations have been largely characterized by apathy, indifference and skepticism; while, at the same time, many of the civil defense plans have been so far-reaching and unrealistic that they have not gained essential support.

This Administration has been looking hard at exactly what civil defense can and cannot do. It cannot be obtained cheaply. It cannot give an assurance of blast protection that will be proof against surprise attack or guaranteed against obsolescence or destruction. And it cannot deter a nuclear attack.

We will deter an enemy from making a nuclear attack only if our retaliatory power is so strong and so invulnerable that he knows he would be destroyed by our response. If we have that strength, civil defense is not needed to deter an attack. If we should ever lack it, civil defense would not be an adequate substitute.

But this deterrent concept assumes rational calculations by rational men. And the history of this planet, and particularly the history of the 20th century, is sufficient to remind us of the possibilities of an irrational attack, a miscalculation, an accidental war, [or a war of escalation in which the stakes by each side gradually increase to the point of maximum danger] which cannot be either foreseen or deterred. It is on this basis that civil defense can be readily justifiable—as insurance for the civilian population in case of an enemy miscalculation. It is insurance we trust will never be needed—but insurance which we could never forgive ourselves for foregoing in the event of catastrophe.

Once the validity of this concept is recognized, there is no point in delaying the initiation of a nation-wide long-range program of identifying present fallout shelter capacity and providing shelter in new and existing structures. Such a program would protect millions of people against the hazards of radioactive fallout in the event of large-scale nuclear attack. Effective performance of the entire program not only requires new legislative authority and more funds, but also sound organizational arrangements.

Therefore, under the authority vested in me by Reorganization Plan No. 1 of 1958, I am assigning responsibility for this program to the top civilian authority already responsible for continental defense, the Secretary of Defense. It is important that this function remain civilian, in nature and leadership; and this feature will not be changed.

The Office of Civil and Defense Mobilization will be reconstituted as a small staff agency to assist in the coordination of these functions. To more accurately describe its role, its title should be changed to the Office of Emergency Planning.

As soon as those newly charged with these responsibilities have prepared new authorization and appropriation requests, such requests will be transmitted to the Congress for a much strengthened Federal-State civil defense program. Such a program will provide Federal funds for identifying fallout shelter capacity in existing structures, and it will include, where appropriate, incorporation of shelter in Federal buildings, new requirements for shelter in buildings constructed with Federal assistance, and matching grants and other incentives for constructing shelter in State and local and private buildings.

Federal appropriations for civil defense in fiscal 1962 under this program will in all likelihood be more than triple the pending budget requests; and they will increase sharply in subsequent years. Financial participation will also be required from State and local governments and from private citizens. But no insurance is cost-free; and every American citizen and his community must decide for themselves whether this form of survival insurance justifies the expenditure of effort, time and money. For myself, I am convinced that it does.

VIII. DISARMAMENT

I cannot end this discussion of defense and armaments without emphasizing our strongest hope: the creation of an orderly world where disarmament will be possible. Our aims do not prepare for war—they are efforts to discourage and resist the adventures of others that could end in war.

That is why it is consistent with these efforts that we continue to press for properly safeguarded disarmament measures. At Geneva, in cooperation with the United Kingdom, we have put forward concrete proposals to make clear our wish to meet the Soviets half way in an effective nuclear test ban treaty—the first significant but essential step on the road towards disarmament. Up to now, their response has not been what we hoped, but Mr. Dean returned last night to Geneva, and we intend to go the last mile in patience to secure this gain if we can.

Meanwhile, we are determined to keep disarmament high on our agenda—to make an intensified effort to develop acceptable political and technical alternatives to the present arms race. To this end I shall send to the Congress a measure to establish a strengthened and enlarged Disarmament Agency.

IX. SPACE

Finally, if we are to win the battle that is now going on around the world between freedom and tyranny, the dramatic achievements in space which occurred in recent weeks should have made clear to us all, as did the Sputnik in 1957, the impact of this adventure on the minds of men everywhere, who are attempting to make a determination of which road they should take. Since early in my term, our efforts in space have been under review. With the advice of the Vice President, who is Chairman of the National Space Council, we have examined where we are strong and where we are not, where we may succeed and where we may not. Now it is time to take longer strides—time for a great new American enterprise—time for this nation to take a clearly leading role in space achievement, which in many ways may hold the key to our future on earth.

I believe we possess all the resources and talents necessary. But the facts of the matter are that we have never made the national decisions or marshalled the national resources required for such leadership. We have never specified long-range goals on an urgent time schedule, or managed our resources and our time so as to insure their fulfillment.

Recognizing the head start obtained by the Soviets with their large rocket engines, which gives them many months of lead-time, and recognizing the likelihood that they will exploit this lead for some time to come in still more impressive successes, we nevertheless are required to make new efforts on our own. For while we cannot guarantee that we shall one day be first, we can guarantee that any failure to make this effort will make us last. We take an additional risk by making it in full view of the world, but as shown by the feat of astronaut Shepard, this very risk enhances our stature when we are successful. But this is not merely a race. Space is open to us now; and our eagerness to share its meaning is not governed by the efforts of others. We go into space because whatever mankind must undertake, free men must fully share.

I therefore ask the Congress, above and beyond the increases I have earlier requested for space activities, to provide the funds which are needed to meet the following national goals:

First, I believe that this nation should commit itself to achieving the goal, before this decade is out, of landing a man on the moon and returning him safely to the earth. No single space project in this period will be more impressive to mankind, or more important for the long-range exploration of space; and none will be so difficult or expensive to accomplish. We propose to accelerate the development of the appropriate lunar space craft. We propose to develop alternate liquid and solid fuel boosters, much larger than any now being developed, until certain which is superior. We propose additional funds for other engine development and for unmanned explorations—explorations which are particularly important for one purpose which this nation will never overlook: the survival of the man who first makes this daring flight. But in a very real sense, it will not be one man going to the moon—if we make this judgment affirmatively, it will be an entire nation. For all of us must work to put him there.

Secondly, an additional 23 million dollars, together with 7 million dollars already available, will accelerate development of the Rover nuclear rocket. This gives promise of some day providing a means for even more exciting and ambitious exploration of space, perhaps beyond the moon, perhaps to the very end of the solar system itself.

Third, an additional 50 million dollars will make the most of our present leadership, by accelerating the use of space satellites for world-wide communications.

Fourth, an additional 75 million dollars—of which 53 million dollars is for the Weather Bureau—will help give us at the earliest possible time a satellite system for world-wide weather observation.

Let it be clear—and this is a judgment which the Members of the Congress must finally make—let it be clear that I am asking the Congress and the country to accept a firm commitment to a new course of action—a course which will last for many years and carry very heavy costs: 531 million dollars in fiscal '62—an estimated seven to nine billion dollars additional over the next five years. If we are to go only half way, or reduce our sights in the face of difficulty, in my judgment it would be better not to go at all.

Now this is a choice which this country must make, and I am confident that under the leadership of the Space Committees of the Congress, and the Appropriating Committees, that you will consider the matter carefully.

It is a most important decision that we make as a nation. But all of you have lived through the last four years and have seen the significance of space and the adventures in space, and no one can predict with certainty what the ultimate meaning will be of mastery of space.

I believe we should go to the moon. But I think every citizen of this country as well as the Members of the Congress should consider the matter carefully in making their judgment, to which we have given attention over many weeks and months, because it is a heavy burden, and there is no sense in agreeing or desiring that the United States take an affirmative position in outer space, unless we are prepared to do the work and bear the burdens to make it successful. If we are not, we should decide today and this year.

This decision demands a major national commitment of scientific and technical manpower, material and facilities, and the possibility of their diversion from other important activities where they are already thinly spread. It means a degree of dedication, organization and discipline which have not always characterized our research and development efforts. It means we cannot afford undue work stoppages, inflated costs of material or talent, wasteful interagency rivalries, or a high turnover of key personnel.

New objectives and new money cannot solve these problems. They could in fact, aggravate them further—unless every scientist, every engineer, every serviceman, every technician, contractor, and civil servant gives his personal pledge that this nation will move forward, with the full speed of freedom, in the exciting adventure of space.

X. CONCLUSION

In conclusion, let me emphasize one point. It is not a pleasure for any President of the United States, as I am sure it was not a pleasure for my predecessors, to come before the Congress and ask for new appropriations which place burdens on our people. I came to this conclusion with some reluctance. But in my judgment, this is a most serious time in the life of our country and in the life of freedom around the globe, and it is the obligation, I believe, of the President of the United States to at least make his recommendations to the Members of the Congress, so that they can reach their own conclusions with that judgment before them. You must decide yourselves, as I have decided, and I am confident that whether you finally decide in the way that I have decided or not, that your judgment—as my judgment—is reached on what is in the best interests of our country.

In conclusion, let me emphasize one point: that we are determined, as a nation in 1961 that freedom shall survive and succeed—and whatever the peril and set-backs, we have some very large advantages.

The first is the simple fact that we are on the side of liberty—and since the beginning of history, and particularly since the end of the Second World War, liberty has ben winning out all over the globe.

A second great asset is that we are not alone. We have friends and allies all over the world who share our devotion to freedom. May I cite as a symbol of traditional and effective friendship the great ally I am about to visit—France. I look forward to my visit to France, and to my discussion with a great Captain of the Western World, President de Gaulle, as a meeting of particular significance, permitting the kind of close and ranging consultation that will strengthen both our countries and serve the common purposes of world-wide peace and liberty. Such serious conversations do not require a pale unanimity—they are rather the instruments of trust and understanding over a long road.

A third asset is our desire for peace. It is sincere, and I believe the world knows it. We are proving it in our patience at the test-ban table, and we are proving it in the UN where our efforts have been directed to maintaining that organization's usefulness as a protector of the independence of small nations. In these and other instances, the response of our opponents has not been encouraging.

Yet it is important to know that our patience at the bargaining table is nearly inexhaustible, though our credulity is limited—that our hopes for peace are unfailing, while our determination to protect our security is resolute. For these reasons I have long thought it wise to meet with the Soviet Premier for a personal exchange of views. A meeting in Vienna turned out to be convenient for us both; and the Austrian government has kindly made us welcome. No formal agenda is planned and no negotiations will be undertaken; but we will make clear America's enduring concern is for both peace *and* freedom—that we are anxious to live in harmony with the Russian people—that we seek no conquests, no satellites, no riches—that we seek only the day when 'nation shall not lift up sword against nation, neither shall they learn war any more'.

Finally, our greatest asset in this struggle is the American people—their willingness to pay the price for these programs—to understand and accept a long struggle—to share their resources with other less fortunate people—to meet the tax levels and close the tax loopholes I have requested—to exercise self-restraint instead of pushing up wages or prices, or over-producing certain crops, or spreading military secrets, or urging unessential expenditures or improper monopolies or harmful work stoppages—to serve in the Peace Corps or the Armed Services or the Federal Civil Service or the Congress—to strive for excellence in their schools, in their cities and in their physical fitness and that of their children—to take part in Civil Defense—to pay higher postal rates, and higher payroll taxes and higher teachers' salaries, in order to strengthen our society—to show friendship to students and visitors from other lands who visit us and go back in many cases to be the future leaders, with an image of America—and I want that image, and I know you do, to be affirmative and positive—and, finally, to practice democracy at home, in all States, with all races, to respect each other and to protect the Constitutional rights of all citizens.

I have not asked for a single program which did not cause one or all Americans some inconvenience, or some hardship, or some sacrifice. But they have responded—and you in the Congress have responded to your duty—and I feel confident in asking today for a similar response to these new and larger demands. It is heartening to know, as I journey abroad, that our country is united in its commitment to freedom—and is ready to do its duty.

B. THE ATLANTIC ALLIANCE AND WESTERN EUROPEAN UNITY

(a) The United States and the Atlantic Alliance

1. Message of President Kennedy to the N.A.T.O. Permanent Council, 15 February 1961[1]

In my Inaugural Address[2] I pledged to the members of this great organization 'the loyalty of faithful friends'.

In the three weeks since I became President I have been increasingly impressed by the magnitude of the perils which confront the United States and free nations everywhere. But I have also been increasingly convinced that we can face down those perils, if we mobilize the unified strength and will of the nations of the Atlantic Community.

We of the Atlantic Community are the single most effective obstacle between tyranny and its desire to dominate the world. Our historic bonds of friendship have been strengthened by common values and a common goal—the creation of a world where free men can live at peace and in dignity, liberated from the bonds of hunger, poverty and ignorance. If we act together, this goal is within our grasp. If we falter, then freedom itself will be in mortal danger.

Therefore I pledge the United States, and my own unremitting efforts, to the support of the principles which guide our effort, to the basic concept of unity which gives us strength, and to the institutions we have created to give working life to our common intent.

Effective collective defense is the first mission of our great alliance in NATO. Our task here is to convince any aggressor that an attack on the territory of NATO members would be met with swift and punishing resistance. While relying also on the growing strength of all, the United States will continue its full participation in the common defense effort. I am convinced that the maintenance of U.S. military strength in Europe is essential to the security of the Atlantic Community and the free world as a whole. Strength in Europe, like strength here in the United States, is an essential condition of peace.

But the interests of NATO, and the Atlantic Community as a whole, are not military alone. The dangers to our security and the challenges to our enterprise take many forms—economic, ideological and political. Through its various instruments the Atlantic Community must equip itself to respond with speed and unity of purpose on every front—by improving our processes of consultation—by expanding the area of our cooperation to include common problems of trade and money, and by uniting in the effort to construct a sound, growing economy for the entire non-Communist world.

This last undertaking—the task of economic development—is vital to the preservation of freedom in the turbulent, emerging continents of Asia, Africa and Latin America; it is also a duty which the strong owe to the weak. It is an undertaking unmatched in scope, in difficulty, and in nobility of purpose.

[1] *Public Papers*, 1961, pp. 90–91.   [2] Above, pp. 1–3.

It is an important and heartening fact that the adventure of assisting the underdeveloped areas has captured the imagination and the idealism of the young on both sides of the Atlantic. This undertaking will require the efforts of all of us—and other nations too. In accomplishing all our economic tasks we must work together in a new intimacy in the OECD, and I hope that through the OECD we shall come firmly to grips with this fundamental problem of aid.

Although the technical task here is economic, our ultimate purpose transcends material considerations. The challenge is to create a new partnership between the old nations in the north and the new nations to the south. In the end, we must build that partnership not merely on a common interest in economic growth, but on a common commitment to the principles of political freedom.

The United States, because of its larger resources, is prepared to bear a heavy share of this burden. But I am confident that the nations of Western Europe will wish to commit an equitable proportion of their own growing resources to the common effort of economic development, as well as to the tasks of the common defense. Without that willingness our effort will surely fail. In all our common enterprises we must establish principles, clearly understood by our governments and our peoples, on which burden-sharing can be based.

We shall also continue to support and encourage the movement toward European integration. This movement is a powerful and unifying force which can multiply free Europe's strength and prestige, can assure increased security and progress for European peoples, and can contribute greatly to meeting the goals of the broader Atlantic Community.

The years ahead will be difficult and dangerous for the friends of freedom. There will be setbacks as well as gains. But if we face candidly the agenda that confronts us, our natural differences will fade and assume tolerable proportions. If we summon to the real tasks we face our resources of mind and will and material strength—if we never lose sight of our common goals—then we will have carried forward in our time the old task of our community: to preserve and extend the values of a civilization which has lighted man's way for more than 2500 years.

2. Speech by President Kennedy to the N.A.T.O. Military Committee, Washington, 10 April 1961[1]

Lord Mountbatten, members of the Military Committee, and Gentlemen:

I want to express my appreciation to you for your generous welcome this morning, and also to extend to you the warm greetings of the United States Government to the Chiefs of Staff of the nations of NATO as you assemble here for a meeting of the Military Committee. We of course take satisfaction in having your representatives with us regularly, in permanent session, but it is especially good, today, to have in Washington the Military Committee itself. Moreover, it is for me much more than a ceremonial pleasure to meet you.

You hold a critical responsibility in the affairs of NATO, and I want to talk with you about the substance of the task and about the necessary relation between you as military officers and others of us as political leaders.

[1] *Public Papers*, 1961, pp. 254–6.

NATO, as you gentlemen know, is at a turning point in military planning. In Supreme Headquarters and in many of the capitals of the alliance, work on our future needs is going ahead. As part of this effort, we in the Government of the United States are now well advanced in a careful study of our own view of the military policy of NATO.

Vice President Johnson explained last week in Paris[1] our belief that there should be a reenforcement of the capabilities of NATO in conventional weapons. NATO needs to be able to respond to any conventional attack with conventional resistance which will be effective at least long enough, in General Norstad's phrase, to force a pause. To this end, we ourselves mean to maintain our own divisions and supporting units in Europe and to increase their conventional capabilities.

In addition to strengthened conventional forces, we believe that NATO must continue to have an effective nuclear capability. We hope to consult closely with our allies on the precise forms which the nuclear deterrent should take in future years. In his address last week, Prime Minister Macmillan pointed out the urgency of this question.[2] The United States means to do its full share in working toward an effective solution of this problem, and we believe that the clarity and firmness of our own commitment to the full defense of Europe can be helpful in this direction.

The proper first forum on these matters is of course the North Atlantic Council, and moreover questions of this importance also require careful discussions in each country at the very highest levels of government.

But before I turn to other matters, let me comment briefly on one further military point. In our studies we have found a serious need for a sensitive and flexible control of all arms, and especially over nuclear weapons. We propose to see to it, for our part, that our military forces operate at all times under continuous, responsible command and control from the highest authorities all the way downward—and we mean to see that this control is exercised before, during, and after any initiation of hostilities against our forces, and at any level of escalation. We believe in maintaining effective deterrent strength, but we also believe in making it do what we wish, neither more nor less.

In stating this doctrine, I am reaffirming principles to which the responsible military leaders of NATO have always adhered—but I am also assuring you that the political leadership of the United States will apply both energy and resources in this direction.

And this brings me to my second main point. NATO is remarkable among the alliances of history in its combination of political, military, economic, and even psychological components. What NATO is, at any time, depends not only upon its forces in being, but upon the resolution of its leaders, the state of mind of its people, and the view of all these elements which is held by those who do not always wish us well.

In this situation, it is clearly necessary that there should be close understanding between political leaders and the senior military officers. In our countries, of course, final responsibility always rests with political authorities, and we also have a tradition of respect for the professional judgment of professional soldiers.

[1] *D.S.B.*, 24 April 1961, pp. 581-3.   [2] Below, pp. 69-78.

But in NATO, from the very beginning, it has been essential that neither class of men should accept any arbitrary division of our problems into 'the political' and 'the military' spheres. The crucial problems have always been mixed. Political leaders have had a duty to share with their senior officers a full understanding of the political purposes of the alliance, and military leaders for their part have had to recognize that in NATO all the important military problems are political problems also.

This recognition of the interconnection between policy and force is an even more compelling necessity today, especially in all the questions which relate to the command, the deployment, and the possible use of nuclear weapons.

In the months ahead, as we share in the framing of NATO's policy and in new decisions which must guide us safely toward the future, we shall need to have the closest and most understanding communication not only from country to country, but from soldier to civilian. Political planning must be aware of military realities, and military plans in turn must be responsive to political considerations —among them such varied and important matters as resource capabilities, national attitudes, and other alliance objectives like our common purpose to advance the economic welfare of the whole free world. Our force goals, our military policy, our deployments, and our war plans themselves must all reflect the purposes and spirit of our great community. Military and political problems are not separable, and military and political men must work ever more closely together.

I hold an office which by our very Constitution unites political and military responsibility, and therefore it is no more than my duty to pledge my own best effort to keep these two kinds of problems together in my mind. I ask the same of you.

In ending, gentlemen, let me turn for one moment from our problems to our accomplishment. NATO has kept the peace of Europe and the Atlantic through 12 dangerous years, and in that time our community has grown in strength and in well-being. This is no small accomplishment. I offer to you, and through you to all of NATO's armed forces, the thanks and congratulations of the people and the Government of the United States of America. Let us continue from this bright past to a future which offers us the high task of guarding a free community's peace, and its security, and its freedom.

Thank you.

3. President Kennedy's speech to the Canadian Parliament, Ottawa, 17 May 1961[1] (extracts)

. . . Ours is the unity of equal and independent nations, co-tenants of the same continent, heirs of the same legacy, and fully sovereign associates in the same historic endeavor: to preserve freedom for ourselves and all who wish it. To that endeavor we must bring great material and human resources; the result of separate cultures and independent economies. And above all, that endeavour requires a free and full exchange of new and different ideas on all issues and all undertakings.

[1] *Public Papers*, 1961, pp. 384–6.

For it is clear that no free nation can stand alone to meet the threat of those who make themselves our adversaries—that no free nation can retain any illusions about the nature of the threat—and that no free nation can remain indifferent to the steady erosion of freedom around the globe.

It is equally clear that no Western nation on its own can help those less-developed lands to fulfill their hopes for steady progress.

And finally, it is clear that in an age where new forces are asserting their strength around the globe—when the political shape of the hemispheres are changing rapidly—nothing is more vital than the unity of the United States and of Canada.

And so my friends of Canada, whatever problems may exist or arise between us, I can assure you that my associates and I will be ever ready to discuss them with you, and to take whatever steps we can to remove them. And whatever those problems may be, I can also assure you that they shrink in comparison with the great and awesome tasks that await us as free and peace-loving nations.

So let us fix our attention, not on those matters that vex us as neighbors, but on the issues that face us as leaders. Let us look southward as part of the Hemisphere with whose fate we are both inextricably bound. Let us look eastward as part of the North Atlantic Community upon whose strength and will so many depend. Let us look westward to Japan, to the newly emerging lands of Asia and Africa and the Middle East, where lie the people upon whose fate and choice the struggle for freedom may ultimately depend. And let us look at the world in which we live and hope to go on living—and at the way of life for which Canadians—and I was reminded again of this this morning, on my visit to your War Memorial—and Americans alike have always been willing to give up their lives in nearly every generation, if necessary to defend and preserve freedom.

First, if you will, consider our mutual hopes for this Hemisphere. Stretching virtually from Pole to Pole, the nations of the Western Hemisphere are bound together by the laws of economics as well as geography, by a common dedication to freedom as well as a common history of fighting for it. To make this entire area more secure against aggression of all kinds—to defend it against the encroachment of international communism in this Hemisphere—and to see our sister states fulfill their hopes and needs for economic and social reform and development—are surely all challenges confronting your nation, and deserving of your talents and resources, as well as ours.

To be sure, it would mean an added responsibility; but yours is not a nation that shrinks from responsibility. The Hemisphere is a family into which we were born—and we cannot turn our backs on it in time of trouble. Nor can we stand aside from its great adventure of development. I believe that all of the free members of the Organization of American States would be heartened and strengthened by any increase in your Hemispheric role. Your skills, your resources, your judicious perception at the council table—even when it differs from our own view—are all needed throughout the inter-American Community. Your country and mine are partners in North American affairs—can we not now become partners in inter-American affairs?

Secondly, let us consider our mutual hopes for the North Atlantic Community.

Our NATO alliance is still, as it was when it was founded, the world's greatest bulwark of freedom. But the military balance of power has been changing. Enemy tactics and weaponry have been changing. We can stand still only at our peril.

NATO force structures were originally devised to meet the threat of a massive conventional attack, in a period of Western nuclear monopoly.

Now, if we are to meet the defense requirements of the 1960's, the NATO countries must push forward simultaneously along two lines:

First, we must strengthen the conventional capability of our Alliance as a matter of the highest priority.

To this end, we in the United States are taking steps to increase the strength and mobility of our forces and to modernize their equipment. To the same end, we will maintain our forces now on the European Continent and will increase their conventional capabilities. We look to our NATO Allies to assign an equally high priority to this same essential task.

Second, we must make certain that nuclear weapons will continue to be available for the defense of the entire Treaty area, and that these weapons are at all times under close and flexible political control that meets the needs of all the NATO countries. We are prepared to join our Allies in working out suitable arrangements for this purpose.

To make clear our own intentions and commitments to the defense of Western Europe, the United States will commit to the NATO command five—and subsequently still more—Polaris atomic-missile submarines, which are defensive weapons, subject to any agreed NATO guidelines on their control and use, and responsive to the needs of all members but still credible in an emergency. Beyond this, we look to the possibility of eventually establishing a NATO sea-borne force, which would be truly multi-lateral in ownership and control, if this should be desired and found feasible by our Allies, once NATO's non-nuclear goals have been achieved.

Both of these measures—improved conventional forces and increased nuclear forces—are put forward in recognition of the fact that the defense of Europe and the assurances that can be given to the people of Europe and the defense of North America are indivisible—in the hope that no aggressor will mistake our desire for peace with our determination to respond instantly to any attack with whatever force is appropriate—and in the conviction that the time has come for all members of the NATO community to further increase and integrate their respective forces in the NATO command area, coordinating and sharing in research, development, production, storage, defense, command and training at all levels of armaments. So let us begin. Our opponents are watching to see if we in the West are divided. They take courage when we are. We must not let them be deceived or in doubt about our willingness to maintain our own freedom.

Third, let us turn to the less-developed nations in the southern half of the globe—those who struggle to escape the bonds of mass misery which appeals to our hearts as well as to our hopes. Both your nation and mine have recognized our responsibilities to these new nations. Our people have given generously, if not always effectively. We could not do less. And now we must do more.

For our historic task in this embattled age is not merely to defend freedom. It is to extend its writ and strengthen its covenant—to peoples of different cultures and creeds and colors, whose policy or economic system may differ from ours, but whose desire to be free is no less fervent than our own. Through the Organization for Economic Cooperation and Development and the Development Assistance Group, we can pool our vast resources and skills, and make available the kind of long-term capital, planning and know-how without which these nations will never achieve independent and viable economies, and without which our efforts will be tragically wasted. I propose further that the OECD establish a Development Center, where citizens and officials, and students and professional men of the Atlantic area and the less-developed world can meet to study in common the problems of economic development.

If we in the Atlantic Community can more closely coordinate our own economic policies—and certainly the OECD provides the framework if we but use it, and I hope that you will join as we are seeking to join to use it—then surely our potential economic resources are adequate to meet our responsibility. Consider, for example, the unsurpassed productivity of our farms. Less than 8 percent of the American working force is on our farms; less than 11 percent of the Canadian working force is on yours. Fewer men on fewer acres than any nation on earth— but free men on free acres can produce here in North America all the food that a hungry world could use—while all the collective farms and forced labor of the communist system produce one shortage after another. This is a day-to-day miracle of our free societies, easy to forget at a time when our minds are caught up in the glamor of beginning the exploration of space.

As the new nations emerge into independence, they face a choice: Shall they develop by the method of consent, or by turning their freedom over to the system of totalitarian control. In making that decision they should look long and hard at the tragedy now being played out in the villages of Communist China.

If we can work closely together to make our food surpluses a blessing instead of a curse, no man, woman or child need go hungry. And if each of the more fortunate nations can bear its fair share of the effort to help the less-fortunate— not merely those with whom we have traditional ties, but all who are willing and able to achieve meaningful growth and dignity—then this decade will surely be a turning-point in the history of the human family.

Finally, let me say just a few words about the world in which we live. We should not misjudge the force of the challenge that we face—a force that is powerful as well as insidious, that inspires dedication as well as fear, that uses means we cannot adopt to achieve ends we cannot permit.

Nor can we mistake the nature of the struggle. It is not for concessions or territory. It is not simply between different systems. It is an age old battle for the survival of liberty itself. And our great advantage—and we must never forget it—is that the irresistible tide that began five hundred years before the birth of Christ in ancient Greece is *for* freedom, and *against* tyranny. And that is the wave of the future—and the iron hand of totalitarianism can ultimately neither seize it nor turn it back. In the words of Macaulay: 'A single breaker may recede, but the tide is coming in.' . . .

4. Speech by President Kennedy at the Armoury, Boston, 29 May 1961[1] (extracts)

. . . I leave tomorrow night on a trip to France. . . . I go to France on this occasion not in order to invoke old memories, even though those memories are important, but to look to the future, of the close relationship which must exist between France and the United States if the cause of Freedom in the Atlantic community is to be preserved. And I go to pay a visit to a distinguished captain of the West, General de Gaulle, who has been involved for more than 20 years in a struggle to protect the integrity of Western Europe; and therefore I go with the good wishes of all of our citizens of our country as we pay a visit to an old friend.

I go also to Vienna, and I know there are some Americans who wonder why I take that journey. I am only 44, but I have lived in my 44 years through three wars, the First World War, the Second World War, and the Korean War. No one can study the origins of any of those three struggles without realizing the serious miscalculations, the serious misapprehensions, about the possible actions of the other side which existed in the minds of the adversaries which helped to bring about all those wars. The War of 1914, where the Austrians gave an ultimatum to Serbia and the Russians then mobilized and the French then in alliance with Russia then mobilized and then the Germans mobilized, and then when the Germans saw the French and the Russians mobilizing attacked through Belgium which brought the British in. One week before the British never would have dreamed they would be at war and I doubt that the French would. No one would have dreamed that two years later the United States would be involved in a war on the continent. In 1939 and 1940, after the loss of Austria and Czechoslovakia, finally the British guaranteed Poland, but there is certainly some evidence that Hitler never believed that the British would come to the assistance of Poland, and he never believed that the United States would again become involved in a great struggle on the plains of Europe. Certainly in the War of 1950 in Korea, the North Koreans never imagined that the United States would come to the assistance, by war-like means, of the Republic of South Korea, and we on our part did not imagine that the Chinese Communists would intervene as we approached to the north of North Korea.

Now we live in 1961, where freedom is in battle all around the globe, where the United States has intimate alliances with more than 40 countries, and where the communists in their meeting in Moscow and in the speech of the Chairman of the Communist Party, in his speech of January 6th, enunciated the Doctrine of the Wars of Liberation, where the possibility of escalation is always with us. I see value in talking to those with whom we're allied, but I also think it valuable at a time when both sides possess weapons of mutual destruction and annihilation—I think it's also valuable that there should be understanding and communication and a firm realization of what we believe.

So I go to see Mr. Khrushchev in Vienna. I go as the leader of the greatest revolutionary country on earth. I know that there is in some areas of the world, and even in some parts of the United States an image of us as a fixed society. Bernard DeVoto once said New England is a finished place, and some people may think that of the United States. That is not my view. When John Quincy

[1] *Public Papers*, 1961, pp. 417–18.

Adams went to call on the British Governor, before the Revolution, about the problem of the British here in this state, they had an amiable conversation until finally Adams mentioned the word 'revolution', and then he wrote in his diary 'It was then I saw his knees tremble.' Now, our knees do not tremble at the word 'revolution'. We believe in it. We believe in the progress of mankind. We believe in freedom, and we intend to be associated with it in the days to come. . . .

(b) Statements of British Foreign Policy

1. Speech by the British Prime Minister, Mr. Macmillan, at the Massachusetts Institute of Technology, 7 April 1961[1]

King William IV once received a deputation with these words: 'If my love for you equalled my ignorance of everything concerning you, it would be unbounded.' I'm afraid your international reputation is too wide for me to be able to advance a similar claim. Indeed the Centenary of the Massachusetts Institute of Technology is an awe-inspiring event. You were founded to teach 'the fundamental principles of positive science, with their leading applications to the industrial arts'. At that time no one could have foreseen the pre-eminent position which the Institute was destined to hold, not only in America but throughout the world. I am therefore all the more grateful for the great honour you have done to my country. First by awarding the atoms for peace prize to one of the most notable figures in British science—Sir John Cockcroft, secondly, by asking me to speak on this occasion. When you founded this Institution 100 years ago both your methods and your timing were right.

In these years the application of scientific techniques to the methods of production, distribution, transport, and the communication of ideas has set the whole human race on the march. This process will go on until it has revolutionized the whole conduct of human life upon this planet and no doubt beyond. You follow the scientific methods—by the ruthless logic of experiment. For you —as Thomas Huxley once said—the only tragedy is a hypothesis killed by a fact. We politicians must seem to your trained and professional minds hopelessly amateur. Sometimes we may have a success more by good luck than by good management. Thus, occasionally, by pure chance we may swing for the bleachers and collect a homer. Yet, for all your natural impatience without shortcomings you must feel a deep desire for your efforts to be matched by some comparable developments in social organisation and political thought. This is the link between your work and that of those who hold high political office. I therefore make no apology for talking to you tonight on a political theme. For if your achievements are not matched by the thoughts and deeds of political leaders, your work will be in vain—it will seep away into the sand. If the world is to progress the unity which science helps to promote must be matched by harmony in international relations.

Meanwhile we must face facts as they are. We must first achieve some unity of political purpose and method in the Western Alliance. Let us start with our two countries. Three years ago, after a visit to Washington, I spoke at Johns

[1] Text provided by the Prime Minister's Office, Admiralty House, London.

Hopkins University. I will only quote one phrase that I used, I said: 'Whether we like it or not—and I do like it—the destinies of the English-speaking world are inextricably intertwined'. At that time I was speaking in the presence of your President—my old friend and comrade President Eisenhower—whose life for twenty years was devoted to the joint purposes of your country and of mine.

Before coming to Johns Hopkins I had spoken also at De Pauw University in my mother's State of Indiana. There I declared my belief that if the progress of humanity was to continue, this word 'interdependence' must be the keynote of the second half of the twentieth century. I want tonight to consider with you what this belief means and how we can translate it into effective action. No easy task—for it calls for something even more rare than intelligence—it calls for decision and resolution. Now I have come to meet and take counsel with a new President at the beginning of his term of office.

In his inaugural address the President used these words: 'My fellow citizens of the world, ask not what America will do for you but what together we can do for the freedom of men.' This noble phrase certainly matched the level of events, and it has set the pattern for our talks together. In the same spirit let us look realistically and objectively at the state of the Free World to-day. How have we been getting on since 1958? To be frank, we have been doing fairly well but not well enough.

The vital centre of the Free World's resistance, our Western Alliance, is no better organised, whether in the field of defence, economics or political relations. If we have broadly held our own we have gained no ground. When I speak of the Free World, I mean the whole non-Communist world. There are of course many groupings of nations outside the Sino-Soviet *bloc*. Some of these are economic, some political, some cultural and some defensive. But the core of the Free World is our Western Alliance, primarily the Atlantic Community. On its strength and vitality all depends. For if we can organise ourselves in imaginative partnership at the centre, the effects of our unity will spread through all the world. Three years ago your President and I declared for interdependence.[1] To-day I say interdependence is not enough. We need unity—a wider unity, transcending traditional barriers; unity of purpose, of method, of organisation.

First, defence. Our Alliance will only be united if it is secure against aggression. Otherwise it can have no life or strength. There are two roads to security. The best, the cheapest, and the most sensible and the only one by which political man could match the successes of scientific man, is disarmament—comprehensive and effective; the only sure guarantee of peace. I do not speak of course of some mere paper treaty not commanding real confidence. I mean genuine disarmament, secured by effective controls—not a sham but a reality. Some day we may reach this goal which, up to now, like a mirage in the desert, always seems to recede the nearer we approach it. Certainly we shall persevere, for the prize is supreme. It is the banishment of fear.

Even if we did not want disarmament on moral grounds, we certainly need it on economic grounds. The cost of defence is a specially heavy burden on Britain and America—whether we think of it in terms of men, money or resources. It

[1] In a 'declaration of common purpose' issued on 25 October 1957; see *Documents*, 1957, pp. 400–3.

weighs upon both our economies partly by our huge internal expenditure and partly by the direct cost in foreign exchange. All this puts a serious strain on our balance of payments. We in Britain spend overseas on defence about $620 millions a year. Of this $210 millions goes across the Exchanges in NATO. The rest we use in the cause of peace throughout the world. The United States are faced with the same problems at home and abroad.

Meanwhile, until disarmament comes the Free World must be secure and united.

Nor, in this age of missiles, must we overlook our conventional forces. Our task is to keep them mobile, hard-hitting and up-to-date. Our military alliances all round the world are not aggressive or offensive. Their purpose is to see that little wars and adventures do not turn into great disasters. We must maintain these Alliances. They are permanent facts in modern life. But since unity is as important as security we must try to share the burden more efficiently. Surely it is illogical that our teams of military planners, scientists and technicians should waste any of their efforts duplicating work and projects. Of course co-operation is not easy. Everyone is in favour of it in principle. In practice they find it rather a nuisance. All the vested interests work the other way. Nevertheless it is a technical not a political problem which it should be in our power to solve.

Standing behind these conventional forces is the great weight of the Western nuclear deterrent power. This guarantees our security but here the implications of unity are more obscure and controversial. The first essential is that the deterrent should deter; this is self-evident and overriding. Secondly, an effective deterrent should not be wasteful. Of course in recent years the relative advantage of the West has greatly diminished. We cannot afford to be too weak either in weapons or in means of delivery. All the same it is almost as important not to try to be too strong. The calculation is not an easy one to make. For as the armament of democracy will never be used aggressively, it may need to be larger than that of a potential aggressor. The very size of the area which we have to protect dictates some dispersal, and perhaps duplication. Yet we cannot afford waste. Moreover, we must take care lest by building up our own security we perpetuate and encourage a nuclear arms race. That is one reason why I so earnestly hope for a successful outcome of the present negotiations in Geneva. The United States and Britain will do all we can to make this agreement with Russia to end nuclear tests.

But of course a Tests ban in itself will not give us nuclear disarmament. Meanwhile, the balance of priorities must be carefully weighed. The nuclear deterrent must take account of our necessarily defensive strategy. It must be effective and not wasteful.

If then our Western deterrent is both credible and efficient, what more do we need? May I suggest to you a third element. Although the nuclear deterrent gives us security, it is not yet so organised as to contribute fully to our unity. All of us here know that America and Britain, who at present control the Western deterrent, regard themselves as trustees for the Free World. I think sometimes we are a little smug about this. It is rather like the trustees of a private fortune, of whom the beneficiary once observed: 'They may be my trustees, but I am not sure whether they trust me.'

Why was it that after the war in my country under successive Governments, Labour and Conservative, we spent so many millions of pounds on a nuclear capacity? I will tell you. Although we in Britain have been accustomed for centuries to fighting our battles as part of an alliance, we have always been ready in the last resort to fight alone. There have been times when the world has not regretted our courage, even if they have judged it desperate. Sometimes people doubted our determination. It was so in 1914 and again in 1939 and I am not altogether surprised because it is very easy to misunderstand our national character. I only ask the doubters to look at the record and draw the moral. So our determination to make our own nuclear contribution was in a sense instinctive. And perhaps, with the Atlantic Ocean between us, it has been no bad thing for the people of Europe to see that at least one European member of NATO shares the nuclear power with you. Besides, because of our geographical position and the advantages of increased dispersal, our British nuclear force contributes far more to the total Western deterrent than its size alone would imply. At any rate this is a matter of history. Now let us turn to the position of our allies.

When Sir Winston Churchill made his famous speech at Westminster College, Fulton, in 1946,[1] he coined a memorable phrase. 'The awful ruin of Europe with all its vanished glories glares into our eyes.' How different is the scene to-day. Thanks largely to American help, poured out through the Marshal Plan and in other ways, the economy of Western Europe is buoyant—even booming. Above all, the spirit of her peoples is alive again. It is natural enough then that there should be some in Europe who feel unhappy that their nuclear defence should be left purely in Anglo-American hands. There are no doubt some who think that you and we might unleash the deterrent rashly; there are others who fear just the opposite—that we might both be too vacillating to use it at all until it was too late. Some fear our finger on the trigger; others fear our thumb on the safety catch. And so there is to-day—we might as well face it—a certain unease in the NATO alliance.

What are we to do about it? We do not want, naturally, to alarm and perhaps endanger the world by appearing gratuitously to encourage the uncontrolled spread of nuclear weapons from country to country. We want a ban—if we can get it—on nuclear tests. We do not want our allies to feel it essential to their honour or their safety to pour out their money in wasteful duplication. Probably the West as a whole does not need an increase in total nuclear power. Nevertheless this is a real problem. We cannot just ignore it. We must find a way of meeting the legitimate feelings of our European allies. Naturally every extension of trusteeship, every increase in the concept of partnership, has its dangers. But the health of our whole NATO alliance depends on finding a way of building a partnership in the nuclear as well as in the conventional field. The prize of this would be great—and a double one. The prevention of uncontrolled extension of nuclear manufacture and secondly the sense of real unity which would follow a new agreement with our allies.

In attacking all these problems in the field of defence we have the advantage of the new and fertile mind of a young and forceful President. In the spirit of

[1] Text in *The Sinews of Peace. Post War Speeches by Winston S. Churchill*, ed. Randolph S. Churchill (London, Cassell, 1948), pp. 93–105.

partnership we must review the burdens and the responsibilities. Some of these are uneven. This could be tolerated in the early years after the war with a shattered Europe to protect. But now, in the 1960s, we must look again at our system if it is to endure. In the same way the question of nuclear power is fundamental. Its organisation is an issue on which the unity of the Atlantic Community may stand or fall. These questions in my view cannot be evaded. They must be faced.

So far I have spoken of unity in the context of our military alliances. Is this enough? Surely not—and for this simple reason. Happily the present struggle in the world is not primarily a military one. The real test will not be on the battlefield but in the market place. It is now almost 15 years since the main structure of our present system for world trade and payments was designed. That was in the heyday of the East-West war alliance. The founders of GATT, the signatories of Bretton Woods and all the architects of our post-war system could not forsee the full economic effects of the great divide. World economic unity would have been hard enough to achieve in a world of 19th century nation States; it became impossible as the full effect of the Sino-Soviet system manifested itself. At the same time a new economic force has appeared in the world. The second Industrial Revolution has already swept through our developed economies. It is still only in its early stages and I am sorry to have to tell this audience that it is largely your fault. For this revolution is of a scientific and technological character. And these technical developments overleap national frontiers. They require for their effective exploitation even larger economic units. I readily admit that in spite of these new factors our international trading and financial arrangements have somehow or another managed to carry a great increase in world production and trade. But no wonder they are now beginning to creak and groan. For they are really an old model. Sooner or later they will have to be traded in. There are now three main problems to be resolved. The first is how to maximise world trade. This is essential to the prosperity of developed and undeveloped countries alike. Secondly, how are we best to organise assistance and capital to build up the less developed countries? Our common humanity cries out to us to help here, and our economic interest in new markets encourages us and finally political necessity compels us. Lastly how are we to finance an ever increasing volume of trade and aid? If our monetary arrangements are bad, or outmoded, we shall not succeed. We shall stagnate instead of expand. And Capitalism must expand or perish. Even Marx knew that.

First, how to organise world trade. Are the present international trading arrangements and institutions, evolved 15 years ago in quite different conditions, really appropriate to the circumstances of the sixties? We all still think too cautiously, and too parochially. We need to think not so much nationally or even in terms of greater economic co-operation between nations but in terms of wider groupings. For the advantages of size, of large areas transcending national boundaries where capital and labour and goods can move without impediment— these are surely more manifest to us year by year. In Britain we are already in the centre of two important trading groups—the Commonwealth and the European Free Trade Association. The Commonwealth trading structure came into being during the great depression between the two wars. It is based on a preferential system between the partners, with free entry into the United Kingdom. But the new developments in Europe are of a different order. The six Common Market countries are successfully forming a full Customs Union which bids fair to be as great in population and strength as that of the United States itself. The Seven—now, with Finland, the Eight—have constituted the European Free Trade Association. Elsewhere in the world similar groupings are in prospect. What then are we to do? Well, there are, of course the pessimists—who observe progress, and deplore it; those who think it is always better to travel despondently than to arrive. These people will no doubt try to reverse these trends: or they will ignore them and pretend that nothing has happened. Surely what we have to do is to use these developments for the benefit of the whole free world. I have no doubt of what our aim should be. We ought to try to work for the largest area of free trade that we can create.

Free trade for a Free World. That may still be but a vision. It may be a long time before it can take practical shape. Yet many new and vital ideas are now being discussed by practical men which a few years ago would have been dismissed as impractical dreams. Some of these policies and plans would be quite revolutionary in their effects. Others are more in the nature of palliatives. There are naturally widely different views and cross currents but there is a new spirit abroad in the world—you can feel it everywhere. The young are intoxicated by it and the old happily reinvigorated. It is the spirit of enterprise and adventure moving into the second half of the twentieth century and soon to knock at the door of the twenty-first. For us in Europe the urgent need is that of bringing together the Six and the Seven—now the Six and the Eight. I believe that we must and we can do this without detriment to our domestic interests or to our Commonwealth association and without injury to any other nation or group of nations. A comprehensive arrangement in Western Europe; not highly protective; looking outwards and not inwards; building up its own strength but ready to help others; this would be a real benefit to the whole Free World, both economically and politically. Economically it would take us nearer to a still bigger area of free trade. It would prevent much duplication of investment. It would stimulate trade and demand. Nor do I believe that a comprehensive European group would harm the United States. United States industry has in the past always maintained its share of expanding trade. The pattern varies across the great range of industry but the broad picture remains. A European settlement will bring great economic benefits. The political gains will be even more significant. The consequences of the economic division of Western Europe are only just beginning to make themselves felt in the political field. Yet if this economic division persists, the political rift will inevitably widen and deepen. This must, sooner or later, affect our military coherence and strength. It will be a canker gnawing at the very core of the Western Alliance.

If new and extended patterns of trade are vital for us and our future they are equally important for the less industrialised countries. These countries have two material needs from us. They want more aid and they want more trade. Of course, in my view, trade is really better than aid both with nations and with individuals. An intelligent and energetic man should be able to earn more money than he will ever be able to beg or borrow from his friends and relations. But trade cannot be confined to primary products, important as these are. Of course there are difficulties for the industrialised countries in accepting increased imports of manufactured goods from developing countries. There is the possibility that sudden or unrestrained increases over a limited range of products can cause too great a disruption for our own producers. We must try to deal with these cases by means of friendly agreement with the country concerned. You have done this with Japan. We have done it with Hong Kong. But the broad rule should be to admit goods as freely as possible subject only to special modifications when these are essential to prevent disruption for our own producers. All the same primary products are still the life blood of many less industrialised and less developed countries. And so expanding trade by the industrialised countries is often the best way to help. For such expanding trade stimulates the demand for primary products. Between 1950 and 1951 commodity prices went up over 20 per cent. That was during the Korean boom. By 1960 they had fallen again below the 1950 level. It would certainly not help the primary producers to try to push prices artificially high. But there are many schemes for particular commodities which have helped to iron out violent fluctuations in the short term and to give some stability to prices. We must study these problems—urgently. In its various aspects trade, then, is of paramount importance. But trade does need supplementing by aid. In this, up to now, the record of the West compares favourably—more than favourably—with that of the Communists. In my speech to the General Assembly of the United Nations last September I gave the figures. They are startling and unanswerable. Yet I am not sure that the West always get the full credit for what we do. For much of our help is provided through such bodies as the World Bank and now the International Development Association. But although these are within the framework of the United Nations, they are boycotted by the Communist countries. I do not see why we should be content to hide our light under this bushel. That is why I welcome our new—and entirely free world—machinery. The newly-constituted O.E.C.D.—and now under an American suggestion to be supplemented by D.A.G.—strange initials, under whose frigid exterior is concealed a rare warmth of kindness and imagination.

Trade and aid are very important. But the medium for both must be money —enough money. Of course economists are apt to make heavy weather about money. Naturally—it's their mystery. But it is really quite simple. Just as each individual country painfully acquired a central banking system, so there ought— ideally—to be a central banking system for all the countries of the Free World. We are still a long way from that although, with the various international institutions which have come into being since the war and with the closer co-operation of Central Banks, we are groping our way forward. The present system is certainly not perfect. As technicians, you wouldn't tolerate it in your sphere. First there is the imbalance of payments. If you will forgive such a frivolous comparison our system now is rather like a children's game. When the family sit round to play rummy, or cooncan, or poker, and one child gets all the chips and another has not enough to go on, something must be done. Either more chips must come out of the Bank (which Father generally keeps) or the winning children must hand over some of theirs to the others. Otherwise the game just stops. So in the modern world, if one country were to accumulate all the reserves and

D.I.A.–D

lock them up, our system could not go on. I do not suggest blame to any particular countries for the present imbalance of world payments and reserves. This imbalance is in a sense only the external result of policies arising from the often contradictory fears of individual countries.

In the United Kingdom we have a horror of mass unemployment. That dates back to the time between the Wars. Now, we have full employment—in many parts of the country more jobs than men. On the other hand we have to worry about other dangers—inflation and balance of payments difficulties. In Germany they have different priorities; they worry more about inflation than about unemployment. That too is for historical reasons—because of their double experience of inflation when, in Voltaire's vivid phrase, paper was reduced to its intrinsic value. All these different national niceties—different in France, Italy and Japan—all create international difficulties. So much for imbalance but then there is the volume of money. For imbalance of payments is only one aspect of the problem of money. Imbalance deals with who has the chips—or the money—at any given moment. But is there enough money? World trade has expanded four times in terms of money since before the last war. Yet the Free World credit base is only twice as big. No wonder some people argue that we just have not got enough reserves in total and must create more so as to finance expanding trade. All sorts of remedies are being suggested. The main difficulty about many of them is what I might call the mental hurdles which they present. It is normal to think of money as something painfully acquired; a dollar represents so many drops of sweat or so many ulcers. There seems to be something immoral in increasing the credit base by mutual agreement. It is done often enough in our internal economies; but the extension to the international field is hard to swallow. All the same, I repeat, expanding trade needs expanding money.

So there are three elements in the economic problem of the free world—trade, development and finance. They are closely linked. The needs of our time demand a new attitude to all of them. An old fashioned or doctrinaire approach is not good enough. We must use the energy and abundance of our free enterprise system to transform our economic life. Above all, we must try to jump—even the older ones among us—the mental hurdles. If the political leaders in the great countries of the world have but the will, the experts will doubtless find the way or rather several ways—for us to choose from. But we must have the will. I will sum up then. We must be ready first to welcome the progressive development of new trading arrangements and to see in them a means of moving towards a wider system of unfettered trade throughout the free world as a whole. Secondly, the industrialised nations must accept their responsibility for raising living standards in the less developed countries, both by trade and aid. Thirdly, we must ensure that the credit system in the free world is adjusted to these needs and that money becomes the servant and not the master of man's needs. This complex of economic questions is the second great problem whose issue may be decisive for our way of life.

I remember one of our great judges remonstrating with a somewhat prolix barrister, pleading in his court, with these words: 'There is in chemistry what is called saturation point—I have reached it.' Nevertheless, at the risk of earning from you a similar rebuke I must repeat—my theme is Unity. In certain spheres, at least, we must reach out beyond interdependence to united action. I have tried to show how we might do this in the military and the economic fields. Should we also attempt to consider a greater political unity or even union. We must try of course to agree on our policies and to unite in pursuing them. But if the West were to become as monolithic as the Soviet *bloc* we should lose that very independence of spirit in which we believe. In any case our diverse national traditions are strong and fruitful. It would be folly to tamper with the loyalties for which men will strive and sacrifice. So when we call for unity in the Free World we should not—at any rate at this moment in history—think in terms of a politically federated or unitary State.

A World Government seems far away, and even a Free World Government is only a distant dream. Nevertheless the nature of the struggle for the minds and hearts of men is such that no one country, not even the greatest, can hope to stand alone. The first lesson for us to accept, therefore, is that our political ideas must never be nationalistic in the narrow sense. It is no longer right to consider policies exclusively in relation to the United States or Britain; even Europe or the Americas or the Commonwealth are not big enough. And that means a revolution in our thought. We in Europe will no longer be able to indulge in dreams of self-sufficiency—let alone the wilder chimera of being a Third Force between the United States and the Soviet *bloc*. You in America will have to resist the temptation to think of Europe as a cross between a bear-garden and an Old Curiosity Shop with certain undoubted tourist attractions. Nor must we forget that the Free World is far larger than any military alliances. There are many nations who would not wish to join us in these groupings but are nevertheless at one with us in the strong determination to preserve their independence and their own way of life. A few weeks ago a meeting of the Prime Ministers of the Commonwealth was held in London. Twenty years ago this body consisted of only five countries, all of European stock. Now there are more than double including members in Asia and Africa. The Commonwealth represents the triumphant evolution of our colonial policy. For we have given these countries the twin benefits of freedom and order. Nowadays the Commonwealth includes some of the most important non-Communist countries, not ranged with us militarily, but spiritually and ideally our partners.

This recent meeting, as you have heard, had its melancholy side. But the decision of South Africa to leave us—I hope only temporarily—has at least underlined the essential characteristic of the Commonwealth to-day. It is an association of many different races and peoples. It is dedicated to the ideal that all peoples, of whatever race, colour or creed, should have full equality of opportunity in their own countries and in the world.

To sum up you and we believe that individual peoples and individual nations should be free to pursue their own ideals, and that this is compatible with widely different cultures and traditions. The Communists, on the other hand, have an ideology which insists that it alone is right, and inspired by this rigid creed, Communism seeks to impose its own system on the world.

Our unity, therefore, cannot be enforced. It must develop freely—not as a result of external conquests, as with some great empires in the past, but through an organic and conscious growth. If then we can reach out towards unity in our defence, in our trading policies, in our economic life and in our political thought, shall we in the West have won the world struggle? At least we shall have put ourselves in a position not to lose. This whole generation are taking part in a great and dramatic debate—conducted, not just by words or thoughts, but with all the formidable apparatus of power. Its result will be judged by the harsh tests of practical success. Nevertheless, the struggle between what we call the Communist *bloc* and the Free World is fundamentally an attempt to decide between two concepts of humanity. I will call them the idealist and the materialist. Will man's destiny be fulfilled when once all men can satisfy their material needs? Or is there some deeper purpose, some higher power of which our bodies are only the transient manifestation?

This great debate goes on across the world. It is not daunted by frontiers nor shut out by censorship. Sooner or later, if not already, men and women in the Communist world will seek once more the answer to the eternal questions. Why are we here; what is life's purpose; is there a right and a wrong; is there God? Our Faith tells us that they will ask these questions and that in due course they will find themselves forced to answer them in the idealist sense. Then the great struggle on which we are now engaged may suddenly seem irrelevant and become a mere disagreement as to the best forms of social organisation. It is against that day that we must prepare and until that day that we must hold on and hold together. This does not mean that we should abandon our efforts to use the United Nations Organisation to the full. For it does at least stand among all nations for the principle of international law, as the basis for international life. Nevertheless, it would be foolish to disregard the pressures now being exercised and the attempts of the Communists to turn the United Nations Organisation not into a forum of negotiation, but into an arena for propaganda.

Therefore, while we must struggle on to make the United Nations a success, we in the Free World must strengthen rather than weaken our own unity. These measures which I have suggested, and others which will become necessary, are the essential framework to buttress our endurance. If these things are not done, then our Western free idealist way will fall apart, and our disunity and weakness will discourage those very elements in the Communist world which otherwise in time under Providence will work its salvation and our release. There is always change and movement in our lives. History does not stand still. Unless we work for greater unity now we shall slide into division. The time is short. Let there be no delay.

2. Speech by the British Foreign Secretary, Lord Home, to the Council on Foreign Relations, Chicago, 16 June 1961[1]

Chicago has in the past been associated in British minds with the political doctrine of isolationism. Yet too the very existence of the Chicago Council on Foreign Relations, and of the English Speaking Union, the presence here to-day of so many distinguished citizens, and the impressive list of speakers of all

[1] Foreign Office Press Release.

nationalities who have addressed you in the past shows how out of date general impressions can be.

Chicago, I had always thought, was a dangerous place for the British—a place where elections were fought on the issue of a certain King George. And yet no city on the North American continent gave Her Majesty the Queen a more wonderful welcome when she visited you in 1959. Long memories and generosity contended; and generosity won.

On this evidence, I decided it was safe for me to accept your invitation. Thank you for it. I am very glad that I came. Not only to meet you and see something of your great city; but to bring our ideas about each other up to date.

I start from one basic premise. If there is to be peace and progress in the world, there must be clarity and understanding between Britain and America. And our understanding depends in its turn upon speaking our minds as friends and allies.

So I should like to talk to you about our outlook on world affairs, telling you where Britain stands upon them in the 20th century world.

Let me begin with the major preoccupation of our day: East-West relations.

It is, I think, common knowledge that the Communists are out to impose their system on the rest of the world: they certainly lose no opportunity of saying so: that, thanks to Western determination to preserve the balance of power by maintaining the nuclear deterrent, they have come to realise that they cannot win their ideological victory by war; and that they are employing instead every form of political, economic and ideological warfare for which they have invented the disarming label 'peaceful co-existence'.

That much is generally known. What is not so generally understood is the pattern and variety of the offensives that they are launching on the political front. Let me enumerate some of them.

At the General Assembly of the United Nations last year they mounted a personal attack on the Secretary-General of the United Nations and proposed his replacement by a triumvirate: one to represent the West, one the East and one the neutral nations. I doubt if the neutrals, with their variety of interests and their distaste for *blocs* think well of this. What all of us must realise is that in practice this means introducing the veto into the heart of the United Nations working machinery, the Secretariat. It does more than that, it declares openly for the first time since the Charter was written that one group of Powers intend to use the Secretariat openly to promote their own political creed. If that practice prevails, it is goodbye to an international civil service and to the United Nations.

It may not be apparent yet that this was no isolated foray. They are now trying to introduce this 'troika' principle right across the board. This is illustrated by their attitude in the Nuclear Tests Conference at Geneva, in the field of disarmament, and the International Control Commission in Laos. What they are saying in effect is that they refuse to accept any sort of international control or action which they cannot render useless by their veto. If that practice prevails the whole concept of internationally controlled agreements will suffer an almost irretrievable setback.

Or take the question of Berlin. There they seem prepared to endanger world peace in order to upset a situation which has existed perfectly well for the last

15 years. The West Berliners seek no change. The Western Powers have no expansionist ambitions there. What is more they have both rights and obligations which cannot unilaterally be abrogated by one partner to the agreement.

The reason why the Russians want a change in Berlin is obvious. For it is in Germany that the Communists are seen to be losing in fair competition with a free society. There are Germans on both sides of the zonal boundaries: equal in gifts and qualities. But one part of the nation has had an alien system imposed on it; while the other has, under a Government of its own choosing, taken the path of freedom.

With what result? With the result that every year a quarter of a million people leave East Germany, voting with their feet since they are denied any other method of expressing their will. So, apparently, the peace of the world is to be endangered simply because this puppet régime cannot survive or even keep its population unless the Iron Curtain is clamped down still more vigorously on free Berlin and on the boundaries.

These forms of political warfare are disturbing enough. What is even more disturbing is the philosophy which lies behind it. It is that when they decide that some action is necessary to advance Soviet interests or to promote the Communist revolution, nobody else is justified in opposing it; nor, whatever its international repercussions, justified in suggesting that the Communists should compromise.

History can seldom have seen a more arrogant use of power.

It is in this context that each of us has to take a public stand. Let it be understood that while Britain will always work for peace and good neighbour policies in international relations, we stand with the United States in the front line against aggressive expanding Communism. The Russians can adopt any political creed they like for themselves but when they export it by subversion backed by force, when it threatens the social and political systems freely chosen by others, it must be opposed.

We are therefore members, with you, of alliances which stretch round the world from the North Cape of Norway to the Pacific Ocean. Our signature is on the treaties. We have accepted, to the full, in spirit and in letter, the obligations of those treaties. They must be interpreted with intelligence but we shall never falter or default on them.

Let me at this point give the lie to the notions which circulate and gain currency whenever the Western nations are faced with a problem. I see the rumour-mongers are starting up their presses again over Berlin.

They are wrong. What we are doing all the time is working out firm and sensible policies to fit every possible contingency. I know of no disunity, only a common purpose to do what is right for our alliances and for free men.

I want to make that clear because I sometimes hear it said in America that we in Britain are 'soft' on Communism. As a matter of recorded history, if you look up Mr. Winston Churchill's famous speech at Fulton, Missouri, you will find that American comment was highly critical of the declaration that an 'Iron Curtain has descended on Europe from Stettin to Trieste'. I remember protesting in the House of Commons against the Yalta Agreements and saying 'The Russians have never receded for one moment from the view that in this matter (that is the East-European satellites) they alone are the judges and what they have taken they will keep.'[1]

So you see we are not so short-sighted nor so gullible. We do not always choose to express our opposition to Communism in the military context. That would be much too simple an answer, but we see the challenge clearly and the need to meet it all along the line. So do not be misled into thinking us soft. Some of our enemies made that mistake. Napoleon called us a nation of shop-keepers. The memorial to him in London is a railway station called Waterloo. Shopkeepers we may be, but neither our principles nor our alliances are for sale.

I cannot however blame you if you fail to appreciate some of our national peculiarities. A band of young men in Britain are persistent demonstrators against nuclear weapons. But to generalise about British opinion from the antics of a few whose minds are as immature as their beards leads you wide of the mark. A much surer yardstick of opinion is to be found in the recent considered vote on the matter in the General Assembly of the Church of Scotland. There, a motion which faced the facts of the nuclear deterrent in general and the Polaris base at Holy Loch in particular was passed by an overwhelming majority: 700 to 16, I believe.

Nuclear devastation is something about which it is right to be sensitive and restive. No Christian could fail to be that. But the British people have lived dangerously for long enough to know that until there is agreed disarmament the peace must be kept by the balance of power; and that the most effective element in that is the nuclear deterrent. Our friends and any potential breaker of the peace are entitled to know that they can rely on that.

But, equally, only a simpleton would contend that the military reposte is the sole answer to Communism.

For though Communism has mammoth military forces, it is not merely a military tyranny. Communists are animated by an idea and by a missionary zeal to proselytize; that can only be defeated in the long run by a more vigorous set of ideas and by greater zeal. Communism is also a method of economic organisation; and can only be beaten in the long run if the free societies demon-strate a more dynamic system which is seen to build a richer and fuller and more satsifying life for their peoples, and if they can and will help the emerging coun-tries to do the same in conditions of freedom which economic advance on Marxist lines would deny.

For this purpose we must look to the buoyancy of our home economies. Each of our countries in the Atlantic Alliance must be solvent and so direct our surplus earnings to stimulate the maximum of useful development.

There is one problem of which the United States and the United Kingdom must take account. Neither of us can run a great programme of overseas investment and aid, and expenditure on military forces overseas, upon a deficit in our balance of payments. When therefore we in Britain draw attention to the cost of our forces in Germany and to the problem of payments across the ex-changes with which they face us it is not because our support for NATO is weakening. Quite the contrary. It is because we want to keep our economy strong so that there will be no question but that we can fulfil our obligations.

[1] On 27 February 1945; H. C. Deb., vol. 408, col. 1306.

The fact is that military flanks can be turned by ideas and strong positions undermined by economic strains. So we must conclude that political rights, social justice and economic advance are the essential complements to military readiness.

Then again there is political wisdom exercised in the international arena. I sometimes detect signs of impatience with the attitude which we adopt towards neutrals.

We do not hold that those who refuse to stand up and be counted among our allies are undeserving of respect. As we interpret it, our duty is to give men and nations freedom of decision. It is inconsistent with this belief if we try to coerce those who wish to be neutral into our alliances. We will never use them for that purpose.

The fact is that the free world can live with neutrals whether they are in Europe, in Asia or in Africa; and the Communists cannot. Tibet and Eastern Europe from Latvia to Hungary prove my point. Always, everywhere, the Communists dragoon peoples to conform with their political rules. In the short run they have some success; in the long run the nations will find who are their real friends.

Again one hears dire mutterings about 'British Colonialism', as if half the world were groaning under the lash of some strange tyranny and it is a liability. The fact is of course that this British Colonialism was responsible in the first half of the 19th century for the abolition of the slave trade. The fact is equally that in our years of colonial rule we sent out to our dependent territories doctors and administrators, agricultural experts and engineers, who lived in bad climates on small pay and were the forerunners of modern 'technical aid'. And in the last 15 years we have brought over 600 million people to independence in societies where the fundamental values of democracy are maintained.

Since the war British Colonialism has established 10 fully independent nations in Asia and Africa. In the next generation (if we are given the time) and the United States must give us time—it will be responsible for the first non-racial societies in Africa. None of these countries has sold itself to the Communists.

Here the example of India is of immense significance. India is a country of over 400 million inhabitants which has inherited from 150 years of British Government freedom for the individual and the rule of law, a sound administrative infrastructure and all the prerequisites of a liberal and parliamentary State. It is economically still far behind the advanced industrial countries. But it is dedicated to the truth that a vast under-developed area can be governed and developed by a liberal democracy. This is the greatest contradiction in the world to-day of the Communist claims.

So neither we nor you, if I may say so, should be on the defensive about British Colonialism. Quite the contrary.

I believe that British Colonialism is already an example in freedom which may be used to prise the Communist empire wide open.

America is unquestionably the main repository of power and the leader of the free forces in the world, but I venture to say that the example of the free Commonwealth and the public contrast of the free Commonwealth with the enslaved Communist empire may be the decisive factor in convincing the un-aligned that the way of the West is the way for them.

There is another area of division which has brought weakness and trouble to the world which Britain may be able to help to resolve. The disunity of Europe has brought two world wars. If that could be ended there would be an immense addition of economic political and military strength to the free world.

What should be Britain's role? The thought has struck me that Britain's rediscovery of Europe has certain things in common with America's emergence from isolation. In the 19th century, you in this vast, splendid country of yours had to devote all your energies to developing your land between the Atlantic and the Pacific. We in Britain had similar energies but since Britain is a small island, we chose to expand our energies overseas. You turned away from the rest of the world while you opened up the West (the British Navy and the Pax Britannica helped, I believe) we tended to turn our back on Europe as we went about our imperial mission.

Now we are in an exciting period or rediscovery. Now we are seeking for a new relationship with the Continent of Europe. There are powerful reasons why we should do so—political and economic.

Politically, we must play our part in healing the ravages of the past. Europe has been too long divided against itself. France and Germany too long at odds. A united Europe would finally cement that rapprochement between France and Germany which has been one of the great features of the post-war world and act as a tremendous magnet for that part of Europe which has been artificially cut off from the mainstream of European development by an alien creed. Interdependence for Britain must include European interdependence.

In the economic sphere, modern industry operates most efficiently in a vast home market. You have discovered this truth for yourselves in continental America. In Europe, we could have a domestic market of more than 250 million people. The generation of wealth in such a market will be tremendous. Its attractions need no underlining.

Modern science and technology can best develop on the industrial basis and the financial power of an economic unit of this magnitude. The Industrial Revolution started in Britain. We don't want to be left out of the second or third industrial revolutions and deny our people scope to develop their talents.

Again we have a particular duty to the Commonwealth and a general duty to develop their talents.

Again, we have a particular duty to the Commonwealth and a general duty to help those who are less well off than ourselves. It will be more difficult for us, if we remain outside, to generate the necessary wealth to provide the capital and skills for the developing countries. In 1960 we in Britain contributed nearly $1 billion ($800 million to be precise) in loans, grants and investment for developing countries overseas. Britain in Europe could contribute more to the Commonwealth than Britain out of Europe.

Of course we could not go into Europe at the sacrifice of our friends. The economies of some of the Commonwealth countries are almost totally dependent on the United Kingdom market. We do not intend to make a choice between our alliances with the United States, our Commonwealth responsibilities, and our European connexions; it is a question of reconciling all three. It is I believe in the interest of all three that we should succeed.

So the international scene as we see it in Britain is like this. There is a cold war and a challenge. It is none of our choosing but so long as it lasts it must be contained. It will involve us in a long haul of endurance and trial. Situations like that in the Congo or in Berlin will test our nerve but if we have the stamina we will get through.

Of course the Communists have no moral rules and we play to the rules. That is no reason why we should merely react to moves from Moscow or Peking. We must have policies of our own and make the other side react for a change.

What should these policies be? The Communists seek to divide and conquer. We should unite to liberate. We should strive to promote every movement towards interdependence in freedom.

For Britain and America that means improving and nurturing our alliances, and especially the idea of Atlantic kinship. For Britain it means doing all in our power to strengthen the Commonwealth cutting across the divisions of race and colour, religion and continent, and stressing the essential unity of mankind. It means promoting the unity of Europe, once the power centre of the world and capable of equal greatness in the future. It means supporting the United Nations in its hour of trouble. We must narrow the divide between rich and poor, between the North and the South, as your President has so graphically put it.

Above all, we must take a good look at ourselves and our institutions. Are they equal to and worthy of the tasks that lie ahead? Are our economic organisations working properly: can our financial institutions both ensure stability and finance growth? Do our societies provide the sort of example that free men should strive to emulate.

If we can forge such a sense of purpose; if we release the energy, courage and imagination that our people have in them, on both sides of the Atlantic, who knows but that one day even Mr. Khrushchev's grandchildren may live in freedom.

(c) Statements of French Foreign Policy

1. Speech by the French Foreign Minister, M. Couve de Murville, to the Consultative Assembly of the Council of Europe, 2 March 1961[1]

Mr. President, Ladies and Gentlemen, it is natural that I should, first of all, try to express my sentiments in addressing this Assembly as Chairman of the Committee of Ministers. The honour that thus falls to my lot is increased by the satisfaction which I feel in knowing that at this Session you have decided to take as the subject of your debates two major problems of the present day: the evolution of European policy, and the creation of the Organisation for Economic Co-operation and Development.

Both of these problems can be counted among the main interests of the Consultative Assembly. The Council of Europe is the first of those European organizations that have grown in number during the last twelve years, and, from its beginnings—like the Organisation for European Economic Co-operation—it has been an institution representing all the countries of Europe. When I say

[1] Council of Europe, *Consultative Assembly, Twelfth Ordinary Session, Official Report,* vol. V (Strasbourg 1961), pp. 114–23.

Europe I mean, of course, free Europe, because Europe geographically is something rather different. No doubt the time will come when the two are the same, because nothing is eternal in this world, not even the suppression of freedom. Then we shall see the end of the division of Europe, which has been the tragedy of our old continent, forever rent asunder and forever springing to life again.

While awaiting that day, to which all true Europeans look forward with longing, free Europe is very much alive and is asserting itself. The Council of Europe exists as a living testimony thereof, and that, indeed, is its true *raison d'être*. Its mission is to show that there is a group of countries stretching from Ireland to Germany, from Norway to Greece, which not only share certain vital political and economic interests, but are the cradle of our civilisation, a civilisation which, although it is not the most ancient, is still the most humane, the most fruitful, the most inspiring, without which the world would lose its meaning and many of its hopes for the future. (*Applause*.)

This Europe of ours, except for a very small number of countries that escaped the storm, has been ravaged by war as perhaps never before in its history, certainly not for many centuries.

It is in its distress, amid the heaps of ruins and faced with an upheaval of the balance of power in the world, that Europe began to realise its need for a fresh start, and to appreciate the basic solidarity of its countries. Economic reconstruction gave the first opportunity of demonstrating these new aspirations towards co-operation, if not unity. The OEEC was born to be the tangible expression of this movement.

Very soon this tendency spread from economics to politics. The Council of Europe was born of the general feeling that Governments and Parliaments must be associated with the development of the idea which was arousing public opinion, that Europe must unite to face its destiny in a new world.

This great institution of yours and ours was cradled in a basic political understanding between those two great allied countries, Great Britain and France. I feel that I may be allowed to recall this without wishing to belittle in any way the credit due to others, since it is always a good thing to remember that such an understanding, which is in the nature of things, is of prime importance in European affairs.

Within a very few years there came about a transformation, one might almost say a revolution, that was to play a decisive part in the development of European policy and to symbolise to some degree the new tendency of relations within the great community in which we are all linked together—I refer to the reconciliation between France and Germany and the establishment of bonds of friendship and trust between these two countries.

The end of what used to be called the historic feud between France and Germany was the indispensable condition for European recovery. It was well that it should come about at a time when a new Germany was rising from the ruins of a past that will never return.

I said a moment ago that Franco-German reconciliation was in a way a symbol of the spirit of the new Europe; that is because it indicates the disappearance of what throughout history has been the tragic factor in the destiny of all our countries, the spirit of domination. Henceforth no single Power or group of

Powers among us can attempt to dominate or even think of doing so. It is now a spirit of partnership that is uppermost among us and will guide us along the new paths we have to tread. These are developments of far-reaching importance which have come about at the same time as similar developments in the relations between those of us that were formerly colonial Powers in Africa and Asia and the peoples that they ruled.

It is on this sound basis that in the last ten years sweeping changes have been made and undertakings have been set on foot, the full implications of which cannot yet be easily measured. It seems to me that we do not always realise this clearly enough in everyday life and discussions, since our view of reality is clouded by all manner of misunderstandings that arise from the very nature of things.

There are two obstacles in particular that are continually met with.

The first of these is vocabulary. The very originality of what some of us—if not all—are trying to do renders ordinary language totally inadequate. The language of our public law describes the institutions and relationships of our States as they have always been. It does not contain any terms that would describe the new relationships that are now being created.

Similarly, none of the oft-quoted historical precedents, ranging from Germany to the United States, is truly applicable, since in the past it was always a matter of uniting a single people. Although in the course of history there are many examples of peoples or nations that have been united under the domination of one of them, there is no example of ancient nations that were determined to retain their identity and yet attempted freely and deliberately to associate together within some wider unit, either economic or political.

The second obstacle is that, since Europe is made up of numerous countries, the movement that is urging us to unite has brought about a multiplicity of plans and hence of new organisations, which gives an impression of confusion, so that there is even talk of fresh divisions, whereas everywhere people are thinking rather in terms of re-grouping.

When such radical changes are taking place we cannot be surprised at this confusion, at inevitable clashes of interest, at disagreements on points of policy, nor even at there being some difficulty in defining one's position. Neither can we expect that developments will be as rapid and as sure as some people hope. There is nothing to be gained in trying to go too quickly, because fundamental changes can only be brought about in the course of time and with the free consent of those directly concerned, and sometimes of others as well.

Of all European undertakings, if I may say so, the most coherent and the most far-reaching in its implications is the association of the six countries that form the European Economic Community.

I should like briefly to explain a few points in this connection to the Assembly, still speaking, of course, from the point of view of the French Government. I think everyone will agree that the Common Market is a flourishing concern, and the steps towards acceleration that were taken on 1st January last are the most recent and most striking testimony of that.[1] It is no doubt precisely this success that has given rise to the reservations and doubts that are expressed on many

[1] See *Survey*, 1959–60, pp. 161–3.

sides and which, paradoxically, cause people to accuse the Common Market of endangering European unity—a unity which would presumably be characterised by the co-existence of our fifteen States without any particular connecting link between them.

If, as was expected at the time when the Rome Treaty was signed, there had been continual obstacles and many delays, probably no one would have made the complaints against the Common Market that are being heard now.

The problem that actually arises—as was only to be expected—is that of relations between the European Economic Community and the other countries of Europe. Between us all there exist traditional trade channels and habits of industrial investment, which should not be upset, in everyone's interest, political and economic.

In the early stages an attempt was made to settle this problem by creating between all our countries a great free trade area, that is to say, in fact, by robbing the Common Market of its substance from the outset. The result at the same time would have been to destroy the germ of political union contained in the European Economic Community, and which we made no attempt to hide.

The idea now appears to have been abandoned, and we are all trying to find another. Our colleagues in the six countries and we ourselves have always said that the Common Market was and would remain open for any other European country to join if they wished. We still believe that for some people at least this is a worthwhile prospect and probably the only satisfactory solution. We still hope that there will be a change of mind in certain quarters whence the response has so far invariably been negative.

Failing direct participation, the idea of association has been suggested. France on her side is always ready to discuss any ideas or proposals that are put to her. Contrary to what some people declare, she is anxious that the Common Market should not be damaging to anyone in Europe, since it would only be damaging to France herself.

We must, of course, stop short of any arrangement which would allow everyone to benefit from increased competition in certain fields, but leave exclusively to the European Economic Community other fields which, because of the very organisation of that Community, are an essential element in the general balance.

Pending a general settlement, much could be done, in our opinion, in a practical way to prevent distortion and facilitate trade. Neither the Common Market nor the other European countries must follow a protectionist policy. Every effort must be made towards the maximum of liberalisation, in particular by the lowering of tariffs. In this field we are hoping for much from the forthcoming negotiations with GATT,[1] in which the Economic Community—as has frequently been announced—is determined to co-operate whole-heartedly.

Ladies and Gentlemen, in the very nature of things the actions of States, in whatever field, always have a certain political character or political effect. This is the case with the Common Market. If the Common Market is to survive it cannot be otherwise. Economic unification, the existence of close links and strict obligations between the various countries, inevitably, whether they will or not, creates special political relationships between them.

[1] The second phase of the GATT tariff talks opened in Geneva on 29 May 1961.

This is becoming very clear now that the Common Market has really taken shape; the problem has in point of fact arisen.

There will no doubt be much talk of the form that these relations should take. I would only say that, since they are to be political relations, it is not easy to imagine how they could possibly be dissociated from the normal political organs of the participating countries, that is to say, their Governments and Parliaments.

A political authority cannot be created out of nothing. Everyone knows the suggestions on this subject that have been made by the French Government to its partners in the Common Market, regarding the establishment of organised political co-operation which might serve as a basis for an association that must inevitably be of a novel character, whatever it might be called.

There have been lively criticisms from all sides. According to some people we were timid and reactionary because, instead of insisting on the creation of a European State out of nothing, we fell back upon outworn formulae of political *entente* between States, from which nothing truly constructive could be expected. According to other people the mere suggestion that a new political group be created was multiplying those dangers of division in Europe that had already arisen from the existence of the Common Market.

It is, I think, easy to reply to criticisms of the first type, not only by pointing out, as I have already done, the necessity for a modicum of realism, but by indicating that the very existence of such doubts and anxieties is enough to show that our plans are not merely academic but have a latent dynamic that inspires hope in some—and in others fear—of further developments.

To critics of the second type I would suggest, first of all, that it is something of a fallacy to say that what tends to unite some of us will run counter to the general aspiration towards European unity. No one has ever suggested, nor even thought, that it would be possible to unite all the Western European countries, either economically or politically, by a stroke of the pen.

We must begin more modestly and in a rather empiric manner. It will be necessary to keep in mind individual characteristics and individual links or obligations in certain matters. In other words, let us make gradually what progress we can, but on two conditions: the first, that no step should be directed against anyone—unity, and not separation, is what we are aiming at; the second, that we should never for a moment lose sight of our ultimate aim—the unity of all Europeans in all fields.

Meanwhile, steps may be taken in both the political and economic fields to prevent friction and maintain the spirit of co-operation and understanding that is the basis of our relationships.

If, for example, the six Common Market countries agree to begin the political co-operation we have in mind, which will necessarily be of a special character owing to their growing economic unity, there is nothing to prevent our using some existing organisation, such as Western European Union, to maintain and develop that close understanding with Great Britain in international politics which is dictated by tradition and common sense.

In other words, if there is good will on all sides it should not be impossible, nor even very difficult, to satisfy everyone, to cater for individual sentiments and interests, to avoid anything that would be contrary to the general European interest, in short to prepare for the future without placing any obstacles in the way of the first steps. It is in this spirit that the French Government has tackled this major problem.

Mr. President, I should like now in the same spirit to say a few words on the second subject in your Orders of the Day, that of the Organisation for Economic Co-operation and Development, because here again, although in this case we have been joined by the United States, we find the same fundamental aim of co-operation between us in the cause of European unity.

After negotiations that lasted throughout the year, Canada and the United States and the eighteen member countries of the European Organisation for Economic Co-operation on 14th December signed the Convention setting up the Organisation for Economic Co-operation and Development.[1] This Convention is now being ratified in our various countries, and we hope that it will come into force by the appointed date, that is to say in the autumn of 1961.

It is perhaps superfluous to recall here the stages in the negotiations which, starting from the communiqué of the four Heads of State or of Governments who met in Paris in December 1959,[2] led to the signing ceremony of 14th December 1960. I only wish to explain briefly what appears to me the significance of this transformation of OEEC and the important part to be played by the new organisation.

The disappearance of the OEEC does not mean that that Organisation is no longer able to deal with the tasks entrusted to it; it means rather that its work has either been satisfactorily accomplished or has ceased to have any object. To understand this it is only necessary to compare the critical situation of European economies in 1948 with their present position.

The countries of Europe have attained a degree of prosperity that has enabled them gradually to renounce all protectionist measures. Currency reserves have been built up again—and almost general financial stability made it possible two years ago to restore the principal European currencies to convertibility and to abolish the European Payments Union. This Union, which rendered great service at a time when international trade was paralysed by the lack of means of payment, was superseded by the more flexible system of the European Monetary Agreement.

The final step along the road of liberalisation of trade and payments has just been taken by several countries which, in submitting to the terms of Article 8 of the International Monetary Fund, have given up certain restrictive practices in external trade.

These results have been achieved by effort on the part of Governments, national effort, and also thanks to that American aid with which the name of General Marshall is associated. The OEEC on its side seconded these efforts. It enabled member States to reach a better understanding of their mutual problems; it formed habits of co-operation; it gave European nations an opportunity for expressing their solidarity when the need arose. These habits and this spirit of co-operation, this feeling of solidarity, should be counted to the credit of OEEC perhaps even more than its actual practical achievements in various fields—and they should be preserved.

[1] *Documents*, 1960, pp. 174–9.   [2] *Documents*, 1959, p. 482.

The time has come in the history of the Organisation when its principal aims have been fulfilled and when, its Members being faced with new and pressing tasks, some new element must be introduced. Among these new and pressing tasks are those resulting from the establishment first of the European Economic Community and then of the European Free Trade Association. The existence of these two groups, while, on the one hand, it may be a powerful factor in promoting trade, on the other hand, raised problems that the OEEC in its present form cannot solve. Moreover, the removal of obstacles to movements of capital and goods has had the general effect of making the economies of our various countries more interdependent. For this reason the need for co-ordination of economic policies is all the greater.

Finally, the question of aid to countries in process of development is steadily growing in importance. Everywhere new independent States are springing up which rightly wish to see a rapid rise in the living standards of their peoples. We cannot remain indifferent to their appeal now that we have once more the means to respond to it.

These problems are, of course, not new. The confrontation of economic policies already existed in the OEEC. Several countries represented here have long been rendering assistance amounting to a considerable portion of their national income to countries in process of development. But the setting up of the OECD means that such tasks will henceforward be regarded as essential and that efforts now started along those lines will be developed and co-ordinated.

It is quite obvious, too, that the exclusively European membership of the OEEC limited its field of action. Neither co-ordination of policies nor aid to countries in process of development could be fully achieved with the presence and participation of the North American countries. Europe has therefore been very glad, I think, to see that America had also understood that a new era of co-operation in the Western world was beginning, and was willing to take part in founding an organisation where the United States, in particular, would be on an equal footing with the countries she had so recently helped toward recovery.

This Organisation, which includes all the countries of free Europe and almost all the industrial nations of the Western world, has three objectives, which are defined thus in the Convention:

First, to achieve the highest sustainable economic growth and employment and a rising standard of living in member countries, while maintaining financial stability, and thus to contribute to the development of the world economy;

Secondly, to contribute to sound economic expansion in member as well as non-member countries in the process of economic development;

Thirdly, to contribute to the expansion of world trade on a multilateral, non-discriminatory basis in accordance with international obligations.

These three objectives are closely linked together. One of the original features of the OECD is that they appear together in the convention setting up the organisation. The expansion of world trade cannot be dissociated from aid to countries in process of development any more than aid to countries in process of development can be dissociated from the prosperity of those countries whose economic potential enables them to provide that aid.

For this work to proceed smoothly—that is to say, without the course taken by one country or group of countries being deterimental to some other—there must be regular and close consultations on all the economic, financial and monetary policies of the twenty participating States.

The OECD will provide the framework for these countries to exchange information regarding their policies, to discuss their schemes and intentions, and to take such decisions as are required for the co-ordination of their activities.

The new Organisation will not be working in a purely European context but in a world context. This is to some degree inevitable because of the economic and commercial importance of the countries that are joined in it. Obviously, twenty nations which alone transact two-thirds of world trade and form a market of 500 million people cannot disregard the consequences to the whole world of any step taken by one and *a fortiori* by all of them.

At the same time the organisation will be able to deal with European problems. Against a wider background these problems can be considered in the same spirit of good will and friendship that has existed in the OEEC from the outset. Even if one reduces them to their true proportions, the problems that arise from the coexistence of two economic groups in Europe are sometimes difficult. But we ourselves are convinced that the new Organisation will place these problems in their proper perspective among its broader tasks and be able to study them and deal with them objectively.

I know, Ladies and Gentlemen, the importance that your Assembly rightly accords to the establishment of links between the Council of Europe and the OECD, and my Government has noted your Recommendation 245 with interest and sympathy.

For several years there has been co-operation between the Council of Europe and the OEEC. The Consultative Assembly was regularly informed of the activities of the Organisation and in return passed on to it for an opinion any economic Recommendations that were being adopted. It is desirable, we feel, that this co-operation should be continued and if possible strengthened.

With the accession of the United States and Canada, the European economic organisation has lost its exclusively European character; thus the terms of the problem have changed, since the difference in composition between the new Organisation and the Council of Europe has been accentuated.

Your Assembly has appreciated the difficulty, and has suggested that an *ad hoc* meeting should be held every year between members of the Consultative Assembly and parliamentary representatives of the five States that belong to the OECD but not to the Council of Europe. These meetings would consider the progress of the new Organisation. They would associate the Parliaments with its work and help to make it better known to the general public.

The French Government considers that there is every advantage to be gained from such a system. It will be for the Council of Ministers of the new Organisation, in agreement with the Council of Europe, to make the necessary arrangements.

In the economic history of Europe the formation of the OECD may be regarded as marking the end of the post-war reconstruction period, and also as indicating the desire to guide the nations of the Western world in the new tasks that lie ahead of them. I am sure that the close relations that will be maintained between this Organisation and your Assembly will facilitate its work and help it to fulfil its aims.

Mr. President, Ladies and Gentlemen, in dealing as I have with the two fundamental aspects of European policy at the beginning of this year 1961, I think I have at the same time indicated the tasks that face our countries.

On the one hand they must, by arduous paths, seek greater unity without losing that diversity that is one source of their riches. On the other hand, they must restore Europe to its place and influence in the world, not with the purpose of an outworn hegemony but for the common well-being of mankind. The Governments would be bitterly disappointing the nations to whom they are responsible if they did not resolutely face this difficult but inspiring future. We have come some distance and now we must go further.

In conclusion, I venture to express the hope that the achievements of the next ten years will not be less than those of the last ten, since we must show how youthful is this Europe that is still called the Old World.

2. President de Gaulle's Fourth Press Conference, 11 April 1961[1] (extracts)

ALGERIA

Question: Mr. President, after simultaneous announcements from Paris and Tunis of the meeting at Evian, the F.L.N. has abruptly changed its mind. Is there a new factor in the situation? How can this change of position be explained? What are the present possibilities of opening discussions? Could these be undertaken or pursued if, in the absence of a cease-fire, a *de facto* truce were at least announced?

Answer: If you will permit, we shall take up at once—since the whole world is waiting for it—the question of Algeria, which I should like once again to discuss thoroughly. In defining France's policy toward Algeria, it can, of course, be said first of all that France intends to see to it that, by one means or another, the fighting and the terrorist attacks are stopped, for nothing constructive can be accomplished while the war continues. It can also be said that France intends to let the Algerian populations freely determine their own destiny, for nothing is or will be valid unless the populations are given the right to determine their own fate.

But, as France sees it, what is primarily at stake is the future of Algeria. The cease-fire, self-determination—these are preliminaries that are designed to open the way for Algeria.

What the Algeria of tomorrow will be, what her future relations with France will be—that is what I want to talk about and outline once again what this country's policy is.

It is a fact that at the moment Algeria is a country in which war rages. It is also a fact that her future is not at all clear. I should like it to be well understood that in France's policy toward Algeria, the following essential idea must be faced squarely: In the world of today and in the times in which we live, France has no interest whatsoever in maintaining under her jurisdiction and under her dependence an Algeria which would choose another destiny, and it

---

[1] *Speeches and Press Conferences, No. 162* (French Embassy, Service de Presse et d'Information, 11 April 1961).

would not be in France's interest to be responsible for the population of an Algeria which would have become mistress of her own fate and would have nothing to offer in exchange for what she would ask.

The fact is that, to say the least, Algeria costs us much more than she is worth to us. Whether in the matter of administrative expenses, economic investments, social welfare, cultural development or the many obligations with regard to the maintenance of law and order—what we furnished to her in effort, money and human ability has no counterpart that anywhere nearly approaches it. It must in the same way be realized that France's present responsibilities in Algeria constitute heavy military and diplomatic burdens for her. And that is why France would consider today with the greatest calm a solution whereby Algeria would cease to be a part of France—a solution which in former times might have seemed disastrous for us but which, I say it again, we consider with a perfectly calm mind.

It would be quite different, of course, if the Algerian masses were bent on remaining part of the French people, for in that case it would be worth any sacrifice to retain within the mother country a fraction of her children. But it is difficult to claim that the Algerian masses, as a whole, wish to be a part of the French people. Consequently, when it is a matter of her fate in relation to us, we will first have to consider our interest and that is why—I repeat it—France has no objection and intends to raise no obstacle to the fact that the Algerian populations would decide to form a State which would be in charge of their country. This State will be such as the Algerians want. For my part, I am convinced that it will be a sovereign one within and without. And, once again, France will raise no obstacle to this.

There are people who will say: 'But it is the rebellion which leads you to think in this way.' I do not deny that the rebellion has confirmed, affirmed in my mind that which was already my thought well before the rebellion broke lose In any case, it is not the present situation of the fighting which induces me to speak as I do, for at no time during the past six years have the army and the police had, as it is said, things under better control, although numerous information organs—is this a liking for catastrophe?—continually bring up the 'fresh outbreaks' of the skirmishes and terrorist attacks. It is a fact that the rebellion, which in the past took a daily toll of about fifty civilians and soldiers, now takes an average of only seven or eight a day, four or five of whom are Moslems. It is not this that makes me speak as I do; I do not deny that the events which have occurred, which are occurring in Algeria have confirmed what I have thought and demonstrated for more than twenty years, without any joy no doubt—and you can well understand why—but with the certainty of serving France well.

Since Brazzaville I have not ceased to affirm that the populations dependent on us should have the right to self-determination. In 1941, I granted independence to the mandated states of Syria and Lebanon. In 1945, I gave to all Africans, including Algerian Moslems, the right to vote. In 1947, I approved the Statute of Algeria which, if it had been applied, would probably have led to the progressive institution of an Algerian State associated with France. At that time I agreed that the protectorate treaties concerning Tunisia and Morocco should come to an end. In 1958, having resumed leadership, I, along with my Government, created the Community, and later recognized and aided the independence of the young States in Black Africa and Madagascar. Not having returned to power in time to prevent the Algerian insurrection, immediately upon my return I proposed to its leaders to conclude the peace of the brave and to open political talks. In 1959, I proclaimed the right of the Algerian populations to self-determination as well as the determination of France to accept the solution, whatever it might be, which would result from this.[1] In 1960, I affirmed many times over that Algeria would be Algerian, I spoke of the birth of its future republic and renewed our offer of discussions. It was not our fault that the Melun contacts did not have any results; at the same time I broke the plots intended to force me to support integration. In 1961, I asked the French people to give me their approval, which was done through a massive 'Yes' vote in the referendum,[2] and, once again, I invited the men of the rebellion to get in touch with our representatives. And, during these same three years, I and my Government have not ceased to act in order to promote a Moslem leadership in Algeria and to put the Moslems in a position to take local affairs into their own hands, until such time as they are able to take over on the government level.

Thus the single college was instituted, numerous deputies and senators were elected—a great majority of whom were Moslems—many communes were established, a great number of Moslems have come to hold most of the mayor's offices, and general councils have been re-elected or instituted. At present the chairman of each of these thirteen councils is a Moslem. Thus the commissions of elected representatives have been set up, composed for the most part of Moslems. Thus a large number—a number which will be further increased—of Moslem prefects and subprefects have been appointed in Algeria, and the proportion of Moslems in all ranks and levels of the army, the police force, the administration and the magistrature has grown.

In short, we are proving every day that an Algeria belonging to herself would in no way be contrary to the policy of France. In conclusion what does this add up to: to decolonization. But if I have undertaken and pursued this task for a long time, it is not only because we could foresee and later because we witnessed the vast movement toward freedom which the world war and its aftermath unleashed in every corner of the globe, and which the rival bids of the Soviet Union and America did not fail to emphasize.

I have done it also, and especially, because it seemed to me contrary to France's present interests and new ambition to remain bound by obligations and burdens which are no longer in keeping with the requirements of her stength and influence.

Moreover, this is true for others as well. It must be recognized that in the great transformation which is taking place from one end of the universe to the other, the itching for independence of erstwhile dominated peoples and also the incitements proffered by all the demagogies of the world are not the only motivating forces. There is another which is not always very clearly perceived because of habits of mind, but which is nonetheless a very positive factor, one that is growing and tending to become the predominant one, especially in France.

[1] *Documents*, 1959, pp. 533–7.   [2] Below, p. 782.

I mean that the reason which once led certain civilized peoples to take under their direct control certain other peoples which were not—these reasons are disappearing even from the minds of the ex-colonizers. It now seems to the most powerful nations that their future, their welfare and the potentialities of their world action depend on their own development and on the cooperation of the formerly colonized countries, much more than on domination imposed on allogeneous peoples.

It was not always like that. We French, we built our empire at a time when our internal activities had reached a sort of ceiling—an industry which was not breaking any new ground, an agriculture which was not making any changes, trade channels which were fixed, salaries and wages unchanged, practically stereotyped budgets, gold currency, interest rates at 3 %, etc. . . . On the other hand, our old ambitions of European hegemony and natural frontiers were countered by the treaties of 1815, and after 1870 by the unity and strength of a threatening Germany. Then we sought in distant extensions a new role for the surplus of our enterprising abilities, a complement to our prestige and soldiers for our defense.

France does not have to be at all sorry for what she has achieved overseas in this capacity and in this form. I have said it often and I repeat: It constitutes a great human accomplishment which—notwithstanding certain abuses and errors and despite all the endless spouting of all sorts of worthless demagogues —will forever be a credit to France. But how many things have changed today.

Now our great national ambition is our own national progress, constituting a real source of power and influence. Now the modern era permits us, nay, compels us, to undertake a vast development. Now, for this development to succeed, we must first of all employ the means and resources at our disposal in our own behalf, in our own country. All the more so as we need these means and resources to ensure our own defense and that of our neighbors against the greatest imperialism that the world has ever known—the imperialism of the Soviet Union. We also need these means to win out in the tremendous economic, technical and social struggle now under way between the forces of humanity and the forces of slavery.

It is a fact: Our interest and, consequently, our policy, lies in decolonization. Why should we continue to cling to costly, bloody and fruitless domination when our country has to undergo complete renovation; when all the under-developed countries, beginning with those which yesterday were our dependencies and which today are our favorite friends, ask for our aid and our assistance? But this aid and this assistance—why should we extend them if it is not worth-while, if there is no cooperation, if what we give finds no return? Yet, it is a matter of exchange because of what is due us, but also because of the dignity of those with whom we are dealing.

This is the basis of France's policy with regard to her future relations with Algeria. If, in the final analysis, the Algerian populations are willing to let themselves be led to a break with France, such that we will no longer have any part to play in their destiny, we shall not oppose this in any way. Naturally, we shall cease immediately to sink in a henceforth hopeless enterprise our resources, our men and our money. We shall invite those of our nationals who are there and who truly run too many risks to leave the organization, by the influences exercised over them by various outside imperialistic forces, finally by the illusions with regard to the French situation instilled in them by certain partisan factions or press clans in Metropolitan France—with whom they have had contact and for whom the Algerian affair is only a grounds for opposition. I admit that it is difficult for an essentially insurrectional organism to tackle, with the minimum necessary serenity and on the desired level, questions such as those of peace, of the organization of a State and of the economic development of a country. But these leaders—since they will not win on the military field where our army at present, I repeat, has the situation in hand; since, on the other hand, they have great responsibilities because of the influence they exercise and the audience they find among a large number of Moslems; since finally, a number of them seem to be called upon to play an outstanding role in the first stages of the new Algeria—the question is, will these leaders, in the final analysis, be capable of adopting a positive stand.

For the moment, France continues to restore law and order, to accomplish her work of progress and to aid Algeria in making her political, administrative and economic structure Algerian from top to bottom.

Naturally we are anxious that, once peace has been re-established and civil liberties restored, the populations may sincerely choose their destiny. After which, if it is not in vain, France will undoubtedly be led by her heart and her reason, to give her aid and friendship.

That is what I wanted to say about Algeria.

I believe someone asked me a question about Ben Bella, and I shall answer it.

This person is under detention. The condition under which he was arrested are already known, and I do not hide the fact that many people bring this subject up to me; they have been bringing it up for a long time. I do not hide the fact that I myself have discussed the subject with President Bourguiba—as he himself has mentioned—when he did me the pleasure of coming here to meet me.[1] I found this meeting to be thoroughly satisfying and encouraging with regard to the future of Franco-Tunisian relations. Besides, it is always gratifying to meet a man of the quality of President Bourguiba. I have also, of course, had occasion to communicate on this subject with the King of Morocco—whose loss Morocco mourns and for whom I grieve, for he was my friend—and also with his son. I have discussed it with others as well who have brought it up to me.

The question is very simple. If talks do get under way between the representatives of the rebellion—of whom Ben Bella is one—and the representatives of the [French] Government, the regulations to which Ben Bella and his associates are now subject would in that case be modified. They would be made considerably more liberal. As soon as—by common accord—the fighting and the terrorist attacks cease, in other words, as soon as the cease-fire is established, we shall certainly not detain Ben Bella and his associates in France any longer. We would send them back where they came from, that is, to Rabat. For as long as the war continues we shall not release one of its leaders; but as soon as the war is over, there will no longer be any prisoners.

This is what I wanted to say to you.

[1] Below, p. 797.

UNITED NATIONS

Question: Mr. President, would you tell us why France, like the Soviet Union, refuses to pay her share of the expenses of United Nations operations in the Congo and, in a more general way, why she has for some time shown such great reservations with regard to the U.N.?

Answer: The United Nations Organization and its institutions were created in 1945 on the basis of a Charter, and with purposes which France at that time approved. I was, myself, at that time at the head of my country and in this capacity I was one of the founders of the United Nations at the request of President Roosevelt and then of President Truman, who were its promoters.

There was an executive council, the Security Council, which was a sort of Government composed of the five big powers, that is to say, the United States, the Soviet Union, Great Britain, China and France. And then there was a kind of non-legislative deliberative parliament, the General Assembly. The General Assembly, at that time, was supposed to debate only on subjects which were submitted to it by the Security Council. I will add that the General Assembly then included only about forty States, which had been in existence for a long time, which were endowed with cohesion and unity, and which were used to international relations and to the traditions, obligations and responsibilities which these relations entail.

In the Security Council each of the members—each of the big powers—had the veto power. And then finally in the General Assembly, in accordance with what France had wanted and had obtained in San Francisco, it was necessary—and still is—to have a two thirds majority in order to pass a resolution.

It seems that all these procedures would enable the States to establish contact with each other, to examine world questions jointly and to promote peace while restricting demagogic activities.

As for the Charter, it was designed to prevent the Organization from interfering in the affairs of each State and it could intervene only on the explicit request of a government.

Finally, among the intentions which had inspired its creation there was the desire, perhaps the illusion of the Western nations—in any case of the Americans—to bring the Soviets to cooperate with the West. We know what has happened.

Today it must be said that the United Nations really do not in any way resemble what they were or ought to have been at the start. First of all, the Security Council no longer comprises—is far from comprising—only the big powers, but also several powers elected in turn, and then there is an undetermined number of delegations attending all debates of the Security Council, depending on the subjects under discussion. As for the General Assembly, at the present time it has assumed all powers. It can deliberate on everything, without and even against the advice of the Security Council, which is thus dispossessed of its essential prerogative. In addition, this General Assembly now includes the representatives of more than one hundred States—soon they will number one hundred twenty—most of which, at least many of which, are improvised States and believe it their duty to stress grievances or demands with regard to the older nations, rather than elements of reason and progress.

As for the Charter, it now inconveniences every one and there is no one who can enforce its application. As regards the hoped-for cooperation between East and West within the United Nations, we can see its results.

So that now the meetings of the United Nations are no more than riotous and scandalous sessions where there is no way to organize an objective debate and which are filled with invectives and insults proffered especially by the Communists and by those who are allied with them against the Western nations.

And then, as the United Nations becomes a scene of disturbance, confusion and division, it acquires the ambition to intervene in all kinds of matters. This is especially true of its officers. It is anxious to assert itself even by force of arms—as it did in the Congo.

The result is that it carries to the local scene its global incoherence, the personal conceptions of its various agents and the individual partiality of each of the States which send their contingents with their own orders—send them, then withdraw them.

Under these conditions, France does not see how she can adopt any other attitude toward the United, or Disunited, Nations than that of the greatest reserve. In any case, she does not wish to contribute her men or her money to any present or eventual undertaking of this organization—or disorganization. Of course we hope that the day will come when common sense will again prevail and when the reasonable nations, noting the results of experience, will wish to resume this great world undertaking on a new basis.

In my opinion, this will be achieved if Europe succeeds in organizing itself and consequently in asserting its power, its reason and its experience in the world. Then Europe will be able to take the necessary steps.

Nuclear Power

Question: Does France still intend to build an atomic force and does she still plan to conduct tests in the Sahara?

Answer: During World War II, the Americans, with the aid of a certain number of European scientists and technicians, began to build atomic bombs, then used them at the end of the war. After which a frightening nuclear arms race was unleashed between the Anglo-Saxons and the Soviets, a race which is going on worse than ever. It is true that the two sides have temporarily suspended their tests. But they no longer have any need for these tests, since those which they have already carried out have enabled them to stockpile means which, in both camps, make it possible to destroy the entire world. Now the race is essentially concerned with the means of launching bombs, which are increasing —so to speak unlimitedly—the destructive capacity of these devices. What is frightening in this race is that it corresponds to the fundamental situation of our world, that is to say to the rivalry between the two camps and that, consequently, it takes on a sort of fatal character.

In any case, no State has ever raised its voice in a positive manner to cast the blame on one or the other of the parties which have manufactured and continue to manufacture these frightening weapons. To my knowledge, no State in the world has broken off relations with London, with Moscow, with Washington because of this. To my knowledge, the United Nations has not called on the United States, on the Soviet Union, or on Great Britain to destroy their atomic armament and their launching facilities. Then, since these two parties do not renounce their nuclear armament—quite the contrary—France, for reasons which concern her own defense and that of several others, has felt compelled to equip herself, in turn, with a force of this sort. It is true that the weapons she is building and which she can build will be only a very small fraction of what the others have built. It is true that the tests she is conducting are very small in number in relation to all the tests which the others have carried out. But all this is disregarded, it is against France and against France alone that the outcry of indignation which you hear is directed.

Since the French tests took place in the Sahara, attempts are made to stir up terror among populations situated vast distances away—for the tests took place in a completely desert region—by invoking the danger of radioactivity.

However, no one has ever discovered, on any one, any effect whatsoever with regard to health because of the three French atomic tests which have already taken place. Moreover, why would the three French atomic tests be much more dangerous than the 120 tests—at least that many—carried out by the two parties which I mentioned a moment ago.

Since the Sahara is in Africa, attempts are made to persuade the African States that their rights are at stake. The Americans have conducted nuclear tests in the Nevada desert and, to my knowledge, there were no ardent protests on the part of the other 47 States. The Russians have carried out their tests in Turkestan, in Siberia; to my knowledge, the 28 Asian States did not raise any protests of any great consequence. The Americans and the British have conducted tests in the Pacific; to my knowledge, the 27 countries—I have counted them— bordering on the Pacific have not considered this an encroachment.

Of course, it is understandable that the powers which possess atomic weapons, that the United States, the Soviet Union and Great Britain, do not wish France to acquire them. Of course, it is understandable that these three powers are finding, among the States which have more or less close ties with them, a response favorable to their arguments and unfavorable to the French plan. Of course, France owes it to herself and to all others to observe the strictest prudence in the tests which she still has to conduct, and that is what she will do, as she has already done in the preceding ones. But, as long as others have the means to destroy her, it is necessary for her to have the means to defend herself.

ATLANTIC ALLIANCE

Question: Do you think that after your talks with the President of the United States, the questions of reciprocal consultations within the Atlantic Alliance could evolve in the direction that you advocated nearly three years ago? And, in a general way, would you give your opinion on the reorganization of the Atlantic Alliance?

Answer: I cannot anticipate what President Kennedy and I will say to each other. In any case, on the question of the Atlantic Alliance, I can repeat and clarify what I have already said.

No one is more convinced than I that it is necessary for the free peoples to be allied in case of a conflict between East and West. Of course, this applies particularly to those who are on one or the other side of the Atlantic. What I question, therefore, is not the Atlantic Alliance, but the present organization of the Atlantic Alliance.

Everyone feels that a change is necessary, and with regard to this change, I can say that, in my view, it must take into account three essential points.

First: the right and the duty of the European continental powers to have their own national defense. It is intolerable for a great State to leave its destiny up to the decisions and action of another State, however friendly it may be. In addition, it happens that, in integration—for it is integration that I mean—the integrated country loses interest in its national defense, since it is not responsible for it. The whole structure of the Alliance then loses its resilience and its strength. And what would it be like in time of war?

Another point: it is necessary to clarify thoroughly the question of the use of nuclear weapons by the two Western powers which possess them, and also the question of the use of their other arms. For the European States of the continent, which are by far the most exposed, must know exactly with which weapons and under what conditions their overseas allies would join them in battle.

Finally the third point: since the Atlantic Alliance was created, the threats of war are no longer limited to Europe. They extend over the entire world, Africa and Asia in particular. Under these conditions, in order to endure, the Atlantic Alliance must be extended to all these new fields. If it did not do so, it would lose the basic, the close solidarity between its members which is indispensable to it. If it does so, then it must revise its organization which does not encompass these extra-European questions.

We shall soon have, I repeat, the great honor and the great pleasure of seeing President Kennedy. I suppose that this is one of the subjects which we will discuss as good friends and good allies. . . .

. . . THE COMMUNITY

Question: Mr. President, one of the last structures of the community—the Senate—has ceased to exist. Furthermore, the foundations for an Afro-Malagasy organization have just been laid in Yaoundé.[1] How do you visualize the future relations between France, the French-speaking African and Malagasy States and the new structures?

Answer: We have followed the work of the Yaoundé conference with the greatest interest. We consider it very important for Africa, for our relations with Africa, and for the world, that the French-speaking African States and Madagascar join their efforts—economic, political and undoubtedly even military. We consider this to be very useful and France, naturally, has no objection to this —quite the contrary.

As regards relations between these States and ourselves, you know that they are not as yet fully defined. Some States belong to the remodeled Community; the others—which do not—are working, however, toward a form of cooperation,

---

[1] See below, pp. 667–77.

and we believe that the agreements establishing this cooperation will be signed shortly. In any case, the spirit in which France views these young States and, I believe, the spirit in which these young States view France, is as friendly and gratifying as it could be. I am happy that you have given me the opportunity to say so.

With regard to the Senate of the Community, it is true that since a certain number of States are no longer explicitly a part of this Community, its Senate—in the form previously provided—no longer has any reason to exist. But I believe that everyone, or almost everyone, feels the need to establish on the parliamentary level an organized system of contact between France and these States. And I believe that this is one of the points on which it will not be difficult, for France at any rate, to come to complete agreement.

3. Speech by M. Couve de Murville to the National Assembly, 20 July 1961[1]

Mesdames, messieurs, c'est dans une conjoncture internationale lourde de préoccupations que se présente le débat de politique extérieure qui s'ouvre maintenant devant l'Assemblée nationale par la déclaration que je vais avoir l'honneur de faire au nom du Gouvernement.

Les espoirs qu'avait pu faire naître, de manière hélas! fugitive, la détente générale esquissée dans les premiers mois de l'année dernière ont été brutalement dissipés après l'échec, dès avant son ouverture, de la conférence au sommet. Depuis lors, la situation n'a cessé de se détériorer, en attendant cette grande crise à propos de Berlin, préparée depuis plus de deux ans et demi, que l'on nous annonce maintenant de sang-froid pour l'automne prochain.

C'est bien entendu, avant tout à ce sujet que je voudrais expliquer complètement les positions qui sont les nôtres.

Aucun des autres problèmes n'a le même caractère de gravité, même si nous en trouvons partout, en Asie, en Afrique, en Amérique latine, et si la France y est partout intéressée, directement ou indirectement.

Plus qu'à aucun moment depuis la fin de la guerre, en effet, ce que l'on est convenu d'appeler « le tiers monde » fait figure d'enjeu dans la compétition internationale.

L'Afrique en fournit naturellement les examples les plus frappants, après le Moyen-Orient, qu'il s'agisse par exemple du Congo ou de la Guinée. Mais tout n'est pas qu'ombre à cet égard car nous ne pouvons que nous féliciter de la manière dont, depuis qu'ils ont accédé en accord avec nous à la pleine indépendance, les Etats de l'ancienne Communauté ont pu affirmer leur personnalité et commencer à jouer leur rôle dans la vie internationale. Cela ne les empêche en aucune manière de continuer à coopérer librement avec la France pour leur développement et pour le maintien de ces liens culturels, économiques et humains qui manifestent la solidité de l'amitié qui les unit à l'ancienne métropole.

Mesdames, messieurs, en Afrique du Nord, la situation est dominée aujourd'hui par les graves événements qui se passent à Bizerte.[2]

---

[1] *Journal Officiel, Débats Parlementaires, Assemblée Nationale*, 1er *séance du 20 juillet 1961*, pp. 1861–4.
[2] For Bizerta, see below, pp. 797–807.

L'Assemblée sait qu'aux termes d'un échange de lettres intervenu le 17 Juin 1958, des accords négociés entre la France et la Tunisie devaient régler le statut provisoire, puis le statut définitif de la base de Bizerte.[1] De nombreuses conversations, traversées de multiples péripéties, ont eu lieu depuis lors sans qu'aucun arrangement formel soit jamais intervenu mais sans, non plus, qu'il y ait jamais eu de rupture. Le Gouvernement français, d'autre part, a, de son propre chef, en 1960 et en 1961, remis à la disposition de Tunis un nombre important d'installations de la base dont, en particulier, les casernes situées dans la ville de Bizerte. Enfin, des négociations ont été engagées il y a plusieurs mois pour déterminer les conditions dans lesquelles l'arsenal de Sidi-Abdallah pourrait être reconverti en un établissement industriel exploité par la Tunisie, à son compte et pour son profit.

Lorsque le président Bourguiba était venu à Rambouillet, en février de cette année, il s'était entretenu de Bizerte avec le général de Gaulle. Le président de la République avait confirmé son désir de régler le problème amicalement avec la Tunisie. Il avait, toutefois, marqué que, dans la situation internationale, ce problème ne se posait pas dans le seul contexte franco-tunisien. Bizerte occupe en Méditerranée une position stratégique essentielle, essentielle pour le monde libre. Tant que subsiste la menace, la France est obligée de s'y maintenir et la crise qui se prépare à Berlin n'a fait, malheureusement, depuis, que confirmer cette évidence.

M. RENE-GEORGES LAURIN: Très bien!

M. LE MINISTRE DES AFFAIRES ÉTRANGÈRES: Aucune impression d'urgence, cependant, moins encore de menace, n'avait été donnée alors par les propos de M. Bourguiba.

C'est il y a quinze jours, de manière publique et brutale, que le Gouvernement tunisien a ouvert un véritable conflit, en organisant des rassemblements populaires, en préparant des mesures de force et en enjoignant au Gouvernement français d'accepter sans délai le principe de l'évacuation de la base puis d'ouvrir des négociations pour fixer rapidement le calendrier de cette évacuation. Faute d'acceptation immédiate, un blocus serait organisé et des mesures de force mises en œuvre.

Le Gouvernement ne pouvait évidemment se rendre à de telles injonctions. Il a répondu le 13 juillet qu'il restait, comme par le passé, disposé à négocier et même désireux de le faire, mais que des négociations n'auraient pas lieu sous la menace ou dans des conditions propres à provoquer des troubles graves.

Le discours prononcé le 17 juillet par le président Bourguiba a alors annoncé la mise à exécution des menaces formulées.

Le lendemain, 18 juillet, par une note qui a été publiée hier soir, le Gouvernement, en renouvelant les indications antérieurement données sur sa volonté de négocier dans des conditions normales, a mis en garde le Gouvernement tunisien contre l'action qu'il annonçait, action qui ne pouvait pas ne pas appeler des mesures de défense en même temps qu'elle ne pouvait pas ne pas altérer gravement pour l'avenir les rapports entre les deux pays et cette coopération à laquelle la Tunisie se déclarait cependant fermement attachée.

[1] *Documents*, 1958, pp. 400–1.

Dans la nuit du 18 au 19 juillet, des barrages ont été installés autour de la base, déclenchant ainsi l'engrenage de la violence. Au début de l'après-midi du 19, le feu était ouvert sur un hélicoptère français. Les forces tunisiennes ont continué à tirer ensuite, d'abord sur les renforts envoyés pour assurer la défense de nos installations, puis sur ce installations mêmes.

L'armée, mise en état de légitime défense, a dû riposter ; elle ne l'a fait qu'après plusieurs heures.

Dans la nuit dernière et ce matin, les attaques tunisiennes se sont poursuivies et le nombre des victimes augmente.

Aujourd'hui même, une nouvelle mise en garde solennelle est faite à Tunis. La chronologie des événements démontre à l'évidence que la responsabilité des incidents, et donc des pertes, incombe exclusivement au Gouvernement tunisien. De même lui incombera entièrement la responsabilité des contre-mesures que nous sommes amenés à prendre. De même, enfin, la responsabilité de la rupture des relations diplomatiques dont il vient de prendre l'initiative.

Nous souhaitons de tout cœur que cesse sans délai cette déplorable épreuve de force qui ne peut avoir d'autre conséquence que de détériorer profondément et durablement les relations de deux nations que la nature et l'Histoire paraissent cependant avoir destinées à coopérer. (*Mouvements divers à droite.*)

En Asie, depuis longtemps, l'attention s'est concentrée sur cette péninsule indochinoise que l'on appelle aujourd'hui le Sud-Est asiatique. La guerre civile qui sévit au Laos est un épisode, entre bien d'autres, de l'affrontement entre l'Est et l'Ouest. La France soutient depuis longtemps que la sagesse et l'intérêt du peuple laotien commandent de mettre ce pays en dehors de la guerre froide, sous un régime de neutralité internationalement garanti. Un accord général s'est enfin réalisé sur cette idée et la conférence de Genève a été convoquée pour la mettre en œuvre. Bien des obstacles sont encore rencontrés car la dégradation de la situation va rendre difficile une véritable neutralité. Mais l'intérêt général est cependant de poursuivre dans cette voie et nous sommes prêts, pour y aider, à maintenir au Laos, dans l'avenir, l'assistance militaire prévue par les accords de 1954 et qui serait, par hypothèse, la seule à subsister une fois l'accord intervenu, ainsi que nos rapports économiques et culturels.

La France a ainsi un rôle utile à jouer dans ce petit pays ami. Il en va de même des autres pays de l'ancienne Indochine, non, certes, pour la domination, mais pour l'aide et la coopération. Jamais nos relations n'ont été meilleures ni plus confiantes avec le Royaume du Cambodge, et la République du Vietnam, avec laquelle nous nous sommes toujours attachés à maintenir nos liens culturels et économiques, ne laisse pas de tourner ses regards vers Paris.

Dans de toutes autres conditions, nous avons aussi notre tache en Amérique latine. Cet immense continent connaît les tourments d'un renouveau politique, économique et social indispensable. Les Etats-Unis lui consentent depuis long-temps une aide technique et financière que personne sans doute ne pourrait remplacer, mais la France, et par delà elle l'Europe occidentale tout entière, est en mesure d'apporter en propre, de son côté, une contribution matérielle et politique considérable.

C'est une œuvre à laquelle nous-mêmes et nos partenaires du Marché commun nous avons décidé de nous attacher dans toute la mesure de nos moyens. La décision en a été prise à Bonn le 18 juillet[1] dans la conférence des Six sur laquelle je reviendrai tout à l'heure.

Afrique, Asie, Amérique latine, partout nous retrouvons les conséquences d'une transformation dramatiquement rapide du monde, et la compétition entre le camp de la liberté et celui du totalitarisme. Pour trouver davantage, c'est-à-dire des motifs immédiats et précis de réelle menace, il faut aller de la périphérie au centre, c'est-à-dire en Europe, et dans cette Europe en Allemagne, car le sort final de ce pays est bien toujours le véritable enjeu.

Les faits sont connus. Ils le sont depuis qu'en novembre 1958 le président du conseil des ministres de l'Union soviétique a lancé sa première injonction aux puissances occidentales d'avoir à régler le problème allemand et celui de Berlin conformément à ses vues.[2] Celles-ci n'ont pas depuis lors changé. La dernière mise en demeure, qui remonte à juin 1961 et a été à toute occasion publiquement répétée depuis, est conçue à peu près exactement dans les mêmes termes.[3]

Seize ans après la fin de la guerre, il est temps, nous est-il dit, d'en faire disparaître les séquelles en réglant d'une manière définitive le statut de l'Allemagne. A défaut d'un tel règlement, ce pays restera un foyer de troubles, et ce, d'autant plus que la République fédérale cultive le militarisme et l'esprit de revanche. En conséquence, l'Union soviétique propose la réunion d'une conférence chargée de discuter les termes d'un traité de paix. Si, au moment de la signature, l'Allemagne n'est pas réunifiée, le traité sera signé avec les deux gouvernements allemands en existence. De toutes manières la réunification de l'Allemagne ne regarde plus les anciens alliés. Elle est l'affaire de ces deux gouvernements. Quant à Berlin, c'est-à-dire Berlin-Ouest, la Russie ne prétend pas changer son régime politique et social; mais le statut d'occupation doit disparaître avec le traité de paix, et Berlin deviendra une ville libre neutralisée dont le statut sera garanti par le traité lui-même.

Si la France, les Etats-Unis et la Grande-Bretagne n'acceptent pas une telle proposition, alors l'Union soviétique agira seule. Elle ne peut contraindre ses trois anciens alliés de la guerre à signer un traité de paix avec les deux Allemagnes. Elle se limitera donc à la partie de l'Allemagne qui dépend d'elle et nous ne doutons pas, en effet, que cette partie de l'Allemagne ne dépende entièrement d'elle. Une conférence sera organisée qui groupera les Etats acceptant une telle formule. Le traité sera signé. Dès sa mise en vigueur, la Russie considérera qu'elle n'a plus aucune responsabilité concernant Berlin-Ouest. Autrement dit, elle reniera tous les accords qui la lient à ce sujet aux puissances occidentales. . . .

Au centre. Comme Bourguiba!

M. LE MINISTRE DES AFFAIRES ÉTRANGÈRES. . . . elle considérera que la République démocratique allemande devient seule compétente pour tout ce qui concerne les communications de nos trois pays avec Berlin-Ouest. Les trois Occidentaux devront s'entendre avec Pankow s'ils veulent assurer le maintien et le ravitaillement de leurs garnisons. Dans le cas où les Occidentaux n'accepteraient pas ce contrôle de l'Allemagne orientale, la Russie prêterait tout

---

[1] Below, p. 187–9.   [2] *Documents*, 1958, pp. 146–64.   [3] Below, pp. 277–280.

son appui à cette dernière pour empêcher qu'il soit porté atteinte à sa souveraineté; tout son appui, cela signifie son appui par les armes.

Telle est la position russe, inlassablement répétée.

C'est, mesdames, messieurs, le 28 Avril 1959, lors du premier débat de politique extérieure de la présente législature, que j'avais, pour la première fois, défini devant l'Assemblée nationale quelle était, en regard, la position de la France et de ses alliés.[1] Cette position n'a pas, elle non plus, été modifiée depuis. Elle a en dernier lieu été rappelée dans une note remise le 18 juillet,[2] c'est-à-dire lundi dernier, à Moscou, en même temps qu'une note américaine et une note britannique. J'en résume maintenant les grandes lignes.

Il est en effet bien regrettable que les alliés de la guerre n'aient pas été, entre 1945 et 1961, capables de s'accorder sur un règlement allemand. Ce n'est pas faute, de la part de l'Occident, de s'y être efforcé. Jamais, cependant, aucune discussion sérieuse n'a pu être engagée avec Moscou. C'est ainsi que, peu à peu, s'est cristallisée une situation qui est proprement le résultat de la guerre froide.

M. Jacques Douzans: Et de Potsdam!

M. le Ministre des Affairs Étrangères: L'on trouve à l'Ouest une Republique féderale construite dans la liberté, et qui a cherché tout naturellement sa place dans le monde libre; à l'Est, une région dominée par un régime communiste qui n'est, en fait, que le représentant de la puissance occupante. Cette division de l'Allemagne est une tragédie. Mais nous savons que l'on ne pourra trouver une solution définitive que le jour où un véritable accord sera possible entre l'Est et l'Ouest. Pourquoi, en attendant, prétendre donner forme juridique, par un traité, à une situation qui, par essence, n'est pas normale? La Russie sait bien que nul à l'Occident ne songe—la République fédérale elle-même l'a solennellement déclaré—à essayer de modifier par la force le *statu quo*. Dès lors y a-t-il autre chose, dans cette proposition que l'on nous fait de conclure un traité de paix avec les deux Allemagnes, que le dessein d'amener les Occidentaux à reconnaître—au moins *de facto*—le régime de la République démocratique allemande, et par là à lui apporter un appui dont il paraît, en effet, avoir bien besoin?

Le Gouvernement soviétique sait bien, à l'avance, que nous ne serons pas prêts à y consentir. Il avance tout aussitôt une solution alternative qui, elle, serait unilatérale.

Que M. Khrouchtchev signe un traité avec la République démocratique allemande, c'est, on l'a dit, un peu comme s'il signait un traité avec lui-même. Nous n'avons pas la prétention de l'en empêcher. Mais, à son tour, il ne peut prétendre nous obliger à accepter les conséquences qu'il déclare en tirer quant à notre statut à Berlin. Les Etats-Unis, la Grande-Bretagne et la France sont puissances occupantes à Berlin, chacune dans leur secteur, non pas du fait de l'Union soviétique, mais en vertu des actes interalliés qui ont suivi la capitulation inconditionnelle de l'Allemagne hitlérienne, actes qui ne peuvent être abrogés par l'une des parties et qui demeurent en vigueur aussi longtemps que les quatre

[1] *Journal Officiel, Débats Parlementaires, Assemblée Nationale*, 29 April 1959, pp. 319–22.
[2] Below, p. 323. The British and American Notes were sent on 17 July.

puissances ne se sont pas mises d'accord pour les modifier ou pour les abroger. Dire qu'un accord passé avec un tiers met fin à ce statut est aussi juridiquement insoutenable qu'il est politiquement inconcevable de vouloir transformer notre actuelle occupation à Berlin en une présence précaire soumise au bon vouloir des autorités de l'Allemagne orientale.

Je voudrais insister sur ce point, car bien des personnes de bonne foi demandent s'il est vraiment important que le contrôle du trafic de nos garnisons soit entre les mains de l'un ou de l'autre, entendez de l'U. R. S. S. ou de la République démocratique allemande, si notre opposition aux prétentions russes n'est pas fondée sur des motifs bien formels, et si, après tout, en 1961, nous sommes vraiment justifiés à nous obstiner à maintenir un statut d'occupation devenu, du simple fait du passage du temps, un peu anachronique.

Pour comprendre, il faut évidemment se demander ce que cherchent les Russes. Comme à l'ordinaire, là n'est pas le plus facile.

Que le sort final de l'Allemagne soit considéré à Moscou comme un problème national essentiel, c'est une évidence; personne ne peut le critiquer. Mais les Russes savent—et la façon dont, dès l'origine, ils ont présenté leur programme le confirme—qu'il n'est pas possible d'en décider maintenant, c'est-à-dire aussi longtemps que dure la guerre froide, et *a fortiori* de la manière dont ils l'envisagent.

C'est pourquoi, leur proposition d'un traité de paix présentée pour la bonne règle, ils se bornent à ce qu'il leur paraît possible de faire de leur propre chef, c'est-à-dire à régler le sort de Berlin, lequel ne fait pas partie de leur zone de domination, mais s'y trouve géographiquement inclus.

Ici encore nous pouvons comprendre leur souci, même s'il n'est en aucune façon le nôtre. Berlin-Ouest, placé au cœur de la R. D. A., est libre et prospère. C'est une anomalie insupportable dans une région de l'Allemagne qui se trouve n'être ni l'une, ni l'autre. (*Très bien! très bien! à gauche, au centre et à droite.*)

En particulier, Berlin-Ouest est un refuge où, par milliers chaque mois, des habitants de la zone orientale vont chercher le moyen d'émigrer en République fédérale. Personne ne doute que, pour le régime de M. Ulbricht, une telle situation soit à la longue une cause de faiblesse. Mais, est-ce la faute des Occidentaux si ledit régime est odieux à la population qui lui est soumise au point de provoquer une fuite constante et massive? (*Applaudissements à gauche, au centre, au centre gauche et sur de nombreux bancs à droite.*)

Que propose-t-on dans ces conditions? C'est ici que nous commençons à ne plus comprendre. On nous dit en effet ceci: Berlin-Ouest vit sous un régime qui n'est pas communiste. Si ses habitants entendent conserver un tel régime, nous Russes, leur reconnaissons ce droit et n'avons aucune idée de les contraindre à en changer. Ce que nous voulons simplement, c'est abolir un statut d'occupation périmé, et le remplacer par un statut de ville libre qui sera, si vous le voulez, internationalement garanti, et par conséquent assurera aux Berlinois exactement les mêmes sécurités qu'auparavant. Si les puissances occidentales demeurent à Berlin, pour des raisons qui leur sont propres et que d'ailleurs nous ne comprenons pas, libre à elles. Nous sommes prêts à leur donner toutes les garanties pour leurs communications avec l'Ouest.

Si tout cela est refusé, alors, à notre regret, nous irons de l'avant par le mécanisme d'un traité avec la R. D. A. Mais cela encore ne signifie pas un blocus de Berlin, ni une injonction aux Occidentaux à se retirer. Il leur suffira de régler avec ladite R. D. A. les conditions de leur trafic.

Autrement dit, d'après ce qu'on nous dit, dans les deux termes de l'alternative qu'il y ait accord ou qu'il y ait solution unilatérale, aucun changement de fait ne serait apporté à Berlin-Ouest, à son régime politique ou au maintien des garnisons occidentales. Quel avantage en résulterait donc pour l'Union soviétique et pour le régime qu'elle a établi à Pankow? Qu'y aurait-il de changé dans le rôle que cet îlot de liberté joue en Allemagne orientale et qui est, pour celle-ci, une cause si évidente de faiblesse? Pourquoi remuer le ciel, la terre, et même les enfers, pourquoi proférer des menaces, entretenir une crise pendant des années, et chercher à créer chez les Occidentaux la dissension et la panique, s'il s'agit seulement de substituer à un statut dont personne, en droit, ne conteste d'ailleurs la validité, un autre statut dont on nous dit qu'il offrirait exactement les mêmes garanties?

Tout cela apparait en vérité bien dérisoire.

Ou bien alors, il s'agit de tout autre chose. Il s'agit, sous couvert de mettre un terme à un anachronisme, de transformer, par la pression environnante, une situation qui serait sans doute moins forte que l'actuelle, de telle façon que Berlin-Ouest perde progressivement sa physionomie et se confonde en fin de compte avec la masse qui l'entoure. Nous n'avons pas de raison d'accepter un changement de statut pour le seul motif qu'une forme différente apparaît plus satisfaisante à certains. Nous en avons moins encore si c'est le fond qui se trouve en jeu.

Ce n'est là qu'une hypothèse. Encore une fois, de tout ce que l'on nous dit officiellement et officieusement, il ne s'agit pas de faire partir nos troupes de Berlin. Alors, vraiment, pourquoi vouloir engager une épreuve de force? Les Occidentaux ne menacent personne. Ils sont certes déterminés à ne pas se laisser couper de Berlin et à prendre, le cas échéant, les mesures indispensables pour assurer leurs communications. Mais ceci suppose que l'on voudrait faire obstacle à leur légitime droit de passage. Créer de toutes pièces, à l'âge thermo-nucléaire, une telle crise internationale, serait à la vérité bien inconsidéré ou bien criminel.

Il est d'autres façons d'aborder sérieusement les problèmes sérieux, et l'Allemagne est, à l'évidence, un problème capital. La France, pour sa part, ne s'est jamais refusée à la négociation. Encore faut-il que celle-ci puisse être utilement engagée. Elle ne peut l'être sous la menace. Elle n'est d'autre part susceptible de conduire à des résultats positifs que si elle prend place, non dans une atmosphère de crise, mais dans un climat de détente qu'il faut, au préalable, créer et laisser se développer. C'est ainsi que nous pourrons discuter valablement des problèmes allemands. Nous souhaitons que le Gouvernement soviétique le comprenne et qu'il s'engage avec nous dans la voie de la raison.

Telle est, dans cette grave affaire, la position de la France. Elle est aussi celle de nos alliés, américains et britanniques. Depuis longtemps, plus encore depuis deux mois, les trois gouvernements sont en contact étroit, et la République fédérale participe régulièrement à ces consultations. L'Assemblée sait que, dans quelques jours, à Paris, va se tenir une nouvelle réunion des ministres intéressés. Rien n'est plus important, dans l'attente de la crise, que de maintenir

D.I.A.–E

un front occidental uni, et de ne donner prise à aucune manœuvre de division. (*Applaudissements à gauche, au centre, au centre gauche et sur de nombreux bancs à droite.*)

A cet égard, la visite que le président des Etats-Unis a faite à la fin du mois de mai au général de Gaulle a présenté une importance décisive, en manifestant la complète communauté de vues des deux chefs d'Etat. Cette visite a été fructueuse, certes, à bien d'autres égards, et nous avons toutes raisons d'en être satisfaits, mais ceci est sans doute l'essentiel.

La menace qui pèse sur l'Europe occidentale donne un relief particulier à cette partie essentielle de notre politique extérieure qu'est notre politique européenne. C'est ce qui ressort nettement de la réunion des chefs d'Etat ou de gouvernement des pays du Marché commun, qui s'est tenue à Bonn, le 18 juillet dernier. Jamais sans doute les nations de l'Europe, déjà rassemblées au sein des Communautés existantes, n'ont mieux compris qu'elles doivent s'unir si elles veulent survivre dans la liberté, jouer leur rôle dans le monde et sauvegarder ce bien inestimable qu'elles possèdent en commun et qui est leur civilisation.

Désormais, c'est concurremment sur deux plans, le plan politique et le plan économique, que va se poursuivre leur effort. Du développement des communautés économiques, j'aurai peu à dire car des débats récents ont déjà permis au Gouvernement de faire connaître ses positions pour l'essentiel.

L'année 1960 avait été pour le Marché commun l'étape du début du véritable désarmement douanier entre les Six et de la mise en place du tarif extérieur commun. Telle était la conséquence de la décision capitale prise en mai l'année dernière au sujet de l'accélération de l'exécution du traité de Rome.

Ainsi a commencé à vraiment prendre figure ce grand marché industriel qui est le premier de nos objectifs. Cette étape doit normalement être suivie d'une autre, celle de la mise en œuvre des autres dispositions du traité qui, s'ajoutant au désarmement douanier, sont nécessaires pour faire des six pays un ensemble économique véritablement cohérent. Il s'agit de ce que l'on a appelé les politiques d'harmonisation, au premier rang desquelles nous plaçons et avons toujours placé la politique agricole commune. Nous ne pouvons concevoir que le Marché commun se maintienne et se développe si, à cet égard aussi, les dispositions du traité ne sont pas entièrement respectées. C'est la position très ferme que le Gouvernement a prise à Bruxelles. D'ici la fin de l'année, de longues et difficiles négociations sont prévues. Nous sommes parfaitement conscients de tous les obstacles qu'il faudra encore surmonter. Mais nous ne pouvons penser que, sur ce point comme précédemment sur les autres, un accord ne soit pas finalement réalisé qui permettra de passer, le 1er janvier 1962, à la seconde étape prévue par le traité.

D'autres problèmes se poseront par la suite, qui seront également difficiles et importants. Au premier rang je placerai celui de l'association du Marché commun avec les pays africains nouvellement indépendants. 1961 est, pour la communauté économique européenne, l'année de l'agriculture. 1962 sera sans doute l'année de l'Afrique. Ainsi, d'obstacles en obstacles et d'efforts en efforts, avancerons-nous dans la voie qui doit conduire l'Europe des Six au but qu'ils se sont fixé sur le plan économique.

Entre temps continuera sans doute à se poser la question des rapports des Six avec les autres Etats de l'Europe occidentale, question devenue maintenant celle de l'adhésion éventuelle de nouveaux membres. C'est, bien entendu, à la Grande-Bretagne que je pense en premier lieu. Depuis plusieurs mois, le Gouvernement de Londres étudie sérieusement les conditions d'une telle adhésion et les conséquences que celle-ci pourrait impliquer, notamment en ce qui concerne le Commonwealth. La décision à prendre appartient à l'Angleterre, et je tiens à dire que nous comprenons parfaitement, pour notre part, les difficultés qu'elle soulève. Notre attitude a été très clairement définie dans la déclaration de Bonn du 18 juillet,[1] aux termes de laquelle les six chefs d'Etat ou de gouvernement souhaitent l'adhésion, aux communautés économiques européennes, d'autres Etats prêts à assumer, dans tous les domaines, les mêmes responsabilités et les mêmes obligations.

Il est dit: dans tous les domaines, et ceci vise naturellement aussi le domaine politique. Telle est la conséquence logique des décisions prises par ailleurs dans les réunions d'avant-hier.

Les traités de Paris et de Rome avaient sans conteste, dès avant même leur signature, un arrière plan politique. L'idée d'union politique était impliquée dans l'entité économique qu'il s'agissait de créer. Elle s'est affirmée de manière de plus en plus évidente, à mesure que le Marché commun, qui est la pièce maîtresse de cet édifice économique, commençait à se mettre en place. Je crois qu'aujourd'hui tous nos partenaires, comme nous-mêmes, sont parvenus à la conclusion que le Marché commun n'est pas concevable dans la durée sans quelque forme d'union politique de l'Europe.

C'est il y a un an exactement que des propositions en ce sens ont été pour la première fois avancées par le général de Gaulle. Bien entendu les problèmes sont entièrement différents de ceux qui se posent dans le domaine de l'économie. Il est apparu dès le départ qu'aucune forme définitive, ni aucun processus systématique ne pouvait être envisagé d'emblée. Seule apparaissait possible une méthode pragmatique et progressive. Il ne peut s'agir que de commencer à organiser entre les Six une coopération politique véritable. Celle-ci prendrait notamment la forme de réunions périodiques au niveau le plus élevé. Ainsi pourrions-nous échanger nos vues, confronter nos politiques, arriver, si possible, à des positions concertées, bref pratiquer une collaboration qui, peu à peu, créerait des habitudes, permettrait de parvenir à une politique commune, en attendant de pouvoir déboucher sur des institutions.

Ce programme a été discuté longuement avec nos partenaires. Il a soulevé des critiques et des oppositions, que chacun connaît et sur lesquelles je ne reviendrai pas, car il s'agit du passé. L'essentiel est en effet qu'un accord général vient de se réaliser; il convient maintenant de se tourner résolument vers l'avenir.

La déclaration publié à Bonn avant-hier, à laquelle je me suis déjà référé, constitue la première étape du développement qui doit conduire à l'union de l'Europe. C'est ce fait qui lui donne son importance.

Tous les trois ou quatre mois, les chefs d'Etats ou de gouvernement tiendront une réunion. En attendant le statut dont la mise à l'étude a été décidée, la

[1] Below, p. 187.

commission qui fonctionne depuis le 10 février continuera à travailler pour préparer ces réunions et faire des propositions sur les questions qui lui sont renvoyées. Une décision en ce sens a été prise le 18 juillet déjà pour ce qui concerne les relations de l'Europe avec l'Afrique et de l'Europe avec l'Amérique latine.

D'autre part, la conférence, à la suite d'un exposé du général de Gaulle sur la défense de l'Europe, a, sur sa proposition, tenu à affirmer la solidarité des Six face aux menaces qui sont proférées et à la crise qui s'annonce à propos de Berlin.

J'ajoute que des décisions ont été prises également pour organiser la co-opération des Six dans le domaine de l'enseignement et de la culture. C'est là un domaine essentiel pour l'Europe, puisqu'il s'agit de la formation de sa jeunesse. Un conseil des ministres de l'éducation nationale a été créé, auquel un très large champ d'activité est ouvert. Par ailleurs, une solution a été trouvée au problème de l'université européenne que le Gouvernement italien avait le désir de voir s'ouvrir à Florence.

Tel est, dans ses grandes lignes, le bilan de la recontre du 18 juillet. Il est à tous égards satisfaisant. La France ne peut que s'en féliciter, dans la conscience qu'il lui incombera, dans la nouvelle organisation, comme dans celles qui existent déjà, un rôle qui doit répondre à l'attente des peuples de l'Europe.

C'est sur cette note que je terminerai mon exposé. Les circonstances du moment sont difficiles. Celles de demain le seront sans doute davantage encore. Comme toujours, lorsqu'il s'agit d'une crise grave, c'est le sort de l'Europe et, par conséquent, le sort de la liberté, qui se trouve être en jeu. Encore faut-il que, pour se défendre, l'Europe s'affermisse et s'unisse.

Pour le surplus, souhaitons que la Russie ne fasse pas de faux calculs fondés sur la conscience qu'elle a de sa puissance militaire et sur ce qu'elle croit être les hésitations ou la mésentente de ses adversaires. Qu'elle comprenne au contraire que, face à un monde occidental résolu et uni, la seule voie qui s'ouvre est celle de la libre discussion et d'une entente de bonne foi. (*Applaudissements à gauche, au centre et sur quelques bancs à droite.*)

4. President de Gaulle's Fifth Press Conference, 5 September 1961[1] (extracts)

BERLIN

Question: Do you believe that a world conflict over Germany and Berlin can be avoided and under what conditions? My additional question concerned the Soviet nuclear tests: do you believe that this makes the search for peace more difficult, less difficult or that it is of no great importance?

Answer: One may, indeed, wonder why the Soviets have suddenly used the pretext of Berlin in order to demand that the city's status be changed, by will or by force; one may also wonder why this Berlin situation, which has seemed tolerable to them for the past sixteen years and which they themselves organized and set up with the United States and Great Britain at the Potsdam meeting at which France, moreover, was not present—one can also wonder why, suddenly,

---

[1] *Speeches and Press Conferences, No. 168* (French Embassy, Service de Presse et d'Information, 5 September 1961).

this situation seems intolerable to them. One may wonder why they are suddenly mixing their demands with frightening threats. One may wonder if there is someone who truly believes that the Federal German Republic, such as it is, is a danger to the present Russia. And one may finally wonder if there is a Soviet citizen who believes this when the Kremlin states that it is in a position to crush totally, immediately, under bombs equivalent to 100 million tons of TNT, whoever would raise his hand against the Communist world.

Actually, there is in this uproar of imprecations and demands organized by the Soviets something so arbitrary and so artificial that one is led to attribute it, either to the premeditated unleashing of frantic ambitions, or to the desire of drawing attention away from great difficulties: this second hypothesis seems all the more plausible to me since, despite the coercions, isolation and acts of force in which the Communist system encloses the countries which are under its yoke, and despite certain collective successes which it has achieved by drawing upon the substance of its subjects, actually its gaps, its shortages, its internal failures, and above that its character of inhuman oppression, are felt more and more by the elites and the masses, whom it is more and more difficult to deceive and to subjugate.

And then, also, the satellites that the Soviet regime holds beneath its sway are feeling to an increasing degree in their national sentiment the element of cruelty in the annexation which they have suffered. It may then be understood that, under these circumstances, the Soviets consider that the Berlin question may be a suitable opportunity to deceive themselves and to deceive others. And, in fact, where Berlin is located, it is relatively easy for them to make demonstrations on the spot, and the measures of restraint which they are taking involve limited risks for them. And, in addition, they may think that the United States, England and France will allow themselves to be somewhat discouraged and somewhat resigned, and therefore that the retreat of these three powers will deal a serious blow to the Atlantic Alliance; that, above all, throughout the world, it will look as if the totalitarian regime, the totalitarian camp, in the face of an uncertain and divided West, is clearly the stronger.

But, in fact, this is not true. Admittedly the Soviets possess terrible nuclear weapons, but the Western powers also have some formidable ones. If the world conflict were to break out, the use of forces of destruction would undoubtedly result, in particular, in the complete disruption of Russia and the countries which are a prey to Communism. What is the good of ruling over dead men? And then, in addition, the rule itself would also come to an end because in this disaster the framework would be broken, the framework of a regime which only keeps going by means of an authoritarian mechanism, a rigidly planned and relentlessly imposed police regime. This, moreover, the Soviet leaders are aware of in spite of all their boasting.

Then the Western powers have no reason not to consider the Soviet demonstrations with a clear eye and a firm heart. It is true, I repeat, that on the spot, in Berlin, the action of force which would be undertaken could bring some advantage to the Soviets, as it would obviously be difficult for the Western powers to act from such a distance on the soil and in the sky of the former German capital. But the Western powers could well fight back on the seas and in the skies traveled by Soviet ships and planes which would also be far from their bases. There would then be an exchange of wrong doings which undoubtedly would not end to the benefit of the Soviets. In short, if the Soviets want, by force, to reduce the positions and cut the communications of the Allies in Berlin, the Allies must maintain by force their positions and their communications. Clearly one thing leads to another, as they say, and if all this tends to multiply the hostile acts committed by the Soviets, to which we shall be obliged to reply, we may end up with a general war. But then, this would be what the Soviets deliberately wanted, and in that case any retreat has the effect of overexciting the aggressor, of pushing him to redouble his pressure and, finally, to facilitate and hasten his assault. In summing up, the Western powers have no better means of serving world peace at present than to remain resolute and firm.

Does this mean that the two camps must oppose each other forever? This is by no means what France believes, because it would really be extremely foolish and extremely costly. If the world conflict is to break out, then modern technical progress will have led to death. If that is not the case, we must try to make peace. Let the Soviets stop issuing threats. Let them help ease the situation instead of hindering it. Let them encourage a peaceful international atmosphere instead of creating a suffocating one. Then it will be possible for the three Western powers to study all the world problems with them and, in particular, that of Germany.

In that case, France could be counted upon to put forth solutions. Indeed France—who, for her part, is not prepared to give way before the threats of the totalitarian empire—nonetheless retains a deep and sincere friendship for the countries which live in this empire. Furthermore, France believes that the future of modern civilization can lie only in understanding, cooperation and, finally, the osmosis between the countries that created civilization and continue to create it, and which have spread it throughout the world and continue to spread it, and, above all, the osmosis of all the European peoples. That is how I can answer you.

Nuclear Disarmament

Question: Do you think that we can avoid a world conflict over the subject of Germany and of Berlin, and under what conditions? Do you believe that the resumption of nuclear tests by the Soviet Union renders the attempt for a peaceful solution more difficult, less difficult or that it is of no great importance?

Answer: I will answer only this: France knows that a conference has been under way for a long time at Geneva between the three States possessing huge atomic weapons. It always seemed to us that this conference should be part of a comprehensive question called disarmament, and more specifically nuclear disarmament. With regard to everything that effectively leads to nuclear disarmament, France would undoubtedly cooperate; this is all I can say for the moment.

Algeria[1]

Questions: What is the position of France concerning the Governments which have recognized the G.P.R.A.?

----

[1] See also below, pp. 782–97.

As a result of the reshaping of the G.P.R.A. and of the speech delivered yesterday in Belgrade by its new President, do you envisage different perspectives?

How do you intend to resolve the Algerian question before the end of this year? By giving independence to Algeria?

Answer: I will answer all this in due time. Rather I shall repeat, once again, that our conception for Algeria is completely different from that which we have held since the conquest, and this is so because all the conditions of this problem —French, Algerian and world conditions—have themselves completely changed. Our objective is not at all one of retaining the political, administrative and economic responsibility for Algeria. That particular policy, if it may have been good in former times, would today be vain and anachronistic, and we do not believe that the interest, the honor and the future of France should be, in this present era, based on continuing the domination of populations—a large majority of whom is not composed of her people—and everything leads and will lead these populations more and more to become free and to be their own masters. This must be understood and must be kept in mind when one finds fault with the ideas of the Head of State on this matter.

Once again we are a country in full revolution which knows that the source of its prosperity and its strength lies in its own development, which needs its own means in order to achieve this development and which does not intend to sink these means indefinitely in fruitless tasks. In brief, we are not at all anxious to be the possessors and the keepers of this region. Naturally, we do not exclude the possibility that this disengagement could result in a form of cooperation like that which took place elsewhere, but this cooperation, as desirable as it may appear to us, and especially so sentimentally—this cooperation is by no means necessary to us; we hold on to it only insofar as it implies exchange and understanding.

This being so, for us the Algerian problem comes down to three essential questions: the institution of an Algerian State, France's relations with this State and, as you suggested, the future of the Sahara.

The institution of an Algerian State. Where can such a State come from? Normally it can only come from self-determination, that is to say from the vote of the inhabitants, because no legitimacy, no Algerian sovereignty existed prior to the conquest on which one can fall back as was done in Tunisia and Morocco. This self-determination means a referendum which will institute the Algerian State, and afterwards elections from which the definitive government will emerge. However, we do not want self-determination, in case it should take place, to originate directly from the French authorities, because then we would still be fruitlessly holding on when the point is disengagement.

Under these conditions, only a provisional Algerian authority can lead the country to self-determination and to elections. And naturally it is necessary that this authority have enough stability, enough support and also that it be in agreement with us on the conditions of the procedure. We assumed—perhaps we can still assume—that the F.L.N., providing that fighting and terrorist attacks had ceased, would become part of such an all organism. Moreover, this was one of the principal objects of the conversations we attempted to hold with its representatives. Failing this, the only conceivable source from which an Algerian

Executive can be formed is the whole of the elected representatives, and the immediate task of this Executive would be to lead the country once more to a referendum and to elections with, no doubt, a strictly local force of law and order being placed at its disposal.

If, in the long run and definitely, in spite of what France proposes and what she intends to propose again, we cannot attain that the Algerians be willing and able to lead Algeria to its own decision, then we would have to draw the inferences of this situation. Indeed, as far as France is concerned, the present situation in Algeria cannot last forever. On the other hand, the success of our armed forces in Algeria assures us complete freedom of our decisions and of our movements, a freedom we are not certain that the international situation will allow us to keep fully indefinitely.

That is why, in the hypothesis which I mentioned, we would be led to relocate in a specified region the Algerians of European stock and those Moslems who would wish to remain with France. Afterwards, we would undoubtedly see our way more clearly. Even more so since those among these elements who would express the desire to do so would be transferred to Metropolitan France, where their settlement and their future situation is about to be organized. As for the territories that we would leave to themselves, it goes without saying that the funds for current operation and investments which we are now devoting to them would be stopped. Others than ourselves would be responsible for the life of the populations.

There is the question of the Sahara. With regard to the Sahara, our line of conduct is that which safeguards our interests and which takes realities into account. Our interests consist in the following: free exploitation of the oil and gas which we have discovered or would discover, disposal of airfields and traffic rights for our communications with Black Africa. The realities, they are that there is not one Algerian—I know this—who does not believe that the Sahara should be a part of Algeria, and that there would not be one single Algerian Government, whatever may be its orientation with regard to France, who would not ceaselessly proclaim Algerian sovereignty over the Sahara. Finally, the fact that, if an Algerian State were instituted and if it were associated with France, the great majority of the Saharan populations would want to belong to it, even if they had not explicitly asked for it in advance.

This is to say that, in the Franco-Algerian debate, whether it is renewed with the F.L.N. or whether it is undertaken with another representative body—that one composed of elected representatives—the question of the sovereignty of the Sahara does not need to be considered, or at least it should not be considered by force. This can serve as a slogan, as a signboard for propaganda. With regard to France, it is a wasted effort. But what concerns us is that there emerge from this agreement—should it take place—an association which safeguards our interests. If neither this safeguard nor association are possible on the Algerian side, we must create, out of all that stone and all that sand, something special as long as and insofar as, for us, the disadvantage be no greater than the advantage.

In any case, of course, the Saharan populations must be consulted on their destiny and under conditions which conform to their dispersion and their diversity. These Saharan populations—since the Sahara, as you well know, is a desert—are exceedingly small and rare in number. . . .

. . . GREAT BRITAIN AND THE COMMON MARKET

Question: Do you approve of the decision made by Great Britain to join the Common Market?

Answer: All along the members of the Common Market, the six of them, have wanted other countries, and in particular Great Britain, to join the Treaty of Rome, to assume the obligations involved in it and, I think, to obtain the advantages deriving therefrom.

We know very well how complex the problem is, but it appears that everything now points to tackling it, and as far as I am concerned, I can only express my gratification, not only from my own country's point of view, but also from the point of view of Europe, and consequently of the world.

BIZERTA[1]

Question: Given your concern in keeping Bizerta at the service of Western defence, have you considered the possibility of negotiating its transfer to the NATO forces?

Answer: Bizerta has never been covered by NATO and I doubt that it ever will be. It does not fall within the scope of the Organization of which you speak.

If you want to form an unbiased judgment on the Bizerta affair, I advise you to look at a map. Then you can see that the location of Bizerta is exceptional; it lies where the Mediterranean narrows between two basins, one on the East and one on the West. For the countries bordering on the latter, that is to say the West, there is the prospect of aggression coming from the other, that is to say the East. They cannot fail not to anticipate it, especially since the world situation is dominated every day, every moment, by the prospect of a war that the East would unleash against the West. And, furthermore, you should look where France is situated on the map. France who—in case of enemy intervention in these regions—would be vitally interested in what would happen, militarily and politically, to the coastal regions lying close to her territory; France who, in any event, would be directly involved in the defense of both sides of the Mediterranean. Therefore, when you consider these facts, you can understand that France will not and cannot, in the present world situation, expose herself, expose Europe, expose the free world to the likelihood of a seizure of Bizerta by hostile forces.

This is why France established a base in Bizerta. This base was held, until the recent events took place, by a garrison just large enough to prevent Bizerta from being taken by a surprise attack. In no way does this base constitute a threat to or put pressure on Tunisia. It faces directly toward the sea and not at all toward the interior. In the middle of these installations, two cities are located: Bizerta and Menzel-Bourguiba, which were normally administered by the Tunisians and occupied by their troops. The arsenal is located right in the Tunisian city. Before the recent events, thousands of Tunisians worked in the

---

[1] See also below, pp. 797–807.

arsenal or on the military grounds, and the channel which linked the base to the sea was held by the Tunisians. When in 1954 France, on her own initiative, concluded with the Bey of Tunis a treaty which replaced the Protectorate, when in 1956 she recognized the independence of Tunisia,[1] and when in 1958 I myself ordered the withdrawal of all the French troops still in that country,[2] we never, for one single instant, left any doubt in the minds of the Tunisians as to the fact that, while taking this friendly step on their behalf, we intended to continue to use the base of Bizerta as long as the world threat remained what it is.

Naturally, this did not prevent us from proposing to the Tunisians, as we do constantly, that they settle with us the conditions for the use of this base. And little by little we handed over to them all kinds of installations and barracks which were not necessary for the possible future use of the services.

Above all, we maintained with Tunisia political, economic, cultural and human relations, of which the least that can be said is that they were not to the detriment of that country.

On the Tunisian side, we might have thought that, even while proclaiming its sovereignty over Bizerta—a sovereignty that in principle was never contested by France and is not contested today—and while declaring that one day the withdrawal of French troops would need to be negotiated, it was understood that the general situation did not include this issue at the present time. The exchange of letters which took place on June 17, 1958 between my Government and that of Tunis, and which settled the question of the withdrawal of the French forces, excluded Bizerta from this withdrawal, and explicity reserved this question. There was therefore reason to believe, on the French side, that this was a sort of commitment to temporize and await developments. When I received the President of the Tunisian Republic at Rambouillet on February 27 and the question of Bizerta came up, I told him quite clearly that, things being as they were, France could not and would not leave Bizerta. And I must say he appeared to accept this. Moreover, after these talks he launched forth into friendly statements towards us. In the meantime he emphasized, on a number of occasions, that the essential question for the Mahgreb was the settlement of the Algerian issue, and that as long as this question had not been settled, he would not raise the Bizerta question so as not to complicate matters still further. Then, for reasons probably connected with what is happening in the Arab world, the Tunisian Republic suddenly changed its tone and its tune. There were threats; then demands, and then aggression.

It must be said that during the Rambouillet talks, the President of the Tunisian Republic called for a change to be made in the frontiers of the Sahara in favor of Tunisia and at the expense of Algeria. This modification of the frontier was, in a way, to provide Tunisia with a future access to the Sahara. Moreover, M. Bourguiba did not hide the fact that this was only a beginning and that he was aiming at the Edjeleh region in the heart of the desert where there are, as you know, large oil deposits. Incidentally, I would point out that the Edjeleh region had never been inhabited by anyone before the French set up their installations and carried out their research there. But this was only another indication of that passionate and sudden interest which is now being taken in the

[1] *Documents*, 1956, pp. 692–3.   [2] ibid., 1958, pp. 400–1.

Sahara desert by people other than very scattered nomads, occasional cave explorers and passing tourists. I should add that everything looked as if the friendly decision that my Government took in 1958—a decision to place the terminus of the Edjeleh oil pipe-line in Tunisia instead of in Algeria like the Hassi-Messaoud pipeline, which gave Tunisia, ultimately at French expense, royalties which were not inconsiderable—gave a right to Tunisia to claim the source of the black gold.

We informed M. Bourguiba at the time that since we were in the act of helping an Algerian State to come into being, a State which could not help having a basic interest in the Sahara, and since we were also in the process of devoting to the desert many of our initiatives and investments, we were not going to stake claims of sovereignty over the stones and the sand heedlessly, and hand them out piece by piece. The question of the Sahara could not be studied normally and settled at that time with Tunisia. It was then that the Tunisian aggression occurred, both on our territory in the Sahara and at our installations in Bizerta. Simultaneously, there were all kinds of sequestrations, confiscations and humiliations inflicted on a number of our compatriots living in Tunisia. Under these circumstances, we could not and did not do anything except maintain the integrity of our territory in the Sahara and re-establish the conditions for use of the Bizerta base. And surely we shall do this again if necessary.

But we have for a long time been issuing constant invitations to the Tunisian Government, and we have done so again recently, to negotiate with us, first the conditions of a *modus vivendi* in Bizerta and later the conditions for using the base during the dangerous period through which the world is passing. It seems that the so-called 'United' Nations discussed and voted a resolution on the subject. I do not think it necessary to point out that, given the present composition of this Organization, the wild or fanciful currents which stir it, and given also the constant violations of its own charter, we do not recognize its having any right of arbitration or of jurisdiction. When all the words squandered there on this subject shall have faded away like so many others before them, the realities will remain. Would that Tunis take them into account and reach with Paris an agreement based on common sense. Such is the wish of France.

GENERAL DE GAULLE'S CONCLUSION

France is now engaged in the greatest effort of regeneration that she has ever undertaken. She is pursuing her technical, economic and social progress. The number of her young people is growing and educational facilities are being expanded for them. Overseas, she is completing her task of decolonization. She is regaining her international stature. She is modernizing her means of defense.

Clearly, all this is not taking place without difficulties and commotions, for the task is an extremely hard one. What is more, we are coming up from far behind. Finally, anything connected with prejudice, private interests, passions and routines is inevitably affected. Since the State has undergone severe crises and a lengthy deterioration, the result is that negligence and inadequacy can still be found in the services which work for it. Among them there have even been dissenters. As freedom is maintained in every field—politics, press, labor unions—it is easy for grievances, criticisms and complaints to have free rein.

Since the groups that harbor old and new grudges, also those that are fundamentally pessimistic, and finally those that pledge obedience to foreign totalitarianism, act simultaneously on all matters, there is sometimes a feeling in the air of various enterprises being made to discourage the public. But all that is nothing more than froth floating on the surface of deep waters. In point of fact, those who, both here and abroad, keep their eyes and their ears open, accept the evidence of our national progress.

However, on the outside, Soviet claims—more virulent than ever—are being raised. Moreover, if France shows herself to be solid and stable within, it can also be noted to what extent she is firm and serene in the face of troubles without.

Undoubtedly, her attitude contains the idea that, since the pretext used by the Soviets for their demonstration—that is, the Berlin affair—is quite ridiculous in relation to the great misfortunes which they risk causing, they will not go to the extreme where they themselves would be destroyed while they ravaged others. At the same time, our people judge, by instinct and by experience, that the best way to aid world peace is not to withdraw before those who threaten it. They know that the first duty which free men must fulfill is not to allow to be subjugated those who wish to remain free. But, also, they believe that the greatest service which a country sure of itself, as ours is rightly so, can render to civilization is to remain ready to establish all contacts, rapprochements, common efforts —which are imperative to the great States on both sides—as soon as the outrages and threats will have ceased and a peaceful atmosphere will enable them to collaborate.

Such is the France of today. Certainly, it may be regretted that the relative means she possesses are limited in comparison to those which she had at other times in history. How often—I can say it—have I myself experienced the distress and disadvantage of this. But the French, provided that they persevere, are on the road to recovering these means. In any case and from now on, right at this moment, in the midst of the peoples who all, yes all, bear their burden, as we ourselves bear ours, I believe that the French nation is truly worthy of France.

5. Address delivered by President de Gaulle over French radio and television, 2 October 1961[1] (extracts)

National renovation—what a vast and arduous undertaking. For France, as she is today, is offered no other choice by the times and the world we live in other than that of great success or downfall without reprieve. Owing to the deepseated unity demonstrated by our people, we are on the road to success. But if, unfortunately, we should once again permit worries, tumult and the incoherence that we know of to take a hold of our affairs, then downfall would be our lot.

At home, our country is in the process of a transformation which destines her —for the benefit of all her children—to a prosperity and a strength worthy of her. But this requires that no private interest prevail over the general interest; that our economy, our government, our technology, our education, our equipment always keep pace with modern standards; that nothing, however, prevail over

[1] *French Affairs, No. 126* (French Embassy, Service de Presse et d'Information, 2 October 1961).

the objectives of the plan, the stability of finances and the soundness of the franc, which are the foundations of our structure. Within the context of this development, of this discipline, many things have already been accomplished and everyone knows it. Many things are being accomplished and everyone sees this. Many things are yet to be accomplished and everyone believes this. But there would be no chance of achieving any real progress nor of preserving what has already been achieved if we were to fall back again into agitation and crises.

As far as Algeria is concerned, we have not ceased, through wind and tide, during the last three years to move nearer to the goal that I laid down in the name of France: exercise by the Algerians of the right to decide their own fate; the setting up, if they so desire—and I have no doubt that they do—of an independent and sovereign Algerian state by means of self-determination; cooperation offered by France to the new Algeria for its existence and its development, which implies in particular that the people of European stock have their rights and guarantees in Algeria. During the same period in which—ever since the upheaval of May 1958—the evolution that was leading the vast majority of Frenchmen and Algerians to this clear and firm solution was taking place, the French army, the French forces of law and order had to, and still have to, control the field. This was done. Finally, at the risk of collapse, it was and still is necessary that, despite the repeated incitements to disobey and to desert tendered by those who went astray, the army remain, then as well as now, attached to its duty. It did so then; it is doing so now. All honor to it.

At present it is possible to construct. We are prepared once again to seek an agreement with the leaders of the rebellion, to bring peace once and for all to Algeria, to settle the conditions for self-determination and to decide upon the basis of a Franco-Algerian cooperation. We wish, at the same time—for one does not exclude the other—to see the representative elements in Algeria take up, on their own initiative, the preparation of that great undertaking that the referendum will be. We are in any case determined to organize as of now a truly Algerian force of law and order which will be at the service of the provisional powers when they assume the responsibility of leading the country to a decision. We declare to the Algerian people that peace, choice and the future of Algeria are within their own reach. We solemnly call upon the French people in Algeria, whatever their regrets for an era that is over, to stand by France, to give forthright assistance to the birth of a new Algeria, of the kind that France desires, that is, one in which the French will have their rightful place. It remains well understood, of course, that, if this were not so, the protection of Frenchmen would be assured in any case, either by relocating them in safety areas, or, for those who should so request, by giving them the means to take their place, in Metropolitan France, in the life of the country.

Yesterday because these were the things we wanted and that we led the great majority of the people gradually to adopt; now and in the future in order to successfully conclude the task—we needed, we need and we shall need a steadfastness and a firmness that of course rule out the uncertainties, the weaknesses and the contradictions of the past, failings that have been condemned by the people and by events.

We have to go about the transformation of the country and the complete change in our relations with Algeria in a period of international danger. Everything that we have to do is very much complicated by this. Since we are France, a country that is essential to Europe and necessary to the free world, it is our duty to stand firm and erect in the face of demands from the totalitarian bloc and to urge our allies to do the same. For nothing would be more dangerous to our cause, or safety, our alliance and our peace than to retreat step by step before those who are menacing us. But, should the threats stop, should there at long last be an easing of international tension and should relations between East and West return to normal, then France will be ready to enter into constructive negotiations between the great powers on world problems: Germany, disarmament, aid to underdeveloped countries, cooperation for human progress. Undoubtedly she could also facilitate the emergence of a Europe balanced between the Atlantic and the Urals, provided that totalitarian imperialism would have ceased to manifest its ambitions there. But this policy that is being pursued by a newly rebuilt France would soon melt into thin air if—making once again of our powers the houses of cards that they were yesterday—we moved toward confusion and then toward subversion. Then our decline and, shortly, our disruption would lead to the dismemberment of Western Europe and give the signal for calamity. . . .

6. Statement to the Senate by M. Couve de Murville, 5 December 1961[1]

Mesdames, messieurs, je voudrais indiquer, en commençant, que je suis reconnaissant à M. Le Bellegou—je le dis comme je le pense—d'avoir posé une question et provoqué ici un débat sur le problème essentiel qui domine aujourd'hui la scène internationale. C'est, pour le Gouvernement, pour moi-même en particulier, une occasion bienvenue, non seulement d'entendre les points de vue qui ont été exposés, mais de définir publiquement devant vous notre position.

Ces occasions n'étant pas fréquentes—et je le regrette autant que M. Le Bellegou, car je suis toujours à la disposition du Sénat—je voudrais demander la permission de traiter le sujet dans son ensemble, faisant à cette occasion, plutôt qu'une réponse à une question, un exposé de politique étrangère.

C'est, monsieur Raymond Guyot, le 28 Novembre 1958 qu'a commencé l'affaire de Berlin lorsque le Gouvernement soviétique a envoyé aux trois puissances occidentales une note[2] dans laquelle il mettait, pour la première fois, en cause le statut de cette ville et notamment le maintien des garnisons française, américaine et britannique. Il lançait ce qui, à l'époque, avait été considéré comme un ultimatum, nous donnant six mois pour régler la question, conformément aux exigences de M. Khrouchtchev.

On connaît la suite: la ferme résistance des Occidentaux, puis le voyage de M. Macmillan en Russie, enfin, la conférence de Genève poursuivie pendant plus de trois mois sans beaucoup de résultats et finalement interrompue à la suite de l'invitation lancée par le président Eisenhower au Premier ministre soviétique de venir lui rendre visite au Etats-Unis.

Cette première rencontre au sommet, suivie de nombre d'autres au cours de

Journal Officiel, Débats Parlementaires, Sénat, 2e Séance du 5 décembre 1961, pp. 2296-7.
[2] *Documents*, 1958, pp. 146-64.

l'automne 1959, aboutit finalement à l'organisation d'une conférence au sommet également en mai 1960. Il n'est pas besoin de rappeler ici ce qui se passa à cette réunion, suite sans doute fatale d'une équivoque créée au cours des six mois précédents sur les possibilités de régler à l'amiable le problème de Berlin dans des conditions satisfaisant les exigences contradictoires de toutes les parties en présence.

Un nouveau délai fut annoncé par M. Khrouchtchev le 16 mai 1960:[1] Il s'agissait d'attendre le résultat des élections présidentielles américaines et le départ de M. Eisenhower, pour permettre au leader soviétique de traiter raisonnablement avec le successeur de celui-ci. Le nouveau terme paraissait être février ou mars 1961, c'est-à-dire un mois ou deux mois après l'installation du futur élu à la Maison Blanche. En fait, c'est au début de juin 1961 que M. Kennedy et M. Khrouchtchev se rencontrèrent à Vienne et que ce dernier put exposer à son nouvel interlocuteur ses vues sur Berlin et sur l'Allemagne.[2] Ces vues étaient, bien entendu, celles-là mêmes qui étaient contenues dans la note de novembre 1958: transformation du statut de Berlin-Ouest en un statut de ville libre et neutralisée, mise en cause des garnisons occidentales, détachement total de Berlin de la République fédérale, contrôle des accès par les autorités communistes de l'Allemagne orientale.

En ce qui concerne cette dernière, je veux dire l'Allemagne orientale, la Russie annonçait aussi son intention de conclure avec elle, avant la fin de l'année en cours 1961 un traité de paix qui automatiquement lui transmettrait les pouvoirs que jusqu'alors l'Union soviétique s'était réservés concernant le contrôle et la garantie des accès occidentaux à Berlin. Nous aurions alors à nous arranger avec cette République démocratique allemande que nous ne reconnaissions pas, et si nous cherchions à passer outre, nous aurions affaire à l'armée russe.

Aucun accord ne pouvait évidemment se faire sur de telles bases entre M. Kennedy et M. Khrouchtchev. Une violente campagne d'intimidation fut alors organisée par l'Union soviétique, fondée avant tout sur la menace des armes nucléaires et dirigée successivement contre chacun des pays de l'Europe occidentale. Cette campagne devait culminer en septembre par la reprise des expériences atomiques, couronnée de façon spectaculaire par l'explosion de la bombe de cinquante mégatonnes.

Cependant, la panique se développait en Allemagne de l'Est provoquant dans la population—M. Portmann l'a évoqué tout à l'heure—des départs massifs vers la République fédérale, via Berlin-Ouest. C'est dans ces conditions et, je le crois, essentiellement pour arrêter un exode devenu catastrophique pour l'administration de M. Ulbricht, que Moscou prit et exécuta, le 13 août, la décision majeure de couper Berlin en deux et d'interdire totalement l'accès de Berlin-Ouest aux malheureux habitants de la République démocratique allemande. Décision majeure, réussie sans coup férir, qui pèse et continuera à peser sur la situation et l'avenir de l'Allemagne tout entière.

Par là déjà la Russie réalisait plus qu'à moitié son programme. Il n'est pas étonnant dès lors qu'elle ait pu, deux mois plus tard, annoncer qu'elle renonçait au délai fixé en dernier lieu, celui de la fin de l'année 1961, pour la signature de

[1] ibid., 1960, pp. 26–30.   [2] Below, pp. 277–80.

son traité avec l'Allemagne orientale.[1] Trois ans après le 28 novembre 1958, nous repartons donc dans l'affaire de Berlin pour une période indéterminée.

L'affaire n'en reste pas moins grave. Le Sénat sait que le Gouvernement français, pour sa part, n'en a jamais sous-estimé l'importance. Au cours des trois années qui viennent de s'écouler je crois pouvoir dire qu'il a maintenu sa position sans faiblesse, aussi bien quant aux méthodes que quant au fond des problèmes. Quant aux méthodes nous n'avons jamais accepté l'idée qu'il fût possible de négocier sous la menace, fût-ce la menace suprême, celle de la destruction atomique. Nous n'avons pas accepté non plus que les questions à discuter fussent celles-là mêmes et celles-là seulement, que nos interlocuteurs posaient ou imposaient. Une négociation internationale doit être ouverte et libre. On ne peut prétendre contraindre à prendre seulement en considération la solution présentée par l'une des parties. Enfin il nous apparaît que pour être utile une négociation doit être suffisamment préparée et offrir une perspective raisonnable de ne pas s'orienter immédiatement vers la rupture ou vers le renoncement. Nous avions déjà très fermement exprimé cette idée à la fin de 1959 et au début de 1960, lorsqu'il s'agissait d'envisager la réunion d'une conférence au sommet. L'expérience a malheureusement prouvé qu'une préparation insuffisante ou superficielle ouvre la voie aux échecs les plus spectaculaires.

Quant au fond, nous avons toujours dénoncé le caractère fallacieux du réglement définitif et pacifique de la question allemande que le Gouvernement soviétique a imaginé et qu'il entend nous faire accepter: consacrer la division de l'Allemagne par un traité de paix, signé, à défaut des deux Allemagnes, par celle de l'Est, laquelle n'a évidemment rien à refuser à la Russie; neutraliser Berlin-Ouest ensuite en éliminant progressivement la présence occidentale.

Certes il s'agit, pour ce qui est de la division de l'Allemagne, de consacrer le *statu quo*. Nous n'avons jamais eu l'idée, et la République fédérale d'Allemagne pas davantage, qu'il fût concevable de chercher à changer, par la force, les situations acquises. Mais proclamer ces situations acquises comme l'état final des choses, contrairement d'ailleurs aux principes de l'autodétermination, n'est-ce pas tout simplement, sous prétexte de juguler un prétendu esprit de revanche —qui paraît aujourd'hui préoccuper davantage M. Guyot qu'autrefois un pacte trop célèbre ses prédécesseurs. . . . (*Applaudissements à droite et sur divers bancs au centre et à gauche.*)

M. Louis Namy: Parlez-nous de Munich!

M. le Ministre: Vous m'avez compris!

. . . N'est-ce pas chercher à détacher l'Allemagne occidentale de l'Occident en réduisant le peuple allemand au désespoir, c'est-à-dire à l'aventure? Et puis, si nous devons reconnaître les faits accomplis, pourquoi borner cette reconnaissance aux faits accomplis qui conviennent à la Russie? Après tout, la situation de Berlin si étrange qu'elle soit—mais qu'est-il de normal dans la situation de l'Allemagne?—la situation de Berlin est un de ces faits accomplis qui résultent de la guerre et de la capitulation nazie. Est-il moins respectable que les autres parce qu'il est un inconvénient pour M. Ulbricht?

---

[1] Below, p. 224.

Face aux exigences de la Russie, nous disons pour notre part: se réunir avec l'Union soviétique pour discuter du problème allemand et de tous les autres grands problèmes qui nous séparent d'elle, bien entendu, cela est nécessaire et cela devra avoir lieu. Encore faut-il que cela se fasse dans l'atmosphère qui convient aux solutions positives, c'est-à-dire dans la détente, dans l'objectivité, loin des menaces et des imprécations. Encore faut-il que dans une telle atmosphère, les problèmes soient librement débattus.

Encore faut-il, enfin, si, comme il est probable, les solutions définitives ne sont pas concevables aujourd'hui pour l'Allemagne, encore faut-il que le *statu quo* et les aménagements à y apporter soient conclus de telle sorte qu'ils respectent les droits et les intérêts légitimes de toutes les parties en présence. Il est clair à cet égard que, pour les Occidentaux, leurs droits et leurs intérêts à Berlin sont fondamentaux et qu'ils ne peuvent être abandonnés.

Mesdames, messieurs, tels sont les principes qui, depuis trois ans, et encore au cours de ces derniers mois, ont constamment inspiré l'action diplomatique de la France. Ils nous ont guidés, en particulier, lorsqu'il s'est agi de prendre position sur le problème complexe qu'il est convenu d'appeler maintenant la négociation avec l'Union soviétique.

Ce problème, paradoxalement, est de savoir si les Français, les Américains et les Britanniques doivent prendre l'initiative de proposer aux Russes l'organisation d'une conférence à quatre. Je dis paradoxalement car, enfin, ce sont les Russes qui ont posé la question d'un changement de *statu quo*. Retournant en quelque sorte la situation, il s'agirait pour nous de leur demander de discuter des conditions qu'ils mettraient à notre maintien à Berlin, c'est-à-dire de discuter des concessions que nous aurions à leur faire pour qu'ils acceptent, dans une certaine mesure et peut-être pour un certain temps seulement, que nos garnisons puissent rester et qu'ainsi la liberté de Berlin-Ouest demeure plus ou moins garantie.

Nous n'avons pas envisagé de nous engager à l'aveugle lorsque, en août, puis en septembre, nous nous sommes rencontrés avec nos alliés pour en discuter. Tous ensemble, nous nous sommes mis d'accord sur la conclusion qu'il ne fallait rien précipiter. Nous avons constaté, d'autre part, qu'il était essentiel d'abord de bien marquer à Moscou le sérieux et même le danger de son entreprise à un moment où les Occidentaux, pour leur part, manifestaient leur volonté de résister à la menace en prenant des mesures pour renforcer la défense de l'Europe. On sait quel a été, à cet égard, l'effort considérable décidé aux Etats-Unis.

Je voudrais dire également à M. Le Bellegou que la France, de son côté, a fait l'effort maximum compatible avec ses obligations présentes en Algérie. Je ne sais pas si les critiques portées contre l'O. T. A. N. sont de nature, comme il a été dit, de mettre en péril la sécurité occidentale, mais ce qu'on est bien obligé de constater c'est que, de tous les pays européens, la France, si critiquée, est la première à avoir pris des mesures sérieuses et que ce fait est unanimement reconnu par ses alliés comme par le commandement interallié.

En septembre, à New York, puis à Washington, on a, du côté américain, procédé à certaines prises de contact avec le ministre des affaires étrangères soviétique. Je ne peux pas dire que ces sondages aient éclairci d'une façon définitive la situation. Sans doute, ont-ils permis de mieux comprendre les procédures envisagées du côté russe. En ce qui concerne, en revanche, l'avenir de Berlin-Ouest, aucune explication complémentaire n'est venue donner l'impression que les positions fussent moins éloignées les unes des autres.

Enfin, il est apparu que l'on était enclin, à Moscou, à évoquer, à défaut d'un réglement général de la situation allemande, certains problèmes touchant à la sécurité européenne ou à la reconnaissance de la République démocratique allemande, problèmes dont la seule évocation montre les intentions lointaines de l'Union soviétique.

A la suite de ces conversations russo-américaines, une certaine pause est intervenue au moment des élections allemandes, car il fallait alors attendre la constitution du nouveau gouvernement de Bonn. Entre temps s'est tenu le XXIIe congrès du parti communiste de l'Union soviétique qui a apporté au contexte international un certain nombre d'éléments nouveaux. Puis les consultations occidentales ont repris avec le voyage à Washington du chancelier Adenauer et l'entretien du général de Gaulle avec M. Macmillan. Elles sont aujourd'hui en plein développement. Le chancelier Adenauer viendra dans quelques jours à Paris et, la semaine prochaine, les ministres des affaires étrangères des trois puissances et le ministre allemand vont se rencontrer, puis l'ensemble du problème sera évoqué à la réunion annuelle du conseil de l'Alliance atlantique.

J'indique en passant, pour répondre à une observation de M. Portmann, que je ne vois dans tout cela nulle trace de l'absentéisme de la France.

Quoi qu'il en soit, ces réunions auront une importance décisive et nous devons, pour le moment, en attendre les résultats.

Il est naturellement essentiel—on l'a dit tout à l'heure et je le souligne à mon tour—que dans une conjoncture aussi sérieuse le front des Occidentaux demeure ferme et uni. Il le sera dans la mesure où, tous ensemble, nous serons conscients de véritables données du problème et nous manifesterons à leur sujet une volonté unanime.

De quoi, en définitive, s'agit-il en effet?

On dit beaucoup, depuis quelque temps, qu'il faut engager une discussion avec la Russie strictement limitée à Berlin et à ses accès. Je répète que personne aujourd'hui ne peut dire qu'un accord sur un tel sujet serait possible et nous considérons, pour notre part, que le risque serait grand d'un échec qui nous laisserait dans une situation plus tendue encore. En outre, même si des prévisions optimistes apparaissaient justifiées, quelle conviction pourrions-nous avoir que le lendemain, le mois suivant, l'année suivante, tout ne recommencerait pas? En effet, ce n'est plus—cela n'a sans doute jamais été—Berlin seul qui est en cause, c'est l'ensemble de l'Allemagne et par conséquent, le sort de l'Europe elle-même. (*Applaudissements à droite, au centre et sur plusieurs bancs à gauche.*)

Déjà, on voit l'effort de la Russie se tourner dans d'autres directions, celle de la Finlande en particulier, et, au-delà de la Finlande, vers les Etats scandinaves. C'est notre sort à nous, Français, qui est en cause en même temps que celui de l'alliance atlantique elle-même. Neutraliser l'Europe centrale et, d'abord, l'Allemagne est l'objectif évident de la politique soviétique. C'est la remise en cause de tout l'équilibre sur lequel, depuis dix ans et plus, nous cherchons à fonder l'avenir de l'Europe et par conséquent la paix du monde, je veux dire la constitution d'une Europe occidentale étroitement unie pour l'économie, la défense et la politique, et solidement alliée aux Etats-Unis d'Amérique.

Nous avons conscience que là est le danger et que, par conséquent, là est l'essentiel. Le temps viendra à coup sûr—il doit venir—où nous nous en expliquerons avec l'Union soviétique, et ce sera la véritable négociation. (*Applaudissements à droite, sur de nombreux bancs au centre et sur quelques bancs à gauche.*)

(d) Statements of Federal German Foreign Policy

1. Address by the Federal German Foreign Minister, Herr von Brentano, to the United States Council on Foreign Relations, New York, 15 February 1961[1]

President Kennedy in his impressive State-of-the-Union message to Congress[2] frankly expressed his concern about the present situation of the Western alliance system and, in particular, of NATO. We, too, are moved by the same anxieties, and so are the other allies of the United States in Europe. We should therefore reflect and consider in common where the mistakes lie and how they can be remedied. We must not shrink from criticism, even if it is painful; we cannot ignore any demands, even if they concern some of us directly.

I shall refrain from outlining the familiar facts about the origin and development of NATO. I would only recall that the Soviet Union in the years preceding the foundation of NATO forcibly brought more than a hundred million people in Europe under the sway of Communism and absorbed about 600,000 square miles of territory into its sphere of power. Its latest attempt to continue this policy of expansion in Europe began with the Berlin blockade which came to an end almost simultaneously with the establishment of NATO. I believe that the attitude of the Soviet Union to Berlin now and in the near future will be an index of its assessment of the solidarity and capacity for resistance of the Western world.

There is no doubt that the economic and military power of the Soviet bloc has been steadily increasing in the past 12 years. In 1949 the Soviet Union's atomic armament was still in its infancy, whereas that of the United States was already well advanced. Today various signs indicate that the Soviets are equal to the United States in some spheres of nuclear armament and rocket development. The same applies in many other spheres of armament—we need, for example, think only of the Red submarine fleet. This increase in military strength is coupled with a considerable development of the Soviet Union's economy, a development which has been enhanced by the integration of the economies of the satellite states into the Soviet system. On this basis there has been a steadily growing self-assurance on the part of the Soviets and this, in turn, has led to a world-wide political activity and expansion. It is not yet possible to judge whether the rise of Chinese Communism will effect the build-up of the Soviet position of power advantageously or adversely. It may be that serious tensions exist between the Soviet Union and Red China, perhaps ultimately rooted in

[1] H. von Brentano, 'Goals and Means of the Western Alliance', xxxix, *Foreign Affairs*, No. 3, April 1961. Reprinted by permission of the Council on Foreign Relations.
[2] See above, pp. 3–8.

conflicting ideological trends. These differences may affect the future attitude of the Soviet Union towards the Western world. But I think it would be dangerous and premature to record these possible tensions and differences at present as credit items for Western policy.

On the Western side the picture is not so clear. In the economic sector the past 12 years have without doubt led to a significant rise and recovery. Appreciable defense efforts have produced a certain feeling of security. Thanks not least to American help, the free part of Europe has acquired a vitality which is of considerable weight in the over-all potential of the free world. But do not let us deceive ourselves: the equilibrium so laboriously maintained up to now between East and West may change at any time to the disadvantage of the West. The so-called non-committed world, the emerging peoples of Africa and Asia, are vacillating. In their quest for independence they are apt to overlook the real dangers threatening their freedom in the future. And even the free states of the world are in danger of subordinating their security to the maintenance and improvement of living standards and of forgetting that social welfare alone cannot resist political and military pressure supported by superior atomic missiles. This holds good not only for security but also for science and technology. The achievements of American and European scientists in the past hundred years were brilliant and unique; but this would soon become a futile recollection if technical developments in the West were now to lag behind those in the Soviet empire.

That is the position we are in at present. What is NATO's part in this set-up? Has NATO failed? Or can it contribute to the solution of the problems confronting us?

Let us take a look at the Treaty of Washington[1] which is NATO'S constituent instrument and constitution. Only the first five articles of this brief and impressive document are of essential importance. Only one of them, namely Article 5, deals with the obligation to furnish military assistance. Articles 1 to 4, on the other hand, contain far-reaching commitments mainly of a political or economic nature which are regarded by the public at large—if known to it at all—as at most political trimming. Even in informed quarters, including our governments, NATO is frequently looked upon as a merely military alliance which owes its special importance perhaps to the extent of the danger threatening us, but which, apart from that, is no different from any other military coalition. And therein lies an error to which many a mistake, many a failure in recent years, may be traced. Anyone who regards the strongest link uniting the West as nothing more than a military alliance is easily inclined to regard the problems of the world today merely, or largely, from the angle of military security. And, paradoxically enough, this way of looking at things harbors a grave danger precisely for military vigilance and defense preparedness. Whenever the opponent alters his tactics, temporarily suspends the military threat, and operates publicly with apparent pliancy and readiness to compromise, the military danger recedes from the popular consciousness, and there is a noticeable tendency to neglect defense efforts. Visible signs of this dangerous development are the efforts to restrict national defense budgets and curtail the duration of military service.

[1] Of 4 April 1949; *Documents*, 1949–1950, pp. 257–61.

The one-sided picture of NATO as a military defense alliance also contains the danger that the military authorities and their purely military demands may gain a predominant influence on politics. And this touches the very core of the Western world. For us, politics can never be a function of military thought, but must be the responsible organization of all the vital forces in the nation, a task to which defense must be clearly subordinated.

An alliance such as NATO, to which such comprehensive and far-reaching tasks and aims have been entrusted in the preamble as well as in the individual articles of the Treaty, cannot and must not be confined solely to the military sector, to the more passive work of organizing defense: it must regard as its main function the active shaping of a better future. Every decision, every measure we prepare or take, should aim at contributing to a peaceful order both at present and as desired for the future. Seen in this light, the tasks imposed on us by the cold war fall into their logical position and assume their right proportions, as do also any military and other measures serving to deter or, if need be, to wage a hot war. The purpose of these measures is to secure the present peaceful order and keep the way open for achieving a still better order.

In spite of the strong emphasis on NATO's military function, it cannot be said, unfortunately, that NATO's military strength is adequate. Gone is the early momentum which was due not least to the shock of the glaring Communist aggression in Korea, and which culminated in the military decisions of the NATO Council at Lisbon in February 1952.[1] People do not like to be kept in a state of constant over-all strain. Elections and internal political struggles take their toll. All that is part of the concomitants, known to us all, of the democratic way of life, which in our view is the only form of government capable of preserving man's freedom and, therefore, the only form of government offering any prospect of lasting stability. But as the motto of the integrated headquarters of the European NATO forces says, 'Vigilia pretium libertatis'—the price of freedom is vigilance—and vigilance demands a considerable measure of discipline, restrictions and even sacrifices for freedom. Inhibitions are therefore all too understandable. Nevertheless, we must demand such sacrifices from our peoples, our parliaments, our states. Just as the individual must fit himself into his family, so must governments and states in the interest of preserving their independence consciously recognize a certain interdependence.

The danger of war can be reduced without any loss of freedom only if we are at least as strong as our potential opponent. Today this means more than an adequate proportion of divisions or cannon. The brains behind the conduct of war, i.e. political leadership, are today at least as important as physical armaments. We are faced by a politically fanatical opponent who manipulates his instruments of military power with an iron hand and with a uniform, concentrated power of command. We are 15 free states with 15 independent armed forces. Each state has, in turn, its internal and external tasks and problems requiring the services of those forces. Only a part of those forces are at the disposal of NATO. All of this may be politically understandable and inevitable. But it is far from rational that the armed forces at the disposal of NATO are not all under one supreme commander invested with clear-cut authority.

[1] See *Documents*, 1952, pp. 4–7.

We have four different command areas (Europe, the Atlantic, the Channel, Canada/U.S.A.) the commanders of which are not subordinate to one single supreme commander but to a committee, the Military Committee, to which another committee, the Standing Group, is superior, subordinate or equal in questions of military planning, but not in questions of command. And all these bodies are theoretically subordinate to the political guidance of the NATO Council which would scarcely be capable of action in an emergency, since the permanent members, the NATO ambassadors, are dependent on instructions from their respective capitals. The said commanders, *e.g.* General Norstad for Europe, have no power of command whatsoever over the armed forces of the Alliance in time of peace, and but a limited power of command in time of war. A British battalion cannot even be transferred from North Germany to South Germany; this is due not only to lack of power of command but also to the fact that logistics lie within the sphere of national competency. That is, the equipment, weapons, vehicles, spare parts, ammunition, etc., stored in South Germany are suitable for the United States units but not for the German, British or French units under the same commander.

The longest distance between the Iron Curtain and the Atlantic Ocean is 500 miles. It can be covered by modern bombers in a few minutes. Yet, that narrow area is still subdivided into several air-defense zones under different commands, simply because national sensibilities have not permitted any other solution so far.

I have mentioned but two examples from a long list of deficiencies in the Organization. I do not intend to set forth the military problems in detail, but am only concerned with the political problem namely, that our policy of deterrence cannot be very convincing or effective as long as we prepare and organize our defenses all too inadequately.

We have been all the more gratified, therefore, by the new conception of setting up a uniform NATO atomic force as proposed to the NATO Council in December last year by the United States Government as part of long-term planning.[1] This would at last be a step towards creating a concentrated NATO power of command—or an integrated NATO force, if I may be permitted a frequently misused expression which I have so far purposely avoided. No final decisions have been made as yet. There are many grave problems to be solved first, perhaps not least in the field of United States legislation. The inescapable question of a reorganization of the command structure raises difficult political and military problems. It will be our task in the near future to solve them. One of these problems concerns the increase of European co-determination in the field of atomic defense. But we have to understand quite clearly that the answer to that question has to take account of one imperative necessity: it must under no circumstances lead to a weakening of NATO's military strength.

II

Let us now turn from the theoretical military battlefield to the very real battlefield of the cold war. Here a dramatic battle of truly historic significance is

[1] See *Documents*, 1960, pp. 131–3; *Survey*, 1959–60, pp. 129–32.

being fought between the two blocs representing antagonistic ideologies, one of them aggressive, expansionist and missionary—a struggle for men's souls and for the shaping of the national systems of all those territories which have not yet taken a definite stand or do not want to do so at all.

While we of the West can contemplate only defense in the military sphere, we should definitely take the initiative in the cold war. We shall not make any progress toward a better order in the world and the realization of our ideals if we seek illusive security behind a political Maginot Line and are content to await the enemy's attacks and only to react instead of acting.

We are indeed fighting in a good cause. Why do we always seem to be ashamed of it? Are not our ideas of freedom and justice and peace and prosperity noble and convincing? For more than two thousand years, many have suffered and died for those ideals. Are we no longer able to convey them to others? We should not be so proud as to consider political propaganda beneath our dignity. If the citizens of a newly created state are taken in by the most primitive Soviet propaganda and act accordingly, all our fine education is of no avail, and that state takes its stand with World Communism against the West. The members of NATO have to this day been unable to agree on any concerted action in a field which for want of a better term is called 'psychological warfare', and this in spite of the fact that we would have the advantage of being able to make propaganda based on truth and reality without resorting—as the Communists must— to lies and slander. The makers of the North Atlantic Treaty were fully aware of that task when stipulating in Article 2 that the member States 'will contribute toward the further development of peaceful and friendly international relations by strengthening their free institutions' and 'by bringing about *a better under-standing* of the principles upon which these institutions are founded'.

It is in this light that we also have to look at one particular aspect of our relations with the less developed or, as we call them, the developing countries. It is certainly not incumbent on NATO to carry out joint actions in such countries. But it is definitely one of the urgent and typical tasks of our Alliance to subject to joint consideration every measure which seems likely to forestall Soviet activity and help the peoples in those developing countries to achieve and preserve true freedom.

This brings us to the question of political consultation, an obligation accepted by all but fulfilled consistently by only a few. Article 4 of the NATO Treaty lays down unequivocally that 'the Parties will consult together whenever, in the opinion of any of them, the territorial integrity, political independence or security of any of the Parties is threatened'. This text is both so clear and so comprehensive that practically all political questions of worldwide importance ought to be the subject of consultation within the NATO Council. And yet it happens again and again either that questions of vital importance to the West are not discussed within NATO at all, or that in spite of consultation, differences between NATO partners remain unbridgeable. It is no use tinkering with methods and trying, for instance, to introduce a binding obligation to consult. We are faced here with a dilemma which may be due to the fact that the actions and policies of a nation, a state, can in the last resort be determined only by its own innate forces which sometimes are intelligible to that nation alone and which, though certainly influenced by individual and collective decisions, have their roots in the national life of the people concerned. The subjective limit of loyalty to an alliance seems to be reached as soon as a nation feels that vital interests of its own are at stake; and this is particularly dangerous in the case of NATO, as that alliance is meant to secure the existence of us all. It is a matter of political wisdom not to formulate or construe agreements in so inflexible a manner that this limit will be reached or even drawn. Such political wisdom has been applied by the men who drafted the North Atlantic Treaty. We should not, in too perfectionist a mood, expect our allies to do more than they—or we—are able and willing to grant.

Awareness of the limitations of our Alliance may make it easier for us to find the place that NATO might occupy in the future system of peace that we are striving for. I am thinking, first, of the shaping of the free world, *i.e.* of the internal system of the West, and secondly of the future of the world in general.

III

As regards the internal Western system, NATO is to us a wall protecting us from hostile interference so that we may shape and organize our internal situation according to our own ideas. We have not yet found a final pattern; indeed, we may never find one, but we should never tire of seeking better solutions. However, there have been a number of successes and results that may encourage us to continue on the road we have followed so far. In saying this I have in mind, among other things, certain developments in the Federal Republic of Germany. After the complete collapse of the ignominious Third Reich we have succeeded in establishing Germany a solid democratic system. That was possible only because the free world was ready to admit Germany to the community of free nations, thus clearing the road for reconstruction by the German people. Today our Federal Republic is an integral part of the free world, and the German people are determined to strengthen that link and never again to let it give way. That there is an evil spirit of intolerance and injustice in the other part of Germany, that concentration camps still exist there, is, God knows, not the fault of the Germans. The régime there is instituted and maintained solely by the Soviet Union.

I am also thinking of the fundamentally new relations of friendship uniting the Germans and the French after centuries of feuds—a relationship that is based equally on feelings, rational considerations and conviction.

Let me mention also the bold idea of a supranational community which constitutes a first attempt at transforming and perhaps overcoming the ancient concept of the nation-state by introducing new and superior institutional forms of relationship between different peoples. The Schuman Plan, the Common Market and Euratom may not be perfect solutions, but they may constitute a solid foundation on which to erect the structure of a political community. In my view the contrast between the 'Six' and the 'Seven' that causes Americans and Europeans so much concern at present is not a proof of failure but a challenge to advance towards a closer union by means of new solutions. We are firmly convinced that the O.E.C.D. which has just been created will also serve this objective. In the final analysis all these endeavors are nothing but an attempt to give organizational form to an existing spiritual, political and economic reality.

As I have said, NATO in my view is not necessarily an element of the internal system of the West but rather a guardian to safeguard in undisturbed development. All the greater, on that account, is NATO's importance as a stabilizing factor in the endeavor of the free nations to shape the future of the world in general. In the Preamble to the North Atlantic Pact the following is laid down:

> The Parties to this Treaty reaffirm their faith in the purposes and principles of the Charter of the United Nations and their desire to live in peace with all peoples and all Governments.
>
> They are determined to safeguard the freedom, common heritage and civilization of their peoples, founded on the principles of democracy, individual liberty and the rule of law. . . .
>
> They are resolved to unite their efforts for collective defence and for the preservation of peace and security.

NATO's point of departure, therefore, is an avowal of faith in the United Nations. From the very first, the founders of NATO stated clearly that NATO was created in conformity with the Charter of the United Nations and would be active only within that framework. This condition, by the way, was also given due consideration by the Federal Republic of Germany. Contrary to the wishes of its people and government, our Federal Republic is not a member of the United Nations; yet on its accession to the North Atlantic Treaty it solemnly declared its readiness to conduct its policy in conformity with the principles laid down in the United Nations Charter and to undertake the obligation contained in Article 2 of that Charter.

Some day when all the nations have made the Charter of the United Nations the basis of their policy, NATO may become superfluous; but at the present stage the United Nations urgently needs NATO and the balance of power it creates in opposition to the system that, as President Kennedy has stated, desires to make the United Nations an arena for the cold war.

However, the common attitude of NATO partners towards the United Nations is, as regards the political reality, not identical with a uniform attitude within the United Nations, where differences exist and have frequently been expressed. There are clashes of opinion not only between individual NATO states but also within these states. The divergent views about the future of colonial regions which have acquired freedom and independence are a typical example. Nobody will deny the fundamental claim which all peoples have to self-determination and freedom. But in political practice that claim is bound up with the necessity to safeguard the freedom of those peoples. We would fail to do justice to our responsibilities towards the emergent nations if we allowed them to pass from a state of misunderstood freedom into the total slavery of Communism. The fate meted out to the peoples in Eastern and Central Europe shows that Communism is, in fact, an atrocious form of neo-colonialism. Similar problems are presented by the question of what attitude we should take towards those European states still under Soviet domination.

Thus, in the end, it all leads up to the problem of the possibilities and limitations of political consultation. With all due recognition of the momentous factors governing the political views of individual member states, we simply cannot afford to be disunited. An argument that is not supported by other nations is of no use. We would do well in this case to support a view that, while perhaps not in complete conformity with our own view, points in the right direction and has prospects of being accepted. I have the impression that Western States sometimes oppose their allies more rigidly than they oppose their opponents. I think it would be a wiser policy to confront the opponent with a unanimous view even if unanimity has to be reached by means of a compromise with a friend.

No matter whether future summit conferences or other East-West negotiations are being considered or whether disarmament or United Nations problems are being discussed, the West will have to realize more clearly than before the danger inherent in its disunity. Every one of us should abstain from carrying his point to the last extremity if such a renunciation would make it possible to achieve the unity of the free world. We should be prepared at least to listen to the arguments of our friend; the arguments of the opponent we will have to face anyway. Therefore, we should not hestitate in NATO to bring forward for consultation particularly those questions on which we have to expect opposition and criticism.

Although we acknowledge the democratic principle of the equality of all members, which also is applicable in international organizations, it is nevertheless a fact that the Soviet Union recognizes only one power as being of equal rank to it, namely, the United States of America. That fact burdens the United States with a particular responsibility, but it also entitles it to an exceptional position among its allies. I do not suppose that this is denied by any of them. This circumstance entitles the United States to demand that its allies make the same sacrifices and efforts it is prepared to make itself. NATO certainly is not a club for the defense of Europe by the United States but rather an emergency community based on reciprocity. Throughout the years past we have seen impressive evidence of American assistance and loyalty to the alliance, which, of course, reflected at the same time a sound assessment of the American national interest—the Marshall Plan, the undertaking to station American forces in Europe, and, more recently, the declaration of the readiness of the United States to maintain American atomic weapons on the Continent as long as NATO is in force.

In April 1949, the former Secretary of State, Mr. Dean Acheson, gave a clear definition of the term 'mutual assistance' which might well be accepted by the other partners of the alliance. He said: 'Article 3 [of the North Atlantic Treaty] does not bind the United States to the proposed military assistance program nor indeed to any program. It does bind the United States to the principle of self-help and mutual aid. Within this principle, each Party to the Pact must exercise its own honest judgment as to what it can and should do to develop and maintain its own capacity to resist and to help others.'[1] It is in this spirit that during the past months the German Federal Government has

[1] *Strengthening the Forces of Freedom, Selected Speeches and Statements of Secretary of State Acheson, February 1949–April 1950* (Washington U.S.G.P.O. 1950), p. 89.

investigated in what way it could best contribute to aiding the United States to overcome its balance of payments difficulties.

Speaking in New York in 1955, I pointed out that 'the Soviet version of détente policy has the attractiveness of all comfortable or, I dare say, all faint-hearted ideas'. And I continued: 'I think that, should the free world be so faint-hearted as to fall in with the Soviet plans, we would very soon enter a period of disintegration of the free world, and the efforts we shall finally have to make in order to safeguard our own vital rights will be many times greater than the efforts required at present to attain our objectives.'

I fear that the situation is actually worse today than it was at that time, and that we all share in the responsibility for it. Great efforts are required of every one of us. We expect the United States to go ahead of us, nor as a protecting shield behind which we can enjoy an easy life, but as the leader of a community of free nations which are eager to secure to coming generations a decent life in peace and freedom.

IV

I shall now try to sum up my ideas in a few propositions.

1. NATO was founded as an answer to a distinct political and military threat; particularly the events in Prague and the Berlin blockade made the menace visible in its full significance. Perhaps the free world was only then becoming fully aware of what had previously happened in Poland, in Rumania, in Bulgaria and in Hungary.

2. The political and military threat to the free world has not diminished. The interpretation given by the Soviet Union to the concept of coexistence, too, shows that Moscow has not abandoned its aim of achieving world revolution. On the contrary, one is forced to conclude that the danger has increased. The military strength of the Soviet Union has increased many times over since 1949. In addition to the European 'theatre of war', we now have, in Asia, Korea, Laos and Tibet; in Africa, the Congo; in Latin America, Cuba (to mention only a few examples).

3. NATO has proved its worth. The increasing strength of NATO has stopped the advance of Communism at least in Europe. Communism has ceased to make any progress in the area covered by NATO.

4. NATO will be able to do justice to its future task only if it is possible at least to maintain the balance in weapons technology. This requires unremitting and additional armaments efforts by the NATO partners.

5. The solidarity of the Communist bloc calls for a similar solidarity within NATO. Although NATO is based on voluntary cooperation between sovereign states, the armed forces of the Alliance will, in view of technical developments, be able to fulfill their defense function only if all those concerned are prepared to effect a maximum of integration.

6. Comprehensive integration presupposes within NATO the consummation of joint political intentions. Military strength cannot be an end in itself. The preparation and utilization of such strength requires unified political leadership. The critical remark formulated by a shrewd French politician during the discussions on the European Defense Community also applies to NATO. 'There

have been states without an army, but surely never an army without a state.'

7. If it is necessary to reorganize the command authority within NATO in order to ensure a maximum of integration, it is just as necessary to strengthen political cooperation within NATO.

8. This necessity also arises from the incontestable interdependence of political problems in all parts of the world. Whatever happens in Africa or Asia, first affects those states directly concerned there, *i.e.* for instance, the members of SEATO; but any such developments also indirectly affect every NATO member state, because every engagement involving one of them weakens NATO as a whole. Consultation should lead to a homogeneous political attitude among the member states.

9. This applies very particularly to the United States, which has undertaken world-wide commitments. We should all draw the logical conclusions from the clear, courageous statement by Secretary of State Dean Rusk to the effect that the power of the United States has restricted its sovereignty. He rightly emphasizes that any decision of the United States should take into consideration the needs and hopes of those who have cast in their lot with the United States. This demands, however, the same attitude on the part of all the partners in the Alliance towards the United States.

10. This consideration results logically in the right and duty of the United States, as the strongest power in the free world and the firmest link in the chain of defense alliances, to undertake more vigorously than ever the task of leadership.

11. The other member states consequently have the obligation not to do anything likely to weaken NATO. Thus, for example, European policy should lead only to a strengthening of the West. It is in this spirit and for this reason that the Community of the 'Six' has come into being. Their task is not to develop a defense conception of their own; that task can and should be accomplished only within the framework of NATO. The growing economic potential and the increasing political important of that Community is also at the service of NATO. The tension between the Community of the 'Six' and the Free Trade Area of the 'Seven' is a serious drawback. To eliminate this tension is one of the tasks of the O.E.C.D. Here, too, the United States has a specific function of leadership.

12. Development assistance is not one of NATO's specific tasks. But, on the other hand, it should be recognized that the free world is engaged in conflict with Communism in the less developed countries. Hence, development tasks should also be viewed from the aspect of foreign policy and coordinated accordingly. The O.E.C.D. should, then, in the common interest, undertake or arrange for the implementation of such measures bilaterally or multilaterally.

13. Another of NATO's tasks is to prepare disarmament negotiations or, to be more exact, all negotiations on effective armament controls. Even if such negotiations are carried out under other auspices, for example within the United Nations, as has been the case so far, NATO should participate in the preparations.

14. The necessity of such cooperation, however, applies not only to armament controls. Political coordination within NATO should as far as possible extend to cooperation with other alliance systems, *e.g.* with SEATO. I am thinking,

for example, of the participation of the Secretaries-General of these two organizations in the respective sessions of the Councils of Ministers.

15. It seems just as necessary to extend political coordination to the questions that are discussed and decided within the United Nations. The NATO allies should not confront each other in the United Nations as opponents. The attempt by the Soviet bloc to abuse the United Nations in this sense must be frustrated. The United Nations should be, and should remain, an instrument for the use of the free nations of the world to secure and propagate freedom.

I am aware that the scope of a brief article enables me to give only sketchy answers to some of the questions confronting the Western world. But perhaps I shall succeed in initiating a useful discussion by this analysis of our present position and by raising provocative questions regarding future developments.

2. Press conference given by the Federal German Chancellor, Dr. Adenauer, 10 March 1961[1] (extract)

The Soviet Memorandum

The memorandum of the Soviet Government[2] which Herr Smirnov, as you know, gave to me on February 17, and which was only published a few days ago, is different in tone—and I would like to emphasize that—compared with earlier declarations made by the Soviet Government. The tone is conciliatory, the contents of the memorandum rather less so. The gist of the whole is as follows:—You began the war, and you lost the war. That is nothing new. Then, however, comes the declaration that the end of the war actually established the frontiers [of Germany], and that it is now a matter of providing a legal foundation for this actuality. The memorandum says this in so many words.

In connection with this I should like to remind you that we have still not concluded any Peace Treaty, with the United States, Britain and France, as these four who are united one with another in relation to the conclusion of any Peace Treaty. Naturally the contents of a Peace Treaty are of the utmost importance for Germany and the German people. But they have also a very important meaning for the three western powers that I have just named, so that on no account can we enter into any negotiations with the Soviet Union on a Peace Treaty without previously getting into contact with the three western states, and reaching an agreement with them on general terms. I say this so that you may see the whole complicated nature of this question. You will agree with me that time is necessary to deal with this whole question at all.

The question arises further whether it would be right at the present moment, when apparently a series of contacts are in progress between the Soviet Union and the U.S.A., to begin again on this very delicate question. I would like to say expressly that for us it is in the first instance a matter of the recovery of the personal freedom of 17 million Germans in the Soviet zone through a Peace Treaty. Above all it is for us impossible, and I mean for all Europeans, [to

---

[1] *Bulletin des Presse und Informationsamtes der Bundesregierung*, No. 50/S.457, 14 March 1961. The translation, which attempts to preserve the curious flavour and structure of the German original, was prepared in Chatham House.

[2] See below, p. 272–277.

accept] that a new colony should be set up in the centre of Europe's heart—if I may use that expression. I may also mention that the Soviet Union has publicly recognized the right of self-determination. We are convinced that if the inhabitants of the Soviet zone could vote freely, they would vote in an overwhelming way for freedom and not for a continued subordination to the Soviet system.

That is the question of the Soviet zone. Now for the question of Berlin: it was not a happy decision that established the zonal frontiers in the manner in which they are now established. If we think back a little and remember that parts of the present Soviet zone including Berlin, were put in this very difficult situation because areas in Germany were handed over to the Russians and that as consequence this brought the separation of Berlin from the territory of the three other zones which later became the Federal Republic, then it is clear that many decisions which were then made without further consideration in the heat of the moment can now have extraordinarily far reaching and unwelcome consequences. One must be the more careful, therefore, if the whole complex of questions is soon—when I know not—to be opened. That Berlin's freedom is threatened by such a re-arrangement as the Soviet Union suggests, is clearly obvious.

It would like, however, to mention that a part of Berlin, the so-called Soviet sector, has already lost its freedom so that this question must be raised and negotiated upon: what is the state of the present Soviet sector in Berlin? I can also answer the question in that the freedom of Berlin is in reality extraordinarily imperilled by the Soviet demand that a Peace Treaty should be concluded with two German states. You have surely read that the American Secretary of State yesterday held a conference in which,[1] according to the report of the German Press Agency, he was showered with questions about the future of Berlin. The declarations that he then made agree completely with our point of view.

To further questions the Chancellor answered as follows:—

We should oppose any discussion of [*the conclusion of*] a Peace Treaty with two German states; this would imply the legal recognition of Germany's division. We must certainly, if God will, obtain a Treaty of Peace, and we want this. I should also emphasize that we want good neighbourly relations with the Soviet Union. Perhaps the whole question could be solved if the right to national self-determination of the population is taken as the starting point. It is of the first importance that in this whole complex of questions the decisions to be taken concern 17 million people, their lives, their whole fate and that of their children. All this would be much easier to solve, so I believe, even the question (for example the negotiations between the two German states) which you just raised, if a plebiscite could be held as to what the population of the Soviet zone wanted. Do they want this system or that system? In relation to the status of Berlin, Chancellor Adenauer referred to a DPA Report about the Press Conference given by Dean Rusk in which he held by the original rights of Berlin. On the question of the nature of special concessions to the Soviet Union, should it be possible to improve the fate of the Soviet population in this way, the Chancellor replied that if one was going to talk at all about future negotiations, one simply could not say beforehand, we are ready to concede this or that.

[1] *D.S.B.*, 27 March 1961, pp. 431–9.

Relations with Poland

Chancellor Dr. Adenauer made the following remarks on this:—

I believe that one cannot compare Poland with the other eastern states just like that. Poland is a special case, and so is the attitude of the Polish population itself to the relationship between Germany and Poland. In general I desire that the relationship between Federal Germany and Poland should in time become a good one, and from the evidence of returning prisoners of war, I have gained the impression that this desire is also shared by the population of Poland. The attitude of the Polish people towards returning prisoners of war was excellent. I believe that we Germans should always have it in mind to establish a good relationship with Poland, notwithstanding when it may be possible, or whether it may take a long time to achieve, and in my view it may take years.

Questions were then asked about negotiations. One cannot actually call them negotiations. The question has been allowed to rest for the moment, and I would prefer not to give any answer. The question was asked whether without re-opening diplomatic relations it might come to some kind of non-aggression pact or the like in order to allay Polish anxieties over alleged German *revanchism*. The answer was given: I could very well imagine it coming to that. A question was asked whether diplomatic relations between Poland and Germany were in any way possible so long as Germany remained divided. The Federal Chancellor answered: I do not believe Poland lays any weight on the establishment of diplomatic relations.

Relationship with the United States

In relation to the desire of the U.S. concerning the balance of payments and long term participation in aid to the under-developed countries, Dr. Adenauer declared: There will be negotiations on the balance of payments not only with the United States. There will be also negotiations in the next few weeks with Mr. Selwyn Lloyd, who comes on behalf of Great Britain, on the balance of payments with Great Britain. This is a general problem, and I hope very much, in the interest of all, on the one side and the other, that these discussions will be carried on successfully on a multilateral basis.

We agree with the U.S. that aid to the under-developed countries must be given on a long term basis and that this problem arises not only from motives of humanity, but is also a policy problem of the first importance,—the way things have developed in the last few years—whether we can erect a dam against communist infiltration. From this it follows that there must be some kind of organic relationship between the various countries involved in development programmes, so that these programmes can be divided among them on a systematic basis. I hope very much that as soon as possible there will be such a meeting of the different countries which are ready to give aid so that this extraordinarily difficult task can be properly taken care of.

On the alleged turning of public opinion in the U.S. against the Federal Republic, the Chancellor made the following remarks:— This raises a problem which I have always kept in front of me. We Germans lean towards preferring to forget those things which happened in our past which were other than pleasant

—and this is easy to understand. We lean more towards preferring to forget these things than do those countries which were affected by them. We Germans cannot expect that the years of National Socialism will disappear without further ado from the minds of those affected by it. That was always my opinion and I am therefore not surprised when a change in the attitude towards us by other countries becomes apparent. So far as the present Administration is concerned, we have not been able to establish that any change in those attitudes towards us has taken place. I find the statements that especially President Kennedy made towards the NATO Council[1] are excellent, very clear and very firm.

That the new Administration in the U.S. desires to undertake an examination of all the problems, including the inter-American problem which confronts it is good and correct and justified. This must naturally take time. And I believe that a careful examination of the whole situation by the new Administration of the U.S., even if it takes a few months, is much better than such an examination not taking place at all. For this reason I do not see any change in attitude towards us; rather I hold this examination to be necessary, intelligent and correct in the interest of the matter itself. Naturally this examination brings a certain hesitation in the whole diplomatic field, but that is not a bad thing. On the contrary it is much more intelligent, as I have already said, for the new Administration not to make up its own mind without putting itself into the picture over the whole previous set of events or over everything which has already happened. I am not afraid that this examination will lead to any sizeable alteration in the attitude of the U.S. towards us; if this attitude rests upon facts, upon political and geographical facts, which remain the same whatever Administration now heads the government of the U.S. . . .

. . . The question of the atomic armament of NATO is at the moment being examined by the new Administration in the U.S. We are informed that this examination will soon have reached its conclusions. I take the view that if controlled disarmament does not take place, NATO must be armed with atomic weapons and that in this case the German armed forces must naturally be armed in the same way as the other armed forces in NATO. I have already declared on behalf of the Federal Government[2]—this was some years ago— that we will accept any agreement on disarmament reached by other states. . . .

[1] See above, pp. 62–4.

[2] The reference is to Dr. Adenauer's statement of October 1954 included in the Final Act of the Nine Power Conference held at London, 28 September to 3 October 1954. See *Survey*, 1954, pp. 144. The text of this statement which was omitted from the accompanying volume of *Documents*, 1954, is appended below:
'The Federal Chancellor declares:
'that the Federal Republic undertakes not to manufacture in its territory any atomic weapons, chemical weapons or biological weapons, as detailed in paragraphs I, II and III of the attached list;
'that it undertakes further not to manufacture in its territory such weapons as those detailed in paragraphs IV, V and VI of the attached list. Any amendment to or cancellation of the substance of paragraphs IV, V and VI can, on the request of the Federal Republic, be carried out by a resolution of the Brussels Council of Ministers by a two-thirds majority, if in accordance with the needs of the armed forces a request is made by the competent supreme Commander of N.A.T.O.;
'that the Federal Republic agrees to supervision by the competent authority of the Brussels Treaty Organization to ensure that these undertakings are observed.'
Cmd. 9289, *Final Act of the Nine-Power Conference held in London, September 28–October 3 1954* (London, H.M.S.O., 1954), para. 15, pp. 6.

Policy in Europe

On the development of European policy and the European integration on which a question was posed, Dr. Adenauer made the following comments:—

On the European Coal and Steel Community and equally with the creation of the Common Market, the starting point was always that at the end of these developments which were in the first instance concerned with economic matters, a political union of Western Europe must come. We remain firmly of this opinion today as in the past, and I believe that we do not stand alone among the six States.

To say with any certainty how and when this will come I believe to be impossible. I take the view—and I have spoken in this sense on my visit to Paris—that one should not take a theoretical approch to this but a pragmatical one, that one should create facts, one after the other, and that at the end it will happen of itself that a state of European unity has been obtained that is tolerable for everybody, that is good for everybody, even for the whole world.

3. Address given by the Federal German Minister of Defence, Herr Strauss, at Georgetown University, Washington, 27 November 1961[1] (extract)

In every alliance in history the question has been posed as to how the sovereignty of the individual member states and the necessity and the obligations of alliance as a whole could be reconciled, one with the other; but it is only in our world in which we live today, that this question has arisen as a true contradiction in terms, not only because all decisions must be taken unanimously as in NATO, but also because the changes which have taken place in the 20th century and especially after the Second World War, make it necessary that in practice a satisfactory solution must always be found for a general formula which could be expressed as follows:— As much sovereignty as possible, as much commitment to the alliance—that is abandonment of sovereignty—as is necessary. In the many conferences of NATO and almost innumerable meetings of the various Committees and Commissions it is daily proved how difficult it is to translate a general formula in individual cases into a practicable procedure.

There are two factors which have to be taken account of as developments or changes:

1. The line of historical development which one can subsume under the concept: Great Power- World Power-Power Blocs, which distinguishes the period from the 17th to the 20th century.

2. Hand-in-hand with this the technological revolution consequent on modern scientific research and the application of the results of that research.

For our purposes this can perhaps be expressed differently:—

1. The phenomenon of World Communism whose standard-bearers are the Soviet Union and her satellites and Red China, in which state power and party system are identical and there is a special close relationship between them, all with the clearly formulated aim: the achievement of world domination.

---

[1] *Bulletin des Presse und Informationsamtes der Bundesregierung*, No. 224/S.2097, 1 December 1961. Translation made in Chatham House.

D.I.A.–F

2. Man's breakthrough into the innermost foundation of organic matter—into the atomic nucleus—which puts cosmic energies into human hands, together with the break-out from man's own planet into the universe, or to be more correct and accurate, into the areas of the universe adjoining the earth.

In order that the alliance of the 15 free nations of the West shall be true to its obligations, and, more importantly, be able to remain true to them, the question of the relationship of national sovereignty and alliance requires a continued examination; above all it requires the readiness to draw conclusions from experiences which are often obvious.

If sovereignty—independence in foreign relationships as in domestic policies—is the highest form of state power then it need not stand in contradiction to international law, as even sovereignty has its limits when faced with higher ideals. . . .

In this connection something should be said about the nature of independence. The Mandates Commission of the League of Nations expressed itself in 1931 on the preconditions on which a mandate could be ended,[1] that is under which the mandated area could become a single sovereign state, and named especially among the five points it regarded as essentials the ability to maintain its territorial integrity and political independence.

From this we come to the three great tasks of the state:

> to secure its external security;
> to create a state of order based on law at home;
> to create the pre-conditions for the welfare of its citizens.

It is obviously not true that the question of independence for the medium and small sized states was raised only with the cries of world communism and with the consequences of the technological revolution; in reality there has always been a graduated scale of independence—and one generally recognized. . . .

. . . One must clearly recognize two facts:—

1. That sovereignty or independence are not the highest norms and aims, but means to give the individual man a life of law and liberty, the nations a historical existence under the principal of the right of self-determination, by which these two aims must be brought into agreement with one another.

2. That, independent of the limitations of sovereignty set by the basic rights of man and the provisions of international law, in practice the power-relationships between the individual states have created a certain scale of limitations to sovereignty in the past.

For this reason one should guard against appealing to the conception of sovereignty in the same way as against a hypocritical usage which speaks of sovereignty and means pseudo sovereignty; by this I understand especially the application of the Soviet conception of sovereignty to the satellite states and its misuse towards the emancipated coloured peoples, as well as its misuse in propaganda for the neutralisation of certain zones.

We Europeans, but not only we Europeans, should recognize certain realities

---

[1] League of Nations, *The Mandates System, Origins—Principles—Application* (Geneva, 1945), pp. 118–20.

which must go beyond the facts mentioned above, especially in relation to the power-relationships of the powers of which I spoke:

1. The hegemony of one European state as Napoleon and Hitler under different circumstances strove to achieve, belongs as much to the past as does the concept of a European Balance of Power. Europe is no longer the centre of the earth, and the Balance of Power in Europe is meaningless, since the scales have been overturned.

2. The means of modern technology have crumpled the earth into a small unit—the more tragic it is for humanity that they should be witness to that phenomenon which has armed communism with the most modern weapons of destruction.

3. The historical catastrophe of the Soviet irruption into Europe brought about or made possible by Hitler, has basically altered conditions in Europe.

4. The power relationships of the powers express themselves today no longer in size of one's territory and the number of one's population; rather are the differences between them made stronger by the factor of modern technology, so that completely new proportions arise which can work particularly strongly in the economic and military fields and therefore lead to a change in political relationships. Khrushchev has clearly recognized this and attempted to reconcile the doctrine of Marxism-Leninism with these factors and contrarywise to put those facts into the service of Marxism-Leninism.

5. The revolutionary developments in the techniques of war make the medium and small states more and more incapable of guaranteeing their independence by their own force; has compelled them to enter into alliances and to accept a certain voluntary cut in the independence of their foreign policy. Thus concern for interests in common brings about a lessening of the possibilities of pursuing interests peculiar to the individual state.

6. From this necessity, recognition must grow that independence can only be protected by a policy of alliances, and that the political-geographical conditions are present to compel an enduring policy of alliance within Europe—but also a policy of alliance with America, which excludes a change of alliance according to the classic diplomatic game of the past.

7. From this comes the final conclusion, which may be a paradox, that a voluntary limitation of sovereignty by the individual partners in the alliance is necessary, since in view of the present situation sovereignty without an alliance is no longer possible. Khrushchev has drawn the moral in this too if he advocates the sovereignty of the European nations and wants to persuade them to abandon a policy of alliances.

III

In the military field these considerations make themselves felt when one attempts to employ the lines of thought just mentioned for the building up and for the strengthening of the reality of the alliance. In earlier times the reality of an alliance consisted in the co-operation of national armies as agreed by treaty, these forces operating beside one another. Neither in the first nor in the second World War was there a common strategic planning system between Germany and her allies to say nothing of a common High Command. There was not even a co-ordination of strategy. On the other side the Entente only achieved a common Supreme Command in 1918 with Marshal Foch under the strong pressure of the German offensive. In the same way it was only with the preparation of the invasion of Europe in the Second World War that Eisenhower headed a common Supreme Command. In both wars there was a certain co-operation with the Russians which did not go much beyond agreement from time to time on individual planned actions.

In addition the limited effects of the weapons in both cases made it possible that the military potential of the opponents of Germany could be mobilized after the outbreak of war without interference from the air by a potential enemy.

Here also conditions have altered completely.

The highest political-military aim of the alliance must be to prevent the outbreak of war not to win one that has already broken out. In addition, the revolution in arms technology has created weapons the speed, range, and effect of which have almost no more limits whatever on the earth. Therefore, it is not the development of war potential after the outbreak of war that makes a defence policy possible although this has a certain deterrent effect; it is rather a question of the front-line strength capable of employment at any time for any act of military defence on a smaller or larger scale, and which can meet the first blows coming from an aggressor with a counter-stroke still capable of destroying him, (second-stroke capability).[1]

The breakthrough of modern technology with atomic energy, electronics and rocket systems, when brought together with the experience of the appeasement policy towards Hitler, and the shock of Pearl Harbour, have created new conditions. The desire to be able to stand up to them led to the decision to found N.A.T.O., that is an American-European Defence Community.

The American President a few days ago, when dealing with the sovereignty of the partners at his evening address in connection with the visit of the Federal Chancellor, said: 'an alliance is a very difficult system to operate'.[2]

Many traditional, affectionately-regarded anachronisms which have stiffened into pre-conceived ideas must be overcome and new forms of co-operation found in their place. In view of the pre-conditions mentioned above it is necessary: to create in peacetime already a common High Command in Europe, which in view of the global peril must one day lead to an Atlantic High Command; collective striking forces banded together to create blanced striking forces as the means of defence available to the medium and small member-states are no longer sufficient to maintain adequate balanced striking forces within their own boundaries (one can think of the problem of air defence against aircrafts and rockets); that is we must aim at a division of labour which covers not only the tasks, the nature and the size of the striking forces, but also the research, development and production for the armament of these striking forces; to abandon national defence plans to a very wide degree and to adjust the tasks of the national General Staffs and their size to the changed conditions of the day; to create a common

---

[1] In English in the original.
[2] *Public Papers*, 1961, pp. 737–8. President Kennedy's remarks were actually made at a luncheon-party given in Dr. Adenauer's honour at the White House on 21 November 1961.

system of logistics for the forces of the alliance; to work out a series of defence plans which will establish and continue to maintain the right balance between conventional and nuclear weapons, while, despite this, making the value of their contributions credible to the medium and small partners in the alliance; which will avoid any conflict of interest over the relative value of what is to be defended; which will distribute the burdens and risks in equal measure; which will recognize the basic equality of rights of the different partners, and which above all, will create a force in being which will attain the highest aim, the prevention of an outbreak of war, without the sacrifice of the freedom of one partner in the alliance to the Soviet pressure for expansion.

IV

The Soviet Union's policy towards Germany as well as their pressure on the northern flank of N.A.T.O. shows that they are concerned to secure concessions in order in this way to break up the external unity of the western alliance in matters of foreign and defence policy as well as to dissolve its moral unity. In other words, Moscow is speculating on an alleged conflict of interest. We have observed this for years. They want to convince the Western nations that their security interests are opposed to that of Germany or at least do not run in conformity with them; this is, for example, expressed in the thesis that 'the Germans alone must pay for losing the war'. On the other hand, they are trying to suggest to the Germans that they have been in tow in the wake of the interests of the United States.

In this connection the question was recently posed to me whether there was really no 'conflict of interests' to be observed in N.A.T.O.

I gave the following answer:

'To believe that there can be any differences between the elementary interests of the individual partners of our Atlantic Community is a highly dangerous illusion. It is quite clear that the alliance will be unavoidably drawn into a mortal crisis which it would not survive if Soviet policy and propaganda succeeded in spreading the opinion in the West that they can manoeuvre on the periphery of the world without unavoidably involving the interest of the centre in immediate peril. Every infraction on the European periphery—even if this is only a moral infraction—would set up chain reactions which are unforeseeable and would in any case reach to the centre. It is therefore the task of everyone in the Atlantic Community—especially in the Federal Republic—to keep these emotions under control, to avoid hectic comments under any circumstances and to watch that the discussions which are certainly necessary and which also guarantee a free community, do not give rise to some illusion likely to convince the East that there are any basic differences in interest and that these will, in the long run, govern the course of the Alliance more than their common interests. Let us all be clear about this: Europe can only remain free on the side of America.'

The strategy of terror was a relatively simple matter so long as the United States possessed the monopoly of atomic weapons, and even when the U.S. lost that monopoly but continued to dispose of an overwhelming superiority including the means of delivery. This is complicated and threatens to lose its effectiveness if parity is attained on both sides, which will be the case in the foreseeable future. How then will the relationship between America and Europe present itself within and in the Alliance?

We live in the middle of a great conflict which we must survive and which we can only survive together. In view of the strategic relationship caused by the technological revolution not only does Europe today depend on America as it had done in the past, but the north American countries depend in their turn on the European contribution. In the past, America covered the whole alliance strategically; but is it not an open fact that in the future Europe must provide protection for America in the same way as America does for Europe? The one-way street will of necessity turn into a street with traffic going in both directions —a change in relationships. Unfortunately, the European contribution is not as great as it could be if the means applied were to be applied to a common N.A.T.O. strategy, and even more if these means were to a measurable extent to be increased.

Just at this point, however, a problem arises today the psychological depth and the political and pragmatic consequences of which one is inclined to under- rather than to overestimate. This concerns the fact that possession and control of nuclear weapons seems to have become the symbol, even the characteristic criterion of sovereignty.

Naturally in this connection the question will be posed with justice whether N.A.T.O. cannot have its own sovereignty, or whether—from the tendency to arrive at a common power of decision—the deterrent has not developed from a force de frappe into a farce de frappe, as there are 15 fingers on the trigger.

As the non-members of the so-called atomic club are practically defenceless if the deterrent power of nuclear weapons is not at their disposal; as on the other hand the extension of power and control over atomic weapons to more and more nations justly meets considerable political objections, a system of guarantees and formulas must be found which will give to the small and medium partners in N.A.T.O. the consciousness and the role of partnership. Both the former and the present American Administration have recognized the importance of the problem and put forward proposals for their solution.

I want to emphasize two points very clearly: that it is not in the remotest way a matter of not trusting the United States, rather that this concerns the structure of the alliance and its future development.

It would exceed the scope of this address, were I to name possible solutions and formulas. Further this would upset the discussions to come, as each public comment would make the quiet handling of this question more difficult and alarm the negative critics and know-it-alls who know all possible ways in which a question cannot be solved.

But on one thing clarity must prevail. Whatever formula is found, whatever solution is sought, any decision that strengthens the structure and the development of the alliance will demand in every case a certain abandonment of national-state rights, and a legal diminution of sovereignty which from a technical point of view has long been diminished, if it has not been abolished.

V

This is not a matter of the working out or discussion of hair-splitting legal formulations, it is really a matter of an eye for the most important relationships; it is a matter of the readiness to draw certain conclusions and to set aside conditions which may be dear to us, but are all the same anachronistic.

The American President in his message on the State of the Union on 30 January 1961 said the following:—[1]

'In Europe our alliances are unfulfilled and in some disarray. The unity of N.A.T.O. has been weakened by economic rivalry and partially eroded by national interest. It has not yet fully mobilized its resources nor fully achieved a common outlook. Yet no Atlantic power can meet on its own the mutual problems now facing us in defence, foreign aid, monetary reserves, and a host of other areas; and our close ties with those whose hopes and interests we share are among this Nation's most powerful assets.'

I hold the conviction that these aims set out by the American President can no longer be obtained with the weapons of a conventional policy. We must come to an alteration in the structure of the Alliance and with this must also change the relationships between the members and the Alliance as a whole. The methods of consultation and co-ordination are no longer adequate to solve the problems of the era of nuclear energy and space travel in a divided world threatened by communism.

In handling the theme which I have posed myself I must try and reach a conclusion. My concern with the problems of N.A.T.O., my anxiety for the future of the free world, and the search for victory in a war forced on us by communism, have driven me to seek a permanent solution. . . .

. . . Today we confront the question what we must do to make the Alliance into a political institution. We can only promise a voluntary abandonment of our sovereign rights; with this we can give our alliance a superiority which not only compares with the technical advantages of the compulsorily centrally-organised powers of the communist bloc, but also exceeds them.

I therefore call for an extension of the military alliance into the economic sphere and advocate the gradual creation of a common Atlantic market of which the O.E.C.D. is a starting point of development. I therefore advocate the creation of a competent and responsible office which should carry out these tasks which can no longer be undertaken at the equivalent national level.

The role which history and destiny demands of us runs from co-operation and co-ordination to confederation, and from there to partial federation. This aim does not stand in contradiction to the uniting of Europe, rather it is a continuation of this road. For many European states such a decision would perhaps be easier and could be sooner attained than the decision to enter the United States of Europe. Among the tasks with which this pioneer institution, which must be under parliamentary control, should deal and over which it should have power, must be especially included questions of N.A.T.O.'s strategy, of control over atomic weapons, of ability to dispose of their employment, the question of

[1] Above p. 3.

the control of armaments and disarmament, of the guidance of aid to the under-developed states, of certain economic functions necessary for the creation of a Common Market, of the conclusion and rational examination of the scientific-technical potential of the Alliance and not least the common intellectual-psychological defence against communism which must reach from the arousing of an Atlantic consciousness to the systematic support of the enslaved peoples.

I speak for the creation of an Atlantic Union; we confront perhaps the greatest task which can be given a generation. We must find an answer—the opponent's trumpets sounds to world revolution 'to the last battle'. Fear is a bad counsellor. We are stronger—in ideas and in materials—if we reach the correct decisions.

Exceptional problems demand exceptional solutions. The peoples of the free nations ask: 'Will it come to war? Will we submit to communism?'

The enslaved peoples ask: 'Are we forever condemned to the yoke of communism?'

War or slavery, is that the unavoidable alternative which is written with letters of fire on the wall? No!

Only great decisions alter the world—the great idea must be shown to the people and then it must be translated into reality through careful labour and with tenacious energy. If that is the sacrifice which will save us from war and communism then we must make it. The price which otherwise is demanded is higher than the abandonment of national sovereignty and of the primacy of individual economic interest.

This is what I call a strategy of freedom and peace in which lies concealed the solution of the fateful questions of our time which seem insoluble.

4. Statement of Policy of the Federal German Government to the Bundestag, 29 November 1961[1] (extracts)

Defence

. . . Let me now come to foreign policy. Since its creation the Federal Republic has concerned itself with attaining good relations with all states. It has succeeded in establishing friendly relations with most countries and in making them closer and firmer from year to year.

This is true of many states in Asia. Relations with Latin America have also developed in a most friendly way. The governments of that continent have in the last few months almost unanimously spoken up for the demands of the German people, for re-union and self-determination, in the last instance at the 16th Plenary Session of the United Nations, for which I would like to express our thanks at this point. . . .

. . . In the scope of our efforts for a peaceful co-existence with all peoples come also our efforts to help the under-developed countries. We have already achieved considerable success. For the years 1961/62 alone capital assistance is envisaged at the level of five milliard Marks all told. To extend this public assistance we are trying to secure the initiative of private enterprise also. We expect investments from the private side of the economy to have a great effect

[1] *Frankfurter Allegemeine Zeitung*, 30 November 1961. Speech by the Federal Chancellor, Dr. Adenauer.

in the sphere of aid to the under-developed countries. We will proceed with aid to the under-developed countries without political strings. We cannot, however, leave out of our considerations that the German people would not understand it if we entered into a development-partnership with states that do not recognize our rights to self determination. Cultural work abroad must not be confused with publicity work. But even this work, which has been taken up on a larger scale since the beginning of the Berlin crisis and which has brought us considerable success—especially through the Visit to Berlin programme— needs to be reinforced and improved. Co-operation with the three western powers has developed very happily. We must, however, do even more to bring the Berlin and the German questions more immediately before public opinion, so that it can recognize that it concerns its own vital interests. . . .

. . . The Federal German Republic supports the aims of the Charter of the United Nations even though we do not belong to U.N.O. We are, however, a member of all its special organs and work in active co-operation with many organisations of the United Nations, especially in those of a humanitarian character. We have each year undertaken greater financial obligations especially for the development projects of the United Nations.

European Union

A special welcome development—despite all world crises—is to be seen in the field of European Union. Our labours which began eleven years ago for the integration of Europe have already led to the creation of a centre of power in Europe to which great importance both in economical and political matters must be attached, and which has also contributed to the internal stability of the member states.

The basis for this policy of European Union was the German-French Entente. The close German-French friendship which has meanwhile arisen is considered by the Federal Government as one of the greatest achievements of recent history, and as a guarantee of the peace, security and welfare of Europe. The Federal Republic which is coming together with five other European states into an even closer community, desires and hopes that Great Britain together with other European states will enter as soon as possible into the European Community. A healthy, strong and free Europe will only be created by certain sacrifices and through unceasing labours. Europe is, however, our hope. If we succeed in creating this, it would contribute decisively to the achievement of peace and freedom for us and for our children.

In the negotiations before us three principles must be observed which should not be abandoned: the security of the Federal Republic; the maintenance of the existing political, legal and economic ties between Berlin and the Federal Republic, free access by the civilian population and the maintenance of a common German policy, that is the re-unification of our land in peace and freedom, the non-recognition of that part of Germany occupied by the Soviets and of the government in power there, and the regulation of frontier questions in a real treaty of peace which must be concluded with a common German government and towards whose coming into existence we will apply ourselves with all our strength.

The Federal Government knows that these aims cannot be attained by force. Any attempt in this direction would lead to the destruction of our country and a great part of the outside world. It would be the end of any German policy. The Federal Government has, therefore, publicly declared more than once, that it abandons for all times the use of force or the threat of force as a means to achieve her political aims. It renews this guarantee at this instance and is ready to make this abandonment of force the basis of international negotiations in any form that may seem appropriate.

Reunion in Peace and Freedom

The re-establishment of Germany's unity in peace and freedom remains the unshakeable aim of German foreign policy, even though we can today give no date for its realization. The right to self-determination will not be withheld permanently from any peoples. The unnatural division of our people has led again and again to periods of tension and crisis. The Federal Government demands the re-establishment of the unity of Germany on the basis of the right to self-determination, a right which has become a general and binding principle of international law and is anchored in statutes of the United Nations.

The Federal Government will therefore set itself against anything happening which may hinder re-unification. It refuses decisively any recognition of the Communist régime in central Germany. Those who exercise authority in central Germany have not founded their government on the basis of the rights of self-determination. They are purely a deputy organisation of the Soviet occupying-power. There is even a fundamental difference between them and governments that work with totalitarian means: in the Soviet-occupied zone not only do people oppose the régime by an overwhelming majority, but also the existence of a separate German part-state. This is it above all that differentiates the Soviet-occupied zone from all other states in the world. This is the reason why the Federal Government must regard the taking up of diplomatic relations with the régime in the Soviet-occupied zone or the signature of a so-called separate Peace Treaty as an unfriendly act against the German people and the taking up of an attitude against the reunion and for the division of Germany. With the forceful measures of 13 August 1961 in Berlin, with the evacuation along the demarcation line and the increase of terror in the whole of Germany, the régime in power has furnished renewed proof of its inhuman brutality. Basic human rights are continuously infringed. The moral necessity of those separated from us by barbed wire and concrete walls is indescribable. The Federal Government emphatically demands above all the restitution of law in the whole of Germany. Above all the blockade measures in Berlin must be rescinded again. The wall of shame must disappear! Free communication routes between Berlin and West Germany must be guaranteed.

I now come to a question which is of the utmost importance for the destiny of the German peoples and of some importance to all peoples of Europe: the question of European security. In this question there are certain principles for the Federal Government which it cannot abandon. We refuse all measures of regional security in Europe if they are declared to be preliminary steps to an agreement on general disarmament, as the main demands of the West—the maintenance of a balanced East-West power relationship—can only be fulfilled on a world-wide basis. The Federal Government is, however, ready to take part in considerations to serve the end of diminishing or setting aside the danger of sudden attacks in so far as these are a matter of world-wide measures. I repeat: the Federal Government is not ready to agree to measures which under the title of 'European Security' would in reality increase insecurity. It is ready not only to agree to such matters as may be designed to enable a solution of the political problems in Europe, but also to agree to those that may serve towards a guarantee of a just peace.

General Controlled Disarmament

One of the most important aims of German foreign policy is controlled disarmament. The Federal Government welcomes the programme submitted in September by the American government to the United Nations for general and complete disarmament in a world at peace.[1] It considers this programme to be a realistic basis for continued disarmament talks. The Federal Government especially regrets that the negotiations for a controlled ban on nuclear tests, which at one moment seemed to stand at the verge of positive conclusion, have again been delayed by the attitude of the Soviet Government. The Federal Government urgently desires a treaty between the atomic powers on the controlled cessation of these tests. It hopes that the re-commencement of these negotiations in Geneva on 28 November will lead to success.

The prospects of keeping and guaranteeing world peace through disarmament are unfortunately not encouraging. On the contrary, the crisis evoked by the Soviet Union clearly shows that the free peoples must stand united against any military threat.

For this reason the Federal Government regards the strengthening of N.A.T.O. as the question of the hour, strengthening through improved political consultations and through military reinforcement. In the view of the Federal Government the plan for a N.A.T.O. nuclear striking force should be realized as soon as possible. The setting up of such striking force is necessary so as to raise the defensive powers of the forces in N.A.T.O. to the same level of technology as those possessed by one opponent. With this demand the Federal Government weakens at the same time any reproach of wishing to obtain atomic weapons for her own use. The Federal Government has never raised this demand. If we consider the reinforcement of N.A.T.O. as our foremost task, which must be fulfilled, it comes to be a question of proving our co-operation through practical measures; that is, we must try our utmost to fulfil our obligations towards N.A.T.O. With this aim we will have to prolong the date of service at the colours to 18 months, and we must continually review this and adapt our legislation in such a way as to maintain our internal and external security. The Basic Law[2] needs extension to cover the possibility that the existence of the free democratic foundations of our State are threatened. The Federal Government will soon submit to the Bundestag other draft laws which should also serve

[1] See below, p. 389.
[2] An English translation of the Basic Law of 1949 is available in a Department of State publication, *Germany 1947–1949, The Story in Documents* (U.S.G.P.O., Washington, 1950), pp. 283–305.

as advance preparations for the possibility of crisis. I need only mention the protection of the population in their homes and factories, the regulation of the preparation of our economy, food and transport for the special needs of a crisis, and the introduction of civil conscription, so as to guarantee the protection of and provision for the civilian population as well as the maintenance of all public services in case of an emergency. . . .

. . . Many of the matters which the Federal Government must take up must dig deeply into the life of the individual German. The Federal Government knows this well. It must demand such sacrifices from her peoples, as correspond to the gravity of the situation. The alliance of the free peoples is an indivisible whole. The Federal Government is especially aware of the obligations which have developed as a result of the Federal Republic's membership of N.A.T.O. It is deeply convinced that the security and peace of the German people can only be maintained in close collaboration with her allies.

Conversations in Washington

The meeting which I had with the President of the United States a few days ago[1] is an obvious expression of the close and fruitful ties which have developed between the members of the North Atlantic Alliance. It is obvious that in this Alliance the United States of America must play an exceptional role of leadership. I am therefore happy and thankful to have had, right at the beginning of this Federal Government's period of office, an opportunity for an open and cordial exchange of views on current questions. They have made it again clear that, as has been the case for many years, the relationship not only of the governments but also that of the American and German peoples towards one another is based on mutual trust and friendship. The conversations in Washington have again brought proof that we—Americans and Germans—can rely upon another. I will shortly be meeting President de Gaulle and Mr. Macmillan when the annual conference of N.A.T.O. members takes place in Paris in December. These meetings serve the aim to strengthen the cohesion and solidity of our alliance. The stronger we tie ourselves into this community, the more we realize and fulfil our rights and duties in common, the stronger we will be. We must fulfil the limits set by the organisation of the North Atlantic Pact. We must strengthen our common defences and our economic co-operation and bring our policies closer one to another. Then we will be able not only to meet the demands of the future, but also to lay the foundation stone for a future in which peace and freedom will be realities.

In front of us are great and difficult tasks. These can only be solved if we pool all our powers. The community of German endeavours should find visible expression. The Federal Government is confident that every member of this high House will recognize the basic principles of her foreign policy and defence policy as agreeing with the central desires of the German people. Only if we follow these basic principles—this is the view of the Federal Government—can the life of the German peoples be secured for the future.

[1] For the resultant joint communiqué, see below, p. 152.

(e) Bilateral Negotiations on the North Atlantic Alliance

1. Joint statement issued by President Kennedy and Dr. Adenauer, Washington, 13 April 1961[1]

During the past two days the President and the Chancellor have had a most cordial and useful exchange of views on a number of subjects of interest to their two Governments.

Their informal conversations have included among other things, discussions of; the problem of a divided Germany including Berlin; the current nuclear test ban talks; political and military developments pertaining to NATO; aid to developing countries; European economic cooperation; East-West relations; and the situation in some critical areas of world politics.

Also participating in the talks were Secretary of State Dean Rusk and German Foreign Minister Heinrich von Brentano.

The President and the Chancellor reaffirmed the position of their Governments that only through the application of the principle of self-determination can a just and enduring solution be found for the problem of Germany including Berlin. They renewed their pledge to preserve the freedom of the people of West Berlin pending the reunification of Germany in peace and freedom and the restoration of Berlin as the capital of a reunified country.

The President and the Chancellor agreed that intensified political cooperation in NATO is indispensable in order to coordinate the efforts of the Allies for the preservation of peace and security in the world.

The President and the Chancellor reaffirmed their support of NATO as the keystone of the common defense of the North Atlantic area. They underlined the conviction of their Governments as to the necessity for the Alliance to maintain and develop further all military means required to enable them to deter effectively a potential aggressor from threatening the territorial integrity or independence of any ally.

Furthermore, the problems of general and controlled disarmament were discussed. The President and the Chancellor are convinced that reasonable, freely negotiated measures to reverse the growth of uncontrolled national armaments will serve to lessen the danger of war and that concurrently measures should be negotiated to secure a life in freedom to all nations. The goal is a general and total peace.

The President and the Chancellor agreed on the importance of a concerted aid effort by the industrialized free world nations in an amount commensurate with their resources and on a basis corresponding to the magnitude of the task. They pledged the support of the United States and the Federal Republic to the fulfillment of the objectives adopted by the member nations of the Development Assistance Group at their meeting in London two weeks ago.

The President and the Chancellor welcomed the prospective establishment of the Organization for Economic Cooperation and Development as constituting a step of vital importance in the development of an Atlantic Community. The new possibilities which it opens for economic cooperation and economic policy

[1] *Public Papers*, 1961, pp. 265–6.

coordination and the means of achieving closer interdependence were also discussed.

In this connection, the President and the Chancellor agreed that continuing attention should be paid to the balance of payments problem.

The important role of the European Economic Community as a powerful and cohesive force in the core of the Atlantic Community was stressed. The dynamic political and institutional potential of the EEC was agreed to be an important element of present strength for the Atlantic Community.

The fruitful exchange of views which the President and the Chancellor have had, as well as the frank and cordial atmosphere in which the talks were conducted have contributed significantly to deepening the ties of friendship and understanding between the two countries and to the strengthening of the free world community.

2. Joint statement issued by President Kennedy and Dr. Adenauer, Washington, 22 November 1961[1]

The President and the Chancellor have had an extended exchange of views during the past three days on a number of problems of vital concern to their Governments. These exchanges took place in a frank and cordial atmosphere and established that there is substantial unanimity of view both on the substance of the problems and how to deal with them.

The visit of the Chancellor afforded an opportunity to the Foreign Ministers and the Defense Ministers of the two countries to participate in the discussion and exchange views among themselves.

Berlin, over which the Soviet Union has created an international crisis, was the subject of earnest consultation. The President and the Chancellor reaffirmed their clear determination to insure the continuance of a free and vigorous life for the population of Berlin. They are in accord on the basic elements which will permit a peaceful resolution of this crisis through negotiation if there is reasonableness on the part of the Soviet Union. They agreed on the measures which should be taken in pursuing this objective in a manner consistent with the legitimate interests of all parties concerned. At the same time they also agreed on the necessity for maintaining and increasing the ability of the NATO Alliance to cope with any military developments. These discussions will be continued through the already announced meetings between Chancellor Adenauer, Prime Minister Macmillan and President de Gaulle and concluded in the Foreign Ministers meeting and the NATO Ministerial Meeting scheduled in mid-December in Paris.

The President and the Chancellor reaffirmed the ultimate goal of their Governments of achieving by peaceful means the reunification of Germany on the basis of self-determination. They were also in agreement that this objective could be realized without prejudice to the legitimate interests of the Soviet Union and Germany's neighbors.

The President and the Chancellor reviewed the state of the North Atlantic Treaty Organization. They welcomed the measures now in progress to strengthen

[1] *Public Papers*, 1961, pp. 738–40.

the Alliance, but recognized the need for a sustained effort to further improve the ability of the Alliance to resist aggression.

The President and the Chancellor noted Soviet charges accusing the NATO Alliance of aggressive intent, and singling out the Federal Republic of Germany and its democratically elected government as the principal object of its false and unwarranted attack. In this regard, the President and the Chancellor reaffirmed that:

(1) The North Atlantic alliance is an alliance for defense against aggression which abides fully by the requirements of the Charter of the United Nations. The peaceful characteristics of its members and their freedom from coercion make it manifestly impossible for NATO to commit aggression against anyone.

(2) The Federal Republic of Germany has demonstrated that it looks to its legitimate security interests entirely within the North Atlantic Alliance, and to this end has integrated its entire effective defense establishment into the multi-national NATO framework. The Chancellor, in emphasizing the defensive aspects of West German armed forces, noted that the Federal Republic is the only nation of its size all of whose forces are under international command.

While agreeing on the need to take all measures essential to strengthen the defensive posture of NATO, the President and the Chancellor recognized the necessity of not permitting Soviet pressure over Berlin to deflect them from urgently required constructive tasks vital to the welfare of their peoples and those of other nations.

The President reaffirmed the strong support of the United States for the movement toward European unity through the European Economic Community, the European Coal and Steel Community, and EURATOM. The President and the Chancellor agreed on the important role that the development of the European communities can play in further strengthening and complementing the entire Atlantic community. They agreed particularly on the importance and significance of proposals now being considered for a European Political Union pursuant to the Bonn Declaration of July 1961.[1]

They welcomed the recent decision by the OECD Council of Ministers[2] to increase the combined gross national product of the OECD member countries by 50 percent in 1970 and pledged themselves to work toward this goal.

The President and the Chancellor also discussed the urgent need to increase the flow of development assistance to the less-developed countries. They noted that the Development Assistance Committee of the OECD provides an excellent means of stimulating a greater effort in this field. They considered that in many cases the application of combined resources from several capital exporting countries to specific development assistance problems would be a valuable method of assisting the less-developed countries.

It is the view of the President and the Chancellor that the fruitful exchange of views which they have had will facilitate the close cooperation between the United States and the Federal Republic and result in further strengthening the ties of friendship and mutual understanding which have characterized their relations in the post-war period.

[1] Below, p. 187.   [2] Below, p. 156.

3. Joint statement by President Kennedy and Mr. Macmillan issued at the close of their talks in Bermuda, 22 December 1961[1]

The President and the Prime Minister have had two days of valuable discussions surveying the world situation. Their discussions centred mainly on the question of Berlin, on nuclear problems and on the situation in the Congo. Their talks will form the basis of continued United States-United Kingdom cooperation during the coming months on a great variety of questions.

The President and the Prime Minister examined the situation concerning Berlin in the light of the decisions taken at the meetings of the Foreign Ministers of the Four Powers and of the NATO Council in Paris. In particular they discussed the steps to be taken in regard to the renewal of diplomatic contacts with the Soviet Union. The President has agreed as a consequence of the Paris meeting that the initial contact would be made by the U.S. Ambassador in Moscow and the Prime Minister has indicated that the British Ambassador would be available to play whatever part might be found helpful. The President and the Prime Minister agreed that the purpose should be to ascertain whether a reasonable basis for negotiation can be found. The other governments directly concerned will of course be fully consulted throughout. Consultations with the other governments concerned are continuing.

The President and the Prime Minister considered the problems of the nuclear arms race. They took note of the new situation created by the massive series of atmospheric tests conducted in recent months by the Soviet Government after long secret preparations. They agreed that it is now necessary, as a matter of prudent planning for the future, that pending the final decision preparations should be made for atmospheric testing to maintain the effectiveness of the deterrent.

Meanwhile, they continue to believe that no task is more urgent than the search for paths toward effective disarmament, and they pledge themselves to intensive and continued efforts in this direction.

Serious progress toward disarmament is the only way of breaking out of the dangerous contest so sharply renewed by the Soviet Union. The President and the Prime Minister believe that the plans for disarmament put forward by the United States in the current session of the United Nations General Assembly offer a basis for such progress, along with the treaty for ending nuclear tests which the two nations have so carefully prepared and so earnestly urged upon the Soviet Government.

The President and the Prime Minister reviewed recent developments in the Congo. They noted with satisfaction that, as an encouraging step toward understanding, a useful meeting had been held at Kitona between Mr. Adoula and Mr. Tshombe. They expressed their strong hope that further progress would be made through the efforts of both parties. It seemed to them of first importance that the present discussions should be actively continued in appropriate ways. They agreed on the importance of avoiding any renewal of armed action while genuine efforts at consultation are going forward.

In general discussion of the economic situation the President and the Prime

[1] *Public Papers*, 1961, pp. 817–18.

Minister took note of progress in the negotiations between the United Kingdom and the European Economic Community and expressed the hope that these would be brought to a successful conclusion.

(f) N.A.T.O. and O.E.C.D.

1. Final communiqué of the N.A.T.O. Ministerial Council, Oslo, 10 May 1961[1]

The North Atlantic Council held its spring ministerial meeting in Oslo from May 8 to May 10, 1961, under the chairmanship of its new Secretary General, Mr. D. U. Stikker.

Since the Atlantic countries united twelve years ago, in accordance with the United Nations Charter, to insure their common defense, their alliance has safeguarded peace and freedom. But the menace which drew them together is now not only military but also has world-wide political, economic, scientific and psychological aspects.

The North Atlantic alliance threatens no one. It will never be used for aggression. It seeks to eliminate war and the causes of war. But it is resolved to defend the right of its peoples to live in freedom.

In the world as it is today the unity and strength of the Atlantic alliance is essential to peace and the survival of liberty. Its collective resources—moral and material alike—are fully adequate to this task. Confident in their strength, in the will of their peoples and in the truth of the ideals they uphold, the fifteen Atlantic nations dedicate themselves anew to building a world free from the false doctrine of continuing and inevitable conflict.

During the meeting the ministers reviewed developments in the international situation. Aware of the intensified efforts of the Communist bloc to foment and to exploit conflicts and to extend its domination over an ever-increasing area, the ministers reaffirmed their resolve to meet this challenge.

For their part, the Atlantic nations are ready to make their contribution toward achieving an equitable and just settlement of outstanding political questions. They deplore Soviet unwillingness to reciprocate.

The ministers noted with regret the lack of progress on the reunification of Germany. They reaffirmed their conviction that a peaceful and just solution for the problem of Germany, including Berlin, is to be found only on the basis of self-determination.

With particular regard to Berlin, they reiterated their determination, as expressed in the declaration of 16 December, 1958,[2] to maintain the freedom of West Berlin and its people. As to the often-repeated threat by the Soviet Union to sign a separate peace treaty, they reaffirmed the statement in the 1958 declaration that 'the denunciation by the Soviet Union of the inter-Allied agreements on Berlin can in no way deprive the other parties of their rights or relieve the Soviet Union of its obligations'.

Disarmament by stages under effective international control remains one of the principal objectives of the governments of the alliance. The Council expresses the hope that the initiation by the United States of consultations with the

[1] N.Y. Times, 11 May 1961.   [2] Documents, 1958, pp. 373–4.

U.S.S.R. for the purpose of arriving at a mutually acceptable procedure will permit the resumption of negotiations about the end of July.

They agreed that the position of those members of the alliance participating in the disarmament discussions will be developed in close consultation in the North Atlantic Council.

With regard to the Geneva negotiations on the suspension of nuclear tests, the Council noted with approval that the United States and the United Kingdom had tabled [submitted] a comprehensive draft treaty offering a basis for agreement. They regretted that the negative attitude of the Soviet Government has raised new difficulties. They expressed the hope that that Government will move promptly to join in an effective treaty as a first and significant step toward disarmament.

The task of helping the less-developed areas of the world to raise their social and material standards is one of the major challenges of our time. It is a challenge which the members of the Atlantic alliance gladly accept; and in their examination of the world situation the ministers gave high priority to this question. They took note with satisfaction of the large volume of free world aid—dwarfing that granted by the Sino-Soviet bloc—and reaffirmed their determination to increase these efforts.

The ministers discussed the problems of long-term planning within the alliance in the nonmilitary sphere on the basis of a report presented by the Council in Permanent Session, dealing with the future development and role of the alliance in the political, economic, civil emergency planning and other fields. Proceeding from this report, they gave guidance to the permanent council for strengthening the cohesion of the alliance.

The Council recognized that much progress had been made in developing an increased unity of purpose and harmonization of action by its members. It emphasized the importance for this purpose of close, constant and frank consultation in order to make effective the growing unity of the Atlantic alliance.

The ministers invited the Council in Permanent Session, in close cooperation with the military authorities, to continue its studies of all aspects of the military posture of the alliance, with a view to improving its deterrent and defensive strength. They requested the Council to submit these studies when ready and to report to the ministerial meeting in December.

The ministers gave special attention to the economic problems affecting Greece and Turkey. Bearing in mind the important contribution made by these two countries to the common defense, they considered ways and means of assisting efforts being made by Greece and Turkey to speed up development programs and improve the living standards of their peoples.

2. Final communiqué of the O.E.C.D. Ministerial Council, Paris, 18 November 1961[1]

The First Ministerial Council of the OECD, meeting in Paris on November 16 and 17 under the chairmanship of the Canadian Minister of Finance, the Honorable Donald M. Fleming, surveyed the economic prospects of the vast

[1] *D.S.B.*, 18 December 1961, pp. 1018–20.

community of member nations comprising more than five hundred million people in Europe and North America and examined its world responsibilities.

The Ministers noted the substantial economic growth that had taken place in most members countries during the past decade. They agreed on the desirability of establishing a target for further growth. Under conditions of price stability and the necessary provision for investment, rapid growth facilitates the harmonious development of world economy, helps to promote a liberal world trading system, provides a necessary foundation for rising living standards, and ensures a high level of employment. It will enable industrialized member countries to contribute more effectively to the development of less-advanced countries both through the provision of financial and technical assistance and through a widening of their export markets and the increase of their export revenues.

Accordingly the Ministers set as a collective target the attainment during the decade from 1960 to 1970 of a growth in real gross national product of fifty percent for the twenty member countries taken together. The rate of growth may vary from year to year and from country to country. Moreover, being a collective target, individual countries may fall short of or exceed it in varying degrees.

Each country will have to make its contribution to collective growth in accordance with its own special circumstances. This contribution will be supported and made more effective by simultaneous expansion in other countries. The setting of a joint target for economic growth is itself recognition of the increasing interdependence of the separate economies of the twenty member countries. Given their needs, it is desirable that member countries in the process of development should have a relatively higher rate of growth. A fifty percent increase in output during the decade will call for deliberate national economic policies and their coordination through the Organization's procedures of consultations and cooperation.

In this respect the Ministers put particular emphasis on the necessity of a proper equilibrium in the external payments of member countries as a condition for the fulfillment of the growth target mentioned above. It was therefore necessary to develop still further the close coordination of financial and economic policies and the mutual sense of responsibility between deficit and surplus countries in order to attain the common objective of accelerated economic growth while further improving the international payments mechanism. The various means already available to relieve temporary pressures on particular currencies were of great value, but they should be further developed.

Price stability is of the highest importance in order to assure to the population the full benefit of economic growth and to maintain equilibrium in international payments. Excess demand should, therefore, be prevented and efforts made to improve productivity and labor mobility. The gains through higher productivity should be fairly distributed, and increases in the level of money incomes should be kept generally in line with increases in productivity, which alone provide the means to a durable increase in the standard of living. In countries with payments deficits it is particularly important that the competitive position is not undermined through cost increases. Liberal import policies are another means of assuring price stability. The surplus countries have a special responsibility to use this and other means available to them which contribute to both external and internal equilibrium.

The Ministers emphasized that a special effort must be made to promote growth in less-developed member countries and thus endeavour to reduce the very great disparities in incomes per head. In these countries there are great possibilities for achieving a higher standard of living through more intensive use of natural and human resources. They stressed their conviction that more investment and more training are necessary conditions for such a development. To induce a real increase in the inadequate growth rates of such member countries the Ministers instructed the Organization to encourage and assist such countries in their efforts, including the preparation and achievement of sound development plans.

In order to achieve the growth target, increasing use of scientific training and research is needed. Their utilization in agriculture and industry should be closely studied. The Organization should further develop its work in these fields.

The Ministers noted that, thanks to increased productivity and mechanization, agricultural production had risen considerably in the OECD countries and they recognized that agriculture would also play an important role in attaining the collective growth target. The Ministers agreed that necessary adjustments within agriculture should be carefully studied. They thought that increased productivity within agriculture should contribute to general price stability. In addition, agriculture could, in many countries, make manpower available for the expansion of industry. In this connection the importance was recognized of insuring that the agricultural population should share in the rising standard of living resulting from economic growth. The Ministers agreed with the OECD Ministers of Agriculture meeting of October 1961 that agricultural policies should be the subject of continuous consultation and confrontation within the Organization in order to insure that industrial and agricultural production developed harmoniously.

The Ministers were determined that increased production should lead to a significant increase in the aid to the less-developed countries. In 1960, the aid to the less-developed countries. In 1960, the aggregate flow of resources, both public and private, from member countries and Japan, a member of the Organization's Development Assistance Committee, amounted to about $7.5 billion. The Ministers agreed that a further increase of development assistance was needed and they welcomed the intention of the Development Assistance Committee to institute, beginning in 1962, an annual review of aid efforts and policies of its member countries. The main purpose should be to increase the efforts and to adapt them better to the needs and circumstances of the recipient countries through exchange of experience regarding bilateral aid. The Ministers expressed the desire that the Development Assistance Committee should encourage greater cooperation among donor countries in their bilateral aid efforts and that a common approach should be applied increasingly to specific problems of economic development assistance. They also recognized the need for full cooperation with and support of multilateral institutions providing development aid, and they welcomed the work going on to define measures to encourage private capital exports to less-developed countries.

The Ministers recognized that successful economic expansion in less-developed countries can best be achieved through carefully prepared programs based on an assessment of needs and resources. They therefore, welcome individual and regional efforts by less-developed countries in drawing up such programs. The Ministers instructed the Organization to study the functions and structure of the contemplated OECD development center which could help, in coordination with existing institutions, to meet the urgent need for more knowledge and for qualified persons to assist in the development efforts.

The Ministers stressed the importance of reducing barriers to the exchange of goods and services, in particular on the part of the more industrialized countries, as a means of promoting economic growth and of providing expanding markets. They emphasized the need to seek ways and means, both in the OECD and in other international forums, to reduce barriers to trade among OECD countries and between OECD countries and the rest of the world. The main instrument of the Organization in achieving this aim should be periodic confrontations of trade policies. The Ministers underlined the significance of the negotiations between the European economic community and other European countries. The arrangements adopted should safeguard the legitimate interests of other countries. They expressed their satisfaction that the countries engaged in negotiations were willing to keep the OECD informed of the progress of the negotiations. The aim of the Organization should be to contribute to the maximum freedom of trade and to enable the less-developed countries to obtain increasing export revenues.

In conclusion, the Ministers noted that these measures were but first steps in a collective effort that must extend increasingly beyond the relationships among their own countries and the material well-being of their citizens. Member countries will pursue together the three objectives of the OECD convention pertaining to economic growth, aid and trade in order to ensure a sound expanding free world economy.

3. Final Communiqué of the N.A.T.O. Ministerial Council, Paris, 15 December 1961[1]

The North Atlantic Council met in ministerial session in Paris from 13 to 15 December, 1961. A thorough examination was made of the problems confronting the alliance. The world-wide Communist threat to freedom, the problem of relations between the North Atlantic alliance and the Soviet bloc, in particular Berlin, were its central concern.

The aim of the peoples of the Atlantic community is a stable order in which no man and no nation need fear for their existence, their liberty or their future. World peace cannot indefinitely rest on a precarious balance of mutual terror.

The alliance seeks peace and disarmament. But this desire has consistently been frustrated by the Soviet bloc. The Western powers have presented a series of plans for general and complete disarmament.

[1] *N.Y. Times*, 16 December, 1961.

The Soviet Government has, however, so far refused to accept an effective and universally applicable system of international control, without which no nation could have confidence in a disarmament agreement.

It envisages only verification of the arms destroyed, while rejecting control of the arms that remain. It is still the earnest hope of the alliance that despite previous disappointments disarmament negotiations when resumed will yield useful results.

On the question of the abolition of nuclear tests, the Soviet Union has argued, evaded and obstructed for over three years, and through more than 300 meetings. The Soviet Union, while professing to negotiate in good faith, must for many months past have been secretly preparing the longest series of nuclear tests yet carried out, culminating in the largest nuclear explosion yet known.

At the same time as the Soviet Union has been attempting to intimidate the peoples of the free world with demonstrations of its nuclear strength, it has intensified its efforts to get the whole of Berlin at its mercy, to impose a discriminatory status on Germany, to perpetuate her divided state, and to break up the Atlantic alliance.

With these ultimate aims in mind, the U.S.S.R. has artificially provoked a crisis over Berlin. Disregarding the obligations it has undertaken, the Soviet Union has cut Berlin in two. Walling-in of the people under its control has once more demonstrated to the world the real nature of the Communist system and the irresistible attraction of a free society.

Ministers expressed their sympathy with all those for whom the raising of this wall in Berlin has meant the separation of families and the denial of escape to freedom in the West.

They also expressed their admiration of the courage and attachment to freedom of the people of Berlin, and reiterated their conviction that a just and peaceful solution of the problem of Germany, including Berlin, must be found on the basis of self-determination.

In the spirit of the agreed policy of the alliance, the ministers recalled their communiqué on Berlin of 16 December, 1958, and reaffirmed their determination to protect and defend the liberties of West Berlin, and ensure to its people the conditions for a free and prosperous life.

Established rights and obligations, solemnly confirmed in international agreements, cannot be extinguished unilaterally by the stroke of a pen—by the signature by the Soviet Government of a 'peace treaty' with a regime which represents no one but its Soviet masters.

The three Western powers who bear special responsibilities for Berlin stand by their clear obligation to protect those who have put their trust in them. Acting in close co-operation with their NATO allies, they have taken the necessary measures to maintain their rights and to fulfill their obligations.

Confirming their agreement on this policy, the members of the alliance reaffirmed the responsibilities which each member state has assumed in regard to the security and welfare of Berlin and the maintenance of the position of the three powers in that city. They agreed to maintain close consultation on this question.

The Council heard statements on Berlin by the foreign ministers of the countries most directly concerned, and was informed of the intention to resume diplomatic contacts with the Soviet Union, in accordance with the aims which the West is pursuing for the maintenance of world peace and in the hope that these contacts might serve to determine whether a basis for negotiation could be found.

Their colleagues approved the resumption of diplomatic contacts and expressed the hope that a negotiated settlement could be achieved. After full discussion of the situation, the Council agreed that the alliance must continue on its resolute course, combining strength and firmness of purpose with a readiness to seek solutions by peaceful means.

Ministers noted the improvements made by member countries in their force contributions, particularly in response to the aggravation of the military threat arising from the deterioration in the Berlin situation.

Units have been reinforced and their state of readiness enhanced. A mobile task force has been established. There have been advances in cooperative programs for defense research and production, as well as in communications and infrastructure. Ministers also noted the progress made by the Council in its study of the long-term problems of improving the deterrent and defensive strength of the alliance.

They instructed the Permanent Council to continue its examination of these urgent questions at an early date.

The North Atlantic Treaty alliance threatens no one. In the world as it is today the alliance must more than ever look to its defense, in view of the ever-increasing military capability of the Communist bloc and its manifest intention to expand its domination.

So long as the Communist bloc is unwilling to agree to real disarmament, the countries of the alliance must continue to strengthen their forces and modernize equipment so as to be able to deal with any form of attack.

Only by an increased defense capability can the alliance continue to deter Communist aggression. This will require still further dedication and effort from the NATO nations. But the clear and growing threat they face leaves no alternative.

In considering civil emergency planning, particularly the protection of the civilian population, the Council recognized that such measures represented an essential element in the defense effort of NATO countries.

In the economic field, the Council noted that a mission of high-ranking personalities had been set up in conformity with a decision taken at the last ministerial meeting to study ways and means of assisting the efforts of Greece and Turkey to speed up their development programs and improve the living standards of their peoples. The mission will report to the Council before the end of April, 1962.

Ministers emphasized the importance for member states, not only of raising the living standards of their peoples, while maintaining an economic structure capable of supporting an adequate defense system, but also of expanding aid to the developing countries. The economies of the NATO countries are far stronger now than when the alliance was formed. Ministers stressed the need to strengthen and deepen cooperation between all member countries in order to continue this progress.

The next ministerial meeting of the Council will be held at Athens from 3 to 5 May, 1962.

(g) *The European Economic Community, the European Free Trade Area, and Great Britain*

1. Communiqué of the meeting of Heads of State and Heads of Government of Member States of the E.E.C., Paris, 11 February 1961[1]

Les chefs d'Etat ou de gouvernement et les ministres des affaires étrangères de la République fedérale d'Allemagne, de Belgique, de France, d'Italie, du Luxembourg et des Pays-Bas se sont réunis à Paris le 10 et le 11 février 1961.

Des liens particuliers unissent dejà les six Etats sur le plan économique et ils se renforceront encore par la mise en œuvres des traités de Paris et de Rome. Les six gouvernements sont désireux de rechercher dans un esprit de bonne volonté et d'amitié tous les accords susceptibles de maintenir et de développer les échanges avec les autres pays européens, en particulier avec la Grande-Bretagne, ainsi qu'avec les autres pays du monde. Ils s'efforceront, dans le même esprit, de trouver des solutions aux problèmes qui résultent de l'existence de deux groupements économiques en Europe.

La conférence avait pour objet de rechercher les moyens propres à organiser une coopération politique plus étroite. En établissant des liens dans d'autres domaines, il s'agit de jeter les bases d'une union qui se développerait progressivement. Cette union, limitée pour le moment aux Etats membres de la Communauté économique européenne, pourra s'étendre par la suite.

Il a été constaté que l'établissement en Europe d'un nouveau type de relations fondé à la fois sur le développement d'un marché unique par l'abolition de toute mesure de protection douanière et l'harmonisation des économies et sur une coopération politique dans un esprit d'amitié, de confiance et d'égalité constitue l'un des faits majeurs de la période actuelle. Au milieu des crises et des remous qui secouent le monde, l'Europe occidentale, ravagée naguère par les rivalités nationales et les conflits, doit devenir une zone d'entente, de liberté et de progrès. Ainsi l'action de l'Europe se fera-t-elle mieux sentir dans le monde pour l'avantage de tout pays libre et en particulier pour le développement de la coopération avec les Etats-Unis.

Il a été décidé de charger une commission composée de représentants des six gouvernements de présenter à la prochaine session des propositions concrètes concernant les réunions des chefs d'Etat ou de gouvernement et des ministres des affaires étrangères, ainsi que toute autre réunion qui paraîtrait souhaitable. Cette commission étudiera aussi les autres problèmes concernant la coopération européenne, notamment ceux qui sont en rapport avec le développement des Communautés. Il a été décidé de tenir la deuxième réunion le 19 mai 1961 à Bonn.[2]

---

[1] *Le Monde*, 12/13 February, 1961.
[2] The meeting was held in July; see below, p. 187.

2. Communiqué of the E.F.T.A. Ministerial Council meeting, Geneva, 16 February 1961[1]

The Council of the European Free Trade Association met at Ministerial level in Geneva from 14th to 16th February, 1961.

The Ministerial Council decided to bring forward by six months to 1st July, 1961, the date by which the next 10 per cent reductions are due to be made in the tariffs applied within EFTA. In this connection they agreed to conclude at an early date the examination, required by the Convention, of the arrangements relating to trade in fish, with the declared aim of effectively increasing this trade.

Ministers agreed that the Council at official level should pursue the examination of the possibility of advancing the subsequent stages of the timetable for reducing and eliminating the tariffs applied within EFTA. They agreed that this examination should be carried out at the same time as the studies which have in any case to be carried out during 1961 in accordance with other provisions of the Convention. They had particularly in mind the review which has to be undertaken of progress in the dismantling of quantitative restrictions; the studies which have to be made in connection with the gradual abolition of subsidised agricultural exports, and the facilitation of the expansion of trade in agricultural goods so as to provide reasonable reciprocity to the EFTA countries mainly concerned.

The Council also agreed on the procedure for the review of the development of agricultural trade provided for in the Convention and established 1st July, 1961, as the target date for this review.

Ministers reached agreement on the form of Association to be offered to Finland, including both the commercial and the institutional arrangements. Discussions with Finland will begin immediately. Ministers are confident that negotiations to establish a final text of an Agreement can be completed in a very short time.

To strengthen Europe it is essential to maintain and fortify all elements of cohesion and strength that exist already, the E.E.C., EFTA, the United Kingdom's links with the rest of the Commonwealth, and the other European countries, Members of O.E.E.C., who do not belong either to EFTA or to the E.E.C. The E.E.C. and EFTA are important achievements in strengthening Europe. But the mere co-existence of these two groups is not sufficient to realise Europe's economic potential, to enable it to play its full part in the world, and make a greater contribution to the advance of the technically less-developed countries. EFTA's wish is to take part, with the E.E.C., in the creation of a single European market which could comprise over 300 million people, one of the largest free markets in the world. This would greatly strengthen the future O.E.C.D. Only in these ways would it be possible to prevent the wasteful use of productive resources, the misdirection of enterprise and investment and the extension of European division to Africa.

The Ministers noted with satisfaction that, in the Communiqué issued on 11th February,[2] the Heads of State and of Governments of the E.E.C. have

---

[1] *E.F.T.A. Bulletin*, March 1961, pp. 8–9.   [2] Above, p. 162.

proclaimed their intention of trying to find a solution of the problems resulting from the existence of two economic groups in Europe. Given this will, such a solution can be found. For their part, they are ready to begin negotiation with the Members of the European Economic Community whenever they wish. They therefore welcome the contacts between representatives of the United Kingdom and of countries of the E.E.C. to explore the basis for future negotiations between all the countries concerned. They welcomed also the continuing opportunities presented with the framework of the GATT for the broadly-based reduction of barriers to trade, not only within Europe, but also between Europe and the United States and other countries of the world.

Ministers agreed that the Consultative Committee, which includes representatives of the main sectors of economic life in Member States, should meet for the first time early in May.

It was agreed to hold the next regular meeting of the Council at Ministerial level in London during the second half of June.[1]

3. Speech by the British Lord Privy Seal, Mr. Heath, to the Council of the Western European Union, Paris, 27 February 1961[2] (official summary)

Mr. Heath had been very glad that Recommendation No. 53 should have been placed on the agenda, since this would provide an opportunity for a thorough discussion of the question of European unity in its widest aspect, political as well as economic. Though this question had been raised so many times in so many places over the past years, never before had it been thoroughly discussed in the W.E.U. Council. He therefore welcomed a substantial examination on the present occasion.

The widespread interest in the subject was not confined to Governments; public opinion, and also parliamentary circles, were closely concerned with it, as was shown by the almost unanimous adoption of Recommendation No. 53 at the last session of the Assembly.

Mr. Heath wished to take this opportunity of making a full and frank statement of the British Government's views on the matter. He would greatly welcome in return an expression of the views of his colleagues. He proposed to take the test of Recommendation No. 53 as a convenient basis for his statement, though his remarks would cover a wider field.

Recommendation No. 53 covered three points:

a) Britain's relations with the European Economic Community;
b) Britain's relations with the other two communities (ECSC and Euratom);
c) Political consultation in Europe, in a rather special context.

a) *Britain's relations with the European Economic Community*

In the W.E.U. Council, discussions were always carried on against the background of the world situation as a whole, such as the challenge of the East, increased threats to the West in such places as Laos and the Congo, the coming

[1] For the communiqué of which, see below, p. 178.
[2] Text supplied by the Western European Union office, London.

challenge in Germany over Berlin, disarmament, the evolution of the United Nations and the attack on its Secretary-General, the direction in which the newly-emergent nations would look in the future, etc. All these problems served to emphasise the vital need for unity in Europe.

Against this background, the United Kingdom Government were very much in tune with the anxieties expressed by the Assembly and therefore welcomed their recommendation. His Government agreed with them that Britain was an essential part of Europe and 'should participate fully and jointly with the other member States in the development of European unity' (cf. first paragraph of Recommendation No. 53). They were ready to play their part. The development of two separate economic groups in Europe was bound to hamper the expansion of production and trade in Western Europe and lead to a wasteful use of resources, in particular in investment. This must bring about, sooner or later, ill-feeling which, in its turn, would have political consequences detrimental to European unity. The British Government had, therefore, been bending their efforts over the past year to finding a solution.

However, because they realised that another breakdown, such as had taken place in 1958,[1] would be disastrous, they had not wished to start any formal negotiations until they could be reasonably certain that a real basis for a successful outcome existed. They had as a result been seeking over the past five months a fresh approach which could provide such a basis for negotiation.[2]

The Council would recall that the British Prime Minister had seen Chancellor Adenauer, President Fanfani and General de Gaulle. Mr. Heath himself had had opportunities of discussing these matters with his six colleagues and he was most grateful to them for their help and guidance. Furthermore, the British Government had discussed the problem with the Commonwealth Finance Ministers in September, and had kept in touch with the Ministers of EFTA. Finally, there had been informal and exploratory talks with German and Italian officials, and now similar talks with French experts were starting in London. They welcomed these talks.

The results so far were reasonably encouraging; a good deal of common ground had been found, and there now existed an understanding of the British point of view.

During these informal talks, a number of points had been made on the British side, which formed the basis of their new approach to the problem. The main one was that if the Six could meet their Commonwealth and agricultural difficulties, the United Kingdom could then consider a system based on a common or harmonised tariff on raw materials and manufactured goods imported from countries other than the Seven or the Commonwealth.

Mr. Heath stressed that this represented a fundamental change of principle in the British position since never before had they envisaged adopting a common tariff. He hoped that this would be recognised as a major contribution to the solution of the problem.

Mr. Heath added that his Government also visualised special arrangements

[1] The breakdown of the European Free Trade Area negotiations in December 1958; see *Survey*, 1956–58, p. 488.
[2] For developments in the latter part of 1960, see ibid., 1959–60, pp. 156–7.

for tropical and agricultural products, because they believed that this was important not only for economic reasons, but also to prevent an extension of the division of Europe into Africa, and particularly into the newly emergent territories there.

In addition, in response to German and Italian enquiries at their talks, the British Government had made it clear that as part of an overall settlement, the United Kingdom would see no difficulty of principle in the way of discussions between the Six and the Commonwealth countries concerning possible reductions in the tariff preferences which Britain now enjoyed in those countries. This too was an important point.

As regards method, his Government had suggested that the best approach was to start by isolating the individual technical problems and trying to find solutions for each of them. That is to say, to look at the major groups of commodities one by one, and see what the requirements were for each country. When that had been done, it would be easier to see what sort of framework would be required to cover the agreed arrangements.

Recommendation No. 53 proposed that the United Kingdom should accede to the European Economic Community as a full member. The British Government did not wish at present to express a view on this, chiefly because they could not see clearly what their general relationship with the Six would be until they had learned more from them about their attitude to these problems. His Government was therefore keeping an open mind on this question. They fully recognised that common institutions would be necessary to control a common or harmonised tariff. They accepted this and were not afraid of any such institutions. He must however stress that no arrangements would be satisfactory to his Government which did not involve a political as well as an economic relationship with the Six.

Mr. Heath went on to make it clear that in all these discussions his Government had been speaking for themselves alone and that they had no mandate from their partners in EFTA. However, they had always said that the interests of these partners must be safeguarded; these interests had therefore been borne very much in mind, and the EFTA partners had been kept fully informed. The recent EFTA Council communiqué[1] showed that the British Government had the firm support of their partners there in what had been done, and also demonstrated the latter's readiness and will to work for a solution.

As regards the Commonwealth, the United Kingdom had every hope that an arrangement on the lines mentioned would be acceptable to them. Of course, further discussion would be necessary, but the countries of the Commonwealth recognised the importance of European unity. Mr. Heath recalled that their Prime Ministers were to meet in ten days' time, when these views would doubtless be confirmed.

Summing up on this point, Mr. Heath considered that the series of explorations and informal exchanges should be continued until it was possible to see clearly enough ahead to justify more formal negotiations. But they could not, of course, give away their full negotiating position now.

He did not claim that his Government's approach was a revolutionary one,

[1] Above, p. 163.

he did maintain however that it was the sensible way to proceed and he hoped the Council would share this view.

b) *Britain's relations with the other two communities*

(E.C.S.C. and Euratom)

Mr. Heath recalled that the second part of Recommendation No. 53 suggested negotiations with a view to British accession to both these communities at the same time as to E.E.C.

In June 1960, Mr. Profumo had told the Assembly that in the context of a wider economic arrangement, the United Kingdom would be ready to consider any proposal for joining these two communities.[1]

He feared that his Government's purposes in this matter had been some-what misunderstood. It had apparently been thought that Britain was trying to get something for nothing and to impede the linking-up of the three Communities. He could not say too strongly that this was not at all the case. On the contrary, his Government had intended to demonstrate their desire to come closer to their European Allies since they looked on all these matters as parts of the central problem which was to keep Europe united.

c) *Political consultation in Europe*

Mr. Heath wished first to make a general statement of principle. The British Government had no desire whatever to weaken the ties of the Six-Power Community or to dilute or impede the flow of this great European Organisation towards greater forms of unity.

They understood very clearly the impulsions and historic necessities which lay behind this movement; he himself had tried to explain in his country the momentum which it had gained and there was now widespread understanding of it. The United Kingdom had too great an interest in seeing it prosper to tolerate any policy of obstruction to it. They recognised it as a real force which they understood and accepted. They sought therefore to take part in it, to fulfil, to enlarge and strengthen it, and not to dilute it.

He then divided the question into four main heads:

i) The United Kingdom recognised, of course, that political discussions between the Six relating to, or arising from, the business of the Communities, were the sole concern of the Six Governments. The United Kingdom would not be entitled, nor would they expect, to take part in such discussions unless or until they had joined, or formed some association with, the communities.

They had no wish to see the identity of the communities weakened while a solution of their relationship with them was being sought. They were not trying to force their way into meetings where they did not have the same responsibilities as the other participants.

ii) On the other hand, when an acceptable arrangement with the six-Power Communities was reached, the United Kingdom would not be afraid of

---

[1] Assembly of Western European Union. *Proceedings, Sixth Ordinary Session, First Part, June 1960, vol. II, Minutes and Official Report of Debate* (Strasbourg, W.E.U., 1960), p. 137.

the resulting institutions. They would expect to participate in them to the full extent required by the arrangements agreed upon.

iii) In the meantime, when political discussions took place on broad European and world-wide problems in which the United Kingdom was also concerned, they were interested, and his Government believed that the United Kingdom should participate. He considered that the Western countries would run into very great dangers, both in Europe and in the world as a whole, if they could not concentrate and organise their discussions so as to unite their policies and strengthen their alliances.

iv) Until such time as the relationship of the United Kingdom and the Six on the economic and political planes had been settled, he considered that the W.E.U. Council, which was, after all, the European nucleus from which NATO had sprung, could provide the forum for any necessary discussion of broad European problems. He thought it was a matter for regret that W.E.U. had not been more fully used in the past, and recalled in this connection the recent statement of Chancellor Adenaeur. The British Government had always been very ready to use W.E.U. more extensively, and the present discussions could be a beginning of most fruitful exchanges of view.

He wished, however, to stress that the British Government would not like to be excluded from European discussions of political questions in which they had a direct interest, such as East-West relations, the political future of Europe, questions of security and disarmament, relations with other continents, and so on. He did not think anyone could deny that they had an important contribution to make to such discussions, and that it would be damaging to European, as well as to wider Western interests, if there were any growth of divergencies between the United Kingdom and other European countries on such issues.

Political consultations could take many forms. Sometimes they could require decisions to be taken in common, for example consultations in NATO about problems of East-West relations. In this case, it was necessary to reach agreement and formulate a united policy.

At other times, the object of such consultations was to exchange views and build up a body of understanding so that policies could be harmonised as much as possible. If a Europe was to be built up which was capable of carrying the weight and influence to which it was entitled by the skills and energies of its peoples, the Allies must pool their ideas and efforts to the utmost extent.

Mr. Heath then turned to the third part of Recommendation No. 53, which related to a possible Conference of Heads of Governments and the question of the British Prime Minister taking part. He thought it would be clear from what he had already said how his Government regarded the general question of their participation in institutions, meetings and discussions, what their attitude to this suggestion would be. He could only repeat what the Prime Minister himself had said in the House of Commons, namely, that if the United Kingdom were to receive a unanimous invitation from the Six to join them in such meetings, they would be disposed to accept it.

In conclusion, Mr. Heath hoped that if anyone still harboured doubts about the British will to find a solution to this problem, these doubts had now been dispelled. Furthermore, if anyone questioned the ability of the United Kingdom to make a settlement, Mr. Heath hoped he had demonstrated that they had taken firm steps towards this such as had never been taken previously.

4. Speech by Mr. Heath to the House of Commons, 17 May 1961[1] (extract)

. . . Looking at the problem of Western unity, I wish to turn now to the question of Europe. The problem with which we have to deal in Europe is a fundamental one. It is the question of what are to be the relations of ourselves and the Commonwealth and the E.F.T.A. partners with the new Europe that is emerging. This I believe to be a most fundamental question and I propose to devote the rest of my speech to it.

After the war, Europe was weak. It was disunited, its buildings destroyed, and its economies in ruin. Over the next ten years it slowly and gradually made its recovery, economically with the help of Marshall Aid and O.E.E.C., militarily through N.A.T.O., and politically through such organisations as the Council of Europe. Throughout that period we played our full part in all these organisations—and when I say 'we' I refer to Governments of both sides of the House. We played our full part in working for the recovery of Western Europe.

Today, Europe is strong. The pattern has changed and a fresh relationship has to be established between ourselves and the other countries of Europe and the six countries of the Economic Community. What is that relationship to be? This is one of the major problems of our time and it confronts us with decisions of immense importance to ourselves, to Europe and to the Commonwealth. It is only right that these decisions should be taken with as full a knowledge as possible of all that is involved. There must be no misunderstandings. We must weigh all the factors carefully, but, above all, we must set them in the right perspective.

The Government are often urged to enlighten the House and the country about these issues. That is perfectly right, but it is not always easy to do so on an issue of this kind. Our own tradition of parliamentary government is one in which the Government take a decision, submit it to the House and await its verdict. But in a situation like this, which is evolving, in which one is trying to establish relations with a number of other countries, and in which, later, it may be necessary to undertake negotiations, it is by no means easy to enlighten the House and the country to the extent which is being asked at the moment and to the extent to which we should like to do. Nevertheless, as this is one of the great issues of our time I believe it right to try to set before the House, as fairly as I can, what the issues are and what we are trying to do to reach a solution to them.

We see today in Europe a powerfully developing group of nations in the European Economic Community. Its strength is shown by its size of over 170 million people compared with 50 million in the United Kingdom and rather under 90 million in E.F.T.A. as a whole. Their reserves of manpower are much greater. In ten years' time the populations under the age of 45 in France and Germany

---

[1] H.C. Deb., vol. 640, cols. 1386–1400.

alone will be double that of the United Kingdom. The gross national product of the Six is two and a half times that of the United Kingdom. Their rate of industrial growth is much higher. The internal trade of the Six rose by 30 per cent. in 1960 compared with 16 per cent. for the internal trade of the Seven.

The Six have a strong balance of payments position and large resources. Their prospects are already attracting increased investment both from the United States and from the United Kingdom. In the past, over 50 per cent. of the investment in Europe from the United States came to the United Kingdom. In 1960, it was down to 41 per cent., and in 1961 over 50 per cent. of the United States' investment in Europe is expected to go to the Six.

I gave these facts to the House as an indication of the strength and the size of the new group which has emerged in Europe. It has established itself, and it is showing every sign of future success.

What, then, we must ask ourselves, is to be the impact of this group on ourselves, on our Commonwealth and on our partners in E.F.T.A.? We now see opposite to us on the mainland of Europe a large group comparable in size only to the United States and the Soviet Union, and as its economic power increases, so will its political influence.

Throughout our history—I am trying to put these facts before the House because I think that they are necessary for making a balanced judgment—we have recognised the need to establish a relationship with the other countries on the mainland. Usually, it has been because we feared their military hostility. Our relationship has been part of the balance of power. Today, that is certainly not the case. It is the great *blocs* of the Communist world and the Western Powers which confront each other. But the problem remains for us to establish a relationship with the new and powerful group on the mainland of Europe.

In the political sphere we see the growth of political consultation between the countries of the Six. There is regular consultation at the level of Foreign Ministers. There is frequent and regular consultation between Ministers of other kinds at other levels, and between, for example, the governors of the State banks; and proposals are being considered for more formalised consultation at the level of heads of Government.

This is not in any way blameworthy, as is sometimes suggested. It is the perfectly natural development of the cohesion of a group such as we see now developing in Europe. From the point of view of political consultation, we have consultation in Western European Union, in which the Six and the United Kingdom sit. At the last meeting of Western European Union the members of the Six told me that they had postponed some of their political consultation from their own meeting the day before until we were present, so that we could take part in it. That was, I think, an indication of their desire that we should take part in some form of permanent political consultation with them. Western European Union is being used meantime as a substitute until more permanent arrangements can be made.

This development poses for us and the rest of Europe considerable political problems. I am talking now not only of the next six months, or the next two or three years, but of a much longer period. We can then see the danger which faces us of a decline in political influence in the world at large and in our Commonwealth. So the first point that I want to emphasise is the political factor involved in this new arrangement of the European countries which has come about since Europe recovered from the after-effects of the war. That is the political background to this problem.

What will be the economic consequences for us of its development? Until the creation of the Economic Community our trade with Europe was increasing. It amounted to 15 per cent. of our trade. During the past five years our exports to the Six have increased at nearly twice the rate of our total export trade. This trade is bound to be affected by the creation of the common tariff round the markets of the Six and the gradual abolition of their internal tariffs.

This will be particularly the case, first, because most of our trade with them is in industrial products, and, secondly, because our markets were in those countries such as the Federal Republic of Germany, which have to raise their tariffs to reach the common tariff level. The creation of a group of this kind means, in any case, that they have all the advantages of mass production with a large market. This, again, poses economic problems for us of competition. More than that, it also means that the Six will be better able to compete in third markets of the world. This will be a challenge to our export trade as a whole. What I have already described also means that the Six will prove a continuing attraction for investment on both sides of the Atlantic. I am not telling the House that our trade is in immediate danger. What I am trying to do for the House is to look into the future over a longer period and see how these things may well develop.

Those are the consequences of the division today between the European Economic Community and the rest of Western Europe. The results of a closer unity between the group and ourselves and our partners in E.F.T.A. would, of course, be the reverse. It is not only that we would together be able to share the benefits and advantages of this new development. We would also be able to contribute very much to it ourselves. On the political side, one of the major political achievements of the Six has been to create a Franco-German rapprochement which is invaluable. Our presence would undoubtedly consolidate this and contribute towards the balanced development of the Community.

These, then, are most powerful reasons why we should use all our strength and energy to find a solution to the problem of a closer relationship between ourselves and our partners and the European Economic Community. It is against these political factors that we should place the very real difficulties of finding a solution in the economic and commercial field.

Of course, if we examine these, we shall find some things which we do not like—some individual things which may be disadvantageous to us and some which they do differently from the way to which we are accustomed. But, against this, we must weigh the very formidable political and material advantages to be gained from a closer association, and we must weigh it all in the context of the future position of our country and the Commonwealth, and of the future position of Europe as a whole and its influence throughout the world.

I would now like to tell the House something of what has been done since we started a new approach to this problem nine months ago. At the meeting then between Chancellor Adenauer and my right hon. Friend the Prime Minister it was decided that we would explore through diplomatic channels, by official and ministerial talks, to see whether a basis for negotiations could be found.

Two things were necessary. The first was to create the will on both sides in Europe to find a solution. The second was to find the technical means whereby the differing interests could be reconciled. On the question of creating a will to find a solution, I believe that there is now a greater will in Europe than ever before to find a means of settling this problem. We have many friends in Europe, and all of them are anxious that these things which now divide us should be removed.

We have made good progress with the technical talks and have covered a lot of ground. Some hon. Members—and I can quite understand it—may ask why it is that this work has still to be done. The reason is that the earlier solutions which were proposed to this problem, in particular, the Free Trade Area, by their nature excluded the sort of problems which we have been closely examining with great energy over the past few months. The Free Trade Area solution excluded by its nature anything to do with agriculture and Commonwealth trade, and institutional problems. Therefore, it is only since we made the new approach last September that this work has been done.

At the meeting of W.E.U. Ministers at the end of February, I was able to report on the progress which had been made.[1] Again, hon. Members may ask why this should be done in W.E.U. It was done there, first, because the Union has as its object to help create closer unity in Europe, and, secondly, because it is the only forum in which members of the Six and ourselves together meet as of right.

I reported our view of the political position in Europe. Briefly, it was this: discussion amongst the Six themselves about their own problems is a matter for the Six. We have no desire to force our way into it. On the other hand, if an arrangement is made between the two groups, or in some other way there is political discussion, then, of course, we will play our full part in it. If there are political discussions on Europe of a nature outside the domestic affairs of the Six, about Europe's influence in the world, then we believe that we should be present, that we have long played our part and have much to contribute. Lastly, as my right hon. Friend the Prime Minister has told the House,[2] if he was invited to attend a conference of heads of Government he would be disposed to accept.

That statement made our political position, as far as Europe is concerned, absolutely plain to all its members, and I am sure that there is no doubt about it today. As far as the economic position is concerned, all I put forward was a report. It was not a series of proposals for negotiation which were to be accepted or rejected. It was a report on the way things had been going in the talks so far and the position that we had reached. I told the members of the Six that if they were able to meet our problems with regard to the Commonwealth and to domestic agriculture, we could then consider a system based on a common or harmonised tariff on raw materials and manufactured goods imported from countries other than the Six, the Seven or the Commonwealth. This was an important change on our part, because it meant that over that sector, excluding the Commonwealth and E.F.T.A., we were accepting the common tariff and its implications. That is the context in which we have been working.

[1] See above, pp. 164–9.   [2] On 16 February 1961; H.C. Deb., vol. 634, col. 1759.

I now want to mention to the House four matters which we are very concerned about. The first is our trade with the Commonwealth. The second is our domestic agriculture. The third is our E.F.T.A. partners. The fourth is the institutional question. We have always made it plain—and I repeat it now—that we shall keep in close touch throughout with other Commonwealth Governments, and will have full consultation with them before we decided on the course to follow.

We have been examining imports from the Commonwealth under four heads —raw materials, tropical products, manufactured goods and temperate food-stuffs. Very few raw materials present any difficulty since, with a few exceptions —I think that there are five main ones—they are imported duty free both into the E.E.C. and into the United Kingdom.

Tropical products present a more complex problem which is, indeed, world wide. It vitally affects the interests of countries outside Europe, including those which have no links with European countries. This must be borne in mind. I have good hopes that progress can be made as far as tropical products are concerned.

The difficulties lie with manufactured goods and temperate foodstuffs. Together, they represent about half our imports from Commonwealth countries, and we have been and still are studying the complex problems involved. But I must tell the House that we cannot yet see clearly what can be done. In our talks with the Six we have naturally been asked what we think should be done, in the context of an overall settlement, in regard to the preference at present enjoyed by United Kingdom exports in some Commonwealth countries. We have replied that we should see no difficulty of principle in the way of discussions between the Six and the Commonwealth countries concerned about possible reductions in tariff preferences, as part of a satisfactory overall settlement so as to put it in general balance.

This has helped confidence. This is where we showed, in our desire to reach an arrangement, that we are not trying to get the best of all worlds and that we are not putting forward the Commonwealth as a reason why we should not have an arrangement with the Six.

Our second main concern is domestic agriculture. If a settlement is to be reached, all the E.E.C. countries now consider that agriculture cannot be excluded altogether. In trying to place the position fully before the House, I must make it plain that that is their view. There must be further discussion before a clear picture emerges, but I want to make three points about it today.

First, while the Rome Treaty lays down the general scheme for a common agricultural policy—a scheme which is different from ours—its detailed implementation has not yet been decided. Secondly, there are indications—and these have come since my statement to the W.E.U. ministerial meeting—that the Community might be ready to consider the possibility of modifications in its present proposals for a common agricultural policy in order to go some way to meet us.

Lastly, while there might be difficulties in one or two commodities—just as there would be problems in industry—British agriculture as a whole, as its post-war record shows, is in a sound state to contemplate participation in a common agricultural policy, provided that that participation is on equal terms as part of an enlarged European Economic Community. The British farmer is efficient and competitive.

The next point I want to make is that the Common Market in agriculture will be introduced gradually, and it will be a long time—perhaps eight years or more —before it comes into full effect. We have, of course, given firm pledges to our farmers, and any change in the method of support we consider would have to take full account of them.

Thirdly, I want to talk about our E.F.T.A. partners. I am very glad that it was possible to reach agreement about the association of Finland with E.F.T.A., and it is also very pleasing to us that so soon after reaching this agreement it was possible for the President of Finland to visit this country. A shadow has been cast over our memories of his visit by the sudden death, shortly after his return to Helsinki, of the Finnish Foreign Minister, with whom I had talks last week in London. That is a matter of great regret to us.

In these exploratory talks we have been speaking only for ourselves. We have always made it plain that the interests of E.F.T.A. must be safe-guarded. We have kept the member countries of E.F.T.A. fully informed of all stages of the ideas that have been put forward and examined. We shall continue to do this, and we shall also consult them before we take any final decisions. Some anxiety has recently been expressed by the Press of some of the E.F.T.A. countries that the United Kingdom, or another E.F.T.A. country might suddenly decide 'to go it alone' without consideration for its partners. This would break up E.F.T.A., and leave the other countries in a weak position in which to make their own arrangements.

The United Kingdom will not abandon its E.F.T.A. partners in that way. We all wish to find a solution—

MR. A. C. MANUEL (Central Ayrshire): In what way?

MR. HEATH: I was referring to the allegations that have been made in the Press that we would 'go it alone'. We are not prepared to abandon our E.F.T.A. partners in any way in trying to find a solution, which may not be the same one for each of us, but we should all help each other to find a solution.

That was the original purpose for which E.F.T.A. was formed. If E.F.T.A. were to disintegrate because some members were looking for solutions on their own without thought of their partners, that would be deplorable. If, on the other hand, E.F.T.A. eventually disappears because we have each found an arrangement that suits us in a wider Europe, E.F.T.A. will have achieved its purpose.

We have also been examining the question of institutions, and this ought to be faced frankly and openly. It is necessary that we should understand what is involved in them. The Treaty of Rome set up a permanent commission under a Council of Ministers. What I wish to emphasise is that the activities are limited to commercial and tariff policy on behalf of the Council of Ministers which takes the decisions in these matters.

The operations of the Community affect two particular aspects of national sovereignty and, again, there should be no misunderstanding, in looking at these problems, as to what is involved. First, the power to make commercial agreements passes to the Commisssion when it is that sector. Secondly, an appeal from commercial decisions lies to the international court. It is only right that those two things should be mentioned; they are both important, and we should face them frankly and openly.

I now wish to deal with the particular point mentioned in the Amendment standing in the name of the Leader of the Liberal Party—[HON. MEMBERS: 'Where is he?'] This is an important matter which is constantly brought before us. He suggests that we can make progress in solving this problem only by first announcing that we propose to sign the Treaty of Rome and then start to negotiate such derogations as may be possible.

I do not believe that to be the case. The signature of the Treaty of Rome does not, of itself, solve any of the difficulties that I have been describing to the House. They would still remain to be resolved. If it were necessary to do this to convince Europe that we were genuine, there might be some argument for it, but that, I am quite convinced, is not the case. Neither have any of the members of the Six, in our talks, asked us to follow this procedure. They realise that it is reasonable that we should see the broad lines of a settlement before any request is made to start negotiations—

MR. ARTHUR HOLT (Bolton, West): Neither the Leader of the Liberal Party nor any other leader has stated what the right hon. Gentleman has ascribed to my hon. Friend. To say that we should apply is quite different from saying that we should sign before commencing negotiations. We have only said that we should apply for entry first, and negotiate later.

MR. HEATH: It is only reasonable, and is accepted by Europe as reasonable, that we should first see what the broad lines of a possible settlement are, and that is the procedure that we have been following—

MR. HAROLD DAVIES (Leek): We have listened to a quite important speech, to a very dramatic statement. Would the right hon. Gentleman let the House know whether or not his party and the Government would take a dramatic and major step like this without first discussing it with the British electorate? This problem is of such magnitude that the whole life of our people might be changed by it. The issue is one which should be put forward in a General Election programme—not pushed through Parliament without discussion at the polls.

MR. HEATH: I am putting forward these points today so that the House might consider the great issues involved; and I am sure that the country, too, will be the better able to do so. I am sorry if, perhaps, from some points of view in the House, I am devoting so much time to this issue, but I think that it is right to do so. [AN HON. MEMBER: 'On this Motion?'] Yes, on this Motion, because this matter of European unity is of the greatest possible importance.

I have tried to describe the European position and I now want to say a brief word about the United States position, because its trading arrangements may well be affected by any solution we may reach. The new Administration in Washington have made their attitude quite clear. The United States is prepared to accept additional discrimination against its goods provided that the arrangement reached can be shown to strengthen the political unity of Europe. It does not feel itself obliged to accept further discrimination from a purely trading arrangement which carries no political advantage. This is a position we can all understand and appreciate. At the same time, it is for the countries of Europe themselves to decide what action they want to take in those circumstances.

As to the attitude of the Six, there is now evidence of a desire throughout the Community that we should reach a settlement. M. Couve de Murville, with whom I had most useful talks last October, which were followed by talks between the Prime Minister and President de Gaulle, has now publicly stated that it is open to us to accede to the Treaty of Rome, which is what the French Government would prefer, or to form some kind of association with it. This view is shared by France's partners in the Community. I therefore submit to the House that what remains is for us to pursue as vigorously as we can our discussions with the members of the Six about the nature of any settlement that is possible, and the means of dealing with our particular problems.

There are really four courses that are open. The first is to abandon the search for a solution. That would be a counsel of despair. The second course is to try to make an economic arrangement between the two separate groups, which will continue to retain their identity. We have, of course, been exploring this, and exploring it fully. It would mean some additional discrimination against the outside world without the corresponding political advantages necessary to offset it. As far as we can see at the moment, it is not a solution that particularly commends itself to the members of the Six.

The third course is for the United Kingdom, and other members of E.F.T.A.—not as a group, but individually—to make a form of association with the Community. In that course, one has to consider the degree of political participation which would be involved, which I emphasised at the beginning of my speech. One would also have basically to consider the influence of an association on the economic policies of the group. On this, again, there is much exploratory work to be done because the first form of association between the Economic Community and another country, that with Greece, has only just been made and has not yet been published.

The fourth course is that of full membership, provided that proper arrangements are made for Commonwealth trade and for our agricultural system to reconcile them with trade and agriculture in Europe, and proper arrangements for our E.F.T.A. partners. If we are to reach agreement there must be give-and-take on both sides. We shall not secure all we would like, but we shall share in great benefits which are not now available to us. To be lasting, any settlement must be fair to both sides.

This is an urgent matter. As the Community develops and its policies crystallise so it will become more difficult to fit into the arrangements which are made. So long as uncertainty exists, businessmen and those engaged in industry and commerce cannot make their plans, either for sales promotion or for investment. On the political side consultations cannot fully develop until this problem is solved. Nevertheless, it is bound to take time, in a matter as complex and as difficult as this, to find a solution to these problems.

As we have so often repeated, we are resolved not to start negotiations until we can see the prospect of a successful outcome from them.

MR. WOODROW WYATT (Bosworth): Negotiations have started.

Mr. Heath: We have *not* started negotiations, but have been carrying out exploratory talks without any commitment of any kind.

I have tried to put as fully as I can the aspects of these European matters, the political and economic aspects of the problem. We recognise that there are for the people of this country very deep human feelings involved in great matters of this kind. Those are feelings which sometimes are buried. They survive from times long ago but today they often colour, perhaps subconsciously, our attitude towards these things. After a point, human beings come to dislike change. Working out a new relationship with Europe involves major decisions and changes. It would be much easier if none of these developments had come about and if no decisions had to be made about them in future, but no nation which allowed that attitude to govern its actions could survive in the world today.

For all of us it is perhaps the Commonwealth which most permeates our thoughts on this problem. Our love for the Commonwealth is deeply bred within us and the question immediately raises itself: will our connection with the Commonwealth in any way suffer if we establish a new relationship with Europe? We must face this situation frankly and openly. Those who have been handling this matter have thought long and deeply about it. I believe that we can maintain our close connection with the Commonwealth and I believe that is what Europe itself desires. The personal ties which link individuals within the Commonwealth and the channels of trading which are so well established, the network of consultation which has grown up over the years, the Prime Ministers' conference, all these can be maintained.

Indeed, with the strengthening of our economic position we should be more able to help in developing the Commonwealth and to strengthen the ties which bind its members together. These then, are the issues which are involved.

Sir Harry Legge-Bourke (Isle of Ely): I am very sorry to interrupt my right hon. Friend, but could he say whether Her Majesty's Government have yet come to any view as to the likelihood of the Common Market countries going on to a common currency? If so, what are likely to be the consequences of that for sterling?

Mr. Heath: I could have dealt with the individual matters concerning the institutions. There are a number of other matters of Article III of the Treaty of Rome, of which financial and investment questions are one. On those other questions the members of the Six are only beginning to formulate policies and they are in the early stages. These are matters we shall have to explore in our talks.

I hope that hon. Members will realise the complexities and difficulties of finding a reconciliation between these matters and policies in the different countries. This is the problem that we are discussing in Europe today. I believe that it is one of the greatest which confronts our generation. It is technical and complex and its aspects must be kept in perspective. Above all, I think that the technical and commercial matters I have mentioned must be set among the great political issues I have described. They must be set in the context of the unity of Europe and the contribution they can make towards the freedom of Europe, on the unity and freedom of which peace depends.

5. Communiqué of the E.F.T.A. Ministerial Council meeting, London, 28 June 1961[1]

The Council of the European Free Trade Association met at Ministerial level in London from 27th to 28th June, 1961, under the chairmanship of the President of the Board of Trade, the Rt. Hon. Reginald Maudling.

The aim of the European Free Trade Association has been, from the outset, not only to create a free market between its Members, but ultimately also to achieve the economic integration of Europe as a whole, in the form of a single European market comprising 300 million consumers, following liberal policies towards the outside world. This purpose is stated in the Stockholm Convention and has been re-affirmed at every Ministerial Meeting since July, 1959. Ministers agreed that a generally increased awareness of the dangers of the present split in Europe has led to signs of willingness to make a new effort to bring to an end the division which, during recent years, has become an obstacle to European economic co-operation. An ending of this division would enable the European countries to give their full attention to the serious problems of economic relations between Europe and the rest of the world, and in particular the relationship between Western Europe as an industrialised region, and the developing countries of other Continents. A new effort to bring to an end this European division will necessitate a readiness to make some modification of policy on all sides, but it must respect the basic political positions not only of the several States of Europe, but also of the European Economic Community.

Experience gained in recent years has provided a basis for a re-examination of the problems of European integration. This re-examination has shown that while some EFTA countries could not accept obligations of a political nature, all members of EFTA are willing to undertake, in order to achieve an integrated European market, obligations which go beyond those which they have accepted among themselves in the Stockholm Convention.

Ministers agreed that the aim of any solution must be to promote unity and solidarity in Europe; to strengthen the European economy and to build an integrated market upon solid and permanent foundations. To this end, Ministers agreed that there must be effective institutions to supervise the implementation of undertakings necessary to achieve a solution acceptable to all parties.

Ministers considered whether their common objective—a single European market embracing all the Members of EFTA—could be achieved by way of negotiation for membership of, or association with the European Economic Community. They concluded that it was premature to judge whether this was possible or was likely to be successful; they decided to re-examine the question at their next meeting.

Ministers agreed that if such a course should then appear possible, the Members of EFTA should co-ordinate their actions and remain united throughout the negotiations. Ministers resolved that the European Free Trade Association, the obligations created by the Convention between the Members, and the momentum towards integration within the Association, would be maintained at least until satisfactory arrangements have been worked out in negotiations to

[1] *E.F.T.A. Bulletin,* July 1961, pp. 8–9.

meet the various legitimate interests of all Members of EFTA, and thus enable them all to participate from the same date in an integrated European market. They agreed that a partial solution which created new economic division within Western Europe could not in any circumstances be regarded as satisfactory.

Ministers recalled their discussion at the Geneva Meeting of the Council from 14th to 16th February, 1961,[1] and their decision to advance the date for the next ten per cent reduction of import duties from 1st January, 1962 to 1st July, 1961. They agreed that there would be advantage in a further acceleration of the time-table for the dismantling of tariff protection within EFTA, and decided to consider the matter further at their next meeting.

During the course of their meeting the EFTA Ministers received the Finnish Ambassador in London, His Excellency Leo Tuominen, representing the Finnish Government. The Chairman of the EFTA Council expressed the pleasure of all the EFTA Ministers at the recent entry into force of the Association Agreement with Finland, and the prospect of fruitful economic co-operation which it held out.

The Finnish Ambassador declared in reply that his Government felt great satisfaction at the link now created between Finland and the EFTA countries by the new Agreement which was of the utmost importance for his country.

6. Address by the President of Ghana, Dr. Nkrumah, to Parliament, Accra, 4 July 1961[2] (extract)

. . . Recently a new threat has loomed up to the cause of African unity which is no less ominous for being unobtrusive. It is the creation of the European Common Market. I want to take this opportunity to make the policy of my Government absolutely clear on this matter.

We naturally do not oppose any arrangement which the nations of Europe may wish to make among themselves to seek for themselves greater freedom of trade within Europe; but we are most decidedly and strongly opposed to any arrangement which uses the unification of Western Europe as a cloak for perpetuating colonial privileges in Africa. We therefore naturally protest against any economic or political grouping of the European powers which aims at exerting political and economic pressures upon the newly emergent countries of Africa; or which discriminates against the trade of those countries which are not willing to participate in these exclusive and unfair arrangements. The operation of the European Economic Community, as at present conceived, will not only discriminate against Ghana and other independent States of Africa economically, but what is more important, it will perpetuate by economic means the many artificial barriers which were imposed on Africa by the European colonial powers.

Any form of economic union negotiated singly between the highly industrialised

[1] See above, p. 163.
[2] Supplement to *Ghana Today* for 19 July 1961, pp. 4–5. For French African reactions to the E.E.C., see below, pp. 647–57.

States of Europe and the newly emergent countries of Africa is bound to retard the industrialisation, and therefore the prosperity and general economic and cultural development of these countries. For it will mean that those African States which were inveigled into joining this union will continue to serve as protected overseas markets for the manufactured goods of their industrialised partners, and the source of cheap raw materials.

Let me assure my brothers, the leaders of those African States who are exposed to these temptations, that the subsidy which they will receive in return for assuming these obligations will be small compared with the losses which they will suffer from perpetuating their colonial status—losses which are to be measured not only in terms of their own retarded economic and cultural development, but in the harm which they do the peoples of Africa as a whole. It is true that by joining they obtain a preferential market for their cash crops and minerals in the territories of the European Economic Union. But the advantages of this are largely illusory since most of the commodities which they export are goods for which the European partners would in any case have to buy from them. On the other hand, they deprive themselves of the advantages of meeting their own requirements in the world market and will be bound to have to pay considerably more for everything they buy—quite apart from the hindrances which the common market is bound to impose on their own internal industrial development. I am aware that the Rome Treaty introduces explicit safeguards concerning tariff protection by the overseas territories of the European Economic Union. But in the circumstances, I am by no means confident that these safeguards will prove effective. The ex-French colonies of Africa have plenty of direct experience of the difficulties they have encountered in setting up manufacturing industry in those cases where this operates to the disadvantage of industries in France itself. Without going into detail, I should like to refer in this connection to the well-known case of the flour mills of Dakar.

It is true of course that the producers of raw materials are always at a disadvantage in bargaining *vis-à-vis* the industrial countries, in the efforts to obtain a fair price for their exports. This naturally follows from their economic weakness which can only be alleviated through unity of action between the different raw material producing countries, but not through exclusive trading arrangements between the strong and the weak. The case of Daniel and the lions may occasionally come out right, but it is not a safe basis for economic planning. So far as Africa is concerned these objectives can only be achieved by close economic association between African States—which in turn pre-supposes close political co-operation between them—and it is on account of its retrograde effect to the cause of African unity that the Government of Ghana is so completely opposed to the European Economic Community in its present form.

I appeal in all sincerity to the leaders of all African States to place the interests of African unity in the forefront of their consideration. I realise that many of these countries find themselves in a difficult position. They are strongly dependent on foreign contributions simply to maintain the machinery of their Governments. Many of the newly created States have deliberately been made so weak economically (by being carved up into many separate countries) that they are not able to maintain out of their own resources the machinery of an independent

Government, the cost of which cannot be reduced beyond a certain minimum. It would be wrong, therefore, for us to criticise their leaders because they have not been able immediately to escape from the impossible position in which they were placed when the transfer of power took place. Their frontiers were not of their own choosing and they were left with an economic, administrative and educational system, which each in its own way was so designed as to perpetuate the colonial relationships.

It is not surprising that in such circumstances these States find it extremely hard to formulate an independent policy, or to envisage the loss of the contributions which they were offered in exchange for continued conformism to the policies of the colonial powers. Their remedy is clear. They must form bigger units than their colonial masters designed them to have. They should help in building up the common market of a united Africa, rather than serve as appendages to the European Common Market.

I am of the firm belief that the senior member of the Commonwealth, the United Kingdom, should not join the European Economic Community unless she succeeds, first, in eliminating from the present arrangements all those features which involve discriminatory trading relations between the European members and their colonies or ex-colonies; second, unless she can give assurances that her own treatment of her colonies and ex-colonies will be no less favourable than those which exist at present; and third, unless she can ensure that whatever financial assistance is offered by the European powers to the newly emergent States of Africa is given unconditionally, and not in the form of a bribe for joining the common market. When the representative of the United Kingdom Government came to see me last week in order to elicit the views of the Ghana Government on this question I made our own attitude clear and also the reasons for it.[1] I wish to say now that if the United Kingdom were to join the common market on conditions in which the position of Ghana as a member of the sterling area was prejudiced, we shall almost certainly be forced to leave the sterling area in order to safeguard our trading position.

Quite apart from our attitude to the common market as governed by our overriding interest in the future of Africa, I should be very sorry to see the United Kingdom becoming a member of the European Economic Community on account of its disruptive effects on the Commonwealth. The free association of peoples which is known as the Commonwealth is an important force for good in the world. Despite all the differences in the political outlook of the different members and the differences caused by their political and ideological alignments and non-alignments, the existence of the Commonwealth is an important stabilising force in this troubled and unstable world. Now that South Africa has been excluded,[2] the members have in common a civilised outlook and a reasonableness of temper in the conduct of international negotiations, and the mutual feeling of trust in their honesty of purpose and the reliability of their word, which makes the Commonwealth an important instrument in the maintenance of world peace. If the senior partner of the Commonwealth were to opt out from membership by

[1] The British Minister of Labour, Mr. Hare, visited Accra at the end of June, before going on to Freetown, Lagos, and Salisbury.
[2] Below, pp. 701–5.

joining a close European federation, I am sure that the other members of the Commonwealth would have to consult on how they could continue this association in some other form. . . .

7. Statements issued during the Commonwealth tour made by the British Minister for Commonwealth Relations, Mr. Sandys, July 1961[1]

(*i*) *Joint statement of Mr. Sandys and the Prime Minister of New Zealand, Mr. Holyoake, Auckland, 6 July 1961*

1. The Prime Minister of New Zealand, Mr. Holyoake, and other New Zealand Ministers have during the last four days had discussions with the British Secretary of State for Commonwealth Relations, Mr. Duncan Sandys.

2. Mr. Sandys explained that British Government were concerned about the future consequences both economic and political of continued division in Europe and were therefore re-examining their relationship with the European Economic Community. Before determining their attitude they were seeking views of other Commonwealth Governments.

3. New Zealand Ministers stated that while they supported the objective of economic and political unity in Europe they had to have regard to the effects of possible developments upon New Zealand's economic well being. They emphasized that their agriculture, which was New Zealand's basic industry, had been developed to supply the British market and that New Zealand's economy was highly dependent on the sale of foodstuffs in that market at remunerative prices. They therefore stressed the grave consequences for New Zealand's economy if Britain should join the Common Market without having taken steps to protect New Zealand's vital interests.

4. Mr. Sandys assured them that the British Government fully understood the dependence of New Zealand's agriculture on the British market. At the same time it had to be recognised that even if Britain did not join the Common Market New Zealand might in any case be faced with difficult problems in finding outlets for its increasing agricultural production. There were limits to the British Market. Mr. Sandys said that the British Government had not yet come to any decision whether or not to enter into negotiations to join the Common Market and would not do so until the views of all Commonwealth countries had been fully considered. He made it clear that in the course of any such negotiations the British Government would seek to secure special arrangements to protect the vital interests of New Zealand and other Commonwealth countries and that Britain would not feel able to join the E.E.C. unless such arrangements were secured.

5. New Zealand Ministers made it clear that they could not at present see any effective way of protecting New Zealand's vital interests other than by maintenance of unrestricted duty free entry. Mr. Sandys explained the difficulties of reconciling unrestricted duty free entry into Britain for all New Zealand's exports with the concept of the Common Market and said that it might therefore be

[1] Cmnd. 1449, *Commonwealth Consultations on Britain's Relations with the European Economic Community* (London, H.M.S.O., July 1961), pp. 4–8. Hereafter cited as Cmnd. 1449.

necessary in any negotiations to explore other methods of securing comparable outlets for New Zealand exports. New Zealand Ministers said that while adhering to the views they had expressed they would be willing to examine any such alternative methods for protecting New Zealand interests which might emerge in the course of negotiations. Until specific proposals had been put forward they would necessarily have to reserve their position.

6. Mr. Sandys gave an assurance that if Britain entered into negotiations with the European Economic Community the New Zealand Government and other Commonwealth Governments would be closely consulted on all matters affecting their interest before and during the negotiations and that arrangement would be made for the results to be thoroughly discussed with them before the British Government took any decision to join the European Economic Community.

7. New Zealand Ministers welcomed the assurances that Mr. Sandys had given, namely that the New Zealand Government would be closely consulted before and during any negotiations, that in any such negotiations the British Government would seek to secure special arrangements to protect the vital interests of New Zealand, that Britain would not feel able to join the European Economic Community unless such arrangements were secured and that the results of any negotiations would be thoroughly discussed with the New Zealand Government before the British Government took a decision to join the European Economic Community. In the light of these assurances they informed Mr. Sandys that they would understand it if, after considering the views of Commonwealth countries, the British Government should open negotiations with the European Economic Community. In that event New Zealand would be prepared to participate in the subsequent consultations envisaged.

(ii) Joint statement of Mr. Sandys and the Prime Minister of Australia, Mr. Menzies, Canberra, 11 July 1961

The Prime Minister of Australia, Mr. Menzies, and other Australian Ministers have during the last few days had discussions with the British Secretary of State for Commonwealth Relations, Mr. Duncan Sandys.

Mr. Sandys explained the various considerations which had led the British Government to re-examine its attitude towards, and relationship with, the European Economic Community (the Common Market) established by the Treaty of Rome.

In the course of several meetings the political and economic implications of such a step were fully discussed.

The Australian Government considered that should Britain join the European Economic Community it might well be that she will become increasingly involved in not only the economic policies of the Community, but also in matters of an international and political kind. Mr. Sandys emphasised that the British Government was convinced that the objective of closer unity in Europe was in no way incompatible with the maintenance and further development of Commonwealth ties which constitute a valuable unifying influence in a much divided world.

Australian Ministers pointed out that they thought the ultimate political implications of the Treaty of Rome are extremely significant and will tend to possess a developing character in the achievement of some kind of European unity. They saw merit in such unity since a continuing division in rival economic groups would be a source of danger and weakness, while a powerful and experienced group of free European nations can do much to preserve the world's peace. However, they emphasised that, although avoidance of a divided Western Europe was a desirable objective, it should not be accomplished at the cost of division within the Commonwealth or elsewhere in the free world. Australian Ministers expressed their concern at the weakening effect they believed this development would have on the Commonwealth relationship.

Mr. Sandys stressed the importance the United Kingdom attaches to maintaining their relationship unimpared. Indeed, the British Government believed that a closer association of Britain with the continent of Europe might well be an added source of strength not only to Britain but to the Commonwealth as a whole.

Full exchanges occurred on the economic advantages and disadvantages which would ensue if Britain were to accede to the Treaty of Rome, and the possible effects of this on the trade and industry of Britain and Australia. It was recognised that the issue of Britain's accession to the Treaty of Rome was primarily a matter for Britain and was one which the British Government alone could decide, but Australian Ministers explained the serious adverse consequences for Australian producers and for the Australian balance of payments which would confront Australia if the United Kingdom were to enter the Common Market on a basis which failed to safeguard Australian interests for the future.

Mr. Sandys assured the Australian Government that the British Government fully shared its concern to maintain the long-established flow of trade between their two countries. If negotiations took place, the intention would be to secure special arrangements to protect these important trading interests.

Mr. Sandys made it clear that he did not ask the Australian Government to express an opinion on the question whether Britain should join the Common Market. The British Government itself had as yet reached no decision on this issue. The immediate question was whether or not to open negotiations with the European Economic Community.

As the whole question is of major importance for Britain and for decision by her, Australian Ministers did not feel entitled to object to the opening of negotiations by the British Government should it reach the conclusion that this was desirable, but they made it clear that the absence of objection should in the circumstances not be interpreted as implying approval. They further stressed that as in any such negotiations various Australian export industries would be materially involved, Australia should be in a position to negotiate direct on Australia's behalf when details and arrangements affecting items of Australian trade were being discussed.

Mr. Sandys said he well understood the position of the Australian Government and he appreciated its understanding of Britain's problem.

It was agreed that these talks, which had been conducted in a most helpful and constructive spirit on both sides, had resulted in a more complete understanding of the important and complex issues involved.

(iii) *Joint statement of Mr. Sandys and Canadian Ministers, Ottawa, 14 July 1961*

Mr. Duncan Sandys, the British Secretary of State for Commonwealth Relations, met yesterday and today under the Chairmanship of Mr. Donald Fleming, Canadian Minister of Finance, with Mr. Howard Green, Secretary of State for External Affairs, Mr. George Hees, Minister of Trade and Commerce, and Mr. Alvin Hamilton, Minister of Agriculture. Mr. Sandys also had a meeting with the Prime Minister, Mr. Diefenbaker.

Mr. Sandys explained the British Government's assessment of the potential advantages and disadvantages of Britain either joining or staying out of the European Economic Community. The British Government had as yet reached no decision on this issue. The immediate question was whether or not to open negotiations with the Community.

The Canadian Ministers recognised that this is a matter for decision by the British Government.

Mr. Sandys said that if, following the present preliminary exchanges of views, the British Government should decide to open negotiations, they would then consult fully with the other members of the Commonwealth.

The Canadian Ministers indicated that their Government's assessment of the situation was different from that put forward by Mr. Sandys. They expressed the grave concern of the Canadian Government about the implications of possible negotiations between Britain and the European Economic Community, and about the political and economic effects which British membership in the European Economic Community would have on Canada and on the Commonwealth as a whole.

Mr. Sandys said that before the British Government reached any decision, they would carefully consider the views of the Canadian Government together with those of other Commonwealth Goverments.

8. Statements issued during the Commonwealth tour made by the British Minister of Aviation, Mr. Thorneycroft, 11 and 14 July 1961[1]

(i) *Joint statement of Mr. Thorneycroft and Pakistani Ministers, Karachi, 11 July 1961*

On the 10th and 11th of July Mr. M. Hafizur Rahman, Minister for Commerce and Acting Minister for Finance, and Mr. A. K. Khan, Minister for Industries, assisted by the Secretaries of Commerce, Finance and Industries and other officials of the Ministry of Commerce, held discussions with the Rt. Hon. Peter Thorneycroft, British Minister for Aviation, who was assisted by Mr. Andrew of the Board of Trade, Mr. Martin of the Commonwealth Relations Office, Mr. Carter (United Kingdom Senior Trade Commissioner in Pakistan) and other officials of the United Kingdom High Commission in Pakistan. In addition, officials assisting Mr. Thorneycroft and officials of the Ministries of Commerce and Industries had discussions.

Frank and free discussions were held on the possible effects of the United Kingdom joining the Common Market. Mr. Thorneycroft explained that the

[1] Cmnd. 1449, pp. 9–12.

British Government had not yet come to any decision whether or not to enter into negotiations to join the Common Market and would not do so until the view of all Commonwealth countries had been fully considered. He further pointed out that the British Government were concerned about the continued division in Europe and were therefore re-examining their relationship with the European Economic Community.

The Pakistan Ministers stated that while they supported the objectives of economic and political unity in Europe they had to have regard to the possible repercussions upon Pakistan's economic well-being particularly her development programme. They emphasised that Pakistan's economy had in the past remained more or less stationary because of her dependence on exports of primary commodities, mainly jute. Pakistan had therefore now to develop other avenues of exports which comprised not only primary commodities, but also semi-manufactured and manufactured goods based on her raw materials. The Pakistan Government was therefore concerned about the adverse consequences that were likely to follow on the United Kingdom joining the Common Market without any arrangement under which the interests of Pakistan could be safeguarded.

Mr. Thorneycroft undertook that full account would be taken throughout by the United Kingdom of the interests of Pakistan as explained in the discussions and particularly her position as a developing country. Mr. Thorneycroft gave an assurance that if the United Kingdom entered into any negotiation with the European Economic Community the Pakistan Government would be closely consulted on all matters affecting their interests before and during the negotiations, and that arrangements would be made for the results to be thoroughly discussed with them before the British Government took any decision to join the Community. The representatives of the Pakistan Government welcomed this assurance of close consultation on the basis of which the Pakistan Government would be in a position to get a more concrete picture of the future association of the United Kingdom with the Common Market and which would enable the Pakistan Government also to plan her own further course of action for her future associations with the United Kingdom and the European Economic Community.

(ii) *Joint statement of Mr. Thorneycroft and Indian Ministers, Delhi, 14 July 1961*

Shri Morarji Desai, the Minister of Finance, Shri K. C. Reddy, Minister of Commerce and Industry, and other Indian Ministers held discussions on 12th, 13th and 14th July with the British Minister of Aviation, the Right Hon. Peter Thorneycroft, about the issues involved in any negotiation by the British Government to join the European Economic Community. Mr. Thorneycroft had also a brief discussion on the main policy matters arising out of this question with the Prime Minister of India on 13th July.

Mr. Thorneycroft explained that although the British Government had reached no decision, they were concerned about the economic division of Europe which was emerging; and they were therefore examining carefully the problems that would arise if they decided to join. He drew attention to the economic consequences of continued division and to the importance of maintaining a new and expanding European economy, both as a market for the products of developing countries and as a source of investment funds for them. On the other hand, acceptance of a common tariff would inevitably give rise to the question how far the traditional facilities of duty-free entry into the United Kingdom and the system of preferences could be maintained in favour of India and other Commonwealth countries.

It was recognised that the question whether Britain should enter into negotiations with a view to acceding to the Treaty of Rome was primarily a matter for Britain; and the British Government alone could take a decision on it. Indian Ministers suggested that the accession of the United Kingdom to the 'Treaty of Rome' might weaken existing Commonwealth links and injure the economies of the developing countries of the Commonwealth in particular. They drew attention to the importance of avoiding further differences and complications in areas outside Europe.

Indian Ministers and officials emphasised the serious damage which was likely to be caused to India's export trade if the United Kingdom were to join the Community without securing agreement on special measures necessary adequately to safeguard it. They pointed out that the principal exports of India as well as of many other developing countries were subjected to high tariffs, internal taxes and quantitative restrictions of a discriminatory character in some of the countries of the E.E.C., while these products were being admitted duty-free and without restrictions to the United Kingdom. If the United Kingdom joined the European Economic Community without suitable provisions for the future trade of the Commonwealth with special emphasis on the types of products which come from the developing countries, India and other developing Commonwealth countries would find it extremely difficult to maintain and expand their export trade. This is a matter of vital concern to developing countries like India since the earnings of their export trade provide the external resources for their economic development. It was common ground that the credits which India was receiving from the United Kingdom as well as other countries could only be repaid through an expansion of India's exports. The Ministers examined in detail the exports which might be affected and the wider commercial policy implications of any change in the present position. They attached great importance to the maintenance and expansion of intro-Commonwealth trade. Mr. Thorneycroft assured the Indian Ministers that the interests of India as they had been explained to him would be kept fully in mind in any negotiations for entry into the European Economic Community. If negotiations were embarked upon, the British Government would keep in the closest touch with the Government of India in all matters affecting their interests. The Ministers agreed that arrangements should be made for such consultations and for further discussion between the two Governments before the British Government took any decision to join the Community.

9. The 'Bonn Declaration'. Joint statement of the Heads of States and Governments of the E.E.C. States, Bonn, 19 July 1961[1]

Les chefs d'Etat ou de gouvernement de la République fédérale d'Allemagne, de la Belgique, de la France, de l'Italie, du Luxembourg, ainsi que le provident du conseil et le ministre des affaires étrangères des Etats-Unis désireux d'affirmer les

[1] *Le Monde*, 20 July 1961.

valeurs spirituelles et les traditions politiques qui forment leur patrimoine commun, unis dans la conscience des grandes tâches que l'Europe est appelée à remplir au sein de la communauté des peuples libres pour sauvegarder la liberté et la paix dans le monde, soucieux de renforcer les liens politiques, économiques, sociaux et culturels qui existent entre leurs peuples, notamment dans le cadre des communautés européennes, et d'avancer vers l'union de l'Europe.

Convaincus que seule une Europe unie, alliée aux Etats-Unis d'Amérique et à d'autres peuples libres, est en mesure de faire face aux dangers qui menacent l'existence de l'Europe et celle de tout le monde libre, et qu'il importe de réunir les énergies, les capacités et les moyens de tous ceux pour lesquels la liberté est un bien inaliénable, résolus à développer leur coopération politique en vue de l'union de l'Europe et à poursuivre en même temps l'œuvre déjà entreprise dans les communautés européennes.

Souhaitant l'adhésion aux communautés européennes d'autres Etats européens, prêts à assumer dans tous les domaines les mêmes responsabilités et les mêmes obligations, ont décidé:

1) De donner forme à la volonté d'union politique, déjà implicite dans les traités qui ont institué les communautés européennes, d'organiser à cette fin leur coopération, d'en prévoir le développement, de lui assurer la régularité que créera progressivement les conditions d'une politique commune et permettra finalement de consacrer l'œuvre entreprise dans des institutions:

2) De tenir, à intervalles réguliers, des réunions qui auront pour objet de confronter leurs vues, de concerter leurs politiques et de parvenir à des positions communes affin de favoriser l'union politique de l'Europe, renforçant ainsi l'alliance atlantique. Les dispositions pratiques nécessaires seront prises pour préparer ces réunions. D'autre part la poursuite d'une collaboration active entre les ministres des affaires étrangères contribuera à la continuité de l'action entreprise en commun. La coopération des Six doit dépasser le cadre politique proprement dit, elle s'étendra en particulier au domaine de l'enseignement, de la culture et de la recherche, où elle sera assurée par des réunions périodiques des ministres intéressés;

3) De charger leur commission de leur présenter des propositions sur les moyens qui permettraient de donner aussitôt que possible un caractère statutaire à l'union de leurs peuples.

Les chefs d'Etat ou de gouvernement ont la conviction qu'en organisant ainsi leur coopération ils favoriseront par là même l'exécution des traités de Paris et de Rome. Ils estiment également que leur coopération facilitera les réformes qui, dans l'intérêt d'une plus grande efficacité des communautés, apparaîtraient opportunes.

A cet effet, ils ont décidé:

1) De faire mettre à l'étude les divers points de la résolution de l'Assemblée parlementaire européenne du 29 juin 1961, relative à la coopération politique entre les Etats membres des communautés européennes;[1]

---

[1] *Journal Officiel des Communautés Europeennes, 4e année, No. 50*, 22 July 1961. pp, 970–1/61. Text as follows:
L'Assemblée parlementaire européenne,
    ayant pris connaissance des résultats de la première conférence des chefs de gouvernement et des ministres des affaires étrangères qui a eu lieu à Paris les 10 et 11 février 1961,

2) D'associer davantage l'opinion publique à l'effort entrepris, en invitant l'Assemblée parlementaire européenne à étendre aux domaines nouveaux, avec la collaboration des gouvernements, le champ de ses délibérations.

10. Statement by Mr. Macmillan to the House of Commons, 31 July 1961[1]

With permission, I wish to make a statement on the policy of Her Majesty's Government towards the European Economic Community.

The future relations between the European Economic Community, the United Kingdom, the Commonwealth and the rest of Europe are clearly matters of capital importance in the life of our country and, indeed, of all the countries of the free world.

This is a political as well as an economic issue. Although the Treaty of Rome is concerned with economic matters it has an important political objective, namely, to promote unity and stability in Europe which is so essential a factor in the struggle for freedom and progress throughout the world. In this modern world the tendency towards larger groups of nations acting together in the common interest leads to greater unity and thus adds to our strength in the struggle for freedom.

I believe that it is both our duty and our interest to contribute towards that strength by securing the closest possible unity within Europe. At the same time, if a closer relationship between the United Kingdom and the countries of the European Economic Community were to disrupt the long-standing and historic ties between the United Kingdom and the other nations of the Commonwealth the loss would be greater than the gain. The Commonwealth is a great source of stability and strength both to Western Europe and to the world as a whole, and I am sure that its value is fully appreciated by the member Governments of the

---

est d'avis:

—que des réunions périodiques des chefs de gouvernement ou des ministres responsables de la politique étrangère des Etats membres des Communautés européennes pourront contribuer efficacement et dans les meilleures formes à renforcer cette coopération;

—que cette initiative constituerait un progrès dans l'intégration européenne:

   —si elle comportait une participation des exécutifs des Communautés à la discussion de toutes les questions intéressant l'exécution de leur tâche;

   —si elle laisse intacts le fonctionnement et les compétences de ces Communautés et de leurs institutions, sur la base des traités de Rome et de Paris et renforce les Communautés;

   —si les gouvernements font rapport à l'Assemblée au moins une fois par an, sur l'état de la coopération politique;

   —si elle contribuait à réaliser le projet de convention de l'Assemblée parlementaire européenne relatif aux élections européennes directes, la proposition de fusion des exécutifs des Communautés et celle de la création de l'Université européenne;

   demand aux gouvernements de déterminer les étapes de la réalisation progressive d'une union politique étroite, en précisant la durée de ces étapes et plus particulièrement de la dernière, a fin de parvenir, sur le plan de la Communauté, à un minimum de structure politique européenne, fonctionnelle et vivante;

   considère que les objectifs prévus dans les alinéas précédents constituent un ensemble équilibré et souhaite que la réalisation soit décidée simultanément;

   charge son président de faire connaître le texte de cette résolution à la prochaine conférence intergouvernementale.

[1] H.C. Deb., vol. 645, cols. 928–31. Britain's formal application for negotiations to be opened with a view to Britain's joining E.E.C. was transmitted to the President of the E.E.C. Council, Herr Erhard, on 9 August after both Houses of Parliament had approved the Government's decision. Negotiations opened in Brussels on 8 November.

European Economic Community. I do not think that Britain's contribution to the Commonwealth will be reduced if Europe unites. On the contrary, I think that its value will be enhanced.

On the economic side, a community comprising, as members or in association, the countries of free Europe, could have a very rapidly expanding economy supplying, as eventually it would, a single market of approaching 300 million people. This rapidly expanding economy could, in turn, lead to an increased demand for products from other parts of the world and so help to expand world trade and improve the prospects of the less developed areas of the world.

No British Government could join the European Economic Community without prior negotiation with a view to meeting the needs of the Commonwealth countries, of our European Free Trade Association partners, and of British agriculture consistently with the broad principles and purpose which have inspired the concept of European unity and which are embodied in the Rome Treaty.

As the House knows, Ministers have recently visited Commonwealth countries to discuss the problems which would arise if the British Government decided to negotiate for membership of the European Economic Community. We have explained to Commonwealth Governments the broad political and economic considerations which we have to take into account. They, for their part, told us their views and, in some cases, their anxieties about their essential interests. We have assured Commonwealth Governments that we shall keep in close consultation with them throughout any negotiations which might take place.

Secondly, there is the European Free Trade Association. We have treaty and other obligations to our partners in this Association and my right hon. Friends have just returned from a meeting of the European Free Trade Association Ministerial Council, in Geneva, where all were agreed that they should work closely together throughout any negotiations. Finally, we are determined to continue to protect the standard of living of our agricultural community.

During the past nine months, we have had useful and frank discussions with the European Economic Community Governments. We have now reached the stage where we cannot make further progress without entering into formal negotiations. I believe that the great majority in the House and in the country will feel that they cannot fairly judge whether it is possible for the United Kingdom to join the European Economic Community until there is a clearer picture before them of the conditions on which we could join and the extent to which these could meet our special needs.

Article 237 of the Treaty of Rome envisages that the conditions of admission of a new member and the changes in the Treaty necessitated thereby should be the subject of an agreement. Negotiations must, therefore, be held in order to establish the conditions on which we might join. In order to enter into these negotiations it is necessary, under the Treaty, to make formal application to join the Community, although the ultimate decision whether to join or not must depend on the result of the negotiations.

Therefore, after long and earnest consideration, Her Majesty's Government have come to the conclusion that it would be right for Britain to make a formal application under Article 237 of the Treaty for negotiations with a view to joining the Community if satisfactory arrangements can be made to meet the special needs of the United Kingdom, of the Commonwealth and of the European Free Trade Association.

If, as I earnestly hope, our offer to enter into negotiations with the European Economic Community is accepted we shall spare no efforts to reach a satisfactory agreement. These negotiations must inevitably be of a detailed and technical character, covering a very large number of the most delicate and difficult matters. They may, therefore, be protracted and there can, of course, be no guarantee of success. When any negotiations are brought to a conclusion then it will be the duty of the Government to recommend to the House what course we should pursue.

No agreement will be entered into until it has been approved by the House after full consultation with other Commonwealth countries by whatever procedure they may generally agree.

11. Declaration by the Danish Government, 31 July 1961[1]

The Government have considered the situation which has arisen by the decision of the British Government to make an application to join the European Economic Community.

The Government, which for some time have realised that this step might be taken, see in this decision a possibility that the increasing economic and political division of Western Europe may be replaced by a development towards a strengthening of the economy and the cohesion of our countries.

On this basis the Government, after consultations with the Foreign Affairs Committee of the Danish Parliament and with other EFTA countries, have decided likewise to apply for negotiations with the European Economic Community with a view to Denmark joining the Community on terms which will meet the special needs of the various economic sectors and of the Danish community as a whole, including those of Greenland and the Faroe Islands.

The Government intend to carry out the negotiations under full consideration of the interests of her EFTA partners and with a view to maintaining Nordic cooperation. As has been the case during previous market negotiations the Government will maintain close consultation with the interested Danish organisations.

Before making a formal approach to the European Economic Community the Government will submit the matter to the Danish Parliament.

12. The 'Geneva Declaration'. Statement of the Ministerial Council of E.F.T.A., Geneva, 31 July 1961[2]

At their meeting in London on 27th and 28th June, EFTA Ministers decided to re-examine at their next meeting the question whether their common objective —a single European market—could be achieved by way of negotiation for membership of, or association with, the European Economic Community, and they

[1] *E.F.T.A. Bulletin*, August–September 1961, p. 8.
[2] *E.F.T.A. Bulletin*, August–September 1961, p. 7.

agreed on the lines on which such negotiation should be co-ordinated in EFTA. This examination was carried further at the Ministerial Meeting in Geneva on 28th July. In this connection, Ministers recalled the repeated statements by the Members of the European Economic Community of their willingness to accept other countries as Members or in an associated status.

EFTA Governments consider that the decision of the United Kingdom Government to take the initiative announced by the Prime Minister in the House of Commons this afternoon, which was followed by a similar statement of the Danish Government, provides an opportunity to find an appropriate solution for all EFTA countries and thus to promote the solidarity and cohesion of Europe. In reaching this conclusion, the Members of EFTA reaffirmed the decisions recorded in the London Communiqué.[1]

The Members of EFTA consider that it is the duty of all concerned not to miss this new opportunity. EFTA, for its part, will, on the lines set out in the London Communiqué, do everything in its power to seize it. All Member States of EFTA declare their intention to examine with the European Economic Community, the ways and means by which all Members of EFTA could take part together in a single market embracing some 300 million people.

The Council of EFTA will consider at future meetings, what further action should be taken by the Members of EFTA in the light of these developments.

The Council invited the Chairman, Dr. Bruno Kreisky, to inform the European Economic Community of this declaration.

*　　*　　*

The Council instructed the Secretary-General to inform the Finnish Government of these decisions.

13. Joint statement of Ministers of the E.F.T.A. 'neutral' countries, Vienna, 19 October 1961[2]

The Ministers of the neutral EFTA countries[3] met on 19th October, 1961, in Vienna in order to consult about the ways and means appropriate to achieve the objective laid down in the Decision of the EFTA Council of 31st July, 1961[4] the creation of an integrated European market.

On the basis of previous studies, the Ministers were able to establish that, as regards the form of the future relationship with the E.E.C., they see in the same light the problems posed by the neutrality status of their countries. They however found themselves also confirmed in their view, that neutrality does not constitute an obstacle to their participation, through association in appropriate form, in the economic integration of Europe, and to their taking the measures necessary for the functioning of an integrated European market.

The Ministers subsequently conferred about further steps as regards the formal offer to the E.E.C. of negotiations and the conduct of the negotiations. In order to attain the goal of a simultaneous entry into force of an overall solution for all the EFTA countries, the Ministers concluded that, in the light of satisfactory

[1] Above, p. 178.   [2] *E.F.T.A. Bulletin*, November 1961, p. 4.
[3] Sweden, Switzerland, and Austria.   [4] Above, p. 191.

progress with the integration negotiations, it would be justified to follow up with formal steps by the individual countries, before the end of the year, their readiness to negotiate—already indicated in the EFTA Declaration of 31st July, 1961. Before taking final decisions in this regard, the neutral EFTA countries will co-ordinate their actions with the other EFTA members during the next EFTA Ministerial meeting, which is due to take place in the course of November, and they will initiate consultations with their parliamentary bodies or report to them.

The Secretary-General of EFTA, who took part in the meeting, undertook to inform the other EFTA members about the proceedings of the meeting.

14. Communiqué of the E.F.T.A. Ministerial Council, Geneva, 21 November 1961[1]

The EFTA Council met at Ministerial level in Geneva on the 20th and 21st November under the chairmanship of its Vice-Chairman, Mr. J. O. Krag, Danish Minister for Foreign Affairs. The Ministerial meeting was the first since the joint declaration of intention to take part in a single European market, issued at Geneva on 31st July.[2]

Ministers took note of statements by Mr. Heath and Mr. Krag about the United Kingdom and Danish negotiations with the European Economic Community, and of the intention of the Austrian, Swiss and Swedish Governments to seek an appropriate form of Association with the Community. They also received reports on the positions of the Norwegian and Portuguese Governments.

Ministers expressed satisfaction with the steps taken or contemplated in this field and with the manner in which Member Governments were keeping each other informed. They will continue to consult on the action each Member State takes to implement the decision that each Member should seek an appropriate relationship with the European Economic Community.

Ministers decided that the next reduction in tariffs of 10% within EFTA, due according to the Stockholm Convention to take place on the 1st July 1963, should be advanced to 1962. This decision will be implemented by Denmark, Portugal, Sweden, Switzerland and the United Kingdom on the 1st March 1962, and by Austria and Norway not later than the 1st September 1962. The decision is subject to confirmation by the Danish Government.[3]

The next meeting of the Council at Ministerial level is expected to take place in Geneva in the second half of February 1962.

---

[1] *E.F.T.A. Bulletin*, December 1961, p. 5.   [2] Above, p. 191.
[3] Confirmation was received on 27 November.

C. THE SOVIET BLOC

(a) The Soviet-Albanian rift

1. Report by the First Secretary of the Albanian Communist Party, Mr. Enver Hoxha, to the Fourth Congress of the Party, Tirana, 14 February 1961[1] (extracts)

(i) *The International Situation and the Foreign Policy of the People's Republic of Albania*

1. The consolidation of the world socialist system and the further decline of the world capitalist system . . .

Our Party of Labor has always regarded as its foremost duty and promoted with all its strength the preservation and the constant consolidation of the unity of the great socialist family on the basis of the Leninist principles of equality, noninterference, mutual respect, close cooperation, and fraternal, mutual assistance. In the most difficult moments when international reaction, headed by U.S. imperialism and utilizing all its agents, especially the Yugoslav revisionists, was attacking the Soviet Union and the unity of the socialist camp, our party and government have raised ever higher the banner of unity. They were, are, and always will be prepared to face any obstacles and fulfill to the end their international duty, just as the other fraternal countries will fulfill their duties toward our country if the need should arise. (*Stormy applause, ovations*) One for all and all for one. The banner of our unity is the banner of our victories, of the victory of peace and socialism in the world.

The Albanian people are rightly pleased that the People's Republic of Albania, guided by our Party of Labor, has also made and continues to make its modest contribution to this precipitous rise in the international authority of the world socialist system, to the ever-growing superiority of the forces of socialism over the forces of capitalism, and to the historic struggle for the victory of Communism.

But, while the world socialist system is precipitously advancing, developing, and flourishing and is daily demonstrating an ever-increasing and indisputable superiority, the world capitalist system is decaying and disintegrating and is daily demonstrating its reactionary and antisocial character, its inability to solve the social problems of its time. The death knell of capitalism is now tolling.

The collapse of the system of colonial enslavement under the impact of the national liberation movement is the heaviest blow to imperialism since the formation of the world socialist system.

It is clear, comrades, that all these magnificent victories of the world socialist system and the national liberation movement of dependent and colonial peoples have decisively weakened the dominating position, the influence, and the prestige of the capitalist system and have at the same time sharpened on an unprecedented scale its all-round contradictions and general crisis.

---

[1] W. E. Griffith, *Albania and the Sino-Soviet Rift* (Cambridge, Mass., 1963), pp. 197–222. Hereafter cited as *Albania and the Sino-Soviet Rift*.

The creation of the world socialist system and the disintegration of the imperialist colonial system have greatly narrowed the sphere of imperialist domination and, consequently, the sphere in which its laws are operative. This has sharpened all the contradictions which are gnawing at the capitalist system from within, both class and national, internal and external. The attempts to save capitalism from its irreconcilable contradictions, to preserve its decadent foundations through the militarization of the economy and the arms race are carrying the capitalist order toward its inevitable doom and further tightening the knot of its contradictions. The economy of the capitalist countries has entered a blind alley from which it cannot escape, and it is becoming more and more unstable. Not only have the periodic economic crises not disappeared, as the bourgeois ideologists and their revisionist colleagues maintain, but they are becoming more frequent and today seriously threaten many capitalist countries. The decay of capitalism is clearly evident in the most powerful capitalist country, the United States of America, where widespread unemployment has become chronic, production growth rates are declining, the arms race has assumed unprecedented proportions, the fascist and racist tendencies in everyday life are becoming more and more evident, and the military circles are increasingly determining the policy of the government.

All this clearly shows that the international situation is developing in favor of socialism and to the disadvantage of capitalism, that socialism is becoming stronger every day while capitalism is becoming weaker, that the socialist camp is much stronger than the imperialist camp. This is the principal characteristic of our times. The Moscow Declarations of 1957 and 1960 state that the main content of our time is the transition from capitalism to socialism, that our age is the age of the struggle between two opposing social systems, of the socialist and national liberation revolutions, of the breakdown of imperialism, of the liquidation of the colonial system, and of the triumph of socialism and Communism.

Our Party of Labor has always had and continues to have a correct Marxist-Leninist grasp of this question. But does this mean that the hands of the imperialists are already tied because the forces of socialism surpass those of capitalism? That we are now in a position to impose our will on them, whereas they are in a position to do nothing? That we are now in a position to guarantee peace, while they are not in a position to unleash war?

The Marxist-Leninist dialectical method and the materialist conception of history give us the correct answer: Both the overestimation of our forces and the underestimation of the enemy forces on the one hand, and the underestimation of our forces and overestimation of the enemy forces on the other, lead to grave errors. The first weakens vigilance and leads to adventurism, while the second leads to opportunist errors and attitudes. Therefore, our party has always stressed that the balance of power in the world has changed in favor of socialism, that the forces of socialism are stronger than those of imperialism, that the forces of peace are stronger than the forces of war; but at the same time it has not underestimated the forces of imperialism. The correct line of our party on this matter has found accurate expression in its attitude toward the problems of war and peace, toward imperialism, and so forth. Our party has always maintained that it is possible to prevent world war, that today world war is not fatalistically inevitable, but at the same time it has maintained that the danger of war exists, for as long as imperialism exists so too will the basis for aggressive war. On the one hand, we are concentrating all our efforts on strengthening the socialist camp, on preserving and tempering its unity, and on increasing its defensive power; on the other hand, while consistently following the Leninist policy of peaceful coexistence between states with different social systems, we have at the same time always unmasked imperialism and in particular American imperialism, its war preparations, and its aggressive nature. Hence our slogan: 'Let us hold a pick-axe in one hand and a rifle in the other.' (*Stormy applause, ovations.*)

To view this problem differently means openly to contradict the Moscow Declarations of 1957 and 1960 and to pass over to the rightist positions of revisionism and opportunism.

Peace cannot be ensured by making concessions to the imperialist or by flattering them. All the endeavors of the socialist countries in the field of international relations, the policy of peaceful coexistence with capitalist countries consistently followed by the great Soviet Union and the other socialist countries, and the permissible tactics and compromises on our side should help strengthen us and weaken the enemy in order to compel him to abandon the arms race, the production and testing of atomic weapons, the creation of military bases, and preparations for a third world war.

Imperialism, headed by the United States of America, confronts us as a serious threat to peace.

Therefore, in the face of this savage enemy of all humanity, which is trying to plunge the world into another world war that would result in incalculable misery and ruin from the use of existing nuclear weapons, the socialist camp must be militarily as well as politically and morally prepared to deal with any kind of imperialist adventure. The popular masses throughout the world must rise to stay the hand of the imperialists, to unmask the intrigues of the imperialists and their lackeys—the revisionists—who are trying to sow discord among the peoples, to deceive them, and to catch them unprepared, by surprise. (*Fervent applause*) The peoples must strengthen their vigilance. This is the way, and the only way, to halt the imperialists and to make them incapable of unleashing war. The enemy cannot be trusted, and this is the case with imperialism—especially American imperialism.

The existence and the struggle of two opposing world systems determine the existence of two opposing lines in international politics; on the one hand, there is the peaceful and consistent policy of the glorious Soviet Union, People's China, and the other socialist countries, which daily finds ardent and ever-increasing support among the peoples of the whole world, and, on the other hand, there is the aggressive warmongering policy of the imperialist powers, chiefly the United States of America, which is endangering world peace. These two opposing lines in international politics have been clearly evident even in recent years.

To those who doubt our sincerity in the struggle for peace, who allege that socialism needs a world war in order to conquer everywhere, we reply that we repudiate this bourgeois propaganda charge of the so-called 'export' of socialist revolution just as we resolutely oppose the imperialist export of counter-revolution. To those who think that socialist countries stand for peace because they are weak and fear for the fate of their system, we reply that there is no doubt whatsoever that should the mad imperialists, disregarding all consequences, unleash a third world war, it would result in the utter destruction of imperialism, in the liquidation of capitalism as a social system. (*Fervent applause*)

(ii) *The foreign policy of the People's Republic of Albania*

Albania is the only country building socialism under conditions of hostile capitalist encirclement.

Friendship with the Soviet Union has been, is, and will always remain the cornerstone of the foreign policy of the new Albania. (*Stormy applause, ovations*)

Friendship and fraternal cooperation with the Chinese People's Republic have been further consolidated on the basis of Marxism-Leninism, the common struggle for socialism and peace, and mutual fraternal aid and support.

With all the other socialist countries—Poland, Czechoslovakia, the German Democratic Republic, Hungary, Romania, Bulgaria, Korea, Mongolia, and Vietnam—our people are linked by indestructible friendship.

Our party and government have always paid particular attention to relations with neighboring countries and especially to the situation in the Balkan and Adriatic area. Our policy has always aimed and still aims at the transformation of this area into one of peaceful and fruitful cooperation. The proposal advanced by the government of the Soviet Union and the People's Republic of Albania to transform the Balkans and the Adriatic area into a zone of peace, free of atomic arms and rocket bases, is directed toward this goal. The implementation of this proposal would at the same time be a contribution to the efforts for general and complete disarmament, within the framework of which even the disarmament of the Balkan countries would be acceptable and practicable. We must emphasize that the negative factors in the situation in this area are the Balkan Pact, an appendage of NATO, the installation of American rockets in Italy, Greece, and Turkey, and the frequent visits of the American Sixth Fleet to the ports of those countries and those of Yugoslavia.

The People's Republic of Albania has continued its efforts to develop relations with neighboring countries on the basis of equality, noninterference, mutual respect and benefit. On the initiative of our government, normal relations have been re-established with Yugoslavia. At its Third Congress, our party declared that despite the great damage caused by the hostile policy of the Yugoslav leaders, we were ready to establish correct and neighborly relations. And we have made sincere efforts to establish and develop normal good neighborly relations, trade, cultural, and tourist exchanges, and so forth. But the Yugoslav leaders have never abandoned their hostile policy toward our country and have continued their brutal intervention in our affairs, their attempts to liquidate our party, our people's power, our freedom and national independence. This is clearly demonstrated by the facts, the organization and activation of various groups of agents, the dispatch of whole gangs of saboteurs from Yugoslavia, and the endless provocations along our border. The Yugoslav leaders in their public speeches and press as well as through farcical legal proceedings, which have particularly increased of late, miss no opportunity to slander and attack our party, our government, and our people, but this mud falls on their own faces.

The tragic fate of the Albanian population living in Yugoslavia is familiar to all. Our party will continue to speak out against the persecutions, the deportations to Turkey, and the chauvinist extermination policy pursued in Yugoslavia toward our brothers in Kossovo, Maccdonia, Montenegro, and the Dukagjini highlands. Our party considers this its lofty humanitarian duty, deriving from the principles of Marxism-Leninism, and will continue to do so as long as Yugoslavia has not guaranteed the Albanian population of one million inhabitants its full rights as a national minority, on the basis of the principles of international law. In the future, just as in the past, we will be for normal neighborly relations on the basis of peaceful coexistence and reciprocity. To this end, our People's Republic is prepared to continue developing normal relations, but on the condition that the Yugoslav government does not obstruct them and abandons without delay its hostile activities against the People's Republic of Albania.

In regard to our relations with Greece, they have not changed at all owing to the reactionary and shortsighted policy of the Greek ruling circles, who have blindly submitted to the American imperialists and coordinate their hostile policy toward Albania with that of the ruling circles of Yugoslavia. We have made numerous attempts to normalize our relations with Greece, we have taken unilateral initiatives, we have given the Greek government sufficient opportunities to respond to our readiness and good will by the repatriation of Greek citizens sheltered in Albania, by the clearing of the Corfu Channel, by our proposals for the normalization of the border situation, of trade, and so on. But the Greek rulers have continued their policy of criminal provocations along the border, of insane campaigns on the so-called state of war between our two countries and their absurd claims to southern Albania, of plots against the territorial integrity of our fatherland. Naturally, they have received and will always receive the answer they deserve. While always maintaining a high level of vigilance, we shall also continue in the future our policy of normalizing relations with Greece on the above-mentioned principles, but of course much depends in this respect on the Greek government, which must abandon without delay its hostile activities toward the People's Republic of Albania.

We very much love and respect the fraternal peoples of Yugoslavia and Greece, and we will work relentlessly to strengthen the sincere friendship we feel for our fraternal neighbors. We are convinced that they do not and never will approve the criminal actions of their governments against a peaceful people who seek to live in peace and to maintain good neighborly relations with them. We appeal to the neighboring peoples of Yugoslavia and Greece to constrain their governments and to check them in their activities against our fatherland, because these actions may lead to the disruption of peace in the Balkans. We believe that the governments of Yugoslavia and Greece know full well the Albanian people and its people's power, and realize that if they should raise the sword against our outstretched hand, we would be certain to break that sword. (*Stormy applause, ovations*) In our time the old order in the Balkans has been overthrown just as it has been overthrown in the world. In the Balkans there exist and flourish three socialist states, Bulgaria, Roumania, and Albania, which are as united as flesh and blood to one another and to the other countries of the socialist camp headed by the Soviet Union. (*Stormy applause, ovations*)

The vital interests of the peoples of this region strongly demonstrate to the socialist and nonsocialist countries the necessity for coordinating their joint struggle for the preservation of peace and cooperation between states on the basis of nonintervention, equality, and mutual interests. We sincerely favor a policy of good neighborly relations and are convinced that such a policy is in the interest of Albania as much as in the interest of the neighboring countries. But let the rulers of our two neighbors have no illusions that they may take Albania by surprise, that they may isolate Albania or have isolated her, as they fancy, or that they may soon be able to settle accounts with her. The Albanian people have suffered much throughout their history, and they are not easily lulled to sleep. They cannot be deceived by the Greek and Titoist bluffs.

The present Yugoslav state is not a 'neutral' or 'non-bloc' state, as Belgrade propaganda claims or as the professed of secret friends of the Tito regime try to present it. This 'neutrality' and 'extra-military bloc' attitude of the Yugoslav state bears no resemblance whatsoever to such neutral states as the United Arab Republic, India, Indonesia, Switzerland, or Austria. Present-day Yugoslavia is a state that participates in the aggressive NATO bloc through the Balkan Pact. The Balkan Pact, which binds together Yugoslavia, Greece, and Turkey, obliges NATO as well as Yugoslavia to come to the aid of one another at any time with all the means at their disposal. The Yugoslav leaders themselves have more than once declared that this treaty was signed because, allegedly, Yugoslavia was in danger of 'being attacked' by the countries of the socialist camp. This has always been and will always be an absurd fabrication because the socialist countries have never had and never will have any intention of attacking Yugoslavia or any other country. But the reverse has been and remains true, that is, that the members of the Balkan Pact, closely linked to the NATO powers, are preparing for aggression, particularly against the socialist countries of the Balkans. It suits the policy of the Belgrade revisionist clique to claim today that the military articles of this treaty 'have lost their value'. This humbug can, of course, deceive no one except those who wish to be deceived and indirectly wish to deceive others in order to support Titoism.

On the basis of the Balkan Pact, military and operational plans are openly or secretly coordinated, especially those of Yugoslavia and Greece; both their armies are equipped with modern weapons openly given by American imperialism on credit and gratuitously; aggressive bases have been set up, and many times each year groups of top-ranking officers of the general staffs of these states meet to co-ordinate military plans and to attend maneuvers and war games conducted in their territories. Greece and Yugoslavia are feverishly making military preparations. American imperialism goes so far in these preparations as to finance the military highways which are being built in Yugoslavia. It is a crime against world peace, it is a crime against the socialist camp, it is a crime against the socialist countries of the Balkans, and in particular it is a crime against Albania to fail to unmask publicly the aggressive plans of the Titoists and to conceal them under a smokescreen of false 'neutrality', under fallacious and anti-Marxist slogans alleging that the renegade Titoist clique is carrying on the construction of socialism in Yugoslavia. We have unmasked and will continue to unmask the diabolical and divisive role as well as the plots of the ruling Yugoslav group, the Titoist renegades, against peace, against the socialist camp, and against Albania, because we feel very deeply the responsibility we have toward the defense of peace, socialism, our camp, and our fatherland. (*Stormy applause, ovations.*)

Titoist Yugoslavia is conspiring together with her ally Greece and in conjunction with NATO and the American Sixth Fleet in the Mediterranean against the freedom, independence, and sovereignty of our country. This is proven by the facts.

I can tell the Congress, the people, and the party that these two neighboring countries, Yugoslavia and Greece, in collaboration with certain Albanian traitors, who are either in our country or have deserted to Yugoslavia and in conjunction with the American Sixth Fleet in the Mediterranean, some months ago organized an attack against Albania with the aim of liquidating the People's Republic of Albania. Their criminal plot failed completely. (*Stormy continued applause, lengthy ovations.*) The conspirators and the facts are in the hands of the people's justice. This odious plot failed because our heroic party, our people, our army, and the state security forces were guarding, vigilantly as ever, the defense of our fatherland and people. (*Stormy applause, ovations.*)

Our relations with Italy have been developing more or less normally, especially in the field of trade. The conclusion of an agreement on reparations is a step forward. But the installation of rockets on Italian soil must be mentioned as a negative factor. We cannot help but feel uneasy about the transformation of Italian territory into an imperialist base for aggression against our country and the other countries of the socialist camp. We are anxiously following the actions of the Italian government in this respect, and, as we have stated, we cannot stand by with our hands folded.

We think that trade, cultural relations, and communications between our two countries can be developed successfully and to our mutual advantage if the ruling circles of Italy show a more realistic understanding of these problems. We think that it would be in the interest of friendly relations between our two neighboring countries and in the interest of peace in this area if Italy should give up her role as a den for Albanian war criminals, for this does not conform to normal relations between two countries.

2. Speech by Mr. Hoxha at the Embassy of the Chinese People's Republic, Tirana, 1 October 1961[1]

Twelve years ago the great fraternal Chinese people proclaimed their People's Republic. The first of October has become in China a day of great rejoicing for the working masses, who, justifiably proud, set a high example of peaceful and creative effort with the splendid victories which they score from year to year. All the peoples of the socialist camp as well as the whole of progressive mankind rejoice with great China. The anniversary of the proclamation of the Chinese People's Republic is also a day of rejoicing for the Albanian people and the Albanian Party of Labor, the sincere and loyal friends of the fraternal Chinese people. Permit me, dear comrade Ambassador, in the name of the Central Committee of the Albanian Party of Labor, the Presidium of the People's Assem-

---

[1] *Albania and the Sino-Soviet Rift*, pp. 222–7.

bly, the government of the Albanian People's Republic, and the entire Albanian people to extend to you, and through you to all the Chinese people, the Chinese Communist Party, and the government of the Chinese People's Republic the most heartfelt fraternal congratulations on the occasion of your great day.

The proclamation of the Chinese People's Republic and the establishment of a proletarian dictatorship in a country comprising a vast territory and one-quarter of the world's population marked a decisive step forward in the development of forces throughout the world in favor of socialism and to the detriment of imperialism. They marked the acceleration of the further disintegration and collapse of capitalism. The liberation of the great Chinese people has given an incomparable impetus to the just liberation struggle of the peoples of Asia, Africa, and Latin America.

Under the wise guidance of their glorious Communist Party, led by their distinguished son, Comrade Mao Tse-tung, the heroic Chinese people have achieved in the years since the proclamation of the republic brilliant and historic victories in socialist construction. By creatively applying Marxism-Leninism, the glorious Chinese Communist Party is transforming the Chinese People's Republic into a mighty socialist country. The Chinese people are successfully implementing the three red banners: the general line of the party on socialist construction, the great leap forward, and the people's communes. They have displayed a high level of creative initiative in all realms of socialist construction. Thus in the industrial sector, during the three years of the great leap forward, China fulfilled ahead of schedule the main targets of the second five-year plan, created an extensive modern industrial base, and increased by several times the productive capacity of the main industrial branches. In the agricultural sector, land reclamation, construction, and a series of other projects have been developed on a large scale, thus creating favorable conditions for the further expansion of agricultural production. During the same period education and culture have rapidly progressed. There is no doubt that the brilliant successes achieved so far represent a very solid basis for further and more rapid progress.

These brilliant successes are the result of the colossal efforts of this great and talented people and of their invincible unity with the glorious Chinese Communist Party. These successes are an inspiration to other peoples still suffering under the savage yoke of capitalism in their struggle for freedom, independence, and social progress.

The Chinese People's Republic, consistently pursuing the wise Marxist-Leninist policy of the strengthening of friendship and unity with the Soviet Union and the other countries of the socialist camp, supports with all its strength the revolutionary efforts of the oppressed peoples in their struggle against imperialism and colonialism, and resolutely struggles against the imperialist policy of aggression and war.

As a mighty socialist country, China is playing an ever greater role on the international scene. It is making an important contribution to the triumph of the principles of peaceful coexistence between states with different social and political systems and to the settlement through negotiations of international disputes, while remaining steadfast in the front ranks of the struggle against imperialism, particularly American imperialism, and for the consolidation of friendship between peoples, for an international détente, and for the preservation of world peace.

The wise Marxist-Leninist peace policy of the Chinese People's Republic is greatly appreciated by all the peace-loving peoples who see in her, just as in the Soviet Union, a firm and consistent supporter of the freedom and independence of peoples, an unflinching fighter against all forms of oppression, exploitation, and injustice. That is why the correct policy of the Chinese People's Republic cannot be obscured by the accusations and vile slander of the United States imperialists and their allies, nor by that of the modern revisionists and, primarily, by the Yugoslav revisionists.

The Kennedy government with its Western partners, while hypocritically speaking about peace in order to deceive the peoples, is pursuing its old policy against peace, is stepping up in an unprecedented manner the arms race and its feverish preparations for war, and is thus creating a very tense international situation. The imperialist states, with the United States at the head, have continually sabotaged the talks on disarmament and the cessation of nuclear tests, proposed by the Soviet Union, and strongly supported by the Chinese People's Republic and all other socialist countries. While rejecting the constructive proposals of the Soviet Union and the just and legitimate measures of the German Democratic Republic regarding the peaceful settlement of the German problem and, on this basis, the question of West Berlin, the American imperialists and their allies, particularly the revanchist Bonn government, have lately launched a vast bellicose campaign; they have further increased their aggressive activities and provocations as well as their efforts to create a war psychosis.

The Albanian Party of Labor, our government, and our people have supported the decision of the Soviet government to proceed with nuclear weapons tests as well as the signing of a peace treaty with Germany and the normalization of the situation in West Berlin as a free and demilitarized city.

Events are increasingly and even more clearly exposing the aggressive nature of imperialism. Therefore in the present international situation the peoples must more than ever increase their vigilance. All the peace-loving forces must strengthen their unity in order to check the aggressive plans for the preparation and unleashing of war by the imperialists and particularly by the American imperialists, those vicious assassins of peace and sworn enemies of mankind. The bellicose and warmongering plans and activities of the imperialists must be opposed and assailed without mercy. The demagogical efforts of the imperialists and their revisionist agency, with the Belgrade revisionist clique at the head, must be unmasked without vacillation. The Marxist-Leninist parties have waged and will continue to wage a resolute principled struggle against modern revisionism, which represents the main danger to the Communist movement. In this struggle between Marxism-Leninism and revisionism, Marxism-Leninism will be victorious while revisionism is doomed to inevitable failure and destruction. The revisionists may succeed in duping some Marxists but not the overwhelming masses. The revisionists may deceive for a while but not for always. The conscience of Communists is not an object for bargaining which may be bought and sold on the market. The clear-thinking minds of Marxists cannot be easily muddled by the tricks of acrobats and charlatans. Marxism-Leninism is merciless when it comes to renegades. Therefore the revisionists, whatever their guise, are terribly afraid because they know the fate that awaits them.

The American imperialists and their allies, terrified by the growing authority of the Chinese People's Republic throughout the world, are pursuing their war-like policy and flagrantly trampling underfoot the most elementary rules of international law and the fundamental principles of the United Nations Charter. They have tried by every possible means for twelve years to deny the Chinese People's Republic the restoration of its legitimate rights in the United Nations. They have invented the so-called 'two Chinas' policy as a diabolical tactical maneuver to keep alive the political corpse of Chiang Kai-shek, whom the Chinese people ousted from their fatherland in their heroic struggle, and to perpetuate the occupation of Taiwan. But whether the American imperialists and their lackeys like it or not, there exists today only one China, one and indivisible, the great Chinese People's Republic, a mighty socialist state which is progressing and thriving with each passing year and without the participation of which no important international problem can be solved.

The Albanian people, the Albanian Party of Labor, and our government condemn with the greatest resolve the machinations of the United States imperialists and those of their lackeys aimed at denying the Chinese People's Republic its legitimate rights in the United Nations. They support without reservation the policy of immediately granting to the Chinese People's Republic its rightful seat in the United Nations. We consider Taiwan and the other neighboring islands as an integral part of the Chinese People's Republic; that is why we have supported and will continue to support in the future the issue of their complete liberation.

Dear comrades and gentlemen, the Albanian people and the Chinese people are bound to one another by everlasting fraternal friendship based upon the principles of Marxism-Leninism and proletarian internationalism. This great friendship, which deepens, grows stronger, and flourishes with each passing day, has been tempered by our common struggle for the preservation of the purity of Marxism-Leninism, for the resolute unmasking to the end of the war-mongering American imperialists and their lackeys, the modern revisionists with the dangerous Belgrade clique in the lead, for our common goals and ideals, for the construction of socialism and the preservation of universal peace. The builders of this indestructible friendship are our Marxist-Leninist parties which are struggling resolutely and without hesitation, no matter what the obstacle or difficulty, for the implementation of the Moscow Declaration of 1960 and for the consolidation of the unity of the socialist camp, with the Soviet Union at the head, and the unity of the international Communist and workers movement, which the hirelings of imperialism and modern revisionism are vainly trying to disrupt.

The fruits of this great friendship between our peoples are perfectly reflected in the expansion and many-sided consolidation of contacts and fraternal co-operation between our peoples and our two socialist countries. We note with great pleasure that during the last few years, particularly during 1961, coopera-tion in all realms between the Albanian People's Republic and the Chinese People's Republic has assumed greater momentum in the interest of our two

D.I.A.–H

peoples and of the socialist camp. The Chinese People's Republic has given and continues to give to the Albanian people substantial and generous international aid for the construction of socialism in Albania. The Albanian Party of Labor, the Albanian government, and the Albanian people have always been and will always be greateful to the great Chinese people, to the glorious Chinese Communist Party, and to the government of the Chinese People's Republic for this fraternal and disinterested aid.

Comrades and gentlemen, the Albanian people, under the wise and brave guidance of the Albanian Party of Labor, distinguished by a spirit of fervent patriotism and self-denying industry, are resolutely marching forward and have already scored brilliant successes in the construction of socialism and the strengthening of the international position of the Albanian People's Republic and its defensive capacity, fearing neither geographical encirclement by the capitalists and revisionists nor the constant hostile probes of the imperialists and their tools against our fatherland.

The imperialists, the Belgrade revisionists, and all the enemies of our party and people have tried by sword and fire, by means of various plots and blockades, to strangle our party and to subjugate our people. These enemies think they can easily liquidate Albania because it is a small country. But they have miscalculated, they have failed, and they will continue to fail shamefully because they have come up against and will always come up against a rocklike impregnable fortress, heroically and gallantly defended by a brave people and party. Those who tried to dig a grave for Albania have fallen into the grave themselves. The new socialist Albania is marching valiantly forward, as befits a socialist country which lives and struggles in the great century of Leninism. Its body shows the scars of the wounds inflicted by the swords and bullets of its enemies, but its brow is clear and bright, with neither wrinkles nor blemishes, its eye is the eye of an eagle, and its heart is as pure and ardent as the revolution. It is for this reason that all the progressive peoples and Communists throughout the world love, respect, and defend Albania and its heroic party. It is for this reason that he who raises a hand against Albania will be struck down not only by this courageous land but by all the Communists of the world, by all the peoples of the socialist camp with the Soviet people at the head, and by all honest and progressive people. Let the enemies of our people and party remember that they will not take us by surprise. We are prepared for everything, and we are ready to cope successfully with any situation. We know and understand their tricks, their plots, their machinations against our people and against our party. Herein lies the strength and maturity of our people and our party. We do not deceive ourselves with illusions and dreams; we are perfectly aware that the cares of mankind and our people cannot end before the extinction of imperialism and its agent—revisionism. And since we are not afraid to face up to our cares and to abolish them forevermore, we reap successes constantly, while our enemies reap failures.

With indescribable enthusiasm, the workers of our country have mobilized all their forces as never before for the fulfillment and overfulfillment of the targets of the third five-year plan. This is best demonstrated by the brilliant successes achieved in the fulfillment of the plan for the first nine months of this year.

The historic decisions of the Fourth Congress of our party best reflect the correct and consistent Marxist-Leninist policy of the Albanian Party of Labor. Inspired by these decisions, the Albanian people, as a worthy and inseparable member of the mighty socialist family, will in the future work even more resolutely for the construction of socialism in our free and sovereign fatherland.

Our people are confidently advancing along the path of socialism because everywhere in the world they have the support of friends and sincere and loyal brothers, primarily the fraternal peoples of the Soviet Union, the Chinese people, and the other peoples of the socialist countries. An ardent, pure, sincere, and immortal friendship that will live through the centuries has been forged in the hearts of our party and our people for the Soviet Union and the glorious party of Lenin and Stalin. This is not to the liking and confuses the plans of the Belgrade revisionists, who brand us as anti-Soviet and as Pharisees. But the party says to the people: Let the dogs bark; concentrate on your glorious work because you are in the right, and strengthen this friendship because our friendship with the Soviet Union is the cornerstone of our present and of our even brighter future. Our party and people will, as ever, struggle with all their might to consolidate their fraternal friendship with the Soviet Union, the Chinese People's Republic, and all the other socialist lands. They will struggle further to strengthen the unity of the socialist camp and to defend the lofty interests of their fatherland and of socialism in the southwestern corner of our camp, on the shores of the Adriatic and Ionian Seas.

On this great festive day of indescribable rejoicing for the fraternal Chinese people, permit me to drink this toast:

To the great, heroic, and talented Chinese people;

To the glorious Communist Party of China, headed by the beloved Comrade Mao Tse-tung;

To the President of the Chinese People's Republic, Comrade Liu Shao-chi;

To the government of the Chinese People's Republic, and Comrade Chou En-lai;

To the unbreakable friendship between our fraternal peoples;

To the powerful socialist camp, headed by the Soviet Union;

To peace and friendship among peoples;

To your health, Comrade Ambassador.

3. The 22nd Congress of the Communist Party of the Soviet Union, 17–27 October 1961

(i) *Speech by Mr. Khrushchev to the twenty-second congress of the Communist Party of the Soviet Union, 17 October 1961*[1] (extracts)

Comrades, the chief content of the period following the Twentieth Congress of the C.P.S.U. has been the competition between the two world social systems— the socialist and capitalist systems. This has become the pivot, the main feature

---

[1] *Report of the 22nd Congress of the Communist Party of the Soviet Union, delivered by N. S. Khrushchev, First Secretary of the Central Committee.* Soviet Booklet No. 80 (London, 1961), pp. 7–8, 12–33, 78–80, 97.

of world development in the present historical period. Two lines, two historical tendencies in social development, are becoming more and more evident. One of them is the line of social progress of peace and creative activity. The other is the line of reaction, oppression and war.

If we imagine the whole globe as the scene of this competition, we see that socialism has been winning one position after another from the old world. In the first place, capitalism has been seriously cramped by socialism in a decisive sphere of human activity, that of material production. The socialist system's share in world production has increased and its rates of development greatly exceed those of the most advanced capitalist countries. It is obvious to everyone that the socialist countries are able to develop colossal productive forces and create a real abundance of material and spiritual values.

While conducting an unswerving policy of peace we have not forgotten the threat of war from the imperialists. Everything necessary has been done to ensure the superiority of our country in defence. The achievements of socialist production and Soviet science and technology have enabled us to effect a real revolution in military matters. Our country and the entire socialist camp now possess vast power, ample to provide a reliable defence for the great gains of socialism against the inroads of imperialist aggressors. The growing defensive might of the Soviet Union and the other socialist countries and the world peace forces have not allowed the imperialists to divert the competition between the two systems from the path of peace on to that of armed conflicts, of war. The Soviet Union, while pursuing the Leninist policy of peaceful coexistence, has resolutely exposed and checked imperialist provocations.

The fact that it has been possible to prevent war, and that the Soviet people and the peoples of other countries have been able to enjoy the benefits of a peaceful life must be regarded as the chief result of the activities of our Party and its Central Committee in increasing the strength of the Soviet state and in implementing a Leninist foreign policy, as a result of the work of the fraternal parties of the socialist states and the greater activity of the peace forces in all countries.

In recent years, as we know, the imperialists have made a number of attempts to ignite the fires of a new war and test the strength of the socialist system. During the past five years the U.S. and its closest allies have frequently resorted to brutal force, have resorted to arms. But on each occasion the Soviet Union and all the socialist countries have checked the aggressor in good time. Of particular, fundamental importance, were the actions of the socialist countries in defence of the peoples struggling for their liberty and independence. The masses are coming to realise more and more that the Soviet Union and all the socialist countries are a reliable support in the struggle the peoples are waging for their liberty and independence, for progress and peace.

In the course of the peaceful competition between the two systems capitalism has suffered a profound moral defeat in the eyes of all peoples. Ordinary people are becoming convinced daily that capitalism cannot solve any of the urgent problems facing mankind. It is becoming ever more obvious that these problems can be solved only through socialism. Faith in the capitalist system and the capitalist path of development is dwindling. Monopoly capital is losing influence and resorting more frequently to the intimidation and suppression of the people, to methods of open dictatorship to force through its domestic policy and to aggressive acts against other countries. The people, however, are offering increasing resistance to reaction.

It is no secret that intimidation and threats are not a sign of strength but are evidence of the weakening of capitalism and the deepening of its general crisis. As the saying goes, 'If you can't hang on by the mane, you won't hold on by the tail!' The reactionaries in some countries are still able, in defiance of constitutions, to dissolve parliaments, cast the best representatives of the people into prison and dispatch gun-boats and marines to subdue the 'unruly'. All this may put off for a time the fatal hour of capitalist rule. Such measures of repression, however, expose, to a still greater extent, the predatory nature of imperialism. The imperialists are cutting off the branch on which they are sitting. There are no forces in the world that can stem mankind's advance along the road of progress.

Events show that our Party's policy, worked out by the Twentieth Congress, was a correct and true one; the Congress noted that the main feature of our epoch was the emergence of socialism beyond the bounds of one country and its transformation into a world system. In the period since that Congress there has been further important progress—the world socialist system is becoming a desicive factor in the development of society.

The Party drew the conclusion that the collapse of colonialism is inevitable. Under the powerful blows of the national liberation movement the colonial system has, to all intents and purposes, fallen to pieces.

The Party propounded the important thesis that wars between states are not inevitable in the present epoch, that they can be prevented. The events of the past years serve to confirm this, too. They show that the mighty forces that stand watch over peace have today effective means of preventing the imperialists from launching a world war. The superiority of the forces of peace and socialism over those of imperialism and war has become more evident.

To put it briefly, comrades, on a world scale, for us those six years have been good years. . . .

. . . The socialist countries have shown the way for new standards of international life by demonstrating to the whole world an example of really equal, fraternal relations between peoples. Under the influence of the ideas of socialism, the working people's struggle for emancipation and the general democratic movement of the peoples are merging into a common world-wide torrent that is washing away the supports of imperialism.

As socialism wins new victories, the unity of the peoples, both within each socialist country and in the world socialist system as a whole, grows stronger.

In the same way as a mighty tree with deep roots does not fear any storm, so the new, socialist world does not fear any vicissitudes or upheavals. The counter-revolutionary insurrection in Hungary, organised by internal reaction with the support of the imperialist forces, and the intrigues of enemies in Poland and the German Democratic Republic showed that in the period of socialist construction the class struggle may, from time to time, grow stronger and take on sharp forms. In the future, too, the remnants of internal reaction may, with imperialist backing, attempt to sever one country or another from the socialist system and to restore the old bourgeois régime. The reactionary forces speculate on the difficulties that are inevitable in an undertaking as new as the revolutionary transformation of society, and continue sending their agents into the socialist countries.

The ruling circles of certain imperialist powers have elevated subversive activities against the socialist countries to the level of state policy. The United States of America spends, with open cynicism, hundreds of millions of dollars on espionage and sabotage against the socialist countries, and organises so-called 'guerilla units' made up of criminal elements, cut-throats, who are prepared to undertake the vilest of crimes for money. For several years in succession provocative 'captive nations weeks' have been held in the United States. The paid agents of the monopolies call 'captive' all those peoples that have liberated themselves from imperialist bondage and have taken the path of free development. Truly, imperialist demagogy and hypocrisy knows no bounds! Monopolists who howl about 'captive nations' are like the crook who has his hands in somebody's pocket and shouts 'Stop thief!'

The intrigues of the imperialists must always be kept in mind. Our gigantic successes in building the new way of life must not lead to complacency and relaxation of vigilance. The greater the achievements of socialism and the higher the living standards in each socialist country, the more solidly the people will gather around the Communist and Workers' parties. That is one aspect of the matter, and a very encouraging one. There is, however, something else to be borne in mind. As the unity of the peoples of all socialist countries grows the hopes the imperialists have of restoring the capitalist régime, of the socialist countries degenerating, are gradually fading away. World reaction, therefore, is more and more turning to the idea of striking a blow at the socialist countries from outside in order to win capitalist world dominion through war or, at least, to check the development of the socialist countries.

The most rabid imperialists, who act in accordance with the principle 'after us the deluge', openly voice their desire to set out on a new war venture. To intimidate the peoples the ideologists of imperialism are trying to instil into them a kind of philosophy of hopelessness and despair. 'Better death under capitalism than life under communism' they cry hysterically. They, you see, do not like free peoples to prosper. They are afraid that the peoples of their countries will also take the path of socialism. Blinded by class hatred, our enemies are prepared to plunge all mankind into the holocaust of war. The possibilities for the imperialists to implement their aggressive plans are, however, becoming fewer. They behave like the feeble and covetous old man whose strength is exhausted, whose physical capacity is low, but whose desires remain.

The imperialists, of course, may set out on dangerous adventures, but they have no chance of success. They are prepared to try other ways as well. To weaken the socialist community the imperialists try to bring about quarrels between the peoples of the fraternal countries or introduce discord into the relations between them, to revive the remnants of national strife and artificially heat up nationalist sentiment.

A great historical responsibility rests with the Marxist-Leninist parties, with the peoples of the socialist countries—to strengthen tirelessly the international brotherhood of the socialist countries and friendship between nations.

As long as the imperialist aggressors exist we must be on the alert, we must keep our powder dry and improve the defences of the socialist countries, their armed forces and their state security organs. If the imperialists, in contradiction to all common sense, dare attack the socialist countries and hurl mankind into the abyss of a world war of annihilation, that mad act will be their last, it will be the end of the capitalist system.

Our Party has a clear understanding of its tasks and its responsibility and will do everything in its power to ensure that the world socialist system continues to grow stronger, gather fresh strength and develop further. We are confident that socialism will be victorious in the competition with capitalism. We are confident that the victory will be won in peaceful competition and not through war. We have taken our stand, and always shall take our stand on the peaceful coexistence of states with different social systems; we shall do everything to strengthen peace throughout the world.

(2) Sharpening of the contradictions in the capitalist countries. Growth of the revolutionary struggle and upsurge of the national-liberation movement

Comrades, the Twentieth Congress of the Party analysed the situation in the capitalist countries and drew the conclusion that they were moving steadily towards new economic and social upheavals. That conclusion has been borne out. In the years that have followed there has been further sharpening of the contradictions both within the capitalist countries and between them, colonial empires have been collapsing and the struggle of the working class and the national-liberation movements of the peoples have assumed huge proportions.

The general trend—the further decay of capitalism—has continued to operate ruthlessly. Although there has been some growth in production, the economy of the capitalist countries has become still more unstable and reminds one of a man sick with fever, so often do its temporary recoveries give way to depressions and crises. The United States, the chief capitalist country, has experienced two critical recessions in five years; in the post-war period as a whole there have been four such recessions. The crisis of 1957–1958 involved countries whose share in capitalist industrial output amounts to almost two-thirds of the whole. With the incomes of the monopolies increasing to a fabulous degree, real wages have increased very slightly and far more slowly than the productivity of labour. The social gains achieved by the working class in the past are gradually dwindling away. In general, the condition of the working people, especially in the under-developed countries, is growing worse.

During the past five or six years mankind has made great progress in the development of science and technology, particularly in the fields of atomic energy, electronics, jet propulsion and rocketry. As Lenin pointed out, the evils of capitalist production hamper the rational use of those achievements. As far back as 1913 he wrote: 'Whichever way you turn, at every step you come up against problems that mankind is fully capable of solving *immediately*. Capitalism is in the way. It has amassed enormous wealth and has turned people into the *slaves* of that wealth. It has solved the most complicated technical problems, but the application of technical improvements is hampered by the poverty and ignorance of the people, by the stupid miserliness of a handful of millionaires.

'Under capitalism, the words civilisation, freedom and wealth call to mind a rich glutton who is rotting alive but will not let that which is young live on.' (*Collected Works*, Vol. 19, p. 349.) How apt those words of Lenin's sound today!

The application of scientific and technical achievements, far from eliminating the insuperable contradictions of capitalism, deepens them still more. Capitalist automation has only just begun, but millions of workers have already been thrown out of production. The imperialists expected to find a way out of these difficulties by militarising the economy. Their expectations were not justified.

Militarisation, of course, has brought prosperity to the branches of industry producing arms. Direct war expenditure for the past five years in the United States alone has exceeded 220,000 million dollars, and all the NATO countries together have spent over 500,000 million dollars on the arms race during the past ten years. Militarisation, however, gave rise to new disproportions, had a serious effect on other branches of the economy and deprived millions more working people of their employment. During the past five years the number of totally unemployed in the United States has rarely been less than three million. In Italy, Japan and a number of other countries, mass unemployment has acquired a permanent character. The greater the amount of money spent on war production, the more unstable becomes capitalist economy and the more acute its contradictions. A glaring contradiction in present-day capitalism is the increasing employment of human labour to produce means of destruction. A social system that creates such contradictions is discrediting and outliving itself.

No wonder the American millionaire Harriman proposed abolishing the word 'capitalism'. 'Plagiarising from Khrushchev,' he said, 'we should "bury" the word "capitalism".' He was forced to admit that people outside America think of the word 'capitalism' as a synonym for imperialism, for exploitation of the poor by the rich, for colonialism. It is a dishonoured word, and one that breeds terror. Indeed, there is no getting away from the truth! Not even the most thorough cleansing could remove the blood and filth from that sullied word. There is an apt folk saying that 'you can't make a leopard change its spots'. We can only welcome the efforts of Mr. Harriman who has taken up a spade to dig a grave for the word 'capitalism'. But the peoples of the capitalist countries will draw a more correct conclusion and as well as the word will bury the capitalist system with all its evils, a system that is rotten through and through.

In recent years there have been some significant changes in the alignment of forces in the capitalist world.

First, the United States of America has lost its absolute supremacy in world capitalist production and commerce. The U.S. share of the industrial output of the capitalist world dropped from 56·6 per cent in 1948 to 47 per cent in 1960, its exports fell from 23·4 per cent to 18·1 per cent and its gold reserves from 74·5 per cent to 43·9 per cent. The result is that the United States today occupies approximately the same position among the capitalist countries as it did before the war.

Secondly, there has been a noticeable weakening of the position of Britain and France; these states, like Belgium and Holland, are losing their colonies for ever. They have been unable to recover their pre-war position in world industry.

Thirdly, the defeated countries have made a big leap forward, especially West

Germany and Japan. The share in capitalist world industrial output of West Germany, Japan and Italy combined is now about 17 per cent, that is, larger than in 1937, on the eve of the Second World War.

West Germany has drawn level with Britain in industrial output, and as far as exports are concerned takes second place after the United States. In the post-war years U.S. monopolies have invested huge sums of money in the economies of West Germany and Japan. For a number of years these two countries were actually relieved of the burden of their own war expenditure because the United States provided them with armaments at the expense of the American taxpayers. West Germany and Japan have made huge investments in the key branches of the economy to renew their constant capital and reorganise production along modern lines. As a result they are already serious rivals in the world market to Britain, France and even the United States.

The contradictions that existed between the imperialist powers before the war have reappeared and new ones have emerged. The struggle between British and West German imperialism for supremacy in Western Europe is growing fiercer. French imperialism, in its struggle against British imperialism, is attempting to find support in yesterday's enemy, the West German monopolies. This unnatural alliance, like a marriage of convenience, is more and more frequently operating against France herself. There are profound contradictions dividing the United States and Britain and other imperialist states. They are manifested in NATO and other aggressive blocs.

It is becoming more and more obvious that the imperialist powers and their leaders fear an easing of international tension because in a tense situation it is easier for them to form military blocs and keep the peoples in fear of an alleged threat coming from the socialist countries. The imperialists are seeking to involve all countries in the arms race, to tie the economies of other countries to their own and direct them towards militarisation. This line of action is most clearly demonstrated by United States policy towards West Germany and Japan. U.S. imperialists are deliberately drawing West Germany into the arms race. In the event of an outbreak of war it is to their advantage to pay for the new adventure mainly in the blood of the German people. At the same time they hope that this policy will damage the economy of West Germany and weaken her as a rival in the world market. Approximately the same policy is being pursued in respect of Japan.

In their talks the leaders of the Western Powers do not conceal that their policy is one of arming West Germany. Their argument is something like this— if West Germany does not rearm and does not spend money on armaments, she may become a still more powerful and dangerous rival. In short, there are some acute contradictions in the imperialist camp.

In their fear of the future the imperialists are trying to unite their forces and to strengthen their military, political, commercial and customs alliances. The reactionaries count on aggression against the socialist countries as a way out. In the pre-war period they placed great hopes on Hitler Germany. Today the role of the chief aggressive force belongs to the United States of America which has become the centre of world reaction. The U.S. imperialists are acting in alliance with the West German militarists and revenge-seekers and threatening the peace and security of the peoples. In our times, however, it has become dangerous for them to seek a way out of their contradictions in war.

The position of imperialism in Asia, Africa and Latin America, where until recently the colonialists oppressed hundreds of millions of people, is becoming shakier. The revolutionary struggle of the peoples of those continents is rapidly gaining momentum. In the course of the past six years twenty-eight countries have won political independence. The sixties of our century will go down in history as years of the complete disintegration of the colonial system of imperialism.

It must not be forgotten, however, that although the colonial system has collapsed, its remnants have not been eliminated. Many millions of people in Asia and Africa are still suffering under colonial slavery and are struggling for their liberation. For seven years the blood of Algerian patriots has been flowing in the fight for freedom. The French monopolies do not want to end the war in Algeria although that 'dirty war' against a peaceful people is costing thousands of lives and is a heavy burden on the French and Algerian peoples. Portugal, a small state with an area no more than two-thirds of our Vologda Region, holds in bondage colonies with an area nearly twenty-five times its own size. The Dutch colonialists stubbornly refuse to return to the Indonesian people their ancient land of West Irian. The United States is maintaining its grip on the Chinese island of Taiwan and the Japanese island of Okinawa. Against the will of the Cuban people it is retaining its hold on the military base of Guantanamo which is on Cuban soil.

The forces of imperialism are opposing any effort on the part of the peoples to achieve liberty and independence, democracy and progress. Under the pretence of various commitments, the imperialists strive to smother the national-liberation movement, and intervene brazenly in the internal affairs of young countries by entering into deals with their reactionary forces. That was the method they used in Iran, Pakistan and the Congo and are now using in Laos and Kuwait.

Throughout this period the Soviet Union, in fulfilment of its internationalist duty, has been helping the people who struggle against imperialism and colonialism. There are those who do not approve of this position. But we cannot help that. Such are our convictions. Our people won freedom in a long and stubborn fight against oppression by the landlords and the capitalists and against the intervention of international imperialism. We remember well enough what that struggle cost us, we remember the sacrifices that had to be made for the sake of victory. From the bottom of our hearts we wish success to those who are struggling for their liberty and happiness against imperialism. We believe that it is the inalienable right of peoples to put an end to foreign oppression and we shall support their just fight. Colonialism is doomed and a stake will be driven into its grave. Such is the will of the peoples, such is the course of history.

The countries that have liberated themselves from the colonial yoke have achieved certain successes in national and cultural regeneration. But economic progress in the majority of the newly-free countries of Asia and Africa is still slow. The masses of the people are still living in miserable conditions, while the wealth of their countries flows in streams of gold into the coffers of foreign banks and corporations. The U.S. monopolies are making two or three dollars profit on every dollar they spend in the underdeveloped countries. The U.S. monopolists have recently announced that they wish to allocate 500 million dollars to 'aid' the Latin American countries. What is 500 million dollars among twenty countries over a period of five years? These are the miserly alms that the rich man throws to those whom he has been robbing for many years. The peoples who have been plundered have the right to demand from the colonialists, not aid, but the return of the property stolen from them.

Today the colonialists, sensing that their rule is coming to an end, are putting on a good face in a losing game. They assert that they are leaving the colonies of their own accord. Who will believe them? Anyone can see that they are taking this step because they know that all the same they will be driven out in disgrace. The more prudent of the colonialists are getting out, so to say, five minutes before they are given 'a kick in the pants', to put it in popular language.

The colonial powers are imposing unequal treaties on the liberated countries, are locating military bases on their territories and are trying to involve them in military blocs, one of the new forms of enslavement. Almost a half of the states that have emerged as a result of the disintegration of the colonial system are shackled by burdensome, unequal treaties. At the centre of this refurbished but no less disgraceful colonialism stands the United States of America. Its closest allies and at the same time its rivals are British colonialism and West German imperialism, the latter unceremoniously pushing the British and French monopolies out of Africa and the Middle East.

The countries freed from colonial oppression have entered a new phase of development. The struggle for political independence united all the national forces that suffered under the colonialists and shared common interests. Now that the time has come to eradicate the roots of imperialism and introduce agrarian and other urgent social reforms, the differences in class interests are coming more and more into the open. Broad sections of the working people and also that considerable section of the national bourgeoisie which is interested in the accomplishment of the basic tasks of the anti-imperialist, anti-feudal revolution, want to go farther to strengthen independence and carry out social and economic reforms. Within the ruling circles of those countries, however, there are forces that are afraid to go farther in their collaboration with the democratic, progressive section of the nation. They would like to appropriate the fruits of the people's struggle and hamper the further development of the national revolution. These forces compromise with imperialism outside the country and feudalism within, and resort to dictatorial methods.

The example of Pakistan shows what this policy leads to. That country spends two-thirds of its budget revenue for war purposes, its national industry is not developing and foreign capital rules as if it were in its own backyard. The sad fate of Pakistan, whose people we wish nothing but good, should set the public thinking in some other countries where influential forces are wrecking national unity and are persecuting progressive leaders, especially the Communists, who have shown themselves to be the stoutest defenders of national independence.

To adopt the path of anti-communism means splitting the forces of the nation and weakening them in face of the imperialists, the colonialists.

And contrariwise—the sounder the unity of the democratic national forces, the more radical the implementation of urgent social and economic reforms, the stronger is the young state. Why did the Cuban people, for instance, rally so solidly around their government? Because the Cuban peasants obtained land and extensive material support from the government. Because the Cuban workers are working for themselves and not for the American monopolies now that industry has been nationalised. Because the small and medium producers in Cuba have been given protection against the arbitrariness of the monopolies. The Cuban people as a whole acquired broad democratic rights and liberties, the road was opened up to a better way of life, to happiness and prosperity! In the hour of danger, when the American imperialists organised the invasion of Cuba, the entire people stood like a solid wall in defence of the gains of their revolution. Under the leadership of that courageous patriot and revolutionary, Fidel Castro, the Cubans speedily routed the American mercenaries and hurled them into the Bahia de Cochinos, which being translated means 'the Bay of Swine'. The proper place for them!

Imperialist agents are more and more frequently advising the peoples of the liberated countries not to be in a hurry with their reforms. They would like the peoples of the underdeveloped countries believe that they cannot avoid the lengthy path travelled by the capitalist countries of Europe and America before they reached the present level of economic development. They conceal, however, that that path was a bloody and tortuous one for the peoples. They prefer to say nothing about the roads and prisons in England, France and Germany from the seventeenth to the nineteenth centuries being filled with vagabonds and homeless people, about the workers in those countries being forced to work from 14 to 18 hours a day even in the middle of the nineteenth century, or about the last plots of land being taken away from the English peasantry to make way for sheep pastures, so that, as was said at the time, 'the sheep ate the people'.

The capitalist path of development would be still longer and more arduous for the peoples of the colonies at whose expense the Western Powers achieved their own affluence. Why should this long and arduous road be imposed on peoples today, in the middle of the twentieth century? Communists believe that the age-old backwardness of peoples can be overcome through socialism. We do not, however, impose our ideas on anybody; we are firmly convinced that sooner or later all peoples will realise that there is no other road for them to happiness and well-being.

Comrades, the increasing contradictions of imperialism confront the working class of the capitalist countries with the grave alternative of either throwing itself upon the mercy of the monopolies and continuing in a miserable plight, or fighting for its rights and its future. The workers prefer to fight, and are fighting with great tenacity.

Bourgeois prophets have announced the advent of an era 'class peace'. They have claimed that the time of class struggles is a thing of the past and that Marxist theory in general is obsolete. Events have shown the utter absurdity of such prophecies. Strikes by the working people are growing in number and scale and in 1960 alone involved over 53 million people. The mass actions of the French and Italian working people, the Belgian workers' strike, the prolonged strike of

American steel workers, in which more than 500,000 people took part, and the strike of British engineering workers will for ever go down in the history of the working-class movement. The Japanese proletariat, for its part, has demonstrated its militant strength on more than one occasion.

New contingents of the working class have stepped into the world arena in recent years. There are upwards of 100 million industrial and office workers in Asia, Latin America and Africa, or about 40 per cent of the wage labour employed in the non-socialist world. This young working class is asserting itself more and more as a revolutionary force.

The struggle which the working people of the capitalist countries are waging for their economic and social rights is becoming ever more acute. For today they are faced, as a rule, not by individual employers but by powerful monopolies which, moreover, have the entire power of the state to support them. More and more often, the working people's actions assume a political character. Over 40 million people, or roughly 73 per cent of the total number of strikers, took part in political strikes in 1960. Powerful actions by the working class and the masses of the people last year brought about the fall of the governments in Japan, Italy and Belgium. The working people of France, who rallied to the working class, foiled an attempt by the militarist 'ultras' to impose a fascist régime on that country.

The social situation that has taken shape in the major capitalist countries during the last five years has also been marked by a growing peasant movement. In France, Italy, West Germany and elsewhere, monopoly domination is ruining the peasantry, and they are participating ever more actively in the struggle against the monopolies.

The experience of recent years has provided more evidence that the working people owe all their gains to joint action. Nevertheless, the split within the working class persists because of the subversive activity of Right-wing Social-Democratic leaders, who are making frantic efforts to divert their parties and the working class from the struggle against capitalism. Right-wing Socialist leaders and many trade union bosses have long since betrayed the interests of the working class and faithfully serve monopoly capital. But among the Social-Democratic rank and file, among the officials and even within the leadership there are many honest people who sincerely want to take part in the common struggle for working-class interests. They have lately been putting up increasing resistance to the policy of the Right-wing leaders.

That is the reason why Communists, while continuing to lay bare the ideological bankruptcy and disruptive actions of the Right-wing Social-Democratic officials, want to co-operate with all the sound elements among the Socialists and join them in the struggle for peace, democracy and socialism. This is not a temporary tactical slogan but the general policy of the Communist movement, a policy prompted by the fundamental interests of the working class.

Progress in the working-class movement is inseparably bound up with the activity of the Communist parties. The Communist movement has entered on the highroad of constructive activity. In our day the political influence of Communists makes itself felt in every country with a more or less advanced working-class movement. Over the last years the close-knit family of Communists has increased by another twelve parties and the total number of Communists, by seven million.

The Communist parties are growing all over the world despite the fact that the reactionaries are conducting vicious anti-communist campaigns. Communists are blacklisted, deprived of jobs, declared 'foreign agents' or imprisoned. In thirty-six capitalist countries, the Communist parties are compelled to operate deep underground. But the peoples are learning from experience that the Communists are the most loyal and reliable defenders of their interests. Communist ideas cannot be stopped by any barriers; they cannot be shot or put behind even stout prison bars. They are conquering the minds and hearts of people and are becoming an invincible force.

Of course, the Communist parties in some major capitalist countries are as yet small. But that by no means detracts from their historical role. Whatever the situation, the Communists, who are strong because they realise that theirs is a just cause, stand in the leadership of the working class. For example, it is well known that the number of Communists in the United States is small. But that big capitalist power, for all its enormous military and police machinery, is afraid of the Party of Communists, and obstructs its activities in every possible way. That indicates that the small contingent of U.S. Communists is working as befits Marxists-Leninists. Truly, a small body often harbours a great soul!

The Communists of the socialist countries never forget the difficulties and hardships falling to the lot of their brothers in the capitalist countries, who are fighting for the victory of the working class, for the cause of all working people. Today, on behalf of the delegates to this Congress, of all Soviet Communists, we send the most heartfelt fraternal greetings to our fellow-Communists in the capitalist countries, who bear aloft the victorious banner of Marxism-Leninism, to all those in the dungeons of reaction who have not bowed their heads to the enemy, to all those who are fighting courageously for the interests of their peoples.

The decisions of the Twentieth Congress, backed by the fraternal parties, added to the great creative power of the Communist movement and helped restore the Leninist spirit and style to the activities of the fraternal parties and the relations between them. The meetings of Communist and Workers' parties held in recent years were important milestones marking the progress of the world Communist movement. International Communist meetings are one of the forms evolved by the fraternal parties to ensure their militant co-operation.

It is indisputable to Marxists-Leninists that the fundamental interests of the international Communist movement require consistent unity of action, and the Communist and Workers' parties are loyal to it. Only the leaders of the League of Communists of Yugoslavia, who are plainly affected by national narrow-mindedness, have turned from the straight Marxist-Leninist road on to a winding path which has landed them in the bog of revisionism. The Yugoslav leaders responded to the 1957 Declaration of the fraternal parties, which resounded throughout the world as a charter of Communist unity and solidarity, with a revisionist anti-Leninist programme, which all the Marxist-Leninist parties subjected to a severe and just criticism.[1]

[1] *Documents*, 1957, pp. 527–39. An English version of the Yugoslav programme was published in 1959 by the International Society for Socialist Studies, London.

Revisionist ideas pervade both the theory and practice of the leadership of the League of Communists of Yugoslavia. The line they have adopted—that of development in isolation from the world socialist community—is harmful and perilous. It plays into the hands of imperialist reaction, foments nationalist tendencies and may in the end lead to the loss of socialist gains in the country, which has broken away from the friendly and united family of builders of a new world.

Our Party has criticised, and will continue to criticise, the Yugoslav leaders' revisionist concepts. As internationalists, we cannot but feel concern about the destinies of the fraternal peoples of Yugoslavia, who fought selflessly against fascism and, on the achievement of victory, chose the path of socialist construction.

The historic November 1960 meeting[1] convincingly reaffirmed the will and resolve of the Communist parties to uphold the purity of Marxism-Leninism, strengthen the unity of their ranks, and continue their determined struggle on two fronts—against revisionism, which constitutes the main danger, and against dogmatism and sectarianism. The propositions on the necessity for each party to observe decisions adopted collectively and not to permit any action likely to undermine Communist unity are of tremendous importance in bringing about greater solidarity of the working-class parties.

The achievements of socialist construction in the Soviet Union and the People's Democracies are proof of the great power and vitality of Marxism-Leninism. They show mankind what can be achieved when the workers and peasants have taken their destiny into their own hands and are equipped with the most progressive revolutionary theory.

Socialism results from the creative activity of the broadest masses marching under the banner of Marxism-Leninism. Communists are opposed to the forcible, artificial implantation of any particular socio-political system in other countries. We are convinced that in the end the socialist system will triumph everywhere; but this in no way implies that we will seek to achieve its triumph by interfering in the internal affairs of other countries.

Attempts are made to blame us Communists for any action by the masses against their oppressors. Whenever the working people of a capitalist or colonial country rise to fight, the imperialists claim that it is the 'handiwork of the Communists', or 'the hand of Moscow'. To be sure, we are glad to have the imperialists attributing to Communists all the good actions of the peoples. By so doing the imperialists are unwittingly helping the people to gain a better understanding of Communist ideas. These ideas are spreading throughout the world. But, of course, this is not happening because the Soviet Union and the other socialist countries impose them on the peoples. You cannot bring in ideas on bayonets, as people used to say in the past, or in rockets, as it would now be more appropriate to say.

Certainly, warring classes have always sought the support of kindred forces from outside. For a long time the bourgeois class had an advantage in this respect. The world bourgeoisie, acting in concert, stamped out revolutionary

---

[1] The Statement of the Moscow meeting was published in *World Marxist Review* for December 1960.

centres everywhere and by every means, including armed intervention. It goes without saying that even at that time the international proletariat was not indifferent to the struggle of its class brothers; but more often than not, it could express its solidarity with them only through moral support. The situation has changed since then. The people of a country who rise in struggle will not find themselves engaged in single combat with world imperialism. They will enjoy the support of powerful international forces possessing everything necessary for effective moral and material support.

The imperialists, who are alarmed by the scale of the revolutionary struggle, continue their attempts to interfere in the internal affairs of peoples and states. That is the reason they have reserved, in military pacts and agreements, the 'right' to armed intervention in the event of so-called internal unrest, that is, to suppress revolutions and popular actions against reactionary régimes. The imperialists claim at every turn that the Communists export revolution. The imperialist gentlemen need this slander in order to camouflage their claims to the right to export counter-revolution.

These gentlemen use a strange logic. They are apparently still under the spell of the times when they were able to strangle the liberation movement of the peoples. But those times have gone, never to return. The Communists are against the export of revolution, and this is well known in the West. But we do not recognise anybody's right to export counter-revolution, to perform the functions of an international gendarme. This, too, should be well known.

Imperialist attempts to interfere in the affairs of insurgent peoples would constitute acts of aggression endangering world peace. We must state outright that in the event of imperialist export of counter-revolution the Communists will call on the peoples of all countries to rally, to mobilise their forces and, supported by the might of the world socialist system, firmly repel the enemies of freedom and peace. In other words, 'as ye sow, so shall ye reap'.

(3) Peaceful coexistence is the general line in Soviet foreign policy. The peoples are the decisive force in the struggle for peace

Comrades, important changes have come about in the alignment of world forces during the period under review. The world socialist system has become a reliable shield against imperialist military ventures not only for the peoples of the countries that are friendly to it, but for the whole of mankind. And the fact that the socialist community of nations has a preponderance of strength is most fortunate for all mankind. The peace forces, furthermore, have grown all over the world.

A few years ago there were two opposing camps in world affairs—the socialist and imperialist camps. Today an active role in international affairs is also being played by those countries of Asia, Africa and Latin America that have freed, or are freeing, themselves from foreign oppression. Those countries are often called neutralist though they may be considered neutral only in the sense that they do not belong to any of the existing military-political alliances. Most of them, however, are by no means neutral when the cardinal problem of our day, that of war and peace, is at issue. As a rule, those countries advocate peace and oppose war. The countries which have won their liberty from colonialism are becoming a serious factor in the struggle against colonialism and imperialism, and the basic issues of world politics can no longer be settled without due regard for their interests.

In the capitalist countries, too, the masses are taking more and more vigorous action against war. The working class and all working people are fighting against the arms race and the disastrous policy of the war-mongers.

Thus the aggressive policy of the imperialist powers is now being opposed by growing forces. *The struggle which the countries of socialism and all the forces of peace are carrying on against preparations for fresh aggression and war is the main content of world politics today.*

In these past years, the forces of war and aggression have jeopardised world peace more than once. In 1956 the imperialists organised, simultaneously with the counter-revolutionary rising in Hungary, an attack on Egypt. In the second half of 1957 the imperialists prepared an invasion of Syria that threatened a big military conflagration. In the summer of 1958, in view of the revolution in Iraq, they launched an intervention in the Lebanon and Jordan and, at the same time, created a tense situation in the area of Taiwan, an island which belongs to the People's Republic of China. In April–May 1960 the U.S. imperialists sent their military aircraft into Soviet air space and torpedoed the Paris summit meeting. Last spring they organised an armed invasion of Cuba by mercenary bands and tried to bring Laos under their sway, to involve her in the aggressive SEATO military bloc. But all those imperialist sorties failed.

It would be a gross error, however, to imagine that the failure of aggressive schemes has brought the imperialists to their senses. The facts show just the opposite. The imperialists continue their attempts to aggravate the international situation and to lead the world to the brink of war. In recent months they have deliberately created a dangerous situation in the centre of Europe by threatening to take up arms in reply to our proposal to do away with the vestiges of the Second World War, conclude a German peace treaty and normalise the situation in West Berlin.

In view of the aggravation of the international situation, we were compelled to take appropriate steps to safeguard our country against the encroachments of aggressors and save mankind from the threat of a new world war. The Soviet Government was compelled to suspend the reduction of the armed forces planned for 1961, increase defence expenditure, postpone the transfer of servicemen to the reserve and resume tests of new and more powerful weapons. We were compelled to adopt these measures; they were unanimously supported by our people and correctly understood by the peoples of other countries, who know that the Soviet Union will never start a war. The Soviet people are only too familiar with the ways of aggressors. We have not forgotten the years of the Great Patriotic War, we remember Hitler Germany's treacherous, wanton attack on the Soviet Union. In the presence of the war menace created by the imperialists, there is no room for complacency and carelessness.

Some people in the West assert that the measures taken by the Soviet Government to strengthen the country's defences mean renunciation of the policy of peaceful coexistence. That, of course, is nonsense. The policy of peaceful co-existence follows from the very nature of our system.

I should like to recall the following fact. When our country was beating back the furious attacks of the Whites and foreign interventionists, the Soviet Government was discussing the question of the Soviet coat of arms. The first sketch contained a sword. Lenin raised a sharp objection. 'Why the sword?' he asked. 'We need no conquest. The policy of conquest is utterly alien to us; we are not attacking but repulsing domestic and foreign enemies; ours is a defensive war and the sword is not our emblem.' As everyone knows, the hammer and sickle, symbols of peaceful, constructive labour, have become the emblem of our country.

The principles of peaceful coexistence, laid down by Lenin and developed in our Party documents, have always been the central feature of Soviet foreign policy. The Soviet Government's foreign policy is convincing evidence of the loyalty of the Party and the Soviet people as a whole to the peaceful course charted by Lenin.

But it is hard to remove the war menace by unilateral action, in the same way as it is hard to put out a fire if one person pours water upon it while another pours oil. The Western Powers, who should be interested in avoiding thermo-nuclear disaster no less than we are, must, for their part, show readiness to seek ways of settling disputed issues on a mutually acceptable basis.

Certain pacifist-minded people in the West are ingenuous enough to believe that if the Soviet Union made more concessions to the Western Powers, there would be no aggravation of international tension. They forget that the policy of the imperialist powers, including their foreign policy, is determined by the class interests of monopoly capital, in which aggression and war are inherent. When, under the pressure of the masses, the partisans of a more or less moderate policy gain the upper hand, there occurs an international détente and the clouds of war are dispelled to some extent. But when the pressure of the masses slackens and the scales tip in favour of those groupings of the bourgeoisie that capitalise on the arms race and see war as an additional source of profit, the international situation deteriorates.

Hence the peaceful coexistence of countries with different social systems can be maintained and safeguarded only through the unrelenting struggle of all peoples against the aggressive aspirations of the imperialists. The greater the strength of the socialist camp and the more vigorously the struggle for peace is waged within the capitalist countries, the more difficult it is for the imperialists to carry out their plans of aggression.

Peace and peaceful coexistence are not quite the same thing. Peaceful co-existence does not merely imply absence of war; it is not a temporary, unstable armistice between two wars but the coexistence of two opposed social systems, based on mutual renunciation of war as a means of settling disputes between states.

Historical experience shows that an aggressor cannot be placated by con-cessions. Concessions to the imperialists on matters of vital importance do not constitute a policy of peaceful coexistence but a policy of surrender to the forces of aggression. To that we will never agree. It is high time the imperialists understood that it is no longer they who are the arbiters of mankind's fate, and that socialism will exist, develop and gain strength whether they like it or not. But for the time being the imperialist gentry do not seem to have understood this. One may well expect of them foolhardy actions that would spell disaster for hundreds of millions of people. That is why we must curb the aggressors and not aid and abet them.

The peace supporters in many countries, who have associated in various bodies and movements, have made an important contribution to the struggle against the forces of aggression and war. Everyone will remember how, in the early fifties, hundreds of millions of people called for a ban on atomic weapons and how indignantly the peoples of Europe protested against the establishment of the notorious European Defence Community and West Germany's participation in it. The pressure which the people exerted on parliaments and governments produced a powerful effect.

The work being done by peace supporters is particularly important now that the danger of a new war has increased. In the present situation, men of goodwill can no longer confine themselves to mere utterances in favour of peace. It should be evident that despite the numerous actions of the general public in defence of peace, the forces of aggression and war are becoming even more brazen. Indeed, a few years ago no Western politician would have made bold, without risking his career, to hint about rearming the Bundeswehr. But now the militarisation of West Germany is going full blast, and the Bundeswehr has become the biggest armed force in Western Europe. Strauss, West German War Minister, cynically boasts that the Federal Republic of Germany is not merely a member of NATO, but has the upper hand there. Moreover, something unheard-of has happened: the governments of Britain and France, that is, governments of countries which in the past suffered from German militarism, have granted the Bundeswehr training grounds and barracks on their territories and have placed their armed forces under the command of former Hitler generals. As a result, Bundeswehr soldiers are trampling British soil, which in two world wars they were unable to reach by armed force.

We share the bitterness and indignation of French and British patriots, who see West German revenge-seekers marching across their homeland.

It is said that even a gale of words won't make a windmill turn. Still less will talk of peace stop the aggressors' war machine. It is necessary to act resolutely and vigorously to stay the criminal hand of the warmongers in good time, before it is too late. Obviously, the struggle for peace, like any struggle, requires sustained effort and perseverance. When fighting one not only delivers but also receives blows. But is that something to be afraid of at a time when the fate of mankind is at stake? *It must be realised that it depends above all on the peoples themselves, on their resolve and vigorous action, whether there is to be peace on earth or whether mankind will be hurled into the catastrophe of a new world war.* It is necessary to heighten the vigilance of the peoples with regard to the intrigues of imperialist warmongers. Vigorous anti-war action by the peoples must not be put off till the war starts; such action must be launched immediately and not when nuclear and thermonuclear bombs begin to fall.

The strength of the peace movement lies in its mass scope, its organisation and resolute actions. All the peoples and all sections of society, with the exception of a handful of monopolists, want peace. And the peoples insist that a peace policy be pursued and must use all forms of struggle to achieve that end. The peoples can and must render harmless those who are obsessed with the insane ideas of militarism and war. It is the peoples who are the decisive force in the struggle for peace.

(4) Seek settlement of international problems by peaceful means. Expose the intrigues and manoeuvres of the warmongers. Improve relations between countries

Comrades, the situation calls for the settling of fundamental international problems without delay, in keeping with the principles of peaceful coexistence. Following the Twentieth Congress the Soviet Union put forward an extensive and realistic programme of action that would ensure the maintenance and consolidation of universal peace. The purpose of that programme is, in a nutshell, to deliver mankind from the dangerous and burdensome arms race, do away with the vestiges of the Second World War and remove all obstacles to a healthier international climate.

The struggle for general and complete disarmament is a major component of the foreign policy of our Party. The Soviet Union has persevered in this struggle for many years. We have always resolutely opposed the arms race, for in the past competition in this field not only imposed a heavy burden on the peoples but inevitably led to world wars. We are opposed to the arms race still more firmly now that a tremendous technical revolution has taken place in warfare and the use of modern weapons would inevitably lead to hundreds of millions of people losing their lives.

The stockpiling of these weapons, which is taking place in an atmosphere of cold war and war hysteria, is fraught with disastrous consequences. It would only need an addle-brained officer on duty at a 'button' somewhere in the West to lose his nerve for events to occur that would bring great misfortune to the peoples of the whole world.

It should be plain that the idea of our programme for general and complete disarmament is not the unilateral disarmament of socialism in the face of imperialism or the other way round, but a universal renunciation of arms as a means of settling controversial international problems. Since they do not dare to say they are against disarmament, the ruling circles of the capitalist countries, primarily of the United States, Britain and France, have invented the tale that the Soviet Union is against control over disarmament. We exposed this manoeuvre of the capitalist powers and openly declared that we were prepared in advance to accept any proposals for the most rigid international control they might make, provided they accepted our proposals for general and complete disarmament.

To mislead people, the imperialists are hypocritically raising a racket over the fact that we were compelled to carry out experimental blasts of nuclear weapons. But the racket did not prevent the peoples from seeing that we had taken this step only because the Western Powers, after bringing the solution of the disarmament problem and negotiations on nuclear weapons tests to a dead end, had set the flywheel of their war machine turning at top speed in order to achieve superiority in strength over the socialist countries. We forestalled them and thus retained the superior postition of the socialist camp, which is defending peace.

We were forced to take these measures. It was known that the United States had for a long time been preparing to resume tests, and as for France, she had carried them out repeatedly. In the present conditions, the need for the people's struggle to get rid of the arms race is all the more obvious. The disarmament problem affects the vital interests of every nation and of mankind as a whole. When it has been solved there will be no more need for nuclear weapons and hence for their manufacture and testing.

The elimination of the vestiges of the Second World War is of tremendous importance for the maintenance and strengthening of peace. The fact that a peaceful settlement with Germany has still not been achieved sixteen years after the defeat of the Hitler invaders is something that cannot be tolerated. The Western Powers, headed by the United States, are alone to blame for this unpardonable delay. As soon as the war was over they set out to revive German militarism, in complete disregard of the interests of the peoples.

The absence of a peace treaty has already played into the hands of the Bonn revenge-seekers. With help from the U.S. imperialists, they have re-established their armed forces with an eye to further aggression. It is the West German militarists' cherished dream to profit by the unstable situation in Europe so as to set their former enemies—the powers of the anti-Hitler coalition—against each other. They dream of absorbing the German Democratic Republic, enslaving other neighbouring countries and taking vengeance for the defeat they sustained in the Second World War.

We have always held that a peace treaty would make permanent the German frontiers defined in the Potsdam agreement, tie the hands of revenge-seekers and discourage them from adventures. The socialist countries have waited long enough for a treaty to be signed, in the hope that common sense would gain the upper hand in Washington, London and Paris. We are still ready to negotiate with the Western Powers mutually acceptable and agreed solutions.

Recently, while attending the U.N. General Assembly, Comrade Gromyko, the Soviet Foreign Minister, had conversations with the Secretary of State and the President of the United States. He also had talks with the Foreign Secretary and the Prime Minister of Britain. We gained the impression from those conversations that the Western Powers are showing some understanding of the situation and are inclined to seek a solution to the German problem, and to the issue of West Berlin, on a mutually acceptable basis.

But there is something strange about the Western countries, above all with the United States. In those countries one thing is said in the course of talks between statesmen and another reported by the press, although it is plain that the press is informed about the tenor of the talks. The Western press presents the issue of a German peace treaty in an unreasonable, unrealistic vein. It makes the accusation, for example, that someone wants, in settling the German problem, to take the orchard and give an apple in exchange. Perhaps those who say so like this figure of speech. But in this particular instance the figure does not do justice to the real state of affairs.

Everyone knows that the Soviet Government proposes signing a German peace treaty. Peace treaties are concluded to clear the way, as far as possible, to normal relations between countries, to avert the threat of a new war and ease international tension.

We proceed from the actual situation which has arisen since Hitler Germany was defeated, and from the existence of the two German states and the post-war frontiers. Any war, however trying and cruel, must end in the signing of a peace treaty. One has to render account and to pay for aggression, for starting wars. That being so, where does the orchard or the apple come in?

Some Western politicians offer us would-be advice by declaring that the signing of a peace treaty would endanger the Soviet Union and the other socialist countries. What are we to make of that? Since when have wars been considered to endanger one side only? The times when the imperialist powers dominated have gone for ever. The Soviet Union today is a mighty socialist power. The great socialist community, which posseses developed industry and agriculture and advanced science and technology, is making good progress.

I think that the imperialist circles will guess that, since we have advanced industry and agriculture, the arms of our Soviet Army, naturally, conform to the latest standards.

We consider that at present the forces of socialism, and all the forces championing peace, are superior to the forces of imperialist aggression. But even granting that the U.S. President was right in saying a short time ago that our forces were equal, it would be obviously unwise to threaten war. One who admits that there is equality should draw the proper conclusions. It is dangerous in our time to pursue a policy of strength.

A German peace treaty must be signed, with the Western Powers or without them.

The treaty will also normalise the situation in West Berlin by making it a free, demilitarised city. The Western countries and all the other countries of the world must enjoy the right of access to West Berlin in keeping with international law, that is, must reach an appropriate agreement with the Government of the German Democratic Republic, since all communications between West Berlin and the outside world pass through her territory.

Certain spokesmen of the Western Powers say that our proposals for the conclusion of a German peace treaty this year constitute an ultimatum. But they are wrong, for it was as far back as 1958 that the Soviet Union proposed concluding a peace treaty and settling the issue of West Berlin on that basis by transforming it into a free city. A long time has passed since then. We did not rush the settlement of the issue, hoping to reach mutual understanding with the Western Powers. It is fair to ask, therefore, why this talk about an ultimatum? In proposing the conclusion of a German peace treaty, the Soviet Union presented no ultimatum, but was prompted by the necessity to have this pressing issue settled at last.

The Soviet Government insists, now as before, on the earliest possible solution of the German problem; it is against that problem being shelved indefinitely. If the Western Powers show readiness to settle the German problem, the issue of a time limit for the signing of a German peace treaty will no longer be so important; in that case, we shall not insist on signing a peace treaty absolutely before December 31, 1961. The important thing is to settle the matter—to eliminate the remnants of the Second World War by signing a German peace treaty. That is the fundamental issue, the crux of the matter.

The solution of these problems will pave the way to further steps in the sphere of peaceful co-operation, both multilateral and bilateral, between states. What else has to be done for the further strengthening of peace, in addition to the conclusion of a German peace treaty?

The problem of *a considerable improvement of the United Nations machinery* has long been awaiting solution. That machinery has grown rusty in the cold war years and has been operating fitfully. The time has come to clean it, to remove the crust that has formed on it, to put fresh power into it, with due regard to the changes that have occurred in the international situation in recent years. It is high time to restore the legitimate rights of the People's Republic of China in the U.N. The time has come for a decision on the question of the German people's representation in the United Nations. As matters stand now, the most reasonable solution would be to conclude a peace treaty with both German states, whose existence is a reality, and to admit them into the U.N. It is time to grant genuinely equal rights in all U.N. agencies to the three groups of states that have come into being in the world—socialist, neutral and imperialist. It is time to call a halt to attempts to use the U.N. in the interests of the military alignment of the Western Powers.

The problem of the full abolition of colonial tyranny in all its forms and manifestations must be solved in accordance with the vital interests of the peoples. At the same time real and not verbal aid must be rendered to the peoples, and consequences of colonialism, must be remedied. The peoples must be helped to reach, as speedily as possible, the level of the economically and culturally developed countries. We see the way to achieve that goal first of all in making the colonial powers restore to their victims at least part of their loot. The Soviet Union and other socialist countries are already rendering the peoples disinterested, friendly support and assistance in the economic and cultural fields. We shall continue to help them.

The solution of pressing regional political problems could play a fairly important part in achieving a healthier international atmosphere. We attach great importance to the problem of establishing atom-free zones, first of all in Europe and the Far East. A non-aggression pact between the countries in the Warsaw Treaty Organisation and those in the North Atlantic military bloc could go a long way towards promoting security. An agreement could also be reached on the establishment of zones separating the armed forces of military groupings and a start could be made to reduce the armed forces stationed on foreign soil. And if the countries in military blocs were to come to the reasonable conclusion that all military alliances must be disbanded and armed forces withdrawn within their own national boundaries, it would be the best, the most radical solution of the problem.

In short, given mutual desire, many useful steps could be taken that would help the nations reduce the war danger and then remove it altogether.

We see a way to a better international situation in *more extensive business relations with all countries*.

Our relations with the socialist countries have been, and will continue to be, relations of lasting fraternal friendship and co-operation. We shall expand and improve mutually beneficial economic and cultural ties with them on the basis of agreed long-term plans. Such co-operation will enable us all to proceed even faster along the road of socialism and communism.

Our people derive deep satisfaction from our expanding co-operation with the great Asian powers of India and Indonesia. We rejoice in their successes and realise their difficulties and we readily expand business co-operation which helps them promote their economy and culture. Successfully developing on similar lines are our relations with Burma, Cambodia, Ceylon, the United Arab Republic, Iraq, Guinea, Ghana, Mali, Morocco, Tunisia, Somalia and other Asian and African countries that have freed themselves from foreign tyranny.

We will develop business relations with the Syrian Arab Republic.

After long and painful trials a government which declared itself to be successor to the Patrice Lumumba Government was set up in the Congo. The Soviet Government is prepared to help the Congolese people solve the difficult problems facing them in the struggle to overcome the consequences of colonial oppression.

Our relations with Latin American countries have similarly made progress in the period under review, despite the artificial barriers raised by internal reaction and the U.S. imperialists. The heroic people of Cuba, who have broken down those barriers, are establishing co-operation on an equal footing with other countries. And even though the U.S. imperialists stop at nothing—not even to overthrowing lawful governments—as long as they can prevent Latin American countries from pursuing an independent policy, events will nevertheless take their own course.

We shall continue assisting newly-independent nations to get on to their feet, grow strong and take up a fitting place in international affairs. Those nations are making a valuable contribution to the great cause of peace and progress. In this the Soviet Union and the other socialist countries will always be their true and reliable friends.

We attach great importance to relations with the major capitalist countries, first and foremost the United States. U.S. foreign policy in recent years has invariably concentrated on worsening the international situation. This is deplored by all peace-loving peoples. As for the Soviet Union, it has always held that the only way to prevent a world war of extermination is to normalise relations between states irrespective of their social system. That being so, there is a need for joint efforts to achieve this. No one expects the ruling circles of the United States to fall in love with socialism, nor must they expect us to fall in love with capitalism. The important thing is for them to renounce the idea of settling disputes through war and to base international relations on the principle of peaceful economic competition. If realistic thinking gains the upper hand in U.S. policy, a serious obstacle to a normal world situation will be removed. Such thinking will benefit not only the peoples of our two countries but those of other countries and world peace.

We propose to expand and promote normal, businesslike economic and cultural relations with Britain, France, Italy, West Germany and other West European countries. Some progress has been achieved in this respect in recent years, and it is up to the other side to improve the situation.

The Soviet Union pays special attention to the promotion of relations with its neighbours. Differences in social and political systems are no hindrance to the development of friendly, mutually advantageous relations between the U.S.S.R. and such countries as Afghanistan or Finland. Our relations with Austria and Sweden are progressing fairly well. We have sought, and will continue to seek, better relations with Norway and Denmark. Relations with our Turkish neighbour have been improving lately. We should like them to go on improving.

The Soviet Union would also like to live in peace and friendship with such of its neighbours as Iran, Pakistan and Japan. Unfortunately, the ruling circles of those countries have so far been unable, or unwilling, to disentangle themselves from the military blocs imposed on them by the Western Powers, nor have they been using the opportunities for business co-operation with our country. Their governments' present policies imperil their peoples. Outstanding in this respect is the Shah of Iran, who has gone to the point of agreeing to turn almost half the country into a zone of death in the interests of the aggressive CENTO bloc.

The Soviet Union has exerted considerable effort to improve its relations with Japan. But the government of that country, which is bound to the United States by an unequal military treaty, still refuses to eliminate the vestiges of the Second World War. The absence of a Soviet-Japanese peace treaty seriously handicaps wider co-operation between our two countries. The Japanese people are becoming increasingly aware of the great loss Japan is incurring as a result. We hope that common sense will win sooner or later and that our relations with Japan will make proper progress to the benefit of both countries.

The role *of economic ties* as an important element of peaceful coexistence is growing. In the period under survey, Soviet foreign trade has almost doubled in volume. We have stable commercial relations with more than eighty countries. But a great deal more could be achieved in this field if the Western Powers stopped their obstructionist practices and frequent arbitary actions, which damage business co-operation with the socialist countries. Incidentally, these outmoded practices do more harm to them than to us. Whoever resorts to discrimination, trade barriers and even blockades inevitably exposes himself as a support of war preparations and an enemy of peaceful coexistence.

Our country's *cultural relations* have expanded considerably in recent years and we now maintain such relations with more than a hundred countries. Over 700,000 Soviet people go abroad every year, and over 700,000 foreigners visit our country. We are willing to continue these mutually beneficial international contacts on a large scale. They can and must play a role in promoting co-operation and understanding among people.

Contacts with the leaders of other countries have become an important factor in Soviet foreign policy. It will be recalled that, despite pressure of business, Lenin, who guided the foreign policy of the Soviet state, received and had talks with American, British, French, Finnish, Afghan, and other foreign personalities. It was his intention to attend the 1922 Genoa Conference. The Central Committee of the Party has regarded it as its duty to follow this Lenin tradition. In pursuing an active foreign policy, members of the Presidium of the Central Committee of the C.P.S.U. have often visited countries of the socialist community. They have paid sixty-five visits to twenty-seven non-socialist countries. I have had to travel far and wide myself. It cannot be helped—such is the need.

We have received many distinguished foreign guests, including the heads of state or government of European, Asian, African and Latin American countries. Party and government leaders of the socialist countries have been frequent and welcome visitors to our country. We are prepared to continue meetings with one or a number of heads of state or government.

Comrades, events have shown that the foreign policy of our Party, worked out by the Twentieth Congress, is correct. We have achieved major victories by pursuing that policy. While our strength has increased very appreciably, we shall persevere in our Leninist policy in an effort to bring about the triumph of the idea of peaceful coexistence. *There is now a prospect of achieving peaceful coexistence for the entire period in which the social and political problems now dividing the world will have to be solved.* The indications are that it may actually be feasible to banish world war from the life of society even before the complete triumph of socialism on earth, with capitalism surviving in part of the world.

V. I. Lenin taught us to be firm, unyielding and uncompromising whenever a fundamental question of principle was involved. In the most trying conditions, at a time when the only socialist state had to resist the attacks of the whole capitalist world, when the enemy attacked us at the front, in the rear and from the flanks, Lenin spoke with the imperialists in firm, resolute terms, while following a flexible course and always retaining the initiative.

What are the tasks which the present international situation sets before Soviet foreign policy?

We must continue:

—steadily following the principle of the peaceful coexistence of states with different social systems as a general line of the Soviet Union's foreign policy;

—strengthening the unity of the socialist countries through fraternal co-operation and mutual assistance, and contributing to the might of the world socialist system;

—promoting contacts and co-operating with all who champion world peace. Together with those who want peace we must oppose those who want war;

—strengthening proletarian solidarity with the working class and all working people of the world, and rendering the fullest moral and material support to the peoples fighting to free themselves from imperialist and colonial oppression or to consolidate their indepenence;

—vigorously extending business ties, economic co-operation and trade with all countries that are willing to maintain such relations with the Soviet Union;

—pursuing an active and flexible foreign policy. We must seek the settlement of pressing world problems through negotiations, expose the intrigues and manoeuvres of the warmongers, and establish business co-operation with all countries on a reciprocal basis.

Experience has proved that the principle of the peaceful coexistence of countries with different social systems, a principle advanced by the great Lenin, is the way to preserve peace and avert a world war of extermination. We have done, and will continue doing, everything in our power to enable peaceful coexistence and peaceful economic competition to triumph throughout the world. . . .

. . . The policy of the 20th Congress encountered ardent approval from the international Communist movement, from the fraternal Marxist-Leninist parties. This was reflected in the decisions of Congresses and other materials of the fraternal parties and in the documents of the conferences of representatives of Communist and workers parties in 1957 and 1960.

Thus the statement of the Moscow conference of 1960 pointed out that 'the historic decisions of the 20th Congress of the CPSU . . . initiated a new stage in the international Communist movement and contributed to its further development on the basis of Marxism-Leninism'.

At the same time it should be noted that, as it later turned out, our party's policy of overcoming the harmful effects of the cult of the individual did not meet with due understanding from the leaders of the Albanian Party of Labor; indeed, they began to conduct a struggle against this policy.

Everyone knows that until recently the relations between the Soviet Union and the People's Republic of Albania and between the Communist Party of the Soviet Union and the Albanian Party of Labor were friendly and good. The peoples of our country gave Albania comprehensive, disinterested help in developing its economy, in socialist construction. We sincerely wanted and want to see Albania a flourishing socialist republic and its people happy and enjoying all the benefits of the new life.

For many years the Albanian leaders signified their complete unity of views with the Central Committee of our party and the Soviet government on all questions of the international Communist movement. They repeatedly declared their support of the 20th Congress policy. Enver Hoxha, First Secretary of the Central Committee of the Albanian Party of Labor, stated this in his speeches at the 20th and 21st Congresses of our party. At the Third Congress of the Albanian Party of Labor, held soon after the 20th Congress, the criticism of the cult of the individual as well as measures to overcome its harmful consequences were fully and completely approved.

We Soviet people believed the Albanian leaders and considered that mutual understanding and unity of views existed between our party and the Albanian Party of Labor.

The facts show, however, that recently the Albanian leaders, despite their former declarations and the decisions of their own Party Congress, sharply changed political course without any excuse and took the path of acute deterioration of relations with our party, with the Soviet Union. They began to depart from the commonly agreed line of the whole world Communist movement on the major questions of our times, something which became particularly manifest from the middle of last year.

Now the Albanian leaders do not conceal the fact that they do not like the course, taken by our party, of firmly overcoming the harmful consequences of the Stalin cult, of sharply condemning the abuse of power, of restoring Leninist norms of Party and state life.

Evidently the Albanian leaders in their hearts disagreed with the conclusions of the 1957 and 1960 conferences of fraternal parties, which, as everyone knows, approved the decisions of the 20th Congress and our party's policy of overcoming the harmful consequences of the cult of the individual. This stand of the Albanian leaders is explained by the fact that they themselves, to our regret and distress, are repeating the methods that occurred in our country in the period of the cult of the individual.

We are following events in Albania with a feeling of anxiety for the destinies of the heroic Albanian people. We are pained to see that rank-and-file Albanian Communists and the whole Albanian people, who are vitally interested in friendship and co-operation with all the socialist countries, are obliged to pay for the mistaken line of the Albanian leaders. We are deeply troubled by this situation and have persistently sought and are seeking ways of overcoming the differences that have arisen.

The course drawn up by the 20th Congress of our party is a Leninist course, and we cannot concede on this fundamental question to either the Albanian leaders or anyone else. To depart from the 20th Congress line would mean not heeding the wise instructions of Lenin, who discerned the danger of the appearance of the Stalin cult even when it was in embryo. It would mean disregarding the costly lessons of history, forgetting the price that our party paid for not having heeded in time the instructions of its great leader.

Now the Albanian leaders, opposing the 20th Congress policy, are trying to pull our party back to ways that they like but that will never be repeated in our country. Our party will continue firmly and unswervingly to carry out the line of its 20th Congress, a line that has withstood the test of time. No one will succeed in diverting us from the Leninist path! (*Stormy, prolonged applause*)

If the Albanian leaders hold dear the interest of their people and the cause of building socialism in Albania, if they really want friendship with the CPSU, with all the fraternal parties, they should renounce their mistaken views and return to the path of unity and close cooperation in the fraternal family of the socialist commonwealth, the path of unity with the whole international Communist movement.

As for our party, it will continue, in keeping with its internationalist duty, to do everything it can so that Albania may march shoulder to shoulder with all the socialist countries.

From the rostrum of the 22nd Congress we declare that purity of the Marxist-Leninist teaching and irreconcilability with any kind of distortions of its great principles are law for our party. (*Prolonged applause*) Communists hold the cause of the revolution, the cause of the people, above all else, and its leaders are worthy of the name only when they express the vital interests of the working people and follow the true path. Such leaders and chiefs are forged in the course of the struggle itself, they win authority by their service to the people, to the cause of Communism, they serve the people and should be under the people's control. (*Stormy applause*)

. . . . The Party regards communist construction in the U.S.S.R. as the fulfilment of its internationalist duty to the working people of all countries. It will continue to work untiringly to strengthen the world socialist system and the unity of the entire international Communist and working-class movement. Our Party will develop fraternal contacts with all Communists and Workers' parties and, together with them, will conduct a determined struggle for the purity of Marxism-Leninism, against the various manifestations of opportunism, against present-day revisionism as the gravest danger, against dogmatism and sectarianism.

Loyalty to the great theory of Marxism-Leninism and ties with the people were in the past, are in the present, and will be in the future the foundation of our victories, a gurantee of the triumph of communism!

Comrades, this Congress is to examine and discuss magnificent plans for the building of a communist society. These are plans for peaceful creative work, for a gigantic, economic and cultural growth, for higher living standards. All the countries of the mighty socialist community are making great headway. Great and clear-cut prospects are ahead of us.

The peoples building socialism and communism do not need war. They adhere to and translate into practice the principle of peaceful coexistence inherited from the great Lenin.

In the name of the Communist Party and the Soviet people, we solemnly proclaim from the rostrum of the Twenty-Second Congress: 'The Soviet Union will continue to pursue unswervingly a Leninist peaceful foreign policy, and will try to establish mutual trust and co-operation with all states irrespective of their social system. The Soviet Union will continue to strive for the easing of international tension and for general and complete disarmament under strict international control.'

We have appealed and again appeal to the governments and peoples of the countries that fought together with the Soviet Union against nazi Germany, to put an end to the vestiges of the Second World War and remove everything that hinders the strengthening of peace and friendship between nations, everything that holds the threat of a new war. The Soviet Union's proposals to conclude a peace treaty with Germany and, on that basis, to settle the question of West Berlin, involve no damage to the interests of other states. The proposals show nothing but solicitude for the strengthening of peace between peoples. We should like to believe that in the end reason will triumph.

Under the conditions obtaining today, when there are terribly destructive weapons in the hands of the great powers, it is criminally dangerous to play with fire by fomenting war. We call on the governments of all countries to strive towards mutual understanding and co-operation, towards the peaceful solution of outstanding international issues. It is the sacred duty of the peoples to conduct a persistent and energetic struggle, using all available means, for the preservation and consolidation of peace on earth.

(ii) *Speech by the Chinese Prime Minister, Mr. Chou En-lai, to the twenty-second Congress of the Communist Party of the Soviet Union, Moscow, 19 October 1961*[1] (*extracts*)

. . . Together with the peoples of the other socialist countries, the Soviet people are exerting enormous efforts to uphold world peace, relax international

[1] *Diversity in International Communism, A Documentary Record, 1961–1963*, ed. A. Dallin with J. Harris and G. Hodnett (New York and London, 1963), pp. 45–54. Hereafter cited as *Diversity in International Communism*.

tension, bring about general disarmament, maintain the peaceful coexistence of states with different social systems, and extend support to the national democratic movement in Asia, Africa, and Latin America. A short while ago the Soviet Union advanced proposals that a German peace treaty be concluded and the situation in West Berlin normalized on that basis. In the face of the serious situation that had resulted from intensification of the arms race and military preparations, the breakdown of the conference on the cessation of nuclear testing, and the rejection of disarmament by the United States, the Soviet Union was forced to take very important steps, such as the resumption of test explosions of nuclear weapons. These proposals and these steps represent important moves to uphold world peace and protect the security of the socialist camp, and to put a stop to imperialist military adventures; they are fully consistent with the interests of the peoples of the whole world. The Chinese people fully support all of these important moves by the Soviet Union aimed at defending world peace. (*Applause.*)

The way in which the present international situation is developing fully substantiates the scientific Marxist-Leninist analysis given in the 1960 Statement of representatives of Communist and workers parties.

The forces of the socialist camp and its international influence are growing very rapidly. The strides in construction in all the countries of the socialist camp are reinforcing the positions of peace and socialism all over the world. The burgeoning national democratic movement in Asia, Africa, and Latin America, supported by the socialist camp, has already become a great force in the struggle against the new and the old colonialism and internal reaction. The class struggle in the capitalist world is becoming ever sharper, the capitalist system is continuing its decline and decay, and the imperialist camp, headed by the United States, is day by day nearer the point of breaking up. This means that the preponderance of the forces of socialism over the forces of imperialism, of the forces of peace over the forces of war, is today becoming more and more apparent in the world arena. The correlation of forces in the world has created a situation that is extremely favorable for the people's struggle for universal peace, national liberation, democracy, and socialism. (*Applause.*)

The struggle of the peoples of the socialist countries for the cause of revolution and construction, the revolutionary struggle of the peoples of the capitalist countries, the liberation movement of oppressed nations, and the general democratic movement and struggle of the masses for peace all over the world are today flowing together into a common stream which is undermining and demolishing the imperialist system. The Cuban revolution is advancing with giant strides and successfully parrying the aggressive and interventionist intrigues of the United States. The Laotian people, despite U.S. interference, have won tremendous victories in the struggle to uphold their independence and neutrality. The peoples of the southern part of Vietnam and the southern part of Korea are engaged in a selfless struggle for the peaceful unification of their countries. The Algerian people are steadily gaining strength in the struggle for their independence. The peoples of the Congo, Angola, and Cameroon and other African peoples still being oppressed by the new and the old colonialism have engaged colonialism in fierce combat, seeking to smash its chains. In Japan and Brazil, everywhere the fiendish grip of American imperialism extends, the patriotic struggle of the peoples against that imperialism, their struggle to uphold national independence, is building up.

In the principal capitalist countries the masses of workers and peasants are waging a struggle against oppression, a struggle to win and defend democratic rights and to improve their living conditions. The struggle of the masses to defend world peace is spreading to every corner of the globe. No matter how savagely the imperialists and reactionaries of various countries may behave, and no matter how tortuous the path of struggle may be, the oppressed nations and peoples, encountering support from the socialist camp, are certain to win out over imperialism; the forces of peace, with the socialist camp and the international working class as their nucleus, are certain to win out over the forces of war. Inevitable doom awaits the imperialists and all reactionaries. (*Applause*.)

As the Statement of the Moscow Conference points out, however, as long as imperialism lasts, the soil for aggressive wars will remain. The worst enemy of peace is American imperialism. It is the bulwark of present-day colonialism and international reaction, the prime force of aggression and war. The whole world sees today that the Kennedy administration is even more insidious and adventurous. Seeking to make itself more attractive with an 'olive branch', it spouts 'peace', 'progress', and 'the prosperity of mankind', while under the cloak of 'peace' it is actually making even more frenzied efforts in the arms race and in preparing for war. This administration has been the direct organizer of an attack on Cuba and has provoked civil war in Laos, and it is preventing the reaching of an agreement at the Geneva conference. It is this administration which, making use of the so-called Berlin crisis, is raising a frantic war clamor and threatening war, incessantly engineering military provocations in Berlin, Cuba, Laos, South Vietnam, and South Korea, and on territory belonging to our country—Taiwan. It is this administration which is appropriating the largest sums the United States has ever spent for military purposes in time of peace, which is making intensive preparations for local wars and nuclear war against the peoples of the whole world. The face of American imperialism as the common enemy of the peoples of the whole world has been completely exposed.

All the actions of American imperialism indicate that we still face the danger of war and that the peoples of all lands must redouble their vigilance. The struggle against imperialist aggression and the defense of the world peace remain, as they have been, a task of extreme urgency for the peoples of all countries. If the socialist camp, the international working class, the national liberation movement, and all peace-loving peoples and states make common cause, form a united front to combat the policy of aggression and war being pursued by the imperialist circles headed by the United States, and wage an unflagging struggle, world peace is certain to be preserved. (*Applause*.)

Our country steadfastly upholds solidarity with the Soviet Union and the other socialist countries and, together with them, is carrying on an unflagging struggle for world peace and the progress of mankind. We are actively supporting the liberation struggle of oppressed nations and oppressed peoples and resolutely opposing the policy of aggression and war being pursued by the imperialist circles headed by the U.S.A. We stand at all times for the peaceful coexistence of countries with different social systems on the basis of the Five Principles and are exerting tremendous efforts to achieve it. In recent years China has concluded treaties of friendship or treaties of friendship and non-aggression with many countries of Asia and Africa, including Yemen, Burma, Nepal, Afghanistan, Guinea, Cambodia, Indonesia, and Ghana. The conclusion of these treaties not only strengthens and develops the friendly relations between China and these countries but also makes a useful contribution to the defense of world peace.

The Moscow conferences of representatives of Communist and workers parties held in 1957 and 1960 were conferences of great historic importance for the international Communist movement. The 1957 Declaration and the 1960 Statement are the common program of action for the Communist and workers parties. The Declaration and the Statement point out that the solidarity of the socialist camp and of the international Communist movement is the guarantee of victory in the struggle of the peoples of all countries for universal peace, national liberation, democracy, and socialism. Upholding this great solidarity is an internationalist duty for us as Communists. (*Applause*.)

The Declaration and Statement point out that the solidarity of the socialist camp and of the international Communist movement is the nucleus for even broader cohesion on a world-wide scale. This solidarity of ours is cemented by common ideals and a common cause. It has been reinforced and developed in the joint struggle against common enemies. It rests on the foundation of Marxism Leninism and proletarian internationalism. This solidarity of ours has stood up under testing, and there are no forces capable of undermining it. Our socialist camp of twelve fraternal countries, from the Korean People's Democratic Republic to the German Democratic Republic and from the Democratic Republic of Vietnam to the People's Republic of Albania, constitutes a single whole. Our socialist countries and our Communist parties fraternally support and cooperate with one another on the basis of independence and complete equality. We must unite as closely as possible, must cherish our solidarity as the apple of our eye, and on no account permit any statements or actions detrimental to that solidarity. (*Applause*.)

We hold that if, unfortunately, disputes and disagreements have arisen among the fraternal parties and fraternal countries, we should resolve them patiently, being guided by the spirit of proletarian internationalism and by the principles of equality and the achievement of unanimity through consultation. Open unilateral condemnation of a fraternal party does not make for unity, does not help settle the issues. Openly exposing disputes between fraternal parties and fraternal countries for enemies to see cannot be regarded as a serious, Marxist-Leninist approach. Such an approach can only pain friends and gladden foes. The Communist Party of China sincerely hopes that the fraternal parties between which the disputes and disagreements exist will reunite on the basis of Marxism-Leninism and on the basis of mutual respect for independence and equality. I think that this is the position that we Communists should take on this question.

At present the imperialist circles headed by the United States, using the struggle against communism as a façade, are engaged in aggressive and expansionist activities. American imperialism and the Yugoslav revisionist group are doing all they can to drive a wedge into the progressive forces of the world and to undermine their solidarity. Under the circumstances the solidarity and unity of the whole socialist camp and of the whole international Communist movement take on supreme importance. In solidarity there is strength. If there is solidarity any difficulty can be surmounted. In the face of the solidarity of the forces of world socialism, the solidarity of oppressed nations and peoples and of the peace-loving peoples and states of the whole world, the mad designs of the imperialists and their stooges are all sure to founder. (*Applause.*)

(iii) *Speech by the First Vice-Chairman of the U.S.S.R. Council of Ministers, Mr. Mikoyan, to the twenty-second Congress of the Communist Party of the Soviet Union, Moscow, 20 October 1961*[1] *(extracts)*

. . . Comrades! The XX Congress was a turning point in the life of our party and of the entire world Communist movement. The political course of that Congress and its theoretical instructions have already produced fine shoots. This has been proved by the historical experience of the past few years.

The ideological orientation of the XX Congress was not something that manifested itself in the space of a day before the Congress or within the few days of its proceedings. It evolved over a span of two years preceding the Congress in the process of critical reexamination of certain ideological principles, reorganization of the practical work of the Party and the state, and the elimination of the harmful consequences of the cult of the individual.

Disagreements on basic questions of party policy and practice had arisen within the Central Committee in this period. Molotov, Kaganovich, Malenkov, and Voroshilov showed conservatism in their thinking and proved incapable of correctly assessing the postwar international and domestic situation, of comprehending the new line of conduct that was required of Marxist-Leninists. They rejected everything new and opposed the theses that were later advanced by the Central Committee at the XX Congress of the CPSU. The fractionalist antiparty group, of which Molotov became the chief ideologist, was later joined by Bulganin, Pervukhin, Suburov, and Shepilov. . . .

. . . The result of his underestimating forces of socialism and consequently overestimating the forces of imperialism was that Molotov made serious mistakes on questions of international development—on peaceful coexistence and the possibility of preventing a world war, and on the multiplicity of the forms of transition to socialism in various countries.

In general, Molotov rejects the line of peaceful coexistence, reducing the concept to nothing more than a state of peace, or rather the absence of war at a given moment, and denying the possibility of preventing a world war. In its substance this view approximates that of the foreign adversaries of peaceful coexistence, who interpret it as a variant of the 'cold war', as a state of 'armed peace'.

This conception is at odds with the Leninist understanding of relations between the two systems and would have led to repudiating the broad development of economic relations between them and to the curtailment of contacts and cultural ties. Finally, it would to all intents and purposes have meant accepting

[1] *Diversity in International Communism*, pp. 55–63.

the inevitability of war and abandoning the active quest for agreements aimed at reducing international tension and at disarmament. It is no accident, therefore, that he should reject the historic thesis of the XX Party Congress on the possibility of preventing world war in this age.

He disputes the advisability of the personal meetings our party and government leaders have been holding with leaders of the capitalist states, considering them a pure infatuation ascribable to excessive faith in personal contacts and talks. In defiance of this point of view, the Party undertook to broaden contacts between Soviet and foreign state and public organizations and figures. And experience has shown how right the Party was in these moves: I need only refer to the enormous political response to the meetings and speeches abroad of N. S. Khrushchev and other figures and to the great good they have done and continue to do. (*Applause*.)

The Soviet people are building a communist society in the fraternal family of the peoples of the socialist countries.

The welding of all the forces of socialism, of all the Communist and workers parties, is the most important factor in our common advance. The Communist and workers parties have placed a high assessment on our party's vanguard role in the international Communist movement and on the importance of the XX Congress. Our party feels the moral support of the fraternal parties in all its work. (*Applause*.) Unfortunately, this does not apply to the leaders of the Albanian Party of Labor.

For many years the leaders of the Albanian Party of Labour on any and all occasions vowed their friendship with our party and the Soviet people and professed to support the decisions of the XX Congress. But as recent events have shown, these vows and protestations of theirs were insincere. For more than a year now the Albanian leaders, having abruptly altered their political policy, have been waging a fight against the decisions of the XX Congress of the CPSU and attacking our party and its Leninist Central Committee, headed by N. S. Khrushchev, and other Communist parties. The actions of the Albanian leaders indicate that they are departing from internationalist positions and back-sliding onto the path of nationalism.

Where nationalism and alienation from the socialist camp lead to is shown by the experience of Yugoslavia's revisionism, which is being given effect in practice and has found expression in concentrated form in the anti-Leninist Program of the League of Communists of Yugoslavia. It would be worth while for the Albanian leaders to give this some thought.

The facts indicate that a deplorable situation has developed in the Albanian Party of Labor. Just how far Hoxha and Shehu have descended can be seen from the fact that they not only failed to publish the draft Program of the CPSU (this is, of course, their internal affair) but presented a distorted account of it in their press. What are we to make of this? Why, even *The New York Times*, as well as many other bourgeois organs, carried the draft Program in full. Even in Greece, Albania's neighbor, where bourgeois reactionaries are in power, progressive forces managed to have our Program published in a printing that was enormous for that country. But the Albanian people and the Albanian Communists are deprived of an opportunity to read this historic document. The Albanian leaders today see even the publication of the Program of the CPSU as a danger to them. The people have an expression for a situation of this kind: 'How far can you go!'

Developments are showing that those who persist in revisionism and dogmatism arrive, even though from different directions, at one and the same thing— estrangement from Marxism-Leninism and from the socialist camp and the world Communist movement.

The Albanian leaders' disagreement with our party's Leninist policy as laid down by the XX Congress is also to be explained by the fact that Enver Hoxha and Mehmet Shehu have long been cultivating in their party practices and methods that are incompatible with Marxism-Leninism. How Mehmet Shehu, for example, interprets the norms of party life is plain from his statement at the recent Congress of the Albanian Party of Labor that anyone who disagreed with the leadership on a question would get (and I quote) 'a spit in the face, a punch in the mouth, and, if need be, a bullet in the brain'.

Several prominent figures in the Albanian Party of Labor have only recently been expelled from the Party and subjected to repressive action: Liri Belishova, member of the Politburo, together with her husband, and Mago Como, member of the Central Committee and a government minister (both of them were also deprived of their deputies' credentials), and also Koco Tashko, veteran of the international Communist movement and the oldest member of the Albanian Party of Labor, who has been active since as far back as the Comintern days of the 1930's and who has never had a disagreement with the Party; until recently Enver Hoxha considered him his closest friend. Now he has been expelled from the Party. These people have been victimized merely because they did not wish to leave the tried and tested path of Albanian-Soviet friendship.

Albanian seamen who had been studying in our country recently returned home. In talks among themselves they voiced perplexity over what could have caused the sudden deterioration of relations between Albania and the USSR. Many of them landed in prison for this.

Albanian students who were studying in our country went home for their vacations, and afterwards many of them were not permitted by the Albanian authorities to continue their studies in the USSR. This naturally caused dissatisfaction among them, and again many of the malcontents were subject to repressive action.

On the one hand, the Albanian leaders persecute those who want to maintain friendship between our parties and peoples, and on the other hand they hold a Soviet-Albanian friendship month to deceive their people. This was in September.

It will be said that these are their internal affairs and must not be interfered in. But after all, the persecution and acts of repression are directed against Albanians who uphold the traditional friendship with the Soviet Union. And this is something that directly concerns us; we cannot remain indifferent in the matter, and are obliged to state our opinion.

The Albanian leaders are now extolling the cult of Stalin and seeking to use his name as a cover-up for actions that are incompatible with Leninism.

Can anyone really think that friendship between us is possible on the 'basis'—

if I may be excused for using the term—on which the Albanian leaders are now operating? No, they have to understand clearly that only by renouncing this course and taking positions that are mandatory for Communist parties can they count on the friendship of the party of Lenin—the friendship of the Soviet people. This is the only way it can be! (*Stormy, prolonged applause.*)

Comrades, problems of foreign policy have occupied and will continue to occupy an important place in our party's activities. These problems cannot be separated from our domestic policy. What counts most for us is to ensure peaceful conditions for the building of a communist society. . . .

(iv) *Declaration of the Central Committee of the Albanian Communist Party, Tirana, 20 October 1961*[1]

At the XXII Congress of the Communist Party of the Soviet Union, N. Khrushchev publicly attacked the Albanian Party of Labor. The anti-Marxist calumnies and attacks of N. Khruschchev are of use only to the enemies of communism and of the Albanian People's Republic—to the various imperialists and to the Yugoslav revisionists. N. Khrushchev, in revealing to the enemies the disagreements which have long existed between the leadership of the Communist Party of the Soviet Union and the Albanian Party of Labor, has brutally violated the Moscow Statement of 1960, which emphasizes that the disagreements arising between fraternal parties must be settled with patience, in the spirit of proletarian internationalism, and on the basis of the principles of equality and mutual consultation. In publicly attacking the Albanian Party of Labor, N. Khrushchev has in effect undertaken an open attack against the unity of the international Communist and workers movement, against the unity of the socialist camp. The responsibility for this anti-Marxist act and for all the consequences which derives from it falls entirely upon N. Khrushchev.

The Albanian Party of Labor, guided by the interests of the unity of the world Communist movement and of the socialist camp, has endeavored with great patience, from the moment our disagreements with the Soviet line first arose, to settle them in the correct Marxist-Leninist way, by the path designated in the Moscow Statement. N. Khrushchev, however, has chosen the anti-Marxist path of aggravating these disagreements, the path of attacks and slanders, of pressures and threats, the path of public denunciation of our disagreements.

The Albanian Party of Labor warmly welcomed the declaration of Comrade Chou En-lai, head of the delegation of the Communist Party of China to the XXII Congress of the Communist Party of the Soviet Union, which stated that unilateral criticism and revelation to the enemy of disagreement between fraternal parties cannot be considered a serious and Marxist-Leninist attitude. But even after this statement of principle on the part of the representative of the Chinese Communist Party, the most virulent attacks and calumnies continue from the rostrum of the XXII Congress of the Communist Party of the Soviet Union against the Albanian Party of Labor and the Albanian People's Republic. These attacks have come as much from certain members of the Soviet leadership as from certain leaders of the Communist and workers parties of other countries,

[1] *Diversity in International Communism*, pp. 85–88.

who also thus assume a heavy historical responsibility as splitters of the unity of the international Communist and workers movement.

In these conditions—in the face of the organized anti-Marxist attack by N. Khrushchev and his followers, in the face of these calumnies and inventions which have as their goal the discrediting of our party, in the face of the serious danger to the future destiny of the international Communist and workers movement and of the socialist camp—the Albanian Party of Labor cannot keep silent. By means of supporting facts and documents, it will make known to the entire Communist and workers movement, as well as to world public opinion, where the truth lies, on what side justice is to be found about the relations between the Albanian Party of Labor and the leadership of the Communist Party of the Soviet Union; it will unmask the anti-Marxist and anti-Albanian activities of N. Khrushchev and his group.

The unity of the socialist camp and of the international Communist and workers movement is seriously endangered by the anti-Marxist plots of N. Khrushchev and his followers. In this situation, in order to defend the highest interests of the people and the fatherland and their socialist victories, in order to defend the purity of Marxism-Leninism and the unity of the ranks of the Communist movement and the socialist camp, the Albanian Party of Labour has assumed and will continue to assume with a clean conscience all responsibility for all its actions, both before the international Communist and workers movement and before the Albanian people.

The struggle which is imposed upon our party and our people will be long and difficult. But difficulties have never alarmed our party and our people. Our party and our people have been firmly tempered in the struggle against the numerous and continual slanders and attacks and plots of the various imperialists and of the Yugoslav revisionists. They will not waver nor will they be brought to their knees in the face of the slanderous attacks, blackmail, and pressures exerted by N. Khrushchev and his followers. The Party and the people, in a unity of steel, will as always mark out resolutely the path before them and will triumph in taking the correct path, the path of the triumph of Marxism-Leninism and of the cause of socialism and communism. We will gain the victory because we are not alone. With us, with the great cause of Marxism-Leninism, stand the Communists and the peoples of the Soviet Union, for whom we feel an indestructible affection and friendship which we will keep intact in our hearts through all storms and tempests; with us are the Communists and the peoples of China; with us are the Communists of the world and the peoples of the other socialist countries. The victorious flag of the Party, the invincible flag of Marxism-Leninism, will always fly proudly over new socialist Albania.

(v) *Speech by Mr. Khrushchev to the twenty-second Congress of the Communist Party of the Soviet Union, 27 October 1961*[1] *(extracts)*

Some people attack us, accusing us of oversimplifying or softening the picture when in assessing the international situation we underline the need for peaceful

[1] *Diversity in International Communism*, pp. 71–81. See also *Report on the Programme of the Communist Party of the Soviet Union and Reply to Discussion*, Soviet Booklet, No. 81 (London, 1961).

coexistence in present-day circumstances. We are told that those who lay stress on peaceful coexistence somehow underestimate the nature of imperialism and even end up contradicting Lenin's assessment of imperialism.

Vladimir Ilyich Lenin's classical definition of imperialism is well known. This definition of Lenin's discloses the reactionary and aggressive nature of imperialism as the final stage of capitalism. Imperialism is inseparably linked with wars, with the struggle for the division and redivision of the world, for enslaving people and bringing them under the rule of monopoly capital. It is capable of any adventurous undertaking.

This appraisal of the nature of imperialism retains full validity today. Far from disavowing it, our party reaffirms it and is guided by it in all its policy, in its working out of the strategy and tactics of revolutionary struggle. This is impressively shown in the draft of our party's new Program. At the same time the Party is obliged, if it hews to creative Marxism, to take into account the great changes that have occurred in the world since Lenin gave his analysis of imperialism.

We are living through a period in which there are two world systems, a period in which the world socialist system is developing rapidly. The time is not far off when it will surpass the world capitalist system in the production of material wealth. As for the science and culture, the countries in the world socialist system have already greatly surpassed the capitalist countries in a number of fields. At present the world socialist system is mightier than the imperialist countries militarily as well.

This being the case, it cannot be maintained that nothing has happened, that nothing has changed in the world in the past few decades. Only people who are out of touch with life, who are blind to the great changes that have occurred in the balance of forces in the world arena, can maintain this.

It is a fact that the essence of imperialism, its aggressive nature, has not changed. But the possibilities open to it today are no longer what they were in the period when it exercised undivided sway. The situation today is such that imperialism cannot dictate its will to all, or pursue its aggressive policy unimpeded. . . .

Under present circumstances the principle of the peaceful coexistence of states with different social systems assumes vital importance.

The only people who fail to see this are the hopeless dogmatists who, having learned by rote general formulas on imperialism, stubbornly turn away from life. This continues to be the position of the diehard Molotov. He and his like fail to appreciate the changes in the world situation, the new developments in life. They have not kept up with the times and have long since become a drag, a needless burden. (*Applause.*) . . .

Comrades! The Central Committee's report and also speeches by delegates to the Congress have referred to the erroneous position of the leaders of the Albanian Party of Labor, who have taken the path of combating the line of our party's XX Congress and undermining the foundations of friendship with the Soviet Union and other socialist countries.

The representatives of the fraternal parties have declared in their speeches that they share our alarm over the state of affairs in the Albanian Party of Labor and roundly condemn the dangerous actions of its leaders, which are prejudicing the fundamental interests of the Albanian people and the solidarity of the entire socialist commonwealth. The speeches by delegates and by representatives of the fraternal parties are convincing evidence that our party's Central Committee was absolutely correct in reporting to the Congress, openly and as a matter of principle, on the abnormal state of Soviet-Albanian relations.

We were obliged to do this because our repeated attempts to normalize relations with the Albanian Party of Labor have unfortunately borne no fruit. I should like to emphasize that the Central Committee of our party has shown a maximum of patience and has done everything in its power to restore good relations between our parties.

The members of the Presidium of the Central Committee of the CPSU have tried time and again to get together with the Albanian leaders and discuss the issues that have arisen. Back in August, 1960, we twice proposed a meeting to the Albanian leaders but they avoided it. They were equally persistent in declining to have talks with us at the time of the Moscow Conference of fraternal parties in November, 1960.

When, at the insistence of the Central Committee of the CPSU, such a meeting did take place, Enver Hoxha and Mehmet Shehu disrupted it and moved on to actions that can only be described as provocative. The leaders of the Albanian Party of Labor made a deliberate show of walking out on the November conference, indicating their refusal to defer to the collective opinion of the fraternal parties. To our subsequent suggestions that we meet, exchange views, and resolve our differences they again responded with a rude refusal, and they stepped up their campaign of attacks and slander against our party and its Central Committee.

There are no expedients that the leaders of the Albanian Party of Labor shrink from using in their efforts to hide from their people the truth about what our party and people are doing. Albania is the only country in the socialist camp in which the draft Program of the CPSU was not published in full. The Albanian press carried only sections of the draft, deliberately creating a distorted impression of our party's activities. This fact speaks for itself. After all, even communism's adversaries were unable to pass over our Program in silence.

We can understand why the Albanian leaders are concealing the CPSU Program from their party and people. They fear the truth like the plague. The Party Program is something sacred for us, our lodestone in the building of communism.

Had they published it in full the working people of Albania would have been able to tell truth from slander, would have seen that all our party's activities, all its plans accord with the vital interests of the peoples, including the interests of the Albanian people, who are friendly to us. (*Prolonged applause.*)

Our great party has more than once been subjected to bitter and filthy attacks from open and covert enemies of communism. But it must be said outright that we do not recall an instance in which anyone shifted with such dizzying speed from protestations and vows of eternal friendship to unbridled anti-Soviet slander as the Albanian leaders have done.

Presumably they expect in this way to lay the groundwork for earning handouts from the imperialists. The imperialists are always willing to pay thirty pieces of silver to those who cause a split in the ranks of the Communists. But pieces of silver have never brought anyone anything but dishonor and shame. (*Applause.*)

Clearly, the Central Committee of our party could not fail to tell the Congress the whole truth about the reprehensible stand taken by the leadership of the Albanian Party of Labor. Had we not done so, they would have gone on claiming that the Central Committee of the Communist Party of the Soviet Union was afraid to let the Party know of its differences with the leadership of the Albanian Party of Labor. Our party and the Soviet people should know how the Albanian leaders have been acting. And let the Congress, which is empowered to speak for the whole Party, state its attitude on this matter, pronounce its authoritative opinion.

It has been emphasized at our Congress that we are prepared to normalize relations with the Albanian Party of Labor on the basis of Marxist-Leninist principles. How have the Albanian leaders responded to this? They have lashed out at our party and its Central Committee with a blatant, mud-slinging statement.

Comrade Chou En-lai, head of the delegation of the Communist Party of China, voiced concern in his speech over our having openly raised the issue of Albanian-Soviet relations at the Congress. As far as we can see, his statement primarily reflects alarm lest the present state of our relations with the Albanian Party of Labor affect the solidarity of the socialist camp.

We share the anxiety of our Chinese friends and appreciate their concern for the strengthening of unity. If the Chinese comrades wish to apply their efforts to normalizing the Albanian Party of Labor's relations with the fraternal parties, it is doubtful whether there is anyone better able to facilitate accomplishment of this purpose than the Communist Party of China. This would really redound to the benefit of the Albanian Party of Labor and accord with the interests of the entire commonwealth of socialist countries. (*Prolonged applause.*)

It is true, of course, that Communists should so frame their interparty relations as not to provide the enemy with the slightest opening. But unfortunately the Albanian leaders have grossly flouted this requirement. For a long time now they have been openly attacking the line of the XX Congress, providing the bourgeois press with food for all sorts of speculation. It is they, the Albanian leaders, who have been shouting from the rooftops about having a position of their own, views of their own that differ from the views of our party and the other fraternal parties. This showed clearly at the Fourth Congress of the Albanian Party of Labor, and has been particularly clear of late.

Why did the Albanian leaders launch a campaign against the decisions of our party's XX Congress? What treason do they see in them?

Above all, the resolute condemnation of the Stalin cult and its harmful consequences is not to the liking of the Albanian leaders. They are displeased that we should have resolutely denounced the arbitrary rule, the abuse of power from which many innocent people suffered, among them eminent representatives of the old guard who had been with Lenin in building the world's first proletarian state. The Albanian leaders cannot refer without vexation and rancor to the fact that we have put an end for good to the situation where one man at his own pleasure arbitrarily decided all-important questions relating to the life of our party and country. (*Prolonged applause.*)

Stalin is no longer among the living, but we have thought it necessary to denounce the disgraceful methods of leadership that flourished in the setting of the Stalin cult. Our party is doing everything possible to prevent phenomena of this sort from ever again recurring.

One would have supposed that the Leninist line of the XX Party Congress, which was supported by the fraternal parties would have met with support from the leadership of the Albanian Party of Labor too, since the cult of the individual is incompatible with Marxism-Leninism. Actually, the Albanian leaders heaped encomiums on the Stalin cult and launched a violent campaign against the decisions of the XX Party Congress, in an effort to make the socialist countries swerve from this sound course. This, naturally, was no accident. All that was reprehensible in our country in the period of the cult of the individual is manifested in its worst form in the Albanian Party of Labor. It is now an open secret that the Albanian leaders remain in power by resorting to force and arbitrary rule.

For a long time now there has existed in the Albanian Party of Labor an abnormal, evil situation in which any person objectionable to the leadership is liable to meet with cruel persecution.

Where today are the Albanian Communists who built the Party, who fought the Italian and German fascist invaders? Nearly all of them are victims of the bloody misdeeds of Mehmet Shehu and Enver Hoxha.

The Central Committee of the CPSU has received more than one letter from Albanian Communists appealing to us to restrain the Albanian leaders from dealing savagely with the finest sons and daughters of the Albanian Party of Labor. The delegates to the Congress can form their own idea of the Albanian leaders' moral complexion by having a look at some of these letters.

The Albanian leaders reproach us with meddling in the internal affairs of the Albanian Party of Labor. I should like to tell you what form this so-called meddling took.

A few years ago the Central Committee of the CPSU interceded with the Albanian leaders over the fate of Liri Gega, a former member of the Politburo of the Central Committee of the Albanian Party of Labor, who had been sentenced to death along with her husband. This woman had for a number of years been a member of leading bodies of the Albanian Party of Labor and had taken part in the Albanian people's struggle for liberation. In approaching the Albanian leaders at the time, we were guided by considerations of humanity, by anxiety to prevent the shooting of a woman, and a pregnant woman at that. We felt and still feel that as a fraternal party we had a right to state our opinion in the matter. After all, even in the blackest days of rampant reaction, the tsarist satraps, who tortured revolutionaries, scrupled to execute pregnant women. And here, in a socialist country, they had sentenced to death and they executed a woman who was about to become a mother; they had shown altogether unwarranted cruelty. (*Stir in the hall. Shouts of 'Shame! Shame!'*)

People of integrity today incur punishment in Albania just for daring to come out for Soviet-Albanian friendship, which the Albanian leaders are fond of talking about in such high-sounding and florid terms.

Comrades Liri Belishova and Koco Tashko, prominent figures in the Albanian Party of Labor, were not only expelled from the Party's Central Committee but are now being called enemies of the Party and the people. And all this merely because Liri Belishova and Koco Tashko had the courage honestly and openly to voice their disagreement with the policy of the Albanian leaders and took a stand for Albanian solidarity with the Soviet Union and the other socialist countries.

People who today advocate friendship with the Soviet Union, with the CPSU, are regarded by the Albanian leaders as enemies.

How is all this to be squared with the vows and protestations of friendly feelings for the CPSU and the Soviet Union that have been heard from Shehu and Hoxha? It is obvious that all their spouting about friendship is nothing but hypocrisy and deception.

This is the atmosphere that prevails in the Albanian Party of Labor, and this is why the Albanian leaders oppose the Leninist line of the XX Party Congress. After all, to put an end to the cult of the individual would in effect mean that Shehu, Hoxha, and others would have to give up their key positions in the Party and government. And this they do not want to do. But we are certain the time will come when the Albanian Communists and the Albanian people will have their say, and then the Albanian leaders will have to answer for the harm they have done their country, their people, and the cause of socialist construction in Albania. (*Stormy, prolonged applause.*)

Comrades! Our party will continue to combat revisionists of all shades as it has in the past. Steadfastly conforming to the principles of the Declaration and the Statement of the conferences of Marxist-Leninist parties, we have exposed and shall continue unremittingly to expose the revisionism that has found expression in the Program of the Yugoslav League of Communists. We shall also constantly combat dogmatism and all other deviations from Marxism-Leninism. (*Applause.*) . . .

I would like to say a few words about the following question. In many speeches at the Congress, and not infrequently in our press as well, when mention is made of the activity of our party's Central Committee a certain special emphasis is placed on me personally, and my role in carrying out major party and government measures is underlined.

I understand the kind feelings guiding these comrades. Allow me, however, to emphasize emphatically that everything that is said about me should be said about the Central Committee of our Leninist party and about the Presidium of the Central Committee. (*Stormy, prolonged applause.*) Not one major measure, not one responsible pronouncement has been carried out upon anyone's personal directive; they have all been the result of collective deliberation and collective decision. (*Stormy applause.*) And this concluding speech, too, has been considered and approved by the executive collective. (*Prolonged applause.*) Our great strength, comrades, lies in collective leadership, in collegial decisions on all questions of principle. (*Stormy applause.*) . . .

Here at the Congress much has been said, for instance, about the furious energy displayed by the antiparty fractionalists Molotov, Kaganovich, Malenkov, and others against the Leninist Party Central Committee and against me personally. Speaking against the course set forth by the XX Congress, the schismatics concentrated their main fire against Khrushchev, who did not suit them. Why against Khrushchev? Well, because Khrushchev had been promoted by the will of the Party to the post of First Secretary of the Central Committee. The fractionalists badly miscalculated. The Party smashed them both ideologically and organizationally. (*Stormy applause*.)

The Central Committee of our party has displayed an exceptionally high political maturity and a truly Leninist understanding of the situation. It is characteristic that literally not one member or candidate member of the Central Committee and not one member of the Inspection Commission supported the miserable handful of schismatics. (*Prolonged applause*.)

While resolutely pronouncing themselves opposed to all the disgusting phenomena of the cult of the individual, Marxist-Leninists have always recognized and will continue to recognize the authority of leaders.

But it would be incorrect to single out this or that leader, to set him apart from the executive collective or to exalt him inordinately. This is contrary to the principles of Marxism-Leninism. It is known with what impatience Marx, Engels, and Lenin spoke out against those who eulogized their contributions. Yet it is difficult to overestimate the great role of the founders of scientific communism, Marx, Engels, and Lenin, and their contributions to the working class and to all mankind. (*Prolonged applause*.)

Feelings of self-praise and any special emphasis on or excessive exaggeration of the role of individual leaders are utterly alien to true Marxist-Leninists. They find it simply insulting when someone tries obtrusively to set them apart, to isolate them from the executive nucleus of comrades. (*Stormy applause*.)

We Communists highly value and support the authority of correct and mature leadership. We must safeguard the authority of the leaders who are recognized by the Party and the people. But each leader must also understand the other side of the matter—never to plume himself on his position, to remember that in holding this or that post he is merely fulfilling the will of the Party and the will of the people, who may have invested the greatest power in him but never lose control over him. (*Applause*.) The leader who forgets this pays heavily for his mistake. I would add that he will pay while he is alive; or even after his death the people will not forgive him, as we can see from the condemnation of the cult of Stalin. (*Applause*.) A person who forgets that he is obliged to fulfill the will of the Party and of the people cannot, properly speaking, be called a true leader; there must be no such 'leaders' either in the Party or in the state apparatus. (*Applause*.)

Of course, for many reasons great power is concentrated in the hands of the man who holds an executive post. A leader advanced by the Party and the people must not abuse his power. In the reports to the Congress you have heard about the measures that we have implemented and that we shall carry out in order that a revival of the ugly phenomena of the cult of the individual may never recur in the future. But there is one thing that no statutory provision can prescribe: The collective of leaders must thoroughly understand that a situation must not be permitted to arise whereby any authority, even the most deserving one, can cease to heed the opinions of those who have advanced him. (*Applause*.)

It is wrong, comrades, it is simply impossible to permit the inception and development of instances when the merited prestige of an individual may assume forms in which he fancies that everything is permissible to him and that he no longer has need of the collective. In such a case this individual may stop listening to the voices of other comrades who have been advanced to leadership, just as he was, and may begin suppressing them. Our great teacher V. I. Lenin resolutely fought against this, and the Party paid too dear a price for not heeding his wise counsel in good time.

So let us be worthy disciples of Lenin in this important matter. (*Stormy, prolonged applause*.) . . .

4. Speech by the First Secretary of the Albanian Communist Party, Mr. Hoxha, 8 November 1961[1] (extracts)

All our people, young and old, are now joyfully celebrating two wonderful dates: the twentieth anniversary of the founding of the glorious Albanian Party of Labor and the forty-fourth anniversary of the victory of the Great October Socialist Revolution.

It is not by chance that we celebrate them together. The two outstanding events—the triumph of the Great October Revolution in Russia on November 7, 1917, and the founding of the Albanian Communist Party on November 8, 1941, are closely intertwined in the history of our people; they are two bonds in the historical destiny of our country. . . .

In the past our people did not have capable leadership thoroughly determined to lead their fight and struggle successfully. They found such leadership only in the creation of the Albanian Communist Party (today our APL). (*Stormy applause. All rise. Ovation*.) . . .

In the past our people did not have any strong and loyal support in the international arena, aid and support with which to meet successfully the aggression of the imperialists and to liquidate the great socioeconomic and cultural backwardness to which foreign occupation and the rule of reactionary and exploiting classes had doomed Albania. Our people received such support with the triumph of the Great October Socialist Revolution, with the birth of the first socialist state in the world, the glorious Soviet Union. (*Stormy applause*.) . . . With the aid of the glorious Soviet army, which smashed the war machine of Nazi Germany in World War II, it became possible to liberate our country from fascist slavery. The aid and unstinting internationalist support of the Soviet Union after the liberation of the country was the decisive external factor which enabled our country to stand as firm as granite against all the plots of the imperialists and their tools, to overcome all difficulties, and to go securely forward on the road to socialism. Here lies the roots of the deep, everlasting, unbroken friendship of our people with the glorious, fraternal peoples of the Soviet Union. (*Stormy applause*.) . . . Neither the maneuvers of imperialists, nor the intrigues of Tito's renegade band, nor the slanders, pressures, blackmail, and blockade of Nikita Khrushchev have been, are, or will be able to break off this friendship

---

[1] *Diversity in International Communism*, pp. 88–132.

(*Applause*.)   The life-giving Albanian-Soviet friendship will live for ages! In celebrating the forty-fourth anniversary of the October Socialist Revolution, the revolution that shook the old world to its foundations and laid the foundation of a new world, the Party and our people send their very best wishes to the fraternal Soviet people and the Communist Party of the Soviet Union for ever newer and greater victories, for the glory of the great Communist cause. (*Stormy applause*.) . . .

The great historic victories which our people won in the struggle for liberation of the country and for the construction of socialism in a free, independent, and sovereign Albania are due to the internationalist aid and support which the Soviet Union, in the first place, the Chinese People's Republic, and other countries of the socialist camp gave and are giving to our country. The Party and the Albanian people will remain ever grateful for this generous help. This help is a wonderful expression of the eternal friendship which binds our people with the glorious peoples of the Soviet Union, with the great Chinese people, and with all the peoples of the other socialist countries. We shall always cherish this sacred friendship highly, since it is our common strength, a sound guarantee of our invincibility. . . .

The APL recognizes and understands the profound changes that have taken place in the world, the new conditions and phenomena that have appeared. . . .

. . . Correct, revolutionary, Marxist-Leninist conclusions must be drawn from the changes that have occurred in the world—conclusions that do not generate pacifist and reformist illusions, that do not weaken the struggle against imperialism but continually strengthen this just struggle. . . .

. . . Let us consider the problem of the war and peace. Shall I say that the change in the balance of forces in favor of socialism has brought a change in the nature of imperialism, that imperialism is bound hand and foot, that it is not capable of doing anything, of launching wars and undertaking other aggressive actions? Such a conclusion is not only wrong but extremely harmful. Underestimating the forces of the enemy and overestimating our forces leads to relaxing our guard and encourages dangerous adventures, just as underestimating our forces and overestimating the forces of the enemy leads to unfounded concessions, mistakes, and an opportunistic stand.   Proceeding from the actual relationship of forces in the world today, our party has always said and still says that in the question of war and peace two possibilities have to be considered and prepared for: the banning of war, and the launching of war by the imperialists. Our firm conviction that at the present time world war and other imperialistic aggressive wars can be banned rests not at all on the 'good intentions' of the leaders of imperialism but on the colossal economic, political, and military force of the powerful socialist camp, on the unity and struggle of the international working class, on the resolute struggle of all peoples of the world against the imperialist warmongers, on the unity and cohesion of all peace-loving forces. (*Stormy applause*.)

During all the years of its existence, the people's regime, the government of the Albanian People's Republic, has resolutely and consistently followed a line of foreign policy that fully corresponds to the interests of our people and country, to the interests of the defense of national freedom and independence, and to the interests of the whole socialist camp and to the cause of peace and progress of human society. The basis of the foreign policy of the APL has always been and is the continuous strengthening of the ties of friendship, fraternal collaboration, and mutual aid and support with the countries of the socialist camp headed by the Soviet Union; the rendering of support to the anti-imperialist and anti-colonial national liberation struggle of oppressed peoples and nations and the revolutionary struggle of workers in capitalist countries; efforts to ensure relations of peaceful coexistence between the Albanian People's Republic and capitalist countries, especially neighboring countries; efforts to maintain and strengthen peace in the whole world, especially in the Balkan and Adriatic area; unmasking the policy of war and aggression that is followed by imperialist powers, headed by the United States of America, and their partners and tools around our country, such as the Italian imperialists, the monarcho-fascist Greeks, and the Yugoslav revisionists.

In foreign policy, our party and government have always gone arm in arm with the other socialist countries in an effort to maintain and consolidate peace in the world. They have always approved and strongly supported the general line of the foreign policy of the Soviet Union and all the other socialist countries for solving the most important international problems. And this foreign policy of the Albanian People's Republic has always been approved by the Soviet Union and other socialist countries, which have always considered it as a correct policy, favoring our common cause.

But recently N. Khrushchev and his friends sharply changed their attitude towards us, first calling us 'adventurers and warmongers' and then accusing us of 'rapprochement' with imperialism. (*Laughter.*) Those who accuse us have no argument, no single fact, only slander and fiction, to prove that the foreign policy of the Albanian People's Republic has changed. Nothing has changed in our foreign policy. There has been no change in our stand on the problems of war and peace, on the relations with other states, particularly with neighboring states on the struggle against imperialism, and on unmasking Yugoslav revisionists.

The twenty-year life and the revolutionary struggle of the APL refute all these slanders and base fictions which have deeply angered and enraged our people, who have fought and are fighting heroically against imperialism and its lackeys. Those who accuse and slander the APL and its leadership are not able to present a single fact to prove their case, whereas we can present many facts and documents to show clearly their deviation from the Marxist-Leninist position and their wavering in the battle against imperialism. We have never had any illusions about our enemies, we have not embraced and kissed them, we have not flattered them or rubbed elbows with them, we have never bowed before them. (*Stormy applause. All rise. Ovation.*) Our party and government have always maintained a resolute stand, based on Marxist-Leninist principles, in regard to the enemies of peace and socialism; they have harshly and constantly unmasked imperialists, whether they be American or English, French or Italian, and their policy of war and aggression; they have been implacable with regard to the class enemy. They have shown their solidarity and have supported, with all their strength and without wavering, the just cause of peoples who have risen up in a struggle against imperialism. They have always given support to the fraternal peoples of Algeria,

Cuba, the Congo, Laos, etc., in their sacred struggle against imperialism, resolutely condemning all aggressive attempts of imperialism.

For all this 'good' that the Party has done to imperialism during these twenty years (*laughter*), imperialism and its tools have rewarded it with a savage and uninterrupted fight against the Albanian People's Republic, by plots and continuous provocations, by diversions, blackmail, and incessant slanders.

We are accused of being afraid of imperialism (*laughter*), of being afraid to accept responsibility for solving important international problems. The question involved here is the signing of a peace treaty with Germany and settling the West Berlin question. The APL and government of the Albanian People's Republic never have been and are not afraid of imperialism, they never have been and are not afraid of their responsibility as a socialist country and member of the Warsaw Pact, and they have carefully and honorably discharged their international duties. (*Stormy applause*.) The whole world knows the position of the APL and of the government of the Albanian People's Republic on the German question; it has been stated in many well-publicized documents. The APL and the government of the Albanian People's Republic have always supported and now support firmly the efforts of the USSR and the GDR for a peaceful solution of the German problem. The viewpoint of our party and government has been and is that the signing of a peace treaty with Germany and the solution of the West Berlin question on this basis are necessary, long overdue steps that are also in the interest of peace and security in Europe. We have been and are for solving these problems as soon as possible, because any delay only benefits our enemies. The declaration of the Central Committee of the APL on the German question stated directly that 'in any situation and at any dangerous moment we shall fight to the end alongside the Soviet Union and the other fraternal countries, regardless of any sacrifice, and on every occasion, as always, we shall show our solidarity to the end and shall honorably discharge our obligation'. This has been, is, and will be the point of view of our party and government. (*Stormy applause*.)

The question arises: Who is really afraid of the responsibility for solving the German question? Who has dragged it out? We, who have been and are for its solution as soon as possible, or our accusers, who have retreated in this question and have dragged out its resolution from year to year?

Or let us take the problem of disarmament. It is public knowledge that our government has supported the proposal of the Soviet Union for complete and general disarmament, since as long as arms exist and the armaments race continues, as long as there is no complete and general disarmament, there will not be any kind of assurance of the preservation of peace. The Soviet government, together with our government, has proposed making the Balkan and Adriatic area a peace zone, without atomic arms or rocket bases. But the proposal of the Soviet Union and of the socialist countries for complete and general disarmament and for the creation of peace zones was rejected by the imperialist powers. In such a situation, our government has supported and fully supports the decision of the Soviet government for the resumption of nuclear weapons tests as a very important and necessary measure for the guarantee of security of the Soviet Union and of the entire socialist camp, to restrain the imperialist forces, headed by the United States and the Bonn revanchists, who have intensified to the maximum the unrestrained armaments race and the insane preparations for a new world war. We realize that the disarmament problem is a difficult one, that great efforts will be needed for its solution, and that a resolute struggle must be waged without wavering by the socialist countries and by all peace-loving forces to impose the solution on imperialism. But N. Khrushchev, instead of following any such correct road, seeks to disarm a socialist country surrounded by enemies on all sides, the Albanian People's Republic. By weakening the defensive powers of Albania, he harms not only the interests of our country but of the entire socialist camp. And all this is done at a time when the American Sixth Fleet cruises in the Mediterranean like a sea monster, when American rocket bases are established in Greece and Italy, when the NATO forces are feverishly continuing the armaments race, when the imperialists and West German revanchists rattle their sabers and gravely endanger the peace of the world. No fault or responsibility for this falls on the Albanian government. But in any case, N. Krushchev should not have reached the point of openly inciting the imperialists and the various reactionaries against a socialist country such as the Albanian People's Republic. In spite of all this, the defense of the boundaries of Albania is completely secured. (*Stormy applause. All rise. Ovation.*)

In a situation where there exist in the world states with different social systems, the only correct principle for regulating relations among them is the principle of peaceful coexistence, the principle defined by Lenin and applied by Stalin. Our party has always considered and considers that the policy of peaceful coexistence corresponds to the vital interests of all peoples, both of the socialist countries and the capitalist countries, corresponds to the aim of further strengthening the positions of socialism and peace in the whole world. Therefore this principle has been the basis of the relations of our state with the other, nonsocialist states.

It is absurd to accuse our party and socialist state of being against peaceful coexistence. This slander is refuted in all the practical aspects of our state's foreign policy. We do not oppose the principle of peaceful coexistence, but do not agree with some opportunistic views of N. Khrushchev and his followers, who consider peaceful coexistence the general line of the foreign policy of socialist countries, the main road to victory of socialism on a world scale; who for the sake of peaceful coexistence retreat from the struggle to unmask imperialism; who are ready to abandon the political, ideological struggle against the Yugoslav revisionists on the pretext that Yugoslavia supports the Soviet Union in some matters of foreign policy. Such a notion of peaceful coexistence is distorted and anti-Marxist, because it leads to a denial of the class struggle. Correct execution of the policy of peaceful coexistence, by pointing out and unmasking imperialism and its policy of war and aggression, should aid in carrying out the struggle of the working class in capitalist countries and the national liberation movement in colonial and dependent countries. For their part, the successes of the working class and national liberation revolutionary struggle, by narrowing and weakening the positions of imperialism, strengthen the cause of peace and peaceful coexistence. Communist parties in capitalist countries, along with the struggle to impose the policy of peaceful coexistence on the bourgeois governments of their countries, at the same time carry on a class struggle to overthrow the bourgeois regimes and for the transition to socialism according to the concrete conditions in each country. . . .

. . . It is strange that Nikita Khrushchev and his followers demand that we apply peaceful coexistence to our Greek neighbors. They accuse us of not going along with the proposal for disarmament of the Balkan countries; they accuse us of not making efforts toward a 'Balkan understanding'; they join in the chorus of Tito and Karamanlis as though we were the 'warmongers of the Balkans' at the very time when Greece continues to consider itself in a 'state of war' with Albania, when it makes territorial claims against our country and plots to attack Albania, when monarcho-fascist Greece has become a fortress, armed to the teeth by American imperialists, against our socialist country. The accusations of our critics are baseless, since no one in his right mind would think that tiny Albania, surrounded by wolves which for seventeen years in a row have tried to swallow her whole, does not want peace and disarmament.

Everybody knows, and experience has shown, how much monarcho-fascist Greece has disarmed, to what extent the hopes of those who believed in this have been fulfilled; but if we had failed to criticize Nikita Khrushchev (and we made this criticism in a comradely fashion) when he raised the hopes of Sophocles Venizelos for 'the autonomy of southern Albania', it would have been treason on our part. N. Khrushchev did not like our just criticism. This is the least of evils. But he twisted our criticism into a counteraccusation, accusing us of slandering the Soviet Union, which liberated us and protects us. This, of course, is Machiavellian. However, the devil showed his horns again later. When the Americans, Greeks, and Turks were conducting large-scale military maneuvers along the Albanian and Bulgarian borders, N. Khrushchev said in a statement to [C.L.] Sulzberger, a *New York Times* reporter, on September 10, 1961: 'You [Americans] have also established bases in Greece and from there are threatening our ally Bulgaria.' Has not monarcho-fascist Greece also established missile bases against Albania? When did Nikita Khrushchev decide that Albania cannot be an ally of the Soviet Union? This is astounding. Are these trifling matters? Should the First Secretary of the Central Committee of the CPSU and Prime Minister of the USSR, even if he were engaged in mortal combat with socialist Albania, be allowed to say openly to Greek reactionary elements that Albania is not an ally of the Soviet Union and to send President Kennedy the news that 'relations between the Soviet Union and Albania have deteriorated'?

Therefore, according to some, we are the ones who look at things as 'sectarian nationalists', while others, who speculate with the interests of our people, are Marxists. Tomorrow these same critics may make us responsible for the election defeat of the Greek Progressive Party, the EDA. (*Laughter.*) Can these so-called Marxists think that we ought to hand over the keys of our country to the Greek monarcho-fascists so that their line of 'peaceful coexistence' may triumph and power may be taken over in Greece 'in a peaceful and parliamentary way'? (*Laughter.*) No, they cannot expect that of us. Let the so-called Marxists not forget the internationalism of the great APL and the Albanian people in saving tens of thousands of heroes of the Greek people and of the Greek Communist Party who, we are sure, do not spit on the horse after they have crossed the river. (*Stormy applause.*)

Our party and government have followed this foreign policy. These are our views on the problems of present world development. It is precisely for these positions, for these views that they criticize us, that N. Khrushchev attacked us at the XXII Congress of the CPSU. In this way, he first unilaterally brought our differences out into the open, giving weapons to the enemy and taking upon himself a great historical responsibility as a dissenter from the unity of the international Communist movement and the socialist camp. Our APL has never openly aired our differences, it has spoken of them only at party meetings. But now that N. Khrushchev has made them public, our party is obligated to make public its view. (*Stormy applause.*)

In his speeches at the XXII Congress of the CPSU, Nikita Khrushchev, accusing our party, said that Albanian-Soviet relations had deteriorated through the fault of the Albanian leadership. . . . it is absurd and incredible that any-one can believe it was the Albanian leaders who 'without any reason' and 'with dizzying speed' changed their attitude toward the Soviet Union and the CPSU. Equally incredible is the slander that the Albanian leaders have joined the im-perialists and sold out for thirty pieces of silver. (*Laughter.*) . . .

. . . Throughout all its revolutionary history, the APL has always fought and is fighting resolutely against imperialism and its agents; it never has held, is not holding, and will not hold out its hand in the past, present, or future, to anyone for alms, least of all to the imperialists and their allies. (*Stormy applause. All rise. Ovation.*) It has received and is receiving from its friends and brothers of the countries of the socialist camp not alms but only internationalist aid in credit, and it will continue in the future to accept only from those socialist countries that want to offer such aid to it. We beg for alms from no one. If, for one reason or another, N. Khrushchev and his followers do not wish to aid us, they wait in vain for us to go to the imperialists and their allies for 'alms'. Our people have friends and comrades in socialist countries that have not left us and will not leave us in the lurch. (*Stormy applause. All rise. Ovation.*) But indepen-dently of this, we say to N. Khrushchev that the Albanian people and their party will live on grass if necessary, but never will they sell out for thirty pieces of silver because they would rather die on their feet with honor than to live on their knees in dishonor. (*Stormy applause. All rise. Ovation.*) . . .

. . . N. Khrushchev, who talks so much about democratic methods, patience, and internationalism, employs the most anti-Marxist methods against our country, methods which are thoroughly alien to relations between socialist countries. . . .

. . . Thus, in the economic field all credits that the Soviet Union had granted our country for the Third Five-Year Plan were cut, and this was done to sabotage the economic plan of our country; all the Soviet specialists who were working in Albania and whom our economy needs and whom we officially asked to stay were withdrawn unilaterally and without any reason; with an ultimatum that, starting this year, we repay old debts (although, according to existing documents, this should start after 1970), the Soviet side has broken off almost all trade on a clearing basis; scholarships were taken away from all Albanian civilian and military students in the Soviet Union, etc., etc. Economic pressures have been accompanied with pressures and restrictive measures in the military sphere. . . . about a year and a half ago, the Soviet press declared a blockade of silence against Albania. Whereas it does not let the slightest occasion go by to write about any positive word that by chance has escaped from any English lord, the Soviet press has not written a line either about the APL or Albania, as though there did not exist on the face of the earth either the People's Republic of Albania or the Albanian people who are constructing socialism and are fighting for peace, finding themselves in the jaws of the wolf, surrounded on all sides by imperialists and their tools. The icy silence was broken only at the XXII Congress of the CPSU by N. Khrushchev, and it was broken solely and simply to slander and pour out bile on the APL and the Albanian People's Republic.

Some leaders of the socialist countries of Europe have also followed Nikita Khrushchev in these anti-Marxist and hostile actions toward the Albanian people. Altogether they are doing their utmost to isolate Albania economically, and militarily by creating a 'cordon sanitaire' around her. N. Khrushchev forgets that in the century of the triumph of Leninism there can be no 'cordon' to isolate a people and a party that are fighting resolutely for the triumph of socialism and communism: there can be no 'cordon', however organized and strong, that can resist Marxist-Leninist truth. Any 'cordon' will be smashed and its organizers fall in shame! (*Stormy applause. All rise. Ovation.*)

The First Secretary of the Central Committee of the CPSU and the Chairman of the Council of Ministers of the USSR was not satisfied with this. Seeing that all his pressures, blockades, and blackmail did not yield the results he desired, did not bring our party and people to their knees, he openly issued a call from the rostrum of the XXII Congress to overthrow the leaders of the APL with a counter-revolutionary putsch, to liquidate the Party, which is something he refrains from doing even with regard to the governments of capitalist countries, since he considers it meddling in their internal affairs. . . .

Who is really defending the Soviet Union and its prestige? Is it Nikita Khrushchev, who with his own unprincipled attacks and slanders against J. V. Stalin has discredited the glorious Soviet Union, presenting it as a country where savage terror reigned, like Hitler's Germany; or is it the APL, which has defended and is defending the Soviet Union from the savage attacks of imperialist and revisionist propaganda to which Nikita Khrushchev has given arms? Who is defending the Soviet Union and its prestige—Nikita Khrushchev, who by his anti-Marxist activities, attacks, pressures, and blockades against the People's Republic of Albania has given arms to the imperialists to stain the Soviet Union in the eyes of the world, or the APL, which has shown and is showing that his anti-Marxist actions have nothing in common with the internationalist principles and traditions of the glorious Soviet Union and Lenin's great party, that they are an unfortunate and passing illness in their healthy body? . . .

. . . Our party and people, as always, will fight for the cause of socialism and communism, united in the socialist camp, hand in hand with the fraternal peoples of the Soviet Union, with the fraternal Chinese people, with all the peoples in the countries of the socialist camp. . . .

(b) Sino-Soviet Relations

1. Communiqué on the trade talks between the Soviet Union and the People's Republic of China, Moscow, 8 April 1961[1]

Following their preliminary talks in Peking, the Government trade delegations of the People's Republic of China and the USSR held talks in Moscow recently. The talks have concluded successfully.

Taking part in the talks from the Chinese side were: Yeh Chi-Chuang, head of the Chinese Delegation and Minister of Foreign Trade, Li Chiang, Vice-Minister of Foreign Trade, Chou Hua-Min, Assistant Minister of Foreign Trade, Cheng To-Pin, Commercial Counsellor of the Embassy of the People's Republic of China, to the USSR, other members of the delegation and responsible functionaries of the Chinese Ministry of Foreign Trade.

Taking part in the talks from the Soviet side were: N. S. Patolichev, head of the Soviet Delegation and Minister of Foreign Trade, P. N. Kumykin, Vice-Minister of Foreign Trade, M. I. Sladkovsky, Director of the Eastern Department of the Ministry of Foreign Trade, I. A. Eremin, Soviet Trade Representative to the People's Republic of China, other members of the Soviet delegation and responsible functionaries of the Ministry of Foreign Trade of the USSR.

N. S. Khrushchev, First Secretary of the Central Committee of the Communist Party of the Soviet Union and Chairman of the Council of Ministers of the USSR, received the Government trade delegation of the People's Republic of China. The meeting between the delegation and Khrushchev took place in an atmosphere of cordial, fraternal friendship. Khrushchev told the delegation the achievements made by the Soviet Union in the fields of economy, science and technology and the measures taken by the Central Committee of the Communist Party of the Soviet Union and the Soviet Government for the further enhancement of agriculture.

Speaking of the trade talks which took place successfully, Khrushchev was firmly convinced that the talks would facilitate the further consolidation of the close economic and trade relations between the People's Republic of China and the Soviet Union and would contribute to the further strengthening of the fraternal friendship of the two countries.

Leader of the Government trade delegation of the People's Republic of China Yeh Chi-Chuang conveyed the fraternal regards of comrade Mao Tse-Tung, Chairman of the Central Committee of the Chinese Communist Party, comrade Liu-Shao-Chi, Chairman of the People's Republic of China, and comrade Chou En-Lai, Premier of the State Council, to N. S. Khrushchev, members of the Presidium of the Central Committee of the Communist Party of the Soviet Union and the Soviet Government, and expressed thanks for the warm, friendly reception accorded to the Government trade delegation of the People's Republic of China.

N. S. Khrushchev also requested comrade Yeh Chi-Chung to convey to comrade Mao Tse-Tung, comrade Liu Shao-Chi, comrade Chou en-Lai and other Leaders of the Chinese Communist Party and Government the fraternal

[1] *H.N.A.*, 9 April 1961.

regards of the Central Committee of the Communist Party of the Soviet Union, the Soviet Government and himself.

As a result of the talks conducted between the Government delegations of the People's Republic of China and the Soviet Union in the spirit of cooperation and full mutual understanding, the volumes of goods to be supplied mutually were agreed upon and a protocol on goods exchange between China and the Soviet Union for 1961 was signed on April 7th, 1961.

The agreed goods exchange volumes include many kinds of goods needed by the national economy of the two countries.

As in previous years, the People's Republic of China will supply the USSR in 1961 non-ferrous metal ores, tin, mercury, lead, pig iron, cement, tung oil, chemicals, wool, raw silk, tea, woollen and silk piecegoods, products of sewing industry and knit-wear, other industrial and handicraft products.

The Soviet Union will supply the People's Republic of China with forging and pressing equipment, power-generating and electrical-technical equipment, oil equipment, metal-cutting machine tools, excavators, pumps and compressors, tractors, motor vehicles, oil products, ferrous and non-ferrous rolled metals, chemicals, and other traditional goods which the Soviet Union exports to the People's Republic of China.

During the talks, both sides also discussed the question concerning the unpaid account of the People's Republic of China to the Soviet Union in 1960 trade as a result of the serious natural calamities suffered by the People's Republic of China in agriculture. The Soviet side expressed full understanding for the temporary difficulties experienced by the People's Republic of China and proposed to the Government of the People's Republic of China the above-mentioned account be paid within five years, in instalments and without interest.

The Chinese side accepted with gratitude the proposal that the Soviet Union will, before the end of August this year, supply the People's Republic of China 500,000 tons of sugar in the form of credits. The sugar will be repaid between 1964 to 1967 interest-free.

The two sides, in a friendly and fraternal atmosphere, also agreed on certain other questions concerning the further development of trade relations between China and the Soviet Union.

The protocol on exchange of goods between China and the Soviet Union and other agreements and documents were signed for the Chinese side by Yeh Chi-Chuang, Minister of Foreign Trade of the People's Republic of China; for the Soviet side by N. S. Patolichev, Minister of Foreign Trade of the Soviet Union.

Present at the signing ceremony, on the Chinese side, were Chang Teh-Chun, Charge d'Affaires ad interim of the Chinese Embassy in the Soviet Union, Li Chiang, Chinese Vice-Minister of Foreign Trade, Chou Hua-Min, Assistant Minister of Foreign Trade, Cheng To-Pin, Commercial Counsellor of the Chinese Embassy in the Soviet Union, and other members of the Chinese delegation; on the Soviet side, comrade A. N. Kosygin and D. S. Polyansky, V. Novikov, Vice-Chairman of the Council of Ministers of the Soviet Union, S. A. Skachkov, Chairman of the State Foreign Economic Relations Committee under the Council of Ministers, G. M. Pushkin, S. A. Borisov,

P. N. Kumikin and I. F. Semichastnov, Vice-Ministers of the Soviet Union, M. I. Sladkovsky, Director of the Eastern Department of the USSR Foreign Trade Ministry, I. A. Eremin, Soviet Commercial Representative to China, and other members of the Soviet delegation.

The Government trade delegation of the People's Republic of China visited places of historical interest in Moscow. The Exhibition of Achievements in the Soviet National Economy, many industrial enterprises and buildings, and saw art performances of the theatres in the capital.

The delegation had paid homage to the Lenin-Stalin mausoleum and laid wreaths there.

At the invitation of the Soviet Foreign Trade Minister N. S. Patolichev, the Government trade delegation of the People's Republic of China will visit several areas and cities in the Soviet Union to understand the achievements in building Communism by the Soviet People and their life.

(c) North Korea between Russia and China

1. Treaty of Friendship, Co-operation and Mutual Assistance between the Soviet Union and the Democratic People's Republic of Korea, Moscow, 6 July 1961[1]

The Presidium of the Supreme Soviet of the Union of Soviet Socialist Republics and the Presidium of the Supreme People's Assembly of the Korean Democratic People's Republic.

Striving to develop and strengthen the friendly relations between the Soviet Union and the Korean Democratic People's Republic, relations based on the principle of socialist internationalism,

Wishing to contribute to the maintenance and consolidation of peace and security in the Far East and throughout the whole world in accordance with the aims and principles of the United Nations,

Fully determined to render assistance and support to each other in case of an armed attack by some state or a coalition of states on one of the Contracting Parties,

Being certain that the strengthening of friendship, good-neighbourliness and cooperation between the Soviet Union and the Korean Democratic People's Republic meets the vital interests of the peoples of both states and will in the best way be conducive to their further economic and cultural development,

Have resolved with this end in view to conclude this Treaty and have appointed as their plenipotentiaries:

The Presidium of the Supreme Soviet of the Union of Soviet Socialist Republics—Nikita Sergeyevich Khrushchev, Chairman of the Council of Ministers of the U.S.S.R.;

The Presidium of the Supreme People's Assembly of the Korean Democratic People's Republic—Kim Il Sung, Chairman of the Cabinet of Ministers of the K.D.P.R.

[1] *Soviet News*, 8 July 1961.

Both plenipotentiaries, after exchanging their credentials, which were found to be in due form and full order, agreed on the following:

Article I

The Contracting Parties declare that they will continue in the future as well to take part in all international actions aimed at ensuring peace and security in the Far East and throughout the world and will make their contribution to the cause of the accomplishment of these noble tasks.

In the event of one of the Contracting Parties becoming the object of an armed attack by some state or a coalition of states and thus finding itself in a state of war, the other Contracting Party will immediately render it military and other assistance with all means at its disposal.

Article II

Each of the Contracting Parties undertake to conclude no alliance or to participate in no coalitions or actions and measures directed against the other Contracting Party.

Article III

The Contracting Parties will consult each other on all important international issues affecting the interests of both states, being guided by the striving to contribute to the consolidation of peace and general security.

Article IV

Both Contracting Parties undertake, in the spirit of friendship and co-operation and in accordance with the principles of equality and also mutual respect for state sovereignty, territorial integrity and non-interference in the integrity and non-interference in the internal affairs of each other, to develop and strengthen the economic and cultural contacts between the Union of Soviet Socialist Republics and the Korean Democratic People's Republic, to render each other all possible assistance and carry out the necessary co-operation in the economic and cultural fields.

Article V

Both Contracting Parties maintain that the unification of Korea must be carried out on a peaceful and democratic basis and that such a settlement is in line both with the national interests of the Korean people and the cause of maintaining peace in the Far East.

Article VI

The Treaty goes into force on the day of the exchange of the instruments of ratification, which will take place in Pyongyang.

The Treaty remains in force for a period of 10 years. If one of the Contracting Parties does not declare, one year before the expiration of this term, its desire to denounce the treaty, it will continue to remain in force for the next five years and will be prolonged in accordance with this rule.

2. Treaty of Friendship, Co-operation and Mutual Assistance between the People's Republic of China and the Democratic People's Republic of Korea, Peking, 11 July 1961[1]

The Chairman of the People's Republic of China and the Presidium of the Supreme People's Assembly of the Democratic People's Republic of Korea, Determined, in accordance with Marxism-Leninism and the principle of proletarian internationalism and on the basis of mutual respect for State sovereignty territorial integrity, mutual non-aggression, non-interference in each other's internal affairs, equality and mutual benefit, and mutual assistance and support, to make every effort to further strengthen and develop the fraternal relations of friendship, cooperation and mutual assistance between the People's Republic of China and the Democratic People's Republic of Korea, to jointly guard the security of the two peoples, and to safeguard and consolidate the peace of Asia and the world, and deeply convinced that the development and strengthening of the relations of friendship, cooperation and mutual assistance between the two countries accord not only with the fundamental interests of the two peoples but also with the interests of the peoples all over the world, have decided for this purpose to conclude the present treaty and appointed as their respective plenipotentiaries:

The Chairman of the People's Republic of China: Chou En-Lai, Premier of the State Council of the People's Republic of China.

The Presidium of the Supreme People's Assembly of the Democratic People's Republic of Korea: Kim Il Sung, Premier of the Cabinet of the Democratic People's Republic of Korea.

Who, having examined each other's full powers and found them in good and due form, have agreed upon the following:

Article One

The Contracting Parties will continue to make every effort to safeguard the peace of Asia and the world and the security of all peoples.

Article Two

The Contracting Parties undertake jointly to adopt all measures to prevent aggression against either of the Contracting Parties by any state. In the event of one of the Contracting Parties being subjected to the armed attack by any state or several states jointly and thus being involved in a state of war, the other Contracting Party shall immediately render military and other assistance by all means at its disposal.

Article Three

Neither Contracting Party shall conclude any alliance directed against the other Contracting Party or take part in any bloc or in any action or measure directed against the other Contracting Party.

Article Four

The Contracting Parties will continue to consult with each other on all important international questions of common interest to the two countries.

[1] *H.N.A.*, 12 July 1961.

Article Five

The Contracting Parties, on the principles of mutual respect for sovereignty, non-interference in each other's internal affairs, equality and mutual benefit and in the spirit of friendly cooperation, will continue to render each other every possible economic and technical aid in the cause of socialist construction of the two countries and will continue to consolidate and develop economic, cultural, and scientific and technical cooperation between the two countries.

Article Six

The Contracting Parties hold that the unification of Korea must be realised along peaceful and democratic lines and that such a solution accords exactly with the national interests of the Korean people and the aim of preserving peace in the Far East.

Article Seven

The present Treaty is subject to ratification and shall come into force on the day of exchange of Instruments of Ratification, which will take place in Pyongyang.

The present Treaty will remain in force until the Contracting Parties agree on its amendment or termination.

(d) Soviet Foreign Policy

1. Speech of the Prime Minister of the Soviet Union, Mr. Khrushchev, Moscow, 6 January 1961[1] (extracts)

Now that a world socialist system has come into being and the anti-imperialist, national liberation revolutions are on a mighty upward swing, it is necessary to determine the further course and prospects of world development. This cannot be done unless there is a profound understanding of the essence, content and character of the decisive tasks of the present epoch.

The question of the character of the epoch is not an abstract, narrow theoretical question. Inseparably linked with it are the general strategy and tactics of world communism and of each Communist Party. . . .

In defining the essence and character of the present epoch as a whole, it is absolutely essential that we should be clear about the main peculiarities and distinguishing features of its present stage. The period after the October Revolution, seen from the point of view of its chief motive forces, is clearly divided into two stages. One of them began with the victory of the October Revolution. It was, to use Lenin's phrase, the period of the establishment and development of the national dictatorship of the proletariat, that is to say, a dictatorship of the proletariat within the national confines of Russia alone.

Although the Soviet Union has been exerting a tremendous influence on international affairs ever since it came into being, imperialism largely determined the course and character of international relations. But even at that time imperialism proved to be incapable of crushing the Soviet Union, of preventing

[1] *Soviet News*, 21 January 1961.

it from becoming a mighty industrial power, a bulwark of progress and civilisation, a centre of attraction for all the forces combating imperialist oppression and fascist enslavement.

The second stage in the development of the present epoch is bound up with the emergence of the world socialist system. It has been a revolutionary process of historic significance. The October Revolution broke one link in the imperialist chain. Then the imperialist chain was broken all along the line. In the past, we spoke of breaking one or more links in the imperialist chain, while at the present time that all-embracing chain of imperialism no longer really exists. The dictatorship of the working class has gone beyond the confines of a single country and become an international force. Imperialism has lost not only the countries where socialism has triumphed. It is rapidly losing nearly all its colonies. Naturally, as a result of such blows and losses the general crisis of capitalism has become much more acute, and the balance of forces in the world has changed radically in favour of socialism.

The principal distinguishing feature of our time is the fact that the world socialist system is becoming the decisive factor in the development of human society. This also finds direct expression in the sphere of international relations. The prerequisites have arisen in present conditions for socialism to determine to an ever greater degree the character, methods and trends of international relations. That does not mean that imperialism is an 'insignificant factor' which can be ignored. Not at all. Imperialism is still very strong. It controls a powerful military machine. . . .

At the present time imperialism has, in peacetime, built up a gigantic war machine and a ramified system of military blocs and has subordinated its economy to the arms race. The American imperialists want to bring the whole world under their sway, and threaten mankind with a rocket and nuclear war. imperialism is increasingly marked by decay and parasitism. In their evaluation of the prospects of international development Marxist-Leninists do not, and must not have any illusions with regard to imperialism.

The facts illustrating the policy of barefaced acts of provocation and aggression pursued by the imperialists are simply innumerable. That is nothing new. The novel factor is that all the imperialist intrigues are not only being conclusively exposed, but also firmly repelled, and attempts made by the imperialists to start local wars have been thwarted.

The present balance of world forces enables the socialist camp and the other forces of peace, for the first time in history, to set themselves the entirely realistic task of preventing the imperialists from starting a world war—for fear of seeing their own system destroyed.

In connection with the possibility of preventing a world war, I should like to deal with the prospects of the further development of the general crisis of capitalism. It is common knowledge that both the First and the Second World Wars had a tremendous influence on the rise and sharpening of the general crisis of capitalism. Does this lead to the inference that world war is an indispensable condition for the further intensification of the general crisis of capitalism? That inference would be utterly incorrect, because it distorts the Marxist-Lenninist theory of socialist revolution and inverts the true causes of revolution. A proletarian revolution is not the result solely of military cataclysms; first and foremost, it is the effect of the development of the class struggle and of the internal contradictions of capitalism. . . .

There is every reason to infer that both economically and in the sphere of international affairs the principal capitalist power has entered a phase of mounting difficulties and crises—the phase of its decline.

As for the economy of the other capitalist countries, it, too, is characterised by increasing instability.

Although at the present time the capitalist world is not split into two imperialist camps, as was the case on the eve of the two world wars, it is none the less far from being united and is being rent by bitter internal conflicts. The display window of so-called 'Atlantic solidarity' screens an unprepossessing picture of internal strife and conflict and increasing resistance to United States leadership and dictation. The rebirth of German militarism and revenge-seeking in the heart of Europe is renewing the tangle of Anglo-German, Franco-German and other imperialist contradictions. One has only to compare the present state of capitalism with what it was at the end of the Second World War, to see clearly that the general crisis of capitalism has become much deeper. . . . 'a new stage has begun in the development of the general crisis of capitalism'. A peculiarity of this stage is that it arose, not owing to world war, but in competition and struggle between the two systems, at a time of a growing change in the balance of forces in favour of socialism and a marked aggravation of all the contradictions of imperialism, at a time when the successful struggle of the peace forces to maintain and promote peaceful co-existence had prevented the imperialists from wrecking world peace by their aggressive actions, in an atmosphere of increasing struggle by the broad masses of the people for democracy, national liberation and socialism. This is an indication of the further advance and aggravation of the general crisis of capitalism.

Our comrades-in-arms in the Communist Parties of the capitalist countries take this into consideration when charting their further tactical line in the struggle for the working-class cause. And we can confidently say that the immediate future holds new successes in store for the joint forces of world socialism, the working class and the national liberation movement. . . .

The countries of the world socialist system are drawing ever closer to one another; their co-operation in all fields of endeavour is growing. This is a natural development. There are no insoluble contradictions between the socialist countries, nor can there be any. The more developed and economically stronger countries are rendering disinterested fraternal assistance to the economically less developed countries. For instance, more than 500 enterprises have been built in fraternal socialist countries with Soviet help. The loans and credits granted by us to these countries exceed 7,800 million roubles. At the same time we consider it our duty to note that the fraternal socialist countries, for their part, are assisting in the development of the Soviet economy. . . .

The consolidation of the common economic basis of the world socialist system and the creation of the material basis for the more or less simultaneous transition of all the peoples of the socialist system to communism, will proceed all the faster the more fully the internal resources of each country of this system and the advantages of the socialist international division of labour are utilised and the basis provided for catching up in the level of economic development. . . . the problem of preventing a thermonuclear world war is the most burning and vital problem for mankind.

The attitude of the Communist Party of the Soviet Union to the questions of war and peace is known to all. It has been expounded on more than one occasion in the decisions of its congresses and in other party documents.

Wars came into being after society broke up into classes. This means that the grounds for all wars will be completely abolished only after the division of society into hostile, antagonistic classes has been abolished. With the victory of the working class throughout the world, and with the triumph of socialism, which will destroy all social and national causes giving rise to wars, mankind will be able to rid itself of that terrible scourge.

Today we must distinguish between the following kinds of war: world wars, local wars, and wars of liberation, or popular uprisings. This is necessary in order to work out correct tactics in regard to these wars.

Let us begin with the problem of *world wars*. Communists are the most resolute opponents of world wars, as they are of wars between states in general. Only the imperialists need such wars to seize foreign territories, to enslave and plunder the peoples. Before the world socialist camp came into existence, the working class was unable to exert a decisive influence on deciding the question of whether there would be a world war or not. In those circumstances the finest representatives of the working class put forward the slogan of turning imperialist war into a civil war, that is to say, of the working class and all the working people using the situation to take power. Such a situation developed during the First World War, and it was utilised in a classical way by the Bolshevik Party, by Lenin.

In our time the conditions are entirely different. The world socialist camp, with its powerful economy and armed forces exerts an ever-growing influence on deciding questions of war and peace. To be sure, acute contradictions and antagonisms between the imperialist countries, and an urge to profit at the expense of others who are weaker, exist even now. However, the imperialists are compelled to heed the Soviet Union and the entire socialist camp, and are afraid to start war between themselves. They try to tone down the differences existing among them. They have created military blocs and have involved many capitalist countries in them. In spite of the fact that those blocs are rent by internal struggles, their members are united, as they themselves admit, by their hatred of communism and, naturally, by the common nature and aspirations of the imperialists.

In present-day conditions wars between the capitalist, imperialist countries are not the most probable, although such an eventuality should not be discounted either. The imperialists are preparing war chiefly against the socialist countries, above all against the Soviet Union, the most powerful of the socialist states. They would like to undermine our might and thereby restore the former rule of monopoly capital.

Our task is to raise insurmountable obstacles to war being started by the imperialists. Our possibilities of curbing the warmongers are increasing and we can, therefore, avert a world war. It stands to reason that we cannot fully preclude war since there exist imperialist countries, but it is now much more difficult for the imperialists to start a war than it was previously, before the emergence of the powerful socialist camp. The imperialists can start a war, but they are forced to give thought to its consequences.

I have had occasion to say that even a maniac like Hitler, had he known how utterly his bloody venture would fail, had he known that he himself would have to commit suicide, would have thought twice before starting a war against the Soviet Union. Yet there were only two socialist countries at that time—the Soviet Union and the Mongolian People's Republic. However, we defeated the aggressors, using also the contradictions between the imperialist states.

Today the situation is entirely different. The imperialist camp is now opposed by the socialist countries, which constitute a mighty force. It would be wrong to belittle the strength of the socialist camp, its influence on world developments and, consequently, on deciding the question of whether there is to be war or not. Now that there is a mighty socialist camp possessing powerful armed forces, the peoples can undoubtedly prevent war and thereby ensure peaceful co-existence, if only they rally all their forces for an active struggle against the bellicose imperialists.

Now about *local war*. There is much talk in the imperialist camp today about local wars, and the imperialists are even making small-calibre atomic weapons to be used in such wars. A special theory on local wars has been devised. Is that mere chance? Of course not. Certain imperialist groups fear that a world war might end in complete failure for capitalism, and therefore bank on local wars.

There have been local wars in the past and they may break out again. But the opportunities for starting even such wars are dwindling. A small-scale imperialist war, no matter who among the imperialists starts it, may develop into a thermo-nuclear world war, a rocket war. We must therefore fight against both world and local wars.

An example of a local war started by imperialists was the aggression of Britain, France and Israel against Egypt. . . .

I have said that local wars may recur. It is therefore our task to be always on the alert, to summon the forces of the socialist camp, and also the peoples of other countries and all peaceloving forces, to prevent wars of aggression. If the peoples of all countries are united and rallied, if they struggle untiringly and join forces, both within each country and on an international scale, wars can be prevented.

Now for *wars of national liberation*. An example of such a war is the armed struggle of the Viet Namese people, or the war of the Algerian people, now in its seventh year.

These wars began as uprisings of colonial peoples against their oppressors, and developed into guerrilla wars.

There will be wars of liberation as long as imperialism exists, as long as colonialism exists. They are revolutionary wars. Such wars are not only per-missible but inevitable, for the colonialists do not of their own free will grant independence to peoples. The peoples can therefore win their freedom and independence only through struggle, including armed struggle.

Why was it that the United States imperialists, who were eager to help the French colonialists, did not venture to intervene directly in the war in Viet Nam. They did not do so because they knew that if they gave France armed assistance, Viet Nam would receive the same kind of assistance from China, the Soviet Union and other socialist countries, and that this could develop into a world war. The outcome of the war is known—North Viet Nam won.

A similar war is being waged in Algeria. What kind of war is it? It is an uprising of the Arab people against the French colonialists. It has assumed the form of a guerrilla war. The imperialists of the U.S.A. and Britain are helping their French allies with arms. Moreover, they have allowed France, a party to N.A.T.O., to transfer troops from Europe to fight against the Algerian people. The Algerian people, too, receive assistance from neighbouring and other countries which sympathise with their love of freedom. But that is a war of liberation, a war of independence waged by the people. It is a sacred war. We recognise such wars; we have helped and shall go on helping the peoples fighting for their freedom.

Or take Cuba. There was a war there too. But it, too, started as an uprising against an internal tyrannical régime, backed by United States imperialism. Batista was a puppet of the United States and the United States helped him actively. However, the U.S.A. did not directly intervene with its armed forces in that war. Led by Fidel Castro, the people of Cuba won.

Can such wars recur? Yes, they can. Can such uprisings recur? Yes, they can. But they are wars in the nature of popular uprisings. Can conditions in other countries reach a point where the people's patience is stretched to the limit and they take up arms? Yes, they can. What should our attitude be with regard to such uprisings? It should be most favourable. These uprisings must not be identified with wars between states, with local wars, because the insurgent people are fighting for their right to self-determination, for their social and independent national development; these uprisings are directed against decayed reactionary régimes, against the colonialists. Communists support such just wars fully and without reservations, and march in the vanguard of the peoples fighting for liberation.

Comrades, mankind has reached a stage in history when it is in a position to solve problems that previous generations were not equal to solving. This also applies to the most burning of all problems—the problem of preventing a world war.

The working class, which today governs a vast area of the world and in time will rule the whole world, cannot allow the doomed forces to drag hundreds of millions of people into the grave with them. For a world war in present-day conditions would be waged with rockets and nuclear weapons, that is to say, would be the most devastating war in history.

Among the hydrogen bombs already tested there are bombs each of which is several times more powerful than all the explosives used in the Second World War and, indeed, ever since mankind has been in existence. Scientists have estimated that the explosion of one hydrogen bomb in an industrial area can kill up to 1,500,000 people at once and bring death to another 400,000 people through the resultant radiation. Even a medium hydrogen bomb would be enough to wipe out a large city. British scientists have arrived at the conclusion that four megaton bombs, one each on London, Birmingham, Lancashire and Yorkshire, would kill at least 20 million people.

According to data supplied by United States experts to the Senate, the losses to be expected in the United States in 24 hours of nuclear war would total from 50 to 75 million people. The well-known American physicist, Linus Pauling, says that the areas likely to receive powerful nuclear blows are inhabited by a total of about a thousand million people and that 500 to 750 million people may perish within 60 days of an atomic blow. Nuclear war would also bring untold calamities to the peoples of those countries not directly bombed; in particular, many millions would die as a result of the disastrous effects of radiation.

We know that if imperialist madmen began a world war the peoples would wipe out capitalism. But we are definitely against war, primarily because we are concerned with the destinies of mankind, with its present and future. We know that the first to suffer in the event of war would be the working people and their vanguard—the working class.

We remember how Lenin put the question of the destiny of the working class. In the early years following the revolution, when the world's first state of workers and peasants was in a ring of fire, he taught that 'if we save the working man, the main productive force of mankind, that is, the worker, we shall regain everything, but we shall perish if we fail to save him. . . .' (*Collected Works, vol. 29, pp. 334–335, Russian edition*.)

There exists in the world today, not one state of workers and peasants, but a whole system of socialist states. It is our historic duty to safeguard peace and the peaceful development of this great creation of the international working class. The victory of socialism on a world scale, inevitable by virtue of the laws of historical development, is no longer far off. War is not needed for this victory.

A sober-minded appraisal of the inevitable consequences of nuclear war is indispensable for the consistent pursuit of the policy of averting war and mobilising the masses of the people to fulfil this task. For recognition by the masses of the people of the danger of a devastating war strengthens their will to fight against war. It is necessary, therefore, to warn the people against the highly dangerous consequences of a new world war and thereby to rouse their righteous anger against those who are plotting this crime. The possibility of averting war does not come from heaven. Peace cannot be pleaded for. It can be secured only by an active, purposeful struggle. That is why we have been waging this struggle, and will continue to wage it. . . .

The policy of peaceful co-existence is thus, as far as its social content is concerned, a form of intense economic, political and ideological struggle between the proletariat and the aggressive forces of imperialism in the world arena.

The struggle against imperialism can succeed only if its aggressive actions are firmly resisted. The imperialist adventurers cannot be stopped by mere admonition. There is only one way in which they can be curbed: continuous promotion of the economic, political and military power of the socialist countries, vigorous consolidation and reinforcement of the world revolutionary movement, and mobilisation of the people for the struggle to ward off the war danger.

The central committee of the C.P.S.U. and the Soviet government will persevere in doing everything to increase the military might of our country, since the imperialists are continuing the arms race.

In rebuffing the aggressive actions of imperialism, our party and government always display firmness and self-control. In upholding the interests of the socialist camp, we invariably strive to direct developments in such a way as not to allow imperialists provocateurs to start a new world war.

We see it as our task to expose the aggressive nature of all the military-political groupings of the imperialists, such as N.A.T.O., S.E.A.T.O. and Cento, and to work for their isolation and eventual abolition. We have repeatedly declared that we are prepared on this condition to abolish the Warsaw Treaty Organisation. All the peoples of the world stand to gain from the abolition of military groupings.

This would be a major and real contribution to peace and to creating a sounder international atmosphere, and a great achievement of the policy of peaceful co-existence. All their efforts notwithstanding, the imperialists have in recent times failed to draw a single new state into their military blocs. It is significant that all the new independent states have declared their intention to pursue a policy of non-participation in military blocs.

Of special importance for the promotion of peace in Europe, and not only in Europe, is the struggle against revived West German militarism. The Soviet Union is waging this struggle together with the German Democratic Republic, Poland, Czechoslovakia and other socialist countries along various lines, the most important of them being the struggle for a peace treaty. The initiative of the socialist states in putting forward a programme for the peaceful settlement of the German question and the solution, on this basis, of the problem of West Berlin, has done much to unmask the United States, the Federal Republic of Germany and the other N.A.T.O. countries as opponents of a *détente*. The international position of the German Democratic Republic—the outpost of socialism in Western Europe—has been strengthened.

The positions of the United States, Britain and France have proved to be especially vulnerable in West Berlin. These powers still try to cling to the old positions, but they cannot fail to realise that the occupation régime in that city will end sooner or later.

It is necessary to continue, step by step, to bring aggressive-minded imperialists to their senses, to compel them to reckon with the real situation. And if they balk, we shall take resolute measures, we shall sign a peace treaty with the German Democratic Republic, for we are fully determined to conclude a German peace treaty, at long last, to pull out of the heart of Europe the thorn that the occupation régime in West Berlin is.

Comrades, if prevention of a new war is *the* question of our day, disarmament provides the most radical way to it. The meeting of Marxist-Leninist parties has declared that the realisation of the Soviet programme for general and complete disarmament would be of historic importance to the future of mankind.

Our struggle for disarmament is *not* a tactical move. We sincerely want disarmament.

The struggle for disarmament is a most important factor in preventing war. It is an effective factor in the fight against imperialism. In this fight the socialist camp has the majority of mankind on its side.

When we advance the slogan of struggle for 'a world without weapons and without wars', we bear in mind, of course, that in the present conditions, when two differing world social systems exist, there are still forces in the imperialist camp, and quite strong forces at that, which not only refuse to support this slogan but are waging a struggle against it.

The question of the struggle for communism is a class question. In the case of the struggle for peace, that is a problem whose solution may unite not only the forces of the working class, the peasantry and the petty bourgeoisie, but even that part of the bourgeoisie which sees the real danger of thermo-nuclear war.

The fight for disarmament is an active fight against imperialism, for narrowing its war potential. The peoples must do everything to achieve the prohibition and destruction of nuclear weapons and all other types of weapons of mass annihilation. Peace will then be ensured and the peoples will secure most favourable prospects for modelling their lives in keeping with their wishes and interests.

A primary condition for progress in disarmament is the mobilisation of the people and their growing pressure on the imperialist governments.

Two trends are to be observed in the policy of the capitalist camp in relation to the socialist countries: the 'bellicose-aggressive' and the 'moderate-sober'. Lenin drew attention to the need for establishing contacts with those circles of the bourgeoisie which gravitate towards pacifism, 'be it even of the poorest kind'. He said that in the struggle to preserve peace we must also use 'sensible representatives of the bourgeoisie'.

The correctness of these words is confirmed by current events as well. Fear for the future of capitalism haunts the ruling classes of the imperialist camp. The more reactionary circles are showing increasing nervousness and an inclination to adventurist practices and aggression, with the help of which they hope to mend their shaky affairs. At the same time, there are also forces among the ruling circles of these countries which realise the danger that a new war presents to capitalism. Hence the two trends: one towards war, the other towards accepting, in one form or another, the idea of peaceful co-existence.

The socialist countries take both of these trends into account in their policy. They work for negotiations and agreements with the capitalist countries on the basis of constructive proposals and promote personal contacts between statesmen of the socialist and capitalist countries. Every opportunity should be used, as before, to expose the 'cold warriors', those who want to keep up the arms race, and to show the masses of the people that it is really in good faith that the socialist countries are fighting to safeguard world peace.

The knowledge that it is the communists who advocate basing relations between countries upon the principle of peaceful co-existence, the knowledge that it is they who are the most ardent and consistent fighters for peace, is taking root in the minds of the peoples. We must take pride in the fact that peace and communism are being increasingly associated in the minds of the peoples.

The communists thus believe that if all the progressive and peaceloving forces of modern times—the socialist countries, the international working class, the national liberation movement, the newly-established national states, and all

D.I.A.–K

peace champions—vigorously attack the forces of war, they can fetter them and prevent a new military world catastrophe. More sections of the population must be drawn into the struggle for peace every day, overcoming the passive attitude which unfortunately prevails among some sections of society in bourgeois countries.

Comrades, the peoples that have gained national independence have become another mighty force in the struggle for peace and social progress.

The national liberation movement is striking more and more telling blows at imperialism, helping to reinforce peace and speeding the development of mankind along the path of social progress. At present, Asia, Africa and Latin America are the most important seats of revolutionary struggle against imperialism. Some 40 countries have won national independence since the war. Nearly 1,500 million people have cast off colonial slavery.

The national liberation movement is an anti-imperialist movement. Imperialism has become much weaker with the collapse of the colonial system. Vast territories and large masses of people have ceased, or are ceasing, to serve as a reserve for it, as a source of cheap raw materials and cannon fodder. Asian, African and Latin-American countries, supported by the socialist countries and all progressive forces of the world, are inflicting defeats upon the imperialist powers and coalitions more and more frequently. . . .

The successes of the national liberation movement are due in large measure to the victories of socialism and, in turn, strengthen the international positions of socialism in the struggle against imperialism. It is this truly Leninist conception of these historical processes that forms the basis for the policy of the Communist Parties and socialist countries, a policy aimed at strengthening the close alliance with the peoples who are fighting for independence or have already won it.

Bourgeois and revisionist politicians allege that the national liberation movement develops independently of the struggle which the working class wages for socialism and independently of support from the socialist countries, and that the colonialists themselves bestow freedom on the peoples of the former colonies. These fabrications are used to isolate the newly-independent states from the socialist camp and prove that they must play the role of a 'third force' in the international arena instead of opposing imperialism. Needless to say, this is an outright falsehood. . . .

The imperialist powers, above all the United States, are doing their utmost to tie the countries that have cast off the colonial yoke to their system and thereby strengthen the positions of world capitalism, to supply it, as bourgeois ideologists put it, with fresh blood, to rejuvenate and consolidate it. If we look the facts in the face, we have to admit that the imperialists have powerful economic levers to exert pressure on the newly-free countries. They still succeed in enmeshing some politically independent countries in the web of economic dependence. Now that it is no longer possible to establish outright colonial régimes, the imperialists resort to disguised forms and methods of enslaving and plundering the countries that have attained freedom. At the same time, the colonial powers back internal reactionary forces everywhere in countries which recently achieved freedom; they try to set up puppet dictatorial régimes in these countries and to involve them in aggressive blocs. Although there are sharp contradictions between the imperialist countries, they often take joint action against the national liberation movement. . . .

The correct application of Marxist-Leninist theory in the newly-free countries consists precisely in seeking forms that take account of the pecularities of the economic, political and cultural life of the peoples in order to unite all the sound forces of the nation, to secure the leading role of the working class in the national front, in the struggle for the resolute destruction of the roots of imperialism and the remnants of feudalism, for clearing the way for the ultimate movement towards socialism.

Today, when imperialist reaction is striving to foist the policy of anti-communism on the young independent states, particular importance is attached to the truthful explanation of the communist views and ideals. Communists support the general democratic measures of the national governments. At the same time, they explain to the masses of the people that these measures are far from being socialist.

To no one else are the aspirations of the peoples who are smashing the fetters of colonialism as near and as understandable as to the working people of the socialist countries, to the communists of the whole world.

Our very world outlook and the interests of working mankind for which we are fighting, impel us to do our best to ensure that the peoples take the correct road to progress, to the flowering of their material and spiritual forces. By our policy we must strengthen the peoples' confidence in the socialist countries.

The aid given by the U.S.S.R. and other socialist countries to the countries which have won independence pursues but one aim—to help strengthen the position of these countries in the struggle against imperialism, to promote the development of their national economy and the improvement of the peoples' life. . . .

The internationalist duty of the victorious working class consists in helping the people of the economically underdeveloped countries to smash the chains of colonial slavery to the last link and render them all-round aid in their struggle against imperialism, for the right to self-determination and independent development. However, it does not at all follow that socialist help exerts no influence on the prospects of the further development of countries which have recently achieved freedom.

The Soviet Union has been and remains a sincere friend of the colonial peoples; it has always championed their rights, interests and strivings for independence. We shall continue to strengthen and develop our economic and cultural co-operation with countries which have become independent. . . .

For us Soviet communists, sons of the October Revolution, recognition of the necessity of the revolutionary transformation of capitalist society into socialist society is axiomatic. The road to socialism lies through the proletarian revolution and the establishment of the dictatorship of the proletariat. As regards the forms of transition to socialism, these, as pointed out by the 20th Congress of the C.P.S.U., will become more and more varied. Nor does that necessarily mean that the transition to socialism will everywhere and in all cases be connected with an armed uprising and civil war. Marxism-Leninism proceeds from the premise that the forms of transition to socialism may be peaceful and non-peaceful. It is in the interests of the working class, of the masses of the people, that the revolution be carried out in a peaceful way. But if the ruling classes oppose the revolution with violence and refuse to submit to the will of the people, the proletariat must crush their resistance, resort to arms and launch a resolute civil war.

We are convinced that with the growth of the might of the world socialist system and the better organisation of the working class in the capitalist countries, increasingly favourable conditions for socialist revolutions will arise. The transition to socialism in countries with developed parliamentary traditions may be effected by utilising parliament, and in other countries by utilising institutions conforming to their national traditions. In this case it is a question of using the parliamentary form and not the bourgeois parliament as such, in order to place it at the service of the people and to fill it with new meaning. Thus, it is not a matter of electoral combinations or simply skirmishes round the polls. The reformists indulge in this sort of thing. Such combinations are alien to us communists. For us the rallying and consolidation of the revolutionary forces of the working class and of all working people and the launching of mass revolutionary action are an absolute condition for winning a stable majority in parliament. To win a majority in parliament and transform it into an organ of people's power, provided a mighty revolutionary movement exists in the country, means smashing the military-bureaucratic machine of the bourgeoisie and setting up a new, proletarian people's state in parliamentary form.

It is quite obvious that in those countries where capitalism is still strong and still commands a huge military and police machine, the transition to socialism will inevitably take place in conditions of a sharp class struggle. The political leadership of the working class, headed by the communist vanguard, is the decisive condition no matter what the forms of the transition to socialism are. . . .

Of course, it is for the proletariat itself in each country and for its communist vanguard to decide on the forms and methods of struggle to be employed by the working class of the respective country in the concrete historical situation. . . .

The struggle against revisionism, against any deviation from Leninism, remains as important as ever. It is a struggle aimed at strengthening the socialist camp, at consistently applying the principles of Marxism-Leninism. . . .

The communist movement faces yet another danger—dogmatism and sectarianism. At present, when all forces must be united to fight imperialism, to prevent war, to overthrow the omnipotence of the monopolies, dogmatism and sectarianism may do great harm to our cause. Leninism is uncompromising towards dogmatism. Lenin wrote: 'It is necessary to grasp the indisputable fact that the Marxist must take guidance in living facts, in the precise fact of *reality*, and not hang on to the theory of the past day which, like any theory, does no more at best than outline the basic, the general factors, and that no more than merely *approaches* the understanding of the complexities of life.' (*Collected Works, Vol. 24, p. 26, Russian edition.*)

Dogmatism nourishes sectarian bigotry, which hampers the unity of the working class of all progressive forces, with the Communist Parties. Dogmatism and sectarianism are irreconcilably at variance with the creative developemnt of revolutionary theory and its creative practical application and they lead to the isolation of communists from the broad masses of the working people, doom them to passive waiting or reckless ultra-leftist actions in the revolutionary struggle, and prevent them from utilising all opportunities in the interests of the victory of the working class and of all the democratic forces. . . .

Comrades, the battle between the communist and all the people's forces, on the one hand, and the imperialist forces, on the other, is entering a new stage. In these circumstances, the unity of the socialist camp, of the entire international communist movement, acquires paramount importance. Our solidarity on the principles of Marxism-Leninism, of proletarian internationalism, is the main condition for the victory of the working class over imperialism. The behest of the great Lenin to advance shoulder to shoulder is sacred to us. The unity of our ranks multiplies our forces tenfold. Unity, unity and once more unity—such is the law of the world communist movement.

The very essence of Leninism implies that no Marxist-Leninist party must allow, either in its own ranks or in the world communist movement, any actions likely to undermine its unity and solidarity. . . .

The Communist Party of the Soviet Union does not lead other parties. There are no 'superior' or 'subordinate' parties in the communist movement. All the Communist Parties are equal and independent, all are responsible for the destiny of the communist movement, for its setbacks and victories. Every Communist and Workers' Party is responsible to the working class, to the working people of its country, to the entire international working-class and communist movement.

The role of the Soviet Union does not lie in it leading the other socialist countries, but in it being the first to blaze the trail to socialism, in it being the most powerful country in the world socialist system, in it having accumulated vast positive experience in building socialism, and being the first to embark on the full-scale building of communism.

At the present time, when there is a large group of socialist countries each facing its own specific tasks, when there are 87 Communist and Workers' Parties each with its own tasks, it is impossible to lead all the socialist countries and Communist Parties from any single centre. It is impossible, and what is more, it is not necessary. Tempered Marxist-Leninist cadres capable of leading their parties, their countries, have grown up in the Communist Parties.

And, indeed, it is well known that the C.P.S.U. does not issue directives to other parties. The fact of being called 'the head' means no advantages for our party or the other parties. Just the reverse. It only creates difficulties. . . .

The Communist Party of the Soviet Union is firmly determined to strengthen unity and friendship with all the fraternal parties of the socialist countries, with the Marxist-Leninist parties of the whole world. In this connection I want to emphasise our invariable efforts to strengthen the bonds of fraternal friendship with the Communist Party of China, with the great Chinese people. In its relations with the Communist Party of China our party always proceeds from the premise that the friendship of the two great peoples, the unity of our two parties, the biggest parties in the international communist movement, are of exceptional importance in the struggle for the triumph of our common cause. Our party has always exerted and will continue to exert every effort to strengthen this great friendship. We have one common goal with People's China, with the Chinese communists, as with the communists of all countries—to safeguard peace and build communism. Our common interests are the happiness and well-being of the working people; and a firm common basis of principle—Marxism-Leninism.

The Communist Party of the Soviet Union and the Soviet people will do their utmost to increase further the unity of our parties and our peoples, so as not only to disappoint our enemies but to jolt them even more strongly through our unity, to attain the realisation of our great goal, the triumph of communism. . . .

D. EAST-WEST RELATIONS

(a) The Berlin Crisis

1. Aide-mémoire of the Soviet Government to the Federal German Government, 17 February 1961[1] (extract)

The Soviet government believes that both sides should spare no efforts to achieve mutual understanding on major political issues of interest to the U.S.S.R. and the Federal Republic of Germany which have been touched upon during talks. It has welcomed Mr. Adenauer's words about his desire to disencumber relations between our two countries. In Moscow the fact was also welcomed that the trade agreement was signed after all.

But we would be wrong to fail to draw the conclusion from the experience of the trade talks that, provided there is a real desire to improve relations between our countries, no artificial obstacles should be raised to the development of co-operation, in which both the U.S.S.R. and the Federal Republic of Germany should be equally interested. The Soviet government has always sought the all-round improvement of relations with the Federal Republic. Moreover, it has wanted these relations not only to develop successfully but also to grow into strong, friendly co-operation, in view of the fact that the state of Soviet-German relations has always been of tremendous importance for the destinies of peace in Europe.

2. The Soviet government considers that the question of a peace treaty with Germany is now the main issue in Soviet-West German relations and attaches prime importance to the urgent solution of this problem. The government of the Federal Republic of Germany should be quite familiar with the U.S.S.R.'s position. It has been stated in detail, in particular in N. S. Khrushchov's message of January, 1960, to the Federal Chancellor.[2] Without indulging in repetition, it is necessary to point out, nevertheless, that the absence of a peace treaty has a most harmful effect not only on the situation in Germany but also on the entire European climate.

There is no getting away from the fact that year by year in Western Germany voices demanding a revision of the existing frontiers in Europe are becoming

---

[1] *Soviet News*, 7 March 1961. For the Federal German reply of 12 July, see below, p. 320.
[2] ibid., 2 February 1960.

more and more loud and insistent, although it is clear to all that this is fraught with the danger of a new war. As the armaments of the Federal Republic of Germany, grow, so these voices are becoming increasingly strong. The Federal government cannot be unaware of the reaction these demands has on the peoples of the Soviet Union, Poland, Czechoslovakia and other European states, to be sure.

The situation is completely abnormal in West Berlin, which is still being used for subversive activities against the German Democratic Republic, the U.S.S.R. and other socialist states.

This cannot go on: The alternative is either to move towards an increasingly dangerous worsening of relations between states, towards armed conflicts, or to conclude a peace treaty.

3. In the West, apparently they are now beginning to realise the need to sign a peace treaty, to end the state of war and to normalise relations among states. Nevertheless some statesmen are trying to take the following line during talks:

They say: 'This is not a propitious time—preparations for presidential elections are underway in the United States; we should wait until they are over.' And after the elections they say: 'The President and the new United States government have just assumed their duties, they have not yet grasped things, therefore some time should be allowed to pass.'

Others reason that it would be untimely to attempt to solve this problem now in view of the forthcoming elections in the Federal Republic of Germany. After these elections they will apparently say: 'The elections have just ended and in the heat of the election campaign many irresponsible speeches were made; again we must allow time for political passions to settle, for inflammatory speeches to be forgotten.'

If such a course is adopted this can go on *ad infinitum*.

Some public leaders in the Federal Republic of Germany intimate that possibly the Christian Democratic Union would agree to the signing of a peace treaty and to the present frontiers, but, they say, in the Federal Republic there are millions of displaced persons and if the government recognised the frontiers these persons would not support the party now in power.

These leaders know that promises to displaced persons to secure a revision of the frontiers are castles in the air, that they are unreal, but nevertheless they exploit their hopes; and not only do they exploit them but they also incite feelings of revenge and foster hopes for a revision of the frontiers.

Every sober-minded statesman realises that the frontiers established as a result of the Second World War are final, and any government seeking to change them is apparently getting ready to wage war for this purpose. All this goes to show that we must obviously sign a peace treaty. It is now obvious that all the time-limits have expired for understanding the need to sign a peace treaty and thereby solve the problem of the occupation status of West Berlin, making it a free city.

In the Federal Republic of Germany they sometimes say that conditions are not yet ripe for the solution of this problem, since, they say, a peace treaty can be concluded only with an all-German government, that is, after the unification of Germany. Such a position would be understandable if Germany really stood on the threshold of unification.

In fact, however, exactly the opposite is the case. The government of the Federal Republic of Germany stubbornly resists all co-operation and *rapprochement* with the German Democratic Republic and follows an openly hostile policy towards it, and thus blankly closes the only possible way towards restoring the country's unity. In these conditions how is it possible to make the signing of a peace treaty contingent on the formation of an all-German government? To accept such a viewpoint would mean to put off a peace settlement with Germany for many years.

It is equally impermissible to make the solution of the problem of the peace treaty contingent on an agreement on disarmament, as the government of the Federal Republic of Germany does. The peace treaty and disarmament are independent questions. Moreover, they are complex enough in themselves and should not be further complicated by putting the peace treaty in artificial dependence on disarmament or disarmament on the peace treaty. Attempts to tie these major international issues into one knot can mean only one thing—a desire to prevent a solution of either.

Speaking about disarmament as such, the position of the government of the Federal Republic of Germany on this question is essentially that of waiting until a comprehensive agreement which concerns all peoples, including the German people, is worked out by other powers.

Meanwhile the Federal government prefers to dedicate itself to the maximum building up of its own armaments and to taking an active part in the armaments of the western powers—its partners in military groupings.

The continuous annual increase of military appropriations, support for·plans for converting N.A.T.O. into a fourth nuclear power, negotiations with Britain about establishing Bundeswehr military bases in that country, the signing of an agreement with a number of N.A.T.O. member countries on the joint production of rocket weapons and the further extension of military co-operation—these and many other facts indicate that while leaving it to others to surmount the tremendous difficulties on the road to general and complete disarmament, the government of the Federal Republic of Germany is itself working in a diametrically opposite direction.

Naturally, in these conditions no professions, however eloquent, of devotion to the idea of disarmament will convince anyone of the sincerity of those who make them so often.

The present policy of the government of the Federal Republic of Germany cannot but warrant the assumption that it hopes to achieve its aims by force and that it is for this purpose that extensive military preparations are going on in the Federal Republic and its government is insistently clamouring for nuclear weapons, in defiance of the efforts of the peoples fighting for general and complete disarmament.

The Federal government proclaims that it has exclusively peaceable intentions. We are ready to believe this: Sign a peace treaty, which would eliminate mistrust in the Federal Republic's policy in many countries of the world! If the Federal government were really prepared to guide itself by principles of peaceful co-existence it would seem that there should be nothing to prevent it from putting its signature to this document.

The Soviet Union asks no sacrifices of the Federal Republic of Germany. The only thing we suggest is that the situation which has existed in Europe since the war be acknowledged, that the immutability of the frontiers established after the war be legally sealed, and that the situation in West Berlin be normalised, taking into account, within reason, the interests of all sides.

What does the Federal Republic stand to lose, compared with what it has today, from such a settlement? Roundly, nothing. On the other hand, by taking part in the signing of a peace treaty the Federal Republic would not only play an important role in creating the prerequisites for carrying out the general national task of the German people. Such a step would also lead the Federal Republic out of the blind alley into which it has run in its relations with a number of European states.

4. It is well known that the Soviet proposals envisage the solution of the problem of West Berlin as a free city on the basis of the conclusion of a peace treaty with the two German states. This circumstance opens before the Federal Republic of Germany broad opportunities for safeguarding its interests in West Berlin, inasmuch as in that case its representatives would appear as a party in the peace negotiations.

In any case, as far as the Soviet government is concerned, it is prepared to display the utmost understanding of the wishes of the Federal government and take them into account during negotiations with all the other parties concerned.

An entirely different situation would arise if the Federal government continued to insist on its negative position with regard to a peace treaty with Germany. By this very fact it would deny itself the possibility of directly defending its interests.

The Soviet position still does not rule out the possibility of an interim settlement for West Berlin pending the conclusion of a peace treaty with Germany—on the understanding, however, that a strictly specified time-limit for the conclusion of such a treaty is fixed in advance. But it should be taken into consideration that the working out of an interim agreement on West Berlin can be done only by the parties directly concerned, which does not apply to the Federal Republic of Germany, as is well known.

Should no peace treaty with both states be concluded within the agreed time-limit, the Soviet Union, together with the other states wishing to do so, will sign a peace treaty with the German Democratic Republic. That will also mean ending the occupation régime in West Berlin, with all the attendant consequences. In particular, questions concerning the use of the lines of communication by land, water and air passing through the territory of the German Democratic Republic will in that case be settled only on the basis of appropriate agreements with that republic.

5. The Soviet Union is sometimes threatened with war in retaliation for the conclusion of a peace treaty with the German Democratic Republic. But, as the head of the Soviet government, N. S. Khrushchov, has repeatedly declared, only madmen could venture on such a step just because the Soviet Union and other states had signed a peace treaty designed to improve the situation in Central Europe. However, if anyone should risk an act of aggression against the socialist countries, he would, with the present balance of forces, have to expect the grave

consequences which such a venture would unavoidably entail. The Soviet Union and her friends have everything they need to uphold their just cause in a fitting manner.

6. The need for a peace treaty is increasingly appreciated by responsible officials of the states concerned. It is impossible to put off the matter any longer, for it has been put off far too long. . . .

The Federal Republic, one of the legal successors of the Germany guilty of starting the Second World War, does not want to conclude a peace treaty now and is hindering the solution of this problem. This cannot fail to worry people in other countries which had fallen prey to German aggression.

7. Some individuals in the Federal Republic of Germany claim that we are seeking to dictate to the West Germans. Not at all. We stretch out a hand of friendship to the entire German people. The Soviet draft of a peace treaty with Germany is not an ultimatum. Should the government of the Federal Republic disagree with any particular point of our draft, it is welcome to make its own suggestions on this subject or put forward a draft peace treaty of its own.

The Soviet government is prepared to discuss any constructive proposals of the government of the Federal Republic which would take account of the present situation and contribute to concluding a peace treaty. It is not behind the back of the German people or at the expense of their legal rights that we want to conduct peace talks. We want them conducted with the direct participation of the Germans themselves and with due respect and regard for their national interests. While drafting its proposals for a peace settlement with Germany, the Soviet government has maintained close contact with the German Democratic Republic. We are prepared to enter into appropriate negotiations with the government of the Federal Republic at any time.

8. There is every indication that changes for the better are in the making. There is a tendency for world tensions to decrease, although not so rapidly as one would like them to, and conditions are arising for the solution of disputed problems by peaceful means, through negotiations.

The defeat of the Republican Party in the United States election has everywhere been rightfully taken as the American people's condemnation of the perilous and futile policy which the Eisenhower government practised in its latter years. . . .

9. The Soviet Union, and also the states friendly to it, are adamant in their determination to secure a peace settlement with Germany. Whether or not this problem will be adjusted with the participation of the Federal Republic of Germany depends on the Federal government alone.

We will do everything to come to terms on this matter with our former allies in the war against nazi Germany. But no one should forget that the great powers have certain wider interests which impel them towards settling the unresolved issues. It is these wider interests, rather than the German issue, that ultimately determine their stand in negotiations. If, however, they should still refuse to share in a peace settlement, we would sign a German peace treaty together with the states that wish to do so.

The Soviet side would like you, Herr Federal Chancellor, to consider and duly appreciate all this, and muster the courage to tell your people the truth: that it is necessary to eliminate the vestiges of the war and to conclude a peace treaty. Should the Federal government still oppose a peace settlement with Germany, it would have to face the facts of reality. The reality will consist in the Soviet Union and other states concerned signing a peace treaty. We will sign the treaty with the German Democratic Republic. That will settle the question of West Berlin as a free city, will fix the German frontiers and settle, by force of law, all the questions liable to settlement through a peace treaty.

One would expect that a realistic assessment of the present situation would restrain the Federal government from taking rash steps and enable it to take the right decision.

It is hoped in Moscow that the Federal Chancellor will exercise all his personal influence and his rich experience as a statesman to ensure that the Federal Republic would make a worthy contribution to a peace settlement with Germany, and thereby to the consolidation of peace and security in Europe. Such a position of the government of the Federal Republic of Germany would, at the same time, create the surest prerequisites for a fundamental change in relations between the Federal Republic and the Soviet Union in favour of friendship and constructive co-operation.

The Soviet Union, for its part, is prepared to do everything in its power to achieve mutual understanding on these matters and to discuss them at length with the government of the Federal Republic of Germany.

2. Aide-mémoire of the Chairman of the Council of Ministers of the U.S.S.R., Mr. Khrushchev to President Kennedy, Vienna, 4 June 1961[1]

The years' old delay with the peace settlement in Germany has largely pre-determined the dangerous course of developments in Europe in the post-war period. Major decisions of the Allies on the eradication of militarism in Germany, which once were considered by the Governments of the United States and the USSR as the guarantee of stable peace, have been implemented only partially, and now are actually not being observed on the greater part of German territory. Of the Governments of the two German States which appeared after the war, it is only the Government of the German Democratic Republic that recognises and adheres to these Agreements. The Government of the Federal Republic of Germany publicly proclaims its negative attitude to these Agreements, cultivates sabre-rattling militarism, and advocates the revision of the German frontiers and the results of the Second World War. It tries to substantiate its aggressive plans by a powerful military basis, to kindle the dangerous fires of conflicts on German soil and to set the former Allies in the anti-Hitler coalition at logger-heads.

The Western Powers have allowed the Federal Republic of Germany to start accumulating armaments and setting up an army, which are clearly in excess of the defence needs. The NATO Powers took new dangerous steps when they gave

[1] Cmnd. 1552, *Selected Documents on Germany and the Question of Berlin 1944–1961* (London, H.M.S.O., 1961), pp. 443–7. Hereafter cited as Cmnd. 1552.

the Federal Republic of Germany permission to build warships of up to six thousand tons displacement and also to use the territory of Great Britain, France, and Italy for military bases of the Federal Republic of Germany.

The Soviet Government sincerely desires to remove the sources of tension between the United States and the USSR, and to proceed to constructive friendly co-operation. The conclusion of a German peace treaty would allow the two countries to come much closer to the attainment of this goal. The USSR and the United States fought together against the Hitlerite Germany. Their common duty is to conclude a German peace treaty, and thereby create a reliable guarantee that German soil will never again give birth to forces which could plunge the world into a new and even more devastating war. If the desire of the Soviet Union to consolidate peace and to prevent the unleashing of a new world war in Europe does not run counter to the intentions of the United States Government, then it will not be difficult to reach agreement.

Proceeding from a realistic evaluation of the situation, the Soviet Government stands for the immediate conclusion of a peace treaty with Germany. The question of a peace treaty is one that concerns the national security of the USSR and of many other States. The time has already passed when the situation in Germany could be left unchanged. All the prerequisites for the conclusion of a peace treaty matured a long time ago, and such a treaty must be concluded. The crux of the matter consists in who will conclude it and when, and whether this will involve unnecessary complications.

The Soviet Government is not pursuing the task of harming the interests of the United States or other Western Powers in Europe. It does not propose to change anything either in Germany or in West Berlin to the benefit of any single State or of a group of States. The USSR deems it necessary in the interests of consolidating peace to formally recognise the situation which developed in Europe after the war, to formalise juridically and to secure the inviolability of the existing German borders, to normalise the situation in West Berlin on the basis of reasonable regard for the interests of all the parties concerned.

In order to facilitate agreement on a peace treaty the Soviet Union does not insist on the immediate withdrawal of the Federal Republic of Germany from NATO. The two German States could for a certain period, even after the conclusion of a peace treaty, remain in the military groupings to which they now belong.

The Soviet proposal does not bind the conclusion of a peace treaty with the recognition of the German Democratic Republic or the Federal Republic of Germany by all the parties to this treaty. It is up to each Government to decide whether it will or will not recognise this or that State.

If the United States is not prepared to sign a single peace treaty with the two German States, a peaceful settlement could be achieved on the basis of two treaties. In that case the States that participated in the anti-Hitlerite coalition would sign a peace treaty with two or one German State at their own discretion. These treaties need not be completely identical, but they must contain the same provisions on the most important points of a peaceful settlement.

The conclusion of a German peace treaty would also solve the problem of normalising the situation in West Berlin.

Deprived of a stable international status, West Berlin at present is a place where the Bonn revenge-seeking circles unceasingly maintain a tense situation, and engineer all kinds of provocations that are very dangerous for peace. We are duty bound to prevent such a development when the strengthening of West German militarism could lead to irreparable consequences due to the unsettled situation in West Berlin.

At present, the Soviet Government does not see a better way to solve the West Berlin problem than by transforming it into a demilitarised free city. The implementation of the proposal to turn West Berlin into a free city, with the interests of all parties taken into consideration, would normalise the situation in West Berlin. The existing occupation régime has already outlived itself and has lost all connexion with the purposes for which it was established, as well as with the treaties concluded by the Allies on Germany on the basis of which it existed. The occupation rights will naturally cease to exist upon the signing of a German peace treaty, whether it is signed with both German States or only with the German Democratic Republic on whose territory West Berlin is situated.

The Soviet Government believes that the free city of West Berlin should maintain unobstructed contacts with the outside world, and that its internal life should be determined by the freely expressed will of its population. The United States, as well as other countries, would naturally have every possibility to maintain and develop their relations with the free city.

In general, West Berlin, as the Soviet Government sees it, should be strictly neutral. Of course, it cannot be permitted that West Berlin should continue to be used as a base for inciting hostile activity against the USSR, the German Democratic Republic, or any other State, or that it should remain a dangerous hot-bed of tension and international conflicts.

The USSR proposes that reliable guarantees should be established against interference in the affairs of the free city on the part of any State. As a guarantee of the free city, token troop contingents of the United States, Great Britain, France, and the USSR could be stationed in West Berlin. The USSR would have no objections either against the stationing there for the same purpose of contingents of neutral States under the United Nations aegis. The status of a free city could be registered in due form by the United Nations and formalised by the authority of that international organisation. The Soviet side agrees to discuss any other measures that could guarantee the freedom and independence of West Berlin as a free demilitarised city.

All this considered, the settlement of the West Berlin problem should naturally take into account the necessity of respecting and strictly observing the sovereign rights of the German Democratic Republic which is known to have declared its readiness to join such an agreement and respect it.

The Soviet Government proposes to decide right now without any delay on the convocation of a peace conference to conclude a German peace treaty and to solve the problem of West Berlin as a free city on this basis. If for some reason the Governments of the United States and other Western Powers are not ready at present for this, an interim decision could be taken for a specified period of time.

The four Powers will appeal to the German States to come to an agreement in any form acceptable for them on problems connected with a peace settlement with Germany and its reunification. The four Powers will declare in advance that they will recognise any agreement achieved by the Germans.

In the event of a favourable outcome of the negotiations between the German Democratic Republic and the Federal Republic of Germany, a single German peace treaty would be agreed upon and signed. If the two German States fail to reach agreement on the above-mentioned issues, steps will be taken to conclude a peace treaty with the two German States or with one of them at the discretion of the States concerned.

To avoid delay of a peace settlement it is necessary to fix a time-limit, in the course of which the Germans should seek possible ways for agreements on problems of internal competence. The Soviet Government considers that not more than six months are needed for such negotiations. Such a period is quite sufficient for the German Democratic Republic and the Federal Republic of Germany to establish contacts and to negotiate, since an understanding of the necessity of putting an end to the vestiges of the Second World War in Europe has matured during the sixteen post-war years.

The Soviet Government is prepared to consider any constructive proposals of the United States Government on a German peace treaty and on normalising the situation in West Berlin. The Soviet Government will show a maximum of goodwill so that the question of a German peace treaty could be settled by mutual agreement between the USSR, the United States, and other States concerned. The signing of a German peace treaty by all the participants of the anti-Hitlerite coalition and the settlement of the question of a neutral status for West Berlin on this basis would create better conditions for trust between States and for the solution of such important international problems as disarmament and others. If the United States does not show that it realises the necessity of concluding a peace treaty, we shall deplore this, and, since it is impossible and dangerous to delay the conclusion of a peace treaty, we shall be obliged to sign one not with all States but only with those that wish to sign it.

The peace treaty will formally define the status of West Berlin as a free city and the Soviet Union, like the other parties to the treaty, will, of course, strictly observe it; measures will also be taken to ensure that it is observed by other countries. At the same time, this will mean putting an end to the occupation régime in West Berlin with all its implications. Notably all questions of communications by land, water, or air through the German Democratic Republic will be settled only by appropriate agreements with the German Democratic Republic. That is but natural since control over such communications is an alienable right of every sovereign State.

The conclusion of a German peace treaty will be an important step towards the final post-war settlement in Europe which the Soviet Union is persistently striving for.[1]

---

[1] At the end of their meeting at Vienna, President Kennedy and Premier Khrushchev issued the following joint statement on 4 June:

President Kennedy and Premier Khrushchev have concluded two days of useful meetings, during which they have reviewed the relationships between the U.S. and the USSR, as well as other questions that are of interest to the two States. Today, in the company of their advisers, they discussed the problems of nuclear testing, disarmament, and Germany. The President and

3. Address given by President Kennedy over American radio and television, 6 June 1961[1]

Good evening, my fellow citizens:

I returned this morning from a weeklong trip to Europe and I want to report to you on that trip in full. It was in every sense an unforgettable experience. The people of Paris, of Vienna, of London, were generous in their greeting. They were heartwarming in their hospitality, and their graciousness to my wife is particularly appreciated.

We knew of course that the crowds and the shouts were meant in large measure for the country that we represented, which is regarded as the chief defender of freedom. Equally memorable was the pageantry of European history and their culture that is very much a part of any ceremonial reception, to lay a wreath at the Arc de Triomphe, to dine at Versailles, and Schönbrunn Palace, and with the Queen of England. These are the colorful memories that will remain with us for many years to come. Each of the three cities that we visited—Paris, Vienna, and London—have existed for many centuries, and each serves as a reminder that the Western civilization that we seek to preserve has flowered over many years, and has defended itself over many centuries. But this was not a ceremonial trip. Two aims of American foreign policy, above all others, were the reason for the trip: the unity of the free world, whose strength is the security of us all, and the eventual achievement of a lasting peace. My trip was devoted to the advancement of these two aims.

To strengthen the unity of the West, our journey opened in Paris and closed in London. My talks with General de Gaulle were profoundly encouraging to me. Certain differences in our attitudes on one or another problem became insignificant in view of our common commitment to defend freedom. Our alliance, I

---

the Chairman reaffirmed their support of a neutral and independent Laos under a government chosen by the Laotians themselves, and of international agreements for insuring that neutrality and independence, and in this connection they have recognized the importance of an effective cease-fire. The President and the Chairman have agreed to maintain contact on all questions of interest to the two countries and for the whole world. (*Public Papers*, 1961, p. 438.)

On leaving Vienna, President Kennedy passed through London, where he held talks with Mr. Macmillan at the end of which, on 5 June 1961, the following joint statement was issued:

After his visits to Paris and Vienna, President Kennedy paid a short private visit to London on June 4 and 5. This gave the President the opportunity to review the world situation with the Prime Minister in the light of his talks with President de Gaulle and Mr. Khrushchev. The President and Mr. Macmillan were thus able to continue the close personal contact begun in Washington two months ago.

Their discussion covered the major problems, both economic and political, and revealed once again the close agreement of the two governments in pursuing their common purposes.

Occasion was given to review the need for economic collaboration and expansion in the general interest of developed and under-developed countries alike.

On Laos, the President and the Prime Minister noted with satisfaction the agreement in Vienna on the need for an effective cease fire which, in their opinion, should lead to progress in Geneva towards an agreement permitting the establishment of a neutral and independent Laos.

Particular attention was also given to the nuclear tests conference and to the question of disarmament.

The situation in regard to Germany was reviewed and there was full agreement on the necessity of maintaining the rights and obligations of the allied governments in Berlin. (*Public Papers*, 1961, p. 441.)

[1] *Public Papers*, 1961, pp. 441–6.

believe, became more secure; the friendship of our nation, I hope—with theirs—became firmer; and the relations between the two of us who bear responsibility became closer, and I hope were marked by confidence. I found General de Gaulle far more interested in our frankly stating our position, whether or not it was his own, than in appearing to agree with him when we do not. But he knows full well the true meaning of an alliance. He is after all the only major leader of World War II who still occupies a position of great responsibility. His life has been one of unusual dedication; he is a man of extraordinary personal character, symbolizing the new strength and the historic grandeur of France. Throughout our discussions he took the long view of France and the world at large. I found him a wise counselor for the future, and an informative guide to the history that he has helped to make. Thus we had a valuable meeting.

I believe that certain doubts and suspicions that might have come up in a long time—I believe were removed on both sides. Problems which proved to be not of substance but of wording or procedure were cleared away. No question, however sensitive, was avoided. No area of interest was ignored, and the conclusions that we reached will be important for the future—in our agreement on defending Berlin, on working to improve the defenses of Europe, on aiding the economic and political independence of the underdeveloped world, including Latin America, on spurring European economic unity, on concluding successfully the conference on Laos, and on closer consultations and solidarity in the Western alliance.

General de Gaulle could not have been more cordial, and I could not have more confidence in any man. In addition to his individual strength of character, the French people as a whole showed vitality and energy which were both impressive and gratifying. Their recovery from the postwar period is dramatic, their productivity is increasing, and they are steadily building their stature in both Europe and Africa, and thus, I left Paris for Vienna with increased confidence in Western unity and strength.

The people of Vienna know what it is to live under occupation, and they know what it is to live in freedom. Their welcome to me as President of this country should be heartwarming to us all. I went to Vienna to meet the leader of the Soviet Union, Mr. Khrushchev. For 2 days we met in sober, intensive conversation, and I believe it is my obligation to the people, to the Congress, and to our allies to report on those conversations candidly and publicly.

Mr. Khrushchev and I had a very full and frank exchange of views on the major issues that now divide our two countries. I will tell you now that it was a very sober 2 days. There was no discourtesy, no loss of tempers, no threats or ultimatums by either side; no advantage or concession was either gained or given; no major decision was either planned or taken; no spectacular progress was either achieved or pretended.

This kind of informal exchange may not be as exciting as a full-fledged summit meeting with a fixed agenda and a large corps of advisers, where negotiations are attempted and new agreements sought, but this was not intended to be and was not such a meeting, nor did we plan any future summit meetings at Vienna.

But I found this meeting with Chairman Khrushchev, as somber as it was, to be immensely useful. I had read his speeches and of his policies. I had been advised on his views. I had been told by other leaders of the West, General de Gaulle, Chancellor Adenauer, Prime Minister Macmillan, what manner of man he was.

But I bear the responsibility of the Presidency of the United States, and it is my duty to make decisions that no adviser and no ally can make for me. It is my obligation and responsibility to see that these decisions are as informed as possible, that they are based on as much direct, firsthand knowledge as possible.

I therefore thought it was of immense importance that I know Mr. Khrushchev, that I gain as much insight and understanding as I could on his present and future policies. At the same time, I wanted to make certain Mr. Khrushchev knew this country and its policies, that he understood our strength and our determination, and that he knew that we desired peace with all nations of every kind.

I wanted to present our views to him directly, precisely, realistically, and with an opportunity for discussion and clarification. This was done. No new aims were stated in private that have not been stated in public on either side. The gap between us was not, in such a short period, materially reduced, but at least the channels of communications were opened more fully, at least the chances of a dangerous misjudgment on either side should now be less, and at least the men on whose decisions the peace in part depends have agreed to remain in contact.

This is important, for neither of us tried to merely please the other, to agree merely to be agreeable, to say what the other wanted to hear. And just as our judicial system relies on witnesses appearing in court and on cross-examination, instead of hearsay testimony or affidavits on paper, so, too, was this direct give-and-take of immeasurable value in making clear and precise what we considered to be vital, for the facts of the matter are that the Soviets and ourselves give wholly different meanings to the same words—war, peace, democracy, and popular will.

We have wholly different views of right and wrong, of what is an internal affair and what is aggression, and, above all, we have wholly different concepts of where the world is and where it is going.

Only by such a discussion was it possible for me to be sure that Mr. Khrushchev knew how differently we view the present and the future. Our views contrasted sharply but at least we knew better at the end where we both stood. Neither of us was there to dictate a settlement or to convert the other to a cause or to concede our basic interests. But both of us were there, I think, because we realized that each nation has the power to inflict enormous damage upon the other, that such a war could and should be avoided if at all possible, since it would settle no dispute and prove no doctrine, and that care should thus be taken to prevent our conflicting interests from so directly confronting each other that war necessarily ensued. We believe in a system of national freedom and independence. He believes in an expanding and dynamic concept of world communism, and the question was whether these two systems can ever hope to live in peace without permitting any loss of security or any denial of the freedom of our friends. However difficult it may seem to answer this question in the affirmative as we approach so many harsh tests, I think we owe it to all mankind to make every possible effort. That is why I considered the Vienna talks to be useful. The somber mood that they conveyed was not cause for elation or relaxation, nor was it cause for undue pessimism or fear. It simply demonstrated how much work we in the free world have to do and how long and hard a struggle must be our fate as Americans in this generation as the chief defenders of the cause of liberty. The one area which afforded some immediate prospect of accord was Laos. Both sides recognized the need to reduce the dangers in that situation. Both sides endorsed the concept of a neutral and independent Laos, much in the manner of Burma or Cambodia.

Of critical importance to the current conference on Laos in Geneva, both sides recognized the importance of an effective ceasefire. It is urgent that this be translated into new attitudes at Geneva, enabling the International Control Commission to do its duty, to make certain that a cease-fire is enforced and maintained. I am hopeful that progress can be made on this matter in the coming days at Geneva for that would greatly improve international atmosphere.

No such hope emerged, however, with respect to the other deadlocked Geneva conference, seeking a treaty to ban nuclear tests. Mr. Khrushchev made it clear that there could not be a neutral administrator—in his opinion because no one was truly neutral; that a Soviet veto would have to apply to acts of enforcement; that inspection was only a subterfuge for espionage, in the absence of total disarmament; and that the present test ban negotiations appeared futile. In short, our hopes for an end to nuclear tests, for an end to the spread of nuclear weapons, and for some slowing down of the arms race have been struck a serious blow. Nevertheless, the stakes are too important for us to abandon the draft treaty we have offered at Geneva.

But our most somber talks were on the subject of Germany and Berlin. I made it clear to Mr. Khrushchev that the security of Western Europe and therefore our own security are deeply involved in our presence and our access rights to West Berlin, that those rights are based on law and not on sufferance, and that we are determined to maintain those rights at any risk, and thus meet our obligation to the people of West Berlin, and their right to choose their own future.

Mr. Khrushchev, in turn, presented his views in detail, and his presentation will be the subject of further communications. But we are not seeking to change the present situation. A binding German peace treaty is a matter for all who were at war with Germany, and we and our allies cannot abandon our obligations to the people of West Berlin.

Generally, Mr. Khrushchev did not talk in terms of war. He believes the world will move his way without resort to force. He spoke of his nation's achievements in space. He stressed his intention to outdo us in industrial production, to outtrade us, to prove to the world the superiority of his system over ours. Most of all, he predicted the triumph of communism in the new and less developed countries.

He was certain that the tide there was moving his way, that the revolution of rising peoples would eventually be a Communist revolution, and that the so-called wars of liberation, supported by the Kremlin, would replace the old methods of direct aggression and invasion.

In the 1940's and early fifties, the great danger was from Communist armies marching across free borders, which we saw in Korea. Our nuclear monopoly helped to prevent this in other areas. Now we face a new and different threat. We no longer have a nuclear monopoly. Their missiles, they believe, will hold off our missiles, and their troops can match our troops should we intervene in these so-called wars of liberation. Thus, the local conflict they support can turn in their favor through guerrillas or insurgents or subversion. A small group of disciplined Communists could exploit discontent and misery in a country where the average income may be $60 or $70 a year, and seize control, therefore, of an entire country without Communist troops ever crossing any international frontier. This is the Communist theory.

But I believe just as strongly that time will prove it wrong, that liberty and independence and self-determination—not communism—is the future of man, and that free men have the will and the resources to win the struggle for freedom. But it is clear that this struggle in this area of the new and poorer nations will be a continuing crisis of this decade.

Mr. Khrushchev made one point which I wish to pass on. He said there are many disorders throughout the world, and he should not be blamed for them all. He is quite right. It is easy to dismiss as Communist-inspired every anti-government or anti-American riot, every overthrow of a corrupt regime, or every mass protest against misery and despair. These are not all Communist-inspired. The Communists move in to exploit them, to infiltrate their leadership, to ride their crest to victory. But the Communists did not create the conditions which caused them.

In short, the hopes for freedom in these areas which see so much poverty and illiteracy, so many children who are sick, so many children who die in the first year, so many families without homes, so many families without hope—the future for freedom in these areas rests with the local peoples and their governments.

If they have the will to determine their own future, if their governments have the support of their own people, if their honest and progressive measures—helping their people—have inspired confidence and zeal, then no guerrilla or insurgent action can succeed. But where those conditions do not exist, a military guarantee against external attack from across a border offers little protection against internal decay.

Yet all this does not mean that our Nation and the West and the free world can only sit by. On the contrary, we have an historic opportunity to help these countries build their societies until they are so strong and broadly based that only an outside invasion could topple them, and that threat, we know, can be stopped.

We can train and equip their forces to resist Communist-supplied insurrections. We can help develop the industrial and agricultural base on which new living standards can be built. We can encourage better administration and better education and better tax and land distribution and a better life for the people.

All this and more we can do because we have the talent and the resources to do it, if we will only use and share them. I know that there is a great deal of feeling in the United States that we have carried the burden of economic assistance long enough, but these countries that we are now supporting—stretching all the way along from the top of Europe through the Middle East, down through

Saigon—are now subject to great efforts internally, in many of them, to seize control.

If we're not prepared to assist them in making a better life for their people, then I believe that the prospects for freedom in those areas are uncertain. We must, I believe, assist them if we are determined to meet with commitments of assistance our words against the Communist advance. The burden is heavy; we have carried it for many years. But I believe that this fight is not over. This battle goes on, and we have to play our part in it. And therefore I hope again that we will assist these people so that they can remain free.

It was fitting that Congress opened its hearings on our new foreign military and economic aid programs in Washington at the very time that Mr. Khrushchev's words in Vienna were demonstrating as nothing else could the need for that very program. It should be well run, effectively administered, but I believe we must do it, and I hope that you, the American people, will support it again, because I think it's vitally important to the security of these areas. There is no use talking against the Communist advance unless we're willing to meet our responsibilities, however burdensome they may be.

I do not justify this aid merely on the grounds of anti-Communism. It is a recognition of our opportunity and obligation to help these people be free, and we are not alone.

I found that the people of France, for example, were doing far more in Africa in the way of aiding independent nations than our own country was. But I know that foreign aid is a burden that is keenly felt and I can only say that we have no more crucial obligation now.

My stay in England was short but the visit gave me a chance to confer privately again with Prime Minister Macmillan, just as others of our party in Vienna were conferring yesterday with General de Gaulle and Chancellor Adenauer. We all agreed that there is work to be done in the West and from our conversations have come agreed steps to get on with that work. Our day in London, capped by a meeting with Queen Elizabeth and Prince Philip was a strong reminder at the end of a long journey that the West remains united in its determination to hold to its standards.

May I conclude by saying simply that I am glad to be home. We have on this trip admired splendid places and seen stirring sights, but we are glad to be home. No demonstration of support abroad could mean so much as the support which you, the American people, have so generously given to our country. With that support I am not fearful of the future. We must be patient. We must be determined. We must be courageous. We must accept both risks and burdens, but with the will and the work freedom will prevail.

Good night, and thank you very much.

4. Address given by Mr. Khrushchev over Soviet radio and television, 15 June 1961[1]

Dear Comrades, Friends, as you know, I recently returned from Vienna where for two days I met and had comprehensive talks with John F. Kennedy, the President of the United States of America.

[1] *Soviet News*, 17 June 1961.

Much has been published in our press, and also in the entire world press, on this subject. Many of you have already read the memorandums which were handed to President Kennedy. The first memorandum dealt with the question of ending nuclear weapon tests, and the other with the conclusion of a peace treaty with Germany, and a solution of the West Berlin problem on that basis.

Obviously many of you have also read President Kennedy's radio and television speech which was published in full in our newspapers. Thus, Soviet public opinion is well informed about the views which the United States President expounded and his appraisal of our meeting.

Today I should like to express some thoughts, some considerations of my own about the meeting and talks with President Kennedy in Vienna.

As you already know, this meeting was preceded by an exchange of views through diplomatic channels and also by an exchange of messages between the President of the United States and myself. We agreed on such a meeting as took place in Vienna on June 3 and 4. This meeting was a good opportunity for the first personal contact and exchange of views on basic problems between myself, as Chairman of the U.S.S.R Council of Ministers, and the new President of the United States.

On the way to Vienna we spent a few days with our Czechoslovak friends and, of course, had very thorough talks with Comrade Antonin Novotny, President of the Czechoslovak Socialist Republic and first secretary of the Communist Party of Czechoslovakia, and other Czechoslovak leaders.

I have had occasion to visit fraternal Czechoslovakia several times and I have always been conscious there of an exceptionally warm and cordial attitude. That was also the case on this occasion. We were welcomed everywhere as dear friends, as brothers, linked by a community of vital interests and aims.

I avail myself of the opportunity to thank once again the government of the Czechoslovak Socialist Republic and all our dear friends, Czechs and Slovaks, who gave us such a cordial and hospitable welcome during our stay in their wonderful country, which is confidently advancing along the road of building communism.

This is how things are in the relations between our socialist countries—the great common cause of building a new, socialist world has created a bond of kinship between us, has united us in one closely knit family. In upholding and defending the interests of their peoples, the leaders of our countries are at the same time upholding and defending the interests of all the peoples of the socialist countries, the great cause of socialism and lasting peace on earth.

In going to Vienna for our meeting with the President of the United States, we, of course, considered in the first place how this meeting would affect, not only the relations between our two countries, but also the relations between the countries of the new socialist world and the capitalist countries.

We consider that such meetings are indispensable because, in present conditions, questions which defy solution through conventional diplomatic channels insistently require meetings between heads of government.

Such meetings are indispensable, on condition, of course, that these heads of government strive towards safeguarding peace between states. For our part, we are doing everything in our power to ease international tension and solve the major problems in the relations between states.

Before taking up specific questions which were discussed in my talks with the President of the United States, I should like to thank cordially the Federal President of Austria, Dr. Schärf, Federal Chancellor Dr. Gorbach, and Vice-Chancellor Dr. Pittermann for all they did to ensure that the Vienna meeting took place in most favourable conditions for both sides, and we are grateful to the citizens of beautiful Vienna for their kind and cordial attitude towards us, representatives of the Soviet Union.

And now, dear comrades, allow me to state our point of view on questions discussed between myself and President Kennedy. I should like to state some considerations as to what, in our opinion, is the best way of solving those disputed or outstanding problems in the relations between states—problems which have become ripe for settlement or even over-ripe, and which insistently call for a solution.

One of those fundamental, paramount questions is that of general and complete disarmament.

It is well known that the Soviet Union has been working persistently and steadily for a solution of the disarmament problem. For decades the Soviet state had been raising this problem before the entire world.

It will be recalled that as long ago as 1922, at the Genoa conference, the Soviet Union, on the initiative of the great Lenin, proposed general and complete disarmament. In 1927 we raised this question before the League of Nations. At that time we were not able to ensure the solution of this problem and the imperialists subsequently started a world war.

Since the Second World War, which brought so much suffering and such disasters to the peoples, we have redoubled our efforts for a solution of the disarmament problem at the earliest possible moment. Both within the United Nations and outside it we miss no opportunity for pressing for a positive solution of the disarmament problem and removing the danger of a new world war.

The Soviet Union has taken part in the work of the United Nations Atomic Energy Commission which has been entrusted with the task of working out an agreement to ban nuclear weapons.

We have also conducted negotiations with the commission on conventional armaments. Starting with 1950, when the joint disarmament commission was set up, the Soviet Union took an active part in its work. For four years our representatives sat on the sub-committee of this commission in London and New York. Many were the proposals submitted, many were the speeches heard, without a single step forward being taken towards the solution of the disarmament problem.

A ten-power disarmament committee met in Geneva last year, this time composed differently from the bodies that preceded it. Represented on it were five socialist and five western states. However, this committee likewise failed to achieve any positive results in view of the unwillingness of the western powers to accept disarmament.

It is said that if the mounds of paper written on at the commissions and sub-committees on disarmament had been dumped into Lake Geneva, it would have overflowed its shores. A lot of paper has been wasted without even coming near to a realistic solution of the disarmament problem.

The question is, why is it that all these commissions and sub-committees have failed to achieve any success? For the simple reason that the western powers were plainly not prepared for serious negotiations, did not want and, to be frank, do not want disarmament to this day. It is clear that no government can afford to appear openly before the peoples with such an attitude! The western powers are afraid to tell public opinion directly and squarely that they do not want to negotiate disarmament with the Soviet Union in a businesslike way.

The capitalist monopolies are making big profits out of the arms race and have a stake in it continuing. But in order to conceal all this, they, it seems, need at least a pretence at negotiations. And so they have chosen the diplomatic approach: without refusing to negotiate outright, at the same time they do not accept concrete proposals on disarmament.

They keep dragging their feet, as the saying goes. A whole system has been worked out for preventing the objective from being reached, for definitely leading disarmament to a dead end.

The proposals on general and complete disarmament which, on the instructions of the Soviet government, I submitted to the United Nations General Assembly for consideration constitute a good basis for the solution of the disarmament problem. These proposals of ours, if accepted, would forever relieve the peoples of the grave burden of the arms race and of the threat of a nuclear-rocket war of extermination.

We said then, and I emphatically repeat it now, that if the western powers agree to general and complete disarmament, the Soviet Union is ready to accept any system of control they may conceive.

But in spite of this, the western powers claim that it is the attitude of the Soviet Union on control that is hindering agreement on disarmament and that they cannot come to terms with us on these questions.

I repeat once again: the Soviet Union stands for strict and effective international control. We are prepared to accept your proposals on control, Mr. President of the United States, provided you accept our proposals on general and complete disarmament. And then there will be no deadlock in the disarmament talks.

We want honest disarmament: we want to ensure equal terms for all nations during disarmament, so that no one may ever take advantage of disarmament to gain benefits for himself, to the detriment of the security of other nations. Our proposals envisage strict control at every phase in the implementation of the disarmament agreement. We consider that if complete disarmament is carried out, the most thorough control will be needed. Control agencies should have access everywhere without the so-called veto, without any bans, without any restrictions. Access should be open at any time and to any place, and we are prepared to provide this to the control agencies.

Only on the condition of general and complete disarmament with the strictest control it is possible to achieve trust and create real conditions for the peaceful co-existence of states in which no country or group of countries could arm secretly for the purpose of attacking other countries.

That is our point of view. What clearer statement need be made to prevent the western representatives from reiterating that the Soviet Union does not accept control!

All the fabrications to the effect that the Soviet Union does not want control show only one thing—how freely the people are deceived in the so-called 'free world'. Our world, the world of the socialist countries, is, however, excellently informed and knows that we stand for effective control. But in the 'free world', with its 'freedom of information', they are free to dupe society, to reiterate definitely false contentions in order to mislead people.

Talks between the U.S.S.R. and the United States on problems of disarmament will begin in Washington on June 19. I should like to believe that on this occasion, at last, we shall meet with a constructive approach on the part of the United States.

Now I should like to dwell on another question on which we exchanged opinions with President Kennedy—the question of the talks on banning tests of nuclear weapons.

For nearly three years we have been negotiating with the United States and Britain on this question. At the very outset of the discussions we submitted a draft treaty to the western powers for their consideration. Although this draft meets the interests of all those taking part in the talks and although during the negotiations we have met half way a number of the wishes expressed by the western powers, the talks have failed to produce any concrete results.

Now new difficulties have arisen. The western powers resolutely refuse to accept our proposal on the forms of control.

What is the essence of our proposal? Allow me to state it briefly. At first we thought it possible to accept the proposal of the western powers that the executive body of the system controlling the observance of the test ban should be headed by one man, appointed by agreement between the sides. But the events in the Congo made us wary and taught us, it might be said, a lesson. The government of the Republic of the Congo appealed to the United Nations for assistance in the struggle against the Belgian colonialists who were seeking to restore their colonial domination over that country. The Security Council and the General Assembly passed a number of good resolutions in this connection. But what happened after that?

Mr. Hammarskjöld, who poses as a neutral person, taking advantage of his position as Secretary-General of the United Nations, interpreted and implemented these decisions of the Security Council and the General Assembly in such a way as to please the colonialists. Is this not attested to by the foul assassination of the Prime Minister of the Congo Republic, Patrice Lumumba—the head of the very same government which requested assistance from the armed forces of the United Nations against the outrages of the colonialists?

The tragedy of the Congolese people has clearly shown the consequences which may result from arbitrary actions of the executive body of the United Nations in the person of a single Secretary-General. We must do our utmost to prevent a repetition of such actions. That is what the interests of the peoples, the interests of the preservation of peace demand.

Precisely because of that the Soviet government has arrived at the firm conviction that control over the observance of a nuclear weapon test-ban treaty must be exercised with the participation of representatives of the three existing groups of states—the socialist countries, the member-countries of western military groupings, and states following a neutral policy—and at that, the representatives of these three groups of states may adopt only agreed decisions.

The Soviet Union has never demanded, nor does it demand, any special status for itself. We do not seek to dominate the control commission, but neither shall we allow anyone to dominate us. We demand for ourselves precisely the same rights as the other parties to the treaty will have. What we want is that there should be no abuses on the part of the control organisation.

And what do the western powers want? They want to impose upon us a 'neutral' person of some kind as the sole interpreter and executor of the treaty. In other words, they want to foist upon us in this post some new Hammarskjöld, so that he would supervise control over all the territory of our country. Frankly speaking, they want such a man to allow them to conduct espionage within our territory in the interests of the West. To this, of course, we cannot agree and will never agree, because this concerns the security of our country.

It is clear to everyone, of course, that the ending of nuclear weapon tests would not be enough to prevent a nuclear-rocket war. We can ban nuclear weapon tests, but the existing stocks would remain, the production of these arms could continue and, consequently, the stockpiling of them would go on. Thus, the danger of a nuclear-rocket war would keep mounting. It is quite obvious that the ending of nuclear weapon tests alone would not be some kind of a dam to bar the way to the arms race.

Judging by everything, it is difficult to reach agreement on the ending of nuclear weapon tests at the Geneva talks due to the position taken by the western powers.

The main thing at present is to solve without delay the problem of general and complete disarmament. We told the United States President: Let us solve both problems jointly—the problem of tests and the problem of general and complete disarmament. Then it will be easier to reach agreement on the setting up of an executive control body.

In conditions of general and complete disarmament the question of international security will appear in a new light: there will be no armies and no danger of one state attacking another. Under these conditions the Soviet government will be ready to accept the western powers' control proposals.

We shall agree that provisions should be made for a control system without any restrictions by any side whatsoever, including the country in whose territory it is carried out. This will remove any danger of control being used for spying against some state. And this is perfectly logical, because if there are no armies, no arms race, states will have no military secrets, and then the western representatives will be able to enter any door, any plant or institute in our country, just as our representatives will in their countries.

In assessing the possibilities of an agreement to end nuclear weapon tests in conditions when there is no agreement on general and complete disarmament, we must not ignore this important circumstance either:

At a time when negotiations to end nuclear tests are under way between the three powers—the Soviet Union, the United States of America and Britain—France is staging tests in defiance of the protests of world public opinion and governments and ignoring repeated decisions passed by the United Nations, decisions urging states to refrain from such tests.

Thus a peculiar situation exists: while we seek agreement with the western powers in Geneva, an ally of these powers—France—continues testing nuclear arms and declares that the Geneva talks do not put her under any obligation. Consequently, France, a member of N.A.T.O.—that aggressive military bloc which does not conceal that it is directed against the Soviet Union—is able to perfect nuclear weapons in the interests of her western allies.

Moreover, we must reckon with the fact that France's example may be followed by other countries, when they have the appropriate scientific and technical prerequisites.

Of course, we understand the peculiar logics of the western powers, which, apparently, have no confidence in their allies in military blocs and wish to ensure their independence by relying on their own nuclear weapons. The President of France, General de Gaulle, says, for instance, that he wants to have his own nuclear arms so as to enable France to conduct an independent policy.

But other countries ensnared in the western blocs may state that they do not want to place reliance on the nuclear test-ban treaty in conditions when the states possessing nuclear weapons will retain them after the signing of such an agreement. Obviously, they can also repeat the arguments now used by France in order to justify the holding of tests, can strive to develop their own nuclear weapons and join the so-called 'nuclear club'.

These, of course, are logics injurious to the cause of peace. They can be used and are already being employed by those circles in the West which do not want to renounce nuclear arms, continuing to bank on these weapons of mass annihilation.

All this brings us to the conclusion that we must link the solution of the problem of ending nuclear weapon tests with the problem of general and complete disarmament. In the existing conditions, it seems, no other way out can be found.

In the course of the exchange of views with the President, we set forth in detail our viewpoint concerning the interdependence of the solution of the problem of general and complete disarmament and the ending of nuclear weapon tests. We should like the United States government to understand our views correctly. This would help to find a basis for agreement.

The peoples expect the governments to expedite the solution of the problem of general and complete disarmament in order to safeguard peace. This is why entire world public opinion raises its voice demanding that the governments which do not show interest in the solution of this problem should stop sabotaging and dragging out the talks. It is high time to take the disarmament problem out of the labyrinth of empty talk, where it has remained for many years already.

Permit me to turn now to the German question, which occupied an important place in our talks with President Kennedy.

The Soviet government has repeatedly stated its position on this question. And the western powers cannot complain that they have an insufficient knowledge of our proposals. We have done and are doing everything to convince the governments of Britain, the United States of America, France, and other states which took part together with us in the war against Hitler Germany that the absence of a peace treaty with Germany has created a profoundly abnormal and dangerous situation in Europe.

It has always been recognised that peace treaties should be concluded after the end of wars between states. This has already become a custom and, if you wish, a standard of international law. Instances of this can also be found in international practice after the end of the Second World War. Peace treaties with Italy and the other states that fought on the side of Hitler Germany were signed more than 14 years ago. The United States of America, Britain and the other countries concluded a peace treaty with Japan in 1951.[1] But the governments of the selfsame countries won't hear of the conclusion of a peace treaty with Germany!

Can such a situation continue in the future? After all, the peoples of Europe are vitally interested in the conclusion of a peace treaty with Germany. It has been long awaited by the peoples of Poland, Czechoslovakia and all the other states bordering on Germany. This treaty is essential to both German states: the German Democratic Republic and the Federal Republic of Germany.

The population of these countries live in hope that a line will be drawn, at long last, under the Second World War and the German people will maintain relations with neighbouring states on the basis of mutual confidence.

The question seems to be clear. A peace treaty with Germany is indispensable. Moreover, of course, there can be no question of any new changes of frontiers. We proceed from the premise that the peace treaty with Germany will put a seal on what has already been established by the Potsdam Agreement. The government of the German Democratic Republic has repeatedly stated that it recognises as final the eastern frontier of Germany along the Oder-Neisse line, established by this agreement, and regards it as a frontier of peace between the German and the Polish peoples.

Indeed, the governments of the western powers obviously understand, too, how senseless it would be to raise now the question of revising Germany's frontiers. Their representatives have often told us this during our conversations.

The President of France, General de Gaulle, for instance, has publicly stated that the German people 'must not question the present frontiers in the west, east, north and south'. Even Chancellor Adenauer, that champion of the cold war and specialist in stirring up passions among states, has come out with a statement to the effect that the Federal Republic of Germany does not strive to alter the frontiers through war, through the use of force.

Then why not sign the peace treaty, if everyone realises clearly that the present frontiers of Germany cannot be altered without war, and that war, as the western governments declare, is not wanted by them?

A simple operation, it would seem—to put a seal on what actually exists already and what has long been demanded by the peoples! What is it then that keeps the western governments from this step?

The reason obviously lies in the fact that certain people pay lip-service to

[1] *Documents*, 1951, pp. 611–25.

peace while actually wishing to keep alive the smouldering embers of the Second World War, so as to choose a suitable moment to kindle the conflagration of a new war. For this purpose more and more new divisions are being formed in Western Germany and Chancellor Adenauer is demanding atomic weapons for his army.

What is the purpose of all this? After all, neither a big army nor atomic weapons are needed to retain what Western Germany possesses today. However, there are forces there which still covet what does not belong to them and which cannot resign themselves to the existing frontiers. What would an attempt to change the frontiers at present mean? It would mean war, and a thermonuclear war at that.

This is why the position of the enemies of a peace settlement with Germany cannot fail to put the peoples on their guard. They have the right to say: If you are for peace, prove this by deeds—sign a peace treaty and pursue a policy in conformity with it.

In his conversations with me, President Kennedy—and as a matter of fact, other western representatives too—referred to the fact that the western powers have some kind of obligations to the residents of West Berlin and that these obligations cannot be affected even by the conclusion of a German peace treaty.

It is natural to ask, however, what obligations they feel must be maintained if all of them follow from the surrender of Hitler Germany and from the provisional Allied agreements and, consequently, can be valid only until the peace treaty is signed? What is more, there are in general no special Allied commitments with regard to West Berlin.

The Allied obligations applied to the entire territory of Germany and it was precisely these agreements that were grossly violated by the western powers. They turned Western Germany into a militarist state, founded a military bloc directed against us, and in this bloc Federal Germany plays a primary part. The generals who commanded Hitler's troops, who committed atrocities in the Soviet Union, Poland, Czechoslovakia, Albania, Yugoslavia, France, Greece, Belgium, Norway and other countries now hold a commanding position in N.A.T.O.

It has always been the case that after the signing of a peace treaty the conditions of surrender lose their force on the entire territory which the treaty covers, and throughout this territory the occupation terms are lifted.

Consequently West Berlin, which is situated on the territory of the German Democratic Republic, will after the signing of the peace treaty be free of all the conditions established as a result of the surrender of Hitler Germany and the introduction of the occupation régime there.

It should be said that when the question of a peace treaty with Germany, and consequently of the normalisation of the situation in West Berlin, arises the representatives of the western powers in many cases depart from legal grounds and start appealing to questions of prestige. But these attempts are beneath criticism. I should like to mention a fairly recent case.

We fought together with the United States against Japan. Our peoples shed their blood together. The Soviet army routed the main nucleus of the Japanese army—the Kwantung army in Manchuria. The Soviet Union, together with the other countries that fought against Japan, took part in drafting the measures for controlling Japan's postwar development. A Far Eastern Commission was set up in Washington and also an Allied Council for Japan with headquarters in Tokyo. In these bodies Soviet representatives took a most active part on an equal footing. Then it came to the conclusion of a peace treaty with Japan. Our allies disregarded the views of the Soviet Union and signed a separate peace treaty with Japan.

I shall not dwell on the reasons which at that time determined the position of the Soviet Union on the question of a peace treaty with Japan, since now we are speaking of a different matter—of the way the United States treated its ally in that case. It unilaterally abolished the Allied Council for Japan and deprived the Soviet representatives of all rights. Our representatives were left virtually in mid-air—they were being pushed out of Tokyo by every means, yet we had certain rights and obligations which stemmed from the surrender of Japan and were stipulated in the corresponding agreements.

So you see that at that time the Americans disregarded both the rights of the Soviet Union and the international agreements. Relying on its superiority in atomic weapons, it sought to dictate conditions not only to conquered Japan but also to its allies in the war against Japan.

More than two years ago we published our draft of a peace treaty with Germany. It contains nothing detrimental to the interests of our former allies, or, incidentally, to the Germans themselves.

The Soviet Union, which suffered greater losses than all the rest of the allies in the anti-Hitler coalition taken together, proposes the conclusion of a peace treaty in order to normalise the situation in Europe, to normalise relations with both German states. Meanwhile the United States, Britain and France, together with Federal Germany, do not want to sign a peace treaty; they seek to preserve an uncertain and dangerous situation. They refuse to eliminate the remnants of the last war through the conclusion of a peace treaty and insist on retaining the occupation régime and their troops in West Berlin.

Every person, if not deprived of common sense, understands that the signing of a peace treaty is the way to improve relations between states. The refusal to sign a peace treaty and the perpetuation of the occupation régime in West Berlin are directed at continuing the cold war, and who can say where the borderline lies between a cold war and a war in the full sense of the word? Surely it is clear that a cold war is a period of preparation, of gathering forces for war?

I speak of all this so that everyone should understand the gravity of the danger incurred by any further delay in the conclusion of a German peace treaty.

When we suggest signing a peace treaty with Germany and turning West Berlin into a free city we are accused of wanting to deprive the western powers of access to this city. But that is an incorrect and unworthy argument. Granting West Berlin the status of a free city would mean that all countries of the world wishing to maintain economic and cultural ties with that city would have the right and possibility to do so freely.

Of course, agreement would have to be reached with the country across whose territory the communications pass that link West Berlin with the outside world. This is normal. Otherwise the sovereignty of the state inside which West Berlin is situated would be jeopardised.

The governments of the western powers claim that they have pledged themselves to defend the freedom and well-being of the population of West Berlin. In the four-power agreements on Berlin, however, nothing is said of these obligations of the United States, Britain and France.

The idea of ensuring freedom for the population of West Berlin can in itself arouse no objections from anyone. None other than the Soviet Union suggests that the political and social régime in West Berlin should be the one which its population wants.

That means that no hand is lifted against the freedom of West Berlin, nor are there any obstacles to access to the city. We have repeated in the past and we repeat again, a peace treaty will create all the necessary conditions for ensuring the liberty of the free city of West Berlin and its unhampered ties with the outside world. Naturally, in solving the problem of access to West Berlin it is essential to abide by the generally-accepted international standards, that is, to use the territory of the country through which the roads of access pass only by agreement with its government.

Such a situation is recognised as normal by everyone. So why should it be considered abnormal to ask the consent of the German Democratic Republic to pass through its territory to West Berlin? After all, the land routes to West Berlin pass through its territory, the waterways also run through its territory, and so, too, do the air routes.

Consequently, after the conclusion of a peace treaty countries wishing to maintain ties with West Berlin will have to reach agreement with the German Democratic Republic on ways of access to West Berlin and communications with that city.

We are not suggesting anything unusual. That is the way it has been in relations between equal states for hundreds of years, perhaps even many hundreds of years. We did not invent this, it exists not only *de facto* but also *de jure*, and has long ago become the general rule.

When the Soviet government suggests concluding a peace treaty and normalising on this basis the situation in West Berlin, it wants only peace, it wants to remove from relations between states everything that causes friction and could cause dangerous conflict.

It is not the socialist countries but the western powers that are throwing down a challenge to the world, when, contrary to commonsense, they declare that they will not recognise the conclusion of a peace treaty and will seek to preserve the occupation régime in West Berlin, which—if you please—they conquered! That is not a policy of peace, it is trampling on the most elementary standards in relations between states, it is a desire to preserve a state of extreme tension in international relations, and moreover, it is a threat of war.

The Soviet Union and our friends do not want war and we will not start a war. But we will defend our sovereignty, will fulfill our sacred duty to defend our freedom and independence. If any country violates peace and crosses the frontiers—land, air or water—of another that country will assume full responsibility for the consequences of the aggression and will receive a proper rebuff.

The world press has published many comments on our meetings and talks with President Kennedy. Among these comments there are many sensible statements made in the United States, in Britain, in France and in Western Germany —not to mention the German Democratic Republic and the other socialist countries.

But there are also hate-ridden persons, deprived of common sense, who oppose negotiations with the Soviet Union and call for a crusade against communism. They are organising new provocations all the time. And it was by no means accidental that numerous gatherings of revenge-seekers, at which belligerent speeches were made by Adenauer and other leaders of the Bonn government, were timed in Federal Germany to coincide with the Vienna meeting.

The opponents of a normalisation of the international situation have now launched another big provocation in West Berlin, where from the beginning of June committees of the West German parliament have been meeting and where a session of the Bundesrat is scheduled for June 16, although West Berlin never has been and is not now a part of Federal Germany. Evidently in Western Germany itself a shortage of *lebensraum* for provocations is being felt.

To what lengths of folly persons blinded by their hatred for socialism can go is revealed by a statement of the Canadian-American inter-parliamentary group published a few days ago. These parliamentarians howl like hyenas and threaten nuclear war. They have not seen war on their territory. I do not know whether they have personally taken part in a war or not, but it is absolutely clear that they have no idea what a modern thermonuclear war is like, if they can try to push their countries, and others with them, into a conflict. Today, any war, even if it begins as a conventional, non-nuclear war, can develop into a devastating nuclear-rocket war. The peoples should put straitjackets on the madmen who are pressing for war.

The peoples of Europe know what war is. We have had to take part in two world wars. Twenty years ago a war was forced on the Soviet people, the most sanguinary and hard war in our history. The enemy reached the threshold of Moscow, he reached the Volga and occupied and devastated a considerable part of Soviet territory. But the Soviet Union withstood the drive of the enemy and won that war. We went to Berlin and punished those who unleashed the war.

We do not want another world war—we want peace. The Soviet people have achieved good mutual understanding with the Germans of the German Democratic Republic. The best relations have developed between the Soviet Union and the German Democratic Republic, and the conviction has grown that we should be friends, not enemies and that this friendship is beneficial and advantageous to both peoples. The Soviet people wish to have good relations also with the Germans of Western Germany.

Our people want to be friends with the French. We fought together with them against Hitler Germany, and each of us has learned from his own experience what fascism means, what war means.

We want friendship with the British, the Americans, the Norwegians and other peoples of the anti-Hitler coalition, together with whom we fought for peace on earth. We have no reason to quarrel with any people; we want to live in friendship and concord with all peoples.

To that end the Soviet Union is proposing to sign, jointly with other countries, a peace treaty with Germany. And this peaceful step is called a threat or even an act of aggression! Such talk can come only from those who seek to slander us or distort our intentions, to poison the minds of the peoples with lies.

We ask everyone to understand us correctly: the conclusion of a peace treaty with Germany cannot be postponed any longer, a peace settlement in Europe must be attained this year.

We call on all countries that fought against Germany to take part in the peace conference when agreement is reached on convening it. The question that remains now is not whether to sign a peace treaty or not, but whether the peace treaty will be signed with the two existing German states—the German Democratic Republic and the Federal Republic of Germany—or with one of the German states, whether all countries that fought against Germany will take part in the peace settlement or only a part of them.

The governments of certain countries have announced in advance that they will not take part in a peace conference. The Soviet Union will, of course, regret it if some countries evade signing a German peace treaty. We have always wanted and still want all countries of the anti-Hitler coalition to take part in the peaceful settlement of the German question.

But even should certain countries refuse to take part in the negotiations on the conclusion of a peace treaty, this will not stop us, and together with other countries which desire it, we shall sign a peace treaty with the two German states. Should Federal Germany not agree to sign a peace treaty, we shall sign it with the German Democratic Republic alone, which has long declared its desire to conclude a peace treaty and has agreed to the formation on her territory of a free city of West Berlin.

There are some in the West who threaten us, saying that if we sign a peace treaty it will not be recognised and that even arms will be brought into play to prevent its implementation. Evidently they forget that times are different now. Even in the past the 'positions of strength' policy was useless against the Soviet Union, but now it is more than ever doomed to failure.

The Soviet Union is against the use of force in relations between states. We stand for a peaceful settlement of controversial questions between states. However, we are capable of giving a proper rebuff to any use of force and we have what is needed to defend our interests.

During the meetings in Vienna there was also an exchange of views on the situation in Laos and on a peaceful settlement of the Laotian question.

The communiqué says on this matter that the President of the United States and the Prime Minister of the U.S.S.R. 'reaffirmed their support of a neutral and independent Laos under a government chosen by the Laotians themselves, and of international agreements for ensuring that neutrality and independence, and in this connection they have recognised the importance of an effective cease-fire'.

The Laotians are a peace-loving people. Having taken the road of independent development, that country threatened no one and was not a source of tension. That lasted until the imperialists decided to turn Laos into their military springboard, into a base for preparing aggression.

An uprising was organised against the legitimate government of Prince Souvanna Phouma. The rebels received arms and military advisers from the

United States. Peace in the country was disrupted, a war started—a war which, because of outside interference, threatened to develop into a big conflagration. An extremely dangerous situation for peace developed in South-East Asia.

Now the American side does not hide the fact that the responsibility for the dangerous events in Laos lies with the previous United States Administration and that its policy in that part of the world was not always wise. In March of this year Mr. Kennedy stated that the government he heads would seek to create a neutral and independent Laos. As far as the Soviet Union is concerned, we have stood in the past, and we stand today, for Laos being an independent and neutral state, not a tool in the hands of military blocs, and for no one interfering in the internal affairs of that country.

Thus, before the meeting in Vienna there existed sufficient grounds for finding a basis for agreement on a peaceful settlement in Laos.

During the discussions with President Kennedy on the Laotian question, it appeared that our approach was similar.

I declared that in order to settle this question it was essential to ensure the formation of an independent and neutral Laos. At the same time it was necessary to make a clear distinction between external problems and internal ones. The domestic policy of Laos cannot and must not be determined either by the U.S.S.R. or the United States, or by other countries. If any countries were to establish how Laos should live and what government it should have, then it would not be an independent neutral Laos, but a Laos governed from outside. And that is impermissible. The three political forces acting in Laos must themselves form a government which will uphold the principles of independence and neutrality. The Soviet Union will welcome such a policy and will do everything in its power for it.

I told President Kennedy all this. And it seemed to me that the President received with understanding what I told him. He declared that our two countries should influence the corresponding political groupings in Laos in order to achieve agreement between them on the formation of a single government and its programme on the basis of recognition of independence and neutrality. We consider such an approach sensible.

We are firmly convinced that no one should interfere in the internal affairs of Laos, because the interference of any one side could be fraught with very dangerous consequences. It is essential to approach the settlement of the Laotian problem carefully and cautiously and not permit anything which might complicate the possibility of a peaceful settlement in Laos.

In this connection we drew attention to the fact that the use of American officers and military advisers in the rebel forces meant interference in internal affairs on the side of a definite political grouping. Such an approach is contrary to recognition of the policy of the neutrality of Laos and constitutes open interference in that country's domestic affairs. The sooner the American side renounces such interference the better. If the present policy of connivance with the rebels continues, then the course of events could lead to bad consequences.

It is all the more impermissible that certain persons in the United States have not abandoned their plans for bringing marines into Laos and waging war there

D.I.A.—L

with the help of special military units. In the United States these units are, for some reason or other, called guerrilla units.

In reality they are nothing but forces for the purposes of wrecking and sabotage, intended for action against the peoples of those countries whose régimes do not suit the ruling circles of the United States. It can be said in advance that those who seek to try such methods have not weighed all the consequences for themselves.

If the United States government really seeks peace in Laos it should promote the speedy success of the talks in Geneva. No one should delay these talks under invented pretexts of various kinds, claims that in Laos there has been a breach of the cease-fire agreement. If there have been such instances, then it has not been the national patriotic forces that have been responsible. The American side and its military advisers in Laos are well aware of this.

We shall continue our efforts to ensure a peaceful settlement in Laos. And we urge all the other states taking part in the talks in Geneva to do the same.

We are proceeding on the basis of the concept that if one really seeks, not war, but peace, then relations between states with different social systems should be built on the basis of peaceful co-existence.

It emerged from our talks with President Kennedy that we understand the peaceful co-existence of states differently. The President's idea is to build up something like a dam against the peoples' movement to establish in their countries social systems which the ruling circles of the western powers consider unsuitable.

If one takes such a view of them one must conclude an agreement and assume obligations to control other states, to prevent any changes of the existing systems in those states, even if the peoples rebel against those systems. It turns out that if the people of a country want to change their social and political system, this should not be allowed.

Naturally this is an absolutely wrong concept and we, of course, cannot agree with it. It is not in anyone's power to halt the peoples' striving for freedom. All régimes which are built on the oppression and exploitation of peoples are unstable and cannot exist forever. And no matter how cunningly a system of exploitation and oppression is built up, the peoples will still win freedom and overthrow the oppressors. The changing of the social and political life of society is an inevitable process. It does not depend on agreement between statesmen. If anyone were to display such folly and seek to get agreement on this question, he would thereby be displaying his own worthlessness and lack of understanding of the events and the changes taking place in the world.

It is impossible to bar the peoples' advance to progress, to a better life. This has been proved by the entire course of human development. At one time slavery existed; it was replaced by feudalism, and then the place of feudalism was taken by capitalism. One system replaced another, because the new system was the more progressive.

One could cite the example of the United States itself, which emerged in the struggle against the colonial yoke of Britain. The American people waged a bitter liberation struggle and won independence by force of arms. At one time the United States considered such a course of events to be normal. Yet now, when people rise to struggle against reactionary régimes, against their oppressors, the United States tries to interfere in the affairs of those countries in order to preserve the old régimes.

The representatives of imperialist states want to find a way to prevent liberation ideas, the ideas of Marxism-Leninism, from spreading further. When the people of a capitalist or colonial country, showing their discontent with the existing system, seek to change it, to establish a new system corresponding to their interests, then the governments of the imperialist countries immediately announce that this is a communist intrigue, the hand of Moscow, and so on. They are not averse to using such inventions as a pretext for interfering in the internal affairs of other countries.

The assistance of imperialist states to reactionary forces in other countries is fraught with great danger and could lead to great complications. The Soviet people and other freedom-loving peoples firmly stand for non-interference in the domestic affairs of any country. This is an essential condition for ensuring peace. Every people has the right to independence and a free national existence and no state should interfere in the internal affairs of other countries. A class struggle is under way in the capitalist countries. The peoples are fighting against their oppressors, against reactionary régimes. It is impossible to regulate these processes by agreement. Anyone who might want to reach an agreement on this question, would only be showing that he did not understand history, did not understand the laws of development of society.

We believe that the most important thing that the western powers, and particularly the United States, should recognise is that socialism is now firmly established in the world and it is not in anyone's power to change this fact. It is common knowledge that the ruling circles of the western powers have in the past harboured plans for abolishing the socialist system and do so at the present time. But these attempts failed in the past and will fail again. It is essential to proceed on the basis of the fact that two social systems exist in the world, and to build relations between the socialist and capitalist systems in such a way as to ensure peaceful co-operation between them. This is the only sensible path to be taken in the relations between states in order to ensure peace.

That is what I wanted to say, comrades, about our talks with the President of the United States. I must point out that on the whole I am pleased with these talks. If you were to ask me whether it was worth while negotiating this meeting, whether it was worth holding it, I would reply without hesitation: This meeting was worth while and moreover, it was necessary.

In our talks with the President of the United States neither side evaded bringing up and discussing the most acute questions. It can be said that we had frank talks. We listened with attention to the position of the United States government and set out in detail the position of the Soviet government on a number of major international problems. That in itself is quite important. Of course, no one thought that we would reach complete agreement—after all, the paths followed by our two countries are too widely divergent to expect that. But I have the impression that President Kennedy understands the great responsibility that rests with the governments of two such powerful states. I should like to hope that the awareness of this responsibility will remain in the future, so that outstanding international problems may be solved, so that the rocks that bar the way to a lasting peace, to better relations between the Soviet Union and the United States of America, may be removed.

At the present time the relations between our countries leave much to be desired, and this situation has not developed through the fault of the Soviet Union. But we would like to believe that there will come a time when Soviet-American relations will improve, and this will have a favourable influence on the entire international situation.

In Vienna we worked to what might be called a crowded timetable. The realisation that we represented the great Soviet Union gave us energy and made our task easier. We knew that our Leninist foreign policy enjoys the whole-hearted support of the Soviet people, of the peoples of the socialist countries.

The sympathies of hundreds of millions of people all over the world are on our side.

The Soviet government will continue to carry out in all consistency the Leninist policy of peaceful co-existence, the policy of strengthening peace and friendship between peoples.

Thank you, dear comrades.

Good-bye, Goodnight.

5. Statement by Mr. Macmillan to the British House of Commons, 27 June 1961[1]

42. MR. DONNELLY asked the Prime Minister if he is aware of public anxiety at the new decision of Her Majesty's Government, as communicated to President Kennedy since the London talks, to modify the British commitments in Berlin; and if he will now state current British policy in this matter.

THE PRIME MINISTER. There has been no such decision, as my noble Friend the Foreign Secretary made clear on 20th June.[2]

Her Majesty's Government, in concert with their allies, have over the years made a number of comprehensive proposals for the just and equitable solution of the problem of Germany and Berlin, culminating in the Western Peace Plan presented at the Geneva Foreign Minister's Conference in 1959.[3] All these proposals have been rejected by the Soviet Government, who prefer instead to manufacture an artificial crisis for the purpose of gaining their own ends. We and our allies have certain obligations in Germany, and we do not intend to abandon them. Among these obligations is the preservation of the freedom of the people of West Berlin. The Soviet Government must come to realise that we intend to defend this, and that we cannot countenance proposals inconsistent with it. If they wish to discuss the issue with us, we are prepared to do so, but they must understand that it can only be on the basis I have described. The House will appreciate from what I have said that there is no question whatever of any modification of British commitments in Berlin.

6. President Kennedy's press conference of 28 June 1961[4] (extracts)

. . . I should like to comment briefly on Germany and Berlin.

Soviet and East German leaders have followed the recent Soviet *aide-mémoire*

---

[1] H.C. Deb., vol. 643, col. 199.   [2] H.L. Deb., vol. 232, cols. 494–5.
[3] See *Documents*, 1959, pp. 34–39.   [4] *Public Papers*, 1961, pp. 476–84.

with speeches which were apparently designed to heighten tension. It is of the greatest importance that the American people understand the basic issues involved and the threats to the peace and security of Europe and of ourselves posed by the Soviet announcement that they intend to change unilaterally the existing arrangements for Berlin.

The 'crisis' over Berlin is Soviet-manufactured.

The Soviets illegally blockaded the city in 1948 and lifted the blockade in the spring of 1949. From that time until November 1958, almost a decade, the situation in Berlin was relatively peaceful.

The peoples of West Berlin developed a thriving and vital city. We carried out our responsibilities and exercised our rights of access to the city without serious incident, although we were never completely free from irritating difficulties that were put in our way.

In November 1958, the Soviets began a new campaign to force the Allied Powers out of Berlin, a process which led up to the abortive summit conference in Paris of May last year.

Now they have revived that drive. They call upon us to sign what they call a 'peace treaty', with the regime that they have created in East Germany. If we refuse, they say that they themselves will sign such a treaty.

The obvious purpose here is not to have peace but to make permanent the partition of Germany.

The Soviets also say that their unilateral action in signing a 'peace treaty' with East Germany would bring an end to Allied rights in West Berlin and to free access for that city.

It is clear that such unilateral action cannot affect these rights, which stem from the surrender of Nazi Germany.

Such action would simply be a repudiation by the Soviets of multilateral commitments to which they solemnly subscribed and have repeatedly reaffirmed.

About the exercise of the rights of the principal powers associated in World War II: If the Soviets thus withdraw from their own obligations, it is clearly a matter for the other three allies to decide how they will exercise their rights and meet their responsibilities.

But the Soviets say that when we do so, we will be subject to the designs of the East German regime and that these designs will be backed by force.

Recent statements by leaders of this regime make it very plain that the kind of 'free city' which they have in mind is one in which the rights of the citizens of West Berlin are gradually but relentlessly extinguished—in other words, a city which is not free.

No one can fail to appreciate the gravity of this threat. No one can reconcile it with the Soviet professions of a desire to coexist peacefully.

This is not just a question of technical legal rights. It involves the peace and the security of the peoples of West Berlin. It involves the direct responsibilities and commitments of the United States, the United Kingdom, and France. It involves the peace and the security of the Western world.

In the interests of our own vital security, we and other Western countries entered in a defense arrangement in direct response to direct Soviet moves following World War II.

These alliances are wholly defensive in nature. But the Soviets would make a grave mistake if they suppose that Allied unity and determination can be undermined by threats or fresh aggressive acts.

There is peace in Germany and in Berlin. If it is disturbed, it will be a direct Soviet responsibility.

There is danger that totalitarian governments not subject to vigorous popular debate will underestimate the will and unity of democratic societies where vital interests are concerned.

The Soviet Government has an obligation to both its own people and to the peace of the world to recognize how vital is this commitment.

We would agree that there is unfinished business to be settled as concerns Germany. For many years, the Western nations have proposed a permanent and peaceful settlement of such questions on the basis of self-determination of the German people.

Moreover, we shall always be ready to discuss any proposals which would give increased protection to the right of the people of Berlin to exercise their independent choice as free men.

The proposals which have now been placed before us move in the opposite direction and are so recognized throughout the world.

Discussions will be profitable if the Soviets will accept in Berlin, and indeed in Europe, self-determination which they profess in other parts of the world, and if they will work sincerely for peace rather than an extension of power.

[3.] I have a second statement. The Soviet Union's refusal to negotiate seriously on a nuclear test ban at Geneva is disheartening to all those who have held high hopes of stopping the spread of nuclear weapons and the pace of the arms race. It also raises a serious question about how long we can safely continue on a voluntary basis a refusal to undertake tests in this country without any assurance that the Russians are not now testing.

Consequently, I have directed that the President's Science Advisory Committee convene a special panel of eminent scientists to take a close and up-to-date look at the serious questions involved, including two questions in particular.

First, what is the extent of our information on whether the Soviet Union has been or could be engaged in secret testing of nuclear weapons?

Second, to the extent that certain types of tests can be concealed by the Soviet Union, what technical progress in weapons could be under way in that area without our knowledge?

These answers will be received and reviewed by myself, by the Joint Chiefs of Staff, and the National Security Council in the light of what they mean to the security of the free world.

In the meantime, our negotiating team will remain at Geneva, our draft treaty is on the table there, and I urge the leaders of the Soviet Union to end their intransigence and to accept a reasonable and enforceable treaty which is our wholehearted desire.

[4.] And lastly, Chairman Khrushchev has compared the United States to a worn-out runner living on its past performance and stated that the Soviet Union would out-produce the United States by 1970.

Without wishing to trade hyperbole with the Chairman, I do suggest that he reminds me of the tiger hunter who has picked a place on the wall to hang the tiger's skin long before he has caught the tiger. This tiger has other ideas.

Premier Khrushchev states that the Soviet Union is only 44 years old but his country is far older than that, and it is an interesting fact that in 1913, according to the best calculations I can get from governmental and private sources, the Russian gross national product was 46 percent of the United States gross national product.

Interestingly enough, in 1959 it was 47 percent. Because, while the Soviet Union was making progress and improving the material standards of her people in the ensuing years, so was the tiredout runner, and, on a per capita basis, the Soviet product in 1959 was only 39 percent of ours.

If both countries sustain their present rate of growth, $3\frac{1}{2}$ percent in the United States and 6 percent in the Soviet Union, Soviet output will not reach two-thirds of ours by 1970 and our rate will be far easier to sustain or improve than the Soviet rate, which starts from a lower figure.

Indeed, if our growth rate is increased to even $4\frac{1}{2}$ percent, which is well within our capability, it is my judgment that the Soviet Union will not outproduce the United States at any time in the twentieth century.

This faster growth rate is a primary object of the various measures I've submitted and will submit in the future, tax incentives, education, resource development, and all the rest.

Mr. Khrushchev obviously sees the future differently than we do and he has urged his people to work hard to develop that future. We in the United States must work hard, too, to realize our potential.

But I believe that we can maintain our productive development and also our system of freedom. We invite the U.S.S.R. to engage in this competition which is peaceful and which could only result in a better living standard for both of our people.

In short, the United States is not such an aged runner and, to paraphrase Mr. Coolidge, 'We do choose to run.'

[5.] Q. Would you care to comment on recurrent reports that the administration is considering a partial mobilization to meet the threat in Berlin?

THE PRESIDENT. No such proposal has been placed before me at the present time. As you know this matter of what steps we would take to implement our commitments to Berlin have been a matter of consideration. Mr. Acheson, the former Secretary of State, was named to consider this matter in the middle of April. His report will be coming in—we're going to discuss it this week and we will be considering other proposals which might be put forward in order to make meaningful our commitment. But the proposals are still—have not still come to the White House officially and I'm therefore not able to comment because we have not seen any such proposal as you suggested at the present time, though of course we will be considering a whole variety of measures which might be taken. . . .

[13.] Q. Mr. President, how do you feel now in retrospect about summit meetings and do you foresee any more of them in the future?

THE PRESIDENT. Well I've never described the meeting in Vienna as a summit meeting. I think the meeting in Vienna was useful to—certainly to me in meeting my responsibilities, and perhaps it was also to Mr. Khrushchev. Because, as I've said from the beginning, these issues which we're now talking about are extremely serious issues which involve the well-being of a great many people besides even the people of the United States, and decisions have to be made on the basis of the best information we can get, and they involve the security of the United States and they involve also the peace of the world, and therefore if those decisions can be made more educated by such a meeting it was useful. Now there are no plans to have any further meetings that I know of. . . .

[18.] Q. Do you feel that the Berlin threat is serious enough for you to plan a personal meeting with the British and French to map our strategy there if the situation becomes indeed very hot?

THE PRESIDENT. It is a matter which we discussed with General de Gaulle and Mr. Macmillan. In addition, they've had—Lord Home was here—the French Government has had a representative, as well as the British Government, talking about the response in the *aide-mémoire*. I've no doubt that we will have close exchanges with Mr. Macmillan and General de Gaulle and when the matter reaches a point where a meeting would be useful, we would have it.

[19.] Q. On your statement this morning about a committee to go into the extent of information on Soviet testing, is there any suggestion here, sir, that we have an intelligence gap in this field? Or to specify, did not the Eisenhower administration pretty well know what the Soviets have been doing in nuclear testing during this——

THE PRESIDENT. No, there's—in what way?

Q. I just wondered if you had information about what testing they may have been doing.

THE PRESIDENT. No, we do not—this is a matter which the committee will look into. But in answer to your question, I have not seen any information, nor did the previous administration have any knowledge, which would state that the Soviet Union had been testing—information either by seismography or by any other means. What is of concern is, it is possible to test without those evidences being secured? Is it possible to test underground, for example, without a determination being made that such a test is being carried on? That's the matter which we wish to have explored. But it would be inaccurate to state that we have information that would indicate to us that the Soviet Union is now testing. What we're concerned about is that our information is quite incomplete and we want to know whether it's possible that they could be testing without our knowing and what the chances are that that might be true. . . .

[21.] Q. Realizing that the Acheson and other contingency reports have not been finished, could you, nevertheless, give us at least a hint this morning in what areas the public may be involved in supporting your strong stand on Germany? I ask that question against this background: that it's generally considered that your words to Mr. Khrushchev in Vienna were highly impressive, but it's necessary to follow them up with decisions and deeds.

THE PRESIDENT. Yes, well, that's the matter which is now engaging the attention of the United States Government; it is one of the matters which will be discussed at the Security Council tomorrow. But as of now, no report of the deliberations of the Pentagon and others as to what actions might be usefully taken have officially—have been finalized.

In addition, I would point out that we are talking about matters of extreme seriousness and I think we should wait until a judgment has been reached as to what action we should take before it's useful to discuss it publicly. As of today, these considerations and recommendations have not yet come to the White House. One of the matters which will be discussed, as I say, tomorrow will be this matter at the Security council.

7. Speech by Mr. Khrushchev to graduates of the Soviet military academies, Moscow, 8 July 1961[1]

Dear Comrades, today we are marking the graduation from our military academies of a new detachment of highly-skilled officers.

May I, on behalf of the central committee of our party, the Presidium of the Supreme Soviet, and the Soviet government, heartily congratulate the graduates of the academies and wish you great successes in that important activity you are called upon to conduct in military units.

The Soviet people love their own army, they are proud of those who dedicate their lives to building the armed forces, to strengthening the defence capacity of our great homeland.

I congratulate the professors and teachers, the entire staff of the academies, who have worked hard to impart to the students the necessary knowledge, to help them master the latest achievements of modern military science.

We salute the officers from the socialist countries who have finished their training at military academies this year. We wholeheartedly wish you fruitful work in strengthening the fraternal armies for the good of your peoples, for the sake of the interests of the entire socialist camp.

Comrades, you have finished your studies and will soon be sent to military units. Each of you can and must make his worthy contribution to the great and honourable cause of strengthening the armed forces of the Soviet Union. You must always bear in mind that the Soviet people, the Communist Party and the government have entrusted the Soviet troops with the defence of the achievements of the October Revolution, the achievements of socialism, attained under the leadership of the party of the great Lenin.

The armed forces of the Soviet Union and the fraternal socialist countries stand guard over our splendid present and the still brighter future to which our peoples are advancing under the banner of Marxism-Leninism.

Our entire country is preparing for the 22nd Congress of the Communist Party of the Soviet Union. The special importance of the 22nd Congress lies in the fact that it will adopt a new party programme which will lay down the principal tasks in economic and cultural developments, in foreign policy and in the communist education of the people. The programme will chart concrete ways for the Soviet people's advance towards communism.

Before long all Soviet citizens will be able to acquaint themselves with this highly important document and to rejoice in the future of their country, which in

[1] *Soviet News*, 10 July 1961.

the next two decades will achieve magnificent successes in advancing the economy and culture and raising the living standards of the Soviet people. In its economic development the Soviet Union will outstrip the major capitalist countries.

Comrades, the Soviet Union is a profoundly peaceloving state. There is no other country in the world which has done so much to safeguard lasting peace and international co-operation.

The Soviet Union has been exerting tremendous efforts in order to reach agreement on disarmament with strict international control. The idea of general and complete disarmament, advanced by the Soviet government, has been unanimously approved by the United Nations General Assembly and has met with broad support in all countries of the world.

However, as the talks have shown, the ruling circles of the western powers, while paying lipservice to the idea of disarmament, do not really want it. Recently they have even been afraid of mentioning general and complete disarmament. They are seeking to confine the matter to control over armaments, to placing under their control, above all, the up-to-date types of Soviet armaments and military equipment.

The western powers are even frustrating agreement on the ending of nuclear weapon tests by refusing us an equal status in the control agency. They would like to see a system of verification of the cessation of nuclear tests functioning in our country while we would essentially be kept out of participation in the work of control agencies. We would simply have nothing to do but submit to the decisions of an international administrator, a kind of new Hammarskjöld.

Today it is acknowledged in the West that the forces of the Soviet Union and other socialist countries are not inferior to the forces of the western powers.

However, the proper conclusions are not drawn from this fact: given equal forces, there must also be equal rights and equal opportunities. Yet our partners, acknowledging that the balance of power has not tilted in their favour, nevertheless want to dominate in international agencies and impose their will there.

In the solution of the disarmament problem and other international issues, the Soviet government is not seeking to place the western powers in an unequal position. But we will never forego our interests.

The Soviet Union has always been ready to examine in a businesslike manner all proposals which are made by governments and statesmen of various countries. We believe that it would be a good thing to revert to some proposals which various countries have made in recent years, for many of them are extremely realistic and their implementation would promote the cause of peace.

Let us take, for instance, the Polish proposal for a nuclear-free zone in the centre of Europe;[1] the proposal for the withdrawal of foreign troops from alien territories to within their national frontiers; the conclusion of a non-aggression pact between the N.A.T.O. countries and the Warsaw Treaty Organisation; on averting a surprise attack and the establishment in Europe of a zone of reciprocal inspection and aerial survey on both sides of the line dividing the armed forces of N.A.T.O. and the Warsaw Treaty.

---

[1] *Documents*, 1957, pp. 155–9. This and the subsequent proposals formed part of Mr. Khrushchev's disarmament plan set before the United Nations fourteenth General Assembly; cf. ibid., 1959, p. 108.

Would the acceptance of such proposals hurt anyone? No, it would facilitate a relaxation of international tension, elimination of the cold war, and better mutual understanding. However, even if these measures were implemented general and complete disarmament remains the most cardinal problem the solution of which would radically improve the entire international climate, would make people confident that there would be no third world war. The Soviet Union will do its utmost to have this problem solved for the good of mankind.

Our country wants to have good relations with all states. One must have a sober approach to the settlement of international disputes. We want to eliminate the vestiges of the Second World War, to put an end to the cold war and thus help to reach agreement on disarmament. It is time to draw a line under the past, which must not be allowed to stand in the way of the future.

Permit me, comrades, to dwell in greater detail on such an important question as the conclusion of the German peace treaty, to let you know what our policy is and what situation is now taking shape.

The Soviet government, together with the governments of the other socialist countries has proposed to our allies in the war with fascist Germany that a German peace treaty be concluded and on this basis the situation in West Berlin made normal. We have also urged the head of the West German government, Chancellor Adenauer, to show understanding and good will in order to solve this vital problem of our time. The socialist countries have said openly that they want to conclude a peace treaty this year, since over 16 years have passed since the end of the war—a more than adequate period for preparing a solution of this problem.

What are the western reactions to this? The governments have not yet replied officially. But many reports on this matter have appeared in the organs of the western press which are close either to governmental circles, military staffs or ruling parties. Unfortunately, voices are being heard expressing a great deal of nonsense and little common sense. We are threatened, we are told that they will stand 'firm', will resort to force in order to break through to West Berlin when the German peace treaty is signed.

Recently threatening notes have also been heard in statements by leaders of western governments. General de Gaulle, the President of France, recently declared that one French division would be shipped from Algeria to Europe in the autumn in order to reinforce N.A.T.O.

Mr. Macmillan, the Prime Minister of the United Kingdom, also has not yet found better, more constructive words than statements on 'firmness' for the sake of preserving the vestiges of the war and the occupation in Germany.

The Soviet government stands on positions of peace and peaceful co-existence on positions of respect for sovereignty and non-intervention in the domestic affairs of other states. We have stood by this firmly and will continue to do so. Our firmness, therefore, has a definite, peaceful trend.

When others in one breath mention firmness and the necessity of mobilisation, the shipment of more troops to Europe and the like—this is quite a different course. This is obstinate unwillingness to heed the demands of the time and the voice of reason, an attempt to resort to arms in the old fashion, believing that this is the weightiest argument in solving pressing international problems.

Replying to our proposals for the conclusion of a peace treaty, proposals which, it would seem, are perfectly natural, the West begins to count divisions. And Chancellor Adenauer is shouting himself hoarse for nuclear weapons. What does Adenauer need nuclear weapons for? Twice German militarism has engineered world wars. Now, when the wounds of the Second World War are still being felt, he calls for nuclear weapons. The Bundeswehr needs them, not for peace, but for unleashing a third world war.

Many of you, comrades, fought in the Second World War and saw for yourselves how much suffering it brought; you experienced for yourselves the meaning of war. You all understand what a war would mean now. God forbid that it should break out! Here it is not the number of divisions that will be decisive. In nuclear war the note will be struck by rockets, by atom and hydrogen bombs. And it is not so important how many divisions will be shipped from Algeria —one or ten, it makes no difference.

Herr Adenauer did not fight and, evidently, wants to make up for it in his old age. He has also indicated against whom to fight. As recently as last Sunday the Bonn Chancellor again described the Soviet Union as the 'potential enemy' and demanded that the Bundeswehr should become equal in armaments with this enemy. At the same time he cursed those who are advocating neutrality in Western Germany.

Did the Chancellor think what he was saying? He loves to pass himself off as a victim of Hitler, yet he is following in Hitler's footsteps. Adenauer, evidently, has no idea what modern war means, otherwise he would not play about so recklessly with the destinies of human beings.

One must call not for war but for peace, one must not worsen the atmosphere, must not bring matters to a conflict. Let us sit down at a table and calmly discuss all questions without resorting to threats. We propose that a peace conference be convened and we shall go there with our draft treaty. Let the western powers make their proposals and submit their draft for a peace settlement. We shall discuss all proposals and accept those which in the best way facilitate the strengthening of peace and which pay due regard to the interests and sovereignty of all states.

West Berlin is an island inside the German Democratic Republic, an island where the capitalist order has been preserved. We do not want to intervene in the domestic affairs of the city's population or do anything to affect the prestige of the United States, the United Kingdom and France.

Is it possible to find a solution such as would satisfy all countries that fought against Germany and would not disturb the established way of life in West Berlin? Yes, it is possible, and we propose such a solution—to grant West Berlin the status of a free city, to give it a guarantee, either by the four great powers—the United States, the United Kingdom, France and the Soviet Union —or by neutral countries, or by the United Nations Organisation.

If the western powers have a better version of guarantees let them propose it.

However, it is only natural that any West Berlin solution must take into consideration that the city lies in the centre of a sovereign state and that all communications of West Berlin with the outside world pass across the territory of that state. It is accepted in international relations that access to one country or other across the territory of another state has always required appropriate agreement with the authorities of that state.

For instance, the Soviet and British governments have set up a regular air service between Moscow and London. The route of the flights passes through Copenhagen. But no one would have permitted us to fly via Copenhagen had we not reached an understanding with the Danish government. This is so normal and legitimate that there is nothing puzzling about it. So why should there be a different procedure for flights over the territory of the German Democratic Republic or for using her roads and railways?

In proposing to conclude a German peace treaty and on this basis to solve the problem of West Berlin, we are threatening no one. We do not demand either changes in the postwar social and political conditions in one state or another, or the establishment of new frontiers. The Soviet Union does not seek any gains for itself in the peace settlement, does not seek to humiliate anyone or infringe anyone's interests.

The socialist countries do not encroach upon the right of the West Berliners freely to determine the social and economic order under which they want to live. No one is going to create obstacles to access to West Berlin. The city will be able to establish and maintain contacts with any other state and to the extent it considers advantageous to it.

The Soviet government agrees with President Kennedy's recent statement that any new West Berlin solution must not infringe the rights of the population of that city to make an independent choice, as free people. Our proposal fully accords with this demand.

The Soviet government is ready for the most far-reaching guarantees as regards West Berlin. I have more than once mentioned various forms of guarantees, but the N.A.T.O. countries, which are whipping up hysteria over West Berlin, studiously hush up this part of our proposals.

The capitalist 'free' press, sensing the weakness of the western positions, is shouting that the Soviet Union wants to seize West Berlin, to gain some advantages at the expense of others.

By such fabrications it seeks to conceal from the public the genuine nature of the Soviet proposals. We do not encroach on West Berlin or the freedom of its population. We are for the freedom of West Berlin on a foundation of freedom and not on a foundation of occupation. We want nothing but the elimination of the vestiges of the Second World War in order to improve the entire climate in Europe. That is precisely why the Soviet Union insists on the conclusion of a German peace treaty.

The Soviet Union regrets that the leaders of the western powers show no desire to co-operate with us in the conclusion of a German peace treaty. Either they do not understand the importance of a peace settlement with Germany for the future of the world, or, what is more likely, cannot rise above the narrow interests of their military blocs.

This is clear and understandable to all who search for reasonable solutions. But there are people who depict our proposals as a 'threat' and then say that they will reply with force to this 'threat'. Is this a sober policy? It is not without reason that it is being justly criticised in the western countries themselves.

Many people there assess the situation correctly and urge the leaders of the United States, the United Kingdom and France to abandon prejudice and to examine how remote western policy is from the real conditions in which states live.

One can refer to such prominent authorities in the western world as the United States General MacArthur, who in a recent speech in Manila called for outlawing world war.[1] Or to the British Field Marshal Montgomery, who suggests the withdrawal of all foreign troops from Europe, the closing down of foreign military bases, the withdrawal of foreign troops from Berlin, and so on.[2] These are the voices of men who have fought in war; they know the meaning of war and have a correct idea of the calamity a new world war would bring to mankind should it break out.

We urge that the method of intimidation be discarded. War must not be tolerated—it will take a toll of far too many human lives. The first shots might be fired on the frontier where troops face each other. But who can guarantee that these shots will not be echoed by nuclear explosions throughout the world, that a war will not begin which mixes up the front and the rear? Everyone must be aware of this. Those who threaten us ought to know that we are able to rebuff aggressors. We have means for this.

The Soviet Union has made tremendous progress in the economy, culture and technology. Our people created and built up armed forces that bore the brunt of the struggle against fascism and crushed German militarism.

This gives us the right—I think I shall be understood correctly—to appeal to leaders of the countries that were our allies in the last war, to the President of the United States, Mr. Kennedy, the President of the French Republic General de Gaulle, the Prime Minister of the United Kingdom Mr. Macmillan, urging them to display wisdom in the solution of the German problem, to attend a conference together with other peaceloving states and to conclude a peace treaty.

Common sense—and once again common sense—is needed above all now. And it must find expression in peaceful deeds, in the desire to eradicate tension. No other step in our time can be more peaceable than the conclusion of a peace treaty and the elimination of the vestiges of the last war.

We propose peace, we want reason to prevail in the relations between states, we want peaceful co-existence and competition on which system can secure greater material and spiritual blessings for the peoples. The peoples must themselves decide which system accords with their vital interests—the communist system or the capitalist one.

Proposing the conclusion of a peace treaty, the Soviet government does not want a position in which some would gain and others lose. Let us record what exists. No one's sovereignty will be affected by the conclusion of a German peace treaty.

The militarist revenge-seeking circles in Western Germany, of course, will dislike the peace treaty. It will tie their hands, make it more difficult to collect forces for fresh gambles. But therein, of course, lies the meaning of the peace treaty, to cut short the dangerous play of the West German revenge-seekers who

---

[1] *N.Y. Times*, 6 July 1961.   [2] *Sunday Times*, 18 June 1961.

hope to take advantage of unstability in Europe and to set the great powers at loggerheads.

I repeat, there are no serious reasons which could really prevent a peace settlement with Germany, but nevertheless the opponents of an international détente and the conclusion of a peace treaty seek to justify such a position by all kinds of untenable arguments.

They declare, for instance, that the division of Germany prevents a peace settlement. If the western powers really wanted to help the Germans to be united, far from being obstructive, they would advise the government of the Federal Republic of Germany to enter into negotiations with the government of the German Democratic Republic. They would support the proposal of the government of the German Democratic Republic for setting up a confederation of the two German states.

If the absence of an all-German government really prevented the conclusion of a peace treaty, the western powers and the Federal Republic of Germany would accept the proposal the Soviet Union is now making—that the Germans should meet before the signing of a German peace treaty to hammer out common views both on the question of a peace settlement and on the reunification of the country.

It is the business of the Germans themselves to restore Germany's national unity. No state has the right to interfere in this matter because no one except the Germans themselves can solve this problem. We do not intend to conduct any talks on this question. Let the governments of the Federal Republic of Germany and the German Democratic Republic reach agreement on this question and we shall recognise any decision which they take.

But if anyone counts on liquidating with our hands the socialist system in the German Democratic Republic, he is living in a world of illusions. The German Democratic Republic has a loyal and reliable friend in the Soviet Union.

There are many questions in Germany that have not been settled. This, apparently, is now acknowledged by everyone, and hence the logical conclusion —we must settle these matters and not wait until they cause a conflict. Problems of an international nature must be solved at an appropriate forum. Inter-German problems can be settled only by the German themselves.

The Soviet government will regret it very much if any one of our former allies does not sign, together with us, the German peace treaty and if Western Germany refuses to accept the hand of reconciliation held out to her by the socialist states.

We cannot tolerate the solution of this problem, vitally important for so many states and peoples, being dragged out for many more years merely because certain circles want to reserve for themselves opportunities for revenge and for perpetuating an occupation régime in a part of German territory. The Soviet Union will be confronted with the need to reach agreement with the German Democratic Republic and the countries that want to conclude a peace treaty with this peaceloving German state.

The procedure for concluding a peace treaty with the German Democratic Republic will conform strictly to existing international practice and custom. After the conclusion of the treaty, the Soviet Union will lay down all the obligations it has hitherto discharged on the communication lanes with West Berlin.

In short the government of the German Democratic Republic will enjoy full sovereignty over all its territory, just like any other independent state.

You, Comrades, are military men and you know very well what it means to disregard the provisions of a peace treaty and to try to violate the sovereignty of the German Democratic Republic. Many of you will be serving in the forces which, under the Warsaw Treaty, are stationed on the territory of the German Democratic Republic and this means that you will have to rebuff the aggressive forces if they decide to frustrate a peace settlement by force of arms. I draw your attention to the fact that it is precisely a peace treaty to which some people are threatening to reply with force and to cause a dangerous international crisis.

The Soviet government is displaying persistence in the conclusion of the German peace treaty, convinced that if measures are not take now to normalise the situation in Germany and West Berlin, the people may be confronted with the fact of aggression launched by the West German militarists. There is no guarantee that some venture of the West German successors of Hitler will not light the fire of a big war. Then it will be too late to carry out an investigation into what prevented the timely conclusion of a peace treaty and why in spite of all the warnings of the peace-loving forces, militarism in Western Germany was allowed to get on to its feet and take up arms again.

Remember how Hitler pushed the world to the brink of war and then unleashed war. He advanced gradually, step by step, methodically towards this goal; he extorted concessions from the western powers. He was encouraged by the ruling circles of Britain, France and America. They believed that with the help of fascism they would be able to defeat the Soviet Union, to destroy communism.

There are not a few documents and books describing how Hitler Germany prepared the Second World War. Recently I read, for instance, the book by the French journalist Géneviève Tabouis, *Twenty Years of Diplomatic Struggle*. This book gives a very good picture of the backstage side of the collusion of the German militarists with the reactionary forces of the other countries of monopoly capital.

Evidently the frantic monopolists and the West German revenge-seekers would not be averse to embarking once again on this road with a view to settling disputed questions through war. The monopolists regard the question of communism, its development, as the main issue. Their reason is obscured by hatred of communism, of the countries of socialism. They may lose all self-control and the imperialists may unleash a new war. Adenauer is repeating what Hitler did in his day when preparing for war. And actually the same countries that encouraged Hitler are now encouraging Adenauer.

But they forget that the situation has changed radically since then. In those days the Soviet Union and People's Mongolia were in the midst of capitalist encirclement. Now the mighty socialist camp, a camp which unites over one thousand million people, is growing and becoming stronger.

The colonial system is collapsing and ever more new and independent states are emerging and embarking upon the road of a peaceful policy. Today it is not the forces of imperialism but the forces of peace and socialism that determine the main laws, the main direction of international and social development.

The Soviet Union is displaying the maximum good will in order to achieve understanding with our former allies and the Federal Republic of Germany. But the language of threats and intimidation to which the West often resorts is not conducive to a businesslike atmosphere for negotiations. Moreover, under such circumstances, concluding a peace treaty with the German Democratic Republic, with all the attendant consequences, may prove to be the only way out of the existing situation.

We shall sign the peace treaty and order our armed forces to administer a worthy rebuff to any aggressor if he dares to raise a hand against the Soviet Union or against our friends.

The Soviet government is sincerely striving to achieve a lasting peace. But we must not forget that the safeguarding of peace does not depend only on our own desire, on our own efforts. A lasting peace can be ensured only if efforts to achieve this goal are also exerted by the governments of other states, if the peoples of the whole world fight for this.

We say that a new world war is not inevitable. However, it must not be considered that the possibility of war has already been ruled out completely, inasmuch as the imperialist powers still exist. That is why we must be ready for any contingencies and well prepared. The Soviet people, and our young people above all, must be vigilant and ready to defend the country, to rebuff the aggressor if he dares to attack our homeland.

We must perfect our weapons and improve our skill in handling arms, so that they fire without fail and with pinpoint accuracy. This must be remembered primarily by you yourselves—the commanders and leaders of our forces. The Soviet army must be ready at any moment to defend reliably the peaceful construction of communism in the Soviet Union and to do its international duty of rendering aid to the other socialist countries.

The Soviet armed forces today have everything necessary in order to carry out successfully the responsible tasks set before them. They possess the necessary quantities of thermonuclear weapons and the most efficient means of delivering them—close combat, intermediate and intercontinental missiles.

It is best for those who are thinking of war not to imagine that distances will save them. No, if the imperialists unleash a war, it will end with imperialism's complete collapse and ruin. Mankind will end, once and for all, the system which gives rise to aggressive wars.

Comrades, the government of the Soviet Union is attentively following the military measures taken recently by the United States of America and its N.A.T.O. allies. We cannot ignore such facts as the building up of armed forces in the western countries, the steps to increase considerably the number of strategic nuclear bombers, which are constantly kept in the air. The forces of Western Germany are being equipped with the latest weapons and increased numerically.

The United States President, Mr. Kennedy, has proclaimed in his recent Messages to Congress a so-called 'new course'. It provides for stepping up the programme of developing rocket-missile strategic weapons and an increase in the military preparedness of all services. For this purpose President Kennedy has proposed that military allocations be increased as compared with the draft budget submitted by the previous President by more than 3,500 million dollars.

This means that the military expenditures in the fiscal year of 1961–62 will exceed 53,000 million dollars. The military expenditures in the Federal Republic of Germany have increased by 18 per cent. this year. A considerable growth of military expenditures is characteristic of Britain, France and other N.A.T.O. countries.

This is how the western powers are replying to the Soviet Union's unilateral reduction of armed forces and military expenditures carried out over several past years.

Would it be correct for us, in these conditions, to continue to reduce our armed forces unilaterally?

Taking into account the existing situation, the Soviet government has been compelled to instruct the Ministry of Defence to suspend temporarily, pending special orders, the reduction of armed forces planned for 1961.

In view of the growing military budgets in the N.A.T.O. countries, the Soviet government has taken a decision to increase defence expenditures in the current year by 3,144 million roubles, thereby raising the total military expenditures in 1961 to 12,399 million roubles.

These are forced measures, Comrades. We are taking them owing to the emerging circumstances, because we cannot neglect the interests of the Soviet people's security.

Comrades, we are firmly convinced that the solution to many pressing problems concerning the improvement of the international situation depends to a great extent on the improvement of relations between the Soviet Union and the United States of America. Of course, we realise that the improvement of Soviet-American relations is not a simple task. It cannot be achieved without a desire on the part of both sides and practical steps by both sides.,

Interesting in this light is a statement made by the President of the United States, Mr. Kennedy, at a press conference on June 28, when he dwelt on peaceful economic competition between our two countries.[1] We appreciate such an approach. This, of course, is much better than competing in the development of ever more destructive types of weapons. We have always said this and we go on repeating it.

The Soviet Union is still lagging behind the United States as regards the level of its economic development, and we frankly admit this. But our country has inexhaustible potentialities for overcoming this lag quickly and for becoming richer than the United States.

The Soviet people are convinced that the time is not far off when the Soviet Union will overtake and outstrip the United States of America as regards basic economic indices. This is not wishful thinking, but concrete plans based on concrete calculations.

Our desire to be richer than the United States, to overtake it in economic development, does not, of course, signify a threat to the United States. Some people call this our challenge to the United States. But this is a challenge to peaceful competition. What is bad about that? Irrespective of who wins this competition, the peoples of both countries will benefit from it, because they will enjoy the blessings of peaceful labour.

[1] Above, p. 302.

In his statement at the press conference President Kennedy acknowledged that the socialist system permits the Soviet Union to overtake the United States. He believes, it is true, that this will happen in a more distant future than is indicated by us. He questions the feasibility of our plans, but facts, life itself, eloquently show that he is not right about this.

I shall not enter into polemics with Mr. Kennedy. Simple calculations will be sufficient. The volume of the Soviet Union's industrial production was equal to 60 per cent. of American output in 1960. The average annual rates of industrial growth in our country have amounted to 10.6 per cent. during the past 16 years. If Soviet industrial output continues to grow annually by 10 per cent., in 1966 the Soviet Union will be producing 106 per cent. of the present American output and in 1970 it will be producing 156 per cent.

In order to increase by 56 per cent. in 10 years, United States industrial output must increase by $4\frac{1}{2}$ per cent. annually. However, even if the Americans succeed in ensuring an annual increment of $4\frac{1}{2}$ per cent., as Mr. Kennedy would like it to be, we shall overtake them just the same in 1970.

If the Americans retain the rate of their industrial output at 2 per cent., which they have averaged in the postwar years, the Soviet Union will outstrip America already in 1967. If American industrial output increases by three per cent. annually, we shall leave them behind in 1968.

Approximately the same figures could be adduced with regard to the prospects for agricultural development in our two countries.

Forecasts with regard to economic development give rise to most of the arguments, of course. I, for instance, am sceptical about Mr. Kennedy's statements, which he made during the election campaign, criticising Eisenhower for the low rates of American economic development. He promised an economic upsurge with the advent of the new Administration in the United States, and less unemployment.

Back in those days, speaking to Mrs. Roosevelt, I said that if the Democratic Party came to power and Mr. Kennedy became President, he would hardly be able, in my opinion, to achieve more in the economic sphere than Eisenhower's government.

As a matter of fact, that is precisely what has happened. Look, for instance, at unemployment. Last October the United States had three and a half million people without work. In June of this year, eight months later, the number of unemployed had not declined, but had increased to five and a half million.

Under the capitalist system economic development depends very little on the President. Every capitalist disposes of his capital himself and throws workers out into the street if that benefits him.

Such are the laws of capitalism—draconic laws, but laws which still operate. The socialist system, of course, does not and cannot have all this.

We can argue about the prospects for economic development in this or that state. We can make various guesses, but these arguments are not a reason for war between states.

So let us allow history, Mr. Kennedy, to determine who is making correct forecasts and who is making a mistake.

An important role in developing good relations among nations is played by economic, cultural and other contacts, and the Soviet Union is striving to develop them. We have favourable trade relations with Great Britain, France, Italy, Japan, and Western Germany. This trade benefits both sides.

Our trade relations with other countries are developing, too. But the same cannot be said about trade with the United States. In actual fact we do not have any trade with the United States and this is not to the advantage of the two countries. I should like to be understood correctly. We stand for the development of trade with the United States of America, but not because we cannot do without it. The Soviet Union will not only keep going, but will continue its rapid advance, fulfilling and overfulfilling the economic plans that are drafted.

But it is possible to speak earnestly about the improvement of relations and the creation of an atmosphere of confidence between the two strongest powers in the world if one of them is pursuing a policy of economic discrimination in relation to the other? Of course not. If the United States had displayed good common sense and given up the policy of artificially restricting trade relations with the Soviet Union, that would have promoted the improvement of friendly relations, an improvement in the international climate.

Soviet policy is a policy of peaceful co-existence. That is why we tell President Kennedy, General de Gaulle, Mr. Macmillan: Let us compete in this sphere. This would be sensible. If we were to conclude a peace treaty with Germany, shake hands and declare that we would devote our efforts to economic competition, all the people of the world would heave a sigh of relief. This would be a good prologue for further talks and for the realisation of mankind's age-old dream of lasting peace on earth. We are ready for this and we offer our hand to the western governments.

Comrades, the Soviet army has won many glorious victories over the enemies of our homeland. Today it is the most up-to-date, the mightiest army in the world. The technical basis of our Soviet army, navy and air forces has been changed radically during the past few years, thanks to the concern displayed by the party and the people. Our armed forces will go on developing and improving continuously; they will continue to be equipped with the mightiest weapons, until a plan for general disarmament is adopted.

However, no matter how up-to-date and strong military equipment is, it can serve its purpose only if it is placed in the reliable and skilful hands of servicemen who are ideologically steeled, courageous and boundlessly loyal to their country.

Responsibility for fulfilling the tasks facing the Soviet armed forces rests, above all, on the officer cadres. In order to be up to the mark, officers must persistently master Marxist-Leninist theory.

A Soviet officer must always and everywhere be a model of political maturity and high morality, and he must do his military duty faultlessly. At the same time a very exacting attitude is needed constantly in the armed forces more than anywhere else, together with the iron will on the part of the commanders and unswerving observance of the principle of undivided command. To command means to be an organiser of the masses, to guide the people skilfully towards goals that have been set.

Officers must make sensible use of their great rights in order to increase combat preparedness, to strengthen discipline and order in their units and ships.

Military discipline is called the mother of victory. And it must be said that the experience of war fully confirms this truth. New equipment and new types of weapons, far from reducing the importance of military discipline, immeasurably increase it.

In our day an officer must have high military-technical training; he must possess a wide range of theoretical views. He can successfully do his duty if he keeps abreast of the development of military theory and practice.

It is sufficient to give yourself airs for a short time and you will be among those who are lagging behind. A critical attitude towards the results of one's work, an irreconcilable attitude towards shortcomings, and honesty and truthfulness towards the party and the people must be inherent qualities of all our officers.

The Soviet army has always been strong, thanks to the consciousness of its personnel, their allegiance to the sacred ideals of our party. The soldiers' high level of ideological conviction, their readiness to fight honestly for the Soviet homeland, for our people, for the noble and high ideals of socialism, constitute the great advantages of our army over the armies of the capitalist states.

It is imperative to continue persistently rearing the troops on the ideas of Marxism-Leninism, in the spirit of Soviet patriotism, friendship between the peoples and proletarian internationalism.

The strength of our army, created under the guidance of the great Lenin, lies in its unbreakable bonds with the people. It owes all its successes and victories to the party. Guidance by the party, the party's constant solicitude for strengthening the armed forces, constitutes the foundation of foundations of military affairs and signifies the strengthening of the defence potential of the Soviet Union.

Enhancing the role and influence of the party organisations in the army and the navy must continue to be the foundation of our military policy. It is the task of commanders, political workers and all chiefs in their work to draw skilfully on party organisations, steadily to channel the creative energy and activity of communists and members of the Young Communist League into improving the combat preparedness of the Soviet armed forces.

Difficult and honorable is the work of our officers. They bear full responsibility for their subordinates, for their education and training. The need for constant combat preparedness on the part of the troops demands intense work from commanders and political workers and from the entire personnel.

The people have entrusted their armed forces with the task of vigilantly standing guard over our great Soviet homeland, confidently advancing towards communism. Show yourselves worthy of this great trust.

Dear Comrades, may I once again heartily congratulate you on graduating from the military academies and wish you big successes in your noble work for the sake of peace and the security of our socialist homeland.

Long live the powerful and prosperous Soviet homeland!

Long live the gallant Soviet armed forces and their officer cadres!

Glory to the Communist Party of the Soviet Union—the organiser and inspirer of all our victories!

8. The Federal German Government to the Government of the Soviet Union, 12 July 1961[1]

The Federal Government has carefully examined the memorandum of the Government of the U.S.S.R. of 17 February 1961.[2] The Federal Government takes the following attitude:—

The Federal Government has learned with satisfaction of the efforts of the Soviet Government to improve its relations with the Federal Republic in every way. This desire for an improvement in relations is shared by the Federal Government. If the government of the Soviet Socialist Republic, however, raises the question of a solution of the German question in this connection, it should be mentioned that the responsibility for the re-establishment of the unity of Germany and with it the solution of the German question lies in the first instance with the governments of France, Great Britain, the U.S.S.R. and the United States. In view of this responsibility the Federal Government expresses the hope that these Four Powers will remain in contact with one another. For its own part it is determined to support the relevant efforts of the Four Powers to the utmost.

The Federal Government welcomes the offer of friendship made by the Government of the Soviet Socialist Republic to the whole German people. The reference to the whole German people is considered by the Federal Government to be the expression of a corresponding attitude on the part of the U.S.S.R. towards the German problem. It is an irrefutable fact that in spite of all developments which have occurred as a result of World War II, the German people continues as a whole; that there is only one German people. Any policy which in the course of attempting to solve the German question, neglects this fact, cannot claim to be considered as realistic.

The unsatisfactory state of the German question—as it is expressed in the memorandum of the government of the U.S.S.R.—can be attributed to the fact that it is still forbidden, even 16 years after the end of the war to give the German people as a whole a common political system. A sober assessment of the present situation, as is more than once called for in the memorandum of 17 February 1961, leads to the conclusion that this condition can only be altered if the German people are allowed to exercise the right of self-determination. The Government of the U.S.S.R. has in past months expressly demanded the right for self-determination for a number of peoples. If the Soviet government would allow this right to the whole German people—to whom it offers its friendship— that would constitute a valuable and permanent basis for this friendship.

The Federal Government finds its conception of the dominating importance of the right of self-determination for the German question confirmed by the Geneva directive of 23 July 1955 of the Heads of Government of France, Great Britain, the U.S.S.R. and the United States.[3] In a realistic assessment of the circumstances of the German problem, the four heads of government based their directive on the right to self-determination of the German people, in agreeing that the German question and the question of the re-unification of Germany

---

[1] *Frankfurter Allgemeine Zeitung*, 13 July 1961. (Translation prepared in Chatham House.)
[2] See above, pp. 272–7.   [3] *Documents*, 1955, pp. 48–49.

should be solved by free elections. The four heads of government took this decision in the full knowledge of their common responsibility for the solution of the German problem. To this day nothing has altered in this responsibility of the four powers. The principles contained in the afore mentioned directive of 23 July 1955 for a way to the solution of the German problem remain unaltered.

In the memorandum of 17 February 1961 the government of the U.S.S.R. refers to the urgency of the conclusion of a Peace Treaty with Germany and places the first importance on the formation of a government of the German people which shall be capable of negotiating, legitimised by a democratic decision of the German people, and whose sovereignty shall encompass the whole German people. Such a government can only be created by the German people if it is made possible for it to exercise a right of self-determination by a free decision of will. The timing of the conclusion of a Peace Treaty with Germany depends therefore on the readiness of the government of the U.S.S.R. to concede to the German people the right of self-determination. The Federal Government would welcome the taking of such a decision by the Soviet government at the earliest possible date, so that the negotiations on a Peace Treaty with a government for all Germany should be made possible.

The Federal Government, in agreement with its allies, is of the opinion that only a government, based on the right of self-determination would be legitimised to conclude a Peace Treaty for Germany. A Treaty of Peace that does not correspond with those requirements would not be worthy of the name. Furthermore, even apart from the legal impossibility of concluding peace with a divided Germany, such a procedure would not be accepted by the German people, which clearly desires the re-establishment of its unity. The German people would see in the conclusion of the Peace Treaty as proposed by the U.S.S.R. only a deepening of the division of Germany. When the government of the U.S.S.R. states that such a Peace Treaty does not demand any sacrifice from the Federal Republic, it overlooks that it demands the sacrifice of the main desire of the German people, namely its re-unification.

A separate Peace Treaty with one part of Germany would conflict with the right to self-determination of all nations which is recognized in Article 1, para 2 of the Charter of the United Nations, signed by the Soviet Union, as one of the guiding principles of the United Nations, and which the U.S.S.R. is pledged to respect. The right to self-determination exists for the German people as the unalterable basic right of all peoples, who hold fast to their national unity, and express their desire for this in free elections.

The Soviet Government in its memorandum urges the Federal Government to make counter-proposals for a Peace Treaty. The Government of the U.S.S.R., however, only considers such proposals constructive, which themselves are based on the unalterability of the division of Germany. Proposals which are based irrevocably on the division of Germany cannot be constructive, as they will never lead to a permament peace settlement. Only proposals which have as their aim the overcoming of Germany's division, can be a constructive contribution to a peace settlement. The West have advanced such proposals without success in every Four Power Conference on Germany in the last few years—on the last occasion at the Geneva Foreign Ministers Conference in 1959. The Western

Peace Plan then published, which offered a complete basis for a permanent peace settlement was unfortunately turned down by the government of the U.S.S.R., as all preceding constructive proposals of the West had been.

A Peace Treaty with a generally-recognised government, based on the right of self-determination of the German people, would settle all problems touching Germany, including the question of her frontiers. The question of Berlin raised by the Soviet Government would also be clarified as Berlin could fulfil its natural position as capital city of Germany. Here too a unitary organism is artificially divided against the will of the German people. This fact must be given its proper value when one is judging the present position of Berlin. In the view of the Federal Government a Peace Treaty based on the division of Germany would in no way lead towards a reduction of international tension. On the contrary, such a Treaty would lead to an increase in tension as it would make the division of Germany permament. The Federal Government, however, is looking for possibilities of decreasing tension. It is, as has often been stated, of the view that general and controlled disarmament is the real way to diminish international tensions all over the world. An international détente attained by such disarmament would also create favourable conditions for a permanent just settlement of the German question based in the rights of self-determination of the German people.

In the Past the Federal Government has often and repeatedly declared itself ready to join a Great Power agreement on a general and controlled disarmament at any time. The Federal Government is attempting to further the cause of disarmament by giving its agreement in advance to any disarmament agreement of the Four Powers.

The Federal Government regrets that allegations are contained in the memorandum of the U.S.S.R. which lack any basis in fact. Such allegations are not well suited to serve the efforts of the Soviet Government to improve its relations with the Federal Republic. In the memorandum of 17 February 1961 the idea is expressed that the Federal Government hopes to attain its ends by force. It arms itself to settle the question of Germany's frontiers by war. The Federal Government rejects such allegations with the utmost emphasis. It has repeatedly declared and here and now declares again that it will not use force either to bring about re-unification, or to settle the frontier question.

The accusations of the Soviet Government are the less comprehensible as it must be known to them that the whole striking force of the Bundeswehr is integrated into N.A.T.O. which was created for the sole purpose of western defence and serves no aggressive purposes. The Federal Republic of Germany exercises its lawful defence responsibilities entirely within the scope of the N.A.T.O. alliance. There are no nuclear weapons under the control of the Federal Republic of Germany or of its armed forces. Furthermore, the Federal Government points out that the Federal Republic has contracted on its own initiative to renounce the creation of atomic weapons.

The Federal Government has also noted with surprise the allegation contained in the memorandum of 17 February 1961 concerning the election campaign in the Federal Republic. The Federal Government rejects these allegations decisively. As the Government of the U.S.S.R. has made the domestic affairs of the Federal Republic the basis for its statement, the Federal Republic considers it necessary to declare once more that it is in agreement with all parties in the Bundestag to do everything in its power towards the re-unification of the German people in peace and freedom. The Federal Republic emphasises once again that it wished to achieve this only by peaceful means. It does, therefore, not intend to raise a feeling of enmity towards the U.S.S.R. amongst the peoples of Federal Germany. Such an action would be contrary to the basic principles of the Federal Republic's policy, that is to abandon any negotiation which might lead to an increase in international tension. The Federal Republic would like to recommend the U.S.S.R. to refrain from such actions in a like manner.

9. United States Note in reply to the Soviet aide-mémoire of 4 June, 17 July 1961[1]

The United States Government has given careful consideration to the Soviet Government's *aide-mémoire* received on June 4, 1961, in Vienna. It has consulted with its British and French Allies and has found itself in full agreement with them. It has also consulted the Government of the Federal Republic of Germany, and the other members of the North Atlantic Treaty Organisation.

The United States Government fully concurs with the Soviet Government that a peace settlement is long overdue. It is clear from the public record of efforts on the part of the Western Powers to reach agreement with the Soviet Union on the terms of such a peace settlement that it is the Soviet Union which has blocked all progress. The United States first suggested in 1946 that a special commission be appointed to draft a German peace treaty.[2] It has continued its efforts throughout all the intervening years but without avail because of Soviet efforts to obtain special advantages for itself and the Soviet bloc in any such settlement at the expense of a lasting peace.

The United States Government would like to be able to believe the Soviet Government's statement that it sincerely desires to remove the sources of tension between the United States and the Soviet Union and to proceed to constructive friendly co-operation. This aim is close to the hearts of the American people and their Government, it found its expression in wartime co-operation, and the United States was deeply disappointed when Soviet post-war actions disrupted the conditions for its continuation. The conclusion of a German treaty in peace and freedom and based on the freely expressed will of the German people would, indeed, allow the U.S.S.R. and the United States to come much closer to the attainment of this goal.

With regard to Berlin, the United States is not insisting upon the maintenance of its legal rights because of any desire merely to perpetuate its presence there. It is insisting on, and will defend, its legal rights against attempts at unilateral abrogation because the freedom of the people of West Berlin depends upon the maintenance of those rights. The support and approval of the people of West

---

[1] *D.S.B.*, 7 August 1961, pp. 224–30. For the text of the British and French Notes to the Soviet Government of the same date see Cmnd. 1552, pp. 448–9, and *Le Monde*, 18 June 1961. For President Kennedy's commentary on this Note see *Public Papers*, 1961, pp. 521–3.

[2] See *The United States in World Affairs*, 1945–7 (New York and London, Harper, 1947), pp. 119, 125, 133.

Berlin for the system under which they live has been made amply clear over the years. Their overwhelming support for their Government in free elections is a dramatic example of this. That the United States is not wedded to one particular arrangement for Berlin is demonstrated by the all-Berlin solution which was proposed at Geneva in 1959.[1] It has accepted the possibility of practical arrangements intended to improve the present situation in Berlin until such time as an over-all solution of the German problem can be achieved. It is sorry to note that all the proposals it has made to that end have been rejected by the Government of the U.S.S.R. However, the United States also supports the clearly expressed wish of the West Berliners that no change be made in the status of their city which would expose them, at once or gradually over a long time, to the domination of the regime which at present controls the surrounding areas.

The United States Government continues to believe that there will be no real solution of the German problem, nor any real tranquillity in Central Europe, until the German people are reunified in peace and freedom on the basis of the universally recognised right of self-determination. It is because of this conviction that the United States Government, with its Allies, has repeatedly proposed solutions for the German problem based on these principles—unfortunately without evoking a positive response from the Soviet Government.

Thus, they proposed to the Soviet Government on May 14, 1959 the Western Peace Plan;[2] which was acclaimed throughout the world as a constructive offer. The detailed proposals in the peace plan were intended as a practical step-by-step approach to the problem of a Central European settlement based on the principle of self-determination, to which the Soviet Government professes to adhere but which is conspicuous by its absence in Soviet proposals.

The Soviet *aide-mémoire* argues that the time has already passed when the situation in Germany could be left unchanged. The United States Government is persuaded that a change for the better is to be desired. But at the same time it is certain that world opinion has noted that in the decade between the end of the Soviet blockade of Berlin and the renewed threat to Berlin in the Soviet Note of November 27, 1958[3] the German problem did not disturb world peace. And just as the world could not fail to note who was responsible for disturbing the peace on those two occasions, it will surely condemn any attempt by any one of the four Powers to change the existing situation in West Berlin against the will of the other three and against the overwhelming desire of the vast majority of the people of Berlin and Germany, who are most directly concerned.

To justify the action it wishes to take, the Government of the U.S.S.R. alleges that without a peace treaty there is danger of conflagration in Europe. The U.S. Government does not consider that this argument has any merit. Minor incidents which occur from time to time in the present situation are settled through exercise of those quadripartite responsibilities which, in themselves, constitute the most effective protection against any local aggravation of the situation growing into a real threat to the peace.

Contrary to the unfounded assertion in the Soviet *aid-mémoire*, the Western Powers vigorously carried out the programme to eradicate Nazi militarism, to

[1] *Documents*, 1959, pp. 56–57.   [2] *Documents*, 1959, pp. 34–39.
[3] ibid., 1958, pp. 146–64.

eliminate vestiges of the Third Reich, to prevent the rebirth of aggressive forces, and to chart a course by which Germany could recover its respect and play a constructive role in international affairs. The Federal Republic of Germany is the proof of the successful achievement of these aims by the West.

The Federal Republic's foreign and military policies accept significant restraints. It has undertaken not to manufacture atomic, chemical and biological weapons, and has accepted international control to ensure that this undertaking is honoured. All the Federal Republic's combat forces are completely integrated to NATO, which has only defensive—not aggressive—aims. The Federal Republic does not seek, or intend to develop, an independent nuclear capability or the transfer of nuclear weapons to its national jurisdiction. It looks to its legitimate defence requirements entirely within the NATO framework. In addition, the Federal Government has publicly stated that the Federal Republic does not contemplate the use of force to achieve reunification or to alter existing boundaries. It has also consistently taken significant steps to integrate itself peacefully and firmly into the Western European Community—steps which would never be taken by a government bent on a militaristic course.

After the end of World War II, the United States and its Western Allies demobilised their military forces in the expectation of a peaceful world order. However, post-war Soviet policies compelled the organisation of the military defence of the North Atlantic Treaty Area. Without the armed threat to Western Europe, the purely defensive alliance to which the United States is fully committed and in which the Federal Republic participates might well never have developed. The pursuit by the U.S.S.R. of its unilateral objectives in Eastern Europe convinced the present members of NATO that Soviet power would be extended into any area Westward which did not have the ability to defend itself. Should the U.S.S.R. make unilateral moves in its German policy, contrary to binding international agreements, the NATO countries could only interpret such moves as a purposeful threat to their national interests.

The Soviet Government, in its *aide-mémoire*, is presenting the Western Powers with a demand that they accept its solution of the German problem. Despite the protestations of the Soviet Government that it does not intend to harm the interests of the United States or other Western Powers in Europe, it remains the firm conviction of the Western Powers that the end result of the Soviet proposals would harm not only their interests, but also those of the German people, and—since they endanger the peace—those of the entire world.

The counterpart of the Soviet position is that unless the Western Powers accept its German solution, the Soviet Government will try to obtain what it wants by unilateral action.

The Soviet Government thus threatens to violate its solemn international obligations, to determine unilaterally the fate of millions of Germans without their consent, and to use force against its World War II Allies if they do not voluntarily surrender their rights and vital positions. The Soviet Government must understand that such a course of action is not only unacceptable, but is a more serious menace to world peace, for which it bears full responsibility before all mankind.

At the end of World War II, the victorious Powers entered into a number of agreements to settle the German problem, based on the principle that questions concerning Germany as a whole were a matter for joint action by the victorious Powers. A peace settlement with Germany is foremost among those questions. The Potsdam Agreement of 1945, for instance, refers to 'the preparation of a peace settlement for Germany to be accepted by the Government of Germany when a government adequate for the purpose is established'.[1]

Under international law, the Soviet Government cannot ignore these agreements in order to conclude unilateral arrangements with a part of Germany; nor would such action invalidate the rights of the United States Government and the other Governments responsible for the settlement of the German question, since these rights derive absolutely from the unconditional surrender of Nazi Germany, and were not granted by, or negotiated with, the Soviet Union. This has repeatedly been acknowledged by the Soviet Government, as recently as at the Vienna meetings and in Chairman Khrushchev's address on June 15, 1961.[2] For the same reason, the United States Government does not admit that its rights and obligations toward Germany as a whole can be affected by unilateral negotiations of peace settlements with a part or parts of Germany.

The obligation to maintain the unity of Germany was affirmed by the victorious Powers from the beginning. It was acknowledged by the Soviet Union in 1955, at a conference attended by Chairman Khrushchev, in the Geneva directive of the four Heads of Government, which says:

'The Heads of Government (of France, the United Kingdom, the Soviet Union, and the United States), recognising their common responsibility for the settlement of the German question and the reunification of Germany, have agreed that the settlement of the German question and the reunification of Germany by means of free elections shall be carried out in conformity with the national interests of the German people. . .'[3]

What the Soviet Union proposes, unless the three Powers formally abandon their efforts to reunify Germany, is to determine by itself the fate of Germany through an agreement with the authorities of the so-called 'German Democratic Republic', which is not freely chosen, but has been created by the Soviet Union as an instrument of Soviet foreign policy.

By its signature of the United Nations Charter and in numerous statements, the Soviet Government is committed to respect for the principle of self-determination. But, in contradiction of this, by denying freedom of choice to seventeen million East Germans it has not permitted freedom of choice to the German people as a whole. And it is now proposing to perpetuate that denial by concluding a final settlement with a regime which is not representative of these people, does not enjoy their confidence, and is, in fact, no more than its own creation and an extension of its own authority. Under these circumstances, the part of Germany subject to that regime cannot be regarded as an independent sovereign state, and a 'peace treaty' with the part of Germany's territory termed 'German Democratic Republic' by the Soviet Government could have no validity in international law, nor could it affect in any way whatsoever the rights of the Western Powers.

According to the thesis repeatedly expounded by the Soviets, the 'separate

[1] Cmnd. 1552, p. 49.   [2] Above, p. 286.   [3] *Documents*, 1955, p. 48.

peace treaty' would, upon its conclusion, terminate the rights of the West in, and with regard to, Berlin. These assertions are untenable and fallacious from a legal point of view, both because such a separate treaty would be legally ineffective, and because neither the Soviet Union nor East Germany can, for the reasons stated above, unilaterally deprive the three Western Powers of their original rights in, and regarding, Berlin. Rights of access to Berlin are inherent in the rights of the Western Powers to be in Berlin. The procedures for the exercise of these rights have been defined in numerous agreements between the four Governments and were confirmed by the Soviet Government in the Paris Agreement of June 20, 1949[1] on the termination of the Berlin blockade, and in practice over many years. They cannot be unilaterally abrogated by any act of the Soviet Government. If any one of the four withdraws from these arrangements, then it is clearly the responsibility of the other three to make such dispositions with respect to the exercise of their access rights as they deem appropriate.

The Soviet Union further asserts that a 'peace treaty', whether signed by all the interested parties or not, would bring about the establishment of West Berlin as a 'demilitarised free city'. As proposed, this would bring with it the cessation of the rights of the Western Allies in Berlin, including the right of access.

The United States considers entirely unfounded the Soviet claims that this unilateral act could deprive the other three participants in the joint occupation of Berlin of their basic rights in the city—rights derived from the Nazi surrender as indicated, and expressed in binding and valid agreements, to which the Soviet Union is a party. The agreements of September 12, 1944, and May 1, 1945[2] establishing the occupation arrangements for the city were joint undertakings by the occupying Powers, all of whom derived rights and obligations from them. The obligation of the Soviet Union to assure the normal functioning of transport and communication between Berlin and the Western zones of Germany was reaffirmed in the Four Power Agreement of June 20, 1949. This legal situation was thus jointly created by the Four Powers and cannot be altered except by the common consent of all of them.

The United States wishes particularly to reiterate, in discussing the legal aspects of Berlin's status, that Soviet references to Berlin as being situated on the territory of the so-called 'German Democratic Republic' are entirely without foundation. This can be readily and clearly established by reference to the attached copy of the Protocol of September 12, 1944.[3] The protocol makes clear that Berlin was not a part of, or located on, the territory to be occupied as a zone by any one of the Powers under the agreement. With respect specifically to the area now constituting the so-called 'GDR' the Protocol clearly stated that a specified area, described by metes and bounds, 'will be occupied by armed forces of the U.S.S.R., with the exception of the Berlin area, for which a special system of occupation is provided below'. The Protocol subsequently clearly specified that 'the Berlin area will be jointly occupied by armed forces of the U.S., U.K., and U.S.S.R., assigned by the respective Commanders-in-Chief'. The Soviet Government approved the Protocol on February 6, 1945,[4] and since

---

[1] *Documents*, 1949–50, pp. 160–1. [2] Cmnd. 1552, pp. 27–29, 35–36.
[3] Omitted; for text, see n. 2. [4] At the Yalta Conference.

that time there have been no legal alterations in the special status of Berlin.

The Soviet Union claims that the 'free city' of West Berlin would be able to maintain freely its communications with the outside world and determine its domestic order by the free expression of the will of its people. Since, however, the 'free city' would in fact be isolated within the so-called 'German Democratic Republic', which according to the Soviet proposal would control all access to and from the city, it is of significance to examine the stated intentions of the leaders of that regime with respect to West Berlin.

The United States notes in particular the statements made by Mr. Ulbricht on June 15[1] in which he made clear his regime would seek to close Tempelhof Airport, West Berlin's principal airport and a vital part of its communications with the outside world. In addition, Mr. Ulbricht announced he 'considered it a matter of course' that the refugee centres in West Berlin would be closed. These camps are maintained by West Berlin for the constant stream of refugees fleeing from East Germany, and Ulbricht's statement makes clear the degree to which his regime intends to interfere in West Berlin where it suits his purpose. In view of such statements, it is not surprising if neither the West Berliners nor the Western Powers are reassured by professions of peaceful intent. In this connection, it is relevant to ask why the Soviet Union has chosen to raise the question at all if it has not had in mind a fundamental change in West Berlin.

It is evident that the present status of the city, which the Soviet Union chooses to characterise as an 'occupation regime' which 'has already outlived itself', is actually an arrangement that—under the existing abnormal division of Germany —does not constitute any threat to peace. Attempts by the Soviet Union to destroy that arrangement, in pursuit of its political goals, are certain to jeopardise gravely the very peace in the name of which the Soviet action is taken. With respect to the nature of these goals in Berlin itself, it is significant that the Soviet Union, having previously occupied East Berlin and violated its Four Power status by establishing there an alleged 'G.D.R.' Government, now proposes that its troops will be among those stationed in a 'free city' of West Berlin. The Soviet Government would thus seek to extend its post-war empire by the absorption of the Eastern sector of Berlin and to shift the Four Power principle from all of Berlin to the Western part of the city alone.

The immediate cause of this threat to peace arises from the announced intention of the Soviet Government to present the three Western Powers with a *de facto* situation based on the false assertion that they would no longer be entitled to remain in Berlin, or to have free access thereto. Such a move could lead to highly dangerous developments, and would be totally devoid of legal effect. The United States considers the exercise of its rights together with its British and French Allies, in order to maintain the freedom of over two million people in West Berlin, a fundamental political and moral obligation.

The international dispute arising out of Soviet claims would have the gravest effects upon international peace and security and endanger the lives and well-being of millions of people. It would be irresponsible on the part of the nations directly concerned not to use available means to settle such a dispute in a peaceful manner.

[1] *Neues Deutschland*, 16 June 1961.

As in the past, the United States Government is always prepared to consider in agreement with its Allies a freely negotiated settlement of the unresolved problems of Germany. Such a settlement must be in conformity with the principle of self-determination and with the interests of all concerned. The United States Government for its part has never contemplated confronting the Soviet Union with a *fait accompli*. It hopes that for its part the Soviet Government will renounce any idea of taking such action, which, as noted, would have unforeseeable consequences. It thinks it necessary to warn the Soviet Government in all seriousness of the grave dangers of such a course, and to express the hope that the Soviet Government will rather aim, as does the United States Government, at the creation of conditions in which a genuine and peaceful settlement of outstanding problems can be pursued.

Peace and freedom are not merely words nor can they be achieved by words or promises alone. They are representative of a state of affairs.

A city does not become free merely by calling it free. For a city or a people to be free requires that they be given the opportunity without economic, political or police pressure to make their own choice and to live their own lives. The people of West Berlin today have that freedom. It is the objective of our policy for them to continue to have it.

Peace does not come automatically from a 'peace treaty'. There is peace in Germany today even though the situation is 'abnormal'. A 'peace treaty' that adversely affects the lives and rights of millions will not bring peace with it. A 'peace treaty' that attempts to affect adversely the solemn commitments of three great Powers does not bring peace with it.

There is no reason for a crisis over Berlin. If one develops it is because the Soviet Union is attempting to invade the basic rights of others. All the world will plainly see that the misuse of such words as 'peace' and 'freedom' cannot conceal a threat to raise tension to the point of danger and suppress the freedom of those who now enjoy it.

10. President Kennedy's press conference of 19 July 1961[1] (extracts)

THE PRESIDENT. [I.] I have a statement on Germany and Berlin. I'll read a few paragraphs of it and it will be available for distribution right after the press conference.

The Soviet *aide-mémoire* is a document which speaks of peace, but threatens to disturb it. It speaks of ending the abnormal situation in Germany, but insists on making permanent its abnormal division. It refers to the Four Power Alliance of World War II, but seeks the unilateral abrogation of the rights of the other three powers. It calls for new international agreements, while preparing to violate existing ones. It offers certain assurances, while making it plain that its previous assurances are not to be relied upon. It professes concern for the rights of the citizens of West Berlin, while seeking to expose them to the immediate or eventual domination of a regime which permits no self-determination. Three simple facts are clear:

1. Today there is peace in Berlin, in Germany, and in Europe. If that peace is

[1] *Public Papers*, 1961, pp. 513–23.

destroyed by the unilateral actions of the Soviet Union, its leaders will bear a heavy responsibility before world opinion and history.

2. The people of West Berlin are free. In that sense it's already a 'free city'—free to determine its own leaders and free to enjoy the fundamental human rights reaffirmed in the United Nations Charter.

3. Today the continued presence in West Berlin of the United States, the United Kingdom, and France is by clear legal right, arising from war, acknowledged in many agreements signed by the Soviet Union, and strongly supported by the overwhelming majority of the people of that city. Their freedom is dependent upon the exercise of these rights—an exercise which is thus a political and moral obligation as well as a legal right. Inasmuch as these rights, including the right of access to Berlin, are not held from the Soviet Government, they cannot be ended by any unilateral action of the Soviet Union. They cannot be affected by a so-called 'peace treaty', covering only a part of Germany, with a regime of the Soviet Union's own creation—a regime which is not freely representative of all or any part of Germany, and does not enjoy the confidence of the 17 million East Germans. The steady stream of German refugees from East to West is eloquent testimony to this fact.

The real intent of the June 4 *aide-mémoire* is that East Berlin, a part of a city under four power status, would be formally absorbed into the so-called German Democratic Republic while West Berlin, even though called a 'free city', would lose the protection presently provided by the Western Powers and become subject to the will of a totalitarian regime. Its leader, Herr Ulbricht, has made clear his intention, once this so-called 'peace treaty' is signed, to curb West Berlin's communications with the free world and to suffocate the freedom it now enjoys.

The world knows that there is no reason for a crisis over Berlin today—and that if one develops it will be caused by the Soviet Government's attempts to invade the rights of others and manufacture tensions.

A city does not become free merely by calling it a 'free city'. For a city or a people to be free requires that they be given the opportunity, without economic, political, or police pressure, to make their own choice and live their own lives. The people of West Berlin today have that freedom. It is the objective of our policy that they will continue to enjoy it.

Peace does not come automatically from a 'peace treaty'. There is peace in Germany today even though the situation is 'abnormal'. A 'peace treaty' that adversely affects the lives and rights of millions will not bring peace with it. A 'peace treaty' that attempts to affect adversely the solemn commitments of three great powers will not bring peace with it. We again urge the Soviet Government to reconsider its course, to return to the path of constructive cooperation it so frequently states it desires, and to work with its World War II Allies in concluding a just and enduring settlement of issues remaining from that conflict. . . .

[ii.] Q. Mr. President, in your consideration of the military requirements now in dealing with the Berlin situation, and of the allied military reevaluation, are you basing your judgment on the assumption that it is conceivable that we might fight a ground war in Europe over Berlin?

THE PRESIDENT. I'm making my judgment on what I consider to be the relative power balance between the Communist bloc and ourselves, the attitude which the Communist bloc is now taking, and what possible needs we might have in protecting our commitments and vital interest. . . .

Now, in answer to your question, I think that we'll make public—and you can make perhaps a better calculation after we give our figures—and as I said before those figures should not be discussed, in my opinion, until at least those who share this burden with us have a chance to be informed.

This alliance—NATO alliance—is going to move through very difficult periods in the coming months. Every country has its own strategic and tactical problems and carries particular burdens which other countries do not. If this alliance is going to move in concert, in my opinion we have to improve our consultation.

It took us, as you know, some time before we were able to come to a conclusion on the language of the *aide-mémoire*. We're going to have to improve our consultation so that we can come to decisions more quickly. But I think we should realize—as anyone who has studied the history of alliances—how enormous a task it is to have 15 countries moving down a stream all together over an issue which involves the security of them all. So we will inform them, and then the Congress, of what we plan to do, and the Congress will make the final judgment. . . .

[17.] Q. Mr. President, in your reply to the Soviet *aide-mémoire*, you stressed several times the lack of the right of self-determination among the peoples of Eastern Europe, and within the week you have issued a proclamation looking to the freedom of captive nations. Can you conceive in the event of any popular uprisings in Eastern Europe of a more active role for the United States in support of those uprisings than was the case in Hungary in 1956?

THE PRESIDENT. I think—I'll stand on the statement which we made at this time. . . .

[19.] Q. Mr. President, Soviet Ambassador Menshikov is reported to have said that he did not think the United States people were either prepared or ready to go to war over Berlin. Do you think Ambassador Menshikov is sending back a correct assessment of the mood and temper of the American people?

THE PRESIDENT. Well, I saw that this report came out of some function. I don't know how accurate it is, and whether that represents Mr. Menshikov's view. But I don't think that it's possible that anyone could read the *aide-mémoire* or the other statements which have been made by other governments and this Government without realizing that this is a very basic issue, the question of West Berlin, and that we intend to honor our commitments.

[20.] Q. Mr. President, tomorrow as you doubtless know marks the end of your first 6 months in the Presidency. In view of Laos, Cuba, and now Berlin, I wonder if there is anything you would care to tell us about the vicissitudes of the Presidency.

THE PRESIDENT. Well, I will say that we've had a—I think I said in the State of the Union address about the news will be worse instead of better. I would also say that Mr. Khrushchev would probably agree with that, in the sense that I think we are always conscious of the difficulties that we have. But there are a good many difficulties which should be taken into calculation in considering future bloc actions, in considering their own problems—whether it's the food

D.I.A.—M

shortage in China or the difficulties in other parts of the bloc empire, relations between certain bloc countries, and all the rest.

Now, as far as the United States, we've been pleased with the progress we've made internally, as far as the economy, the progress the country has made. We do feel we still have this problem of rather chronic unemployment. I'm glad that some of these bills which have been discussed for a number of years have passed. I'm hopful that we can add education to that and long-term borrowing authority for foreign aid. My judgment is that the American people and this Government and the Congress must realize that we're in a long struggle which we'll be involved with for a great many years against very powerful countries, nearly a billion people in them, with strong economies in some cases, and that we cannot look for success on every occasion.

But I think if we have the patience and willingness to take some setbacks without taking unwise actions, recognizing that there are also other successes which may not be as dramatic to us but certainly come within Mr. Khrushchev's calculations, that we can move through this period, I hope, protecting our vital interests and our commitments and also maintaining the peace. But no one should think that it's going to be easy.

11. Address given by President Kennedy over American radio and television, 25 July 1961[1]

Good evening:

Seven weeks ago tonight I returned from Europe to report on my meeting with Premier Khrushchev and the others. His grim warnings about the future of the world, his *aide-mémoire* on Berlin, his subsequent speeches and threats which he and his agents have launched, and the increase in the Soviet military budget that he has announced,[2] have all prompted a series of decisions by the Administration and a series of consultations with the members of the NATO organization. In Berlin, as you recall, he intends to bring to an end, through a stroke of the pen, *first* our legal rights to be in West Berlin—and *secondly* our ability to make good on our commitment to the two million free people of that city. That we cannot permit.

We are clear about what must be done—and we intend to do it. I want to talk frankly with you tonight about the first steps that we shall take. These actions will require sacrifice on the part of many of our citizens. More will be required in the future. They will require, from all of us, courage and perseverance in the years to come. But if we and our allies act out of strength and unity of purpose—with calm determination and steady nerves—using restraint in our words as well as our weapons—I am hopeful that both peace and freedom will be sustained.

The immediate threat to free men is in West Berlin. But that isolated outpost is not an isolated problem. The threat is worldwide. Our effort must be equally wide and strong, and not be obsessed by any single manufactured crisis. We face a challenge in Berlin, but there is also a challenge in Southeast Asia, where the borders are less guarded, the enemy harder to find, and the dangers of commun-

[1] *Public Papers*, 1961, pp. 533–40. [2] On 8 July; cf. above, p. 307.

ism less apparent to those who have so little. We face a challenge in our own hemisphere, and indeed wherever else the freedom of human beings is at stake.

Let me remind you that the fortunes of war and diplomacy left the free people of West Berlin, in 1945, 110 miles behind the Iron Curtain.

This map makes very clear the problem that we face. The white is West Germany—the East is the area controlled by the Soviet Union, and as you can see from the chart, West Berlin is 110 miles within the area which the Soviets now dominate—which is immediately controlled by the so-called East-German regime.

We are there as a result of our victory over Nazi Germany—and our basic rights to be there, deriving from that victory, include both our presence in West Berlin and the enjoyment of access across East Germany. These rights have been repeatedly confirmed and recognized in special agreements with the Soviet Union. Berlin is not a part of East Germany, but a separate territory under the control of the allied powers. Thus our rights there are clear and deep-rooted. But in addition to those rights is our commitment to sustain and defend, if need be—the opportunity for more than two million people to determine their own future and choose their own way of life.

II

Thus, our presence in West Berlin, and our access thereto, cannot be ended by any act of the Soviet government. The NATO shield was long ago extended to cover West Berlin—and we have given our word that an attack upon that city will be regarded as an attack upon us all.

For West Berlin—lying exposed 110 miles inside East Germany, surrounded by Soviet troops and close to Soviet supply lines, has many roles. It is more than a showcase of liberty, a symbol, an island of freedom in a Communist sea. It is even more than a link with the Free World, a beacon of hope behind the Iron Curtain, an escape hatch for refugees.

West Berlin is all of that. But above all it has now become—as never before—the great testing place of Western courage and will, a focal point where our solemn commitments stretching back over the years since 1945, and Soviet ambitions now meet in basic confrontation.

It would be a mistake for others to look upon Berlin, because of its location, as a tempting target. The United States is there; the United Kingdom and France are there; the pledge of NATO is there—and the people of Berlin are there. It is as secure, in that sense, as the rest of us—for we cannot separate its safety from our own.

I hear it said that West Berlin is militarily untenable. And so was Bastogne. And so, in fact, was Stalingrad. Any dangerous spot is tenable if men—brave men—will make it so.

We do not want to fight—but we have fought before. And others in earlier times have made the same dangerous mistake of assuming that the West was too selfish and too soft and too divided to resist invasions of freedom in other lands. Those who threaten to unleash the forces of war on a dispute over West Berlin should recall the words of the ancient philosopher: 'A man who causes fear cannot be free from fear.'

We cannot and will not permit the Communists to drive us out of Berlin, either gradually or by force. For the fulfillment of our pledge to that city is essential to the morale and security of Western Germany, to the unity of Western Europe, and to the faith of the entire Free World. Soviet strategy has long been aimed, not merely at Berlin, but at dividing and neutralizing all of Europe, forcing us back on our own shores. We must meet our oft-stated pledge to the free peoples of West Berlin—and maintain our rights and their safety, even in the face of force—in order to maintain the confidence of other free peoples in our word and our resolve. The strength of the alliance on which our security depends is dependent in turn on our willingness to meet our commitments to them.

III

So long as the Communists insist that they are preparing to end by themselves unilaterally our rights in West Berlin and our commitments to its people, we must be prepared to defend those rights and those commitments. We will at all times be ready to talk, if talk will help. But we must also be ready to resist with force, if force is used upon us. Either alone would fail. Together, they can serve the cause of freedom and peace.

The new preparations that we shall make to defend the peace are part of the long-term build-up in our strength which has been underway since January. They are based on our needs to meet a world-wide threat, on a basis which stretches far beyond the present Berlin crisis. Our primary purpose is neither propaganda nor provocation—but preparation.

A first need is to hasten progress toward the military goals which the North Atlantic allies have set for themselves. In Europe today nothing less will suffice. We will put even greater resources into fulfilling those goals, and we look to our allies to do the same.

The supplementary defense build-ups that I asked from the Congress in March and May[1] have already started moving us toward these and our other defense goals. They included an increase in the size of the Marine Corps, improved readiness of our reserves, expansion of our air and sea lift, and stepped-up procurement of needed weapons, ammunition, and other items. To insure a continuing invulnerable capacity to deter or destroy any aggressor, they provided for the strengthening of our missile power and for putting 50% of our B-52 and B-47 bombers on a ground alert which would send them on their way with 15 minutes' warning.

These measures must be speeded up, and still others must now be taken. We must have sea and air lift capable of moving our forces quickly and in large numbers to any part of the world.

But even more importantly, we need the capability of placing in any critical area at the appropriate time a force which, combined with those of our allies is large enough to make clear our determination and our ability to defend our rights at all costs—and to meet all levels of aggressor pressure with whatever levels of force are required. We intend to have a wider choice than humiliation or all-out nuclear action.

[1] Above, pp. 39, 51.

While it is unwise at this time either to call up or send abroad excessive numbers of these troops before they are needed, let me make it clear that I intend to take, as time goes on, whatever steps are necessary to make certain that such forces can be deployed at the appropriate time without lessening our ability to meet our commitments elsewhere.

Thus, in the days and months ahead, I shall not hesitate to ask the Congress for additional measures, or exercise any of the executive powers that I possess to meet this threat to peace. Everything essential to the security of freedom must be done; and if that should require more men, or more taxes, or more controls, or other new powers, I shall not hesitate to ask them. The measures proposed today will be constantly studied, and altered as necessary. But while we will not let panic shape our policy, neither will we permit timidity to direct our program.

Accordingly, I am now taking the following steps:

(1) I am tomorrow requesting the Congress for the current fiscal year an additional $3,247,000,000 of appropriations for the Armed Forces.[1]

(2) To fill out our present Army Divisions, and to make more men available for prompt deployment, I am requesting an increase in the Army's total authorized strength from 875,000 to approximately 1 million men.

(3) I am requesting an increase of 29,000 and 63,000 men respectively in the active duty strength of the Navy and the Air Force.

(4) To fulfil these manpower needs, I am ordering that our draft calls be doubled and tripled in the coming months; I am asking the Congress for authority to order to active duty certain ready reserve units and individual reservists, and to extend tours of duty;[2] and, under that authority, I am planning to order to active duty a number of air transport squadrons and Air National Guard tactical air squadrons, to give us the airlift capacity and protection that we need. Other reserve forces will be called up when needed.

(5) Many ships and planes once headed for retirement are to be retained or reactivitated, increasing our airpower tactically and our sealift, airlift, and anti-submarine warfare capability. In addition, our strategic air power will be increased by delaying the deactivation of B-47 bombers.

(6) Finally, some $1.8 billion—about half of the total sum—is needed for the procurement of non-nuclear weapons, ammunition and equipment.

The details on all these requests will be presented to the Congress tomorrow. Subsequent steps will be taken to suit subsequent needs. Comparable efforts for the common defense are being discussed with our NATO allies. For their commitment and interest are as precise as our own.

And let me add that I am well aware of the fact that many American families will bear the burden of these requests. Studies or careers will be interrupted;

---

[1] A letter to the President of the Senate transmitting amendments to the Department of Defence budget was released by the White House on 26 July. On 17 August the President approved the Department of Defence Appropriation Act, 1962 (Public Law 87–144; 75 Stat. 365).

[2] On 26 July the White House released the text of identical letters to the President of the Senate and to the Speaker of the House of Representatives transmitting a request for authority to call reservists and to extend tours of duty. Also released was the text of a proposed joint resolution granting such authority, which was enacted on 1 August 1961 (Public Law 87–117; 75 Strat. 242).

husbands and sons will be called away; incomes in some cases will be reduced. But these are burdens which must be borne if freedom is to be defended—Americans have willingly borne them before—and they will not flinch from the task now.

IV

We have another sober responsibility. To recognize the possibilities of nuclear war in the missile age, without our citizens knowing what they should do and where they should go if bombs begin to fall, would be a failure of responsibility. In May, I pledged a new start on Civil Defense.[1] Last week, I assigned, on the recommendation of the Civil Defense Director, basic responsibility for this program to the Secretary of Defense,[2] to make certain it is administered and coordinated with our continental defense efforts at the highest civilian level. Tomorrow, I am requesting of the Congress new funds for the following immediate objectives: to identify and mark space in existing structures—public and private—that could be used for fall-out shelters in ease of attack; to stock those shelters with food, water, first-aid kits and other minimum essentials for survival; to increase their capacity; to improve our air-raid warning and fall-out detection systems, including a new household warning system which is now under development; and to take other measures that will be effective at an early date to save millions of lives if needed.

In the event of an attack, the lives of those families which are not hit in a nuclear blast and fire can still be saved—*if* they can be warned to take shelter and *if* that shelter is available. We owe that kind of insurance to our families—and to our country. In contrast to our friends in Europe, the need for this kind of protection is new to our shores. But the time to start is now. In the coming months, I hope to let every citizen know what steps he can take without delay to protect his family in case of attack. I know that you will want to do no less.

V

The addition of $207 million in Civil Defense appropriations brings our total new defense budget requests to $3.454 billion, and a total of $47.5 billion for the year. This is an increase in the defense budget of $6 billion since January, and has resulted in official estimates of a budget deficit of over $5 billion. The Secretary of the Treasury and other economic advisers assure me, however, that our economy has the capacity to bear this new request.

We are recovering strongly from this year's recession. The increase in this last quarter of our year of our total national output was greater than that for any postwar period of initial recovery. And yet, wholesale prices are actually lower than they were during the recession, and consumer prices are only $\frac{1}{4}$ of 1% higher than they were last October. In fact, this last quarter was the first in eight years in which our production has increased without an increase in the overall-price index. And for the first time since the fall of 1959, our gold position has improved and the dollar is more respected abroad. These gains, it should be stressed, are being accomplished with Budget deficits far smaller than those of the 1958 recession.

[1] See above, p. 51.
[2] In a statement issued on 20 July; text in *Public Papers*, 1961, p. 525.

This improved business outlook means improved revenues; and I intend to submit to the Congress in January a budget for the next fiscal year which will be strictly in balance. Nevertheless, should an increase in taxes be needed—because of events in the next few months—to achieve that balance, or because of subsequent defense rises, those increased taxes will be requested in January.

Meanwhile, to help make certain that the current deficit is held to a safe level, we must keep down all expenditures not thoroughly justified in budget requests. The luxury of our current post-office deficit must be ended. Costs in military procurement will be closely scrutinized—and in this effort I welcome the cooperation of the Congress. The tax loopholes I have specified—on expense accounts, overseas income, dividends, interest, cooperatives and others—must be closed.

I realize that no public revenue measure is welcomed by everyone. But I am certain that every American wants to pay his fair share, and not leave the burden of defending freedom entirely to those who bear arms. For we have mortgaged our very future on this defense—and we cannot fail to meet our responsibilities.

V

But I must emphasize again that the choice is not merely between resistance and retreat, between atomic holocaust and surrender. Our peace-time military posture is traditionally defensive; but our diplomatic posture need not be. Our response to the Berlin crisis will not be merely military or negative. It will be more than merely standing firm. For we do not intend to leave it to others to choose and monopolize the forum and the framework of discussion. We do not intend to abandon our duty to mankind to see a peaceful solution.

As signers of the UN Charter, we shall always be prepared to discuss international problems with any and all nations that are willing to talk—and listen—with reason. If they have proposals—not demands—we shall hear them. If they seek genuine understanding—not concessions of our rights—we shall meet with them. We have previously indicated our readiness to remove any actual irritants in West Berlin, but the freedom of that city is not negotiable. We cannot negotiate with those who say 'What's mine is mine and what's yours is negotiable.' But we are willing to consider any arrangement or treaty in Germany consistent with the maintenance of peace and freedom, and with the legitimate security interests of all nations.

We recognize the Soviet Union's historical concern about their security in Central and Eastern Europe, after a series of ravaging invasions, and we believe arrangements can be worked out which will help to meet those concerns, and make it possible for both security and freedom to exist in this troubled area.

For it is not the freedom of West Berlin which is 'abnormal' in Germany today, but the situation in that entire divided country. If anyone doubts the legality of our rights in Berlin, we are ready to have it submitted to international adjudication. If anyone doubts the extent to which our presence is desired by the people of West Berlin, compared to East German feelings about their regime, we are ready to have that question submitted to a free vote in Berlin and, if possible, among all the German people. And let us hear at that time from the two and one-half million refugees who have fled the Communist regime in East Germany—voting for Western-type freedom with their feet.

The world is not deceived by the Communist attempt to label Berlin as a hot-bed of war. There is peace in Berlin today. The source of world trouble and tension is Moscow, not Berlin. And if war begins, it will have begun in Moscow and not Berlin.

For the choice of peace or war is largely theirs, not ours. It is the Soviets who have stirred up this crisis. It is they who are trying to force a change. It is they who have opposed free elections. It is they who have rejected an all-German peace treaty, and the rulings of international law. And as Americans know from our history on our own old frontier, gun battles are caused by outlaws, and not by officers of the peace.

In short, while we are ready to defend our interests, we shall also be ready to search for peace—in quiet exploratory talks—in formal or informal meetings. We do not want military considerations to dominate the thinking of either East or West. And Mr. Khrushchev may find that his invitation to other nations to join in a meaningless treaty may lead to *their* inviting *him* to join in the community of peaceful men, in abandoning the use of force, and in respecting the sanctity of agreements.

VII

While all of these efforts go on, we must not be diverted from our total responsibilities, from other dangers, from other tasks. If new threats in Berlin or elsewhere should cause us to weaken our program of assistance to the developing nations who are also under heavy pressure from the same source, or to halt our efforts for realistic disarmament, or to disrupt or slow down our economy, or to neglect the education of our children, then those threats will surely be the most successful and least costly maneuver in Communist history. For we can afford all these efforts, and more—but we cannot afford *not* to meet this challenge.

And the challenge is not to us alone. It is a challenge to every nation which asserts its sovereignty under a system of liberty. It is a challenge to all those who want a world of free choice. It is a special challenge to the Atlantic Community —the heartland of human freedom.

We in the West must move together in building military strength. We must consult one another more closely than ever before. We must together design our proposals for peace, and labor together as they are pressed at the conference table. And together we must share the burdens and the risks of this effort.

The Atlantic Community, as we know it, has been built in response to challenge: the challenge of European chaos in 1947, of the Berlin blockade in 1948, the challenge of Communist aggression in Korea, in 1950 Now, standing strong and prosperous, after an unprecedented decade of progress, the Atlantic Community will not forget either its history or the principles which gave it meaning.

The solemn vow each of us gave to West Berlin in time of peace will not be broken in time of danger. If we do not meet our commitments to Berlin, where will we later stand? If we are not true to our word there, all that we have achieved in collective security, which relies on these words, will mean nothing. And if there is one path above all others to war, it is the path of weakness and disunity.

Today, the endangered frontier of freedom runs through divided Berlin. We want it to remain a frontier of peace. This is the hope of every citizen of the Atlantic Community; every citizen of Eastern Europe; and, I am confident, every citizen of the Soviet Union. For I cannot believe that the Russian people —who bravely suffered enormous losses in the Second World War—would now wish to see the peace upset once more in Germany. The Soviet government alone can convert Berlin's frontier of peace into a pretext for war.

The steps I have indicated tonight are aimed at avoiding that war. To sum it all up: we seek peace—but we shall not surrender. That is the central meaning of this crisis, and the meaning of your government's policy.

With your help, and the help of other free men, this crisis can be surmounted. Freedom can prevail—and peace can endure.

I would like to close with a personal word. When I ran for the Presidency of the United States, I knew that this country faced serious challenges, but I could not realize—nor could any man realize who does not bear the burdens of this office—how heavy and constant would be those burdens.

Three times in my life-time our country and Europe have been involved in major wars. In each case serious misjudgments were made on both sides of the intentions of others, which brought about great devastation.

Now, in the thermonuclear age, any misjudgment on either side about the intentions of the other could rain more devastation in several hours than has been wrought in all the wars of human history.

Therefore I, as President and Commander-in-Chief ,and all of us as Americans, are moving through serious days. I shall bear this responsibility under our Constitution for the next three and one-half years, but I am sure that we all, regardless of our occupations, will do our very best for our country, and for our cause. For all of us want to see our children grow up in a country at peace, and in a world where freedom endures.

I know that sometimes we get impatient, we wish for some immediate action that would end our perils. But I must tell you that there is no quick and easy solution. The Communists control over a billion people, and they recognize that if we should falter, their success would be imminent.

We must look to long days ahead, which if we are courageous and persevering can bring us what we all desire.

In these days and weeks I ask for your help, and your advice. I ask for your suggestions, when you think we could do better.

All of us, I know, love our country, and we shall all do our best to serve it.

In meeting my responsibilities in these coming months as President, I need your good will, and your support—and above all, your prayers.

Thank you, and good night.

12. Communiqué of the meeting of representatives of the Warsaw Treaty States, Moscow, 5 August 1961[1]

A meeting of the First Secretaries of the Central Committees of the Communist and Workers' parties of the Warsaw Treaty countries was held in Moscow

---

[1] *N.Y. Times*, 6 August 1961.

on August 3 to 5 to discuss questions connected with the preparations for the conclusion of a German peace treaty.

The meeting was attended by representatives of the Communist and Workers' parties of the Warsaw Treaty countries and also by representatives of the fraternal parties of the Socialist countries of Asia.

The participants in the meeting had a broad exchange of opinions on foreign policy and economic questions concerning preparations for the conclusion of a German peace treaty.

All the participants agreed unanimously that the question of the conclusion of a German peace treaty and the normalization through it of the situation in West Berlin is long ripe for solution and brooks no delay.

It was emphasized that to delay the conclusion of the German peace treaty for an indefinite period is deliberately to contribute to an intensification of the threat of a new war in Europe and not only in Europe.

The meeting's participants expressed readiness to contribute by every means to the attainment of a peaceful settlement with the two German states, coordinated with the Western powers. The German peace treaty should record the situation which has developed in Europe after the war, record in legal form the immutability of the present German frontiers, normalize the situation in West Berlin, create better requisites for rapprochement and cooperation between the two German states, secure conditions for the peaceful development of both Germany herself and all the countries of Europe.

The meeting's participants proceed from the fact that such a peaceful settlement would not prejudice any country and would conform to the interests of all those who really seek to preserve and colsolidate universal peace.

The participants in the meeting unanimously reaffirmed that West Berlin, as a free, demilitarized city, would be able to maintain its unhindered communications with the outside world in case of the conclusion of a peace treaty with both German states. Not a single Socialist country presses for a change in the social order existing in West Berlin. Reliable and effective guarantees will be furnished by the peace treaty to insure strict nonintervention in the affairs of West Berlin and access to it.

The meeting expressed the inflexible determination of all its participants to achieve a peace settlement with Germany before the end of this year. At the same time it was unanimously resolved that, should the Western powers continue to evade the conclusion of a German peace treaty, the states concerned will be impelled to conclude a peace treaty with the German Democratic Republic which will draw a line beneath the last war and safeguard conditions for stabilization of the situation in that part of Europe.

A peace treaty will also resolutely protect the sovereign rights of the German Democratic Republic, including her rights on land, water and in the air.

The situation in West Berlin will also be settled on the basis of the above mentioned peace treaty. As a free city, it must lead its independent life and enjoy in conformity with agreements which will be concluded with the German Democratic Republic, the rights to unhindered communications with the outside world.

The meeting instructed the appropriate competent bodies to prepare all necessary foreign political and economic measures ensuring the conclusion of a German peace treaty and observance of its provisions, including those provisions which refer to West Berlin as a free city.

The meeting took place in an atmosphere of a complete unanimity and demonstrated the unshaken determination of the Socialist countries to liquidate the vestiges of World War II.

13. Statement of the Council of Ministers of the German Democratic Republic, Berlin, 12 August 1961[1]

On the basis of the declaration of the member states of the Warsaw Treaty and the decision of the People's Chamber of the German Democratic Republic, the Council of Ministers of the German Democratic Republic adopts the following resolution;

The maintenance of peace requires that the way be barred to the activities of the West German revanchists and militarists and, by the conclusion of a German peace treaty, the way opened to the safeguarding of peace and the re-birth of Germany as a peace-loving, anti-imperialist, neutral state. The Bonn government's view that the Second World War is not yet ended, is accompanied by the demand for freedom for militarist provocations and civil war measures. This imperialist policy conducted in the guise of anti-communism, is the continuation of the aggressive aims of fascist German imperialism in the period of the Third Reich. The Bonn government drew the conclusion from the defeat of Hitler Germany in the Second World War that the rapacious policy of German monopoly capital and its Hitler generals should be given another chance in which a German national policy is renounced and West Germany is converted into a NATO state and a US satellite.

This new threat to the German people and other European peoples by German militarism could become acutely dangerous because the basic provisions of the Potsdam Agreement on the eradication of militarism and nazism were continuously violated in the West German Federal Republic and in the frontline city of West Berlin.

The policy of revenge was intensified in West Germany with mounting territorial demands against the German Democratic Republic and Germany's neighbour states in close connection with the accelerated armament and atomic arming of the West German Bundeswehr. The Adenauer government is carrying on systematic preparations for civil war against the German Democratic Republic. Citizens of the German Democratic Republic who visit West Germany are increasingly exposed to terrorist persecution. West German and West Berlin espionage centres organize the systematic enticement of citizens out of the German Democratic Republic as well as a regular commerce in human beings.

As is to be learned from official government documents and from the basic declarations of the CDU/CSU party (the Adenauer party) leadership, it is the aim of this aggressive policy and disruptive activity to incorporate the whole of

[1] German Democratic Republic, Ministerrat, *Declaration of the Governments of the Warsaw Treaty States, Decision of the Council of Ministers of the German Democratic Republic* (Berlin, 1961), pp. 7–8.

Germany into a western military bloc of NATO, and to extend the military rule of the Federal Republic to the German Democratic Republic. By all kinds of deceptive maneuvres, such as so-called 'free elections', the West German militarists first aim at extending their military bases as far as the Oder River in order then to start the big war.

The West German revanchists and militarists are misusing the peace policy of the U.S.S.R. and the Warsaw Treaty states on the German question in order to injure the German Democratic Republic and all the other states of the socialist camp by enticement and diversionist activities.

For all these reasons and in accord with the decision of the political advisory commission of the Warsaw Treaty states on the safeguarding of European peace, the protection of the German Democratic Republic and in the interest of the security of the socialist camp, the Council of Ministers of the German Democratic Republic adopts the following measures:

The forms of control which are customary on the frontiers of every sovereign state will be introduced along the frontiers of the German Democratic Republic including the borders of the western sectors of Greater Berlin in order to end the hostile activity of the revanchist and militarist forces of West Germany and West Berlin. A reliable guard is to be instituted along the West Berlin border in order to stop subversive activity. These frontiers may be passed by citizens of the German Democratic Republic by special permission only. As long as West Berlin has not been transformed into a demilitarized, neutral, Free City citizens of the capital of the German Democratic Republic require a special pass to cross the borders to West Berlin. Peaceful citizens of West Berlin may visit the capital of the German Democratic Republic (democratic Berlin) by showing the West Berlin identity card. Revanchist politicians and agents of West German militarism may not enter the capital of the GDR (democratic Berlin). There is no change in the control procedure for citizens of the West German Federal Republic entering democratic Berlin. The entry of foreign citizens into the capital of the German Democratic Republic is not affected by these regulations.

The regulations previously in force for citizens of West Berlin travelling abroad and using the lines of communication through the German Democratic Republic remain unaltered.

This decision makes no change in the previous regulations governing transit traffic between West Berlin and West Germany through the German Democratic Republic.

The Minister of the Interior, the Minister of Transport and the Mayor of Greater Berlin are instructed to issue the necessary regulations.

This decision on measures for the safeguarding of peace, the protection of the German Democratic Republic, especially its capital Berlin, and for the guarantee of the security of other socialist states will remain in force until the conclusion of a German peace treaty.[1]

[1] On 22 August 1961 the Ministry of the Interior of the German Democratic Republic issued orders on access to East Berlin on the following lines:

(1) *Permits for West Berliners*

West Berlin citizens now require a permit (*Aufenthaltsgenehmigung*) to visit East Berlin. The permit will specify the crossing-point to be used. Applications for permits stating reasons for the visit must be submitted to the East Berlin Police Presidium. West Berliners will apply at

14. Joint declaration of the Governments of the Warsaw Treaty States, 13 August 1961[1]

For several years already, the member states of the Warsaw Treaty have attempted to bring about a peace treaty with Germany. These states are of the opinion that this problem is ripe for decision and can tolerate no further delay. As is known the Soviet Government, with the approval and full support of all Warsaw Treaty states, has proposed to all countries which participated in the war against Hitler Germany that a peace treaty be signed with both German states which could include the peaceful solution of the West Berlin problem by converting West Berlin into a demilitarized Free City. This proposal takes into consideration the real situation that has developed in Germany and Europe during the post-war period. It is not directed against the interests of any side, but its only purpose is to eliminate the vestiges of the Second World War—and to strengthen world peace.

Until now, the governments of the western powers have not shown their readiness to reach a solution to this problem through negotiations. Moreover, the western powers have answered these peaceful proposals of the socialist countries with intensified war preparations, with a campaign of war hysteria and with threats of military force. Official representatives of several NATO countries have announced an increase in their armed forces and plans for partial mobilization. In some NATO countries, plans have in fact been published for the invasion of GDR territory.

Aggressive forces are using the absence of a peace treaty to force the militarization of West Germany and to strengthen the Bundeswehr at a more rapid rate, equipping it with the most modern weapons. West German revanchists are openly demanding that they be supplied with nuclear and atomic weapons. The governments of the western powers which support the rearmament of West Germany in every way are thereby guilty of breaking the most important inter-

---

West Berlin branch offices of the East German State Travel Bureau. East Berlin citizens may apply on behalf of their prospective visitors through their local police office. A fee of one West mark will be charged for a permit.

(2) *Special Crossing-Points*
Until a peace treaty is signed, separate crossing-points are established for
    (*a*) foreigners, including members of the Diplomatic Corps and the Western occupation forces,
    (*b*) West Germans, and
    (*c*) West Berliners.

Category (*a*) may use only one crossing-point (Friedrichstrasse) 'in the interests of speedier clearance'. Category (*b*) may use two crossing-points (Bornholmerstrasse and Heinrich-Heine-Strasse), and category (*c*) four crossing-points (Chausseestrasse, Invalidenstrasse, Oberbaumbruecke, and Sonnenallee). West Berliners must be in possession of an identity-card and visitor's permit. West Berlin children may only cross the border in the company of their parents, and must be entered on the latter's identity-card.

(3) *Banned Area along Sector Border*
All persons are once more warned, in the interests of their own safety, to keep 100 metres away from both sides of the sector border. (Cmnd. 1552, p. 472.)

[1] German Democratic Republic, Ministerrat, *Declaration of the Governments of the Warsaw Treaty States, Decision of the Council of Ministers of the German Democratic Republic* (Berlin, 1961), pp. 5–6.

national agreements which provide for the elimination of German militarism and the prevention of its rebirth in any form.

The Western powers have not only ignored the need to normalize the situation in West Berlin but continue to strengthen it as a centre of diversion against the GDR and other socialist countries. There is no place on earth where so many foreign espionage and diversionist centres are concentrated and where they can operate so unrestrictedly as in West Berlin. These centres send agents into the GDR to commit various diversionary acts, recruit spies and incite hostile elements to organize acts of sabotage against the GDR and to spread unrest.

The ruling circles of the Federal Republic and the espionage agencies of the NATO countries make use of the present transport situation on the West Berlin border to undermine the economy of the German Democratic Republic. By means of deception, corruption and extortion, government organs and armament trusts in the Federal Republic have caused a certain unstable part of the GDR population to go to West Germany. These victims are forced into the West German armed forces, they are recruited for the espionage organs of various countries and are then returned to the GDR to commit acts of espionage and sabotage. Indeed a special fund has been set up in order to carry out these diversionist activities against the German Democratic Republic and other socialist countries. West German Chancellor Adenauer recently called on the NATO governments to increase this fund.

It is characteristic that the diversionist activities originating in West Berlin have increased in the recent past, after the Soviet Union, the German Democratic Republic and the other socialist countries had made proposals for an immediate peace settlement with Germany. These diversionist activities not only harm the German Democratic Republic but also infringe on the interests of other socialist countries. In view of the aggressive aims of the reactionary forces of the Federal Republic and their NATO allies, the Warsaw Treaty states are obliged to take appropriate measures to guarantee their security and especially the security of the German Democratic Republic which is vital to the interests of the German people themselves.

The governments of the Warsaw Treaty states turn to the People's Chamber and the government of the GDR and to all workers of the German Democratic Republic with the proposal that such measures be taken as will insure that the diversionist activities against the socialist countries are stopped, and that around the entire area of West Berlin including its border with democratic Berlin reliable guards and effective controls are established. Of course, these measures will not affect the prevailing regulations for controlling traffic and lines of communications between West Berlin and West Germany.

The governments of the Warsaw Treaty states understand, of course, that such protective measures along the West Berlin borders will bring about some inconvenience for the population but in view of the present situation, the responsibility for these measures lies solely with the western powers and above all with the government of the Federal Republic. The fact that the West Berlin borders have remained open in the past was based on the hope that the western powers would not misuse the good will of the government of the GDR. They have, however, disregarded the interests of the German people and the population of

Berlin by using the open West Berlin border for their malicious diversionist activity. The present abnormal situation must be ended by a strengthened guard and control along the West Berlin border.

At the same time the governments of the Warsaw Treaty states consider it necessary that these measures be removed as soon as a peace settlement with Germany is reached and, on that basis, the solution to current problems is found.

15. The three Western Commandants in Berlin to the Soviet Commandant, 15 August 1961[1]

During the night of August 12–13, the East German authorities put into effect illegal measures designed to turn the boundaries between the West Sectors of Berlin and the Soviet Sector into an arbitrary barrier to movement of German citizens resident in East Berlin and East Germany.

Not since the imposition of the Berlin blockade has there been such a flagrant violation of the Four-Power Agreements concerning Berlin. The Agreement of June 20, 1949[2] in which the U.S.S.R. pledged itself to facilitate freedom of movement within Berlin and between Berlin and the rest of Germany, has also been violated.

The disregard of these agreements and of the wishes of the population of this city, for the welfare of which the four Powers are jointly responsible, freedom of circulation throughout Berlin has been severely curtailed. Traffic between the East Sector and the Western Sectors of Berlin has been disrupted by the cutting of S-Bahn and U-Bahn service, the tearing-up of streets, the erection of road-blocks, and the stringing of barbed wire. In carrying out these illegal actions, military and paramilitary units, which were formed in violation of four-Power Agreements and whose very presence in East Berlin is illegal, turned the Soviet Sector of Berlin into an armed camp.

Moreover, the East German authorities have now prohibited the many inhabitants of East Berlin and East Germany who were employed in West Berlin from continuing to pursue their occupations in West Berlin. They have thus denied to the working population under their control the elementary right of free choice of place of employment.

It is obvious that the East German authorities have taken these repressive measures because the people under their control, deeply perturbed by the threats on Berlin recently launched by Communist leaders, were fleeing in large numbers to the West.

We must protest against the illegal measures introduced on August 13, and hold you responsible for the carrying out of the relevant agreements.

16. The British Embassy in Moscow to the Soviet Minister of Foreign Affairs, 17 August 1961[3]

The British Embassy presents its compliments to the Minister for Foreign Affairs, and, upon instructions of its Government, has the honour to direct the

---

[1] Cmnd. 1552, pp. 468–9. [2] *Documents*, 1949–50, pp. 160–1.
[3] Cmnd. 1552, pp. 469–70. Identical Notes, *mutatis mutandis*, were presented by the United States and French Embassies on the same day. For texts see *D.S.B.*, 4 September 1961, p. 397, and *Le Monde*, 18 August 1961.

most serious attention of the Government of the U.S.S.R. to the following:—

On August 13, East German authorities put into effect several measures regulating movement at the boundary of the Western Sectors and the Soviet Sector of the city of Berlin. These measures have the effect of limiting, to a degree approaching complete prohibition, passage from the Soviet Sector to the Western Sectors of the city. These measures were accompanied by the closing of the sector boundary by a sizable deployment of police forces and by military detachments brought into Berlin for this purpose.

All this is a flagrant, and particularly serious, violation of the quadripartite status of Berlin. Freedom of movement with respect to Berlin was reaffirmed by the Quadripartite Agreement of New York of May 4, 1949, and by the decision taken at Paris on June 20, 1949 by the Council of the Ministers for Foreign Affairs of the Four Powers.[1] Her Majesty's Government has never accepted that limitations can be imposed on freedom of movement within Berlin. The boundary between the Soviet Sector and the Western Sectors of Berlin is not a state frontier. Her Majesty's Government considers that the measures which the East German authorities have taken are illegal. It reiterates that it does not accept the pretension that the Soviet Sector of Berlin forms a part of the so-called 'German Democratic Republic', and that Berlin is situated on its territory. Such a pretension is in itself a violation of the solemnly pledged word of the Government of the U.S.S.R. in the Agreement on the Zones of Occupation in Germany and the Administration of Greater Berlin. Moreover, Her Majesty's Government cannot admit the right of the East German authorities to send their Armed Forces into the Soviet Sector of Berlin.

By the very admission of the East German authorities, the measures which have just been taken are motivated by the fact that an ever-increasing number of inhabitants of East Germany wish to leave this territory. The reasons for this exodus are known. They are simply the internal difficulties in East Germany.

To judge by the terms of a Declaration of the Warsaw Pact Powers published on August 13, the measures in question are supposed to have been recommended to the East German authorities by these Powers. Her Majesty's Government notes that the Powers which associated themselves with the U.S.S.R. by signing the Warsaw Pact are thus intervening in a domain in which they have no competence.

It is to be noted that this Declaration states that the measures taken by the East German authorities are 'in the interests of the German people themselves'. It is difficult to see any basis for this statement, or to understand why it should be for the members of the Warsaw Pact to decide what are the interests of the German people. It is evident that no Germans, particularly those whose freedom of movement is being forcibly restrained, think this is so. This would be abundantly clear if all Germans were allowed a free choice, and the principle of self-determination were also applied in the Soviet Sector of Berlin and in East Germany.

Her Majesty's Government solemnly protests against the measures referred to above, for which it holds the Soviet Government responsible. Her Majesty's Government expects the Soviet Government to put an end to these illegal

[1] *Documents*, 1949–50, pp. 157, 160–1.

measures. This unilateral infringement of the quadripartite status of Berlin can only increase existing tension and dangers.

17. The Soviet Government to the Government of the United States, 18 August 1961[1]

In connection with the Note of the United States government of August 17, 1961,[2] the government of the Union of Soviet Socialist Republics finds it necessary to state the following:

1. The Soviet government fully understands and supports the actions of the government of the German Democratic Republic, which has established effective control on the border with West Berlin in order to block the way to the subversive activities being conducted from West Berlin against the G.D.R. and other countries of the socialist commonwealth.

In its measures on the frontiers the government of the German Democratic Republic has merely exercised the ordinary right of every sovereign state to defend its interests. Any state introduces on its frontiers with other states a régime such as it considers necessary and meeting its lawful interests. As is well known, the régime of state frontiers is one of the internal questions of any state and its settlement does not need recognition or approval by other governments. Therefore the attempts of the United States government to interfere in the internal affairs of the German Democratic Republic are absolutely groundless and irrelevant.

2. The government of the United States of America is, undoubtedly, quite familiar with the causes which made the introduction of control over the traffic on the border between the German Democratic Republic and West Berlin necessary and even inevitable. The United States government itself made quite a few efforts to create these causes.

West Berlin has been turned into a centre of subversive activities, sabotage and espionage, into a centre of political and economic provocations against the German Democratic Republic, the Soviet Union and other socialist countries. The former and present West Berlin municipal leaders have cynically called West Berlin 'an arrow in the living body of the German Democratic Republic', 'the frontline city', 'a trouble spot' and 'the cheapest atom bomb planted in the centre of a socialist state'.

The gates of West Berlin were flung wide open to international criminals and agents-provocateurs of all shades in order to intensify international tension and extend the scope of provocations and subversive actions against the countries of the socialist commonwealth.

3. It is well known that over 80 subversive sabotage and espionage organisations and centres have established their headquarters in West Berlin and are operating with impunity there. The full names and addresses of persons engaged in hostile activities incompatible with the status of West Berlin, which lies in the territory of the German Democratic Republic, were repeatedly given in documents delivered to the western powers at the appropriate time, but the West

---

[1] *Soviet News*, 21 August 1961.
[2] See p. 345, n. 3. The same Note, *mutatis mutandis*, was directed to the British and French Governments.

Berlin authorities and the occupation bodies of the three powers have not lifted a finger to put an end to these criminal activities.

The reason, apparently, is that West Berlin has become a den of adventurers, rogues, paid agents, terrorists and other criminals serving the intelligence services of the entire imperialist world, including the Central Intelligence Agency of the United States, the British secret intelligence service, the Frence Service of External Documentation and Counter-Espionage, and the West German subversive intelligence organisations with their numerous branches and ramifications. Things reached a point where West Berlin became the residence of the so-called 'American Committee for the Liberation of the Peoples of Russia'.

The question inevitably arises: Do such actions have anything in common with observance of the quadripartite status established in Berlin immediately after the rout of nazi Germany, to which the government of the United States refers in its Note? One must have an excessively great sense of humour to claim that the activities in West Berlin accord with the quadripartite obligations.

The Soviet side repeatedly made representations to the American authorities in connection with the spy tunnel dug by American agencies in the Alt-Glienicke area of West Berlin to communication lines of the Soviet troops and communication lines of the German Democratic Republic inside G.D.R. territory. That huge tunnel was equipped with special apparatus and devices for listening in on and recording conversations on the aforementioned communication lines.

The American authorities, including the U.S. State Department, caught red-handed, did not even reply to these representations. Does this constitute observance of the solemn commitments assumed by the United States of America in the quadripartite agreements concluded by the Allied powers with regard to Germany?

But the spy-tunnel in Alt-Glienicke is a mere trifle in comparison with the tunnel which has been daily and hourly driven from the territory of West Berlin to undermine the socialist system in the German Democratic Republic and other socialist states.

4. It must be well known to the government of the United States that, with the assistance of the occupation authorities, the ruling circles of the Federal Republic of Germany have turned West Berlin into the main base of incessant economic sabotage against the German Democratic Republic.

At the expense of the taxes levied upon the population of the Federal Republic of Germany a speculative rate for the exchange of western marks into the G.D.R. currency was arbitrarily introduced and artificially maintained in West Berlin. No city in the world has ever known such shameless speculation in currency as West Berlin, and this under the wing of the occupation authorities. The buying up of valuable goods and foodstuffs in the German Democratic Republic and their export to West Berlin and the Federal Republic of Germany has been organised on an enormous scale, which has done tremendous harm to the population and the national economy of the German Democratic Republic.

The open frontier with West Berlin annually cost the working people of the German Democratic Republic at least 3,500 million marks.

West Berlin lived an unhealthy, feverish life, actually at the expense of the population of the German Democratic Republic and those thousands of millions in subsidies which were pumped from the pockets of the taxpayers of the Federal Republic of Germany—its factory and office workers and farmers. The lion's share of these funds got into the hands of black marketeers, saboteurs and subversive organisations. This was the pay for the role which the 'frontline city' of West Berlin played for the benefit of the N.A.T.O. military bloc in the 'cold war' against the socialist countries.

From West Berlin, government bodies and concerns of the Federal Republic of Germany directed a whole army of recruiters, who used deceit, bribery and blackmail to impel a certain part of the population of the German Democratic Republic to move to Western Germany. There these people were made to serve in the Bundeswehr and to work in military production, and were drawn into various subversive organisations.

5. Implementing their aggressive militarist policy, hostile to the cause of peace, the ruling circles of the Federal Republic of Germany converted West Berlin into an arena for open revenge-seeking gatherings and pogrom demonstrations directed against the neighbouring peaceful socialist states.

The government of the Federal Republic of Germany has made no secret of its efforts to draw the population of West Berlin into its war preparations. West German recruiting centres, providing mercenaries for the Bundeswehr, are operating on the territory of the city. It is known that there are 20,000 West Berliners serving in the West German army at the present time. Recruitment of soldiers from among the West Berlin population apparently plays by no means the least role in Bonn's plans for that part of the city.

The government of the Federal Republic has tried to adapt to its military plans the economy of West Berlin as well. It cynically announced the extension to West Berlin of the laws making it binding on the city's industries to fulfil military orders for the Bundeswehr.

Propaganda against the Soviet Union, the German Democratic Republic and other socialist countries—propaganda characterised by incitement and slander—has been conducted and continues to be conducted systematically by radio and television in West Berlin. The radio and television in West Berlin are subordinated to one task—to sow enmity among the nations, to foment war hysteria, to try to organise disorders, to transmit coded instructions to agents of western intelligence services.

The governments of the United States, Britain and France have themselves admitted that West Berlin is not part of the Federal Republic of Germany and cannot be administered by its organs. The Soviet government has more than once drawn the United States government's attention to the impermissible actions of authorities of the Federal Republic in West Berlin which are incompatible with either the present status of the city or the interests of tranquillity in Europe.

Nevertheless over 50 government institutions of the Federal Republic of Germany are now operating in West Berlin and interfering without ceremony in all the affairs of the city, while the organs of the Bundestag and the Bundesrat present their lawless claims to this part of the city.

But why is all this happening? The explanation is to be found in the connivance and direct encouragement on the part of the western occupation authorities, who have long since bartered away their commitments under the quadripartite agreements to which they refer, for the services they get from Western Germany as a member of the aggressive N.A.T.O. military bloc.

Therefore they have not even once responded to any of the just demands of the Soviet Union and the government of the German Democratic Republic that measures be taken to prevent international provocations organised by militarist and revenge-seeking forces of the Federal Republic of Germany from West Berlin.

6. The German Democratic Republic has for many years been extremely tolerant in the face of this absolutely revolting and impermissible situation. Carrying out its consistently peaceful and democratic policy, it has made enormous sacrifices in order to facilitate the reaching of agreement between the two German states on the question of a peace settlement and Germany's reunification in accordance with peaceful and democratic principles.

Nevertheless, subversive activities from West Berlin against the German Democratic Republic and the other socialist countries have been further extended especially in recent times, following the submission of proposals for the immediate conclusion of a peace treaty with Germany and the normalisation of the situation in West Berlin on that basis. The enemies of peace and tranquillity in that area have not let slip a single opportunity to hamper the plans for socialist construction in the German Democratic Republic and to prevent the rise in the living standards of its population, and this has been done by every means, stopping at nothing to complicate the situation in the republic.

It is quite understandable, therefore, that the government of the German Democratic Republic, seeking to prevent the complication of the present international situation and responding to an appeal from the socialist states that are members of the Warsaw Treaty, has taken appropriate measures to protect its national interests and the interests of the security of the other socialist states.

7. In concluding their historic agreements at the end of the Second World War and after the rout of nazi Germany, the U.S.S.R., the United States, Britain and France jointly mapped out a programme for reviving the life of Germany along democratic and peaceful lines. This programme has been carried out on the territory of the German Democratic Republic.

Western Germany, unfortunately, as the Soviet government has repeatedly pointed out, has followed the road of reviving militarism and chauvinist and revenge-seeking forces dangerous to the cause of peace, and forces which inspired and organised nazi aggression are again prospering there.

The western powers have themselves contributed to this and have flagrantly violated all the foundations of the post-war four-power agreements. In its Note of August 17, the government of the United States tries to refer to the quadripartite agreements on Germany which that government has itself violated. But it is possible in destroying the whole to retain a part of the agreement which one finds to one's own advantage? And have the United States government and its organs in West Berlin guided themselves in practice by the principles of the four-power agreements which they now invoke?

Did the separate monetary reform extended to West Berlin from Western Germany accord with the four-power principles? Or the establishment of

Bizonia and a separate magistracy in West Berlin? Can these quadripartite principles, in the opinion of the United States government, be reconciled with the separate tripartite occupation status for West Berlin or the Paris agreements on the rearming of the Federal Republic of Germany and its inclusion in N.A.T.O.? Or are the aforementioned subversive actions against the U.S.S.R., the German Democratic Republic and other countries, which are conducted from West Berlin perhaps also in conformity with the principles of four-power cooperation?

It is sufficient to ask these questions in order to realise the entire groundlessness and absurdity of the references by the United States government to the aforementioned agreements.

8. The references of the western powers to the Allied agreements are also unwarranted because these agreements were concluded for the period of Germany's occupation and for the purposes of occupation. Much has changed in the course of the past sixteen and a half years; the face of Germany itself has changed. Two independent states have sprung up on its territory with their capitals and their borders—the socialist peaceloving German Democratic Republic and the capitalist militarist Federal Republic of Germany.

No one has the right to interfere in the affairs of these two German states as long as they fall under the internal jurisdication of those states. One can recognize or not recognize these real facts—they will not cease to exist because of that.

The United States Government tries in its Note to present the striving to perpetuate the occupation of West Berlin (and this 16 years after the end of the war!) as concern for the Germans and almost as a practical expression of the right to self-determination. Such attempts cannot, of course, be taken seriously.

And if the protective measures on the border of the German Democratic Republic with West Berlin create certain temporary inconveniences for the population of the city, the responsibility for this must be placed entirely on the occupation authorities and the government of the Federal Republic of Germany, which have done everything to prevent an improvement in the situation in that area with due consideration for the lawful interests of all states. In view of this, the protest made in the Note of the United States government is groundless and is categorically rejected by the Soviet government.

9. As has already been stated earlier, the measures taken by the government of the German Democratic Republic are provisional. The Soviet government has repeatedly emphasised that the conclusion of a peace treaty with Germany and the normalisation of the situation in West Berlin on that basis will not infringe the interests of any of the sides and will benefit peace and the security of all peoples. It is to this that the Soviet government summons the government of the United States.

18. The Soviet Commandant in Berlin to the three Western Commandants, 18 August 1961[1]

With reference to your letter of the 15th August 1961,[2] I have been instructed to communicate the following:—

[1] Cmnd. 1552, pp. 470–1.   [2] Above, p. 345.

As has been stressed repeatedly, the Headquarters of the garrison of Soviet troops in Berlin does not interfere in the affairs of the capital of the German Democratic Republic. The problem which you have raised with me lies entirely within the competence of the Government of the German Democratic Republic. The measures taken at the boundary of the German Democratic Republic and West Berlin have been carried out by the Government of the German Democratic Republic in exercising the common right of every sovereign country for the protection of its lawful interests. Any country may establish on its boundaries such a system as it considers necessary and appropriate to the circumstances. Your remarks in connexion with these measures are, therefore, quite misplaced. Of course, the Commandants of the United States, British, and French Sectors in West Berlin know full well the reasons which necessitated the introduction of an effective control on the boundary with West Berlin. It was pointed out many times that over eighty diversionary subversive and spying organizations have been established, and carry on, under the protection of the Occupation Authorities, subversive work against the German Democratic Republic, the U.S.S.R., and other Socialist countries. The Commandants are doubtless also aware of such facts as the transporting in planes from the Federal German Republic through the air-corridors into West Berlin for the participation in rallies and demonstrations of West German revanchists and militarists, and of every kind of attempt by the Government of the Federal German Republic to include West Berlin in the sphere of its military preparations.

Equally well known is the rôle assigned to West Berlin in the plans of the Federal German Republic and N.A.T.O. countries with regard to the undermining of the economy of the German Democratic Republic, and for the carrying on of hostile and firebrand propaganda against the countries of the Socialist community. Politicians of the Federal German Republic have frankly called West Berlin a 'front-line city', the duty of which they said is to hinder peaceful development in the German Democratic Republic and in other Socialist countries. All this was carried on despite the repeated serious warnings with regard to the consequences of such hostile actions. Nothing was done by the authorities of the United States, Great Britain, and France to put an end to the using of West Berlin territory for such inadmissible international provocations.

Quite naturally the German Democratic Republic was forced to take measures, in view of such provocative activities of the revanchist and militarist circles, which would put an end to these activities. These measures are aimed at the protection of the interests of the entire Socialist community of States, of which fact these States made mention in their Joint Statement to the German Democratic Republic. As was pointed out in the Declaration of the countries participating in the Warsaw Pact, the entire responsibility for the situation thus created and certain inconveniences which are borne by a portion of the population in connexion with these protective measures lies squarely and fully on the revanchist-militarist circles of the Federal Republic of Germany, and also on the Western Powers carrying out occupation functions in West Berlin. Therefore, this responsibility lies on you as well as General Delacombe, as the person at the head of an occupation authority. Consequently I categorically reject the assertions contained in your letter of the 15th August as being completely unfounded.

19. The Soviet Ministry of Foreign Affairs to the British Embassy in Moscow, 23 August 1961[1]

The Ministry of Foreign Affairs of the U.S.S.R. present their compliments to the British Embassy, and, on instructions from the Soviet Government, state the following:—

The Soviet Government have more than once drawn the attention of the British Government to the unlawful and inadmissible interference by the Federal Republic of Germany into the affairs of West Berlin. It is generally known that West Berlin does not constitute a part of the Federal Republic of Germany and that the competence of the latter's authorities cannot extend to it. This is admitted by the Governments of the Western Powers.

Nevertheless, the British Government has not taken due steps to avert the provocative activity of certain circles of the Federal Republic of Germany in West Berlin. With the connivance of the occupying organs of the three Powers in West Berlin, this activity not only has not stopped, but, of late, especially in connexion with the proposal for an urgent peaceful settlement with Germany and the solution on this basis of the question of West Berlin, has abruptly intensified. This activity is attaining such proportions as to create a danger of violation of peace and tranquillity in this area.

In West Berlin for a long period Bonn's Minister for so-called All-German questions, Lemmer, has been operating. He has set up his residence there, in which provocations of various kinds are being prepared, and from which the direction of subversive work against the German Democratic Republic and other Socialist countries is being exercised. Revanchists, extremists, subverters, spies, and saboteurs of all kinds are being sent from the Federal Republic of Germany to West Berlin. In order to send them there, the Western Powers are using the air-corridors as well. Thus the United States, Britain, and France are patently abusing their position in West Berlin, profiting from the absence of control on the air communications. As a result there has been gross violation of the Agreement reached in 1945[2] under which, as is well known, air-corridors were assigned to the three Western Powers, temporarily, for the supplying of the needs of their military garrisons, not for the subversive and revanchist aims of West German militarism, and not for the conducting of those subversive actions which are being demonstratively carried out before the eyes of the whole world, including the Germans themselves, by West German figures who have recently been turning up almost daily in West Berlin. By the air-corridors to West Berlin, official representatives of the Government and Bundestag of the Federal Republic of Germany are also arriving who set off directly from the airport on demonstrative tours of 'inspection' round the city, and make provocative hostile statements against the German Democratic Republic and the Soviet Union. Last week alone, Gerstenmaier, the Chairman of the Bundestag of the Federal Republic of Germany; Krone, the Chairman of the Christian Democratic Union-Christian Social Union fraction in the Bundestag; Ollenhauer, the Chairman of the Social Democratic Party; Mende, the Chairman of the Free Democratic Party; and others assembled there. Their arrival was accompanied by the organisation of

---

[1] Cmnd. 1552, pp. 473–4.   [2] ibid., pp. 60–64.

rallies and demonstrations at which calls for aggression against peace-loving neighbouring States, and for reprisals against the democratic forces of East Berlin were openly proclaimed.

The intensified intrigues of the ruling circles of the Federal Republic of Germany in West Berlin are testimony of their strivings intentionally to render the situation in this area more acute so as to evoke complications and conflicts, and to attempt to bring the Western Powers into collision with the Soviet Union to the advantage of the West German militarists and revanchists. All this is taking place before the eyes and with the benevolent support of the Occupation Authorities of the three Powers in West Berlin who, it would seem, ought to have taken into account the dangerous consequences of the above-mentioned provocative activity of those circles of the Federal Republic of Germany who have founded their policy on ideas of revanche.

In continuing to connive at the interference of the authorities of the Federal Republic of Germany into the affairs of West Berlin and at the utilisation of the territory of the city for acts of international provocation, the Government of Great Britain bears full responsibility for the possible consequences.

The Government of the U.S.S.R. insists that the Government of Great Britain, which is exercising at the present time occupation functions in West Berlin, should forthwith take steps to terminate the unlawful and provocative activities of the Federal Republic of Germany in this city.

20. The British Government to the Government of the Soviet Union, 26 August 1961[1]

The Government of the Soviet Union objects in its Note to the use by the Western Allies of their air-corridors to Berlin. Her Majesty's Government must protest strongly against the suggestion that the purposes for which the Western Allies use the air-corridors are within the competence of the Soviet Union.

These corridors were established in 1945 by decision of the Four-Power Allied Control Council[2] as the manner in which the unrestricted right of air access to Berlin would be exercised by the Western Powers. There has never been any limitation whatsoever placed upon their use by the aircraft of the Western Powers. Her Majesty's Government will hold the Government of the Soviet Union responsible for any interference with the safety of these aircraft in the corridors.

The Government of the U.S.S.R. in its Note accuses the Western Powers of violating the Four-Power Agreements of 1945. In particular, it reproaches them for 'their connivance at the interference of the authorities of the Federal Republic of Germany in the affairs of West Berlin and at the use of the territory of the city for international provocations', and insists 'that the Government of Great Britain, which at present exercises occupation functions in West Berlin, take steps to stop the illegal and provocative actions of the Federal Republic of Germany in that City'.

This demand is at the very least surprising. Indeed, since the night of August

[1] Cmnd. 1552, pp. 474–6. U.S. Note in *D.S.B.*, 11 September 1961.
[2] ibid., pp. 60–64.

12 to 13, the authorities of East Germany, with the concurrence of the Soviet Union, as the Note of the Soviet Government dated August 18 attests,[1] have not ceased taking unilateral measures which do precisely violate the Four-Power Agreements and the freedom of movement within the city of Berlin.

First they erected barricades, strengthened from day to day, to stop the traffic from East to West, in order, in fact, to put an end to the increasing exodus of refugees. For some days, the same authorities have been attempting to establish unilateral and arbitrary control over access to East Berlin by the inhabitants of West Berlin and the Federal Republic of Germany. And they have just limited to a single point the possibilities of movement of the Allies from West to East. Moreover, the inhabitants of East Berlin who worked in West Berlin have been denied the pursuit of their occupations.

If there are 'illegal and provocative actions', they are certainly those of the authorities of East Germany in taking such measures. As the British Note delivered to the Soviet Government on July 17 stated,[2] if there is a crisis in Berlin, it is certainly the doing of the Soviet Union.

Did not the number of refugees increase considerably from the day on which the Soviet Government made apparent the imminence of the implementation of its plan for a separate 'peace treaty' and a 'free city'?

The Soviet Government protests against the presence in West Berlin of personalities from the Federal Republic such as, for example: 'Gerstenmaier, the President of the Bundestag of the Federal Republic of Germany; Krone, the Chairman of the Christian Democratic Union-Christian Social Union Bundestag fraction, Ollenhauer, the President of the Social Democrat Party; Mende, the President of the Free Democratic Party, and others'.

Her Majesty's Government does not understand the position of the Soviet Government. West Berlin has a wide variety of ties with the Federal Republic that are in no way incompatible with the four-Power status of Berlin.

These accusations are all the more inadmissible since, for a long time and even quite recently, the Soviet Union, as well as the East German authorities, have been trying to integrate East Berlin completely into East Germany by isolating it from the outside, and attempting to make it the capital of East Germany.

The fundamental fact is that the whole of Berlin has a quadripartite status. Her Majesty's Government note that the Soviet Government explicitly recognizes the rights and responsibilities of the Western Powers in Berlin. Unlike the Soviet Government, the Western Powers have always taken great care to see that the special status of the city as a whole is protected and preserved in accordance with Four-Power Agreements. The Western Powers have established thorough procedures and safeguards for this purpose, and the Soviet Government is well aware of this. Her Majesty's Government are willing, as always, to consider any legitimate complaints which the Soviet Union may put forward, but the allegations in the Soviet Note are false.

Accordingly, it is up to the Soviet Union and not her Majesty's Government to take measures to allay the state of tension and unrest which has developed in Berlin. The whole world will be concerned at the scarcely veiled threat of

[1] Above, p. 347.   [2] Above, p. 323, n. 1.

aggression against the Allied air-routes to and from West Berlin. Her Majesty's Government must serve a solemn warning to the Soviet Union that interference by the Soviet Government or its East German régime with free access to Berlin would have the most serious consequences for which it would bear full responsibility.

21. The British Ambassador in Bonn to the Soviet Ambassador to the German Democratic Republic, 26 August 1961[1]

I should like to draw your serious attention to the recent measures taken by the East German authorities related to travel from West to East Berlin. In addition to purporting to limit even more severely the crossing-points for residents of West Berlin and the Federal Republic of Germany, these measures would limit foreigners, diplomats, and civilian or military members of the Allied Forces to a single crossing-point. The regulations issued by the East German authorities also warn persons to remain 100 metres from the sector boundary.

These flagrantly illegal measures have as their purpose the further sealing-off of East Berlin and East Germany from the free world. They are in clear violation of the quadripartite status of Berlin.

I should in particular like to remind you of your responsibility for unrestricted access by the Allied Forces to East Berlin. In allowing the East German authorities to attempt to limit them to one crossing-point, you have condoned an action which violates solemn agreements to which your Government was signatory. I solemnly protest against the measures described above, and insist that you take the necessary steps to ensure continued unrestricted access to East Berlin without hindrance as to place or time. I also urge you with the utmost seriousness to warn the East German authorities of the dangers of their pretensions to prohibit movement within 100 metres of the Western side of the sector boundary. Any attempt to enforce this illegal prohibition could only have the most serious consequences.

22. The Soviet Ministry of Foreign Affairs to the British Embassy in Moscow, 2 September 1961[2]

The Ministry of Foreign Affairs of the U.S.S.R. presents its compliments to the Embassy of Great Britain and, in answer to its Note of August 26, 1961,[3] on behalf of the Soviet Government, states the following:—

In its Note the British Government again advances as the main question the question of the so-called quadripartite status of Berlin. The Soviet Government adduced in its Note of August 18[4] abundant material witnessing to the fact that, over the course of many years, the Western Powers destroyed, by all their actions, this quadripartite status, by converting West Berlin into a base for diversionary, spying, speculative, and subversive activity against the German Democratic Republic, the Soviet Union, and other Socialist States. The British

---

[1] Cmnd. 1552, p. 476. Identical Notes were sent that day by the American and French Ambassadors in Bonn to the same addressee. For texts see *D.S.B.*, 18 September 1961, and *La Documentation Française*, 12 September 1961.
[2] Cmnd. 1552, pp. 477–9.   [3] Above, preceding document.   [4] Above, p. 351.

Government puts on a pretence of not noticing the irrefutable arguments and facts adduced by the Soviet Government. There is, evidently, nothing that it can say on the subject of these facts and arguments. By this same token, it confirms that it cannot either refute or challenge them and, in consequence, cannot challenge the justness and well-foundedness of the position of the Soviet Union which is insisting on the liquidation of this inadmissible situation in West Berlin and the immediate prevention of the subversive and criminal activity of the authorities of the Federal Republic of Germany from the territory of West Berlin, which activity is a danger to the cause of peace.

In the above-mentioned British Note, an attempt is again made to turn the internal measures of a third sovereign State, the German Democratic Republic, into a subject for discussion. Such actions are a gross contradiction of the generally accepted norms of international law. If Great Britain does not have normal relations with the German Democratic Republic, this is far from giving her any foundation for any sort of interference in the internal affairs of the German Democratic Republic. If the contrary assertion is to be admitted as well-founded, this means substituting arbitrariness for law in international life, and substituting chaos for international law and order in relations between States. The arguments contained in the British Note on the subject of the measures taken by the Government of the German Democratic Republic on the frontier with West Berlin are imbued with the fusty air of an occupation which has long since outlived itself, and with unwillingness to look actual reality in the face. The old Germany no longer exists: the Socialist German Democratic Republic and the capitalist Federal Republic of Germany have come into being in place of it. Any realistic policy on the part of the States cannot fail to take into account the existence of these two sovereign German States which came into being not yesterday, nor yet to-day, but twelve years ago. No invocations, however much they may be repeated in Bonn or in the other capitals of the Western Powers, can set aside this fact.

The British Government does not deny in its Note that the air-corridors which pass across the territory of the German Democratic Republic are being utilised for the transportation from the Federal Republic of Germany to West Berlin of revanchists, militarists, spies, and diversionaries who operate against the German Democratic Republic and other Socialist countries. At the same time, the British Government asserts that the Western Powers, in accordance with the decisions of the Control Council in Germany, have an 'unrestricted right' of transportation by air into West Berlin—of people of the foregoing sort, it is to be understood—and that 'there has never been any limitation in respect of their (the air-corridors) use by the aircraft of the Western Powers'. Such assertions cannot be justified either from a juridical point of view or as regards their substance. It is apparent from the documents of the Control Council that the air-corridors between Berlin and the Western Occupation Zones of Germany which are now in use were temporarily provided solely for meeting the needs of the military garrisons of Britain, the United States, and France in West Berlin, and for ensuring the communications of these garrisons with and the transportation of their personnel and freight to the headquarters of the occupation forces of the corresponding Powers in West Germany. This is referred to, in particular, in the unanimously adopted decision of November 30, 1945 of the Control Council on the Report of the Military Air Directorate.[1]   No quadripartite decisions on uncontrolled commercial air-flights along the air-corridors or on the transportation along them of any German personnel or of persons not serving with the Occupation Authorities of the three Powers or, *a fortiori*, of West German revanchists and militarists were passed by the Control Council, and such decisions do not exist in actuality.   It is well known that the question of the establishment in the territory of Germany of air-route not directly connected with the discharge by the four Powers of their occupation functions was under discussion at one time in the organs of the Control Council.   However, the Control Council recognised itself to be not competent to settle such a question.   And, in general, the agreements to which the British Government refers were concluded prior to the formation of the sovereign German States who have already received wide international recognition.   Apart from this fact, these Agreements were concluded during the period of the occupation of Germany, about the termination of which appropriate statements were issued by the Occupying Powers, apart from West Berlin, where the occupation régime has been for some reason retained by the three Western Powers up to the present moment.

The British Government strives in its Note to present the matters as if the present wide variety of ties between West Berlin and the Federal Republic of Germany 'are not incompatible with the quadripartite status of Berlin'.   The Soviet Government has already had the opportunity of showing what is the character of these 'variety of ties'.   It is quite evident that ties of this kind have nothing more in common with the quadripartite agreements, references to which are contained in the British Note, than the spying and diversionary tunnel in Alt-Glienicke, the activity of revanchist organisations and subversive centres in West Oerlaik, currency speculation, and other similar crimes.

The Western Powers have frequently recognised and, judging by the British Note, do not now deny that West Berlin is no part whatsoever of the Federal Republic of Germany, cannot be administered by its authorities, and, consequently, cannot serve as a residence for such authorities.   The question, however, arises of how to reconcile with this official British position the creation and functioning in West Berlin, under the cover of the Occupation Authorities, of West German agencies and establishments, the holding there of sessions of the Parliament of the Federal Republic of Germany and of its organs, the extension to West Berlin of the operation of Bonn laws, the claims of the Government of the Federal Republic of Germany to represent West Berlin in its external relations, etc.   It is clear that these are incompatible things.   It is difficult to escape the impression that, in taking up such a position, the three Western Powers are trying to shield their West German Allies, who are carrying out in West Berlin activity which is provocative and dangerous for the cause of peace, and who are now trying to hide behind the backs of the Occupation Authorities of the Western Powers.

The Soviet Government has more than once stated that it does not in the least intend to limit the international ties of West Berlin in general and with the

[1] Cmnd. 1552, pp. 63–64.

Federal Republic of Germany in particular. West Berlin, as a free city, will have the right and the opportunity to maintain diplomatic, economic, and cultural links with any country of any continent after the conclusion of a peace treaty. However, it cannot be a subversive centre against the German Democratic Republic on whose territory it is situated. The free city of West Berlin will, it stands to reason, have the right of unhindered communication with the outside world, but this right will not be connected with the occupation; it will be based on appropriate agreements with the Governments of those countries through whose territory its communications will pass.

Confirming its Note of August 23, 1961,[1] the Government of the U.S.S.R. insists that the British Government, which at the present time is exercising occupation functions in West Berlin jointly with the Governments of the United States and France, put an end to the unlawful and provocative actions of the Federal Republic of Germany in this city. The Soviet Government considers it necessary to warn the British Government that it bears full responsibility for the possible consequences of the continuation of such provocative activity. The British Government will be displaying too casual an approach to this entire question of the use of the communications with West Berlin for the provocative purposes indicated in the Note of August 23 of the Government of the U.S.S.R. if it adheres to the point of view expressed in the British Note of August 26.[2]

23. The British Government to the Government of the Soviet Union, 8 September 1961[3]

Air-access to Berlin along the three corridors from West Germany is and has been unrestricted since the end of World War II in 1945.

West Germans who make use of this means of transportation to Berlin do so in pursuit of a variety of business, cultural, political, or other objectives, individually chosen, in a manner which is familiar and well understood in societies where free men regulate their own lives in accordance with free choice. That the U.S.S.R. should characterise such activities as criminal does not make them so. Moreover, these ties with the Federal Republic and the outside world are of vital importance to the viability and well-being of West Berlin. The attitude of the U.S.S.R. and the East German authorities towards freedom of travel is plainly shown in the recent actions by which a prison-wall was built across the heart of Berlin. The authorities of the East German régime have fired on and even killed their fellow countrymen who were seeking no more than to enter West Berlin.

Rights with respect to air-access to Berlin derive from precisely the same source as do the rights of the U.S.S.R. in East Germany and East Berlin, namely, the joint military defeat of the German Reich and the joint assumption of supreme authority over Germany. These rights are confirmed by the circumstances under which the four Powers entered Germany, by their subsequent discussions and agreements, and by open and established practice over a period of fifteen

---

[1] Above, p. 353. [2] Above, p. 354.
[3] Cmnd. 1552, pp. 479–82. The United States and France sent identical Notes the same day. See *D.S.B.*, 25 September 1961, and *La Documentation Française*, 26 September 1961.

years. The Soviet Note refers to the Report of the Air Directorate of the Allied Control Council (which the Note incorrectly designates as the Military Air Directorate) and to the decision of the Council itself regarding flight in the corridors. These documents reveal both the nature of the rights of the respective parties and arrangements as to the exercise of these rights. Paragraph 1 of the Air Directorate Report states that 'because of the increasing number of flights between the Greater Berlin area and the respective occupied Zones of the four Allied Powers in Germany . . . there is a real need to ensure safety of flights . . . by means of air-corridors under strict rules of flight for all aircraft using the corridors'. Paragraph 3 proposes six air-corridors, three to points in the Western Zones, and three to points outside Germany 'which could be used by aircraft of the four Allied nations with full freedom of action'.

The Co-Ordinating Committee of the Allied Control Authority on November 22, 1945 approved the following request from the Air Directorate:—'to confirm the proposal for the establishment of air-corridors West of Berlin as follows:— Berlin—Hamburg, Berlin—Bückeburg, Berlin—Frankfurt-on-Main, each twenty English miles wide. Flight over these routes (corridors) will be conducted, without previous notice being given, by aircraft of the nations governing Germany'.[1]

Lt.-General Kutsevalov represented the U.S.S.R. On November 30, 1945, the Control Council itself approved the document, with Marshal Zhukov acting for the U.S.S.R.[2] Contrary to what is alleged by the Soviet Government, which now finds this decision inconvenient, there is no reference in this decision or in the report of the Air Directorate to any limitation upon the use of the air-corridors either as regards their duration or as regards the goods or persons to be transported by aircraft of Allied nations.

Thus, from the earliest days, the Soviet Union recognised that the air-corridors were to be used 'by aircraft of the four Allied nations with full freedom of action'. This understanding is confirmed in the records of subsequent quadripartite meetings. For example, at the meeting of the Air Directorate on April 30, 1946, the Soviet Delegate, Lt.-General Kutsevalov, stated:

'The Soviet Delegation thinks that the existing system of air-routes through the Soviet Zones of occupation in Germany is fully sufficient, not only to meet the requirements of the Allied troops in the Sector of Greater Berlin, but also to carry out successfully all the Allied transportation needs for commercial cargoes regardless of their volume.'

In February 1947, in connexion with preparations for the Council of Ministers Meeting, the Western Powers renewed a recommendation for establishing additional air-corridors for civil flights to Berlin by aircraft of nations other than the four Powers. The Soviet Union objected, on the ground, as stated in the U.S.S.R. report dated February 5, 1947, that the quadripartite decisions establishing the three air-corridors provided adequate facilities to meet existing requirements.[3] The Soviet Union thus recognised that the air-corridors were

---

[1] Cmnd. 1552, pp. 60–63.   [2] ibid., pp. 63–64.
[3] Committee on Foreign Relations, United States Senate. *Documents on Germany, 1944–1961* (Washington, U.S.G.P.O., 1961), pp. 73–74.

legitimately used by the civil aircraft of the Allied Powers. The practice of the Western Powers is equally significant in confirming the understanding as to air-access. Civil aircraft of the Allied nations had been flying to and from Berlin on special charter-flights from the early days of the occupation. British European Airways inaugurated regular flights to Berlin on September 1, 1946; and in the first year of operation carried out 286 round-trip flights. In 1948 there were 549 round-trip flights by all carriers; in 1949 there were 4,776; in 1950 there were 6,974. All of these flights were processed as a matter of routine through the Berlin Air Safety Centre on which the Soviet Union is represented. Civil air-flights to Berlin continued unrestricted throughout the Berlin blockade and thereafter.

For the rest, the Soviet Note consists merely in the repetition of many charges and allegations which Her Majesty's Government cannot accept, and which it has discussed at length in its Notes of July 17, 1961 and August 26, 1961,[1] as well as in many previous communications on the subject of Germany and Berlin.

The Soviet Government claims that the quadripartite status of Berlin was destroyed by acts of Her Majesty's Government and its Allies. But it is plain to see what divides Berlin in two. It is the wall of barbed wire and concrete built on the sector-border by East German authorities in violation of solemn obliga-tions freely and repeatedly undertaken by the U.S.S.R. This may be 'the true reality' which people living in the U.S.S.R. or under the East German authorities must 'look in the face', but Her Majesty's Government cannot admit that the arbitrary application of force can alter the legal or moral foundation of rights and obligations.

The Soviet Government refers to certain relations between West Berlin and West Germany. The relationships referred to are in fulfilment of the obligation undertaken by the four Powers in Paris on June 29, 1949,[2] after the Berlin blockade, to work for 'facilitation of the movement of persons and goods and the exchange of information between the Western Zones and the Eastern Zone and between Berlin and the Zones'. The policies of the U.S.S.R. have been in flagrant violation of this undertaking. Indeed, the Soviet Note's criticism of normal and peaceful relations between these two parts of the same country is peculiarly inappropriate in view of the fact that the East German authorities with Soviet support have for many years maintained their headquarters in East Berlin, and have stationed military and para-military units there, thus violating the agreed status of Berlin and seeking illegally to annex East Berlin by force. The governing authorities of West Berlin are chosen by the people of West Berlin in free elections and those authorities have freely approved relations between West Berlin and West Germany. Those relations are consistent with the legal status of Berlin.

The Soviet Government again implies that its proposed 'peace treaty' with the East German authorities can somehow alter the status of West Berlin. But such a 'peace treaty' can at most have certain limited effects on the relationship between the Soviet Union and its Zone of occupation. The three Western Powers recognised the principle involved when, in their Convention on Relations

[1] Above, p. 323, n. 1 and p. 354. [2] *Documents*, 1949–50, pp. 160–1.

with the Federal Republic of Germany signed in Paris on October 23, 1954,[1] they specifically retained the rights and responsibilities exercised or held by them relating to Berlin and to Germany as a whole, thus safeguarding the positions of all countries concerned, including the Soviet Union. Indeed, the Soviet Foreign Minister, commenting on this very Convention as recently as May 25, 1959,[2] made clear the view of the Soviet Government that agreements 'concluded not with all the Powers who fought against Germany but only with a group of those Powers, and not with the whole of Germany but only with a part' cannot seriously be regarded 'as some sort of likeness to, or substitute for, a peace treaty'.

Her Majesty's Government is forced to conclude that the sweeping claims of the Soviet Government as to the effects of a 'peace treaty' between the Soviet Union and the so-called German Democratic Republic are merely an effort to provide camouflage for the exploitation of certain advantages which the Soviet Government thinks it has because of the geographic location of Berlin. The Soviet Note gives a foretaste of what the 'freedom' of West Berlin would be like as a consequence of a 'peace treaty' with the East German régime. Although the Note asserts again that the 'free city of West Berlin, of course, will have the right to maintain unobstructed communications with the outside world . . .' the inference is plain that the right would not extend to anyone to whom the U.S.S.R. or the East German authorities may choose to deny it by labelling him as a revanchist, militarist, spy, diversionist, or subversive. The people of the world are by now sufficiently accustomed to the upside-down use of words in the Soviet lexicon not to be deceived by the cynical efforts to mislead them with such labels. Thus, in Soviet usage, a 'revanchist' seems to be anyone who believes in self-determination for the German people; a 'militarist' seems to be one who would afford the people of the Federal Republic and of West Berlin the right to arms and defence after the Soviet Government had created military forces in East Germany to supplement the vast Soviet forces maintained in that territory; a 'spy' would seem to be anyone who is curious about what goes on in the world; a 'diversionist' may be anyone who publicly opposes Soviet views as to right policy; while a 'subversive' appears to be anyone who favours freedom of speech, assembly, and movement.

As of to-day there is free and peaceful movement of goods by air between West Germany and West Berlin. Any change in this situation will be the result of aggressive action against established rights by the Soviet Government and the East German régime. It is the duty of all States, especially in times like these of increasing tensions and dangers to international peace, to refrain from unilateral action to alter existing agreements, and practices further increasing such tensions. Her Majesty's Government wishes to repeat in the most solemn terms the warning already given in its Note of August 26, 1961,[3] against any action to interfere with flights in the air-corridors to West Berlin.

---

[1] Cmnd. 1552, pp. 208–9.
[2] Department of State, *Foreign Ministers Meeting, May–August 1959, Geneva* (Washington, U.S.G.P.O., 1959), p. 186.
[3] Above, p. 354.

24. The Soviet Ambassador to the German Democratic Republic to the British Ambassador in Bonn, 11 September 1961[1]

With reference to your letter of the 26th of August,[2] I should like to direct your attention to the fact that the Soviet Government, in its Notes to the British Government of the 18th and 23rd of August and also of the 1st of September,[3] gave an exhaustive explanation of all the problems upon which you touch again. It remains for me to stress once more that the problems about which you approached me lie entirely within the competence of the Government of the German Democratic Republic, in so far as the establishment of a régime on its frontiers is an internal matter for any sovereign State.

The regulation of visits into the German Democratic Republic and its capital by nationals of foreign countries is at the discretion of the Government of the German Democratic Republic which is, as is well known, an independent sovereign State. If there is any matter that you would like to raise in this respect, then, according to accepted standards, you should contact the authorities of the German Democratic Republic. I may add that Soviet citizens abide strictly by the regulations and laws in force on the territory and borders of the German Democratic Republic.

Furthermore, the reference in your letter to the quadripartite status of Berlin is without any foundation whatsoever, as you, Mr. Ambassador, are well aware of the fact that, as a result of the unilateral measures taken at the time by the three Western Powers, this status was destroyed, and at the present time the occupation régime remains only as a sort of gangrenous rudiment in West Berlin.

In connexion with the introduction of controls on the boundary with West Berlin of which you speak in your letter, no undesirable consequences could arise, if, of course, the situation is not artificially aggravated, and if you were, as is customary in international relationships, to respect the decisions of the competent authorities of another country. I have, nevertheless, to state that the three Powers are making demonstrative transfers of troops through the territory of the German Democratic Republic, and are moving military units right up to the boundary between West Berlin and the German Democratic Republic. All these dangerous actions exacerbate the situation, and help to encourage the Fascist and revanchist elements in West Berlin to further provocations (attempts at destroying the defences along the boundary, the insulting of the People's Police guarding the boundary, etc.).

I must therefore, with all firmness, warn you and the Officer Commanding in your name the British troops in West Berlin, of the extremely serious consequences which could result from such provocations and from the support of provocateurs by the occupation authorities in West Berlin.

I hope, Mr. Ambassador, that you will give your full attention to the aforesaid, and that you will take the necessary steps in the interests of the creation of normal conditions in West Berlin.

---

[1] Cmnd. 1552, p. 483.   [2] Above, p. 356.
[3] Above, pp. 347, 353, 356. This last note was presumably drafted in Moscow on 1 September and arrived in London on 2nd.

D.I.A.–N

25. Speech by Marshal Malinowski to the twenty-second Congress of the Communist Party of the Soviet Union, 24 October 1961[1]

Comrades, the 22nd Congress of our Communist Party indeed marks a great stage in the heroic history of the Soviet people. Like a bright sun it will illuminate for whole decades the future of our motherland, the future of the whole of mankind. Allow me, on behalf of the gallant Soviet armed forces, to convey to you—delegates to the historic Congress of the Party—ardent militant greetings. (*Prolonged applause.*) Communists and servicemen of the armed forces, together with the whole Soviet people, fully approve the Party's foreign and the domestic policies, outlined by the Party in its Draft Programme—the plans for the building of the brightest and most just communist society. (*Prolonged applause.*)

These grandiose plans have been received with unprecedented creative enthusiasm in the Army and Navy. The troops developed a large-scale pre-Congress competition in which the personnel of all types of armed forces took part, and which yielded remarkable results. In the Army and Navy the ranks of first class servicemen and experts in the various categories increased considerably, and new leading lights have appeared, spreading advanced experience to the broadest masses of servicemen. All this helps to raise the combat readiness of the armed forces.

Comrades, the results of the self-denying work of Soviet people during the period after the 20th and 21st Congresses of the CPSU, the majestic prospects of our country's development along the path to communism, are thoroughly and deeply elucidated in the report of the CPSU Central Committee delivered by that faithful Leninist, that outstanding leader of the Party and of the State, our dear Nikita Sergeyevich Khrushchev. (*Prolonged applause.*) They are vividly revealed in the CPSU's new Draft Programme.[2] It speaks with Lenin-like wisdom of the root problems of contemporary social life, vital problems of Party and State development; the aims and tasks of all our work are precisely defined there.

The plans for communist construction outlined by the Party and the first results already achieved in carrying them out are striking in their grandeur and scope. They testify vividly to the superiority of the socialist over the capitalist system, to the irresistible force of communism. The capitalist world has nothing to offer in opposition to the progressive movement of communism. Capitalism has no future, no ideas which could capture the imagination and lead the peoples. The history of recent decades confirms objectively the conclusion of Marxism-Leninism as to the doom and inevitable death of the capitalist system, which is growing decrepit.

However, capitalism, which has outlived itself, in its death throes threatens mankind with terrible calamities. The imperialist Powers are making mad plans for an armed attack on the Soviet Union and other socialist States. On various hypocritical pretexts they reject the Soviet proposals for general and complete disarmament and are constantly increasing the strength of their armed forces. They threaten to reply with force to our just proposals to conclude a German peace treaty and on this basis to liquidate the abnormal situation in West Berlin.

---

[1] *S.W.B.*, SU/778/C/8–16.

[2] *Programme of the Communist Party of the Soviet Union adopted by the 22nd Congress of the C.P.S.U., October 31, 1961* (Moscow, Foreign Languages Publishing House, 1961).

The U.S. President, Kennedy, proclaims his determination to preserve vitally important interests in Berlin. But where is the U.S.A. and where is Berlin? What kind of vitally important interests of the U.S.A. can there be there? Nevertheless, the U.S. President increases the military budget by over 6,000 million dollars, that is, by 14 per cent; he promises by the end of 1964 to increase by 50 per cent [*indistinct passage*] by 50 per cent the number of strategic bombers which are to be kept on runways ready to take off 15 minutes after the proclamation of a state of emergency, to double the number of the Minuteman rockets. He is increasing the strength of ground forces, increasing the output of rifles from 9,000 to 44,000 a month, and increasing by 150 per cent the armed forces for fighting guerrilla movements in captive countries. And all this, according to him, is being carried out in order to attain parity with the Soviet Union.

Speaking on 12th October of this year in North Carolina,[1] President Kennedy was forced to admit that the times have changed, that the U.S.A. is passing through an unusual period—Angola and Algeria, Brazil and Bizerta, Syria and South Vietnam, Korea and Kuwait, the Dominican Republic, Berlin and the United Nations itself—all these are problems about which we could not even dream 20 years ago, and all this in conditions where two Powers standing face to face are capable of destroying each other. We agree with U.S. President Kennedy. Much has changed in 20 years, and a different epoch has arrived. If one adds to this other burning problems, such as the Congo, the Republic of South Africa, Cyprus, Iran, West Irian, Cuba, the Palestine question, the lynching of negroes, the chronic unemployment, the deficit of over 5,000 million dollars to be observed in the U.S.A., then the prospects for the American imperialists are certainly not cheerful. (*Applause*.)

Although war is not fatally inevitable at present, the danger of war will remain while imperialism survives. Mankind has not yet had time to breathe freely after the recent nightmares of the second world war when, through the fault of the aggressors, the sinister clouds of war are once again gathering in the West, threatening to darken the cloudless sky with the mushroom-like atomic whirlwinds of death. The imperialists have now chosen as a pretext for a new wave of war hysteria the Soviet proposals for the conclusion of a German peace treaty. In reply to the Soviet Union's peaceful initiative, the Western Powers have turned the rudder of their policy even more sharply towards the preparation and unleashing of a new war. They are gravely increasing international tension.

As a counter-measure to the increasing practical preparation for war carried out by the Western Powers on the pretext of a Berlin crisis, the Party Central Committee and the Soviet Government have been compelled to take a number of measures known to you to increase the defensive capacity and security of the Soviet Union. The reduction of armed forces, which was being carried out by us according to plan, has been temporarily stopped. Defence expenditure has been somewhat increased. The routine release from the Army and Navy to the reserve of soldiers, sailors, NCOs and petty officers who have completed their terms of active service has been temporarily stopped. Tests of nuclear weapons are being carried out.

Needless to say in military units themselves several essential concrete measures

[1] *Public Papers*, 1961, pp. 666–9.

have been carried out, aimed at placing the armed forces in a heightened state of combat readiness. By strengthening our military might we are carrying out our international duty to the peoples of all countries. We are not planning to attack any one at all, but at the same time we declare firmly that we shall destroy any aggressor who lights the torch of a world war. (*Stormy applause.*)

The social and political essence of present-day wars has been profoundly revealed in the Party Programme. In it the attitude of the Communist and Workers' Parties to such wars is shown. The Programme's postulates on these questions are of fundamental significance for a correct definition of our methods of military development and the solution of problems connected with the pre-paration of the people and the Army for defence of the socialist motherland. In all this work, we military have been guided by the decisions of the Party Central Committee and the Soviet Government. The basic, concrete tasks of the armed forces and the direction of military development in our country under present conditions were concisely and expressively set out in his historic report at the fourth session of the U.S.S.R. Supreme Soviet in 1960 by our Supreme Com-mander-in-Chief, Nikita Sergeyevich Khrushchev.[1] (*Stormy applause.*)

The report has also provided a profound analysis of the character of modern war which forms the basis of Soviet military doctrine. One of the important theses of this doctrine is that a world war, if it should nevertheless be unleashed by the imperialist aggressors, will inevitably assume the character of a nuclear rocket war—that is, a war in which the main means of striking will be nuclear weapons and in which the main means of delivering them to their targets will be rockets. In view of this a war will both begin differently from hitherto and will be waged in a different way. The use of atomic and thermonuclear weapons, combined with the unlimited possibility of delivering them to any target in a matter of minutes by means of rockets, makes it possible to achieve decisive military results at any range and over immense territory in a minimum of time. Besides concentrations of the enemy's armed forces, industrial and vital (*zhiz-nennyy*) centres, focal points of communications and everything which supports the war will be targets for crushing nuclear strikes. A future world war, if it is not averted, will assume an unprecedentedly destructive character. It will lead to the death of hundreds of millions of people, and whole countries will be turned into lifeless, ash-strewn deserts. It must be said that this is also well understood by the ruling circles of the West, which are therefore striving to reach their own aggressive goals by resorting to small local wars fought with conventional and tactical atomic weapons. In spite of the fact that in a future war the decisive place will belong to rocket and nuclear weapons, we nevertheless conclude that final victory over an aggressor can only be achieved as a result of the combined action of all types of armed forces. This is why we pay due attention to the improvement of all types of weapons and teach troops to handle them skilfully to win a decisive victory over the aggressor. (*Applause.*) We also consider that in modern conditions a future world war will be fought, in spite of huge losses, by mass armed forces in all their millions.

The Praesidium of the Central Committee of the Party and the Soviet Govern-ment have required and still require us to devote special attention to the initial

[1] *Documents*, 1960, pp. 63–67.

phase of a possible war. The importance of this phase is inherent in the fact that the very first mass nuclear strikes are capable of predetermining to a vast extent the whole subsequent course of the war and of causing losses in the rear and among troops that could put the people and the country in an exceptionally difficult position. In any realistic appraisal of the position it should be reckoned (*sleduyet schitat*) that it is actually a surprise nuclear attack on the Soviet Union and the other socialist countries for which the imperialists are preparing. This is why Soviet military doctrine regards it as the most important—the principal and primary—task of the armed forces to be constantly prepared to parry a surprise attack by the enemy unerringly and thwart his criminal plans. The essential point is that, in present conditions, any armed conflict will inevitably develop into a universal nuclear rocket war should the nuclear Powers be involved in it. We are thus forced to prepare our armed forces, the country and the whole people to fight an aggressor primarily and mainly in conditions of nuclear warfare.

Our country is great and vast; it is less vulnerable than the capitalist countries; but we are fully aware that it would be for us an exceptionally hard war. We are firmly convinced that in such a war, should the imperialists force it on us, the socialist camp will prove victorious, whereas capitalism will be destroyed for ever. (*?Prolonged applause*.) Permit me to remind you now of certain figures. An official document of the U.S. Congress states that there might be 263 thermonuclear strikes each equivalent to some 5,000,000 tons of TNT against the most important targets in the U.S.A. in the initial phase of a war. According to the Americans' calculations, 132 major military objectives will be destroyed by these strikes, together with many important industrial enterprises of various kinds and 71 large towns. The total area of radioactive contamination would at the same time amount to almost half the country's territory. As a result of all this half the population would be subjected to the nuclear onslaught. According to the U.S.A.'s health service, in the event of a nuclear attack on American towns the number of killed alone would amount to 53,000,000 out of a population of 188,000,000. Moreover, a number of calculations similar to those given above are cited with regard to other countries. Thus, for example, they calculate that no more than eight nuclear warheads, each [equivalent to] 5,000,000 tons, are necessary to put Western Germany out of action. We are particularly surprised by the bellicose stand and warlike threats of Chancellor Adenauer and his War Minister, Strauss. And what is the worth of the threat by the Lord Privy Seal, the Conservative Heath, in a speech in the British House of Commons on behalf of the Government. You must realise, you madmen, that it only needs a few nuclear bombs in the multi-million range to destroy your small and densely populated countries and for you to perish immediately in your lair! (*Tempestuous applause*.) On 21st October this year—that is, quite recently—the West Virginia Employers' Council was addressed, not apparently without President Kennedy's knowledge, by the Assistant U.S. Defence Secretary, Roswell Gilpatric,[1] who, boasting the U.S.A.'s power, threatened us with force. What can one say to this, one more threat, to this petty statement? Just one thing: the threat does not frighten us. (*Stormy applause*.)

[1] U.S.I.S. press release, 23 October 1961.

We heartily approve the proposal of our Party and Government for the conclusion of a peace treaty with Germany and are ready to carry out any task that the armed forces are given. (*Applause*.) We warn our enemies that if we are forced to fight we shall have fully enough means to deliver nuclear blows to an even considerably larger number of the most varied objectives of any aggressor. (*Applause*.) American experts have taken as the unit of calculation a charge of only 5,000,000 tons, but, as you already know, we have nuclear warheads of a few tons up to 100,000,000 tons of TNT in power and our ballistic rockets have shown themselves to be so splendid that no one can have any doubts as to their ability to life and deliver such warheads to any point of the Earth from which an attack may be made on the Soviet Union and other socialist countries. (*Stormy applause*.)

It is obvious that in the light of these more precise details, the U.S. specialists must make substantial corrections in all their calculations both as regards the power of nuclear charges and the number, as possessed by the Soviet Union. This should also be seriously considered by all countries which allow their territory to be used for military bases and for the construction of rocket sites by the aggressors. These countries have small territories, a high population density, and for them the outbreak of nuclear war would be the most complete catastrophe.

Now permit me to report to the Congress on the state of combat readiness of the armed forces of the Soviet Union. Since the 20th Congress of the Party five and a half years have passed. For our armed forces this was a period crowded with significant events, connected with their re-armament with new and modern equipment, the wide introduction in the forces of rocket-nuclear weapons. This was a genuine turning-point in the development and accumulation of the strength of our Army and Navy. During the past few years, on the basis, mainly, of the wide introduction of nuclear-rocket weapons, we have considerably perfected all the—so to speak—old types of the armed forces. But the chief thing is that, on the initiative of Nikita Sergeyevich Khrushchev and on the decision of the Central Committee of the Party and the Soviet Government, a new type of armed forces has been created—the strategic rocket forces.

These, comrades, are forces in constant combat readiness. They already have such a number of launching installations, rockets and warheads for them of multi-million power that, if necessary, we are in a position greatly to exceed the calculations of the U.S. scientists and military, of which I have spoken earlier, and to deal an annihilating defeat to the aggressor and his country. (*Applause*.) I must emphasise that the strategic rocket forces were created at a time when a numerical reduction of the armed forces as a whole was being effected. In reducing—and this was expedient—the numbers of our forces and particularly, the administrative apparatus and auxiliary organs, we at the same time considerably strengthened and are continuing in every way to develop such a type of the armed forces as anti-aircraft and anti-rocket defence forces. Our land forces have become fully modern as regards their technical equipment—and also the Navy, the Air Force, the military air transport branch, which in a future war will be called upon to play a very important part.

The radical reorganisation of the armed forces which has been carried out demanded the revision of the theory of military art, of regulations and manuals, and the re-training of personnel, particularly officers and generals. At the present time the stage of reorganisation has on the whole been completed. As a result, the might of the Soviet armed forces has grown immeasurably. A directing and organising role in the reorganisation of the armed forces was played by the Leninist Central Committee of our Party, headed by Nikita Sergeyevich Khrushchev. The correct military-technical policy of the Central Committee, the successes of industry, the outstanding achievements of Soviet science and technology, have made it possible in a relatively short period to create a powerful and qualitatively new material and technical basis for arming the Army and Navy with modern military equipment and, in the first place, with rocket equipment. (*Applause.*)

I consider it my duty to express, on behalf of the servicemen of the Soviet armed forces, profound gratitude to all the toiling people, to our remarkable workers, engineers, technicians, designers and scientists whose creative and selfless work has made it possible to provide the Army and Navy with the most modern and powerful equipment, and enabled us to be the first in the world to launch artificial Earth satellites and space ships and successfully to launch rockets with a startling accuracy at great distances into the waters of the oceans. (*Prolonged applause.*)

I must report to you that the volume of production of rocket armaments in recent years has increased to such an extent that we are equipped not only completely, but also with a large surplus, with rockets of various types and targets. (*Applause.*) Now our rocket forces are fully in a high state of combat readiness, they are constantly on combat duty and are able successfully to discharge the tasks entrusted to them. I may add that practical live rocket launchings carried out by the rocket forces in 1961 yielded convincing results. Of all launchings of medium-range rockets over 90 per cent were classed as excellent or good. (*Applause.*) As regards inter-continental rockets, they all fulfil their tasks only with mark 'excellent' or 'good'. It may seem strange, but rockets land more accurately at long distances than at short distances. (*Merry animation in the hall; applause.*)

These, comrades, are real, graphic data about the might, about the exceptional military capacities of our rocket troops, and we make no secret of it. The soldiers of the rocket troops correctly understand their tasks and their very great responsibility to the homeland. They continually increase their military skill. Before the Congress socialist competition developed widely among these troops. I think it will be of interest to Congress delegates to learn that at the present time there are in the rocket troops about 1,800 excellent sub-units (*podrazdeleniya*), and these are great masters of their craft, masters of hitting without a miss any point of the globe. (*Stormy prolonged applause.*)

Good results in socialist competition in honour of the 22nd CPSU Congress were achieved by a large number of units and detachments of other arms of the armed forces also. The land forces have been reduced considerably in recent times. However, their military capacities have increased considerably. They are capable of waging active, highly manoeuvrable military operations at unprecedently high speeds to an immense operational depth in conditions of enemy use of nuclear weapons. The land forces, particularly in the frontier regions, are in a state of permanent combat readiness. The main strength of the land forces is now their rocket detachments and tactical operation units (*chasti operativno-takticheskogo naznacheniya*) armed with nuclear and other rockets, with a range of from several to many hundreds of kilometres.

Target practice has confirmed the high degree of the military potential of these rocket troops, their accurate marksmanship, the high acceleration off the the rocket launching pad, their ability to travel under their own power over great distances without loss of fighting strength.

We are not relaxing attention, either, to the conventional types of weapons, in particular, the artillery. Our motorised infantry division is now in number of personnel considerably smaller than a division at the end of the last war, but its fire-power, not counting rocket weapons, has more than quadrupled. (*Applause*.)

As for tanks, there are more of them in our modern motorised infantry and tank divisions than in a mechanised or tank corps at the time of the Great Fatherland War, or in the corresponding divisions of any NATO country. Our land forces, which won fame in combat in the Great Fatherland War, are prepared to discharge with honour any task assigned to them by the Party Central Committee and the Soviet Government. (*Applause*.)

Notable successes have been achieved by our glorious paratroops. Their skill and valour were observed by many of you at this year's air display. These troops are well trained for drops, including from new types of aircraft, by day or night. So that we should have an idea of the possible scale of action of paratroops in contemporary conditions, I will say that during manoeuvres our military air transports alone dropped over 100,000 paratroops, not counting the conveyance of men and freight, and that these air transports can carry motor vehicles, weapons and rockets. It must be reckoned that, if the need arises, our civil air fleet, the splendid qualities of which you all well know, will come speedily to the aid of the military transport aviation. No doubt, not a few delegates came to the Congress in TU-104, IL-18, AN-10 and other marvellous aircraft. (*Applause*.)

The Central Committee of the Party has shown and continues to show particular concern for the country's anti-aircraft and anti-rocket defences. In the period that has elapsed since the 20th Party Congress, the armament and also the organisation of troops of the country's anti-aircraft defences has radically changed. Now the anti-aircraft defence is based primarily on the might of anti-aircraft rocket troops, which work in conjunction with new fighter aircraft. The following facts graphically indicate the superiority of anti-aircraft rockets over anti-aircraft artillery. During the last war an average of 4,600 shells was expended on the destruction of one enemy aircraft by anti-aircraft artillery. Modern aircraft, however, capable of immense speed and height, twice exceeding the height reached by shells of anti-aircraft weapons, can be brought down by one, or at the most two, rockets. I must report in particular that the problem of destroying rockets in flight has also been successfully solved. (*Stormy applause*.)

Among our anti-aircraft defence troops the number of those with 'excellent' marks in military and political training is growing and the number of such sub-units is increasing. By the opening of the Congress they numbered about 1,200; this is a reliable guard for our own towns against raids by modern vultures. The anti-aircraft defence units and troop formations are constantly and vigilantly carrying out their military duties. (*Applause*.)

In the Air Force, during the period under review, obsolete military piston-engined aircraft have been completely replaced by modern jet machines, including supersonic long-range bombers. Cannon and machine-gun aircraft armament has been replaced by rockets. In recent years the speed and ceiling of our military aircraft have been raised by 1.5 to 2.5 times. Rocket-carrying aircraft are being introduced more and more extensively; they are capable of striking rocket and nuclear blows at an aggressor from a long distance without entering the zone of his anti-aircraft defence. This has greatly increased the military capabilities of our Air Force.

Our air forces, in co-operation with the country's anti-aircraft defence troops, have raised their combat readiness with regard to their ability both to repulse an air attack by an aggressor and to deal him, in conjunction with the strategic rocket troops, powerful nuclear blows. The air display this year was much praised by the workers of our country.

Our Navy has also undergone marked changes. Its power has grown and it has become a truly modern Navy capable of undertaking any active operations assigned to it far beyond our territorial waters.

Submarines for various purposes constitute the Navy's main force. In conditions of rocket-nuclear warfare, they are incomparably more effective than surface vessels. We regard as the basis of our submarine fleet our atomic submarines, armed with powerful rocket-nuclear weapons. (*Applause*.) The naval rocket-carrying air force is called upon to carry out military operations in co-operation with submarines.

Nikita Sergeyevich Khrushchev reminded the over-zealous admirals of the West that modern military technology makes it possible to take under fire the vital centres and to destroy the naval vessels, of any aggressor from submarines by means of ballistic and self-guided rockets. I should like to note in this connection that our rocket-carrying submarines have learned to operate well under the ice of the Arctic and accurately to take up position for launching rockets, which is very important for hitting reliably objectives on land and at sea. (*Applause*.)

Comrades! In 1961 we carried out a large number of varied military exercises both by our own forces and jointly with the fraternal armies of the Warsaw Treaty Powers. Chief attention in all exercises was paid to the study of rocket and nuclear weapons and other new military equipment, to the conduct of military operations with the aggressor using weapons of mass destruction. The main common task posed to all our armed forces in their military training was to study and work out ways of repelling a sudden nuclear attack by an attacker and of exploding his aggressive plans by striking a timely and devastating blow at him. Stress was laid on the conduct of exercises in conditions approximating to those of a modern war, the possible actual situation which could materialise in the initial stages of war in the event of an attack by an aggressor. New means of troop control (*upravleniye*), including electronic computers, were used during the exercises on a wide scale.

In view of the worsening of the international situation this year, we checked and controlled by means of inspections and field training all units of all branches of the armed forces. This made it possible to better expose any defects, to render the troops practical assistance on the spot and to determine in greater detail the true state of combat, readiness and speed of mobilisation of the armed forces.

All this makes it possible to report with complete confidence to the 22nd Congress of the Party that our armed forces are at present technically well equipped. Their organisational structure, the level of their military and operational training, fully satisfy the great demands of the Praesidium of the Party Central Committee and the situation which has arisen in the world. (*Prolonged applause.*)

Our command cadres, the entire officer corps of the Soviet armed forces, are a picked detachment of sons of the Soviet people, politically mature, highly-trained in a military, political and technical sense, boundlessly devoted to the cause of the Party, and capable of fulfilling at any moment their duty in the defence of the beloved homeland.

The Soviet officer is the representative of the Party and Government in the Army and Navy. He is a commander vested with undivided authority (*komandiryedinonachalnik*), and his orders are a law to his subordinates. At the same time, he is a painstaking educator of his subordinates, an exponent of the Party's ideas. (*Prolonged applause.*)

It is significant that the proportion of Communists and of Komsomol members among our officers, generals and admirals amounts to nearly 90 per cent. (*Applause.*) One in four among them has had a higher education. The number of our engineer-technical cadres is constantly growing. Among the rocket troops, for example, 72 out of every 100 officers are engineers and technicians. Almost all officers at regimental level and above have gained valuable military experience in the battles of the Great Fatherland War. (*Applause.*)

Fresh detachments of highly-trained officers—ardent patriots of their country—are joining our ranks every year. Young officers are working hard and persistently to perfect their many-sided knowledge, military skill, and, like Majors Yuri Gagarin and Herman Titov, are always ready to accomplish any feat to the glory of the fatherland. (*Applause.*) We have wonderful soldiers, who are the world's best, and sailors, N.C.O.s and Petty Officers who obey their commanders unquestioningly. Inherent in them are such remarkable qualities as high political consciousness, unshakable loyalty to their Party and people, courage, steadfastness and heroism, and readiness for self-sacrifice in the defence of their dear country. They have at heart the immortal ideas of the great Party of the Communists and are prepared to defend them unsparingly with their very lives. (*Prolonged applause.*)

We, the military, have a special score to settle with the members of the anti-Party group. I see in this hall high-working military commanders who were in prison, although guiltless. All Army Communists approve unanimously and with particular fervour the rout of the anti-Party group of Molotov, Malenkov, Kaganovich, Voroshilov, Bulganin, Pervukhin and Saburov, and cordially thank our Party Central Committee for its firm Leninist line in the struggle against the anti-Party group; in the first place they thank Nikita Sergeyevich

Khrushchev, the outstanding champion of the restoration of Leninist principles and norms in the leadership of Party and State. (*Prolonged applause.*)

The former Minister of Defence, Zhukov, displayed adventurism and Bonapartist aspirations towards a single-handed seizure of power. In the army he implanted his own personality cult and pursued a policy aimed at winding up Party political work, to its detriment. The Party Central Committee cut short this harmful activity in time and removed Zhukov from his post.

In this connection a very important role in strengthening the Army and Navy was played by the decisions adopted in 1957 at the October plenum of the CPSU Central Committee which laid down measures by the Party to strengthen the leadership of the armed forces and fundamentally to improve Party political work in them. (*Applause.*)[1] As a result of the practical implementation of the decisions of the October plenum and subsequent decisions of the CPSU Central Committee, Leninist principles for the leadership of the armed forces were fully restored; the role of political organs and of Party organisations in the armed forces rose; the Army's links with the people were strengthened; Party political work with personnel improved considerably.

In the armed forces there was a sharp increase of Party membership from among the best soldiers; the membership of the Komsomol rose; Communists and Komsomols today comprise 82 per cent of the personnel of the armed forces. (*Applause.*) In this lies the tremendous strength of our Army and Navy, the foundation of the high political morale of the troops—the guarantee of the successful solution of the problems facing them in ensuring the Motherland's security.

Comrades! One of the essential factors in the might of our armed forces is the close and inviolable unity of the Army and the people. The expansion and strengthening of contacts of Army and Navy Party organisations and political organs and Military Councils with local Party, administrative, Komsomol and trade union organisations renders inestimable help to the armed forces in the patriotic education of soldiers, and helps them to realise and feel even more deeply their vital unity with the people. This joint work must be continued and improved. (*Applause.*)

Comrades! The Soviet Union is a peaceful country. We are threatening nobody. We defend world peace with all our strength. But the calamities of the past war are too fresh in our minds, in the minds of all Soviet people—calamities which brought so many casualties and so much suffering. Therefore we have no right to forget for one minute the severe lessons of this war—the bestial face of imperialism—and we are forced to keep our powder dry. (*Prolonged applause.*)

Comrades delegates! Soviet soldiers, with the same thoughts and feelings as the whole people, greeted the 22nd Congress of the CPSU with remarkable successes in the improvement of their military skill. Never before have the armed forces of the U.S.S.R. been as powerful as they are now. Shoulder to shoulder with our glorious armed forces the fraternal armies of all socialist countries stand guard over the security of the socialist camp. (*Applause.*) The ever stronger unity of the socialist countries and the military co-operation of their armed

[1] See *N.Y. Times*, 3 November 1957.

forces are a decisive factor in the curbing of the imperialist aggressors and the preservation of peace.

Dear comrades, allow me, on behalf of all personnel of the Army and Navy, firmly to assure the 22nd Congress of the great Party of Communists that the mighty and glorious U.S.S.R. armed forces, under the leadership of their own Leninist Party, basing themselves on the wholehearted support of the people, will continue worthily to discharge their sacred military duty. (*Stormy prolonged applause. All rise.*)

(b) Disarmament

1. Statement by the Commonwealth Prime Ministers, London, 17 March 1961[1]

1. The aim must be to achieve total world-wide disarmament, subject to effective inspection and control.

2. In view of the slaughter and destruction experienced in so-called 'conventional' wars and of the difficulty of preventing a conventional war, once started, from developing into a nuclear war, our aim must be nothing less than the complete abolition of the means of waging war of any kind.

Principles

3. An agreement for this purpose should be negotiated as soon as possible, on the basis of the following principles—

   (a) All national armed forces and armaments must be reduced to the levels agreed to be necessary for international security.

   (b) Once started, the process of disarmament should be continued without interruption until it is completed, subject to verification at each stage that all parties are duly carrying out their undertakings.

   (c) The elimination of nuclear and conventional armaments must be so phased that at no stage will any country or group of countries obtain a significant military advantage.

   (d) In respect of each phase there should be established, by agreement, effective machinery of inspection, which should come into operation simultaneously with the phase of disarmament to which it relates.

   (e) Disarmament should be carried out as rapidly as possible in progressive stages, within specified periods of time.

   (f) At the appropriate stage, a substantial and adequately armed military force should be established, to prevent aggression and enforce observance of the disarmament agreement; and an international authority should be created, in association with the United Nations, to control this force and to ensure that it is not used for any purpose inconsistent with the Charter.

4. On the basis of the above principles, it should be possible, given goodwill on both sides, to reconcile the present differences of approach between the different plans put forward.

---

[1] Cmnd. 1694, *Documents relating to Disarmament and to the establishment of the 18-Nation Committee.* (London, H.M.S.O., 1962), pp. 7–9. Hereafter cited as Cmnd. 1694.

Negotiations

5. The principal military Powers should resume direct negotiations without delay in close contact with the United Nations, which is responsible for disarmament under the Charter. Since peace is the concern of the whole world, other nations should also be associated with the disarmament negotiations, either directly or through some special machinery to be set up by the United Nations, or by both means.

6. Side by side with the political negotiations, experts should start working out the details of the inspection systems required for the measures of disarmament applicable to each stage, in accordance with the practice adopted at the Geneva Nuclear Tests Conference.

7. Every effort should be made to secure rapid agreement to the permanent banning of nuclear weapons tests by all nations and to arrangements for verifying the observance of the agreement. Such an agreement is urgent, since otherwise further countries may soon become nuclear Powers, which would increase the danger of war and further complicate the problem of disarmament. Moreover, an agreement on nuclear tests, apart from its direct advantages, would provide a powerful psychological impetus to agreement over the wider field of disarmament.

8. Disarmament without inspection would be as unacceptable as inspection without disarmament. Disarmament and inspection are integral parts of the same question and must be negotiated together; and both must be made as complete and effective as is humanly possible. It must, however, be recognized that no safeguards can provide 100 per cent protection against error or treachery. Nevertheless, the risks involved in the process of disarmament must be balanced against the risks involved in the continuance of the arms race.

9. It is arguable whether the arms race is the cause or the result of distrust between nations. But it is clear that the problems of disarmament and international confidence are closely linked. Therefore, while striving for the abolition of armaments, all nations must actively endeavour to reduce tension by helping to remove other causes of friction and suspicion.

2. Joint statement by the delegates of the United States and the Soviet Union of agreed principles for disarmament negotiations, New York, 20 September 1961[1]

Having conducted an extensive exchange of views on disarmament pursuant to their agreement announced in the General Assembly on 30 March 1961,

Noting with concern that the continuing arms race is a heavy burden for humanity and is fraught with dangers for the cause of world peace,

Reaffirming their adherence to all the provisions of the General Assembly resolution 1378 (XIV) of 20 November 1959,[2]

Affirming that to facilitate the attainment of general and complete disarmament in a peaceful world it is important that all States abide by existing international agreements, refrain from any actions which might aggravate international

---

[1] Cmnd. 1694, pp. 9–11. Also printed in G.A.O.R., Sixteenth Session, Annexes, Agenda item 19, p. 2.

[2] *Documents*, 1959, p. 115.

tensions, and that they seek settlement of all disputes by peaceful means,

The United States and the U.S.S.R. have agreed to recommend the following principles as the basis for future multilateral negotiations on disarmament and to call upon other States to co-operate in reaching early agreement on general and complete disarmament in a peaceful world in accordance with these principles.

1. The goal of negotiations is to achieve agreement on a programme which will ensure that (a) disarmament is general and complete and war is no longer an instrument for settling international problems, and (b) such disarmament is accompanied by the establishment of reliable procedures for the peaceful settlement of disputes and effective arrangements for the maintenance of peace in accordance with the principles of the United Nations Charter.

2. The programme for general and complete disarmament shall ensure that States will have at their disposal only those non-nuclear armaments, forces, facilities, and establishments as are agreed to be necessary to maintain internal order and protect the personal security of citizens; and that States shall support and provide agreed manpower for a United Nations peace force.

3. To this end, the programme for general and complete disarmament shall contain the necessary provisions, with respect to the military establishment for every nation, for:

(a) Disbanding of armed forces, dismantling of military establishments, including bases, cessation of the production of armaments as well as their liquidation or conversion to peaceful uses;

(b) Elimination of all stockpiles of nuclear, chemical, bacteriological, and other weapons of mass destruction and cessation of the production of such weapons;

(c) Elimination of all means of delivery of weapons of mass destruction;

(d) Abolishment of the organization and institutions designed to organize the military effort of States, cessation of military training, and closing of all military training institutions;

(e) Discontinuance of military expenditures.

4. The disarmament programme should be implemented in an agreed sequence, by stages until it is completed, with each measure and stage carried out within specified time-limits. Transition to a subsequent stage in the process of disarmament should take place upon a review of the implementation of measures included in the preceding stage and upon a decision that all such measures have been implemented and verified and that any additional verification arrangements required for measures in the next stage are, when appropriate, ready to operate.

5. All measures of general and complete disarmament should be balanced so that at no stage of the implementation of the treaty could any State or group of States gain military advantage and that security is ensured equally for all.

6. All disarmament measures should be implemented from beginning to end under such strict and effective international control as would provide firm assurance that all parties are honouring their obligations. During and after the implementation of general and complete disarmament, the most thorough con-

trol should be exercised, the nature and extent of such control depending on the requirements for verification of the disarmament measures being carried out in each stage. To implement control over and inspection of disarmament, an International Disarmament Organization including all parties to the agreement should be created within the framework of the United Nations. This International Disarmament Organization and its inspectors should be assured unrestricted access without veto to all places as necessary for the purpose of effective verification.[1]

7. Progress in disarmament should be accompanied by measures to strengthen institutions for maintaining peace and the settlement of international disputes by peaceful means. During and after the implementation of the programme of general and complete disarmament, there should be taken, in accordance with the principles of the United Nations Charter, the necessary measures to maintain international peace and security, including the obligation of States to place at the disposal of the United Nations agreed manpower necessary for an international peace force to be equipped with agreed types of armaments. Arrangements for the use of this force should ensure that the United Nations can effectively deter or suppress any threat or use of arms in violation of the purposes and principles of the United Nations.

8. States participating in the negotiations should seek to achieve and implement the widest possible agreement at the earliest possible date. Efforts should continue without interruption until agreement upon the total programme has been achieved, and efforts to ensure early agreement on and implementation of measures of disarmament should be undertaken without prejudicing progress on agreement on the total programme and in such a way that these measures would facilitate and form part of that programme.

3. Mr. McCloy, adviser on disarmament questions to President Kennedy to the Soviet Deputy Foreign Minister, Mr. Zorin, 20 September 1961[2]

At the 18 September 1961 session of our bilateral discussions on disarmament you indicated that the draft of a joint statement of agreed principles[3] which I submitted to you on behalf of the United States Government on 14 September 1961 would be acceptable to the Government of the Soviet Union provided the following clause were omitted from paragraph 6:

'Such verification should ensure that not only agreed limitations or reductions take place but also that retained armed forces and armaments do not exceed agreed levels at any stage.'

This sentence expresses a key element in the United States position which

---

[1] The following sentence was dropped from the original draft at the close of paragraph 6:

Such verification should ensure that not only agreed limitations or reductions take place but also that retained armed forces and armaments do not exceed agreed levels at any stage.

See also below, document following.

[2] Cmnd. 1694, pp. 11–12. Also printed in G.A.O.R., Sixteenth Session, Annexes, Agenda item 19, p. 6.

[3] Above, preceding document.

we believe is implicit in the entire joint statement of agreed principles that whenever an agreement stipulates that at a certain point certain levels of forces and armaments may be retained, the verification machinery must have all the rights and powers necessary to ensure that those levels are not exceeded.

It appears from your statements that the Soviet Union will be unwilling to agree to a joint statement of agreed principles unless the above-mentioned clause is omitted therefrom. My Government has authorized me to inform you that, in the interests of progress toward resuming disarmament negotiations, it is willing to remove the above-mentioned sentence from paragraph 6 of the joint statement of agreed principles since it is an item to which the Soviet Union has not agreed.

This is done upon the express understanding that the substantive position of the United States Government as outlined in the above-quoted sentence and in our memorandum of 14 September 1961 remains unchanged, and is in no sense prejudiced by the exclusion of this sentence from the joint statement of agreed principles.

The United States continues to adhere to and will continue to advance the principle contained in the omitted sentence as a necessary element in any comprehensive disarmament negotiations or agreement.

4. Report by the Soviet Foreign Minister, Mr. Gromyko, on the Soviet-American talks, 22 September 1961[1]

In fulfilment of the resolution of the United Nations General Assembly of April 21, 1961, the Soviet government considers it its duty to inform the members of the United Nations of the course and results of the exchange of views on questions of disarmament between the U.S.S.R. and the United States which took place in Washington, Moscow and New York in June, July and September, 1961. The great interest among the United Nations member-states in this exchange of views is quite understandable.

There is no more acute or more urgent task in our day than the preservation and consolidation of peace. The thoughts and aspirations of all peoples are directed towards this noble goal. They link with peace their most cherished aspirations and hopes for a peaceful life, tranquil labour and the wellbeing of their children. The peoples rightly see a true and reliable way to this in general and complete disarmament, which will destroy the material means of waging war and will thus make war impossible.

It is not surprising, therefore, that the question of general and complete disarmament, which was first raised at the 14th session of the United Nations General Assembly on the initiative of the Soviet government, immediately met with wide support on the part of all United Nations member-states, which unanimously recognised it as the most important question of our time and demanded that the governments exert the maximum efforts toward its speediest solution.

Concerned over the failure of the ten-power committee in Geneva which,

---

[1] *Soviet News*, 25 September 1961. Also in G.A.O.R., Sixteenth Session, Annexes, Agenda item 19, pp. 7–12.

because of the western powers, could not accomplish its task of working out an agreement on general and complete disarmament, many countries belonging to the United Nations found it necessary that measures be taken to prevent a recurrence of delays in the solution of this most important international problem. They spoke in favour of the General Assembly approving specific directives for working out a treaty on general and complete disarmament.

Seeking to promote a solution to the problem of disarmament, the Soviet Union submitted proposals concerning such directives for subsequent talks. A large group of neutralist powers, including India, Indonesia and Ghana, also submitted a draft resolution concerning the basic principles of general and complete disarmament. Already at that time the Soviet government announced its favourable attitude to that draft.

It will be recalled that the 15th session of the General Assembly nevertheless could not reach agreement on directives because of the stand of the former Administration of the United States which openly came out against any decisions on general and complete disarmament. The new American Administration declared, for its part, that it was not yet ready to consider in substance the questions of disarmament, and expressed the wish for time to study the problems of disarmament.

Meeting the wishes of the new government of the United States half way, the General Assembly agreed not to consider the question of disarmament in substance in the second part of its 15th session. In so doing, it also took into account the important circumstance that agreement had been reached between the Soviet Union and the United States on bilateral exchanges of views on questions of disarmament. It will be recalled that the Assembly, in a special resolution, approved the holding of such exchanges, expecting that the talks would contribute to the solution of the problem of disarmament and the achievement of the necessary agreement.

The Soviet government hereby submits to the General Assembly a report on the bilateral Soviet-American talks on questions of disarmament.

1. *General and Complete Disarmament—The Most Reliable Way of Ridding Mankind of the Threat of War*

The Soviet government attached great importance to direct negotiations between the U.S.S.R. and the United States, considering that in the course of these talks both sides would sincerely strive to bring their positions closer together to the greatest possible extent. For it is well known that a solution to the problem of disarmament depends in a large measure on agreement between these two powers. It is impossible to ignore the fact that the Soviet Union and the United States of America today have the largest armed forces and the most powerful modern types of armaments, including rocket nuclear weapons. If the U.S.S.R. and the United States reached agreement between themselves on the basic questions of disarmament, this would unequestionably give a great impetus to the solution of the entire problem of disarmament and predetermine agreement on the liquidation of the entire military establishments of states.

The Soviet government made extensive preparations for bilateral exchanges of views. It considered, in so doing, that the new form of talks would enable the sides not only to understand each other better and determine where their positions coincided and where they differed but also to map together specific ways of solving the problems of disarmament. The Soviet government sincerely desired that the talks would from the very start assume a businesslike character, and that positive results would be achieved. This is why the Soviet government proposed to the American government to exchange, first of all, views on the substance of the problem of general and complete disarmament and consider specific proposals on this question, especially since the need for solving the problem of disarmament on the basis of the general and complete disarmament of states had already been recognised by the United Nations General Assembly.

Being desirous of giving the United States government an opportunity of making a closer study of the Soviet Union's position, the delegation of the U.S.S.R., on June 27, handed to the American side a statement by the Soviet government concerning general and complete disarmament [the text of this document will be published in the magazines *International Affairs* and *New Times*].[1]

In the course of subsequent talks, the Soviet delegation handed to the U.S. delegation a memorandum of July 19, 1961, on the need for general and complete disarmament, and a memorandum of July 21, 1961, expressly on control over general and complete disarmament [the text of this document will be published in the magazines *International Affairs* and *New Times*].[2] These documents substantiated in detail the programme for general and complete disarmament under strict international control submitted by the head of the Soviet government N. S. Khrushchov, to the General Assembly of the United Nations on September 23, 1960.[3]

What are the motives which prompt the government of the U.S.S.R. to insist on the immediate realisation of general and complete disarmament?

Never in history has there been such an acute and urgent need for the most resolute measures to save mankind from the threat of devastating war. The impetuous development of science and military techniques has led to the creation of monstrous nuclear bombs, each of which is capable of wiping a big industrial or cultural centre off the face of the earth.

Intercontinental ballistic rockets have appeared capable of delivering such bombs inexorably, in a matter of minutes, to any point on the globe. The establisment by western powers of a series of military blocs—N.A.T.O., S.E.A.T.O. and Cento—directed against peaceloving states, the dense network of American military bases on foreign territories, the fomenting of the cold war, which has poisoned relations among states, and the constant intensification of the arms race have already accumulated a vast amount of inflammable material for a tremendously dangerous war.

Especially dangerous are the recent developments when, in reply to the Soviet Union's proposal for a peace treaty with Germany and the normalisation on this basis of the situation in West Berlin, the western powers have started sabre rattling, threatening to unleash a military conflict.

The most reliable way to ridding mankind forever of this threat is precisely

---

[1] *International Affairs* (Moscow) for October 1961, pp. 134–40.
[2] ibid., pp. 140–4.   [3] *Documents*, 1960, pp. 93–94.

general and complete disarmament. It is necessary to destroy all means of waging war, to abolish the military machines of states and to prevent their re-establishment in whatever form.

While the states possess armies and weapons, the threat of war cannot be considered to have passed. While there remain armaments and armed forces, even if reduced, limited or truncated, the possibility will remain of a military conflict, of the use of armed force by one state against another or one group of states against another.

The Soviet government regards general and complete disarmament as a feasible task. What are the grounds for this assumption? First of all, it is a fact that the implementation of disarmament would preclude any possibility of this or that state securing a military advantage and would guarantee equal conditions for all countries. If all states disarm, if no state has a military machine at its disposal, the threat to the security of all states will be removed.

General and complete disarmament disposes of many of the obstacles which arose when partial disarmament measures were proposed and when individual states feared that the implementation of those measures might upset the balance of forces at some stage and prejudice their security. If in the past many states were suspicious of various disarmament plans, seeing in them an intention by the other side to secure some unilateral advantages, general and complete disarmament will remove all these apprehensions, as all will gain by it, and no one will lose.

There is no need to say that the very readiness of states to embark on such disarmament would not fail to have an immediate favourable effect on the entire international situation. This readiness would show that the states have no intention of attacking anyone and are determined to strengthen trust and build the relations among them on the basis of the principles of peaceful co-existence, to live in peace and friendship.

The fact should likewise be taken into consideration that the conclusion of an agreement on general and complete disarmament would also greatly facilitate international control over disarmament measures. When the threat to their security is removed by general and complete disarmament, the states will have no reason to hide anything, and the doors for checking compliance with the commitments assumed will be flung wide open to international inspection.

In these conditions control will not obstruct, but will cement mutual confidence, enabling every state to see for itself that the other parties to the agreement are also fulfilling their commitments in good faith.

Need it be stressed that the destruction of the means of warfare would radically alter the entire situation in the world: the arms race and the cold war, which make the peoples live in constant fear for their future, would give way to stable peaceful co-existence and the pooling of efforts to harness the as yet unexplored forces of nature, nuclear energy, all the natural wealth of our planet, and outer space, which man has already begun courageously to penetrate. All the thoughts of men will then be directed, not to preparations for destructive war, but to the creation of material and cultural values and to joint struggle against disease and natural calamities which still do great harm to the peoples.

In working out a plan for the implementation of general and complete disarmament in three consecutive stages, the Soviet government was guided by the desire that the very first steps along this road should produce the greatest positive effect and reduce to the minimum the threat of nuclear war—which is the most dangerous to mankind—if not eliminate it altogether. The Soviet Union therefore proposes that disarmament be started, not only with a substantial reduction of the armed forces and conventional armaments of states, but also with the destruction of all means of delivering nuclear weapons, the dismantling of foreign military bases, and the withdrawal of all troops from foreign soil.

It is not hard to see that the complete liquidation of means of delivering nuclear weapons would practically eliminate the threat of one country attacking another with atomic and hydrogen weapons. This, in turn, would provide more favourable conditions for a rapid solution, in the next stage, to the task of the complete prohibition of nuclear weapons, including the ending of their production, their removal from armaments and the destruction of all stockpiles of these weapons.

In renouncing weapons which are its principal means of defence against aggression, the Soviet Union is entitled to demand that the interests of its security be taken into consideration, and that military bases on foreign soil be dismantled simultaneously with the destruction of means of nuclear delivery. A glance at the map of military bases which the United States and other members of western military blocs have pushed up to the frontiers of the socialist states is enough to show that if rockets were destroyed while military bases on foreign soil were left intact, the United States and its allies in military blocs would find themselves in a privileged position.

The liquidation of the means of delivery, simultaneously with the closing down of military bases, is an indispensable condition for ensuring the practical equality of states during disarmament. The Soviet Union does not demand any advantages for itself, but neither can it agree to others obtaining unlawful advantages. This is why the disarmament measures are so balanced, both within the framework of the entire programme of general and complete disarmament and at every stage of the programme, that their implementation should not give any advantages to any country or group of countries.

In the course of bilateral exchanges of views, the Soviet delegation emphasised the great importance of agreement that a single treaty be worked out and concluded embracing all stages of the programme of general and complete disarmament and providing for specific time limits for both the individual stages and the programme in general.

Only given an agreement setting specific time limits for disarmament measures under effective control is it possible to speak of the commitments to be assumed by the states as specific. Only then can one be confident that the opponents of disarmament will not be able to delay or even wreck disarmament measures by pleading the vagueness of commitments under the appropriate treaty.

Taking into consideration the urgency of the disarmament problem, the Soviet government expressed the conviction in the course of its talks with the U.S.A. that the states should exert the maximum efforts to accomplish disarmament in a short time. The Soviet Union proposes that general and complete disarmament, be completed in four to five years. This is a realistic time limit, one that takes into account the possibilities of states in liquidating their military machines and converting their economy and their entire life to peaceful lines.

The Soviet Union is prepared to consider any other proposals on the time limits of the programme of general and complete disarmament. It believes, however, that in any case the agreed time limit should be definite and as brief as possible.

2. General and Complete Disarmament Should Be Effected Under Strict International Control

In the course of the talks, the Soviet side set forth in detail the Soviet position on the question of international control over disarmament.

The Soviet government considers that agreement on general and complete disarmament should ensure firm confidence that no side would violate its commitments. The Soviet Union is, therefore, in favour of strict international control over disarmament and will never agree to any disarmament measures without effective control over their implementation.

As has already been stressed by the Soviet government, the Soviet state has reasons for abiding by this position, if only because it is impossible—as experience shows—to rely on the good faith of some western powers.

The government of the U.S.S.R. and its head, N. S. Khrushchov, have repeatedly declared that if the western powers accept the proposal for general and complete disarmament, the Soviet Union will unconditionally accept any western proposals for control over disarmament. These clear statements make it obvious to all that it is not the Soviet Union's position that is preventing a solution to the problem of control over disarmament, but the efforts of the western powers to use this problem to raise an artificial obstacle to disarmament, the spurious nature of their positions on disarmament and control, their reluctance to accept either disarmament or control over disarmament.

In upholding effective control over disarmament, the Soviet Union resolutely objects to control over armament. Such control, far from limiting the arms race in any way, would create conditions for its unhampered continuation and, consequently, for the further stockpiling of weapons of all kind, including nuclear and rocket weapons. Divorced from disarmament measures, control would become an international system of legalised espionage, making possible the collection of information in which the War Ministries of certain states are interested. Such control would serve, not disarmament, but preparations for a new war.

The system of control envisaged in the Soviet programme for general and complete disarmament is an effective and reliable system. The Soviet Union wants the process of disarmament in general, and every disarmament measure individually to be carried out under effective international control from start to finish. It follows from this that the tasks of control, its functions and powers, should extend continuously as disarmament proceeds, spreading to ever new areas. Only bad faith and unwillingness to seek agreements can explain the western claims that the Soviet Union proposes to start disarmament first, and only then establish control.

What does the Soviet Union propose in the sphere of control? The international control organisation should start fulfilling its functions simultaneously with the coming into force of a treaty on general and complete disarmament. It will consist of all states that are signatories to the treaty, whose representatives will meet periodically for conferences to consider questions connected with effective control over disarmament. The conference will elect a control council which will have its organs in all countries that are parties to the treaty, staffed with international personnel.

The Soviet government considers that the control council, which is to direct the entire control system, should consist of representatives of socialist countries, representatives of states belonging to western military-political alliances, and representatives of neutral states. In proposing this composition, the Soviet Union proceeds on the basis of the situation that exists in the world today, and seeks to make the control organisation a reliable and really impartial control organ and not a tool of any group of states.

It was by these considerations that the Soviet government was guided in working out the propositions concerning control in its programme for general and complete disarmament and seeking to ensure that the international control organ has the necessary means and facilities for accomplishing the tasks entrusted to it.

Accordingly, the first stage will see the establishment of on-the-spot international control over the liquidation of rocket weapons, military aircraft, surface warships and submarines, and other means that can be used for the delivery of atomic and hydrogen weapons. There will be control over the dismantling of foreign military bases and the withdrawal of military personnel and troops to within the confines of their national territories, and also over the disbandment of troops and the destruction of armaments. Measures for control in the second and third stages of the Soviet disarmament programme have been worked out in the same way, on the basis of close conformity to the disarmament measures.

The Soviet government considers that even after the realisation of general and complete disarmament the control organisation should continue in operation and effect constant supervision so that no state could secretly resume military production and start rebuilding armed forces.

The states will submit to the control organisation information concerning the points where the contingents of police (militia) are located, their strength at every point, and also all considerable movements by them near state frontiers. International inspection groups will see that the numerical strength of the police (militia) and its armaments conform to the agreed quotas for each country.

The Soviet proposals are fully in keeping with all the demands that can be made on an international system of strict control over disarmament, but if the United States and other western powers do not agree with them, for some reason, and submit their proposals to strengthen control, the Soviet government will be prepared to consider them.

The Soviet Union is ready, as hitherto, to sign at once an agreement on general and complete disarmament with the establishment of any, the strictest, international control, up to and including the broadest all-embracing control in conditions of general and complete disarmament.

3. *Position of U.S.A. in Washington and Moscow Stages of Talks*

In the first two stages of the bilateral talks, in Washington and Moscow, the American delegation refused altogether to consider a programme of general and complete disarmament, insisting on the working out of only general principles.

The statement on principles submitted by the United States delegation on June 19, 1961,[1] did not even mention the need to solve the problem of general and complete disarmament, even though the unanimously adopted resolution of the General Assembly of November 20, 1959,[2] for which the United States, too, had voted, proclaimed this problem to be the most important one before the world at the present time, and urged the governments to exert every effort for its constructive solution.

Instead of general and complete disarmament, the American side put forward the idea of 'total universal disarmament', which provided neither for the abolition of armaments and armed forces, nor for the prohibition of nuclear and other weapons of mass destruction, nor for the dismantling of military bases on foreign soil.

Simultaneously, the American delegation in the first two stages of the talks tried to replace general and complete disarmament by such measures as the termination of the production of fissionable materials for military purposes, control over the launching of devices into outer space, etc., even though these measures actually have nothing in common with disarmament.

Indeed, the termination of the manufacture of fissionable materials for military purposes would be meaningless without a ban on nuclear weapons and the destruction of stockpiles of those weapons, and would boil down to the establishment of control over the atomic industry, and not only the atomic industry, which would enable the western powers to obtain the information they want about Soviet nuclear weapons. The raising of the question of control over the launching of devices into outer space separately from disarmament cannot be regarded otherwise than as an effort to obtain access to information about Soviet rockets.

The American side laid the main emphasis on the need to establish 'international armed forces', and submitted proposals aimed at the establishment of such forces in circumvention of the Security Council. It was also proposed that the strength of these forces should increase with the reduction of the national armed forces and that the 'international armed forces' could be armed with nuclear weapons.

The American government accompanied these proposals with a demand for the abolition of the rule of unanimity in adopting decisions on the use of 'international forces'—a rule envisaged by the United Nations Charter—seeking thereby to violate the main principle which underlies the U.N. Charter and which the states that played the leading role in establishing the United Nations regarded as the cornerstone of its activities.

It is obvious that the establishment of 'international armed forces' on these terms could not offer any guarantees that these forces would be used in the

[1] cf. below, U.S. Note of 17 June 1961, p. 437.
[2] *Documents*, 1959, p. 115.

interests of peace and would not become a tool of the expansionist policy of some state or group of states. The experience of the use of U.N. armed forces in the Congo is an eloquent warning in this respect.

In putting forward its proposal for the establishment of international armed forces, the American side completely by-passed the question of their command and the need to prevent their use for unlawful purposes. What is more, the demand to abolish the rule of unanimity, provided for in the United Nations Charter, in deciding on the use of 'international armed forces' gave wide scope for the arbitrary use of these forces in the interests of the western military bloc against the vital interests of the peaceloving states, to suppress the national liberation movement in the colonial and dependent countries, to preserve and implant reactionary régimes hated by the peoples.

It is clear that because of this position of the U.S. government it was impossible to reach any agreement on the programme of general and complete disarmament in the first two stages of the talks.

Guided by a desire to get the talks out of the deadlock in some way, the Soviet government, at the end of the Moscow stage of the negotiations, expressed readiness to reach agreement on at least the basic principles of general and complete disarmament. With this aim in view, the Soviet side submitted on July 27 this year the draft of a 'Joint Soviet-American Statement on the Basic Principles of a treaty on General and Complete Disarmament' [the text of this document will be published in the magazines *International Affairs* and *New Times*].[1]

The document contained recommendations concerning directives for a future organ for negotiations providing the basis for a draft treaty on disarmament. But the U.S. representatives turned down the draft of the joint document submitted by the Soviet Union.

In view of this position of the United States government, it proved impossible in the bilateral Soviet-American talks in Washington and Moscow to reach agreement even on the basic principles of general and complete disarmament.

4. *Closing Stage of Talks and Co-ordination of Basic Principles*

In the last stage of the bilateral talks, in New York, the U.S. government somewhat modified its position on the question of general and complete disarmament, and submitted on September 6 this year a new document, a statement of principles, which was then amended additionally by the American side and submitted in its final form on September 14.[2]

In this statement, the government of the United States recognised the need for agreement on a programme ensuring general and complete disarmament and including: disbandment of armed forces; dismantling of military bases; termination of armaments production; liquidation of all stocks of nuclear, chemical, bacteriological and other weapons of mass destruction and all means of their delivery, termination of the manufacture of these weapons; abolition of organisations and institutions designed for the organisation of national military estab-

[1] *International Affairs* (Moscow) for October 1961, p. 145.
[2] See also above, p. 378.

lishments; discontinuation of military training and closing of all military educational establishments; and an end to expenditures on military purposes.

The American document said also that general and complete disarmament should be effected in stages and in established periods, and that at no stage should any military advantage be obtained by any state or group of states.

Acceptance by the United States of these propositions, on which the Soviet side had insisted throughout the talks, marked a step forward compared with the former position of the American government. Taking this into consideration and being guided by a desire to contribute to the utmost to settling the problem of general and complete disarmament, the Soviet government arrived at the conclusion that it would be possible to submit the statement of principles, as a joint proposal of the U.S.S.R. and the United States, to the U.N. General Assembly as draft directives for the working body for the drafting of an agreement on general and complete disarmament.

The Soviet government agreed to this even though the American draft of the statement of principles contained many insufficiently clear formulations which allowed—as also followed from verbal explanations by the U.S. representative in the bilateral talks—for various interpretations, including interpretations which have nothing in common with the tasks of disarmament. The Soviet side declared, however, that one important proposition in the American draft was utterly unacceptable and could raise insurmountable obstacles to agreement on a programme of general and complete disarmament. It envisaged that control should be established, not only over the implementation of disarmament measures, but also over the armed forces and armaments that would remain in the possession of states at various stages of disarmament. In practice, this would mean the establishment of control over armament and not disarmament, which could benefit only a potential aggressor, and to which states which have no aggressive intentions naturally cannot agree.

On September 19, 1961, the government of the United States, on the insistence of the Soviet side, agreed to delete from the statement of principles the aforementioned provision aimed at the establishment of control over armament. As a result, it became possible to submit to the General Assembly a joint Soviet-American proposal concerning general principles.

The joint Soviet-American statement concerning agreed principles for talks on disarmament was submitted by the Soviet and American delegations to the General Assembly on September 20, 1961. It should be stated, however, that serious difficulties might arise in the coming talks on the drafting of an agreement on general and complete disarmament if the United States and its allies do not renounce their position which is aimed at the establishment of control over armament. Although the United States has deleted this proposition from the document on principles it has not abandoned the line of replacing disarmament by control over armament. This is evident, in particular, from the letter of September 20, 1961, from the U.S. representative in the bilateral talks to the representative of the U.S.S.R., which openly states that control over the remaining armed forces and armaments at every stage of disarmament is a key element of the United States position.

The Soviet government considers it necessary to declare that the question of whether there should be disarmament under control or whether there will be control over armament is very much a matter of principle.

5. *Question of Composition of Disarmament Committee*

Another task of the U.S.S.R. and the United States in their bilateral talks was to reach agreement on the composition of the working body which should continue the talks on a treaty on general and complete disarmament.

The Soviet government reminded the other side in the course of the talks that it considered it useless to continue the talks on general and complete disarmament in the ten-power committee which met in Geneva in the spring and summer of 1960. Represented in that body, it will be recalled, were five socialist countries and five western powers. This composition proved unsatisfactory, and the committee's sterility was due to a considerable extent to the fact that it did not include representatives of one of the three main groups of states which have been formed in the world today, namely, the group of neutralist states.

And yet the direct participation in talks on disarmament of representatives of states which follow a neutralist policy is not only useful but necessary, even though the neutralist states themselves do not possess large armed forces. The peaceful policy of these states, which represent about a thousand million people, is an important reserve of the cause of peace, and this reserve should be used in settling the problem of removing the threat of war.

That is why the Soviet Union proposed, already at the 15th session of the U.N. General Assembly, that, together with the former ten members, a group of neutral countries should be included in the disarmament committee as equal partners in the talks. The question of the number of neutral states to be included in the committee and what states should be chosen for the purpose is to be agreed upon.

The Soviet government stressed in the course of the bilateral talks with the United States that the working disarmament body would be effective and capable of accomplishing its tasks only if it included representatives of all three groups of states—the socialist countries, the states belonging to western military blocs and the neutralist countries, all of them enjoying equal rights.

The U.S. government's proposals concerning the composition of the working body, which it submitted in the course of the bilateral Soviet-American exchanges of views, do not conform to these important principles. The government of the United States of America proposed that the ten-power committee be revived. The Soviet side could not accept this proposal as it provided for the continued exclusion of neutralist states from the disarmament negotiations.

The U.S. government then proposed that two or three citizens of neutral countries be included in the ten-power committee as chairman and vice-chairmen, who could not participate on a footing of equality in the consideration and solution of questions of disarmament. It is clear that this proposal could not be accepted either, as it actually barred the neutralist states from participation in the work of the disarmament committee.

Finally, the U.S. government proposed that the ten-power committee be enlarged by adding ten other states, the majority of which are open supporters of the policy of the western powers, or even military allies of theirs. It was only on the condition of the Soviet Union's consent to the inclusion of these countries that the U.S. government would agree to the inclusion of the few neutralist states which figured in its proposal. It goes without saying that this proposal could not provide the basis for agreement either.

Thus it proved impossible in the course of the bilateral Soviet-American talks to reach agreement on the composition of a working body to prepare an agreement on general and complete disarmament. The Soviet government considers it necessary for the General Assembly to adopt a decision on this subject which will ensure the equal participation in the disarmament talks of all states which have the right to this, and without which talks on disarmament cannot be productive.

In informing the United Nations member-states of the course and results of the bilateral talks, the Soviet government would like to stress that the situation which has developed in the solution of the disarmament problem requires most serious attention. The General Assembly should exert the maximum efforts to ensure a successful solution to this question, this most important problem ever faced by mankind. As for the Soviet government, it will continue to do everything possible for the earliest practical solution of the question of general and complete disarmament in the interests of world peace.

5. Declaration by the Government of the United States: 'A Programme for General and Complete Disarmament in a Peaceful World', 25 September 1961[1]

The Nations of the world,

Conscious of the crisis in human history produced by the revolutionary development of modern weapons within a world divided by serious ideological differences;

Determined to save present and succeeding generations from the scourge of war and the dangers and burdens of the arms race and to create conditions in which all peoples can strive freely and peacefully to fulfil their basic aspirations;

Declare their goal to be: a free secure, and peaceful world of independent States adhering to common standards of justice and international conduct and subjecting the use of force to the rule of law; a world where adjustment to change takes place in accordance with the principles of the United Nations; a world where there shall be a permanent state of general and complete disarmament under effective international control and where the resources of nations shall be devoted to man's material, cultural and spiritual advance;

Set forth as the objectives of a programme of general and complete disarmament in a peaceful world:

(a) The disbanding of all national armed forces and the prohibition of their re-establishment in any form whatsoever other than those required to preserve internal order and for contributions to a United Nations Peace Force;

(b) The elimination from national arsenals of all armaments, including all weapons of mass destruction and the means for their delivery, other than

[1] Cmnd. 1694, pp. 12–18. Also printed in G.A.O.R., Sixteenth Session, Annexes, Agenda item 19, pp. 22–25.

those required for a United Nations Peace Force and for maintaining internal order.

(c) The establishment and effective operation of an International Disarmament Organization within the framework of the United Nations to ensure compliance at all times with all disarmament obligations;

(d) The institution of effective means for the enforcement of international agreements, for the settlement of disputes, and for the maintenance of peace in accordance with the principles of the United Nations.

Call on the negotiating States:

(a) To develop the outline programme set forth below into an agreed plan for general and complete disarmament and to continue their efforts without interruption until the whole programme has been achieved;

(b) To this end to seek to attain the widest possible area of agreement at the earliest possible date;

(c) Also to seek—without prejudice to progress on the disarmament programme—agreement on those immediate measures that would contribute to the common security of nations and that could facilitate and form a part of that programme;

Affirm that disarmament negotiations should be guided by the following principles:

(a) Disarmament shall take place as rapidly as possible until it is completed in stages containing balanced, phased and safeguarded measures, with each measure and stage to be carried out in an agreed period of time.

(b) Compliance with all disarmament obligations shall be effectively verified from their entry into force. Verification arrangements shall be instituted progressively and in such a manner as to verify not only that agreed limitations or reductions take place but also that retained armed forces and armaments do not exceed agreed levels at any stage.

(c) Disarmament shall take place in a manner that will not affect adversely the security of any State, whether or not a party to an international agreement or treaty.

(d) As States relinquish their arms, the United Nations shall be progressively strengthened in order to improve its capacity to assure international security and the peaceful settlement of differences as well as to facilitate the development of international co-operation in common tasks for the benefit of mankind.

(e) Transition from one stage of disarmament to the next shall take place as soon as all the measures in the preceding stage have been carried out and effective verification is continuing and as soon as the arrangements that have been agreed to be necessary for the next stage have been instituted.

Agree upon the following outline programme for achieving general and complete disarmament:

STAGE I

A. *To Establish an International Disarmament Organization:*

  (*a*) An International Disarmament Organization (IDO) shall be established within the framework of the United Nations upon entry into force of the agreement. Its functions shall be expanded progressively as required for the effective verification of the disarmament programme.

  (*b*) The IDO shall have:

    (1) A General Conference of all the parties;

    (2) a Commission consisting of representatives of all the major Powers as permanent members and certain other States on a rotating basis; and

    (3) an Administrator who will administer the Organization subject to the direction of the Commission and who will have the authority, staff, and finances adequate to assure effective impartial implementation of the functions of the Organization.

  (*c*) The IDO shall:

    (1) ensure compliance with the obligations undertaken by verifying the execution of measures agreed upon;

    (2) assist the States in developing the details of agreed further verification and disarmament measures;

    (3) provide for the establishment of such bodies as may be necessary for working out the details of further measures provided for in the programme and for such other expert study groups as may be required to give continuous study to the problems of disarmament;

    (4) receive reports on the progress of disarmament and verification arrangements and determine the transition from one stage to the next.

B. *To Reduce Armed Forces and Armaments:*

  (*a*) Force levels shall be limited to 2·1 million each for the United States and U.S.S.R. and to appropriate levels not exceeding 2·1 million each for all other militarily significant States. Reductions to the agreed levels will proceed by equitable, proportionate, and verified steps.

  (*b*) Levels of armaments of prescribed types shall be reduced by equitable and balanced steps. The reductions shall be accomplished by transfers of armaments to depots supervised by the IDO. When, at specified periods during the Stage I reduction process, the States party to the agreement have agreed that the armaments and armed forces are at prescribed levels, the armaments in depots shall be destroyed or converted to peaceful uses.

  (*c*) The production of agreed types of armaments shall be limited.

  (*d*) A Chemical, Biological, Radiological (CBR) Experts Commission shall be established within the IDO for the purpose of examining and reporting on the feasibility and means for accomplishing the verifiable reduction and eventual elimination of CBR weapons stockpiles and the halting of their production.

C. *To Contain and Reduce the Nuclear Threat:*

(*a*) States that have not acceded to a treaty effectively prohibiting the testing of nuclear weapons shall do so.

(*b*) The production of fissionable materials for use in weapons shall be stopped.

(*c*) Upon the cessation of production of fissionable materials for use in weapons, agreed initial quantities of fissionable materials from past production shall be transferred to non-weapons purposes.

(*d*) Any fissionable materials transferred between countries for peaceful uses of nuclear energy shall be subject to appropriate safeguards to be developed in agreement with the IAEA.

(*e*) States owning nuclear weapons shall not relinquish control of such weapons to any nation not owning them and shall not transmit to any such nation the information or material necessary for their manufacture. States not owning nuclear weapons shall not manufacture such weapons, attempt to obtain control of such weapons belonging to other States, or seek to receive information or materials necessary for their manufacture.

(*f*) A Nuclear Experts Commission consisting of representatives of the nuclear States shall be established within the IDO for the purpose of examining and reporting on the feasibility and means for accomplishing the verified reduction and eventual elimination of nuclear weapons stockpiles.

D. *To Reduce Strategic Nuclear Weapons Delivery Vehicles:*

(*a*) Strategic nuclear weapons delivery vehicles in specified categories and agreed types of weapons designed to counter such vehicles shall be reduced to agreed levels by equitable and balanced steps. The reduction shall be accomplished in each step by transfers to depots supervised by the IDO of vehicles that are in excess of levels agreed upon for each step. At specified periods during the Stage I reduction process, the vehicles that have been placed under supervision of the IDO shall be destroyed or converted to peaceful uses.

(*b*) Production of agreed categories of strategic nuclear weapons delivery vehicles and agreed types of weapons designed to counter such vehicles shall be discontinued or limited.

(*c*) Testing of agreed categories of strategic nuclear weapons delivery vehicles and agreed types of weapons designed to counter such vehicles shall be limited or halted.

E. *To Promote the Peaceful Uses of Outer Space:*

(*a*) The placing into orbit or stationing in outer space of weapons capable of producing mass destruction shall be prohibited.

(*b*) States shall give advance notification to participating States and to the IDO of launchings of space vehicles and missiles, together with the track of the vehicle.

F. *To Reduce the Risks of War by Accident, Miscalculation, and Surprise Attack:*

(*a*) States shall give advance notification to the participating States and to the IDO of major military movements and manoeuvres, on a scale as may be agreed, which might give rise to misinterpretation or cause alarm and induce countermeasures. The notification shall include the geographic areas to be used and the nature, scale and time span of the event.

(*b*) There shall be established observation posts at such locations as major ports, railway centres, motor highways, and air bases to report on concentrations and movements of military forces.

(*c*) There shall also be established such additional inspection arrangements to reduce the danger of surprise attack as may be agreed.

(*d*) An international commission shall be established immediately within the IDO to examine and make recommendations on the possibility of further measures to reduce the risks of nuclear war by accident, miscalculation, or failure of communication.

G. *To Keep the Peace:*

(*a*) States shall reaffirm their obligations under the United Nations Charter to refrain from the threat or use of any type of armed force—including nuclear, conventional, or CBR—contrary to the principles of the United Nations Charter.

(*b*) States shall agree to refrain from indirect aggression and subversion against any country.

(*c*) States shall use all appropriate processes for the peaceful settlement of disputes and shall seek within the United Nations further arrangements for the peaceful settlement of international disputes and for the codification and progressive development of international law.

(*d*) States shall develop arrangements in Stage I for the establishment in State II of a United Nations Peace Force.

(*e*) A United Nations peace observation group shall be staffed with a standing cadre of observers who could be dispatched to investigate any situation which might constitute a threat to or breach of the peace.

STAGE II

A. *International Disarmament Organization:*

The powers and responsibilities of the IDO shall be progressively enlarged in order to give it the capabilities to verify the measures undertaken in Stage II.

B. *To Further Reduce Armed Forces and Armaments:*

(*a*) Levels of forces for the United States, U.S.S.R., and other militarily significant States shall be further reduced by substantial amounts to agreed levels in equitable and balanced steps.

(*b*) Levels of armaments of prescribed types shall be further reduced by equitable and balanced steps. The reduction shall be accomplished by transfers of armaments to depots supervised by the IDO. When, at specified periods during the Stage II reduction process, the parties have agreed that the armaments and armed forces are at prescribed levels, the armaments in depots shall be destroyed or converted to peaceful uses.

(c) There shall be further agreed restrictions on the production of armaments.

(d) Agreed military bases and facilities wherever they are located shall be dismantled or converted to peaceful uses.

(e) Depending upon the findings of the Experts Commission on CBR weapons, the production of CBR weapons shall be halted, existing stocks progressively reduced, and the resulting excess quantities destroyed or converted to peaceful uses.

C. *To Further Reduce the Nuclear Threat:*

Stocks of nuclear weapons shall be progressively reduced to the minimum levels which can be agreed upon as a result of the findings of the Nuclear Experts Commission; the resulting excess of fissionable material shall be transferred to peaceful purposes.

D. *To Further Reduce Strategic Nuclear Weapons Delivery Vehicles:*

Further reductions in the stocks of strategic nuclear weapons delivery vehicles and agreed types of weapons designed to counter such vehicles shall be carried out in accordance with the procedure outlined in Stage I.

E. *To Keep the Peace:*

During Stage II, States shall develop further the peace-keeping processes of the United Nations, to the end that the United Nations can effectively in Stage III deter or suppress any threat or use of force in violation of the purposes and principles of the United Nations:

(a) States shall agree upon strengthening the structure, authority, and operation of the United Nations so as to assure that the United Nations will be able effectively to protect States against threats to or breaches of the peace.

(b) The United Nations Peace Force shall be established and progressively strengthened.

(c) States shall also agree upon further improvements and developments in in rules of international conduct and in processes for peaceful settlement of disputes and differences.

STAGE III

By the time Stage II has been completed, the confidence produced through a verified disarmament programme, the acceptance of rules of peaceful international behaviour, and the development of strengthened international peace-keeping processes within the framework of the United Nations should have reached a point where the States of the world can move forward to Stage III. In Stage III, progressive controlled disarmament and continuously developing principles and procedures of international law would proceed to a point where no State would have the military power to challenge the progressively strengthened United Nations Peace Force and all international disputes would be settled according to the agreed principles of international conduct.

The progressive steps to be taken during the final phase of the disarmament programme would be directed toward the attainment of a world in which:

(a) States would retain only those forces, non-nuclear armaments, and establishments required for the purpose of maintaining internal order; they would also support and provide agreed manpower for a United Nations Peace Force.

(b) The United Nations Peace Force, equipped with agreed types and quantities of armaments, would be fully functioning.

(c) The manufacture of armaments would be prohibited except for those of agreed types and quantities to be used by the United Nations Peace Force and those required to maintain internal order. All other armaments would be destroyed or converted to peaceful purposes.

(d) The peace-keeping capabilities of the United Nations would be sufficiently strong and the obligations of all States under such arrangements sufficiently far-reaching as to assure peace and the just settlement of differences in a disarmed world.

6. Memorandum from the Soviet Government to the United Nations, 26 September 1961[1]

There is no task more vital and urgent today than that of preserving peace. The efforts of all states, all members of the United Nations Organisation, of all people throughout the world, must be directed at preserving peace and ruling out war for ever from the life of human society. A correct and reliable way towards this is provided by general and complete disarmament, which will completely demolish the military machines of states and secure a world without arms, a world without wars.

The Soviet government is working persistently for immediate agreement on general and complete disarmament and has repeatedly made proposals on this question incorporating all positive elements of the position of the western powers. The programme of general and complete disarmament, submitted by the head of the Soviet government, N. S. Khrushchev, to the 15th session of the United Nations General Assembly on September 23, 1960,[2] is a good basis for such agreement, because it envisages a radical solution of the disarmament problem and the complete freeing of mankind from the burden of armaments. The Soviet Union is prepared to sign at any time a treaty on general and complete disarmament, with the establishment of any and the most strict international control.

Regarding general and complete disarmament as the main means of ensuring lasting peace, the Soviet government, at the same time, does not rule out the possibility of agreement on a series of measures which would contribute to the easing of international tension, would strengthen confidence between states and thereby facilitate general and complete disarmament. It stands to reason that the guiding principle, both in the choice and carrying out of such measures, must be to see to it that no state or group of states should be able to gain military advantages and that security is ensured to all states in equal measure.

[1] *Soviet News*, 6 October 1961. [2] *Documents*, 1960, pp. 93–94.

D.I.A.–O

The implementation of such measures must not divert attention from the main task, that of general and complete disarmament. On the contrary, every such measure taken separately and in their entirety must contribute to creating an atmosphere conducive to the conclusion of such a treaty and its effective implementation. Along with considering the disarmament problem as a whole and a number of other important international problems, it is possible and necessary to adopt a series of simple decisions easy for millions to understand, decisions which would lessen the danger of an outbreak of war and on which the states could agree already in the nearest future.

Acting in this spirit, the Soviet government proposes that an understanding be reached on carrying out the following measures, or at least some of them:

1. *The Freezing of National Military Budgets*

Military preparations and the uncurbed arms race place a heavy burden on the backs of the working people. They increase international tensions and amplify the danger of war. In an endeavour to rid the world of this peril, the Soviet government proposes that, without waiting for the solution of the problem of general and complete disarmament, certain concerted measures be taken to fix for the states a budget ceiling on military spending that would not be above their military appropriations as on January 1, 1961. It is quite obvious that these measures would not undermine the security of any state.

After all, it is an open secret that today more than enough armaments—including nuclear weapons—have been stockpiled to inflict colossal destruction. Meanwhile, the continuing multiplication of military spending, besides impairing normal economic advancement, is also increasing tremendously the area of suspicion and mistrust in relations between states and is thus adding more and more complications to the solution of the problem of general and complete disarmament.

The freezing of military budgets would make a considerable contribution to the effort to prevent the intensification of the arms race. It is well known that the Soviet Union has more than once taken definite unilateral measures to cut its armed forces and armaments and consequently reduce budgetary military spending. The Soviet government is prepared to continue along this road, provided the United States and the other western powers, for their part, also take the corresponding steps in this direction. There need be no doubt that this peace bid would have the support of all states.

2. *Repudiation of the Use of Nuclear Weapons*

Before concluding an agreement on general and complete disarmament, which would end the very existence of A- and H-bombs and the means of delivering them, the states manufacturing nuclear weapons could announce, by way of morally paving the way for such an agreement, their decision not to use nuclear weapons—in the same way as a number of states declared in their time that it was impermissible to use poison gas and bacteriological weapons.

It is common knowledge that the agreement prohibiting means of chemical and biological warfare has stood the test of time. Unquestionably, the existence of this agreement contributed in no small degree to the fact that even during the fierce fighting of the Second World War millions of people, including women, children and old people, were saved from agonising death from poison gas or artificially induced epidemics, even though the belligerents then had at their disposal the appropriate types of weapons.

Now, if mankind was able to save itself from one manifestation of barbarism why could we not try to follow suit as regards another, still more terrible manifestation of barbarism as the use of modern nuclear weapons, which condemn to death hundreds of millions of people, without distinction, without any division of front and rear, of soldiers and civilians?

The Soviet government is of the opinion that the draft resolution on the conclusion of an appropriate international convention, which Ethiopia and other Afro-Asian countries put before the General Assembly at its 15th session, would be a suitable basis for solving the problem of prohibiting the use of nuclear weapons. But if the western powers are not yet prepared to assume, together with the Soviet Union, a pledge to repudiate unreservedly the use of nuclear weapons, we could then agree, as a beginning, to undertake not to use nuclear weapons first.

3. The Prohibition of War Propaganda

All the states could contribute greatly to the amelioration of the international climate by calling jointly for an end to all kinds of propaganda for war, enmity and hatred between peoples.

After all, it was as long ago as 1947 that the United Nations General Assembly decided to ban war propaganda.[1] However, this decision is still not being abided by in many countries. It is no secret that in certain countries, in the press, over the radio and television and in public utterances by prominent figures, the idea of the arms race is being justified and feelings of hatred and enmity for other peoples are being whipped up.

It is well known that this propaganda is looked upon in different ways. In some countries it is considered almost an expression of freedom of speech. We, however, calling a spade a spade, look upon calls for war—even those expressed in a veiled form—as one of the worst crimes, since they gravely undermine confidence in relations between states, facilitate the speeding up of military preparations and exacerbate the danger of a war which would bring death to millions upon millions of people.

Still, however war propaganda is assessed, one thing is clear, and this is that it stands in the way of the establishment of peaceful relations between states. If measures to stop it are taken universally, this will benefit, not one particular country, but all the states, all the peoples.

We can institute different measures to see to it that this propaganda is not allowed. In the Soviet Union and in other socialist countries special laws have been passed forbidding war propaganda. Other countries could also take analogous steps. The adoption of a joint declaration or statement calling for an end to war propaganda, as inimical to the cause of peace and understanding between peoples, would be of great political significance.

[1] In Resolution 110 (II). Text in G.A.O.R., Second Session, Resolutions, p. 14.

4. *On the Conclusion of a Non-aggression Pact between the NATO and Warsaw Treaty Countries*

In its search for possibilities of mutual understanding on measures opening up, for the future at least, prospects for overcoming the division of the world into blocs, the Soviet Union has repeatedly proposed the conclusion of a non-aggression agreement between the N.A.T.O. countries and the states belonging to the Warsaw Treaty. Such an agreement could be based on the renunciation by the contracting parties of the use of force and threat of force, and an obligation by them to settle arguments that may arise between the parties to the agreement by peaceful means exclusively. The parties to the agreement could hold mutual consultations on questions connected with the implementation of the agreement.

Such a measure would undoubtedly improve the situation in Europe and strengthen the peoples' confidence in the possibility of living in really peaceful conditions. Without the solution of this problem mutual suspicion will be preserved, complications will be possible at any time and, moreover, a chronic threat of a military conflagration will remain.

The signing of a non-aggression pact would not disturb the existing 'balance of forces' between the blocs by a single soldier or a single gun. Such a measure would not even raise the problem of the abolition of blocs on a practical plain, although, in the Soviet government's opinion, this would be the best solution possible. At the same time the proposed agreement would be an expression of the absence of aggressive intentions on the part of states belonging to different blocs and would help to improve the international situation.

This agreement would be a serious deterrent to a potential aggressor who, in the event of aggressive war being unleashed, would find himself in international isolation, with all the consequences arising therefrom.

5. *On the Withdrawal of Troops from Foreign Territories*

The Soviet Union comes out for the withdrawal of troops from foreign territories. It has more than once proposed that the United States and other western powers should come to agreement on the withdrawal of foreign troops from the territory of Europe, having in mind that Soviet troops would leave Germany, Hungary and Poland, and the United States, Britain, France and Canada would recall their troops stationed on the territories of other N.A.T.O. countries.

However, the experience of the past talks shows that the United States is obviously not ready to accept the Soviet proposals on the complete withdrawal of foreign troops from the territories of European states. Under the circumstances, the Soviet Union thinks that there is a necessity of solving at least the problem of cutting down the strength of foreign troops on the territories of N.A.T.O. countries and the countries belonging to the Warsaw Treaty. As a first step, all foreign troops in Germany could be reduced by one-third, or in any other agreed amount, in a certain specified time, with proper control established over the implementation of this measure.

The reduction of foreign troops on German territory would be particularly important for peace. More inflammable material which can give rise to war has been amassed in the heart of Europe than anywhere in the world. It is precisely there that there is a danger of the flame of a world conflagration being kindled. It is necessary to put an end to the whipping up of war-like passions in this powder magazine of Europe. The reduction and then the withdrawal of all foreign troops from German territory would promote the normalisation of the situation in Germany and Europe as a whole, which would be of tremendous benefit to the consolidation of universal peace.

In the Soviet government's opinion, the situation existing in connection with the question of a peace treaty with Germany should not hamper the examination of this matter.

6. *On Measures Against the Further Spread of Nuclear Weapons*

In the Soviet government's opinion, there is a possibility at present for concluding an agreement under which nuclear powers would pledge themselves not to pass nuclear weapons to other countries, while states not possessing nuclear weapons would undertake not to manufacture these weapons or buy them from nuclear powers.

Obviously, there is no need to emphasise what an acute danger to peace can be created by the expansion of the circle of powers possessing nuclear weapons or the secret of their manufacture, irrespective of whether it would be an 'individual' possession or the passing of such weapons within the framework of one or another military bloc system.

One must clearly realise the possible consequences of handing over atomic weapons to the Federal Republic of Germany, where many people are dreaming of revenge and would not hesitate to do anything to achieve their aggressive ends. What would the countries neighbouring on the Federal Republic of Germany— and not only those neighbouring on the F.R.G.—have to do then? In that case the Soviet Union and other countries would naturally be forced to adopt serious counter-measures with a view to safeguarding their security. It is not hard to imagine what course the development of events in Europe would take under those circumstances.

The solution of the disarmament problem would become much more complicated with the expansion of the circle of nuclear powers. If the solution of this problem—particularly the problem of the elimination of nuclear weapons and control over their elimination creates such difficulties even now, what could be expected if nuclear weapons were possessed, not by three or four, but by, let us say, ten states of the East and West? It is clear that in such a case the world would be thrown a long way back in its attempts to solve the disarmament problem.

7. *On Setting up Atom-free Zones*

Another effective way of hampering the spread of nuclear weapons on our planet is *to agree that certain geographical zones should be free from the deployment and manufacture of such weapons by anyone.*

It is generally known that the governments of different countries have come out with a whole number of plans and projects on atom-free zones in the last few years. There are proposals for setting up atom-free zones in the areas of Europe that cause the greatest anxiety. There is a proposal of the Chinese People's Republic for setting up an atom-free zone in the area of the Far East and the Pacific basin. An analogous plan has been put forward with regard to Africa and is supported by many African states. All this shows how attractive the plans for atom-free zones are to the peoples and governments of many countries. One can say that ideas for setting up such zones literally fill the air.

The Soviet government considers it necessary to facilitate the practical implementation of these plans. It is doubtful whether anyone would deny that the appearance of such zones would not fail to make the outbreak of military conflicts less possible, would not fail to avert the danger of nuclear and rocket weapons being spread to new countries and continents, would not fail to facilitate the establishment of an atmosphere of confidence in relations between states. At the same time useful experience would be amassed in organising control and inspection—even if it were meanwhile on a regional scale—which would have a positive influence in setting up control over general and complete disarmament.

The Soviet government is of the opinion that the transformation of the entire African continent—where a large number of states are actively conducting a neutralist policy and resolutely coming out against nuclear weapons—into a nuclear-free zone could be easily carried out in practice. At the last session of the General Assembly, Ghana and six other African states advanced a proposal for transforming Africa into a nuclear-free zone and for excluding it from the sphere of production, deployment and stockpiling of atomic and hydrogen weapons. The Soviet Union, it will be recalled, supported this proposal and, just as in the past, is prepared to render every assistance in its implementation.

The process of setting up atom-free zones could be started in Central Europe, in respect of which there are detailed proposals of the Polish government, backed by Czechoslovakia and the German Democratic Republic. If the deployment and production of rocket-nuclear weapons were banned on the territories of the Federal Republic of Germany, the German Democratic Republic, Poland and Czechoslovakia, then a belt of relaxed tension could be formed between the N.A.T.O. and Warsaw Treaty organisations. The implementation of this measure would contribute greatly to the improvement of the entire atmosphere in Europe and to preventing the threat of war.

The setting up of atom-free zones is even more realistic inasmuch as no one would receive any military advantages whatsoever from it and the existing correlation of military forces in the world in that case would not be violated either.

8. *On Measures for Lessening the Danger of Surprise Attack*

Striving to remove the danger of an outbreak of war, the Soviet Union as long ago as in 1958 proposed that agreement be reached and a number of concrete measures be carried out to avert surprise attack, which would make it possible to lessen considerably the threat of an outbreak of war. Certainly, the possibility of an attack with the employment of destructive rocket-nuclear weapons could be fully precluded only under conditions of general and complete disarmament, when the war machines of states would be completely demolished. The Soviet government is, however, of the opinion that already now a number of measures could be carried out, the implementation of which would be of benefit to the cause of peace.

Naturally, measures for averting surprise attack should lead to the removal and not to the intensification of suspicion between states. It is important that in this nothing should be done aimed at attaining military advantages for any group of countries or the collection of intelligence and no harm should be caused to the security of states taking part in carrying out one measure or another.

Among the most feasible measures which could be carried out in the nearest future is the setting up of ground control posts at railway junctions, big ports and highways, to see to it that there should be no dangerous concentrations of armed forces and military materials.

The Soviet government is of the opinion that the setting up of such ground control posts could be one of the effective means for lessening the danger of a surprise attack. No one is likely to refute the fact that, even with the existence of nuclear weapons, preparations for a modern large-scale war are inevitably connected with the necessity of concentrating at definite points large military formations with a great amount of armaments and equipment.

Simultaneously with this, a corresponding reduction and withdrawal of armed forces and armaments from territories situated at a definite distance either side of the demarcation line could be carried out.

The measures suggested by the Soviet Union ensure sufficient opportunity for detecting symptoms of an intended concentration of troops in the most dangerous areas, and for warning beforehand of preparations for an attack. At the same time they take into account the interests of the security of both sides to an equal degree. The implementation of these measures would be a good basis for expanding co-operation between states in strengthening European security and would facilitate the carrying out of general and complete disarmament.

* * *

The Soviet government does not consider as exhaustive the measures it has enumerated aimed at delivering international relations from the burden of the cold war. It will attentively study any and all constructive considerations in this respect and is prepared to exchange opinions on these problems in any form which might be considered most suitable.

7. Resolution of the General Assembly adopted 20 December 1961[1]

The General Assembly,

Noting with concern that the continuing arms race is a heavy burden for humanity and is fraught with dangers for the cause of world peace,

Conscious of its responsibilities, under the Charter of the United Nations, for disarmament,

Recalling its resolution 1378 (XIV) of 20 November 1959,[2] in which it called

---

[1] G.A.O.R., Sixteenth Session, Supplement No. 17, pp. 7–8, Resolution 1722 (XVI) sponsored jointly by the United States and the Soviet Union.
[2] *Documents*, 1959, p. 115.

upon Governments to make every effort to achieve a constructive solution of the problem of general and complete disarmament and expressed the hope that measures leading towards the goal of general and complete disarmament under effective international control would be worked out in detail and agreed upon in the shortest possible time,

Being deeply concerned that the objectives of that resolution be achieved as early as possible,

I

Noting with satisfaction the report submitted to the General Assembly by the Union of Soviet Socialist Republics and the United States of America following their exchange of views on questions relating to disarmament and to the resumption of negotiations in an appropriate body,[1]

1. *Welcomes* the joint statement of the Governments of the Union of Soviet Socialist Republics and the United States of America of agreed principles for disarmament negotiations included in that report;

2. *Recommends* that negotiations on general and complete disarmament should be based upon those principles;

II

Deeming it essential that negotiations on general and complete disarmament under effective international control be resumed at the earliest possible time,

Recognizing that all States have a deep interest in disarmament negotiations,

1. *Endorses* the agreement that has been reached on the composition of a Disarmament Committee, whose membership will be: Brazil, Bulgaria, Burma, Canada, Czechoslovakia, Ethiopia, France, India, Italy, Mexico, Nigeria, Poland, Romania, Sweden, Union of Soviet Socialist Republics, United Arab Republic, United Kingdom of Great Britain and Northern Ireland and United States of America;

2. *Recommends* that the Committee, as a matter of the utmost urgency should undertake negotiations with a view to reaching, on the basis of the joint statement of agreed principles and taking into account, *inter alia*, paragraph 8 of those principles, agreement on general and complete disarmament under effective international control;

3. *Requests* that the Committee submit to the General Assembly a report on such agreement as soon as it has been reached, and in any case submit to the Disarmament Commission, not later than 1 June 1962, a report on the progress achieved;

4. *Requests* the Secretary-General to render the necessary assistance and provide the necessary services to the Committee.

[1] G.A.O.R., Sixteenth Session, Annexes, Agenda item 19, pp. 1–2.

(c) Anglo-American-Soviet Negotiations for a Ban on the Testing of Nuclear Weapons

1. Statement to the Geneva Three-Power Conference by the British delegate, Mr. Ormsby Gore, 30 March 1961[1]

If no other representative wishes to speak, I should like to make some remarks in my capacity as United Kingdom representative. During these past two weeks, while the United States delegation has been developing the Western proposals and positions of March 21[2] in greater detail, I have not thought it necessary to make parallel statements on behalf of the United Kingdom delegation. Mr. Dean has fully and clearly explained the joint Western position on each group of subjects, and the United Kingdom has been fully in accord with what he has said. Today, however, when the exposition of the Western proposals has been completed and we are about to take our short Easter holiday, I should like to review the significance of these past two weeks and sum up the state of affairs in this Conference.

The first important point is that the two Western delegations have now laid out before the Soviet delegation, clearly and in detail, a comprehensive treaty offer. We have described the treaty that our Governments would be prepared to sign in a matter of weeks, as soon as the actual drafting could be completed. Such a treaty would mark the triumphant success of this long Conference; it would be fair and we believe it would be effective and workable; and it would of course not only bring an inestimable benefit to the world, but would surely be an immense encouragement to further agreements in the field of disarmament. This treaty, we believe, is now there for the taking.

The second point I wish to stress is the extent to which the two Western Governments, in making this offer, have modified their positions to meet the desires and interests of the Soviet Union. I have mentioned already, and must do so again, a tendency in Soviet Press statements to suggest that the West has not really modified its positions or at least has not modified them on the points of greatest importance to the Soviet Union. I hope and believe that this suggestion does not represent any official Soviet view, because nothing could be further from the truth. I will quote a paragraph from the Soviet representative's opening statement at our meeting on March 21, just before he heard our new proposals. The paragraph reads:

'At the present time agreement could speedily be reached on all outstanding questions on the basis of the proposals submitted by the Soviet Union. These Soviet proposals ensure effective control over compliance with the treaty on the prohibition of nuclear tests, and at the same time—and this is

[1] Cmnd. 1397, *Text of the Draft Treaty on the Discontinuance of Nuclear Weapon Tests tabled by the Delegations of the United Kingdom and the United States at the 292nd meeting of the Conference on the Discontinuance of Nuclear Weapon Tests at Geneva on April 18, 1961, together with statements by the United Kingdom and United States Delegates at the 281st, 292nd and 300th meetings of the Conference* (London, H.M.S.O., 1961), Appendix I. Hereafter cited as Cmnd. 1397.

[2] United States Disarmament Administration, *Geneva Conference on the Continuance of Nuclear Weapon Tests, History and Analysis of Negotiations* (Washington, U.S.G.P.O·, 1961), pp. 467–75.

very important for the agreement—the interests of both the sides participating in the negotiations are taken into account. This applies to the Soviet proposals on such very important issues as the duration of the moratorium; the control of the nuclear detonations which the United States wishes to carry out as part of a scientific research programme on underground explosions; the composition of the control commission; the number of control posts and the time limits for their establishment; the inspection quota; the staffing of control posts and inspection teams; the control of nuclear detonations for peaceful purposes and so on.'

Let us see what the West has done on these 'very important issues'—those were the Soviet representative's words, 'on such very important issues' as those he listed.

First, the duration of the moratorium. We have moved more than half-way to meet the Soviet Union by lengthening the duration of the moratorium to three years, by correspondingly lengthening the period of the seismic research programme, and by declaring our understanding that, for practical purposes, the research programme can begin simultaneously with the early signature of a treaty. We have thereby brought the timing of the research programme closely into line with the timing of the programme proposed by the Soviet experts in May 1960.[1] Our scientists are prepared to say, and no Soviet expert has disputed it, that the research programme can be completed within the three year period. The Soviet Union has in turn accepted that the moratorium should cover the period of the research programme. There can therefore be no Soviet objection to our latest proposal on this 'very important issue', to use Mr. Tsarapkin's words.

Next, the Soviet representative mentioned the control of the nuclear detonations which the United States wishes to carry out as part of a scientific research programme on underground explosions. Here we have gone the whole way to meet the Soviet Union by declaring our general acceptance of the four safeguards proposed by the Soviet Union. All last summer and autumn the Soviet representative was tell us that this was perhaps the most crucial issue for further progress in the Conference. This obstacle to agreement is now removed.

The next item on our Soviet colleague's list was the composition of the control commission. Here again we have gone the whole way to meet the Soviet Union: we have agreed, in the context of a satisfactory treaty, to accept parity between the Western and the Soviet sides on the commission. I have seen it suggested in Soviet Press statements that this move by the West is too hedged around with 'ifs' and 'buts' and conditions. That is, to my mind, an absurd suggestion. The sole condition is, in effect, that we reach an acceptable treaty, and that is a condition which attaches to every proposal, Soviet and Western, that has been made at this table. Nothing is going to be realized in practice unless we agree upon a treaty which all three of us can sign.

The fourth matter which Mr. Tsarapkin mentioned was the number of control posts and the time limits for their establishment. I must say that the Soviet delegation has always taken a very narrow and self-interested view of the number

---

[1] *Documents*, 1960, p. 103.

of control posts, thinking only of how to reduce the number in the Soviet Union. Little as we agree with that approach, which is quite contrary to our own approach, we have offered to reduce the number of posts we propose in the Soviet Union from twenty-one to nineteen. To be very precise, we have gone one-third of the way to meet the Soviet Union on a subject where it has never taken a single step to meet us. And we must recall that the Western delegations made substantial concessions to the Soviet Union last September and October on the phasing of the establishment of control posts and on the number of Western-based posts to be set up in the first phase. Since before that time the Soviet delegation has made no move on the subject, whereas we have moved twice.

Next on Mr. Tsarapkin's list came the inspection quota. This is the sole point on the Soviet representative's list where we have felt unable to make any major change from our previous position. We have felt so because it is obvious that the control commission must have an inspection capability which constitutes an effective deterrent to violation of the treaty in the underground environment. Without this, control would have no meaning, and the treaty would be worthless and constitute a dangerous and wholly objectionable precedent in the disarmament field. The Soviet proposal for three inspections a year in each of our three countries would provide no deterrent to a determined violator. We maintain our figure of twenty because we believe that would assure us of a really substantial deterrent. And yet even here we have moved to meet the Soviet Union; we have agreed that each of our countries should be liable to twenty inspections, so that there would be forty inspections in the West—and we are quite prepared to have them—as against only twenty in the Soviet Union.

Next the Soviet representative listed the staffing of control posts and inspection teams. Under that heading we have made one quite important modification of our position—at least, it must be important if we recall how strongly and how often the Soviet delegation has insisted on the point in the past. I refer to the new principle we have suggested for staffing the third third at control posts. This was described by Mr. Dean in his statement on March 28. We have offered the Soviet Union numerical parity, at every control post in the system, between nationals on the one hand, of the United States and the United Kingdom and of countries associated with either of them, and, on the other hand, nationals of the Soviet Union and of countries associated with it. Thus the Soviet demand for equality, precise equality, in this matter is fully met. Apart from this we have not seen any reason to modify our positions as regards the heads of control posts and the leadership and staffing of inspection teams; it is clear that the Soviet proposals on those points would amount to self-inspection, and we cannot accept that.

Finally, the Soviet representative mentioned the control of nuclear detonations for peaceful purposes. On that subject the West has gone substantially the whole way to meet the Soviet Union by withdrawing the so-called 'black box' proposals and agreeing to apply the same four safeguards to peaceful detonations as to research explosions.

Thus the Soviet representative's list of very important issues contained seven items. On three of those items we have met the major concerns of the Soviet Union 100 per cent. On three others we have made important moves towards the

Soviet positions, and even on the inspection quota we have taken a substantial step.

Moreover, we have made an important declaration in favour of an immediate and total ban on high altitude testing, not mentioned in the list of the Soviet representative; and we have agreed to a veto on the control organization's budget. On both those matters, over and beyond the Soviet representative's list, our positions are in accord with the Soviet Union's declared positions.

It is impossible, therefore, to contest the fact that the Western proposals of March 21 represent a major effort on the part of the United States and United Kingdom to overcome the Soviet hesitations and meet the desires of the Soviet Union wherever they can be met without seriously endangering the prospect of real control over the fulfilment of the treaty.

From the Soviet side, in these past two weeks, we have been sorry to hear nothing constructive or forward-looking. We are considerably disappointed by the tone, as well as the content, of the statement with which the Soviet representative opened our new session on March 21. As I said at the time, that statement contained only two new points, and they were both retrograde in tendency. I have seen no reason to revise that view; indeed, it has been reinforced by the knowledge that nowhere in the world outside the Soviet bloc has there been anything but dismay at the latest attitude adopted by the Soviet Union since the resumption of our meetings. As regards the specific proposal to reopen the agreements reached about the administrator and replace him by a triumvirate, I can say that my Government fully concurs both with my initial reaction to that proposal and with what our United States colleague has just said on the subject. The proposal was made, of course, before the Soviet delegation had heard the new Western positions. It was made, therefore, before the Soviet representative knew that the West was offering parity on the control commission, which is the supreme directing body of the control organization; and also before the further Western offer, which is important in this context, of a parity arrangement for staffing the third third at control posts. In view of those Western moves we are convinced that the Soviet delegation has no need to press its proposal on the administrator, and will not press it if the Soviet Government has the interests of a successful and workable treaty at heart.

Since March 21 we have of course heard little of any kind from the Soviet delegation. My Soviet colleague's initial reaction when I urged the possibility of a fresh Soviet approach to participation in the seismic research programme was discouraging. However, I prefer to await a more considered response on that subject. Apart from this we have no complaint if the Soviet representative has wanted to hear the full exposition of the Western treaty offer before giving us his reply. Our exposition is now completed. It has covered practically all the outstanding issues on the treaty; on the one or two that have not been mentioned the Soviet delegation already knows the views of the West. The next step in our work must therefore be the Soviet delegation's reply to all that has been said in these two weeks. We hope that that reply will not be long delayed; indeed, we shall look for it immediately after the Easter break.

On the nature of the Soviet reply very much now depends, not only for us but for the whole world and the whole effort to make progress in the field of disarmament. The choice now lies with the Soviet Union whether the treaty, which is already in sight, can soon become a reality. If the Soviet Union would come to meet us on those few points where the Soviet positions still do not offer us the assurance of real control, then in a matter of weeks the world might be welcoming the signature of a treaty.

2. Draft treaty on the discontinuance of nuclear weapons tests, submitted to the Geneva Conference by the United States and Britain, 18 April 1961[1]

Preamble

The Parties to this Treaty

Pursuing the aim of reducing international competition in armaments and in the development of new weapons of war;

Endeavouring to take a practical step towards the achievement of the objectives of the United Nations in the field of disarmament, including the eventual elimination and prohibition of nuclear weapons under effective international control and the use of atomic energy for peaceful purposes only;

Desirous of bringing about the permanent discontinuance of nuclear weapon test explosions;

Recognizing that the establishment and continuous operation of effective international control is essential to the achievement of this objective;

Hoping that all other countries will also join in undertakings not to carry out nuclear weapon tests and to ensure the satisfactory operation of that control throughout the world;

Confident that a discontinuance of such tests under effective control will make possible progress towards agreement on measures of disarmament

Have agreed as follows:

ARTICLE 1

Obligations to Discontinue

1. Each of the Parties to this Treaty undertakes, subject to the provisions of this Treaty and its Annexes:

A. to prohibit and prevent the carrying out of nuclear weapon test explosions at any place under its jurisdiction or control; and

B. to refrain from causing, encouraging, or in any way participating in, the carrying out of nuclear weapon test explosions anywhere.

2. The obligations under paragraph 1 of this Article shall apply to all nuclear weapon test explosions except those underground explosions which are recorded as seismic events of less than magnitude 4·75.

ARTICLE 2

Establishment of Control Organization

1. For the purpose of assuring that the obligations assumed in this Treaty are carried out by the Parties, there is hereby established a Control Organization, hereinafter referred to as 'the Organization', upon the terms and conditions set forth in this Treaty and the Annexes thereto.

[1] Cmnd. 1397, pp. 6–22.

2. Each of the Parties agrees to cooperate promptly and fully with the Organization established under paragraph 1 of this Article and to assist the Organization in the discharge of its responsibilities pursuant to the provisions of this Treaty and the provisions of any agreements which the Parties shall have concluded with the Organization.

ARTICLE 3
Elements of Control Organization

1. The Organization established under Article 2 of this Treaty shall consist of: a Control Commission, hereinafter referred to as 'the Commission', a Detection and Identification System, hereinafter referred to as 'the System'; a Chief Executive Officer, hereinafter referred to as 'the Administrator'; and a Conference of Parties to the Treaty, hereinafter referred to as 'the Conference'.

2. The Headquarters of the Organization shall be located at Vienna.

ARTICLE 4
Composition of Control Commission[1]

1. The Commission shall consist of the following Parties:

A. The Union of Soviet Socialist Republics, the United Kingdom of Great Britain and Northern Ireland, and the United States of America, as original Parties to this Treaty; and

B. Eight other Parties to the Treaty elected by the Conference as follows: Three Parties associated with the U.S.S.R.; two Parties associated with either the United Kingdom or the United States; three Parties not associated with any of the original Parties.

2. The Parties referred to in paragraph 1 B of this Article shall be elected and shall serve for a period of two years; they shall be eligible for re-election.

3. The Parties elected to the first elected Commission shall serve from the time of their election until the end of the third regular session of the Conference. The Parties elected at the third regular session of the Conference, and those elected biennially thereafter, shall serve from the end of the Conference at which they were elected until the end of the Conference which elects their successors.

4. Each member of the Commission shall have one representative.

ARTICLE 5
Parties or Other Countries Associate–with the Original Parties

The determination whether a Party or other country is at any time to be regarded for the purposes of this Treaty as associated with any of the original Parties shall be made by the Preparatory Commission or by the Commission. However, in any case in which advice is jointly tendered by the three original Parties, the determination shall be made in accordance with that advice.

[1] A footnote in the text reads as follows:
The above revised text is submitted in the context of the statements made by the United States and United Kingdom Representatives at the 274th, 286th, and 289th meetings, to the effect that the United States and United Kingdom Governments are prepared to accept the above text provided expressly, and not otherwise, that agreement is reached by this Conference upon a control system which is reliable, rapid and effective—such as is set forth in other articles and annexes of the present draft treaty proposal—and provided that agreement is reached upon all other treaty articles and annexes.

ARTICLE 6
Functions of the Control Commission

1. The Commission shall establish procedures and standards for the installation and operation of all elements of the System, and shall maintain supervision over the System to ensure its timely installation and effective operation in accordance with the terms of this Treaty and its Annexes. The Commission shall determine, after consultation with the Parties concerned, the extent to which existing launching, tracking, and data receiving and transmission facilities should be used in the installation and operation of the satellite systems.

2. A. The Commission shall appoint the Administrator; this appointment shall require the concurring votes of the original Parties.

B. (i) Subject to the approval of the Commission in each case, the Administrator shall appoint five Deputy Administrators, including one First Deputy Administrator who shall act in place of the Administrator in case of absence or vacancy.

(ii) Approval by the Commission of the appointment of the First Deputy Administrator shall require the concurring votes of the original Parties.

(iii) Appointment by the Administrator of two Deputy Administrators shall be made upon the recommendation, or with the approval, of the Government of the U.S.S.R.; appointment of the two other Deputy Administrators shall be made upon the recommendation, or with the approval, of the Governments of the United Kingdom and the United States.

C. The term of office of the Administrator shall be a period of three years. The initial term of office of the First Deputy Administrator shall be a period of two years; subsequently, the term of office of the First Deputy Administrator shall be a period of three years. The term of office of the other Deputy Administrators shall be a period of three years.

D. The Administrator and the Deputy Administrators shall be eligible for reappointment. An Administrator or Deputy Administrator appointed to fill a vacancy which has occurred before the expiration of the term provided for by this Article shall hold office only for the remainder of his predecessor's term but shall be eligible for reappointment.

3. The Commission shall establish procedures for disseminating to all Parties and interested scientific organizations data produced by the System.

4. The Commission shall submit to the Conference an annual report and such special reports as the Commission deems necessary on the operation of the system and on the activities of the Commission and the Administrator in carrying on their respective responsibilities. The Commission shall also prepare for the Conference such reports as the Organization may make to the United Nations.

5. Except for the location of the Headquarters of the Organization, the Commission shall decide upon the location of components of the System. Such decisions shall be taken in agreement with the Party exercising jurisdiction or control over the territory on which the component is to be located. If any location recommended by the Commission should be unacceptable to the Party concerned, the Party shall provide, without undue delay, an alternative location

which in the judgment of the Commission meets the requirements of the System, in accordance with the provisions of this Treaty and its Annexes.

6. The Commission shall lay down permanent flight routes, for use by special aircraft sampling missions, over the territory under the jurisdiction or control of each Party. Such flight routes shall be laid down in agreement with the Party concerned and in accordance with the standards set forth in Article 7 of Annex I. If a permanent flight route which the Commission desires to lay down should be unacceptable to the Party concerned, the Party shall provide, without undue delay, an alternative route which in the judgment of the Commission meets the requirements of the System.

7. The Commission may conclude agreements with any State of authority to aid in the carrying out of the provisions of this Treaty and its Annexes.

8. The Commission shall ensure that the most effective and up-to-date equipment and techniques are incorporated in the System and, to this end, shall ensure that an adequate research and development programme is carried out.

9. The Commission shall establish procedures for the implementation of Article 13 on detonations for peaceful purposes.

10. In addition to the functions referred to in the preceding paragraphs of this Article, the Commission shall perform such other functions as are provided for in this Treaty and its Annexes.

ARTICLE 7
Procedures of the Control Commission

1. The Commission shall be so organized as to be able to function continuously.

2. The Commission shall meet at such times as it may determine, or within twenty-four hours at the request of any member. All members shall be notified in advance of meetings of the Commission. The meetings shall take place at the Headquarters of the Organization unless otherwise determined by the Commission.

3. The Commission shall adopt its own rules of procedure including the method of selecting its chairman.

4. Any Party to the Treaty which does not have a representative on the Commission may participate, without vote, in the discussion of any question brought before the Commission whenever the latter considers that the interests of that Party are specially affected.

5. Except as otherwise expressly provided in this Treaty, decisions of the Commission shall be made by a simple majority of the members present and voting. Each member of the Commission shall have one vote.

ARTICLE 8
The Conference

1. The Conference consisting of representatives of Parties to this Treaty shall meet in regular annual session and in such special sessions as shall be convened by the Administrator at the request of the Commission or of a majority of Parties to the Treaty. The sessions shall take place at the Headquarters of the Organization unless otherwise determined by the Conference.

2. At such sessions, each Party to the Treaty shall be represented by not more than three delegates who may be accompanied by alternates and advisers. The cost of attendance of any delegation shall be borne by the State concerned.

3. The Conference shall elect a President and such other officers as may be required at the beginning of each session. They shall hold office for the duration of the session. The Conference, subject to the provisions of this Treaty, shall adopt its own rules of procedure. Each Party to the Treaty shall have one vote. Decisions on budgetary matters shall be made pursuant to Article 15 and decisions on amendments pursuant to Article 23. Decision on other questions, including the determination of additional questions or categories of questions to be decided by a two-thirds majority, shall be made by a simple majority of the Parties to the Treaty present and voting.

4. The Conference may discuss any questions or any matters within the scope of this Treaty or relating to the powers and functions of any organs provided for in this Treaty and may make recommendations to the Parties or to the Commission or to both on any such questions or matters.

5. The Conference shall:

A. elect States to serve on the Commission in accordance with Article 4;

B. consider the annual and any special report of the Commission;

C. approve the budget recommended by the Commission in accordance with paragraph 1 of Article 15;

D. approve reports to be submitted to the United Nations as required by any relationship agreement between the Organization and the United Nations or return them to the Commission with the recommendations of the Conference;

E. approve any agreement or agreements between the Organization and the United Nations or other organizations as provided in Article 17. Or return such agreement with its recommendations to the Commission for resubmission to the Conference;

F. approve amendments to this Treaty in accordance with Article 23.

6. The Conference shall have the authority:

A. to take decisions on any matter specifically referred to the Conference for this purpose by the Commission;

B. to propose matters for consideration by the Commission and request from the Commission reports on any matter relating to the functions of the Commission.

ARTICLE 9

Administrator and International Staff

1. The Administrator shall be the chief executive officer of the System and the head of the staff of the Organization. He shall be responsible to the Commission and, under its supervision, shall carry out its policy directives. He shall have executive responsibility for the installation and operation of the System under procedures and standards established by the Commission. He shall provide to the Commission such advice, reports and assistance as the Commission may request.

2. The Administrator and the staff shall not seek or receive instructions concerning the performance of their duties from any authority external to the

Organization. They shall refrain from any action which might reflect on their status as international officials and employees responsible only to the Organization. Each Party undertakes to respect the international character of the responsibilities of the Administrator and staff and not to seek to influence them in the discharge of their duties.

3. Except as otherwise provided in this Treaty, the Administrator shall appoint, organize and direct the staff of the Organization in accordance with the following provisions:

A. The staff shall include such qualified scientific, technical and other personnel as may be required to carry out the functions of the Organization with the highest standards of efficiency, technical competence and integrity.

B. The staffing of individual components of the System shall be designed so as to ensure maximum operating efficiency.

C. In keeping with the foregoing stipulations, the staff of the Organization shall be recruited on as wide a geographical basis as possible from personnel recommended by, or acceptable to, the governments of the countries of which they are nationals and acceptable to the Administrator, subject to the following provisions:

(i) The permanent administrative, scientific and technical staff of the Headquarters of the Organization shall, as a whole and at all levels, be composed in equal proportions of nationals of the U.S.S.R., nationals of the United Kingdom or the United States, and nationals of other countries. In cases where deputies, other than the Deputy Administrators, to senior officials of the Organization Headquarters are appointed, a national of the U.S.S.R. shall have a deputy who is a national of the United Kingdom or of the United States, and a national of the United Kingdom or the United States shall have a deputy who is a national of the U.S.S.R.

(ii) In land control posts situated on territory under the jurisdiction or control of any of the original Parties, the scientific and technical staff of each post shall be composed in equal proportions of nationals of the U.S.S.R., nationals of the United Kingdom or the United States, and nationals of other countries. In the appointment of nationals of other countries, preference shall be given, subject to other provisions of sub-paragraph C of this Article, to nationals of countries exercising jurisdiction or control over territory upon which control posts are to be established.

(iii) In land control posts situated on territory under the jurisdiction or control of Parties other than the original Parties, no more than one-third of the scientific and technical staff of each post shall be composed of nationals of the country exercising jurisdiction or control over the territory on which the control post is situated.

(iv) The supporting and auxiliary staffs of each land control post shall, wherever possible, be composed of nationals of the country exercising jurisdiction or control over the territory on which the control post is located.

(v) The scientific and technical staffs of control posts on ships or in areas not under the jurisdiction or control of sovereign states and the members of the staff of the Organization selected by the Administrator for the purposes of paragraph 3 of Article 11 of Annex I shall be composed in equal proportions of nationals of the U.S.S.R., nationals of the United Kingdom or the United States, and nationals of other countries.

(vi) The chief or acting chief of each control post shall be a national of a country other than that exercising jurisdiction or control over a territory on which the control post is situated. If the country exercising jurisdiction or control over such territory is associated with an original Party, the chief or acting chief of the control post shall be a national of other than such original Party or a country associated with it.

(vii) The chief or acting chief of each control post situated on territory under the jurisdiction or control of the United States or the United Kingdom shall be a national of the U.S.S.R.; the chief or acting chief of each control post situated on territory under the jurisdiction or control of the U.S.S.R. shall be a national of the United States or the United Kingdom.

(viii) The scientific and technical staffs of on-site inspection groups shall be composed of technically qualified personnel who are not nationals of the country exercising jurisdiction or control over the territory in which the event under investigation may have occurred. The Party exercising jurisdiction or control over such territory may designate one or more observers to accompany the inspection group.

(ix) The scientific and technical staff of any on-site inspection group despatched to conduct an inspection on territory under the jurisdiction or control of the U.S.S.R. shall be composed of nationals of the United States or the United Kingdom; the scientific and technical staff of any on-site inspection group despatched to conduct an inspection on territory under the jurisdiction or control of the United States or the United Kingdom shall be composed of nationals of the U.S.S.R.

(x) The U.S.S.R. or the United Kingdom and the United States may authorize the Administrator to depart from the requirements of sub-paragraphs (i) through (ix) above, insofar as they concern the appointment of their respective nationals to scientific and technical staff positions, either in favour of the nationals of another Party or other Parties or without restriction. In each case, the original Party or Parties concerned shall furnish the Administrator in writing with the authorization, including the period of its duration. Notwithstanding the authorization made under this paragraph, the nationals so appointed shall be considered, for the purposes of sub-paragraphs (i), (ii) and (v) to be nationals of the original Party authorizing the departure.

(xi) In making appointments under sub-paragraphs (i), (ii), (iii) and (v), the Administrator shall ensure that the administrative, scientific and technical staff of the Headquarters of the Organization, and the scientific and technical staff of each control post, shall be so composed that the total number of nationals of the U.S.S.R. and of countries associated with it shall be equal to the total number of nationals of the United States and the United Kingdom and of countries associated with either of them.

(xii) Any adjustment to the proportions in sub-paragraphs (i), (ii) and (v) above, which may be unavoidable for practical reasons, shall be kept to the minimum, and a compensating adjustment shall, whenever possible, be made elsewhere in the System.

D. Regulations governing the appointment, remuneration and dismissal of staff shall be approved by the Commission.

4. The Administrator shall prepare for the Commission the budget estimates of the Organization.

5. The Administrator shall develop and arrange for the execution of a program of research and development for the continuing improvement of the equipment and techniques used in all components of the System, and shall from time to time make recommendations to the Commission regarding improvements to be incorporated in the System. The program may, with the approval of the Commission, include detonations performed to test the effectiveness of the System. Any nuclear detonations for this purpose shall be conducted under the procedures set forth in Article 14.

6. The Administrator shall prepare recommendations for approval by the Commission regarding:

A. specific sites for all components of the System;

B. specific flight patterns for routine air sampling flights;

C. the number and base location of inspection groups;

D. the equipping of all components of the System and the standards and specifications which equipment to be used therein must meet.

7. A. When special aircraft sampling missions are undertaken, the Administrator shall appoint two qualified members of the Organization staff to accompany each aircraft as technical operators. The technical operators shall, in accordance with the provisions of Article 7 of Annex I, verify the execution of the agreed flight plan; operate the sampling equipment; direct sampling operation; make appropriate arrangements for the safe delivery to the Organization of the samples collected; and report on the mission to the Administrator.

B. (i) The technical operators shall not be nationals of:

(a) any Party exercising jurisdiction or control over territory in which the event under investigation may have occurred; or of

(b) any original Party which may be associated with the Party in paragraph 7 B (i) (a) of this Article; or of

(c) any Party which may be associated with any original Party to which paragraphs 7 B (i) (a) or 7 B (i) (b) of the Article may refer;

nor, subject to the provisions of sub-paragraph B (ii), shall they be nationals of any Party exercising jurisdiction or control over territory in the air space over which samples may be taken.

(ii) On flights investigating events which may have occurred in territory under the jurisdiction or control of the U.S.S.R., the technical operators shall be nationals of the United Kingdom or the United States. On flights investigating events which may have occurred in territory under the jurisdiction or control of the United Kingdom or the United States, the technical operators shall be nationals of the U.S.S.R.

C. Any Party exercising jurisdiction or control over territory in which the event under investigation may have occurred or in the air space over which samples are to be taken may designate an observer to accompany the technical operators on the flight.

8. The Administrator shall determine when special aircraft sampling missions are required in accordance with the terms of Article 7 of Annex I and shall have authority to order the despatch of such missions. For missions whose purpose is the collection of samples over the territory of a Party or Parties, the Administrator shall select routes from among the permanent flight routes laid down by the Commission in accordance with paragraph 6 of Article 6; before despatch of the mission, the Administrator shall notify all Parties over whose territories it will fly and shall inform them of the routes selected.

9. The Administrator shall forward to the Commission within twenty-four hours after receipt all reports submitted to him by inspection teams and special aircraft missions, together with any relevant data and analyses.

10. The Administrator shall encourage and facilitate the participation by personnel of components of the System in programs of basic scientific research, to the extent that such participation would not interfere with their primary duties.

11. In addition to the functions referred to in the preceding paragraphs of this Article, the Administrator shall perform such other functions as are provided for in this Treaty and its Annexes.

ARTICLE 10

On-Site Inspection of Seismic Events

1. A. The Administrator shall certify immediately by public notice at the Headquarters of the Organization whenever he determines that an event eligible for on-site inspection in accordance with the provisions of Article 8 of Annex I has occurred. This certification shall include a specification of the time of origin and location of the seismic event, the area eligible for inspection (hereinafter referred to as the 'certified area'), and the data and analysis upon which the determination of eligibility was made. The Administrator shall make every effort to make this certification within seventy-two hours after the occurrence of the event.

B. Whenever the Administrator is informed through the Organization that a seismic event of seismic magnitude of 4·75 or above which is located by the System has occurred, and if the event is not immediately rendered ineligible for on-site inspection in accordance with the provisions of Article 8 of Annex I, he shall immediately make public at the Headquarters of the Organization all data relating to such a seismic event which could be of assistance:

(i) to any Party exercising its right to request an on-site inspection under paragraphs 2 and 3 of this Article; or

(ii) to the Commission in its decision whether to issue a directive under paragraph 4 of this Article.

The Administrator shall make every effort to make this data public within seventy-two hours after the occurrence of all events referred to in this sub-paragraph, except for those events which have subsequently been found ineligible for on-site inspection in accordance with sub-paragraphs 3 C and 3 D of Article 8 of Annex I.

2. A. If any portion of the certified area lies in territory under the jurisdiction or control of any of the original Parties, the Administrator shall immediately despatch an inspection group to carry out an on-site inspection of such portion of the certified area in accordance with Annex I, provided that:

(i) The U.S.S.R. requests the inspection of such portion of the certified area which lies in territory under the jurisdiction or control of the United Kingdom or the United States, and the current annual number of inspections for the Party liable to inspection is not exhausted; or

(ii) The United Kingdom or the United States requests the inspection of such portion of the certified area which lies in territory under the jurisdiction or control of the U.S.S.R. and the current annual number of inspections for the U.S.S.R. is not exhausted; and

(iii) The request for inspection is made to the Administrator not later than fifteen days after the Administrator has made public all data relating to the seismic event in question, as specified in paragraph 1 B of this Article.

B. An original Party requesting an on-site inspection pursuant to this paragraph shall simultaneously inform the other original Parties.

3. A. If any portion of a certified area lies in territory under the jurisdiction or control of a Party other than an original Party, any Party may, not later than fifteen days after the Administrator has made public at the Headquarters of the Organization all data relating to the seismic event in question as specified in paragraph 1 B of this Article, request the Commission to direct an on-site inspection of such portion of the certified area.

B. The Commission shall consider and decide upon any such request within forty-eight hours after its receipt. If a certified area lies in territory under the jurisdiction or control of more than one Party, other than an original Party, the Commission shall make a separate decision as to the inspection of that portion of the certified area on the territory of each Party concerned. If the current annual number of inspections of the Party liable to inspection is not exhausted, and if the Commission decides that the request to direct an on-site inspection should be complied with, the Commission shall direct the Administrator to carry out an on-site inspection of the certified area lying in that Party's territory in accordance with Annex I.

C. If any portion of a certified area lies in territory under the jurisdiction or control of a Party represented on the Commission, that Party shall not particpate in the decision as to the inspection of such portion of the certified area.

D. If any portion of a certified area lies in territory under the jurisdiction or control of a Party associated with an original Party, that original Party and

Parties associated with it which are represented on the Commission shall not participate in the decision as to the inspection of such portion of the certified area.

4. S. If any portion of a certified area lies in an area not under the jurisdiction or control of any sovereign state, the Administrator shall decide whether to undertake an on-site inspection. The Administrator shall notify the Commission of his decision whether to undertake an on-site inspection and shall make every effort to do so within seventy-two hours after the occurrence of the event. After the Administrator notifies the Commission that he has decided to undertake an on-site inspection, he shall proceed to have the inspection carried out unless he is otherwise directed by the Commission within forty-eight hours of such notification.

B. The Commission may direct the Administrator to inspect a certified area not under the jurisdiction or control of any sovereign state, if the Administrator has not already proceeded to do so, not later than fifteen days after the Administrator has made public at the Headquarters of the Organization all data relating to the seismic event in question as specified in paragraph 1 B of this Article.

C. All on-site inspections under this paragraph shall be carried out in accordance with Annex I.

5. The number of on-site inspections which may be carried out in territory under the jurisdiction or control of each of the original Parties, pursuant to paragraph 2 of this Article, shall be twenty inspections in each annual period.

6. A. The number of on-site inspections which may be carried out in each annual period in territory under the jurisdiction or control of a Party other than an original Party, pursuant to paragraph 3 of this Article, shall be, with respect to each such Party, two, or such higher number as the Commission may, after consultation with the Party, determine by a two-thirds majority of those present and voting.

B. Pending the determination of a Party's number by the Commission, the provisional number for that Party shall be one inspection in each annual period for each 500,000 square kilometers or remaining fraction thereof of territory under its jurisdiction or control, except that for each Party the provisional number shall be at least two inspections in each annual period. Inspections carried out under a Party's provisional number shall be deducted from the number subsequently determined for that Party for the annual period in which such inspections were initiated. In the case of acceding Parties, the Preparatory Commission shall, after consultation with such Parties, promptly recommend, for subsequent approval by the enlarged Preparatory Commission an appropriate number of inspections to be carried out in each annual period within territory under the jurisdiction or control of such Parties.

7. The number of on-site inspections for each Party shall be reviewed by the Commission within three years after this Treaty enters into force and annually thereafter. In light of each such review, which shall take full account of practical experience in the operation of the System and of measures taken to maintain or improve its effectiveness, the Commission may fix revised numbers, provided that no number (A) shall be less than two, (B) nor less than twenty per cent. of the average annual number of events of seismic magnitude 4·75 or above which are located by the System in accordance with paragraph 2 of Article 8 of Annex I,

provided that when criteria for the identification of seismic events eligible for on-site inspection are agreed, no less than thirty per cent. of the events remaining unidentified after the application of such criteria, occurring in territory under the jurisdiction or control of the Party to which the number relates. Such average annual number shall be based on data from control posts and research programs undertaken by the Commission in accordance with the provisions of Article 6 for a period prescribed by the Commission.

8. The liability of a Party to on-site inspections pursuant to paragraph 2 or 3 of this Article shall commence from the date on which the Treaty enters into force for that Party. The annual period in which the number of on-site inspections for each Party may be carried out shall commence on the date of entry into force of the Treaty and thereafter on the anniversary of that date in each succeeding year. In the case of a Party which deposits its instrument of ratification or acceptance after the date of entry into force of the Treaty, the number of on-site inspections which may be carried out in territory under its jurisdiction or control in the period remaining before the next anniversary of the date of entry into force of the Treaty shall bear the same proportion to its number determined in accordance with paragraph 6 of this Article, as that period bears to one year, but shall not be less than two. If the number of on-site inspections calculated in accordance with the preceding sentence includes a fraction, that fraction shall, if it is smaller than one-half, be disregarded, or, if it is one-half or greater, be regarded as equivalent to one.

9. Notwithstanding any other provision of this Article, the Commission may direct the Administrator to carry out on-site inspection in territory under the jurisdiction or control of any Party either at the request of such Party or pursuant to an agreement made by such Party prior to or subsequent to signature of the Treaty. Inspections carried out under this paragraph shall not be deducted from a Party's number. Inspections carried out pursuant to paragraphs 2 and 3 of this Article shall take priority over inspections carried out under this paragraph.

10. The Administrator shall make available to all Parties to the Treaty within twenty-four hours after receipt all reports submitted to him by on-site inspection groups, together with any relevant data and analyses.

ARTICLE 11

Installation and Operation of the System in Parties' Territories

Each of the original Parties and all other Parties to this Treaty agree to accept on territory under their jurisdiction or control components of the System which is established on the basis of the 'Report of the Conference of Experts to Study the Methods of Detecting Violations of a Possible Agreement on the Suspension of Nuclear Tests' of August 20, 1958,[1] the 'Report of the Technical Working Group on the Detection and Identification of High-Altitude Nuclear Explosions' of July, 1959,[2] and the 'Conclusion of Technical Working Group II Regarding

---

[1] Cmnd. 551, *Report of the Conference of Experts to Study the Methods of Detecting Violations of a Possible Agreement on the Suspension of Nuclear Tests* (London, H.M.S.O., 1958).

[2] United States Disarmament Administration, *Geneva Conference on the Discontinuance of Nuclear Weapon Tests, History and Analysis of Negotiations* (Washington, U.S.G.P.O., 1961), pp. 367–75.

Possible Improvements of Techniques and Instrumentation' of December 18, 1959,[1] and shall be installed and shall operate in accordance with the provisions of this Treaty and its Annexes.

ARTICLE 12

Undertakings Concerning Co-operation with the System

1. Each of the Parties undertakes to assure that adequate and expeditious transportation is available from the point of entry, or within its territory, to the site of any element of the System or any area where an on-site inspection is to be conducted.

2. Each of the Parties undertakes to enter into appropriate arrangements with the Commission for the utilization of existing meteorological and commercial aircraft flights over ocean areas for routine air-sampling purposes.

3. Each of the Parties undertakes to enter into appropriate arrangements with the Commission to have aircraft immediately available for special flights, carried out pursuant to the provisions of Article 9 and Article 7 of Annex I, over territory under its jurisdiction or control or to permit such special flights by aircraft forming part of the System.

4. Each of the Parties undertakes to enter into appropriate arrangements with the Commission for the utilization of existing weather or geophysical exploration vessels for use as components of the System.

5. Each of the Parties undertakes to give inspection groups, despatched pursuant to the provisions of Article 10, immediate and undisputed access to the area in which an on-site inspection is to be conducted, to refrain from interference with any operation of an inspection group and to give such groups the assistance they may require in the performance of their mission.

6. Each of the Parties undertakes to enter into appropriate arrangements with the Commission: for the design, construction, and provision of necessary satellite vehicles; for the provision and use of launching sites and launching vehicles; for the establishment and operation of stations to track satellites and to receive and analyze data from such satellites; and for the establishment and carrying out of a research program to measure background levels in space and to develop the necessary equipment and techniques to put effective space monitoring control systems into operation.

ARTICLE 13

Detonations for Peaceful Purposes

1. Each of the Parties to this Treaty undertakes to detonate, or assist others in the detonation of, nuclear devices for peaceful purposes only in accordance with the provisions of this Article. The detonations carried out pursuant to the provisions of this Article shall not be regarded as a violation of Article 1.

2. A Party intending to carry out or assist in such a detonation shall provide the Commission, at least four months in advance of the proposed detonation date, with a plan containing the following information.

A. The date, site and purpose of the proposed detonation;

B. The procedure it will follow to comply with paragraph 4 of this Article;

[1] ibid., pp. 384–413.

C. The expected yield of the device;

D. The measures to be taken to ensure that there will be no substantial fallout outside the immediate vicinity;

E. The measurements to be taken and any experimentation to be conducted therewith.

3. Within two months after the receipt of the plan, the Commission shall authorize the Party to proceed with, or assist in, the proposed detonation, unless the Commission shall find that such detonation would not be carried out in accordance with paragraph 4 of this Article. If, as a result of observations at the proposed site, the Commission determines that there is a lack of compliance with paragraph 4, it shall immediately so notify the Party planning to conduct or assist in the detonation. The Party shall thereupon refrain from carrying out or assisting in the detonation until notified by the Commission that it has determined that the detonation will be carried out in accordance with paragraph 4.

4. Each of the original Parties shall be given an adequate opportunity at a designated inspection site to inspect externally and internally any nuclear device to be detonated pursuant to this Article and to examine detailed drawings of the device, provided that such detailed drawings may not be reproduced or taken away from the inspection site. The device to be detonated shall, after inspection and reassembly, be under the continual surveillance of members of the Organization staff until detonation.

5. Members of the Organization staff shall, in addition to maintaining surveillance of the device to be detonated, observe all preparation for, and the actual firing of, the device and shall at all times have unrestricted access to the vicinity of the detonation to ensure that the device employed is the one provided in accordance with paragraph 4 of this Article.

6. Representatives of the original Parties shall be given adequate opportunity to accompany and to participate with members of the Organization staff in the exercise of their functions under paragraphs 4 and 5 of this Article.

7. The Commission may, with the concurring votes of the original Parties, provide for any other system of safeguards to ensure that nuclear detonations for peaceful purposes are carried out in accordance with the objectives of this Treaty.

ARTICLE 14

Periodic Review of the System

1. Three years after the coming into force of this Treaty, the Commission shall review the System established under this Treaty in order to:

A. evaluate its effectiveness for verifying compliance with the obligations set forth in Articles 1 and 13 of this Treaty;

B. determine in the light of experience and scientific progress whether any specific improvements should be made or new elements added to the System:

C. consider such measures to improve or maintain the effectiveness of the System as may be proposed by any Party to the Treaty in the light of experience in the operation of the Treaty.

2. The System may be reviewed by the Commission annually thereafter for the same purpose upon request of the Conference or any of the original Parties.

ARTICLE 15

Finance

1. Annual budget estimates for the expenses of the Organization shall be submitted to the Commission by the Administrator. After receipt of these estimates, the Commission shall submit a proposed budget to the Conference. The Conference may approve the budget as submitted or return it to the Commission with recommendations. If the budget is returned, the Commission shall then submit a further budget to the Conference for its approval.

2. The expenses of the Organization shall be borne by the Parties in accordance with a scale fixed by the Conference on the basis of recommendations submitted by the Commission as part of each annual budget. The annual contributions of the U.S.S.R. and the United States shall be equal.

3. Any Party desiring to pay its assessments, in whole or in part, by supplying materials, services, equipment or facilities shall make its offer in writing to the Commission. Within ninety days after receipt of the offer, the Commission shall determine whether to accept the offer, in whole or in part, and shall notify the Party of its decision. The Commission shall not accept such an offer unless the materials, services, equipment or facilities offered by the Party meet the standards prescribed by the Commission and are readily usable.

4. Subject to the rules and limitations approved by the Conference, the Commission shall have the authority to exercise borrowing powers on behalf of the Organization without, however, imposing on the Parties to this Treaty any individual liability in respect of a loan or loans entered into pursuant to this authority.

5. Decisions of the Commission and of the Conference on all financial questions shall be made by a majority of those present and voting. However, decisions by the Commission on the scale of contributions to be recommended and on the total amount of each annual budget shall require the concurring votes of the original Parties.

ARTICLE 16

Privileges and Immunities

The privileges and immunities which the Organization, its staff and the representatives of Parties shall be granted by the Parties, and the legal capacity which the Organization shall enjoy in the territory of each of the Parties, shall be as set forth in Annex II of this Treaty.

ARTICLE 17

Relationships with Other International Organizations

1. The Commission, with the approval of the Conference, is authorized to enter into an agreement or agreements establishing an appropriate relationship between the Organization and the United Nations.

2. The Commission, with the approval of the Conference, shall arrange for the Organization to be brought into an appropriate relationship with any international organization which may in the future be established among any of the Parties to this Treaty to supervise disarmament and arms control measures.

ARTICLE 18

Annexes

The Annexes to this Treaty form an integral part of this Treaty.

ARTICLE 19

Parties to the Treaty

1. The essential Parties to this Treaty shall be:

A. The Union of Soviet Socialist Republics, the United Kingdom of Great Britain and Northern Ireland and the United States of America, referred to herein as the 'original Parties'.

B. Any other State whose adherence is decided by the Commission to be necessary for the achievement of the fundamental Treaty purpose of securing an effectively controlled permanent discontinuance of nuclear weapon test explosions on a world-wide basis or to permit the installation of elements of control as required by the provisions of Annex I. If any State which is proposed to be the subject of a decision in accordance with the preceding sentence is associated with an original Party for the purposes of this Treaty, that original Party and any State associated with it for the purposes of this Treaty shall abstain from voting in the decision.

2. The signature and ratification or the acceptance of this Treaty by all the States designated in paragraph 1 A and any State whose adherence is decided to necessary in accordance with paragraph 1 B shall be required for the fulfilment of the provisions of this Article.

3. Any other State desiring to adhere, whose adherence the Preparatory Commission or the Commission decides would contribute to the achievement of the purposes of this Treaty, may become a Party.

ARTICLE 20

Signature, Ratification, Acceptance and Entry into Force

1. This Treaty shall be open for signature by the states referred to in paragraph 1 A of Article 19. The signatory states shall become Parties to this Treaty by deposit of instruments of ratification.

2. Instruments of ratification and instruments of acceptance by states adhering pursuant to paragraphs 1 B and 3 of Article 19 shall be deposited with the Government of . . . ., hereby designated as Depositary Government.

3. Ratification or acceptance of this Treaty shall be effected by states in accordance with their respective constitutional processes.

4. This Treaty, apart from Annex III, shall enter into force when all the original Parties have deposited instruments of ratification thereof.

5. The Depositary Government shall promptly inform all signatory states of the date of deposit of each instrument of ratification and of each instrument of acceptance and the date of entry into force of this Treaty. The Depositary Government shall promptly inform all Parties of the dates on which states become Parties to this Treaty.

6. Annex III of this Treaty shall come into force on the day after this Treaty shall have been signed by the original Parties.

ARTICLE 21

Registration

1. This Treaty shall be registered by the Depositary Government pursuant to Article 102 of the Charter of the United Nations.

2. Agreements between the Organization and any Party to this Treaty or any other State or public international organization shall be submitted for registration by the Commission with the United Nations.

ARTICLE 22

Duration

This Treaty shall remain in force indefinitely subject to the inherent right of a Party to withdraw and be relieved of obligations hereunder if the provisions of the Treaty and its Annexes, including those providing for the timely installation and effective operation of the control system, are not being fulfilled and observed.

ARTICLE 23

Amendments

Amendments to this Treaty and its Annexes shall enter into force for all Parties to the Treaty when they have been adopted by a vote of two-thirds of the members of the Conference and ratified in accordance with their respective constitutional processes by two-thirds of the Parties to this Treaty, including all the original Parties.

ARTICLE 24

Authentic Texts

This Treaty, of which the English and Russian texts are equally authentic, shall be deposited in the archives of the Depositary Government. Duly certified copies of this Treaty shall be transmitted by the Depositary Government to the Governments of the other signatory States and to the Governments of States which become Parties to this Treaty pursuant to paragraphs 1 B and 3 of Article 19.

IN WITNESS WHEREOF the undersigned, duly authorized, have signed this Treaty.

DONE at————————————————, this——————day of———————— one thousand nine hundred and sixty-one.

3. Statement by the United States delegate to the Geneva Conference, Mr. Dean, 18 April 1961[1]

On behalf of the United States and United Kingdom delegations I shall now table a proposal for a complete draft treaty on the discontinuance of nuclear weapon tests.

[1] Cmnd. 1397, pp. 48–51. For the statement by the British delegate, Mr. Ormsby Gore see ibid., pp. 51–53.

The Western delegations, on March 21 last, presented in the Conference broad, new and major proposals which we believe should make it possible promptly to reach agreement on a treaty.[1]

Following our meeting on March 21, 1961, the United States and United Kingdom delegations have explained in considerable detail the proposals which we then presented.

In an effort further to clarify the positions of the two Western delegations, we are now tabling exact treaty language for a complete draft treaty.

The draft treaty which we now table is complete. It covers, we believe, every necessary element of an over-all agreement for the discontinuance of nuclear weapon tests. We strongly believe that it represents a sound, fair, equitable and workable treaty. We believe that its provisions call for an adequate control system and a system which does not impose undue burdens upon any party to the treaty.

The draft treaty which we present today is a treaty which the Governments of the United States and the United Kingdom are prepared to sign immediately to end tests underground above the seismic scale of magnitude 4·75, in the sensible atmosphere, in the oceans and in outer space.

Its signature would, of course, be accompanied, as we have previously agreed, by unilateral declarations on the part of the three original parties undertaking a moratorium of an agreed duration on underground tests below the treaty threshold level of 4·75 and by agreement that seismic research programmes undertaken by any of the original parties subsequent to signature of the treaty would involve application of agreed safeguards to such nuclear explosions as may be included in those research programmes. It is to be hoped that at the end of the seismic research programmes our then knowledge will permit us to lower the treaty threshold.

This draft treaty represents our best and most advanced ideas for an agreement which will achieve discontinuance of nuclear weapon tests under adequate international control.

The delegations of the United Kingdom and the United States will, of course, stand ready to explain their views fully and to give careful consideration to any ideas which the delegation of the U.S.S.R. may have with respect to achievement of the objective of a sound treaty for the protection of the people of the world.

We are prepared to discuss this draft patiently and in detail. It represents our best thought but we are by no means inflexible about it. We are entirely open to reason. We shall listen carefully.

This draft treaty is presented by the Western delegations in a sincere effort to assist our negotiations to reach a successful conclusion.

I should like now to read the draft treaty into the verbatim record of the Conference, and also to distribute it as a Conference document:

[*At this point the United States Delegate read into the record the draft treaty text.*]

I realize that this document in its bulk—some sixty-seven pages and about

---

[1] See above, p. 403, n. 2.

15,000 words—presents, in size at least, a rather formidable aspect, but I can assure my colleagues that they should not be disheartened.

While the draft treaty which I am presenting today does constitute a complete version which the two Western Governments would be prepared to sign immediately, I can say that a large percentage of its contents is made up of texts upon which we here have already reached agreement or which have been before this Conference for quite some time.

To assist in using and reading through this treaty draft, I will quickly point out those parts which do not contain anything new in substance, and direct particular attention to those parts which do present new positions on the part of the Western delegations.

To run through the headings of the articles, of which in this version there are twenty-four in the main part of the treaty, I might note that the preamble and the articles on establishment of the organization, the elements of the control organization, the conference, privileges and immunities, relationships with other international organizations, annexes, registration, duration, amendments and authentic texts all have been unchanged in substance and remain as they have been agreed by the three participants in this Conference.

In connexion with the article on the elements of the control organization, I should like to point out that, as has been previously agreed, the article calls for a single administrator to be the chief executive officer of the control organization.

Also in this category are Annex II on privileges and immunities and, except for a few minor amendments, Annex III.

The article on procedures of the control commission is unchanged from that which has been before the Conference since it was tabled by the United Kingdom delegation in December 1958.[1]

The major changes which appear in this text for the most part incorporate the moves in positions of the Western delegations which I described on behalf of the two delegations in the statement which I made on March 21 at our two hundred and seventy-fourth meeting. In particular, this applies to Article 4 on the composition of the control commission, the article on detonations for peaceful purposes with its new safeguards provisions, the article on finance and the quota provisions of the on-site inspection article.

In the same category are the major additions which appear in the new version of draft Annex I which now contains complete textual provisions on high altitude controls, appearing chiefly in Articles 11 and 19 of Annex I, as well as in Article I, as well as in Article 12 of the treaty—the article which relates to undertakings concerning co-operation with the system.

Annex I now also incorporates the new Western position on the placement of control posts.

The remainder of the articles which I have not yet mentioned incorporate revisions or new texts which the two Western delegations today propose in order to complete this single composite treaty.

[1] Sub-committee on Disarmament of the Committee on Foreign Relations, United States Senate, *Conference on the Discontinuance of Nuclear Weapons Tests, Analysis of Progress and Positions of the Participating Parties, October 1958–August 1960* (Washington, U.S.G.P.O., 1960), pp. 50–52, 55.

In this category I can mention Article 1, which now incorporates a threshold provision, a new version of the article on parties to the treaty, the signature article and a very important new article under which we spell out the procedure by which will be determined the category of parties or countries 'associated with original parties' as that term is employed in various articles of this new version.

In particular, we have introduced the 'associated' State concept in the article on control commission composition, the article on on-site inspection of seismic events, the articles on parties, and the article on administrator and international staff.

This latter article, Article 9, which has over the many months of this Conference grown into the giant among the articles of the treaty, represents in this up-to-date version a drawing together of all of the paragraphs which have been either agreed upon among the three of us or which have been the subject of a series of amendments over the past months.

We have also included certain new ideas with respect to this most difficult question of staffing, ideas which incorporate the concept of associated parties or countries.

As for Annex I, in addition to the provisions on high altitude control which I have just mentioned there are new provisions relating to regional offices and to the view of criteria for on-site inspections. Finally, as a part of this draft, there is a series of small amendments to Annex III on the preparatory commission. All of these, I think, are minor and self-explanatory.

In closing I should like to draw particular attention to a drafting change which my delegation has incorporated in the agreed article on authentic texts. The text of this article as it now reads in its agreed form refers to the predicted date of signature of the treaty as occurring in the year 1959. We have changed this date in our new version to the year 1961. I sincerely trust that in this change my colleagues will find no basis for argument and that this will be the last change of this nature we will have to make in this article.

I sincerely hope we can look forward to a signature of this treaty by representatives of the three Governments participating in this Conference at some date within the near future.

May I end on this note of hope. I commend this document to the serious attention of my Soviet colleagues. It is a document that represents a most earnest and sincere effort on the part of the Western delegations to present as a whole and in a clear and precise form a complete treaty text which we consider to be sound, fair and equitable for all States which might become parties to it, a treaty which will measure up to the noble purposes for which our three delegations convened here many months ago, a treaty which will effectively, fairly and dependably control the obligation to discontinue the testing of nuclear weapons in the manner upon which we all agree and which the world will applaud.

My delegation will await with interest any comments which the Soviet representative may have on the new draft treaty, in the hope that we all will be able now seriously to begin and soon complete whatever negotiation remains to be done before we finally achieve agreement on a complete treaty and also each announce the beginning of the moratorium on underground testing below the treaty threshold.

We submit this complete draft of a nuclear test ban treaty to the Soviet Government with high hope. We believe it meets the aspirations of the world. In deep humility we commend its provisions to the Soviet Union.

With agreement, we can all look forward to a hopeful and peaceful world. Without it the future of mankind remains clouded and uncertain. For our part, we believe that that future should be clear, certain and unclouded.[1]

4. Statement by Mr. Dean to the Geneva Conference, 28 April 1961[2]

The three hundredth meeting of the Conference is called to order. I should like to make some remarks in my capacity as representative of the United States.

Where do we stand today? When I arrived in Geneva in March with our far-reaching major proposals for a nuclear test ban treaty which the United Kingdom and the United States are prepared to sign, I hoped that by this date we would all surely be immersed deeply in serious negotiations. I had every expectation that the Soviet Union would be as anxious to conclude a reasonable test ban treaty incorporating effective control measures as are the United Kingdom Government and my own Government. I have still not reached a contrary conclusion, but the doubts in my mind are increasing, and I am concerned by the trend of our affairs.

The significant fact today is that this is the three hundredth meeting of the Conference. How much thought, effort and patient hard work are hidden in that single number of 300? How many months have passed since October 31, 1958—some months of hope and anticipation of success, other months of frustration and pessimism.

I am concerned because there has been no contribution to our work over the past twenty-seven meetings by the Soviet Union. Indeed, it has made backward movements. Yet, despite this completely unreasonable attitude, the Soviet representative continues to say that he seeks a treaty: he continues to acknowledge the sound reasons of national interest which should make each of our countries anxious for success in our talks.

We have never forgotten the strong words in favour of an effectively controlled treaty expressed on many occasions by Premier Khrushchev, not least of all in his letters of April 23, 1959 and May 15, 1959, to President Eisenhower.[3] And yet, despite this, nothing happens on the Soviet side to move the negotiations forward towards a sound and workable treaty.

I have, on occasion, thought that our Conference is like the vault of a great national museum. Inside are great treasures to be had, treasures worth more than the most famous paintings—the treasure of better East-West relations, the treasure of a first step towards bringing the awesome weapons of today under control, the treasure of establishing a pattern of international co-operation. But those treasures will not stay intact for ever; they are fragile, perishable and in danger of dissolving into the dust of yesterday—of what might have been.

[1] For the supporting statement of the British delegate see Cmnd. 1397, pp. 51–53.
[2] Cmnd. 1397, pp. 54–59. For the statement by the British delegate, Sir Michael Wright, see ibid., pp. 59–62.
[3] *Documents*, 1959, pp. 125–7 and 133–5.

D.I.A.–P

Yet this museum vault, as is usually the case with such strong rooms, cannot be opened with only one key. There are two keys held by separate custodians and unless they both get to the vault at the right time with the right key the treasures will remain beyond human vision and human grasp. And while we all wait here for these two custodians—one of the East and one of the West—finally to get together, the priceless contents of our civilization may disappear for ever in clouds of radio-active particles.

I cannot doubt that my Soviet colleague would abhor this result as much as I. Yet he is a trusted agent of one of the sides owning an indispensable key—a key which, to all appearances, I regret to say, he has not yet been authorized to produce at our Conference table. I must beseech him therefore to take the most careful account of where we all stand; to see, if he can, and then to understand, how, in all honesty and sincerity, the situation looks to the world at this three hundredth meeting.

Although I personally have tried to help my country on several occasions, I am not a full-time professional public servant. My occupation—the practice of law—is a full-time job of itself. When I was asked to accept the honour of leading the United States delegation at this nuclear test ban treaty Conference I first investigated, before deciding upon my answer, what the situation was in which I would work. I wanted to know the purpose of my Government, the policy it wished to pursue and the proposals which it would be ready to put forward. The fact that I undertook this job is clear evidence not merely of my own personal desire to conclude a just and reliable treaty with effective international controls for the benefit of mankind, but also of the very real and sincere determination of President Kennedy and his Administration to support every reasonable effort to achieve this noble and humane end.

In the weeks in Washington during February and early March when we were preparing for the resumption of the Conference my Government painstakingly reviewed every treaty issue. We were convinced that our major and far-reaching proposals to the Soviet Union had to be made in the utmost good faith so that our desire for the success of the Conference would be plainly evident for all to see. The parallel preparations of the United Kingdom Government took the same course, and as a result, after joint consultations, the Western Powers were able to return with an agreed upon group of far-reaching moves and initiatives to settle the thorny problems which had arisen.

We set our offer before the Soviet delegation across the board at the very first meeting after the recess, namely, on March 21 last.[1] We then took several weeks to explain and expound our positions in detail. On April 18, 1961, we tabled every one of these proposals in precise and detailed treaty language, all combined in a draft text which also greatly improves upon old language and which we are ready to sign at any time.[2] Since then we have spent ten days in pointing to significant details of the revised drafts of the treaty articles and annexes. We have announced our desire—which remains as strong as ever—to enter with our Soviet colleagues into earnest negotiations on our detailed proposals in an effort to inject some impetus into our work.

It is impossible to belittle the major steps we have taken since March 21

[1] See above, p. 403, n. 2.   [2] Above, p. 407.

because they deal with so many of the most controversial issues of this Conference. Let me list them again.

First, we have agreed that the research programme should be extended to three years.

Second, the moratorium is correspondingly to be extended to three years, with the last three to six months given over to consultations among the original parties on what should be done about the treaty threshold of magnitude $4\cdot75$ in the post-moratorium period.

Third, both the research programme and the moratorium are to start on the signature of the treaty.

Fourth, President Kennedy has made known his entire willingness to request the necessary amendments in United States legislation to make it possible to adopt the four steps requested by the U.S.S.R. which would involve an unprecedented declassification of United States secret information but which the U.S.S.R. considers essential to ensure that research nuclear detonations cannot be used by any party to gain additional weapons development information.

Fifth, we are prepared to apply these safeguard procedures to all nuclear detonations for peaceful purposes.

Sixth, although we would prefer twenty-one, it will be agreeable to us if the number of control posts in U.S.S.R. territory is reduced from twenty-one to nineteen.

Seventh, while adhering to our figure of a quota of on-site inspections of twenty per year for the U.S.S.R., we are ready to grant the U.S.S.R. twenty in the United States and twenty in the United Kingdom, or a total of forty, or twice our own request from the U.S.S.R.

Eighth, we have proposed a total ban of nuclear tests at high altitudes and have tabled complete treaty texts to cover the establishment of the corresponding control arrangements.

Ninth, the Western Powers have agreed that all original parties will have the right to exercise a veto in the control commission in voting on the total annual control organization budget, which will include the scale of contributions. In the latter regard, the United States and the U.S.S.R. we suggest are to contribute equal shares, with the United Kingdom paying a smaller share.

Tenth, a new formula has been offered which guarantees East-West parity at every control post in the control system, as well as at the headquarters in Vienna.

Eleventh, the parties article has been redrafted to make it still clearer that either each nuclear side will be able to ensure that important associates of the other nuclear side adhere to the treaty or the first side will, if the adherence does not take place, have the option of itself invoking the duration article.

Twelfth, on the understanding that the other provisions to be adopted will add up to a reliable, workable, and effective treaty and control system, we have agreed that there shall be East–West parity in the control commission, with four seats each for East and West and three for neutral States, thus giving a total of eleven.

Just to review these new proposals is to demonstrate again how far we have offered to move to meet the Soviet Union in order to obtain a nuclear test ban treaty.

Of course, we make no secret of the fact that we have not conceded every Soviet demand which would make the treaty unworkable and we have no intention of doing so. However, we have urged and will continue to urge the Soviet representative to come forward with corresponding initiatives of his own so that we can get down to the brass tacks of settling those important points which still remain unresolved.

The Soviet response so far has been threefold. First, where the West has entirely accepted some major Soviet demand the U.S.S.R. generally agrees that it is still willing to let us settle the problem on the basis proposed first by the Soviet Union without any move whatsoever by it. Second, Mr. Tsarapkin has graciously informed us that in those instances where we have yet to adopt the Soviet position he will not budge a millimetre. However, he will be patient with us for a while until we announce our full and complete capitulation. Third, the U.S.S.R. has put forward a totally new demand for a three-man administrative council—acting only by unanimity—which would replace the single administrator on whom we previously agreed at the twenty-fourth meeting, and would make possible a total veto for each nuclear side, as well as for the neutral States, over all control operations.

I am sure that Mr. Tsarapkin fully realizes that this plan will never prove acceptable to the United Kingdom and the United States Governments and will have to be withdrawn.

The problems of the second category, where the U.S.S.R. is demanding new Western concessions, go to the very heart of control effectiveness. The Soviet Union wants only a token number of annual on-site inspections, namely, three on each original party's territory. The United States and the United Kingdom, basing themselves on the agreed scientific studies, want a realistic number which will actually tend to deter potential violators, namely, twenty on each original party's territory.

Again, on criteria, the U.S.S.R. insists on a formula which would make it questionable whether even one event per year would be certified as eligible for inspection. This has no appeal to the West, which wants scientifically reasonable criteria.

The Soviet delegation refuses to consider any more than fifteen control posts on Soviet territory, even though we have already moved to meet its demand by coming down from twenty-one to nineteen and have proved, by the Soviet delegation's own arithmetic that the number cannot be reasonably fewer than sixteen in Soviet Asia, two in Europe and one on a Soviet island. Similarly, we have been told that no control operations can start for four years from the date of entry into force of the treaty, even though a beginning would be technically feasible within two years upon the completion of phase I A of the installation of the control system.

On important matters such as the staffing of inspection teams and special aircraft flights and the choice of the head of teams and control posts, the U.S.S.R. is adhering to old demands that nationals of the country being inspected or controlled play a dominant role. However, the Western Powers have not been and will not be willing to accept arrangements permitting self-inspection.

In addition to all this there are various other matters which are essential to a sound and workable treaty. I might mention the Soviet demand for a veto right by the original parties over parts of the budget as well as over the whole.

Then too, there is Soviet insistence that each original party shall contribute equally to control system costs, even though on questions of exercising power in the organization East–West parity is to prevail.

Finally, we cannot forget not only Soviet urging for a still longer moratorium period, extending to four or five years, but also Soviet insistence that the moratorium, in practice, should be never-ending, without regard to whether or not below-threshold control capabilities do or do not improve through the seismic research programme which we are undertaking at our own expense in order to improve the area of the treaty.

Now what does this all add up to?

One thing that strikes me is that Mr. Tsarapkin has often attempted to justify the do-nothing attitude of his delegation by claiming that since the U.S.S.R. made all the concessions in 1959 and 1960, and that since those concessions covered seventy per cent of the treaty, it has the right calmly to accept all of the major and far-reaching United States and United Kingdom proposals without even saying 'Thank you', and then sit back and await even further concessions from the United States and the United Kingdom in 1961. I am afraid, however, that this claim, to use one of Mr. Tsarapkin's favourite expressions, is 'totally without foundation'.

Let me examine briefly the situation with regard to Soviet concessions.

First, the Soviet representative has claimed that, owing to many Soviet compromises, he has removed the so-called Soviet veto list on which unanimous votes by the original parties were to be essential on the control commission before any important decision could be taken. The veto list was tabled by the U.S.S.R. on January 30, 1959,[1] and Mr. Tsarapkin's first statements about its withdrawal were heard in June 1959.[2] In fact, however, it has recently reappeared in even more virulent form in the shape of the Soviet demand for a three-man administrative council, so it is on a 'Now you see it, now you don't' basis.

As I have described at length at the two hundred and nienty-fourth and two hundred and ninety-ninth meetings, this is the most complete demand for a veto over control operations that has ever faced our negotiations. It is clear that there has been no Soviet move forward in this area.

Second, our ears have been filled with many Soviet assertions that the U.S.S.R. saved the Conference on March 19, 1960,[3] when it agreed to accept United States demands for a treaty with an underground threshold in the first phase, on the sole condition that a moratorium on testing be announced to prevent testing below the threshold during the period when research work would be carried out to investigate the possibilities for discovering improvements in seismic detection and identification capabilities. As it turns out, however, the

[1] United States Disarmament Administration, *Geneva Conference on the Discontinuance of Nuclear Weapon Tests, History and Analysis of Negotiations* (Washington, U.S.G.P.O., 1961), pp. 334–5.
[2] *N.Y. Times*, 12 and 17 June 1959.　　　[3] *Documents*, 1960, pp. 98–100.

more we probe into this Soviet offer the more it seems that it really did nothing more than suggest a comprehensive treaty in disguise.

The U.S.S.R. is now trying to commit the Western Powers to a moratorium which, in practice, will never be able to end no matter how the seismic research efforts turn out. We have asked Mr. Tsarapkin about this directly at three meetings, but he has not yet replied. Until he tells us something to the contrary it would appear that we have no Soviet concession here either.

Third, there has been a great fuss about the Soviet plan for a veto-free quota of on-site inspections each year. In practice, however, little in the way of concessions seems involved. By setting up criteria which will keep seismic events from becoming eligible for inspection, by offering only a nominal three inspections for each year of 365 days—just think of it, three inspections for an entire year—by calling for the staffing of inspection teams in large part by nationals of the country being inspected and, finally, by insisting that all control operations, including inspections, be started only after an unreasonable delay of four years, the practical effect is to make the Soviet minimal move on a quota meaningless. And to limit the number of on-site inspections to three a year in a country the size of the Soviet Union—approximately twenty-two million square kilometres—is really to say that there can be no inspections at all for most of any year.

To be sure, the U.S.S.R. has made a few moves, such as agreeing in principle to permitting peaceful uses detonations, accepting nuclear detonations in the research programme, and adopting the thirds staffing arrangement at control posts. However, the latter item, I should note, involved just as much of a concession to the U.S.S.R. by the West, as *vice versa*, since the final formula has amounted virtually to splitting the difference between the original positions of the two sides.

The foregoing summary should make it evident to all that the West, having done a great deal itself in recent weeks to advance the work of the Conference, has every right to expect much action on the part of the Soviet Union. In simple terms, Mr. Tsarapkin, the books of this Conference are woefully unbalanced in the eyes of the world, and the U.S.S.R. is greatly in debt to the United States and the United Kingdom. The Soviet Union simply must take the initiative to meet these Western proposals. We repeat, we are prepared to enter with great patience into earnest negotiations with our Soviet colleague both on our detailed proposals and on any constructive proposals that he may put forward in an effort to solve this problem. But only the Soviet Union has it in its power to rectify this situation. And, as I said at the outset today, time will not stand still for ever if the U.S.S.R. does not come forward with a constructive initiative.

In one way or another this Conference has lived through 300 meetings—which must be a record of sorts of this type of endeavour. It taxes my imagination to think that the Conference might still be floundering in the same sea of indecision innumerable meetings hence. To me it seems much more likely that within some reasonable period our fate will have been determined and our success or failure written down upon the pages of history.

I appeal to the leaders of the Soviet Government to see that the pages of history will not say that our efforts have been in vain, that the hopes of mankind for a workable nuclear test ban treaty have been disappointed and that the great moral forces for disarmament have suffered a grievous [*sic*] blow.[1]

5. Soviet Aide-mémoire of Mr. Khrushchev to President Kennedy, Vienna, 4 June 1961[2]

The Soviet government considers it necessary to present its considerations on the question of ending atomic and hydrogen weapon tests. It is known that negotiations between representatives of the U.S.S.R., the United States and Great Britain at Geneva have been going on for more than two and a half years. However, there are still great difficulties in the road to the conclusion of an agreement.

The Soviet Union has done and is continuing to do everything it can to come to terms with the United States and Great Britain on a treaty to end nuclear weapon tests. It is known that in order to remove obstacles to agreement it has made substantial concessions to the western partners in the talks, having accepted a number of proposals submitted by them.

The position of the Soviet government at the Geneva talks is simple and clear. The Soviet Union wants nuclear weapon tests of all kinds to be ended everywhere and for all time. But the Soviet government cannot agree and will never agree to the test-ban treaty becoming an empty scrap of paper which could be used as a cover for further experiments with nuclear weapons for the purpose of improving them and developing new means of mass destruction. There can be no exemptions from the treaty: all kinds of nuclear weapon tests must be banned —in the air, underwater, underground and in outer space.

In view of the present unsatisfactory position at the Geneva conference, the Soviet government should like to state once more its position on fundamental issues which remain unresolved to this day.

Question of a Moratorium

It is known that the Soviet government agreed to the American proposal that the treaty should temporarily exclude from the ban underground tests of nuclear weapons below a definite threshold value. Now we must reach agreement on a moratorium on underground nuclear explosions temporarily not covered by the treaty.

It goes without saying that the agreement on a moratorium must be of such a nature that no state could violate it arbitrarily and resume test explosions of nuclear bombs. In view of this, the Soviet government is firmly convinced that the expiration of the moratorium, an agreement on which would be reached by the parties concerned, should not absolve states of their commitment not to hold underground nuclear explosions.

Question of Control

The Soviet Union, just as the United States, considers that strict international control must be established over the cessation of the tests. However, it is quite

[1] For the statement of the British delegate, Sir Michael Wright, supporting his United States colleague, see Cmnd. 1397, pp. 59–62.

[2] *Soviet News*, 13 June 1961.

obvious that this control can be effective only if it rests on the mutual consent of the sides and not on the desire to take advantage of the control machinery to impose the will of one group of states upon another group.

The Soviet government has examined all aspects of the question how to safeguard equal rights of the sides in the implementation of control, and has drawn the firm conclusion that the staffing of the control agencies must be based on equal representation of the sides. It is precisely in conformity with this principle that the Soviet Union proposes that an understanding should be reached on the composition of the chief executive agency—the administrative council.

The refusal to accept the proposal on instituting an administrative council of three equal representatives, one each from the principal groups of states—the socialist states, the countries belonging to western military blocs, and the neutralist states—is being justified by allegations that the Soviet Union seeks to obtain some special rights in the control organisation. This assertion, of course, has no foundation whatsoever.

What is the real meaning of the Soviet proposal? It is precisely to preclude the possibility of one side obtaining any special advantages or prejudicing the security of one or another group of states. We want to safeguard, not formal, but real equality of the sides while putting into effect the treaty on a ban on nuclear weapon tests.

The control commission, on which all the principal groups of states will be represented, can adopt sound, just decisions, taking into consideration the interests of all states. However, it is not enough to take such decisions. It is imperative to guarantee their impartial implementation. Impartiality cannot be guaranteed if the implementation of the decisions is entrusted to one man alone.

The history of contemporary international relations knows many instances when one man, being under the influence of some grouping of states or acting for its benefit, has carried out already agreed decisions in an incorrect way. Of course, this benefited only one group of states, whose interests this man furthered, but harmed other states. For it is well known that while there are neutral states there are not—nor can there be—neutral men.

Agreement on the cessation of nuclear weapon tests directly affects the interests of the safety of states, and the government of the United States will undoubtedly agree that maximum caution must be observed in solving this kind of problem. In present conditions, when the world is divided into military blocs, when large armies are maintained, when the threat of a nuclear conflict continues to hang over the world, it is impermissible that questions affecting the interests of the security of states and the destinies of peoples should depend on the decisions of one man.

Furthermore, the appointment of one man for implementing decisions adopted on control can be regarded as dictatorship, a desire to impose one's will. Indeed, it can hardly be expected that the western powers would consent to the appointment of this man from some socialist country. They would rather suggest for this post a man from a neutral country.

But is there any guarantee that such a man would take a neutral, impartial stand with regard to the socialist countries? We cannot agree to such an approach. The Soviet Union cannot tolerate dictatorship from any side. We want to have equal conditions for all and we shall never consent to being placed in an unequal position.

We are confident that the government of the United States subscribes to the opinion that any international agreement must contain guarantees precluding ill-intentioned and unjustified actions against a state, party to the agreement. This is the inalienable and lawful right of each state, each government. In proposing that a collegial executive body of representatives of the three groups of states should be instituted, the Soviet Union proceeds from the desire to guarantee to the states the implementation of precisely this right.

Objecting to the Soviet proposal on the composition of the administrative council, the representatives of the United States and the United Kingdom at the Geneva conference have alleged that it is tantamount to establishing a right of 'veto' with regard to inspections. But such allegations cannot be assessed in any other way than as a continuation of the old line of distorting the position of the U.S.S.R. on control questions.

One might recall in this connection that the Soviet government, as early as May, 1959,[1] explaining its proposal on the establishment of quotas of inspections, emphasised that on-the-spot inspections within the limit of the agreed quotas must be effected at the request of the side interested in the inspection without any voting in the control commission or any other agency.

All that is needed are objective readings of instruments at control posts indicating that a phenomenon has taken place in some part of a given country which must be suspected of being a nuclear explosion. If there is such an objective reading, the Soviet proposal envisages that neither the control commission nor any other body of the control organisation can interfere with the satisfaction of the demand of the side for an inspection. Hence, no obstacles to inspection, to which the United States representatives refer in speaking of the so-called 'veto', can be created by the administrative council.

Of course, there are other questions too, and many of them are bound to arise in the course of carrying out the treaty on the discontinuance of nuclear weapon tests, on which the executive agency will have to take decisions. A situation cannot be tolerated in which unilateral decisions would be taken and conditions for arbitrariness created. The danger of arbitrariness increases several times over if there is a single administrator. The possibility of arbitrariness and unilateral decisions is completely precluded if the structure of the executive agency proposed by the Soviet government is adopted. It follows that the question of a 'veto' is artificially conceived.

The Soviet government is convinced that the adoption of the Soviet Union's proposal on the composition of the administrative council would remove one of the big obstacles to agreement on the treaty.

There is still another question on which there are divergencies. This is the question of the size of the quota of inspections. The Soviet government hopes that the government of the United States will also adopt a realistic approach to the question of the number of on-the-spot inspections. Our proposal for three inspections a year each on the territory of the U.S.S.R., the United States and

[1] *Documents*, 1959, pp. 133–5.

the United Kingdom provides quite adequate guarantees against violations of the treaty on the discontinuance of nuclear weapon tests.

The demand for an excessive number of inspections, on which the United States and the United Kingdom insist, cannot but suggest the idea that in this case concern is by no means being shown for the establishment of effective control.

In assessing the position of states on questions of inspection, one cannot, of course, disregard the circumstance that while there are military groupings of states in the world, inspections can be used for intelligence purposes.

Such is the position with regard to the talks on the cessation of nuclear tests.

We have set forth with the utmost frankness our considerations on the ways to overcome the difficulties that have arisen. Our approach provides a sound foundation for the conclusion in the near future of a treaty on the discontinuance of nuclear weapon tests.

At the same time, objectively assessing the situation existing around the problem of banning nuclear tests, one should, evidently, acknowledge that it appears that the parties to the Geneva talks now find it difficult to agree on the cessation of nuclear tests.

Would it then not be better for our countries to take up the main, cardinal question—the question of general and complete disarmament? In this connection we welcome President Kennedy's statement in his latest message to Congress to the effect that the conclusion of a treaty on an effective ban on nuclear tests would be the first major step towards disarmament. Indeed, let us solve both problems in their interdependence, then the main obstacle will be eliminated which the western powers now see in the Soviet proposal for setting up a three-member administrative council.

The Soviet government, as is well known, has already more than once emphasised that the Soviet government, for its part, is willing unconditionally to accept any western control proposals, if the western powers accept the proposal for general and complete disarmament.

The Soviet government reaffirms its readiness and in that case agrees to sign a document which will include the western proposals on the cessation of nuclear tests.

We can take this step because the question of the security of states would be on a different level in conditions of general and complete disarmament: there would be no armies, nor would there be threats of attack by one state on another.

When all states disarm and have no means of attack on other countries, then conditions will indeed be created under which each country will have proper guarantees of its security. No state will have the possibility of secretly setting up armed forces which will threaten any other state or group of states. In these conditions we are ready to accept any control proposed by the western powers.

Now, when an arms race is under way in the world and antagonistic military groupings exist, we must preserve our armed forces in the interests of the security of our country and our allies. If the armed forces of states are maintained, no control can be separated from intelligence. Control will not be associated with intelligence only when armed forces are abolished and armaments destroyed. Then, indeed, universal control will be necessary to see to it that no state or group of states could secretly manufacture arms or arm themselves to prepare aggression against other states. Strict and effective control against the arming of states cannot be avoided.

At the same time it must be acknowledged that in present conditions control is by no means a guarantee against some country attacking another, because arms and armed forces are not only being maintained but also strengthened, strengthened especially in the field of nuclear weapons, which the United States President has himself admitted. Cessation of nuclear weapon tests does not mean discontinuance of their manufacture and stockpiling, and the risk of war is not reduced. In these conditions, each state has the right to suspect that intelligence agencies might be set up on the plea of control.

If general and complete disarmament is effected, the states will maintain only agreed, restricted contingents of militia or police necessary for maintaining internal order and protecting the personal safety of citizens. These forces cannot create a threat of attack on other countries.

In the case of necessity these contingents can be used by the Security Council if some state nevertheless takes aggressive actions. Of course, all main groups of states must be equally represented in the leadership of such international forces, i.e., it must be really an international leadership.

The Soviet government is profoundly convinced that in our time the most realistic way of solving the disarmament problem is general and complete disarmament under effective international control. This has been acknowledged by the majority of the world's states, as is borne out both by the resolution of the 14th session of the General Assembly[1] and the discussion of disarmament problems at the 15th session of the United Nations General Assembly.

The Soviet government expresses the hope that the government of the United States will take into consideration the ideas set forth in this memorandum and, for its part, will facilitate a solution of the problem of general and complete disarmament, including the tasks of discontinuing for good all nuclear weapon tests.

6. The United States Embassy in Moscow in the Soviet Ministry of Foreign Affairs, 17 June 1961[2]

The Embassy of the United States of America presents its compliments to the Ministry of Foreign Affairs of the Union of Soviet Socialist Republics and has the honor to state the following:

An international agreement for the discontinuance of nuclear weapons tests is and will continue to be a prime objective of the United States Government. The United States and the United Kingdom have proposed a treaty that will achieve this goal. This proposed treaty is the result of almost three years of painstaking effort on the part of the United States and the United Kingdom to work out an effective agreement with the Soviet Union to which we hope other governments would promptly adhere. This agreement would point the way toward ending the arms race in safety and in trust; it would remove any hazards involved in testing.

[1] *Documents*, 1959, p. 115.   [2] *D.S.B.*, 3 July 1961, pp. 18–22.

It would restrict the number of countries producing nuclear weapons, thereby reducing the possibility of nuclear war.

During more than two years of negotiations, prior to their resumption on March 21, 1961, the areas of disagreement between the parties had apparently been substantially narrowed. In fact, it appeared that more progress had been made in this negotiation than in any other in the general field of disarmament. Each side had modified its position in response to the position of the other side. The United States, therefore, redoubled its efforts to find common ground in the hope that this might lead to an agreement.

Beginning with the opening day of the resumed sessions on March 21, the United States and the United Kingdom delegations advanced a series of new proposals.[1] Building upon the base established by the almost three years of arduous negotiation, the United States and the United Kingdom, in an effort to move toward the Soviet point of view, proposed: (1) to fix the number of on-site inspections in the Soviet Union, the United States and the United Kingdom somewhere between twelve and twenty depending upon the annual incidence of suspicious seismic events; (2) to reduce the number of control posts on Soviet territory; (3) to establish a control commission with equal representation for both sides; (4) to institute means for controlling nuclear tests in outer space; (5) to extend to three years the proposed moratorium on those weapons tests which the control system cannot presently detect and which, therefore, will be excluded from the treaty pending the outcome of a research program; and (6) to open up for internal and external inspection the nuclear devices to be used in research on test-detection or for peaceful engineering uses.

There was, unfortunately, no corresponding movement on the part of the Soviet Union to this narrowing of differences between the parties, as might have been anticipated in view of the many Soviet statements as to the importance of arriving at a prompt agreement banning nuclear weapons tests. Instead, since the resumption of the test ban negotiations on March 21, 1961, the Soviet Union has withdrawn its agreement to a single impartial administrator of the control system, and reiterated without change all of its other positions on outstanding issues. It now argues that reaching agreement on a test ban should be subordinated to the solution of other disarmament problems in spite of the fact that it was the Soviet Union that had insisted on separating the two questions at the outset.

The Soviet proposals would prevent achievement of the objective of effective control. They would amount to adoption of the principle of self-inspection and would permit any country, if it wished, to evade the agreement with impunity. At the same time, the Soviet Union proposes, as an alternative to complete acceptance of its position, to choke off negotiations at Geneva, on which so much work has been done, and to merge them into the general disarmament negotiations in which we would have to start all over again.

The positions taken by the Soviet delegation at Geneva and at Vienna and summarized in the Soviet *aide-mémoire* of June 4, 1961,[2] make it appear that the Soviet Union does not want an agreement banning nuclear weapons testing. Nothing in the statements of the Soviet Union explains such a major change in

[1] See above, p. 403, n. 2. [2] Above, p. 433.

its position on a question of fundamental importance to the peoples of the world. In this situation, the United States Government has an obligation to declare its position and to state clearly its disagreement with the Soviet *aide-mémoire*.

The United States believes that a treaty prohibiting nuclear weapons tests, like other agreements in the field of disarmament, must contain effective provisions for control. It has sought to devise a treaty which will provide for such effective control and at the same time assure that no party to the treaty and no operator of the control system could hurt the interests of another party or abuse the authority granted by the treaty. Through long and patient negotiations the United States and the United Kingdom had worked out arrangements with the Soviet Union which delineated the requirements of such a control system and which had appeared to be acceptable to both sides.

The Soviet Union, in its *aide-mémoire* of June 4, 1961, states that it too favors effective international control. But the Soviet proposals and the position taken in the Soviet *aide mémoire* negate the entire concept of effective international control. Moreover, by insisting on vesting control of the inspection system in an unworkable, three-headed administrative council, the Soviet Union has undone all that had been apparently successfully achieved during the long series of previous negotiations to reconcile the requirements of an effective system of inspection with the Soviet concern about security and secrecy. This proposal was a retrograde step from the position previously taken by the Soviet Government in favor of a single, impartial administrator to be chosen by both sides, with his duties prescribed by the treaty.

The *aide-mémoire* mentions that it is necessary only to have the testimony of objective readings of instruments for a party to demand that an inspection be made and that there is no way for the administrative council to put obstacles in the way of inspection. The *aide-mémoire* passes over the fact that there must be some authority within the control system to certify which seismic events, according to objective criteria, are eligible for inspection, and to arrange, direct, and dispatch an inspection team. Under the proposed treaty and certification for inspection, and the dispatch of the inspection teams, would be done by the administrator. Under the Soviet proposal, any member of the administrative council could block the certification of the event as eligible for inspection by simply failing to agree that the criteria have been met. Any member could, in addition, obstruct or delay the dispatching of an on-site inspection team and hence render it ineffective. No matter what explanation is attempted, the fact remains that the Soviet proposal for a tripartite administrative council involves a built-in veto over the operation of the control system.

The Soviet *aide-mémoire* on June 4, 1961, attempts to justify the Soviet position by contending that one man at the head of the inspection system might take arbitrary action against Soviet interests.

The United States representative at Geneva has inquired of the Soviet representative what particular functions of the proposed administrator give the Soviet Union concern. He has pointed out that the powers and duties of the administrator are precisely set out in the treaty. Moreover, he has pointed out that the administrator would receive directions from the control commission set up by the treaty on which both sides in the negotiations would have equal representation and which would have responsibility for all politically important decisions which had not been determined by the treaty itself. There is no reason, therefore, for any signatory nation to fear that positive acts of the administrator could impair its security. What it ought to fear are the possibilities for obstruction, nullification, and confusion, which a three-headed council would multiply intolerably.

The Soviet *aide-mémoire* suggests that the 'Western' powers would most likely nominate for the administrator a person from a 'neutral' country and questions whether such an official even though chosen by unanimous consent 'would take a neutral' stand with regard to the Communist countries. It states that 'there do not and cannot exist, any neutral persons' and questions whether a single administrator could 'ensure impartial implementation' of an agreement.

The United States cannot accept the idea that there are no men in the un-aligned countries with sufficient objectivity and sense of duty to carry out explicit provisions of international agreements. It is the firm belief of the United States that there are such men and they play an important role in the hope for developing a more stable world order. No one should be misled by the fact that the Soviet proposal purports to assign a role to the neutral as a member of the three-man administrative council. It is a role which could be effectively exercised only with the concurrence of the U.S.S.R.

The Soviet proposal for a tripartite administrative council is not, of course, the sole point at issue in the Geneva negotiations. The present Soviet proposals for on-site inspection of possible violations of the nuclear test treaty are completely unworkable. The need for rapid and efficient on-site inspection of such events has been agreed in principle since the 1958 experts conference.[1] However, the technical criteria proposed by the Soviet delegation for judging the eligibility of such disturbances are entirely contrived and would in themselves rule out any possibility for inspection of many events which could in fact be nuclear explosions.

Beyond this, the Soviet Union has proposed that the number of on-site inspections be tightly restricted to three per year. This number represents a completely inadequate sampling of the more than 100 large seismic events which, on the average, will occur every year in the Soviet Union. Only a small percentage of this number can be identified as earthquakes. Any one of the remainder might be a clandestine nuclear test.

The United States has proposed that the number of inspections in the Soviet Union, the United States and the United Kingdom should vary between a maximum of twelve and a maximum of twenty, depending upon the actual number of events that occur. This could hardly represent a threat to the security of the Soviet state or present an opportunity for veiled espionage. To begin with, the inspections would be carried out by international inspection teams whose freedom of movement would be narrowly circumscribed to a very small area and which would operate only in response to carefully defined objective instrument readings. The location of the areas to be inspected would be determined solely by earth tremors which are not within the control of the party requesting inspection. In addition, the United States has proposed a provision which would

---

[1] cf. *Survey*, 1956–58, pp. 561–2.

allow the Soviet Union to assign any number of observers to accompany each inspection team to insure that its members will not engage in espionage activities. If the Soviet Union cannot accommodate this degree of carefully supervised activity in its territory by an international body, the prospect for any appreciable progress towards effectively controlled disarmament in a peaceful world is indeed dim.

The Soviet Union still insists that the chief of any control post established in its own territory be a citizen of the U.S.S.R. The United States believes that this is fundamentally contrary to the aim of objective international surveillance. The Soviet Union insists as well that on-site inspection teams operating in its own territory be staffed in large measure by its own nationals and headed by one of its nationals. This would frustrate completely the purpose of on-site inspection of suspicious events.

The United States is at a loss to understand the Soviet position on the moratorium on small underground tests. It has been clear that under the present state of scientific knowledge the type of control system contemplated in the treaty could not be relied upon for determining whether or not such tests had taken place. The moratorium was proposed to allow time for a joint research program to be pursued vigorously and cooperatively to develop techniques for detecting these small underground tests so that the treaty could be extended to cover them. The Soviet Union has abandoned its original commitment to join in this program and repudiated the position of its scientists that the program is necessary. The present Soviet position means that the Soviet Government attaches no importance to the detection of these explosions and amounts to a demand for a permanent unpoliced ban on small underground nuclear tests. For its part, the United States has allocated a large sum for, and is prepared to carry out, a research program to improve detection techniques so that the treaty can be extended to cover all tests as quickly as possible. The United States calls upon the Soviet Government to join with it in this program.

The *aide-mémoire* of the Soviet Government asks whether it is not better 'to start with the main, cardinal, question, i.e., the question of general and complete disarmament' and suggests that both problems be solved 'interdependently'. Quite apart from this being a total reversal of the Soviet position which originally insisted on treating the test ban separately, the delays and complexities involved in merging the test ban negotiations into the general disarmament discussions are unacceptable.

The delay in reaching a test ban agreement which would result from merging the test ban negotiations into the comprehensive disarmament negotiations suggests that the Soviet Union is attempting to continue a situation in which the United States accepts an unenforced commitment not to test. This would leave the Soviet Union, with its closed society, its Government unaccountable either to a parliament or to an informed public opinion, and its action shrouded in a veil of secrecy, free to conduct nuclear weapons tests without fear of exposure. For almost three years, the United States has been willing to assume the risk of not testing nuclear weapons without the certainty that the Soviet Union has likewise stopped its testing. The national security and defenses of the free world do not allow this risk to be assumed indefinitely.

If the Soviet proposal means that progress in a test ban negotiation be delayed pending agreement in other fields of disarmament it is equally objectionable. The United States believes that the progress already made in the negotiations should be continued, not stopped, and that the chances for reaching agreement on banning nuclear weapons tests should not be pushed further into the future or be made dependent upon progress in other areas of disarmament. The United States believes that the most expeditious and effective way to reach final agreement on a test ban treaty is to keep the test ban talks separate from other disarmament discussions. Moreover, a successful conclusion of the test ban negotiations would facilitate to a great degree progress on other disarmament steps.

To throw away the progress made toward a test ban agreement would mean a setback to the world's hopes for disarmament. It would mean the further proliferation of nuclear weapons and the testing of such weapons by an ever-greater number of countries. In view of the east of clandestine nuclear testing under an unpoliced ban, it means that each government will face an increasing need to take whatever steps may be necessary in its own defense, including nuclear testing. These are the consequences of failure to agree and for which the U.S.S.R., which seems bent on making success impossible, would have to take the responsibility.

There are wider consequences for which the U.S.S.R. would also have to take the responsibility. After World War II, the leading powers joined in establishing a world organization because of a common conviction, resting upon the evidence of history, that a world made up of numerous, separate sovereign powers, acting without regard to their responsibilities in the international community, was a world in which wars were too easily bred. There was a widespread feeling that states must be willing to place some limit upon the free exercise of sovereign powers in the interests of the larger community of nations. This has been the trend of history. Now, the Soviet Government apparently desires to return to a period of history when the sovereign state admitted no limitations to its actions. The positions maintained by the Soviet Union at Geneva appear to mean that, even with all that is at stake, the Soviet Union is not ready to abate in some small degree its regime of secrecy and jealously-guarded sovereignty.

This attitude offers small prospect for a constructive outcome of the Geneva test ban negotiations. It also offers little hope for the development of the kind of world, under an international rule of law, in which general disarmament can take place. The United States urges the U.S.S.R. to give careful consideration to the U.S. position as stated in this note. An effective test ban treaty promptly concluded at the negotiations in Geneva is of the utmost importance to the peoples of the world. To a world grown impatient with protracted tensions and unease, it would signify the willingness of the major powers to subordinate a narrow concept of their national interests to the higher aim of creating a more peaceful and stable world order. It would brighten the prospects for agreement in other areas of conflicting interests. An effective test ban treaty should be signed without delay.

7. The Soviet Ministry of Foreign Affairs to the United States Embassy in Moscow, 5 July 1961[1]

The Ministry of Foreign Affairs of the U.S.S.R. pays its respects to the Embassy of the United States of America and has the honour of stating the following:

The Soviet government has considered the reply of the United States government of June 17, 1961,[2] to the memorandum on the question of the discontinuance of nuclear weapon tests, handed to the United States President, Mr. J. Kennedy, during his meeting with N. S. Khrushchev, Chairman of the Council of Ministers of the U.S.S.R., in Vienna on June 4 this year.[3]

It follows from this reply that the United States government, unfortunately, has not agreed to the Soviet government's proposals aimed at facilitating and speeding up the solution of the problem of discontinuing for ever the tests of atomic and nuclear weapons.

The entire contents, and the very tenor of the reply Note of the United States government show that instead of a businesslike and constructive exchange of opinions the government of the United States has taken a different course, the course of distorting the Soviet proposals and of idle allegations about the Soviet Union's position. The United States government is clearly striving to exacerbate the polemics and to introduce at the same time elements which have no bearing on the question under discussion.

All this, apparently, is being done in an effort to free the United States of responsibility for the futility of the Geneva talks. There is no sign of even a shadow of desire to facilitate agreement on banning nuclear tests. On the contrary, the American Note suggests the idea that the United States government has now only one concern—how to justify in the eyes of public opinion the resumption of nuclear weapon tests now being prepared in the United States, and on what pretext to burn the bridges leading to an agreement between the powers on banning such tests.

Indeed, the American press makes no bones about the fact that the United States Defence Department, the Pentagon and the American Atomic Energy commission are eagerly waiting for the day when a signal will be given to them to continue nuclear tests.

It is for this reason, obviously, that the United States government is trying to present in a distorted light the whole course of the three-power talks in Geneva.

The Soviet government finds it necessary to recall the basic facts pertaining to the talks on the question of discontinuing atomic and hydrogen weapon tests and, specifically, to the position of the sides at the Geneva conference.

For many years the Soviet Union has been consistently coming out for the world to be freed for ever of any nuclear explosions, which intensify the atomic arms race and jeopardise the life and health of the people. It was none other than the Soviet Union who was the first of the atomic powers to raise the question of the necessity of ending without delay the dangerous experiments with nuclear weapons.

Wishing to facilitate an international agreement on this question, the Soviet

---

[1] *Soviet News*, 10 July 1961.　　　[2] Above, p. 435.　　　[3] Above, p. 433.

Union, as far back as March, 1958, unilaterally discontinued nuclear weapon tests, although the U.S.S.R. was known to have staged less experimental explosions than the United States and Britain. What was the reply of the governments of the United States and Britain to this? They replied with an unprecedentedly intensive series of experimental explosions of nuclear bombs. But the Soviet Union adhered to its line for the discontinuance of nuclear tests everywhere and without delay.

In 1959 the Soviet government took a decision not to resume nuclear explosions, provided the western powers, on their part, did not stage such explosions.[1] The Soviet Union strictly abided by its commitment in spite of the fact that France—an ally of the United States and Great Britain in the N.A.T.O. military bloc—is regularly staging nuclear tests.

The three-power Geneva conference itself was convened precisely as a result of the Soviet Union's insistent efforts. The whole history of the Geneva talks is, in the first place, the history of the Soviet Union's tireless search for mutually acceptable solutions with regard to the prohibition of all nuclear weapon tests. It is known that the Soviet government, with a view to reaching agreement, accepted a number of American and British proposals on important points of the treaty which was being drafted. And if definite progress was made at the Geneva conference, it was primarily a result of the good will and sincere striving of the Soviet Union to advance the cause of the discontinuance of tests.

And what was the position of the government of the United States and of other western powers? On various artificial pretexts they blocked the solution of this problem. Who does not know that it was precisely the western powers, and the government of the United States of America in the first place, which for a long time came out against the test ban talks in general.

If the Geneva conference is regarded, not through a distorting mirror, as the United States government is trying to do, but in a true light, then it will be evident to any more or less objective observer that in point of fact the United States has been making efforts throughout the Geneva conference to prevent an agreement on the discontinuance of nuclear weapon tests from being outlined. Many facts go to show that, but for the position of the United States and Great Britain aimed at thwarting agreement, the work of the Geneva conference would have long ago been completed and an agreement signed.

A favourable situation was, for instance, taking shape in 1958 after the conference of experts of the United States, Britain, the Soviet Union and other countries who thoroughly discussed the methods of detecting nuclear explosions and outlined unanimous recommendations on the question of control over the discontinuance of atomic and hydrogen weapon tests. It remained only for the governments which are taking part in the talks and which approved these recommendations to conclude quickly on this basis an agreement on ending all nuclear weapon tests.

At the conference of representatives of the U.S.S.R., the United States and Great Britain, which opened in Geneva, agreement was reached on a number of articles of the draft treaty on the discontinuance of tests. But this, apparently, seriously alarmed those circles in the United States of America which feared,

[1] *Documents*, 1959, p. 137.

and still fear, the very prospect of nuclear tests being banned. Indeed, it is a fact that the American government backed out and made attempts to revise and, in point of fact, to reject the recommendations of the scientist-experts which had been approved by this government itself.

The United States government worked hard to discredit these recommendations. Its representatives specially pressed the point that the system of control over underground explosions, worked out by the experts in 1958, would, allegedly, be inadequate. On the basis of this far-fetched argument the United States at first demanded exclusion from the treaty of all provisions referring to the prohibition of underground nuclear weapon tests. In view of the Soviet Union's resolute objections, they then came out with a proposal to exclude from the treaty the question of underground nuclear weapon tests below a certain magnitude.

The United States representatives invariably tried to justify their demands by alleging that the control system evolved by the experts was unreliable. Meanwhile, the scientist-experts who had worked out the recommendations are of the opinion that now all possibilities already exist for detecting any violation by states of an agreement on the discontinuance of tests, and consequently, for ensuring that the states fulfil their commitments.

But even if the control system is to some extent inadequate, this can by no means be pleaded as an obstacle to reaching agreement, because with the progress of science and engineering better and better instruments will be designed and, consequently, the system of control will be improved. Therefore that part of the draft treaty which was agreed upon includes a provision that two years after the treaty on the discontinuance of tests goes into force, and then annually, the control organisation will be able to introduce improvements in the control system on the basis of the experience accumulated and of scientific progress.

The United States government is deliberately ignoring this important provision, agreement on which was reached as a result of prolonged efforts. The references to a technical inadequacy of control methods show once again that the United States is not interested in honest agreement on a treaty which would end nuclear tests once and for all and is looking for all sorts of loopholes to circumvent the treaty and convert it into a scrap of paper.

Is this not proved by the fact that the United States, trying to impose such a treaty, demands that the cessation of underground tests of atomic bombs of small magnitude (the so-called moratorium on such explosions) be established for only three years? But what meaning would there be in an agreement on a moratorium such as is suggested by the United States? In fact it would result in the U.S.S.R.'s territory being placed under control and in three years' time the United States would have the possibility of resuming nuclear weapon tests on some artificial pretext.

It is clear to everyone that control over the discontinuance of nuclear tests would, under such conditions, turn into the collection of espionage information.

Thus the United States' position on the question of underground tests already renders agreement impossible. But this is not the only question on which the United States government has demonstrated its unwillingness to conclude an agreement.

In its Note the United States government has tried to advertise the proposals advanced by the United States delegation at the Geneva conference recently. But in doing so it carefully passes in silence the fact that the United States government's position has not changed on the essential points, namely, on the question of recognising the fully equality of the sides and ensuring them equal conditions of control without which agreement is unthinkable. If there is a serious approach to the conclusion of an agreement, then, first of all, all these barriers must be removed, because only in such a case will the Geneva conference be able to break out of the deadlock and will the road to agreement be cleared.

In this connection it is impossible to pass in silence the United States government's objections to the proposals of the Soviet government for the control organisation to be headed, not by one administrator, but by an administrative council consisting of equal representatives of the three main groups of states: the socialist states, the capitalist states affiliated with western military blocs, and the neutral states.

In proposing the establishment of an administrative council with such a composition, the Soviet government proceeded from the real facts of international life today, from the need to create equal conditions for the representatives of all three groups of states and preclude any possibility of the executive authority in the control organ being abused and being detrimental to the security of the countries which sign the treaty.

The United States government also admits in its Note of June 17 that the control system must be organised in such a way that not one of the signatories to the treaty and not one of the persons in the control system could damage the interests of one or another side or abuse the authority they are invested with on the strength of the treaty. But the United States government contradicts itself by insisting that the executive authority in the control organ should be placed in the hands of one person.

Indeed, experience shows that there is no such person as one who could have an unbiased approach to this or that international event, to this or that social system. This is not surprising, because no person can live in a society without being influenced by one ideology or another and by relations existing between different groups inside that society. That is why, while neutral countries do exist, there are not and cannot be any neutral persons.

Examples—and very instructive ones at that—are not far to seek. The tragedy of the Congo graphically showed to the whole world how dangerous it is to entrust the task of fulfilling important decisions to one person. Only the politically blind can fail to see that it is precisely with the help of Hammarskjöld, who poses as a neutral person, that the colonialists have been and are committing monstrous crimes on Congolese soil. It was none other than Hammarskjöld who, to please the colonialists, turned upside down the Security Council's decisions aimed at protecting the national independence of the Congo.

Using Hammarskjöld and the United Nations officials appointed by him as catspaws, the colonialists are stifling the liberation forces in the Congo and making short work of Congolese patriots. Is it possible to regard Hammarskjöld's behaviour in the Congo as neutral when he is violating elementary justice, giving protection to the murderers of Patrice Lumumba, that passionate fighter for the independence of the Congo?

No, on the question of the Congo, as well as on other international matters, Hammarskjöld is not neutral, although he is a representative of neutral Sweden. In fact he has been, and remains, a proponent of the policy of only one group of states, namely, the capitalist states. And after all this the United States government is trying to impose a man similar to Hammarskjöld as the only administrator in the organ which is called upon to exercise control over the discontinuance of nuclear weapon tests!

It goes without saying that no state to which the cause of peace is dear will be willing to repeat the experiment with another Hammarskjöld—all the more so on questions affecting the most vital interests of the peoples, the interests of their security.

How is it possible to preclude any unilateral actions in the control organ which would infringe the lawful interests of any signatory states of the treaty? The Soviet government asked itself this question and on the basis of an exhaustive study of this problem arrived at the firm conclusion that only an executive organ consisting of equal representatives of the three main groups of states could ensure fair and unbiased control over the fulfilment of commitments assumed by the states.

Objecting to the equal co-operation of representatives of the three main groups of states in the main executive organ of the control organisation, the United States government again claims that such co-operation would render this organ, inefficient and would be tantamount to introducing the right of 'veto'. But speaking of the right of 'veto', it is precisely the United States government that wants to invest the sole administrator with such a right. Indeed, the United States wants the person placed at the head of the control organ to decide whether this or that phenomenon the checking of which is demanded by a signatory of the treaty is subject to inspection or not.

The result is that this administrator would actually have the right of 'veto', which would enable him not only to hamper inspection where it was needed but also to prevent it in general. And since an administrator cannot be neutral, his decisions could not be expected to be objective. The state whose interests would be unlawfully infringed by the administrator would, naturally, not agree to his demands. This, in fact, would paralyse the work of control and render it ineffective.

The legitimate question therefore arises: Who in fact is insisting on introducing the right of 'veto' and on establishing an inefficient control organ—the Soviet Union, which suggests the establishment of a tripartite administrative council on an equal footing, or the United States, which is demanding that the control organ should be placed at the disposal of one person who, as the United States expects, must serve as a tool of the western powers?

In the view of this there can be no other opinion than that the United States government is striving to establish an organ in which it would be guaranteed unilateral privileges and which would be dominated by the 'veto' right possessed by the placeman of one group of states, the actions of which—for instance, in the United Nations—and international law are incompatible concepts, as has been proved by experience.

The position of the Soviet Union completely precludes the possibility of any arbitrariness in carrying out inspection. The Soviet Union's proposals for annual quotas of on-the-spot inspections clearly state that within the limits of the agreed quotas inspection is carried out at the request of the opposite side, and no one—neither the control commission nor the administrative council, nor any other organ of the control organisation—can prevent the rights of states to inspection within the quota from being exercised, if objective indications of the instruments testify to the existence of a suspicious phenomenon.

The Soviet government and its head, N. S. Khrushchev, have repeatedly declared that the Soviet Union has not demanded for itself and does not demand any special position or domination in the control organ. The Soviet Union seeks to secure for itself the same rights as will be enjoyed by all other participants of the treaty.

The United States government points out in its Note that for nearly three years the United States has been taking the 'risk' of abstaining from nuclear weapon tests without having an international agreement on this matter and that it cannot continue to take this 'risk' endlessly.

If this is how the question is put, it must be said that it was the Soviet Union and not the United States that was running the risk. Indeed, it is well known that whereas the U.S.S.R. is staging no experimental explosions of nuclear weapons, the United States' ally in the military N.A.T.O. bloc—France—is carrying out nuclear weapon tests and thus has the possibility of improving this weapon also in the interests of the United States of America, as her ally in this bloc.

General and complete disarmament would be the cardinal solution of the problem, ensuring the prevention of another world war. In conditions in which the western powers, seeking unilateral military advantages, have brought the test ban talks to a deadlock, the way out of the existing situation is to be sought in linking the solution of the problem of general and complete disarmament with that of the discontinuance of nuclear weapon tests. The advantage of such a solution is that it removes the main obstacle which the western powers now see in the Soviet proposals for setting up a three-member administrative council.

As Chairman of the U.S.S.R. Council of Ministers N. S. Khrushchev stressed at the meeting of the United Nations General Assembly, if the western powers accept the proposal for general and complete disarmament, the Soviet government, for its part, is prepared to accept unconditionally any proposals by the western powers for control.

Objecting to the interlinking of the solution of the problem of the discontinuance of nuclear weapon tests and the problem of general and complete disarmament, the United States government pretends not to notice this agreement by the the Soviet Union to the forms of control suggested by the western powers, in conditions of general and complete disarmament being implemented.

Noteworthy also are the statements made by the United States government in its Note of June 17 that if both questions were considered simultaneously an agreement on the question of discontinuing nuclear weapon tests would be endlessly put off and that it would be necessary 'to start everything from the beginning', and so on.

It inevitably follows from these words that the United States and their western allies in military blocs intend to delay endlessly the conclusion of a treaty on general and complete disarmament, thus assuming grave responsibility for all the consequences. The Soviet government cannot agree that everything would have to be started from the beginning again in the talks on general and complete disarmament.

Nearly two years have passed since the Soviet Union advanced the proposals for general and complete disarmament. This problem was discussed in detail for several months in the ten-power disarmament committee which was in session last year.

The Soviet government had hoped that the new American Administration would revise the policy of the Eisenhower government on this issue, a policy which cannot be described in any other way than obstructionist. But in view of the statements contained in the United States Note, and in the light of some other facts, it is necessary to recognise that these hopes have not been justified so far.

The U.S.S.R. government would like to express the hope that both great powers—the U.S.S.R. and the United States—will find a common language on the disarmament problem.

General and complete disarmament has now become a pressing historical necessity, the surest way to lasting peace on earth. And though the question of ending the tests is of considerable importance and an agreement on it would be an important step toward disarmament, it should be clearly realised that ending nuclear tests cannot in itself eliminate the menace of atomic war and put an end to the arms race.

General and complete disarmament is necessary if the great task of ridding mankind of wars and the burden of armaments is to be accomplished. It is necessary to break up and destroy the military establishments of states.

The Soviet government agrees that the successful conclusion of the talks on the discontinuance of nuclear tests would contribute to progress in other disarmament measures and it has, for its part, done everything possible to achieve this, and is continuing to do so. But it follows from the Note of June 17 that the government of the United States of America now wants to use the outcome of the three-power Geneva conference, which is dealing only with the question of ending nuclear tests, as a preliminary condition for the solution of a much broader and more important problem, that of general and complete disarmament.

Thus, while on the one hand the United States government has made considerable efforts to lead the Geneva conference into an impasse, on the other hand it is now making the fate of the talks on the problem of disarmament in general conditional upon the outcome of the talks in Geneva.

This is strange logic, to say the least. It can only play into the hands of those who want to sabotage both the talks on general and complete disarmament and the talks on ending nuclear tests.

It is to be regretted that the government of the United States has found it possible, in its Note, to take the slippery road of attacks on the social system of the Soviet Union. What is this—a manifestation of animosity towards communism or an attempt to divert attention from the weakness of the United States' position on questions of disarmament?

The Soviet government has no intention of starting a discussion with the government of the United States on the question of which form of society, the socialist or the capitalist, is an 'open' one and which is a 'closed' one.

The government of the U.S.S.R. proceeds from the assumption that if the feelings the sides have with regard to each other's social system are given free rein in considering the question of disarmament, the question of ending nuclear tests or, in general, any question of inter-governmental relations, we shall then have to admit that any possibility of agreement is, in effect precluded, in advance.

The Soviet government has always abided by this viewpoint and considers it to be the only correct one. However, since the United States government has touched upon this question, we should like to say with the utmost clarity that Soviet society is indeed firmly and reliably closed to the activities of exploiters and oppressors of all stripes who grow rich on the sweat and blood of the people. It is closed to all who are enemies of the social and state system of the U.S.S.R. But it opens up unlimited possibilities for the satisfaction of the needs and desires of the working people, who enjoy all fullness of power in the Soviet Union and are the absolute masters of the fruits of their labour.

And to whom is American society open? It is open only to the exploiters, to a handful of monopolies which have put the entire powers of the state in the service of their selfish interests.

It ill becomes the government of a country whose system is founded on the brutal exploitation of man by man to preach democracy to the Soviet people.

If the claims the American leaders like to make, that all secrets are open to everyone in the United States, that the public there is informed of every step of the government and other official agencies, if these claims are correct, how then would the United States government reply to these questions, for instance:

Did the American people, or even such a highly placed body as the United States Congress, know of the provocative flights by American U-2 planes over the U.S.S.R.? They didn't, apparently, before the flights were exposed and those responsible caught redhanded.

Was it with the approval of the American people that atomic bombs were dropped on Hiroshima and Nagasaki? No, the American people knew nothing of the preparations for this inhuman act and, as far as is known, they condemn it.

Lastly, were the American people consulted when the recent aggression against Cuba was prepared and organised from the territory and with the support of the United States? No, it was kept a close secret from the American people.

All these facts apparently fit easily within the meaning of the 'free' and 'open' society so much vaunted in the American government's Note, but there is no place for them within a truly free and a truly open society.

It has long been known that some foreign military headquarters are eagerly waiting for the Soviet Union to open its state frontiers and thus facilitate espionage operations on Soviet territory.

The western governments frequently bow to the demands of these bodies and follow their line even at international talks. Is this not the reason, specifically, for the pressing demands of the western powers for the utmost increase in the number of on-the-spot inspections which are to oversee compliance with the cessation of nuclear tests on the territory of the U.S.S.R.? Everything goes to show that the government of the United States is prepared to sacrifice to the interests of intelligence the achievement of agreement on the ending of nuclear tests.

The Soviet government has repeatedly declared that it is prepared to introduce in its country all the control measures necessary to carry out the agreement on the ending of nuclear weapon tests. But the Soviet government considers it necessary to stress once more that it will never agree to control being divorced from disarmament and constituting control over armaments, which the United States has been pressing for for many years in the United Nations, among other places.

The Soviet Union declares, at the same time, that it will never agree to any disarmament measures without effective control over their implementation. The Soviet government will not agree to disarmament without control, as bitter experience has taught it not to rely on the word of its western partners in agreements.

The Soviet government abides firmly by the views put forward in its memorandum of June 4 this year. It would like the government of the United States to have a correct understanding of the viewpoint of the Soviet Union, as this would help find the basis for agreement on both the problem of general and complete disarmament and the question of ending the tests of atomic and hydrogen weapons.

8. The United States Embassy in Moscow to the Soviet Ministry of Foreign Affairs, 15 July 1961[1]

The Embassy of the United States of America presents its compliments to the Ministry of Foreign Affairs of the Union of Soviet Socialist Republics and has the honor to state the following:

The United States Government has examined the reply of the Soviet Government of July 5, 1961 to the note of the Government of the United States of June 17, 1961 on the question of the nuclear test ban negotiations. Apparently in an effort to avoid the question of halting nuclear weapons tests under effective international control, the Soviet note contains a multitude of irrelevant and unwarranted comments. The United States Government sees no point in replying to these comments.

Instead, the United States Government prefers to confine its reply to the Soviet Government to the central issue in the nuclear-test negotiations. This issue is clear; it is whether the Soviet Union is now willing and prepared to reach an accord which would halt nuclear-weapons tests under effective international control. For its part, the United States is fully prepared to accept all the necessary international controls in its territory to insure that nuclear testing is effectively halted. It fails to understand why the Soviet Union considers that these same controls, which are strictly limited in scope to fit technical and organizational requirements, would jeopardize its national security.

[1] *D.S.B.*, 31 July 1961, pp. 184–6.

In an effort to achieve a basis for final agreement at the earliest possible time, the Governments of the United States and the United Kingdom have made numerous proposals designed to accommodate Soviet positions on international inspection and control. In many cases these proposals have met the Soviet position completely. Yet the reaction of the Soviet Government to our efforts to narrow the gap between the two sides has been to create new obstacles to agreement and lately to propose that a treaty banning nuclear weapon tests should await agreement on, and perhaps indeed implementation of, general and complete disarmament.

The United States stands ready to negotiate a general disarmament agreement as rapidly as this can be done. It is clear that an immediate agreement to end nuclear weapon tests would aid in the achievement of such a disarmament agreement and, equally clear, that failure to reach agreement on a test ban would in all likelihood hinder efforts to conclude swiftly an accord on disarmament. The fact that the Soviet Union resists so strenuously the limited control measures required by a nuclear test ban treaty can only cause grave concern for the possibilities of achieving effectively controlled disarmament.

This contrast between the attitudes of the Governments of the United States and the United Kingdom, on the one hand, and the Soviet Government on the other has been and is being brought into sharp relief in the conference proceedings on the question of how the control system should be managed and directed.

An issue which the Soviet Government had long described as one of the most important facing the conference was the issue of the composition of the control commission. The United States and the United Kingdom have agreed to equality of representation with the Soviet Union on this supreme supervising organ of the control system. There would be four representatives from each of the two sides and three neutral representatives, The Soviet Union and its allies would participate directly in the control commission in its task of setting the guidelines for operation of the control system and maintaining supervision over it.

Despite this significant move, which gave the Soviet Union an equal voice with the United States and the United Kingdom in guiding the affairs of the control system, the Soviet Union demanded still greater powers to impose its will on the control organization. Retreating from an agreed provision of the treaty, the Soviet Union has unfortunately chosen to advance the proposal that day-to-day administrative and executive authority over the international control system be exercised by a three-man administrative council. This council, on which each of the two nuclear sides and nonassociated states would be represented, could take action only by unanimous consent so that the implementation of both the decisions of the control commission and the provisions of the treaty itself could be freely frustrated or vetoed. The effect of this proposal would be the paralysis of the entire control organization and would surely make a mockery of effective international inspection.

It cannot be argued that this new Soviet proposal was necessary to protest Soviet security interests. Under agreed provisions of the treaty, the Soviet Union has received ample assurance that administration of the control system will be competent and impartial. The administrator is made accountable to the policy-making control commission and works under its continuous supervision. His appointment and the appointment of his first deputy requires the concurring vote of the Soviet Union. The Soviet Union has the right to nominate two deputy administrators. The staff of the control organization is appropriately divided so as to provide quality between the two nuclear sides. Decisions as to the total amount of each annual budget, and the decisions as to amendment of the treaty, require the concurring vote of the Soviet Union. From this it is abundantly clear that concern over the administrator's activities could not have been the motivating cause for this Soviet demand for a tripartite administrative council.

In an attempted justification for its tripartite administrative council proposal, the Soviet Government states that 'there is no one person who can live in a society and not be influenced by one or another ideology and by mutual relations which exist between different groups within society. Neutral countries exist, but there are not and cannot be neutral people.'

The Government of the United States believes that this rejection of the idea of an international civil servant acting impartially under guidance from international policy-making organs constitutes nothing less than an attack upon the executive capacity of any international organization for effective action.

There are, of course, many people who are capable of exercising independent judgment in behalf of the international community; the whole history of international organizations bears witness to this fact. The United States rejects this Soviet contention categorically and is convinced that nations which do not wish to submit to the domination of great powers will also reject it.

This is a striking example of the Soviet Union's attempt to sabotage the Geneva nuclear test ban negotiations. It is not the only example, however, as was pointed out in the June 17 note of the United States Government. The Soviet refusal to accept more than three on-site inspections a year; the demand that international control posts and inspection teams in Soviet territory be headed by Soviet nationals; the Soviet insistence on criteria for on-site inspection which would seldom, if ever, permit an on-site inspection to be made regardless of how suspicious a detected event might be—all these are examples of the Soviet resistance to negotiating an effective nuclear test ban agreement in Geneva.

For its part, the United States Government must express its profound regret at the turn of events that has taken place in the test ban conference. The United States still regards the reaching of an agreement as a prime objective of its national policy. It repeats its readiness to negotiate in a reasonable spirit with the Soviet Government on the terms of a test ban treaty. Despite the lateness of the hour, the United States believes that the Soviet Government cannot be insensible to the demands of millions of people everywhere that agreement be reached urgently to ban nuclear weapons tests under effective control.

A binding treaty with effective controls would guarantee against hazards involved in testing; it would be a first step along the road towards accord on disarmament and towards the improvement of East-West relations; and it would inhibit the spread of nuclear weapons manufacturing capability. The prize we seek is too valuable and the consequences of our failure to win it are too serious to permit the luxury of indulging in narrow and temporary national interests. The United States Government makes common cause with all humanity when it urges the Soviet Government to allow the negotiators at Geneva to get on with their work.

9. The Soviet Ministry of Foreign Affairs to the United States Embassy in Moscow, 9 August 1961[1]

The Foreign Ministry of the U.S.S.R. acknowledges receipt of the Note of the United States Embassy of July 15, this year, on the question of ending nuclear weapon tests and considers it necessary to state the following:

Having studied the United States Note, the Soviet government is compelled to conclude that the government of the United States stands by its former positions and shows no readiness to solve the problem of ending nuclear weapon tests on a mutually acceptable basis.

From this Note and from other official documents of the United States government, and also from the negotiations which have been going on for years, it is evident that the efforts of the United States are in fact aimed mainly at legalising the holding of tests in any agreement—if such an agreement were signed—and creating an international control agency which would be a pliant tool in the hands of the western powers and would be used by their general staffs to collect the intelligence information they require.

Such an attitude on the part of the U.S.A. makes impossible the signing of an agreement to end nuclear tests and is plainly not designed to achieve this end. The responsibility for this situation rests with the governments of the United States and Great Britain.

The Soviet government has stated its position very fully in its aide-mémoire of June 4 and its Note of July 5 this year. It firmly intends to continue adhering to this position in the future too.

Objectively assessing the situation existing on the problem of ending nuclear weapon tests and guided by the desire to relieve mankind for ever of the threat of a nuclear war, the Soviet government has proposed a reliable and realistic course leading to the ending for all time of all kinds of nuclear weapon tests.

This course is the interdependent solution of the problem of ending nuclear weapon tests and the problem of general and complete disarmament. The conclusion of a treaty on general and complete disarmament would completely remove those obstacles which the western powers have erected to the conclusion of an agreement on the ending of nuclear weapon tests.

This proposal of the Soviet Government accords with the demands of the peoples of all countries—that an end be put to the dangerous arms race, and that the threat of a devastating nuclear war be averted.

As for the Soviet Union, it is ready at any moment to sign a treaty on general and complete disarmament of the states and to accept any proposals of the western powers concerning international control over the implementation of such an agreement.

The Soviet government is entitled to insist that the United States government should closely study the Soviet Union's proposals aimed at the earliest solution of the problem of general and complete disarmament, and thus also of the

_____
[1] *Soviet News*, 14 August 1961.

problem of ending all nuclear weapon tests for all time, and should make its contribution to the great cause of consolidating peace among the nations.

10. Soviet Government statement, 30 August 1961[1]

The peoples are witnessing the ever-increasing aggressiveness of the policy of the N.A.T.O. military bloc. The United States and its allies are spinning the flywheel of their military machine ever faster, whipping up the arms race, to an unprecedented extent, increasing the strength of armies and making the tension in the international situation red-hot. Matters have reached a point where the leading statesmen of the United States and its allies are resorting to threats of having recourse to arms and unleashing war as a counter measure to the conclusion of a peace treaty with the German Democratic Republic.

Being faced with these facts, which cannot fail to cause anxiety, the Soviet government considers it its duty to take all necessary measures so that the Soviet Union may be completely prepared to render harmless any aggressor if he tries to launch an attack. The tragedy of the first months of the Great Patriotic War, when Hitler attacked the U.S.S.R., having ensured for himself a superiority in military equipment, is too fresh in peoples' memories to allow this to happen now. This is the reason why the Soviet government has already taken a number of serious measures to strengthen the security of the U.S.S.R. For the same reason, after a thoughtful and comprehensive examination of this question, it has taken a decision to carry out experimental explosions of nuclear weapons.

Being fully conscious of the importance and responsibility of this serious step, the government of the Soviet Union considers it necessary to explain to the Soviet people and to all mankind the meaning and significance of the decision, the sole aim of which is to do everything possible to prevent the catastrophe which a third world war would represent for the hundreds of millions of inhabitants of our planet.

Those who are preparing a new world holocaust are sowing illusions that a new war, if it were unleashed, would, so they allege, be waged without thermonuclear weapons. But this is deception of the peoples.

The experience of history teaches us that it has never been possible to keep the fire of war within predetermined limits. Wars have stern and inexorable laws of their own. An aggressor starts a war in order to bring his victim to its knees and to impose his will on it. But even the aggressor is aware that in the event of defeat the fate that he was preparing for his victim will befall him. Therefore every state that takes part in a war, regardless of whether it is attacking or defending, will stop at nothing to achieve victory and will not accept defeat without having used and expended every means of waging war in its possession. Under these conditions any armed conflict, even if insignificant at first, would inevitably grow into a universal rocket and nuclear war if the nuclear powers were drawn into it.

The desire of peoples to put an end to the arms race and to free themselves for ever from devastating wars is especially near and dear to the Soviet people,

_____
[1] *Soviet News*, 31 August 1961.

who have recently seen a war in their own house and paid with unparalleled losses for the restoration of peace. But everything which people went through in past wars pales in comparison with the horrors which can be let loose on them by merely a few thermonuclear bombs. And today, not a dozen, not a hundred, but thousands of such bombs are in the arsenals of the great powers. As one of the nuclear powers, the Soviet Union has accumulated enough sicentific and technological knowledge about the destructive power of new types of weapons, about means of delivery of thermonuclear charges to their target, and about the consequences of using such weapons to be fully aware of the character of modern war.

The Soviet government was the first to raise its voice in favour of general and complete disarmament, in favour of stopping nuclear weapon tests. It has repeatedly submitted to the United Nations specific proposals that ensure the achievement of that aim. From the rostrum of the United Nations, in the messages and statements of the head of the Soviet government, N. S. Khrushchev, and wherever representatives of the socialist camp have met representatives of the western countries there has been heard the sincere and ardent appeal of the Soviet Union that agreement be reached to destroy, once and for all and under the strictest international control, all types of armaments to the last bomb and to the last shell, to disband armies to the last soldier, to abolish completely General Staffs and military institutions.

It will not be an exaggeration to consider that even today mankind could be living in a world without weapons or armies had the governments of the United States, Britain and France and some other member-states of the western military blocs manifested a reciprocal striving for this.

The opponents of disarmament still pretend that the different approach of the Soviet Union and the western powers to the question of control is an obstacle to an agreement on disarmament. No one denies that the establishment of international control over disarmament, which involves the most sensitive interests of states, the interests of their security, is a complicated and delicate matter. The question of control has for years been a stumbling block in the way of agreement on disarmament. This has been so because control has been used by the western powers as a pretext for turning down any proposal on disarmament.

Even before, they were never anxious to achieve control over disarmament. This was most explicitly said from the rostrum of the United Nations by the former President of the United States, Dwight D. Eisenhower, who unequivocally stated that it was not a question of control over disarmament but of control over armaments.

In order not to allow the essence of the matter—disarmament itself—to be ruined, the Soviet government has stated openly that it is ready to accept in advance any proposal of the western powers on international control. Only one thing was expected of the western powers and this was that they should accept our proposals on general disarmament and submit their own proposals on general control.

Yet strange though it was, those who had hitherto expressed so much concern about international control, seemingly lost the power of speech when given unlimited opportunities to formulate and execute their ideas regarding a system of international control.

What can be the explanation for the fact that no specific proposals on that subject have as yet followed from the western powers? This can be explained only by fear that the Soviet Union will accept their proposals on control and then the western powers would either have to agree to general and complete disarmament or would utterly expose themselves as opponents of disarmament and as opponents of control over disarmament.

The main thing in our day is disarmament, general and complete, and an agreement on such disarmament would cover the question of nuclear tests.

Indeed, when the arms race is stopped and when the weapons that have been stockpiled are destroyed, there will be no incentives for the improvement of weapons and consequently no incentives for carrying out experimental nuclear tests. But, on the other hand, merely an agreement on stopping nuclear weapon tests cannot by itself put an end to the arms race. The states that already possess atomic weapons will inevitably feel tempted to act in violation of such an agreement and seek ever new ways and loopholes for perfecting weapons, to say nothing of the fact that the tests carried out by three or four powers are quite sufficient for unlimited stockpiling of the most dangerous thermonuclear weapons of the existing types.

The states which do not yet possess thermonuclear weapons will in their turn try to create them, in spite of an agreement prohibiting nuclear tests.

Incidentally, they can put forward arguments which the champions of nuclear disarmament will have difficulty in parrying. Indeed, is it realistic to expect that a situation will continue for long in which some states that are far advanced in developing atomic power for military purposes will continue to manufacture mountains of atom and hydrogen bombs on the basis of the experiments already carried out, while others will watch idly how they are lagging further and further behind the nuclear powers as regards their military strength, and consequently in the capacity for ensuring their security?

Experience proves the contrary.

There was a time when a monopoly of atomic weapons existed in the world and the United States tried to retain it. Taking advantage of the fact that it had in its hands weapons of which no other state had the equivalent at that time, the United States was testing atom bombs whenever and wherever it liked, without paying heed to what the peoples thought or said about it. The United States did not shrink even from testing this monstrous weapon on human beings —children, women, old people—dropping atom bombs on the Japanese cities of Hiroshima and Nagasaki, on the land of an enemy who had actually already been routed. Brandishing the atom bomb, those who at that time determined the policy of the United States were trying to dictate their will almost to the entire world and trying to blackmail the socialist countries. An extremely dangerous situation arose.

The Soviet people were compelled to mobilise all their material and spiritual resources to break the atomic monopoly of the United States, which had become a threat to peace, and to create within the shortest possible period of time their own nuclear weapons.   Soon the circle of nuclear powers expanded. Britain also joined it.

The peoples realised in time what a danger was involved in the inclusion in the arms race of ever new countries, and they enthusiastically responded to the demand that nuclear tests be stopped. The Soviet Union became the standard-bearer of those demands. For many years it consistently and unswervingly fought for the cessation of all kinds of nuclear tests everywhere and for all time.

For this purpose it discontinued nuclear tests unilaterally, although such an action on its part involved a certain risk, since the United States and Great Britain had by that time carried out a greater number of nuclear explosions than the Soviet Union. It was due to the initiative and efforts of the Soviet Union that negotiations between the three nuclear powers began in Geneva, in the course of which the Soviet government patiently sought mutually acceptable solutions, repeatedly taking important steps forward to meet the wishes of the United States and Great Britain.

Yet with what line did the western powers counter the clear and honest attitude of the Soviet government?

They responded to the Soviet Union's unilateral ending of nuclear tests by carrying out a series of explosions of nuclear bombs unprecedented in its intensity.

The government of the United States and Britain responded to the attempts repeatedly made by the Soviet Union to bring the positions of the negotiating parties closer together, by going back on their own proposals which they had supported only the day before. They did their utmost to prevent agreement. In fact they deleted the unanimously adopted conclusions and recommendations of scientific experts, including their own experts—American and British—concerning the methods of identifying nuclear explosions and ensuring appropriate control over the observance of a treaty on the discontinuance of nuclear tests.

The governments of the western powers have persistently put forward, and continue to put forward, the demand that a treaty on the discontinuance of nuclear tests should not provide for the prohibition of underground nuclear explosions. Meanwhile it is obvious to every informed person that the carrying out of such explosions, even if it is claimed that they are conducted for peaceful purposes, is nothing but a concealed form of perfecting existing nuclear weapons or putting the finishing touches to new types. If a nuclear explosive device is effective, for example, for 'shifting earth'—and the western powers want to secure for themselves the right to carry out such explosions—the same explosive device will also be effective for military purposes. Thus, while coming out in words in favour of the discontinuance of nuclear tests, the United States and Britain are in fact showing concern for something quite different—for inserting into the treaty a loophole for the further improvement of thermonuclear weapons by conducting underground explosions or explosions for so-called peaceful purposes.

The Soviet government has proposed an agreement that in the international control body the socialist states, the capitalist member-states of military blocs, and the neutral states should be equally represented and enjoy equal possibilities of control. In contrast to this, the western powers have made proposals the implementation of which would give them an advantage over the Soviet Union and would permit those powers to have complete command in the control body and cover the territory of the Soviet Union with a network of espionage centres under the guise of control posts and teams.

The entire course of the negotiations in Geneva proves that the western powers are pursuing the aim of actually legalising those types of nuclear tests in which they are interested and of establishing an international control body which would be an obedient tool in their hands and would, in fact, be an appendage of the General Staffs of western powers. The hypocritical statements made by representatives of the United States and Great Britain about the ending of tests and international control have proved to be nothing but camouflage.

In order to help the negotiations out of the deadlock the Soviet government has proposed that the solution of the question of the discontinuance of nuclear weapon tests be linked with the problem of general and complete disarmament. This important proposal was set forth in the aide-mémoire handed over at the Vienna meeting of N. S. Khrushchev, Chairman of the U.S.S.R. Council of Ministers, and John Kennedy, the President of the United States.

This initiative of the Soviet government has opened up additional possibilities for achieving mutually acceptable solutions to the whole complex of disarmament questions, and what is especially important, has removed obstacles in the way of establishing the widest and most comprehensive international control, including control over the discontinuance of nuclear tests.

What has been the reaction of the western powers to the new attempt of the Soviet Union to facilitate mutual understanding? Instead of a business-like examination of the Soviet proposal, the governments of the United States and Britain have preferred to engage in distorting its content and in idle fabrications concerning the Soviet Union's intentions. At the same time responsible representatives of the United States have begun dropping hints that the United States will resume nuclear weapon tests in the immediate future.

The Soviet government considers it its duty to draw the special attention of the peoples of the world to the fact that now in the United States there is much ado about projects for developing a neutron bomb. Such a bomb would kill everything living but at the same time would not destroy material objects. Only aggressors dreaming of plunder, of seizing foreign lands and foreign property can mobilise the efforts of scientists for the development of such weapons. While exterminating people, they want to use the fruits of the labour of the victims killed by them, the riches created by those people. This is the morality of monsters. The plans for developing a neutron bomb expose the inhuman essence of modern imperialism, which is no longer satisfied with merciless exploitation of the working people and which is ready, for the sake of profit, to commit crimes which, by their monstrous nature, would eclipse the memory of the gas-chambers and murder-vans of the Hitler hangmen.

It is an open secret that the United States is standing on the threshold of carrying out underground nuclear explosions and only waiting for the first suitable pretext to start them. However, it is clear to everyone that since the United States government has the intention of resuming nuclear weapon tests, this is only a question of time.

D.I.A.—Q

The Soviet government cannot ignore the fact that France, an ally of the United States in N.A.T.O., has already been carrying out nuclear tests for a long time. While the Soviet Union refrained from nuclear tests, trying to achieve agreement with the United States and Great Britain at the conference table on the complete discontinuance of those tests, France was conducting explosions of nuclear devices, one after another.

She is continuing to do this in spite of the appeal of the United Nations to all states to refrain from such tests, in spite of the protests of broad circles of the public in all countries of the world, in spite of the warnings of the Soviet Union that it will be forced to resume tests if France does not stop her experiments with nuclear weapons.

Had they not drawn proper conclusions from the fact that nuclear tests are being conducted by France, the Soviet Union and its allies would have found themselves in an inequitable position as compared with the United States, Britain, France and the other countries which are their partners in a single military bloc. Let those people in the United States and Britain who may be confused by the experimental explosions of Soviet nuclear weapons imagine that it was not their ally, France, but an ally of the U.S.S.R.—let us, say, Czechoslovakia—who was carrying out thermonuclear weapon tests, while other powers were refraining from tests.

What, in that case, would be the reaction of the United States, Britain and other N.A.T.O. countries? Would they put up with a situation in which obvious harm was being done to the interests of their security? But nuclear tests are not being conducted by Czechoslovakia or some other socialist country. They are being carried out by France, who is a member of N.A.T.O. How, then, can it be demanded that the Soviet Union should not take counter measures to strengthen its security? No government which has a real concern for the vital interests of its people and the defence potential of its country can act differently.

The yield of the French explosions set off in the Sahara may as yet be comparatively small, but their political repercussions are several times more dangerous.

The blast wave of the French nuclear tests has struck at the hopes of people in the most remote corners of the globe, causing general anger and indignation. It has also reached Geneva, actually sweeping away from the conference table the proposals aimed at putting an end to nuclear weapon tests once and for all. The continued nuclear weapon tests and also the active part played by the French government in the aggressive N.A.T.O. military bloc are often, and not without reason, associated with the shameful colonial war in Algeria and the attack on Bizerta, in Tunisia.

The legitimate question arises: Where were the governments of the United States and Britain when France was exploding nuclear devices on the African continent, challenging the United Nations and the people of the whole world? Instead of influencing their partner in the military bloc and keeping her from conducting nuclear explosions, they actually encouraged the French government.

This is sufficiently borne out by the fact that the United States and Britain refused to support the resolution of the United Nations General Assembly calling on the states not to carry out nuclear tests.

The Soviet government, however, would be telling only part of the truth if it passed in silence over the fact that not only states participating in the western military bloc, but also many other countries that voted in favour of that resolution actually reconciled themselves to the fact that the French government was going against the will of the United Nations, against the will of the peoples. Certainly, the Soviet government knows that among those states there are quite a few sincere supporters of the cessation of nuclear tests.

But if at the present time the nuclear arms drive is being stepped up again, the governments of those countries should admit directly and honestly that a certain share of the responsibility for the situation rests with them, since they failed to administer a timely rebuff to those French circles which are driving the world to the continuation of nuclear tests.

The harmful effects of thermonuclear weapon tests on living organisms are well known in the Soviet Union and every measure is therefore being taken to minimise those effects. Yes, any experiments with nuclear weapons instil alarm in people and make their hearts ache. And if the Soviet Government has nevertheless decided to carry out nuclear tests, it has been with a heavy heart. It has been compelled to do this, reluctantly, with regret, and only as a result of the most careful and comprehensive study of the question.

The Soviet government has been compelled to take this step, the significance of which it fully appreciates, under pressure of the international situation created by the imperialist countries.

The policy of the leading N.A.T.O. powers—the United States, Britain, France and the Federal Republic of Germany—and of this aggressive bloc as a whole, leaves the Soviet Union no other choice.

The Soviet people, the Soviet government cannot fail to take into account the fact that, as was the case 20 years ago, ominous clouds of war are once again hanging over the approaches to our motherland, that Western Germany and the present allies of the German militarists are feverishly engaged in military preparations.

Not only the governments of the United States, Britain and France, but also the governments of a number of European countries whose people suffered a great deal from the Hitler invasion are now with their own hands helping the West German revenge-seekers to equip themselves for the new adventures. The governments of smaller N.A.T.O. states—Belgium, Denmark, Holland, Norway, Greece and other countries taking part in this military bloc—also bear their share of responsibility for the policy of arming Western Germany. They will be unable to hide behind the backs of their senior N.A.T.O. partners and they will have to answer themselves for all the grave consequences of this short-sighted and dangerous policy.

Adenauer and the forces that stand behind him are pursuing the course of turning Western Germany into a militarist state, armed to the teeth. The main goal of the foreign policy of that state is revenge and the revision of the frontiers established in Europe as a result of the Second World War.

Now the government of the Federal Republic of Germany is trying to make up for the first years after the unconditional surrender of Hitler Germany, when the United States, Britain and France had not yet fully departed from the allied agreements providing for Germany's demilitarisation.

The 16 postwar years are a sufficient span of time to judge whether the peoples of Western Germany have learned the proper lessons—as is the case in the German Democratic Republic—from the militarist past, from the disastrous defeat in two world wars unleashed by Germany.

Unfortunately there is too much evidence pointing to the fact that the Germans who live in Western Germany are again succumbing to the opium of revenge and are permitting latter-day Fuehrers to carry them away along the path of war. What other explanation could there be for the fact that at every election to the Bundestag the population of the Federal Republic of Germany votes for Chancellor Adenauer and those politicians who are stubbornly dragging Germans to new acts of aggression? Germans voting for Adenauer cannot but know that Adenauer and those who adhere to his policy in Western Germany have adopted those very slogans of anti-communism and revenge-seeking under which Hitler came to power and subsequently unleashed the Second World War.

It goes without saying that every nation is free to place at the helm of the state those political figures it wants. But no one can deprive other nations, which have already on a number of occasions witnessed the seeds of militarism and aggression ripening in Germany, of the right to raise their warning voices against the tragic events of the past being repeated—voices which must be heard by every German. No matter how bitter it may be to realise, not only the Germans of Western Germany, but also the peoples of other countries that are taking part in the military blocs of the western powers are not yet equal to the demands of the time and do not display proper activity to stop at once the preparation of a new war. This conclusion suggests itself from the very fact that in elections they also vote for candidates and parties which form governments pursuing the policy of building up armaments.

Shunning the efforts aimed at eliminating the 'cold war' and safeguarding peace, they fail to muster the necessary determination to deny their trust and support to governments which have shown by all their activities that they are opponents of general and complete disarmament and supporters of the arms drive and the whipping up of war hysteria.

If those peoples do not take the opportunity to put a curb on the governments which are pushing the world to a universal catastrophe, if they do not unite their efforts with other peoples so as to assert their will to achieve disarmament, to expel war finally from the life of human society, there is only one conclusion that can be drawn: the peoples of these countries have not yet awakened, have not realised the importance of the responsibility that rests with them for safeguarding peace.

The more tangible is the danger of a military conflict being set ablaze by Western Germany, the more urgent and pressing becomes the signing of a German peace treaty, which would protect the peoples from fresh encroachments by the German militarists. It is common knowledge that this is precisely the aim of the Soviet Union. Nevertheless, in response to the Soviet Union's declared determination to conclude a German peace treaty and thus draw a final line under the Second World War, it is being threatened with the unleashing of a third world war.

A new demonstration of strength in response to the Soviet proposals concerning the Germany peace treaty is the dispatch to West Berlin of additional troops and armaments by the United States and Britain.

As for the reinforcement of the military garrisons of the western powers in West Berlin, this has no special significance and it has been undertaken obviously as a provocation and only as a provocation. Those who took the decision to send that military contingent to West Berlin know this better than anyone. The Soviet government would not be doing its sacred duty to the peoples of its country, to the peoples of the socialist countries and to all peoples striving for a peaceful life if, in the face of the threats and military preparations that have gripped the United States and certain other N.A.T.O. countries, it did not make use of the available possibilities for perfecting the most effective types of weapons that can cool the hotheads in the capitals of certain N.A.T.O. powers.

The Soviet Union has worked out designs for creating a series of super-powerful nuclear bombs equivalent to 20, 30, 50 and 100 million tons of T.N.T., and powerful rockets similar to those with the help of which Major Y. A. Gagarin and Major H. S. Titov made their unrivalled space flights round the earth, can lift and deliver such nuclear bombs to any point on the globe from which an attack on the Soviet Union or other socialist countries could be launched. It would be unjustifiable thoughtlessness not to draw appropriate conclusions from the situation that has arisen owing to the aggressive policy of the N.A.T.O. military bloc, and not to take care of strengthening the security and might of the Soviet state, the great socialist camp and all peaceloving states.

The Soviet government addresses this statement not only to the friends of the Soviet people who correctly understand the Soviet Union's peaceloving policy, but also to those people in foreign countries who might perhaps judge too severely the carrying out by the Soviet Union of tests of new types of nuclear weapons. The Soviet government is taking this step in the firm belief that the peoples will understand the forced nature of this measure and its inevitability in the present conditions. In order to discourage the aggressor from criminal playing with fire, it is necessary to make sure that he knows and sees that there is a force in the world which is ready to administer an armed rebuff to any encroachment on the independence and security of the peaceloving states and that the weapon of retribution will reach the aggressor in his own den.

The Soviet government is speaking about all this not only in order to make absolutely clear the motives that have prompted it to carry out nuclear tests at the present moment.

It is giving a reminder of this, in the first place, in order that the peoples of the world may know from where the menace comes, in order that they may clearly see the manoeuvres of the enemies of peace so that they can unite their forces to combat this danger. Let all who cherish peace know that they may confidently rely on the Soviet Union, on the titanic efforts it is undertaking to bring the initiators of war hysteria to their senses and to stop the ever-accelerating drive towards a new war.

Being invariably guided by the Leninist principles of peaceful co-existence, the Soviet Union does not threaten anyone and, of course, does not intend to attack anyone. The Soviet government solemnly declares that the armed forces of the U.S.S.R. will never be the first to resort to arms.

The Soviet people would be happy if the arms race could be stopped, if the necessity of nuclear weapon tests could disappear forever and the peoples could free themselves for good from the heavy burden which they have had to shoulder ever since war became the sinister companion of human society.

If every people, whether the people of a large or a small country, of one with a highly developed industry or one only beginning to develop its economy, of a country which is a member of military blocs of states or a country following a neutral policy, had demanded with the full power of their voice that the military machinery of states be at last smashed and that mankind be delivered from the danger of destructive nuclear war, this would have been achieved.

Expressing the vital interests of the Soviet people and, as it is convinced, the interests of all sincere champions of disarmament and peace, the Soviet government addresses the peoples and the governments of all countries of the world with its appeal that the efforts to carry out in practice the idea of general and complete disarmament and to eliminate forever the danger of nuclear weapons from the life of mankind be increased tenfold. It reaffirms the readiness of the Soviet Union to sign at any time an agreement on general and complete disarmament which would put an end to nuclear weapon tests.

The Soviet government's entire policy is directed towards the establishment of relations between states based on the principle of peaceful co-existence, so that the peoples may freely develop trade, mutually enrich each other with spiritual values, and compete, not in producing the maximum of means of destruction, but in creating the material wealth so necessary for the people.

The draft programme of the Communist Party of the Soviet Union, which defines the practical tasks of the Soviet Union for the next 20 years, is imbued with this noble aspiration.

The Soviet government is confident that the efforts of the Soviet people in the struggle for the consolidation of international security will not be wasted and will merge with the efforts of other peoples directed towards the establishment of firm and unbreakable peace on earth, for the triumph of the ideas of peace and progress.

The cause of peace and friendship among the nations will triumph and the calculations of the aggressive forces will be thwarted.

11. Statement from the Office of the President of the United States, 30 August 1961[1]

The Soviet government's decision to resume nuclear weapons testing will be met with deepest concern and resentment throughout the world. The Soviet government's decision to resume nuclear weapons testing presents a hazard to every human being throughout the world by increasing the dangers of nuclear fallout. The Soviet government's decision to resume nuclear weapons testing is in utter disregard of the desire of mankind for a decrease in the arms race. The Soviet government's decision to resume nuclear weapons testing presents a threat to the entire world by increasing the dangers of a thermo-nuclear holocaust. The Soviet government's decision to resume nuclear weapons testing

[1] *Public Papers*, 1961, pp. 580–1.

indicates the complete hypocrisy of its professions about general and complete disarmament.

For three years world attention has centered on the negotiations in Geneva for a treaty to secure an end to nuclear testing. Until last March it appeared that slow but encouraging progress had been made. At that time, the Soviet Union reversed its own earlier positions on key issues, refused to discuss seriously the genuine efforts made by the United States and the United Kingdom to meet known Soviet views, and blocked the path toward a nuclear test ban treaty. In order to avoid missing any possible opportunity to arrive at an agreement, the United States and the United Kingdom remained at the negotiating table. Only this week Ambassador Dean has made additional proposals in the hope of moving toward a test ban under effective international control. Urgent discussion of this issue had been scheduled at United States initiative at the forthcoming session of the General Assembly in the hopes that constructive debate could show the way to surmount the impasse at Geneva.

The pretext offered by the announcement for Soviet resumption of weapons testing is the very crisis which they themselves have created by threatening to disturb the peace which has existed in Germany and Berlin. It is not the first time they have made such charges against those who have dared to stand in the way of Soviet aggression. In addition, the announcement links the Soviet resumption of testing with threats of massive weapons which it must know cannot intimidate the rest of the world.

The purpose and motivation of this Soviet behavior now seems apparent: The Soviet Government wished to abandon serious negotiations in order to free its hand to resume nuclear weapons testing.

The United States continues to share the view of the people of the world as to the importance of an agreement to end nuclear weapons tests under effective safeguards. Such an agreement would represent a major breakthrough in the search for an end to the arms race. It would stop the accumulation of stock piles of even more powerful weapons. It would inhibit the spread of nuclear weapons to other countries with its increased risks of nuclear war.

These results, with their prospects for reducing the possibility of a nuclear war, have been blocked by the Soviet unilateral decision to resume nuclear testing. The Soviet Union bears a heavy responsibility before all humanity for this decision, a decision which was made in complete disregard of the United Nations. The termination of the moratorium on nuclear testing by the Soviet unilateral decision leaves the United States under the necessity of deciding what its own national interests require.

Under these circumstances, Ambassador Arthur Dean is being recalled immediately from Geneva.

12. Joint statement by President Kennedy and Mr. Macmillan, 3 September 1961[1]

The President of the United States and the Prime Minister of the United Kingdom propose to Chairman Khrushchev that their three governments agree,

[1] *Public Papers*, 1961, p. 587.

effective immediately, not to conduct nuclear tests which take place in the atmosphere and produce radioactive fallout.

Their aim in this proposal is to protect mankind from the increasing hazards from atmospheric pollution and to contribute to the reduction of international tensions.

They urge Chairman Khrushchev to cable his immediate acceptance of this offer and his cessation of further atmospheric tests.

They further urge that their representatives at Geneva meet not later than September 9 to record this agreement and report it to the United Nations. They sincerely hope that the Soviet Union will accept this offer, which remains open for the period indicated.

They point out that with regard to atmospheric testing the United States and the United Kingdom are prepared to rely upon existing means of detection, which they believe to be adequate, and are not suggesting additional controls. But they reaffirm their serious desire to conclude a nuclear test ban treaty, applicable to other forms of testing as well, and regret that the Soviet Government has blocked such an agreement.

13. Statement by President Kennedy, 5 September 1961[1]

In view of the continued testing by the Soviet Government, I have today ordered the resumption of nuclear tests, in the laboratory and underground, with no fallout. In our efforts to achieve an end to nuclear testing, we have taken every step that reasonable men could justify. In view of the acts of the Soviet Government, we must now take those steps which prudent men find essential. We have no other choice in fulfillment of the responsibilities of the United States Government to its own citizens and to the security of other free nations. Our offer to make an agreement to end all fallout tests[2] remains open until September 9.

14. Statement by Mr. Khrushchev, 9 September 1961[3]

The Soviet government has familiarised itself with the joint statement of the United States President and the Prime Minister of Great Britain of September 3 this year on the tests of nuclear weapons.[4] How can this statement be assessed?

First of all, one's attention is drawn to the fact that the leaders of the United States and Britain have not uttered a single word about the gravity of the period we are living through, about the tense international atmosphere, although they should realise, it seems, that the situation as regards nuclear tests cannot be regarded in isolation from this atmosphere.

It is precisely from the governments of the United States and Britain, which decide matters in the western military blocs, that the peoples have a right to expect a clear and direct reply: When will they finally discontinue their sabre-rattling, when will they finally cease pushing the world to a nuclear war catastrophe?

Leaving all this aside, Mr. Kennedy and Mr. Macmillan not only divorce the

[1] *Public Papers*, 1961, pp. 589–90. The first underground weapons test was made on 15 September.
[2] Above, preceding document.   [3] *Soviet News*, 11 September, 1961.   [4] Above, p. 465.

question of nuclear weapon tests from the problem of disarmament, of which it is a part, but are trying to consider it in isolation, as though in a test tube, unrelated to important events of international life.

Each line of the statement by the President of the United States and the Prime Minister of Great Britain reveals a desire to ensure—cost what it may—for the western powers and their allies in aggressive military blocs unilateral military advantages to the detriment of the security interests of the Soviet Union and the other socialist states. Moreover, the leaders of the United States and Britain are even trying to present the case as though their joint statement has been dictated by concern for the easing of international tension, for the interests of all mankind.

But no matter what high-sounding words the leaders of the United States and British governments choose in an attempt to whitewash their line on the question of nuclear weapons, it is impossible with the help of such words to present an aggressive policy as a peaceful one, to present brutality as humanism.

To make clear the purposes of this statement, let us see what its specific content is.

The statement advances the proposal that the Soviet Union, the United States of America and Britain should immediately reach agreement not to hold nuclear weapon tests in the atmosphere, provided, however, that the question of experimental blasts of this weapon underground and in outer space should not be affected by this agreement.

It is not very difficult to guess the meaning of this proposal. We are offered that the United States and Britain, let alone France, which remains completely outside this proposal, should retain the opportunity to go on improving their nuclear weapons. But even this is not enough for them. They want to try to see whether it is possible to tie the hands of the Soviet Union even stronger in the raising of its defence potential. In other words, they want to kill two birds with one propaganda stone: to sanctify by the Soviet Union's consent their war preparations in the sphere of nuclear armaments, while at the same time tripping up their partner in the negotiations—the Soviet Union.

Indeed, it is common knowledge that the programme of developing new types of nuclear weapons which has been drawn up in the United States now requires precisely underground tests, that is to say, the kind of experiments to which the American-British proposal is to give the green light. For several years the United States has striven at the Geneva negotiations of the three nuclear powers to have underground nuclear blasts legalised, which has been one of the main obstacles to the conclusion of a treaty on the complete discontinuance of nuclear tests.

After all, it is an open secret that the United States has long since planned underground nuclear tests, and appropriate pits and huge underground galleries in the state of Nevada are kept in readiness there.

If any further proof were needed that the aims pursued by the joint statement of the United States President and the Prime Minister of the United Kingdom were too thin, it was furnished by Mr. Kennedy himself when he issued instructions to resume underground nuclear tests on September 5,[1] that is to say, the day after the message was sent to the Soviet Union.

The government of the United States was so impatient that evidently it did

1 Above, p. 466.

not even think, if only for appearances' sake, of waiting for the Soviet government's reply to the American-British statement. Does this not show that from the very outset it was not going to concert its actions with the reply of the Soviet government to this statement?

This is not the first time that the governments of the United States and Britain have sought to confine a nuclear tests ban to tests in the atmosphere alone. They made similar proposals, for instance, in 1959.[1] Why has the Soviet government been an opponent—and still is—of such an approach to the question of discontinuing nuclear weapon tests? Because agreement on the cessation of one kind of tests only—in the atmosphere—would do a disservice to the cause of peace.

It would mean deceiving the peoples. Such agreement could create harmful and dangerous illusions among the peoples that steps were being taken to put an end to the arms race while in fact nothing of the kind would have been done. In fact, states would continue, in a sort of legalised way, to improve existing types of atom and hydrogen weapons, using for this purpose underground tests, including those for so-called peaceful purposes, and tests in outer space.

Besides, the possibility would be preserved of designing new, and more destructive types of nuclear weapons on the basis of the data obtained, as a result of these experiments. Of course, the military circles of the N.A.T.O. member-states would just rub their hands with satisfaction, since they know full well that the implementation of such a plan would only add grist to the mill of the N.A.T.O. bloc—a potential aggressor.

Thus, the nuclear arms race would continue and its dangerous consequences would in no way be less than they are now. The conclusion of an agreement, starting a kind of race in underground nuclear tests—and, if one wished, in outer space or under water—could be assessed by the peoples, and with good reason at that, as a dishonest deal. Of course, the Soviet government cannot and will not make such a deal. Such a deal is wanted by those who build their policy on deceiving the peoples, on playing at talks.

The Soviet Union is a champion of the cessation of all kinds of nuclear weapon tests, without any exception, everywhere and for all time to come. It was precisely as a result of its efforts that representatives of the U.S.S.R., the United States and Britain three years ago opened talks on the discontinuance of nuclear tests. The Soviet government went to those talks hoping that the western powers, too, would accept an agreement on the cessation of tests.

During the talks the Soviet Union made a number of concessions to the United States and the United Kingdom, yet, with each meeting, and there have already been over 300 of them, hopes for success disappeared just as a mirage disappears in the desert when one approaches the desired object. Bitter though it is to realise this, looking at things realistically one must draw the conclusion that the Geneva talks are today as far from accomplishing their purpose as they were three years ago.

Nor can one overlook the fact that while the United States and Britain have been stalling at the Geneva talks, their partner in a military bloc, France, has become a nuclear power. The French government has staged a series of nuclear

[1] *Documents*, 1959, pp. 124–5.

explosions and clearly intimated that it would not regard itself bound by any commitments with regard to the cessation of nuclear weapon tests.

The Soviet government has pointed out more than once that a false situation for the Geneva talks was created in connection with the French nuclear tests. The Soviet Union warned that it would be compelled to resume tests if France did not stop her test explosions. However, it became clear that there was a certain distribution of roles between the N.A.T.O. allies: the United States and the United Kingdom were holding talks with the U.S.S.R. on the cessation of tests, thus retarding the improvement of Soviet nuclear weapons, while France was exploding one nuclear device after another.

If there still were gullible people who might have believed the assurances that France was staging nuclear tests by herself and not working hand in glove with the United States in this respect, in the interests of the entire N.A.T.O. bloc, the agreement just approved by the United States President on co-operation between the United States and France in using atomic energy for military purposes has dispelled any illusions on this score. It is clear that the results of nuclear tests, held by any N.A.T.O. power, go into the common imperialist N.A.T.O. pool.

Now, too, Mr. Kennedy's and Mr. Macmilan's statement refers only to three nuclear powers—the U.S.S.R., the United States and the United Kingdom. And what about France? The authors of the statement proceed from the assumption that France will continue nuclear tests as hitherto. Aren't they asking too much of the Soviet Union in expecting that it would tolerate such an impermissible situation?

The situation is worsened by the fact that the N.A.T.O. powers in recent months have sharply turned the wheel of their policy towards preparing a military clash.

To start with, the United States government demanded a sharp increase of military appropriations in the spring of this year. Today the United States military budget amounts to more than 50,000 million dollars. Never before has any state spent such tremendous amounts of money on military purposes in peacetime. This was followed by a build-up of the United States armed forces, the call-up of 250,000 reservists, the reinforcement of the American garrison in West Berlin, the decision of the United States government to speed up the production of new types of submarines and rockets and to recommission even old American ships and planes. There are many such facts and it is impossible to list all of them.

Not only the United States is engaged in military preparations, but so too are its allies in military blocs, above all Western Germany, whose leaders, obsessed by the ideas of militarism and revenge-seeking, are probably working harder than anyone else to pit the great powers against each other in connection with the conclusion of a German peace treaty, to light a spark which may produce the flame of a third world war.

But what makes it most suspicious is the attitude of the governments of the United States, Britain, France and the Federal Republic of Germany to the proposal to conclude, at long last, a German peace treaty. In reply to the proposal to sit down at one table and settle in a calm atmosphere and in a businesslike way the question of reaching a peaceful accommodation with Germany and normalising on this basis the situation in West Berlin, the western governments have started a whole avalanche of military measures. Blunt threats against the Soviet Union and the socialist countries are being made with increasing frequency.

All this has compelled the Soviet Union, as stated earlier by the Soviet government, to show concern for the further strengthening of its defences.

In face of the feverish war preparations of the N.A.T.O. powers directed against the Soviet Union and the socialist countries, we had no other alternative but to take measures which are prompted by the need to counter the threats, by the necessity of being ready to take up arms against aggression. Such a necessity arose against our will; it was created, not by us, but by the policy of brandishing arms and inciting war which is now being carried through by the chief N.A.T.O. powers, especially in connection with the question of the conclusion of a German peace treaty. The Soviet Union has resumed nuclear weapon tests because it would border on utter thoughtlessness in the existing situation to disregard the possibility of aggression against it.

In deciding to resume tests, the Soviet government, of course, was aware that at first some people might not be able to assess the entire complexity of the international situation and would show a certain lack of understanding of this step taken by the Soviet Union. We realised in advance that some people in the West would not disdain to exploit this in order to try to earn propaganda capital. Nevertheless the Soviet Union could not act otherwise. Weighing all the pros and cons, the Soviet government, with an aching heart, had to resume test explosions.

We do not doubt that the overwhelming majority of mankind rightly assesses the Soviet government's measures. Strengthening the defence potential of the Soviet Union means at the same time strengthening the peace forces throughout the world. The aggressor must know that there is a dependable force capable of defending peaceful labour, freedom and the independence of the peoples.

The joint American-British statement touches upon the question of the growing danger of contamination of the atmosphere with radioactive substances. It goes without saying that these are undesirable phenomena. The Soviet Union is taking all measures to reduce to a minimum the harmful effects of tests on living organisms.

However, it is legitimate to pose the question why neither the government of the United States nor the government of Britain complained over the contamination of the atmosphere when for a number of years the roar of the explosions of atom and hydrogen bombs continued far from the vital centres of those states on Bikini, Eniwetok and Christmas Islands—and when a tremendous amount of radioactive fallout not only poisoned the earth's atmosphere but also contaminated the waters of the Pacific and passed, through products of the sea, into the bones and blood of innocent people?

Why have the governments of the United States and the United Kingdom found no words to condemn the actions of the French government, which for almost two years has been contaminating the earth's atmosphere, staging nuclear tests in the Sahara?

Concern over the contamination of the earth's atmosphere, expressed in the American-British statement, if checked, turns out to be artificial and ostentatious. Would it not be more honest to tell the peoples what really is in store for them if events continue developing further in the direction in which they have been developing in recent months as a result of the growing aggressiveness of the policy of the N.A.T.O. powers? Yet matters are taking such a turn that mankind might be caught up in the tornado of a nuclear-rocket war and tens and hundreds of millions of people may perish in the inferno of such a war unless the policy of the western powers is changed in time.

The present policy of the N.A.T.O. powers creates a situation in which we must fear, not radioactive fall-out, but lest nuclear weapons themselves, with all their deadly and destructive force, are dropped on the heads of the people. If we put on the scales the harm of nuclear tests to the peoples' health and the consequences of the combat application of nuclear weapons, everyone will see the alternative facing mankind today and how hypocritical are the statements of the western powers concerning experimental nuclear blasts.

No, the Soviet Union cannot permit the lives of millions upon millions of people to be risked. The Soviet government would not be discharging its duties if it did not show proper concern for the security of the Soviet people.

And if it is now confronted with the grim necessity of resuming tests of nuclear weapons, this is being done only to safeguard our people—and indeed all mankind—from experiencing themselves, as was the case with the Japanese cities of Hiroshima and Nagasaki, live explosions of these weapons.

The Soviet Union is trying to prevent people from becoming victims of atomic, hydrogen or neutron bombs, which are spoken of increasingly frequently in the West by those who counterpose to the genuine humanity of socialist society and our foreign policy their own man-hating policy according to which people are merely fuel to stoke the furnace of nuclear war, and the material and cultural treasures created by the peoples—potential booty, spoils of war for imperialist aggressors.

It is common knowledge that the Soviet Union has held several times less nuclear tests than the United States, Britain and France. And yet we have every reason—both from the standpoint of morality and from the standpoint of safe-guarding our national interests—to hold as many tests as the western powers.

For the leaders of the western powers themselves often say that while the arsenals of nations are bursting with stockpiled arms, the security of each of them depends to a large extent on the balance of forces. And there is much truth in this. What the western leaders consider just in the security interests of their states, which no one threatens, is much more just with regard to the Soviet Union and the entire socialist commonwealth, which have to live in an atmosphere of threats and sabre-rattling by imperialists.

To disperse the stormclouds of war and normalise the relations among states it is necessary to solve the key problem of our time—the problem of general and complete disarmament.

This idea, which has won the hearts of all who cherish peace, is now courageously advocated not only by the Soviet Union, by the socialist countries, but also by many independent states of Asia, Africa and Latin America. Evidence of this is the results of the conference of 25 non-aligned states which has just ended in Belgrade,[1] a conference which has made a fine contribution to curbing the forces of war and strengthening the forces of peace.

Those who can squarely face the truth will recognise that nuclear tests can now be ended everywhere and forever only on the basis of general and complete disarmament. Once this problem is settled, no one would have the temptation to test nuclear weapons on land, underground, in the atmosphere or in outer space, and, indeed, there would be nothing to test, as the weapons, and above all nuclear-rocket weapons, would be sent to the scrap heap. Life itself has linked these two questions into one indivisible whole.

Unfortunately, the United States government—as shown by the bilateral Soviet-American talks—does not want even to approach general and complete disarmament, with the establishment of rigorous international control over the activities of states in this field. But then the government of the United States and also the government of Britain—which, judging by everything, abides by the same position—must assume responsibility also for the fact that the question of ending nuclear tests will remain unsettled.

In reply to the proposal to limit ourselves to renouncing the holding of nuclear tests in the atmosphere, we can only say to the President of the United States and the Prime Minister of Great Britain: Let us direct the minds and energy of our peoples not to military preparations, not to inflaming the cold war, not to quests for spurious propaganda moves, but to getting down together to settling the main problem of our time—general and complete disarmament. Let us seek seriously, in good faith, a solution to the problem of a German peace treaty in order to arrest in time the sliding of states into the chasm of nuclear-rocket war. Then everything will fall into its place, not only will there be no nuclear tests but also no threat of nuclear war itself.

One need not be a prophet to predict that the Russians and the Americans, the Czechoslovaks and the British, the Arabs and the Indians, all peoples of the world, will remember forever with gratitude the statesmen and the governments who spare no effort to achieve general and complete disarmament and rid mankind forever of wars.

If, on the other hand, this problem remains unsettled, the peoples will curse those leaders who used their position and authority to preserve the fever of war preparations and the abiding threat of nuclear-rocket war. Nor will they ever forgive them if everything is not done to draw a line under the Second World War, to conclude a peace treaty with Germany, which would relieve the peoples of Europe—and not only of Europe—of fear and concern for the future, and would bring them a tranquil and peaceful life.

General and complete disarmament with the elimination of national military establishments as a whole, the immediate conclusion of a German peace treaty, and a line drawn under the Second World War—such, in the present conditions, is the straight road to ridding the peoples of wars and the calamities and misfortunes which they bring to mankind. It is to embark on this road that we urge the governments of the United States and Great Britain.

[1] cf. below, pp. 596–636.

15. Joint statement by President Kennedy and Mr. Macmillan, 9 September 1961[1]

President Kennedy and Prime Minister Macmillan note with deepest regret that the Soviet Union has not accepted their proposal of September 3, that tests in the earth's atmosphere producing fallout be stopped without delay.

This action contrasts vividly with the Soviet Union's own repeated expressions of concern as to the health hazards of such testing.

The President and the Prime Minister reaffirm the readiness of the United States and the United Kingdom to negotiate a controlled nuclear test ban agreement of the widest possible scope.

16. Statement by President Kennedy, 2 November 1961[2]

The United States is carefully assessing the current series of nuclear tests being conducted by the Soviet Union. I do not have to dwell on the irresponsible nature of these Soviet actions. The Soviet Union has shown its complete disregard for the welfare of mankind, first, by breaking off the nuclear test cessation negotiations at Geneva, which had been underway since October 31, 1958, and second, by contemptuously exploding in the atmosphere a large number of nuclear weapons ranging into many megatons, including a device which, by their own admission, exceeded 50 megatons.

I do not suggest that we can dismiss these Soviet nuclear tests as mere bluff and bluster. To a certain extent this does enter into the Soviet campaign of fear, but these tests are, no doubt, of importance to Soviet leaders and scientists in developing and improving nuclear weapons.

This much can be said with certainty now:

1. In terms of total military strength, the United States would not trade places with any nation on earth. We have taken major steps in the past year to maintain our lead—and we do not propose to lose it.

2. The United States does not find it necessary to explode 50 megaton nuclear devices to confirm that we have many times more nuclear power than any other nation on earth and that these capabilities are deployed so as to survive any sneak attack and thus enable us to devastate any nation which initiates a nuclear attack on the United States or its Allies. It is essential to the defense of the Free World that we maintain this relative position.

In view of the Soviet action, it will be the policy of the United States to proceed in developing nuclear weapons to maintain this superior capability for the defense of the Free World against any aggressor. No nuclear test in the atmosphere will be undertaken, as the Soviet Union has done, for so-called psychological or political reasons. But should such tests be deemed necessary to maintain our responsibilities for Free World security, in the light of our evaluation of Soviet tests, they will be undertaken only to the degree that the orderly and essential scientific development of new weapons has reached a point where effective progress is not possible without such tests—and only within limits that restrict the fall-out from such tests to an absolute minimum.

In the meantime, as a matter of prudence, we shall make necessary

[1] *Public Papers*, 1961, p. 596.   [2] *Public Papers*, 1961, pp. 692–3.

preparations for such tests so as to be ready in case it becomes necessary to conduct them.

In spite of the evidence which shows very clearly that the Soviet Union was preparing its own tests while pretending to negotiate their cessation at Geneva, the United States maintains its determination to achieve a world free from the fear of nuclear tests and a nuclear war. We will continue to be ready to sign the nuclear test treaty which provides for adequate inspection and control. The facts necessary for such a treaty are all evident—the argument on both sides have all been made—a draft is on the table—and our negotiators are ready to meet.

17. Resolution adopted by the General Assembly of the United Nations, 9 November 1961[1]

The General Assembly,

Recalling its resolutions 1252 (XIII) of 4 November 1958, 1402 (XIV) of 21 November 1959 and 1577 (XV) and 1587 (XV) of 20 December 1960,

Noting with regret the recent initiation of nuclear weapons testing and the rejection of the proposal of the Governments of the United States of America and the United Kingdom of Great Britain and Northern Ireland that further nuclear tests in the earth's atmosphere should be suspended,

Noting that the negotiations at Geneva on the discontinuance of nuclear weapons tests have been recessed pending completion of the discussion of this matter by the General Assembly,

Recognizing that a permanent and continuing cessation of nuclear weapons testing in all environments would be guaranteed only by an effective and impartial system of verification in which all States have confidence,

1. *Reaffirms* that it is urgently necessary to reach an agreement prohibiting all nuclear weapons tests under effective control which would be a first step towards reversing the dangerous and burdensome arms race, would inhibit the spread of nuclear weapons to other countries, would contribute to the reduction of international tensions and would eliminate any health hazards associated with nuclear testing;

2. *Urges* the States negotiating at the Conference on the Discontinuance of Nuclear Weapons Tests at Geneva to renew at once their efforts to conclude at the earliest possible time a treaty on the cessation of nuclear and thermo-nuclear weapons tests on the following basis:

(*a*) The treaty should have as its objective the cessation of all nuclear weapons tests in all environments under inspection and control machinery adequate to ensure compliance with its terms;

(*b*) International control machinery should be organized so as to be representative of all parties to the treaty and should be staffed and operated to guarantee its objectivity and effectiveness, avoiding self-inspection, under procedures which would ensure that its facilities will be used exclusively for purposes of effective control;

(*c*) The day-to-day executive and administrative operations of the control system established under the treaty should not be susceptible to obstruction by

---

[1] G.A.O.R., Sixteenth Session, Supplement No. 17, p. 4. Resolution 1649 (xvi), see also below p. 481.

the exercise of a veto, and administrative responsibility should be concentrated in the hands of a single Administrator acting impartially and functioning under the supervision of a commission composed of representatives of parties to the treaty;

3. *Requests* the negotiating States to report to the Disarmament Commission by 14 December 1961 on the progress of their negotiations;

4. *Calls upon* all States, upon the conclusion of a treaty which will ensure that nuclear weapons tests will be permanently prohibited under effective controls, to ratify or to adhere to that treaty.

18. The United States Embassy in Moscow to the Soviet Ministry of Foreign Affairs, 13 November 1961[1]

The Embassy of the United States of America presents its compliments to the Ministry of Foreign Affairs of the Union of Soviet Socialist Republics and has the honor to state the following:

The Geneva Conference on the Discontinuance of Nuclear Weapon Tests recessed on September 9, 1961. The relevant portion of the joint communique[2] agreed to by the Soviet, British, and American delegations is as follows:

The representatives of the United States and of the United Kingdom proposed a recess until after the completion of the General Assembly debate on the nuclear tests question.
The Conference went into recess.

The United Nations General Assembly has now completed its debate on the nuclear test issue. Thus, the condition under which the Geneva conference recess was proposed last September has now been fulfilled. Further, the General Assembly has overwhelmingly adopted a resolution calling for resumption of negotiations on a nuclear weapon test ban.[3]

The United States Government therefore formally proposes to the Government of the Union of Soviet Socialist Republics that the meetings of the Conference on the Discontinuance of Nuclear Weapon Tests be resumed on November 28, 1961.

In this connection the United States Government notes that the General Assembly resolution 1649 (XVI) of November 8, 1961, calls for a progress report on nuclear test ban negotiations to be submitted to the United Nations Disarmament Commission no later than December 14, 1961. The United States Government will consider any other date which the Soviet Government may wish to suggest with respect to prompt resumption of nuclear test ban negotiations which would also permit fulfillment of the requirement laid down in the General Assembly resolution cited above.

[1] *D.S.B.*, 11 December 1961, p. 965.
[2] United States Disarmament Administration, *Geneva Conference on the Discontinuance of Nuclear Weapon Tests, History and Analysis of Negotiations* (Washington, U.S.G.P.O., 1961), pp. 640–1.
[3] G.A.O.R., Sixteenth Session, Supplement No. 17, p. 4, Resolution 1649 (XVI).

19. The Soviet Ministry of Foreign Affairs to the United States Embassy in Moscow, 21 November 1961[1]

The Ministry of Foreign Affairs of the U.S.S.R. presents its compliments to the Embassy of the United States and in reply to its Note of November 13, 1961, considers it necessary to state the following:

Throughout the entire postwar period since the emergence of new weapons for the mass extermination of human beings—nuclear weapons—the Soviet Union has consistently strived, and is striving, for a ban on the use of these weapons and an end to their manufacture and the destruction of stockpiles of such weapons, and hence for the cessation of all kinds of nuclear tests for all time.

To rid mankind of the threat of the outbreak of a nuclear-rocket war is the aim the Soviet government has been invariably pursuing. The well-known Soviet proposals on general and complete disarmament, now under consideration at the United Nations, serve this aim.

The Soviet government, as before, is ready to do everything in its power to bring nearer the day when nuclear weapons will never again threaten human life. It is for this reason that on November 14 it voted at the 16th session of the United Nations General Assembly for the draft resolution to ban the use of nuclear weapons.[2] The Soviet government would welcome corresponding efforts on the part of the governments of the United States and Great Britain.

The Soviet government's stand on nuclear tests is undoubtedly well known to the governments of the United States and Great Britain, since it has been thoroughly and comprehensively set forth in a number of documents of the Soviet government and in statements by Nikita Khrushchev, Chairman of the Council of Ministers of the U.S.S.R., published after the suspension of these talks.

Noteworthy in this respect is Nikita Khrushchev's speech at a reception on November 7,[3] on the occasion of the 44th anniversary of the October Socialist Revolution, in which he expounded the Soviet government's position on this question, giving due consideration to the present international situation and proceeding from the Soviet Union's sincere desire to rid mankind of the threat of nuclear war as soon as possible.

If at this moment the governments of the United States and Great Britain feel that a resumption of talks in Geneva between the governments of the U.S.S.R., the United States and Great Britain on the discontinuance of nuclear tests can help to narrow the gap between the viewpoints of the sides, the Soviet government is ready to attempt once more jointly to push ahead this matter, proceeding from the assumption that the three powers taking part in the talks have proclaimed general and complete disarmament as their common goal.

In doing so the Soviet government proceeds from the assumption that, in accordance with the agreement on the principles of general and complete disarmament achieved between the governments of the U.S.S.R. and the United

---

[1] *Soviet News*, 22 November 1961.
[2] In the First Committee. Text in G.A.O.R., Sixteenth Session, Supplement No. 17, pp. 4–5, Resolution 1653 (XVI).
[3] *Soviet News*, 9 November 1961.

States, in the near future the 16th session of the United Nations General Assembly, as is to be hoped, will adopt a decision on the resumption of talks on general and complete disarmament in their entirety and on setting up the negotiating body.

It goes without saying that if during the talks any power starts to test nuclear weapons, then by force of circumstances to which the Soviet government has more than once drawn attention, the other side would be compelled to draw appropriate conclusions also with regard to nuclear tests.

Taking all this into account, the Soviet government expresses its consent to the resumption of the Geneva three-power nuclear test-ban talks as from November 28, 1961.

20. Statement by the Soviet Government, 27 November 1961[1]

The Soviet government is firmly and consistently upholding the cause of general and complete disarmament. This task has been set the peoples of our planet by the entire progress of historical development.

In our time, when the states have monstrous means of destruction and extermination, concern for the life and well-being of the present and future generations is closely linked with the struggle for general and complete disarmament. Mankind today has no alternative to scrapping the entire military machine and creating a world without armies and without armaments. Otherwise the peoples will be engulfed in a whirlwind of nuclear rocket war and within a few minutes, not only will individual towns and populated centres be wiped from the face of the earth, but whole countries would also be devastated.

The 22nd Congress of the Communist Party of the Soviet Union, after comprehensive analysis of the specific features of the present international situation, reaffirmed with complete conviction that the preservation of peace in our time was a realistic and feasible task. The correct, reliable road to this lies through the implementation of general and complete disarmament under effective international control. The Soviet Union believes in the force of ideas and not in the force of arms. That is precisely why the Soviet government proposes that all weapons, conventional and thermonuclear, be dumped in the deepest part of the ocean.

Unquestionably, if this matter had depended on the Soviet Union alone, the disarmament problem would have been solved long ago—the armies would have been disbanded, the stockpiles of weapons would have been destroyed and their production would have been stopped. It is obvious, however, that the Soviet government cannot solve this problem single-handed, divorced from the realities of international life, when the aggressive N.A.T.O. bloc is feverishly building up its armed forces, perfecting its weapons and openly threatening us with war. In these conditions the Soviet government could not and cannot disregard the interests of its own security, the security of all peaceloving states.

The Soviet Union must perforce seek a solution to the disarmament problem by agreement with the western powers, which unfortunately, in actual fact, are not as yet striving for this. The Soviet government believes, however, that this

---

[1] *Soviet News*, 28 November 1961.

state of affairs cannot last indefinitely. Sooner or later the western powers, if they do not intend to bring matters to the point of self-destruction, will have to accept general and complete disarmament.

The Soviet government notes with satisfaction that the idea of general and complete disarmament, put forward by N. S. Khrushchev at the 14th session of the United Nations General Assembly, enjoys worldwide support, although the western powers are evading the signing of an appropriate agreement.

An encouraging factor is the joint statement on agreed principles for disarmament talks, submitted by the Soviet Union and the United States for examination at this session of the General Assembly. The Soviet government is proceeding on the assumption that the present session of the General Assembly, as might be hoped, will on the basis of this statement take a decision on the resumption of the talks on the whole complex of the problems of general and complete disarmament and on setting up a body for holding such talks.

Agreement on general and complete disarmament will also remove the difficulties with regard to the introduction of an international control system. The Soviet government has pointed out more than once that it is ready to accept any control proposed by the western powers if they accept general and complete disarmament. In a situation in which there are no armaments or armies, the states will have no reason to worry about the use of control for espionage and intelligence purposes. In a totally disarmed world, control will become solely a means of verification. It will be really effective and comprehensive.

The implementation of general and complete disarmament as such would also solve the question of ending nuclear tests inasmuch as nuclear weapons themselves would be destroyed and therefore the nations would have no reason to carry out tests and, indeed, would have nothing to test.

The Soviet government is convinced that it is precisely this road that ensures the most reliable solution to the question of ending all nuclear weapon tests for all time.

In pressing insistently for the main goal of general and complete disarmament, the Soviet government considers it necessary to make the utmost use of all means, all possibilities in order to facilitate the attainment of this goal. It is because of this that it has agreed to the resumption of nuclear test-ban talks and has sent to Geneva its delegate who has been instructed to try once more to reach agreement on this question with the representatives of the western powers.

The Soviet government has given thorough consideration to the question of the resumption of the Geneva talks and, what is most important, to the question of how to ensure the success of these talks. Do the peoples need yet another fruitless conference? They are entitled to concrete and positive results and are justifiably demanding such results.

They might ask: 'Is there a way out of the present situation?' Yes, there is. The Soviet government has come to the conclusion that what is needed now is a new approach to nuclear tests which would exclude the difficulties and obstacles which have stood in the way of agreement in the past.

The entire experience of the three-year talks in Geneva has shown that the talks were bound to be deadlocked because our partners tried to obtain unilateral advantages for themselves to the detriment of the interests of the security of the other side. In the last analysis this blocked a solution to the problem of ending nuclear tests. On such a basis, which in the end discredited itself, one cannot, of course, secure an end to nuclear tests, especially at the present time, when the member states of the N.A.T.O. bloc are engaged in all-out war preparations and are threatening to retaliate with war to the conclusion of a German peace treaty.

The question arises: In the existing situation is it possible, nevertheless, to solve the problem of ending nuclear weapon tests so as to take a real step towards the accomplishment of the main task—general and complete disarmament? Yes, it is possible.

With this aim in view the Soviet government is submitting for the examination of the governments of the western powers the following proposal: to conclude, already at the present time, an appropriate agreement on the cessation of nuclear weapon tests in the atmosphere, under water and in outer space, that is to say, in those spheres where the implementation of control is not attended by any serious technical difficulties.

The observance of these pledges could be mutually checked, effectively and with sufficient reliability, by the already existing national technical facilities. It is well known that until now national means of detection have successfully coped with their tasks and in practice tests of nuclear weapons, whether by the Soviet Union, the United States, Britain or France, have not remained unregistered or undetected by them.

It was about such a real possibility of exercising control that the United States President, Mr. John Kennedy, and the British Prime Minister, Mr. Harold Macmillan, spoke in their joint statement of September 3, this year, when, as is known, they suggested the banning of nuclear tests in the atmosphere, relying on the existing means of detection which, they feel, are quite adequate and need no additional international machinery.

This approach suggested by the leading statesmen of the United States and Britain can also be extended to tests of nuclear weapons held both under water and in outer space, since the possibility of controlling such tests is likewise not limited in any way, technically, and such control could be fully effected by the already existing national means of detection. Moreover, public opinion throughout the entire world would also keep a careful watch over the observance of the agreement of the powers not to hold nuclear tests, which would also be a very important deterring factor.

As regards nuclear weapon tests underground, in the opinion of the Soviet government, the states should undertake not to hold such tests pending an agreement on a system of control over underground explosions as an integral part of an international system of control over the implementation of a programme of general and complete disarmament.

The way of solving the problem of ending nuclear tests proposed by the Soviet Union makes it possible to rid mankind of all nuclear explosions without delay, while at the same time no state would enjoy an advantage and the national security of states would not be prejudiced. Given such an approach, all suspicions which legitimately arose in connection with the wide possibilities of the control system worked out being used for intelligence purposes, would be completely eliminated.

It goes without saying that the success of the Geneva talks would undoubtedly be facilitiated by the consent of all nuclear states not to hold any nuclear tests as long as the talks are in progress. Although the Soviet government has held far fewer nuclear weapon tests than the United States, Britain and France, nevertheless, it is ready to give such a pledge if other states do likewise.

The Soviet government also considers that the time has now come to secure France's participation in the talks on the ending of nuclear weapon tests.

It is high time to put an end to the double game of the western powers in which some members of N.A.T.O. negotiate on a test ban, while others, with the tacit approval of their allies, continue to explode nuclear bombs and to perfect these weapons, strengthening the military potential of the N.A.T.O. bloc.

It goes without saying that if any western power, including France, starts holding nuclear tests, the Soviet Union, by force of circumstances, will again be confronted with the necessity of drawing all the appropriate conclusions for itself.

Wishing to direct the Geneva talks which are now opening into a practical channel, the Soviet government has drawn up a draft agreement on the cessation of atomic and thermonuclear weapon tests which it is submitting for the consideration of the western powers.

The Soviet government expresses confidence that the proposals which it is submitting open up a real possibility of an early agreement on the cessation of nuclear weapon tests and will help to create a favourable atmosphere for solving the problem of general and complete disarmament, the relaxation of international tension and the strengthening of peace.

Draft Agreement on Ending Tests of Atomic and Thermonuclear Weapons

The governments of the Union of the Soviet Socialist Republics, the United States of America, the United Kingdom of Great Britain and Northern Ireland and the French Republic, proclaiming as their principal aim the earliest achievement of an agreement on general and complete disarmament which would remove forever the danger of the outbreak of war, would put an end to the arms race and would eliminate the incentive to produce and test weapons of all kinds, including atomic and thermonuclear weapons;

And taking into consideration the fact that the renunciation by states of the holding of atomic and thermonuclear weapon tests would facilitate agreement on general and complete disarmament,

Have agreed with this object in view on the following:

Article 1

The states which are parties to the agreement solemnly pledge themselves not to hold tests of any types of atomic and thermonuclear weapons in the atmosphere, in outer space and under water.

Article 2

With the object of conducting observation on a reciprocal basis over the fulfilment of the commitment contained in Article 1 of this agreement, the states which are parties to the agreement shall use their national systems of detecting atomic and thermonuclear explosions.

Article 3

The states which are parties to the present agreement assume the obligation not to hold any underground tests of nuclear weapons pending agreement between them on a system to control such tests as a constituent part of an international control system over the realisation of an agreement on general and complete disarmament.

Article 4

The present agreement comes into force immediately after it is signed by the governments of the Union of Soviet Socialist Republics, the United States of America, the United Kingdom of Great Britain and Northern Ireland and the French Republic, and is open to the adherence of any state.

21. Report of the British and American Governments to the United Nations Disarmament Commission, 19 December 1961[1]

Following a searching and exhaustive discussion of nuclear testing, the sixteenth United Nations General Assembly passed Resolution 1649 (XVI) urging resumption of the test ban negotiations at Geneva.[2]

In accordance with the resolution, the United Kingdom and the United States immediately proposed to the Soviet Government that the Geneva conference resume its meetings on November 28, 1961. Shortly thereafter the Soviet Government agreed.

Resolution 1649 (XVI) provided the following guidance to the negotiations:

It is recognised that a permanent and continuing cessation of nuclear weapons testing in all environments would be guaranteed only by an effective and impartial system of verification in which all states would have confidence.

It reaffirmed that it was urgently necessary to reach an agreement prohibiting all nuclear weapons tests under effective control, which would be a first step toward reversing the dangerous and burdensome arms race, which would inhibit the spread of nuclear weapons to other countries, which would contribute to the reduction of international tension and which would eliminate any health hazards associated with nuclear testing.

Finally, it urged the three negotiating states to renew at once their efforts to conclude at the earliest possible time a treaty on the cessation of nuclear and thermo-nuclear weapons tests on the basis:

(1) That the treaty should have as its objective the cessation of all nuclear weapons tests in all environments under inspection and control machinery adequate to ensure compliance with its terms;

(2) That international control machinery should be organised so as to be

---

[1] United States Arms Control and Disarmament Agency, *International Negotiations on Ending Nuclear Weapon Tests, September 1961–September 1962* (Washington, U.S.G.P.O., 1962), pp. 182–6.
[2] G.A.O.R., Sixteenth Session, Supplement No. 17, p. 4. See above, pp. 474–5.

representative of all parties to the treaty and should be staffed and operated to guarantee its objectivity and effectiveness, avoiding self-inspection, under procedures which would ensure that its facilities would be used exclusively for purposes of effective control; and

(3) That the day-to-day executive and administrative responsibility should be concentrated in the hands of a single administrator acting impartially and functioning under the supervision of a commission composed of representatives of parties to the treaty.

The Soviet announcement that it would return to the negotiating table[1] raised the hopes of many people around the world that the Soviet Union at last was ready to negotiate an effective test ban treaty. Even before the conference resumed, however, the Soviet Union dashed these hopes by presenting a draft test ban agreement[2] which would in effect be a moratorium without any international controls, a proposal which the Soviet Union knew ran counter to the declared positions of the Western Powers and to General Assembly Resolution 1649.

This Soviet proposal amounted to an uncontrolled agreement on the suspension of all nuclear tests. It repudiated every previous agreement for international inspection and control undertaken by the U.S.S.R. during three years of patient and laborious negotiations at Geneva. It abandoned, as well, commitments made in other international forums and in correspondence between the Heads of Government of the United States, the United Kingdom and U.S.S.R., in which the Soviet Union continually professed its willingness to accept effective, reliable, workable, and impartial international controls to guarantee fulfilment of its disarmament obligations.

For example, in June, 1957, the Soviet Government submitted a proposal to the United Nations sub-committee on disarmament calling for an international commission to control a cessation of nuclear tests.[3] The same proposal provided for the establishment of control posts in the United States, the United Kingdom, the U.S.S.R. and in the Pacific Ocean.

The Soviet Union also discarded agreement on the report of the 1958 Geneva Conference of Experts convened to study the technical basis of an agreement on the suspension of nuclear tests. Even the draft treaty proposed by the U.S.S.R. on October 31, 1958[4]—when the Geneva Conference on the Discontinuance of Nuclear Weapons Tests was first convened—called for the establishment of a network of control posts in accordance with the recommendations of the conference of experts.

In addition, the November 27 draft agreement[5] proposed by the Soviet Union, further repudiates the Soviet-accepted recommendations of the group of experts from both sides convened during the Geneva test ban conference to study methods to detect high-altitude tests. These experts—including Soviet scientists —recommended that earth and solar satellites to be placed in orbit and that additional equipment be installed at ground control posts to detect space tests.

---

[1] Above, p. 476.   [2] Above, pp. 480–1.   [3] *Documents*, 1957, pp. 139–40.
[4] United States Disarmament Administration, *Geneva Conference on the Discontinuance of Nuclear Weapon Tests, History and Analysis of Negotiations* (Washington, U.S.G.P.O., 1961), pp. 313–14.
[5] Above, p. 480.

The new Soviet draft asked states to rely on existing national systems to detect tests in space.

Also repudiated by the latest Soviet *volte-face* are the preamble, 17 draft treaty articles, and two annexes agreed by the three Powers during the course of the test ban negotiations. These agreements recognised the need for the establishment and continued operation of an effective international inspection and control system. In doing so they provided for:

(1) The establishment of a control organisation to include a control commission, a detection and identification system, and a single administrator;

(2) The installation and operation of the control system;

(3) The composition of the control commission; and

(4) Arrangements designed to ensure the signatory states' cooperation with the control system for, inter alia, transportation, aircraft flights, air sampling and on-site inspection.

Throughout the Geneva Conference on the Discontinuance of Nuclear Weapons Tests, the Soviet Union has constantly attempted to hamper the establishment of an effective, reliable inspection and control system. Yet even the U.S.S.R. admitted on many occasions to the principle of international inspection and control whatever differences it may have had as to the details of on-site inspection, international control posts, and international inspection teams. Now the Soviet Union has abandoned the very principle of international verification and control to which it has been committed throughout the negotiations.

The Western delegates to the resumed conference at once indicated their wish to avoid all polemics and immediately begin work to negotiate a meaningful treaty. They called Soviet attention to the draft of a treaty presented to the conference in April 1961 by the United States and the United Kingdom which consisted of 24 articles and three annexes.[1] The draft treaty was complete and much of it already agreed. The remainder consists of compromise proposals put forward by the West to meet the Soviet point of view. The Western Powers have never insisted that these articles be accepted by the Soviet Union as they stand; and while the West considers them fair and responsible proposals, they remain open to negotiation.

The Soviet draft agreement, on the other hand, with which the United States and the United Kingdom were suddenly confronted on their return to the conference, in effect rejected not only the numerous provisions for international supervision already agreed at Geneva but even the small amount of control contained in the Soviet Union one-page treaty tabled at the very first meeting in 1958. This constituted an extraordinary step backwards and must be considered an affront both to the other members of the conference and to the majority of members of the United Nations who voted for Resolution 1649 (XVI). Nevertheless, in the course of the resumed negotiations, the United States and United Kingdom delegations, in order to leave no doubt about the Soviet position, questioned the Soviet delegation closely.

The Soviet delegation said that the Soviet Union was no longer prepared to accept impartial international verification because of the tension existing in international relations. He was, however, unable to say:

[1] Above, pp. 407–23.

(a) How the international situation had deteriorated since June 4, 1961, when the Soviet Government had most recently stated in a Note to the United States Government that it was prepared to accept international control for a nuclear test ban treaty;[1]

(b) Why the Soviet Union had continued during the period immediately before its test series to adhere to agreed treaty articles embodying the principle of international control which it was obviously planning to repudiate as soon as its tests were concluded;

(c) Why the United States and United Kingdom were confronted with this sudden change in the Soviet attitude only a day or two before the conferences began and then only through the international Press.

The Soviet contentions that the international situation compelled it first to resume testing and then to change its attitude in the conference is patently untenable. The Soviet-manufactured crisis in 1961 corresponds closely to the tense situation created by the Soviet Union in 1958 when the conference began.[2] It is precisely the existence of tension and the absence of confidence engendered by Soviet actions over Berlin and elsewhere which makes international verification of a test ban all the more necessary.

Moreover, the Soviet series of tests has contributed to tension in the international situation and it is notable that the Soviet Union is only proposing a test ban agreement without international supervision at a moment when it has concluded its massive series of tests and is unashamedly boasting about them and threatening to renew them.

The Soviet proposal for an agreement simply on the word of the parties is all the more unacceptable in that the Soviet Union had previously given its word that it would not be the first among the three members of the nuclear test ban conference to resume testing and had solemnly voted in the United Nations on the 20 December, 1960, for a moratorium on further nuclear weapon testing.[3]

The Soviet Government argues that its new proposals resemble those made by President Kennedy and Prime Minister Macmillan on September 3.[4] But the Soviet Government rejected them. In any case, the Western proposals on that date were made in an emergency in an attempt to save the world from the dangers of the Soviet test series and in the hope that they would lead to a sound treaty under international control. Experience of Soviet actions since then have, however, gone far to destroy that hope.

The United States and the United Kingdom are continuing their efforts at Geneva to persuade the Soviet Union to reverse its present position and open the way to fruitful negotiations on the basis recommended by the United Nations General Assembly in Resolution 1649 (XVI).

The United States and the United Kingdom undertake to continue to keep the Disarmament Commission, and through it, the General Assembly, informed of the progress of the Geneva negotiations.

---

[1] Above, p. 433.   [3] *Documents*, 1960, pp. 108–9.
[2] Over Berlin; cf. *Survey*, 1956–8, pp. 584–8.   [4] Above, p. 465.

(d) *The Soviet attack on the Secretary-General of the United Nations*

1. Speech by the Soviet Foreign Minister, Mr. Gromyko, to the General Assembly, 21 March 1961[1] (extracts)

. . . 74. The events in the Congo raise with new urgency the question whether the United Nations with its present structure can perform as a truly international organization its duty of guarding international security and the freedom and independence of peoples. The events in the Congo would alone have been quite sufficient proof that the United Nations present structure is monstrous and cannot be allowed to remain.

75. The disgraceful part played by the head of the executive staff of the United Nations in the events in the Congo once again confirms the wisdom of the Head of the Soviet Government, Mr. Khrushchev, in asserting at the first part of the fifteenth session of the General Assembly, the need to reorganize the structure of the United Nations on sound lines.[2] The Soviet Union firmly maintains this position, and considers re-organization of the structure of the United Nations even more urgent.

76. Why does the Soviet Government insist that the Secretary-General should no longer have supreme power and that the United Nations should have three secretaries, each representing one of the main groups of countries in the world today—the States members of the military blocs of the Western Powers, the socialist States, and the neutral countries? We insist on this because we want all countries to have equal opportunities in the United Nations. We are doing this because we cannot be content that the United Nations only has the façade of an international organization, and in fact continues to serve the interests of one group of States only.

77. There now exists in the United Nations the intolerable situation that Mr. Hammarskjöld is using his post of Secretary-General to usurp the prerogatives of its organs one after another and in a number of cases is acting for them and attempting to supplant them by his own person. This suits some people down to the ground. When there is mutual understanding between Mr. Hammarskjöld and those whose interests he is serving, it is even very convenient for some people to pursue their policy through him. Then discussion is superfluous, there is no need for a vote, and the veto is not a stumbling block. It is true that there is a small 'but'. Mr. Hammarskjöld's actions are making co-operation impossible between the Members of the United Nations, and especially between the three Powers who are permanent members of the Security Council. However, apparently this does not worry the people who are directing Mr. Hammarskjöld's action nor indeed Mr. Hammarskjöld himself. If he is allowed to go on as he is going, he will probably soon fancy that he is Prime Minister of the World Government and, given half the chance, will assert '*L'Organisation, c'est moi*'.

78. Why does the Secretary-General, the head of the executive body, the Secretariat, and thus an official of the United Nations, although he holds a responsible post, presume to disregard the interests of many States, although as

[1] G.A.O.R., Fifteenth Session, 965th plenary meeting, 21 March 1961, pp. 31–32.
[2] *Documents*, 1960, pp. 239–42 and 246–55.

everyone knows, in the United Nations decisions are taken by the States and not by the Secretariat? This is happening because Mr. Hammarskjöld is the henchman of one group of States—which incidentally is the smallest both in number of countries and size of population—but still is able to have his own way in the United Nations thanks to the lopsided, crazy structure both of the Secretariat and of the other organs of the United Nations. We naturally do not mind this group having its representatives in the executive body of the United Nations; we want the other two groups of States now existing in the world scene to have their representatives in it.

79. Nobody can reproach us on the ground that replacement of the supreme office of Secretary-General by a representative body would give the Soviet Union or the socialist states in general any one-sided advantage. No; we should not secure preferential position for ourselves, and are not seeking advantages at the expense of other States. We have right, justice, and common sense on our side, and will spare no effort to see that the activity of the United Nations is determined, not by the interests of any one group of countries, but by the general interests of the co-operation of States, irrespective of their political and social system.

80. Even now people still sometimes say: imagine not one but three persons guiding the activities of the executive body of the United Nations: how then will this body reach the agreement necessary for the adoption and implementation of decisions? However, this is superficial reasoning. Naturally, the smaller the group discussing a question, the smaller the chance, ostensibly, of disagreements arising. And if the number of participants is reduced to one, it may be assumed that he will never vote against himself.

81. It is also true that it is more complicated to work out agreed decisions than to bypass States, including permanent members of the Security Council, as Mr. Hammarskjöld is doing over the Congo. In our view it is better to make more efforts, show more patience, self-control and common sense, and finally come to an agreed decision, than to rely on the very risky method of imposing decisions to suit one group of countries and disregarding the legitimate interests of others. Such methods may lead to an even more dangerous situation than that with which the United Nations is confronted today in the Congo. The States whose legitimate interests are being disregarded will not hesitate duly to protect those legitimate interests.

82. The trouble is of course neither only nor mainly Mr. Hammarskjöld himself. Ultimately it is for the Western Powers to decide whom to appoint as their representative. We are demanding the removal of Mr. Hammarskjöld because all his actions as Secretary-General have been directed against the interests of the socialist countries and, we are convinced, of many other countries as well. Those who sympathize with him can give him a farewell dinner—not on the United Nations budget of course; out of voluntary contributions. But you will not see us there. The leadership of the executive body, the Secretariat, which would replace the single post of the United Nations Secretary-General should, in our opinion, be a kind of cross-section of the present world situation. It must reflect the real world, and not be an anachronism.

83. The Soviet Union is prepared to do everything in its power not to weaken

but to strengthen the United Nations as a true international organization, serving the cause of international co-operation.

84. The lessons of the events in the Congo give food for deep thought on the future fate of the United Nations: either it will gain enough strength to stop the aggression against the Congo; or else a fate is in store for it similar to that of the unfortunate League of Nations. Comparison with the situation faced by the League of Nations a quarter of a century ago is irresistible. Then Italian fascism launched an attack against Ethiopia. The Emperor Haile Selassie appealed for help from the rostrum of the League of Nations. But those who were managing affairs in that international organization did not want to extend a helping hand to Ethiopia, and did not want to curb the aggressor. It will be useful to recall that the Soviet Union then resolutely condemned this aggression, and sounded a warning against the serious consequences for peace which would ensue if the aggressor were not resisted. In reply we heard that Ethiopia was a distant under-developed country, on account of which it was not worth risking serious complications with the Fascist States. Everybody knows the outcome of the policy, which was followed for many years; of acquiescence in aggression. Only a few years afterwards it led to the Second World War.

85. Historical parallels, naturally, are always inaccurate. Who, however, would dare to deny that in our time any unpunished aggression is likely to produce an even more dangerous situation than that which arose out of the attack on Ethiopia? The main reason is that we all live in a world full of nuclear missiles, and the consequences of a policy of non-resistance to aggression in this world are even more dangerous than just before the Second World War.

86. In conclusion, the Soviet delegation would like to express the hope that during the present session of the General Assembly decisions will be adopted whereby the Congolese problem will be solved in accordance with the national hopes of the people of the Congo and the needs of peace, and that there will arise again in the United Nations a desire to re-establish its authority as a truly international organization guarding the peace, freedom and independence of the nations.

2. Statement by the Secretary-General of the United Nations, Mr. Hammarskjöld, to the General Assembly, 5 April 1961[1] (extracts)

. . . 6. On Tuesday, 21 March 1961, the Foreign Minister of the Soviet Union said in the Assembly, in words which merit to be put again on record:

'The Soviet Government has already declared that it considers Hammarsk-jöld to be responsible for the murder of Patrice Lumumba and his comrades. Today we are reiterating this accusation from the rostrum of the United Nations. For we cannot reconcile ourselves to this villainy which was perpetrated with the connivance of the international Organization of which our country is a Member, perpetrated with the sanction and assistance of the highest official in the United Nations executive body. We cannot reconcile ourselves to the fact that a prominent post in the United Nations is held by a man who has sullied himself by this murder. It is not only he who wields the

[1] G.A.O.R., Fifteenth Session, 977th plenary meeting, 5 April 1961, pp. 191–4.

knife or revolver that is the murderer: the main criminal is the one who placed the weapon in his hand.' [*965th meeting, para. 39.*]

Later the Foreign Minister requested the removal of the present incumbent from the post of Secretary-General 'as an accomplice and organizer of the slaughter of the leading statesmen of the Republic of the Congo' [*ibid., para. 43*].

7. Following up the same theme, the Foreign Minister of the Byelorussian Soviet Socialist Republic said:

'Having betrayed the interests of the Congolese people, having entered into a plot with the colonialists, having become a co-participant in the murder of Patrice Lumumba and his colleagues, Mr. Hammarskjöld has lost all the confidence and has brought upon himself the condemnation and contempt of all decent human beings. He has placed himself outside the United Nations.' [*970th meeting, para. 200.*]

8. Members of the Assembly will have noted that these accusations, couched in the most general and condemning terms, were put forward without attempts to give them credence by the indication of any single substantive fact on which they might be based.

9. I have no reason to comment on these accusations in personal terms. The record is there. It proves that the Secretariat and the United Nations Command have acted loyally in support of the interest of the whole of the Congolese people, that they have taken a completely independent, in fact, defiant, stand against so-called colonialists—as well as against others who have tried to intervene in the Congo—and have done what could be done for the protection of Mr. Lumumba by the means at the disposal of the Secretary-General. However, the statements I quoted, and some others of the same character, require comments from another viewpoint.

10. Where, in any parliament, jealous of its democratic traditions, its integrity and its respect for the human person, could such allegations be made without those making them trying to justify their case or, especially, without the parliamentary body requesting them to do so? The United Nations General Assembly has been called a parliament of nations. Are the peoples of the world less jealous of the integrity of the General Assembly than the members of a nation are of the integrity of its democratic institutions?

11. We, all of us, who give what we may have to give to the work of this Organization, do so because of our faith in what it stands for and in the vital necessity of this experiment in organized international co-operation for mutual aims. We do so with pride in the integrity of the efforts made. When we come under responsible criticism, we accept it as a valuable contribution to the common effort, aimed at improving its quality. However, when criticism takes such a direction as to negate the very ideals for which the Organization stands and for which we consider it a privilege to work, one may be led to ask whether the spirit of this Organization will justify for long the faith on which the efforts are and must be based.

12. As an international civil servant entitled to express his views on the development of international co-operation in the forms provided by the United

Nations and related agencies, I consider it my duty to voice these concerns. I would have expressed them with equal conviction but with a greater sense of freedom if the developments to which I refer had not, as in this case, happened to refer also to me as a person.

13. As regards the Secretary-Generalship and my way of conducting my office, the critics have in this debate brought forward one new viewpoint, a viewpoint which seems to reveal awareness of the weakness of the arguments previously used, and to show also what the basic considerations are which, over the last few months, have led to the repeated and increasingly violent attacks. In the same speech on 21 March, Mr. Gromyko said:

'Having without any legitimate grounds taken the whole affair into his own hands, Hammarskjöld began to decide on his own what should and what should not be done . . . He began to determine on his own choice which countries should send their troops to the Congo and in what numbers; he placed those troops under his own command and became indeed, some sort of United Nations field marshal.' [*965th meeting, para. 9.*]

Further he said:

'An intolerable situation has, indeed, taken shape in the United Nations at present where Hammarskjöld, taking advantage of his office of Secretary-General, is usurping the prerogatives of its bodies, one after another, and in some cases has acted for these bodies trying to supplant them by his own person . . .

'If Hammarskjöld is allowed to follow this course, he may assume himself to be the Prime Minister of a World Government. . . .' [*Ibid., para 77.*]

From the context, it is to be assumed that also these latter remarks mainly refer to the Congo operation.

14. It is with some hesitation that I take your time for comments on this new element in the continued attack, since I am certain that all Members, who have followed the development of the Congo operations, are aware of the groundlessness of the allegations, and since I also believe that they give a realistic interpretation to the motives for the introduction of this new point. . . .

23. I believe that every Member of this Assembly knows why over the years, and again in the Congo crisis, the Security Council or the General Assembly have found it convenient to entrust, in very general terms, executive action on highly explosive problems to the Secretary-General. If the Soviet Union regrets its participation in these decisions, that is its right, but it is its opinion now that the Secretary-General, in anticipation of its own afterthoughts, should have refused to respond to requests for which it had voted?

24. The same theme has been taken up and further elaborated [*968th meeting*] also by another member of the Soviet group, the Foreign Minister of the Ukrainian SSR. He brought out four quotations from the Secretary-General's reports to the General Assembly which he considers as evidence of my 'usurpation' of power, against the Charter, and as supporting the theses of the Foreign Minister of the Soviet Union.

25. The first two quotations are from the reports of 1954 and 1956. It may

surprise some that the significance of these statements of mine had not been discovered until March 1961 and, especially, that they were not noted at my re-election in 1957.

26. However, the most important quote or, as the spokesman said, 'the most blatant expression' of my 'authoritative tendencies' is, according to him, to be found in my report to the General Assembly in 1959. The way in which the text is treated in the intervention may suffice as comment on all the observations of the speaker in this context. He said that the Secretary-General was 'compelled to recognize that in the United Nations Charter there was no basis for his unilateral actions'. Let us compare this with the text the speaker discussed. I quote the passage to which he seems to refer, in full:

> 'There have been, in the first place, various decisions taken in recent years by the General Assembly or the Security Council under which the Secretary-General has been entrusted with special diplomatic and operational functions, which he is responsible for carrying out within the wide framework of general terms of reference laid down in the resolutions and, naturally, in the Charter itself. This, also, represents an evolution of the procedures of the United Nations for which no explicit basis is to be found in the Charter. . . .' [A/4132/Add.1, p. 3.]

27. The Members of the General Assembly will thus see that the text referred to discusses action taken by the Secretary-General at the direct request of the General Assembly or the Security Council, and that the statement regarding the lack of an explicit Charter basis for such action refers not to the Secretary-General's response to the requests but to the decisions of the General Assembly and the Security Council.

28. I would invite the Members to make for themselves a comparison between what I have said and what I have now been said to have said. The speaker was kind enough to provide the Assembly with the necessary references, so I need not repeat them here. If the texts are studied. Members will find that also in this context it is now one of the main accusations against the Secretary-General that he has acted in accordance with requests for which the accusers have voted.

29. It is with regret that I have found it necessary to take the time of the General Assembly for comments on some points raised, as they have no relation to the situation in the Congo, although they have figured broadly in the speeches of one group of delegates.

30. Naturally, the methods illustrated by the points discussed have been applied also to the writing of the history of the Congo operation. One can admire the ingenious way in which, with a skilful combination of unrelated facts, a careful choice of data, and appropriate changes of emphasis and lighting, the representative of Romania, for example, has built up history which to the uninformed may have a semblance of veracity. But such admiration cannot hide the fact that the skill shown has no application to the way in which United Nations organs must deal with a serious international problem, however effective they may have proven for political puposes in this or that national setting.

31. At this point it may be appropriate for me to give a few comments of a mainly legal and technical nature regarding the two specific questions raised

before the Assembly by the representative of the Soviet Union in his intervention last Monday [*973rd meeting*].

32. The Soviet Union insists that expenditure for an operation like the one undertaken in the Congo and, of course, previously the operation started during the Suez crisis, from the financial point of view should fall under Articles 43 and 48 of the Charter; the principle is supposed to be that all expenditure for the maintenance of peace and security should be decided upon by the Security Council. Members of the General Assembly will undoubtedly have noted the implications of this principle.

33. A decision on action, be it for the maintenance of peace and security or for other aims within the Council's competence, is governed by the unanimity rule in the Security Council. No one can question the right of the Security Council to take decisions in pursuance of articles 43 or 48 or any other provisions under which it has competence. However, once the Council has taken a valid decision which imposes responsibilities on the Organization and requires implementation by the Secretary-General, then the costs which are involved are clearly expenses of the Organization within the meaning of Article 17, paragraph 2, of the Charter and therefore must be apportioned by the General Assembly. True, the Council retains the right to revoke or change its decisions, but as long as the decisions require expenditures by the Organization then Article 17, paragraph 2, must be considered applicable.

34. If this provision of the Charter were to be disregarded and the apportionment of expenses left to the Security Council, this would obviously involve an extension of the unanimity rule in that the approval of all the permanent members would be required for the continued financing of peace and security operations, In short, each permanent member would then have a continuing veto over the implementation decided on by the Council. This would enable each such member to prevent operations, even though the Council itself did not adopt a new decision revoking or modifying its previous action. I leave it to the Members of the General Assembly to draw their own conclusions regarding what this new line would have meant, for example, in the Suez crisis, or would mean for the future development of the Organization and its possibilities to render service in the essential area of international peace and security.

35. The complaint has also been made that the Congo operation has not been run by the Department of Political and Security Council Affairs, allegedly because the Department now is headed by a Soviet citizen.

36. In this context I wish to bring to your attention the following: The request for action was, in this as in other similar cases, addressed to the Secretary General, which obviously means the Secretary-General and not another member of the Secretariat, however qualified. The Secretary-General is the only member of the administration in which Members have chosen, by election, to vest political responsibility; he cannot and does not delegate such responsiblity, be it to a citizen of the Soviet Union or a citizen of the United States or, indeed, a citizen of any other Member country. The Secretary-General naturally must have the freedom to choose the collaborators who, among those available, he finds can best assist him in a special task. Nationality has to be taken into account, but the resources of the Secretariat are not such that nationality can be permitted to be

decisive. Nor does the choice automatically follow from the posts normally held by those assigned. Through the fifteen years of existence of the United Nations this has been the rule applied.

37. Were the Under-Secretary in charge of the Political Affairs Department, whoever he is, to be considered as automatically in charge of field operations, on his own personal responsibility, the logical conclusion would seem to be that he should be appointed with the approval of the main organs of the United Nations, in analogy with the principle established in Article 97.

38. The new stands on financing and on administration to which these short observations refer are obviously entirely consistent with the objectives of the proposal to put a group of three in the place of the Secretary-General.

39. All the various efforts of members of the Soviet group to build up a case against me have one and the same purpose, that is to try to achieve some progress in the direction indicated by Mr. Khrushchev's demand that I leave the post of Secretary-General. My position regarding this demand is well known from previous debates, especially from the recent debate in the Security Council. It can be summed up briefly as follows. I do not consider that I am entitled to present the General Assembly with a *fait accompli* by resigning because I have been requested to do so by a big Power and its like-minded supporters. On the other hand, I regard the will of the General Assembly in this respect as my law, and the General Assembly may thus consider itself as seized with a standing offer of resignation, were the Assembly to find it to be in the best interest of the Organization that I leave.

40. Members of the Assembly, in determining their position regarding this question, will undoubtedly wish to take into account the reduction of the usefulness of the Secretary-General caused by the withdrawal of co-operation with him by one of the permanent members of the Security Council. But they may also wish to consider the possibility to reconcile the view that a big Power, by withdrawing its co-operation, at any time should be able to break the term of office of the Secretary-General—thus *de facto* extending its right of veto from the election, as based on Article 97, to his conduct of business through the whole of his established term of office—to reconcile this with the spirit of Article 100 of the Charter and its demand that the Secretary-General, in order to preserve the international and independent character of the office, should be protected against pressures. In doing so, they will have to look at the reasons given for the withdrawal of co-operation as, obviously, the question of Article 100 does not arise if those reasons are found to be valid in terms of the Charter, while, on the other hand, the question does arise in a very pointed form if the reasons for withdrawal of confidence are found to be of a partisan nature, contrary to the principles of the Organization.

41. With this clear and unambiguous background, responsibility for the impact and consequences of the Soviet demand that the Secretary-General be dismissed rests where it should be, with the General Assembly and in particular with that vast majority of Members who have an overriding interest in the proper functioning of this Organization and who cannot be suspected of reflecting any bloc interests.

42. So far the Assembly has not been seized with the issue in a form requiring

its formal consideration. If the Assembly does not, on such a basis or otherwise, give expression to its wish for action in accordance with the Soviet demand I must, with my standing offer of resignation before it, conclude that it neither expects me to proceed on the basis of that offer nor desires in any other way to avail itself of the possibility it opens. . . .

3. Statement by the United States Secretary of State, Mr. Rusk, 14 July 1961[1]

Throughout history men have dreamed of a world organization capable of preserving the peace. After World War I the League of Nations was established for this purpose but failed because of internal weakness and defiance by aggressive powers. After World War II the United Nations was created to preserve the peace and security which are now essential as the alternative to the destruction of civilization.

It is therefore particularly regrettable that Chairman Khrushchev persists in his assault on the United Nations. In Moscow this week he stated flatly: 'To preserve the situation which now exists in the United Nations means to pave the way to the ruin and death of that international organization.'[2]

No one else wants the 'ruin and death' of the United Nations. The reason he objects to the United Nations, as he said, is 'the situation which now exists' there.

The basic situation 'which now exists' in the United Nations is that the organization has acquired a capacity to act to preserve the peace and security of the smaller nations which make up the great majority of its membership. This does not appear to suit the plans of the Soviet Union.

Mr. Khrushchev contends that he wants an organization in which 'all countries belonging to the United Nations have equal rights and enjoy equal opportunities'. This is what we have now—and what he does not like. To destroy these equal rights and opportunities, Mr. Khrushchev last year launched his proposal for a three-headed Secretary General, which he repeated on Monday.[3]

Under this proposal, the executive organ of the United Nations would not be administered by international civil servants but by 'three persons *representing the three principal groups of states*'. This reflects Mr. Khrushchev's pretenses that the world is divided into three blocks. There is only one bloc in the United Nations which takes its order from a single authority: the Communist bloc, which represents 10 per cent of the members. The other 90 per cent are free to think and decide for themselves although they tend to group themselves by cultural and political sympathies and common interests.

The so-called 'troika' proposal flies in the face of everything we know about effective administration. But the real point of it is that a majority of the members of the United Nations—countries in Asia, the Middle East, Africa and Latin America—would have a total of one vote among them in the executive direction of the United Nations—and that vote could be nullified by a veto. The United Nations would be powerless to act on any proposal that did not suit the purposes of the Soviet Union.

Thus Mr. Khrushchev's assault against the United Nations is, in reality, an

[1] *D.S.B.*, 31 July 1961, pp. 183–4.
[2] In a speech at a luncheon in honour of Dr. Nkrumah; text in *Soviet News*, 13 July 1961.
[3] Tuesday, not Monday, in the speech cited in n. 2.

attack on the 'equal rights and equal opportunities' now enjoyed by all members of the General Assembly—and the protection afforded them by the United Nations' peace-keeping machinery.

An impressive majority of the members already has answered Mr. Khrushchev's assault on the integrity of the United Nations when they rejected his outrageous demand, during the Fifteenth General Assembly, to replace the Secretary General with a three-headed directorate. Mr. Khrushchev made it very clear on Monday that he will continue to press his attack. There is no way that the Soviet Union can impose his proposal. This would mean an amendment of the Charter which requires the consent of the United States and other permanent members of the Security Council. We would not consent, nor would the necessary two-thirds of the General Assembly. The United Nations will not destroy itself.

4. Mr. Hammarskjöld's Introduction to the Annual Report of the Secretary-General of the United Nations, 17 August 1961[1]

I. THE CHOICE

Debates and events during the year since the publication of the last report to the General Assembly have brought to the fore different concepts of the United Nations, the character of the Organization, its authority and its structure.

On the one side, it has in various ways become clear that certain Members conceive of the Organization as a static conference machinery for resolving conflicts of interests and ideologies with a view to peaceful coexistence, within the Charter, to be served by a Secretariat which is to be regarded not as fully internationalized but as representing within its ranks those very interests and ideologies.

Other Members have made it clear that they conceive of the Organization primarily as a dynamic instrument of governments through which they, jointly and for the same purpose, should seek such reconciliation but through which they should also try to develop forms of executive action, undertaken on behalf of all Members, and aiming at forestalling conflicts and resolving them, once they have arisen, by appropriate diplomatic or political means, in a spirit of objectivity and in implementation of the principles and purposes of the Charter.

Naturally, the latter concept takes as its starting point the conference concept, but it regards it only as a starting point, envisaging the possibility of continued growth to increasingly effective forms of active international cooperation, adapted to experience, and served by a Secretariat of which it is required that, whatever the background and the views of its individual members, their actions be guided solely by the principles of the Charter, the decisions of the main organs, and the interests of the Organization itself.

The first concept can refer to history and to the traditions of national policies of the past. The second can point to the needs of the present and of the future in a world of ever-closer international interdependence where nations have at their disposal armaments of hitherto unknown destructive strength. The first one is firmly anchored in the time-honoured philosophy of sovereign national States

[1] G.A.O.R., Sixteenth Session, Supplement No. 1A.

in armed competition of which the most that may be expected in the international field is that they achieve a peaceful coexistence. The second one envisages possibilities of inter-governmental action overriding such a philosophy, and opens the road towards more developed and increasingly effective forms of constructive international cooperation.

It is clearly for the governments, Members of the Organization, and for these governments only, to make their choice and decide on the direction in which they wish the Organization to develop. However, it may be appropriate to study these two concepts in terms of the purposes of the Organization as laid down in the Charter, and, in this context, also to consider the character and significance of the decisions of the Organization as well as its structure.

II. Charter Purposes and Principles

The purposes and principles of the Charter are set out in its Preamble and further developed in a series of articles, including some which may seem to be primarily of a procedural or administrative nature. Together, these parts of the Charter lay down some basic rules of international ethics by which all Member States have committed themselves to be guided. To a large extent, the rules reflect standards accepted as binding for life within States. Thus, they appear, in the main, as a projection into the international arena and the international community of purposes and principles already accepted as being of national validity. In this sense, the Charter takes a first step in the direction of an organized international community, and this independently of the organs set up for international cooperation. Due to different traditions, the state of social development and the character of national institutions, wide variations naturally exist as to the application in national life of the principles reflected in the Charter, but it is not too difficult to recognize the common elements behind those differences. It is therefore not surprising that such principles of national application could be transposed into an agreed basis also for international behaviour and cooperation.

In the Preamble to the Charter, Member nations have reaffirmed their faith 'in the equal rights of men and women and of nations large and small', a principle which also has found many other expressions in the Charter.

Thus, it re-states the basic democratic principle of equal political rights, independently of the position of the individual or of the Member country in respect of its strength, as determined by territory, population or wealth. The words just quoted must, however, be considered as going further and imply an endorsement as well of a right to equal economic opportunities.

It is in the light of the first principle that the Charter has established a system of equal votes, expressing 'the sovereign equality of all its Members', and has committed the Organization to the furtherance of self-determination, self-government and independence. On the same basis, the Charter requires universal respect for and observance of human rights and fundamental freedoms for all 'without distinction as to race, sex, language or religion'.

It is in the light of the latter principle—or, perhaps, the latter aspect of the same basic principle—that the Charter, in Article 55, has committed the Members to the promotion of higher standards of living, full employment and conditions of economic and social progress and development as well as to solutions of international economic and related problems. The pledge of all Members to take joint and separate action, in cooperation with the Organization, for the achievement of these purposes has been the basis for the far-reaching economic and technical assistance channelled through or administered by the Organization, and may rightly be considered as the basic obligation reflected also in such economic and technical assistance as Member governments have been giving, on a bilateral basis, outside the framework of the Organization.

It would seem that those who regard the Organization as a conference machinery, 'neutral' in relation to the direction of policies on a national or international basis and serving solely as an instrument for the solution of conflicts by reconciliation, do not pay adequate attention to those essential principles of the Charter to which reference has just been made. The terms of the Charter are explicit as regards the equal political rights of nations as well as of individuals and, although this second principle may be considered only as implicit in the terms of the Charter, they are clear also as regards the demand for equal economic opportunities for all individuals and nations. So as to avoid any misunderstanding, the Charter directly states that the basic democratic principles are applicable to nations 'large and small' and to individuals without distinction 'as to race, sex, language and religion', qualifications that obviously could be extended to cover also other criteria such as, for example, those of an ideological character which have been used or may be used as a basis for political or economic discrimination.

In the practical work of the Organization these basic principles have been of special significance in relation to countries under colonial rule or in other ways under foreign domination. The General Assembly has translated the principles into action intended to establish through self-determination a free and independent life as sovereign States for peoples who have expressed in democratic forms their wish for such a status. Decisive action has in many cases been taken by Member governments, and then the United Nations has had only to lend its support to their efforts. In other cases, the main responsibility has fallen on the Organization itself. The resolution on colonialism, adopted by the General Assembly at its fifteenth session, may be regarded as a comprehensive restatement in elaborated form of the principle laid down in the Charter. Results of developments so far have been reflected in the birth of a great number of new national States and a revolutionary widening of the membership of the Organization.

The demand for equal economic opportunities has, likewise, been—and remains—of special significance in relation to those very countries which have more recently entered the international arena as new States. This is natural in view of the fact that, mostly, they have been in an unfavourable economic position, which is reflected in a much lower *per capita* income, rate of capital supply and degree of technical development, while their political independence and sovereignty require a fair measure of economic stability and economic possibilities in order to gain substance and full viability.

In working for the translation into practical realities in international life of the democratic principles which are basic to the Charter, the Organization has thus assumed a most active role and it has done so with success, demonstrating both the need and the possibilities for such action.

Further, in the Preamble to the Charter it is stated to be a principle and purpose of the Organization 'to establish conditions under which justice and respect for the obligations arising from treaties and other sources of international law can be maintained'. In these words—to which, naturally, counterparts may be found in other parts of the Charter—it gives expression to another basic democratic principle, that of the rule of law. In order to promote this principle, the Charter established the International Court of Justice, but the principle permeates the approach of the Charter to international problems far beyond the sphere of competence of the Court. As in national life, the principle of justice—which obviously implies also the principle of objectivity and equity in the consideration of all matters before the General Assembly or the Security Council—must be considered as applicable without distinction or discrimination, with one measure and one standard valid for the strong as well as for the weak. Thus, the demand of the Charter for a rule of law aims at the substitution of right for might and makes of the Organization the natural protector of rights which countries without it might find it more difficult to assert and to get respected.

The principle of justice can be regarded as flowing naturally from the principles of equal political rights and equal economic opportunities, but it has an independent life and carries, of itself, the world community as far in the direction of an organized international system as the two first-mentioned principles. It has deep roots in the history of the efforts of man to eliminate from international life the anarchy which he had already much earlier overcome on the national level, deeper indeed than the political and economic principles which, as is well known, were much later to get full acceptance also in national life. Long before the United Nations and long before even the League of Nations, governments were working towards a rule of justice in international life through which they hoped to establish an international community based on law, without parliamentary or executive organs, but with a judicial procedure through which law and justice could be made to apply.

The Charter states and develops the three principles mentioned here as a means to an end: 'to save succeeding generations from the scourge of war'. This adds emphasis to the concept, clearly implied in the Charter, of an international community for which the Organization is an instrument and an expression and in which anarchic tendencies in international life are to be curbed by the introduction of a system of equal political rights, equal economic opportunities and the rule of law. However, the Charter goes one step further, drawing a logical conclusion both from the ultimate aim of the Organization and from the three principles. Thus, it outlaws the use of armed force 'save in the common interest'. Obviously, the Charter cannot, on the one side, establish a rule of law and the principle of equal rights for 'nations large and small', and, on the other hand, permit the use of armed force for national ends, contrary to those principles and, therefore, not 'in the common interest'. Were nations, under the Charter, to be allowed, by the use of their military strength, to achieve ends contrary to the principle of the equality of Members and the principle of justice, it would obviously deprive those very principles of all substance and significance. One practical expression of this approach, which may be mentioned here, is that the organs of the United Nations have consistently maintained that the use of force, contrary to the Charter as interpreted by those organs, cannot be permitted to yield results which can be accepted as valid by the Organization and as establishing new rights.

In the Charter, the right to the use of force is somewhat more extensive than may seem to be the case from a superficial reading of the phrase 'save in the common interest'. Thus, apart from military action undertaken pursuant to a decision of the Security Council for repression of aggression—that is, for upholding the basic Charter principles—the Charter opens the door to the use of armed force by a nation in exercise of its inherent right to resist armed attack. This is a point on which, both in theory and in practice, the development of international law is still at a very early stage. As is well known, no agreement has been reached on a definition of aggression, beyond that found in Article 2, paragraph 4, of the Charter,[1] and the Organization has several times had to face situations in which, therefore, the rights and wrongs in a specific case of conflict have not been clarified. It would be a vitally important step forward if wider agreement could be reached regarding the criteria to be applied in order to distinguish between legitimate and illegitimate use of force. History is only too rich in examples of armed aggression claimed as action in self-defence. How could it be otherwise, when most cases of armed conflict are so deeply rooted in a history of clashes of interests and rights, even if, up to the fatal moment of the first shot, those clashes have not involved recourse to the use of armed force?

In recognition of this situation and in the light of historical experience, the Charter makes yet another projection into international life of solutions to conflicts tested in national life, and establishes the final principle that the Organization shall 'bring about by peaceful means and in conformity with the principles of justice and international law, adjustment or settlement of international disputes or situations which might lead to a breach of the peace'. This principle, as quoted here from Article 1 of the Charter, is further developed specifically in Article 33, which requires parties to any dispute, the consequence of which is likely to endanger the maintenance of international peace and security, to 'seek a solution by negotiation, enquiry, mediation, conciliation, arbitration, judicial settlement, resort to regional agencies or arrangements, or other peaceful means of their own choice'. It is in this sphere that the Security Council has had, and is likely to continue to have, its main significance, both directly as a forum before which any dispute threatening peace and security can be brought up for debate and as an organ which directly, or through appropriate agents, may assist the parties in finding a way out and, by preventive diplomacy, may forestall the outbreak of an armed conflict. It seems appropriate here to draw attention especially to the right of the Security Council under Article 40 to 'call upon the parties concerned to comply with such provisional measures as it deems necessary or desirable' for the prevention of any aggravation of a situation threatening peace and security, and to the obligation of Members to comply with a decision on such measures.

It is in the light of the approach to international coexistence in our world

---

[1] 'All members shall refrain in their international relations from the threat or use of force against the territorial integrity or political independence of any state, or in any other manner inconsistent with the Purposes of the United Nations.'

today, which is thus to be found in the Charter, that judgment has to be passed on the validity of the different conceptions of the Organization which in recent times have become increasingly apparent. As already pointed out, the basic principles regarding the political equality of nations and their right to equal economic opportunities are difficult to reconcile with the view that the Organization is to be regarded only as a conference machinery for the solution, by debate and joint decisions, of conflicts of interest or ideology. It seems even more difficult to reconcile these principles with a view according to which equality among Members should be reflected in the establishment of a balance between power blocs or other groupings of nations. The same difficulty is apparent as regards the principle of justice and the principle prohibiting the use of armed force. It is easier to apply the conference concept to the principle of prevention of conflict through negotiation, but also on this point the difficulties become considerable if it is recognized that such solutions as may be sought by the Organization should be solutions based on the rules of equality and justice.

III. Respect for Authority of the Organization

The General Assembly, the Security Council and other collective organs of the United Nations have features in common with a standing international diplomatic conference, but their procedures go beyond the forms of such a conference and show aspects of a parliamentary or quasi-parliamentary character.

While decisions of a conference, in order to commit its participants, must be based on their subsequent acceptance of the decisions, the organs of the United Nations act on the basis of voting, with the decisions being adopted if supported by a majority. However, the decisions of the Assembly have, as regards Member States, only the character of recommendation (except for financial assessments and certain other types of organizational action) so that obligations like those arising out of an agreement, coming into force after a conference, do not normally flow from them. But although the decisions, legally, are only recommendations, they introduce an important element by expressing a majority consensus on the issue under consideration.

Naturally, such a formula leaves scope for a gradual development in practice of the weight of the decisions. To the extent that more respect, in fact, is shown to General Assembly recommendations by the Member States, they may come more and more close to being recognized as decisions having a binding effect on those concerned, particularly when they involve the application of the binding principles of the Charter and of international law.

Both those who regard a gradual increase in the weight of decisions of the General Assembly as necessary, if progress is to be registered in the direction of organized peaceful coexistence within the Charter, and those who oppose such a development, have to recognize that, with certain variations in individual cases, the practice still is very close to the restrictive Charter formula. Experience shows that even countries which have voted for a certain decision may, later on, basing themselves on its character of merely being a recommendation, refuse to follow it or fail to support its implementation, financially or in other respects.

What has been said applies generally to the collective organs of the Organization, but, as is well known, the Charter has gone one step further beyond the conference concept, in the direction of the parliamentary concept, in the case of the Security Council. In Article 25, Member States of the United Nations have agreed to 'accept and carry out the decisions of the Security Council in accordance with the present Charter', thus by agreement, making the decisions of the Council mandatory, except, of course, when such decisions take the form of 'recommendations' within the terms of Chapter VI or certain other articles of the Charter. They have further, in Article 49, undertaken to 'join in affording mutual assistance in carrying out the measures decided upon by the Security Council'.

This agreed mandatory nature of certain Security Council decisions might have led to a demand for unanimity in the Council, a unanimity which was the rule for the Council of the League of Nations. Even so, however, the arrangement would have gone beyond the conference principle with its requirement that no decision reached in an international organ should be binding on an individual Member short of his agreement. With the present arrangements, requiring a majority of seven and the concurring votes of the permanent members, a bridge between the traditional conference approach and a parliamentary approach is provided by the commitment in Article 25 to agree to the carrying out of the decisions in the Council which should be considered as giving the Council its authority by general delegation as indeed stated in Article 24, paragraph 1.[1]

What clearly remains within the Council of the traditional conference and agreement pattern is the condition that its decisions of a non-procedural character must be supported by the unanimous vote of the five permament members, thus avoiding for those members the risk of being bound by a decision of the Council which has not met with their agreement. It may be observed that this special position for the permanent members, apart from other reasons, has the justification that, without such a rule, the other Members of the Organization, in complying with a Security Council decision, might find themselves unwillingly drawn into a big Power conflict.

In spite of the delegated authority which the Council may be considered as exercising, and the condition that decisions must be agreed to by the permanent members, the experience of the Organization, as regards the implementation of Council decisions, is uneven and does not indicate full acceptance in practice of Article 25. In this case also, examples can be given of a tendency to regard decisions, even when taken under Chapter VII, as recommendations binding only to the extent that the party concerned has freely committed itself to carry them out; there is here a clear dichotomy between the aims of the Charter and the general political practice at its present stage of development. Such cases refer not only to Members outside the Council, or, perhaps, Members inside the Council, who have not supported a specific decision, but also to Members within the Council who have cast their votes in favour of a decision but who later on are found to reserve for themselves at least a right to interpret the decision in ways which seem to be at variance with the intentions of the Council. The ambiguity of this situation emerges with special force in cases where such attitudes have

---

[1] 'In order to ensure prompt and effective action by the United Nations, its Members confer on the Security Council primary responsibility for the maintenance of international peace and security, and agree that in carrying out its duties under this responsibility the Security Council acts on their behalf.'

been taken by permanent members of the Council, who are considered to shoulder the responsibility for the maintenance of peace and security which is reflected in the special position they hold within the Council. Obviously, the problem whether the intended legal weight is given to decisions of the Security Council arises in practice not only in cases of non-compliance but also in cases of a refusal to shoulder the financial consequences of a decision of the Council.

These observations—which have been limited to a reminder of the Charter rules and a factual reminder also of the experiences in practice—point to a situation which in any evaluation of the United Nations must be given the most serious consideration by Members. For the judgment on the various concepts of the United Nations which are put forward, it is one thing to note what the Charter stipulates; it is an entirely different but ultimately more important question as to what the situation is in practice and what, in fact, is the weight given to decisions of the Organization when they go beyond the conference pattern of agreement.

For those who maintain the conference concept of the Organization, it is natural to side-step the mandatory nature of decisions by the Security Council. For those who take a different view, it is equally natural and essential to work for a full and general acceptance of the Charter rules. Were those to be right who hold that the Charter on the points discussed here, and, maybe, also as regards the five basic principles discussed in the first part of this Introduction, is ahead of our time and the political possibilities which it offers, such a view still would not seem to justify the conclusion that the clear approach of the Charter should be abandoned. Rather, it would indicate that Member nations jointly should increase their efforts to make political realities gradually come closer to the pattern established by the Charter.

In the light of such considerations, the significance of the outcome of every single conflict on which the Organization has to take a stand, and the weight given to its decisions in such a conflict stand out very clearly. A failure to gain respect for decisions or actions of the Organization within the terms of the Charter is often called a failure for the Organization. It would seem more correct to regard it as a failure of the world community, through its Member nations and in particular those most directly concerned, to cooperate in order, step by step, to make the Charter a living reality in practical action as it is already in law.

Were such cooperation, for which the responsibility naturally rests with each single Member as well as with all Members collectively, not to come about, and were the respect for the obligations flowing from Article 25 of the Charter, to be allowed to diminish, this would spell the end of the possibilities of the Organization to grow into what the Charter indicates as the clear intention of the founders, as also of all hopes to see the Organization grow into an increasingly effective instrument, with increasing respect for recommendations of the General Assembly as well.

What this would mean for the value of the Organization as protector of the aims, principles and rights it was set up to further and safeguard, is obvious. The effort through the Organization to find a way by which the world community might, step by step, grow into organized international cooperation within the Charter, must either progress or recede. Those whose reactions to the work of the Organization hamper its development or reduce its possibilities of effective action, may have to shoulder the responsibility for a return to a state of affairs which governments had already found too dangerous after the first World War.

IV. Executive Action and an International Secretariat

The growth of the United Nations out of the historic conference pattern—which, as observed earlier in this Introduction, at all events naturally remains the starting point in all efforts of the Organization—is clearly reflected in what, in the light of experience, may seem to be a lack of balance in the Charter. While great attention is given to the principles and purposes, and considerable space is devoted to an elaboration of what may be called the parliamentary aspects of the Organization, little is said about executive arrangements. This does not mean that the Charter in any way closes the door to such arrangements or to executive action, but only that, at the stage of international thinking crystallized in the Charter, the conference approach still was predominant, and that the needs for executive action, if the new Organization was to live up to expectations and to its obligations under the Charter, had not yet attracted the attention they were to receive in response to later developments.

The key clause on the executive side may be considered to be Article 24, in which it is said that 'in order to assure prompt and effective action by the United Nations, its Members confer on the Security Council primary responsibility for the maintenance of international peace and security'. On that basis the Security Council is given the right, under Article 29, to establish such subsidiary organs as it deems necessary for the performance of its functions, the right under Article 40 to decide on so-called provisional measures, the right to use, for the purposes of the Charter, under certain conditions, armed forces made available to the Council, the right under Article 48 to request from governments action on the Council's behalf, as well as the right to request of the Secretary-General to 'perform such . . . functions as are entrusted to him' by the Council.[1]

The various clauses here briefly enumerated open a wide range of possibilities for executive action undertaken by, and under the aegis of, the Security Council. However, no specific machinery is set up for such action by the Council, apart from the Military Staff Committee, with planning responsibilities in the field of the possible use of armed force by the Security Council under Chapter VII of the Charter. In fact, therefore, the executive functions and their form have been left largely to practice, and it is in the field of the practices of the Organization that cases may be found in the light of which it is now possible to evaluate the ways in which the Organization may develop its possibilities for diplomatic, political or military intervention of an executive nature in the field.

The forms used for executive action by the Security Council—or when the Council has not been able to reach decisions, in some cases, by the General Assembly—are varied and are to be explained by an effort to adjust the measures to the needs of each single situation. However, some main types are recurrent. Sub-committees have been set up for fact-finding or negotiation on the spot. Missions have been placed in areas of conflict for the purpose of observation and local negotiation. Observer groups of a temporary nature have been sent out.

[1] Quoted from Article 98.

And, finally, police forces under the aegis of the United Nations have been organized for the assistance of the governments concerned with a view to upholding the principles of the Charter. As these, or many of these, arrangements require centralized administrative measures, which cannot be performed by the Council or the General Assembly, Members have to a large extent used the possibility to request the Secretary-General to perform special functions by instructing him to take the necessary executive steps for implementation of the action decided upon. This has been done under Article 98, as quoted above, and has represented a development in practice of the duties of the Secretary-General under Article 97. The character of the mandates has, in many cases, been such that in carrying out his functions the Secretary-General has found himself forced also to interpret the decisions in the light of the Charter, United Nations precedents and the aims and intentions expressed by the Members. When that has been the case, the Secretary-General has been under the obligation to seek guidance, to all possible extent, from the main organs; but when such guidance has not been forthcoming, developments have sometimes led to situations in which he has had to shoulder responsibility for certain limited political functions, which may be considered to be in line with the spirit of Article 99 but which legally have been based on decisions of the main organs themselves, under Article 98, and thus the exclusive responsibility of Member States acting through these organs. Naturally, in carrying out such functions the Secretariat has remained fully subject to the decisions of the political bodies.

This whole development has lately become a matter of controversy, natural and, indeed, unavoidable in the light of differences of approach to the role of the Organization to which attention has been drawn earlier in this Introduction. While the development is welcomed by Member nations which feel a need of growth as regards the possibilities of the Organization to engage in executive action in protection of the Charter principles, it is rejected by those who maintain the conference concept of the Organization. The different opinions expressed on the development are only superficially related to this or that specific action and the way in which it is considered to have been carried through. They are also only superficially related to the choice of means used for translating decisions into action. The discussion regarding the development of executive functions is basically one confronting the same fundamentally different concepts of the Organization and its place in international politics, which could be seen also in the different attitudes towards the legal weight of decisions of the Organization.

It is in this context that the principle embodied in Article 100 of the Charter is of decisive significance. This principle, which has a long history, establishes the international and independent character of the Secretariat. Thus, it is said that the Secretary-General and the staff of the Secretariat 'shall not seek or receive instructions from any government or from any other authority external to the Organization', and that they 'shall refrain from any action which might reflect on their position as international officials responsible only to the Organization'. In the same Article, the Members of the United Nations undertake to respect 'the exclusively international character of the responsibilities of the Secretary-General and the staff and not to seek to influence them in the discharge of their responsibilities'.

The significance of the principle stated in Article 100 is a dual one. It envisages a Secretariat so organized and developed as to be able to serve as a neutral instrument for the Organization, were its main organs to wish to use the Secretariat in the way which has been mentioned above and for which Article 98 has opened possibilities. But in doing so, the principle also indicates an intention to use the Secretariat for such functions as would require that it have an exclusively international character.

In the traditional conference pattern, participants in a meeting are mostly serviced by a Secretariat drawn from the same countries as the participants themselves, and constituting a mixed group regarding which there is no need to demand or maintain an exclusively international character. It is therefore natural that those who favour the conference approach to the United Nations tend to give to Article 100 another interpretation than the one which the text calls for, especially in the light of its historical background and its background also in other clauses of the Charter.

There is no reason to go more deeply into this special problem here. Suffice it to say that, while the Organization, if regarded as a standing diplomatic conference, might well be serviced by a fully international Secretariat but does not need it, the other approach to the Organization and its role cannot be satisfied with anything less than a Secretariat of an exclusively international character, and thus cannot be reconciled with a Secretariat composed on party lines and on the assumption that the interests represented in the main organs in this manner should be represented and advocated also within the Secretariat. Thus, again, the choice between conflicting views on the United Nations Secretariat is basically a choice between conflicting views on the Organization, its functions and its future.

In order to avoid possible misunderstandings, it should be pointed out here that there is no contradiction at all between a demand for a truly international Secretariat and a demand, found in the Charter itself, for as wide a 'geographical' distribution of posts within the Secretariat as possible. It is, indeed, necessary precisely in order to maintain the exclusively international character of the Secretariat, that it be so composed as to achieve a balanced distribution of posts on all levels among all regions. This, however, is clearly something entirely different from a balanced representation of trends or ideologies. In fact if a realistic representation of such trends is considered desirable, it can and should be achieved without any assumption of political representation within the ranks of the Secretariat, by a satisfactory distribution of posts based on geographical criteria.

The exclusively international character of the Secretariat is not tied to its composition, but to the spirit in which it works and to its insulation from outside influences as stated in Article 100. While it may be said that no man is neutral in the sense that he is without opinions or ideals, it is just as true that, in spite of this, a neutral Secretariat is possible. Anyone of integrity, not subjected to undue pressures, can, regardless of his own views, readily act in an 'exclusively international' spirit and can be guided in his actions on behalf of the Organization solely by its interests and principles, and by the instructions of its organs.

V. Scope of the Organization's Activities

After this brief review of the principles of the Organization, of the character of its decisions and of its structure, especially as regards arrangements for executive action, presented only as a background for the consideration of what basic concepts and approaches should guide the development of the Organization, it may be appropriate, in conclusion, to give attention to the activities of the Organization and their relevance to the current international situation.

For years the Organization has been a focal point for efforts to achieve disarmament. This may still be considered as the main standing item on the agenda of the General Assembly. However, in recent years these efforts of the Organization have been running parallel to other efforts which are either outside of it or only loosely tied to the work of the United Nations. This may be justified on the basis that a very limited number of countries hold key positions in the field of armaments, so that any effort on a universal basis and by voting, to reach a decision having practical force, would be ineffective, unless founded on a basic agreement between those few parties mostly concerned. Therefore, direct negotiations between those countries are an essential first step to the solution, through the United Nations, of the disarmament problem, and do not in any way derogate from the responsibilities or rights of the Organization.

The situation may serve as an example of a problem which has become increasingly important in the life of the Organization: the right way in which to balance the weight of the big Powers and their security interests against the rights of the majority of Member nations. Such a majority naturally cannot expect the big Powers, in questions of vital concern to them, with their superior military and economic strength, automatically to accept a majority verdict. On the other hand, the big Powers cannot, as members of the world community and with their dependence on all other nations, set themselves above, or disregard the views of, the majority of nations. An effort to balance the big Power element and the majority element is found in the Charter rules regarding the respective competence of the General Assembly and the Security Council and regarding the special position of the big Powers within the Council. Other efforts to solve the same problem are reflected in the way in which the disarmament problem has been attacked in recent years. No fully satisfactory or definitive formula has been found, but it must be sought, and it is to be hoped that when the time comes for a Charter revision, agreement may be reached on a satisfactory solution.

What is true of the disarmament problem is, of course, true also of those more specific questions in which security interests of big Powers are or may be directly involved, as for example the Berlin problem. The community of nations, represented in the United Nations, has a vital interest in a peaceful solution, based on justice, of any question which—like this one—unless brought to a satisfactory solution, might come to represent a threat to peace and security. However, the problem of the balance to be struck between the rights and obligations of the big Powers and the rights and obligations of all other nations applies, in a very direct way, also to this problem which is now so seriously preoccupying the minds of all peoples and their leaders. The United Nations, with its wide membership, is not, and can, perhaps, not aspire to be a focal point in the debate on an issue such as the Berlin question, or in the efforts to solve it, but the Organization cannot, for that reason, be considered as an outside party which has no right to make its voice heard should a situation develop which would threaten those very interests which the United Nations is to safeguard and for the defense of which it was intended to provide all Member nations with an instrument and a forum.

Reference has already been made in this Introduction to the work of the Organization devoted to furthering self-determination, self-government and independence for all peoples. In that context it was recalled that the General Assembly, at its last session, adopted a resolution regarding the colonial problem which elaborates the basic principles of the Charter in their application to this problem.

This is, likewise, a question which for years has been before the General Assembly and it is likely to remain a major item until a final result is achieved which reflects full implementation of the basic principles in the direction indicated by last year's resolution. Experience has shown that peaceful progress in that direction cannot be guaranteed solely by decisions of the General Assembly or the Security Council, within the framework of a conference pattern. Executive action is necessary, and neither the General Assembly nor the Security Council—which has had to deal with situations in which the liquidation of the colonial system has led to acute conflict—has abstained from such action in support of the lines upheld. As in the past, executive action by the Organization in the future will undoubtedly also be found necessary if it is to render the service expected from it under the terms of the Charter.

It is in conflicts relating to the development towards full self-government and independence that the Organization has faced its most complicated tasks in the executive field. It is also in the case of executive action in this context that different concepts of the Organization and of its decisions and structure have their most pointed expressions. As regards this specific aspect of the work of the United Nations, the front line has not been the usual one between different bloc interests, but more one between a great number of nations with aims natural especially for those which recently have been under colonial rule or under other forms of foreign domination, and a limited number of powers with other aims and predominant interests. This seems understandable if one takes into account that a majority of nations wishes to stand aside from the big Power conflicts, while power blocs or big Powers tend to safeguard their positions and security by efforts to maintain or extend an influence over newly emerging areas. The United Nations easily becomes a focal point for such conflicting interests, as the majority looks to the Organization for support in their policy of independence also in their relation to such efforts, while power blocs or countries with other aims may see in the United Nations an obstacle in the way of their policies to the extent that the Organization provides the desired support. How this is reflected in the attitude towards the development of the executive functions of the United Nations can be illustrated by numerous examples. It may be appropriate in this context to say in passing a word about the problem of the Congo and the activities of the United Nations in that country.

Different interests and Powers outside Africa have seen in the Congo situation a possibility of developments with strong impact on their international position. They have, therefore, naturally, held strong views on the direction in which they would like to see developments in the Congo turn and—with the lack of political traditions in the country and without the stability which political institutions can get only by being tested through experience—the doors have been opened for efforts to influence developments by supporting this or that faction or this or that personality. True to its principles, the United Nations has had to be guided in its operations solely by the interest of the Congolese people and by their right to decide freely for themselves, without any outside influences and with full knowledge of facts. Therefore, the Organization, throughout the first year of its work in the Congo, up to the point when Parliament reassembled and invested a new national Government, has refused—what many may have wished—to permit the weight of its resources to be used in support of any faction so as thereby to prejudge in any way the outcome of a choice which belonged solely to the Congolese people. It has also had to pursue a line which, by safeguarding the free choice of the people, implied resistance against all efforts from outside to influence the outcome. In doing so, the Organization has been put in a position in which those within the country who felt disappointed in not getting the support of the Organization were led to suspect that others were in a more favoured position and, therefore, accused the Organization of partiality, and in which, further, such outside elements as tried to get or protect a foothold within the country, when meeting an obstacle in the United Nations, made similar accusations. If, as it is sincerely to be hoped, the recent national reconciliation, achieved by Parliament and its elected representatives of the people, provides a stable basis for a peaceful future in a fully independent and unified Congo, this would definitely confirm the correctness of the line pursued by the United Nations in the Congo. In fact, what was achieved by Parliament early in August may be said to have done so with sufficient clarity. It is a thankless and easily misunderstood role for the Organization to remain neutral in relation to a situation of domestic conflict and to provide active assistance only by protecting the rights and possibilities of the people to find their own way, but it remains the only manner in which the Organization can serve its proclaimed purpose of furthering the full independence of the people in the true and unqualified sense of the word.

The United Nations may be called upon again to assist in similar ways. Whatever mistakes in detail and on specific points critics may ascribe to the Organization in the highly complicated situation in the Congo, it is to be hoped that they do not lead Members to revise the basic rules which guide the United Nations' activities in such situations, as laid down in the first report of the Secretary-General to the Security Council on the Congo question, which the Council, a year ago, found reason, unanimously, to commend.

Closely related to a policy aiming at self-government and independence for all is the question of economic and technical assistance, especially during the first years of independence of a new Member State. The United Nations and its agencies and affiliated organs have at their disposal only very modest means for the purpose, but a rich experience has been gathered and the personnel resources are not inconsiderable.

Last year the Economic and Social Council and the General Assembly had to consider proposals designed to open up new possibilities for the Organization to respond to the demands of Member governments facing all the problems of newly achieved independence. Naturally, the problems which are of special importance for such countries are basically the same as those which face all countries which have been left behind in economic development. Therefore, the urgent attention requred by newly independent countries in this respect can in no way justify a discrimination in their favour against other countries with similar difficulties.

This year the General Assembly will have before it proposals initiated by the Scientific Advisory Committee and endorsed by the Economic and Social Council, for a conference under United Nations aegis, intended to provide possibilities for a break-through in the application of the technical achievements of present times to the problems of the economically less developed countries. It is sincerely to be hoped that, in the interest of international cooperation and the acceleration of the economic progress of those countries, this proposal will meet with the approval of the General Assembly.

So far, the economic and technical activities of the United Nations have been less influenced by the conflict between different concepts of the role of the Organization than its activities in other fields. However, it is impossible to isolate the economic and technical problems from the general question discussed in this Introduction. While receiving countries should have full freedom to take assistance from whatever source they find appropriate, they should not be barred, if they so wish, from getting all the assistance they need through United Nations channels or under United Nations aegis. The Organization is far from being able to meet all such demands, as donor nations continue to show a strong preference for bilateral approaches on a national or a group basis. Again, the problem arises of the basic concept of the United Nations. With the conference approach to the work of the Organization a choice is made also in favor of bilateral assistance, while the alternative, approach opens the door to a development under which international assistance, in implementation of the principle of equal economic opportunities for all, would be channelled through the Organization or its related agencies to all the extent that this is desired by the recipient countries and is within the capacity of the Organization.

Basic to the United Nations approach to economic and technical assistance is the principle, under all circumstances, that, although the Organization has to follow its own rules and maintain its own independence, its services are exclusively designed to meet the wishes of the recipient government, without the possibility of any ulterior motives and free from the risk of any possible influence on the national or international policies of that government. Whatever development the executive activities of the Organization may show in the field, there should never be any suspicion that the world community would wish or, indeed, could ever wish to maintain for itself, through the United Nations, a position of power or control in a Member country. Were political groups in a country really to believe in such a risk, the explanation would seem to be that, as has indeed happened in the case of governments of Member countries with long established independence, they may find it difficult to accept the judgment of the majority of the nations of the world as to what in a specific situation is necessary in order to safeguard international peace and security, when such a judgment appears to be in conflict with the immediate aims of the group. With growing respect for the decisions of the Organization and growing understanding of its principles, the risks for such misinterpretations should be eliminated.

This Introduction has limited itself to general observations on questions of principle, leaving all problems of detail to the report itself. This has seemed appropriate in view of the fact that the Organization has now reached a stage in its development where Member nations may find it timely to clarify their views on the direction in which they would like to see the future work of the Organization develop.

5. Statement by Mr. Rusk, 22 September 1961[1] (extracts)

. . . The United Nations is at a critical crossroads as a result of the unexpected and tragic death of Secretary-General Hammarskjöld. The United Nations is now engaged in urgent peace-keeping action in the Congo, in the Middle East, and elsewhere throughout the world. Its widespread activities—political, economic, social and humanitarian—demand strong, uninterrupted executive leadership. The Secretariat must continue to be directed with vigor, confidence and integrity.

It is unfortunately clear, however, that an immediate agreement cannot be expected on the naming of a permanent Secretary-General. The United States therefore believes that action must be taken now to assure that the functions of the office of the Secretary-General are performed effectively and fully while agreement is sought on the appointment of a new Secretary-General.

An outstanding world leader should be named immediately to perform the functions of the office of the Secretary-General for a temporary period, during which efforts to elect a permanent Secretary-General should proceed in accordance with Article 97 of the Charter.[2]

The authority of the office of the Secretary-General must not be compromised. A 'troika' or a panel in any form and at any level of the Secretariat would paralyze the executive of the United Nations and weaken it irreparably. Whoever is appointed should perform the full functions of the office.

The General Assembly has full authority to make such a provisional appointment. By the terms of the Charter, the Assembly has the power to regulate appointments in the Secretariat. That power necessarily includes provisional arrangements for carrying on the functions of the Secretariat's chief officer in emergencies. It has used that power before on at least two important occasions.

The first of these was in 1946 prior to the formal election of a Secretary-General, when the General Assembly adopted the proposal of its President that the Executive Secretary of the United Nations Preparatory Commission be

---

[1] *D.S.B.*, 16 October 1961, pp. 626–7.
[2] 'The Secretariat shall comprise a Secretary-General and such staff as the Organisation may require. The Secretary-General shall be appointed by the General Assembly upon the recommendation of the Security Council. He shall be the chief administrative officer of the Organisation.'

authorized to carry on the duties of Secretary-General pending the appointment of the Secretary-General.[1]

The second occasion was in 1950, when the Security Council was deadlocked in attempting to choose a successor to the first Secretary-General, Mr. Trygve Lie. In November of that year, by a vote of 46 to 5 with 8 abstentions, the General Assembly decided that the present Secretary-General should be continued in office for a period of 3 years.[2]

The vital interest of the members of the United Nations are heavily involved in this question. The Assembly must move rapidly to fill the void. Events cannot permit drift and indecision in the leadership of the United Nations.

We must not allow the prestige and authority of the organization to be dissipated by delay or by diminution of the effectiveness of an office that has become one of the United Nations' unique contributions to the peace of the world. . . .

6. Statement by the Soviet delegation to the United Nations, 2 October 1961[3]

In the past few days reports have appeared in the American press flagrantly distorting the position of the Soviet delegation on the temporary solution of the problem of the leadership of the United Nations secretariat. Attempts are being made to present the Soviet position as aimed at little less than using the veto in the everyday work of the secretariat's governing body.

All these reports are aimed at deluding the public and, at the same time, whitewashing the position of the circles which continue to uphold the vicious practice of subordinating the United Nations apparatus to the will of one country or group of countries. These circles seek to preserve—contrary to the United Nations Charter—the one-sided orientation of the organisation's administrative leadership and to liquidate its international character.

The Soviet Union's principled stand on the question of a radical reorganisation of the structure of the United Nations and its secretariat was reaffirmed in the statement by Andrei Gromyko, the head of the Soviet delegation, at the 16th session of the United Nations General Assembly.[4]

Under present conditions, as was pointed out in that statement, the delegation of the U.S.S.R. believes it possible to adopt an agreed provisional decision which would ensure uninterrupted administrative leadership of the United Nations secretariat, pending the adoption of a permanent decision, and 'would not deepen the gulf between states but provide an even more solid basis for their co-operation within the United Nations' framework'.

In the course of the exchange of opinions that the Soviet delegation had recently with representatives of different countries, including the United States, it advanced a conciliatory proposal on the provisional leadership of the United Nations secretariat.

[1] See G.A.O.R., First Session, 2nd plenary meeting, 11 January 1946, pp. 49–50. The Executive Secretary of the Preparatory Commission was Mr. Gladwyn Jebb of Britain, the President of the Assembly M. Spaak, of Belgium.

[2] Resolution 492 (V), in G.A.O.R., Fifth Session, Supplement No. 20, p. 79.

[3] *Soviet News*, 3 October 1961.

[4] On 26 September 1961; see G.A.O.R., Sixteenth Session, 1016th plenary meeting, 26 September 1961, pp. 102–3.

The essence of this proposal is that the General Assembly, on the Security Council's recommendation—as is provided for by the United Nations Charter —should invite as a leader of the United Nations secretariat for a definite term (until April, 1963) a person well known in United Nations circles, and that both the Security Council and the General Assembly should issue an appeal to this person and to his three deputies, who now work in the leading section of the secretariat and are highly skilled international officials from the U.S.S.R., the United States and one of the Asian or African countries, urging them to act in the spirit of concord.

The Soviet delegation has explained that it does not envisage the use of the veto by any of these assistants of the temporary head of the United Nations administrative apparatus.

However, he must co-operate daily with his assistants, as they must with him, and must strive for the achievement of mutual agreement on the basic questions of the secretariat's work.

These proposals have stemmed from the numerous wishes expressed in recent times by many delegations in the course of the 15th session of the General Assembly and in various United Nations bodies engaged in administrative matters.

The Soviet delegation believes that all those who are interested in normalising the work of the United Nations and in the businesslike day-to-day co-operation of all countries represented in the United Nations, cannot but support the proposals it has advanced giving due regard to the views of the basic groups of nations, and will reject all attempts at imposing on the General Assembly a one-sided decision in circumvention of the Security Council, which can only undermine the very foundation on which the United Nations rests.

7. Statement to the House of Lords by the British Foreign Secretary, Lord Home, 17 October 1961[1] (extracts)

. . . The same kind of considerations and difficulties as I have outlined in the case of disarmament apply to the future of the United Nations. It can be no more than a world debating society, with a very limited function in international policing, unless the Russians are prepared to take the risk that some of the majority decisions in the Assembly will cut across their Communist ambitions; and as yet there is no sign of that whatever. On the contrary, it was because the Communist objectives were thwarted in the Congo by the United Nations that the Russians added the Troika to the Veto. Under the pressure of almost universal disapproval, the Russians seem prepared now to allow one man to fill the gap between now and 1963 to act as Secretary-General of the United Nations. That is an advance since I first went to Washington and New York this autumn. But we must be clear about this: that although they allow one Acting Secretary-General, they still insist that no man can be impartial and, therefore, that there can be no true international civil servant. For this reason they seek to surround the Secretary-General with a group of advisers whom he would be bound to

---

[1] H.L. Deb., vol. 234, cols. 334–7.

consult on all major issues; and those advisers, in the minds of the Russians, would take their instructions from their own Governments.

My Lords, we in this country are perfectly willing to see Under-Secretaries under the Secretary-General of the United Nations chosen because of their knowledge of wide geographical areas. Indeed, there is merit in that proposal. There might be five Under-Secretaries, or there might be seven; or their might be more. But what we are not prepared to accept is the concept that the servants of the United Nations should take their orders from the national Governments of which they are citizens. If that were so, there would be a complete loss of confidence in the impartiality of the United Nations; indeed, it would be the end of the organisation.

I have lately had the opportunity of studying the reaction of the United Nations Assembly to the persistent use of the platform of the United Nations by the Russians and the Communist *bloc* to advance their own purposes in the cold war. There is hardly a delegation in the United Nations which does not detest Russian policies: the suppression of the independence of Hungary and East Germany: their attitude on nuclear tests: their censorship of all news circulating within the Soviet Union: their attitude to the inspection of armaments. But, my Lords, there are far too few in the United Nations Assembly who stand up and back up their convictions by speech or vote. On the contrary, a sort of complex has assailed the Assembly which compels them to vent their feelings on the democracies rather than on the Communist powers.

Speech after speech I listened to, while I was in New York this year, giving glaring examples of the double standard which is applied. Speeches and resolutions are directed against us, the United Kingdom, as 'colonialists'. They know perfectly well, particularly the Afro-Asian countries, that we have given independence to 600 million peoples in the last few years, and that that process continues rapidly. Yet resolution after resolution is framed and passed condemning the United Kingdom as colonialist, and there is never a protest against the Russian conduct of their own empire, which consists of one occupied country after another. The same is true of self-determination. That is pursued, so far as the Africans and the Asians are concerned, with a sort of holy fervour; but when it comes to self-determination for the Eastern Europeans, that is said to be something rather different. On nuclear tests, I heard speaker after speaker equating the attitude of the Soviet Union with that of the United States of America, making no allowance for the fact that it was the Soviet Union who broke the moratorium and tested in the atmosphere. But the performances of the Soviet Union and the United States were put by these speeches on the same level. I heard one speech from the representative of a country to whom we have given a great deal of assistance saying that technical aid agreements could be as bad as the old colonialism. I think it is necessary constantly to call attention to this inability of the countries in the Assembly of the United Nations, or a great many of them, to apply principles with impartiality.

This is not a matter on our part of injured pride or of feeling that there is ingratitude for what we have done: we have all lived long enough to know that there is no gratitude in international politics. But the democracies are the backbone of the United Nations. The democracies are the people who observe and support the rules of the Charter. And we cannot remain silent and be made the victims of attacks by people who know that they are unfair but deliver them, and know that they can deliver them safely, because they know that we are nice, tolerant people. We cannot allow—and I have no intention ever to allow—the case of the democracies to go by default, because if we do that in the Assembly of the United Nations any longer, the political standing of this country as a liberalising influence in the world will be fatally impaired. If that were to happen, it would do great damage not only to the United Kingdom but also to the small nations, particularly the Afro-Asian nations themselves. It would deal a mortal blow to their hopes of a just and free world and imperil the organisation which would give them assistance and aid. In the long run, they would find themselves without friends and therefore seal their own doom.

Nevertheless, with all its faults and with all the difficulties it causes for us, I conclude that we must show patience and more patience, and support the United Nations. And we must support it for these reasons: because any organisation which has as its main purpose the strengthening of peace is a British interest; because every move which the United Nations makes (in the words of the authors of the Charter)

'to harmonise the interests of the nations'

is incompatible with the Communist plan to divide the world; and because, despite the fact that nationalism and racialism and Communism are to-day in the ascendant, the facts of life are against them and the world is moving very fast towards inter-dependence. Provided we can secure that the United Nations is served by a truly impartial Civil Service, there are functions which it can well perform and which will be of great service to the world. For all those reasons, I come down in favour of the United Kingdom's strong support for the Organisation. . . .

8. Statement by the Acting Secretary-General of the United Nations, U Thant, 3 November 1961[1]

25. Speaking for the first time in this hall not in my familiar role as the delegate from Burma, but in the role of Acting Secretary-General of the United Nations, my first thought is to thank my fellow delegates for the honor they have done me, and the confidence they have placed in me, in electing me to this high office. May I at the same time thank you, sir, for your very gracious words of welcome, as also the President and the members of the Security Council for unanimously recommending my name to the General Assembly for election as Acting Secretary General.

26. Most of my colleagues present in this hall know me personally. They know that I come from a relatively small country in Asia. They also know that my country has steadfastly pursued over the years a policy of nonalignment and friendship for all other nations whatever their ideologies. In my new role, I shall continue to maintain this attitude of objectivity and to pursue the ideal of universal friendship.

[1] G.A.O.R., Sixteenth Session, 1046th plenary meeting, 3 November 1961, p. 551.

27. Having been the permanent representative of my country at the United Nations for the last four years and more, I am not unaware of the heavy responsibilities I am undertaking today. The debates in the General Assembly have already shown that the international climate can hardly be described as sunny. The organization is also facing a serious financial problem. In the Congo operation, which is one of the major undertakings in the history of the organization, we continue to encounter serious difficulties which clamor for an urgent solution.

28. If I am to discharge these responsibilities, surmount these difficulties, and resolve these problems, I shall need, in the first instance, the understanding and unstinting cooperation of all my colleagues, I have enjoyed such friendly cooperation from you all for so long as a delegate that I would fain hope that in my new role I shall receive it in even greater measure. For my part, I shall endeavor to cooperate with you all in every possible way. In addition to your cooperation, I shall also need the loyal support of my colleagues in the Secretariat.

29. I know how hard the Secretariat has had to work during the last sixteen months, especially in connection with the Congo operation. The Secretariat has shown itself capable of meeting all demands on it so far and I count on the continued assistance and team spirit of my colleagues in the Secretariat, especially in the difficult days ahead that we shall face together.

30. In particular, it is my intention to invite a limited number of persons who are at present Under Secretaries, or to be appointed as Under Secretaries to act as my principal advisers on important questions pertaining to the performance of functions entrusted by the United Nations Charter. In extending this invitation I am fully conscious of the paramount consideration of securing the highest standards of efficiency, competence and to the importance of as wide a geographical basis as possible, as laid down in Article 101 of the Charter. I intend to include among these advisers Dr. Ralph J. Bunche and Mr. Georgi Petrovich Arkadev. It is also my intention to work together with these colleagues in close collaboration and consultation in a spirit of mutual understanding. I am sure that they will seek to work with me in the same manner. Of course this whole arrangement is without prejudice to such future organizational changes as experience may reveal to be necessary.

31. Once again I thank the President, my fellow delegates in this hall, and the President and members of the Security Council for entrusting me with these heavy responsibilities. In discharging these responsibilities, I shall count on the support of all men and women of goodwill all over the world, whose overriding interest in the peace, security and progress of the world it will be my task to reflect and serve.

9. Speech by Lord Home to the Berwick-on-Tweed branch of the United Nations Association, 28 December 1961[1]

In order that none of us may have any doubts as to the purposes for which the United Nations was founded I will remind you of the obligations which were assumed by the member countries which signed The Charter. They resolved to

---

[1] Foreign Office press release.

'save succeeding generations from the scourge of war which twice in our lifetime
has brought untold sorrow to mankind' and they pledged themselves never to
use force for the resolution of conflicts 'save in the common interest' but to be a
'centre for harmonising the actions of nations'. The United Nations was founded
to provide security as the basis of peace and that is the purpose for which it exists
today.

Since the beginning of this century nations have been groping their way
towards interdependence. Inevitably, since man's oldest habit is to fight, the
organisation of peace must be a slow and frustrating business. The League of
Nations broke on the stresses and strains between its members. The United
Nations started with better prospects—first because the United States of America
was a member and secondly because many who were previously resigned to war
as inevitable have now realised that what Byron called 'that immortal fry of
almost everybody born to die' could literally come true.

Why then, if there is such a universal urge for peace and the machinery to
achieve it is ready to hand, is there a crisis of confidence in the United Nations?

The answer is that for the first time since its foundation a number of countries
have voted publicly and without shame in favour of the use of force to achieve
national ends.

Four countries which were members of the Security Council supported a
resolution condoning the use of force by India against Goa. Had the debate been
in the Assembly many more countries—perhaps even a majority—would have
voted the same way.

The significance of such action is this. Whatever the provocations suffered by
India or the excuses made by her or for her there is no doubt at all that her
actions were a direct breach of the Charter and of international law.

When the United Nations approves that, it could be as Mr. Adlai Stevenson
said, 'the beginning of the end'.

Many of us had foreseen this crisis of confidence. For years the Russians had
been frustrating the proper working of the United Nations but lately a new and
dangerous practice had begun to prevail.

Resolutions have been persistently passed by the Assembly, in particular on
colonialism, which could only be described as reckless and careless of peace and
security. Everyone has seen the chaos in the Congo and everyone knows that it
derives from a premature grant of independence to a country whose people were
totally unprepared for their new responsibilities. Yet many delegates were instructed by their governments to sponsor and vote for resolutions which could
only multiply and magnify that chaos in other places.

I will quote resolution 1514 of December 14, 1960,[1] which says:

> 'Immediate steps shall be taken in Trust and non-self-governing territories
> or in all other territories which have not yet attained independence to transfer
> all powers to the peoples of these territories without any conditions whatever'

and the resolution goes on:

> 'Inadequacy of political, economic, social or educational preparedness
> should never serve as a pretext for delaying independence.'

[1] *Documents*, 1960, pp. 404–6.

Such a resolution and others like it reveal an almost total lack of responsibility and certainly pay no heed to the main purpose of the United Nations which is to ensure order and security of peace.

Then again, although countries are free enough with their votes, they are not nearly so ready to pay their legally assessed subscriptions without which the organisation cannot be solvent or efficient.

Eighty-seven out of 104 are in serious arrears with their payments. The Soviet and their satellites do not pay anything towards the operations in the Congo or on the Israel-Egypt border, and France does not pay towards the Congo expenses.

When, therefore, we have reached a stage when a large part of the organisation which is dedicated to peace openly condones aggression: when an organisation which was founded to sustain law and order encourages policies which must endanger it or when a refusal by many to carry their share of the cost brings a prospect of power without responsibility, it is an understatement to say that there is cause for anxiety.

Tonight, therefore, I would like to analyse some of the causes of the present discontent and discuss with you what we can and should do to save an organisation in which so many of the hopes of men reside.

One of the main causes of the present troubles is an apparent difference of aim and purpose between the 51 founder members and many of the 53 newly independent countries which were elected to membership subsequently to the United Nations' foundation.

As the words which I gave at the beginning indicate the founder members laid the whole emphasis on the organisation of peace through collective security. They set up a Security Council to bear the primary responsibility for maintaining the peace. They named the great powers as permanent members in the expectation that they would agree on how to keep international order and would deal together with any breach of the peace by the smaller powers by united decision and coordinated action.

In the event of disagreement between the great powers each was armed with a veto on action by the others.

The best there could be was collective security collectively imposed—the worst (so it was supposed) stalemate and the status quo.

The supposition was wrong, for almost immediately the Russians showed themselves determined to use their veto to further the international objectives of Communism. Russia's decision to subordinate the main purposes of the Charter to her own national ends was the first breach in the spirit of the Charter and the first threat to the life of the United Nations.

For years the Russians have used the platform of the United Nations to prosecute the cold war using racialism, nationalism and the exuberant individualism of newly independent countries to further their ends. All this put the United Nations under serious stress and strain.

Now another breach is beginning to appear and the origin of it is somewhat similar. A large number of new countries are putting their campaign for acceleration of independence for colonial territories before the main purpose of the Charter which is to provide peace and security. They are more concerned to impose their views on 'colonialism' on others than to fulfil their primary duty which is to 'harmonise the actions of nations'.

I would not equate their motives with those of the Communists, although far too often they find themselves bed-fellows, but the effect of their actions is to weaken the Charter and to call in question the good faith of the United Nations. Unwittingly they play the Communists' game.

This leads me to illustrate how this concentration on colonialism leads to the adoption of a double standard of behaviour by many of the newly elected countries.

Russia's Empire is occupied by military force and ruled by fear. No one who has witnessed what has happened in Hungary and East Germany can have any doubt that Russia's colonialism is the most cruel and ruthless in history. In the United Nations her technique is undisguised—it is that of the bully.

By contrast the British record is one which has freed 600 million people in fifteen years and transformed them from colonial dependence to complete independence within the Commonwealth, where they are equal partners and in no way subordinate. We are moving fast—perhaps faster than in prudence we ought—in the direction in which the new countries want to go. The United Nations members know that to be true but they seldom condemn the Russians and constantly harass us. It seems as if pushing at an open door is not good enough for them. To cooperate with the metropolitan power in completing the process of independence in an orderly way: to ensure that new nations get a good start in international life is apparently emotionally unsatisfying and politically unrewarding.

Since we in Britain are agreed on independence anyway, the only way to pick a quarrel is over timing. Self-government today regardless of whether there is anyone capable of governing—independence tomorrow even though it would mean other Congos.

The double standard as applied to Europeans and Russians, and Europeans and Afro-Asians became so blatant that I felt bound to draw attention to it in the U. N. Assembly. I said:

The United Nations, and in particular this Assembly, must show itself to be impartial, must be seen to be impartial. I'm only going to ask this question; I'm not sure of the answer. Is there growing up, almost imperceptibly, a code of behaviour where there is one rule for the Communist countries and another for the democracies? One rule for the bully, who deals in fear, and another for the democracy because their stock in trade is reason and compromise?

But if the United Nations is to be the body which we wish to see, which guards the weak and is jealous of the independence of small nations, then they must not yield to the temptation to put public pressure always upon the reasonable nations because they feel that in the last resort those nations will be decent and, therefore, will give way. That would be to deny justice to others which they themselves wish to enjoy.

This evidence of a serious falling away from the principles of the Charter places Britain in an appalling dilemma.

Peace, for ours is a most vulnerable island, is the first of British interests. We practise the rule of law and if it is important for us at home it is equally so abroad where we have to earn our living. We want above all to cooperate with all nations without exception. Our safety lies in making and keeping friends and the more the better.

All our instincts and interests therefore combine to urge support for the kind of United Nations for which the founders drew up the Charter. The question which many sober and responsible observers of its practice are asking is whether we can continue to do so and whether the United Nations of the authors of the Charter has had its day?

Let me put the other side of the balance sheet.

1. Whatever its faults the aims of the United Nations are sound and its aspirations true. Britain cannot afford lightly to discard an instrument dedicated to peace which is struggling to put together the elements of peace-keeping machinery however elementary it may appear. Man is not so far removed from the jungle that he can dispense with any discipline there may be to hand.

2. The Communists aim is constant but there is a change working within the Communist societies. From being monolithic it has become through doctrinal disputes what the egg-heads would call polycentric.

Nor need we expect that the Communist powers will always get their way in the United Nations. Already Russia's campaign to achieve a troika in the secretariat has been defeated by the common sense of the Assembly.

3. Colonialism (except in the Russian Empire) is transient and after a few more years of emotionalism it should no longer distort the outlook of members of the United Nations.

4. Some of the decisions of the Security Council have certainly helped to promote the main purpose of the Charter which is peace and security. Luck, because the Soviet was absent from the meeting, enabled collective action to be taken in Korea. United Nations police have helped to keep the peace on the Israel-Egypt frontier. Although we have been, and I believe, rightly, critical of their methods in the Congo, the United Nations have kept the cold war out of that country.

The late Secretary-General too had many acts of conciliation to his credit which prevented disputes in their early stages from becoming acute. The Secretariat can unquestionably do a lot in the field of pacification.

5. Much quiet, unostentatious but valuable work is being done in the fields of education and farming, medicine and labour relations and technical assistance of all sorts. In an unspectacular way the groundwork is being laid for one world.

There then is the loss and the profit. There is no easy way out of our dilemma and we shall not be tempted to look for one—there are no soft options in international affairs.

But having drawn up the balance sheet between pessimism and hope I come down decidedly on the side of hope. And more than that, on a determined effort by ourselves and those who feel like us to bring the United Nations back to working the Charter as it was meant to be. Peace and security must be reinstated as its primary aims.

I have gone into these matters at some length first because the United Nations is of such importance in the life of Britain and for mankind and secondly because I believe that the making of policy should be shared by the people.

I am quite certain that the United Nations Association in this country have a real and honourable task to perform. The Government looks to you to keep the aims and principles of the Charter before the people of this country. That, as I have said, is bound to involve some criticism of its practice but where does loyalty lie, with those who urge upon it actions which tax it beyond its strength or with those who insist that its actions should remain within the compass of the Charter?

In return the Government ask your understanding and informed support as they try to steer a safe and realistic course for our country, neither sailing off into the blue of Utopia nor foundering upon the reefs of cynicism.

With our native blend of idealism and common sense we shall get there in the end.

E. INTERNATIONAL FINANCIAL DIPLOMACY

1. Speech by Lord Cobbold, Governor of the Bank of England, at the Mansion House, 20 October 1960[1] (extracts)

. . . In the monetary field the past twelve months have been notable for three things; a strong swing in the pendulum of monetary policy, the introduction of a new technical device, and a heavy movement of international funds between different markets.

From early 1958 until late 1959 monetary policy had been directed towards countering a mild recession. It was on this occasion at the Mansion House last year that the first notes of caution were sounded that demand might again be running too fast and that the economy might again be in danger of getting overloaded. During the first half of 1960 these dangers became more apparent and monetary policy was progressively tightened to help in combatting them.

It is too early to assess exactly the part played by monetary measures, individually or collectively, in restraining the boom which was gathering force in the spring. But experience since September, 1957, suggests that monetary policy in general, and Bank Rate in particular, exercises greater influence now, when there is more underlying stability in the economy, than it could in the early years after the war, when the economy was distorted and inflationary pressures overwhelming. Indeed it may well be the case that, had the Radcliffe Committee taken its evidence two years later, witnesses would have ascribed considerably more force to monetary measures than they did at the time. The one proviso remains, now as in earlier years, that monetary policy can only carry a part of the burden of economic adjustment, and cannot be affective if it is expected to work against, rather than in support of government policies in fiscal and other fields.

The Special Deposits Scheme, as the Chancellor has said, is not particularly mysterious, and indeed it is very similar to schemes which have been in use elsewhere. I am not myself enamoured of any of these technical devices. Their usual

[1] Bank of England Quarterly Bulletin, No. 1, December 1960, pp. 19–20.

purpose is to correct an excess of liquidity, which it would be better to prevent at the source. But prevention is not always possible, and Special Deposits have this year proved a useful addition to our monetary armoury. Without going too far into technicalities I would add two comments on this subject. Experience so far has confirmed us in the view which we expressed to the Radcliffe Committee that this device is to be preferred to other similar arrangements having approximately the same effect. And I still have the feeling that any prolonged or frequent use of this system (or indeed of any form of credit squeeze on the banks, voluntary or compulsory) is both unfair to the organised banking community, and in the long run liable to be ineffective, unless some similar restraint can be applied to wider categories of short-term lenders.

In the exchange markets significant changes had already taken place in 1959. The greater sense of stability of currencies and the higher degree of convertibility had meant that different levels of interest rates in different centres were having more effect on the movement of funds from one country to another than in earlier post-war years.

This tendency has become more pronounced in recent months. It is a sign of freer trade and payments and of more international confidence. Provided that movements do not get too big and that there is no underlying disequilibrium, it need not bother us unduly. I see no cause to cheer when these short-term money movements cause our reserves to rise: nor shall I see cause to complain if our reserves fall because they go the other way. This is what reserves are for. And a good deal of what now looks like short-term money may in fact turn out to be more permanent investment.

I hope that we shall all get more used to regarding the International Monetary Fund as a second line of reserves for this sort of purpose. Too little importance has been attached to the very large increase in their facilities which was arranged last year, and to the part which they can play in offsetting these movements. Provided that countries are pursuing proper financial policies the Monetary Fund will doubtless be willing to stand behind them. I should like to see countries draw on these facilities as a matter of ordinary business when they need to reinforce reserves, and repay when reserves are rising: recent advance repayments by Her Majesty's Government have been an instance of this policy. If drawing on the Monetary Fund is regarded as only a last resort, then half its utility is lost because it will come to be seen as a crisis measure which may cause as much nervousness as it allays.

Yet we cannot be wholly confident that these movements of funds between markets can always be kept within reasonable bounds. Any major and persistent movement which went unchecked might threaten stability. The mere fact that interest rates are materially higher in some countries with a balance of payments surplus than in some others with a deficit suggests that, in the Central Banks and Treasuries of the world, we have still a good deal of hard thinking to do on this subject.

What judgment should we make, then, of our present position? Sterling is strong in the markets, but our underlying balance of payments, and particularly our exports, are not as good as they should be. Investment demand is still heavy, and, though there are soft spots, consumer demand as a whole is at least maintained. The rising boom of the early summer and the upsurge of bank credit of the past eighteen months have gone 'off the boil', but business remains very active and demand for credit brisk.

It would be unwise to make any changes until we are satisfied that it would not risk starting the pot boiling again. It would be equally unwise (having also in mind developments in other centres) to maintain too much rigidity for too long in our credit restrictions, merely for fear that minor adjustments might be misinterpreted as a change of direction.

I have been speaking of monetary technicalities, because that is my trade. But the fundamental issues for the next decade are different. What really matters is whether the British people and British Governments will choose to live within their means, or to live right up to them and sometimes beyond them. Shall we be content to limit demands on our resources to what we can manage without causing shortages, price rises and too large a bill for imports? Shall we be content to limit our overseas spending and lending to what we earn? If the decisions on these fundamental issues are right, then the monetary technicians can help to keep an even balance. If the decisions on these issues are wrong there are no monetary gimmicks or international credit schemes which can put them right. . . .

2. Statement by the United States Treasury, 27 October 1960[1]

We have been asked concerning reports on the United States position with respect to the London gold market. Any buying and selling by the Bank of England in the London market is of course the responsibility of the British authorities. It is well known that over the years since the market was opened in 1954, the British authorities have entered that market as buyer and seller in accordance with their best judgment. The United States Treasury has no criticism of such policy.

In accordance with the Treasury statement issued on Thursday, October 20th[2] reaffirming long standing practice, the United States buys gold from the Bank of England at the official price.

As is known the Secretary of the Treasury and Mr. M. H. Parsons, a Director of the Bank of England, conferred in Washington early this week, as in this meeting and by other means it is the continuing intention of financial officials of the United Kingdom and the United States to keep each other informed on matters of mutual interest.

3. Special Message of President Kennedy to the United States Congress on Gold and the United States Balance of Payments Deficit, 6 February 1961[3] (extracts)

The gold outflow of the past three years has dramatically focused world attention on a fundamental change that has been occurring in the economic position of the United States. Our balance of payments—the accounting which shows the result of all of our trade and financial relations with the outside world

---

[1] *Bank of England Quarterly Bulletin*, No. 1, December 1960, p. 10.
[2] *N.Y. Times*, 21 October 1960.   [3] *Public Papers*, 1961, pp. 57–66.

—has become one of the key factors in our national economic life. Mainly because that balance of payments has been in deficit we have lost gold.

This loss of gold is naturally important to us, but it also concerns the whole free world. For we are the principal banker of the free world and any potential weakness in our dollar spells trouble, not only for us but also for our friends and allies who rely on the dollar to finance a substantial portion of their trade. We must therefore manage our balance of payments in accordance with our responsibilities. This means that the United States must in the decades ahead, much more than at any time in the past, take its balance of payments into account when formulating its economic policies and conducting its economic affairs.

Economic progress at home is still the first requirement for economic strength abroad. Accordingly, the first requirement for restoring balance in our international payments is to take all possible steps to insure the effective performance of our own economic system—to improve our technology, lower our production and marketing costs, and devise new and superior products, under conditions of price stability. The real wealth of a nation resides in its farms and factories and the people who man them. A dynamic economy producing goods competitively priced in world markets will maintain the strength of the dollar.

Thanks to our international reserves we have time, if we use it wisely, in which to strengthen our domestic economy and make it fully competitive with that of other nations. Our situation is one that justifies concern but not panic or alarm.

In my message on February 2,[1] I dealt with the measures for reviving our domestic economy. The steps I now propose will strengthen our dollar position and insure that our gold reserves are employed effectively to facilitate the commerce of the free nations and to protect the stability of their currencies. Because these steps supplement the policies for strengthening our domestic economy, and because we can take them calmly and deliberately, they are not for that reason any less important or less urgent. Those that are within the present authority of the Executive will be the subject of vigorous action. Where action by the Congress is required I urge early consideration and approval.

For the past decade our international transactions have resulted in a deficit—payments that were in excess of receipts—in every year except that of the Suez crisis, 1957. The surplus of our exports over our imports, while substantial, has not been large enough to cover our expenditures for United States military establishments abroad, for capital invested abroad by private American businesses and for government economic assistance and loan programs. All of these outlays are essential. Our military establishments in foreign countries protect the national security. Private investment promotes world economic growth and trade and, through the return of profits to our country, will strengthen our balance of payments in future years. Our economic assistance programs, much the smallest of these three items in its effect on payments balance, is vital in the continuing struggle against tyranny and oppression, and the poverty on which they feed.

Over the period 1951 to 1957 the deficit in our balance of payments averaged about $1.0 billion annually. These did not result in a net outflow of gold from the United States; foreign monetary authorities, banks and private individuals

[1] *Public Papers*, 1961, pp. 41–53.

held these earnings as dollars or claims on dollars. Thus our gold reserves were $22.8 at the end of 1950 and $22.9 at the end of 1957. But during these years the dollar holdings by foreign countries increased from $8.4 billion at the end of 1950 to almost $15 billion at the of 1957.

These earlier deficits in our balance of payments were, in fact, favorable in their world effect. They helped to restore foreign monetary systems by enabling foreign countries to earn the dollars which they needed to rebuild their international reserves. They made it possible for the industralized countries of Western Europe to restore the convertibility of their currencies, thus freeing world trade and payments from exchange control. This was of benefit to the export trade of the United States. However, this growth in foreign dollar holdings placed upon the United States a special responsibility—that of maintaining the dollar as the principal reserve currency of the free world. This required that the dollar be considered by many countries to be as good as gold. It is our responsibility to sustain this confidence.

In 1958 and 1959 the deficit in our balance of payments sharply increased— to $3.5 billion in 1958 and to $3.8 billion in 1959. This came about mainly because of lagging exports and rising imports. There was no significant increase in our outlays for military expenditures, private investment or government economic assistance. However in these years, unlike the period 1951–57, the deficit resulted in large transfers of gold to foreign accounts as well as a further increase in foreign dollar holdings. For the two years together, 1958 and 1959, gold transfers to foreign accounts were $3.0 billion while foreign dollar holdings by foreign countries increased by another $4.3 billion. These gold transfers did not make the underlying balance of payments fundamentally worse. They did reflect a decision by foreigners to take more of their earnings in gold and to hold less in dollars.

Last year, 1960, the surplus of our exports of goods and services over our imports increased from $2.2 billion in 1959 to $5.8 billion. This was caused, principally, by an increase—amounting to more than $3 billion—in our exports. This once more reduced what may be called our basic deficit—it was only about $1.5 billion for the year. However, during 1960 there was a large movement abroad, a high rate of growth and good investment prospects in Europe and some speculative fears concerning the future value of the dollar all played a part. It is estimated that this outward flow of short-term funds was between $2 and $2.5 billion, and this was the crucial factor in raising the over-all deficit to $3.8 billion. Of this, $1.7 billion were transferred in the form of gold and $2.1 billion took the form of increased foreign dollar holdings.

An outward movement of short-term funds such as that which occurred in 1960 should not be considered a part of the basic deficit. Such movements are quickly reversible in response to changes in interest rates and other business factors here and abroad. Moreover, insofar as short-term funds transferred to foreign financial centers consist of U.S. owned capital, they create United States claims against the recipient country. In the new era of convertible currencies upon which we have entered, we may expect that short-term money will continue to flow back and forth. I have requested the Secretary of State and the Secretary of the Treasury to work for still closer cooperation between the monetary and

D.I.A.–S

financial authorities of the industrialized free nations with a view toward avoiding excessive short-term money flows which could be upsetting to the orderly development of international trade and payments.

In sum our basic deficit of $1.5 billions is of manageable proportions. And it is this basic deficit which affects the real strength of our currency. But the time has come to end this deficit. It must be ended by responsible, determined and constructive measures.

There are other factors which lend basic support to our monetary and financial position. Our gold reserve now stands at $17.5 billion. This is more than $1\frac{1}{2}$ times foreign official dollar holdings and more than 90% of all foreign dollar holdings. It is some $\frac{2}{3}$ of the gold stock of the entire free world.

Of this $17.5 billion, gold reserves not committed against either currency or deposits account for nearly $6 billion. The remaining $11.5 billion are held under existing regulations as a reserve against Federal Reserve currency and deposits. But these, too, can be freed to sustain the value of the dollar; and I have pledged that the full strength of our total gold stocks and other international reserves stands behind the value of the dollar for use if needed.

In addition, the United States has a quota in the International Monetary Fund of $4.1 billion. This can be drawn upon if necessary and our access to the Fund's resources must be regarded as part of our international reserves.

Finally beyond its liquid international reserves, the government and citizens of the United States hold large assets abroad. Western European countries whose currencies are now strong owe us long-term government debts of $2.9 billion. Our private short-term assets abroad now are estimated at $4\frac{1}{2}$ billion. Our long-term private investments in foreign countries—including both plants owned directly by American companies and securities of foreign business and governments owned by Americans—total over $44 billion, exceeding foreign investments in the U.S. economy by some $28 billion. In any reckoning of international assets and liabilities, the United States has a strong solvent position.

In short, powerful resources stand behind the dollar. Our gold and monetary reserves are large; so are the physical and monetary assets we hold throughout the world. And, in the years ahead, if the program I previously outlined is pursued, the dollar will have the added strength of the reviving power of the American economy itself.

Certain firm conclusions follow:

1. The United States official dollar price of gold can and will be maintained at $35 an ounce. Exchange controls over trade and investment will not be invoked. Our national security and economic assistance programs will be carried forward. Those who fear weakness in the dollar will find their fears unfounded. Those who hope for speculative reasons for an increase in the price of gold will find their hopes in vain.

2. We must now gain control of our balance of payments position so that we can achieve over-all equilibrium in our international payments. This means that any sustained future outflow of dollars into the monetary reserves of other countries should come about only as the result of considered judgments as to the appropriate needs for dollar reserves.

3. In seeking over-all equilibrium we must place maximum emphasis on expanding our exports. Our costs and prices must therefore be kept low; and the government must play a more vigorous part in helping to enlarge foreign markets for American goods and services.

4. A return to protectionism is not a solution. Such a course would provoke retaliation; and the balance of trade, which is now substantially in our favor, could be turned against us with disastrous effects to the dollar.

5. The flow of resources from the industrialized countries to the developing countries must be increased. In all that we do to strengthen our balance of payments, we must be especially mindful that the less developed countries remain in a weak financial position. Help from the industrialized countries is more important than ever; we cannot strengthen our balance of payments at the expense of the developing countries without incurring even greater dangers to our national security.

6. The United States must take the lead in harmonizing the financial and economic policies for growth and stability of those industrialized nations of the world whose economic behaviour significantly influences the course of the world economy and the trend of international payments.

To carry forward these policies I propose a program for action, which may be divided into two parts. The first part describes those measures which will improve domestic monetary arrangements and strengthen international cooperation in economic and monetary policy. These measures will help us better to meet short-term demands on reserves such as those of recent years. The measures in the second group are designed to correct the persisting basic deficit in our balance of payments.

I. MEASURES TO EASE THE SHORT-TERM DEMAND PROBLEM

1. *Measures to Improve International Monetary Institutions*

Increasing international monetary reserves will be required to support the ever-growing volume of trade, services and capital movements among the countries of the free world. Until now the free nations have relied upon increased gold production and continued growth in holdings of dollars and pounds sterling. In the future, it may not always be desirable or appropriate to rely entirely on these sources. We must now, in cooperation with other lending countries, begin to consider ways in which international monetary institutions—especially the International Monetary Fund—can be strengthened and more effectively utilized, both, in furnishing needed increases in reserves, and in providing the flexibility required to support a healthy and growing world economy. I am therefore directing that studies to this end be initiated promptly by the Secretary of the Treasury.

2. *Use of United States Drawing Rights in the International Monetary Fund*

The United States has never made use of its drawing rights under the International Monetary Fund to meet deficits in its balance of payments. If and when appropriate, these rights should and will be exercised within the framework of Fund policies. The United States will also support continued efforts in the Fund to facilitate drawings by other members in the currencies of industrialized countries whose payments positions are in surplus and whose reserves are large. This will help to reduce the burden now borne by the dollar.

3. *Special Interest Rates for Dollar Holdings by Foreign Governments and Monetary Authorities*

(a) The Federal Reserve Act should now be amended to permit the Federal Reserve System to establish separate maxima for rates of interest paid by member banks on time and savings deposits held in this country by foreign governments or monetary authorities (Section 19, paragraph 14). This authority, when exercised, would enable American banks to make a maximum competitive effort to attract and hold dollar balances which might otherwise be converted into gold. At the same time domestic rates, when desirable for reasons of domestic policy, could be held at a lower level. I will shortly send to the Congress a draft of the needed legislation.

(b) I have directed the Secretary of the Treasury to use, whenever it appears desirable, the authority already extended to him by the Second Liberty Bond Act to issue securities, at special rates of interest, for subscription and holding exclusively by foreign governments or monetary authorities. The exercise of this authority could provide an additional inducement to hold foreign official balances in dollars.

(c) As a final means of holding or attracting foreign dollars, the Congress should enact a measure designed to unify the tax treatment accorded the earning assets of foreign central banks. At present, income derived by foreign central banks of issue from bankers acceptances and bank deposits is exempt from tax under section 861 of the Code. Income from United States Government securities, however, is taxable to foreign central banks in the absence of applicable tax treaty provisions or a special ruling exempting a particular bank from taxation under particular circumstances. Suggested legislation will shortly be forthcoming.

4. *Prohibition on Holding of Gold Abroad by Americans*

The recent Executive Order forbidding the holding of gold abroad by Americans[1] will be maintained. It was fully justified on grounds of equity. It will also help to prevent speculation in the gold market. I am directing the Secretary of the Treasury to keep me advised on steps being taken for effective enforcement. I place everyone on notice that those few American citizens who are tempted to speculate against the dollar will not profit in this manner.

II. Measures to Correct the Basic Payments Deficit and Achieve Longer-Term Equilibrium

1. *Action by the Senate to Approve the Organization for Economic Cooperation and Development*

I earnestly request early action by the Senate approving United States membership in the Organization for Economic Cooperation and Development.

[1] Executive Order No. 10905 of 14 January 1961; see *D.S.B.*, 6 February 1961, pp. 195–6.

The OECD, in which the industrialized countries of Western Europe, the United States and Canada will be joined, is of vital importance for assisting, on a co-operative basis, the developing countries of the free world. It will also provide a solid framework within which we can carry out intensive and frequent international consultations on the financial and monetary policies which must be pursued in order to achieve and maintain better balance in the international payments position.

2. *Export Promotion*

The Department of Commerce will provide energetic leadership to American industry in a drive to develop export markets. Firms and industries will be encouraged to step up their efforts to develop exports and given every assistance in doing so. As American industry comes to realize the vital role of export earnings for our foreign policy, I have little doubt of its response.

We will promptly increase our commercial representatives and facilities abroad. This is a joint program of the Departments of Commerce and State which must proceed with drive and conviction in order to produce effective results. The budget which has already gone to Congress requests $1,250,000 for the State Department to add 41 Foreign Service Commercial Attaches overseas, together with 48 experienced foreign nationals and supporting American staff.

The new budget requests will also allow an increase in overseas commercial facilities. The Commerce Department is doubling its Trade Mission program from 11 to 18 per year and will provide more useful information to our overseas posts. I am ordering rapid completion of our two new foreign trade centers at London and Bangkok and have requested the departments to explore whether three more could be added next year in Africa, Latin America and Europe.

3. *Cost and Price Stabilization*

Our export promotion efforts, no matter how well devised or energetically pursued, will not be effective unless American goods are competitively priced. Our domestic policies—of government, of business and of labor—must be directed to maintaining competitive costs, improving productivity and stabilizing or where possible lowering prices. Measures to achieve these ends which are important for the domestic economy are even more vital for our international competitive position. I have already stated my intention of creating an Advisory Committee on Labor and Management Policy to encourage productivity gains, advance automation and encourage sound wage policies and price stability.[1]

4. *Export Guarantees and Financing*

Our Export-Import Bank must play an increasingly important role in our export promotion efforts. Last year the Export-Import Bank announced a widening of the facilities which it offers for extending credit to American exporters. Despite the improvements made, these facilities are not yet adequate, nor are they comparable to those offered by foreign countries, especially those

[1] In the special message to Congress on economic recovery and growth of 2 February 1961; see *Public Papers*, 1961, p. 52.

offered to small and medium-sized exporting concerns and those offered for the financing of consumer goods. I am directing the President of the Export-Import Bank, by April 1, to prepare and submit to the Secretary of the Treasury, as Chairman of the National Advisory Council on International Monetary and Financial Problems, a new program under the Export-Import Bank to place our exporters on a basis of full equality with their competitors in other countries. Also, I have asked the Secretary of the Treasury to initiate and submit by the same date a study of methods through which private financial institutions can participate more broadly in providing export credit facilities.

5. *Foreign Travel to the United States*

Foreign travel to the United States constitutes a large potential market hitherto virtually untapped. American travelers annually spend some $2 billion in foreign countries. Foreign travelers only spend about $1 billion in this country. Economic conditions in many foreign countries have improved to the point where a strong travel promotion effort by this country can be expected to yield significant results. . . .

6. *Agricultural Exports*

Our agricultural industry, which is of unparalleled efficiency, must make its full contribution to our payments balance. I am directing the Secretary of Agriculture to report on all feasible and internationally desirable means of expanding our exports of farm products, and to emphasize the need for export expansion as a primary objective of our new farm programs.

7. *Policy on Economic Assistance*

Our foreign economic assistance programs are now being administered in such a way as to place primary emphasis on the procurement of American goods. This assistance, accompanied as it is by the export of American products, does not therefore have a significantly adverse effect on our balance of payments. (Not more than 20% of the funds expended for economic grants, development loan assistance, technical assistance and contributions to international organizations, which amounted to $2.6 billion in 1960, is today available for expenditures outside the United States, and we intend to keep an even closer review of these items.) These restrictions will be maintained until reasonable over-all equilibrium has been achieved. Then the United States will discuss with other capital-exporting countries the desirability of instituting common policies for world-wide procurement in the administration of economic development or assistance programs.

8. *Tariffs, Restrictions and Discriminations Against American Exports*

Quota discriminations against American exports have largely disappeared with the return of currency convertibility. We will press for prompt removal of the few restrictions that still exist, as well as for the maximum liberalization of remaining non-discriminatory quotas in other industralized countries, which apply mainly to agricultural exports. In the tariff negotiations now going forward under GATT[1] we shall seek the fullest possible measure of tariff reduction by foreign countries to the benefit of our exports.

9. *Promotion of Foreign Investment in the United States*

We shall press those Western European countries with strong reserve positions to eliminate the restrictions they still maintain limiting the opportunities for their citizens to invest in the United States and other foreign countries. Also, we are initiating, through the Department of Commerce, a new program to bring investment opportunities in the United States to the attention of foreign investors in the industrialized countries.

10. *Abuse of 'Tax Havens'. Taxation of American Investment Abroad*[2] . . .

11. *Foreign Assistance Contribution to the Less Developed Countries and the Common Defense*

It is indispensable that the industrialized countries of the free world join in undertaking systematic budgetary contributions for economic assistance to the less developed countries and the common defense. These contributions should be fully commensurate with their economic and financial positions. Some countries are fulfilling this responsibility; it is a matter of disappointment that others have not yet undertaken to do so. Such actions are important in the short run to achieve a better balance in international trade and payments. Even more important, they are essential to the continuing and effective discharge of our common responsibilities for free world security, economic growth and stability.

12. *Reduction of Customs Exemption for Returning American Travelers*[3] . . .

13. *Centralized Review of Dollar Outlays*

Through the Bureau of the Budget, it has long been our sound financial practice to centralize the review of total spending of the Departments and Agencies of the Government of the United States, including their spending abroad. Under present circumstances, foreign outlays must be examined in a new perspective. Accordingly, I am instructing the Director of the Bureau of the Budget, in consultation with the Secretary of the Treasury, to develop special procedures for analyzing that part of the requests of departments and agencies for spending authority which will involve overseas outlays to insure that our budgetary decisions will be taken with full understanding of their projected impact on the country's balance of payments.

14. *U.S. Military Expenditures Abroad*

National security expenditures abroad constitute one of the largest items in the outflow of dollars, amounting to about $3.0 billion a year. We must maintain a fully effective military force wherever necessary and for as long as needed. While it is clear that we must exercise maximum prudence in our dollar outlays

[1] The first phase of the two-part GATT conference in Geneva, which began on 1 September 1960.
[2] Not reproduced.   [3] Not reproduced.

abroad, it has become clear that the present limitation on dependents[1] was not the best way to accomplish this savings, and that this limitation was seriously hurting morale and recruitment in the armed forces. At the same time, the Secretary of Defense has informed me that equivalent dollar savings could be made through other measures, including limitations on expenditures abroad by military personnel for tourism and the purchase of durable consumer goods. Accordingly I have directed him to rescind the limitation on dependents and instead to put these measures into effect immediately.

I have also asked him to review the possibilities for savings in the logistic support of our forces, including the combined use of facilities with our allies. We shall also, where appropriate, urge the purchase of the newer weapons and weapons systems by those of our allies who are financially capable of doing so. We shall continue the policy inaugurated last November[2] of emphasizing United States procurement for our military forces abroad wherever practicable, even though some increased budgetary cost may be incurred. Since foreign procurement of this nature has amounted to almost $1 billion a year, significant savings in dollar outflow can be expected—and I am asking the Secretary of Defense to report on these and the other savings by no later than April 1st, to see if further steps are needed then.

CONCLUSION

These measures, combined with increasing confidence in the dollar abroad and steady economic growth at home, can cure the basic long-term deficit in our balance of payments and check the outflow of gold. They symbolize a new dimension of this nation's foreign and domestic economic policies—a new area of difficult problems—but they are problems which can be met by forceful and timely legislative and executive action.

4. Statement of the British Chancellor of the Exchequer, Mr. Selwyn Lloyd, to the House of Commons, 25 July 1961[3] (extracts)

In my Budget speech on 17th April I referred to the unsatisfactory balance of payments and the probable expansion of home demand with its effect upon costs, and upon our competitiveness.[4] I provided for a very large surplus of over £500 million above the line, but I clearly indicated that I thought the situation might require further measures. I asked for two new powers—the regulators.

In the three months since the Budget, home demand has continued to increase and is likely to increase even more than was then foreseen. There are labour shortages in most areas. Investment is rising strongly. The building industry already has more demand upon it than it can satisfy, and parts of the engineering industry are coming under increasing pressure.

Simultaneously with the increase of pressure on our domestic resources, we are faced with a critical external situation. This is the third successive year in which our overall balance of payments has been in deficit, and this is, clearly, not a situation which can be allowed to continue.

[1] By the presidential directive of 16 November 1960; see *Documents*, 1960, pp. 135–7.
[2] See ibid.   [3] H.C. Deb., vol. 645, cols. 218–29.   [4] H.C. Deb., vol. 638, cols. 796–7.

In 1960, the deficit on current account was about £350 million and there was also a net movement overseas of capital funds, by way of Government loan and private investment, of about £200 million. This was not reflected in the reserve figures because of a large flow of funds to London. Indeed, during 1960 the reserves rose by £177 million and, in addition, we strengthened our position with the International Monetary Fund to the tune of about £130 million.

During the first half of 1961 our current account was still in deficit though at a substantially lower rate than last year's rate. There have, however, been heavy withdrawals of short-term balances and, in spite of the Ford transaction and the prepayment of German debt, our reserves of gold and dollars have fallen by about 164 million over the past six months. This fall would have been much greater but for the special arrangements made with the central banks.

If rising personal demand and rising investment demand are not matched by increased production, the burden falls on the balance of payments. We have less for exports and we import more. In addition, prices go up, our competitiveness suffers, and it becomes more difficult to sell our goods abroad.

In my view, therefore, our aims at the present time should be as follows: First, we should maintain investment in productive industry with a view to the long-term growth of the economy. At the same time, we must make ourselves more competitive. Both are vital for a long-term improvement in the balance of payments.

Secondly, we must see that public expenditure is brought under better control.

Thirdly, we must take action designed to protect our position in the immediate future.

The proposals which I shall now outline are, in part, long-term and matters to which I have been giving consideration for some time; in part, they are required by the exigencies of the present situation. . . .

Other Measures to Relieve Strain on Balance of Payments

Before I deal with the private sector at home, I wish to say something about overseas expenditures.

Government expenditures overseas—defence, aid and administrative—are running at present at a rate which will certainly rise to some £480 million next year and quite possibly, on present trends, to £500 million. I do not believe that we can sustain such a level. My aim is to hold that figure down to £400 million in the year 1962–63. This compares with £330 million in 1958–59.

Defence

It is right that we should carry heavy burdens for the sake of maintaining our commitments to our friends and allies around the world. But the defence programme must be carefully examined, particularly in relation to the overseas payments which it involves. The Minister of Defence has put in hand another review of the whole of this programme to see what can be done to lighten the burden.

In fulfilment of commitments to N.A.T.O., we are spending some £80 million a year across the exchanges in Western Europe. Of this sum, over £65 million goes on the maintenance of our forces in Germany, in accordance with our obligations under the revised Brussels Treaty. I have come to the conclusion that the strain upon the balance of payments caused by this expenditure cannot be allowed to continue next financial year. We have, therefore, invited the North Atlantic Council to review the financial conditions under which our forces are maintained. Such a request is provided for under the terms of the Treaty. It does not affect our determination to stand by our N.A.T.O. obligation in the defence of West Berlin and the review will relate to the next financial year.

OVERSEAS AID TO UNDERDEVELOPED COUNTRIES

Assistance to underdeveloped countries from United Kingdom Government funds has risen steadily from some £80 million in 1957–58 to £150 million in 1960, and disbursements are expected to increase still further this year to about £180 million. Most of these disbursements are being made under commitments to other Governments and to international organisations, and these commitments will be honoured. I am bound, however, to take steps to contain the increase and to see it does not rise much above the present level. There is no question of cutting back, but even to sustain this level is a considerable challenge. It will not be easy. The figure of £180 million compares, I say again, with a figure of £80 million in 1957–58 when our balance of payments was better.

OVERSEAS ADMINISTRATIVE EXPENDITURE

Finally, there is the cost of our diplomatic and various administrative services overseas. The total expenditure on these is not large in comparison with that of the commitments which I have been discussing. But, even so, these services must make their contribution towards the reduction in total expenditure overseas which our present situation demands. I look for a saving here of 10 per cent. in the financial year 1962–63.

PRIVATE INVESTMENT OVERSEAS

I now come to private investment overseas. The volume of investment in the non-sterling area, which is subject to control, has been rising steadily. It is true that it produces earnings in the long run. But these earnings do not always benefit the balance of payments in the short term—partly because of the tendency to invest further in the overseas enterprise concerned and partly because of local restrictions on remittances. I therefore propose a more severe test than at present. The test for new investment in the non-sterling area will be that it will produce clear and commensurate benefits to United Kingdom export earnings and to the balance of payments.

REMITTANCE OF OVERSEAS PROFITS

The powers to control investment in the non-sterling area apply equally to investment made out of profits earned overseas by British companies and their subsidiaries. I am not satified that in all cases an adequate proportion of profits earned overseas is being repatriated to this country. I propose to request United Kingdom firms operating overseas to look at their policies in order to ensure that a higher proportion of earnings is remitted home. So far as non-sterling investment is concerned, I propose to reinstitute on a selective basis the examination of company accounts by the exchange control authorities to ensure that this policy is followed.

Monetary and Credit Policy

I now come to measures designed to affect the private sector here at home. The Bank of England have called upon the clearing banks for further special deposits. In the case of the London clearing banks the call is for 1 per cent., of which half is to be deposited by 16th August and the balance by 20th September, 1961. In the case of the Scottish banks the call is for a percentage equal to one-half of that called for from the London clearing banks. In making this call the Governor of the Bank of England has made it clear that it is the intention that the impact should fall on advances.

The banks have been asked that, when reviewing existing commitments or considering new lending, they should be particularly severe on proposals related to personal consumption, including finance for hire purchase, as well as finance for speculative building, property development, or for other speculative purposes, so that all possible room should be left for the finance vitally needed for exports and productive industry. I am sure that, despite the difficulties, the clearing and Scottish banks will as usual give their full co-operation.

The Governor is also drawing the attention of the other United Kingdom banks, including the foreign and overseas banks and the accepting houses, to the action taken with the clearing and Scottish banks. He will see the British Insurance Association and ask that the insurance companies should observe a similar policy in their lending. I look to these institutions, also, to give me their support. It is not my intention to force a down-turn of private investment in productive industry. I am not proposing any change in the initial or investment allowances. At the same time, the demands made by private investment, particularly on the building industry, are growing rapidly and it is right that some less essential forms of development should be postponed. I do not rule out further measures if they appear necessary.

The Government do not intend to alter the present hire-purchase restrictions.

Bank Rate

With my approval, the Bank of England is announcing a rise in the Bank Rate from 5 per cent. to 7 per cent. I have agreed to this partly because of the need to restrain credit internally, and partly because of the unsettled international situation.

The effect of all this will be to make credit more expensive and more difficult to get. The impact will be felt particularly on credit for personal consumption and property development. . . .

I.M.F. Drawing

Finally, I have decided to take action to fortify our reserves by a substantial drawing from the International Monetary Fund. This is being put in hand. The actual amount will be announced shortly when the discussions with the Fund are concluded. I would remind the House that such drawings have to be repaid within a period of three to five years, and this means that it is all the more necessary for the policies and measures I have outlined to be pursued with resolution.

I believe that these measures will protect our position in the immediate future and will form the basis for a long-term improvement in the balance of payments. They mark the first steps, following upon the five-year review, to establish a better relationship between public expenditure and the national resources. They will enable essential investments in productive industry to continue. At the same time, they will assist to restore our competitive power, to expand our exports, and to promote soundly based growth in the economy. . . .

5. Sixteenth Annual Meeting of the Board of Governors of the International Monetary Fund, Vienna, 18–22 September 1961

(i) *Statement of Dr. Per Jacobsson, Chairman of the Executive Board and Managing Director of the International Fund, in presentation of the Annual Report*[1]

May I begin by saying how much pleasure it gives me that this year's Annual Meeting is being held in Vienna. For me, personally, our presence here brings back memories of quite a long time ago—of the time of the League of Nations Reconstruction Scheme for Austria after the First World War. In the summer of 1925 I served as one of the secretaries to Mr. Walter Layton (now Lord Layton) and the late Professor Charles Rist, who had been asked by the League Council to report on the economic position of Austria. These two experts came to the conclusion that Austria was economically viable; but when they made their report at the League of Nations Headquarters in Geneva there were those who thought that they had been too optimistic and dubbed them, after a vaudeville show then running in London, 'the co-optimists'. This time, however, the optimists proved right. Whatever the vicissitudes through which this country has had to pass, it has undoubtedly established itself as a proud and independent nation, thanks to the fortitude, resilience, and vitality of its people: qualities are deeply rooted in them as those of charm and good humor, which are perhaps more readily apparent.

A year ago, when our Annual Meeting was held in Washington, 68 countries were members of the International Monetary Fund. Today we have 73 members. Thus in the last 12 months 5 new members have joined the Fund—Laos, Nepal, New Zealand, Nigeria, and Portugal. A number of other countries have applied for membership, and it is expected that several will be able to sign the Articles of Agreement in the next few months. The increase and expected increase in membership reflect the emergence in recent years of many new countries, particularly in Africa, all of which we shall be glad to welcome as members of the Fund; but I think it also indicates a growing appreciation of the usefulness of the Fund as a center for consultation and as an institution capable of rendering valuable service to all its members. I would think that the usefulness of the Fund has been made even more evident by the intense activity in the year since our last Annual Meeting. In this year, not only have the financial operations of the

---

[1] International Monetary Fund, *Summary Proceedings of the Sixteenth Annual Meeting of the Board of Governors, September 1961* (Washington, D.C., n.d., 1961), pp. 13–32.

Fund been larger than in any other year of the Fund's history, but there has also been very considerable activity in other ways.

It might be of some interest to examine the developments of this last year against the background of the situation at the end of 1959 and early in 1960. Many countries were, of course, faced with difficulties, but world economic activity was generally at a high level and showed signs of increasing. The adoption of external convertibility by a number of European countries at the end of 1958 had clearly been successful, and there had been an almost all-round increase in their gold and foreign exchange reserves. The rise in the general price level had been much less accentuated during 1958 and 1959, holding out the hope that the postwar inflation had at last been contained.

The improvement in the monetary position was underlined by the acceptance early this year of the formal convertibility of their currencies, under Article VIII of the Fund Agreement;[1] by 11 countries: Belgium, France, the Federal Republic of Germany, Ireland, Italy, Luxembourg, the Netherlands, Peru, Saudi Arabia, Sweden, and the United Kingdom. This was greatly to be welcomed, and brought the total number of countries which have accepted the obligations of Article VIII to 21. It is also satisfactory that we have now started regular consultations with Article VIII countries in accordance with the view expressed by the Executive Directors in their decision of June 1 last year.

The growing freedom for the international movement of funds, as a result of the increased convertibility of currencies, and the greater stability of prices—so welcome in themselves—have, however, created new problems which the world has not had to face since the start of the Second World War. Some of these problems were discussed at our last Annual Meeting, others have developed since that time. I believe that much of the disquietude that arose in this new situation was not really justified, but while it lasted it certainly exerted a disturbing influence. In the United States, mainly under the impact of a change in inventories once prices had become more stable, industrial production declined after the spring of 1960 and unemployment increased to the highest percentage since the end of the War. In the spring of this year, however, business activity began to recover, so that the setback proved to have been of short duration. Even so, it was not without influence on the international monetary situation. As was natural in a period of recession, interest rates in the United States declined; and with boom conditions and fairly high interest rates ruling in most European countries, it was to be expected that there would be an outflow of funds from the United States. This outward movement coincided with growing misgivings about the competitive power of the U.S. economy, and also with some apprehensions connected with the election. A temporary flight from currencies into gold led to a steep rise in the price of gold in London, which in turn intensified these fears and gave an impetus to fresh rumors and speculations. All this occurred at a time when there was a remarkable and continuing improvement in the basic position of the U.S. balance of payments. Imports were tending to fall as a result of the decline in business activity, but exports had risen substantially, and

[1] The Articles of Agreement of the International Monetary Fund are printed as Annex A to Cmd. 6546, *United Nations Monetary and Financial Conference, Bretton Woods, New Hampshire, U.S.A., July 1 to July 22, 1944, Final Act* (London, H.M.S.O., 1944).

there was a trade surplus of more than \$4.5 billion for the whole of 1960. Together with the net income from investments and services, the United States had available some \$6 billion to meet government expenditure abroad, including military expenditure and official assistance of all kinds. Thus the only uncovered foreign payments were of a capital nature—private long-term investments abroad and the outflow of short-term funds. Towards the end of the year and in the early months of 1961, the net income from trade and services rose further and was sufficient to cover practically all the long-term private investment abroad at the current rate, in addition to government expenditure abroad.

It was in this improving situation early in February that the President of the United States made his statement that steps would be taken to safeguard the value of the dollar, and that the dollar price of gold would be maintained.[1] In addition, the President declared that 'the United States has never made use of its drawing rights under the International Monetary Fund to meet deficits in its balance of payments. If and when appropriate, these rights should and will be exercised within the framework of Fund policies'. Assisted by reductions in discount rates in Europe and a determination to avoid any great decline in short-term rates in the United States, the outflow of short-term capital subsided, and, with certain advance repayments from abroad, there was a substantial improvement in the over-all balance of payments position of the United States.

The U.S. trade balance was helped by the strong boom which continued in most industrial countries in Europe, as well as in Japan. Compared with 1959, these countries increased their imports by about 20 per cent in 1960, and this was sufficient to lift the volume of world trade by about 10 per cent. Even such a large increase in European and Japanese imports was not sufficient to raise the general level of raw material prices, which in fact declined slightly over the year. Since many of the less developed countries are dependent on the export of only one or two primary products, even a relatively moderate decline in the prices of these products may create difficulties in their balance of payments; and with only slender reserves to fall back on, many have turned to the Fund for financial assistance. Thus the general weakness in the prices of raw materials and foodstuffs has been reflected in the work of the Fund, which has had an unusually large number of transactions with the less developed countries.

In all, 32 countries from all the continents of the world have received financial assistance from the Fund or have had drawing rights under stand-by arrangements during the period since our last meeting. With the exception of the United Kingdom, all of these countries can be said to depend largely on the export of primary products. But the balance of payments difficulties which these countries have experienced have not as a rule been due solely to weakness in the prices of their export products, for many have also suffered from excessive internal demand connected with their own credit and fiscal policies. As long as the general level of prices on world markets was still rising, it was possible to expect that in the individual countries a certain amount of credit expansion would be absorbed by rising prices; but now that the general price level is more stable, an expansion of credit beyond the current requirements of the economy is likely to be reflected with little delay in a deficit in the balance of payments. In several cases, the

[1] Above, pp. 521–30.

situation has been rendered more difficult by the continued maintenance of complex and discriminatory exchange systems. With the widespread desire to establish or maintain orderly monetary conditions and to simplify exchange systems, Fund assistance has generally been requested in support of fiscal, monetary, or exchange programs and the assistance has been given in the form of stand-by arrangements. In fact, of the 22 countries which have drawn from the Fund during the past year, all but 3 have entered into stand-by arrangements.

It would clearly be impossible for me to discuss in detail all these financial operations of the Fund. I should, however, like to mention briefly a few which have had unusual features and which seem to me to be of particular interest.[1] . . .

Turning now to the transaction with the United Kingdom last month, I would like to describe briefly the background of the international movements of funds which preceded it. I have already referred to the large movements of funds out of the United States last autumn and winter—partly to take advantage of high interest rates in Europe. A part of this flow went to the United Kingdom, where a construction boom and a marked increase in investment in plant and equipment had led to a substantial demand for finance and, consequently, to a high level of interests rates. The inflow of funds from the United States and other centers led to an increase in reserves, in spite of the deteriorating position of the current account of the U.K. balance of payments. The British Government used part of the increase in reserves to repay in advance the drawing made from the Fund in 1956, and also to reduce the Fund's holdings of sterling to 75 per cent of quota.

Following the statement made by the President of the United States in February,[2] the outflow of funds from the United States was sharply reduced, but there was still a movement of funds into a number of countries on the Continent in Europe, especially Germany, due at least in part to continued rumors about the revaluation of the deutsche mark. The revaluation of the deutsche mark and of the Dutch guilder by 5 per cent early in March, however, gave rise to a new crop of rumors about further currency changes. All this proved very damaging to confidence, particularly in sterling, because of the deterioration in the current account of the U.K. balance of payments. The authorities in the countries concerned strongly denied the rumors, but to small avail. It was even believed that the Swiss franc would be revalued, despite the growing deficit in the current account of the Swiss balance of payments, to which the Swiss National Bank drew attention.

In this situation, a number of central banks—members of the Bank for International Settlements in Basle, as well as the Federal Reserve System in the United States—decided to cooperate more closely in the spot and forward exchange markets and in the granting of credits. In this way, substantial resources were provided in aid of sterling, but this in itself did not arrest the outflow of funds from London. Steps were needed to remove the imbalance in the British economy and to obtain the external resources required while the steps

---

[1] Dr. Jacobsson then dealt with the standby arrangement of $75 million made to Yugoslavia at the end of 1960; with a similar arrangement with Chile, made in February 1961; and with transactions with Australia, Brazil, and India.

[2] See above, pp. 521–30.

were taking effect. Using, inter alia, certain powers proposed in the budget that had been submitted in April and voted in July, the British Government introduced toward the end of July a comprehensive series of fiscal and monetary measures, and certain other policies, designed to eliminate the deficit in the current account of the balance of payments without imposing any restrictions on trade or current payments and, in particular, to restore confidence in sterling at the existing rate of exchange.[1] The measures adopted by the United Kingdom showed the Government's determination to deal with both the immediate situation and developments over a longer period, particularly in relation to future budget expenditure and to the level of costs.

In support of these measures, the United Kingdom drew from the Fund the equivalent of $1.5 billion in nine currencies: U.S. dollars, deutsche mark, French francs, Italian lire, Netherlands guilders, Belgian francs, Japanese yen, Canadian dollars, and Swedish kronor—the first time the last currency had been drawn from the Fund—and, in addition, entered into a stand-by arrangement for the equivalent of a further $500 million. The U.K. authorities announced that, of the amount drawn, the equivalent of some £200 million would be used during the following month or two for repayment of credits. This transaction with the United Kingdom was by far the largest ever entered into by the Fund; and in order to replenish its holdings of the currencies drawn, the Fund sold gold valued at $500 million to the countries concerned, in the proportion of one third of the U.K. drawing in each currency. . . .

With all the activity during the past year, drawings on the Fund have totaled the equivalent of nearly $2.5 billion. So large a use of resources has had a marked effect on the Fund's holdings of currencies suitable for transactions at the present time. Even after the replenishment of these holdings by the sale of gold at the time of the drawing by the United Kingdom, the Fund's holdings of several convertible currencies are very low. In addition, it has to be remembered that there are open balances under stand-by arrangements equivalent almost $1.1 billion.

It had, indeed, become apparent at the end of last year, at the time of the strong outflow of short-term funds from the United States, that if the Fund were faced with substantial drawings by a number of countries with large quotas, its available holdings of convertible currencies would in all probability be inadequate. This has been borne out by the experience of the last few months. The Fund can, of course, make use of its gold holdings, but these are not necessarily revolving, and once they have been used for the replenishment of currency holdings they may not readily be restored by repurchases in gold. Therefore, the Fund should generally be careful in the use of its gold and should take into account other possibilities for replenishing its currency holdings, for instance, by the borrowing of particular currencies under Article VII of the Fund Agreement.

However, borrowing of currencies is not a method of replenishment that can suddenly be improvised. For this and other reasons, the whole complex of problems connected with such borrowing needs to be closely examined and brought to an effective solution. Consideration of these problems should be set against the wider background of the international monetary system. In the vivid

[1] See above, pp. 530–4.

discussions on the merits and demerits of the present system which have taken place in recent years and months, attention has largely been devoted to the tensions which may result from the international flow of funds in a world of convertible currencies. As you know, a number of suggestions have been put forward advocating more or less radical changes in the existing monetary arrangements. It has been valuable that these matters have been so vigorously discussed, and the first question we have to ask ourselves is whether the present system can be regarded as operating in a manner sufficiently satisfactory to be worth maintaining. If that question is answered in the affirmative, then we must consider whether any particular measures should be taken to strengthen the existing institutional arrangements so as to provide sufficient safeguards to meet any dangerous tensions that may arise.

On the whole, I believe the system has worked well. It would indeed be difficult to conclude otherwise in the light of the great gains that have been made in recent years. In the purely monetary sphere, external convertibility has been established for a broad range of currencies; and with the better distribution of reserves, there is an increasing measure of freedom for capital movements. There has been a parallel development in the ever-growing liberalization of trade and, under conditions of relatively stable prices, international trade has been increasing at an annual rate of about 4 per cent in recent years, reflecting by and large a corresponding rate of growth in world production. These are no mean achievements.

But in spite of these achievements there have been periods of tension and unease. I do not think that the movements of short-term funds from one country to another have impaired the financing of trade or the flow of goods, but it is largely the fears that these movements have aroused that have led to the questioning of the soundness of our present system. In some quarters, doubts have been expressed whether the system under which countries hold part of their international reserves in currencies (which is known as 'the gold exchange standard') will work satisfactorily in the longer run, and whether this system might not break down as it did in the interwar period. I do not think we need draw that conclusion, for it is important to remember that the currency failures which occurred in the early 1930's were caused not by inflation, but by widespread deflation—by a fall in prices which made itself felt first in the United States and then in Europe. I am sure there will be no similar deflation now, for there has been such a change in the objectives of the authorities that sufficient measures would surely be taken to prevent such a calamity, if it seemed to be threatening. Secondly, in the 1930's the exchange reserves of many of the European countries had been acquired by large-scale short-term borrowing, and they melted away when the short-term loans were not renewed; today, most countries are the true owners of their exchange holdings. A third difference is that the International Monetary Fund today stands behind the nations' reserves, supplementing them within the framework of its principles and practices and working at all times to promote international monetary consultation and collaboration. There was no similar international agency in the interwar period.

Today two currencies, the U.S. dollar and sterling, are the main reserve currencies. There is no doubt in my mind that the authorities in the United States and the United Kingdom are determined to pursue policies which will ensure confidence in the stability of their currencies. Of the outstanding short-term U.S. liabilities, about two thirds are in the hands of foreign central banks and governments, and the remainder is largely held by commercial banks and business firms. For sterling, the proportion is very much the same. There are thus substantial amounts of these currencies in private hands, and with convertibility, liquid resources owned by business firms and banks can now, with little or no difficulty, be shifted from one country to another. There is indeed no lack of international liquidity in private hands, but for this very reason it is important that there should be adequate resources in official hands to meet the possible impact of international movements of private funds.

As indicated in the Report of the Executive Directors before you, the Fund has been studying in the course of this year a broad range of problems, some of general import and some of a more detailed technical, legal, or institutional character connected with this situation. It is possible to summarize the main issues that have been considered in the form of three questions. To begin with, what are the payments difficulties for which the Fund's resources may be made available under its Articles of Agreement?[1] Secondly, how can the Fund best use its resources to meet these difficulties? And, finally, what resources are required to meet the difficulties, and are the Fund's available resources adequate to do so?

On the first question, the Executive Directors have discussed the extent to which the Fund's resources may be used for helping to meet those deficits in the balance of payments of members that go beyond the current account and are attributable, in whole or in part, to capital transfers. From a purely practical point of view, there is of course great difficulty in separating current and capital payments under a system of convertible currencies. After a thorough examination of the various aspects of the problem, the Executive Directors have clarified the understanding of the Articles of Agreement, and in that way elimated any doubt, which had not already been dissipated by the practice of the Fund, that the Fund's resources can be used for capital transfers, in accordance with Article VI and the other provisions of the Articles. If a country facing an outflow of capital were to turn to the Fund for assistance, the test to be applied by the Fund would be in accordance with its accepted principles, i.e., that appropriate measures were being taken so that the disequilibrating capital outflow would be arrested and that assistance provided by the Fund would be repaid within a maximum period of three to five years.

The answer to the second question—how the Fund can best use its resources —must take into account the strengthening of the current position and reserves of several member countries and the increased number which have accepted the obligations of Article VIII. This has made possible the use of a much wider range of currencies held by the Fund, thus increasing the volume of its usable resources. The Fund has therefore sought to diversify the use of its currency holdings in such a manner as to ensure that transactions with the Fund, and their repayment, will be conducted in those currencies which will be most helpful to the world payments position. In pursuing this objective, the Fund has been

---

[1] Annex A to Cmd. 6546. See above, p. 535, n. 1.

guided increasingly by the principle that drawings should be made in the currencies of those countries that have a strong payments and reserve position, while it is to be hoped that repayments will generally be made in those currencies that can be strengthened by their use in this way. There are a number of technical and legal problems to be faced in evolving a satisfactory program for the use of a wider range of currencies in Fund transactions and repayments. Some have already been resolved, others will need further attention. A measure of the success already achieved is shown by the fact that during the last year drawings have been made in 11 different currencies.

As a result of sales of their currencies by the Fund, a number of countries have now acquired increased drawing rights because the Fund's holdings of their currencies have been reduced considerably below 75 per cent of quota. The Fund must always take account of the fact that, should there be a reversal in the payments position, the existence of these increased drawing rights could give rise to appreciable demands on the resources of the Fund.

I come now to the third question—the adequacy of the Fund's resources. It will be apparent from what I have said about the Fund's evolving policies on the currencies that should be drawn that the answer to this question cannot be settled simply by adding up the Fund's holdings of gold and currencies, or even gold and convertible currencies, at any particular time. What is important is to ensure that the Fund has enough of those currencies which it would be appropriate to use at any particular time, given the economic conditions of that time and the purposes for which it is appropriate to use the Fund's resources.

I have already referred to the fact that the intense activity over the last year has reduced the Fund's holdings of certain currencies to a very low level, despite the recent sale of gold. But this is more than a transitory problem confined to the present circumstances, and is more than just the question of the Fund's own liquidity. It is vital to consolidate and defend the system of convertibility built up over the last few years, and to avoid the risk of any relapse into restrictions and currency disorder. In order that the Fund may play its part in this effort and meet the expectations of its members, it must be in a position to provide resources that are adequate beyond doubt to meet any needs that may arise. And in a world in which market fears and expectations play a large role, resources—national and international combined—must not only be adequate to meet demands that may be made on them, but must also be large enough to convince the public that they are adequate to defend currencies from ill-advised speculation. A substantial reduction in the Fund's holdings of major international currencies could itself become a disturbing factor, long before the point of exhaustion is reached, unless there existed satisfactory arrangements for replenishing these holdings.

All these questions have to be evaluated in the light of the swift changes in the balance of international payments that have occurred in recent years. In the circumstances, I cannot conclude that the composition and size of the Fund's resources are adequate to support a healthy international financial structure without further strengthening. The need for additional resources might be remedied by an increase in particular quotas, but in present circumstances I believe it can be handled more acceptably by firm borrowing arrangements.

These would be concluded, in particular, with the main industrial countries, because of the major role they play in the swings in international trade and payments. This does not mean that other countries would have no interest in the conclusion of such arrangements, for the maintenance of a stable and convertible exchange system is as important to them as it is to the industrial countries.

Some of the problems arising from the use to be made of the Fund's borrowing powers under Article VII of the Fund Agreement have already been discussed in general terms by the Executive Directors, but many aspects still remain to be considered. An essential step in the conclusion of any borrowing plan is for the authorities in the individual countries to obtain the power to lend to the Fund if they do not already possess it. However, in my opinion, it would not be sufficient to leave the actual borrowing transaction to an ad hoc agreement between the Fund and the lending country under these powers. There is great merit in an assurance that additional resources are available to the Fund for its transactions. The ready availability of resources is in itself a contribution to stability and strength. It has time and again been the experience of the Fund that assurance to a member that it has an access to the resources of the Fund under the provisions of a stand-by arrangement is in itself a stabilizing factor of great importance; often it has not been necessary for the member to use all, or indeed any, of the drawing rights thus assured. There is good reason to believe that the same sort of benefit would be obtained from credit facilities granted to the Fund.

At the same time, adequate provision would have to be made for general safeguards for the lending members. There would, of course, be consultation between the Fund and the prospective lender, and it should be part of the arrangement that the Fund would not borrow from a member country unless the country's payments and reserve position permitted this. Moreover, the arrangement would be such that any member that had lent its currency to the Fund would be able to obtain repayment readily if its own payments position changed. There would, of course, be no question of any weakening of the principles that the Fund has worked out for the appropriate use of its resources. These have stood the test of time in a great variety of circumstances, and we know that they are endorsed by the members of the Fund.

I believe that it should not be difficult to arrive at an agreement that will give due weight to the various aspects of borrowing, and thus to establish a workable system which would be beneficial and acceptable to all members of the Fund. There are, however, a number of decisions of policy still to be taken.

As is said in the Annual Report of the Executive Directors,[1] the approach to the increase in the Fund's resources by means of borrowing 'looks beyond the immediate needs and endeavors to equip the Fund to handle flexibly the many and varied situations that may arise under a system of freely convertible currencies'.

When we consider the Fund's role in the monetary system, it is valuable to keep in mind the two complementary aspects of the Fund's financial activities: on the one hand, the granting of financial assistance by the Fund to help countries to meet an unbalanced position; on the other hand, the assurance that the

[1] International Monetary Fund, *Annual Report of the Executive Directors for the fiscal year ending April 30, 1961* (Washington, D.C., I.M.F., 1961).

country receiving the assistance will be taking the necessary measures to restore a proper balance. For such measures to be effective, it is indispensable that the authorities in the country receiving the assistance must be convinced that the restoration of the balance is in their true interest. As the Duke of Vienna said in 'Measure for Measure', the only play of Shakespeare to be set in this City of Vienna: 'The satisfaction I would require is likewise your own benefit.' It is precisely when this identity of interest is fully realized that the programs which are supported by Fund assistance can be carried out in a spirit of mutual confidence and the desired success achieved. For that result, the countries must feel that stability is essential for their welfare as the only true foundation for sustained growth. In taking this view, they can be encouraged by the evidence that those countries which have persisted in their efforts, and accepted the transitional difficulties of carrying out a stabilization program, have succeeded in staging an impressive rate of growth.

One of the requirements for economic progress is the availability for investment of real resources, and these cannot for any length of time be obtained by inflationary methods of financing. This is an old truth, but it seems that it has to be rediscovered over and over again. To obtain genuine resources requires, of course, effort. At the time when the richer countries are making considerable efforts to provide resources for the aid of the less developed countries, these countries in turn will have to make the maximum effort to mobilize their own resources, and, through stability, create the conditions for domestic and foreign resources to be used in the most effective manner. In creating these conditions, a great many countries have had the support of the Fund, and there can be no doubt that the Fund has thus contributed to the growth in production and trade that has occurred during the last few years.

All this seems clear enough, but I believe it is not convincing to all minds. While I think that nobody will want to maintain that sustained growth can be based on monetary disorder, there seems not seldom to be a lingering fear that stability will mean reduced economic activity, and even stagnation. It is true, of course, that stability is not enough, for the real national objective should be economic growth. Economic growth can be compared with the construction of a good house, with stability as its foundations. A good house can only be erected on a solid foundation. Preparing the foundation, however, is not sufficient. There must be further initiative and activity, and the necessary resources must be acquired to complete the building. In some countries, it seems that the restoration of monetary stability has almost by itself led to a resurgence of activity, and soon produced the savings to finance it. But this is not always the case; in many countries, special domestic efforts are needed, and for these efforts to be effective they have often to be supplemented by international assistance, technical and financial. To introduce monetary stability is often only the beginning of the efforts needed to achieve growth. While the subsequent efforts largely fall outside the sphere of Fund activities, the Fund does not underrate their importance and, insofar as it can, is anxious to assist these efforts in every possible way.

Broadly speaking, the financial assistance given by the Fund helps individual countries to keep in line with general monetary trends in the world economy, while avoiding measures that would be disturbing to international trade. This is an important task, but it does not exhaust the scope of monetary action. Our monetary system has to serve an expanding economy. It is not suggested that credit measures alone can engender a high rate of growth; the fiscal and economic structure and the whole range of social and market practices are of vital importance. It may, for instance, be important to remove maladjustments due to mistaken budgetary policies, or in the cost and price structure, which would retard growth. The conditions under which foreign trade is carried on are also important—and with the new trading arrangements now being established, particular attention must be paid to these aspects. The Fund in its work is naturally interested in these questions, but pays particular attention to matters of monetary policy.

Under modern conditions, the gold flow does not set fixed limits to the possible expansion of credit or international liquidity. Within each country, the credit volume may be expanded in response to demand; and the monetary authorities can also take positive action to stimulate, and provide the basis for, credit expansion. Since the Second World War, on the whole, the problem has been rather to contain the expansion of credit than to stimulate it. All countries have been more or less involved in this process, but those countries that are responsible for a high proportion of the world's production and trade must necessarily play a major role. They are aware, however, that even they cannot act independently of the general trend, and are therefore bound to act in cooperation with each other. Sometimes similar, sometimes complementary, policies will have to be pursued according to the ever-changing situation. The methods of cooperation will vary; there will be direct contacts, but there will increasingly be reliance on international institutions.

In Article I of the Articles of Agreement, which sets out the purposes of the Fund, financial assistance by the Fund is only one of the purposes. It is also the objective of the Fund to promote exchange stability and orderly exchange arrangements; to assist in the establishment of a multilateral system of payments; to facilitate the expansion of international trade, and thereby to increase the productive resources of members; and to act as a center of collaboration and consultation. Indeed, without the close contact between the Fund and the competent authorities in member countries, it is difficult to see how any of the purposes of the Fund could be achieved. This has been proved time and again to be the case in the annual consultations with Article XIV countries. Already excellent results have been obtained in the consultations that have been begun with Article VIII countries. Here it is a question of voluntary cooperation, and for that reason I believe that these consultations will be more, and not less, effective. The cooperation has to be inspired by the notion that countries have a common interest as partners in the international monetary system. This system has to be strengthened where it is vulnerable; but the policies pursued must be such that the system plays its proper role in the process of economic expansion. To observe, on the one hand, the necessary monetary discipline and, on the other, to respond to the needs of expansion is no easy task. It raises many problems, but it is my impression that these problems are now being tackled more effectively than ever before, and with greatly increased chances of success.

(ii) Statement of the Governor for the United States, Mr. Dillon[1] (extracts)

. . . Last year, the Fund's advisory activities continued on a broad scale. Wherever member countries have sought to deal effectively with financial instability—by strengthening their fiscal resources, by controlling money and credit, or by otherwise improving their financial institutions—they have been able to rely on the staff of the Fund for expert and objective advice.

The stabilization programs many members of the Fund have worked out and put into operation, usually with Fund advice, have at times been criticized on the ground that they have supposedly imposed a choice between stagnation and economic growth. I do not believe that this is a correct appraisal of the role played by financial stabilization in economic development. I agree with the opinion expressed by Mr. Jacobsson in his brilliant opening statement: that the aim of a well-designed stabilization program is to eliminate inflation, not only as a source of balance of payments disequilibrium, but also as an obstacle to economic growth. Financial stability can thus assist economic growth which, together with social progress, must be the major objective of development policy.

Of course, financial stability cannot of itself cure all the problems of economic growth that beset the developing countries. Effective development planning, basic internal reforms, and adequate capital from both external and internal sources—all are necessary. This is well recognized by the Fund, which is, as it should be, the partner of economic development institutions, national and international, in coordinated efforts to increase the flow of external assistance and to help the developing countries make the best use of their own domestic resources. . . .

During the past year, as Mr. Jacobsson has reminded us, there has been active discussion and examination in governmental circles, among economists, and in the financial press, of the adequacy of existing international monetary arrangements. These discussions have been very helpful. Mr. Jacobsson has now proposed that each of the principal industrial countries commit itself to lend its currency to the Fund up to a stated amount. I strongly agree that an arrangement of this sort should be worked out to ensure the Fund access to the additional amounts that would be needed should balance of payments pressures involving these countries ever impair or threaten to impair the smooth functioning of the world payments system.

At the same time, for its regular requirements, the Fund can, and should be expected to, borrow from one or another of the participating countries under Article VII whenever its supply of any of these particular currencies becomes low. It would also appear reasonable to consider the possibility that such loans be credited against any commitment which the lending country may have undertaken as its part of the multilateral arrangement. These special bilateral borrowings would thus replenish the Fund's supply of particular currencies in strong demand and, in this way, would help to avoid undue drains on its gold reserve.

I have no fixed opinions on the details of the multilateral borrowing arrangement. I am confident, on the basis of the encouraging views I have heard expressed in the past few days, that practical means can be found to give effect to

[1] *I.M.F. Summary Proceedings, 1961*, pp. 48–55.

the agreement in principle which so evidently exists. There are four important aspects which I do wish to emphasize:

First, the aggregate amount the participating countries should look forward to committing to the project should be large enough to add decisively to the Fund's capacity to play its essential role.

Second, to be effective, the additional resources must be promptly available in case of need.

Third, safeguards will be required to ensure that there will be effective consultation between the Fund and the lenders, and that the Fund will only actually borrow under the commitment arrangements after taking full account of the current reserve position of the lending country. In addition, each country which actually lends to the Fund should, in case the need develops, be able automatically to obtain repayment from the Fund.

Fourth, I concur in Mr. Jacobsson's judgment that there must be no weakening of the policies that have guided the Fund in the use of its resources; nor should the new arrangements change in any way the existing rights and duties of members of the Fund, both as drawers of currencies and as providers of currencies.

This is an important project. The Fund should push ahead promptly in its current consultations with the prospective lending countries in order that the Executive Board may carry the project to completion so that the participating countries may obtain the necessary legislative authority from their parliaments early next year. With this done, the monetary system of the free world will be substantially strengthened, for the Fund will then clearly be in a position to meet the changing needs of the new world of convertible currencies.

Speaking for my country, I want to say that the United States regards the work in which we are engaged here in Vienna as having a direct and important bearing upon the future course of free world growth and progress. I have confidence in the ultimate outcome of our deliberations because I have confidence in the vitality of the free economies upon which the work of the Fund is founded. Our mutual goal is a world of expanding opportunities for every human being to pursue his legitimate aspirations in peace and freedom. The International Monetary Fund is playing an important role in helping us to achieve it.

(iii) Statement of the Governor for France, M. Wilfred Baumgartner[1]

First, I want to thank my friend, Mr. Jacobsson, once more for another year of sustained efforts. We are glad that he will stay at the head of an organization which, in the face of new difficulties, has remained the guardian of the monetary order. It is this task that the Fund must pursue, adapting itself, to be sure, to the requirements of a situation in constant evolution, while observing as well the line of conduct marked out from the beginning by its Articles of Agreement and, since a long time ago, by its policy.

I am sometimes reproached in my own country for the caution with which I speak of the results achieved. In France, understatement has not fully acquired freedom of the city. But before this assembly of specialists I think I can say that the threats which seemed at the beginning of the year to hang over the monetary order have been staved off with some success.

[1] I.M.F. Summary Proceedings, 1961, pp. 60–64.

The decisions taken successively, first in the United States in order to facilitate the recovery of business and restore the balance of payments equilibrium,[1] then in Germany and in the Netherlands with the revaluation of the deutsche mark and the guilder, and finally in the United Kingdom for strengthening internal economic policy, happily contributed to dissipate the widespread rumors about the weakness of the western monetary system and to reduce the resulting capital movements.

Since, at the same time, a substantial number of countries have accepted the obligations of Article VIII of the Agreement, and the liberalization of trade generally has recorded new progress, notably in France, it can be asserted that the past year, despite the difficulties encountered, was finally a year of progress.

Naturally, in expressing this reassuring opinion, I am far from thinking that we are now safe from any hazard. We may well have other worries, and we must be ready to face them. Since a year and a half ago, many plans have been published to assure the strength of the international payments system. I must say that they seem to me unrealistic in general, undoubtedly because there is no panacea in this field.

As we all know, the most effective contribution we can make to the maintenance of the monetary order is for each country to apply nationally a sound policy and to ward off, in a world in expansion, the recurrence of inflationary pressures. The disequilibria which occur in balances of payments call first for internal measures. The contribution of the International Monetary Fund, as well as, eventually, measures of mutual assistance, can and should be only of a complementary nature. Such has been the constant doctrine of our organization, the appropriateness and effectiveness of which need no further demonstration.

The developments of the past year also bear witness to the very great usefulness of the cooperation among central banks which has materialized in Europe through the periodic meetings in Basle, at the Bank for International Settlements.

We have seen in the recent past that, although speculation does not hesitate to attack one currency or another, it can be held in check by the proclaimed cooperation of the main central banks.

Is it necessary to go farther in this field and to organize a second line of defense at somewhat longer term? That is a subject on which much has been said in recent months. It is a problem which, because of the fact that it concerns essentially the currencies of the industrial countries, could eventually be decided outside the International Monetary Fund. In that respect, our institution has clarified the provisions of Article VI of the Agreement concerning capital movements. We have finally been able to approve it, but not without indicating that the meaning of the texts should not be stretched in one direction or another according to the impulses or needs of the moment.

Mr. Jacobsson, in his opening address, indicated that he could not conclude that the Fund's resources were appropriate to its needs. It appears to me that a distinction should be made here between what I would call the normal needs of the Fund and the exceptional needs which might arise from the capital

---

[1] See also this chapter, document 3 above, p. 521.

movements, also exceptional, which have recently been discussed. It is only for these exceptional needs that a strengthening of the Fund's resources might appear desirable.

I would almost say that what the Fund may need in this connection is more an assurance as to possible means of intervention than means meant to be actually used. In other words, the existence of a second line of defense is without doubt more important than its utilization is desirable.

We must indeed be aware of the dangers that an automatic compensation of capital movements would create from the very point of view of safeguarding the international payments system. While recognizing that the world cannot, in the present state of affairs, fail to apply the system of the gold exchange standard, we must remain conscious of the risks of this system.

That is why, although France recognizes the importance of the problem raised by Mr. Jacobsson and is prepared, in principle, to associate itself with the joint efforts that it calls for, we do not intend any more, I believe, than some other European countries to commit ourselves or commit this institution by way of an automatic and rigid solution.

As a matter of fact, things may change quickly in this field. Let me take, for instance, the case of my country. Heavily in debt some time ago, it has been able to repay within two years more than a billion dollars of its external debts. Moreover, vis-à-vis the Fund, its situation has changed radically. Not only has it repaid all the drawings previously made, but it has provided currency for the drawings of other countries. The improvement of its position thus exceeds $600 million. What is true of France is also true of its neighbors. It can be noted in passing that, out of all the currencies utilized by the Fund, the contributions of Germany, France, Italy, the Netherlands, and Belgium added together balance and now even exceed the contributions of the United States. But, again, things may change.

Be that as it may, today France, like other countries, could possibly go a little beyond its present outlay, but under certain conditions.

Mr. Jacobsson, in this connection, mentioned the question of reversibility. This reversibility appears to me to go without saying. It goes without saying that just as the member countries have the right in our practice to an automatic drawing within the gold tranche, so the lending countries should, if their situation happens to change, obtain immediately the repayment of their exceptional contributions. If I in my turn mention this point, it is mainly to show that it illustrates the danger of widespread inflation which automatic compensation of capital movements might entail.

And that leads me to the point which I consider as essential. It seems to me necessary that as regards assistance which will not be granted individually by certain countries directly under Article VII, but which by extension of the same provisions would be included in a borrowing arrangement set up by the main industrial countries, each country should remain judge of the advisability of the use of its own currency. Mr Jacobsson spoke in this connection of consultations. Mr. Dillon spoke of safeguards. I prefer Mr. Dillon's expression, and that is the point to which attention should be given in the coming negotiations, which must be initiated but may be delicate.

To sum up and conclude, it seems to me that no country can wish to escape its duty of international cooperation, which may arise from the very progress that we have made in the convertibility of currencies. But care must be taken to avoid this convertibility being one day jeopardized by insufficiently precise procedures. . . .

(iv) *Statement by the Governor for Germany, Dr. Karl Blessing*[1] (*extracts*)

. . . Let me now say a few words on the international monetary system. When we reached a state of widespread convertibility at the end of 1958, we were all quite proud of this achievement. Convertibility certainly meant a big step forward, but it has also confronted us with new problems, problems which we must learn to deal with. The greater freedom on the exchange markets and the closer integration of the various money and capital markets have brought about a situation in which actual or merely anticipated disequilibria in the balance of payments of various countries rapidly induce international capital movements. Furthermore, it became evident that an isolated and autonomous monetary and credit policy applied in contrast to the requirements of the balance of payments was practically impossible.

It would be a mistake to try to evade these problems by backing away again from the freedom achieved and by imposing some sort of control on capital movements. It also would be wrong, in my view, to resort to flexible exchange rates, because this would hamper world trade and might provoke even larger speculative capital movements. If we want to come nearer to the generally recognized aim of a growing integration of world markets and a further increase in world trade, we have to maintain a system of stable exchange rates as provided by the Fund Agreement. This, however, can only be achieved effectively if domestic policies are better coordinated between the various countries and if monetary, fiscal, and economic policies of both the surplus and the deficit countries are better adjusted to the requirements of the respective balance of payments situations. In fact, it means that we have to submit voluntarily to a monetary discipline similar to that inherent in the automatism of the old gold standard.

I should like to add that we cannot afford a monetary order under which we all march in step into creeping inflation. We must get away from creeping inflation which has dominated the past decade. We must seek to attain price stability than hitherto. The big countries have a special responsibility in this respect, since inflationary impulses originating with them are apt to spread to the entire international monetary system. I am aware that this is not music in the ears of those who believe that easy money and creeping inflation are basic conditions of high rates of growth, but I am more than ever convinced that sustained growth can only be achieved by refraining from inflationary practices.

Lately, there has been an eager search for new and better monetary systems, even involving a complete transformation of the International Monetary Fund. Some people are afraid of a coming shortage of international liquidity; others feel that the gold exchange standard should be abandoned because of its inflationary character. I have the impression that such ideas, stimulating and

[1] *I.M.F. Summary Proceedings, 1961*, pp. 64–69.

thought-provoking as they may be, bring with them the danger that the pre-requisites of any workable international monetary order, namely, monetary discipline at home and readiness for international cooperation, tend to become neglected. I do not believe in the magic of panaceas; I do not believe that monetary discipline can be replaced by new schemes and inventions. I do not share the opinion that we are in urgent need for greater international liquidity, nor do I share the view that the gold exchange standard is an evil in itself, or that it confronts us with the danger of a serious crisis.

The demand for more international liquidity is more or less the result of disequilibria in the international payments situation. In a better balanced world economy, there is, as history proves, less need for high reserves. And if the gold exchange standard is well managed and kept under adequate control, there is no danger in the system as such. I quite agree with what Mr. Jacobsson has said on this subject in his introductory statement. What we need is not a fundamental change but a gradual improvement of the present international system based on monetary discipline at home and on close cooperation on an international level.

In the interest of this close international cooperation, I attach great importance to the ideas outlined in the Managing Director's speech. I consider it desirable that confidence in the Fund's lending power be strengthened by replenishing the Fund's holdings of a number of convertible currencies within the framework of a general replenishment plan, using the power of the Fund to borrow from its members under Article VII, Section 2. I think that firm commitments for granting such credits in case of need should be given by the various countries, but it should be made quite clear that participants in the scheme will only be called upon to provide such additional credits to the Fund if and for such time as their over-all balance of payments position permits such lendings. Since the plan is based on voluntary action, it is indispensable that members whose currencies are used should be fully consulted in advance of transactions. The main purpose of such a general replenishment scheme should, of course, be to make sure that the Fund will be well equipped to deal with critical situations in the international monetary system, such as a major crisis in key currency countries which would adversely affect all of us. I would not exclude, however, the use of the borrowing powers of the Fund also for other purposes, if the need for it can be clearly demonstrated. A replenishment of the Fund's resources through borrowing under Article VII would be justifiable only if these additional means are used for sound and noninflationary purposes. In my view there can thus be no question of any weakening of the Fund's established lending principles. I welcome the suggestion of Mr. Jacobsson that the Executive Directors go ahead with their study of all aspects of the plan, and I hope that they will be able to work out concrete proposals in the not too distant future.

(v) Statement of the Governor for the United Kingdom, Mr. Selwyn Lloyd[1] *(extracts)*

. . . I have been glad to note both from the Annual Report and from Mr. Jacobsson's statement that the Fund has been considering and developing new techniques to deal with changing conditions affecting international payments.

[1] *I.M.F. Summary Proceedings, 1961*, pp. 100–6.

I am sure that it is right that we should discuss possible wide-ranging new approaches to these problems, but I propose to concentrate my remarks today on three matters of immediate importance. These all arise in my judgment from the fundamental problem of imbalance in international payments to which I drew particular attention in my speech last year.

Last year, I expressed my concern lest the method of operation of the Fund should aggravate the problem of imbalance by reason of the tendency for members to take drawings in only a very few currencies. We have travelled a long way since then. The moves to Article VIII, to which I have referred, have helped by increasing the number of currencies in which it is permissible, under the Fund Agreement, to make repayments to the Fund. Equally important in practice has been the establishment of the convention that, in the first place, countries making substantial drawings should, before making their formal request for Fund assistance, consult the Managing Director as to the currencies most suitable for drawing; and, in the second place, that the Managing Director should, for his part, contrive that drawings are taken in the currencies of the countries that are accumulating or have accumulated relatively large reserves. There was a clear example of this policy in the case of the recent drawing by the United Kingdom which was made in no less than nine currencies.

Another aspect of the present payments situation is greater freedom of exchanges has increased the relative importance of capital movements, and this is partly because controls have been relaxed and partly because of speculative factors and disparities in interest rates which have encouraged the ebb and flow of funds. This situation calls for continuous direct cooperation between the countries mainly concerned, and I welcome the evidence of this in recent months. But the Fund also has an important part to play, and I am glad to note that the Executive Board has clarified a previous decision in such a way that use of the resources to finance capital transfers is not precluded. This will help the Fund to maintain the flexibility and effectiveness of its operations.

Finally, there is the question whether the Fund has adequate supplies of the currencies needed for its operations. The resources arising from the original contributions, together with those deriving from the quota increases made following the meeting in New Delhi in 1958, are a substantial provision against most contingencies. Moreover, there exists the possibility of replenishing the Fund's resources by the sale of gold, as was done this year. We agree, however, with Mr. Jacobsson's view that the Fund's gold should be used sparingly. If, however, this view is accepted, we are confronted with the problem which he foresaw in his statement. A country with a fundamentally sound economy but a temporary balance of payments problem must be able to turn to the Fund with confidence that the Fund will be able to help, with resources which are adequate both in amount and in kind. The prudent course, therefore, is to make special provision now for circumstances in which additional supplies of certain currencies may be needed.

The founders of this institution in their wisdom provided a possible remedy in the form of the powers under Article VII to replenish the Fund's holdings by borrowing; and the Managing Director and the staff have already carried out useful studies of ways in which those powers might be used. In the light of those studies, the Executive Board have begun to examine the practicability of credit arrangements of a stand-by nature between the Fund and certain countries which would enable it to borrow their currencies whenever—but not until—the need arose.

Let us be in no doubt that such arrangements are a matter of fundamental importance. Without them, as I believe, it will not be possible to ensure the effective functioning of the present system of international payments. As Mr. Jacobsson said in his speech, this is a matter of deep interest and concern to all members of the Fund. All have a common interest in the effective functioning of the system. All must be confident that, if and when they need help, the Fund will have the means to help. But obviously also the arrangements will be of particular concern to those members whose currencies are likely to be needed by the Fund in greater amounts than are available under their quotas. I am sure that we should all recognize this and the consequent need to have safeguards for effective consultation between the Fund and the lending countries.

The United Kingdom welcomes the work already done by the Executive Board on this important subject, and what has been said on it by previous speakers, and is ready to play its part in a scheme based on the principles to which a general assent seems to be emerging. In our view, it is essential that as a result of this meeting the Executive Board should feel empowered to work out and agree upon a detailed scheme with the minimum of delay.

(vi) Statement of the Governor for the Netherlands, Dr. M. W. Holtrop[1]

Somerset Maugham, the British author, opens one of his books with a quotation from the Upanishad, reading: 'The sharp edge of a razor is difficult to pass over; thus the wise say the path to Salvation is hard.'

I have always been struck by the appropriateness of this simile in describing the toils of monetary authorities. If their salvation be in the fulfillment of that threefold object of economic policy—a sufficient rate of growth, implying full employment, stability of prices, and balance of payments equilibrium—they have to tread a narrow and ever continuing path, from which they can swerve neither to left nor right without falling into the traps of either inflation or deflation, overemployment or underemployment, deficit or surplus.

Looking back to the experience of the past year, I do not feel that we can be quite satisfied with our achievements in keeping to that narrow path. It is true that in the main industrial countries prices have been fairly stable. Yet price inflation has not come to a stop. Less reason for satisfaction has been given in the field of employment, in which we have been faced by the contrast between the buoyancy of employment in Europe as against the continuance of underemployment in the United States. Outright unsatisfactory has been our performance in the pursuit of balance of payments equilibrium, where we have been met with deficits, creating doubt about the stability of the two main reserve currencies and with surpluses causing changes in the parities of the deutsche mark and the Dutch guilder.

How is it, we may well ask, that we find it so hard to keep to the narrow path? Is it that we do not know the rules that should control our course? Is it that,

---

[1] *I.M.F. Summary Proceedings, 1961,* pp. 111–18.

knowing them, we do not apply them, perhaps for lack of proper instruments of policy? Or is it that our institutional arrangements are deficient and in want of being overhauled?

It is remarkable, and perhaps flattering for the monetary managers, that the criticism which has been uttered in connection with this unsatisfactory state of affairs has been directed far more to the alleged deficiency of our institutional arrangements than to a possible lack of proper management. It is the intrinsic character of the gold exchange standard that has especially been the object of discussion.

The gold exchange standard is being blamed by some for having an inherent tendency of creating too much liquidity, thus having an inflationary bias, and by others for having been unable—or at least for being unable in the long run—to create sufficient liquidity, thus having a deflationary bias. Thirdly, it is being blamed for being inherently unstable.

I should like to say a word about these charges.

Among those who blame our present monetary system for having an inflationary bias, there are some who argue that this is due to an intrinsic deficiency of the gold exchange standard as compared with a pure gold reserve standard. Though I would agree that our recent experience with the gold exchange standard has been on the inflationary side, I think it is necessary to reject the thesis that this is due to the intrinsic properties of the system. International monetary equilibrium demands that the volume of international liquidity should conform to the volume of the liquid reserves that the different countries, on the average, want to have, not in order to *spend* them, but to *hold* them. Whether the addition to existing reserves comes from the production of gold or from an increase in the currency liabilities of a so-called key-currency country does not make any difference. What matters is that this addition is not in excess of the amount the reserve-holding countries actually desire to add to their reserves. If it is, the excess will tend to be spent and spent again, thus creating an inflationary situation. If, on the other hand, the creation of international liquidity lags behind the true demand for more reserves, a deflationary atmosphere will result.

There is no intrinsic reason why the gold exchange standard, more than a pure gold reserve standard, should lead to an oversupply of liquidity. The history of the gold standard provides us with periods both of abundance and of shortage of gold. The gold exchange standard may just as well bring periods of oversupply and of shortage of reserve media.

Meanwhile we must admit that, of late, the key-currency countries have been running too high a deficit and that, consequently, we are presently faced with an oversupply of liquidity. I come to this conclusion because it seems obvious to me that the surplus countries are presently not accumulating reserves they really want to hold, but rather reserves they tend to spend. Even if we find that they occasionally follow restrictive, or even deflationary policies, they evidently do not do so in order to increase their reserves, but to combat the inflationary consequences of excessive boom and overemployment. Their further policies, such as the discouraging of capital imports, the stimulating of capital exports, the prepayment of foreign debt, and the pursuit of other forms of compensatory financing, are clear evidence that they prefer not to increase reserves.

The Netherlands, in this respect, is a good example. On the basis of the over-all balance of payments surplus—not including transactions of the banks and compensatory transactions of the Government—during the period from the beginning of 1959 to the end of August 1961, they might have added $900 million to reserves. Yet, the actual addition to net reserves of the central bank and commercial banks—not deducting the drawings by the Fund—was only $160 million. The remainder was absorbed by prepayment of debt, by allowing foreign bond issues on the capital market, and by a very important increase in foreign lending by the banks.

I would conclude, therefore, that we have of late been faced with a situation of oversupply of international liquidity due to balance of payments deficits of the key-currency countries that exceeded the desired increment of reserves by the main reserve-holding countries. This has been a situation of fact; it was not a necessary concomitant of the gold exchange standard as such. The recent important improvement in the basis balance of payments situation of the two-key-currency countries as a matter of fact holds out the hope that this oversupply will not be continued.

In the face of recent experience, it is somewhat difficult to switch over to the consideration of the reverse problem, implied in the thesis that the gold exchange standard is incapable of creating sufficient liquidity. Discounting the contention that this has already been shown by experience, we must yet, I think, give serious consideration to the argument that, in the long run, the present key-currency countries might not prove to be willing, or to be in a position, to increase their currency liabilities to the extent of satisfying the demand for additional reserves of the reserve-holding countries. In the light of the present situation, this problem does not at all seem urgent. Eventually it may, however, deserve our close attention.

There is a connection between this problem and the third point of criticism directed at the gold exchange standard, namely, its alleged inherent instability, due to the right of conversion of key-currency into gold, enjoyed by the holders of official reserves. Although in the year of uncertainties in the field of exchange stability which now lies behind us, monetary authorities have generally not changed their reserve holding habits, it cannot be denied that the power of the authorities in the reserve-holding countries to switch back and forth from non-interest-bearing gold to interest-bearing key currency creates a potential threat to the stability of the system. Paradoxically, one might even say that the system's stability is based upon uncertainty. For if it were inconceivable that the dollar price of gold might wish to hold only dollars and the gold exchange standard would tend to be transformed into a dollar standard, the United States having to buy almost all the world's gold. It is very doubtful that this would be a desir-able development. If, on the other hand, it were almost sure that the dollar price of gold would be raised, few monetary authorities would wish to continue to hold dollars, and the system would tend to revert to a gold reserve standard, for which no sufficient gold would be available. It is uncertainty, therefore, that presently controls the proper mixture of decisions.

It is an intriguing question whether one should prefer uncertainty to continue its present function, or whether one should try to replace it, as would be conceivable, by some arrangement that would give more certainty but less liberty of action. One might think of arrangements in which the Fund would play an intermediary role. One might also think of an agreement between the main reserve-holding countries and the key-currency countries on fixed limits within which the former shall maintain the proportion of their reserves held in gold and in key currency.

I do not want to elaborate on this special problem and its possible ramifications right now, but I thought it necessary to mention it in order to provide the proper background against which I should now like to say a few words about proposed creation of additional resources for the Fund by way of stand-by agreements preparatory to borrowing under Article VII.

My first impression is that these proposals do not give an answer to the problems I have just discussed. Additional resources would have little bearing on the stability aspect of the gold exchange standard. They would, within the limits of the present suggestions, not offer a solution to the possible long-term problem of an insufficiency of liquidity creation. They might, on the other hand, tend to aggravate the problem of the present oversupply of liquidity.

In my opinion, our present problems are not due to any inherent deficiency of our institutional setup. Therefore, we cannot hope to solve them by changes in our institutions, but only by changes in our policies. A rectification of the present situation of imbalance cannot be brought about by the creation of new resources, but only by a reversal of the tendencies of the past. Both surplus countries and deficit countries will have to concentrate on re-establishing balance of payments equilibrium by the use of internal policies appropriate to that end. Deficit countries will have to determine whether their problem is one of internal demand inflation, that eats away at their capacity for exports, or one of cost inflation, that throttles their competitiveness. To combat demand inflation, monetary and budgetary therapies may be indicated; the suppressing of cost inflation will require the development of quite different instruments of policy. Surplus countries, on the other hand, may have to ask themselves whether their wage standards perhaps still lag behind their productivity and whether, more generally, their internal monetary and budgetary policies tend to reduce, or rather to perpetuate, their surpluses.

In the framework of these necessary mutual endeavors to restore equilibrium, more resources can at their best buy more time for the proper execution of the internal programs of action. If that time be not well used, they will only serve to perpetuate disequilibrium. There could be no greater fallacy than to imagine that the solution of our problems could be found—as it is sometimes suggested—in just feeding the excess reserves of the surplus countries back into the international circuit, so as to enable the deficit countries to continually finance their deficits. This would only create the perfect machine for perpetual inflation.

Does this mean that the idea of creating additional resources should be rejected? I do not think so. But it means that we have very carefully to ask ourselves for what purposes and under what conditions such additional resources might be needed, without their calling into existence the very dangers just described.

It seems to me that the experience of the past year has confronted us with two

D.I.A.–T

potential emergencies which might indeed create a justified need for additional resources. I am thinking of the possibility of (a) a substantial drawing by the United States, to cover a temporary deficit, which could not be financed out of the normal resources of the Fund and (b) drawings either by the key-currency countries or by other convertible countries, with the purpose of cushioning the shock of sudden uncontrollable short-term capital movements of a speculative nature.

In the first-mentioned case, the special position of the United States as a key-currency country might make a call on the Fund preferable to relying fully on its own reserves, however substantial these may be. In the second case, the availability of special resources might help to direct the burden of the drawing toward the countries that happen to be the beneficiaries of the short-term capital movements.

If the possible use of additional resources is explicitly confined to these purposes, their creation may indeed serve to strengthen and not tend to weaken the existing international payments system. The Netherlands Government is, therefore, willing to give serious consideration to the possibility of participating in a collective agreement between a number of industrial countries and the Fund with the purpose of giving the Fund, over relatively short but renewable periods, reasonable assurance of the availability of additional resources in case the afore-mentioned emergencies should indeed arise. Such an agreement would necessarily provide for objective criteria determining the magnitude of any individual country's actual contribution at the moment the Fund would want to call on the stand-by arrangement. It would also have to make provision for the reversibility of the loan agreement in case the lending country should, at a later date, find itself in a deficit position. Finally, it would seem essential that the lending countries, when the Fund should make a call on them, shall have the opportunity, by a collective judgment, to confirm that also in their opinion the special emergency, for which the additional resources have been set aside, has indeed arisen.

I hope that it will prove possible to work out in the coming months an agreement between the Fund and the main reserve-holding countries along these lines. I also hope that, for many years to come, it will not be necessary to put such an agreement into operation. For, as the Managing Director has rightly observed, these additional resources would prove their greatest value if they never would have to be touched.

So favorable an outcome will only be achieved, however, if all countries, whether they are presently running deficits or surpluses, while aiming their internal policies at full employment, sufficient growth, and reasonable price stability, manage to adapt both their policies and their policy instruments to the simultaneous fulfillment of that absolute exigency of stable international financial relationships: the establishment of basic equilibrium in the external balance of payments.

F. SOUTH-EAST ASIA

(a) Laos

1. Mr. Khrushchev to Prince Sihanouk of Cambodia, 7 January 1961[1]

Your Royal Highness,

I have the honour to acknowledge the receipt of your message of January 2, 1961,[2] and can assure you that the Soviet government fully shares your profound anxiety over the situation created in Laos, which is fraught with a serious threat to the national independence of the Laotian people as well as to the cause of peace and security in South-East Asia.

During our recent meeting in Moscow,[3] we discussed at length the events in Laos and the causes which brought about the worsening of the situation in that country. The facts irrefutably show that the main cause of this serious aggravation of the situation in Laos is the crude interference of the United States, which was particularly intensified after Prince Souvanna Phouma had legally and constitutionally formed a government in August, 1960.

The programme of peace, neutrality and national unity which has been proclaimed by this government and which is fully in accord with the Geneva agreements, has been unanimously supported by the Laotian people and has received worldwide recognition. And this is only natural, because there has appeared in Laos a real opportunity to ensure the country's peaceful, democratic and independent development, to settle internal political problems and to tackle the problems of improving the living standard of the population.

The activities of the government of Prince Souvanna Phouma in carrying out the abovementioned programme, however, met with sharp counter-action on the part of the United States of America and certain of its allies in the S.E.A.T.O. military bloc. And you, Your Royal Highness, are also well aware that the United States took the road of engineering the armed uprising by General Phoumi Nosavan in order to overthrow the lawful government of Prince Souvanna Phouma.

For this purpose, the U.S.A. and some of its allies in the S.E.A.T.O. military bloc have given and continue to give the rebels military material, technical and financial aid on a large scale, up to and including the direct participation of military personnel of the United States, Thailand and South Viet Nam in military operations on the side of the rebels. The illegal Boun Oum-Nosavan government has been formed with the consent and participation of the U.S.A. and its allies, who are now attempting to give it a constitutional appearance by using the King and Deputies of the Laotian National Assembly who are captives held by the rebels.

It stands to reason that these manoeuvres will fail to deceive world public

---

[1] *Soviet News*, 27 January 1961.

[2] This message has not so far been published. In it Prince Sihanouk had put forward the idea of a fourteen-nation conference to which the eight signatories of the Geneva Agreement of 1954 would be invited, plus the United States, the three member countries of the International Control Commission (Canada, India, and Poland), and Thailand and Burma.

[3] Prince Sihanouk had visited Moscow in December 1960.

opinion. As far as the Laotian people are concerned, the facts amply show that they consider the government headed by Prince Souvanna Phouma the only lawful national government. The major successes recently achieved by the patriotic forces which rallied round the government of Prince Souvanna Phouma, graphically show the firm determination of the Laotian people to finish with the rebels and to restore peace on the basis of the programme proclaimed by the government of Prince Souvanna Phouma.

The fact that the United States is taking measures, these days, aimed at carrying out direct intervention against Laos in order to destroy its independence and to transform Laos into a S.E.A.T.O. base, not stopping short of shedding the blood of the Laotian people, cannot but arouse grave anxiety on the part of all peaceloving nations. In this connection attention is drawn to the order alerting the U.S. armed forces in the Pacific which has been issued by Eisenhower before his forthcoming retirement from the office of President, to the dispatch of a U.S. naval formation to the South China Sea, to the coast of Indo-China, and to the massing of large military forces of Thailand and South Viet Nam on the Laotian border.

It is absolutely correctly noted in your message that no nation and no people can remain indifferent to the sufferings of a peaceful people who several years ago gained their independence, and who want their sovereign right to decide their own fate to recognised. This is precisely why the just struggle of the Laotian people meets with warm sympathy and full support on the part of all the peaceloving peoples, including the Soviet people and their government, who invariably demand the strict observance and the steadfast fulfilment of the Geneva agreements on Laos, which have been and remain a good basis for the preservation and consolidation of peace thoughout the whole of what used to be Indo-China, including Laos.

Your Royal Highness,

The Soviet government highly appreciates Cambodia's attitude concerning the events in Laos. This attitude was reflected in the joint Soviet-Cambodian communiqué adopted during your recent visit to the U.S.S.R.[1]

It is generally known that in this communiqué both sides expressed their sincere desire to see Laos independent and neutral and approved of the efforts of the government of Prince Souvanna Phouma and the entire Laotian people in conducting a peaceful foreign policy based on the 1954 Geneva agreements. The necessity of rendering support to the lawful government of Prince Souvanna Phouma was noted, as that would help to promote stability in this area of the world.

We welcome your statement that 'Cambodia considers it her duty to come out in defence of the fraternal people of Laos, whose existence is seriously threatened'. The Soviet government hopes that the Royal government of Cambodia will continue, jointly with other peaceloving countries, to render all necessary support to Prince Souvanna Phouma's lawful government of Laos.

The Soviet government fully shares your opinion that today an urgent task of all peaceloving forces throughout the world is to find the means for ensuring

[1] Text in *Soviet News*, 6 December 1960.

the legitimate rights of the Laotian people, to bridle the American aggressors, and to avert the threat of a seat of war appearing in South-East Asia.

As you know, the Soviet government has already warned the United States government of the grave consequences which may arise as a result of the aggressive actions perpetrated by the United States and certain of its allies in the S.E.A.T.O. military bloc against the Laotian people. The Soviet government favours the urgent calling of a conference of states similar to the conference which was held in Geneva in 1954. As you know, the Soviet government, which is one of the chairmen of the Geneva Conference on Indo-China, has addressed the other chairman, the government of Great Britain, with the proposal that the activities of the International Commission for Supervision and Control in Laos be immediately resumed.

The Soviet government favourably views your proposals for holding an international conference of the participants in the 1954 Geneva conference, including the United States, the member-countries of the International Commission on Laos, and countries neighbouring on Laos. The aim of such a conference should be to help the Laotian people in ensuring the peace, unity and neutrality of their country on the basis of the 1954 Geneva agreements.

The Soviet government considers that the conference to discuss the question of Laos with the participation of the abovementioned countries could be convened in one of the neutral countries of Asia—in Cambodia, for instance, if you have no objections.

The Soviet government is prepared, together with the Royal government of Cambodia, to take all the necessary measures for convening an international conference on the Laotian issue and to co-operate closely with the Royal government in the efforts aimed at most speedily facilitating the restoration of peace in Laos and the consolidation of peace and security in South-East Asia.

2. The Chinese Prime Minister, Mr. Chou En-Lai, to Prince Sihanouk, 11 February 1961[1]

Your Royal Highness,

I have the honour to acknowledge receipt of Your Royal Highness' messages dated 20 January and 1 February and pay sincere tribute to the earnest efforts Your Royal Highness has made to uphold the Geneva agreements and restore peace in Laos.

I am glad to learn that the proposal Your Royal Highness put forward on 1 January for the convocation of an enlarged meeting of the Geneva Conference with the participation of fourteen countries concerned has won the support of still more countries. I fully agree to what Your Royal Highness pointed out in your message of 20 January, namely, that only the convocation of an international conference of the countries concerned can put an end to foreign interference in the internal affairs of Laos and restore peace in Laos. The Chinese

[1] *H.N.A.*, 15 February 1961. This letter was sent in reply to two letters that Prince Sihanouk had sent to Mr. Chou En-Lai on 20 January and 1 February containing proposals for an international conference to deal with the Laotian problem. These letters have not so far been published.

government is, in general, not against reactivizing the international commission for supervision and control in Laos, but it is against reactivizing it in the present conditions in Laos. As Your Royal Highness has repeatedly stated, the competence of the International Commission in Laos set up under the 1954 Geneva agreements is strictly limited, and that because the situation in Laos now is greatly different from that during the Geneva Conference, even for the purpose of reactivizing the International Commission for supervision and control in Laos, it is necessary first to convene an international conference of the countries concerned, which will make new provisions on the tasks and functions of the commission in the light of the new situation.

I have noted from Your Royal Highness' message of 1 February that the Thailand government indicated its willingness to accept Your Royal Highness' proposal for the convocation of an International Conference on condition that the conference has certain objectives.[1] As everybody knows, the Thailand government has played a dishonourable role in abetting the rebellion of the Phoumi-Boun Oum clique and expanding the civil war in Laos. Judging from their wording, the objectives advanced by the Thailand government are basically in conformity with the provisions of the Geneva agreements. Paragraph 12 of the final declaration of the Geneva Conference explicitly stipulates that all the participants in the conference undertake to respect the sovereignty, the independence, the unity and the territorial integrity of Laos and to refrain from any interference in its internal affairs.[2] Undoubtedly, the three member states of the International Commission in Laos, which is responsible for the supervision and control of the implementation of the Geneva agreements also agree to these provisions. The present unfortunate situation in Laos has occurred precisely because the U.S. government and its followers the Thailand government and the South Vietnam authorities have violated these provisions of the Geneva agreements. Therefore, so far as those countries are concerned which are willing to participate in an enlarged meeting of the Geneva Conference as proposed by Your Royal Highness to seek a peaceful settlement of the Laotian question, it goes without saying that the abovementioned provision of the Geneva agreements should be made.

Objectives of this meeting. If the Thailand government had genuinely advanced these objectives in accordance with the provisions of the Geneva agreements, it should have immediately ceased to help the U.S. government in carrying out intervention and aggression against Laos and withdrawn from Laos all its armed personnel and military equipment. The Chinese government believes that, if the principles of non-interference in the internal affairs of Laos, respect for the unity and territorial integrity of Laos, etc. are conscientiously observed by the countries concerned, it will undoubtedly facilitate the convocation of an International Conference of the countries concerned and the peaceful settlement of the Laotian question.

Both China and Cambodia are close neighbours of Laos and are following with close concern the development of the situation in Laos. The Chinese government will continue to cooperate with the government of the Kingdom

1 The suggestions of the Thai Government have not so far been published.
2 See *Documents*, 1954, p. 140.

of Cambodia and support all proposals and actions conducive to the restoration of peace in Laos.

3. Declaration by King Savang Vathana of Laos, Vientiane, 19 February 1961[1]

In behalf of our people and on the request of the Royal Government, we, Sri Savang Vathana, King of Laos, appealing to the conscience of humanity, address the following solemn declaration to the countries of the world.

Laos is a peaceful country and the Lao people are dedicated to peace; yet Laos for more than twenty years has known neither peace nor security.

Laos is a sovereign country, independent and a member of the United Nations; yet its existence and its sovereignty have many times been threatened, its territorial integrity placed in doubt.

Political quarrels and personal ambitions have been fostered; divisive tactics have been abetted and encouraged from without so that the country is torn by discord.

Laos is firmly resolved to preserve its territorial integrity and its sovereignty. It is determined to defend its freedom and its independence.

Raising our voice above individual and party quarrels, we declare that Laos entertains no feeling of hostility whatsoever toward any country in the world but, on the contrary, aspires to live in an atmosphere of friendship, understanding and peace.

We further declare that within its borders Laos pursues an ideal of justice, freedom and brotherhood. It is only on this basis that Laos can fruitfully manage its own affairs and offer its people a better standard of living in proportion to the possibilities of today's world.

Consequently we desire to proclaim once more the policy of true neutrality that Laos has always sought to follow. Laos will not join in any military alliance. Within the framework of this neutrality, Laos will not have on its territory either foreign forces or military bases.

It intends to exercise the sovereign right of every independent nation to insure the defense of its national territory and to maintain within it order and respect for law. Laos will also honor the international agreements into which it has freely entered.

Once again I appeal to all countries to respect the independence, sovereignty, territorial integrity and neutrality of Laos.

We ask them to renounce all intervention in the internal affairs of the Kingdom, even in the form of aid, if the latter has not been sanctioned by international agreements entered into by Laos. We further ask them to make such intervention impossible.

We have examined the various proposals which have been advanced for the peaceful settlement of the difficulties which our country is facing. We have appreciated the great value of the initiative taken by our neighbors, the Kingdom of Cambodia and the Union of Burma, in behalf of Lao neutrality.

We are convinced that these proposals, made by countries that have gone

[1] *N. Y. Times,* 20 February 1961.

through the same experience as ourselves, will lead to the solution of the problems that now exist.

This is why, in accordance with the aspiration of the Lao people, we hope that our very close neighbors, the Kingdom of Cambodia, the Union of Burma, and the Federation of Malaya, whose impartiality in the sphere of foreign affairs and whose devotion to the cause of universal peace are recognized and respected by all countries, will form a commission, which would come to Laos in order to establish that this country threatens no one and aspires solely to peace.

This commision would have as its mission the denouncing of all foreign intervention, direct or indirect, open or camouflaged, which would result in the imperiling of the kingdom's independence, integrity and neutrality.

Finally, we ask the Secretary General of the United Nations organization to bring this declaration to the attention of all members of this organization. We hope that the nations of the world recognize the legitimate aspirations of the Lao people and that they will agree to sanction the proposals we have made here in behalf of peace.

4. Exchange of letters between Prince Sihanouk of Cambodia and President de Gaulle, March 1961[1]

(i) Prince Sihanouk to President de Gaulle, 3 March 1961

J'ai pris connaissance avec un grand intérêt de la lettre en date du 14 février 1961,[2] dans laquelle Votre Excellence a bien voulu m'exposer les points de vue de la France sur le développement de l'affaire laotienne et suis heureux de voir que nos deux pays partagent les mêmes préoccupations.

Qu'il me soit permis d'exprimer à Votre Excellence notre inquiétude croissante devant une situation qui, au Laos, s'aggrave de jour en jour malgré un calme trompeur dans les opérations militaires. En effet, les éléments d'appréciation dont je dispose m'amènent à penser que la période actuelle est essentiellement mise à profit pour renforcer l'armement des forces en présence sur une échelle qui, à bref délai, conduira à la reprise de combats de grande envergure.

L'enjeu de ces combats sera alors d'une importance telle que l'intervention effective de forces étrangères deviendra inévitable, mais fatale à l'ensemble du Sud-Est Asiatique et peut-être même à la paix mondiale.

Le projet de réactivation de la Commission Internationale de Contrôle soutenu par la France, la Grande-Bretagne et l'Inde aurait eu, s'il avait pu être réalisé rapidement, certaines possibilités de contribuer au retour de la paix au Laos. Malheureusement, par suite des oppositions rencontrées, j'ai la conviction que cette mesure ne peut plus constituer un moyen efficace pour obtenir le cessez-le-feu et l'arrêt de toute les ingérences étrangères.

Enfin, dernier en date, le projet du gouvernement de Vientiane visant à la création d'une « Commission d'experts de l'ingérence étrangère » composée de la Malaisie, de la Birmanie et du Cambodge, devait également se terminer par un

---

[1] *La Documentation Française, Articles et Documents,* 20 April 1961.
[2] President de Gaulle's previous correspondence with Prince Sihanouk has not so far been published. For Sihanouk's suggestions for a conference, see p. 557, n. 2. De Gaulle had replied to this early in January.

échec, malgré un très fort appui des Etats-Unis.[1] Compte tenu de l'existence de deux gouvernements de fait au Laos, le Gouvernement Royal du Cambodge s'est vu, pour sa part, dans l'obligation de décliner une proposition qui, par son caractère unilatéral même, ne pouvait aboutir à des résultats concrets.

La réunion d'une conférence des pays directement intéressés à une solution des problèmes militaires et politiques du Laos s'avère de plus en plus urgents, alors qu'un précaire équilibre des forces peut être encore maintenu pour un temps que tout permet de prévoir très limité. Aussi ai-je la conviction que la France et la Grande-Bretagne, qui ont donné tant de preuves de leur réalisme, seront en mesure de jouer un rôle déterminant dans le retour de la paix au Laos et dans le maintien de la stabilité du Sud-Est Asiatique.

(ii) President de Gaulle to Prince Sihanouk, 24 March 1961

Monseigneur,

Les événements de ces dernières semaines sont venus confirmer les craintes que Votre Altesse exprimait dans Sa lettre du 3 mars. De cette lettre, j'ai pesé attentivement les termes. Les idées qui s'en dégagent me paraissent représenter une analyse extrêmement clairvoyante de l'évolution de la crise laotienne.

Il ne fait pas de doute, en effet, que les circonstances de divers ordres qui ont retardé les solutions politiques ont été mises à profit pour augmenter l'armement des diverses forces en présence et, par conséquent, préparer la reprise des combats qui n'a pas manqué de se produire. Il en est résulté une situation qui est devenue dangereuse.

La réactivation de la Commission Internationale de Contrôle m'avait paru être, tout d'abord, une première mesure efficace pour la pacification du Laos. Mais cette mesure n'a pas été décidée. J'estime donc, comme Votre Altesse, que la réunion d'une Conférence Internationale, dont comme Votre Altesse le sait, je n'ai jamais, pour ma part, écarté la possibilité, est sans doute désormais la procédure appropriée. Il conviendrait, maintenant, que les puissances intéressées se mettent d'accord pour en préparer la convocation.

Les problèmes immédiats au Laos consistent, à obtenir l'arrêt des fournitures d'armes et la cessation des hostilités, à habiliter un organisme de contrôle effectif et à persuader les Laotiens de s'entendre pour constituer un gouvernement réellement représentatif. A tout le moins, l'arrêt des combats devrait-il être réalisé pour que la Conférence puisse aborder utilement sa tâche, en se proposant comme objectif principal de rechercher, dans l'esprit des Accords de Genève, une solution durable du problème laotien. Il me paraît essentiel que cette solution confirme l'indépendance et l'intégrité du Laos, ainsi que sa neutralité.

Votre Altesse peut être assurée comme Elle a bien voulu le dire à la fin de Sa lettre, que mon gouvernement n'épargnera aucun effort pour apporter sa contribution au rétablissement de la paix et de la stabilité dans cette région si gravement troublée du Sud-Est Asiatique.

Veuillez, je vous prie, agréer, Monseigneur, les assurances de ma très haute considération.

CHARLES DE GAULLE.

[1] A reference to the suggestion in the declaration of King Savang Vathana; see previous document.

5. Communiqué issued by Prince Souvanna Phouma and General Phoumi Nosavan, Pnom-Penh, 10 March 1961[1]

D'un commun accord, en vue de parvenir à résoudre la crise laotienne, la délégation du général Phoumi a rencontré à Pnom-Penh, les 9 et 10 mars, le prince Souvanna Phouma en sa villa. Cette rencontre a été rendue possible grâce au gouvernement royal khmer et au prince Sihanouk.

Les conversations se sont déroulées dans une atmosphère de bonne volonté et de compréhension réciproques.

Les deux parties reconnaissent qu'en politique une stricte neutralité et la neutralisation conventionnelle du pays sont les bases fondamentales pour amener la paix et la concorde nationale.

Les deux parties condamnent avec force les ingérences étrangères et refusent de laisser le peuple du royaume faire les frais d'une meurtrière lutte d'influences à laquelle il est étranger.

Les deux parties sont d'accord pour ramener un climat de confiance réciproque en vue d'une réconciliation nationale: il faut que cessent au préalable les ingérences étrangères. Cette éventualité n'est possible qu'avec l'aide d'une commission internationale impartiale, acceptée par les parties, et qui puisse opérer sur tout le territoire national.

Le général Phoumi estime que le problème du Laos doit être résolu par étapes. Il renouvelle sa confiance au prince Souvanna comme le seul homme d'Etat du Laos pouvant servir de trait d'union avec le Néo-Lao-Haksat[2] en vue de la réconciliation nationale.

Le général Phoumi invite le prince Souvanna à accepter cette tâche.

Le prince assure qu'il fera tout son possible pour cette fin.

Le général Phoumi invite le prince Souvanna Phouma à rentrer au Laos pour se consacrer à cette tâche. Le prince décline l'invitation à se rendre immédiatement à Vientiane et déclare qu'il servira mieux la réconciliation nationale en résidant à Pnom-Penh. Il suggère la réunion à Pnom-Penh des trois groupes dont les forces sont en présence au Laos. Afin de trouver une solution définitive au problème du Laos le général accepte le principe de cette réunion qui ne pourra avoir lieu qu'après la cessation des ingérences étrangères.

Les deux parties considèrent leur rencontre de Pnom-Penh comme une prise de contact préliminaire et décident de se consulter le plus souvent possible pour trouver une solution satisfaisante dans les plus brefs délais.

6. British aide-mémoire to the Soviet Union, 23 March 1961[3]

Her Majesty's Government have studied the Soviet *aide-mémoire* about Laos communicated to Sir Frank Roberts on February 18.[4] In considering this they have also had in mind the proposals which have been made by various other

[1] *Le Monde*, 11 March 1961.
[2] The official name for the political party formed from the Pathet Lao.
[3] *D.S.B.*, 17 April 1961.
[4] Not so far published. The Soviet Note of 18 February was in reply to a British Note of 21 January (also not published) suggesting that the International Control Commission should be accredited to King Savang Vathana.

Governments towards a solution of the Laotian problem. In particular there is the suggestion of His Royal Highness Prince Sihanouk of Cambodia for the holding of an international conference of fourteen nations[1] and the request of His Majesty the King of Laos that an international commission of neutral nations should be sent to Laos to bring about an end to the fighting and to assist in working out a national settlement.[2] Her Majesty's Government have also been made aware by the United States Government of the exchange of views which has taken place between the United States and the Soviet Governments.

Her Majesty's Government now wish to make the following proposals. An essential prerequisite for the successful execution of the proposals which follow is that there should be an immediate cessation of all active military operations in Laos. To this end the two co-Chairmen should issue an immediate request for a *de facto* cease fire. If this can be accomplished Her Majesty's Government would agree to the suggestions of the Soviet Government that a message from the co-Chairmen should be sent to the Prime Minister of India asking Mr. Nehru to summon the International Commission for Supervision and Control in Laos to meet in New Delhi as soon as possible. The task of the Commission at this stage would be to verify the effectiveness of the cease fire and report thereon to the co-Chairmen.

Her Majesty's Government are also willing to accept the suggestion of the Soviet Government that an international conference should be convened to consider a settlement of the Laotian problem. To this end they believe that the Geneva Conference should be recalled by the co-Chairmen and they strongly endorse the suggestion made by His Royal Highness Prince Sihanouk of Cambodia that certain other nations should join the Conference and take part in its deliberations as full members. Her Majesty's Government suggest that this Conference should meet as soon as the International Commission can report that the cease fire is effective. They very much hope that this could be brought about without delay say within a period of two weeks.

Finally Her Majesty's Government consider that the question of a neutral Laotian Government of national unity will have to be resolved as soon as possible before an international conference can reach any decisions. Her Majesty's Government cannot recognise the so-called 'government of Prince Souvanna Phouma' as being competent to represent Laos at an international conference. They therefore hope that the various parties in Laos will immediately resume the discussions which were started in Phnom Penh with a view to agreeing on a national government which could represent Laos at the proposed conference. If no Government of national unity has been formed by the time the International Conference convenes it is clear that the Laotian Government cannot be represented as such and that the Conference will have to address itself as its first task to helping the parties of Laos to reach agreement on this point.

7. President Kennedy's press conference, 23 March 1961[3] (extract)

. . . I want to talk about Laos. . . . The position of this administration has been carefully considered, and we have sought to make it just as clear as we

---

[1] Above, p. 557, n. 2   [2] Above, p. 561.   [3] *D.S.B.*, 17 April 1961.

know how to the governments concerned. First: We strongly and unreservedly support the goal of a neutral and independent Laos, tied to no outside power or group of powers, threatening no one, and free from any domination. Our support for the present duly constituted Government is aimed entirely and exclusively at that result, and if in the past there has been any possible ground for misunderstanding of our support for a truly neutral Laos, there should be none now.

Secondly, if there is to be a peaceful solution, there must be a cessation of the present armed attacks by externally supported Communists. If these attacks do not stop, those who support a genuinely neutral Laos will have to consider their response. The shape of this necessary response will of course be carefully considered not only here in Washington but in the SEATO conference with our allies which begins next Monday. SEATO—the Southeast Asia Treaty Organization—was organized in 1954 with strong leadership from our last administration, and all members of SEATO have undertaken special treaty responsibility toward an aggression against Laos.[1]

No one should doubt our own resolution on this point. We are faced with a clear threat of a change in the internationally agreed position of Laos. This threat runs counter to the will of the Laotian people, who wish only to be independent and neutral. It is posed rather by the military operations of internal dissident elements directed from outside the country. This is what must end if peace is to be kept in southeast Asia.

Third, we are earnestly in favor of constructive negotiation—among the nations concerned and among the leaders of Laos—which can help Laos back to the pathway of independence and genuine neutrality. We strongly support the present British proposal of a prompt end of hostilities and prompt negotiation.[2] We are always conscious of the obligation which rests upon all members of the United Nations to seek peaceful solutions to problems of this sort. We hope that others may be equally aware of this responsibility. . . .

8. Communiqué issued by President Kennedy and Mr. Macmillan, Key West (Florida), 26 March 1961[3]

President Kennedy and Prime Minister Macmillan have had a most valuable exchange of views about the situation in Laos. This will be of great assistance to the representatives of the two countries in the discussions at the SEATO meeting which is due to begin in Bangkok tomorrow.

They agree that the situation in Laos cannot be allowed to deteriorate.

They also agree that the recent British note to the Soviet Union contains proposals which, if implemented, would bring to an end the warfare in Laos and would pave the way for Laos to become the truly neutral country, which it is their joint wish to see.[4]

[1] By the South-East Asia Collective Defence Treaty of 8 September 1954. See *Documents*, 1954, pp. 153–6.
[2] Above, p. 564.
[3] *D.S.B.*, 17 April 1961.
[4] A reference to the British *aide-mémoire* to the Soviet Union of 23 March; above, p. 564.

They strongly hope, therefore, that the Soviet Union will make a positive and constructive reply to these proposals.

9. Communiqué of the SEATO Council meeting, Bangkok, 30 March 1961[1] (extract)

Resolution

Having examined the situation in Laos and the Republic of Viet-Nam, the Council unanimously approved the following resolution:

1. Consulting together as provided in the Manila Pact,[2] the SEATO Council has noted with grave concern the continued offensive by rebel elements in Laos who are continuing to be supplied and assisted by Communist powers in flagrant disregard of the Geneva accords.[3]

2. The Council once more makes it clear that SEATO is a defensive organization with no aggressive intentions and reiterates, in the words of the treaty, its 'desire to live in peace with all peoples and all governments'.

3. The Council desires a united, independent and sovereign Laos, free to achieve advancement in a way of its own choosing and not subordinate to any nation or group of nations.

4. It is believed that these results ought to be achieved through negotiations and cannot be hoped for if the present fighting continues.

5. The Council notes with approval the present efforts for a cessation of hostilities and for peaceful negotiations to achieve an unaligned and independent Laos.

6. If those efforts fail, however, and there continues to be an active military attempt to obtain control of Laos, members of SEATO are prepared, within the terms of the treaty, to take whatever action may be appropriate in the circumstances.

7. The Council also noted with concern the efforts of an armed minority, again supported from outside in violation of the Geneva accords, to destroy the Government of South Viet-Nam, and declared its firm resolve not to acquiesce in any such takeover of that country.

8. Finally, the Council records its view that the organization should continue to keep developments in Laos and Viet-Nam under urgent and constant review in the light of this resolution.

10. Aide-mémoire of the Soviet Government to Britain, 1 April 1961[4]

The *aide mémoire* of the government of the United Kingdom on the question of Laos conveyed on March 23, 1961,[5] by the British Ambassador Sir Frank Roberts, has been carefully studied by the government of the U.S.S.R.

The invariable attitude of the Soviet government has been and is that Laos should be a neutral, unified, independent and peaceful state, in conformity with the Geneva agreements, and the Soviet government has long been pressing for

---

[1] *D.S.B.*, 17 April 1961, pp. 549–50.
[2] A reference to the South-East Asia, Collective Defence Treaty, signed at Manila, 8 September 1954. See *Documents*, 1954, pp. 153–6.
[3] ibid., pp. 138–41. [4] *Soviet News*, 5 April 1961. [5] Above, p. 564.

the urgent convocation of an appropriate international conference, as the most effective means of solving the problem of Laos in the interests of ensuring the independence and unity of that country and in the interests of strengthening world peace.

In this connection the Soviet government notes with satisfaction that the United Kingdom government has now consented to the convocation of an international conference to settle the Laotian problem with the participation of the member-countries of the Geneva agreements of 1954, as well as of certain other states, as proposed by the head of state of Cambodia, Prince Norodom Sihanouk. The Soviet government believes that it is essential immediately to reach a definite agreement on the date and place for the convocation of such a conference and, for its part, suggests that it should be called early in April at Pnom Penh.

Like the government of the United Kingdom, the Soviet government regards as desirable the earliest possible termination of hostilities in Laos.

The statement of the Soviet side, made to the Ambassador of Great Britain in Moscow on February 18 of this year, pointed out that in the opinion of the Soviet government the task in Laos is above all to discontinue the military operations there and to achieve a peaceful settlement under which the unity and integrity of Laos would be respected and interference in her internal affairs would be cut short. This is why the Soviet government favours the proposal that the two co-chairmen of the Geneva conference should issue an appeal for a cease-fire in Laos. In conformity with this the interested parties of Laos must, of course, hold talks on questions connected with the cease-fire.

The Soviet government also agrees to the convening of the International Commission for Supervision and Control in Laos. The International Commission for Laos must meet in Delhi as soon as possible and submit its report to the two co-chairmen of the Geneva conference.

Of course, a resumption of the Commission's work must in no way impede the convocation of the aforementioned international conference on Laos.

The *aide mémoire* of the United Kingdom government speaks of the need to settle 'the question of a neutral government of national unity in Laos'. The question of the Laotian government is, naturally, an internal affair of the Laotians themselves. The Soviet government, like the governments of many other European and Asian states, is known to believe that Laos has the lawful government of His Highness Prince Souvanna Phouma, which abides by strict neutrality, stands for the restoration of the unity of the internal forces and enjoys the support of most of the country's population.

The rebellion against this government, started by a group of plotters relying on military assistance from outside, was engineered precisely for the purpose of doing away with the neutrality of Laos in international affairs. Of course, the Soviet government would favour negotiations among various political trends in Laos on measures to strengthen the country's national unity. If the parties to these negotiations do not reach the necessary agreement by the time the international conference on Laos meets, the Soviet government does not rule out that the conference, as has also been proposed by the government of the United Kingdom, may assume, as one of its tasks, the rendering of assistance to the Laotians in reaching agreement.

In conclusion the Soviet government considers it necessary to draw the attention of the government of the United Kingdom to the fact that the settlement of the Laotian problem on the basis of safeguarding the peace, independence and neutrality of that country requires the maintenance of an international atmosphere favouring the solution of this problem.

It goes without saying that the threats of interference in the affairs of Laos by the S.E.A.T.O. military bloc and the tactics of sabre-rattling recently employed by certain powers, far from promoting this, may seriously worsen the position with regard to settling the Laotian problem.

The Soviet government expresses the hope that the government of the United Kingdom will find acceptable the proposals set forth in this *aide mèmoire*—proposals which the Soviet government has drawn up taking due account of the considerations of the United Kingdom government and being guided by a sincere desire to restore peace in Laos as quickly as possible with a view to ensuring the independence and neutrality of that country.

11. Joint communiqué of the Governments of the Soviet Union and Laos, 22 April 1961[1]

At the invitation of the Soviet government, the Prime Minister of the Kingdom of Laos, Prince Souvanna Phouma, paid an official visit to the Soviet Union from April 16 to 22. He was accompanied by his daughter, Princess Moun Souvanna Phouma; State Secretay for Agriculture Prince Sisoumang Sisaleoumsak; Colonel Soukan Vilaisarn; and Mr. and Mrs. Khamchan Pradit.

During Prince Souvanna Phouma's stay in the Soviet Union, the chairman of the Neo Lao Haksat Party, Prince Souphannouvong, and Minister of Information Quinim Pholsena arrived in Moscow.

During his stay in the U.S.S.R. the Prime Minister of the Kingdom of Laos. Prince Souvanna Phouma, was received by N. S. Khrushchev, Chairman of the Council of Ministers of the U.S.S.R. Prince Souvanna Phouma also met L. I. Brezhnev, President of the Presidium of the U.S.S.R. Supreme Soviet, First Vice-Chairman of the U.S.S.R. Council of Ministers A. N. Kosygin, and U.S.S.R. Foreign Minister A. A. Gromyko.

In the course of these meetings and talks, which were held in an atmosphere of friendship, cordiality and mutual understanding, a frank and useful exchange of views took place on the questions of a political settlement in Laos and Soviet-Laotian relations, and on certain major international issues.

The governments of the Soviet Union and of the Kingdom of Laos note that the present serious situation in Laos has resulted from the interference of certain states belonging to the S.E.A.T.O. military bloc, which are rendering military, material and technical, and financial aid to the rebels.

Both sides note that the heroic struggle of the Laotian people against foreign interference and for the implementation of the programme of peace, neutrality and national unity proclaimed by the government of Laos has the warm sympathy and support of the Soviet people and their government, as well as the

---

[1] *Soviet News*, 25 April 1961,

governments of many other countries striving for peace and international co-operation.

The Soviet government has restated its firm and unswerving desire to see Laos a peaceful, neutral and independent state.

The talks revealed the unity of views of the two sides on the basic issues of a political settlement in Laos.

Both governments are of the opinion that real conditions exist for normalising the situation in Laos, in accordance with the national interests of the Laotian people and the interests of peace.

The primary measures towards this should be the convening of an international conference in the nature of the Geneva conference of 1954 with an enlarged composition, as suggested by the head of state of Cambodia, Prince Norodom Sihanouk, a cease-fire, and the resumption of the activities of the International Commission for Supervision and Control in Laos.

The Soviet government fully shares the opinion of the government of Laos that the Geneva agreements on Indo-China of 1954[1] and the Vientiane agreements of 1956–57[2] and also the joint statement of Prince Souvanna Phouma and Prince Souphannouvong of November 20, 1960[3] represent a good founda-

---

[1] Documents, 1954, pp. 138–41.

[2] ibid., 1956, pp. 732–5; and see Survey, 1956–8, p. 273.

[3] On 18–20 November 1960, Prince Souvanna Phouma and Prince Souvannouvong held meetings at Sam Neua, and issued the following communiqué (text in H.N.A., 23 November 1960):

> One. Laos must resolutely follow a line of peace and neutrality. This is because the present world is divided into two camps, the Socialist camp and the Imperialist camp. Laos will not lean to either camp but resolutely stand between the two camps because this line suits best the current Laotian situation and conforms with the people's aspirations. Only in this way can national independence be safeguarded, the unity of the country established, the rights of democracy and freedom realised and all the forces of the Laotian people united to build a progressive and prosperous motherland.
>
> Two. In order to consolidate the position of the government, solve financial and economic difficulties and create favourable conditions for the economic construction of the country, the two princes held that sincere aid without any strings from various countries should be accepted and diplomatic relations with these countries established. Apart from the aid from Britain, France and the U.S., Laos must now request aid from countries following a policy of peace and neutrality and the Socialist countries, should establish economic and cultural relations with all countries with different political systems, and will soon establish such relations with the People's Republic of China and the Democratic Republic of Vietnam.
>
> Three. The two princes unanimously held that the unity of the people of the whole country is a decisive force to realise a policy of genuine peace and neutrality. The Neo Lao Haksat Party reiterates its wholehearted support for the lawful government and will struggle to make Laos a really peaceful and neutral country. The armed forces of the former Pathet Lao fighting units will abide by the policies of the lawful government in order to win victory in the struggle against the Phoumi-Boun Oum traitorous clique and to defend the motherland, religions, the King and the constitution. The Royal government of which Prince Phouma is the Premier guarantees that it will preserve the solid unity and mutual trust between the two sides in order to realise the unity of the entire people.
>
> Four. The two princes unanimously held that it is necessary to form a coalition government of all nationalities and patriotic parties and groups, including the representatives of the Neo Lao Haksat Party, as the foundation for the realisation of the people's aspirations and for the struggle for the independence, unity, prosperity and well-being of Laos. With the exception of Phoumi and Boun Oum, members of the so-called 'Revolutionary Committee' will be given suitable posts in the government if they respect the lawful government and support the policy of peace and neutrality.
>
> On behalf of the lawful government and the Neo Lao Haksat Party, the two princes appealed to the King for a firm stand against the traitorous group and to create favourable

tion for a peaceful settlement in Laos and for the establishment of a government of national unity.

Both sides consider that principles of peaceful co-existence and co-operation, full equality and non-interference in one another's internal affairs should become the basis of relations between all states, regardless of their social system.

In this connection they declare that the use of any kind of political or economic pressure, not to speak of armed forces of foreign states, for the purpose of imposing the will of one state or group of states on any people or country is impermissible in relations between states.

Both sides condemn the policy of interference in the internal affairs of other countries displayed most objectively in the organisation of the external attack on the Cuban people, and demand the immediate cessation of aggressive actions against Cuba which, if continued, may have most serious consequences for universal peace.

The two sides are deeply convinced that the struggle for ending the arms race and for averting the danger of a fatal nuclear war, with all its incalculable calamities, is the most important task of all the peoples of the world. They believe that general and complete disarmament is not only necessary but also realistic, provided all states display a sincere interest in this and show good will.

The solution of the disarmament problem would create conditions for universal security and make available tremendous resources for economic development, for improving the welfare of the population and for rendering aid to less-developed countries.

The two sides express their sincere desire to do everything in their power to help achieve complete and universal disarmament under effective international control, and to implement the resolution of the United Nations General Assembly of November 20, 1959,[1] which approved the idea of the general and complete disarmament of states.

Both governments note the need for the earliest abolition of the colonial system and of all its manifestations, as incompatible with the modern age. They consider that the complete and resolute fulfilment of the provisions of the declaration of the United Nations General Assembly of December, 1960,[2] is highly important for ensuring world peace and security.

This is prompted, in the first place, by the fact that the existence of centres of international tension in a number of areas of the world, in particular in the Far East, in Latin America and in Africa, is, to a considerable extent, due to the colonial policy.

---

conditions for the lawful government to complete its tasks. The two princes called on the people of all strata and nationalities, all political parties and groups and religious groups, the army, police, government functionaries, youth and students to rally closely around the lawful overnment and to firmly oppose the enemy of the policy of peace and neutrality in order to defend the lawful Government, the motherland, religions, the King and the constitution.

Finally, the two princes sincerely appealed to the governments and peoples of all countries in the world to give sympathy and aid to the Laotian government and people in their just struggle to defend the independence and unification of the country and the tranquillity of the people and to contribute to the defence of world peace.

[1] *Documents*, 1959, p. 115.   [2] ibid., 1960, pp. 404–6.

Both sides recognise as abnormal and harmful to the cause of international co-operation the fact that the lawful rights of the Chinese People's Republic have not yet been restored in the United Nations.

During the talks of the Prime Minister of the Kingdom of Laos, Prince Souvanna Phouma, with the leaders of the Soviet government it was noted with satisfaction that the relations and co-operation between the U.S.S.R. and the Kingdom of Laos are based on mutual respect, equality and non-interference in each other's domestic affairs.

The Prime Minister of the Kingdom of Laos, Prince Souvanna Phouma, has expressed deep gratitude to the entire Soviet people, the Soviet government and Chairman of the U.S.S.R. Council of Ministers N. S. Khrushchev for their understanding of the national interests of the Laotian people and for the all-round assistance and support rendered by the Soviet Union to the Laotian people in their just struggle.

Both sides expressed the desire to develop and strengthen friendly relations between the U.S.S.R. and the Kingdom of Laos in the political, economic, cultural and other fields.

In accordance with the desire of the Laotian side, the Soviet government, with a view to developing the economy of the country and raising the material standards of its population, expressed its readiness to help Laos economically and technically in developing its agriculture, in prospecting for minerals and in developing its transport and communications, and also in the fields of health protection, culture and education. The sides agreed that the practical questions of the aid to Laos would be settled more precisely in the future during talks between the governments of the U.S.S.R. and the Kingdom of Laos.

The Soviet government, invariably demonstrating its good will and respect for the people of Laos, has decided to build a hospital and a radio station in Laos as a gift from the Soviet Union to the Laotian people.

The visit of the Prime Minister of the Kingdom of Laos, Prince Souvanna Phouma, to the Soviet Union and the establishment of personal contacts between the statesmen of Laos and the leaders of the Soviet government have demonstrated the consolidation of the friendship between the peoples of the U.S.S.R. and Laos and will be conducive to the further promotion of all-round co-operation between the two countries, for the benefit of the Soviet and Laotian peoples and also in the interests of peace and security throughout the world.

12. Joint Statements of the British and Soviet chairmen of the Geneva conference on Indo-China, Mr. Gromyko and Lord Home, 24 April 1961[1]

(*i*) *The co-chairmen of the Geneva conference on Indo-China, to the participants in civil hostilities in Laos*

The co-chairmen of the Geneva conference on Indo-China, represented by the government of the Soviet Union and Great Britain, are following with great concern the situation which has developed in Laos.

They proceed from the fact that if this situation is not changed the position

---

[1] *Soviet News,* 26 April 1961.

in Laos may become a serious threat to peace and security in South-East Asia. They note at the same time that real conditions exist for normalising the situation in Laos in accordance with the national interests of the Laotian people, on the basis of the Geneva agreements of 1954. The co-chairmen have in view the understanding already reached that an international conference to settle the Laotian problem is to be called in Geneva on May 12 this year.

The co-chairmen call on all military authorities, parties and organisations in Laos to cease fire before the convening of the international conference on Laos, and they call on appropriate representatives to enter into negotiations for concluding an agreement on questions connected with the cease-fire.

The co-chairmen call on the people of Laos to co-operate with the International Commission for Supervision and Control in Laos and to render it assistance, when it arrives in the country on their instructions, in exercising supervision and control over the cease-fire.

(ii) The co-chairmen of the Geneva conference on Indo-China to the Government of India

The co-chairmen of the Geneva conference on Indo-China, represented by the governments of the Soviet Union and Great Britain, are following with great concern the situation which has developed in Laos.

They note that real conditions exist for normalising the situation in Laos in accordance with the national interests of the Laotian people on the basis of the Geneva agreements of 1954.

They have in view the understanding already reached that an international conference for settling the Laotian problem is to be called in Geneva on May 12 this year.

The co-chairmen have addressed to all military authorities, parties and organisations in Laos a call for a cease-fire and for the carrying out by appropriate representatives of negotiations for concluding an agreement on questions connected with the cease-fire.

The co-chairmen propose to the governments of India that it should convene in Delhi the International Commission for Supervision and Control in Laos. They have in view that the commission will discuss the question of the tasks and functions which should be allotted to it after the cease-fire in Laos, and will present an appropriate report to the co-chairmen, who will consider the commission's report and give it directions on going to Laos to carry out the work of controlling the cease-fire.

The co-chairmen in their message on the cease-fire in Laos called upon the population of Laos to co-operate with the International Commission for Supervision and Control in Laos, when it arrives in the country on their instructions, and to render it assistance in exercising supervision and control over the cease-fire.

The co-chairmen are sending a copy of this message to the other two members of the International Commission for Supervision and Control in Laos—the governments of the Polish People's Republic and of Canada.

(iii) The co-chairmen of the Geneva conference on Indo-China to the countries participating in the international conference for the settlement of the Laotian question

The co-chairmen of the Geneva conference on Indo-China, represented by the governments of the Soviet Union and Great Britain, have examined the situation which has developed in Laos and taken note that at present there exist real conditions for the normalisation of the situation in that country.

They have in view that the governments of Burma, Cambodia, Canada, the Chinese People's Republic, the Democratic Republic of Viet Nam, France, India, Laos, the Polish People's Republic, the Republic of Viet Nam, Thailand, the Union of Soviet Socialist Republics, the United Kingdom and the United States of America, have expressed agreement to participate in an international conference, which would have the character of the Geneva conference of 1954 with the broader membership proposed by the head of state of Cambodia, Prince Norodom Sihanouk, for the settlement of the Laotian problem.[1]

The co-chairmen have addressed to all military authorities, parties and organisations in Laos a call for a cease-fire and for the carrying out by appropriate representatives of negotiations for concluding an agreement on questions connected with the cease-fire and have also sent to the government of India a message with a request to convene in Delhi the International Commission for Supervision and Control in Laos.

The co-chairmen express the hope that the government of . . . (*the name of the country concerned*) will send its delegation to the international conference on the Laotian question, which will be held in Geneva and will begin its work on May 12 this year. They have in view that the participating countries will be represented at the conference by Ministers of Foreign Affairs.

13. Statements at the opening of the International Conference at Geneva for the settlement of the Laotian question, 16–17 May 1961

(i) Speech by the Chinese Foreign Minister, Mr. Chen Yi, 16 May 1961[2]

Mr. Chairman, Fellow Delegates,

First of all, please allow me, on behalf of the government of the People's Republic of China and the Chinese people, to greet the opening of this enlarged Geneva Conference. The Chinese government has consistently stood for the peaceful settlement of the Laotian question on the basis of the 1954 Geneva agreements. The Chinese government delegation sincerely hopes that this conference will make contributions in ensuring the neutrality and independence of Laos and safeguarding peace in Indo-China and South-East Asia.

Our present conference is convened on the basis of the 1954 Geneva agreements and on the initiative of Prince Norodom Sihanouk, Head of State of Cambodia. This conference is a continuation and development of the 1954 Geneva Conference. The co-chairmen, the Soviet Union and Britain, have made great efforts to promote its convocation. We are particularly glad that Prince Sihanouk is present at our conference as its initiator. Prince Sihanouk has made consistent efforts to promote the peace and neutrality of Laos. We are con-

[1] See above p. 557, n. 2. [2] *H.N.A.*, 17 May 1961.

vinced that the participation of Prince Sihanouk will certainly play a positive role for our conference.

From the very beginning, Prince Sihanouk's initiative has been welcomed by the Royal Government of Laos headed by Prince Souvanna Phouma, the Neo Lao Haksat and the Laotian people and won the endorsement and support of China, the Democratic Republic of Vietnam, the Soviet Union and Poland. Although this initiative met with the neglect, suspicion or opposition of certain countries, voices for the peaceful settlement of the Laotian question and against the expansion of the war in Laos have prevailed more and more. The series of recommendations for the peaceful settlement of the Laotian question put forward jointly by the Soviet Union and Britain as the co-chairmen of the Geneva Conference[1] have reflected this desire. Now, a *de facto* cease-fire has been realised in Laos; the International Commission for Supervision and Control in Laos, in pursuance of the directives of the co-chairmen of the Geneva Conference, has begun its work; and our enlarged Geneva Conference is eventually taking place here after breaking through the various obstacles. All these are gratifying.

Seven years ago, the question of restoring peace in Indo-China was discussed in this same building and agreements were reached which laid a good foundation for ensuring the peace, neutrality and independence of Laos. Many who are present here today will still remember this. The agreements of that conference stipulate that each member of the conference must undertake to respect the sovereignty, independence, unity and territorial integrity of Laos and to refrain from any interference in its internal affairs. The Royal Government of Laos also declared then that it would not conclude any military alliance with other states and would not allow foreign powers to establish military bases on Laotian territory. It was expected that, with such clear international guarantee, the people of Laos, through their own efforts, would be able to effect the smooth growth of a Laos which is peaceful, neutral, independent, unified, democratic and prosperous.

Unfortunately, however, the 1954 Geneva agreements have suffered increasingly serious violations and the Laotian people's efforts to realize their national aspirations have been continuously frustrated.

It is well-known that the United States of America participated in the 1954 Geneva Conference, but in the end it refused to take part in the agreements reached at the conference. The U.S. government issued a unilateral declaration to the effect that it would refrain from the threat or the use of force to distrub these agreements;[2] yet even this promise was very soon repudiated. Before the ink on the Geneva agreements had dried, the United States hastily rigged up the so-called South-East Asia Defence Treaty Organization. As pointed out then by a number of South-East Asian countries, the majority of the members of this organization are not South-East Asian countries, nor is its purpose one of defence. This organization, assuming the position of an overlord, openly included the three Indo-Chinese states, among which is Laos, into a so-called area under its protection. Over the past years, the United States has all along used this organization as its tool to interfere in the internal affairs of Laos, violate its neutrality and independence and create tension in the whole of South-East Asia.

[1] Above, p. 572.   [2] *Documents*, 1954, pp. 140–1.

The participating nations of the 1954 Geneva Conference undertook to refrain from any interference in the internal affairs of Laos and indicated their wish to see the realization of the desire for national harmony and democratic unity expressed by the Delegate of the Royal Government of Laos. However, in the intervening years the U.S. government has been acting in a diametrically opposite direction. Each time when the people of Laos achieved some progress in their efforts towards this end, the United States invariably carried out obstruction and sabotage by every means. In 1957 when the Royal Government of Laos headed by Prince Souvanna Phouma signed the Vientiane agreements with the Neo Lao Haksat[1] and set up a coalition government, the U.S. government openly expressed serious anxiety over the situation in Laos and indicated that it would reconsider its aid to Laos. Subsequently the Vientiane agreements were wrecked and the coalition government of Laos was overthrown. In 1959, when the Phoui Sananikone government declared that Laos was no longer bound by the Geneva agreements, the United States openly voiced its support.[2] Everybody knows that following that many Laotian patriots were oppressed and persecuted, and even Prince Souphanouvong, Chairman of the Neo Lao Haksat, was arrested. In 1960, Captain Kong Le, with the support of the Laotian people, staged a patriotic *coup d'état*, and Prince Souvanna Phouma resumed power and announced that he would pursue a policy of peace, neutrality, national harmony and State unity. The United States, while recognizing the Royal Government ot Laos headed by Prince Souvanna Phouma, supported the rebel clique of Laos in starting a civil war. Disregarding the notes delivered respectively on 22 November and 2 December 1960 by the legal government under Prince Souvanna Phouma,[3] the United States gave large quantities of military aid to the rebel clique of Laos. Furthermore, the United States instigated certain SEATO members and the remnant Kuomintang troops who had fled to Laos to take part in the Laotian civil war. The United States has even flagrantly set up a 'Military Assistance Advisory Group' to take direct command of the operations of the rebel forces in Laos. Facts of the past seven years have proved that the prolonged instability and present grave situation in Laos have entirely been caused by the United States' violation of the Geneva agreements and its intervention and aggression in Laos.

However, no force can suppress the Laotian people's national aspirations for peace, neutrality and independence. The Royal Government of Laos led by Premier Souvanna Phouma, with the energetic support of the Neo Lao Haksat, has rallied together all the patriotic forces in Laos and led the Laotian people to wage victoriously a just struggle. This struggle has won the resolute support of all the peace-loving countries and people of the world, and as a result, to settle the Laotian question peacefully has become an irresistible trend. Even the United States has now expressed favour for the peace, neutrality and independence of Laos and has sent delegates to take part in the present conference. This is anyhow to be welcomed. It is our hope that the U.S. delegates will seriously

[1] November 1957. See *Survey*, 1956–8, p. 273.
[2] *Documents*, 1959, pp. 250–1.
[3] Souvania Phouma had sent messages to the right-wing rebels calling for representatives to discuss the formation of a coalition government, including Rightists, Neutralists, and pro-Communists. See *N.Y. Times*, 6 December 1960.

work jointly with all the others to seek avenues to a peaceful settlement of the Laotian question.

The peaceful settlement of the Laotian question has two aspects, internal and international. The internal problems of Laos must be settled, and can only be settled, by the Laotian people themselves. The people of Laos, like all the other independent nations of the world, have the right to choose their path according to their own will. We have noted with pleasure that Prince Souvanna Phouma, Premier of the Royal Government of Laos, and Prince Souphanouvong, Chairman of the Neo Lao Haksat, reaffirmed in their joint communiqué of 20 November that 'Laos must firmly follow the line of peace and neutrality' and 'realize the unity of the entire people', and that 'a coalition government comprising representatives of all nationalities and all patriotic political parties including the Neo Lao Haksat' must be established. These propositions reflect the Laotian people's desire for the realization of national harmony and democratic unity, and for the preservation of their national independence. The Chinese government has consistently supported, and will continue to support, this desire.

The international aspect of the Laotian question is to create the necessary international conditions under which the people of Laos will be really able to realize their aspirations free from outside interference. This requires that, in accordance with the principles of the 1954 Geneva agreements, all the participating nations of this conference reach agreement through full consultations and jointly assume obligations to strictly ensure the independence and neutrality of Laos. In view of the experience over the past seven years and the obtaining circumstances, we hold that the principles of respect for the sovereignty, independence, unity and territorial integrity of Laos and of non-interference in its internal affairs, and the stipulations that Laos shall not join any military alliance and that no foreign military bases shall be established in Laos, which were laid down in the 1954 Geneva agreements, should be reaffirmed and strictly and unanimously adhered to. The Laotian people's right to settle their problems themselves should be guaranteed; no foreign power should be permitted to use force or the threat of force against Laos; and no country should be permitted to use aid as a means to violate the neutrality of Laos and interfere in its internal affairs. The military personnel of the United States and of the other countries which are interfering in Laos with U.S. support must be withdrawn; and the remnant Kuomintang troops in Laos must be disarmed and sent out of Laos. If our conference can reach agreement on the questions mentioned above, it will have a good effect not only on ensuring the neutrality and independence of Laos, but also on preserving peace and security throughout South-East Asia and the whole of Asia.

So far as the peace and security of South-East Asia as a whole is concerned, the Laotian question is by no means an isolated one. If the factors which are now threatening the peace and security of South-East Asia are not removed, a settlement of the Laotian question itself cannot be safely ensured. As everybody knows, in Vietnam too, the United States has sabotaged the 1954 Geneva agreements, it has been obstructing the peaceful unification of Vietnam and sending large amounts of military equipment and military personnel into the southern part of Vietnam, and is now even threatening to place southern Vietnam under its direct military occupation. At the same time, the United States has turned Thailand into its main military base and a source of war in South-East Asia. The remnant Kuomintang troops equipped with American weapons are being used to endanger the security of Burma and other South-East Asian countries and to carry out harassing activities against China. The Kingdom of Cambodia, which persists in a policy of peace and neutrality, is constantly subjected to subversive sabotage and military menace by certain member States of the SEATO Military bloc. The aggressive SEATO military bloc has become the principal tool of the United States for encroaching on the sovereignty of different countries, interfering in their internal affairs and incessantly creating turmoil in South-East Asia. This bloc is the root cause of tension not only in Laos but also in the whole of South-East Asia. Only by abolishing this bloc can peace and security in South-East Asia, including Laos, be preserved and consolidated.

It should further be pointed out that, just as we are here to seek a peaceful settlement of the Laotian question and promote the peace of South-East Asia, the U.S. Vice-President Johnson is carrying out activities in South Vietnam, Thailand, the Philippines and intensifying arrangements for aggression and war, thus seriously threatening peace in South-East Asia. The Johnson-Ngo Dinh Diem joint communiqué[1] is a direct violation of the 1954 Geneva agreements. All this cannot but have a most adverse effect on our conference and so arouse our due vigilance.

The Chinese government has consistently pursued a foreign policy of peace and made unremitting efforts to safeguard peace in South-East Asia and the world. In its relations with the South-East Asian countries, as with countries of other regions, China has firmly upheld the five principles of peaceful co-existence.[2] Together with all the other Asian countries present at this conference, China took part in formulating the famous Ten Principles of the Bandung Conference.[3] China has concluded treaties of friendship and mutual non-aggression or of peace and friendship with Burma,[4] Cambodia and several other countries in South-East Asia. China has always stood for extending the application of the five principles of peaceful co-existence and the Ten Principles of the Bandung Conference to relations among all countries, and for the establishment and expansion, first of all, of a peace area in the south-eastern part and the whole of Asia to replace the aggressive military blocs. The Chinese government firmly supports the struggle of the Democratic Republic of Vietnam and the Vietnamese people to uphold the Geneva agreements and to achieve the peaceful unification of their motherland. The Chinese government has consistently supported South-East Asian countries in their just cause of practising a policy of peace and neutrality, safeguarding national independence and opposing interference and aggression from outside.

On the Laotian question, China, as a participant in the 1954 Geneva Conference, has always been faithful to the agreements of the conference and striven to uphold them. Although foreign intervention and aggression in Laos have already posed a direct threat to the security of China and cannot but arouse our

---

[1] Below, p. 593.   [2] *Documents*, 1954, pp. 313–15.   [3] ibid., 1955, p. 436.
[4] ibid., 1960, pp. 499–500.

grave concern, we have still been seeking patiently to settle the Laotian question by peaceful means. The present enlarged Geneva Conference provides another opportunity for the peaceful settlement of the Laotian question. We earnestly hope that the events which took place after the last Geneva Conference due to violations of the agreements and which led to serious consequences in Laos will not recur. The Delegation of the Chinese Government is ready to work jointly with the delegations of all the other countries participating in this conference to make contributions to the peaceful settlement of the Laotian question.

Mr. Chairman and Fellow Delegates! The Laotian people are peace-loving and have never threatened anybody. Intervention and aggression from outside have brought them grave national calamities. All people who uphold justice have a profound sympathy for them. Now the Laotian people have already achieved certain successes in their efforts to rid themselves of such calamities. We ought to support them in their continued efforts until their national aspirations have been fully realized. The peoples of Laos, of Asia and of the whole world are following with close attention the progress of our conference. Our responsibilities are very great. We must not disappoint the hopes of the people of the world. Provided all the countries participating in this conference have the sincerity to truly settle the question, there is no reason why our conference cannot achieve positive results.

I wish the conference success.

(ii) Speech by the United States Secretary of State, Mr. Rusk, 17 May 1961[1]

In late April we received an invitation to an international conference on the Laotian question. On Monday evening last, the co-chairmen announced the opening of the conference and stated that 'this conference is solely concerned with the international aspects of the Laotian question'. We are here to take part on that basis because the Laotian question is urgent, in relation both to the people of that troubled country and to the peace of southeast Asia. We wish to say at the beginning how gratified we were that His Royal Highness Prince Sihanouk was able to open our sessions last evening with wise words aimed at moderation and a genuine attempt to reach a satisfactory solution.

At the outset, Mr. Chairman, I believe it necessary to raise a matter which we believe to be the first order of business in this conference. A number of invited governments, including the United States, considered that this conference could not meet with any hope of success unless there had been achieved a prompt and effective cease-fire. We received on May 12, the date proposed for the opening of our sessions, a report from the ICC, which said that the Commission are satisfied that a general *de facto* cease-fire exists and such breaches as have been informally complained of are either due to misunderstanding or to factors such as the terrain, the nature of disposition of forces, both regular and irregular, of all parties.

Information from Laos indicates that rebel forces continue to attack in a number of localities and that rebel troop movements are occurring which are prejudicial to an effective cease-fire. The most serious of these violations have

[1] *D.S.B.*, 5 June 1961, pp. 844–8.

taken place in the Ban Padong area near Xieng Khouang, where artillery and infantry attacks are continuing against Government forces. The Royal Lao Government has made formal complaint to the ICC chairman.

Surely, Mr. Chairman, the cease-fire and proper instructions to the ICC are matters of first importance. This is something which cannot be postponed. An effective cease-fire is a prerequisite to any constructive result from our proceedings; a failure of a cease-fire would result in a highly dangerous situation which it is the purpose of the conference to prevent. I would urge that the co-chairmen take this up immediately in order that the situation be clarified and the ICC given the necessary authorizations and instructions.

There is another point which affects our ability to come to a satisfactory result. We do not believe that this conference is properly constituted without due provision for the delegates of the constitutional government of Laos. The Royal Laotian Government, empowered by the King and Parliament to govern Laos, represents that country in the United Nations and in other international bodies. It is the only authority resting upon that nation's constitution and the means established by law for registering the wishes of its King and people. We do not see how we can make good progress without the presence here of the Government of Laos, and we regret, though understand, why it does not consider that it can be here under existing circumstances. We believe that this, too, is a matter which requires the immediate attention of the co-chairmen in order that this conference of governments may have the benefit of the participation of the Government of the very country which we are discussing.

Before I turn to what I had intended to say about the questions before the conference, I should like to thank the Secretary of State for Foreign Affairs of the United Kingdom for his constructive and helpful contribution of last evening. We find ourselves in general agreement with his suggestions and hope that the conference can settle down quickly to the detailed provisions required to give them effect.

I also listened with interest to the remarks of the representative from Peiping.[1] He made certain statements about the United States which were not true and not new. We have heard them often before. Indeed, I rather thought that his statement of them on this occasion was less violent than language to which we have become accustomed. To leave open the possibility that those at this table are prepared to find some common basis for the settlement of the Laotian question, I shall comment upon his remarks with the restraint enjoined upon us by Prince Sihanouk.

There is only one problem of peace in southeast Asia, and indeed, in many other parts of the world. It is whether those who have wrapped around themselves the doctrine of the historical inevitability of world domination by their own particular political system merely believe it or will attempt to impose it upon others by all the means at their disposal. The real issue is whether peaceful co-existence is what normal language would indicate it means, or whether it means an all-out and continuous struggle against all those not under Communist control. The real threat to peace in southeast Asia is not from south to north, nor from across the Pacific Ocean. The threats are from north to south and take

[1] Above, pp. 574–9.

many forms. If these threats should disappear, SEATO would wither away, for it has no purpose but to maintain the peace in southeast Asia.

We cannot settle this argument in this conference, for it involves commitments of the Communist world which they would undoubtedly not yield in this discussion, just as it involves the commitments of free peoples who are determined to perfect and cherish freedoms still evolving from more than 2,000 years of struggle against tyranny in all forms. What we *can* do here is to discover whether we can agree that the people of Laos should be permitted to live in their own country without interference and pressures from the outside.

We note the statement made by the representative from Peiping that he 'is ready to work jointly with the delegations of all the other countries participating in this conference to make contributions to the peaceful settlement of the Laotian question'. We ourselves are prepared to work diligently to discover whether there *is* agreement in the conference on the questions before us.

Promptly after assuming office President Kennedy said: 'We strongly and unreservedly support the goal of a neutral and independent Laos, tied to no outside power or group of powers, threatening no one, and free from any domination.'[1] In early exchanges with Chairman Khrushchev, the latter affirmed his commitment to a neutral and independent Laos, and there was useful discussion of the example of Austria. Other spokesmen of other governments, including a number represented here, have declared their desire for a neutral Laos.

The King of that country, on February 19 of this year, declared: 'We desire to proclaim once more the policy of true neutrality that Laos has always sought to follow. . . . Once again we appeal to all countries to respect the independence, sovereignty, territorial integrity and neutrality of Laos.'[2]

I have already indicated that we believe the most immediate problem is to insure an effective cease-fire, to give the ICC the necessary and relevant instructions and to give it the resources required to carry out its vital task.

Next we must turn to the problem of insuring a genuinely neutral Laos. In this task, of course, most of us in this conference act as outsiders. We cannot impose on Laos anything which that country and its people do not truly want for themselves. In this particular instance we are fortunate that the expressed desires of the international community seem to coincide with what the people of Laos themselves want. Almost every nation here has expressed itself in favor of a neutral Laos.

But what does this mean? Neutrality is not simply a negative concept. A neutral Laos should be a dynamic, viable Laos, making progress toward more stable political institutions, economic well-being, and social justice. A truly neutral Laos must have the right to choose its own way of life in accordance with its own traditions, wishes, and aspirations for the future.

It is, of course, too early in the conference to present detailed proposals for achieving this end. But it is not too early to begin considering the broad outlines of a program directed to the goal.

As my Government sees it, such an outline would involve three separate points.

First: A definition of the concept of neutrality, as it applies to Laos, which all

[1] Above, pp. 565–6. [2] Above, p. 561.

of us gathered here could pledge ourselves to respect. This definition must go beyond the classical concept of nonalinement and include positive assurance of the integrity of the elements of national life.

Second: The development of effective international machinery for maintaining and safeguarding that neutrality against threats to it from within as well as without.

Third: Laos will need, if it wishes to take its place in the modern world, a substantial economic and technical aid program. We believe that such aid could be most appropriately administered by neutral nations from the area and that it should be supported by contributions from many states and agencies. We do not believe that a neutral Laos should become a field of rivalries expressed through foreign aid programs on a national or bloc basis. But we do believe that the Laotians should benefit from the enlarged possibilities of better health, broader education, increased productivity which are opening up for mankind in all parts of the world.

A word more is perhaps in order about each of these points.

First, *neutrality*. To be neutral, in the classical sense, means not to be formally alined with contending parties. Certainly we want this classical neutrality for Laos. But in today's world, with modern modes by which one government may subtly impose its will upon another, mere non-alinement is not enough.

Foreign military personnel, except for those specified in the Geneva Accords,[1] should be withdrawn from Laos. But we mean *all*, not just those assisting the forces of the constituted Government of the country at its request. There is no problem about the withdrawal of the limited U.S. military personnel assisting with the training and supply of Government forces if the 'Viet Minh brethren' and other elements who have entered Laos from the northeast return to their homes.

We have no desire to send military equipment into Laos; if international arrangements can be reached about forces and equipment, there would be no problem on our side.

We have no military bases in Laos and want none. We have no military alliances with Laos and want none. We have no interest in Laos as a staging area or as a thoroughfare for agents of subversion, saboteurs, or guerilla bands to operate against Laos' neighbors.

If all those at this table can make the same commitments and support international machinery to protect Laos and its neighbors against such activities, we shall have taken an important step toward peace in southeast Asia.

Finally, neutrality must be consistent with sovereignty. It involves safeguards against subversion of the elements of the state which is organized, directed, or assisted from beyond its borders. In the end we must find a way to let the people of Laos live their own lives under conditions of free choice—and under conditions which permit the continuing exercise of choice to adapt institutions, policies, and objectives to the teachings of experience.

In the Final Declaration of the Geneva Conference of 1954,[1] the parties pledged themselves to respect the sovereignty, the independence, the unity, and the territorial integrity of Laos. The intervening years since 1954 have demon-

[1] *Documents,* 1954, pp. 138–41.

strated as a practical reality that, for Laos, sovereignty, independence, unity, and territorial integrity cannot long be maintained unless others also are willing to respect the neutrality of Laos.

We invite the nations of this conference to join in a solemn recognition and pledge of respect for Laotian neutrality. We invite all here to join in developing adequate machinery for protecting this status and with it the sovereignty, independence, unity, and territorial integrity of Laos as well.

Second, *machinery for keeping the peace.* The Geneva Conference of 1954 spent most of its time in discussing international machinery to supervise and control the introduction of arms and military personnel into the southeast Asian area. Despite those labors, that machinery has not proved effective in controlling military activity and in keeping the peace in the area. It has, however, given us a body of experience upon which we can draw in an effort to build better than our predecessors.

That experience suggests a set of principles or criteria by which we and the world will be able to judge whether the international controls developed here will effectively serve the ends for which they are designed.

The control machinery must have full access to all parts of the country without the need for the consent of any civil or military officials, national or local.

It must have its own transportation and communication equipment sufficient to the task. These must be constantly available to and under the sole orders of the control body.

It must be able to act on any complaints from responsible sources, including personnel of the control body itself, responsible military and civil officials in Laos, the governments of neighboring countries and of the members of this conference.

The control body should act by majority rule with the right to file majority and minority reports. It should not be paralyzed by a veto.

There should be some effective method of informing governments and the world at large about a finding by the control body that the conditions of peace and neutrality, as defined, have been violated.

If we are successful in giving practical meaning to the idea of a neutral Laos with international assurances against aggression and intervention, Lao armed forces could be reduced to the level necessary to maintain its own security.

This is the yardstick by which we can measure the prospective effectiveness of any control machinery for Laos. This is the yardstick which will influence the attitude of the United States toward the work of this conference. In short, pledges and promises must be backed by effective controls, effectively applied to maintain a genuinely neutral Laos.

Third, *economic and technical development for Laos.* The energies of the Lao people have too long been diverted from the constructive work of establishing for themselves and their children a better society and a better life. Schools, hospitals, agricultural improvement, industry, transport and communications, improved civil administration—all are needed, and urgently, if the promise which the 20th century holds out to all men is to be realized for Laos. Such improvement in their way of life is not only the right of the Laotians. It is also, I am convinced, a necessary condition of an independent and neutral Laos.

Unfortunately the resources necessary to permit such improvement at the required speed are not available in Laos itself. It is necessary that as many countries as possible supply the resources needed.

The United States would be willing to contribute to such a program. The United States has already contributed sizable amounts in material support and effort to assist the people of Laos in this program of economic and social development. It is a matter of regret that any portion of this effort has had to be expended to meet the threat to the security of Laos. Certainly one of the prime tasks for this conference is to devise means so that collective assistance efforts for Laos can be dedicated to the peaceful pursuits of people and to bringing the benefits of modern science and technology to the masses.

We believe that such assistance might usefully be administered by an organization of neutral nations of the area. We invite the U.S.S.R. to join with us in underwriting the cost of such assistance. Let us make Laos the scene of a cooperative effort for peaceful construction.

Mr. Chairman, I wish to inform the conference that I am one of several ministers who plan to return to our posts toward the end of this week. It was my announced intention when I first arrived. Our delegation will be led by Ambassador at Large Harriman, one of our most distinguished public servants and most experienced diplomats. But official propaganda has begun to say that my departure means an attempt to sabotage this conference. It is not important that such propaganda is false; it is important that such propaganda bears upon the bona fides of those at the table.

In conclusion, Mr. Chairman, I do hope that all of us at the conference can keep our minds upon the Laotian people, who have suffered much and endured much during the past two decades. Let us find ways to let them lead their own lives in peace. They are few in number and need not be caught up in larger issues. Let us affirm that it is *their* country and not an appropriate target for ambitions with which they need not be involved. We shall contribute what we can to the success of this conference; if each can contribute, a good result can be accomplished.

(iii) Speech by the Soviet Foreign Minister, Mr. Gromyko, 17 May 1961[1]

Dear colleagues, participants in the conference, we have gathered here to find by joint efforts a solution of the Laotian problem, to eliminate the dangerous centre of war which has appeared in the Laos area and threatens to spread far beyond its boundaries.

The Soviet delegation has no intention of dwelling in detail on the history of the events which brought about such a serious worsening of the situation, but we must say forthrightly that had it not been for the interference in the internal affairs of Laos, which took the form of the organisation of a revolt against the lawful government of that country headed by Prince Souvanna Phouma, had it not been for the direct support given to the rebels by the United States, the guns would not have begun speaking in Laos and consequently there would have been no necessity for a cease-fire or for convening another international conference for settling the situation in that country. Such are the facts.

[1] *Soviet News*, 19 May 1961.

In connection with the statement made here by Mr. Rusk to the effect that the United States government is not yet satisfied with the state of affairs as regards the cease-fire in Laos, the question naturally arises: Maybe the United States is displeased with the cease-fire in Laos? Otherwise how can one explain the fact that instead of seriously taking up the basic question confronting the conference —the ensurance of the independence and neutrality of Laos—the United States representatives continue harping on the subject of the cease-fire in Laos. Those taking part in this conference have no right to forget that the cease-fire is only part of a general agreement on the resumption of the work of the International Commission for Supervision and Control in Laos and on calling an international conference for settling the Laotian question.

Another thing to be emphasised is that not only the Soviet Union and the other socialist countries but also the United States and its allies in military blocs must be, to no less extent, interested in creating conditions which would preclude the possibility of a wider and more dangerous conflict in the area of Laos. Were the United States to be guided by other views it would be making a serious blunder.

The Soviet government maintains that the successful outcome of this conference depends primarily on all its participants recognising the necessity for Laos to develop as an independent and neutral state and on agreement being reached on respecting and observing Laos' neutrality. Naturally, we proceed from the assumption that agreements reached in the course of the talks should in no way lead to any interference from outside in the internal affairs of Laos. The Laotian people themselves and no one else should decide on the ways for their country's further development.

Permit me to outline the Soviet Union's position on the essence of the Laotian question. This position is simple and understandable. Our attitude to this problem is determined by the general aims of the Soviet Union's foreign policy —to preserve and strengthen peace, to ensure peaceful co-existence of all countries and peoples and grant them the possibility of shaping their destiny and building their life in accordance with their views and interests independently, without any outside interference.

Following its invariable peace policy, the Soviet government took an active part in working out the decisions of the 1954 Geneva conference, which determined the status of Laos as a neutral state. We unswervingly adhered, and continue to adhere, to these decisions.

From the very beginning of the Laotian conflict the Soviet government and its head, N. S. Khrushchev, personally, have been making strenuous efforts to restore peace in the Laos area. The Soviet Union, discharging the functions of co-chairman of the 1954 Geneva conference, repeatedly called for an end to be put to the violations of Laos' sovereignty and for ceasing all efforts to impose on that country the order and policy against which the Laotian people rose up in arms.

Already towards the end of last year the Soviet government came out with a proposal for the immediate calling of an international conference on Laos of the same type as the 1954 Geneva conference.[1] The Soviet government strove for the

[1] *Documents*, 1960, pp. 527–9.

resumption of the activity of the International Commission for Supervision and Control in Laos. We supported the valuable proposal of the head of state of Cambodia, Prince Norodom Sihanouk, to have the composition of the international conference enlarged to include 14 states.[1] It gives us pleasure to note that this position of the Soviet government met with full understanding and support from the states concerned, which eventually led to the convening and opening of the present international conference.

The Soviet government is convinced that favourable conditions now exist for the peaceful settlement of the Laotian problem. There are ample grounds for drawing such a conclusion.

It seems that now all those taking part in the conference have already expressed their consent to the restoration of the status of Laos as a neutral state. Special note should be taken of such statements on the part of the governments of those countries which formerly adhered to a different position.

Those taking part in the conference have a good basis for working out mutually acceptable decisions—the 1954 Geneva conference. Life has shown that when the Geneva conference's decisions on Laos were fulfilled, peace reigned in that country.

The cease-fire by the belligerents, the resumption of the activity of the International Commission for Supervision and Control in Laos and, finally, the participation in the work of the conference of representatives of the three political forces of that country also create favourable conditions for our talks to yield fruitful results.

In settling the Laotian question, we have before us two groups of questions, namely: a group of international questions and a group of internal questions.

We must make a strict distinction between them and approach them differently.

It goes without saying that all internal questions—in particular such questions as the formation of a government of national unity, the holding of free democratic elections, the reorganisation of a national army—are fully and completely matters for the Laotians themselves to settle. To consider such questions at an international conference would be gross interference in the internal affairs of Laos.

To settle their internal affairs the Laotian people themselves worked out certain legislative principles and standards which have justified themselves in practice and which regulate the social-political relations in the country. I have in mind the constitution of the country, the laws on democratic freedoms adopted by the National Assembly of Laos in October, 1957, the election law of 1957, and the agreement between Prime Minister Prince Souvanna Phouma and the representative of Pathet Lao, Prince Souphanouvong, of November 20, 1960.[2]

As I have already pointed out, besides the internal, there is also another group of questions—international ones pertaining to recognition of and respect for the national sovereignty of Laos, the creation of international conditions which would enable Laos to build its life in accordance with the national interests and traditions of its people. Our conference is called upon to settle precisely this

[1] Above, p. 557, n. 2.   [2] Text in *H.N.A.*, 23 November 1960, and see p. 570, n. 3.

group of questions. There is no doubt that their constructive settlement would provide a foundation for establishing peace in Laos, which, in turn, would be conducive to the settlement of the internal affairs in that country.

Now permit me to tell you how the Soviet delegation sees the practical fulfilment of the tasks confronting the conference.

Obviously, we must first of all agree on how the neutrality of Laos is to be ensured. Under present conditions this is the key to the solution of the Laotian problem.

The Laotian people have already had their say in the matter. At the 1954 Geneva conference the Laotian government already proclaimed neutrality as the basis of its foreign policy. The will and readiness of the Laotian people to carry this principle into life find expression in the statements by the Souvanna Phouma government and the Neo Lao Hak Sat leaders, in the selfless struggle of the Laotian people against all those who are trying to make Laos abandon its policy of neutrality.

What is to be done to help the Laotian people to ensure the true independence and neutrality of their state?

In the Soviet government's opinion it is first of all necessary for our conference to adopt a special declaration on Laos' neutrality. We submit a draft of such a declaration to the conference for consideration.

We suggest that the declaration should record, on the one hand, Laos' obligation to follow a policy of neutrality, non-participation in military blocs and prevention of the establishment of foreign military bases on its territory, and so on, and on the other hand the obligation of the participants in the conference to respect and observe the neutrality of Laos, its independence and territorial integrity, and to take no actions which would directly or indirectly infringe on its sovereignty or could lead to a breach of internal peace in that country. It is also important to include a provision that no state would impose any political conditions on Laos in rendering it any assistance.

The Soviet government considers it expedient to include in the declaration an appropriate clause which would provide for taking measures for removing a threat of Laos' independence and neutrality being violated. In our opinion it is necessary to do so because, as proved by experience, the existence of the 1954 Geneva decisions which defined the neutral status of Laos did not prevent certain countries affiliated with S.E.A.T.O. from embarking on the path of overt interference in the internal affairs of that country.

In this connection we cannot ignore the fact that after the conclusion of the 1954 Geneva agreements there appeared treaties and agreements which stand in direct contradiction with Laos' independence and its status of neutrality. The Vice-Premier and Minister of Foreign Affairs of the Chinese People's Republic, Comrade Chen Yi, justly pointed out in his impressive and brilliant speech[1] that the inclusion of Laos in the sphere of action of the S.E.A.T.O. Treaty can no longer be tolerated. The establishment of a reliable status of neutrality for Laos, situated in the centre of the Indo-Chinese peninsula, would substantially promote the cause of strengthening peace in Asia, and not only in Asia for that matter.

[1] Above, p. 574.

D.I.A.–U

In the Soviet delegation's opinion, an agreement on the withdrawal from Laotian territory of foreign troops and military personnel and on the cessation of military deliveries to that country, apart from that quantity of conventional arms which is necessary for the defence of the country, should be worked out and signed at the conference. A draft of such an agreement is also submitted by the Soviet delegation.

The Soviet draft provides for the withdrawal from the territory of Laos, within 30 days after the signing of the agreement, of all foreign military units, military missions, military advisers, instructors and consultants, including those who serve with the armed forces of Laos, and also all foreign civilians who have any connection with deliveries, servicing, storing and utilisation of military equipment. The draft agreement includes provisions which categorically prohibit admissions to Laos of any foreign military units and military personnel in future as well.

It is clear that without the evacuation from Laotian territory of foreign military units and all foreign military personnel, peace in that country cannot be restored and any talk about ensuring Laos' neutrality would be of no avail.

Noteworthy in this connection is the question of the Chiang Kai-shek bands in Laos.

The Soviet government has made numerous representations to the government of the United States on the subject. In our discussions the American side promised to take measures for withdrawing Chiang Kai-shek units from Laos. A few days ago the United States government assured us that nearly all the Chiang Kai-shek units had been evacuated from Laos, except small individual groups which were hiding in the jungle. It is thus clear that the remnants of Chiang Kai-shek bands still remain on the territory of Laos—in the jungle or elsewhere, it makes no difference—and this cannot but arouse well-justified anxiety on the part of the Laotian people, on the part of all those who strive for peace in Laos. We fully support the demand of the government of the Chinese People's Republic on this matter.

Alongside the immediate withdrawal of foreign military personnel the Soviet draft agreement provides for the discontinuance of the importation to Laos of all kinds of arms, ammunition and war materials. The draft contains an appropriate reservation concerning a definite quantity of conventional arms necessary for the defence of Laos.

The Soviet draft agreement contains basic provisions on the powers of the International Commission for Supervision and Control in Laos and the order of its work. Naturally, our draft is based on the view that Laos is a sovereign state and that international control should not be made an instrument of foreign interference in that country.

The Soviet government submits for the conference's consideration drafts of two documents, the first document is a Declaration on the Neutrality of Laos, the second, an Agreement on the Withdrawal from Laotian Territory of Foreign Troops and Military Personnel and on the Powers of the International Commission.[1]

----

[1] Not printed here.

14. Joint communiqué issued by the three Laotian princes, Zurich, 22 June 1961[1]

The three princes, Souvanna Phouma, Boun Oum and Souphanouvong, high representatives of the three existing forces in Laos, met in Zurich from 19 June, as was agreed among them on 18 June, to discuss the problem of realising national accord through the formation of a government of National Union.

Since that date, the three princes have discussed the political programme of the provisional government of National Union and its immediate tasks.

On these two points, the three princes have agreed as follows:

One. Political Programme

The Kingdom of Laos is resolved to follow the road of peace and neutrality in conformity with the interests and aspirations of the Laotian people and with the 1954 Geneva agreements with a view to building a peaceful, neutral, independent, democratic, unified and prosperous Laos. A provisional government of National Union will be formed, which will apply this policy of peace and neutrality in carrying out the following political programme.

Internal Policy

One. Execute the cease-fire agreement agreed by the three interested parties in Laos and see to it that peace is restablished in the country;

Two. Apply strictly democratic liberties to the benefit of the people and abrogate all provisions of law which are contrary to this, and restore the laws of these democratic liberties of the citizens and the electoral law approved in 1957 by the National Assembly.

Three. Defend the unity, neutrality, independence and national sovereignty of Laos.

Four. Ensure justice and peace to all citizens of the kingdom in order to achieve peace and national accord without descrimination of origin or political obedience.

Five. Realise the unification of the armed forces of the three parties in a single national army according to a programme agreed by the parties.

Six. Develop agriculture, industry and handicrafts, create lines of communication and transport, develop culture and pay full attention to the improving of the standard of living of the people.

External Policy

One. Apply resolutely the five principles of peaceful co-existence[2] in foreign relations, build amicable relations and develop diplomatic relations with all countries, in the first place with the neighbouring countries, on the basis of equality and sovereignty of Laos.

Two. Not to participate in any military alliance or coalition, not to permit

---

[1] *H.N.A.*, 23 June 1961.

[2] The five principles, or Panch Sheela, had been enunciated by Mr. Nehru and Mr. Chou En-Lai on 28 June 1964. These principles were: (1) mutual respect for each other's territorial integrity and sovereignty, (2) non-aggression, (3) non-interference in each other's internal affairs, (4) equality and mutual benefit and (5) peaceful co-existence. See *Documents*, 1954, pp. 313–15.

the establishment of any foreign military base on the territory of Laos, it being understood that those bases which figure in the 1954 Geneva agreements will be the object of a special study; not to permit any country to use Laotian territory for military ends, not to recognise the protection of any military alliance or coalition.

Three. Not to permit any foreign interference in the internal affairs of Laos in any form, demand the withdrawal from Laos of all foreign troops and all foreign military personnel and not to permit the introduction into Laos of any foreign troops and military personnel.

Four. Accept direct and unconditional aid from all countries which desire to help Laos in building an autonomous national economy on the basis of respect for the sovereignty of Laos.

Five. Respect the treaties and agreements which have been signed in conformity with the interests of the Laotian people and the policy of peace and neutrality of the kingdom, notably the 1954 Geneva agreements, and abrogate all those treaties and agreements which are contrary to these principles.

Two. Immediate Tasks

The provisional government of National Union will carry out the following immediate tasks:

One. Form a governmental delegation to participate in the international conference for the settlement of the Laotian question.

Two. Realise a cease-fire and restore peace to the whole country.

Three. Honour commitments undertaken in the name of Laos at the international conference for the settlement of the Laotian question and carry out seriously the agreements concluded among the three interested parties in Laos.

Four. Set free all political prisoners and detainees.

Five. Organise general elections for the National Assembly with a view to forming a definite government.

Six. During the period of transition, the administrative organs established during the hostilities will be left in place provisionally.

Concerning the formation of a government of National Union, the three princes have agreed on the following principles:

One. The government of National Union will comprise the representatives of the three parties and will have a provisional character.

Two. It will be formed according to a special procedure by direct designation and nomination by His Majesty The King without passing through the National Assembly.

The exchange of views is continuing among the three princes on this question and will be the object of a new meeting with the aim of achieving national reconciliation as soon as possible.[1]

---

[1] A further meeting was held in Laos on 6 October 1961 at Hin Heup, and the following communiqué was issued:

The three princes had exchanged views on the formation of the National provisional coalition government during their meetings in Hin Heup on 6 and 8 October. These meetings were held in an atmosphere of trust and mutual understanding.

After the delegations of the three parties held talks in Hin Heup the three princes examined the reports made by the three delegations and arrived at the following agreements:

(b) South Vietnam

1. Mr. Rusk's press conference, 4 May 1961[1] (extracts)

. . . I thought it might be useful if I were to make some comments on the background of the situation in Viet-Nam—that is, not background comments but comments on the background.

Since late in 1959 organized Communist activity in the form of guerrilla raids against army and security units of the Government of Viet-Nam, terrorist acts against local officials and civilians, and other subversive activities in the Republic of Viet-Nam have increased to levels unprecedented since the Geneva agreements of 1954.[2] During this period the organized armed strength of the Viet Cong, the Communist apparatus operating in the Republic of Viet-Nam, has grown from about 3,000 to over 12,000 personnel. This armed strength has been supplemented by an increase in the numbers of political and propaganda agents in the area.

During 1960 alone, Communist armed units and terrorists assassinated or kidnapped over 3,000 local officials, military personnel, and civilians. Their activities took the form of armed attacks against isolated garrisons, attacks on newly established townships, ambushes on roads and canals, destruction of bridges, and well-planned sabotage against public works and communication lines. Because of Communist guerrilla activity 200 elementary schools had to be closed at various times, affecting over 25,000 students and 800 teachers.

This upsurge of Communist guerrilla activity apparently stemmed from a decision made in May 1959 by the Central Committee of the Communist Party of north Viet-Nam which called for the reunification of Viet-Nam by all 'appropriate means'.[3] In July of the same year the Central Committee was reorganized and charged with intelligence duties and the 'liberation' of south Viet-Nam. In retrospect this decision to step up guerrilla activity was made to reverse the remarkable success which the Government of the Republic of Viet-Nam under President Ngo Dinh Diem had achieved in consolidating its political position and in attaining significant economic recovery in the 5 years between 1954 and 1959.

Remarkably coincidental with the renewed Communist activity in Laos, the Communist Party of north Viet-Nam at its Third Congress on September 10, 1960, adopted a resolution which declared that the Vietnamese revolution has as

---

One. The National provisional coalition government should be formed by sixteen members.

Two. The Premier should act concurrently as a member of the cabinet and the Vice-Premier should also act concurrently as a member of the cabinet.

Three. Apart from accepting the reports made by the three delegations, the three princes unanimously agreed to nominate to the King his Royal Highness Prince Souvanna Phouma as Premier of the future National provisional coalition government.

Finally the three princes agreed to ask the three delegations to continue their discussions on the few unsolved questions on the formation of the National provisional coalition government and on the task of the future National provisional coalition government. After these discussions the delegations should report back to the three princes.

The three princes agreed that after reception of the above-mentioned reports from the three delegations, they would meet again at an early date and that the place and time of the meeting would be decided by Prince Souvanna Phouma. (*H.N.A.*, 9 October 1961.)

[1] *D.S.B.*, 22 May 1961, pp. 757–60. [2] *Documents*, 1954, pp. 138–41.
[3] No text of this decision is available, but a reference to this meeting can be found in *H.N.A.*, 14 May 1959.

a major strategic task the liberation of the south from the 'rule of U.S. imperialists and their henchmen'. This resolution called for the direct overthrow of the government of the Republic of Viet-Nam.

The most recent gains by the Pathet Lao in the southern part of Laos have given added seriousness to the security situation in Viet-Nam. Communist control over Lao territory bordering Viet-Nam south of the 17th parallel makes more secure one of the three principal routes by which north Vietnamese armed units have been able to infiltrate the Republic of Viet-Nam. The other two routes are, as is well known, directly across the 17th parallel and by sea along the coastline of the Republic of Viet-Nam. In addition to the obvious fact that the strength of the Pathet Lao has been tremendously increased by the importation of light and heavy arms from the outside, we have no reason to doubt that the north Vietnamese armed units not operating in Laos have been similarly re-equipped and strengthened from the same outside source.

The increased Communist activity in the Republic of Viet-Nam and countermeasures to meet this threat have been matters of urgent and recent discussion, both by the officials of Viet-Nam and the United States. In connection with these the President has authorized an increase in the amount of military assistance, and a number of other measures have been determined upon. Furthermore the United States has undertaken training and advisory measures which are designed to strengthen both materially and militarily the ability of the Viet-Nam armed forces to overcome this increased Communist threat. A part of the effort, of course, must include in a situation of this sort a vigorous civil program as well in the economic and social field. As you may recall, the members of the Southeast Asia Treaty Organization expressed their concern about the situation in Viet-Nam in our recent conference in Bangkok,[1] and it is perfectly apparent that we must all give very serious attention to developments in that country.

Now, I think I will be able to take a few questions.

Q. In your remarks on south Viet-Nam are you, in fact, suggesting that, as the war in Laos draws to a close, the Communists are simply opening up a new theater in southeast Asia?

A. I don't believe this is a shift from one theater to another. I think both of these countries have been under pressure from the Communists from the north, and the pressures in Laos have served to increase the pressures somewhat in Viet-Nam. The most active part of Communist efforts in Viet-Nam is occurring not in the north actually but in the south, the far south, in the Saigon area. But a considerable number of the personnel and also some of the supplies undoubtedly have been coming in from the north by infiltration—some of it through Laos. . . .

. . . *Q. The charge has been made publicly that the south Vietnamese Government is both reactionary and corrupt and that one of the first priorities to shore that area up would be to encourage political reform. Would you care to comment on that?*

A. I think that some of the remarks that I made last evening on foreign aid have some application; that is, questions of defense in a situation such as Viet-

[1] See above, p. 567.

Nam cannot be dealt with solely in military terms. The quality of society, the interest of the people, the mobilization of the energies of the people, the satisfaction of the people in their own system, have a great deal to do with problems of security and the ability to withstand assault and attack and penetration and subversion from the outside.

I have no doubt that a broad program of civil action, improved administration, economic development in Viet-Nam ought to be continued and expanded in order to help with the total situation there, and this is directly related to the defense problem.

Q. Do you think that corruption is the cause of the situation in south Viet-Nam?

A. I don't believe that corruption is the root cause of the situation there, in the face of amounts of determined activity by those coming in from the outside; that is, the initiative in the attack in south Viet-Nam is being taken by those who are attempting to overthrow that government and by those who would be trying to overthrow almost any government you could think of which is not under the control of north Viet-Nam. The economic and social programs and the development of the countryside are relevant to the response to this sort of attack. . . .

2. Joint communiqué issued by the Governments of the United States and South Vietnam, 15 May 1961[1]

Lyndon B. Johnson, Vice-President of the United States, has just completed a visit to the Republic of Vietnam, on behalf of President Kennedy and at the invitation of President Ngo Dinh Diem.

The enthusiastic welcome he received in Vietnam reflected a deep sense of common cause in the fight for freedom in South-East Asia and around the world.

This recognition of mutual objectives resulted in concrete understanding between the Republic of Vietnam and the United States.

It is clear to the Government and the people of Vietnam and to the United States that the independence and territorial integrity of Vietnam are being brutally and systematically violated by Communist agents and forces from the North.

It is also clear to both Governments that action must be strengthened and accelerated to protect the legitimate rights and aspirations of the people of free Vietnam to choose their own way of life.

The two Governments agreed that this is the basic principle upon which their understanding rests.

The United States, for its part, is conscious of the determination, energy and sacrifices which the Vietnamese people, under the dedicated leadership of President Ngo Dinh Diem, have brought to the defence of freedom in their land.

The United States is also conscious of its responsibilities and duty, in its own self-interest as well as in the interest of other free peoples, to assist a brave country in the defence of its liberties against unprovoked subversion and Communist terror. It has no other motive than the defence of freedom.

[1] *D.S.B.*, 19 June 1961, pp. 956–7.

The United States recognises that the President of the Republic of Vietnam, Ngo Dinh Diem, who was recently re-elected to office by an overwhelming majority of his countrymen despite bitter Communist opposition, is in the vanguard of those leaders who stand for freedom on the periphery of the Communist empire in Asia.

Free Vietnam cannot alone withstand the pressure which this Communist empire is exerting against it. Under these circumstances—the need of free Vietnam for increased and accelerated emergency assistance and the will and determination of the United States to provide such assistance to those willing to fight for their liberties—it is natural that a large measure of agreement on the means to accomplish the joint purpose was found in high-level conversations between the two Governments.

Both Governments recognise that under the circumstances of guerrilla warfare now existing in free Vietnam, it is necessary to give high priority to the restoration of a sense of security to the people of free Vietnam. This priority however, in no way diminishes the necessity, in policies and programmes of both Governments, to pursue vigorously appropriate measures in other fields to achieve a prosperous and happy society.

The following measures, agreed in principle and subject to prompt finalisation and implementation, represent an increase and acceleration of United States assistance to the Republic of Vietnam. These may be followed by more far-reaching measures if the situation, in the opinion of both Governments, warrants.

First, it was agreed by the two Governments to extend and build upon existing programmes of military and economic aid and to infuse into their joint actions a high sense of urgency and dedication.

Second, it was agreed that regular armed forces of the Republic of Vietnam should be increased, and that the United States would extend its military assistance programmes to include support for an additional number of regular Vietnamese armed forces.

Third, it was agreed that the United States would provide military assistance programme support for the entire Vietnamese Civil Guard force.

Fourth, it was agreed that the two Governments should collaborate in the use of military specialists to assist and work with Vietnamese armed forces in health, welfare and public works activities in the villages of free Vietnam.

Fifth, it was agreed that the assistance of other free governments to the Government of the Republic of Vietnam in its trouble against Communist guerrilla forces would be welcome.

Sixth, it was agreed that, to achieve the best possible use of available resources by the Vietnamese and the United States, in prosecution of their joint effort against Communist attacks in Vietnam, a group of highly-qualified economic and fiscal experts would meet in Vietnam to work out a financial plan on which joint efforts should be based.

Seventh, it was agreed that the United States and the Republic of Vietnam would discuss new economic and social measures to be undertaken in rural areas, to accompany the anti-guerrilla effort, in order that the people of Vietnam should benefit promptly from the restoration of law and order in their villages and provinces.

Eighth, it was agreed that, in addition to measures to deal with the immediate Vietnam guerrilla problem, the two governments would work together toward a longer-range economic development programme, including further progress in the fields of agriculture, health, education, fisheries, highways, public administration, and industrial development.

These longer-range plans and programmes would be developed in detail after further consideration and discussion.

Their goal would be a Vietnam capable of a self-sustained economic growth.

President Ngo Dinh Diem and Vice-President Lyndon B. Johnson, on behalf of President Kennedy, established a sense of mutual confidence and respect which both believe essential to fulfilment of their objectives.

II. THE 'THIRD WORLD' OF THE 'UNCOMMITTED NATIONS'

A. THE NEUTRALIST MOVEMENT

1. Joint communiqué issued by the Presidents of Jugoslavia and the United Arab Republic, Marshal Tito and Colonel Nasser, Alexandria, 22 April 1961[1]

The President of F.P.R. of Yugoslavia, Marshal Josip Broz Tito, visited the U.A.R. from 17–22 April, 1961, and had talks with the President of the U.A.R., Gamal Abd El-Nasser, concerning the world situation and the direct relations between the two countries.

They reaffirmed the statements they had made together on the occasion of previous visits to the U.A.R. and to F.P.R. of Yugoslavia and on other occasions, regarding the main pending international problems.

On April 19, 1961, the two Presidents made, on the foreign intervention in Cuba, the following joint declaration:

'Having considered carefully the recent and current acts of foreign intervention in Cuba through the supply of arms and other aids to invading elements and the use of foreign territory by these elements;

'We reached most regretfully the conclusion that these acts are an attack against Cuba's independence and constitute a denial of the principles of the United Nations and a breach of international peace, and they call for a firm attitude and for immediate steps by the world community of Nations.

'We, therefore, renew the expression of our countries' and peoples' resentment of these acts and deep concern over them, and their determination to take all available measures and extend every possible help in view to the prompt stopping of foreign intervention in Cuba and the safeguarding of Cuba's independence.

'We are fully aware of the great shock which these recent events have given to the world, and confident that all peace-loving nations will rally around the standard of sanity, decency, and the rule of law in international relations.'

The two Presidents reaffirmed their view that the attempts aimed at settling world problems by relying on force or by interference in the internal affairs of others constitute a direct threat to world peace. They maintained that all countries must exert endeavours towards the establishment of the principles of independence and equality in the relations between States, toward the elimination of the use of force from international relations and toward solving all pending world issues and disputes exclusively by peaceful negotiations.

President Tito and President Abd El-Nasser conferred, further, on the latest development relating to the problems of disarmament, the Congo, Algeria, Palestine and Laos.

They deemed it imperative that efforts be redoubled for attaining complete

---

[1] *President Tito's Visit to Friendly African Countries* (Jugoslavia, Belgrade, 1961), pp. 53–55.

and universal disarmament and diverting all the resources of the world to constructive endeavours and to the peace and happiness of the human race.

Concerning the Congo, the two Presidents deplored the failure of the United Nations to implement its resolutions supporting the independence, the unity and the territorial integrity of that country, and they stressed the necessity of implementing these resolutions without equivocation or further delay. They expressed the view that efforts should be made to extend all possible help to the legal government of the Congo under the premiership of Mr. Antoine Gizenga.

The two Heads of State pursued with anxiety details of the obstacles that hindered the endeavours to stop the war in Algeria; but they emphasized that the only way to peace in Algeria should be the realization of the legitimate rights of the Algerian people, rights for which those heroic people paid a high price in sacrifices throughout seven long years of armed struggle.

The two Presidents reaffirmed their previous statements supporting the full restoration of the rights of the Arabs of Palestine.

As regards Laos, they reiterated their view that the present crisis should be resolved on the basis of scrupulous respect for the independence of that country and for its neutrality and of absolute non-interference in its affairs.

In this respect the two Heads of State reiterated their view on the necessity of the prompt and definitive liquidation of colonialism in every form as one of the main sources of international instability which endangers world peace.

The two Presidents expressed their deep concern over the unfavourable development of international relations and over the dangerous aggravation of these relations caused by the recent developments. In this connection the two Presidents held the view that consultations between the non-aligned countries are indispensable for the purpose of consolidating world peace, safeguarding the independence of all nations and eliminating the danger of intervention in their affairs.

These consultations will also aim at fostering economic, cultural and technical cooperation for the benefit of their peoples and the world community.

The two Presidents resumed their reviewing of the relations between Yugoslavia and the United Arab Republic and expressed their entire satisfaction concerning them and their own and their governments' determination to maintain their progress in every field.

2. Address by Mr. Khrushchev to a parliamentary delegation from the United Arab Republic, Moscow, 3 May 1961[1]

Thank you. I beg you to convey to President Jamal Abd an-Nasir [sic] my overwhelming thanks for the good wishes you convey to me. My thanks, too, to Vice-President Field-Marshal Abd al-Hakim Amir for his good wishes. I wish President Jamal Abd an-Nasir and his Vice-President Field-Marshal Abd al-Hakim Amir continued good health, progress, and success. I wish to thank your Excellency, the President of the parliamentary delegation. I thank you for the good words you addressed to the Soviet people, the Soviet Government, and to

---

[1] *S.W.B.*, Part IV, 10 June 1961. The delegation was led by Mr. Anwar as-Sadat, President of the National Assembly of the U.A.R.

me personally. I thank you and all your colleagues, members of the Arab Parliamentary delegation, and all members of the Arab National Assembly.

The relations, and by this I mean the relations between our two States and our personal relations, are good. We look with understanding on your policy, the policy of independence. As much as we can, we aid you in your struggle to bolster your economy and establish your national sovereignty.

We are glad to have participated to some extent in your struggle for independence. We believe that we also have some share in the defeat inflicted upon Anglo-French imperialism. To some extent we have thus helped to do away with some of the pride of the imperialists. This is a proof that they are not strong and that they do not possess strength in everything. We are very glad to participate in the construction of the High Dam. This construction deals a blow to American imperialism. In the past American imperialism thought that no big undertaking could be accomplished without their participation. We have proved that the people can do great things without the participation of the imperialists. The High Dam will be built according to Soviet plans. Our plans for the High Dam are more progressive and less expensive than previous plans. We are living in an age when everything is progressing in the new socialist world. The socialist world will surpass the capitalist world, that ageing world.

America is actually pursuing a policy of commercial siege against the Soviet Union. America is pursuing this policy of economic siege under the slogan 'We do not give our technique and knowledge to the Soviet Union'. But the entire world knows the result of this siege. Soviet man has travelled around the Earth, while the American man still awaits the opportunity to do so, and I do not believe this will ever take place. This is not because America does not wish it, but because it cannot accomplish it.

What does America want? America is rich and has all the technical means. But our regime has proved to be more progressive. That is why we have triumphed over the Americans. This triumph will continue throughout the centuries. In 1970 we shall catch up with America in the field of production per head of population; in 1965 we shall catch up with America in regard to production volume. Now we produce almost the same amount of steel as the United States. In 1965 our steel production will be about 100,000,000 tons. We have revised our Seven-Year Plan. This year we will produce 71,000,000 tons. Last year we produced 65,000,000 tons. We have effected a 6,000,000 ton increase in one year, while the United States is still where it was, indeed it has gone backward. In the United States, there are now about 7,000,000 workers without work.

We are happy with our success and for this reason we want other people to employ their resources for their own good. We want communism. You say you want Arab nationalism and also socialism. We have different views on many issues. But this should not be a barrier between you and us. History will be our judge. We are communists and you are not connected with this word. But history will teach you. We are not the ones to teach you. Life itself will teach you. If our people live better than you under the communist banner, then how can you declare yourselves averse to communism? The people will tell you to get out. We shall run our own affairs. Faruq for instance, pursued a reactionary policy hand in hand with imperialism. But you, the young officers, have overthrown him. This was right. It is a natural phenomenon.

Communism is more progressive than capitalism. We have proved this by actual work. Our country produces three times as many engineers as America. Communism provides better conditions for learning. The Americans are rich capitalists. But on what do they spend their money? We are not as rich as America but we spend much more on education than the United States. In the United States only the rich study. In our country all are equal. Anyone who wants to study can do so and he does not have to pay anything for learning. We provide him with a place in the dormitories and this is done only in the communist countries.

We shall triumph. We progress and lead you with us. Now you do not want communism. Never mind. We are not angry. In the future you will find that we are right.

[*At this point Anwar as-Sadat said:* 'We respect every principle chosen by any people for their freedom.']

We also follow the same principle. We cannot drive people into paradise with a stick. If this is paradise then people must go to it of their own free will. We respect the principles and systems of all peoples. You have been liberated. Nationalism emanates from your hearts, but this does not mean that happiness lies in nationalism. Nationalism is not the pinnacle of happiness. Happiness occurs when all nations are happy.

You may think that I want to transform you from Arab nationalists into communists. Naturally, I do not propose to do this now but I feel that some of those present here will be communists in the future, because life imposes itself upon man. Communism consists of ideas and ideas cannot be buried in prisons. Man may be imprisoned but he will remain a communist. The Tsar imprisoned Lenin, for example, but Lenin built the biggest State and the people are living in freedom.

I believe that you must not be surprised to see me praising communism to this extent. What else can I praise when I am the Secretary of the Communist Party? Shall I praise the American system? All these systems are past but communism is new. Communist man was the first to see into space. He is Gagarin. But he has had enough publicity.

We work on socialist bases. You Arabs now realise this. You say that you seek socialism. But you do not know much about the socialism which leads to communism. As a scientific phenomenon, socialism is the first step to communism. You are still in the first stage of your thinking, if you want to build up socialism. You are like one who studies the alphabet. You are studying the letter. Socialism is the first letter of the alphabet of the organisation of human society. The letter B is the beginning of communism. If you want socialism, then you must not say that you are averse to communism. You are placing yourselves in a critical position and have fallen into the imperialist trap.

I warn you that I say all this in an honourable way because communism is a sacred thing. We want to be friendly with all people. We leave the socialist systems to the people to decide for themselves. We, the Soviet Union and the communist countries, stand on the side of the peoples who fight against imperialism. You see that we cannot be bought. The imperialists are not our friends. I mean all the imperialists: the United States, France, Portugal, Holland, and Belgium. We boldly opposed Britain and France when they aggressed against Egypt. We also supported Syria and Iraq and now we are supporting Cuba and Laos.

We are developing our economy. We will reduce our daily working hours to six and in the case of hard work to four hours. We feel that we are consolidated and because of this we do not fear helping you to develop your economy. Nobody can do as we do because the United States economy is based on competition . . .[1]

3. The President of the National Assembly of the United Arab Republic to Mr. Khruschev, 9 June 1961[2]

Your Excellency, Nikita Khrushchev, Premier of the Soviet Union:

Mr. Premier, I felt it my duty to send this brief letter to you, filled with my thanks, and those of the UAR Parliamentary delegation, for the cordiality and hospitality accorded us during our visit to the Soviet Union. We saw in this cordiality and hospitality a genuine portrayal of the friendship joining the Soviet and UAR peoples, the friendship that has been nurtured by experiences and events and increased by common understanding and mutual respect.

For us, the visit was an excellent opportunity which has enabled us to see for ourselves the splendid results of the struggle of the peoples of the Soviet Union, of their long patience, and of their unceasing endeavour to develop their system of living and subject the new horizons to the will of man. We have also felt the firm desire of the peoples of the Soviet Union to strengthen the policy of peaceful coexistence, on the grounds that it symbolises the concrete hope of protecting peace and preparing for a comprehensive agreement on disarmament.

Our tour of the Soviet Union strengthened our appraisal of the grand, leading role you play in serving your people, thus serving world evolution in general and pushing events towards the ultimate aim of promoting the welfare and well-being of mankind.

As a matter of fact, I did not wish to miss the opportunity, at the end of my visit to the Soviet Union, of marking down these impressions, for it is my duty to express them sincerely and truly. I also find it necessary to refer to our meeting with you 3rd May 1961, to the conversation we exchanged, and in particular to your address to the UAR Parliamentary delegation.[3]

I wish to emphasise to Your Excellency that we were tremendously pleased to meet you. We felt from your conversation with us, despite our disagreement with you in some parts of it, that you talked frankly to us about your beliefs and views, a matter which we greatly appreciate. Regarding our disagreement with you on several points of your talk, I felt that we ought to make some immediate remarks in defence of our view. Noting that such an action would be outside the limits

---

[1] The final phrase of the speech was not transmitted.
[2] *S.W.B.*, Part IV, 10 June 1961. The date is that of the publication of the letter in *Al-Ahram*.
[3] Above, p. 597.

of our task as a Parliamentary delegation visiting the Soviet Union, I thought it best to place our remarks at your disposal, particularly since: 1. Your Excellence chose to raise the question of the disagreement in our views when we had the honour of meeting you. 2. We had no chance of expressing our views, because we could not convert our meeting with you into an ideological controversy. 3. Our appreciation of your frankness with us requires a similar frankness on our part.

Mr. Premier, Allow me now to move our remarks about your talk with us. First I must point out that there are points in your talk on which we agree with you unreservedly. Your remarks about the ties of friendship which link our peoples, friendship which is based on political and economic co-operation and on an enlightened understanding of each other cultivated by your meetings with President Jamal Abd an-Nasir [sic] and Vice-President Abd al-Hakim Amir, earn our very strong approval. And your ideas about the High Dam, one of our people's greatest dreams being realised with the assistance of the Soviet Union, elicits our gratitude and appreciation. Finally, your comments about the accomplishments of the Soviet Union no one can deny. Many peoples observe them with obvious admiration and noticeable ardour. On all these matters we agree with you unreservedly. Our reservation concerns other topics of your conversation ranging over your opinion on our attitude towards communism, on our socialist trends, and on our devotion to Arab nationalism.

I wish here to record a preliminary remark, that our attitude towards communism, is restricted to our own country. It has been generated by the attitude which the communists have adopted towards the National Revolution. Outside the boundaries of our country our attitude is one based on complete respect for every ideology and its followers. Our disagreement with them in certain aspects by no means diminishes our respect for them as the followers of an ideology in which they believe. Our disagreement with them, if ever it comes to light, springs from our belief in the differences between nations and between the developments of their national history.

However, we have always felt that there are attempts to misrepresent our attitude towards communism in our country. I think the close ties of friendship which bind us to peoples following the communist doctrine, such as the great people of your country, the people of China, and the people of Yugoslavia, are a clear evidence of the truth. More evidence of the truth is our people's great esteem for several heroes and pioneers of the communist world, above all for Marx and Lenin. Your Excellency is one of the foremost personalities in the modern communist world who earns our people's appreciation.

Mr. Premier, We come now to the dispute topics of your talk, when we had the honour of meeting with you on 3rd May 1961. I will take the liberty of quoting your statements, as we heard them from the interpreter, and I will follow them with our remarks.

1. Your Excellency said: 'If our people live better than you, under the communist banner, then how can you declare yourselves averse to communism? The people will tell you: get out, we shall run our own affairs.'

Our remarks on this sentence are as follow: We feel, Your Excellency, that the logical basis of this sentence calls for discussion, for on the basis of this logic, the American people for example, can say to us: 'We live under the banners of capitalism better than you. How then can you advocate socialism?' In fact, using the same argument the American people can tell the Soviet people: 'We are still ahead of you in our standard of living, and consequently our system is better than yours.' This remark centres on the logical construction of the aforementioned sentence.

I also feel that we must take into consideration the comparison between the conditions of peoples and their subjective conditions. We must remember, for example, that the October Revolution has so far spent 43 years trying to achieve its results, while the Arab revolution began only eight years ago. We spent a large part of these years opposing imperialism and in fighting all sorts of horrible wars which imperialism launched against us: wars of nerves, wars of economy, and wars with arms. Yet, under all these circumstances, our people have so far been able to double their national income and to effect radical revolutionary changes in the distribution of the national income. We must also take into consideration the circumstances of imperialist oppression. Before the Revolution, Russia did not experience such oppression. It was one of the world's biggest powers, although its people had become victims of internal exploitation. As for us, both imperialist oppression and internal exploitation combined against us.

It is an established fact that the National Revolution enjoyed the overwhelming support of the people under the circumstances, as can be seen from the genuine sacrifices made by our people in shouldering the responsibilities of doubling the national income. They are now working to double this income every eight years.

2. Your Excellency said: 'You may think that I want to transform you from Arab nationalists into communists. Naturally I do not want to do this now. But I feel that some of those present here will be communists in the future because life imposes itself upon man. Communism consists of ideas and the ideas cannot be buried in prisons. Man may be imprisoned but he will remain a communist. The tsar imprisoned Lenin, for example, but Lenin built the biggest State and the people are living in freedom. I believe that you must not be surprised to see me praising communism to this extent. What else can I praise when I am the Secretary of the Communist Party? Shall I praise the American system? All these systems are past but communism is new. We work on socialist bases. You Arabs now realise this. You say that you seek socialism. But you do not know much about the socialism which leads to communism. As a scientific phenomenon, socialism is the first step to communism. You are still in the first stage of your thinking, if you want to build up socialism. You are like the one who studies the alphabet. You are studying the letter A. Socialism is the first letter of the alphabet of the organisation of the human society. The letter B is the beginning of communism. If you want socialism then you must not say that you are averse to communism. You are placing yourselves in a critical position and have fallen for the imperialist trap.'

Here are our remarks: The Arab nationalism in which we believe neither stands for narrow racialism nor for regional expansion which aims to acquire more land. It is the movement of a people who lived the same history and spoke the same language, and consequently acquired a unity of conscience and thinking.

In trying to eliminate the traces of industrial discrimination which imperialism imposed, Arab nationalism is also trying to do away with all the traces and vestiges which imperialism left on its lands and among its people.

We hope that your statement that you do not propose to transform us from Arab nationalists into communists will also (?apply) to the future, and that the word 'now' which occurred in your statement was only used figuratively without having any literal meaning. Like you, we believe that life will impose itself and that history will, in the end, have its say about the dogmatic experiment of each people in the pursuit of its high ideals.

We do not believe that prisons can make people discard their ideas. Perhaps one of the most cherished characteristics of our national revolution is that even under the most difficult circumstances, it preserved its white nature. If the measures adopted by our revolution were to be compared with the measures adopted by other revolutions for the protection of their aims, it would become evident that our ideas cannot be fought by prisons or bloodshed.

As regards capitalism and communism, we do not (?believe) that the historical development of man runs along the blind alley, of which capitalism is the beginning and communism is the imperative end. We believe that the field for ideological thinking is open to all peoples. All benefit from the rich ideological wealth of the entire human race and all add to the world experience their national assets, which are derived from the historical roots of each of them. The socialism we believe in is based, at the same time, on the liberation and freedom of the individual.

We aim at the destruction of exploitation and work for the elimination of class differences. We work to provide equal chances in the field of health, education, and work for all citizens. On this basis, we work to expand the foundation of the national wealth and to establish a just means for its distribution in a manner in which the individual and the society react to each other creatively. While the land in our country is owned by the peasants on an individual basis, with a maximum limit of ownership, the public ownership in the fields of industry and public utilities has reached 82 per cent of the total ownership in this sector.

Although we fully believe that the inter-class struggle [word indistinct] the society, we believe that the bloody character of the inter-class struggle can be avoided and that the imperative elimination of social anomalies can be accomplished within the framework of national unity. We also believe that there are a number of spiritual factors, including religion, which have their effects in addition to the accepted basis of material development.

As to our belief in Arab nationalism, we do not believe that it contradicts our belief in the unity of world destiny and the imminent solidarity of peoples under the principle of peaceful coexistence. Perhaps we are more sensitive than anybody else with regard to national motives because of two things: first, our belief in the need that our future development must emanate from the potential power of our people and from its suppressed needs and demands over the long centuries of oppression and exploitation; and second, the fact that we are newly experiencing independence and we are very anxious to preserve it, sometimes to the extent of sensitivity.

For all these reasons, we refuse capitalism not only because we hate it, but also because we believe that it contradicts the nature, circumstances, hopes, needs, and requirements of our people. But this refusal does not mean that communism, whose success was proved under the conditions prevalent in other people's countries can be applied and can succeed in our country. Our people refuse to be limited to this choice and believe that the scope of world thinking is now wider than these closed circuits. Our people believe that without isolating themselves from the wealth of world thinking they can, by their skill and creative power, add new things to this wealth. In fact, in its experience with us, imperialism has always fallen into the error that capitalism and communism are the only alternatives for each other. This error always justified, in its eyes, the launching of war against our socialist co-operative ideas and the branding of these ideas as steps leading to communism. From this point, imperialism used to attack the policy of non-alignment which we pursued in the international field and which is, in fact, a true reflection of our national beliefs.

Your Excellency: Because of my awareness of the honour you bestowed upon me when you frankly spoke to me of your views and beliefs, I found it my duty to place my remarks on the statements we heard from you, before you. I once more assert that our differences in views do not in any way whatsoever diminish our profound respect for your beliefs and for you personally. This is, at least, a practical application of the policy of peaceful co-existence for which the Soviet Union has sincerely proved it is working. The UAR has also proved by its actions in all its international relations and commitments that it is faithful to it.

Accept, your Excellency, my great love, respect, and sincere wishes for your good health and happiness, and for the glory and strength of the Soviet people. Signed: Anwar as-Sadat.

4. The Conference of Non-Aligned Countries, Belgrade, 2–6 September 1961

(i) *Address by the President of Ghana, Dr. Nkrumah, Belgrade, 2 September 1961*[1]

Mr. Chairman and Friends,

Humanity has arrived at the crossroads of destiny and we have met in Conference here in this ancient and historic city of Belgrade to decide whether we, the non-aligned nations, shall allow humanity to proceed on the way of tragedy and destruction or on the way of peace and reconstruction. For the first time in modern history a conference such as this has been summoned positively in the interests of peace—solely for peace and nothing else but peace.

We have met at a time when the international situation holds out most unhappy prospects for mankind and threatens the peace and security of the world. The climate of international relations today is gravely overcast by terrifying and ever darkening clouds in Algeria, Angola, South West Africa, South Africa, the Rhodesias, the Congo, Ruanda Urundi, Tunisia, Laos, Brazil, Goa, Korea, and in Germany. What a catalogue of misery, lament and devastation, and how significant it is that so much of this devastation should be taking place in Africa, Asia and Latin America.

Today we stand face to face with the Great Power blocs of the world, the East and the West. Both are committed, each to its own political and economic

---

[1] *Conference of Non-Aligned Countries*, Belgrade, 1961, pp. 98–106.

ideology. Both are militarily powerful and are increasing their military might with every scientific ingenuity. Both are increasingly suspicious of the thoughts and actions of each other. And yet these are the powers which have the power to ensure peace in our troubled world.

It is sad to think that two great communities are set out to destroy each other for no reasonable cause whatever. Furthermore, even if it were possible for any conflict to be restricted to these two power blocs only, it is sadder to think that there should be a conflict at all between them, since the power which they hold could otherwise be used in the peaceful interests of mankind. It is therefore the clear duty of those of us who are pledged to the pursuit of peace to work for the elimination of the causes of war. Let us from this Conference raise the resounding cry for peace. Let us utilize our power and influence to provide a fresh and vigorous outlook and approach to this problem of peace and war in our time. We have come here to interpose our influence between the two existent blocs, for we believe that the time has come when the fate and destiny of mankind should cease to hang so dangerously on the desires and ambitions of the Great Powers. We who have met here should be encouraged by the knowledge that we are echoing the choice of the great majority of the world's population, whose only desire is peace and progress. It is my hope that this Conference will achieve positive results and come out with a clear, bold, fearless and forthright declaration on the issue of peace and war.

Mr. Chairman, I would like to state, with your permission, what I believe to be the basic principles for a non-aligned and neutralist policy. Ghana stands for positive neutralism and non-alignment as against what I might describe as negative neutralism. Negative neutralism consists in believing that armed conflict between the Great Powers can only bring misery and destruction to those who participate in it. I consider this view to be entirely unrealistic. Those who hold it believe that in the world of today a state can secure its safety if it withdraws itself entirely from the international problems of peace and war and avoids taking a definite stand on issues which affect the balance of power in the world today.

Even though we are not here to constitute ourselves into a third bloc, yet, by this very Conference, we are constituting ourselves into a moral force, a distinct moral force which should be a balancing force and influence between the East and the West in the cause of peace. In this respect I propose that the countries that have met here should request their representatives at the United Nations to co-ordinate their efforts and co-operate in the implementation of policies which reflect the declarations or communiqués issued by this Conference. I believe that there exists a sufficient and intense identity of views among us to make it possible for us to act in concert in the complete eradication of colonialism, oppression and racial discrimination, in the achievement of a disarmament agreement, and generally in the cause of peace. Since nuclear war is likely to destroy all of us, whether we are the cause of it or not, negative neutralism is no shield at all; and in my view negative neutralism is a completely impracticable policy, and even dangerous. If ever war comes, the missiles and rockets cannot be prevented from reaching us at our non-aligned doors. Hence, our vested interest in peace. It is sheer madness for anyone to think of going to war in this nuclear age. Only the enemies of mankind can entertain the idea of war. I shudder to think of the horrors and destruction that would follow in the wake of a nuclear war. Imagine half a dozen hydrogen bombs, each equivalent to 100 million tons of T.N.T., dropped on Accra, New Delhi, London, Moscow, Cairo, Peking, New York or Berlin! Again, I shudder at the vision I see. Surely, neither the United States of America nor the Soviet Union could want war.

In this context, what are the problems that divide these two blocs so deeply so as to be incapable of solution and to which nuclear war must be the tragic answer? It is my firm conviction that, besides colonialism, overt or covert, no problem today is more urgent, more pressing than the problem of disarmament; and until this problem of disarmament has been resolved and a disarmament treaty has been signed, we cannot create the necessary atmosphere conducive to the preservation of peace.

Against the background of the present technological and scientific achievements of man, the question of complete and general disarmament becomes most pressing and urgent. As we meet today, America is spending an estimated amount of $47,966 million per year on defence and armaments alone. This is more than half the entire national budget of the nation. Three years ago, the United States Government spent $41,233 million on defence; in 1959–60, the amount of $41,250 million was so spent. Last year, 1960–1961, the figure was $43,211 million. About a month ago, at the request of President Kennedy, the American Congress voted a further increase of $3,454 million in defence expenditure for this year and early next year. Great Britain spent an estimated £1,502 million on defence alone in 1959–60; £1,670 million in 1960–61; and it is estimated to spend £1,655 million for the 1961–62 financial year.

On the other side, the Soviet Union is estimated to be spending equally huge sums of money for her defence programme. In 1959, the Soviet Union spent 96,100 million roubles on defence. Last year, the same amount was spent out of a national budget of 745,800 million roubles. It is a very disquieting experience to compare such vast expenditure on weapons of destruction with a budget expenditure of a country like Ghana of £200 million a year.

Is is not tragic that so much should be spent on armaments, when it has been estimated that one-tenth of the huge rate of expenditure involved would be enough to raise the whole of the less-developed world to the level of a self-sustaining economy?

When we talk of disarmament, we the non-aligned nations of Africa, Asia, Latin America and Europe do not merely draw attention to the destructiveness and madness of the armaments race; we draw attention to the vast possibilities now denied the people of the less developed areas for increased standards of living, the development of housing, agriculture and industry, the planning of cities and the eradication of illiteracy, ignorance, disease and want.

We have recently witness the spectacular conquest of space. It is not inconceivable that in the event of war man will be seriously tempted to extend his destructive operations into space. In that event, not only would the earth itself be destroyed but the inter-planetary world would also be involved in man's catastrophe, the consequences of which no one can yet predict.

I consider, therefore, that this Conference must formulate concrete and realistic proposals on disarmament and make serious representations to the two power blocs. This Conference should urge the Great Powers to sign without further delay a treaty for general and complete disarmament. Since the Great Powers suspect each other so much and since inspection and control on the spot appears to me to be one of the most effective means of obtaining concrete results, the Great Powers should agree to a system of inspection and control where the inspection teams are only composed of certain members of the uncommitted and non-aligned nations. It would eliminate all suspicion, create confidence in the inspection method and help solve this crucial and vital issue. I consider also that the non-aligned nations should be represented at all future conferences on disarmament, that disarmament should be total and complete and that all discussion on disarmament should be held under the auspices of the United Nations.

Mr. Chairman, it is vital to emphasize this problem of disarmament, and I suggest that this Conference should call upon the Powers of the world to disarm. They must disarm in order to ensure that they are unable to strike against each other. And, from this Conference, let us give them a positive maxim: 'If you want peace, stop preparing for war'. Why 'Peace, Peace'— and yet there is no peace?

Only last night, the Soviet Union exploded a nuclear device. This was a shock to me, as it must have been to you all. But it is a shock which forcibly brings home to us the supreme danger facing mankind, the imperative necessity for peace and the urgent need to sign a treaty for complete and general disarmament.

Mr. Chairman and Friends,

The present situation in Berlin creates serious and anxious moments for us all. The accusations and counter-accusations of the two power blocs and the virtual brandishing of arms on both sides is surely not calculated to be conducive to peace.

No one can deny, however, that Berlin is a real problem. It is sixteen years now since the last war came to an end and yet no peace treaty has been signed with Germany. In my view, the conclusion of a peace treaty with Germany is urgent and long overdue. It is imperative therefore that this Conference should carry a firm and positive resolution calling on the Great Powers to sign a peace treaty with Germany without further delay. On the German question let there be no hypocrisy. Everyone knows that there are two Germanies, created as a result of the last war. The circumstances which led to their creation continue to exist. Furthermore, two very different types of political and social systems have now evolved in the two countries—namely, the capitalist system and the socialist system—and this fact is so fundamental in any consideration of the German problem that to my mind it is only reasonable that the world should accept the present facts of the situation; that is to say, there is a State of West Germany and there is a State of East Germany. The nations of the world should therefore recognize the existence of these two States to enable them to co-exist peacefully. Such recognition, I am sure, would contribute tremendously to the preservation of peace.

It is not for us, of course, to advise on the question of German unification, but one could say with some frankness that the solution of this problem, if the Germans themselves are to achieve it without outside interference, must be isolated completely from the cold war. In other words, West Germany must withdraw from NATO and East Germany must withdraw from the Warsaw Pact. It is only then that the Germans themselves will be able to face the critical issues, whether by referendum or otherwise.

The other aspect of the German question, that is to say the issue of West Berlin, ought to present no difficulty at all. West Berlin, as it were, is a sort of island in the East German State. Access to it has been guaranteed over and over again by those who have authority to give such a guarantee. Other Western rights regarding West Berlin have also been emphatically guaranteed. What then is the meaning of these alarms over West Berlin? Must we, or rather must the world, be destroyed over this issue for which a real, ready solution could be found? I am sure that a little good will on both sides and a coming together round the table for peaceful negotiation would be sufficient to clear the war clouds now hanging thick over Europe and the world, and would enable the statesmen of the two power blocs to see the problem more realistically.

The frontiers of Germany as they stand today have existed for the past sixteen years. Any attempt to change these frontiers will lead to unnecessary provocation and is bound to lead to world conflict. The Oder-Neisse frontier which emerged from the last war should therefore be respected.

From this rostrum I make a strong appeal to my two friends, President Kennedy and Premier Nikita Khrushchev, the two men on whom more than on anyone else the fate of the world and mankind depends, to agree to meet again soon, somewhere, to talk about this problem. My Government is prepared to put Accra at their disposal for such a meeting. In any case, I suggest most seriously that this Conference should pass a resolution that if this German question and the Berlin issue continue to drag and linger as a threat to the peace and security of the world then these matters must be brought before the United Nations for solution. I make these proposals in the interest of mankind and of peace.

I now touch upon a question which is no less important than the problem of disarmament—the question of colonialism. As I have said again and again, the question of peace and war is only a reflection of other problems and no final solution to it can be reached unless a massive, deliberate and concerted effort is made to liquidate colonialism completely, thoroughly and finally.

Colonialism is fighting its last battle in Africa today. We speak with deep feeling because we have recent experience of the oppression and degradation which colonialism entails. It is distressing that in this age of enlightenment there should be foreign powers which still regard any territory in Africa as an extension of their own national boundaries, and which refuse to reconcile themselves to the inevitable march of history. It is indeed surprising that nations which regard themselves as civilized should acclaim the unfortunate survival of this pernicious system as a civilizing and useful mission.

What is the record of the so-called civilized nations which have indulged in colonialism and imperialism throughout the ages? From Roman times to the present day it is a shameful record of the most brutal travesty of human decency, dignity and self-respect, a notorious record of extortion of material wealth and distortion of human welfare; a record at once foul and revolting, a decadent system, no longer worthy of our generation and time. It is in recognition of these facts that the United Nations General Assembly has recently passed overwhelmingly a declaration not only condemning colonialism but also demanding the immediate liberation of all territories still under colonial rule.

I have stressed over and over again that colonialism is a fundamental cause of war, because it is an iniquitous system which generates intense hate and produces conflict between nation and nation. For not only is there conflict between the colonizers themselves, because in their eagerness to exploit the resources of the colonies they are driven into the rival camps of the 'haves' and 'have nots', and this becomes a constant source of threat to the peace of the world. Their own grabbing propensities involve them in a constant scramble, like crabs in a pot, climbing over each other's back in order to get the biggest helping. More often than not this scramble ends in physical fighting, with the loss of millions of innocent human lives. When we in Africa deprecate colonialism, therefore, we do this in the general interest of world peace. Colonialism and imperialism and the recent offshoot neo-colonialism, are dead evils which must be eradicated at all costs. Their continued existence makes them a perpetual threat to peace.

We in Ghana have stated time and again that our independence is meaningless unless it is linked up with the total liberation of Africa. The burning desire of the African peoples all over the continent for human rights, for dignity and for independence has never been so manifest as in the past few years.

We have seen the heroic struggle which still continues in Algeria, where the people are determined to regain their sovereignty as a free, independent and self-respecting community. We are familiar with the atrocities and the barbarous repression which the Portuguese have perpetrated on the people of Angola, killing them in thousands for the sake of the selfish economic benefits of Portugal. In South Africa, the masses of the people are struggling against a most pernicious and well organized foreign European minority, who look down on the non-white peoples as inferior and sub-human, with no more status than that of 'hewers of wood and drawers of water'.

We in Ghana are waging a relentless war against colonialism, and we shall not rest until every inch of African soil is free and independent. We must drum it again and again into the ears of those who refuse to listen that Africa is not an extension of Europe, and never will be.

The colonialists must be warned to keep their hands off Africa. Africa is wide awake and will no longer tolerate or submit to any form of domination whatsoever. Today, in the entire continent of Africa, from Algiers to Cape Town, from Lobito to Lusaka, Africa's Freedom Fighters are up in arms and will lay down their lives rather than their arms in the struggle for the total liquidation of colonialism. Protracted constitutional devices designed to defeat the attainment of freedom and independence will no longer be tolerated.

This Conference must urge the United Nations to see that its declaration on the liquidation of colonialism is implemented without further delay. In this regard the United Nations should organize plebiscites in all colonial territories based upon universal adult suffrage, one man one vote, in order to ensure success in this handing over operation. If the United Nations does not do this, peace is severely prejudiced.

I accordingly invite this Conference to endorse my proposal that by 31st December, 1962, all Colonial Powers should withdraw from Africa. It is in their own interest, and in the interest of world peace and security, that they should do so.

I have dwelt so long on the questions of colonialism, imperialism and neo-colonialism because of the fundamental issues which they pose for the peace and the prosperity of the world and mankind.

We know that new dangers threaten the independent African States. That is why we in Ghana have adopted a policy of consistent, persistent and vigorous advocacy of African unity. If Africa were united France would have thought twice before making her despicable attack on Bizerta, for an attack on one would constitute an attack on the African Union.

Under an All-African Union Government the economic development of the continent would present no insoluble problems, and Africa, one of the wealthiest of the continents, would then be able to pool her resources for the greatest good of her peoples and mankind. There would be a single and unified economic plan. Friendly competition among the various states composing the Union would result in the greatest good of the whole continent. Let the voice of every African and African leader ring out this call for unity, for Africa united would be another bulwark for world peace.

The political unification of Africa has assumed even greater importance in view of the new danger facing the continent in the form of the European Common Market. What is this Common Market if it is not a new design for reimposing Europe's domination and exploitation on Africa? Indeed, in a divided Africa each state would fall an easy prey to the greedy Colonial Powers who would swallow them all economically one after another; each state could be forced to enter into alliances and treaties with foreign powers leading to the balkanization of Africa, and thus make the continent a breeding ground for international conflicts and frustrate the realization of a permanent world peace.

This is why I have always opposed, without reservation, military pacts and alliances between African States and Colonial Powers and the establishment of foreign bases in Africa. As I said in my address to the Fifteenth Session of the United Nations General Assembly, Africa should be declared a nuclear-free zone, and I wish the same could apply to the Middle East. This would be a vital contribution to lasting peace.

I now turn to the United Nations. My Government and my people have placed their complete faith in this world organization, for it is our belief that it is the best forum where the many problems of the world, problems of war and peace, can be satisfactorily resolved. It is because of our faith in the United Nations that we are anxious to see it function effectively in the service of mankind. We want to see a United Nations organization fully representative of all the nations of the world, dedicated to the cause of peace, and where countries like my own are not only admitted as members but fully accepted. For my part, however, I seriously consider that the administrative structure of the United Nations in its present form is outmoded and does not reflect the true position and conditions of the world. Sixteen years ago, when the United Nations was set up, Asian, African and Latin American nationalism was of little consequence. Today, a most drastic change has brought to the fore a body of Afro-Asian countries who occupy more than a third of the United Nations seats and thus form a most influential group in the United Nations, representing the greatest majority of the world's population.

Gentlemen, let me repeat here the proposal which I have advanced already in respect of the post of Secretary-General of the United Nations, since we feel that the tragic experiences of the Congo should not be repeated. At that time I said that there should be a subordinate layer of three Deputy Secretaries General, one from the eastern camp, one from the western camp and the other from the uncommitted, non-aligned camp. This reflects the broad stream of political thought of today. Only thus can we restore confidence in the Secretary-Generalship and increase the efficiency and effectiveness of the Secretariat.

In addition to the Secretary-General I propose that there should be set up an executive body elected by the General Assembly whose duty it would be to ensure that the decisions of both the General Assembly and the Security Council would be faithfully and promptly implemented by the Secretariat, for it cannot be denied that an effective Secretariat, working in the true interest of the United Nations Organization, will contribute greatly to the maintenance of peace and security in the world. I invite this Conference to consider these proposals.

One cannot speak of the present structure of the United Nations without raising the anomaly of China's exclusion from this important world forum. With a population of over 650 million people, the People's Republic of China can be a great force for peace, and no discussions of international affairs can really make much sense without the contributions of this substantial portion of the world's population. The present attitude of the United Nations towards China is so unrealistic that one wonders how the United Nations can keep up this farcical situation for so long. The People's Republic of China is a great power and has a place in the counsels of the world and it is only just that she should take her rightful place so that the worthy objectives of bringing the nations together in consultation could be genuinely achieved. We must do everything we can to ensure that the delegation of the People's Republic of China is recognized as the only legal delegation and seated accordingly at the forthcoming Session of the United Nations.

Mr. Chairman, I now wish to re-state the various proposals I have made for the serious consideration of this Conference:

Firstly, we must stand for general and complete disarmament.

Secondly, the existence of two German states must be accepted and recognized.

Thirdly, we must call upon the Great Powers to ensure that a Peace Treaty is signed with Germany without further delay.

Fourthly, we must work for the complete liquidation of colonialism in all its forms and manifestations by the 31st December, 1962.

Fifthly, this Conference should resolve that three Deputies should be appointed for the Secretary-General of the United Nations—one to represent the eastern camp, one to represent the western camp and one to be chosen from the uncommitted non-aligned countries.

Sixthly, we must support the admission of the People's Republic of China at the forthcoming Session of the United Nations General Assembly.

Seventhly, Africa must be declared a nuclear-free zone.

Mr. Chairman, it has been said that 'Peace hath her victories no less renowned from War'. Today we can say without the slightest hesitation that war under any circumstances can never have any renown. All the glory of achievement belongs to peace, and modern man should dedicate himself, all his life and all his energies, to the pursuit of peace.

I have travelled in the West and I have travelled in the East. I can say that I have also travelled extensively in Africa and have visited Asia. Everywhere I have been, Mr. Chairman, the concrete evidence is that peace is construction and that war is destruction. What then is the choice before the world? I have not the slightest doubt that all sane men and all men of goodwill can have but one choice, and that is peace. East or West, if we pursue the true interests of the masses of the world this will not only put a stop to war and liquidate colonialism but will end all forms of exploitation and oppression of man by man and of nation by nation, resulting in peaceful co-existence, and the prosperity and happiness of mankind.

(ii) Address by the Prime Minister of India, Mr. Nehru, Belgrade, 2 September 1961[1]

Mr. Chairman, Distinguished Delegates,

Standing here before this distinguished assembly, I feel moved. I think of the past decades and I see many faces of old comrades and friends who devoted most of their life in the struggle for freedom, and many of them succeeded and many of them have passed away. I see younger faces too, representing their peoples, heads of newly free countries, and I see this great movement of freedom from colonial domination, led by many of the distinguished delegates here, going forward and meeting with success, indeed proving that, in so far as any historical perspective is concerned, the era of classic colonialism is gone and is though dead, of course it survives and gives a lot of trouble yet; but essentially it is over.

I think it was a happy and wise thought of the sponsors of this Conference to have convened it, and it has turned out to be an even happier thought because of subsequent developments. I am glad that we are meeting here in this pleasant and friendly city of Belgrade and more specially under the auspices of the Government and especially the leader, President Tito, of this Government and its people.

I said that it has become an even more important thing that we meet today; it would have been important in any event but it has become more important because of the developments of the last two or three months, when strange things have happened in the world and have suddenly drawn our attention to the abyss stretching out before us and below us. I think that the attention that this Conference has attracted in the world, it would have attracted anyhow; but that

[1] *Conference of Non-Aligned Countries*, Belgrade, 1961, pp. 107–17.

attention is much more today because we meet at this particular crisis in human destiny.

People all over the world are vastly interested to know what we think about this crisis, where our thoughts or actions are going to lead us, what advice we give, what pressure we may exercise in solving this crisis. It is well to remember this because today everything that we have contended against and that we are continuing to struggle against—imperialism, colonialism, racialism and the rest —things which are very important and to which reference has been made repeatedly here, all these things are somewhat over-shadowed by this crisis. For if war comes all else for the moment goes. Therefore it becomes inevitable for us to pay attention to, and not only to pay attention to but to make sure that the dominant note of our thinking and action and what we say and put down is this crisis that confronts humanity. People expect us to do this. The great Powers even also watch us and listen to us, and are watching for what we shall do, and I am quite sure that vast numbers of individuals in every country are thinking of this more even than of the normal subjects that rightly occupy our attention.

We call ourselves a conference of non-aligned countries. Now, the word non-aligned may be differently interpreted but basically it was used, and coined almost, with the meaning non-aligned with the great Power blocs of the world. Non-aligned has a negative meaning, but if you give it a positive connotation it means nations which object to this lining-up for war purposes—military blocs, military alliances and the like. Therefore we keep away from this and we want to throw our weight, such as it is, in favour of peace. In effect, therefore, when there is a crisis involving the possibility of war the very fact that we are unaligned should stir us to action, should stir us to thought, should stir us to feel that now more than ever it is up to us to do whatever we can to prevent such a calamity coming down upon us. So from every point of view and from the point of view of our inception and being as modern nations this problem is dominantly before us. I want to lay stress on this because, since we are engaged with many other difficult problems, which face us as a whole, which face us as individual countries, for all of us have problems, it is a little dangerous with this particular crisis that we might really repeat. I say so with all respect, all the other problems we have before us and put this major problem in the background. That, I think, would be little short of tragedy because we would have failed in our purpose, we would have failed to meet the demands made by humanity on us today when it is facing this crisis. And they will say: 'Yes, what they say is good, we agree, but how does it save us now, today, from the crisis that is the immediate problem? If this does not save us and war comes, what good will their long speeches and declaration have done?' That will be the answer of humanity.

I therefore submit that we must look at things in the proper perspective today. First things must come first, and nothing is more important or has more priority than this world situation of war and peace. Everything else, however vital to us— and other things are vital to us—has a secondary place. If, in this crisis, something we do, some action of ours or some words of ours, helps to some extent to resolve the problem, to remove the fear of war, then we have justified ourselves and strengthened ourselves in order to meet all the other problems that face us.

On the other hand, if we cannot face this matter straightforwardly and clearly in our own minds then somehow we fail mankind in this crisis, we give no lead. Of course we stand for anti-colonialism, anti-imperialism, anti-racialism, and all that. All our lives, the lives of most of us present here, have been spent in that and we shall continue the struggle, but nevertheless the point arises, at this particular crisis, as to what we are going to do. Pass long resolutions and make brave declarations? That is easy enough; we have done it before and we can do it today too; but what else can we do to meet the crisis, because the problem of war and peace has an intimate relation to all those other matters we stand for. It is war or the fear of war that has led to the cold war. It is the cold war which has resulted and is resulting in the old imperialism and the old colonialism hanging on wherever they exist because they deem it advantageous.

So what I wish with all respect to place before this assembly is this: that we must make first things first, and the first thing today is this fear of war, because ever since the last war there have been many ups and downs, many crises, many dangerous situations that have come up. We have got over them somehow or other, but the present situation is by far the most dangerous that has arisen in the last fifteen years or so since the last war ended.

It has become a commonplace for people in every country to refer to the dangers of modern nuclear warfare. Although we talk about it, I am not so sure that even those who talk about it fully and emotionally realize what this means. We talk about the destruction of civilization, the destruction of humanity, the destruction of the human race, if nuclear war comes. Well, if this is so, something much more is required, some greater effort, some greater attempt on our part to do what we can to avoid it. I know that the key to the situation does not lie in the hands of this Conference or in those of other congresses or conferences. The key to the situation today lies essentially in the hands of two great Powers—the United States of America and the Soviet Union. Nevertheless I think that this Conference, or rather the countries that are represented in this Conference, are not so helpless that they can look on while the world is destroyed and war is declared. I think we can make a difference—possibly we can, I cannot guarantee it—and if so we should try our utmost to do it and not talk about other subjects, even though they are important subjects, while the world goes to its doom. That is the thing I would beg this assembly to remember. And I would beg that, in whatever declaration it may make, this should be put foremost and topmost, and perhaps be isolated to show that it is the main thing, that other things may be very important but they are secondary. If this is done it will undoubtedly create a far greater impression than would a mere record of the various other problems that face us, although they are very important problems. I do not deny this, and we should act accordingly, but there is a time and a place to press any subject and today the time and the place and the occasion are here to take up this question of war and peace and make it our own and show the world that we stand for peace and that, so far as we can, we shall fight for it—not fight in the sense of guns, but struggle for it in the ways open to us.

I would like to lay stress on this right at the beginning of the few words that I wish to say to this assembly, because while on the one hand I see the power of the nations assembled here—which is not military power, which is not economic power, but which nevertheless is a power; call it moral force, call it what you will, it does make a difference, obviously, what we in our combined wisdom feel and think and what we are prepared to do—on the other hand, a fear creeps in upon my mind that we may not be able to get out of the rut of meeting together, passing long resolutions and making brave declarations, and then going home and allowing the world to drift to disaster. That itself will be a tragedy when so much is expected by our people, the people whom we represent here, and indeed by so many people outside in other countries who may not be represented here but who are looking up to us.

It is a strange thing that some few years ago—six, seven or eight, if you like—this business of non-alignment was a rare phenomenon. A few countries here and there talked about it and other countries rather made fun of it, or at any rate did not take it seriously. 'Non-alignment? What is this? You must be on this side or that side'. That was the argument. Well, that argument is dead today; nobody dare say that, because the whole course of history of the last few years has shown the growing opinion, the spread of this conception of non-alignment. Why is that so? Because it was in tune with the course of events; it was in tune with the thinking of vast numbers of people, whether the country concerned was non-aligned or not; it was in tune with it because they hungered passionately for peace and did not like this massing up of vast armies and nuclear bombs on either side. Therefore their minds turned to those countries who refused to line up with these people.

Maybe some of us did not approach this question with blank minds, this question of war and peace and whatever lies behind this cold war. We had our opinions, we had our inclinations, but essentially we were against this business of a cold war and all that it implied, and the massing up of weapons and bombs, etc. We talked, everybody talked, and still talk about disarmament. As my friend and colleague, President Nkrumah, has said, disarmament is a most vital thing. I entirely agree with him. The fact is that while we have talked about disarmament the world has gone on arming more and more.

What does all this mean? There is something wrong, some gap between our thinking and the action the world takes. The basic fact is that the world which has talked of disarmament month after month, year after year, has been arming more and more, and it has arrived almost at the final stage when either it disarms or it bursts. There is no choice left today, and in this field of manoeuvring the choice is getting more and more limited. When each party digs in its toes to particular positions, when each great country, even smaller countries, feel their national honour is involved it is difficult to move them. When big countries feel that their national honour is involved they risk war, whatever the consequences. That is what we are getting to. It is possible when these rigid attitudes are taken that an indication from this Conference and all those whom it represents—they are many and they count, in great parts of the world—a positive indication might have some slight effect on these great protagonists who, with their nuclear bombs, threaten each other, and incidentally threaten all of us, because it is now known very well that the effects of war will not be confined to those great Powers or their lives, but other countries which are not in the war will also suffer. Presumably if war comes the countries represented here will not rush into the war; they will remain apart. But what good will it do them to remain apart when they will suffer from it, and when the whole world will suffer?

Therefore, we have arrived at the position today where there is no choice. Well, to say there is no choice between war and peace sounds rather fatuous. I put it this way: there is no choice left between an attempt, between negotiations for peace or war. If people refuse to negotiate they must inevitably go to war. There is no choice. They must negotiate, and I am amazed and surprised that rigid, proud attitudes are taken up by great countries, all being too high and mighty to negotiate for peace. I submit with all humility to them and to others that this is not a right attitude, because it is not their pride that is involved in it but the future of the human race.

I cannot—and I rather doubt if even this assembly can—go into these matters and suggest, 'You must negotiate on these lines', or 'You must come to terms on these lines'. I do not think that is possible for us, or suitable. We may have our ideas, and when the time comes we may even say so, but our indicating 'These are the lines for your settlement, for negotiation' instead of helping may hinder, because we are dealing with proud nations and they may react wrongly. Therefore, we cannot really lay down any terms on which they should negotiate. But it is our duty and function to say that they must negotiate, and any party that does not do so does tremendous injury to the human race.

I am not talking about basic agreements between rival ideas, rival ideologies and rival attempts to increase the power of a nation. I do not think that by one stroke you can solve all these problems, or that anybody can. But at the present juncture one has to see how to lessen these tensions, how at least to remove some of the obstructions to peace, how at least to prevent war coming. If that is done, then other steps will naturally follow.

I believe firmly that the only possible way ultimately to solve these problems, or many of them, is by complete disarmament. Yet it would be absurd for me to say, 'In the next week or month, decide on complete disarmament' because it is not a practicable proposition. Today the situation is such that their fears from each other are leading them towards greater armaments all the time, whether you look at one side or the other. Therefore, although I consider disarmament an absolute necessity for the peace of the world in the future—I think that without disarmament these difficulties, fears and conflicts will continue— nevertheless one cannot expect suddenly, because this Conference wants it, disarmament to appear on the scene in full panoply. We should lay stress on disarmament, of course, but for the present moment the only thing that we can do is to lay stress on the fact of negotiations with a view to getting over these present fears and dangers. If that is done, the next and third step follows and may be taken.

I would venture to say that it is not for us even to lay down what should be done in regard to Germany or Berlin, which are the immediate causes of this present tension. There are some things that seem to me obvious. For instance— and others have referred to it too—it seems to me obvious that certain facts of life should be recognized. The facts of life are, first, that there are two independent entities, powers, countries: the Government of Western Germany (the Federal Republic of Germany) and the Government of Eastern Germany (the

German Democratic People's Republic). That is a fact of life: it is not a matter of my or anyone else's liking or disliking it; it is a fact that has to be recognized. If you ignore the facts of life and the facts of contemporary politics that means that you are ignoring something which will lead you to wrong results.

The second thing (I am expressing my own opinion for the moment) is that as things are we find this great city of Berlin divided by what might be called an international frontier. It is a very awkward situation, but there it is. But anyhow West Berlin is very closely allied to Western Germany, to the Western countries, and they have had these routes of access to them, and I am glad that Mr. Khrushchev himself has indicated that that access will not be limited; it will be open to them as it is now. Now if that is made perfectly clear and guaranteed by all concerned I should imagine that one of the major fears and major causes of conflict will be removed.

I am merely putting this forward to indicate how some of the big things that are troubling people are capable of solution without solving the entire problem. If some things are understood and agreed to definitely, immediately, the fear of war in the near future disappears. Other things can be considered later. So I venture to say that the most important thing for the world today is for these great Powers directly concerned to meet together and negotiate with the will to peace, and not to stand too much on their respective prestige; and I think that if this Conference throws its weight on that, as I am sure it must be prepared to do, it will be a positive step which we take to help.

Take again the United Nations. As far as I remember, when the United Nations was formed one of its early articles said it was formed to save succeeding generations from the scourge of war. That was the main purpose of the United Nations—to save humanity from the scourge of war. Here is a situation arising which threatens war very definitely. What will the United Nations do about it?

I remember I was in Geneva in 1938, in the summer or the autumn, and the old League of Nations was meeting there when the whole of Europe was tense with fear of war. War came a year later, but even in 1938 it was tense because Hitler was marching this way and that way all over Europe. He went to Czechoslovakia and held it and he went to some other place, advancing all the time. There was this fear of war lying all over Europe, but the League of Nations in Geneva was discussing at that time I think the opium traffic. Very important, the opium traffic, undoubtedly; but something else was more important than the opium traffic, and that was war. And war came a year later. It was postponed only: it came in 1939.

Now I do not want the United Nations to function as the League of Nations did. I do not think it will, but I merely mention this. What can the United Nations do? The whole framework of the United Nations, ever since it was formed fifteen years ago, was the recognition of the balance of power in the world. That is why they had certain permanent members in the Security Council vetoing, etc.—all that business. Now of course the world has changed since then, considerably, and there are many more members and this requires a change in the structure, etc., of the United Nations. That is true. Nevertheless the United Nations cannot easily ignore the balance of power in the world. It has to keep that in view. Anyhow, the point is that it is the duty of the United Nations to consider this matter and try its utmost to solve it.

The United Nations meets from time to time for special causes, special discussions. I would have suggested, if it was not meeting as it is, I think, in about two weeks time (or less), its meeting quickly to consider these matters. I am not suggesting the United Nations should sit down and consider Germany, Berlin and all that. No. I say it should meet to consider a situation which might lead to war and take such steps, in its united wisdom, as it can. Fortunately it is meeting. I should say one of the earliest things it should do is to deal with this problem. All other problems are secondary: it should postpone them, or put them lower down on its agenda.

Now I feel strongly that this matter requires our urgent attention and the urgent attention of every government and every organization in the world. Since it so happens by accident—or that circumstances have so dealt with us—that we in this Conference are meeting at this time of grave crisis, we should seize hold of it in so far as we can. I recognize that we cannot issue mandates. I think we are an important Conference. I think we represent countries which individually, and certainly jointly, represent something important and valuable in the world and our voice counts to some extent. That is true.

At the same time we must not overestimate our own importance. After all, we do not control the strings of the world, not only in the military sense but in other senses also. If our mandate ran it would be easy enough—we would issue the mandate. But we know that our mandate does not run all over the place. So we must realize that. We must realize both our actual and our potential strength that we have, and also the lack of strength that we have. Both have to be considered together, when we should decide what to do.

So I am venturing to suggest not any specific course of action but rather a mental outlook that should govern us in approaching this problem: that we should think of this as the most vital and important problem of the day and everything else as being secondary, however important it is. We can deal with other things more effectively and more strongly after we have dealt with this. Otherwise no other problem remains: they are submerged in the terrible disaster of war.

That is the main point I should like to place before this assembly.

Now, Sir, may I add here that this danger of war comes nearer and nearer, has been enhanced and has become nearer to us, perhaps, by the recent decision of the Soviet Government to start nuclear tests. Now I am not in a position, and I suppose no one else here is in a position, to know all the facts which underline these decisions—all the military considerations, political, non-political considerations, whatever they may be—but one thing I know: that this decision makes the situation much more dangerous. That is obvious to me; therefore I regret it deeply because it may well lead to other countries also starting this and then, apart from the danger inherent in nuclear tests—that is radioactive substances falling and all that—all this brings us to the very verge and precipice of war. That is why I deeply regret it, and because of all this it has become even more urgent that this process of negotiation should begin without any delay, without thinking of who is going to ask whom first. The person who asks first will deserve credit; not the person who shrinks from asking others.

I should just like to refer, briefly, I hope, to some of our other problems. Many of the countries represented here have only recently become free or independent. They have tremendous problems and, above all, the problem of making good and to advance their own people, economically, socially, etc., because we must recognize that most of these countries are under-developed—nearly all. We must recognize that they are socially and economically backward countries, and it is not an easy matter to get rid of this inheritance of backwardness and under-development. It requires clear thinking. It requires action. It requires a tremendous amount of hard work, and all of us have to face that. I think that it is right and proper that other countries, the affluent countries, the rich countries, should help in this process. They should do it. They have to some extent done it. I think they should do more of it, but whatever they may do the ultimate burden will lie on the people of our own countries. If it did not, if by some miracle or somebody else's help we stood up, well we would fall down again. When you stand up, you do not stand long when you do not have the strength. The ultimate burden is on us. So it is no good expecting others to do all of our work.

Therefore, this great problem faces each one of our countries, and in facing it we have to think of this modern world which has not only changed greatly but which is changing from day to day: this world of atomic energy and jet and space travel, new forces being let loose and the tremendous value and importance of science today. We have to think of that. We cannot just imitate somebody else and put a little machine here, a machine there, and think we are making progress. We have to catch up with the modern world and with science and technology, keeping our own values intact, I hope.

All these problems can overwhelm us. Why I am venturing to refer to obvious things is that really in considering our other problems we may keep these basic things in view.

There are other countries, some represented here; others whom we know very well which are struggling for their freedom from grasping colonialism or imperialism which will not go. There is Algeria, which has paid a fantastic price in human life and suffering in its struggle for freedom and yet which has not so far succeeded in achieving it. Naturally, everyone present here is wholly desirous of Algeria becoming independent, and I earnestly hope that this will be so.

There is Tunisia, with its recent extraordinary experience, and I am referring particularly to Bizerta.[1] Why Bizerta? Because Bizerta is a foreign base, and the very idea of a foreign base in a country seems quite extraordinary to me. It is bad enough to have bases anyway, but that a country should put its foreign base in another country seems quite extraordinary to me. How can that be tolerated by anybody? I do not understand how anyone can provide for a base in a country which opposes that base, purely from the practical point of view.

There are these problems of Africa, the Congo, and may I say I am glad to learn that possibly by tomorrow we shall have here in this assembly the Prime Minister and the Deputy Prime Minister of the Congo Republic, Mr. Adouala and Mr. Gizenga. There is Angola, the horror of Angola. I do not know how many of the delegates present here have had occasion to read the detailed

[1] See also below, pp. 797–807.

accounts of what has happened in Angola, because Angola has been a closed book. But something is happening in Angola—not only in Angola but round about—which really has a kind of horror which one hardly associates with the modern world—massacres, genocide, and so on. Of course, our minds go out, and we need not only to sympathize; we want to do what we can to put an end to this. Yet we cannot do very much as a rule, although sometimes we may do a little. All these problems face us.

Then there is the situation in East Africa, where conditions are better, of course, and to some extent some countries have been promised independence, such as Tanganyika, I believe, by December, and other countries I hope also. There is the situation in Central Africa—the Rhodesias—where the picture is not good; there is trouble. And further south, in South Africa, you have the supreme symbol of racial arrogance, racial discrimination, *apartheid* and all that, which is an intolerable position to be accepted by any of us. And this is imposed upon South West Africa, in challenge to the United Nations decisions. So all these problems crowd upon us and we have to face them, of course.

For the moment, however, I would repeat that whatever we may do about the other problems—and we should do whatever we can—the problem dominating the issue today is that of this danger of war. The danger of war depends on many factors, but essentially on two major countries, the United States of America and the Soviet Union. It will do us no good, I think, if we start condemning this country or that country. It is not a very easy thing to do anyhow; it has a complicated set of circumstances. But apart from being easy or difficult, if we are to be peacemakers and if we want to help in the cause of peace, it does not help to start by condemnations. We want to win over and to influence and induce them to follow the path of peace, and if we denounce the countries then we cannot influence them, whatever else we can do. We cannot win them over. The times demand, therefore, that we should approach these countries and other countries in a friendly way, in a way to win them over and not merely to denounce them and irritate them and make it even more difficult for them to follow the path we indicate to them.

Let us look at this world today. It is a strange world, perhaps the most fundamental fact of the world being the coming out of these new mighty forces. I am referring to atomic energy, space travel and all that, which is the basic factor of the modern world. We have to think in terms of that, and not get lost in the terms of a world which is past and in slogans that no longer apply. But this is the world that we live in. When power of a new kind comes, all your imperialism and all your old-style colonialism will vanish and will go, I have no doubt. And yet this new power may well dominate over us and dominate certainly the under-developed backward countries, because the sin of backwardness has to pay the penalty by somebody pushing you about. We cannot afford to be backward, therefore we have to build in our own countries societies of free men, societies where freedom is real—because I do think freedom is essential, that freedom will give us strength—prosperous societies where the standards of living are rising. These are for us the essential, basic problems to be thought out in terms of today, in terms of the modern world, space travel, jet travel, atomic energy, not in terms of long ago. When you think in these terms war becomes an even greater folly and anachronism then ever. If we cannot prevent war then for the moment all our other problems are sunk, we cannot deal with them. But if we can prevent war we can go ahead on our other problems, help to liberate parts of the world under colonial and other imperial rule, and more especially build up our own free societies, prosperous societies, welfare states, in our respective countries, because that is to be our positive work. Merely getting angry with some other country achieves nothing, although one does get angry and cannot help it. It is the positive constructive work we do that gives us strength to make our countries free. That is the positive work we have to do.

But we cannot do any of this unless there is no war. If war comes all is doomed. Therefore I venture to submit to this assembly that we must lay the greatest stress on this major danger of today. Not only is this incumbent on us but if we do this we shall be in line with the thinking of millions and millions of people. Strength comes ultimately from being in line with popular thinking. The fact that we are non-aligned has received strength from the fact that millions of people are not aligned, they do not want war, that is why we get indirect strength from this. Today this is the problem of practically the entire population of the world. Let us put ourselves in line with it and deal with it as well as we can, realizing fully of course that our capacity is limited. We must not imagine that we can order about great countries or as small countries do as we like. Our capacity is limited, but we have a certain capacity, a certain strength, call it what you like, moral strength, or other strength. Let us use it properly, rightly, without force but with courtesy and with a friendly approach so that we may influence those who have the power of war and peace in their hands, and thus try if not to prevent war for all time at any rate to push it away so that in the meantime the world may learn the better use of co-operation. Then ultimately the world may put an end to war itself.

I will repeat that I think that essentially we can never succeed unless there is disarmament on the biggest scale. Therefore disarmament is a vital matter, but even that is rather out of reach today, because how can we talk of disarmament when we are told that we are going to have nuclear tests today and tomorrow, and when we are told that all these great countries are becoming more and more heavily armed?

I have ventured to express some of the ideas in my mind. I have not dealt with the various items on the agenda because I feel that the first item overshadows all else. The others should be dealt with no doubt and I hope that when this matter comes up and some kind of resolution or declaration or statement is being issued attention will be paid to this question of world peace being put not only foremost but so that it catches every person's attention and so that it does not get lost in a morass of detail and thus lose all significance and importance.

(iii) *Final Declaration of the delegates to the Belgrade Conference, 6 September 1961*[1]

The Conference of Heads of State or Government of the following non-aligned countries:

---

[1] *Conference of Non-Aligned Countries*, Belgrade, 1961, pp. 253–61.

1. Afghanistan	13. Indonesia
2. Algeria	14. Iraq
3. Burma	15. Lebanon
4. Cambodia	16. Mali
5. Ceylon	17. Morocco
6. Congo	18. Nepal
7. Cuba	19. Saudia Arabia
8. Cyprus	20. Somalia
9. Ethiopia	21. Sudan
10. Ghana	22. Tunisia
11. Guinea	23. United Arab Republic
12. India	24. Yemen

25. Yugoslavia

and of the following countries represented by observers:

1. Bolivia   2. Brazil   3. Ecuador

was held in Belgrade from September 1 to 6, 1961, for the purpose of exchanging views on international problems with a view to contributing more effectively to world peace and security and peaceful co-operation among peoples.

The Heads of State or Government of the aforementioned countries have met in a moment when international events have taken a turn for the worst and when world peace is seriously threatened. Deeply concerned for the future of peace, voicing the aspirations of the vast majority of people of the world, aware that, in our time, no people and no government can or should abandon its responsibilities in regard to the safeguarding of world peace, the participating countries—having examined in detail, in an atmosphere of equality, sincerity and mutual confidence, the current state of international relations and trends prevailing in the present-day world—make the following declaration:

The Heads of State or Government of non-aligned countries noting that there are crises that lead towards a world conflict in the transition from an old order based on domination to a new order based on co-operation between nations, founded on freedom, equality and social justice for the promotion of prosperity; considering that the dynamic processes and forms of social change often result in or represent a conflict between the old established and the new emerging nationalist forces; considering that a lasting peace can be achieved only if this confrontation leads to a world where the domination of colonialism-imperialism and neo-colonialism in all their manifestations is radically eliminated;

and recognizing the fact that acute emergencies threatening world peace now exist in this period of conflict in Africa, Asia, Europe and Latin America and big power rivalry likely to result in world conflagration cannot be excluded;

that to eradicate basically the source of conflict is to eradicate colonialism in all its manifestations and to accept and practise a policy of peaceful co-existence in the world;

that guided by these principles the period of transition and conflict can lay a firm foundation of co-operation and brotherhood between nations, state the following:

I

War has never threatened mankind with graver consequences than today. On the other hand, never before has mankind had at its disposal stronger forces for eliminating war as an instrument of policy in international relations.

Imperialism is weakening. Colonial empires and other forms of foreign oppression of peoples in Asia, Africa and Latin America are gradually disappearing from the stage of history. Great successes have been achieved in the struggle of many peoples for national independence and equality. In the same way, the peoples of Latin America are continuing to make an increasingly effective contribution to the improvement of international relations. Great social changes in the world are further promoting such a development. All this not only accelerates the end of the epoch of foreign oppression of peoples, but also makes peaceful co-operation among peoples, based on the principles of indepedence and equal rights, an essential condition for their freedom and progress.

Tremendous progress has been achieved in the development of science, techniques and in the means of economic development.

Prompted by such developments in the world, the vast majority of people are becoming increasingly conscious of the fact that war between peoples constitutes not only an anachronism but also a crime against humanity. This awareness of peoples is becoming a great moral force, capable of exercising a vital influence on the development of international relations.

Relying on this and on the will of their peoples, the Governments of countries participating in the Conference resolutely reject the view that war, including the cold war, is inevitable, as this view reflects a sense both of helplessness and hopelessness and is contrary to the progress of the world. They affirm their unwavering faith that the international community is able to organize its life without resorting to means which actually belong to a past epoch of human history.

However, the existing military blocs, which are growing into more and more powerful military, economic and political groupings, which, by the logic and nature of their mutual relations, necessarily provoke periodical aggravations of international relations. The cold war and the constant and acute danger of its being transformed into actual war have become a part of the situation prevailing in international relations.

For all these reasons, the Heads of State or Government of non-aligned countries wish, in this way, to draw the attention of the world community to the existing situation and to the necessity that all peoples should exert efforts to find a sure road towards the stabilization of peace.

II

The present-day world is characterized by the existence of different social systems. The participating countries do not consider that these differences constitute an insurmountable obstacle for the stabilization of peace, provided attempts at domination and interference in the internal development of other peoples and nations are ruled out.

All peoples and nations have to solve the problems of their own political, economic, social and cultural systems in accordance with their own conditions, needs and potentialities.

Furthermore, any attempt at imposing upon peoples one social or political system or another by force and from outside is a direct threat to world peace.

The participating countries consider that under such conditions the principles of peaceful co-existence are the only alternative to the cold war and to a possible general nuclear catastrophe. Therefore, by these principles which include the right of peoples to self-determination, to independence and to the free determination of the forms and methods of economic, social and cultural development—must be the only basis of all international relations.

Active international co-operation in the fields of material and cultural exchanges among peoples is an essential means for the strengthening of confidence in the possibility of peaceful co-existence among States with different social systems.

The participants in the Conference emphasize, in this connexion, that the policy of co-existence amounts to an active effort towards the elimination of historical injustices and the liquidation of national oppression, guaranteeing, at the same time, to every people their independent development.

Aware that ideological differences are necessarily a part of the growth of the human society, the participating countries consider that peoples and Governments shall refrain from any use of ideologies for the purpose of waging cold war, exercising pressure, or imposing their will.

III

The Heads of State or Government of non-aligned countries participating in the Conference are not making concrete proposals for the solution of all international disputes, and particularly disputes between the two blocs. They wish, above all, to draw attention to those acute problems of our time which must be solved rapidly, so that they should not lead to irreparable consequences.

In this respect, they particularly emphasize the need for a great sense of responsibility and realism when undertaking the solution of various problems resulting from differences in social systems.

The non-aligned countries represented at this Conference do not wish to form a new bloc and cannot be a bloc. They sincerely desire to co-operate with any Government which seeks to contribute to the strengthening of confidence and peace in the world.

The non-aligned countries wish to proceed in this manner all the more so as they are aware that peace and stability in the world depend, to a considerable extent, on the mutual relations of the Great Powers.

Aware of this, the participants in the Conference consider it a matter of principle that the Great Powers take more determined action for the solving of various problems by means of negotiations, displaying at the same time the necessary constructive approach and readiness for reaching solutions which will be mutually acceptable and useful for world peace.

The participants in the Conference consider that, under present conditions, the existence and the activities of non-aligned countries in the interests of peace are one of the more important factors for safeguarding world peace.

The participants in the Conference consider it essential that the non-aligned countries should participate in solving outstanding international issues concerning peace and security in the world as none of them can remain unaffected by or indifferent to these issues.

They consider that the further extensions of the non-committed area of the world constitutes the only possible and indispensable alternative to the policy of total division of the world into blocs, and intensification of cold war policies. The non-aligned countries provide encouragement and support to all peoples fighting for their independence and equality.

The participants in the Conference are convinced that the emergence of newly-liberated countries will further assist in narrowing of the area of bloc antagonisms and thus encourage all tendencies aimed at strengthening peace and promoting peaceful co-operation among independent and equal nations.

1. The participants in the Conference solemnly reaffirm their support to the 'Declaration on the Granting of Independence to Colonial Countries and Peoples', adopted at the 15th Session of the General Assembly of the United Nations[1] and recommend the immediate unconditional, total and final abolition of colonialism and resolved to make a concerted effort to put an end to all types of new colonialism and imperialist domination in all its forms and manifestations.

2. The participants in the Conference demand that an immediate stop be put to armed action and repressive measures of any kind directed against dependent peoples to enable them to exercise peacefully and freely their right to complete independence and that the integrity of their national territory should be respected. Any aid given by any country to a colonial power in such suppression is contrary to the Charter of the United Nations.

The participating countries respecting scrupulously the territorial integrity of all states oppose by all means any aims of annexation by other nations.

3. The participating countries consider the struggle of the people of Algeria for freedom, self-determination and independence, and for the integrity of its national territory including the Sahara, to be just and necessary and are, therefore, determined to extend to the people of Algeria all the possible support and aid. The Heads of State or Government are particularly gratified that Algeria is represented at this Conference by its rightful representative, the Prime Minister of the Provisional Government of Algeria.

4. The participating countries drew attention with great concern to the developments in Angola and to the intolerable measures of repression taken by the Portuguese colonial authorities against the people of Angola and demand that an immediate end should be put to any further shedding of blood of the Angolan people and the people of Angola should be assisted by all peace-loving, countries, particularly member states of the United Nations, to establish their free and independent state without delay.

5. The participants in the Conference demand the immediate termination of all colonial occupation and the restoration of the territorial integrity to the rightful people in countries in which it has been violated in Asia, Africa and Latin America as well as the withdrawal of foreign forces from their national soil.

[1] *Documents*, 1960, pp. 404–6.

6. The participating countries demand the immediate evacuation of French armed forces from the whole of the Tunisian territory in accordance with the legitimate right of Tunisia to the exercise of its full national sovereignty.

7. The participating countries demand that the tragic events in the Congo must not be repeated and they feel that it is the duty of the world community to continue to do everything in its power in order to erase the consequences and to prevent any further foreign intervention in this young African state, and to enable the Congo to embark freely upon the road of its independent development based on respect for its sovereignty, unity and its territorial integrity.

8. The participants in the Conference resolutely condemn the policy of apartheid practised by the Union of South Africa and demand the immediate abandonment of this policy. They further state that the policy of racial discrimination anywhere in the world constitutes a grave violation of the Charter of the United Nations and the Universal Declaration of Human Rights.

9. The participating countries declare solemnly the absolute respect of the rights of ethnic or religious minorities to be protected in particular against crimes of genocide or any other violation of their fundamental human rights.

10. The participants in the Conference condemn the imperialist policies pursued in the Middle East, and declare their support for the full restoration of all the rights of the Arab people of Palestine in conformity with the Charter and resolutions of the United Nations.

11. The participating countries consider the establishment and maintenance of foreign military bases in the territories of other countries, particularly against their express will, a gross violation of the sovereignty of such States. They declare their full support to countries who are endeavouring to secure the vacation of these bases. They call upon those countries maintaining foreign bases to consider seriously their abolition as a contribution to world peace.

12. They also acknowledge that the North American military base at Guantanamo, Cuba, to the permanence of which the Government and people of Cuba have expressed their opposition, affects the sovereignty and territorial integrity of that country.

13. The participants in the Conference reaffirm their conviction that:

(a) All nations have the rights of unity, self-determination, and independence by virtue of which right they can determine their political status and freely pursue their economic, social and cultural development without intimidation or hindrance.

(b) All peoples may, for their own ends, freely dispose of their natural wealth and resources without prejudice to any obligations arising out of international economic co-operation, based upon the principle of mutual benefit, and international law. In no case may a people be deprived of its own means of subsistence.

The participating countries believe that the right of Cuba as that of any other nation to freely choose their political and social systems in accordance with their own conditions, needs and possibilities should be respected.

14. The participating countries express their determination that no intimidation, interference or intervention should be brought to bear in the exercise of the right of self-determination of peoples, including their right to pursue constructive

and independent policies for the attainment and preservation of their sovereignty.

15. The participants in the Conference consider that disarmament is an imperative need and the most urgent task of mankind. A radical solution of this problem, which has become an urgent necessity in the present state of armaments, in the unanimous view of participating countries, can be achieved only by means of a general, complete and strictly and internationally controlled disarmament.

16. The Heads of State or Government point out that general and complete disarmament should include the elimination of armed forces, armaments, foreign bases, manufacture of arms as well as elimination of institutions and installations for military training, except for purposes of internal security; and the total prohibition of the production, possession and utilization of nuclear and thermo-nuclear arms, bacteriological and chemical weapons as well as the elimination of equipment and installations for the delivery and placement and operational use of weapons of mass destruction on national territories.

17. The participating countries call upon States in general, and States exploring outer space at present in particular, to undertake to use outer space exclusively for peaceful purposes. They expressed the hope that the international community will, through collective action, establish an international agency with a view to promote and co-ordinate the human actions in the field of international co-operation in the peaceful uses of outer space.

18. The participants in the Conference urge the Great Powers to sign without further delay a treaty for general and complete disarmament in order to save mankind from the scourge of war and to release energy and resources now being spent on armaments to be used for the peaceful economic and social development of all mankind. The participating countries also consider that:

(a) The non-aligned Nations should be represented at all further world conferences on disarmament;

(b) All discussions on disarmament should be held under the auspices of the United Nations;

(c) General and complete disarmament should be guaranteed by an effective system of inspection and control, the teams of which should include members of non-aligned Nations.

19. The participants in the Conference consider it essential that an agreement on the prohibition of all nuclear and thermo-nuclear tests should be urgently concluded. With this aim in view, it is necessary that negotiations be immediately resumed, separately or as part of negotiations on general disarmament. Meanwhile, the moratorium on the testing of all nuclear weapons should be resumed and observed by all countries.

20. The participants in the Conference recommend that the General Assembly of the United Nations should, at its forthcoming session, adopt a decision on the convening either of a special session of the General Assembly of the United Nations devoted to discussion of disarmament or on the convening of a world disarmament conference under the auspices of the United Nations with a view to setting in motion the process of general disarmament.

21. The participants in the Conference consider that efforts should be made

to remove economic imbalance inherited from colonialism and imperialism. They consider it necessary to close, through accelerated economic, industrial and agricultural development, the ever-widening gap in the standards of living between the few economically advanced countries and the many economically less-developed countries. The participants in the Conference recommend the immediate establishment and operation of a United Nations Capital Development Fund. They further agree to demand a just terms of trade for the economically less-developed countries and, in particular, constructive efforts to eliminate the excessive fluctuations in primary commodity trade and the restrictive measures and practices which adversely affect the trade and revenues of the newly-developing countries. In general, to demand that the fruits of the scientific and technological revolution be applied in all fields of economic development to hasten the achievement of international social justice.

22. The participating countries invite all the countries in the course of development to co-operate effectively in the economic and commercial fields so as to face the policies of pressure in the economic sphere, as well as the harmful results which may be created by the economic blocs of the industrial countries. They invite all the countries concerned to consider to convene, as soon as possible an international conference to discuss their common problems and to reach an agreement on the ways and means of repelling all damage which may hinder their development; and to discuss and agree upon the most effective measures to ensure the realization of their economic and social development.

23. The countries participating in the Conference declare that the recipient countries must be free to determine the use of the economic and technical assistance which they receive, and to draw up their own plans and assign priorities in accordance with their needs.

24. The participating countries consider it essential that the General Assembly of the United Nations should, through the revision of the Charter, find a solution to the question of expanding the membership of the Security Council and of the Economic and Social Council in order to bring the composition and work of these two most important organs of the General Assembly into harmony with the needs of the Organization and with the expanded membership of the United Nations.

25. The unity of the world Organization and the assuring of the efficiency of its work make it absolutely necessary to evolve a more appropriate structure for the Secretariat of the United Nations, bearing in mind equitable regional distribution.

26. Those of the countries participating in the Conference who recognize the Government of the People's Republic of China recommend that the General Assembly in its forthcoming Session should accept the representatives of the Government of the People's Republic of China as the only legitimate representatives of that country in the United Nations.

27. The countries participating in the Conference consider that the German problem is not merely a regional problem but liable to exercise a decisive influence on the course of future developments in international relations.

Concerned at the developments which have led to the present acute aggravation of the situation in regard to Germany and Berlin, the participating countries call upon all parties concerned not to resort to or threaten the use of force to solve the German question or the problem of Berlin, in accordance with the appeal made by the Heads of State or Government on 5th September, 1961.[1]

The Heads of State or Government of non-aligned countries resolve that this Declaration should be forwarded to the United Nations and brought to the attention of all the Member States of the world Organization. The present Declaration will be also forwarded to all the other States.

(iv) *The delegates to the Belgrade Conference to President Kennedy, 6 September 1961*[2]

Your Excellency,

We, the Heads of State or Government of our respective countries attending the Conference of Non-Aligned Countries held at Belgrade from September 1 to September 5, 1961 venture to address Your Excellency on a subject of vital and immediate importance to all of us and to the world as a whole. We do so not only on our own behalf, but at the unanimous desire of the Conference and of our peoples.

We are distressed and deeply concerned at the deterioration in the international situation and the prospect of war which now threatens humanity. Your Excellency has often pointed to the terrible nature of modern war and the use of nuclear weapons, which may well destroy humanity, and has pleaded for the maintenance of world peace.

Yet we are at the brink of this very danger that menaces the world and humanity. We are fully aware that Your Excellency is anxious as any of us to avoid this dreadful development which will not only end the hopes that we all have cherished for the advancement of our peoples but is a challenge to human survival. We are certain that Your Excellency will do everything in your power to avert such a calamity.

Having regard, however, to the gravity of the crisis that menaces the world, and the urgent need to avert the development that may precipitate it, we take the liberty of urging on the Great Powers concerned that negotiations should be resumed and pursued so that the danger of war might be removed from the world and mankind adopts ways of peace. In particular, we earnestly request for direct negotiations between Your Excellency and the Chairman of the Council of Ministers of the Union of Soviet Socialist Republics, who represent the two most powerful nations today and in whose hands lies the key to peace or war. We feel convinced that devoted as both of you are to world peace, your efforts through persistent negotiations will lead to a way out of the present impasse and enable the world and humanity to work and live for prosperity and peace.

We feel sure that Your Excellency will appreciate that this letter is written because of our love of peace and our horror of war and the compelling desire that a way out must be found before mankind is faced with a terrible disaster.

[1] Not printed here.
[2] *Conference of Non-Aligned Countries*, Belgrade, 1961, pp. 264–5. The same letter, *mutatis mutandis*, was addressed to Mr. Khrushchev. President Sukarno was responsible for delivering the letter to President Kennedy in Washington, and Mr. Nehru took the Russian version to Moscow.

We are sending a letter in identical terms to this to His Excellency Mr. N. S. Khrushchev, Chairman of the Council of Ministers of the Union of Soviet Socialist Republics.

(v) President Kennedy to the Presidents of Indonesia and Mali, Dr. Sukarno and Dr. Modibo Keita, 13 September 1961[1]

Dear Mr. President:

I have studied with care the message from the Conference of Nonaligned Nations which you were good enough to present in person. The United States Government is aware that the nonaligned powers assembled at Belgrade represent an important segment of world opinion, and, especially, that their peoples share with ours a vital stake in the maintenance of the peace. In our continuing deliberations within the United States Government and with our Allies, we will give the message from the conference most careful consideration.

As regards the proposal that I enter into direct negotiations with Premier Khrushchev, we are prepared to use existing and appropriate channels to establish the possibility of surmounting the present impasse. It has been and continues to be our policy to seek to settle our problems with others by peaceful means. We have not attempted to create crises, and we believe it is incumbent upon all responsible governments to explore all possible avenues, including negotiations at the highest levels, for mutually acceptable solutions of current international problems. However, unless such negotiations are carefully prepared beforehand they risk failure and may lead to deterioration of the situation. We therefore feel that a time of great tension is particularly necessary that negotiations of the kind proposed by the Belgrade Conference not only have careful preparation but also a reasonable chance of success.

The Foreign Ministers of the Western powers are meeting in Washington tomorrow. Next week the Secretary of State will head the United States delegation to the General Assembly of the United Nations. We understand that Foreign Minister Gromyko will also be present. This will provide an opportunity for serious talks about Germany and other problems if the Soviet aide proves willing. The channels of diplomacy are open for the exploration of constructive steps toward a reduction of tension. Other means are available when they can serve a useful purpose. Meanwhile, it is clearly of the utmost importance that there be no unilateral acts which will make peaceful progress impossible.

Given a realist approach and a sincere desire on the other side as well as ours to reach a mutually acceptable solution, we see no reason why eventual negotiations should not be successful in coping with the present crisis. However, we do not intend to enter into negotiations under ultimata or threats. It is also clear that we do not propose to discuss either abdication of our responsibility or renunciation of the modalities for carrying out those responsibilities.

Nevertheless, we believe it possible to find a solution which can accommodate vital interests on both sides of the crisis.

The United States has carefully noted the statements in the Belgrade Declaration recognizing that the Berlin and German situations are of vital importance

---

[1] *Public Papers*, 1961, pp. 602–4.

to future developments in international relations.[1] It has consistently been, and will continue to be, our policy to settle differences with realism and responsibility. We would note that this crisis has been initiated by Soviet not by American action. We endorse the Declaration's reference to the rights of all nations to unity, self-determination, and independence, and its condemnation of intimidation, intervention, and interference in the exercise of the right of self-determination. We presume that these principles apply equally to the people of Germany and Berlin.

Our policies in this area have sought to respect these principles. We have absolutely no intention of resorting to force or threats of force to solve the Berlin and Germany problems, but we are determined to honor our commitments and are prepared to meet force with force if it is used against us. While the United States and its Allies are all agreed there must be negotiations on the problem, the Soviet Union must give indication of a readiness to engage in discussion based on mutual respect. The only conditions it has yet exhibited any willingness to consider are conditions which involve the surrender of Western rights.

The United States continues to believe that conclusion of an adequately controlled test ban agreement is a matter of greatest urgency. We wish to reaffirm, however, our belief that test ban negotiations should be resumed separately from negotiations on general and complete disarmament. The Soviet resumption of atmospheric testing has increased the urgency which attaches to the signature of a complete treaty test ban. Complex negotiation on general disarmament should not be permitted to delay the achievement of this significant step forward.

I would emphasize again my regret that the Soviet Union has rejected the offer of the United Kingdom and the United States Governments to halt atmospheric tests creating fallout.

Only after a searching review of vital U.S. security interests and after the utmost provocation did we announce our intent to resume underground tests. The nonaligned nations may be assured of our continued willingness to negotiate an effective treaty; but, meanwhile, the national security interests of our country and of our Allies in the Free World must be protected. The United States looks forward to full consideration of the test ban issue in the forthcoming United Nations General Assembly which we hope will move the Soviet Union to abandon its opposition to effective controls and toward acceptance of a test ban agreement.

The United States is pleased to note that the participants in the recent conference in Belgrade mentioned the importance of an effective system of inspection and control. This is the crux of the matter. It is clear from United States proposals in the nuclear test negotiations that the United States contemplates inspection and control procedures in the disarmament field in which the nonaligned countries, as well as others, would participate.

For some months the United States has been conducting an intensive study of the problem of general disarmament which resulted in a request to Congress to create a disarmament agency.[2] The study has also resulted in the development of a comprehensive plan for general and complete disarmament which is in the

[1] Above, p. 621.   [2] Above, p. 57.

final stage of preparation for public presentation.[1] This plan provides for a program which will insure that the disarmament is general and complete; that war is no longer an instrument for settling international disputes; and that disarmament is accompanied by the creation of reliable procedures for peaceful settlement of disputes and maintenance of peace in accordance with the principles of the United Nations Charter.

The American commitment to these objectives goes deep. Our colleagues in the world community will not find us faint-hearted in this cause.

Talks between the United States and the Soviet Union resumed September 6 in New York in a further effort to bring the two sides closer together and to work out a satisfactory disarmament forum. The proposals put forth by the United States by these talks provide for participation of nonaligned countries in future broad disarmament negotiations. They also provide for negotiations under the auspices of the United Nations if the Soviet Union will agree. The United States believes the General Assembly will have an opportunity to go into the matter since a Committee of the Whole exists in the form of the Disarmament Commission, which can be convened at any time.

In conclusion let me say, Mr. President, that we found elements in the message and in the Declaration which reflected a genuine desire to bring about a relaxation of tensions and which, if applied in a truly neutral and objective manner, could be of positive benefit in easing world tensions.

We respect, as always, the desire of other nations to remain non-aligned. We understand with sympathy and share their passion for peace. We are, as always, prepared to cooperate with all initiatives to bring about an improvement in the world situation. We look forward to continued friendly relations with the governments and peoples participating in the Belgrade meeting.

(vi) Mr. Khrushchev to Mr. Nehru, 16 September 1961[2]

Esteemed Mr. Prime Minister,

I have studied with close attention and interest the letter[3] from the conference of the heads of state and government of 25 non-aligned countries which ended recently and I am deeply touched that you took the trouble to bring it to Moscow and deliver it to me in person. I express heartfelt gratitude to all the distinguished participants in the conference for this letter.

It is gratifying that the views of the Soviet government on the existing world situation coincide in many respects with the considerations set forth in the letter from those who took part in the conference. I was also favourably impressed by the other conference documents, which are full of concern for the fate of the world.

How can one fail to rejoice that the governments of neutral states whose population comprises one-third of mankind have raised their voices in defence of peace and resolutely denounce the policy of war preparations. This will be

---

[1] Above, p. 389.
[2] *Soviet News*, 25 September 1961. Similar letters were sent to the other Heads of State and Government who took part in the conference.
[3] Above, p. 629.

of all the greater importance for world developments since the struggle to prevent war and consolidate peace has been and continues to be the backbone of the entire foreign policy of the socialist states which make up another third of mankind.

This is how broad has become the circle of states which regard concern for peace as their vital cause.

The conference's insistent call for the immediate conclusion of a treaty on general and complete disarmament will unquestionably attract the attention of all people. Yes, this is indeed the most pressing and urgent matter, as it is in this that we have a reliable key to lasting peace on earth.

The Soviet government regards with great respect the conference's considerations and conclusions on a number of other international questions, including the question of the complete and final abolition of colonialism. It can now be confidently said that soon, very soon, the pressure of the joint forces of the peoples will break the resistance of states that are clinging to their colonial possessions which have served them for decades as a source of enrichment, but only because the colonialists have robbed and brutally exploited the colonial peoples. The sweat and blood of these peoples—that is the source of the wealth of the colonial powers. The day is near when colonialism will be wiped off the face of the earth for ever.

In the letter delivered to me the participants in the conference expressed deep concern over the worsening of the international situation and the danger of war. The Soviet government fully shares this concern. Throughout the entire postwar period the threat of war has never, perhaps, been felt so keenly as today. As you are, of course, well aware, this state of affairs has not come about of its own accord. It is a result of the activities of certain forces which are interested in anything rather than lasting peace.

One cannot escape the thought that the policy of the N.A.T.O. powers is being increasingly influenced by circles which simply seek war, drive towards war. They apparently realise that time is working against the old imperialist system founded on domination and oppression, on flouting the basic rights of the peoples, and are considering whether the time has not come to stake everything on an attempt to stop by war the great shifts that are taking place in the life of the peoples throughout the world, and especially on the continents which only yesterday were groaning under the whip of the colonial overseers.

This conclusion imposes itself when you see that the governments of the western powers are intensifying military preparations in every way, are increasing the already inflated military budgets, calling up reservists, and instilling in the population of their countries a spirit of militarism, of which there is already too much in some N.A.T.O. powers. It appears that these countries are not averse to using for the purpose of a general showdown the central question which brooks no delay—the question of a German peace treaty, the conclusion of which would radically improve the situation in Europe, taking into consideration the actual situation that has developed in Germany in connection with the formation of two sovereign German states, and would render an important service to the cause of universal peace.

It is natural that the Soviet people cannot remain passive onlookers when some powers undertake senseless and—I will speak frankly—dangerous, adventurist actions. We have been compelled to take measures which you know of in order to strengthen the security of our country. To have done otherwise would have been to place our country in a dangerous situation in face of a threat by aggressive forces.

I should like to avail myself of this opportunity to declare that we are deeply convinced that the measures we have taken are in the interests, not only of the Soviet people, or of our allies, who like ourselves uphold the cause of peace and the need for drawing a line under the Second World War and concluding a German peace treaty for this purpose, but also in the interests of all other peoples who yearn for a peaceful life. We express satisfaction with the fact that, on the whole, our defensive measures have been understood correctly by very broad circles of the public in many countries.

I should like to tell you openly and frankly, although this will be no news to you, that the Soviet Union would not like to follow in the rut of military rivalry with the western powers. This is not our policy; this is not our road and we should not like to follow along this road unless forced to do so.

Our greatest and most sacred desire is to live in friendship with all states, to live in a world without armaments, in a world without wars.

It is for this reason that we are demanding so persistently that the statesmen responsible for the destinies of the world take the only correct decision: to put an end to the remnants of the Second World War, to smash completely the war machinery of states, and destroy all armaments, including nuclear weapons, which would finally remove the question of nuclear weapon tests; both of these questions are bound up organically, inseparably, and can be solved only simultaneously. It is this that I tried to stress in every way during my recent meeting with President Kennedy in Vienna.

In their letter the participants in the conference of non-aligned countries urge negotiations between the great powers to remove the danger of war. In particular, they suggest direct talks between the Chairman of the U.S.S.R. Council of Ministers and the President of the United States of America.

What can one say to that? You know, of course, that the Soviet Union has always stood for a negotiated settlement of outstanding issues. Naturally now, too, we believe that talks between states, especially between the U.S.S.R. and the United States, as the mightiest and most influential countries, can and must play an important role in cleansing the international atmosphere. For the sake of ensuring peace we are ready for talks at any time, in any place and at any level.

For a long time there has been an urgent need for the statesmen of the nations which fought against Hitler Germany to sit down at a peace conference table and, together with representatives of both German states, in a calm atmosphere, without stirring up passions, work out a peace treaty which would quench the smouldering embers left after the world conflagration which raged a decade and a half ago. These embers do exist, and not just anywhere, but in the centre of Europe, from which spread that conflagration in whose flames tens of millions of people perished. We Soviet people, better than anyone else, know what this tragedy cost and how many lives it carried away.

It goes without saying that negotiations on international problems ripe for solution are needed, and we have said so on more than one occasion. But they are needed, not just for the sake of negotiations. Bitter experience has taught us to speak about this plainly. Talks will be useful only if the statesmen go to these talks with a serious desire and readiness to achieve agreements which will constitute a basis for strengthening peace. The participants in the talks must have the courage to face realities and clearly realise that no one can turn the tide of events which reflect the natural development of human society.

One has to speak about this because some western leaders are not averse to striking attitudes even when the most serious matters are at stake: 'Just look at us, how we don't let ourselves listen to reason.' Is it not a fact that certain western leaders keep interspersing their statements with utterances to the effect that they are maintaining a tough attitude, and savour this word 'tough' in every way?

We, on the other hand, believe that leaders invested with the trust of the peoples, like helmsmen, must look forward, clearly seeing the course their ships of state will take, and in any case should try to see that course and avoid hidden dangers and reefs. Is it not a fact that even a good beginning can take different turns? Negotiations can plot a reliable channel through which these ships will confidently sail into calm waters and avoid the gathering storm.

Yet negotiations, if one dooms them to failure in advance and repeats the incantation about the need for a tough attitude, as certain politicians, in Bonn for example, are doing, can run the ships of state aground, on reefs, and bring down calamities upon the peoples.

I want you to understand me correctly. The Soviet government is ready to take part in negotiations which will really be aimed at the speediest solution of pressing international problems, in the first place in a peace conference on the question of concluding a German peace treaty and normalising the situation in West Berlin on this basis. It is convinced that the sooner such serious negotiations start the better it would be. It would be an expression of great statesmanship if such a treaty were concluded on an agreed basis at the earliest possible date.

In order to strengthen peace and normalise the situation in Europe and throughout the world, it would be a good thing if other countries which have not yet recognised both German states—the German Democratic Republic and the Federal Republic of Germany—would recognise them *de jure* and establish relations with them. The admission of the German Democratic Republic and the Federal Republic of Germany to the United Nations would serve the same purpose.

All this would raise a serious barrier to the revenge-seeking circles in Western Germany, which, as is well known, are rallying forces to change the conditions which have arisen since the Second World War.

The entry of both German states into the United Nations and the establishment of relations with them would stabilise the situation which exists in Germany and this would be a great contribution to the cause of strengthening world peace.

Allow me, Mr. Prime Minister, once again to express satisfaction over the efforts which you personally, together with leading statesmen of other non-aligned countries, are making to cleanse the international atmosphere. I should like to assure you that the Soviet government, faithful to its policy of peace, will for its part continue to spare no efforts to enable the peoples to live without fear of war, in conditions of peace and prosperity.

B. THE EMERGENCE OF AFRICAN RIVALRIES

(a) The International Position

(α) The United Nations

General Assembly resolution regarding the 'consideration of Africa as a denuclearized zone', adopted 24 November 1961[1]

The General Assembly,

Recalling its resolutions 1378 (XIV) of 20 November 1959 on general and complete disarmament, 1379 (XIV) of 20 November 1959 on the question of French nuclear tests in the Sahara, 1576 (XV) of 20 December 1960 on the prevention of the wider dissemination of nuclear weapons, and 1577 (XV) and 1578 (XV) of 20 December 1960 on the suspension of nuclear and thermonuclear tests.[2]

Recalling further its resolution 1629 (XVI) of 27 October 1961,[3] which declared that both concern for the future of mankind and the fundamental principles of international law impose a responsibility on all States concerning actions which might have harmful biological consequences for the existing and future generations of peoples of other States, by increasing the levels of radioactive fall-out,

Concerned about the present rate of nuclear armament and the possible spread of nuclear weapons, as well as the resumption of nuclear tests in the continent of Africa which is being emancipated,

Recognizing the need to prevent Africa from becoming involved in any competition associated with the ideological struggles between the Powers engaged in the arms race and, particularly, with nuclear weapons,

Recognizing further that the task of economic and social development in the African States requires the uninterrupted attention of those States in order to allow them to fulfil their goals and to contribute fully to the maintenance of international peace and security,

Calls upon Member States:

(*a*) To refrain from carrying out or continuing to carry out in Africa nuclear tests in any form;

(*b*) To refrain from using the territory, territorial waters or air space of Africa for testing, storing or transporting nuclear weapons;

(*c*) To consider and respect the continent of Africa as a denuclearized zone.

[1] G.A.O.R., Sixteenth Session, Supplement No. 17, p. 4.
[2] *Documents*, 1959, pp. 115 and 162–3, and ibid., 1960, pp. 108–9.
[3] G.A.O.R., Sixteenth Session, Supplement No. 17, pp. 9–10.

(β) *The United States*

1. Extract from an address by the United States Permanent Representative to the United Nations, Mr. Stevenson, 2 March 1961[1]

. . . In the second half of this 20th century we are living through an historical experience which, in all the annals of man, has proved desperately difficult. This experience is the disintegration of one pattern of imperial power and the establishment of new political facts and relationships and power centers in its place. Whenever such changes occur—the really big changes which resemble some vast seismic disturbance in the earth's political crust—the inevitable outcome is disorder, catastrophe, civil conflict, and war.

Europe lapsed into barbarism after the fall of Rome. Britain's advance into India followed the crumbling and collapse of the Mogul Empire. In China, where man's longest documented record covers the fortunes of his oldest continuous body politic, the rise and fall of imperial dynasties has a rhythm of almost majestic fatality, each new empire rising on the anarchy and ruins of the last and then, in its own turn, falling away.

Times of imperial collapse are always times of trouble. And we are living through the greatest of such disintegrations today. In 15 short years the dominion which Western Europe exercised over most of Asia and Africa until the morrow of the Second World War has all but vanished. All Asia has emerged from colonial or semicolonial control. Africa is in the violent throes of the same process. I doubt if empire on such a scale has ever ended at such breakneck speed. If history is our guide, so rapid and so vast a disintegration must bring the risk of confusion thrice confounded.

And history leaves us in little doubt about the kind of disorder we are likely to endure. We may expect to see new powers jostling to take over the influence and control of the outgoing imperial governments. We may expect to see such efforts sparking local violence and driving it in an outward spiral toward general war. And we may expect, behind local crises and dangers, a general deterioration in international good will, a general increase in distrust and hostility.

Such dangers have marked the collapse of empire before. They mark it now. So the turbulence we see day by day in the world at large, and reflected back to us through the United Nations, is neither surprising nor new. We should and must expect it. And we must get used to it—we who suffer from having had things our way for so long, we are shocked and hurt when other people don't share our views or question our motives. We judge ourselves by our motives; others by their actions.

What is both surprising and new is what the United Nations is trying to do about these risks. Now we come to the wholly new chapter in history, the chapter that gives us at least a marginal hope of escaping the dread fatalities of earlier days. To me, I confess, it is a matter of exhilaration that here, here in America, in the newest of continents and in the midst of perhaps the most far-reaching experiment in free, unimperial government, a new start should be under way in the management of human affairs, a new experiment to defeat and annihilate the set historical patterns and deadlocks of the past.

[1] *D.S.B.*, 20 March 1961, pp. 411–14.

Here at the United Nations the effort is being made to confront the old fatalities of collapsing empires and put in their place wholly new approaches to the dilemmas of our time. It is only when we realize how new they are, how radical, how revolutionary, that we can have any idea of the potential value, the profound historical significance, of what is being attempted at the United Nations, here in New York.

What we are attempting to do today at the United Nations is to roll back every one of the great historical fatalities which, in the past, have made the ending of empire the most perilous condition for the survival of society. We are trying to end the dreary cycle of imperialisms by which the outgoing masters are quickly replaced by new ones who come quickly in to fill the vacuum of power.

The principle which President Wilson declared has since become one of mankind's greatest aspirations—the self-determination of peoples. In the Western World, in this century, the attempt has been made for the first time in history to outlaw imperialism.

This is new. Like all new things, it is difficult. But at least in the last decade, as we have seen the United Nations grow from 50 to nearly a hundred nations, we must admit that for millions of God's children a first step toward freedom has been taken—the step which recognizes their right—their inalienable right—to be free.

But then the dangers and the dilemmas press in. We have done something new in proclaiming the right of small peoples not to be run by other, more powerful states. We have decreed and welcomed the end of colonialism. Indeed it was in these United States that the first practical steps were taken to raise the principle of anticolonialism from a hope to a fact. The shot that echoed round the world from Lexington echoes on to this day.

But have we insured that our new faith can be fully and irrevocably expressed in works? Hitherto, as I have said, the ending of one imperialism has usually spelled, for the small and the weak, the beginning of a new. Are we doing better today? The principle may be new. Is the practice equally so?

This to me is the most urgent issue at stake in Africa today. Do the new nations, sometimes irresolute, sometimes wobbly, know how much they need us in their period of transition to genuine independence? Or are they blinded by their new nationalism, their hatred of the colonialism of the past, both of which are so skillfully exploited by the propaganda of others who are not trying to help them achieve genuine independence and stability? Was it Alexander Hamilton who said that even to be neutral required a stable government? And Wilson warned us that 'Liberty is not itself government. In the wrong hands, in hands unpractised, undisciplined, it is incompatible with government.'

The old colonial system is crumbling. Britain has largely withdrawn, leaving viable new societies behind. The French have helped to bring a large new family of states into the United Nations. But in the Congo the transfer of power has thrown the area into that kind of civil commotion which, in the past, has been the more usual end of imperial control. Here, then, the great question is: Can we, having seen one form of colonialism end, prevent another from being established?

When we in America give our support to the ending of all outside intervention, we mean something definite and practical. We believe that Belgium should complete its withdrawal. We believe that no other foreign power should come thrusting in, especially the new imperialism of the Soviet Union.

In the Congo we seek a solution which brings together and reconciles the Congo's own leaders and forestalls the threatening civil war in which outside intervention would be inescapable. And we do this, not because we have any designs on central Africa but because we don't; because we oppose with all our conviction and experience the risk that, after seeing Western colonialism go, Africa will see Communist imperialism come.

Clearly only one body can prevent this ancient fatality of simply swapping one control for another. It is the United Nations, consulting closely with its Afro-Asian members and barring outside intervention from whatever side.

This is our first aim—to put a genuine end to outside imperial control. Our second stems from it—to prevent local disputes from spiraling into general war. Here, again, we do not have to look far back into history to see the kind of tragedy we must at all costs avert.

At the turn of the last century Turkish imperial power crumbled in the Balkans. Czarist Russia on the one hand, Austria-Hungary on the other, pressed in to take its place. In the small, emergent Balkan states, local factions looked to Moscow or Vienna, as in Africa today they may look to Moscow or Paris or Brussels—or Washington. The defeat of local Balkan leaders began to take on the aspect of a defeat for the powers which backed them. Two small local wars were contained. Then, in 1914, a bullet killed an archduke—as a bullet, this unhappy winter, killed Lumumba. And men stood helplessly by and watched until all the world was engulfed in the horrors of war.

This must not happen now. Africa is the Balkans of today. Any outside power seeking to manipulate its griefs and searchings and first fumbling efforts to stand alone risks bringing down on Africa and on the world the dread possibility of nuclear destruction. Is this really what Mr. Khrushchev has in mind when he demands the withdrawal of the United Nations Force and suggests instead that the Congo should become—as the Balkans once were—the cockpit first of rival factions, then of rival interventions, and finally of a spreading, consuming, horrifying general conflict?

I cannot believe that any statesman conscious of the dread brink upon which all humanity stands can seek to widen the crisis. The United Nations must instead damp down the fires of civil war and reconcile the rival leaders. And in this task the other African states have a role of immense significance to play, for if they can bring their great influence to bear on the various centers of power in the Congo—on Leopoldville, on Elisabethville, on Stanleyville—we may yet see reconstituted a Congo state which, with full U.N. backing, can withdraw itself from the terrifying risks of outside intervention. We in the United States seek no other outcome.

I know it is not easy to reverse the fatalities of history. We are on a melancholy road, which again and again mankind has trodden flat with legions of men marching to destruction. In the Congo today, in Laos, potentially in any area of conflict and civil disturbance, almost nothing is new. The conflicts are old, the rival suspicions and jockeyings for position are old, the brute struggle

for power is as old as man himself. And we know where they have always led—
to war and death.

But today one thing is new. It is the United Nations effort to attempt to
apply peaceful procedures and rational solutions even to the most aggravated
and envenomed of political crises. On a dark scene, in a dark time of troubles,
New York's guest, the United Nations, is proclaiming by deed as well as word
that men can live, not by violence and brute strength but, at last, by reason and
law.

And also I would say to our own people: Support the United Nations with
your approbation, your sympathetic attention, and your prayers. To the smaller
powers, especially the emergent states of Africa, I would repeat that the United
Nations is of first interest above all to weaker states, since without it they have
no ultimate protection against the force of more powerful and predatory
governments.

And to the Soviet Union I would say: There are laws of history more profound
and inescapable than the laws dreamed up by Marx and Lenin, laws which belong
not to class relationships or stages of economic development but to the nature
and destiny of man himself. Among these laws is the certainty that war follows
when new empires thrust into the collapsing ruins of the old. So stay your
ambitions. Think twice about your interventions. Allow the new principles of
international order—the right of peoples to determine their own destiny—to
operate in Africa without your pressure from without. Do not sabotage the only
institution which offers an alternative to imperialism. Do not look backward to
mankind's evil inheritance of violence. Look forward to a world where the
United Nations can be the forum and guardian of peace.

This, I believe, is the hope of the vast majority of mankind. It is above all the
hope of the small powers, whose only protection lies in the international organization of their security. The administration of President Kennedy will go to the
limits of its strength and ingenuity to work with the general consensus of
humanity. It invites all other governments to follow the same path. For let
there be no doubt about the alternatives. They are written in words of flame and
blood on the walls of the world.

Let us, therefore, leave the rivalries and the imperialisms behind and strive
together for the world where nations can be both secure and free.

2. Extracts from an address by the United States Assistant Secretary of State for African Affairs, Mr. Mennen Williams, 26 October 1961[1]

. . . If one general impression must be given, it is that the tasks to be faced
in Africa are of extraordinary magnitude. And I believe that the challenge to us
Americans is far greater than most of us realize. It is great because the stakes are
high, the problems too overwhelming to be neglected.

The challenge is not at all simply a question of lending material assistance,
though that we must do. It confronts us with important moral and political
issues. Our purposes will not be understood, our aid will fall short, if they do

---

[1] *D.S.B.*, 20 November 1961, pp. 861–2, and 864–5.

not involve a wholehearted commitment to the burning desires of African peoples for self-determination and independence, for dignity and equality.

Africa has begun to move. Hope has been liberated. The stored-up dynamism of the African peoples points to a great potential for growth, a distinctively African contribution to the world. What we can and must assist in Africa is the realization of an unprecedented opportunity to enrich the future we all will share.

Too much public discussion, too many news reports, I'm afraid, register on the negative factors at work in Africa. The danger of Soviet penetration is a category under which every possible item is faithfully entered, usually without much background or perspective. Some commentators would apparently feel comfortable about Africa only if the new nations there pretended never to have heard of the Soviet Union and invariably crossed the street to avoid ever striking up an acquaintance. But it is fair to expect African states to forgo diplomatic relations, trade, and other contacts with the Communists when even their former colonial mentors engage in such activities?

It is better to be realistic. We welcome Africa's new independence. We think it is a positive force. We do not wish to control or direct it.

We can indeed legitimately express our concern over certain Soviet activities—inflammatory, disruptive, subversive. We are not blind or passive to the interventionist design which the Communists are working at—scholarships for political training, subsidies for opportunists and propagandists, promissory notes to front-group agitators. This is the old black bag of Communist tricks, familiar around the world. Let us not underestimate it. But let us avoid a fixation about it. Our scrutiny, our labors, must be directed to the primary subjects—the realities of African political, economic, social, and cultural life in today's interactive world.

Our purpose and policy is plain: We want for Africa what the Africans want for themselves. We want an Africa in which independent nations grow in vigor and prosperity, because Africans are determined to assert all the pride and seek all the promise that independence means for them, as for peoples everywhere.

This American point of view is born directly out of our sense of African aspirations and our historic interest in the enlargement of freedom in the world. It does not depend on the stimulus of some outside danger. Our aim now is a fuller understanding of these aspirations, which seek to throw off the burdens of poverty, ignorance, and disease and to assert the dignity and worth of new millions who are now citizens of the greater world. And our aim is to help where we can, where our help is wanted and needed, in bringing the fruits of scientific, technological progress to the task of uplift which is the basic program of every African leader. Our criterion is not whether the Communists are interested in country x but whether country x needs assistance to work toward legitimate goals. As President Kennedy said in his inaugural address,[1] our pledge is made not out of a concern with votes or with communism 'but because it is right' that we help. . . .

The relations of African states with leading Western nations are still in a state

[1] Above, p. 1.

of transition, and distinctions often are not very clearly drawn. Too often 'the West', which is not a monolith, is equated with 'the East', which is an absolutely rigid bloc except in doctrinal squabbles. Because of one colonial experience, a number of African countries are likely to include all Western Powers—including the U.S.—in their sense of grievance over such unresolved problems as Algeria, Angola, or *apartheid*.

At the same time that African feelings are caught up in these effects of historical change and historical hangover, the West is greatly preoccupied with Berlin, which to many Africans seems, by and large, a remote problem. With all of the good will in the world, we cannot, from our vantage point, help but consider certain African nations somewhat unsympathetic in a matter of such profound significance for the future of freedom and self-determination as Berlin so obviously is. My experience, too, is that a good many Africans feel that the United States does not show sufficiently, in a practical way, our concern with the problems which to them seem the really critical ones.

So I believe you may agree that greater mutual understanding, by us, by our allies, and by the Africans, is a vital need. Let me, in this regard, assure my African friends that our commitment to freedom and self-determination is not an expediency but is central to our international policy. We could not otherwise expect to rouse their concern on the same issue when it is at stake elsewhere.

To my American listeners I can only outline a very sizable obligation that America must find the means to meet.

1. Clearly, United States aid to Africa will have to be substantial and widespread; it will have to be increased from all sources, Government and private. It is too little realized that we lag far behind Europe in assistance to African nations. The historical basis for this imbalance has radically altered with the emergence of African states to independence. Yet French aid to Africa last year was much larger than our own.

2. The Peace Corps and similar human-resource and human-commitment programs must be perfected and expanded. We are going to catch an unfavorable headline here and there, out of human fallibility, but such programs are directed at very serious needs and have every prospect of general success.

3. We must devise new methods of cooperating with developed nations who are motivated by a philosophy similar to our own, to continue or to begin to play a part in meeting what is perhaps the greatest challenge of our time—the rising expectations of the peoples of Africa.

4. We must in policy and in action make manifest our commitment to freedom and independence. There is no question as to what the American people in their hearts want for the people of Africa. But sometimes we are slow in acting, sometimes cautious in moving to overcome obstacles. It will be our challenge to measure up in action to the dynamism of the times and the inspiration of our own ideals.

5. We must be understanding and vigorous in our pursuit of the ideal of human dignity. We must banish all vestiges of discrimination from our own national life, and we must be imaginative and faithful in building brotherhood throughout the world. . . .

(γ) *The Communist Bloc*

1. Joint communiqué issued by President Brezhnev and President Touré of Guinea, Conakry, 15 February 1961[1]

At the invitation of the President of the Republic of Guinea, Mr. Sékou Touré, the President of the Presidium of the U.S.S.R. Supreme Soviet, L. I. Brezhnev, made a state visit to Guinea from February 11 to February 16, 1961. . . .

The President of the Presidium of the U.S.S.R. Supreme Soviet and the persons accompanying him[2] had an opportunity of noting with gratification the major achievements of the Guinean people in the development of their truly free and independent country. They also noted with deep satisfaction the solid unity and intense activity of the Democratic Party of Guinea, the government and the entire people of Guinea in the struggle for the complete elimination of the grave consequences of the colonial régime in all spheres of life, for the rapid advancement of the national economy, for raising the cultural level and living standards of the working people, for establishing the democratic basis of the new state, and for peace throughout the world.

During their stay in Guinea the President of the Presidium of the U.S.S.R. Supreme Soviet and the persons accompanying him had friendly meetings and talks with President Sékou Touré, with Speaker of the National Assembly Saifulai Diallo, and with a number of other important political leaders and statesmen of the Republic of Guinea.

These meetings and talks, held in an atmosphere of sincere cordiality, mutual understanding and friendship, revealed a complete identity of views on major international problems.

Both sides believe that averting the danger of another war and safeguarding peaceful co-existence among all peoples is the paramount task of the peace forces in all countries. To accomplish this task, both sides consider it necessary to exert fresh efforts to secure agreement on general and complete disarmament, including the immediate banning of nuclear weapon tests, the prohibition of the use of such weapons and the destruction of stocks of them, and the abolition of military bases on foreign soil.

The implementation of a programme of general and complete disarmament and the elimination of the danger of another devastating world war would make it possible finally to safeguard lasting peace and to direct vast financial and material resources to the development of industry and agriculture and raising the living standards of the peoples, especially of underdeveloped countries of Africa, Asia and Latin America.

Both sides consider that the declaration of the United Nations General Assembly on granting independence to the colonial countries and peoples, the draft of which was originally proposed by the Soviet Union, is a great victory for all progressive mankind.

They point out that, in defiance of the will of the peoples, scores of millions

---

[1] *Soviet News*, 18 February 1961.
[2] The delegation included, among others, the first Deputy Minister of Culture Mr. Kuznetzov.

of people—mainly in Africa—are still in colonial slavery. That is why the task now is to achieve the effective and immediate implementation of all the demands of this declaration, and put an end to the colonial régime in any shape or form.

During the talks it was re-affirmed that the utmost support for the struggle of the oppressed peoples for their national liberation is one of the main principles of the foreign policy of the Soviet Union and the Republic of Guinea.

At the same time, the sides drew special attention to the impermissibility of allowing the abolution of the colonial régime to be reduced to a formal act, meaning, in fact, the preservation of this régime on which history has passed sentence.

Both sides agreed that the imperialist aggression against the Republic of the Congo, under cover of the United Nations flag, is a serious danger to the independence of that country, and a direct threat to the independent existence of all sovereign African states. Both sides believe that the peaceloving peoples must help the Congolese people to expel the colonialists.

Expressing their resolute and full support for the only legitimate government of the Congo, headed from now on by Mr. Antoine Gizenga, Patrice Lumumba's loyal colleague, both sides expressed their profound resentment and indignation at the assassination of the national hero of the Congolese people, the great and immortal son of Africa, Prime Minister Patrice Lumumba, a bestial crime committed by the colonialists and their hangers-on.

The responsibility for this foul crime rests with the colonialist government of Belgium, her allies and the United Nations Secretary-General.

The blood-stained killers of Patrice Lumumba must be immediately and severely punished.

Both sides consider it necessary to take new steps with the object of achieving the immediate release of all members of the legitimate government of the Congo and members of the Congolese Parliament illegally detained, the removal from the Congo of all Belgian military personnel and the military personnel of the other imperialist powers—members of aggressive blocs—and the removal of various placemen of the colonialists who are betraying their homeland.

Lumumba is dead, but the cause of his life, the cause of the struggle for the freedom of the Congolese people and the entire African continent, will triumph.

Resolutely denouncing the colonial war in Algeria, the sides consider that the peace forces of all countries must raise their voice against the continuation of this war and persistently demand that the Algerian people be granted the right to settle their own future. It is the duty of all honest people in the world to render the utmost support to the people of Algeria in their struggle for emancipation from the colonial yoke.

The sides note with great satisfaction the successful development of good and friendly relations between the Soviet Union and the Republic of Guinea, relations resting on the principles of peaceful co-existence, full equality and profound and mutual respect for the national independence, sovereignty and territorial integrity of their countries.

The sides stress the effectiveness of Soviet-Guinean economic, scientific and technical co-operation in promoting Guinea's economic progress and express their desire to strengthen this co-operation.

Being of the opinion that the trade relations between the U.S.S.R. and Guinea are developing successfully, the sides point out that the conclusion of the long-term agreement on goods exchange and payments for 1961–65 provides a good basis for the further growth of goods exchange between the two countries.

The Soviet side declares that it is prepared to expand deliveries to the Republic of Guinea of the goods it needs, in particular machinery and equipment, oil products, consumer goods and foodstuffs, and also to increase purchases of the commodities traditionally exported by Guinea.

Noting the rapid progress in Soviet-Guinean relations in the sphere of education, science and the arts, the sides consider it necessary to develop in every way and further strengthen cultural and scientific co-operation between the two countries.

Both sides regard the visit by the President of the Presidium of the U.S.S.R. Supreme Soviet, L. I. Brezhnev, to the Republic of Guinea as another important step in developing the friendship between the two peoples.

They express their profound confidence that the friendly relations existing between the Soviet Union and Guinea will continue developing and growing stronger, to the benefit of the peoples of the two countries and in the interests of peace in Africa and throughout the world.

> (*Signed*)
> President of the Presidium of the Supreme Soviet of U.S.S.R.
> L. BREZHNEV
> President of the Republic of Guinea
> SÉKOU TOURÉ

2. Statement on President Brezhnev's visit to Ghana, Accra, 19 February 1961[1] (extracts)

The President of the Presidium of the U.S.S.R. Supreme Soviet, L. I. Brezhnev, upon the termination of his official visit to the Guinean Republic, visited the Republic of Ghana at the invitation of President Kwame Nkrumah. . . .

President L. I. Brezhnev met President Kwame Nkrumah and they discussed matters of common interest. The exchange of opinions between them revealed an identity of views on major issues of world politics.

Sharing the deep indignation and the wrath of the peoples of the world aroused by the vile assassination of the national hero of the Congo, the great son of Africa Patrice Lumumba, and his colleagues, Joseph Okito and Maurice Mpolo, President Brezhnev and President Kwame Nkrumah expressed confidence that no intrigues of the colonialists and their henchmen would prevent the courageous Congolese people from taking their destiny into their own hands. The Congo Republic would be free and take a fitting place in the family of independent national states of Africa.

The talks were also concerned with Soviet-Ghanaian relations. Both sides noted with great satisfaction the development and strengthening of friendly relations between the U.S.S.R. and the Republic of Ghana, based on mutual respect for one another's interests, the principles of peaceful co-existence, full

[1] ibid., 21 February 1961. President Nkrumah returned the visit in July.

equality and non-interference in one another's internal affairs. They noted with special satisfaction the successful development of Soviet-Ghanaian co-operation in the economic and scientific-technical fields, as well as in the fields of trade and cultural contacts.

Both sides expressed assurance that the visit by President Brezhnev to the Republic of Ghana would help to strengthen further the friendly relations between the two countries.

3. Treaty of Friendship between Ghana and the People's Republic of China, Peking, 18 August 1961[1]

The Chairman of the People's Republic of China and the President of the Republic of Ghana,

Desiring to consolidate and further develop the profound friendship between the People's Republic of China and the Republic of Ghana, and

Being convinced that the strengthening of friendly cooperation between the People's Republic of China and the Republic of Ghana fully conforms to the fundamental interests of the peoples of the two countries, conduces to the enhancement of the friendship and solidarity between the peoples of the two countries as well as among Asian and African peoples, and is in the interest of world peace,

Have decided for this purpose to conclude the present treaty.

ARTICLE ONE

The contracting parties will maintain and develop the relations of peace and friendship between the People's Republic of China and the Republic of Ghana.

ARTICLE TWO

The contracting parties decide to take the five principles of mutual respect for sovereignty and territorial integrity, mutual non-aggression, non-interference in each other's internal affairs, equality and mutual benefit, and peaceful coexistence and the ten principles laid down at the Asian-African Conference held in Bandung in 1955 as the principles guiding the relations between the two countries.

The contracting parties will settle all disputes between them by means of peaceful negotiation.

ARTICLE THREE

The contracting parties agree to develop the economic and cultural relations between the two countries in the spirit of equality, mutual benefit and friendly cooperation.

ARTICLE FOUR

The present treaty is subject to ratification, and the instruments of ratification shall be exchanged in Accra as soon as possible.

The present treaty shall come into force immediately on the exchange of the

---

[1] *H.N.A.*, 22 August 1961. A number of other agreements were also signed, including an agreement on economic and technical co-operation for which see ibid., 22 August 1961.

instruments of ratification and shall remain in force for a period of ten years.

Unless either of the contracting parties gives to the other notice in writing to terminate the present treaty one year before the expiration of this period, the present treaty shall remain in force indefinitely, subject to the right of either party to terminate it ten years after it comes into force by giving to the other notice in writing of its intention to do so one year in advance.

Done in duplicate in Peking on the eighteenth day of August, 1961, in the Chinese and English languages, both texts being equally authentic.

<table>
<tr><td>Plenipotentiary</td><td>Plenipotentiary</td></tr>
<tr><td>of the</td><td>of the</td></tr>
<tr><td>People's Republic of China</td><td>Republic of Ghana</td></tr>
<tr><td>(Signed) CHOU EN-LAI</td><td>(Signed) KWAME NKRUMAH</td></tr>
</table>

(δ) The European Economic Community

1. Recommendations on Association by the conference between the European Parliamentary Assembly and the representations of the Parliaments of the African States and Malagasy, Strasbourg, 24 June 1961[1]

(a) Recommendation on political and institutional questions

La première conférence de l'Assemblée parlementaire européenne avec les Parlements d'États africains et de Madagascar;

— I —

1. *a*) est unanime à constater que l'association entre les États africains et Madagascar, d'une part, et la Communauté européenne, d'autre part, doit être poursuivie, en tenant compte de la modification intervenue dans la situation politique;

b) se réjouit de l'identité de vues en son sein sur un grand nombre de problèmes de l'Association, et notamment sur le principe de l'égalité absolue entre les partenaires de l'association;

2. constate que l'association trouve sa base dans les principes de la charte des Nations unies, expressément rappelés par le traité de Rome.

L'Association est par conséquent fondée sur:

— la reconnaissance de l'égalité souveraine des États;

— le respect de l'intégrité territoriale et de l'indépendance politique et économique;

— le respect des droits de l'homme et des libertés fondamentales, sans distinction de race, sexe, langue ou religion;

3. approuve aussi, en vue du renouvellement des dispositions sur l'Association, l'objectif de l'Association défini dans les termes suivants:

la promotion du développement économique et social des États associés et l'établissement de relations économiques étroites entre eux et la Communauté

---

[1] *Journal Officiel des Communautés Européennes*, 22 July 1961, pp. 942–50/61. The existing Convention of Association was due to expire at the end of 1962; text in *Traité instituant la Communauté Economique Européenne* (Communauté Economique Européenne, 1957), pp. 273–9. The detailed proposals of the E.E.C. Commission on the revision of the Convention are available as *Association des Etats d'Outre-Mer à la Communauté: Considérations sur le futur régime d'association* (Communauté Economique Européenne, Commission, Brussels, 12 July 1961).

européenne visant en premier lieu à favoriser les intérêts des habitants de ces États et leur prospérité, de manière à les conduire au développement économique, social et culturel qu'ils attendent;

4. déclare que, sur cette base, il faut préparer dès maintenant les nouvelles formes de l'association et de la participation aux organismes directeurs à créer à cet effet;

5. souligne que la nouvelle association devra se réaliser par la conclusion de conventions entre la Communauté européenne et les États associés, individuels ou groupés, en prenant pour base une convention type élaboré en commun et ayant obtenu l'accord de tous les intéressés;

6. estime que la nouvelle Association, dont la durée sera illimitée, devra être ouverte à tous les États africains, étant entendu qu'aucun d'entre eux ne pourra appartenir à un autre groupement économique poursuivant des objectifs incompatibles avec ceux de l'Association;

7. suggère la réalisation des objectifs suivants pour le renouvellement de l'association au terme du 31 décembre 1962;

a) une conférence parlementaire, de composition paritaire, se réunissant au moins une fois par an, alternativement en Europe et en Afrique, la continuité pouvant être assurée par une coopération dans des commissions issues de cette conférence;

b) un conseil d'association paritaire pour traiter toutes les questions intéressant l'Association. Ce conseil d'association sera composé, d'une part, d'un représentant de chaque gouvernement africain et malgache et, d'autre part, du Conseil et de la Commission de la C.E.E., étant entendu que ce conseil d'association pourra instituer tout comité propre à l'assister dans l'accomplissement de sa tâche;

c) une représentation directe des États associés auprès des institutions de la Communauté européenne ainsi que de la Communauté européenne auprès des États africains et malgache;

(*d*) une cour d'arbitrage compétente pour tous les litiges relatifs à l'interprétation et à l'application de la convention d'association;

8. insiste pour que ces objectifs soient atteints pendant la période d'association en cours, étant entendu que faculté sera laissée aux États africains et malgache associés qui le désireraient de participer à ces institutions communes;

9. rappelle la nécessité d'une information sincère aussi bien en Europe sur l'Afrique associée, que dans les États associés sur la Communauté européenne;

— II —

La conférence,

invite l'Assemblée parlementaire européenne, d'une part, et les Parlements des États africains et malgache, d'autre part, à recommander respectivement aux institutions de la Communauté Européenne et aux gouvernements des États associés:

a) d'engager le plus tôt possible les négociations pour le renouvellement de l'Association de telle manière que la nouvelle convention entre en vigueur le 1er janvier 1963;

b) d'envisager la possibilité d'étendre la future association à la C.E.C.A. et à l'Euratom;

c) de se conformer, dans l'élaboration de la convention qui doit régir la nouvelle Association, aux principes énumérés ci-dessus pour assurer le succès de la grande expérience engagée par cette nouvelle coopération de la Communauté européenne et des États africains et malgache.

La conférence,

donne mandat à ses présidents de communiquer la présente recommandation aux gouvernements des États membres de la Communauté européenne ainsi qu'aux gouvernements des États africains et malgache.

(*b*) *Recommendation regarding the implementation of the conference recommendations*

« La conférence invite l'Assemblée parlementaire européenne et les Parlements des États associés à s'employer auprès des gouvernements des États associés et des États membres ainsi qu'auprès des institutions compétentes de la Communauté européenne pour qu'il soit donné aux principes, propositions et suggestions énoncés dans les recommandations de la conférence la suite qu'ils appellent. »

(*c*) *Recommendation on economic and commercial problems*

La conférence de l'Assemblée parlementaire européenne avec les Parlements d'États africains et de Madagascar réunie à Strasbourg du 19 au 24 juin 1961,

— informée des efforts poursuivis par les États associés en vue de mettre en place les structures et de définir les tâches de planification nationales, cohérentes et prévisionnelles, dans lesquelles devront s'insérer leurs différents projets de développement économique et social;

comme aussi du souci manifesté par ces mêmes États d'harmoniser ces planifications par la confrontation, notamment au sein de l'O.A.M.C.E., de leurs objectifs de production, de consommation, d'exportation, de recherche technique appliquée ainsi que de formation des cadres;

— considérant que l'association avec la Communauté économique européenne que les États africains et malgache, devenus indépendants, déclarent vouloir poursuivre, laisse entière la liberté d'action des pays associés en matière économique et commerciale sans autre réserve que celle de ne pas porter atteinte aux règles conventionnelles et à l'esprit de l'association;

attire l'attention de tous les États participants sur la structure actuelle de l'économie et due commerce extérieur des pays associés sur l'étroite solidarité qui les unissait aux anciennes métropoles et sur l'ébranlement que subiraient ces nations si, dans le cadre de l'association avec la Communauté européenne, elles ne pouvaient conserver un soutien au moins équivalent à celui dont elles bénéficiaient jusqu'ici et qui leur est indispensable pour le maintien de leur revenu national;

propose que l'association telle qu'elle est instituée par la quatrième partie du traité de Rome et l'actuelle convention d'association, et telle qu'elle sera prorogée sous la forme d'un nouveau régime à définir par une libre négociation, pour une nouvelle période commençant le 1er janvier 1963, s'inspire des principes suivants et en assûre la réalisation.

I — *Intensification des échanges entre les États membres et les États associés*

La conférence estime que toutes dispositions doivent être prises par les États membres et les États associés en vue d'une intensification des échanges.

A. *Préférence tarifaire*

a) La conférence considère que certaines mesures prises par des États membres de la C.E.E. ont réduit les avantages tarifaires que l'esprit du traité devait valoir aux États associés. A cet égard, la conférence considère tout d'abord que le maintien de taxes intérieures de consommation sur les produits tropicaux ou de toutes autres charges atteignant la consommation de ces produits est gravement préjudiciable aux producteurs et entraîne un freinage de la consommation de ces produits. La conférence demande en conséquence la suppression, ausi rapide que possible, de ces taxes intérieures de consommation sur les produits tropicaux.

La conférence estime en tout cas qu'il importe de supprimer résolument toute fiscalité spécifique qui aboutit pratiquement à annuler une partie appréciable des préférences actuellement reconnues aux États associés.

b) La conférence estime que dans le rapprochement des tarifs nationaux au niveau du tarif extérieur commun, il doit être viellé à ce que les marges de préférence tarifaire soient rigoureusement maintenues, de façon que les États associés conservent au sein de la Communauté les avantages préférentiels qui devaient leur être assurés selon la lettre et l'esprit du traité de Rome.

(*d*) *Recommendation regarding the problems of technical co-operation and cultural exchange*

La première conférence de léAssemblée parlementaire européenne avec les Parlements d'États africains et de Madagascar,

— après avoir pris connaissance des documents de travail concernant la coopération technique et les échanges culturels élaborés tant par les parlementaires européens que par les parlementaires africains et malgaches;

fait siens les principes qui se dégagent de ces documents;

félicite la Commission de la C.E.E. de l'action déjà déployée dans le secteur de la coopération technique et des échanges culturels avec les pays associés;

souhaite qu'à l'avenir les exécutifs des autres Communautés européennes puissent apporter leur concours à cette œuvre;

se réjouit de la concordance de vues qui est apparue à la suite des débats soulevés à propos de ces problèmes tant en commission qu'en séance plénière de la conférence;

est d'avis que la détermination des priorités et l'étendue des projets en matière de coopération technique et culturelle devraient être laissées; dans le cadre de décisions arrêtées de commun accord entre les partenaires de l'association, à l'initiative des États associés eux-mêmes;

approuve, en particulier, les points suivants qui lui apparaissent essentiels et sur lesquels elle tient à attirer plus spécialement l'attention :

1. Un pays riche en ressources naturelles et pauvre en travailleurs qualifiés est condamné à la pauvreté ;

2. l'aide au développement s'étend, en fonction des besoins des États intéressés, à tous les domaines, car la coopération technique et culturelle, les investissements des capitaux et l'accroissement des échanges commerciaux sont des moyens qui concourent tous au même but ;

3. la coopération technique de pré-investissement, c'est-à-dire celle portant sur les opérations préalables à une intervention, conditionne souvent l'efficacité de l'aide financière ;

4. l'aide déjà accordée aus États africains et malgache dans le domaine de la coopération technique et des échanges culturels devra être continuée et renforcée dans la forme institutionnelle qui sera retenue par les instances compétentes—de façon à développer tout spécialement l'enseignement et la formation professionnelle ;

c) En ce qui concerne l'existence des contingents tarifaires, la conférence estime que tout accroissement de consommation devrait bénéficier par priorité aux États associés et qu'en aucun cas il ne devrait donner lieu à l'établissement de contingents tarifaires nouveaux ou à la majoration des contingents existants. La conférence demande instamment qu'aucun contingent tarifaire ne soit établi ou maintenu en contravention avec les dispositions du traité.

d) D'une manière plus générale, la conférence estime que le principe même de la préférence tarifaire ne peut être remis en cause et que le niveau actuel du tarif extérieur commun ne peut être modifié, pour les produits intéressant les États associés si ce n'est après consultation de ces États et dans les cas où des avantages compensatoires seraient consentis. Le maintien du tarif extérieur commun à son niveau est d'autant plus justifié actuellement que des perspectives peuvent se présenter ultérieurement de négociations avec d'autres zones de solidarité telles que le Commonwealth, l'Association européenne de libre-échange ou la Zone de libre-échange latino-américaine, notamment dans le cadre du G.A.T.T.

B. *Coopération économique et préférences commerciales*

a) La conférence estime que les systèmes de régularisation des cours des produits tropicaux actuellement assurés par les caisses de stabilisation ou les fonds de régularisation nationaux, devraient être l'objet d'une régularisation dans le cadre de l'association avec la C.E.E. Cette régularisation devrait être réalisée de façon que soient respectées, dans toute la mesure du possible, les lois naturelles du marché. Réalisée à l'échelon de l'association, elle constituerait un précédent international et une importante contribution aux efforts entrepris à l'échelon mondial.

Une dotation initiale réunissant des contributions de tous les États membres et associés pourrait assurer le début du fonctionnement du système.

b) Indépendamment des mesures de régularisation des fluctuations conjoncturelles, il importe que soient institués :

— un système assurant une garantie minima de débouchés, tendant à prévenir la crise qui pourrait résulter de l'instauration de la libre circulation des marchandises au sein du marché commun, ainsi que de la disparition des contingents bilatéraux;

— le soutien des prix des produits tropicaux actuellement réalisé dans le cadre des États associés par un système garantissant au producteur une rémunération équitable indépendante des fluctuations des cours mondiaux;

— l'obligation, pour les États membres, de favoriser le stockage des produits tropicaux qui s'y prêtent ainsi que son financement, en vue de compléter l'action stabilisatrice des cours des matières premières.

Ces garanties et soutien devraient se réaliser de façon à n'imposer qu'un minimum de coercition aux circuits commerciaux des États membres. Ils pourraient être dégressifs de façon à préparer les États associés à la libre accession aux marchés mondiaux, notamment au fur et à mesure que se réaliseront les programmes de reconversion portant sur les productions excédentaires.

La conférence invite les gouvernements intéressés et la conférence intergouvernementale à mettre au point la réalisation de ces mesures pour lesquelles elle considère que le fonds de développement des pays associés pourrait constituer un instrument fondamental.

II — *Coopération au développement économique et à la planification des États associés*

La conférence considère que la création d'un institut africano-malgache d'étude et de développement pourrait contribuer à cette coordination. Les États membres pourraient participer à cette action en prévoyant une contribution du Fonds commun au fonctionnement de cet institut africano-malgache d'étude et de développement.

III

La conférence de Strasbourg a entendu des échanges de vues sur le problème du droit d'établissement au sein des différents États membres ou associés. La conférence a considéré que la conclusion sur cet échange de vues devrait être post-posée jusqu'au moment où les États associés pourront coordonner leurs vues sur ce problème en fonction des plans de développement qu'ils auront arrêtés.

IV

S'agissant du développement des ressources énergétiques, la conférence attache un grand intérêt au concours que l'Euratom peut apporter aux États associés. Elle considère que les difficultés d'approvisionnement en énergie présentent pour certains de ces États, notamment ceux que la géographie défavorise plus particulièrement, un lourd handicap pour leur développement économique.

Dans cette optique, la conférence estime que l'installation de centrales nucléaires peut s'avérer nécessaire et économique dans certaines régions où l'utilisation de l'énergie classique impliquerait, pour des raisons géographiques, des coûts particulièrement élevés. La conférence a pris connaissance avec intérêt des possibilités de recours à la Communauté européenne de l'énergie nucléaire pour les applications pratiques en matière d'isotopes, la formation des cadres techniques, l'établissement des réglementations sanitaires, etc.

Dans cette même optique du développement des ressources énergétiques, la conférence demande que soit étudiée la possibilité d'approvisionner en gaz et en pétrole, directement et le plus économiquement possible, les États associés que la géographie défavorise.

a) *en ce qui concerne l'enseignement*, la conférence

5. demande que la Communauté européenne s'engage plus activement, à l'égard des États associés, dans un plan d'assistance scolaire, notamment pour la construction, l'équipement et le fonctionnement d'écoles primaires, ainsi que d'établissements secondaires et d'instituts d'enseignement supérieur;

6. souhaite que l'action de la Communauté puisse également se traduire par la mise à la disposition des États associés de personnel, en nombre suffisant, en vue surtout de la formation de cadres enseignants locaux;

7. émet le vœu que les programmes de stages, auprès des services de la Communauté européenne, de ressortissants des États associés, soient de plus en plus développés;

8. préconise que le système des bourses déjà existant, notamment celui en vue d'études post-universitaires spécialisées, soit étendu et que soit accru le nombre des boursiers à admettre dans un plus grand nombre d'écoles et d'universités des pays de la Communauté européenne;

9. se féliciterait de voir mieux adaptés aux conditions locales et harmonisés entre eux les systèmes et les programmes d'enseignement aux différents degrés;

b) *en ce qui concerne la formation professionnelle*, la conférence

10. demande que soit fournie une aide substantielle pour l'édification d'établissements d'enseignement technique et que soit apportée une contribution réelle à l'équipement et au fonctionnement de ces établissements;

11. souhaite qu'un effort particulier soit fait pour assurer une formation professionnelle accélérée aux cadres de base, particulièrement dans le domaine où le besoin de ces cadres se fait spécialement sentir;

12. demande que la formation des cadres de base puisse avoir lieu le plus rapidement possible sur place dans les États associés pour être éventuellement poursuivie et complétée en Europe au moyen d'un système de bourses, de stages dans les différents secteurs professionnels;

13. estime qu'en plus des efforts propres de la C.E.E. les conditions propices devraient être créées, tant de la part des États membres que des États associés, pour que les entreprises et organismes privés des pays membres puissent apporter leur contribution à l'effort commun; il pourrait notamment être envisagé que les contrats passés entre les États associés et les firmes étrangères pour l'exécution de travaux financés par la Communauté européenne soit assortis d'une clause de formation professionnelle et de perfectionnement de cadres;

14. est d'avis que les pays membres et la Communauté européenne, dans la mesure de ses compétences, devraient prendre toutes les mesures susceptibles de faciliter le recrutement et le choix des techniciens à mettre à la disposition des États associés;

c) *en ce qui concerne les échanges culturels proprement dits*, la conférence

15. suggère que dans un règlement à établir soit envisagé chaque année l'accueil d'étudiants africains et malgaches dans la future université européenne;

16. souhaite que la Communauté européenne encourage, dans les universités nationales de l'Europe des Six, la création de chaires et de centres d'études africains et malgaches et qu'à titre de réciprocité les États associés favorisent la création de chaires européennes dans leurs universités;

17. demande que, conformément aux vœux exprimés par les représentants des exécutifs européens, il soit créé un institut euro-africain et malgache de développement qui devra coordonner les efforts publics ou privés en vue d'assister techniquement les États associés et de former leurs experts.

(e) Recommendation on the Development Fund

La conférence de l'Assemblée parlementaire européenne avec les Parlements d'États africains et de Madagascar

ayant pris connaissance des documents de travail présentés sur le Fonds de développement par M. Peyrefitte au nom de l'Assemblée parlementaire européenne et par les parlementaires africains et malgaches,

ayant constaté qu'il n'existe pas de divergences de vues notables entre ces documents,

ayant pris note des imperfections qui caractérisaient, dans sa période de démarrage, le Fonds institué par la convention d'application ainsi que des améliorations récemment apportées à son fonctionnement,

a) est convaincue que la poursuite et l'amplification du concours financier à accorder, par le moyen d'un Fonds, aux États associés est une condition nécessaire au développement de ces États;

b) recommande:

— I —

quant à l'activité de l'actuel Fonds de développement

1. que la Commission de la C.E.E., à laquelle incombe la gestion de ce Fonds, poursuive l'action qu'elle a entreprise en vue d'assouplir et d'accélérer le fonctionnement du Fonds, de manière que l'engagement de la totalité des ressources du Fonds soit effectué avant le 31 décembre 1962, en liaison directe avec les États associés;

2. que la Commission ait les moyens d'aider, dans la présentation des projets, les gouvernements des États associés, en mettant à leur disposition les conseillers techniques indispensables à l'accélération de la procédure préparatoire.

— II —

quant au Fonds de développement à instituer à partir du 1er janvier 1963

1. que le principe de parité préside au régime de ce Fonds

— sur le plan des contributions qui devraient provenir, non seulement des États membres mais aussi des États associés, en fonction de critères à définir d'un commun accord entre les intéressés;

— sur le plan du contrôle administratif et financier et sur le plan d'un contrôle parlementaire dont l'institution apparaît indispensable;

2. que ce principe se traduise dans une nouvelle dénomination du Fonds, qui pourrait être: « Fonds commun de développement»;

3. que les modalités de fonctionnement du Fonds soient conçues suivant des règles souples, tenant compte de la nécessité d'aboutir dans les plus brefs délais à l'approbation ou au rejet d'avant-projets sommaires et de mettre rapidement les moyens nécessaires à la disposition des États associés;

4. que de nouveaux critères de répartition soient définis en commun avec les États associés;

5. que ce Fonds dispose de ressources accrues et soit établi pour une période illimitée;

6. que les modalités d'intervention soient diversifiées (subventions à fonds perdus, prêts à moyen et à long terme, interventions dans la garantie d'emprunts ou d'investissements privés, dans la stabilisation des cours, dans le financement d'activités éducatives et culturelles et de certaines dépenses de fonctionnement), de manière à tenir compte de la variété des besoins des États associés, besoins dont l'inventaire devra être effectué dans le cadre d'une programmation générale avec le concours technique de la C.E.E.

2. Principles and objectives of the new Convention of Association, as agreed by the Eurafrican ministerial conference in Paris, 7 December 1961[1]

I — Problèmes généraux

1. *Principes de l'association*

L'association se fonde sur une volonté mutuelle de coopération librement exprimée par des États souverains traitant sur un pied de complète égalité.

2. *Buts et objectifs de l'association*

Conformément aux principes énoncés par le traité de Rome, l'association a en premier lieu pour but de favoriser les intérêts des États associés et la prospérité de leurs peuples de manière à promouvoir leur développement économique, social et culturel.

A cet effet, la Communauté et les pays partenaires de l'association coopèrent de façon active et étroite en vue d'assurer notamment:

— le développement de la coopération et des échanges entre les États associés et la Communauté,
— la diversification de l'économie et l'industrialisation des États associés,
— le développement de la coopération et des échanges interafricains,
— le renforcement de l'indépendance économique des États associés.

3. *Forme juridique de la nouvelle convention*

La nouvelle convention entre la Communauté et les États associés pourra revêtir la forme d'un accord type complété par des conventions ou protocoles bilatéraux ou multilatéraux.

---

[1] *Assemblée Parlementaire Européenne. Documents de Séance 1961–1962.* Document 139, 19 February 1962, pp. 5–6.

4. *Durée de l'association et de la convention*

L'association pourra être de durée illimitée, mais susceptible d'adaptations dans ses modalités. Tout État associé, de même que la Communauté, disposera du droit de dénonciation selon des modalités à déterminer de commun accord.

La nouvelle convention aura une durée de 5 à 7 ans.

II — *Problèmes économiques et commerciaux*

Dans le cadre des buts et objectifs de l'association, la nouvelle convention assurera des avantages au moins équivalents à ceux que garantit le traité de Rome aux États associés. Elle prévoira les mesures qui, de commun accord, faciliteront l'écoulement des produits tropicaux et en amélioreront la commercialisation et la rentabilité.

La nouvelle convention tiendra compte de la possibilité pour les États associés d'établir des droits de douane qui répondent aux nécessités de leur développement et aux besoins de leur industrialisation ou qui, de caractère fiscal, ont pour but d'alimenter leur budget.

III — *Problèmes de coopération technique et de la formation des cadres*

1. *Coopération technique et formation des cadres en général*

La convention devra prévoir, suivant des modalités à déterminer de commun accord, une action positive de la Communauté en matière de coopération technique et de formation des cadres en général. Au cours des négociations, la question de la création d'instituts de dévelopement—en Europe et en Afrique—sera prise en considération.

2. *Assistance technique liée aux investissements*

La convention devra prévoir, suivant des modalités à déterminer de commun accord, une intervention de la Communauté dans le domaine de la coopération technique préparatoire aux investissements (avant, pedant et après la réalisation des projets spécifiques) en fonction des besoins reconnus des États associés.

IV — *Problèmes de la coopération financière et de la contribution des États membres aux investissements que demande le développement progressif des États associés*

1. *Fonds de développement*

La nouvelle convention devra prévoir la création d'un nouveau Fonds de développement.

Le montant à mettre à la disposition de ce Fonds sera au moins égal au montant dont dispose le Fonds actuel.

Les modalités de fonctionnement du Fonds et notamment la participation des États associés à sa gestion seront déterminées de commun accord.

L'aide financière de la Communauté devra tenir compte des nécessités de l'adaption structurelle de l'économie des États africains.

2. *Mesures pour favoriser le recours aux financements privés*

La nouvelle convention pourra prévoir, suivant des modalités à déterminer de commun accord, des dispositions susceptibles de développer les investissements privés auxquels les États associés apporteraient également leur concours.

V — Problèmes institutionnels

L'association devra prévoir des institutions qui seront organisées en fonction du nouveau statut de droit international des États associés.

Seront notamment prévus:

1. un conseil d'association au niveau ministériel qui examinera, dans des conditions à déterminer de commun accord, les problèmes généraux de l'association;
2. un comité d'association, organe de préparation subordonné au Conseil d'association;
3. une institution au niveau parlementaire.

VI — Procédure et calendrier

Pour la réalisation de ces buts et objectifs, il est prévu la constitution:

1. d'un comité de direction chargé d'organiser et de coordonner l'activité des groupes ainsi que de donner les impulsions nécessaires aux travaux;
2. d'un groupe de travail pour les problèmes institutionnels et administratifs;
3. d'un groupe de travail pour la coopération financière et technique;
4. d'un groupe de travail pour les échanges et l'écoulement des produits, avec constitution de sous-groupes individualisés par produit.

La présidence du comité de direction est assurée par l'État qui préside la Communauté économique européenne, la présidence des groupes et sous-groupes de travail sera alternée entre les États membres et les États associés. Le travail des groupes devra être mené de façon très concrète et tenir compte de tous les éléments de la situation, y compris, notamment, les facteurs extérieurs à la Communauté économique européenne (aide financière des pays tiers et organisations internationales, courants commerciaux avec pays tiers, etc.).

Le calendrier suivant sera observé:

a) date et lieu de réunion des groupes de travail: janvier 1962 à Bruxelles;
b) date et lieu de la deuxième réunion entre les ministres des États membres et les ministres des États associés: 9 et 10 avril à Bruxelles;
c) date et lieu de la troisième réunion entre les ministres des États membres et les ministres des États associés: à fixer par la réunion précitée, mi - 1962.

(b) Pan-Africanism

(α) The Casablanca Group

1. Resolutions of the Casablanca conference, 7 January 1961[1]

(a) The African Charter

Nous, Chefs d'Etat africains réunis à Casablanca du 3 au 7 janvier 1961, conscients de nos responsabilités à l'égard du continent africain.

[1] *Documentation Française, Articles et Documents*, 21 January 1961, pp. 1–4. The Casablanca conference was attended by the Heads of State of Ghana, Guinea, Mali, Morocco and the United Arab Republic; Ceylon, Libya and the Algerian provisional government were also represented. The conference was largely in response to the Brazzaville meeting of French African States, held the previous month. For the latter's resolutions, see *Documents*, 1960, pp. 341–4.

Proclamons notre détermination de faire triompher la liberté dans tout l'Afrique et de réaliser son unité.

Affirmons notre volonté de conserver et de consolider une unité de vue et d'action dans les affaires internationales pour sauvegarder l'indépendance chèrement acquise la souveraineté et l'intégrité territoriale de nos Etats de renforcer la paix dans le monde en pratiquant une politique de non-alignement.

Proclamons notre volonté de libérer les territoires africains encore sous domination étrangère, de leur prêter aide et assistance de liquider le colonialisme et le néo-colonialisme sous toutes leurs formes, de ne pas encourager l'établissement des troupes et des bases étrangères qui met en danger la libération de l'Afrique et de nous employer également à débarrasser le continent africain des interventions politiques et des pressions économiques.

Proclamons la nécessité pour les Etats africains independants d'orienter leur politique économique et sociale dans le sens de l'exploitation des richesses nationales au profit de leurs peuples et d'en assurer une distribution équitable entre tous les nationaux.

Affirmons notre volonté d'intensifier nos efforts en vue de créer une coopération effective entre les Etats africains dans les domaines économique, social et culturel.

Dans le but de consolider la liberté de l'Afrique, de bâtir son unité et d'assurer sa sécurité.

DECIDONS:

1° — La création, dès que les conditions en seront réunies, d'une Assemblée consultative africaine comprenant les représentants de chaque Etat africain, ayant un siège permanent et tenant des sessions périodiques.

2° — La création des quatre comités suivants:

— Le Comité politique africain, groupant les Chefs d'Etat africains ou leurs représentants dûment mandatés, qui se réunit périodiquement en vue de coordonner et d'unifier la politique générale des divers Etats.

— le Comité économique africain, groupant les Ministres des Affaires économiques des Etats d'Afrique indépendants qui se réunit périodiquement, pour arrêter les décisions de coopération économique africaine, et dont une des tâches les plus urgentes est d'établir des relations postales et radiotélégraphiques entre les différentes capitales africaines,

— le Comité culturel africain, groupant les Ministres de l'éducation nationale des Etats africains indépendants, qui se réunit périodiquement en vue de préparer et de développer la culture et la civilisation africaines et d'intensifier la coopération et l'assistance culturelle africaine,

— un haut-commandement africain commun groupant les Chefs d'état-major des Etats africains indépendants, qui se réunit périodiquement dans le but d'assurer la défense commune de l'Afrique en cas d'agression contre une partie de ce continent et de veiller à la sauvegarde de l'indépendance des Etats africains.

3° — La création d'un Bureau de liaison destiné à assurer une coordination efficace entre les différents organismes ci-dessus énumérés, et notamment de provoquer dans un delai de trois mois à partir de la publication du présent document la réunion des experts chargés de régler des modalités pratiques concernant le fonctionnement des organismes précités.

Nous, Chefs d'Etat africains, réunis à Casablanca, du 3 au 7 janvier 1961.

Réaffirmons notre fidélité à la Conférence des Etats africains indépendants réunie à Accra en 1958 et à Addis-Abéba en 1960, et lançons un appel à tous les Etats africains indépendants pour s'associer à notre action commune de consolidation de la liberté en Afrique et d'édification de son unité.

Nous réaffirmons solennellement notre respect inébranlable de la Charte des Nations-Unies et de la déclaration de la Conférence afro-asiatique tenue à Bandoeng dans le but de promouvoir la coopération de tous les peuples du monde et de consolider la paix internationale.

(b) *Algeria*

La Conférence de Casablanca réunie par S.M. Mohammed V Roi du Maroc.

— Considérant que la quinzième session de l'Assemblée Générale des Nations Unies a reconnu le droit du peuple algérien à l'indépendance et de l'autodétermination, sur la base de l'unité de l'intégrité territorriale, ainsi que la responsabilité des Nations Unies dans la mise en application de ce droit en Algérie,

— Considérant que toute aide politique, diplomatique et matérielle apportée au peuple algérien est une contribution à la libération de l'Afrique,

— Considérant que toute aide apportée à la France dans sa guerre en Algérie constitue un acte d'hostilité à l'égard de toute l'Afrique,

— Considérant que le G.P.R.A. est la seule autorité habilitée à représenter et à engager l'Algérie,

— Considérant que la guerre que poursuit la France en Algérie constitue une menace croissante à la paix et à la sécurité de l'Afrique et du monde,

— Considérant que les événements et manifestations qui se développent en Algérie constituent l'affirmation sans équivoque de la volonté du peuple algérien de réaliser son indépendance ainsi que son unanimité et de son union autour du G.P.R.A.,

1° — Déclare sa détermination de soutenir par tous les moyens le peuple algérien et le G.P.R.A. dans leur lutte pour l'indépendance de l'Algérie,

2° — Demande à tous les pays qui soutiennent le peuple algérien dans sa lutte de libération nationale de renforcer leur aide politique, diplomatique et maté rielle,

3° — Dénonce l'assistance adoptée par l'OTAN à la France dans sa guerre de reconquête coloniale en Algérie.

4° — Invite tous les pays à interdire sans délai d'utilisation directe ou indirecte de leur territoire pour des opérations contre le peuple algérien,

5° — Demande le retrait immédiat des troupes africaines servant sous commandement français en Algérie,

6° — Approuve l'engagement de volontaires africains et autres dans l'armée de libération nationale algérienne,

7° — Invite tous les Gouvernements qui ne l'ont pas encore fait, à reconnaitre le G.P.R.A.,

8° — Déclare que la poursuite de la guerre en Algérie est de nature à amener les participants à la Conférence à reconsidérer leurs relations avec la France.

9° — S'oppose au partage de l'Algérie et rejette toute solution unilatérale et tout statut imposé ou octroyé.

(c) The Congo

La Conférence de Casablanca, ayant considéré la situation au Congo:

Déclare l'intention et la détermination des Gouvernements respectivement représentés, de retirer leurs troupes et autre personnel militaire, placés sous le commandement opérationnel des Nations Unies au Congo.

Réaffirme la reconnaissance du Parlement élu et du Gouvernement légalement constitué de la République du Congo qui fut proclamée le 30 juin 1960.

Convaincue que la seule justification de la présence des troupes des Nations Unies au Congo est:

1° — de répondre aux appels du Gouvernement légitime de la République du Congo — à la requête duquel les Nations Unies ont décidé de créer leur commandement opérationnel,

2° — d'exécuter les décisions du Conseil de Sécurité relatives à la situation au Congo,

3° — de sauvegarder l'unité et l'indépendance de la République du Congo et préserver son intégrité territoriale,

Demande instamment aux Nations Unies d'agir immédiatement en vue de:

a) desarmer et dissoudre les bandes illégales de Mobutu,

b) relâcher de prison et libérer tous les membres du Parlement et du Gouvernement légitime de la République du Congo,

c) réunir le Parlement de la République du Congo,

d) éliminer du Congo tout le personnel militaire et paramilitaire belge ou tout autre personnel étranger (n'appartenant pas au Commandement opérationnel des Nations Unies),

e) remettre au Gouvernement légitime de la République du Congo tous les aérodromes civils et militaires, les stations de radiodiffusion et autres établissements, actuellement illégalement retirés à ce Gouvernement,

f) empêcher les Belges d'utiliser le territoire ruanda-urundi sous tutelle des Nations Unies comme base d'agression directe ou indirecte, contre la République du Congo,

Décide qu'au cas où les buts et les principes qui ont justifié la présence du Commandement opérationnel des Nations Unies dans la République du Congo ne seraient pas atteints et respectés, les Etats ici représentés se réservent le droit d'engager toute action appropriée.

(d) The Israeli problem

LA CONFERENCE:

1° — Attire l'attention sur la menace que cette situation fait peser sur la paix et la sécurité du Moyen-Orient et attire l'attention sur le fait qu'il peut en résulter une tension internationale.

2° — Insiste sur la nécessité de trouver une solution juste de ces problèmes, conformément aux résolutions des Nations Unies et aux résolutions des Etats afro-asiatiques réunis à Bandoeng pour restaurer dans leurs droits légitimes les Arabes de Palestine.[1]

3° — Note avec indignation qu'Israël s'est toujours tenu au côté des impérialistes chaque fois qu'une position importante devait être prise en ce qui concerne les problèmes vitaux de leurs pays, notamment l'Algérie, le Congo et les essais nucléaires.

C'est pourquoi, la Conférence dénonce Israèl comme un instrument au service de l'impérialisme du néo-colonialisme non seulement dans le Moyen-Orient, mais aussi en Afrique et en Asie.

4° — Fait appel à tous les Etats d'Afrique et d'Asie pour qu'ils s'opposent à cette nouvelle politique que l'impérialisme est en train de mener pour créer ses propres bases.

(e) The Mauritanian problem

La Conférence tenue à Casablanca:

— Considérant les manœuvres colonialistes destinées à diviser les territoires des Etats africains pour les affaiblir,

— Considérant que la France pour mieux asseoir sa domination au Sahara, en exploiter les richesses et s'assurer des débouchés sur l'Océan Atlantique, a amputé le Maroc de sa partie sud en Mauritanie,

— Considérant que la création d'un Etat factice dit Mauritanie contre la volonté des populations et au mépris des engagements solennels souscrits par la France, constitue une violation des traités et accords internationaux,

— Considérant que l'érection de la Mauritanie en Etat n'est qu'un moyen pour la France d'encercler les Etats Africains, de s'assurer des bases de repli et multiplier le nombre de ses satellites,

— Considérant que, d'une façon générale la multiplication des Etats artificiels en Afrique constitue une menace permanente à la sécurité du continent africain, en même temps qu'un renforcement de l'impérialisme,

— Considérant que l'objectif visé par la France en Mauritanie est l'exploitation économique, et l'utilisation stratégique de cette région — en particulier contre les pays africains, ainsi que le maintien des barrières artificielles en Afrique,

— Considérant que la défense de l'unité et de l'intégrité territoriales de tout Etat africain, constitue en même temps la défense de la liberté en Afrique,

Dénonce et condamne solennellement toute forme d'exploitation économique, politique et militaire en Afrique.

Déclare s'opposer par tous les moyens à toute tentative de division et de satellisation du continent africain.

La Conférence approuve toute action menée par le Maroc en Mauritanie pour y recouvrer ses droits légitimes.

(f) Nuclear tests in the Sahara

La Conférence de Casablanca, réunie du 3 au 7 janvier 1961,

s'élève énergiquement contre la poursuite par la France, sur le territoire africain de ses essais nucléaires en dépit de la révolte de la conscience universelle,

[1] *Documents*, 1955, p. 434.

de la réprobation des pays d'Afrique et des recommandations des Nations Unies.

Dénonce avec force cet acte de provocation dirigé contre les peuples d'Afrique, dans le but de les intimider et de freiner leur marche vers leur libération et la réalisation de leur unité, ce qui constitue un danger permanent pour les populations africaines et une menace constante pour la paix dans le monde.

Dénonce et condamne la collusion entre la France et Israël dans le domaine des essais nucléaires, collusion qui menace la paix dans le monde et particulièrement en Afrique.

Lance un appel à tous les peuples et en particulier aux peuples africains menacés, de tout mettre en œuvre pour arrêter ces essais nucléaires et pour s'opposer à l'utilisation des territoires africains aux fins d'une politique de domination.

Ayant enregistré avec satisfaction le refus du peuple français de laisser se dérouler les expériences sur son territoire, invite tous les pays africains à reconsidérer leurs relations avec la France, devant son obstination de poursuivre ses explosions atomiques en Afrique.

2. Protocol of the African Charter of Casablanca, Cairo, 5 May 1961[1]

Déterminés à mettre en œuvre la Charte africaine issue de la Conférence de Casablanca, réunie du 3 au 7 janvier 1961, et en vertu des dispositions de la dite Charte, les gouvernements des Etats africains signataires ont décidé d'adopter les présents statuts:

ARTICLE PREMIER

La coopération entre les Etats membres de la Charte africaine de Casablanca s'effectue par les organismes suivants:

1) Un Comité politique africain.
2) Un Comité économique africain.
3) Un Comité culturel africain.
4) Un haut Commandement africain commun.
5) Un Bureau de liaison.

Ces organismes d'exécution des dispositions de la Charte ont un caractère permanent.

ARTICLE 2

Le *Comité politique africain* est l'organe suprême compétent pour coordonner et unifier la politique générale des Etats membres. Il est composé des chefs de ces Etats ou de leurs représentants dûment mandatés. Le Comité adopte lors de sa première réunion son règlement intérieur.

ARTICLE 3

Le Comité politique africain doit se réunir en session ordinaire une fois par an. Il peut se réunir également en sessions extrordinaires à la demande d'un Etat membre et après approbation de la majorité.

[1] *Europe France Outremer*, July–August 1961, pp. 75–76.

ARTICLE 4

Le *Comité économique africain* se compose des ministres des affaires économiques des Etats membres ou de leurs représentants. Il doit tenir des réunions périodiques et présenter au Comité politique africain un rapport sur les problèmes traités. Il soumet également au Comité politique un rapport annuel sur ses activités. Le Comité économique adopte lors de sa première réunion son règlement intérieur.

ARTICLE 5

Le *Comité culturel africain* se compose des ministres de l'éducation nationale des Etats membres ou de leurs représentants. Il doit tenir des réunions périodiques et présenter au Comité politique africain un rapport sur les problèmes traités. Il soumet également au Comité politique un rapport annuel sur ses activités.

Le Comité culturel adopte lors de sa première réunion son règlement intérieur.

ARTICLE 6

Le Haut Commandement africain commun se compose des chefs d'états-majors des Etats membres ou de leurs représentants. Il doit tenir des réunions périodiques à l'issue desquelles il soumet un rapport au Comité politique africain.

ARTICLE 7

Les recommandations du haut Commandement deviennent exécutoires après leur approbation par le Comité politique africain.

ARTICLE 8

Le Bureau de liaison a son siège à Bamako, République du Mali, et peut être transféré en tout autre lieu sur décision du Comité politique africain. Il est dirigé par un secrétaire nommé par le Comité politique africain pour une période de trois ans renouvelable. Le secrétaire est secondé par des assistants désignés par le Comité politique africain. Le secrétaire du Bureau de liaison est le plus haut fonctionnaire administratif de cet organisme.

ARTICLE 9

Le secrétaire du Bureau de liaison nomme les fonctionnaires nécessaires au bon fonctionnement des divers comités. Il soumet au Comité politique africain les projets de règlements fixant les conditions de travail.

ARTICLE 10

Le secrétaire doit présenter au Comité politique africain un rapport annuel sur les mesures les plus efficaces pour réaliser le maximum de coordination entre les différents organismes prévus par la Charte africaine de Casablanca.

ARTICLE 11

Le secrétaire ou son représentant assure les travaux du secrétariat dans les réunions des organismes précités.

ARTICLE 12

Le secrétaire prépare le projet du budget et le présente au Comité politique africain avant le début de chaque exercice financier. Le Comité politique détermine les contributions des Etats membres.

ARTICLE 13

Le secrétaire et les fonctionnaires du Bureau de liaison sont considérés comme des fonctionnaires internationaux. Dans l'exercice de leurs fonctions ils doivent recevoir d'instructions d'aucun Etat membre et toutes leurs actions ne doivent pas être incompatibles avec leur statut de fonctionnaires internationaux. Les Etats membres s'engagent à s'abstenir de tout acte de nature à les influencer dans l'accomplissement de leur mission.

ARTICLE 14

Dans tous les Etats membres de la Charte africaine de Casablanca, le secrétaire du Bureau de liaison, ses assistants, le personnel responsable, les envoyés spéciaux et les représentants des Etats membres jouissent pendant la durée de leur mission des privilèges et immunités accordés membres aux du corps diplomatique.

ARTICLE 15

Le siège du Bureau de liaison jouit des privilèges et immunités à convenir. Le secrétaire conclut à cet effet un accord avec l'Etat hôte. Les Comités jouissent, pendant les sessions tenues hors du siège du Bureau de liaison, des mêmes privilèges et immunités.

ARTICLE 16

Tout Etat africain qui accepte les dispositions de la Charte africaine de Casablanca et les présents statuts doit présenter une demande d'adhésion au président du Comité politique africain. Il devient membre après approbation du Comité politique.

ARTICLE 17

1. — Les Etats membres affirment que les devoirs et obligations résultant pour eux de leurs engagements internationaux ne doivent pas être incompatibles avec les devoirs et obligations assumés par eux en vertu des dispositions de la Charte africaine de Casablanca et des présents statuts, et notamment avec la politique de non-alignement proclamée dans la dite Charte.

2. — Les Etats membres s'engagent à notifier au secrétaire les traités et conventions.

3. — La Charte africaine de Casablanca et les présents statuts seront enregistrés auprès du secrétariat des Nations unies en application de l'article 102 de la Charte des Nations unies.

ARTICLE 18

A la demande d'un Etat membre, les présents statuts peuvent être amendés à la majorité des deux tiers des Etats membres en vue de resserrer et de consolider leurs liens.

Les propositions d'amendements doivent être communiquées au secrétaire du Bureau de liaison deux mois avant la réunion du Comité politique africain.

ARTICLE 19

Les présents statuts entrent en vigueur après leur approbation par au moins deux Etats membres.

3. Communiqué issued by the Political Committee of the African Charter of Casablanca, Cairo, 30 August 1961[1]

Le Comité Politique Africain de la Charte africaine de Casablanca a tenu sa première session au Caire les 28 et 29 août 1961. Lors de la première séance, les pays-membres de la Charte ont été représentées par:

S. Exc. Gamal Abdel-Nasser, Président de la République Arabe Unie; S.M. le Roi El-Has II. Roi du Maroc; S. Exc. Modibo Keita, Président de la République du Mali; S. Exc. Ben Youssef Ben Khedda, Chef du Gouvernement Provisoire de la République Algérienne; S. Exc. Akwa Adji, ministre des Affaires étrangères du Ghana, représentant S. Exc. Kwami N'Krumah, Président de la République du Ghana; S. Exc. Beavogui Louis Lansana, ministre des Affaires étrangères de la Guinée, représentant S. Exc. Ahmed Sékou Touré.

Il a ensuite été décidé que le Comité Politique se réunit à l'échelon des Ministre des Affaires étrangères, puis le Comité a approuvé l'ordre du jour et adopté le Réglement Intérieur.

La République Arabe Unie a été élue pour assumer la Présidence de la 1ère session, pour la durée d'un an et M. le Docteur Mahmoud Fawzi, ministre des Affaires étrangères a présidé les travaux.

Le Comité Politique a procédé à la désignation de M. Dris El-Salaoui, ancien ministre du Commerce au Maroc pour assumer les fonctions de Secrétaire du Bureau de Liaison.

Le Comité Politique a adopté à l'unanimité les rèsolutions et les recommandations de la première session du Haut Commandement Africain Commun et qui sont: la création d'un Conseil Suprême du Haut-Commandement Africain, se composant des Chefs d'Etat-Major des forces Africaines, et d'un Etat-Major militaire permanent.

Le Comité a également décidé mettre à la disposition du Haut-Commandement Africain, en cas de nécessité, des contingents appartenant aux pays-membres de la Charte de Casablanca.

Le Comité Politique a également pris note du rapport présenté par le Comité Economique africain sur les résultats de ses travaux exécutés au cours de sa 1ère session tenue à Conakri.

De même, le Comité Politique a pris connaissance du rapport présenté par le Comité Culturel sur les résultats de ses travaux exécutés au cours de sa 1ère session tenue à Tanger.

---

[1] *La Bourse Egyptienne*, 31 August 1961. The Political Committee was set up in May 1961 (see above, p. 662), and consisted of the Heads of State of the Casablanca powers, that is, Ghana, Guinea, Mali, Morocco, and the United Arab Republic. Presidents Nkrumah of Ghana and Touré of Guinea did not, however, attend the August meeting and were represented by their Foreign Ministers.

Les chefs des délégations ont procédé à l'examen des problèmes africains et déterminé leur attitude face aux·derniers événements survenus dans le Continent africain et à l'évolution de la situation internationale et ses répercussions en Afrique.

Les récents événements survenus au Congo ont évidemment retenu l'attention du Comité Politique. Les Chefs des délégations ont réaffirmé leur foi aux principes antérieurement définis, notamment dans la nécessité d'assurer l'unité et l'intégrité du territoire du Congo, et l'avènement d'une politique nationale répondant aux aspirations légitimes du peuple congolais à l'indépendance et à la liberté.

Considérant que le peuple congolais a, par sa lutte pour son indépendance, prouvé son aptitude à présider à ses destinées, les chefs des délégations ont été unanimement d'accord pour éliminer l'ingérence des pays colonialistes dans les affaires intérieures du Congo et laisser le peuple congolais décider seul de son avenir.

Les chefs des délégations ont également examiné les récents développements de la situation en Angola. Ils dénoncent les crimes perpétrés par le Portugal qui jette en prison, exile les populations et maintient la ségrégation raciale pour anéantir le mouvement de libération du peuple angolais et perpétuer l'exploitation des ressources de l'Angola. Ils réaffirment leur appui total au peuple angolais dans sa lutte pour l'indépendance conformément aux principes de la Charte des Nations Unies.

Les Chefs des délégations dénoncent la politique suivie par certains pays qui apportent une aide militaire et économique au Portugal. Ils considèrent que le maintien de cette aide qui permet au Portugal de poursuivre la politique actuelle est un acte d'agression contre le peuple angolais et celui de la Guinée dite portugaise.

Le Comité Politique considère que l'agression commise par la France contre la Tunisie et son peuple pacifique constitue un acte criminel de provocation du colonialisme pour se maintenir dans une partie de l'Afrique contre la volonté du peuple et du gouvernement tunisien.

Le Comité Politique voit dans l'obstination de la France à rester à «Bizerte» et à commettre ses actes d'agression la preuve éclatante du danger des bases militaires, d'où le colonialisme dirige son action pour anéantir les mouvements de libération et porter atteinte à la souveraineté et à l'indépendance des pays.

Le Comité Politique approuve la décision prise par l'Assemblée Générale dans sa séance du 26 août, assurant l'intégrité territoriale de la Tunisie et réclamant à la France d'évacuer le territoire tunisien.[1]

Le Comité Politique a examiné les développements de la situation en Algérie et proclame son appui total au peuple de la République Algérienne et à son Gouvernement dans sa lutte pour l'indépendance, l'unité et l'intégrité territoriale.

Les chefs des délégations dénoncent la politique de segregation raciale pratiquée en Afrique par certains pays européens, politique contraire aux principes des Droits de l'Homme et de sa dignité.

Si les chefs des délégations demandent à ces pays de renoncer à cette politique d'exploitation du Continent africain, ils sont par ailleurs décidés à prendre les

[1] Below, p. 804.

mesures nécessaires pour la dénoncer devant l'opinion publique mondiale.

Les chefs des délégations réaffirment les principes de la Charte de Casablanca et expriment leur souhait de voir d'autres pays africains adhérer à cette Charte afin de conjuguer leurs efforts communs pour assurer le bien-être de leurs peuples, élever leur niveau de vie et garantir leur indépendance et leur liberté.

Les chefs des délégations ont saisi l'occasion de la réunion du Comité Politique pour procéder à un échange des vues sur les moyens propres à développer la solidarité des pays africains et à promouvoir leur unité. Ils ont également étudie les moyens susceptibles de renforcer les liens qui unissent les pays de la Charte et de coordonner leur action dans les domaines politique, économique et culturel.

Les chefs des délégations réaffirment leurs attitudes vis-à-vis des blocs écono-miques européens et leurs dangers sur l'avenir de l'économie africaine; ils jugent nécessaire de promouvoir une politique commune aux pays de la Charte de Casablanca pour parer aux dangers de ces blocs et à leurs répercussions sur le développement des jeunes pays africains.

Les Présidents des délégations dénoncent l'attitude des pays impérialistes qui par le biais du néo-colonialisme utilisent leurs agents pour maintenir leur ingérence dans les affaires intérieures des pays africains et l'exploitation de leurs ressources naturelles.

Il est évident que les Présidents des délégations attachent une importance particulière à la Conférence des Chefs des Etats et des Gouvernements non-alignés qui se réunit à Belgrade le 1er septembre 1961[1] et considèrent cette ren-contre comme un événement historique capital, devant avoir des conséquences primordiales dans le domaine international, pour la liquidation définitive du colonialisme, le renforcement de la paix, en évitant aux peuples du monde les affres de la guerre.

Les Chefs des délégations du Comité Politique Africain réaffirment leur volonté de persévérer dans le sens des principes de la Charte de Casablanca et proclament leur entière adhésion aux résolutions de la Conférence de Casablanca qui s'est tenue du 4 au 7 janvier 1961.

The African and Malagasy Union

1. Documents of the third conference of Heads of State at Yaoundé, Cameroun, 28 March 1961[2]

(a) Communiqué

La Conférence des Chefs d'Etat de Gouvernement d'Afrique et de Madagascar réunie à Yaoundé les 26, 27 et 28 mars 1961, sous la présidence de M. Philibert Tsiranana, président de la République malgache, avait a son ordre du jour des questions d'ordre politique, les unes concernant la situation internationale, les autres les relations entre ces Etats, et des questions d'ordre économique, portant sur les conclusions de la Conference de Dakar du 30 janvier 1961.[3]

La Conférence a consacré six séances à l'examen de ces questions.

[1] Above, p. 604.
[2] *La Documentation Française, Articles et Documents*, 18 April 1961.
[3] A conference of the group's Economic Ministers, appointed by the Brazzaville con-ference (*Documents*, 1960, pp. 341–4) to make recommendations on future economic co-operation.

Elle a adopté une déclaration de politique générale, définissant la position des Etats participants sur les problèmes internationaux, tels que l'Algérie, le Congo, l'admission de la Mauritanie à l'Organisation des Nations Unies, la réunification du Cameroun, la politique de l'Apartheid en Afrique du Sud.

Chaque Etat doit, conformément à cette déclaration, adresser des instructions à sa délégation à l'Organisation des Nations Unies pour soutenir le point de vue dégagé par la Conférence.

La Conférence a également examiné le problème particulier du Ruanda-Urundi, et décidé de soutenir la position la plus conforme à la démocratie et à l'indépendance de ce territoire.

La Conférence a accepté l'invitation lancée par Sir Aladji Abubakar Tafewa Balewa, Premier Ministre de la Fédération du Nigéria, de participer à une Conférence des Etats africains indépendants au Sud du Sahara.

Cette Conférence aurait pour objet l'organisation d'une coopération culturelle, technique et économique entre ces Etats.

Elle pourrait avoir lieu après la Conférence de Monrovia sur le Congo.[1]

Sur les relations entre les Etats participant à la Conferénce, celle-ci a pris un certain nombre de décisions concernant:

A.—La Representation Diplomatique

La République de Côte d'Ivoire a été chargée de préparer un projet d'accord et une étude sur cette question.

B.—La Nationalite et la Citoyennete

La République du Cameroun a été chargé de préparer un projet de convention multilatérale et d'établissement.

C.—L'entraide Judiciaire et le Conseil Economique

La République du Sénégal a été chargée de préparer un projet d'accord et une étude.

D.—Coordination Des Telecommunications

La République du Niger a été chargée de préparer un projet d'accord et une étude.

Ces différents projets seront envoyés à tous les Etats qui feront parvenir à l'Etat rapporteur leurs observations et amendements avant le 15 juin 1961.

E.—La Defense Commune

Une réunion d'experts chargée de metre au point l'Accord de défense se tiendra à Tananarive le 30 juin 1961.

Le siège de l'Organisation a été fixé à Ougadougou.

Sur les conclusions de la Conférence Economique de Dakar, la Conférence a approuvé l'ensemble des résolutions formulées à Dakar et à Yaoundé par les experts.

Elle a pris en conséquence un certain nombre de décisions.

Elle a adopté le Traité de l'Organisation Africaine et Malgache de Coopération Economique à laquelle participent les douze Etats et dont le siège du Secrétariat général a été fixé à Yaoundé.

Les chefs d'Etat et de gouvernement ont signé le traité instituant une Société

---

[1] Below, p. 687.

Commune de Transports Aériens dénommé Air-Afrique et dont le siège administratif a été fixé à Abidjan.

La Conférence a enfin examiné le problème des relations des Etats participants avec la Communauté Economique Européenne à la suite de la Conférence de Dakar et d'une lettre récente adressée par le président de la Communauté Economique Européenne à chacun des chefs d'Etat.

La Conférence a défini les principes d'une négociation concertée des douze Etats avec la Communauté Economique Européenne et a décidé que chaque chef d'Etat les communiquerait au président de la Communauté Economique Européenne et a proposé une date d'ouverture de cette négociation.

Un Comité d'experts chargé de dégager les bases techniques de cette négociation se réunira à Paris le 25 avril à l'ambassade du Cameroun.

La prochaine conférence des chefs d'Etat et de gouvernement d'Afrique et de Madagascar aura lieu du 4 au 10 juillet 1961, à Tananarive.[1]

La Conférence a enregistré avec satisfaction le message de sympathie que lui a adressé le président des Etats-Unis d'Amérique et a donné mandat à son président de répondre au président Kennedy.

Les chefs d'Etat et de gouvernement participant à la Conférence tiennent à adresser au président de la République du Cameroun dont l'allocution de bienvenue a dressé une remarquable bilan de la coopération fraternelle et efficace des douze Etats, au gouvernement, à l'Assemblée nationale et au peuple camerounais tout entier. Leurs remerciements personnels, leurs vœux et ceux de leurs peuples pour le bonheur et la prospérité de la République du Cameroun.

(b) Declaration

Réunie à un moment où les espoirs de paix en Algérie et l'évolution du problème congolais démontrent la justesse de l'appréciation portée et de la position prix sur ces deux problèmes par les Etats de la Conférence.

Soucieuse de la tension internationale entre les grandes puissances, qui se situe, une fois de plus, dans un pays sous-développé, au Laos, confirmant ainsi la tendance de la guerre froide à s'installer dans les pays récemment parvenus à l'indépendance.

Désireuse de metre en garde l'opinion internationale contre le danger, pour la paix mondiale, que constituent de telles situations.

Constate que ces menaces sont encore plus graves pour les jeunes nations indépendantes, dont les territoires risquent de devenir le champ clos des rivalités des grandes puissances.

Rappelant les principes arrêtés à la Conférence de Brazzaville, qui constituent la base de la politique concertée des douze Etats d'Afrique et de Madagascar.

LA CONFERENCE

Salue l'ouverture des négociations directes entre le gouvernement français et le G.P.R.A., qui doit avoir lieu à Evian, comme un nouveau pas important vers la paix en Algérie.

L'ouverture de ces pourparlers illustre l'admission de la thèse sur les

[1] The meeting did not, in fact, take place until September. See below, p. 677.

négociations directes sans préalable, ni partition, définie par les douze Etats à Brazzaville et défendue par leurs délégations à New-York.

La Conférence lance un appel au gouvernement français et au G.P.R.A. pour que les pourparlers d'Evian débouchent, définitivement, sur la paix et l'amité du peuple français et du peuple algérien.

La Conférence se félicite des résultats de la Conférence de Tananarive sur le Congo.[1] Elle souhaite que, continuant cette action, toutes les tendances congolaises s'unissent pour trouver une solution de la crise actuelle, conforme aux intérêts du peuple congolais, préservant en les renforçant, son indépendance et son unité.

Elle condamne toute politique de haine qui dresserait les Congolais contre les autres et dont les conséquences seraient fatalement la division du pays en deux comme en Corée et au Vietnam.

Elle estime que la contribution de l'O.N.U., précieuse à maints égards, pour le peuple congolais, ne doit pas se transformer en une inadmissible tutelle. Toute décision de l'O.N.U. dans tous les domaines doit être prise en accord avec les autorités congolaises.

Dans le cas où cette aide, acceptée par les autorités congolaises, doit revêtir une forme militaire, la Conférence envisagerait, le cas échéant, l'envoi de troupes relevant des Etats participants.

Tels sont les principes que les Etats de la Conférence défendront à la réunion, prévue à Monrovia, sur le problème congolais et à laquelle ils ont décidé de participer.

Les Etats participant à la Conférence prendront, après la réunion de Monrovia, toutes mesures nécessitées par la situation au Congo.

La Conférence enregistre avec satisfaction que la cause de la Mauritanie, parvenue à l'indépendance sur la base de l'autodétermination du peuple mauritanien et par des voies pacifiques, apparait plus clairement à l'opinion internationale et bénéficie de la solidarité croissante des peuples africains et du monde entier ainsi qu'en témoigne l'admission de la République Islamique de Mauritanie à la Conférence Economique de l'O.N.U. pour l'Afrique et à l'Organisation Mondiale de la Santé.

La non-admission de la République Islamique de Mauritanie à l'O.N.U. due au veto soviétique et non à une décision de l'Assemblée générale, ne saurait donc se prolonger.

En conséquence, la Conférence demande aux délégations des Etats participants de soumettre à l'Assemblée générale la résolution, déposée au cours de la précédente session[2] et tendant à un nouvel examen de l'admission de la Mauritanie par le Conseil de Sécurité.

La Conférence décide également de soutenir le point de vue de la République du Cameroun sur le problème du Nord-Cameroun sous tutelle britannique.[3]

La Conférence condamne solennellement la politique d'Apartheid institué en

---

[1] Below, p. 738.

[2] G.A.O.R., Fifteenth Session, Agenda item 20, document A/4656. Mauritania was admitted to membership of the U.N.O. on 27 October 1961, together with Mongolia.

[3] In February 1961 the Northern Cameroons opted by plebiscite to join Nigeria; Southern Cameroons became part of the Republic of Cameroun.

Afrique du Sud et dont le maintien a conduit à la crise du Commonwealth.[1]

La Conférence se félicite de l'audience grandissante du groupe des douze Etats dans le concert international où, sur chaque problème mettant en jeu l'avenir de l'Afrique et la paix mondiale, son opinion, défendue avec calme et fermeté, a constitué une contribution essentielle.

Elle se félicite également des progrès réalisés dans la coopération dans tous les domaines entre les Etats participants qui viennent d'aboutir à la naissance de l'Union Africaine et Malgache.

La Conférence salue les accords en voie de conclusion entre la France et les Etats du Conseil de l'Entente qui prouvent qu'en dominant un formalisme désuet et en s'attachant aux idéaux qui les animent, la France et les Etats participants de la Conférence démontrent ainsi, dans la vie et par l'action, que l'amitié fraternelle dont se réclament leurs peuples, la coopération économique et culturelle sur la base de l'indépendance et l'égalité de leurs Etats, sont les fondements les plus solides d'une communauté d'intérêts, de sentiments et d'action dont la nécessité s'affirme plus que jamais dans un monde qui cherche à préserver la paix et à assurer un avenir heureux à l'humanité.

La Conférence lance un nouvel appel à tous les Etats africains soucieux de l'unité et désireux de coopérer avec les Etats participants sur la base des principes définis à Brazzaville et qu'elle confirme solennellement à Yaoundé.

(c) Resolutions

COMMUNAUTE ECONOMIQUE EUROPEENNE

Les chefs d'Etat Africains et Malgaches, réunis à Yaoundé.

Confirment le maintien de leur participation à la C.E.E. en tant que membres associés;[2]

Considèrent que les rapports entre les Etats membres et les Etats associés doivent se poursuivre dans le respect du traité de Rome;

Regrettent que concernant les produits des Etats associés la Communauté Economique Européenne et certains Etats membres aient pris différentes mesures, contingents tarifaires à droit nul et fiscalité intérieure, qui ne respectent pas l'esprit du traité.

De telles dispositions peuvent en effet être interprétées comme traduisant une orientation nouvelle de la politique de la C.E.E. dans ses rapports avec les Etats associés. Ils demandent en conséquence qu'en attendant l'ouverture d'une conférence réunissant les autorités de la C.E.E. et les représentants des Etats associés, aucune décision intéressant directement ou indirectement l'économie des pays associés, notamment dans le domaine du tarif extérieur commun prévu par le Traité de Rome en faveur des produits tropicaux, ne soit prise, même à titre conservatoire, sans que ces pays aient été entendus par la voix de leurs représentants qualifiés.

Pour ce qui concerne les rapports actuels avec la C.E.E. dans le cadre des conventions en cours, les chefs d'Etat adoptent les principes suivants:

— Négociation concertée avec la C.E.E. pour l'institution de procédures plus

---

[1] See below, p. 701.   [2] For the question of Association, see above, p. 647.

simples et plus efficaces pour le fonctionnement du Fonds Européen de Développement;

— Organisation des marchés prévoyant un soutien et une protection évolutive favorables aux grandes productions tropicales végétales;

— Droit des Etats africains et malgache de prendre toutes mesures tarifaires contigentaires ou autres répondant aux nécessités de leur développement industriel.

Ayant pris les mesures d'application de la décision d'accélération du Traité de Rome, les Etats africains et malgache attendent en contepartie que les Etats membres de la C.E.E. décident en faveur des produits tropicaux une accélération du rythme du traité dans l'esprit de la décision du 12 mai 1960 du conseil des ministres de la C.E.E.[1]

Les chefs des Etats Africains et Malgache, réunis à Yaoundé:

Décident de répondre aux propositions formulées par le président de la Commission de la Communauté Economique Européenne par lettre du 2 mars 1961;

— En transmettant la résolution adoptée à Yaoundé qui traite des relations entre la C.E.E. et les Etats associés;

— En acceptant que la réunion proposée soit fixée au début du mois de juin prochain;

— En demandant que l'ordre du jour de cette réunion comprenne les problèmes posés par la dite résolution.

Investissements Prives

Les chefs des Etats Africains et Malgache, réunis à Yaoundé:

Examinant le problème des investissements privés.

Conscients de l'importance capitale de ces investissements pour le développement économique et social de leurs Etats,

Réaffirment solennellements leur volonté commune d'offrir aux investissements privés toutes garanties de sécurité.

Demandent avec la plus grande insistance l'institution de Fonds nationaux et internationaux de garantie et se déclarent disposés à y participer sous une forme appropriée à déterminer par l'O.A.M.C.E.

Décident: 1) De se communiquer mutuellement, avant le 15 mai prochain, terme de rigueur, la liste détaillée et complète des facilités de toutes sortes accordées sur le territoire de leurs Etats aux investissements privés, que ces facilités soient d'ordre réglementaire, fiscal, domanial ou autre; ainsi que la liste des enterprises ayant déjà bénéficié de ces facilités; 2) Après étude de cette documentation, de rechercher au sein de l'O.A.M.C.E. et compte tenu aussi bien de la diversité des ressources des Etats que de la nature même des investissements privés, l'harmonisation des mesures suivantes:

— Exonération en matière de fiscalité extérieure et intérieure;

— Stabilisation du régime fiscal;

— Convention d'établissement garantissant notamment dans le cadre des réglementations en vigueur, la possibilité de transfert des capitaux investis et des

---

[1] *Documents*, 1960, pp. 154–5.

bénéfices, les avantages accordés aux réinvestissements des bénéfices, ainsi qu'une procédure d'arbitrage.

Les facilités précitées ne devront pas avoir pour conséquences de priver les Etats représentés à Yaoundé, au bénéfice de l'Etat où l'entreprise est installée, des ressources fiscales dont ils disposent. Cela implique pour chaque Etat le droit, après examen des incidences économiques, de maintenir partiellement ou totalement ces ressources, par voie d'imposition ou de convention de ristourne avec l'Etat de production.

Les propositions d'harmonisation devront être soumises par les experts à la Conférence des chefs d'Etat, au plus tard le 15 septembre prochain. A cet effet, la première réunion des experts est fixée pour le 6 juin 1961, à Paris.

3) Avant la réalisation de l'harmonisation envisagée, les Etats membres s'informeront mutuellement à l'intérieur des unions douanières existantes, des projets d'investissements susceptibles de bénéficier des mesures particulières prévues par leurs régimes d'investissements.

TELECOMMUNICATIONS

Les chefs des Etats Africains et Malgache, réunis à Yaoundé:

Considérant que le développement de leurs relations réciproques de télécommunications peut contribuer à créer et à maintenir amitié et compréhension, entre leurs peuples, mais.

Constatant qu'à l'heure actuelle, les liaisons téléphoniques et télégraphiques ont été conçues en fonction d'une répartition géographique dépassée.

Désireux d'harmoniser leurs politiques d'équipement de leurs réseaux nationaux de télécommunications pour apporter une contribution efficace à l'accroissement de leur solidarité sur le renforcement des liens économiques qui les unissent.

Décident la réunion, le 15 juin, à Fort-Lamy, d'un comité d'experts groupant les représentants de l'Union des Postes et Télécommunications des Etats de l'Afrique de l'Ouest, de l'Office Equatorial des Postes et Télécommunications, de la Direction des Postes et Télécommunications du Cameroun.

Ce comité devra proposer à la prochaine conférence des chefs d'Etats des textes organisant une union postale restreinte qui devra être déclarée à l'Union internationale des Télécommunications et à l'Union postale universelle, avant la fin de l'année 1961.

(*d*) *Treaty setting up an African-Malagasy Organization of Economic Co-operation* (*O.A.M.C.E.*)

Le gouvernement de la République du Cameroun, le gouvernement de la République centrafricaine, le gouvernement de la République du Congo (Brazzaville), le gouvernement de la Côte d'Ivoire, le gouvernement de la République du Dahomey, le gouvernement de la République gabonaise, le gouvernement de la République de Haute-Volta, le gouvernement de la République malgache, le gouvernement de la République islamique de Mauritanie, le gouvernement de la République du Niger, le gouvernement de la République du Sénégal, le gouvernement de la République du Tchad,

Considérant la nécessité d'affirmer leur indépendance politique par la promotion économique et sociale de leurs populations;

Constatant qu'il n'y a pas lieu à l'heure actuelle de procéder à la création d'un organisme à caractère supra-national, comportant désaisissement de souveraineté, puisque la réalisation des dits objectifs peut être obtenue par une action concertée respectant la personnalité politique des Etats, menée à leur initiative et sous leur responsabilité;

Considérant que la réalisation de ces objectifs exige une action concertée respectant leur personnalité politique, menée à leur initiative et sous leur responsabilité;

Désireux d'harmoniser leurs politiques économiques et d'apporter ainsi une contribution à l'accroissement de la solidarité africano-malgache par le renforcement des liens économiques qui les unissent dans le respect des engagements internationaux auxquels ils ont souscrits:

Sont convenus de ce qui suit:

Titre I
Dispositions Générales

Article premier. — Il est créé une Organisation africaine et malgache de coopération économique (O.A.M.C.E.), dénommée ci-après l'Organisation.

Art. 2. — L'Organisation a pour objet de renforcer la solidarité profonde et la volonté d'étroite coopération des Etats africains et malgache pour leur permettre d'accélérer l'élévation du niveau de vie de leurs populations.

Elle est ouverte à tout Etat africain dont la politique s'inspire de ce principe.

Art. 3. — A cet effet, l'action de l'Organisation tend à rapprocher progressivement les politiques économiques des Etats membres et à coordonner leurs plans de développement. Cette action peut s'exercer dans tous les domaines de la politique économique, et notamment les suivants:

— la production (coordination des productions agricoles, transformation des techniques) et l'industrialisation ainsi que leur financement (crédit, fiscalité, régime des investissements, fonds africain et malgache de développement et de solidarité);

— les échanges internes et externes (prix et marchés, tarifs douaniers et politique commerciale, circuits commerciaux interafricains);

— la monnaie (coopération africano-malgache et politique monétaire commune vis-à-vis de l'extérieur;

— les relations avec les organisations économiques régionales ou internationales.

Art. 4. — Pour son action, l'Organisation utilise les moyens à sa disposition, et notamment:

— l'élaboration de recommandations aux Etats membres pour l'harmonisation des politiques économiques internes;

— l'entreprise de réalisations communes sur fonds communs et au bénéfice commun lorsqu'elles sont nécessairement à l'échelle plurinationale;

— la coordination des programmes africano-malgaches de recherche scientifique et géologique pouvant aller jusqu'à la création d'instituts plurinationaux et la coopération avec les instituts étrangers ou internationaux;

— la normalisation, la centralisation et la diffusion de la documentation et de l'information;

— la négociation au nom de chacun des Etats membres avec des Organisations ou des Pays tiers.

Art. 5. — Les institutions de l'Organisation sont:

Le Conseil, le Secrétariat général, les comités techniques.

Titre II
LE CONSEIL

Art. 6. — Le Conseil est l'organe suprême de décision de l'Organisation.

Chaque état y délègue un représentant.

Art. 7. — Le Conseil se réunit tous les six mois en session ordinaire, la date d'ouverture d'une session étant fixée par lui au terme de la session précédente.

Il peut se réunir en session extraordinaire sur convocation de son président, l'initiative de celui-ci ou de la majorité de ses membres.

Il siège successivement dans les divers Etats membres, deux mois après l'entrée en vigueur du présent Traité.

Art. 8. — La présidence du Conseil est assurée à tour de rôle par chaque membre pour toute la période s'étendant du début d'une session ordinaire au début de la suivante.

Art. 9. — Les Etats membres s'engagent à participer aux réunions du Conseil ou à s'y faire représenter par un autre Etat membre.

Art. 10. — Les décisions sont prises et les recommandations sont faites par accord de tous les membres.

Chaque membre dispose d'une voix.

Art. 11. — Si un Etat membre n'est pas présent ou représenté à une réunion du Conseil, il est présumé accepter les décisions intervenues en son absence si, dans un délai fixé par le Conseil, il n'a déclaré s'y opposer; dans ce cas, les décisions ne seront pas exécutées. Toutefois, les membres qui ont participé à ces décisions peuvent décider qu'elles leur seront applicables.

Art. 12. — Le Conseil se prononce sur toutes questions dont il juge l'étude opportune pour la réalisation des objectifs communs.

Art. 13. — Le Conseil arrête les règles de fonctionnement des différentes institutions de l'Organisation.

Il nomme le Secrétaire général.

Art. 14. — Le Conseil arrête chaque année le budget de l'Organisation et fixe le montant de la contribution de chaque Etat.

Titre III
LE SECRETARIAT GÉNÉRAL

Art. 15. — Le Conseil est secondé dans sa tâche par un secrétaire général nommé pour deux ans.

Art. 16. — Sous l'autorité du Conseil, le Secrétaire général assure le fonctionnement administratif de l'Organisation.

Le Conseil précise les attributions du Secrétaire général.

Le Secrétaire général présente au Conseil, outre un rapport annuel un rapport à l'ouverture de chaque session du Conseil.

Art. 17. — Le Secrétaire général et le personnel du Secrétariat, placé sous son autorité, ne reçoivent et ne sollicitent de directives que du président du Conseil en exercice.

Art. 18. — Le siège du Secrétaire général est fixé à Yaoundé.

Titre IV
LES COMITÉS TECHNIQUES

Art 19. — L'Organisation comporte les comités techniques suivants :
— un comité de la recherche scientifique et technique ;
— un comité d'études des problèmes monétaires ;
— un comité du commerce extérieur, échanges, coopération douanière ;
— un comité de développement économique et social (études, plans, harmonisation des fiscalités et des régimes des investissements...)

Art. 20. — D'autres comités peuvent être créés, soit à l'initiative de l'Organisation, soit à l'initiative de plusieurs Etats pour l'étude de problèmes généraux régionaux ou spécifiques.

Titre V
COOPÉRATION RÉGIONALE

Art. 21. — Chaque fois qu'il est nécessaire les Etats africains et malgaches, membres ou non de l'Organisation qui en expriment le besoin, en fonction d'intérêts communs spécifiques, peuvent se réunir sous son égide, dans l'esprit de coopération et de solidarité qui préside au présent traité.

Ces Etats, peuvent prendre des décisions spéciales, les concernant dans la mesure où elles ne contredisent pas les décisions de l'Organisation.

Ils peuvent être chargés par l'Organisation de mener des actions régionales.

Ils ont la possibilité de demander la constitution de Secrétariats régionaux ou de Comités techniques consacrés à l'étude de leurs problèmes spécifiques.

Titre VI
DISPOSITIONS DIVERSES

Art. 22. — Chaque année le Conseil au cours de sa dernière session, étudie les moyens de mettre en harmonie les institutions de l'Organisation avec l'évolution de ses objectifs tels qu'ils sont annexées au présent Traité.

Les décisions prises à ce titre par le Conseil sont annexées au présent Traité.

Art. 23. — Les Etats membres prennent toutes mesures propres à assurer l'exécution des dispositions du présent Traité ou celles qui résultant des actes accomplis par les institutions de l'Organisation.

Art. 24. — L'admission d'un nouveau membre fait l'objet d'une décision du Conseil.

Art. 25. — Le présent traité est ratifié ou accepté par les Etats signatairés conformément à leurs règles constitutionnelles respectives.

Les instruments de ratification ou d'acceptation seront déposés auprès du gouvernement de la République du Cameroun désigné comme gouvernement dépositaire.

Art. 26. — Le présent Traité entre en vigueur dès que les instruments de ratification ou d'acceptation auront été déposés par huit Etats auprès du gouvernement de la République du Cameroun.

En foi de quoi, les plénipotentiaires soussignés, dûment habilités, ont apposé leurs signatures au bas du présent Traité.

Fait à Yaoundé, le 28 mars 1961.

Le président de la République du Cameroun.
Le président de la République Centrafricaine.
Le président de la République du Congo.
Le président de la République de Côte d'Ivoire.
Le premier ministre de la République Gabonnaise, chef de l'Etat.
Le président de la République du Dahomey.
Le président de la République de Haute-Volta.
Le premier ministre de la République Islamique de Mauritanie.
Le président de la République Malgache.
Le président de la République du Niger.
Le président du gouvernement de la République du Sénégal.
Le Chef de l'Etat, président du Conseil des ministres de la République du Tchad.

2. Charter of the African and Malagasy Union, Tananarive, 7 September 1961[1]

Article Premier. — L'Union africaine et malgache (U.A.M.) est une union d'Etats indépendants et souverains, ouverte à tout Etat africain indépendant.

L'admission d'un Etat au sein de l'U.A.M. se fait à l'unanimité des membres composant l'Union.

BUT

Article 2. — L'U.A.M. est fondée sur la solidarité qui unit ses membres.

Elle a pour but d'organiser, dans tous les domaines de la *politique extérieure*, la coopération entre ses membres, afin de renforcer leur solidarité, d'assurer leur sécurité collective, d'aider à leur développement, de maintenir la paix en Afrique, à Madagascar et dans le monde.

FONCTIONNEMENT

Article 3. — L'U.A.M. est dotée d'un secrétariat général administratif dont le siège est à Cotonou.

Le secrétaire général administratif est nommé pour deux ans par la Conférence des chefs d'Etat et de gouvernement sur proposition du président de la République du Dahomey.

Son traitement est fixé par la même Conférence, qui vote, par ailleurs, le budget annuel du secrétariat général administratif. La contribution de chaque Etat à ce budget est proportionnelle au budget de fonctionnement de chaque Etat membre.

Article 4. — La politique générale de l'U.A.M. est définie par la Conférence des chefs d'Etat et de gouvernement, qui se réunit, en session ordinaire, deux fois par an. Des sessions extraordinaires pourront avoir lieu, à l'initiative d'un Etat, appuyé par la majorité des membres de l'Union.

[1] *Europe France Outremer*, July–August 1961, p. 74.

Entre ces sessions, il est prévu, suivant la nature des problèmes, des réunions des ministres compétents, des experts ou des délégués permanents à l'O.N.U.

Le vote est acquis à la majorité simple. La discipline est de rigueur dans les problèmes de décolonisation.

Article 5. — Il est créé un Groupe de l'U.A.M. à l'O.N.U.

Ce Groupe se réunit obligatoirement pour se concerter avant toute décision importante.

Article 6. — La présente Charte sera publiée au « Journal Officiel » de chaque Etat membre.

3. Defence Pact of the African and Malagasy Union, Tananarive, 9 September 1961[1]

Preambule

Les Etats parties au présent Pacte.

Réaffirment solennellement leur attachement aux principes de la Charte des Nations Unies et proclament leur désir de vivre en paix avec toutes les Nations.

Reconnaissent *l'égalité souveraine* de tous les Etats et entendent cimenter et renforcer les liens existants entre eux sur la base du respect de leur indépendance et de la non-ingérence dans leurs affaires intérieures.

Déterminés à *sauvegarder la liberté* de leurs peuples, leurs propres civilisations, leurs libertés individuelles et le règne du droit et du respect de l'homme.

Conscients de leur *faiblesse s'ils demeurent isolés* et décidés à unir leurs efforts pour le maintien de la paix et de la sécurité dans leur propre Etat et dans le monde ainsi que pour la promotion de l'Unité Africaine et Malgache.

Ils se sont mis d'accord sur le présent Pacte.

Article Premier. — Les parties s'engagent, en conformité avec la Charte des Nations Unies, à régler par des *moyens pacifiques* tous différends internationaux dans lesquels elles pourraient être impliquées de telle manière que la paix et la sécurité internationales, ainsi que la justice, ne soient pas mises en danger, et à s'abstenir dans leurs relations internationales de recourir à la menace et à toute forme d'agression.

Article 2. — Les parties contribueront au *développement de relations internationales pacifiques et amicales* en renforçant leurs libres institutions; en assurant une meilleure compréhension des principes sur lesquels ces institutions sont fondées et en développant les conditions propres à assurer la sécurité et le bien-être. Elles s'efforceront d'éliminer toute opposition dans leurs politiques, notamment dans les domaines économique, social, culturel et diplomatique et encourageront la collaboration avec chacune d'entre elles et entre toutes.

Article 3. — Afin d'assurer de façon plus efficace la réalisation des buts du présent Pacte, les parties, agissant individuellement et conjointement, d'une manière continue et effective, par le développement de leurs propres moyens et en se prêtant mutuellement assistance, maintiendront et accroîtront leur *capacité individuelle et collective de résistance a toute agression*.

Article 4. — Les parties *se consulteront* sur les mesures à prendre chaque fois que, de l'avis de l'une d'elles, l'intégrité territoriale, l'indépendance politique ou la sécurité de l'une des parties sera menacée.

[1] Union Africaine et Malgache, *Documentation* (Paris, 1963), pp. 97–101.

Article 5. — Les parties conviennent qu'une *agression reconnue* comme telle dans les conditions définies dans un protocole annexe et dirigée contre l'une ou plusieurs d'entre elles, survenant en Afrique ou à Madagascar, sera considérée comme une agression dirigée contre toutes les parties. En conséquence, si une telle agression se produit, chacune d'elles, dans l'exercice du droit de légitime défense, individuelle ou collective, reconnu par l'article 51 de la Charte des Nations Unies, assistera la partie ou les parties ainsi agressées en prenant aussitôt des mesures convenues d'avance, puis après consultation, toutes autres mesures jugées nécessaires, y compris l'emploi de la force armée, pour rétablir et assurer la sécurité en Afrique et à Madagascar.

Article 6. — Les parties conviennent cependant qu'aucune action ne sera enterprise sur le territoire d'un Etat ou diplomatiquement à son bénéfice qu'à sa *requête ou avec son consentement*, sauf que l'ampleur, la violence ou la rapidité de l'agression aient interrompu le libre jeu de ses institutions et l'exercice de sa souveraineté.

Article 7. — Toute agression et toutes mesures prises en conséquence seront immediatement portées à la connaissance du Conseil de Sécurité des Nations Unies.

Article 8. — Les parties conviennent que par « *agression* » on entend non seulement les attaques armées du type nucléaire ou conventionnel mais encore les actions, armées ou non, de forme subversive dirigées animées ou soutenues de l'extérieur.

Article 9. — Les parties conviennent qu'aucun des engagements du présent Pacte ne pourra être interprété comme portant atteinte aux conventions ou accords conclus, en matière de défense, 'ar l'une ou l'autre des parties contractantes avec des *Etats tiers*.

Article 10. — Chacune des parties déclare qu'aucun *des engagements internationaux* actuellement en vigueur entre elle et toute autre partie ou tout autre Etat n'est en contradiction avec le Pacte.

Tout engagement nouveau intéressant la défense devra faire l'objet *d'accords préalables* des parties et les textes définitifs des engagements souscrits seront déposés auprès du Gouvernement de Madagascar.

Article 11. — La politique générale de l'Union ainsi que l'orientation à donner à la Défense seront arrêtées en *Conférence des Chefs d'Etat et de Gouvernement*.

Article 12. — Les parties conviennent de créer un *Conseil Supérieur du Pacte* au sein duquel chacune d'elles sera représentée par un délégué plénipotentiaire.

Ce Conseil sera chargé d'étudier toutes questions relatives à l'application du Pacte et, dans la limite des attributions qui lui sont fixées par la Conférence des Chefs d'Etat et de Gouvernement, d'arrêter les mesures propres à garantir cette application, tant en ce qui concerne la mise en œuvre des dispositions qu'il contient que par la création des organismes civils et militaires nécessaires au bon fonctionnement du Pacte et notamment d'un Etat-Major. Ses décisions seront prises à la majorité des deux tiers des membres du Pacte.

Article 13. — Les parties créent *un Secrétariat Permanent du Pacte* placé à la disposition du Conseil Supérieur, en vue d'assurer la continuité et la rapidité de ses travaux ainsi que la préparation de ses sessions.

Article 14. — Des protocoles particuliers définiront l'organisation, le fonctionnement, les attributions détaillées et le financement du Conseil Supérieur, du Secrétariat Permanent et de tout autre organisme éventuellement créé en application des articles précédents.

Article 15. — Le présent Pacte est *ouvert* aux autres Etats africains qui se déclarent prêts, en y participant, à contribuer à l'union des Etats africains et malgache en vue d'assurer la paix et la sécurité des peuples dans le respect des droits de l'homme.

L'adhésion d'un nouvel Etat au Pacte entrera en vigueur, avec le consentement unanime des Etats signataires du Pacte, après le dépôt des instruments d'adhésion entre les mains du Gouvernement de Madagascar.

Article 16. — L'Union Africaine et Malgache peut, après accord unanime de ses membres, contracter avec tout Etat ou groupe d'Etats, africain ou non, des engagements internationaux concourant aux buts du présent Pacte.

Article 17. — Ce Pacte sera ratifié par les parties conformément à leurs régles constitutionnelles respectives. Les instruments de ratification seront déposés, dans un délai de trois mois après la signature, auprès du Gouvernement de Madagascar qui informera toutes les autres parties du dépôt de chaque instrument de ratification. Le Pacte entrera en vigueur entre les Etats qui l'auront ratifié dès que les instruments de ratification de la majorité simple des signataires auront été déposés. Il entrera en application à l'égard des autres signataires le jour du dépôt de leur instrument de ratification.

Article 18. — Si l'une des parties contractantes avait souscrit ou venait à souscrire *des engagements contraires* aux dispositions du présent Pacte ou à méconnaitre gravement les obligations qui en découlent, elle peut être exclue du Pacte par une décision prise par les autres parties contractantes en Conférence des Chefs d'Etat et de Gouvernement à la majorité des deux tiers.

Toutefois, l'exclusion devra être précédée d'une mise en demeure donnant à la partie en cause un délai raisonnable pour se conformer à ses obligations.

Article 19. — Les parties se consulteront obligatoirement tous les *cinq ans en vue d'une révision éventuelle du Pacte*.

Toutefois, à tout moment, la révision pourra être demandée par l'unanimité des parties.

En tous les cas, la révision ne pourra intervenir que par accord unanime des parties.

Article 20. — Après que le Pacte aura été en vigueur *pendant dix ans*, toute partie pourra s'en retirer. Toutefois, cette mesure ne prendra effet qu'un an après que la partie intéressée aura notifié cette dénonciation au Gouvernement de Madagascar. Ce dernier en informera les Gouvernements des autres parties.

Article 21. — Outre les protocoles évoqués aux articles précédents, des protocoles annexés au présent Pacte règleront en tant que de besoin les conditions de son application.

Article 22. — L'original de ce Pacte sera déposé dans les Archives du Gouvernement de Madagascar.

Des copies certifiées conformes seront transmises par ce Gouvernement aux Gouvernements des autres Etats signataires.

En foi de quoi, les soussignés, Chefs d'Etat ou plénipotentiaires dûment autorisés, ont signé le présent Pacte.

(γ) *The Union of African States*

1. Documents relating to the Conference of Heads of State, Accra, 29 April 1961[1]

(a) Communiqué issued by the Heads of State of Ghana, Guinea, and Mali

Les Chefs d'Etat du Ghana, de la Guinée et du Mali ont tenu à Accra, du 27 au 29 avril 1961, la première réunion des Chefs d'Etat de l'Union.

Ils ont examiné les recommandations soumises par la commission nommées à Conakry le 24 décembre 1960,[2] et ont décidé que soit établie entre les trois républiques du Ghana, de Guinée et du Mali, sous réserve de l'approbation de leurs parlements respectifs, une Union qui s'appellera « Union des Etats Africains » ; une Charte de l'Union comprenant une disposition qui permet à tout autre Etat ou Fédération africaine d'y adhérer fut adoptée.

Les trois Chefs d'Etats ont fait un tour d'horizon de la situation internationale, particulièrement en ce qui concerne le Congo, l'Algérie, les essais nucléaires et le néo-colonialisme.

Les trois Chefs d'Etat après avoir examiné la situation au Congo, ont réaffirmé leur appui total au gouvernement légal dirigé par M. Antoine Gizenga.

Les trois Chefs d'Etat ont réaffirmé leur confiance dans le peuple algérien et le gouvernement provisoire de la République Algérienne qui luttent courageusement pour obtenir une indépendance totale et une souveraineté effective.

Les trois Chefs d'Etat ont marqué leur indignation à l'explosion atomique à laquelle la France vient de procéder sur le sol d'Afrique[3] tout près des Etats de l'Union et ont condamné la France pour son mépris total de l'opinion africaine.

Les trois Chefs d'Etat ont mis tous les pays africains particulièrement ceux qui viennent d'accéder à l'indépendance, ou sont sur le point d'y accéder, en garde contre le néo-colonialisme.

Les trois Chefs d'Etat ont condamné les émeutes fascistes en Algérie.

Ils font appel à tous les Etats africains pour réaliser un front commun de lutte contre la balkanisation et le néo-colonialisme.

Les trois Chefs d'Etats ont noté que deux d'entre eux[4] s'étaient associés à d'autres Etats africains pour convoquer à Monrovia, à partir du 8 mai, 1961, une conférence des chefs des différents Etats africains, afin que les principaux responsables des destinées des pays indépendants d'Afrique puissent étudier sérieusement la conjoncture africaine et arrêter des solutions favorables à l'unité africaine, à la coopération entre Etats, et surtout à la décolonisation intégrale des peuples du continent africain.

Constatant que la plupart des Etats participant à cette conférence seront représentés par d'autres délégués que leurs chefs, les trois Chefs d'Etat de l'Union estiment que la conférence mériterait d'être reportée à une date ultérieure fixée en accord complet entre les Chefs d'Etat qui pourront dans ces conditions participer effectivement à une conférence si importante pour l'avenir commun et solidaire de nos peuples.

[1] *Documentation Française, Articles et Documents*, 25 May 1961.
[2] *Documents*, 1960, pp. 375–6.   [3] At Reggane, Algeria, on 25 April.
[4] Guinea and Mali.

fait à Accra, le 29 avril 1961.

Signé:

MODIBO KEITA,
Président de la république du Mali.

SÉKOU TOURÉ
Président de la République de Guinée.

KWAMÉ N'KRUMAH,
Président de la République du Ghana.

(b) *Charter of the Union of African States*

Le Président de la République du Ghana;
Le Président de la République de Guinée;
Le Président de la République du Mali,
réunis à Accra les 27, 28, et 29 avril 1961;

Considérant:

Les communiqués conjoints:

a) du 23 novembre 1958, à Accra créant une Union entre le Ghana et la Guinée;

b) du 1er mai 1959, à Conakry, établissant les bases pratiques de réalisation de cette union et proposant les principes de base d'une large Communauté africaine n'ayant d'allégeance envers aucune puissance étrangère;[1]

c) le communiqué conjoint des chefs d'Etat de la République du Ghana et de la République du Mali de novembre 1960, à Bamako, dans le sens de la réalisation de l'Unité africaine;

d) le communiqué conjoint des chefs d'Etat de la République de Guinée et de la République du Mali en date du 5 décembre 1960, à Siguri, préconisant une union des deux Etats et décidant de l'intensification des relations d'amitié et de coopération qui les unis sent à la République du Ghana;

e) le communiqué conjoint issu de la rencontre des Présidents Kwamé N'Krumah, Sékou Touré et Modibo Keita à Conakry, le 24 décembre 1960, réaffirmant leur volonté commune de créer une Union entre le Ghana, la Guinée et le Mali et donnant mandat à une commission spéciale de mettre au point des modalités de réalisation concrète de cette Union;[2]

Considérant:

Les conclusions de cette commission spéciale réunie à Accra, du 13 au 18 janvier 1960,

Décident (sous réserve de l'approbation de leurs parlements respectifs):

Titre I
DISPOSITIONS GENERALES

Il est créé entre les Républiques du Ghana, de la Guinée et du Mali une Union qui prend le nom de «UNION DES ETATS AFRICAINS».

L'U.E.A. se considère comme un embryon des Etats Unis d'Afrique, elle est ouverte à tout Etat ou Fédération d'Etats d'Afrique qui en accepte les buts et les objectifs.

[1] *Documents*, 1959, pp. 619–20.   [2] ibid., 1960, pp. 375–6.

Elle réaffirme l'adhesion totale de ses membres à la Charte africaine et aux résolutions de Casablanca.

L'U.E.A. (U.A.S.) se donne comme but:

— de renforcer et de développer les liens d'amitié et de coopération fraternelle entre les Etats membres dans le domaine politique, diplomatique, économique et culturel;

— de mettre en commun les moyens dont ils disposent en vue de la consolidation de leur indépendance, et la sauvegarde de leur intégrité territoriale;

— d'œuvrer conjointement pour la liquidation complète de l'impérialisme, du colonialisme et du néo-colonialisme en Afrique et pour l'édification de l'Unité africaine;

— d'harmoniser la politique nationale et internationale de ses membres pour une grande efficacité de leur action et une meilleure contribution à la sauvegarde de la paix mondiale.

L'activité de l'Union s'exerce principalement dans les domaines suivants:

a) *Politique intérieure:* Elaboration d'une orientation commune des Etats;

b) *Politique extérieure:* Observation stricte d'une diplomatie concertée dans un esprit d'étroite coopération;

c) *Défense:* Organisation d'un système de défense commun permettant de mobiliser tous les moyens de défense des Etats en faveur de tout Etat de l'Union victime d'agression;

d) *Economie:* Définition d'une orientation commune des directives sur la planification économique visant à la décolonisation complète des structures héritées du régime colonial et organisation de l'exploitation des richesses des pays dans l'intérêt des populations;

e) *Culture:* Réhabilitation et développement de la culture africaine et échanges culturels fréquents et divers.

Titre II
Sur le Plan Politique

L'organe suprême de direction de l'U.E.A. (U.A.S.) est la Conférence des Chefs d'Etat de l'Union.

1. — *La Conférence de l'Union:* Elle a lieu une fois par trimestre respectivement à Accra, Bamako, Conakry.

Elle est placée sous la présidence du Chef de l'Etat qui reçoit. Celui-ci fixe la date de la conférence.

2. — La Conférence des Chefs d'Etat de l'Union prend des résolutions qui sont immédiatement exécutoires.

3. — *Commission préparatoire:* La Conférence de l'Union est toujours précédée de la réunion d'une commission chargée de la préparer. Celle-ci peut être convoquée à tout moment par le Chef de l'Etat qui reçoit. Ce Chef d'Etat en fixe le nombre de délégués par Etat en fonction des questions inscrites au projet d'ordre du jour.

La commission préparatoire formule des recommandations à l'intention de la Conférence des Chefs d'Etat de l'Union.

4. — *Comités de coordination des organisations de masses de l'Union:* Il sera créé entre les organisations politiques, syndicales, de femmes et de jeunesse des

D.I.A.–Z

Etats de l'Union, un comité de coordination par nature d'organisation en vue de leur donner une orientation idéologique commune indispensable au développement de l'Union.

Ces Comités seront créés dans les trois mois qui suivent la publication du présent document.

Chacun des comités de coordination prévus ci-dessus, lors de sa première réunion constitutive, établit son règlement intérieur et détermine les moyens pratiques et la méthode à mettre en œuvre pour atteindre les objectifs déterminés en commun.

5. — *Fêtes nationales:* Avant qu'il ne soit institué une fête de l'Union, les fêtes nationales des Etats de l'Union seront marquées par des manifestations dans tous les Etats: cérémonies, meetings publics.

Ces journées pourront être déclarées fériées en tout ou en partie selon les nécessités des pays.

Titre III
SUR LE PLAN DIPLOMATIQUE

Le principe de l'harmonisation de la politique extérieure des Etats de l'Union sera basée sur une diplomatie concertée.

En vue de cette harmonisation:

a) il sera procédé à chaque Conférence des Chefs d'Etat de l'Union à l'analyse par les Chefs d'Etat de la situation politique internationale et à la détermination des directives de l'Union à adresser à l'ensemble des missions diplomatiques des Etats membres;

b) les ambassadeurs, chargés d'Affaires, consuls et chefs de mission des trois pays à l'étranger coordonneront leurs activités par des consultations fréquentes;

c) toute latitude est laissée à chaque Etat de confier sa représentation à l'ambassade d'un autre Etat membre de l'Union. Dans le cas où il n'existerait aucune représentation des trois Etats de l'Union, l'Etat membre désireux de confier ses affaires à la mission diplomatique d'un autre Etat non membre de l'Union, consultera la Conférence de l'Union avant d'y procéder;

d) dans les organismes internationaux, conférences ou rencontres internationales, les délégations des Etats de l'Union se consulteront obligatoirement, arrêteront des dispositions communes que nul n'aura le droit d'ignorer et que tous auront le devoir de défendre.

Titre IV
SUR LA DEFENSE COMMUNE

Pour la sauvegarde de leur souveraineté, les Etats membres s'opposeront à toute installation de bases militaires étrangères sur leur territoire national.

Ils assurent en commun la défense de leur intégrité territoriale. Toute agression contre l'un des Etats est considérée comme une agression contre les autres Etats membres de l'Union.

Il sera organisé un système commun de défense pour permettre d'assurer la défense permanente des Etats de l'Union.

Titre V
SUR L'ECONOMIE
COMMISSION ECONOMIQUE DE L'UNION

La commission économique de l'Union est chargée de coordonner et d'harmoniser la politique économique et financière des Etats de l'Union suivant les directives déterminées ensemble.

La commission économique comprend une délégation de cinq membres par Etat choisis parmi les responsables des secteurs économique et financier de chaque Etat.

Elle tiendra deux sessions annuelles, aux mois de mars et septembre. Chaque Etat sera le siège de la commission économique de l'Union pendant une durée d'un an et en assurera la présidence.

La commission économique de l'Union établira son règlement intérieur lors de sa première session. Les sessions de la commission économique de l'Union ne peuvent durer plus de quinze jours.

Elle arrête au cours des sessions des recommandations qui sont transmises immédiatement aux chefs d'Etat.

Titre VI
SUR LA CULTURE

La réhabilitation de la culture africaine et le développement de la civilisation africaine seront poursuivis sans relâche dans les Etats de l'Union.

L'enseignement bilingue, les échanges de personnels, de programmes de radiodiffusion, la création des instituts de recherches communs seront intensifiés dans les Etats de l'Union.

Titre VII
DIRECTIVES DIVERSES

Les institutions rentreront en vigueur à compter de la date de la publication simultanée de la présente Charte dans les Etats de l'Union.

Des modifications pourront être apportées aux présentes dispositions par la réunion des Chefs d'Etat en cas d'adhésion d'un nouvel Etat ou sur la demande d'un Chef d'Etat en vue de renforcer la cohésion de l'Union.

Tout Etat africain dont le gouvernement acceptera les buts et objectifs de la présente Charte pourra être membre de l'U.E.A. à partir de la date d'une déclaration expresse du Chef de l'Etat. Cette declaration sera transmise aux Chefs des Etats membres de l'Union.

Fait à Accra, le 29 avril 1961.

Ont signé:

MODIBO KEITA,
Président de la République du Mali.

SÉKOU TOURÉ,
Président de la République de Guinee.

KWAMÉ N'KRUMAH,
Président de la République du Ghana.

2. Communiqué issued by the Heads of State, Bamako, 27 June 1961[1]

La deuxième conférence trimestrielle des Chefs d'Etat de l'Union des Etats Africans s'est tenue à Bamako le 26 juin 1961.

Les trois Chefs d'Etat du Ghana, de la Guinée et du Mali ont dans une atmosphère de fraternelle collaboration, procédé au contrôle de l'application des décisions prises à leur réunion d'Accra en avril 1961. Ils ont étudié les nouvelles mesures à prendre pour la complète réalisation des objectifs de la Charte de l'Union des Etats africains. Les trois chefs d'Etat ont en outre échangé leurs points de vue sur divers problèmes notamment la situation politique en Algérie, au Congo, en Angola, la prochaine conférence des Chefs d'Etat des pays non-alignés, l'appui aux divers mouvements de libération nationale en Afrique et l'attitude de l'Union à l'égard du marché européen. Ils réaffirment leur conviction dans la justesse de la mission que s'est assignée l'Union en vue de hâter dans tous les domaines le processus de décolonisation de l'Afrique. Ils considèrent qu'il convient de tout mettre en œuvre pour renforcer l'Union et décident en conséquence:

1° De tenir à Labé, en République de Guinée, le 12 août 1961 la réunion des comités de coordination des partis politiques de trois Etats afin de fixer un calendrier de rencontres des organisations des masses (Jeunesse, Syndicats et Organisations des Femmes).

2° De donner des instructions impératives aux Ministres des Transports des Postes et Télécommunications pour l'exécution immédiate des recommandations arrêtées au cours de leur réunion tenue à Conakry le 5 mai 1961.

Les trois Chefs d'Etat réaffirment leur volonté de continuer à soutenir tous les peuples africains en lutte pour la libération nationale de leur pays, en particulier l'Algérie, le Congo et l'Angola. Ils décident en conséquence de coordonner leurs actions afin de porter une aide efficace à tous les mouvements de libération nationale en Afrique.

En ce qui concerne la prochaine conférence des Chefs d'Etat des pays non alignés prévue en Yougoslavie le 1er septembre 1961, les trois Chefs d'Etat décident de participer à ladite conférence. Ils considèrent que cette rencontre n'atteindra réellement ses objectifs, que dans la mesure où tous ses participants seront effectivement des Chefs d'Etat des pays non alignés. Ils invitent en conséquence le comité préparatoire au respect scrupuleux des critères de participation définie par la conférence préliminaire des Ministres des Affaires étrangères tenue au Caire le 5 juin 1961.

Sur le problème du marché commun européen, les trois Chefs d'Etat réaffirment leurs positions à l'égard de cette institution et décident de continuer leur action commune en vue de la création d'un véritable marché commun africain.

Les trois Chefs d'Etat se réjouissent de leur identité de vue sur tous les problèmes examinés et expriment leur satisfaction pour l'atmosphère de parfaite compréhension dans laquelle s'est déroulée la conférence.

Signé: KWAME N'KRUMAH
Président de la République du Ghana

[1] *La Documentation Française, Articles et Documents*, 13 July 1961.

Signé: SÉKOU TOURÉ
Président de la République de Guinée
Signé: MODIBO KEITA
Président de la République du Mali

(δ) *The Monrovia Conference*

Resolutions adopted by the Monrovia Conference of African Heads of State and Government, 12 May 1961[1]

(*a*) *Resolutions on the means of promoting closer understanding and co-operation towards the achievement of unity in Africa and Madagascar*

La Conférence des Chefs d'Etat et de Gouvernement Africains et Malgache, réunie à Monrovia du 8 au 13 mai 1961.

Ayant constaté l'importance historique de la Conférence de Monrovia en raison du nombre des Etats participants;

Notant avec un profond regret l'absence de certains Etats frères, mais,

Convaincue de leur intense désir de solidarité africaine et exprimant l'espoir qu'il leur sera possible d'assister aux réunions ultérieures;

Soucieuse d'instaurer, dès à présent, une coopération franche et fraternelle entre les Etats Africains et Malgache indépendants;

Considérant la nécessité de la mise en commun de toutes les mesures et de la coordination des efforts afin de surmonter les obstacles qui entravent la croissance des pays africains et malgache en voie de développement;

A. — *Affirme solennellement et adopte* les principes ci-après énoncés qui devront régir les rapports entre Etats Africains et Malgache.

1) Egalité absolue des Etats Africains et Malgache quels que soient l'importance de leurs territoires, la densité du leurs populations, le volume de leurs richesses;

2) Non ingérence dans les affaires intérieures des Etats;

3) Respect de la Souveraineté de chaque Etat et de son droit inaliénable à l'existence et au développement de sa personnalité;

4) Condamnation formelle de l'établissement de foyers de subversion entretenus par des Etats indépendants;

5) Instauration d'une coopération établie aux dimensions de l'Afrique et basée sur la tolérance, la solidarité, les rapports de bon voisinage, des échanges de vues périodiques et le refus de tout leader-ship.

6) L'unité visée en ce moment n'est pas l'intégration politique des Etats Africains souverains, mais l'unité des aspirations et des actions considérées au point de vue de l'identité de la solidarité sociale et politique africaine.

B. — *Demande* instamment que tous les Etats Africains et Malgache s'abstiennent d'encourager directement ou indirectement des groupes dissidents ou des individus appartenant à d'autres Etats dans une action subversive en permettant

[1] *La Documentation Française, Articles et Documents*, 6 June 1961, pp. 1–3. The Monrovia conference was attended by the Heads of State of the Brazzaville group—Cameroun, Central African Republic, Chad, Congo (Brazzaville), Dahomey, Gabon, Ivory Coast, Madagascar, Mauritania, Niger, Senegal, and Upper Volta—together with Ethiopia, Liberia, Libya, Nigeria, Sierra Leone, Somalia and Toga. Tunisia was also represented. The five Casablanca powers refused to attend, and Congo (Leopoldville) and the Sudan were also absent.

que leurs propres pays servent de bases à partir desquels de tels dissidents pourraient opérer ou en aidant fiancièrement de tels dissidents dans d'autres pays ou en employant d'autres moyens à cet égard:

C. — *Retient* le principe de la création d'une organisation consultative interafricaine et malgache dont le rôle essentiel sera de mettre en œuvre les principes ci-dessus énoncés; la création de cet organisme sera décidée à la prochaine Conférence.

1) Qu'une commission d'experts nommés par les Etats respectifs sera créée et que ces experts se réuniront à Dakar, Sénégal, dans les trois mois qui suivront la clôture de cette réunion en vue d'élaborer des plans détaillés pour la Coopération entre les Etats Africains et Malgache en matière d'Economie, d'Education, de Culture, de science et de technique en matière de Communication et de Transport.

D. — *Décide:*

2) Que les institutions techniques et de recherches existantes constituent un organisme efficace pour rassembler les données et distribuer les conclusions des recherches parmi les Etats Africains et Malgache, et que tous les Etats prennent les mesures nécessaires à cet effet;

3) Que tous les Etats Africains et Malgache reconnaîtront leur désir de favoriser la renaissance de la Culture et des traditions africaines en vue de préserver le véritable patrimoine de l'Afrique;

4) Que tous les Etats Africains et Malgache s'efforceront particulièrement d'introduire l'étude du français et l'anglais en plus de celle de leur langue nationale et officielle respective.

E. — *Décide*, enfin, que la prochaine Conférence au sommet des Etats Africains et Malgache se tiendra à Lagos, Nigeria.

(b) *Resolutions on threat to peace and stability in Africa and the World*

(i) La conférence, profondément préoccupée par les menaces graves qui pèsent sur la paix et la stabilité en Afrique et dans le monde.

Considérant que le principe de non ingérence dans les affaires intérieures des Etats Africains et Malgache ne s'applique qu'aux Etats déjà indépendants et souverains;

Affirme sa détermination unanime d'apporter une assistance matérielle et morale à tous les territoires dépendants des puissances coloniales afin d'accélérer leur accession à l'indépendance.

(ii) La Conférence, en ce qui concerne la question algérienne, se félicite de l'évolution de la situation en Algérie et de la décision des deux parties d'entamer les négociations le 20 mai 1961;

Lance un appel à la France et au gouvernement provisoire de la République algérienne pour conclure dans les meilleurs délais un accord mettant fin à la guerre et menant l'Algérie à son indépendance et à son intégrité territoriale.

(iii) La Conférence, en ce qui concerne le Congo.

Réaffirme sa confiance dans l'Organisation des Nations Unies qui, en dépit de ses faiblesses ou de ses erreurs passées, est la seule organisation en mesure de trouver la solution du problème congolais;

Souhaite que tous les Etats Africains et Malgache s'abstiennent d'initiatives telles que la reconnaissance hâtive des régimes sécessionnistes dans la République du Congo et d'une façon générale, de prendre parti pour des groupes rivaux, sous quelque forme que ce soit;

Condamne l'assassinat comme moyen de s'assurer le pouvoir politique;

Condamne les Etats non-Africans qui encouragent ou entretiennent la subversion en Afrique.

(*iii*) La Conférence, en ce qui concerne l'Angola.

Demande à tous les Etats Africains et Malgache de s'engager à apporter sans réserves leur appui matériel et moral aux Africains de l'Angola dans leur lutte pour l'autonomie;

Attire l'attention de la conscience universelle sur les atrocités et la répression sanguinaire dont sont victimes les populations angolaises.

(*v*) La Conférence, en ce qui concerne l'Union Sud-Africaine.

...*Condamne* sans réserves la théorie et la politique de l'apartheid appliquée par le Gouvernement de l'Union Sud-Africaine;

Demande à tous les Etats Africains et Malgache l'application immédiate collective et individuelle, de sanctions politiques et économiques contre le Gouvernement de l'Union Sud-Africaine, non seulement afin de manifester leur indignation contre l'avilissement des habitants non-blancs, mais également afin d'amener le Gouvernement de l'Union Sud-Africaine à abandonner cette politique inique de l'apartheid;

Demande à tous les Etats Africains et Malgache d'apporter, par tous les moyens possibles, leur appui matériel et moral aux Africains et aux Asiens de l'Union Sud-Africaine dans la lutte qu'ils mènent pour reconquérir leur dignité d'hommes;

Affirme que tous les Etats Africains et Malgache participants désirent apporter leur ferme appui à la Résolution permanente du Conseil de Tutelle des Nations Unies qui précise que le Gouvernement de l'Union Sud-Africaine doit se soumettre au Conseil en ce qui concerne le mandat du territoire du Sud-Ouest Africain.

(*vi*) La Conférence, en ce qui concerne le désarmement,

Lance un appel à toutes les puissances atomiques pour qu'elles arrêtent la fabrication, le stockage des armes nucléaires et les explosions de bombes atomiques, en n'importe quelle partie du monde que ce soit.

Décide que le Président devra lancer un appel par écrit, au nom de la Conférence, à la Commission du désarmement atomique siégeant actuellement à Genève, pour lui demander de faire tout ce qui est en son pouvoir pour atteindre les objectifs énoncés au paragraphe précédent;

Prend note des assurances données par le Gouvernement Français selon lesquelles il ne procédera plus à aucune explosion atomique en Afrique.

(*vii*) La Conférence, en ce qui concerne les Nations Unies.

Demande aux membres des Nations Unies d'assurer une répartition géographique plus équitable des sièges au Conseil de Sécurité ainsi qu'au Conseil Economique et Social, et demande également que ces Conseils soient élargis;

Décide d'envoyer un télégramme aux membres du Conseil de Sécurité leur demandant de prendre une décision favorable à l'admission de la Mauritanie à l'Organisation des Nations Unies, conformément à la dernière résolution de l'Assemblée générale;

Condamne toute tentative visant à affaiblir ou à saper l'autorité des Nations Unies;

Précise que tous les Etats Africains et Malgache représentés à la Conférence, sont d'accord pour former à l'avenir, un front commun, en tant que groupe organisé, en face de tous les problèmes mondiaux dont l'Afrique serait appelée à connaître au sein des Nations Unies.

(*c*) *Resolution on the settlement of conflict which may arise between African States*

La Conférence des Chefs d'Etat et de Gouvernement Africain et Malgache, réunie à Monrovia du 8 au 12 mai 1961.

Recommande que

1) Le règlement des conflits se fasse par des voies pacifiques;

2) Une commission soit créée et à laquelle les litiges peuvent être soumis, et qui sera rattachée à l'organisme de coopération des Etats Africains et Malgache;

3) La Conférence décide, à l'unanimité, d'envoyer un appel par écrit, par l'intermediaire de sa commission exécutive, à sa Majesté l'Empereur d'Ethiopie et à Son Excellence le Président de la Somalie, pour qu'ils renouvellent leurs efforts en vue de trouver une sincère et prompte solution à leurs différends frontaliers ou autres.

(*c*) *Decolonization*

(*a*) *General*

General Assembly resolution regarding 'the situation with regard to the implementation of the Declaration on the granting of independence to colonial countries and peoples', 27 November 1961[1]

The General Assembly,

Recalling the Declaration on the granting of independence to colonial countries and peoples contained in its resolution 1514 (XV) of 14 December 1960,[2]

Bearing in mind the purposes and principles of that Declaration,

Recalling in particular paragraph 5 of the Declaration providing that:

'Immediate steps shall be taken, in Trust and Non-Self-Governing Territories or all other territories which have not yet attained independence, to transfer all powers to the peoples of those territories, without any conditions or reservations, in accordance with their freely expressed will and desire, without any distinction as to race, creed or colour, in order to enable them to enjoy complete independence and freedom',

Noting with regret that, with a few exceptions, the provision contained in the aforementioned paragraph of the Declaration have not been carried out,

Noting that, contrary to the provisions of paragraph 4 of the Declaration, armed action and repressive measures continue to be taken in certain areas with

[1] G.A.O.R., Sixteenth Session, Supplement No. 17, p. 65. Resolution 1654 (XVI).
[2] *Documents*, 1960, pp. 404–6.

increasing ruthlessness against dependent peoples, depriving them of their prerogative to exercise peacefully and freely their right to complete independence,

Deeply concerned that, contrary to the provisions of paragraph 6 of the Declaration, acts aimed at the partial or total disruption of national unity and territorial integrity are still being carried out in certain countries in the process of decolonization,

Convinced that further delay in the application of the Declaration is a continuing source of international conflict and disharmony, seriously impedes international co-operation, and is creating an increasingly dangerous situation in many parts of the world which may threaten international peace and security,

Emphasizing that inadequacy of political, economic, social or educational preparedness should never serve as a pretext for delaying independence,

1. *Solemnly reiterates and reaffirms* the objectives and principles enshrined in the Declaration on the granting of independence to colonial countries and peoples contained in its resolution 1514 (XV) of 14 December 1960;

2. *Calls upon* States concerned to take action without further delay with a view to the faithful application and implementation of the Declaration;

3. *Decides* to establish a Special Committee of seventeen members to be nominated by the President of the General Assembly at the present session;[1]

4. *Requests* the Special Committee to examine the application of the Declaration, to make suggestions and recommendations on the progress and extent of the implementation of the Declaration, and to report to the General Assembly at its seventeenth session;

5. *Directs* the Special Committee to carry out its task by employment of all means which it will have at its disposal within the framework of the procedures and modalities which it shall adopt for the proper discharge of its functions;

6. *Authorizes* the Special Committee to meet elsewhere than at United Nations Headquarters, whenever and wherever such meetings may be required for the effective discharge of its functions, in consultation with the appropriate authorities;

7. *Invites* the authorities concerned to afford the Special Committee their fullest co-operation in carrying out its tasks;

8. *Requests* the Trusteeship Council, the Committee on Information from Non-Self-Governing Territories and the specialized agencies concerned to assist the Special Committee in its work within their respective fields;

9. *Requests* the Secretary-General to provide the Special Committee with all the facilities and the personnel necessary for the implementation of the present resolution.

(β) Portugal and Angola

1. Statement to the Security Council by the Permanent Representative of Portugal, Senhor Garin, 10 March 1961[2] (extracts)

. . . 34. I must admit that the action of the delegation of Liberia in pressing for the inscription of an item relating to incidents pertaining exclusively to the

[1] The members of the Special Committee were: Australia, Cambodia, Ethiopia, India, Italy, Madagascar, Mali, Poland, Syria, Tanganyika, Tunisia, U.S.S.R., United Kingdom, United States, Uruguay, Venezuela, and Yugoslavia.

[2] S.C.O.R., Sixteenth Year, 944th meeting, 10 March 1961, pp. 6, 8–9, 19–20.

internal security of Portugal came as a great surprise to my delegation. At the 934th meeting on 15 February 1961, the Liberian representative attempted to by-pass the rules of procedure on this same topic, but he was clearly shown by the President that his motion was out of order. We frankly thought that the matter would rest there.

35. Unfortunately, it would appear at times that a few delegations have nothing more constructive to offer to the international community of nations than their efforts to violate the principles of the Charter of the United Nations, with the vain hope of instilling poison into the national affairs of sovereign Member States.

36. Therefore, my delegation wishes to express the most vehement protest of the Portuguese Government against the action of the Liberian delegation and of the delegations supporting it, an action which makes a mockery of the letter and the spirit of the idea which presided at the foundation of the United Nations. . . .

49. The so-called crisis related by the Liberian representative refers, of course, to the recent disturbance of public order in Luanda, Angola,[1] which occurred without any previous unrest, commotion or demonstration of any sort. In fact, the disturbance involved only small groups of hooligans and hirelings who could not conceivably represent any segment of the population of Luanda, a population which was caught by surprise and reacted with general indignation.

50. In allowing that the Council should occupy itself with this matter, are the Council members perchance accepting a new principle to the effect that the maintenance of public order in cities of sovereign Member States is not essentially within the domestic jurisdiction of those States? It certainly would be a revolutionary new conception for every State. Such a precedent would cause almost unimaginable consequences. For one thing, it would signify that no authority would be recognized to a sovereign State to deal with disturbances of public order within its own territory. Incidents of public disorder occur in every country represented here, and recently we witnessed a disturbance even in this very chamber.[2]

51. Apart from the risk of letting loose anarchy and criminals, it would leave the door open for all kinds of intervention by the international Organization in practically every matter related to the internal jurisdiction of a State for the purpose of political propaganda.

52. The primary function of a State is to guarantee the security of its citizens. Thus the State has more than just the right—it has the obligation—to restore public order whenever disorderly or subversive elements criminally disturb it.

53. In the view of my delegation, a view which is faithful to the letter and spirit of the words written in the Charter, the word 'nothing' written in Article 2, paragraph 7, in the context 'Nothing contained in the present Charter shall authorize the United Nations to intervene in matters which are essentially within the domestic jurisdiction of any State . . .' means exactly 'nothing'. Legally, semantically or otherwise, the word 'nothing' is one of the few in the vocabulary

---

[1] At least thirty-eight people were killed in riots sparked off by the seizure of the liner *Santa Maria*, by the Portuguese opposition leader Captain Henrique Galvao.

[2] A violent negro demonstration in the public gallery soon after the announcement of Lumumba's death in the Congo.

of any language which has but one meaning, nothing, no matter how hard certain delegations may try to distort its meaning for political expediency.

54. If nothing in the Charter authorizes the Organization to intervene in this matter, and, again, if nothing in the Charter recognizes the Council jurisdiction on the matter, even on a pretext falsely invoked, it follows that there is no valid basis whatever, in the light of international law, for the consideration of the matter by the Security Council. Logically, then, if the Security Council should insist on following a path of illegality in this case it would, *ipso facto*, undermine its own authority in doing so.

55. However, even if we leave aside the legal objections to consideration of this subject by the Council, the question inevitably arises, 'Why the anxiety to pick on Portugal?' How many disturbances of public order leading to loss of life have occurred in recent times throughout the world? On what grounds is it now proposed to single out Portugal where, in point of fact, this type of disturbance of public order has occurred more rarely than in almost any other national of the world? Are we to assume that all members favouring the placing of this item on the Council's agenda will, from now on, whenever disturbances of public order occur in their countries, willingly submit to the consideration in this Council of their efforts to maintain law and order in their national territories? If it is to be done, although illegally, in the case of Portugal, it should then be done in the case of all violent disorders against the authority of Member States. Are the members of this Council, and the Members of the General Assembly as well, prepared to accept supervision by the United Nations over the maintenance of public order in their cities, towns and villages, or, if the Members are not willing to submit themselves to the absurdity of such a notion, is my delegation to assume that it is simply a case of singling out Portugal in the most brazen, discriminatory manner? Would not such an attitude on the part of the Council make mockery of Article 2, paragraph 1, which reads: 'The Organization is based on the principle of the sovereign equality of all its Members'? Do any members propose to hide their heads in the sand and refuse to read the Charter when it comes to Portugal, and to raise their heads from the sand and wave the Charter when it comes to themselves? My delegation is beginning to wonder. . . .

97. It is quite apparent, particularly in the light of the recent events in Africa, that the Organization of the United Nations, if it should encourage all ideas and schemes of extremist African nationalism, would in actuality promote a new kind of intolerant racism: anti-white racism, the condemnation of the white man on the basis of the colour of his skin. To the Portuguese, who have always been free of racial considerations in their political and social thinking, this anti-white racism is perhaps one of the most shocking developments of recent times.

98. Three of the members of the Council in their speech before the inscription of the item on the agenda referred erroneously to Portuguese constitutional texts to draw the wrong conclusions. Thus I am compelled to correct their data on the subject. Legal texts of the Portuguese Government dating back to the early seventeenth century were inspired by the concept of equality of rights, regardless of place of birth, religion or race. The present constitution of Portugal, enacted in 1933, which followed the unalterable tradition of Portuguese laws of the previous centuries, defines in article 5 the national territory as an indivisible unit

placing all its parts on a plane of equality. Manifestly, it is not a new juridical conception nor is it an act of political expediency. It is, on the contrary, the very essence of a nation which was born, grew, and defined itself long ago in several continents, unhindered by considerations of race, religion, social origin or caste. This unitary political structure, embodied in the fundamental laws of the country which is much older than the movements of modern constitutionalism, was later expressed in all the Portuguese constitutional texts, namely, the Constitutions of 1822, 1832, 1842 and 1911, whence it took its present shape. It may be evident that Portugal with its overseas components is a political unity like most modern European countries.

99. In this connexion it is appropriate to quote an early seventeenth century ruling of the Royal Council:

'Goa and the other lands overseas with whose Governments this Council is concerned are not distinct nor separate from this realm, nor yet do they belong to it by union but they are members of the same realm as the other provinces such as Algarve . . . and thus he who is born and lives in Goa or in Brazil or in Angola is a Portuguese as he who lives and is born in Lisbon.'

This is a Royal Decree, as I said, of the early seventeenth century.

100. To the territorial unity there corresponds an absolute unity of the Portuguese people who make up an example, certainly an unusual one, of an equal multi-racial society, the acquisition of Portuguese nationality being ruled by one single law which applies equally to everyone as provided by article 7 of the Constitution. As far as we are concerned, there is not the slightest question—the Portuguese overseas provinces are independent with the independence of the nation. We are dealing with historical facts for which it would be vain to seek to fashion either to alien political philosophies or outside standards of measures.

101. The knowledge, by the entire Portuguese population, of all the facts I have pointed out in the course of my statement about the true nature of the events which took place in Luanda, as well as their daily experience with life as it exists in the Portuguese territories, would make it impossible for them to accept, without vehement protest, that this subject should have been taken up in violation of the relevant Articles of the Charter, by this Council. This is likewise the position of my Government. . . .

2. Statement to the Security Council by the Permanent Representative of the United States, Mr. Stevenson, 15 March 1961[1]

Since there are no other speakers, in my capacity as representative of the United States, I shall claim the privilege of expressing the views of my Government on the draft resolution [S/4769].[2]

[1] S.C.O.R., Sixteenth Year, 946th meeting, 15 March 1961, pp. 20–22.
[2] ibid., 945th meeting, pp. 23–24. The resolution was defeated by the abstention of six members of the Council: Britain; Chile; 'China'; Ecuador; France and Turkey. A close version was passed by the General Assembly on 20 April; see below, p. 697, n. 3. America's action in voting for it and for an Assembly resolution on South West Africa the following day (below, p. 705) caused a great stir and were both taken as indications of a dramatic change in the United States policy.

101. When he first raised the question of Angola in the Security Council, the representative of Liberia, Mr. Padmore, recognized that the recent disturbance in Angola was not of itself an immediate threat to the maintenance of international peace and security. At that time he said:

'I believe that there is still time for us to help to build in Angola a future of which neither the Portuguese nor the Africans need be afraid. But we no longer have centuries, or even decades, in which to accomplish what should be a simple humanitarian task.' [934th meeting, para. 7.]

He emphasized several problems with which the United Nations must concern itself: the urgency, in this era of rapid communication, of acting with despatch; the recognition of Angola's problem being a part of the larger African scene; and the desirability of Portugal's availing itself of United Nations cooperation and help in the development of its territories in Africa. It was clear from his remarks that Mr. Padmore was anticipating conditions which, if unchanged, might endanger the peace and security of Africa, if not of the world.

102. It is in a spirit of seeking the constructive elimination of not just the symptoms, but the sources of friction, that the United States approaches this problem. I regret to find myself in disagreement with the representative of China and other members of this Council who present their position with such logic and force. And while we recognize full well that Angola and the conditions therein do not today endanger international peace and security, we believe that they may, if not alleviated, lead to more disorders, with many unforeseen, unfortunate and dangerous consequences.

103. We in the United States deplore the violence which occurred in Luanda and the tragic loss of life, involving all elements of the community. Nothing we can do here will restore these people to life. But perhaps we can discourage further violence, which can only make constructive efforts towards the solution of basic problems more difficult.

104. It is only prudent to view the disorders in Luanda in the context of the dramatic changes which have taken place in so much of Africa in the past few years. Angola is but a part of the over-all picture of evolution on the African continent. The views of the United States have not changed since Jefferson wrote that:

'We hold these truths to be self-evident, that all men are created equal, that they are endowed by their Creator with certain inalienable Rights, that among these are Life, Liberty and the pursuit of Happiness. That to secure these rights, Governments are instituted among Men, deriving their just powers from the consent of the governed.'

Those words reflect, we believe, the basic principles which all Governments would do well to observe and to implement with all of the energy at their command.

105. It is no secret that the General Assembly has been interested for years in conditions within Portugal's African territories. There can be no doubt that the people of Angola are entitled to all of the rights guaranteed them by the Charter, the right of unfettered opportunity to develop their full economic, political and

cultural potentialities. I am sure Portugal recognizes that it has a solemn obligation to undertake the systematic and rapid improvement of the conditions of the people of its territories, an evolution which is contemplated by the Charter.

106. The United States would be remiss in its duties as a friend of Portugal if it failed to express honestly its conviction that step-by-step planning within Portuguese territories and the acceleration thereof is now imperative for the successful political, economic and social advancement of all inhabitants under Portuguese administration—advancement, in brief, towards full self-determination.

107. The practical difficulties facing Portugal in the immediate future are formidable. If the people of Angola are not given reason to believe that they, too, may hope to participate in determining their own future, the tension which exists today will grow and may well result in disorders which will indeed pose a threat to international peace and security. On the other hand, we all know, and know only too well, the tragic events which have occurred in the Congo, that huge, unhappy State which lies just to the north of Angola. I do not think I would be straining the truth to conclude that much of the Congo's problems result from the fact that the pressure of nationalism rapidly overtook the preparation of the necessary foundation essential to the peaceful and effective exercise of sovereign self-government.

108. The important thing for us, then, is to ensure that similar conditions do not exist for the Angola of tomorrow. We believe that a beginning should be made promptly within that Territory to foster that educational, social and economic development of which political development is an integral part and to ensure the rapid attainment of political maturity within this area. As we know, political maturity is the crying need everywhere.

109. On 15 December 1960, by its resolution 1542 (XV), the General Assembly considered that a number of important territories were Non-Self-Governing within the meaning of Chapter XI of the Charter. The Assembly spoke of an obligation which exists on the part of Portugal to transmit information under Chapter XI of the Charter concerning these territories. The Assembly further invited the Government of Portugal to participate in the work of the Committee on Information from Non-Self-Governing Territories. I mention this because, in the view of my Government, the best course of action for Portugal and the best course of action to promote the interests of the people of the Portuguese territories seems to be through co-operation with the United Nations. In our view, the resolution to which I have just referred was an invitation to Portugal to work with Members of this Organization to ensure the more rapid progress of the peoples in Portuguese territory. I stress the words 'work with'. The United States does not read any dark dangers into this resolution. This is a gesture of concern, a gesture of goodwill and, beyond that, an effort toward genuine co-operation in the achievement of goals which are shared by all of us and which are recognized in the Charter of this Organization.

110. Hence, we hope that Portugal will proceed in accordance with the draft resolution now before the Council. In doing so, it would, in the words of Article 73 b of the Charter on the subject of the people of the Non-Self-Governing Territories, work 'to develop self-government, to take due account of the political

aspirations of the peoples, and to assist them in the progressive development of their free political institutions, according to the particular circumstances of each territory and its peoples and their varying stages of advancement'.

111. I hope that what I have said will be taken in the spirit in which it is intended, to encourage the peaceful evolution of a society in Angola in which men of all races can live together in harmony with mutual respect for the different cultures and ways of life which now exist there.

3. Security Council resolution, 9 June 1961[1]

The Security Council,

Having considered the situation in Angola,

Deeply deploring the large-scale killings and the severe repressive measures in Angola,

Taking note of the grave concern and strong reactions to such occurrences throughout the continent of Africa and in other parts of the world,

Convinced that the continuance of the situation in Angola is an actual and potential cause of international friction and is likely to endanger the maintenance of international peace and security,

Recalling General Assembly resolution 1542 (XV) of 15 December 1960 declaring Angola among others a Non-Self-Governing Territory within the meaning of Chapter XI of the Charter as well as General Assembly resolution 1514 (XV) of 14 December 1960,[2] by which the General Assembly declared without dissent that the subjection of peoples to alien subjugation, domination and exploitation constitutes a denial of fundamental human rights, is contrary to the Charter of the United Nations and is an impediment to the promotion of world peace and co-operation and asked for immediate steps to be taken to transfer all powers to the peoples of these Territories, without any conditions or reservations, in accordance with their freely expressed will and desire, without any distinction as to race, creed or colour, in order to enable them to enjoy complete independence and freedom,

1. *Reaffirms* General Assembly resolution 1603 (XV) of 20 April 1961[3] and calls upon Portugal to act in accordance with the terms of that resolution;

2. *Requests* the Sub-Committee on the Situation in Angola, appointed under the terms of the aforesaid General Assembly resolution, to implement its mandate without delay;

3. *Calls upon* the Portuguese authorities to desist forthwith from repressive measures and further to extend every facility to the Sub-Committee to enable it to perform its task expeditiously;

4. *Expresses* the hope that a peaceful solution will be found to the problem of Angola in accordance with the Charter of the United Nations;

---

[1] S.C.O.R., Sixteenth Year, Supplement for April, May, and June 1961, p. 67. S/4835.

[2] G.A.O.R., Fifteenth Session, Supplement No. 16, pp. 30–31, and *Documents*, 1960, pp. 404–6.

[3] G.A.O.R., Fifteenth Session, Supplement No. 16A, pp. 18–19. This resolution called on Portugal to 'consider urgently the introduction of measures and reforms in Angola for the purpose of the implementation of General Assembly resolution 15/4 (XV)'. It was an almost identical version of the resolution defeated in the Security Council on 15 March.

5. *Requests* the Sub-Committee to report to the Security Council and the General Assembly as soon as possible.

4. Report of the United Nations Sub-Committee on Angola, 13 November 1961[1] (extracts)

C. The United Nations and a Peaceful Solution

470. In its resolution of 9 June 1961 (S/4835)[2] the Security Council expressed the hope that a peaceful solution would be found to the problem of Angola in accordance with the Charter of the United Nations.

471. The Sub-Committee is convinced that such a peaceful solution requires efforts both towards the immediate ending of bloodshed and towards the co-ordinated political, economic, and social development of the territory. It feels in particular that measures to remove the legitimate grievances of the population and the establishment of contacts with representatives of Angolan political groups are essential to ensure a cessation of the conflict and to achieve a peaceful solution.

472. The Sub-Committee is convinced that it is in the genuine interest of the Government of Portugal to heed the opinions expressed by the United Nations organs and to take the necessary measures with the co-operation of the Organization. It is further convinced that constructive co-operation between the Government of Portugal and the United Nations is the best means of bringing about a prompt end to the conflict and a peaceful evolution towards the objectives stated in the United Nations resolutions. It feels that rapid measures by the Government of Portugal can still preserve the positive elements of past policies and achievements.

473. The Government of Portugal may well consider the example of other metropolitan Powers which have granted or recognized the right of self-determination and independence to territories which had been administered as overseas territories or provinces and the numerous examples of fruitful relationships which resulted therefrom.

474. The Sub-Committee would express its view that the United Nations cannot but continue its concern with the developments in Angola in view of the provisions of the Charter, the international aspects and repercussions of the situation, and its vital interest with regard to peace in Africa and in the world. The Sub-Committee would hope that the United Nations and its Member States would take further action as appropriate to persuade and assist the Government of Portugal and the Angolan people to embark on a policy of peaceful settlement in conformity with the Charter.

475. The Sub-Committee notes that the representatives of the Angolan groups heard by it, including those accused by the Government of Portugal of responsibility for the recent disturbances, stressed their desire for a peaceful solution of the problem and for co-operation among racial groups within Angola on the basis of equality. This publicly expressed position would seem to provide an opportunity and hope for the achievement of the ends laid down by the General Assembly and the Security Council.

[1] G.A.O.R., Sixteenth Session, Supplement No. 16, pp. 48–49.   [2] Above, p. 697.

476. The Sub-Committee has been told by some of these groups that they had found no channel for discussion with the Government of Portugal and that the latter had eliminated any basis for discussion by its firmly negative attitude on the question of self-determination. The Sub-Committee would express the hope that the Government of Portugal would see fit to accept the path of negotiation for a solution of the Angolan problem.

477. The Sub-Committee would hope that the facilities of the United Nations would be available to those concerned in their search for a peaceful solution.

478. The Sub-Committee feels that a peaceful solution of the Angolan problem requires not only a drastic reform of legislation and administration but also the formulation of plans to prepare the territory for self-government and the exercise of self-determination. It would emphasize, in particular, the need for a rapid and massive expansion of educational facilities in order to enhance the economic, social, and political advancement of the territory.

479. The Sub-Committee would point out that the expenditure of resources on military and security measures, especially when the requirements for development of the territory are so great, does not serve the interests of either Portugal or the Angolan people. Attention should rather be focused on the fulfilment of the basic needs of the people, taking into account the expectations aroused in the population by developments in other territories.

480. The Portuguese authorities face a historic choice: whether to continue to rely on the use of force, with the inevitable miseries, economic losses, and uncertainties; or to respond to world opinion and take measures to reassure the population, ensure the return of the refugees, and build a new relationship with the people of Angola. Much time has been lost in a critical situation, with the casualties and the bitterness mounting in Angola. What is needed is readiness to understand the new forces in the world, courage to accept change, and wisdom to formulate and pursue viable means towards an enduring peaceful solution.

DONE at United Nations Headquarters, New York, this thirteenth day of November, one thousand nine hundred and sixty-one.

(*Signed*) CARLOS SALAMANCA, *Bolivia*
LOUIS IGNACIO PINTO, *Dahomey*
NIK AHMED KAMIL, *Federation of Malaya*
RALPH ENCKELL, *Finland*
OMAR ABDEL HAMID ADEEL, *Sudan*

DANTAS DE BRITO
Secretary

5. General Assembly resolution regarding the 'non-compliance of the Government of Portugal with Chapter XI of the Charter of the United Nations and with General Assembly resolution 1542 (XV)', adopted 19 December 1961[1]

The General Assembly,
Recalling that by resolution 1542 (XV) of 15 December 1960[2] it declared that an obligation exists on the part of the Government of Portugal to transmit

[1] G.A.O.R., Sixteenth Session, Supplement No. 17, p. 38. Resolution 1699 (XVI).
[2] ibid., Fifteenth Session, Supplement No. 16, pp. 30–31.

information under Chapter XI of the Charter of the United Nations concerning Non-Self-Governing Territories under its administration, and that this obligation should be discharged without further delay,

Noting with deep regret that the Government of Portugal has refused and still continues to refuse to submit information on its Non-Self-Governing Territories or to participate in the work of the Committee on Information from Non-Self-Governing Territories, as called for by General Assembly resolution 1542 (XV) and Chapter XI of the Charter,

Recalling further the principles set forth in its resolution 1514 (XV) of 14 December 1960 entitled 'Declaration on the granting of independence to colonial countries and peoples',[1]

Considering that the provisions of the said Declaration and any decision of the General Assembly concerning its implementation are fully applicable to the Territories under Portuguese administration equally with other Non-Self-Governing Territories,

Noting the continuing deterioration of the situation in the Territories under Portuguese administration,

1. *Condemns* the continuing non-compliance of the Government of Portugal with its obligations under Chapter XI of the Charter of the United Nations and with the terms of General Assembly resolution 1542 (XV), and its refusal to co-operate in the work of the Committee on Information from Non-Self-Governing Territories;

2. *Considers* it necessary that, pending the fulfilment of these obligations by the Government of Portugal, the General Assembly must, for its part, continue to discharge its own obligations and responsibilities toward the inhabitants of the Non-Self-Governing Territories under Portuguese administration;

3. *Decides* to establish a Special Committee[2] of seven members to be elected by the General Assembly to examine as a matter of urgency, within the context of Chapter XI of the Charter and relevant resolutions of the Assembly, such information as is available concerning Territories under Portuguese administration, and to formulate its observations, conclusions and recommendations for the consideration of the Assembly and any other body which the Assembly may appoint to assist it in the implementation of its resolution 1514 (XV);

4. *Requests* the Secretary-General, pending the compliance by Portugal with its obligations under Chapter XI of the Charter to transmit information on conditions in the Territories under its administration, to prepare for the use of the Special Committee, on the basis of available information, background papers containing information on conditions prevailing in the Territories under the administration of Portugal;

5. *Authorizes* the Special Committee, in order that information available to it may be as up to date and authentic as possible, to receive petitions and hear petitioners concerning conditions prevailing in Portuguese Non-Self-Governing Territories;

6. *Requests* the Secretary-General to furnish the Special Committee with such

---

[1] *Documents*, 1960, pp. 404–6.
[2] The members of the Committee were: Bulgaria, Ceylon, Colombia, Cyprus, Guatemala, Guinea, and Nigeria.

necessary secretarial and other assistance as it may require in the performance of its tasks;

7. *Requests* Member States to use their influence to secure the compliance of Portugal with its obligations under the Charter and the relevant resolutions of the General Assembly;

8. *Further requests* Member States to deny Portugal any support and assistance which it may use for the suppression of the peoples of its Non-Self-Governing Territories.

(d) South Africa

(α) The Withdrawal from the Commonwealth

1. Statement by the South African Prime Minister, Dr. Verwoerd, to the Commonwealth Prime Ministers' conference in London, 15 March 1961[1]

South Africa is one of the senior members of the Commonwealth and has in the past heartily co-operated with its fellow members.

No self-respecting member of any voluntary organization could, however, in view of what is being suggested and the degree of interference shown in what are South Africa's domestic affairs, be expected to wish to retain membership of what is now becoming a pressure group.

In the circumstances I wish formally to withdraw my request for South Africa to remain a member of the Commonwealth after she becomes a republic on May 31.

My request was made in the expectation that it would be willingly granted, without reservations, as was done also on behalf of South Africa in the previous cases of India, Pakistan, Ceylon, Ghana and Nigeria in spite of our great differences with them which we were prepared to subordinate in co-operation on matters of common concern.

Furthermore, we were influenced by what we considered to be the genuineness of the sentiments expressed at last year's conference of Prime Ministers, to wit, that South Africa was welcome as a member of the Commonwealth.

It is with great regret that I am obliged to take the step of withdrawing my request, and I wish to assure the friendly disposed Prime Ministers of the Commonwealth that South Africa's withdrawal on May 31 will be deeply and sincerely regretted not only by the Government but also by the people of South Africa, and we hope and shall endeavour to co-operate in all possible ways with all those members of the Commonwealth who are willing to maintain their former good relations with us.

I am sure that the great majority of the people of my country will appreciate that in the circumstances no other course was open to us. National pride and self-respect are attributes of any sovereign independent state.

I must admit that I was amazed at, and shocked by, the spirit of hostility— and at this last meeting even of vindictiveness—shown towards South Africa in

---

[1] Text supplied by the South African Embassy, London. South Africa's withdrawal is more fully treated in P. N. S. Mansergh, *Documents and Speeches on Commonwealth Affairs 1952–1962* (O.U.P. for R.I.I.A., 1963), pp. 365–400.

spite of the lengths to which we were prepared to go in the various draft communiques.

It is clear that in the view of the majority of the Commonwealth Prime Ministers, after the lead given by a group of Afro-Asian nations, South Africa will no longer be welcomed in the Commonwealth after May 31 when she becomes a republic.

The character of the Commonwealth has apparently changed completely during the last year. The opposition to South Africa's continued membership is based on alleged discrimination against and oppression of the non-white peoples of South Africa.

I do not intend repeating my strong denial of those allegations at this stage. I do, however, wish to state that it is ironical that these allegations have come from Prime Ministers in whose countries oppression and discrimination are openly practised and where the basic principles of democratic government are flouted.

In this connexion I refer particularly to Ghana, India, Malaya and Ceylon, although certain other Commonwealth countries are also not free from such practices, sanctioned by legal enactments. In other cases, while not expressly permitted by law, little or no attempt is made to discontinue such practices.

In conclusion I wish to state that the proceedings at today's meeting, which have obliged me to take this regrettable step, in my opinion mark the beginning of the disintegration of the Commonwealth.

This free association of states cannot hope to survive if instead of devoting itself to co-operation on matters of common concern, Commonwealth Prime Ministers are going to continue the practice of interfering in each other's domestic affairs and if their meetings are to be made the occasion for attacks on fellow-members.

Such practices have led to the present unsatisfactory conditions prevailing at the United Nations, and they will, I venture to predict, lead to the eventual disintegration of the Commonwealth, which all would regret.

2. Communiqué of the Commonwealth Prime Ministers' conference, London, 15 March 1961[1]

At their meetings this week the Commonwealth Prime Ministers have discussed questions affecting South Africa.

On 13th March the Prime Minister of South Africa informed the Meeting that, following the plebiscite in October 1960, the appropriate constitutional steps were now being taken to introduce a republic form of constitution in the Union, and that it was the desire of the Union Government that South Africa should remain within the Commonwealth as a republic.

In connection with this application the meeting also discussed, with the consent of the Prime Minister of South Africa, the racial policy followed by the Union Government. The Prime Minister of South Africa informed the other Prime Ministers this evening that in the light of the views expressed on behalf of other member Governments and the indications of their future intentions regard-

---

[1] *Commonwealth Survey*, 28 March 1961, p. 319.

ing the racial policy of the Union Government, he had decided to withdraw his application for South Africa's continuing membership of the Commonwealth as a republic.

3. Statement to the House of Commons by the British Prime Minister, Mr. Macmillan, 16 March 1961[1]

The House will know that the Prime Minister of South Africa yesterday decided to withdraw his application for the Union of South Africa to remain a member of the Commonwealth after that country becomes a Republic on 31st May next. Until then, South Africa will remain a member of the Commonwealth. The Prime Minister of South Africa will, therefore, continue to take part in the deliberations of the present Commonwealth Prime Ministers' Conference.

I am sure that I speak for many of us on both sides of the House when I express our deep regret that the Commonwealth ties with South Africa, which have endured for fifty years, are shortly to be severed, and our regret, also, for the circumstances which have made this unavoidable. Remembering that the Commonwealth is an association of peoples of all races, colours and creeds, we must hope that, in the years to come, it will be possible for South Africa once more to play her part in the Commonwealth.

The Prime Minister of South Africa has said that he hopes to co-operate in all possible ways with all those members of the Commonwealth who are willing to maintain good relations with South Africa. He has also said that South Africa will remain a member of the sterling area. We, for our part, welcome these statements, and intend to co-operate fully in matters of common interest.

The House will wish to debate the various implications of the situation with which we are now faced. No doubt arrangements can be made through the usual channels for a debate next week.

The House will appreciate that I do not feel free to go into further details until the Conference is over, and the final communique has been agreed.

Mr. Gaitskell: We welcome the Prime Minister's suggestion that there should be a debate next week. I think that it is clear to all of us that the Commonwealth, in the last few days, has passed through a great crisis, perhaps the greatest crisis in its history, whose impact was bound to be very great, very decisive, not only in the Commonwealth itself, but far beyond it.

I realise that some take the view that what has happened is a step towards the dissolution and decay of the Commonwealth. For our part, on these benches, we take the contrary view. To us, the outcome, bearing in mind all the circumstances, strengthens our faith that the Commonwealth is an institution of great potential value for humanity.

I hope that I may be permitted to put my remarks in the form of a statement —I think that that is usual on such occasions—and not simply as questions. It can hardly be denied—can it?—that the theory and practice of *apartheid*—the advocacy of a permanent division of men according to the colour of their skin, and involving, in practice, different rights, opportunities and status—is a continuous affront to the vast majority of the inhabitants of the Commonwealth.

---

[1] H. C. Deb., vol. 636, cols. 1748–53.

. . . I will confine myself simply to saying this: we wish profoundly that the dilemma thus created has been resolved by a change in the attitude of the South African Government, but, as this apparently proved to be impossible, it was perhaps best that the Prime Minister of South Africa should recognise the hopeless contradiction of South Africa's staying in the Commonwealth under his Government.

I should like to join with the Prime Minister, if I may, in saying to the people of South Africa, whatever colour they may be, that we hope that, in time, the racial theories and policies adopted by the Union today may be changed and brought into line with those practised in the rest of the Commonwealth, and that they will then return as welcome friends to the Commonwealth. . . .

Does the Prime Minister expect that the Prime Minister's Conference will, nevertheless, be issuing a statement on the question of racial policies? Secondly, in view of the decision of the Prime Minister of the Union Government, will the right hon. Gentleman confirm that our attitude to the High Commission Territories remains unchanged, and will he reaffirm our responsibilities to those territories?

The Prime Minister: The communiqué will be settled tomorrow. Of course, I am in the hands of my colleagues as a whole as to how they wish the communiqué to be drawn.

It is the case that the withdrawal of the Union of South Africa from the Commonwealth will have no constitutional effects upon the relationship between the High Commission Territories and the United Kingdom, nor will the withdrawal of South Africa affect our responsibilities and obligations towards those Territories, which have repeatedly been made clear.

Sir J. Duncan: Without anticipating the debate next week, will my right hon. Friend say that the door remains wide open to the Union of South Africa to come back into the Commonwealth if there should be a change of heart?

The Prime Minister: Yes, Sir. I said that, and the Leader of the Opposition repeated it, and I am glad that my hon. Friend has brought it up again.

The tragedy of this event is that we are a comradeship of peoples. There will be very many sad people in South Africa, our friends, our relations, men who have lived there for several generations, others who have only recently gone out. There will be sad people of every kind and every race, and do not let us forget them. We are not a combination of Governments. We are a combination of peoples. Had it been possible to reach agreement, I think that it would have been reached, but it proved not to be so. This seemed the only dignified way out, and I hope that I may be allowed to pay a tribute to the dignity and courtesy of the Prime Minister of South Africa, which was appreciated by all his colleagues, in what was a very good discussion of a very high level. There we are; I agree that we must look to the future.

Mr. Grimond: Is the Prime Minister aware that there will be widespread agreement in this country with the feeling of sympathy which he has expressed with the people of all races in South Africa who, no doubt, regret this decision as much as anybody and also regret the policies which have made it inevitable?

May I ask two questions which the Prime Minister might consider before the debate? Will he consider giving us information, by a White Paper or in some other way, about his view of the position in the Mandated Territories and British citizenship as it affects South Africa? While I appreciate what he has said about the Protectorates, what will be the position of the High Commissionership of the Protectorates which is now situated in South Africa?

The Prime Minister: I have already dealt with the question of the High Commission Territories. A number of questions will have to be dealt with and some of them would have had to have been dealt with anyway, probably by legislation, owing to the change from a monarchy to a republic. There will now have to be another set of questions which are being studied by the Departments concerned. The change does not happen until 31st May, and I hope, in the course of the debate, to explain, at any rate in outline, what our major legislative and administrative problems are following from this event.

Sir H. Oakshott: Will my right hon. Friend recognise that there are many of us who fully share his sorrow at the outcome of this issue, and, if I may say so respectfully, who have watched with great admiration his tireless efforts to try to bring about an accommodation satisfactory to everybody? Is he further aware, as he has indicated, that there are many of us who see a distinction between Governments and peoples, and that if the effects of this decision can be mitigated in the way of trade and commerce, to the advantage of all the peoples of the Union, of all colours and races, that will be very much welcomed by many of us?

The Prime Minister: Yes, Sir.

Mr. M. Foot: In the light of this decision, will Her Majesty's Government review some of the votes which they have cast at the United Nations in recent weeks, in particular their vote this week about South West Africa, since we owe obligations to the people there as well as to those in other parts of Africa?

The Prime Minister: Certainly, but this is a very complicated question, part of which is a question of the interpretation of the legal position and the advisory opinion of the International Court of Justice, given in 1950.[1] Apart from the substance, there are quite complicated legal questions which we are also studying.

(β) *The Onslaught in the United Nations*

1. **General Assembly resolution making an 'appeal to Member States which have particularly close and continuous relations with the Government of the Union of South Africa, with respect to the situation in the Territory of South West Africa', adopted 16 March 1961**[2]

The General Assembly,

Recalling the many resolutions adopted, since its first session, on the question of South West Africa, and especially resolution 1568 (XV) of 18 December 1960,[3]

---

[1] International Court of Justice: *Reports of Judgments, Advisory Opinions and Orders. International Status of South West Africa. Advisory Opinions of July 11th, 1950* (The Hague, I.C.J., 1950).
[2] G.A.O.R., Fifteenth Session, Supplement No. 16A, p. 7. Resolution 1593 (XV). See also above, p. 694, n. 2.
[3] ibid., Supplement No. 16, p. 33.

Noting with concern that up to the present time the Government of the Union of South Africa has ignored those resolutions and has, instead, adopted an attitude contrary to the purposes and principles of the Charter of the United Nations,

Noting with special concern the refusal of the Mandatory Power to implement resolution 1568 (XV),

Likewise noting with concern the continued acts whereby, since 1950, the Government of the Union of South Africa has attempted to bring about the assimilation of the Territory of South West Africa and in particular the so-called referendum of 5 October 1960 in which only the 'European' inhabitants of the Territory were permitted to take part,

Considering that the conduct of the Government of the Union of South Africa constitutes a challenge to the authority of the United Nations,

Considering that attempts at the assimilation of the Mandated Territory of South West Africa, culminating in the so-called referendum of 5 October 1960, are totally unacceptable as having no moral or legal basis and being repugnant to the letter and spirit of the Mandate,

Appeals to those Members of the United Nations which have particularly close and continuous relations with the Government of the Union of South Africa to bring, as a matter of urgency, all their influence to bear on that Government with a view to ensuring that it shall adjust its conduct to its obligations under the Charter of the United Nations and shall give effect to the resolutions adopted by the General Assembly.

2. General Assembly resolution on South West Africa, adopted 7 April 1961[1]

The General Assembly,

Bearing in mind the provisions of the General Assembly's Declaration on the granting of independence to colonial countries and peoples,[2] which declares that immediate steps shall be taken to transfer all powers to such peoples, without any conditions or reservations, in accordance with their freely expressed will and desire, without any distinction as to race, creed or colour, in order to enable them to enjoy complete independence and freedom,

Recalling its resolution 1568 (XV)[3] of 18 December 1960 inviting the Committee on South West Africa to go to South West Africa immediately, *inter alia*, to investigate the situation prevailing in the Territory,

Noting with deep regret, from the preliminary report of the Committee on South West Africa[4] called for under the said resolution, that the Government of the Union of South Africa refuses to co-operate with the United Nations by facilitating the mission of the Committee on South West Africa,

Convinced that it is both the right and the duty of the United Nations to

---

[1] G.A.O.R., Fifteenth Session, Supplement No. 16A, pp. 7–8. Resolution 1596 (XV). A similar resolution, setting up a Special Committee for South West Africa, was adopted at the Assembly's sixteenth session on 19 December 1961; see ibid., Sixteenth Session, Supplement No. 17, pp. 39–40.

[2] *Documents*, 1960, pp. 404–6.

[3] G.A.O.R., Fifteenth Session, Supplement No. 16, p. 33.

[4] ibid., Annexes, Agenda item 43, pp. 16–17.

discharge fully and effectively its obligations with respect to the proper implementation, under its supervision, of the Mandate for South West Africa conferred upon His Britannic Majesty, to be exercised on his behalf by the Government of the Union of South Africa,

Noting with grave concern the continuing deterioration in the situation in South West Africa resulting from the continued application, in violation of the letter and spirit of the Mandate, of tyrannical policies and practices, such as *apartheid*, of the administration of the Union of South Africa in South West Africa,

Reiterating its concern that this situation constitutes a serious threat to international peace and security,

1. *Recognizes and supports* the passionate yearning of the people of South West Africa for freedom and the exercise of national independence and sovereignty;

2. *Rejects* the position taken by the Government of the Union of South Africa in refusing to co-operate with the United Nations in the implementation of General Assembly resolution 1568 (XV) as well as other resolutions concerning South West Africa;

3. *Deplores* the attempts at the assimilation of the Mandated Territory of South West Africa, culminating in the so-called referendum held on 5 October 1960, as totally unacceptable, having no moral or legal basis and being repugnant to the letter and spirit of the Mandate;

4. *Considers* that the full and effective discharge of the tasks assigned to the Committee on South West Africa in paragraph 4 of General Assembly resolution 1568 (XV) is essential to the protection of the lives and property of the inhabitants of South West Africa, to the amelioration of the prevailing conditions in South West Africa, the continuance of which is likely to endanger international peace and security, and to the exercise of the right of self-determination by the people of South West Africa in complete freedom and of their right of accession to national sovereignty and independence with the least delay;

5. *Requests* the Committee on South West Africa, therefore, immediately to proceed to discharge the special and urgent tasks entrusted to it in resolution 1568 (XV) as fully and expeditiously as possible with the co-operation of the Government of the Union of South Africa if such co-operation is available, and without it if necessary;

6. *Requests* the States Members of the United Nations to extend to the Committee on South West Africa such assistance as it may require in the discharge of these tasks;

7. *Decides* to call the attention of the Security Council to the situation in respect of South West Africa which, if allowed to continue, will in the General Assembly's view endanger international peace and security, and to the present resolution, the full implementation of which is necessary to bring that situation to a speedy end;

8. *Takes note with grave concern* of reports of the terrorization of, and armed action against, the indigenous inhabitants, and calls upon the Government of the Union of South Africa to desist from such acts;

9. *Requests* the Committee on South West Africa to submit to the General

Assembly at its sixteenth session a report on the implementation of resolution 1568 (XV) as well as the present resolution.[1]

3. General Assembly resolution, regarding apartheid, adopted 13 April 1961[2]

The General Assembly,

Recalling its previous resolutions on the question of race conflict in South Africa resulting from the policies of *apartheid* of the Government of the Union of South Africa,

Considering that its resolutions 616 B (VII) of 5 December 1952, 917 (X) of 6 December 1955 and 1248 (XIII) of 30 October 1958[3] have declared that racial policies designed to perpetuate or increase discrimination are inconsistent with the Charter of the United Nations and with the pledges of Members under Article 56 of the Charter,

Noting that its resolutions 395 (V) of 2 December 1950, 511 (VI) of 12 January 1952 and 616 A (VII) of 5 December 1952[4] have successively affirmed that the policy of racial segregation (*apartheid*) is necessarily based on doctrines of racial discrimination,

Recalling also that the Government of the Union of South Africa has failed to comply with the repeated requests and demands of the United Nations and world public opinion and to reconsider or revise its racial policies or to observe its obligations under the Charter,

1. *Deplores* such continued and total disregard by the Government of the Union of South Africa and furthermore its determined aggravation of racial issues by more discriminatory laws and measures and their enforcement, accompanied by violence and bloodshed;

2. *Deprecates* policies based on racial discrimination as reprehensible and repugnant to human dignity;

3. *Requests* all States to consider taking such separate and collective action as to open to them, in conformity with the Charter of the United Nations, to bring about the abandonment of these policies;

4. *Affirms* that the racial policies being pursued by the Government of the Union of South Africa are a flagrant violation of the Charter of the United Nations and the Universal Declaration of Human Rights and are inconsistent with the obligations of a Member State;

5. *Notes with grave concern* that these policies have led to international friction and that their continuance endangers international peace and security;

---

[1] The Committee's report was issued in November 1961 as G.A.O.R., Sixteenth Session, Supplement No. 12A.

[2] G.A.O.R., Fifteenth Session, Supplement No. 16A, pp. 5–6. Resolution 1598 (XV). A similar resolution was adopted at the Assembly's sixteenth session, on 28 November 1961; see ibid., Sixteenth Session, Supplement No. 17, pp. 10–11. A resolution calling for non-military sanctions against South Africa was withdrawn before the final vote; text in ibid., Fifteenth Sessions Annexes, Agenda item 72, pp. 6–7. A further sanctions resolution was also withdrawn at the sixteenth session on 28 November; text in ibid., Sixteenth Session, Annexes, Agenda item 76, p. 8.

[3] ibid., Seventh Session, Supplement No. 20, pp. 8–9; Tenth Session, Supplement No. 19, p. 8; Thirteenth Session, Supplement No. 18, p. 7.

[4] ibid., Fifth Session, Supplement No. 20, p. 24; Sixth Session, Supplement No. 20, p. 11; Seventh Session, Supplement No. 20, p. 8.

6. *Reminds* the Government of the Union of South Africa of the requirement in Article 2, paragraph 2, of the Charter that all Members shall fulfil in good faith the obligations assumed by them under the Charter;

7. *Calls upon* the Government of the Union of South Africa once again to bring its policies and conduct into conformity with its obligations under the Charter.

C. INDIAN FOREIGN POLICY AND THE ANNEXATION OF GOA

1. Speech by Mr. Nehru to the Rajya Sabha, 20 February 1961[1] (extracts)

Mr. Chairman, Sir,

. . . Now, I would like to say straightway—that there is not the slightest feeling of complacency in the minds of the Government of India about the conditions in India, internal or external. In fact, the burdens that have to be faced by the country grew bigger and heavier, the problems more difficult. For anyone to consider them and make a charge of complacency, therefore, is not correct, but quite apart from this question of complacency, which nobody in the wide world can have to-day, in no country I would submit from the big ones to the small ones, no country to-day, no leader of public opinion to-day in any part of the world, can view the prospects in the world with complacency. That apart, if we look at the Indian scene, with all its ramifications, complications, knots, troubles, etc., I think it is quite correct to say, as the President has been pleased to say, that we can view it with a certain cautious optimism. By the normal tests, we can certainly be optimistic but there are other things besides the normal tests which trouble us.

Now, I come briefly to our border question. I have noticed, reading the reports of their speeches—I did not have the privilege of being here all the time and I have to go through the reports—that practically every section of the House has praised, has given commendation for our team of officials who went to discuss the border question with the Chinese Officials. That report has been circulated. I am glad of that, because I have been conscious during these months not only of the hard labour but also the ability and scholarship that they brought to bear upon this difficult task. Now, basically this kind of conflict between India and China is obviously a matter of grave import to us and I should say to the world: We are criticised for not taking certain steps. It is said: Why don't you go and have this territory vacated which the Chinese have occupied? While I admire the patriotism and the emotional upsurge of Hon. Members who tell us to go and push the aggressor out, I do not always admire the thought processes which bring about this sudden demand. What is supposed to be the practical aspect of it? The Government has to think of these practical aspects also and not only of the emotional urges that affect us and which the Government also feels. And I would beg this House to consider this question from the practical point of view. It is not an easy matter to indulge in a policy of action which step by step almost

[1] Ministry of External Affairs, *Prime Minister on Sino-Indian Relations*, vol. I (New Delhi Government of India, 1961), pp. 379–84.

inevitably leads to war.   A war between India and China, a war anywhere, according to our thinking, is undesirable. Even a small war may lead to a big one. But a war between India and China is something which no one can welcome. If it is thrust down upon us, that is a different matter. Also, if it is to be war, one has to prepare for it. One does not in a Don Quixotic way go about with a lance in hand to drive out the aggressor. One prepares for it. It is a big thing which, if started, may last our whole lifetime. It is not some police action or an order to a police station to take an area. We have to prepare for it, strengthen ourselves, in many ways and the main thing is to be clear in our minds and to be firm and determined in our resolves. That is the main thing, clear in our minds, not merely emotionally—emotionally we are—but otherwise to be firm and determined as to what our position is, what we want done and to prepare for it, whether it takes a month or a year or several years not to give in and ever to keep that in mind, and meanwhile always to seek methods on one side of solving the problem peacefully and on the other, strengthening ourselves by other methods. That is broadly the policy. According to our thinking our trouble at the border is not a dispute with China. It is a question of words perhaps. It is a dispute of course. When we argue about something, it is a dispute. But my point is, it is not a dispute because we have no doubt about our own position in this matter. So far as we are concerned, we are clear that it is not a normal dispute but it is just a claim on our territory which is ours, and we are convinced that it is ours. Therefore, this has to be clearly understood. Now it is very difficult, even in regard to such matters there may be two opinions. Obviously, rightly or wrongly, the Chinese opinion is different, and presumably most of them believe in it. This series of talks between the officials of India and China has, I think, very largely put an end to any doubt that there might be in people's minds about the real facts of the case. That was necessary. We in India being moved just by emotion hardly knew the facts. Perhaps many people who are most moved knew least about the facts. It is necessary, it was necessary, for this to be built up, this factual case, supported by documents, etc., before the world, before other countries, and indeed before even the people of China, though unfortunately I do not know how many of them will have occasion to study it this way. Therefore, this great gain has come to us. Let us realise that our case in regard to this border stands, if I may use the word, proven, proved for anybody to see. People, let us say, even in Pakistan have made very extraordinary charges against us in the newspapers and other things, and even some others, in regard to this border problem with China. If they do not accept it, all I can say is that they have not cared—to put it mildly—that they do not know the facts and they do not care to study them. They merely give effect to their animus against India because in the ultimate analysis we have to try to settle this, try our utmost not once but many times, peacefully even though it takes time, because the alternative to any kind of peaceful approach, is war, and if war comes down upon us, we have to defend our country of course, but we should avoid war anyhow and more especially in the present context of the world.

Some mention was made by some Hon. Members about China or Chinese forces extending their occupation area in Indian territory. Now I want to make this perfectly clear that the major advance of the Chinese forces into Indian territory in Ladakh took place in the summer of 1959, about a year and half ago. Ever since then there has been no advance anywhere. I cannot guarantee, some little curve in a waste land they may have marched in again, but broadly speaking they have not advanced anywhere, certainly not in N.E.F.A.,[1] certainly not in the middle sector and I think not in the Ladakh area either. Now what is this talk then about 2000 sq. miles of more territory being claimed by China? That is an incorrect thing. One very extraordinary fact which stands out during these past years is the changing position of the Chinese Government in regard to these matters and, what is more, the changing maps that come out from time to time. Premier Chou En-lai in a letter addressed to me on the 17th December 1959 stated that the 1956 map published in China represented the correct boundaries as conceived by the Chinese Government.[2] Throughout this argument we have been asking them to tell us what exactly they stand for, what is their claim, to tell us precisely, not vaguely and generally, to tell us by the precise longitude, latitude, etc., this place, that place, etc. They have never done that. Their maps are vague and so are the claims they advance. So Premier Chou En-Lai said this to me in December 1959. He relied on their 1956 map. This was in response to my letter[3] in which I had pointed out to him the bewildering variety of the delineation in the Chinese maps. The scrutiny of the map which was provided to our officials showed that the line drawn was further west in Ladakh of the 1956 line, that is the map which Premier Chou En-lai had stated as showing their position. That itself was a variation of the previous position which was to some extent set aside by the new map and the new line which the Chinese officials claimed in the western sector specially, and to some extent in the middle sector. Again, another thing happened. Take the middle sector, Uttar Pradesh and Himachal Pradesh and Punjab, etc. They claimed previously odd villages in India on this side of the border. Now they have gone one step further and joined up the odd villages. Previously a village was a bulge in the line. Now they simply joined them up, a series of villages there, so that it becomes a small area rather than a few bulges. That is how these 2000 miles extra in their claim come about. But, as I said, there has been no advance on any territory being occupied ever since the autumn of 1959.

Another thing they claimed, which goes rather counter in regard to the Niti Pass, etc., to the treaty we had with them, Tibetan treaty, I mean. Of course in regard to this border matter our position has been clarified by this report. Some Members said, I believe, that this report bought out certain facts that were not placed before the House previously, that is, that we had hidden them or some such thing. I should like this House to consider one aspect of these questions.

Questions are asked in this House and the other House, questions which we find it difficult to answer because any answer to that question is giving information to people to whom we do not want to give it, to our opponents, to those who are opposing it. It becomes difficult. We do not want to keep anything from the House. What the House knows, the world knows. So we cannot always give precise information in regard to border matters, what we are doing, what steps we take to protect ourselves, what roads we are making, where our armies are

[1] The North-East Frontier Agency.   [2] See *Documents*, 1959, pp. 242–8.
[3] Of 16 November 1959. Ibid., pp. 237–42.

situated and so on. We do not sometimes want the opposite side to know even an argument lest they might take some other steps in regard to it, if they knew it too soon. So there is this difficulty.

Apart from the broad lines of our approach, this involved the collection of material and tremendous labour by way of examination of documents, and many things have come to our notice; many papers have come to us from distant countries, which have gradually added to our information. And there is the vital difference between our stand and the Chinese stand. The Chinese stand has been that our border has not been delimited, has not been marked, let us sit down and consider it, mark it wherever it may be. Having said that, at the same time, they claim large chunks of territory. Suppose a border is not marked but broadly it is well known. A marking of it may involve, let us say, a few hundred yards this way or that way, a mile this way or that way. There is that possibility. But by no stretch of imagination does that involve large chunks of territory being occupied. But apart from that, our stand is that the border is known, is a defined border, it is not an unknown border. It is not marked down or delimited on the ground everywhere; in small bits it is, because it is frightfully difficult in these glacier regions to go about marking them. Anyhow, it was not considered necessary in the past during the British times, and since we became independent, we did not and could not easily do it. Anyhow, our position is that it is a defined border, it is a known border, known by custom, by practice, by usage, by treaty and so on and so forth. So the question of sitting down with the Chinese people to define it and consider the whole matter afresh does not arise, so far as we are concerned. And our case has been strengthened powerfully by the Report presented by our officials.[1] I was glad to find that the Hon. Member opposite who spoke on behalf of the Communist Party gave a great deal of credit to our officials who prepared the Report and said that they had presented a very strong case—I forget his words—almost a case proved to the hilt. I am glad this realisation has come even to doubting minds. But I would add this. It is not enough to realise that and then to proceed to suggest some course of action which does not fit in with that realisation. We must be logical. If that is so, the course of action should fit in with that. It is not good repeating like a manthram, 'Oh! let us sit down, embrace and be friends.' I am always in favour of sitting down and talking and embracing and being friends and all that. But when we are considering a problem like this, we must know the nature of the problem and not give any wrong impression to the public of India or to the public of the world as to where we stand or how this is going to be solved. It is not going to be solved merely by some pious declarations or by pure goodwill. I want goodwill always. The fact of the matter is that our case in regard to the border is almost of foolproof. It does not require high intelligence to realise how strong this case is and that—whatever the reason may be for the Chinese to do it; it is up to them— they were wrong in doing so, in occupying our territory. The question will only be settled when they leave this territory. That is the simple issue and it is not a

[1] Mr. Nehru and Mr. Chou En-Lai had agreed in 1960 that officials from both sides should meet to examine the details of the border dispute. The report, presented to the Indian Parliament on 14 February 1961, claimed that India's view of the position of the boundary was the correct one. The Chinese, it pointed out, were therefore occupying unlawfully some 12,000 square miles of Indian Territory.

question of horse-trading 'All right. You take this, I take this. Let us halve this.' It is not a question of that.

Now another question has been whether I am going to China to discuss it. I say I have no immediate intention of going there. I do not quite know myself about the future, about the steps we may have to take from time to time, and whether any of these steps may involve my having to meet Premier Chou En-lai or going to Peking for this purpose, I cannot say. I cannot obviously commit myself saying 'yes' or 'no' to something which will depend on various developments. But in order to settle this question peacefully, I am prepared to go as far as I can, and it is not a question of my prestige being involved. I may go to China or some other place but the point is there would be no justification for my doing so unless some situation arises when a talk is likely to be fruitful. There is the test. If I say that I will go because I am eager to settle it, that does not help; my saying that I will not go there at all, I am too proud to go, is not a right position which I am not prepared to take. But the question of talks only arises when there is justification for it by something emerging out of talks and what we say about it in regard to this matter being acknowledged, particularly acknowledged by the Chinese Government. That is the position.

I have spoken at some length about this matter because I wanted to make it clear what we stood for. It is a very difficult matter. It is a burden on us, and I would like to share that burden with this House. I would submit that whether it is the Congo or whether it is our border, an adventurous approach, is not helpful; it is very dangerous, and instead of solving problems, we make them even more difficult. I think that even though unfortunately Chinese forces still sit on parts of our territory, in Ladakh chiefly and in other parts, even so. India's case is now much better understood and will be understood in the world, and that is a good background for us to take whatever step we have to take.

I might mention one matter, relatively small but in a sense important. Some questions were asked—I forgot whether in this House or the other—about the evacuation of Longju by the Chinese. Longju, as the House will remember, is in the N.E.F.A. area, about two or three miles from where our forces are present. Longju in fact is a little village, is the only part of N.E.F.A. territory which is occupied by the Chinese forces. And a report came that Longju had been vacated by the Chinese. Also a report came that probably this was done because of an epidemic. I have information from Tibet and this indicates that a rather bad epidemic is raging in many parts of Tibet. What exactly the nature of the epidemic is, I cannot say. But it is raging there, and probably it is the same that occurred in Longju. We have to take care, apart from political and other reasons, to prevent that epidemic coming down through the Himalayan passes to India, and we are taking steps to that end.

2. Exchange of telegrams between U Thant, Acting Secretary-General of the United Nations, President Salazar of Portugal, and Mr. Nehru, concerning Goa, 15 December 1961[1]

(i) U Thant to Dr. Salazar and Mr. Nehru

Having been apprised of the serious situation which has recently developed at

[1] *N.Y. Times*, 18 December 1961.

the border of India and Goa, Damão and Diu, as revealed in letters addressed to the President of the Security Council by the Permanent Representatives of India and Portugal, I respectfully and urgently appeal to Your Excellency and to your Government to insure that the situation does not deteriorate to the extent that it might constitute a threat to peace and security.

I would urge immediate negotiations with a view to achieving an early solution of the problem. I would naturally hope that such negotiations would be in accordance with the principles embodied in the Charter and formulated by the United Nations.

(ii) *Dr. Salazar to U Thant*

I acknowledge receipt of Your Excellency's cable regarding the situation on the frontiers of Goa, Damão and Diu. The Portuguese Government is deeply sensible of Your Excellency's appeal and is in a position to state that, except in the case of an armed aggression, nothing will be done on its part, which may constitute a threat to peace and security.

Rigorous instructions have been given and are being observed to the effect that the Portuguese forces do not undertake nor even reply to any acts of provocation.

The government regrets that the Indian Union, which repeatedly alleges provocations from the Portuguese side, has not thought it possible to accept the proposal, addressed to it on the eighth instant, that international observers may follow the events on the frontiers. These observers would witness if and how violations of frontiers and provocative acts take place.

As regards negotiations, the Portuguese Government has always expressed and confirms its readiness to negotiate with the Indian Union solutions for all the problems arising from the vicinity between the territories of the Portuguese State of India (Goa) and those of the Indian Union, including international guarantee, to be given to the latter, that the Portuguese territory will not be utilized against the security of the Indian Union.

Such negotiations can take place where and how the Government of New Delhi may wish.

(iii) *Mr. Nehru to U Thant*

Thank you for your telegram of 15th December on the serious situation that has developed in and along the borders of the Portuguese colonial possessions of Goa, Diu and Damão on the Indian Continent.

We have in our recent communications to the Security Council given some details regarding the sequence of events which have led to this serious situation and shown how it has been entirely created by Portuguese aggressiveness along the Indian frontiers and an oppressive police régime inside these colonial areas. Portuguese forces continued to shoot indiscriminately at Indian citizens and are committing daily depredations into Indian territory.

We have consistently abided by the provisions of the United Nations Charter. The only solution conforming to the principles and purposes of the Charter, resolutions of the United Nations and the irreversible course of history is for

Portugal to leave its colonies in India and allow the people in these territories to join their countrymen in freedom and democracy.

We have during the last fourteen years been appealing to Portugal to settle this question of ending Portuguese colonial rule on the Indian Continent. Portugal has, however, brusquely rejected all our appeals and also rejected summarily the advice and suggestions in this connection given by other friendly countries.

As you know, Portugal consistently ignored United Nations resolutions on ending colonialism and refused even to recognize the fact that she had colonies and her responsibilities for sending reports to the United Nations. It is hardly possible to negotiate on the basis of the Charter provisions with a government who take their stand on sixteenth-century concepts of colonial conquest by force.

We understand that many of the Portuguese officials in Goa are being withdrawn. This is already leading to serious developments and will progressively lead to chaotic conditions and the growth of unauthorized violence by lawless elements as well as Portuguese soldiery. This will lead not only to grave loss and suffering but also to powerful reactions in India.

This situation is already very serious and is likely to grow more so. The Government of India who have shown considerable restraint in the last many weeks cannot tolerate this state of affairs indefinitely.

I am asking Ambassador Jha to hand over this reply to you and to explain to you in greater detail the serious situation with which we are confronted.

3. Speech by Mr. Adlai Stevenson, United States Permanent Representative at the United Nations, in the Security Council, 18 December 1961[1]

65. I should like to express the views of the United States at this fateful hour in the life of the United Nations. I will not detain you long, but long enough, I hope, to make clear our anxiety for the future of this Organization as a result of this incident.

66. When acts of violence take place between nations in this dangerous world, no matter where they occur or for what cause, there is reason for alarm. The news from Goa tells of such acts of violence. It is alarming news and, in our judgement, the Security Council has an urgent duty to act in the interests of international peace and security.

67. We know, as the world knows, and as has been said countless times in the General Assembly and the Security Council, that the winds of change are blowing all over the world. But the winds of change are man-made, and man can and must control them. They must not be allowed to become the bugles of war.

68. The preamble of the Charter states that the peoples are determined 'to save succeeding generations from the scourge of war', and 'to practice tolerance and live together with one another as good neighbours'. In that connexion, it deserves to be said that all of us at the United Nations owe much to India.

69. The largest contingent in the United Nations effort to establish peace in the Congo are the troops of India. India has also contributed of its resources in the Middle East. Few nations have done more to uphold the principles of this

[1] S.C.O.R., Sixteenth Year, 987th meeting, 18 December 1961.

D.I.A.–AA

Organization or to support its peace-making efforts all over the world, and none has espoused non-violence more vehemently and invoked the peaceful symbolism of Gandhi more frequently. That nation is led by a man whom I regard as a friend, who has been a lifelong disciple of one of the world's great saints of peace, whom many have looked up to as an apostle of non-violence and who only this year addressed this Assembly with a moving appeal for a United Nations Year of International Co-operation.

70. These facts make the step which has been taken today all the harder to understand and condone. The fact is, and the Indian Government has announced it, that Indian armed forces early this morning, on 18 December, marched into the Portuguese territories of Goa, Damão, and Diu. Damão and Diu have been occupied and there is fighting at this moment within the territory of Goa.

71. So here we are, confronted with the shocking news of this armed attack, and that the Indian Minister of Defence—so well known in these halls for his advice on matters of peace and his tireless enjoinders to everyone else to seek the way of compromise—was on the borders of Goa inspecting his troops at the zero hour of invasion.

72. Let it be perfectly clear what is at stake here; it is the question of the use of armed force by one State against another and against its will, an act clearly forbidden by the Charter. We have opposed such action in the past by our closest friends as well as by others. We opposed it in Korea in 1950, in Suez and in Hungary in 1956 and in the Congo in 1960. And we do so again in Goa in 1961.

73. The facts in this case are, unfortunately, all too clear. These territories have been under Portuguese dominion for over four centuries. They have been invaded by Indian armed forces. The Government of India regards these territories as having the same status as the territories of the United Kingdom and France on the sub-continent from which those countries have voluntarily withdrawn. The Government of India has insisted that Portugal likewise withdraw. Portugal has refused, maintaining that it has a legal and moral right to these territories.

74. We have repeatedly urged both of the parties to this dispute to seek by peaceful processes the resolution of a problem which has its roots in the colonial past. I do not at this time propose to concern myself with the merits of the dispute. We are not meeting here today to decide on the merits of this case; we are meeting to decide what attitude should be taken in this body when one of the Members of the United Nations casts aside the principles of the Charter and seeks to resolve a dispute by force.

75. But what is at stake today is not colonialism; it is a bold violation of one of the most basic principles in the United Nations Charter, stated in these words from Article 2, paragraph 4:

> 'All Members shall refrain in their international relations from the threat or use of force against the territorial integrity or political independence of any State, or in any other manner inconsistent with the Purposes of the United Nations.'

76. We realize fully the depths of the differences between India and Portugal

concerning the future of Goa. We realize that India maintains that Goa by right should belong to India. Doubtless India would hold, therefore, that its action is aimed at a just end. But, if our Charter means anything, it means that States are obligated to renounce the use of force, are obligated to seek a solution of their differences by peaceful means, are obligated to utilize the procedures of the United Nations when other peaceful means have failed.

77. Mr. Nehru, the Prime Minister, has often said himself that no right end can be served by a wrong means. The Indian tradition of non-violence has inspired the whole world, but this act of force with which we are confronted today mocks the good faith of India's frequent declarations of exalted principle. It is a lamentable departure not only from the Charter but from India's own professions of faith. What is the world to do if every State whose territorial claims are unsatisfied should resort with impunity to the rule of armed might to get its way? The Indian sub-continent is not the only place in the world where such disputes exist. The fabric of peace is fragile, and our peace-making machinery has today suffered another blow. If it is to survive, if the United Nations is not to die as ignoble a death as the League of Nations, we cannot condone the use of force in this instance and thus pave the way for forceful solutions of other disputes which exist in Latin America, in Africa, in Asia and in Europe. In a world as interdependent as ours, the possible results of such a trend are too grievous to contemplate.

78. This action is all the more painful to my country because we have in recent weeks made repeated appeals to the Government of India to refrain from the use of force. These have included not only a series of diplomatic approaches in Washington and in New Delhi, but also a personal message from President Kennedy to Mr. Nehru on 13 December[1] indicating our earnest hope that India would not resort to force to solve the Goa problem. As a culmination of these efforts, the United States Government last Saturday made an appeal to Mr. Nehru, both through the United States Ambassador in New Delhi and through the Indian Ambassador in Washington, to suspend preparations for the use of force, in connexion with a direct offer of United States help in seeking a peaceful solution of the problem.

79. This resort to armed action is a blow to international institutions, such as the United Nations and the International Court of Justice, which are available to assist in the adjustment of disputes. This is our principal concern. This body cannot apply a double standard with regard to the principle of resort to force. We appeal to India to recognize that its own national interests, as well as those of the entire world community, depend on the restoration of confidence in the processes of law and conciliation in international affairs. Indeed this tragic episode reveals clearly, if nothing else, the need for urgent review of peaceful settlement procedures to deal with the problems of peaceful change. My Government will have more to say about this at an appropriate occasion.

80. The Council has an urgent duty, in our judgement, to bring this dispute back from the battlefield, so fraught with danger for the world, to the negotiating

---

[1] President Kennedy sent letters, which have not so far been published, to Mr. Nehru and President Sukarno, asking them not to use force to gain territory which they regarded as parts of their own country, i.e. Goa and Dutch New Guinea. *N.Y. Times.* 15 December 1961.

table. We earnestly urge the Government of India to withdraw its armed forces from the territories they have invaded. We earnestly appeal for a cease-fire and we earnestly urge the Governments of India and of Portugal to enter into negotiations to achieve a solution. In our judgement, we must ask for an immediate cease-fire; we must insist on withdrawal of the invading forces; and we must insist that the two parties negotiate on the basis of the principles of the Charter; for the law of the Charter forbids the use of force in such matters. There is not one law for one part of the world and another law for the rest of the world; there is one law for the whole world, and it is the duty of this Council to uphold it.

4. Security Council draft resolutions on Goa, 18 December 1961

(*i*) *Draft resolution sponsored by the United States, Britain, France, and Turkey*[1]
   The Security Council,
   Recalling that in Article 2 of the Charter of the United Nations all Members are obligated to settle their disputes by peaceful means and to refrain from the threat or use of force in a manner inconsistent with the purposes of the United Nations,
   Deploring the use of force by India in Goa, Damão and Diu,
   Recalling that Article 1, paragraph 2, of the Charter specifies as one of the purposes of the United Nations to develop friendly relations among nations based on respect for the principle of equal rights and self-determination of peoples,
   1. *Calls* for an immediate cessation of hostilities;
   2. *Calls upon* the Government of India to withdraw its forces immediately to positions prevailing before 17 December 1961;
   3. *Urges* the parties to work out a permanent solution of their differences by peaceful means in accordance with the principles embodied in the Charter;
   4. *Requests* the Secretary-General to provide such assistance as may be appropriate.

(*ii*) *Draft resolution sponsored by Ceylon, the United Arab Republic, and Liberia*[2]
   The Security Council,
   Having heard the complaint of Portugal of aggression by India against the territories of Goa, Damão and Diu,
   Having heard the statement of the representative of India that the problem is a colonial problem,
   Considering that these enclaves claimed by Portugal in India constitute a threat to international peace and security and stand in the way of the unity of the Republic of India,

[1] S.C.O.R., Sixteenth Year, Doc. 2/5033, *In favour:* Chile, China, Ecuador, France, Turkey, United Kingdom, United States. *Against:* Ceylon, Liberia, Russia, United Arab Republic. This resolution was not adopted, one of the negative votes being that of a permanent member of the Council.
[2] ibid., Doc. 2/5038. *In favour:* Ceylon, Liberia, Russia, the United Arab Republic. *Against:* Chile, China, Ecuador, France, Turkey, United Kingdom, United States. Resolution rejected by 7 votes to 4.

Recalling resolution 1514 (XV) and resolution 1542 (XV) of the General Assembly,

1. *Decides* to reject the Portuguese complaint of aggression against India:

2. *Calls upon* Portugal to terminate hostile action and to co-operate with India in the liquidation of her colonial possessions in India.

5. Mr. Nehru's press conference, New Delhi, 28 December 1961[1] (extract)

Question: In the next dangerous international crisis, presumably your Government will again advise the parties to abjure the use of force. In the light of your Government's action in Goa, would you expect your advice to carry as much weight in future as it has in the past?

Prime Minister: That depends on the receptiveness of the other party.

Question: Simply that, would it not involve also your own record as a Government?

Prime Minister: Of course, it always does. I think our record is excellent.

Question: Now that Goa has been liberated, what will be our attitude towards the liberation of West Irian and Taiwan.

Prime Minister: No question of attitude. We have been of the opinion that the Indonesian claim to West Irian is justified and we have hoped that this will be settled between the two Governments concerned. We still hope that that may be done and I believe that some suggestions have been made to that effect and some steps might have been taken. We hope it will be settled in that way.

Question: Can you tell us something about the disposition of the Portuguese in Goa? What would become of the Portuguese in Goa, the troops, armies?

Prime Minister: I suppose the Portuguese will go to Portugal—most of them I don't know, some might stay on for some reason or other. We have no objection to odd people staying on, but so far as the armed forces of Portugal are concerned, they will be not only permitted but encouraged to go back.

Question: Will it be independent of the action taken against Indians in Mozambique and other places?

Prime Minister: We do not tie up the two things, although it is a serious matter—the action taken against thousands of people in Mozambique, Macao and various places, that is, the internment of the Indians there by the Portuguese authorities and seizure of their assets or sealing of their businesses and everything. We have drawn the attention of some friendly Governments to this matter.

Question: Is Britain also one of the Governments?

Prime Minister: Chiefly Britain and the United States.

Question: A vast amount of arms and ammunition dumps were found in a church in Goa, which is described as NATO type and Japanese. A military expert told me that this would have been enough to arm a whole battalion for a 24-hour fierce fighting for one month. Have you sought any clarifications from the NATO authorities or from Japan as to why this vast amount was dumped in Goa.

[1] Ministry of External Affairs, *Prime Minister on Goa* (New Delhi, Government of India, 1962), pp. 22–40.

Prime Minister: There is no doubt that large quantities of arms have been found there—vehicles, arms and vast quantities of dynamite—apparently intended to blow up the whole place. Because of the speed of the operation this was not done, except a few houses here and there, the Governor's house in one place, chiefly bridges were blown up. But that was the intention. Otherwise why collect all this dynamite all over? We have not raised this matter with any other country.

Question: It has been pointed out by an American political scientist that the misunderstanding on the Goa issue is due to the fact that our information agencies in America did not care to put the Goa issue to the Americans in the proper way, particularly the psychological aspect of it. Do you agree?

Prime Minister: It may be partly true. Of course, one can always find explanations. But I should imagine one explanation is that a man's thinking, a nation's thinking, a people's thinking is governed by various factors, not by facts alone. To imagine that you can change their thinking by some facts or figures or information is not quite correct. One starts with certain presumptions. One simple fact I have often laid stress upon is this that geography is one very important factor in a nation's thinking. The world looks different from different parts of the world. Problems look different. The importance of problems becomes different. Something small but nearby is more important than something big and far away.

The second big factor is the conditioning of the people, their past conditioning, history etc., recent history I mean, which makes them think in some particular way or look at problems in some way.

In New York I was asked, I think at a TV interview, if the masses of India, vast numbers of people of India, were excited over the Berlin problem. I said: 'No.' They don't know anything about it. It is obvious. How am I to say that the average peasant is excited over the Berlin problem? The problem of Berlin is one of the biggest and most dangerous today in the world, I admit, for me, for those who understand that, but to say that the masses of people are excited over Berlin is manifestly wrong.

But I said that the masses of our people were excited about a very tiny problem and that is Goa—tiny in the sense of the world sense. In the world sense it is small, but in our sense it is not small. Even the man in the village knows something about it.

You see how one's thinking is governed by a number of factors. It is not a kind of approach in a vacuum. Take this major fact. I know that nothing has happened in India, I say so without any reservations, nothing has happened in India since independence, fourteen and a half years ago, which has excited and thrilled the people of India as this liberation of Goa. Go and ask any 'tongawalla', ask any man you like in the factory—it is not a question of the intellectuals —you will find that they are thrilled by it. Now, that is a fact; whether they have been thrilled rightly or wrongly, that is another matter and you can have your opinions. Why have they been thrilled? It is because of the past conditioning, constant frustration, anger at many things and the fact that it appears to us monstrous, a monstrous imposition, that any foreign power should sit in India.

It does not go down our throats. It is a daily irritant. It has been said in the past again and again by the Portuguese authorities, by Mr. Salazar and others that they have been here 400 years, 451 years. Yes, of course, but they have been there just a few hundred years too long. Why were they here for 400 years? Is it because of the goodwill of the people or by their strength, the goodwill that they have never had in history?

The whole record of Goa is of rebellions and revolts against the Portuguese. They came in the *Mogul* times when the *Mogul* empire was breaking down and they established themselves. During the whole of the British period in India, 250 or 300 years, in some parts of India, they were protected by the British and that is why they were here. They were not here by their own strength obviously. They continued here just like the Indian Princes and others who continued in India because the British gave them protection. Do you think the Indian Princes would have continued all this time? Some may have, but not all of them. They were protected and the Portuguese power was also protected by British alliances and by the fact that Britain was the dominating power in India. That is why they have continued.

Now, when the British power in India disappeared, the whole fabric goes. They remained just as a shadow, and they continued simply because we tolerated the shadow; all substance, all reality went from their remaining in Goa. No country in the wide world would really have tolerated this immediately after that, but it is because of our extreme desire to function in a peaceful and co-operative manner that we did it.

Many people who have criticised our action have told us, 'oh, if you had taken this action in 1947, we would have understood it'. Now, it is a very queer argument. We did not take action in 1947, when we became independent. Therefore, we are barred from taking it afterwards. I do not understand this argument. The point to remember is that they were there simply because of the protection of the British power in India, because obviously otherwise they could not have remained in India. Once that power went, their departure became inevitable, a thing which cannot be avoided.

It is an amazing thing, our not taking any active steps for reasons that we thought adequate, reasons that had nothing to do with Portugal, but reasons of reactions of what might happen on other matters. We never doubted our right to push them out if we wanted to, but we did doubt as to the consequences in the world and in other places. In this tense situation in the world, these things have consequences. That was our drawback, but when it became unbearable, we took action.

Question: Some Western powers, almost all Western powers, have expressed shock and dismay at our action. What is your comment on that?

Prime Minister: Well, it is not for me to comment, but it is an interesting fact to note that nothing that has happened in the last fourteen and a half years since independence has thrilled so much every section of the Indian people, every party, every group, every class. I cannot obviously answer for every individual in India. This is an interesting fact, and a painful fact. Here is something done in India which rouses such tremendous reactions in the whole of India and in Goa. We all know that in Goa this event has been hailed by the people, not by the Hindus only, by the Catholics, Christians. You may have seen in the public Press what the leading dignitary of the Catholic Church in India has said, the Archbishop of Bombay, who is himself a Goan and a Cardinal of the Roman Church. They don't speak irresponsibly. He has welcomed this. I have had telegrams from Bishops in Goa, Catholic Bishops, welcoming this. All these people, in India and in Goa, are governed by facts, by the background.

Here is this solid, mass opinion in India and, as you see, there are some countries in the West condemning us. It really is a matter for careful study, almost psychological study. Why does this happen? I do not like it. If you go a step further, you will find that practically the whole of Africa—the African Africa—rejoiced at this action. Nearly all countries in Asia rejoiced at it. Now, I do not like this division of opinion, to put it very crudely, into white and black. I do not like it at all. It is a bad sign. But there it is. I have been distressed by this more than by anything else.

Only yesterday I was reading an article in a New York newspaper of repute in which they calmly suggest, in polite language, that India should be driven out of Goa and Goa should be restored to the Portuguese. Just think of this and what it means. If an attempt was made, what would happen in India and in the world? There will be hell in the world if this happned—in India of course—but in all the world, and this is casually mentioned that colonial power should be, presumably by force, placed there. Really my head reeled when I read this kind of thing. If out of their thinking this kind of thing emerges it is not surprising that their actions are quite often very wrong, and lead them into trouble.

Why has this Portuguese matter suddenly affected people in various ways? Because in the last 14 or 15 years while we went on talking about it nobody attached much importance. Portugal was sometimes the oldest ally, and sometimes it was looked upon as a museum piece in the world. Whatever its reasons, nobody cared to interest himself in the matter. In fact, Portugal was patted on the back repeatedly by some of the great Powers, and in a sense encouraged. In fact, the NATO alliance itself though it had nothing to do with Goa—encouraged Portugal in its intransigent attitude, apart from arms etc. they may have got. It is a moral encouragement all the time. It amazed us all that at this period this kind of thing was happening. The result is that the time came when it burst, the whole bubble burst. It could not last. It was not what we did or what we did not do. It became a fact of history, the irrepressible force of history functioning. We happened to be its agents for the moment. Here is this enormous mass of human opinion in regard not only to Goa but in regard to the Portuguese colonies.

In the United Nations, in the last two years specially, partly because, of course, more African countries have come to the United Nations—there is resolution after resolution about the removal of colonialism, specially about Portugal, condemning Portugal, for not supplying information about its colonies, saying so definitely and naming Goa, that is, Goa is a colony, not a Portuguese territory, and should be treated as such and that the retention of these colonies is a source of real danger to world peace etc. The thinking of the world has been more and more concentrated in that way. This is what had been happening all this time, when the thing burst.

It simply means that people have got used to thinking according to their own lines. So they do not see where the world is going, what the others think. They are upset by the fact that many African and Asian countries are now in the United Nations and they have a greater voting power, at any rate, as well as some other, I suppose and it obsesses people because the old world is dead, the world of colonialism is dead. It will not come back and if any attempt is made to bring it back, the whole world will go up in flames. It will not be tolerated.

Anybody trying to get back Goa to the Portuguese, I think, will have to face a few hundred million people, and the anger of a few hundred million people is nothing to joke at, even though they may not have powerful weapons. I am amazed, astounded at the calm and casual way people criticise us, and people who, of all persons in the world, have no right to do so. I can understand Mr. Gandhi telling me something about non-violence. But my being preached about non-violence by people who have not the faintest conception of it or respect for it is amazing.

Take this question of non-violence. The word 'non-violence' is seldom used except in some philosophical sense. Mr. Gandhi made it rather popular and some other people have used it too. I think—I am not quite sure—Thoreau used it and some others perhaps. But what it meant is something much more than what is called peaceful methods.

I wonder how many of you remember that in the early days of the last war, may be 1940 or 1941, Mr. Gandhi resigned from the Congress Working Committee at a meeting in Ahmedabad, because the Congress Working Committee could not accept his interpretation of non-violence as a policy for the future in India when India was free. We were all for peaceful methods in our movement. But he said you must now decide that in the future India, when India was free, you must adhere to non-violence which meant keeping no armies, no air force, no nothing hardly a police force. That was his idea of non-violence. And much as we admired Mr. Gandhi and believed in his movement, peaceful non-violent movement, we thought we could not commit the future India to that—we would have liked to do so but we just could not responsibly say so, because it depends upon so many factors, world factors, factors of our own people. People have to be developed to a certain extent to function in this way. We were developing—I believe Indians were perhaps more developed, in that particular way, than others —but still not enough; and we cannot in vacuum do that. We are not prepared to say then that we will not keep an army, a navy, an air force etc. After all we keep it.

Remember that Mr. Gandhi definitely and clearly approved of our action in Kashmir. That was not non-violent action. There is no doubt about it. Mr. Gandhi went a step further. As far as I remember—I speak from memory—I think at the beginning of the Great War, he commended the then Polish Government resisting Hitler, violently and by war. Holding to non-violence, his non-violence was more of the mind and thought—also of action—but more than that. He said, if you have a dagger in your heart, pull it out and use it and not keep it in your mind and heart.

It is difficult for people to understand the almost metaphysical approach to these problems. It is not for me to say what Mr. Gandhi might have done in a particular set of circumstances. We have to judge for ourselves and take the responsibility for it, the blame for it, or the credit for it, whatever it may be.

There are certain things which are worse than, shall I say, maintenance of peace, that is, trying to maintain it by cowardice. Cowardice is not peace. Mr. Gandhi said: 'I want you to carry on non-violently, but if you cannot do it with courage, well, take out a sword and fight.'

The thing Mr. Gandhi would have disliked and abhorred with all his conscience is the cold war, which is a corrupting, corrosive thing in the minds and hearts of men. And if, as is said in the UNESCO constitution, war starts in the minds of men, the cold war may sometimes break out outside. It is a bad thing. It is almost a worse thing than actual war. In actual war you have an outlet and behave and misbehave and destroy. By destroying yourself in the process of the cold war your heart and mind are distorted and perverted. I think that is what we suffer from today.

That is one reason why this Goa affair has excited a number of people. But really it is a serious matter and a painful matter to me that there should be this strong difference of opinion between countries.

I do not mind strong language being used against me or India, though it is very gratifying to see how, now, we are told what a fine image of India there was before the Goa action! The image has been affected! What an unusually great man Nehru was if he had not fallen now! It is something to be told that one was great, even if one is not great now.

But apart from this, it is bad sign for the future, these basic differences of opinion. I am worried. And I may tell you I had no doubt in my mind at any time about our full justification for use of force against the Portuguese in Goa at any time in the last 14 years. I did not want to use it and I did not use it because of certain consequences, not in Goa or India, but outside India and Goa. That has kept me back. There is no doubt that any such thing, however justified, opens a door to certain kinds of action which may be used by others, rightly or wrongly. Therefore, I did not want to do it. That was my main concern and that is why, to the end, I did not want to take this action, almost to the end. It was with great reluctance that I took it. When I decided to take it, of course, it had to be taken efficiently, not half-heartedly. But it was a choice, for me, of a lesser evil, the lesser in the sense of the world.

Looked at from the purely Indian point of view, it was a very desirable and necessary action. Looking at it from the world point of view, which we should in such matter, it had certain possible evil consequences; and we see those. The mere fact of this resentment and anger in peoples' minds outside India is one of the evil consequences that flow from it. It was with difficulty that ultimately I decided.

But as a matter of fact, to be perfectly frank with you, the decision crept up so gradually that the circumstances forced the decision on us. Step by step we were compelled to do it, till there was no choice left, no possibility of withdrawing from that decision. It was not like sitting down and clearly deciding that we will do this and that, but we were driven step by step into it by facts and circumstances, and there was no withdrawing from it.

Question: Did you anticipate all this criticism from the Western powers?

Prime Minister: No, not to this extent. I thought there would be some, of course, but I wonder if there is a definite, shall I say, difference in the thinking of countries which have been under colonial domination and countries which have been among the colonial powers. I wonder, because there seems to be a basic difference in the thinking of countries which have been under colonial domination and countries which have been among the colonial powers. I wonder, because there seems to be a basic difference in thinking.

What has happened in the Congo? What is happening in Katanga even now? What has happened in Angola? In an entirely different sense, of course, what has happened in South Africa—but that is different. The kind of information that has come to us about Katanga and those who are supporting Katanga, I think it is monstrous. We remain quiet, more or less, but I think it is monstrous. Nobody talks about breaking up the U.N. then. It is only when India goes to Goa they say we are hitting at the U.N. When U.N. is in the open field challenged and obstructed in its work in the Congo, in Katanga, when all this is done, all that is fair play.

All this piles up in our mind, piles up and makes us angry and very angry. I am not talking about my mind, I am talking about the mind of Asia and Africa.

I know that the United States of America have been no party to this business in the Congo. I mean to say it has supported the Central Government and all that. I am not criticising the United States for this. I want to make it clear. But there are other countries who obviously have been playing an extraordinarily queer game in the Congo and in regard to Katanga, and nobody has hinted, even gently, that they might be injuring the cause of the United Nations.

It simply shows that the mental approach is different. Something we consider as a great sin is looked upon as a minor misdemeanour which can be passed by and something which we consider a minor misdemeanour is perhaps considered a great sin. So our values differ. Apparently our standards differ. What is said about the failure of the United Nations, I mean the danger to the United Nations, almost looks like the danger coming from the fact that these Asian-African countries, their weight of opinion, well, is becoming more weighty than it was.

Question: Don't you think that the reaction of the United States of America and other Western countries amounts to defending colonialism in general and that it is natural for them to behave like this under the circumstances?

Prime Minister: The sense of perspective is different. At the present moment, I doubt if there is anybody in the wide world who defends colonialism in theory. The biggest colonial powers like Great Britain and France have divested themselves of most of their colonial territories. The process is going on. We may criticise minor matters, for instance how it has been held up in Rhodesia, not so much by the British Government but by the Central African Federation. That is a different matter, but broadly speaking the United Kingdom and France gave up their colonies. Again, so far as France is concerned, Algeria remains. But it is admitted by every body that colonialism must go, except by Portugal which adopted the queer device of passing a statute saying that a bit of India was Portugal. Why they did not say it was a part of the moon requiring some other atomic agency to reach there, I do not know. It is fantastic nonsense. And this kind of thing is swallowed by the great powers. Mr. Dulles comes and tells us about five or six years ago that Goa is part of Portugal. I never heard such amazing stuff in my life, that a bit of India geographically becomes a part of Portugal because the Portuguese Parliament—I do not know if Parliament functions there—because Mr. Salazar thinks so.

What is all this story about the association of free nations? The association of Portugal with NATO has been a greater weakening factor for NATO's influence, moral and other, than anything else. Can any one, even in a drowsy state, describe Portugal as a free nation? Nobody does. Everybody knows that it is one of the most reactionary régimes in the world.

Question: Do you make a distinction between those who are traditionally anti-Indian and those who have been friendly to India? From both sides criticisms have come. You can ignore the former obviously. How do you explain the latter?

Prime Minister: I do not know what you mean by 'making a distinction'? Yes, I make a distinction. I do not generalise. Even I, who am part of the Indian scene, being effected by currents of thought, emotions and urges, I hesitated for long to do this. I did not want to do this. I was compelled step by step by circumstance to do it because every step seemed to me inevitable and the refusal to take that step seemed to me to lead to graver consequences, graver consequences even in terms of peace and war, of violence and non-violence, of peace. I had that choice every time. If we had not taken that step, towards the end, there would have been chaos, absolutely, in Goa. There would have been terrible repression on our people there and we would have had to face an amazing situation—we might have had to shoot down our own people in trying to force our hands or see them being shot down by the Portuguese.

As it was, we went there. The Portuguese administration had really cracked up even before we went there. The whole operation took there, as you know, about 26 hours. It would have taken half that time but for the fact that the roads were mined and vehicles could not go. Our people marched all this distance on foot. It was 30 to 40 miles. That is why it took a little time, otherwise it would have been over in a few hours. But, of course, there was practically no resistance; there was no mind to resist. Not that the Government there did not want to resist. The orders were to resist, but there was no mind to resist. They realised that they had no business to be there. They had to go.

Question: It was said in the Press that Portugal was intending to invite Pakistan to take over Goa if India had not gone in. What is your opinion in regard to that?

Prime Minister: I do not know anything about it.

Question: What have you to say about the future administrative set-up in the light of the visit of the official team to Goa?

Prime Minister: There is nothing much to say about it because we have not decided yet. The first thing to do is to get all the various normal social and other services functioning—the normal apparatus of Government. That is being done fairly rapidly, railways, posts and telegraphs etc. When that is completed, the military authority there will be replaced by the civil authority. That will function for some little time. Later, we will no doubt come up to Parliament for not only the incorporation of Goa into the Indian Union, as we think, as a separate entity under the Central Government but having local autonomy. We have not worked out the details of this yet. In the course of the next month or two months we shall try to do that. But this can only come up before the new Parliament . . . there are one or two things about Goa which I want to make quite clear. There is a report in the Press that the U.A.R. Government had stopped a Portuguese ship from coming with arms to Goa. I do not know where this report emanated from, but it had no foundation of fact at all. There was no Portuguese ship. There was no request by Portugal to let their ship pass through the Suez Canal, and consequently there was no refusal. So, obviously it was quite wrong.

And the other thing that I have seen mentioned in a newspaper article is this— I think I had read it in a Japanese newspaper article—that before we took action we sort of cleared it up with the President of the Soviet Union who was here. Now it is hardly necessary for me to say that it is completely wrong. When Mr. Brezhnev came here for the first time, I had a long talk with him about various matters, but Goa was not mentioned. Anything affecting Goa was not mentioned either by him or by me, although we were full of Goa at that time because, after all, it was four or five days after he left Delhi, that we took action. It was not mentioned, deliberately not mentioned nor was it mentioned or referred to by our Ambassador in Moscow with the Soviet Government. May be three or four years ago we might have talked about Goa and told them what the Goa problem was, but in this connection not a word was said to the Soviet Government, or to the President of the Soviet Union here. He heard of it first of all when he saw a newspaper in Bombay—I think he was travelling from Bombay to Ankleshwar or somewhere. He saw it for the first time. He had no inkling. And he asked one of my colleagues who was accompanying him: 'I am very glad. May I mention this in my next speech at Bombay?'

It might interest you if I remind you again of the background. First of all, all these years, at no time, have we forgotten Goa. It was a constant pricking of our mind and our conscience. If, let me say, suppose we were apt to be complacent, there were enough members of the opposition parties in Parliament and outside to remind us constantly of it. Every year amendments were brought in and we had to answer them. So it was always there. It came to a head in 1955, as you know, when there were shootings of our people (on the Goan border). Then things relatively quietened down but it was all the time there.

What has happened to bring this matter to a head now? Well, a number of things. The whole background has been changing in the last two or three years, the world background, resulting in the resolutions in the U.N. First of all, I would remind you that last year, in December 1960, there was a strong resolution on granting of independence to colonial countries and peoples.[1] I need not read those resolutions but you can see the whole mental background changing. May be some people thought that they were pious resolutions without any meaning, but they were felt strongly by those who voted for it and many of those resolutions were passed almost unanimously.

Then, a week later, the General Assembly of the U.N. on 21st December 1960, passed a resolution specially in regard to Portugal and Portuguese colonies, and Goa is specially mentioned there. This resolution demanded that these

[1] *Documents*, 1960, pp. 404–6.

were colonies and not bits of Portugal, demanded information which Portugal refused to give.

Then we skip a year and on November 14 this year, there was again a resolution of the General Assembly in the U.N. condemning the continuing non-compliance by the Government of Portugal of its obligations under Chapter XI of the Charter and in terms of the General Assembly resolution passed a year before. A special committee of seven members was appointed as a matter of urgency to get this information, such information as was available, about the Portuguese territories.

Then on 28th November this year again, the General Assembly stated that the delay in supplying the information etc. by Portugal was a source of international conflict and disharmony, seriously impeded international cooperation and was creating an increasingly dangerous situation in many parts of the world which might threaten international peace and security. Not only Portugal, but two or three other countries were involved and they called upon those States to take action without further delay. And they decided to establish a sub-committee of 17 members.

So you see this was all leading up. Meanwhile, apart from this, the situation had developed in the Congo and in Angola and it had caused us a very great deal of concern; concern because we found that some of the powers, some of the great powers, were coming in the way of the U.N. action in the Congo, and you have had some evidence of that afterwards—not from Indian sources, but from non-Indian sources—and it was very painful for us. We were involved, of course, in many ways. Our troops were there, too.

What happened in Angola pained us tremendously and in our minds, if I may say so, almost for the first time, Goa and Angola were tied up together, in a sense, vaguely. I cannot justify it, but there it was. Constantly we were thinking of Angola and then we referred back to Goa in our minds, one in a sense as being helpful to the other. So the question of Goa became riper and riper, because of the resolutions of the General Assembly and because of the fact that in spite of those resolutions, the Portuguese refused to accept them, or to take any action or to supply any information, and because of what was happening in Angola.

You will remember that we had a seminar here against Portuguese colonialism, and a number of eminent African leaders came here. The whole context of their speeches etc. was that of tying up Goa with Angola—both Portugal's colonies. How far that was justified, I don't know. It was partly justified, on doubt. But the problem became more and more an allied one in our thinking. So we were keyed up, you might say, long before this happened. Yet, if you had asked me then, there was only a quantitative change, if I may use the word 'change'; we were more eager and more angry, but no qualitative change. We were not thinking of this action then. We were just in a receptive mood—if I may analyse it—because we were searching for something to do and, of course, in Goa and elsewhere round about in India also excitement was growing.

Then some of these things happened, the shooting at one of our merchant ships from Anjadev, the shooting at fishermen, killing one. These, by themselves, were nothing. It was nothing very great and had it happened without any background, we would have thought that some foolish sentry had done it, that somebody got frightened, and would have dealt with it. But in this context of things, when we were keyed up, it had a powerful effect. And it was deliberate, there was no doubt about it.

Immediately, the problem arose before us, for the first time, that we must keep our seaways clear, because our ships are passing that way frequently. Are we going to have potshots at them? It was an intolerable situation. So, we said, we must keep our seaways clear. Then, the next step in our thinking was, what would happen on the land, in the mainland and elsewhere? We must be prepared for any consequence that might happen there. Again, the Portuguese, with quite astounding stupidity—the most remarkable fact about the Portuguese is that stupidity sometimes survives more than intelligence—actually went about having petty excursions into Indian territory, a number of them, small ones, 300 yards, 400 yards, 200 yards coming in, trying to frighten our villagers and shooting at our guards. This is an extraordinary thing. When this happened, in that background again, we said, well, we must protect not only our border but put a stop to this kind of thing. First we had thought about the sea routes and then the land and we said the whole thing is one whole. We must protect this. The next step in thinking was, if you protect this, you must protect it adequately as some half measure may fail, may not succeed.

So step by step we came to the conclusion that we must be prepared for every action. We were convinced of that and yet we slightly hesitated as to when we should take the action and what the nature of it should be. But we should be prepared for it because we did not quite know what might happen. So we ordered our forces to be sent there. And then a number of things happened. Even when our forces were there, these Portuguese excursions went on, petty ones I repeat, but irritating in that particular situation. And we heard stories. In fact, Mr. Salazar himself had publicly announced that he would blow up the whole of Goa and leave it in ruins. Stories came to us, not only of repression in Goa but of the Portuguese Government cracking up, anti-social elements slowly beginning to take advantage of the situation. We saw the whole thing crumbling. And we saw that if this goes on, there would be chaos in Goa and may be the Portuguese authorities blow up most of the important institutes, buildings etc. So we were led step by step to decide that we must intervene.

Now I want to give you some information. We sent several communications to the Portuguese Government through the Embassy of the United Arab Republic. I think first it was on 4th December, about the shooting at S. S. *Sabarmati* and a country craft. On 11th December, another communication was sent about aggression of Portuguese soldiers in the Indian territory and firing by them. On 15th December, yet another note was sent and I would quote a sentence or two from this note. After pointing all this out, we said, 'The Government believe that it is never too late to take the right step and hope that in accordance with the immutable principles of humanity and the irreversible processes of history, the Government of Portugal will leave their Indian colonies forthwith and remove their persistent irritance against international peace. The people of India are determined to ensure that their independence is complete and that there are no longer any vestiges of colonial rule on their territory.' In this note, I think, as far as I remember, a quotation was given from a speech I had delivered in the Rajya Sabha on the 11th December, just two or three days earlier, which said: 'Our patience is certainly exhausted. We still hope that either the Portuguese by themselves or by the advice of their friends, will desist from what they are doing and accept the natural culmination of all this which is their withdrawal from Goa. We can discuss the legalities and modalities later on but the physical handing over should be done.'

Practically, in effect, what we were saying was even less than this namely, let this agreement be arrived at that they were going to leave. When that fact is certain, then let us discuss how, timing etc. If it takes a few months, we will wait for a few months. We have waited for many years but we are not going to discuss anything unless that was clear.

We further informed Portugal that the Government of India have repeatedly stated that when the colonial regime is ended and Goa joins the Indian Union, Goa will retain its identity and will also retain its cultural individuality as regards religion, language, customs etc. All these communications were sent through the UAR Government, copies being sent to the Brazilian Embassy which represents Portugal's interests here.

Thereafter, the Portuguese Government made its reference to the Security Council, I think, on 8th December. It made two or three references. We sent replies to this to the Security Council. I think we sent three messages to the President of the Security Council in reply to these as well as giving all other facts.

Now, when this matter came to a head—as I said, all this came to a head after that firing on our ship and other matter—the only two countries we kept in touch with these matters were the United States of America and the United Kingdom because they are friends of Portugal. We thought they might be able to help. As I said, there was not a word between us and the Soviet Union on the subject or with any other country except that at some later date, we kept some of our Asian and African friends, a few of them, informed of developments. As I have told you the matter was coming to a head almost by its own impetus, and we had to think when it came to a head of taking action, because it was difficult to remain on tip-toe all the time. In the meanwhile whenever any little thing happened, another few Portuguese came into our territory, immediately the tempers rose; in our minds we began to think of a date. Dates in such matters are seldom fixed by Government, because the essence of a date is that it should not be known. All that the Government does is to inform the persons in charge, I mean to say military and other people in charge, of a probable period, and it is for them to fix a date and take action. So in this sense we did inform our defence authorities of a probable date, that is not before this date, sometime after, left to their choice, more or less, within a few days.

Then came a vague approach to us from some Latin-American countries. It was rather vague. Nevertheless, immediately, we postponed that vague date. We thought if there is anything which can be done we would be very happy. We postponed, not for long, but anyhow it was postponed to another date. But soon after, a day or two later, we realised, in fact we were told by the other side that the Latin American approach could not take us anywhere. So that was washed out. That was the first time that we had to postpone this business which was coming to a head; it was not an easy matter.

Then, on 14th December, we had a proposal from the U.S. Government asking us whether we would be agreeable to the Americans taking an initiative in this matter and suggesting to Portugal that they should quit Goa on the understanding that the Government of India would be prepared to take a generous view of Portugal's economic and cultural institutions in Goa. Our answer was that we would be very happy if the U.S. Government could take this initiative and that so far as the Government of India was concerned, they had always taken a generous view on matters of this kind—economic and cultural matters. We referred to what we had already done, our dealings with the British and the French when they left India. We added, however, that the situation was getting rather desperate and any initiative of this kind must be taken quickly.

This was after we had postponed the matter once. Now, because of this enquiry from the U.S. Government, we made a second postponement because if there was the slightest chance, well, we should take advantage of it. But a day or two later we were informed by the U.S. Government authorities that the Portuguese response to the American initiative had been a negative one. They did not accept the suggestion put forward by the U.S. Government or the State Department, whoever it was; I do not know how it was put forward, formally or informally, but we were informed that the response of the Portuguese was a negative one. It was a repetition of stating the Portuguese position, that Goa was not a colony but part of Portugal itself, one of their provinces, and that they would admit nothing else.

There the matter ended. And so we had to think again. We had postponed the matter twice and roughly, vaguely, a third date had to be fixed. It was fixed. There was a compulsion of events about all this, and it became progressively more and more difficult to go about playing a game of going forward and backward and deciding this and that. It appeared to us that if we had really called off the whole thing we would probably have had to shoot down our people in considerable numbers or stand by and witness the Portuguese shooting them.

In the meanwhile, on 15th December—this slightly overlaps; I had told you about the U.S. proposal about their taking the initiative—U Thant, Acting Secretary-General of the U.N., sent a message, a similar, identical message to our Government and to the Portuguese Government suggesting immediate negotiations in accordance with the principles enunciated in the Charter as well as principles formulated by the United Nations in their resolutions.[1]

We replied to the Secretary-General that Portugal had been consistently ignoring the Charter provisions as well as the resolutions of the U.N. and rejecting all our appeals. The Portuguese answer to U Thant was that they were only prepared to negotiate on the basis of Goa being a part of Portuguese territory and of co-existence of India and Portuguese territory side by side. Further, they said they were not prepared to negotiate in accordance with the resolutions of the U.N. So the Portuguese Government closed that door which the Secretary-General of the U.N. had tried to open.

[1] Above, p. 713.

There the matter ended. The Secretary-General said, 'What more can I do?' This was on the 15th.

On 17th December evening, early evening, we got a message from our Ambassador in Washington conveying the suggestion of the U.S. Government that if the Prime Minister, that is, me, could make an announcement that he would delay the use of force by, say, six months, in the meantime they would try to get assurances from some Powers that they would try to evolve some means of solving the Goa problem. It was rather a vague message. One thing we appreciated about it was the anxiety of the United States Government to help in solving this; but it was a vague message. First of all we were to postpone everything by six months and then they would apparently approach other Powers which probably meant the U.K., the so-called oldest ally of Portugal, and then jointly bring some pressure, to do what was not clear, but any how to solve the problem.

Soon after we got this message from our Ambassador, the American Ambassador here saw us in the evening of the 17th, bringing a similar message to us directly. Now, I may mention—it is rather an odd thing—even in this message which was conveyed by our Ambassador it was stated that the U.S. official who conveyed it expected little to happen on the part of Portugal. They live in a world apart and we don't expect much from them. So even he did not give much hope of results. This was rather a vague message. Although we appreciated it very much, still it was vague. On the evening of the 17th December it happened, after one approach by the U.S. Government to Portugal had been rejected by them, with—the latter insisting on Goa remaining a province of Portugal. As a matter of fact, the message came to us so late that almost physically it was not possible for us to reverse the processes that had been started. As you know, it was in the course of the 17th–18th night that our Army in three columns marched in. It was a few hours later. It was almost impossible for us physically. But apart from that if there had been any real thing to hold on to, we would have tried our best even so, although it would have had dangerous consequences. But upsetting all this, stopping all this with great difficulty, and nothing coming out of it except six months' wait was not a feasible proposition for us.

Immediately, the tempers and everything had come up to such a pitch that it would burst and we would have had to face violence all round. I need not elaborate on that.

Then, of course, action started with the result as you know. It was practically over in a day's time, because except for a little bit in Diu and a little bit elsewhere, there was practically no resistance. The casualties would have been practically nil. In Goa mainland the only casualty was one wounded on our side. It was in the island that the Portuguese shot down our people after showing a flag of truce. And something happened in Diu. Even so, I think the casualties were altogether ten. On the Portuguese side too, the casualties were very light.

I have tried to show this to you to indicate how we struggled all the time to find some way of escape, of preventing this happening, although we had no doubt in our mind—I want to make it quite clear—that on the ground of non-violence or peaceful methods we were justified in doing it. That had been our attitude all along. We did not want to do it all the same because of certain consequences elsewhere, outside India and Portugal, and that was an important matter for us. We stuck to it. We tried hard, but step by step, event after event came which pushed us in that direction and made no return possible, except at a cost which was going to be far greater than any cost that we were likely to be called upon to pay if we took action.

Now, I have told you I do not see how non-violence as such in the present day world can be the policy of any nation. Peaceful methods, yes. There is a difference between the two, because non-violence means no army at all. Obviously we cannot have that. I would like that day to come when we can do it, but that day has not come yet. But peaceful methods, yes. But if peaceful methods lead to worse consequences, it is difficult.

It is an odd thing that some of the closest followers of Gandhi have congratulated me on this, and resented the fact that Gandhi's name has been drawn into this by some of our critics. They have said—I am not trying to use their names—that it is entirely in keeping with Gandhi's thinking on such occasions. I would not take the responsibility for saying what Gandhi might have said or might not have said. It is not right for us to exploit his name. But I say it is odd that this question of non-violence has been raised so much by people who have not the remotest connection with non-violence or the non-violent approach.

I would like to say that so far as we are concerned, we adhere firmly and fully to our policies as we have previously declared them, the policy of trying to encourage the forces of peace for the settlement of problems peacefully and of non-alignment.

III. THE MAJOR INTRUSIONS

A. THE CONGO

1. Statement by the Minister of the Interior in Katanga, M. Munongo, 13 February 1961[1]

I have called you here to announce the death of Lumumba and of his accomplices Okito and Mpolo.

Yesterday evening a Katangan from the Kolwezi region—I shall not be more explicit—came to my private residence to inform me that Lumumba, Okito and Mpolo had been massacred yesterday morning by the inhabitants of a small village situated quite a distance from the place where the vehicle had been discovered, so that we are still wondering how the three fugitives could have got there.

On receiving this news I at once informed President Tshombé and the principal authorities of the country.

We flew to the spot this morning, the party consisting of a number of persons capable of identifying the three bodies, the Minister Kibwe, the Minister Kitenge and myself. We were accompanied by a doctor who was to make out a death certificate if the bodies did in fact prove to be those of Lumumba, Okito and Mpolo. They were identified beyond any possibility of doubt and their death was certified. The bodies were immediately buried in a place which we shall not reveal, if only to prevent any pilgrimages being made to it.

Nor shall we disclose the name of the village whose inhabitants put an end to the sorry exploits of Lumumba and his accomplices, for we do not want these Katangans, the name of whose tribe will not even be revealed, to be the object of possible reprisals on the part of Lumumba supporters.

Nor do we wish to be exposed to pressure to make us bring to trial for murder these Katangans who have perhaps acted somewhat precipitately, which is excusable in view of the fact that they believed the fugitives to be armed, but whom we cannot honestly blame for having rid Katanga, the Congo, Africa and the world of a problem which some persons had unduly magnified and which threatened to be a source of trouble to mankind.

This village will receive the 40,000 francs reward promised by the Council of Ministers. I shall tell you nothing more about the circumstances of the fugitives' death. I should be lying if I said that Lumumba's death grieves me. You know how I feel about him: he is an ordinary criminal who is responsible for thousands of deaths in Katanga and tens of thousands in Kasai, not to mention the persecutions and exterminations in Oriental province and Kivu. Mr. Hammarskjöld himself had said that the action against the Baluba of Kasai was nothing less than genocide. It is because of that that I am sure what the outcome of Lumumba's trial would have been: he would have been sentenced to death. Neverthe-

---

[1] S.C.O.R., Sixteenth Year, Supplement for January, February and March 1961, pp. 95–97. S/4688/Add. 1.

less, I should have preferred Lumumba and his accomplices to have been brought to trial. They have only themselves to blame: all they had to do was not to escape in such a strongly pro-Government region at a time when their own friends in the United Nations had whipped up the Katangan peoples to fever-pitch. I am of course aware that the United Nations will say that the whole thing was a plot and that we murdered them ourselves. Such an accusation is inevitable. If Lumumba had died in Katanga of sickness, old age or some other natural cause, we should still have been charged with murder, solely because the death occurred in Katanga. I am going to speak frankly and bluntly, as I usually do. We shall be accused of having murdered them. My reply is: prove it. To demonstrate our good faith, we have placed no obstacles in the way of the journalists' mission.

I also expect the friends of the communist Lumumba to raise the question of the death of the three fugitives in the United Nations Security Council. Even if we had executed them—which is categorically denied and in no way proved—I refuse in advance to recognize any right on the part of the United Nations to take a position on this question.

I shall here recall the cases of Sacco and Vanzetti, Julius and Ethel Rosenberg, and even Caryl Chessman in the United States.[1] I have no wish to compare them to Lumumba and his accomplices, nor to pass judgement on their guilt or innocence. I wish merely to recall that in these famous trials public opinion throughout the world and the highest religious authorities interceded tirelessly for the condemned persons. But in vain. The United States ignored them, considering the matter to be within its exclusive jurisdiction.

There are some who would deny us this right solely because we are black and belong to a young nation. The young nations of Africa, among others, would not understand such a flagrant disregard of the sovereignty of another African nation.

I shall quote other examples, more striking still.

Has the United Nations ever inquired into the fate of the opposition leaders who are periodically executed in one South American country or another? Was it distressed at the death of King Faisal of Iraq?[2] What has it done to protect the tens of thousands of Baluba exterminated by Lumumba's followers in Kasai?[3] Has it opened an inquiry into the poisoning of the Camerounian leader Moumié in Switzerland?[4] Did the defunct League of Nations and the United Nations concern themselves with the fate of the millions of Russians exterminated in the concentration camps of the USSR? What has the United Nations done to protect the life of the brave General Maleter or that of Imre Nagy, the standard-bearer of the Hungarian patriots?[5] Did not the Allies, who established the United Nations, calmly abandon their companion in arms, General Mihailović, executed by his rival Tito?[6]

This enumeration could be continued indefinitely. What I have said is enough

[1] Executed in 1927, 1953, and 1960 respectively.
[2] In the revolution of 14 July 1958; *Survey*, 1956–8, p. 374.
[3] In August 1960, *Survey*, 1959–60, p. 421.
[4] In November 1960.
[5] Executed in 1958; see *Survey*, 1956–8, pp. 531–2.
[6] In 1947.

to strike shame into the United Nations, which prudently lies low whenever a Power is involved and seeks to exercise its alleged authority only when dealing with a weaker country.

Let the United Nations keep before its eyes the image of Mihailović, of Maleter, of Imre Nagy and of so many others whenever it wishes to raise a hypocritically virtuous clamour about individuals who, unlike the majority of those I mentioned just now, are not even worth the trouble.

2. Security Council resolution, sponsored by Ceylon, Liberia, and the United Arab Republic, adopted 21 February 1961[1]

A

The Security Council,

Having considered the situation in the Congo,

Having learnt with deep regret the announcement of the killing of the Congolese leaders, Mr. Patrice Lumumba, Mr. Maurice Mpolo and Mr. Joseph Okito,

Deeply concerned at the grave repercussions of these crimes and the danger of wide-spread civil war and bloodshed in the Congo and the threat to international peace and security,

Noting the report of the Secretary-General's Special Representative (S/4691) dated 12 February 1961 bringing to light the development of a serious civil war situation and preparations therefore,

1. *Urges* that the United Nations take immediately all appropriate measures to prevent the occurrence of civil war in the Congo, including arrangements for cease-fires, the halting of all military operations, the prevention of clashes, and the use of force, if necessary, in the last resort;[2]

2. *Urges* that measures be taken for the immediate withdrawal and evacuation from the Congo of all Belgian and other foreign military and paramilitary personnel and political advisers not under the United Nations Command, and mercenaries;

3. *Calls* upon all States to take immediate and energetic measures to prevent the departure of such personnel for the Congo from their territories, and for the denial of transit and other facilities to them;

4. *Decides* that an immediate and impartial investigation be held in order to ascertain the circumstances of the death of Mr. Lumumba and his colleagues and that the perpetrators of these crimes be punished;[3]

---

[1] S.C.O.R., Sixteenth Year, Supplement for January, February, and March 1961, pp. 147–8. Resolution S/4741. A Soviet draft resolution of 14 February, calling, among other things, for non-military sanctions against Belgium, the arrest of M. Tshombé and General Mobutu of the Congolese National Army, the termination of the United Nations operation within a month and the removal of Mr. Hammarskjöld as the 'accomplice and organizer' of Lumumba's murder, was defeated by 8 votes to 1. Text in *Soviet News*, 16 February 1961.

[2] The interpretation placed on this paragraph by the British delegation was highly important, especially in the light of the events of August–September 1961. In the words of the British Permanent Representative, Sir Patrick Dean, force should not be used 'until agreement has been sought by negotiation, conciliation and other peaceful measures'. Furthermore, force should only be used 'to prevent a clash, between hostile Congolese troops. There can be no question of empowering the United Nations to use its forces to impose a political settlement'.

[3] On 15 April, the Assembly set up a Commission of Investigation into the deaths of the three men, under Resolution 1601 (XV). The Commission's report was not published until

5. *Reaffirms* the Security Council resolutions of 14 July, 22 July and 9 August 1960 and the General Assembly resolution 1474 (ES-IV) of 20 September 1960 and reminds all States of their obligation under these resolutions.[1]

B

The Security Council,

Gravely concerned at the continuing deterioration in the Congo, and the prevalence of conditions which seriously imperil peace and order, and the unity and territorial integrity of the Congo, and threaten international peace and security,

Noting with deep regret and concern the systematic violations of human rights and fundamental freedoms and the general absence of rule of law in the Congo,

Recognizing the imperative necessity of the restoration of parliamentary institutions in the Congo in accordance with the fundamental law of the country, so that the will of the people should be reflected through the freely elected Parliament,

Convinced that the solution of the problem of the Congo lies in the hands of the Congolese people themselves without any interference from outside and that there can be no solution without conciliation,

Convinced further that the imposition of any solution, including the formation of any government not based on genuine conciliation would, far from settling any issues, greatly enhance the dangers of conflict within the Congo and threat to international peace and security,

1. *Urges* the convening of the Parliament and the taking of necessary protective measures in that connexion;

2. *Urges* that Congolese armed units and personnel should be re-organized and brought under discipline and control, and arrangements be made on impartial and equitable bases to that end and with a view to the elimination of any possibility of interference by such units and personnel in the political life of the Congo;

3. *Calls* upon all States to extend their full co-operation and assistance and take such measures as may be necessary on their part, for the implementation of this resolution.

3. Statement by the Indian Prime Minister, Mr. Nehru, regarding the dispatch of Indian troops, 6 March 1961[2]

About a month ago, the Secretary-General of the United Nations asked us to send Indian armed forces to the Congo.[3] We informed him in reply that we had

---

11 November, as U.N. document A/4964. Its conclusions were that the weight of evidence largely contradicted M. Munongo's version (above, p. 734), that the three were most probably killed on arrival in Elizabethville on 17 January and that President Kasavubu and the Katangan Government were jointly responsible for the murders.

[1] *Documents*, 1960, pp. 299–300.
[2] Lok Sabha Debates, second series, vol. LI, no. 15, 6 March 1961, cols. 3234–5.
[3] Following the decision of Indonesia, Morocco, and the United Arab Republic to withdraw their contingents from the United Nations force. For Mr. Hammarskjöld's message regarding this issue, see S.C.O.R., Sixteenth Year, Supplement for January, February, and March 1961, pp. 81–82.

not approved of the way in which the United Nations had been functioning in the Congo. We had no desire, therefore, to send our armed forces to the Congo unless the policy of the United Nations was changed and brought more in line with our views on that subject. With the passage of the recent resolution of the Security Council, which was sponsored by the United Arab Republic, Ceylon and Nigeria,[1] the position has changed to some extent and it appears to us that a more correct and more effective policy would now be pursued. This resolution was drafted in consultation with many Afro-Asian powers and we were also consulted. A certain responsibility, therefore, was cast upon us.

The situation in the Congo has been a changing and confusing one and we were reluctant, as we always are, to send our armed forces outside India. We gave careful thought to these matters and communicated our views about the policy to be pursued in the Congo to the United Nations Secretary-General. When his reply was received it was considered generally satisfactory. After giving very careful thought to all aspects of the question, we decided to place an army brigade at the disposal of the United Nations for service in the Congo. In doing so, however, we informed the Secretary-General that we did not want our force to come into conflict with the forces of any member country of the United Nations, apart from Congolese and Belgian and other mercenaries engaged in the Congo and further that the brigade should function as a unit by itself and not to be attached to other units. We laid stress on the very early withdrawal of the Belgians who are serving in the Congo as this appeared to be the crux of the problem there. We made it clear also that our troops must not be used in any manner against popular movements in the Congo. The transport arrangements will have to be made by the United Nations.

4. Resolution No. 5 of the Tananarive conference, regarding 'relations with the United Nations', 12 March 1961[2]

Après avoir examiné le problème des relations avec l'Organisation des Nations Unies:

Considérant que des dispositions communes ont été prises en vue du maintien de l'ordre dans les limites de la confédération;

Considérant que les autorités présentes s'engagent à mettre tout en œuvre pour respecter les Etats voisins et s'abstenir de toute intervention armée susceptible de provoquer une guerre civile;

Les autorités de droit et de fait de l'ex-Congo belge, réunies à Tananarive le 12 mars 1961:

Considérant comme inapplicables et inacceptables, dans toute leur rigueur les résolutions du 21 février 1961 du Conseil de Sécuritié qui violent les principes de la Charte et portent atteinte à la souveraineté de la confédération et à la volonté exprimée par la conférence de Tananarive qui consacre l'intégrité du territoire;

---

[1] For the text of which see above, pp. 736–7. The third sponsor was Liberia, not Nigeria as stated.

[2] *Congo 1961*, pp. 39–40. The Tananarive conference, held in the Madagascan capital under the auspices of the Brazzaville group of French-speaking African States, was widely regarded as a triumph for Tshombe and Katanga, and a sharp rebuff for the United Nations. Its influence, however, was short-lived.

— réitèrent avec force les termes des diverses déclarations faites par le président de la confédération et les autres autorités de l'ex-Congo belge rejetant ces résolutions du Conseil de Sécurité;

— réaffirment toutefois la volonté de la confédération de collaborer avec l' O.N.U. à la condition que soient respectées les prérogatives de la souveraineté.

Les signataires:

J. KASA-VUBU,
président de la République du Congo.

M. TSHOMBE,
président de l'Etat du Katanga.

A. KALONJI,
président de l'Etat autonome du Sud-Kasaï.

J. ILEO,
premier ministre de la République du Congo.

B. MUKENGE,
président de l'Etat du Nord-Kasaï.

C. KAMITATU,
président de l'Etat de Léopoldville.

J. BOLIKANGO,
vice-premier ministre,
délégué de l'Equateur.

V. MOANDA,
président de l'Etat du Kongo Central.

L. S. BONDEKWE,
président de l'Etat du Congo Oriental.

A. KABANGI,
président de l'Etat du Lomami.

A. OMARI,
président de l'Etat du Maniéma.

E. NDJOKU,
ministre de la Justice
et de la Fonction Publique de l'Etat
de l'Equateur — délégué Mongo.

J. KULUMBA,
ministre de l'Intérieur de l'Etat
de Léopoldville et délégué du Kwango.

5. General Assembly resolution, sponsored by twenty-one powers, adopted 15 April 1961[1]

The General Assembly,

Recalling its resolution 1474 (ES-IV) of 20 September 1960 and the Security Council resolutions of 14 July (S/4387), 22 July (S/4405) and 9 August 1960[2] (S/4426) and, more particularly, that of 21 February 1961 (S/4741)[3] urging the immediate withdrawal and evacuation of all Belgian and other foreign military and paramilitary personnel and political advisers not under the United Nations Command, and mercenaries,

Deploring that despite all these requests the Government of Belgium has not yet complied with the resolutions and that such non-compliance has mainly contributed to the further deterioration of the situation in the Congo,

Convinced that the central factor in the present grave situation in the Congo is the continued presence of Belgian and other foreign military and paramilitary

[1] G.A.O.R., Fifteenth Session, Annexes, Agenda item 85, p. 112. Resolution 1599 (XV), sponsored by Burma, Cambodia, Ceylon, Ethiopia, Ghana, Guinea, India, Indonesia, Iraq, Liberia, Libya, Malaya, Mali, Morocco, Nepal, Saudi Arabia, Sudan, Togo, United Arab Republic, Yemen, Yugoslavia.

[2] *Documents*, 1960, pp. 299–300, 277, 284–6.

[3] Above, p. 736.

personnel and political advisers, and mercenaries, in total disregard of repeated resolutions of the United Nations,

1. *Calls upon* the Government of Belgium to accept its responsibilities as a Member of the United Nations and to comply fully and promptly with the will of the Security Council and of the General Assembly;

2. *Decides* that all Belgian and other foreign military and paramilitary personnel and political advisers not under the United Nations Command, and mercenaries, shall be completely withdrawn and evacuated;

3. *Calls upon* all States to exert their influence and extend their co-operation to effect the implementation of the present resolution.

6. General Assembly resolution, sponsored by seventeen powers, adopted 15 April 1961[1]

The General Assembly,

Having considered the situation in the Republic of the Congo,

Gravely concerned at the danger of civil war and foreign intervention and at the threat to international peace and security,

Taking note of the report of the Conciliation Commission (A/4711 and Corr. 1 and Add. 1 and 2) appointed in pursuance of paragraph 3 of its resolution 1474 (ES-IV) of 20 September 1960,[2]

Mindful of the desire of the Congolese people for a solution of the crisis in the Congo through national reconciliation and return to constitutionality without delay,

Noting with concern the many difficulties that have arisen in the way of effective functioning of the United Nations operation in the Congo,

1. *Reaffirms* its resolution 1474 (ES-IV) and the Security Council resolutions on the situation in the Congo, more particularly the Council resolution of 21 February 1961 (S/4741);[3]

2. *Calls upon* the Congolese authorities concerned to desist from attempting a military solution to their problems and to resolve them by peaceful means;

3. *Considers it essential* that necessary and effective measures be taken by the Secretary-General immediately to prevent the introduction of arms, military equipment and supplies into the Congo, except in conformity with the resolutions of the United Nations;

4. *Urges* the immediate release of all members of Parliament and members of provincial assemblies and all other political leaders now under detention;

5. *Urges* the convening of Parliament without delay, with safe conduct and security extended to the members of Parliament by the United Nations, so that Parliament may take the necessary decisions concerning the formation of a national government and on the future constitutional structure of the Republic of the Congo in accordance with the constitutional processes laid down in the *Loi fondamentale*;

[1] G.A.O.R., Fifteenth Session, Annexes, Agenda item 85, p. 112. Resolution 1600 (XV), sponsored by Burma, Chad, Ethiopia, Iran, Japan, Liberia, Libya, Malaya, Nigeria, Pakistan, Philippines, Senegal, Somalia, Sudan, Tunisia, Turkey, and Upper Volta. A mildly worded Soviet draft, urging the recall of the Congolese Parliament, was defeated; text in ibid., p. 110.
[2] *Documents*, 1960, p. 300.   [3] Above, p. 736.

6. *Decides* to appoint a Commission of Conciliation of seven members to be designated by the President of the General Assembly to assist the Congolese leaders to achieve reconciliation and to end the political crisis;

7. *Urges* the Congolese authorities to co-operate fully in the implementation of the resolutions of the Security Council and of the General Assembly and to accord all facilities essential to the performance by the United Nations of functions envisaged in those resolutions.

7. Agreement on general principles between 'the President of the Republic of the Congo (Leopoldville) and the Secretary-General of the United Nations', 17 April 1961[1]

As a Member of the United Nations, the Republic of Congo (Leopoldville), whose sovereignty should not be in doubt, is under an obligation to respect the Charter of the Organization and to carry out the resolution of the Security Council.

The Republic of the Congo accepts the resolution S/4741 of 21 February 1961, taking into account:

(1) That the United Nations reaffirms its respect for the sovereignty of the Republic of the Congo in the implementation of the resolution;

(2) That the aim of the resolution of 21 February, part A, paragraph 2, and part B, paragraph 2, is to eliminate all deleterious foreign influence. To this effect the President of the Republic of the Congo will receive all possible assistance of the United Nations;

(3) That the United Nations is to assist the President of the Republic so that all foreign personnel, whether civilian, military or paramilitary and all mercenaries and political advisers who have not been recruited or recalled under the authority of the President, be repatriated from the Congo within the shortest possible period of time. To implement the above and taking into account the recognition of the sovereign rights of the Republic and the constitutional powers which he holds, the President of the Republic will re-examine the appointments of foreign civilian, military and paramilitary personnel made under his authority and will take the necessary decisions compatible with the interests of the Republic of the Congo;

(4) That the United Nations is to give to the President of the Republic all possible assistance in:

(*a*) Recruiting the technicians needed by the Republic of the Congo, without however having a monopoly of such recruitments;

(*b*) Training the administrative and technical cadres by granting fellowships and establishing specialized institutes.

The Republic of the Congo recognizes the need to reorganize the national army, it being understood that this reorganization is to be carried out under the authority of the President of the Republic, with United Nations assistance and on the basis of the proposals made by the Chief of State in his letter of 5 March 1961 to the Secretary-General of the United Nations.[2]

[1] S.C.O.R., Sixteenth Year, Supplement for April, May, and June 1961, pp. 46–47. S/4807 Annex 1.

[2] ibid., Supplement for January, February, and March 1961, pp. 199/201. S/4752/Add. 3.

The detailed application of the basic agreement outlined above shall be subject, in each case, to a careful study on the part of the Government of the Republic of the Congo and the United Nations.

Leopoldville, 17 April 1961

[*For the United Nations*]   [*For the Republic of the Congo* (*Leopoldville*)]
(*Signed*) F. C. NWOKEDI   (*Signed*) J. KASA-VUBU
            R. GARDINER   J. BOMBOKO

8. General Assembly resolution regarding the cost estimates and financing of the Congo operations, adopted 21 April 1961[1]

The General Assembly,

Recalling the Security Council resolutions of 14 July, 22 July and 9 August 1960[2] and 21 February 1961,[3] and General Assembly resolutions 1474 (ES-IV) of 20 September 1960[4] and 1599 (XV), 1600 (XV) and 1601 (XV) of 15 April 1961,[5]

Having considered the report of the Secretary-General on the estimated cost of the United Nations operations in the Congo from 1 January to 31 December 1961 (A/4703) and the report of the Advisory Committee on Administrative and Budgetary Questions thereon (A/4713),[6]

Bearing in mind that the extraordinary expenses for the United Nations operations in the Congo are essentially different in nature from the expenses of the Organization under the regular budget and that therefore a procedure different from that applied in the case of the regular budget is required for meeting these extraordinary expenses,

Bearing in mind that the permanent members of the Security Council have a special responsibility for the maintenance of international peace and security and therefore for contributing to the financing of peace and security operations,

Noting with appreciation the intention declared by certain Member States to make substantial voluntary contributions,

1. *Decides* to open an *ad hoc* account for the expenses of the United Nations operations in the Congo for 1961;

2. *Approves* the recommendations of the Advisory Committee on Administrative and Budgetary Questions contained in paragraphs 2, 29 and 30 of its report, subject to paragraph 3 below;

3. *Decides* to appropriate an amount of $100 million for the operations of the United Nations in the Congo from 1 January to 31 October 1961;

4. *Decides further* to apportion as expenses of the Organization the amount of $100 million among the Member States in accordance with the scale of assessment for the regular budget subject to the provisions of paragraph 8 below,

[1] G.A.O.R., Fifteenth Session, Annexes, Agenda items 49/50, pp. 48–49. Resolution 1619 (XV).
[2] *Documents*, 1960, pp. 277, 284–6.
[3] Above, p. 736.
[4] *Documents*, 1960, pp. 299–300.
[5] Above, pp. 739–41.
[6] G.A.O.R., Fifteenth Session, Annexes, Agenda items 49/50, pp. 15–21 and 21–26.

pending the establishment of a different scale of assessment to defray the extra-ordinary expenses of the Organization resulting from these operations;

5. *Urges* the permanent members of the Security Council to make sizable additional contributions;

6. *Appeals* to all other Member States who are in a position to assist to make voluntary contributions;

7. *Calls upon* the Government of Belgium, a State directly concerned with the situation in the Republic of the Congo (Leopoldville), to make a substantial contribution;

8. *Decides* to reduce:

(*a*) By 80 per cent the assessment of Member States whose contributions to the regular budget range from 0.04 per cent to 0.25 per cent inclusive;

(*b*) By 80 per cent the assessment of Member States receiving assistance during 1960 under the Expanded Programme of Technical Assistance, whose contributions to the regular budget range from 0.26 per cent to 1.25 per cent inclusive;

(*c*) By 50 per cent the assessment of Member States receiving assistance during 1960 under the Expanded Programme of Technical Assistance, whose contributions to the regular budget are 1.26 per cent and above;

9. *Decides* to apply the additional contributions of Member States under paragraphs 5, 6 and 7 above to offset the deficit resulting from the implementation of the provisions of paragraph 8.

9. Agreement between the Leopoldville authorities and the Stanleyville authorities, 19 June 1961[1]

1. The typed records of the meetings of 13 to 16 and 19 June 1961 shall be signed by the two parties, who will thereby indicate their approval, and shall serve as basic documents for the arrangements listed hereinafter;

2. After the inspection of the premises by United Nations military authorities, the two parties agree that Parliament shall meet at the University of Lovanium,[2] which place fulfils the conditions required to ensure the absolute safety of the members of Parliament;

3. Armée nationale congolaise forces and police at Leopoldville and in adjoining zones shall not circulate in the city and the said adjoining zones carrying arms, which must be deposited beforehand in armouries under guard of the respective forces. It shall be the responsibility of ONUC to exercise supervision to ensure that no soldier or policeman carries arms in the city or in the adjoining zones, throughout the entire period of the parliamentary session;

4. During the session all the members of Parliament shall be housed in Lovanium itself and shall have no contacts with the outside world.

5. The administrative personnel servicing the assemblies, who will be given special permits issued by the officers of the two Chambers, shall be compelled to stay at Lovanium for the duration of the parliamentary session, under the conditions referred to in the preceding paragraph;

[1] S.C.O.R., Sixteenth Year, Supplement for July, August, and September 1961, pp. 71–72.
[2] A conference of Congolese leaders at Coquilhatville in May had already agreed to reopen the Parliament; text of resolution in *Congo 1961*, p. 392.

6. It shall be the duty of the United Nations to ensure that the members of Parliament, the administrative personnel of the assemblies and the United Nations civilian personnel placed at the disposal of Parliament shall not have with them any weapons, any money or any other negotiable instruments of any kind, either when entering Lovanium or upon their departure;

7. All telephone lines to Lovanium shall be cut off;

8. The free passage of members of Parliament through the Congo shall be ensured by ONUC at the request in writing of the members concerned;

9. United Nations civilian personnel placed at the disposal of members of Parliament during the session shall be required to reside at the seat of Parliament for periods of a fortnight at a time. During each period such personnel shall have no contact with the outside world and shall also be subject to the conditions stipulated in paragraphs 6 and 7 above;

10. The two delegations propose 25 June 1961 as the latest possible date for the opening of Parliament and the United Nations shall take all the necessary steps to ensure that Parliament may open on the date agreed upon by the two delegations;[1]

11. The two delegations propose to Parliament that the vote of confidence in the Government should be taken by secret ballot;

12. The President of the Republic shall convene Parliament on the date appointed by the two delegations;

13. In ordering that the meeting of Parliament may be the reflection of national opinion, the United Nations shall be requested to invite all the other political factions in the Congo to subscribe to this agreement;

14. The United Nations shall also be requested to continue to accord its good offices to the parties concerned in seeking a real and satisfactory solution to the Congolese crisis and to that end it shall be authorized to arrange all the necessary contacts between the Congolese political leaders.

10. Protocol of agreement signed by M. Tshombe, President of the province of Katanga, and the representatives of the Central Government, 24 June 1961[2]

ARTICLE 1

Parliament shall convene at Leopoldville as soon as possible. The Central Government, assisted by the United Nations, shall ensure the safety of the members of Parliament.

ARTICLE 2

A new Government shall be constituted[3] and shall come before the Chambers for a vote of confidence. This new Government shall remain in power until the adoption of the new Constitution. The new Constitution shall be adopted within a period not exceeding three months.

[1] The Chambers did not, in fact, assemble until 22 July, when the Senate met to elect its officers; the Lower House met the following day.

[2] S.C.O.R., Sixteenth Year, Supplement for July, August, and September 1961, pp. 74–75. S/4841/Add. 2. This agreement was soon afterwards repudiated by Katanga.

[3] A Government under the premiership of M. Cyrille Adoula replaced that of M. Joseph Ileo on 2 August.

ARTICLE 3

All custom barriers between Katanga and the rest of the Congo shall be abolished. Goods from Katanga shall be carried along the national route. The Central Government shall ensure the protection of the goods.

ARTICLE 4

All entry and exit dues levied on goods shall be payable in their entirety to the national exchequer. All dues levied at Matadi shall be payable to the Central Government at Leopoldville, and those levied in Katanga shall be payable to the Katanga treasury.

ARTICLE 5

A Commission of national experts, assisted if necessary by foreign experts, shall be established for the purpose of settling the disputes of parastatal companies and of those enjoying special status, such as CSK, CNKI, INEAC, OTRACO.[1]

ARTICLE 6

Currency—During the transitional period, a single currency shall be legal tender, but shall bear two monetary symbols. The two monetary symbols shall be gradually replaced by a single monetary symbol. During this period, Katanga shall be represented on the Currency Council.

ARTICLE 7

Social, educational and administrative problems—In the educational sphere, curricula at secondary, higher and university levels shall be unified, in order that academic grades, established and organized by the central power, may be conferred. In the administrative sphere, the respective States shall be represented in the Commission to be established under the agreement of 17 April 1961 [S/4807, annex I][2] The States shall propose that the commission approve technicians selected by them. In reaching its decisions on such proposals, the Commission shall be guided solely by the interests of the States. Where a proposal is rejected, the State concerned shall be requested to submit further proposals.

ARTICLE 8

Diplomatic representation—Representation abroad is within the exclusive competence of the Head of State. During the transitional period, practical measures shall be taken to ensure that there shall henceforth be only a single diplomatic representation abroad.

ARTICLE 9

Muluba problem—The delegation of Katanga undertakes to release all political prisoners immediately and unconditionally. A Commission of Inquiry assisted by representatives of both parties shall be established by the Central Government. The President of the Government of Katanga agrees to meet Mr. Sendwe outside Leopoldville and in the presence of the Commission of Inquiry.

[1] Comité Spécial du Katanga, Comité National de Kivu, Institut National pour l'Étude Agronomique du Congo, Office d'Exploitation des Transports Coloniaux.
[2] See above, p. 741.

ARTICLE 10

Military problems—With regard to military problems, the two delegations shall refer to the agreement concluded between the headquarters of the Armée nationale congolaise and the authorities of Katanga. This agreement shall be implemented immediately.

ARTICLE 11

The two parties undertake on their honour to ensure the complete implementation of these agreements.

The agreement between Leopoldville and Katanga has been signed on behalf of Leopoldville by: Bolikango, Bomboko, Lihau, Nkayi, Déricoyard, Kabangui, Massa, Kimvayi, Kisolokela, Mahamba, and on behalf of Katanga by: Tshombe and Kimba.

11. The Congolese Prime Minister, Mr. Adoula,[1] to the United Nations chargé de mission in the Congo, Dr. Linner, transmitting the text of Ordnance No. 70 (1961), 'relating to the expulsion of non-Congolese officers and mercenaries serving in the Katanga force', 24 August 1961[2]

I have the honour to refer to my letter of 22 August 1961 by which my Government requested the assistance of the United Nations in putting an end to the aggressive activities of the Katanga gendarmerie and in securing the evacuation of the foreign officers and mercenaries serving in the armed forces of Katanga.

I am taking the liberty of bringing to your attention the text of ordinance No. 70-1961 issued today by the Head of the State on the advice of my Government and ordering the immediate expulsion from the territory of the Republic of the Congo of all non-Congolese officers and mercenaries serving in the Katanga forces who have not entered into a contractual engagement with the Central Government of the Republic of the Congo.

The Government of the Republic of the Congo requests the assistance of the United Nations in implementing this ordinance and in securing, in conformity with part A, paragraph 2, of the resolution adopted by the Security Council on 21 February 1961 and with due respect for considerations of security, the evacuation of the individuals affected by this expulsion order.

(*Signed*) CYRILLE ADOULA
Prime Minister
of the Congo (*Leopoldville*)

Ordinance No. 70 of 24 August 1961 relating to the expulsion of non-Congolese officers and mercenaries serving in the Katanga force
The President of the Republic,
Considering the *Loi fondamentale* of 19 May 1960, in particular its articles 2, 27 and 219;[2]

---

[1] Mr. Adoula's Government was formed on 2 August.
[2] S.C.O.R., Sixteenth Year, Supplement for July, August, and September 1961, pp. 104–5. S/4940 Annex I. On 28 August, United Nations troops in Katanga arrested a large number of mercenaries. While their action was accepted by M. Tshombe, he was careful to reassert Katanga's 'right to self-determination' in his statement of that day; text in ibid., pp. 105–6. See also below, p. 751. See *Congo 1960*, pp. 108, 110, 129–30.

Considering the decree of 4 June 1956 concerning expulsion, local banishment and prescribed residence;

Considering part A, paragraph 2, of the resolution adopted by the Security Council of the United Nations on 21 February 1961 requesting that measures should be taken for the withdrawal and immediate evacuation from the Congo of all military and paramilitary personnel of Belgian and other nationalities not forming part of the United Nations Command as well as of the mercenaries;

Considering the agreement of principle dated 17 April 1961[1] concerning the implementation of that resolution and concerning the assistance to be rendered by the United Nations in that regard;

Considering that it is necessary and urgent to put an end to the aggressive actions of the Katanga Gendarmerie, which are a source of constant suffering to the people and impede the economic rehabilitation of the country;

Considering that these aggressive actions are exclusively attributable to the non-Congolese officers and mercenaries who are commanding and serving in units of the Katanga Forces;

On the proposal of the Ministers of the Interior, of Foreign Affairs and of National Defence;

Orders:

Article 1. All non-Congolese officers and mercenaries serving in the Katanga Forces who have not entered into a contractual engagement with the Central Government of the Republic of the Congo shall be considered as undesirable aliens who by their presence and their conduct are jeopardizing tranquillity and public order in the country.

Article 2. All the non-Congolese officers and mercenaries serving in the Katanga Forces who have not entered into a contractual engagement with the Central Government of the Republic of the Congo are expelled from the territory of the Republic of the Congo and must leave Congolese territory forthwith.

Article 3. The Minister of the Interior and the Minister of National Defence shall be responsible for the fulfilment of this ordinance.

Leopoldville, 24 August 1961.

(*Signed*) JOSEPH KASA-VUBU
President of the Republic of the Congo
(*Leopoldville*)

CYRILLE ADOULA
Minister of National Defence

J. BOMBOKO
Minister for Foreign Affairs

CH. GBENYE
Minister of the Interior

12. Statement to the Federal Parliament by the Prime Minister of the Federation of Rhodesia and Nyasaland, Sir Roy Welensky, 30 August 1961[2]

All Hon. Members will share my grave concern at the turn which events have taken in the Katanga since early Monday morning.

[1] See above, p. 741.   [2] Press release issued by Rhodesia House, London.

D.I.A.—BB

It has not been easy to get accurate information out of Elisabethville since all communications have either been interrupted or taken over by the United Nations. The Government has however, been able to confirm some of the reports. There is no doubt that at dawn on Monday large numbers of United Nation troops in full battle kit and backed by armour took over the town of Elisabethville and other administrative centres in Katanga. Government offices were occupied, as were the Military Headquarters, the Post Office, the Radio Station and the Airport. Road blocks were set up and Elisabethville became in a very short time a military occupied town.

The justification for these extraordinary actions by an organisation set up to preserve peace and to support the maintenance of law and order, was that it had become necessary to arrest and deport large numbers of European officers of the gendarmerie and the so called political advisers. I will deal later with the legality of this action.

Yesterday the situation in Elisabethville appeared to be quiet. Last night and this morning, however, the Federal Government received reliable information that it had begun to worsen. Many of the rumours which are circulating about a possible uprising of the people can be discounted. But let no one be complacent. Large numbers of Katangese people have become uneasy at the high handed activities of the United Nations, normal administration has either broken down completely or is functioning extremely poorly, and the danger has now to be faced that a situation could well arise in Elisabethville which could only be contained by even more drastic measures.

The Federal Government cannot remain aloof to what is happening just across our border. What happens in the Katanga is of vital concern to us. We have all seen and admired the way in which President Tshombe and his Government have, during the past year, maintained law and order in the Katanga, upheld the economy of the area and provided a sound and stable administration. All this has been done in the face of anarchy and disorder in the remainder of the Congo.

The time for equivocation is past and we in the Federation can no longer stay silent. Considerations of our own security as well as considerations of principal now compel me to say frankly and openly what I think.

The success of President Tshombe has not suited a number of countries who are members of the United Nations, and we have watched with growing concern the buildup of United Nations Military Forces in the Katanga and the increasing intransigence of the United Nations authorities in that country. I will make no secret of the fact that I have been urging the British Government, as I urged the Commonwealth Governments at the Prime Ministers' Conference in March, to attempt to persuade the United Nations that neither justice nor stability would be served by trying to impose an external solution on the Katanga people. I have consistently argued that the Katanga and the Congo leaders must be allowed to make their own arrangements and that schemes cooked up in New York should not be forced upon an unwilling people.

I have received assurances that the British Government would not agree to any attempt by the United Nations to take over Katanga by force.[1]

[1] See also Sir R. Welensky, *Welensky's 4000 Days* (London, 1964), pp. 221–9.

Last Friday, however, I got an indication that force was to be employed by the United Nations to subjugate the Katanga Government and to compel it to abdicate its authority and to surrender the last vestiges of its dignity.

I immediately protested to the British Government. I pointed out that such action could bring lawlessness right up to our border.

I said that this was bad enough but that I would view the forcible subjugation of a free people with United Nations aid as the last extremity of policy of empty expediency.

I am quite unable to comprehend how what is happening in Berlin and what is apparently contemplated by the United Nations in the Katanga can possibly be reconciled. No doubt those who are willing to see the United Nations ride rough-shod over a properly elected Government will argue that the two situations are fundamentally different and that one is supported by every legal nicety while the other is not.

I do not accept this view. In terms of basic human rights the two situations are not dissimilar. In each a group of people have expressed the wish to live under a Government of their own choosing. If the West is to allow the Katanga Government to be overthrown by force of arms, then I warn it as solemnly as I can, that its moral position in West Berlin will be immeasurably weakened.

Let me reaffirm the position of the Federal Government. We believe that, left to themselves, the Congo and Katanga leaders can and will reach a satisfactory settlement of their problems. President Tshombe has made it clear that he is anxious to reach agreement and that he is prepared to discuss an economic and monetary union so long as the political and administrative stability achieved by his Government is not jeopardised. All this is to be encouraged.

But the Federal Government does not accept that the United Nations has been given, by the security council resolutions of 21st February or by any other devices, any authority to use force in the way in which it has been and is being used this day in Elisabethville.

The security council resolutions give the United Nations power to use force only to prevent civil war. The resolution is quite specific and I quote it 'the security council urges that United Nations take immediate and all appropriate measures to prevent the occurrence of civil war in the Congo, the halting of all military operations, the prevention of clashes and the use of force if necessary in the last resort.'

Another resolution made at the same time urges that measures be taken for the withdrawal and evacuation from the Congo of all Belgian and other foreign military personnel and political advisers. But it does not authorise the use of force and it was clearly understood that the withdrawal should be by negotiation, and, moreover, that it should be done in such a way as not to jeopardise the efficient operation of the administration, the police and the gendarmerie.

The United Nations have not therefore any possible legal justification for what they are doing—or trying to do. They have no shadow of right—or other than the right of the big stick—to occupy Government offices, to take control of communications, to set up road blocks or to use troops in order to effect the arrest of the gendarmerie officers and political advisers. They have no authority for wholesale arrests of Europeans. No powers to act in this arbitrary and high handed fashion were given by the security council resolutions of 21st February and it follows that no request by the Central Congo Government for the actions taken can give what has been done even the semblance of legality.

What is happening of course is quite clear. The United Nations had decided that they must produce something dramatic for the meeting of the general assembly in mid-September. They therefore planned the elimination of the Tshombe Government as an independent entity and intended by a show of force to soften it up. First, the European advisers and the Belgian officers were to be removed, and then, if riot and disorder did not intervene, there would be nothing organised to withstand the further demands which would be made upon the Government. Well, as I have pointed out, it seems as if the actions taken has only resulted in increasing the tensions and dangers.

Mr. Speaker, Sir, there is nothing wrong in any African country having, European civil service advisers and officers in its police and military forces. This is in fact quite common. In almost all the newly-independent African countries the ex-colonial powers have left behind large staffs of trained men willing and able to maintain the standards of administration and justice. But in the Katanga this has been denied. Not because the properly elected Government of the country does not want it but because it does not happen to suit the plans of those forces in Africa and outside it that have pledged themselves to drive the European out, expecting in the result chaos to profit for themselves.

The House will want to know what the Federal Government proposes to do. We will of course watch the situation closely to the best of our ability. Arrangements are in hand to deal with European and African refugees, and I am taking steps to ensure the safety of our borders. It is not in the public interest for me to disclose precisely what steps are being taken. I hope honourable members will accept my assurance that they will be adequate.

I hope of course that these precautions will prove to be unnecessary and that sane counsels will prevail in New York, Washington, London, Paris and Brussels. If not, then the Federation will do what is necessary and legally possible to give support to its friends.

13. Report by Dr. Linner to Mr. Hammarskjöld 'relating to the implementation of part A, operative paragraph 2, of Security Council resolution S/4741 of 21 February 1961', 14 September 1961[1]

1. Part A, paragraph 2, of the resolution S/4741 adopted by the Security Council on 21 February 1961

'*Urges* that measures be taken for the immediate withdrawal and evacuation from the Congo of all Belgian and other foreign military and paramilitary personnel and political advisers not under the United Nations Command, and mercenaries.'

By far the largest concentration of such personnel, about 500, was to be found in

[1] S.C.O.R., Sixteenth Year, Supplement for July, August, and September 1961, pp. 99–104. S/4940. For the version of Mr. O'Brien (the O.N.U.C. representative in Elisabethville), regarding the events of 13 September, see Chapter 15 of C. C. O'Brien, *To Katanga and Back* (London, 1962).

the Katangese armed forces. Efforts to implement the above provision, which had to be pursued by way of negotiations in view of the lack at this stage of legal authority for the United Nations to take other steps for implementation of the resolution within the Congo, remained for several months without appreciable results.

2. On 24 August 1961, the President of the Republic of the Congo (Leopoldville), upon the advice of the Government, enacted *ordonnance* No. 70, providing for the expulsion of all non-Congolese officers and mercenaries serving in the Katangese forces, not under a contract with the Central Government. The Prime Minister of the Republic of the Congo requested United Nations assistance in the execution of this *ordonnance* and in ensuring the evacuation of the personnel falling under the expulsion decree [*annex I*].[1] These actions gave the United Nations legal rights within the Congo corresponding to the terms of the aforementioned resolution.

3. On 26 August, Mr. Munongo, Minister of the Interior of the Katanga provincial government, announced that the United Nations was planning to disarm the Katangese armed forces and that 1,500 soldiers of the Armée nationale congolaise in United Nations aircraft were on their way to Elisabethville to occupy Katanga. This announcement and similar false rumours created an atmosphere of tension notwithstanding the fact that they were immediately denied by the United Nations. Therefore ONUC was compelled to take security precautions when, on the morning of 28 August, it proceeded to take measures for evacuating foreign military personnel and mercenaries. It placed a surveillance on Radio Katanga, on gendarmerie headquarters and on other key points and installations in the city of Elisabethville. During the few hours that this surveillance lasted, the radio continued to broadcast normally, with the sole exception that no statements of an inflammatory nature, likely to lead to an incitement to civil or tribal disturbances in violation of part A, paragraph 1, of the Security Council resolution of 21 February, were permitted. Moreover an appeal was made to the Katangese gendarmerie to co-operate and to the Katangese population to maintain calm and proceed with their normal occupations. No resistance was encountered from the Katangese forces or police in the execution of the evacuation measures, and life continued normally throughout Katanga.

4. Mr. Tshombe was informed by the United Nations representative of the objectives of the United Nations action. At noon of 28 August Mr. Tshombe stated in a broadcast [*see annex II*][1] that his government had approved of the evacuation of foreign military personnel and had terminated the services of all foreigners in the Katangese armed forces effective that day.

5. In the morning and again in the afternoon of 28 August, United Nations representatives met with the Elisabethville consular corps at their request to discuss repatriation procedures. The Belgian Consul, who presided over these meetings, stated that by arrangement with his colleagues he would undertake the responsibility for ensuring the surrender and repatriation and travel of all personnel required to be evacuated, irrespective of their nationality. He introduced two senior officers who had served in the Katanga gendarmerie and who were

[1] Annex I is printed above, p. 746. For Annex II, see above, p. 746, n. 2.

to assist the United Nations in arranging an orderly withdrawal of all foreign personnel who served in the Katangese armed forces. The United Nations agreed to this evacuation procedure on condition that the evacuation would not thereby be delayed and that the United Nations retained the exclusive authority to decide who should be evacuated and when. On this understanding the United Nations refrained from continuing to search for and apprehend foreign military personnel, and permitted about seventy Belgian officers to stay in the Belgian Consulate building in Elisabethville until transport for them became available.

6. Unfortunately, these arrangements were not scrupulously observed. Only the officers already stationed in the Belgian Consulate building and officers of the Belgian Army placed at the disposal of Katanga by the Belgian Government were dealt with under this procedure, and even in the case of these officers delays or administrative exemptions were proposed. The foreign officers and mercenaries, profiting from this relaxation of evacuation measures, re-infiltrated into the gendarmerie, and there were indications that they began distributing arms to certain political or ethnic groupings. The foreign elements also began exercising pressure on some Katangese Ministers to dissuade them from moving towards political reconciliation to the authority of the Central Government. Finally, the foreign military personnel, together with the so-called 'ultras' among the non-African residents, exercised an adverse influence on the Katangese government, inciting them to terroristic actions and violations of fundamental liberties.

7. Thus, the actions of the political police (Sûreté) which must be regarded as falling under part A, paragraph 2, of the resolution and which is an instrument of Mr. Munongo largely directed by foreign officers, combined with the inflammatory propaganda broadcast on Radio Katanga and the spreading of rumours, caused panic among the Baluba population, who began to throng into United Nations camps, asking for protection. The influx of Baluba refugees, who constitute the economically and educationally most advanced part of the African population of Elisabethville, began on 24 August following the arrest of their spokesman, Mr. Bintu, and a few other leaders. By 9 September the number of refugees had reached 35,000 and created not only a very serious problem for ONUC which had to protect, feed, shelter and care for them, but also a situation likely to lead to tribal and civil war.

8. Information obtained by the United Nations from various sources established that Mr. Munongo and his Sûreté officials were attempting to carry out attacks on ONUC personnel, military as well as civilian. These reports were to some extent confirmed by the occurrence of demonstrations against the United Nations in the first week of September, which resulted in considerable material loss to the United Nations and in injury to a number of United Nations personnel.

9. Of a much more dangerous character, however, was the menace to the security of the United Nations personnel and property constituted by the terroristic conspiracies and activities of some of the foreign officers in the Katangese armed forces who had thus escaped evacuation measures. Most prominent among them were a group of officers of French nationality, some of whom were unable to return to their own country because of their implication in the recent

revolt by French military elements in Algeria. Another group consisted of soldiers of fortune, while a third group were the so-called 'volunteers' recruited from among foreign settlers in the Congo. Information received to the effect that one such group planned to introduce plastic bombs into the building in which the United Nations offices in Elisabethville were located compelled the United Nations on 6 September to move its headquarters to one of the military camps. There was also evidence that these officers were organizing a guerilla group among the gendarmerie personnel, that they were maintaining their hold over certain units of the gendarmerie preventing them from co-operating with the United Nations, and that they organized the attack on the United Nations garage and the burning of United Nations vehicles.

10. The day of 9 September was set as the time-limit as of which all foreign military personnel had to report to a United Nations unit for evacuation. By that date, however, only 273 foreign officers and mercenaries had been repatriated and sixty-five were awaiting repatriation. At least 104 foreign personnel were known to have failed to report or to give any account of themselves [see annex III].[1] The United Nations representative thereupon called once more on the Consuls, asking them to ensure the immediate departure of their nationals, failing which the United Nations would have to resume action for implementing the 21 February resolution by all means at its disposal.

11. In the morning of 11 September the deputy United Nations representative in Elisabethville was arrested on orders given by a non-Congolese officer of the Sûreté. This was the culmination of a long series of wrongful acts by these officers, including the organization of attacks on United Nations personnel or installations, repeated threats, and incitements to violence. Moreover it was impossible to persuade the Baluba refugees to return from the United Nations camp to their homes as long as they were exposed to threats and arbitrary arrests by, or at the direction of, Sûreté officials. The United Nations therefore requested that all the non-Congolese officers of the Sûreté be evacuated within forty-eight hours.

12. At the instigation of the remaining foreign officers, as well as of the local extremists, heavily armed patrols and guard posts began to be maintained by the gendarmerie at all public buildings and other installations in Elisabethville. The police was reinforced by 300 members of Mr. Munongo's Bayake tribe. Arms were also being distributed to individuals and groups who were not properly trained and disciplined to handle them.

13. On 12 September the 'Foreign Minister of the Katanga Government', Mr. Kimba, announced that negotiations had been opened for reinforcing Katangese units with personnel and equipment from Rhodesia.

14. Also on 12 September, United Nations representatives met with Mr. Tshombe and members of his government in an attempt to obtain a lessening of the tension, a withdrawal or at least reduction of the military elements from the streets in Elisabethville, an end to the inflammatory propaganda, redress of refugee grievances which would permit their return to their homes, and assurance that the evacuation of all personnel falling under part A, paragraph 2, of the Security Council resolution of 21 February would proceed promptly. United Nations

[1] S.C.O.R., Sixteenth Year, Supplement for July, August, and September 1961, p. 106.

representatives also attempted to persuade the Katanga government to reconcile their political differences with the Central Government by constitutional means and gave assurances concerning Mr. Tshombe's safety if he wished to travel to Leopoldville for discussions. On all these points the answer of the Katangese government was a negative one; they refused emphatically to permit the evacuation of the foreign officers serving in the Katangese Sûreté.

15. In the early hours of 13 September, the United Nations Force therefore took security precautions similar to those applied on 28 August, and deemed necessary to prevent inflammatory broadcasts or other threats to the maintenance of law and order, while the United Nations resumed carrying out its task of apprehending and evacuating foreign military and para-military personnel. At this point an alert was set since arson was discovered at the ONUC garage. As the United Nations troops were proceeding towards the garage premises, fire was opened on them from the building where a number of foreign officers are known to be staying. United Nations troops were subsequently also resisted and fired at as they were deploying towards key points or while they were guarding installations in the city. United Nations troops returned fire.

16. While it is yet too early to reconstruct from the incomplete reports the whole story of the events of the day, a report transmitted at noon on 13 September by the commander of the United Nations forces in Katanga, Brigadier S. K. Rajah, states that the radio station and post office guarded by United Nations troops were attacked several times and that extensive sniping fire was directed against United Nations troops and the residence of the United Nations representative from houses occupied by non-African residents of the city. Non-Congolese officers and mercenaries were observed leading the attacks, directing fire and handling the weapons. On the other hand there is no evidence of any spontaneous or large-scale actions having been taken against the United Nations by the Congolese personnel of the gendarmerie.

17. Sporadic sniping and occasional bursts from heavier weapons were reported throughout the day and up to the time of writing this report, the Katanga Radio Station was reported substantially damaged by mortar fire directed at it when the United Nations sought to use it to appeal for calm and cessation of fire. Casualties so far ascertained include one Indian soldier and one Swedish officer killed, 6 Indian, 3 Swedish, 4 Irish and one Norwegian personnel wounded.

18. The United Nations representative contacted Mr. Tshombe and attempted to obtain a cessation of the hostilities as soon as possible. A cease-fire was in fact issued by Mr. Tshombe, but was disregarded by the mercenaries involved in the fighting. Throughout the incident, the adjutant of the President, Major Mwamba, assisted the ONUC headquarters in their efforts to contact responsible authorities who could have used their influence to restore calm.

19. To this end, a meeting was arranged between the United Nations representative, the United States Consul, Mr. Tshombe and other political and military leaders to take place at noon. Mr. Tshombe and the Congolese leaders did not come to that meeting, however, and contact between them and the United Nations representative was not re-established up to the time when this report was being drafted. Mr. Kibwe is reported to be in a ONUC camp.

20. In the afternoon of 13 September, the Central Government of the Repub-

lic of the Congo dispatched to Elisabethville a delegation headed by the Commissaire d'État for Katanga, Mr. E. D. Bocheley, to assist the provincial authorities in the restoration of law and order. The United Nations dispatched a team of technical experts to help in the restoration of essential utilities and public services.

14. Mr. Hammarskjöld to M. Tshombe, 16 September 1961[1]

(1) The mandate of the United Nations force in the Congo is, broadly speaking, to help maintain public order. The resolution of 21 February [*S/4741*] defined further two aspects of this mandate which are binding on the Organization and on all Member States and their nationals. I quote the two relevant paragraphs:

'1. *Urges* that the United Nations take immediately all appropriate measures to prevent the occurrence of civil war in the Congo, including arrangements for cease-fires, the halting of all military operations, the prevention of clashes, and the use of force, if necessary, in the last resort;

'2. *Urges* that measures be taken for the immediate withdrawal and evacuation from the Congo of all Belgian and other foreign military and para-military personnel and political advisers not under the United Command, and mercenaries.'

(2) In the same resolution the Security Council declares that it is convinced that the solution of the problem of the Congo lies in the hands of the Congolese people themselves without any interference from outside and that there can be no solution without conciliation. The Council adds that it is convinced further that the imposition of any solution not based on genuine conciliation would, far from settling any issues, greatly enhance the dangers of conflict within the Congo and the threat to international peace and security.

(3) A principle of the United Nations which is absolutely binding upon all is the maintenance of peace and, to that end and in order to protect human life, they are bound to cease all hostilities and to seek solutions to the conflict by means of negotiation, mediation and conciliation.

(4) You have yourself accepted the objectives of the United Nations mission as defined in paragraph (1), that is to say, the maintenance of public order, the prevention of civil war and the evacuation of all the personnel referred to by the Security Council. There should therefore be no difference of opinion between the Organization and you as to the framework within which ways must be sought of putting an end to the present armed conflict.

(5) As regards the idea that a solution to the problem of the Congo should be sought through reconciliation which would naturally have to be achieved within the framework of the constitution of the Republic you have several times given

[1] S.C.O.R., Sixteenth Year, Supplement for July, August, and September 1961, pp. 111–12. Mr. Tshombe's reply of 17 September, proposing conditions for a cease-fire, and Mr. Hammarskjöld's message rejecting these conditions, are also in ibid., p. 113. Mr. Hammarskjöld was killed in an air crash on 17 September *en route* to meet Mr. Tshombe at Ndola, in Northern Rhodesia. A provisional draft cease-fire agreement was signed on 20 September, 'freezing' the military situation and appointing a joint supervisory commission; text in ibid., p. 120. The Protocol of Agreement subsequent to the cease-fire was signed on 13 October; text in ibid., Supplement for October, November, and December 1961, pp. 9–10.

us clear indications that you also accepted this point of view. I am therefore convinced that you do not share the opinion of certain elements who reject the idea of reconciliation, which leads me to the conclusion that your views and those of the United Nations are identical with respect to the principles on which the attempt to find a solution to the political problem should be based.

(6) On the morning of 13 September, you yourself requested a cease-fire and I understand that you made efforts to bring it about. Since the United Nations desires without reservation to avoid hostilities and the shedding of blood, your request was accepted in advance, on condition, of course, that you could establish an effective cease-fire on your side. In so doing, you would remain faithful to the position you have taken, which I mentioned in paragraphs (4) and (5) above. The efforts to bring about a cease-fire have failed for reasons which we do not know, but which seem to derive from the opposition of certain of those responsible for military operations in Katanga. We have unceasingly sought to make contact with you and you even promised us that you would meet United Nations representatives for discussions on Friday evening, but you did not come to the meeting place chosen by common consent. The United Nations, faithful to its principles, still wishes to see established, without delay, the cease-fire which you yourself requested and which it should be possible for you to achieve, given your position of principle as I have described it.

(7) I have been informed of the message received by Mr. O'Brien from Mr. Dunnett, the British Consul, inviting him to meet you tomorrow at 11.30 a.m. at Bancroft in Northern Rhodesia. I suggest that I should meet you personally, so that together we can try to find peaceful methods of resolving the present conflict, thus opening the way to a solution of the Katanga problems within the framework of the Congo. The proposed meeting obviously requires that orders should be given beforehand for an immediate and effective cease-fire. I therefore propose to you that such a cease-fire should be firmly imposed by both sides, so as to make a meeting possible and to come nearer to a solution of the present conflict within the framework established by the Security Council and already accepted by you. As I shall have to go to the meeting place by air, I suggest that the meeting should be at Ndola. I am dependent on our transport facilities and for this reason the hour which you propose is impossible for me. I shall inform you as early as possible tomorrow morning of my time of arrival, allowing for the fact that before I leave I must have your reply to this message, including your decision regarding the cease-fire. The cease-fire will occur automatically on the United Nations side, in view of the fact that according to the instructions given and the rules followed by the Organization, it only opens fire in self-defence.

(8) I am awaiting your urgent reply to this proposal for a meeting and for an immediate cease-fire.

15. Speech (to the House of Lords) by the British Foreign Secretary, Lord Home, 17 October 1961[1] (extract)

. . . Tomorrow my noble friend, Lord Lansdowne, who fulfilled a mission to the Congo, which was not only dangerous but most exacting, with great skill, will talk to your Lordships on his experiences there and in general will give your

[1] H. L. Deb., vol. 234. cols. 337–9.

Lordships the Government's views on the situation in the Congo as it is now.[1] I want to make only three broad references to our policy and to the policy of the United Nations in that country.

The House will remember why the United Nations went into the Congo. They went in because it was necessary to forestall external intervention, which was designed according to the Communist pattern to bring the Congo right into the cold war. And it was according to the Communist pattern for this reason: that the Russians took immediate advantage of a condition of civil war to try to establish a Communist presence in that country. If the United Nations had not gone in, the alternatives were either a Korea situation or an open door to the Communists.

The first objective, to prevent a clash between the big powers in the Congo and the cold war from being imported into the country, was successful. The second objective, to bring the civil war to an end, so that the Congo leaders might settle their own affairs without distraction, was only partly successful— but, of course, it was a much more difficult task. Because private armies were milling around the Congo and making the chances of a constitutional settlement almost impossible, we agreed, on February 21, that in the last resort force might be used by the United Nations to preserve order. I cannot say that at the time I was happy about voting for that resolution, but we did it because we believed that the authority of the United Nations must be sustained. That was the overriding interest. But we made a public reservation, through our permanent representative at the United Nations, which said that while it was proper to use force in the last resort to prevent the spread of civil war, we could not support the use of that force by the United Nations to impose a particular political pattern on the Congo.[2]

We thought that that was wrong, for these reasons; and I have thought about them a great deal. Whatever the merits of the United Nations in its present state or organisation, it would greatly exceed its strength if it tried to do anything of that kind; and if it did get involved and opened itself to the accusation that it was interfering in internal politics, it would excite passions in Africa which would get completely out of control. This was particularly true of the Congo. Lastly, it was true that the rôle of the United Nations in the Congo was to help to keep order; but its first and most important rôle of all was to reconcile interests and therefore not to get involved in imposing political solutions by force. I do not deny that this was an extremely difficult resolution for Mr. Hammarskjöld to interpret, but so certain was I that the advice which we were giving was right (from my knowledge of Africans I know that you cannot hurry them in their constitutional developments) that I repeated this advice to the Secretary-General at regular intervals between February and August of this year.

In my opinion, mistakes were made: mistakes in interpretation of the resolutions and mistakes in their application on the ground; but I hope that the lessons have been learned. The main lesson is not that the United Nations should leave the Congo or that the United Nations should leave Katanga, but that the United Nations should apply all its talents, and they are very great, to helping a reconciliation between Mr. Tshombe and Mr. Adoula.

[1] Below, p. 758.　　　　[2] S.C.O.R., Sixteenth Year, 942nd meeting, paras. 17–24.

Let me make clear the United Kingdom's objectives beyond doubt, because I do not want any ambiguity about this whatsoever. We want to see a unified Congo and we have worked hard all the time and have supported the United Nations in that objective. We have never seen a future for an independent Katanga and we see no future for it now. All our influence, therefore, has been and will be exerted to help the Congolese to work out their own constitutional future and arrive at a united federal constitution or whatever their own decision may be, and to help the United Nations to help them to do so. Now, the thing that it is necessary is to assist Leopoldville and Elisabethville to get together. This is no time for pride or prejudice, and I sincerely trust that after all the treasure and blood that has been expended Mr. Adoula and Mr. Tshombe will agree to meet and settle their troubles in their own way. . . .

16. Speech to the House of Lords by the British Joint Parliamentary Secretary of State for Foreign Affairs, Lord Lansdowne, 18 October 1961[1] (extract)

. . . I will now describe what took place in the Congo at the end of August and my visit to Leopoldville last month. We had received conflicting accounts and rumours about the United Nations action in Elisabethville on August 28. The United Nations intervention of that date was brief and misleadingly successful. With the co-operation of Mr. Tshombe,[2] a considerable number of mercenaries were arrested in the Katanga without resistance. About 100 took to the bush. It was not clear in London what was going on, nor was it clear what prospects there were of reconciliation between the Central and Provincial Governments. Sir Patrick Dean, Permanent Representative to the United Nations in New York, was instructed to ask Mr. Hammarskjöld what was the exact scope and purpose of the United Nations intervention; to find out whether force had been used before other means had been exhausted; and to express the opinion of Her Majesty's Government that there was no mandate for the removal of essential foreign civilians which might lead to a breakdown of the administration of Katanga.

Sir Patrick Dean saw Mr. Hammarskjöld several times in the course of the next week to discuss the position. Mr. Hammarskjöld insisted that nothing that had taken place on August 28 went beyond the terms of the United Nations resolution of February 21. On September 7, after consultation with my noble friend the Foreign Secretary, the Prime Minister decided to send a member of the Government on a fact-finding mission to the Congo the following week. It was originally proposed that I should leave London on September 12.

Meanwhile Mr. Hammarskjöld had decided to visit the Congo and at the invitation of the Central Government he arrived in Leopoldville on September 13. While the late Secretary-General was still in the air, United Nations forces early on the morning of September 13 took over Elisabethville radio station and General Post Office as a preliminary to the arrest of the remaining mercenaries. Your Lordships will remember that it was this action which started the shooting.

---

[1] H. L. Deb., vol. 234, cols. 445–52.
[2] If by 'co-operation' one means acceptance of a *fait accompli*, then Mr. Tshombe can be said to have co-operated with the United Nations.

I do not suppose that anyone will ever know for certain how the first shots came to be fired.

It seemed to us in London, so far as we could judge from the reports which we had received, that the action taken by the United Nations was aimed at the forcible overthrow of the provincial Katangan Government, and therefore went beyond the terms of the February 21 resolution. Our Ambassador in Leopoldville was therefore instructed to see Mr. Hammarskjöld on the evening of September 13 to inquire about the scope and purpose of the further United Nations action. On September 14 I left for Leopoldville with instructions to acquaint myself with the facts at first hand and to report to Her Majesty's Government, to reassure the Government of the Congo that the policy of Her Majesty's Government remained unaltered, and to impress upon Mr. Hammarskjöld that Her Majesty's Government were shocked at the outbreak of fighting in the Katanga and to urge upon him the necessity of bringing the fighting to a close.

I arrived at Leopoldville on the morning of September 15, where I was greeted by Foreign Minister Bomboko. Within 24 hours of my arrival I was able to have meetings with President Kasavubu, Mr. Bomboko and Prime Minister Adoula, who was accompanied by Vice-Premier Gizenga. The Ambassador accompanied me to all these meetings. In all my conversations with the Congolese Ministers I reassured them that it was the wish of Her Majesty's Government to see the Congo independent, united, rich and strong; that we did not support nor ever had supported Mr. Tshombe's pretensions to secession; and that Her Majesty's Government had supported the operation of the United Nations in the Congo and this was costing us a great deal of money. The Government and the people of the United Kingdom had, however, been very shocked by the use of force in what appeared to be an attempt to destroy the Provincial Government of the Katanga.

Prime Minister Adoula insisted that Mr. Tshombe and his Provincial Government had broken the *Loi Fondamentale*, and he referred throughout to the Katanga as being in a state of rebellion against the Central Government. He insisted that he had done everything in his power to promote conciliation and to encourage Mr. Tshombe to take his part in the constitutional, parliamentary life of the country. I was impressed by the balance and moderation of Prime Minister Adoula who is a man who measures his words and expresses himself with great clarity. I am afraid that nothing which I said convinced the Prime Minister that the policy of Her Majesty's Government which I had enunciated was not at variance with what he said were their actions. He instanced, for example, articles in the British Press which appeared to him to support the independence of Katanga. Again I was unsuccessful in convincing Mr. Adoula that Her Majesty's Government did not and could not control the British Press.

From my talk with Mr. Adoula I went straight to see Mr. Hammarskjöld on the morning of September 16. I went, as your Lordships can imagine, with two main purposes in mind: first, to try to get from Mr. Hammarskjöld personally a more precise account of the events of August 28 and September 13; and, secondly, to explain to him how shocked Her Majesty's Government were at the trend of events since September 13. I was therefore very pleased when Mr. Hammarskjöld said to me straight away that he thought that the most important thing was to achieve a cease fire. He showed me a message which he had drafted for transmission to Mr. Tshombe proposing a meeting, and he told me that he had reached the conclusion that Ndola was the most suitable place to meet.

I told him at once that I was sure Her Majesty's Government would entirely support his decision and that I would seek early approval for the use of Ndola both from Her Majesty's Government and from the Federal Government. Mr. Hammarskjöld's plan did not envisage that Mr. Adoula should participate in the meeting. I asked the Secretary-General whether he thought there was still not a chance that Mr. Adoula might also be brought in from the start. Mr. Hammarskjöld did not think that this would be possible, but undertook to discuss it with the Congolese Prime Minister before his message was despatched to Mr. Tshombe.

Mr. Hammarskjöld then explained to me the origins of the United Nations actions on September 13. He said that in the opinion of his officers on the spot it was necessary to act urgently against the remaining foreign mercenaries in the Katanga. The operation of August 28 which had been endorsed by Mr. Tshombe had only been partially successful. Intimidation against the United Nations had been increasing and there had been instances of arson, stone throwing and incitement to violence. There was a danger that with the assistance of these foreigners an organised underground movement might be built up. Mr. Hammarskjöld made it clear to me that the object of the action of September 13 was to complete the work of August 28, and that no further instructions had therefore been required from him. Now I must tell your Lordships that in both my long conversations with Mr. Hammarskjöld I spoke with absolute frankness, and it is my conviction that he spoke with equal frankness to me. Although he did not disagree with my views that his officers had made a quite erroneous appreciation of the resistance that they would encounter, he fully accepted responsibility for the action that they had taken.

As the noble Earl the Foreign Secretary told your Lordships yesterday,[1] and it was certainly my impression also, mistakes were made; and I believe that Mr. Hammarskjöld also shared this view. I emphasised, however, that Her Majesty's Government were not so much concerned with the past as with the achievement of a peaceful reconciliation between Mr. Tshombe and the central Government. I said that I had reluctantly formed the impression that there was an insufficient desire among certain of his officers to bring about the cease-fire. They seemed to me to be carrying out a punitive war, rather than a precautionary police operation.

I also felt obliged to draw the Secretary-General's attention to certain inconsistencies, as I saw them, between his account of the events in the Katanga and the reports which we had had from Elisabethville. There were Press and radio statements attributed to United Nations officers in charge of operations in the Katanga which seemed to me to run directly counter to what he himself had stated to me was the position of the United Nations *vis-à-vis* the Central Government, which the Secretary-General had denied. In order to be precise, I undertook to prepare for the Secretary-General a document setting out in detail the points which had worried me.

[1] See above, p. 756.

At the end of this meeting I had formed the impression that many of the apparently more outrageous aspects of the United Nations action as we had seen them from London were inaccurate or exaggerated. I thought that there had been a gross miscalculation of the effect of the United Nations action, and that this was due to ineptitude and bad judgment. When I left Mr. Hammarskjöld it was in the knowledge that he would be asking Mr. Adoula and his Cabinet for their acquiescence to the despatch of his message to Mr. Tshombe.

At 9.30 a.m. on September 17 I again called on Mr. Hammarskjöld and told him that I should be glad to do anything that I could to facilitate his meeting with Mr. Tshombe at Ndola, and as time was short, and I did not know whether all the arrangements could have been made, I offered to accompany him, in order to assist him on British territory. I added that I appreciated that there was a risk of my accompanying him being misinterpreted. The Secretary-General said that he thought it would be useful if I could precede him to Ndola. It was agreed that I should do this in a United Nations aircraft which he placed at my disposal, and in which I was to fly to Salisbury before he arrived at Ndola.

Before leaving Leopoldville I had word from London that all the necessary arrangements for the meeting had been made, and the Secretary-General was informed of this. None the less, he telephoned to me to proceed to Ndola, and he also informed me that he had received a communication from Mr. Tshombe. Although this communication was not entirely satisfactory he was none the less determined to carry out his mission. In this same telephone conversation, which took place one hour before my departure, the Secretary-General informed me that he had taken note of my personal letter to him, and that as he wished to investigate himself the points which I had raised there would be some delay in his reply. I think it probable that this letter was destroyed in the aircraft in which the Secretary-General was killed. A copy of this letter has since been sent to New York.

I left for Ndola in a United Nations DC 4 at 3 p.m., local time, on September 17. The Secretary-General was to leave Leopoldville in a faster aircraft later that evening. I arrived at Ndola at 10.40 p.m. where I was met by the High Commissioner, Lord Alport, who, with the assistance of the Government of the Federation, had made all the necessary arrangements for the meeting. As my arrival had been announced to Mr. Tshombe, I briefly visited him, Mr. Kibwe and Mr. Kimba, the two Ministers accompanying him. As I had undertaken in no way to interfere in the negotiations which Mr. Hammarskjöld was to carry out I discussed no basic questions but limited myself to expressing the hope that these negotiations would be successful and the belief that a peaceful solution rested with Mr. Tshombe. After conversations with Lord Alport I was informed that the pilot of the Secretary-General's aircraft had been in touch with Ndola Control. I left for Salisbury at about 12.20 a.m. on September 18.

Shortly after my take-off, our pilot endeavoured to establish contact with the Secretary-General's aircraft. He repeated this more than once, but without success. On arrival in Salisbury at half past three in the morning I was informed that there was no further information about the Secretary-General's aircraft. I understood that the 'overdue' procedure had already been put into effect. At 9.30 a.m. I went to see Sir Roy Welensky, and your Lordships will appreciate that our meeting was clouded by the very grave anxiety which we all felt over the disappearance of Mr. Hammarskjöld's aircraft. Sir Roy Welensky confirmed that every possible step had been taken to locate it.

He then proceeded to make the position of his Government on the Congo perfectly clear. He confirmed to me that he shared the objectives of Her Majesty's Government in respect of a united Congo; that he was completely opposed to the secession of the Katanga, and that he had done all he could to encourage Mr. Tshombe to come to terms with Mr. Adoula. Furthermore, he undertook to to send a personal message to Mr. Adoula reaffirming his position. This message I was subsequently able to give to Mr. Adoula on my return to Leopoldville. It was only after my meeting with Sir Roy Welensky that it became clear that the Secretary-General's aircraft had crashed. I then saw Lord Alport, and shortly afterwards returned to Leopoldville, where I arrived again at 9 p.m.

At 11.30 that night I saw Dr. Linner, the Chief Representative of the United Nations in the Congo. In the first instance I saw him alone and offered him my deep sympathy over the tragic death of the Secretary-General. Despite his extreme grief (he was a close personal friend of the Secretary-General) I felt that I must insist that I considered it to be of vital importance that the momentum of Mr. Hammarskjöld's initiative should not be lost. Dr. Linner assured me that it was his intention to arrange for Mr. Khiari to leave for Ndola within a few hours to meet Mr. Tshombe. All the necessary arrangements were immediately made for this meeting, and on September 20 agreement was reached between Mr. Khiari and Mr. Tshombe. The cease-fire started at 00.01 hours on September 21. Later that morning I left Leopoldville for London to report.

After the cease-fire came into effect on September 21 a mixed commission was set up. It has now reported, and its agreed report has been sent to the United Nations for ratification. Meanwhile, there have been many allegations and counter-allegations about breaches of the cease-fire by both sides. It has been said, in particular, that the United Nations have built up their forces since the cease-fire started. Dr. Bunche last week in New York assured my honourable friend the Minister of State that there had been no build-up of United Nations forces in contravention of the cease-fire agreement. Mr. Tshombe is arranging for a delegation to go to Leopoldville to talks with the central Government. I am sure that all your Lordships share the hope of Her Majesty's Government that this will be followed by a meeting between Mr. Tshombe and President Adoula, and that a lasting reconciliation will follow.

My Lords, although, as you will now have realised, much that I had to say to Mr. Hammarskjöld was highly critical of the United Nation's action as I understood it, I left Leopoldville more than ever convinced of the vital importance and great potential of this Organisation. Perhaps I had seen some of its imperfections, but I had also been brought face to face, in deeply moving circumstances, with the single-minded devotion to the cause of peace of its principal officer. At one of our meetings Mr. Hammarskjöld said to me, 'You know, this work of an international Agency is only in its infancy. There is still so much that we all have to learn.'

I should like, my Lords, with deep respect, to pay my personal tribute to a great servant of humanity. Throughout the world there are countless witnesses to his achievements. Let us hope that a peaceful and prosperous Congo may prove to be another one of these.

17. Approval by United Nations Headquarters of the Protocol of Agreement of 13 October, 23 October 1961[1]

1. The protocol of agreement signed at Elisabethville on 13 October 1961[2] is approved by United Nations Headquarters as an accord which is subsidiary to the cease-fire agreement between the United Nations troops and those of the Katangese authorities signed at Ndola on 20 September 1961.[3] The express conditions set forth as the basis for the approval by United Nations Headquarters of the cease-fire agreement of 20 September are equally applicable to the protocol 13 October and constitute the basis on which it is approved. These conditions are the following:

(*a*) The conclusion of the agreement shall in no way affect the resolutions of the Security Council, including that of 21 February 1961, and of the General Assembly;

(*b*) The agreement is of a strictly military nature and applies solely to the United Nations Force in Katanga and to the armed forces of Katanga. It has no political intention or aim;

(*c*) The agreement does not apply outside Katanga.

2. This protocol of agreement is limited to relations between ONUC and Katanga armed forces in Katanga. Approval of it involves no derogation of the unity, territorial integrity or independence of the Congo, affirmed and reaffirmed by resolutions of the Security Council and the General Assembly, of the sovereignty of the Republic of the Congo (Leopoldville), or of the authority of its Central Government.

3. Further, note is taken that it was acknowledged in the discussions between the two parties to the negotiations which led to the formulation and signing of the protocol, that full compliance with the requirements of part A, paragraph 2, of the Security Council resolutions of 21 February 1961 is a condition essential to the effective application of the protocol.

4. This approval is given, finally, on the understanding that the exchange of prisoners will precede the execution of all other provisions of the protocol.

18. Security Council resolution, adopted 24 November 1961[4]

The Security Council,

Recalling its resolutions S/4387, S/4405, S/4426 and S/4741.[5]

Recalling further General Assembly resolutions 1474 (ES-IV) 1592 (XV), 1599 (XV), 1600 (XV) and 1601 (XV),[6]

[1] S.C.O.R., Sixteenth Year, Supplement for October, November, and December 1961, pp. 10–11. S/4940/Add. 11. Annex II.

[2] ibid., pp. 9–10. See also above, p. 755, n. 1.

[3] ibid., Supplement for July, August, and September 1961, p. 120.

[4] S.C.O.R., Sixteenth Year, Supplement for October, November, and December 1961, pp. 148–50. S/5002.

[5] *Documents*, 1960, pp. 277, 284–6, and above, pp. 736–7.

[6] *Documents*, 1960, pp. 299–300, ibid., 1961, pp. 739–40, and G.A.O.R. Fifteenth Session, Annexes, Agenda item 85, p. 112.

Reaffirming the policies and purposes of the United Nations with respect to the Congo (Leopoldville) as set out in the aforesaid resolutions, namely:

(*a*) To maintain the territorial integrity and the political independence of the Republic of the Congo,

(*b*) To assist the Central Government of the Congo in the restoration and maintenance of law and order,

(*c*) To prevent the occurrence of civil war in the Congo,

(*d*) To secure the immediate withdrawal and evacuation from the Congo of all foreign military, paramilitary and advisory personnel not under the United Nations Command, and all mercenaries, and

(*e*) To render technical assistance,

Welcoming the restoration of the national Parliament of the Congo in accordance with the 'Loi fondamentale' and the consequent formation of a Central Government on 2 August 1961,

Deploring all armed action in opposition to the authority of the Government of the Republic of the Congo, specifically secessionist activities and armed action now being carried on by the provincial administration of Katanga with the aid of external resources and foreign mercenaries, and *completely rejecting* the claim that Katanga is a 'sovereign independent nation'.

Noting with deep regret the recent and past actions of violence against United Nations personnel,

Recognizing the Government of the Republic of the Congo as exclusively responsible for the conduct of the external affairs of the Congo,

Bearing in mind the imperative necessity of speedy and effective action to implement fully the policies and purposes of the United Nations in the Congo to end the unfortunate plight of the Congolese people, necessary both in the interests of world peace and international co-operation, and stability and progress of Africa as a whole.

1. *Strongly deprecates* the secessionist activities illegally carried out by the provincial administration of Katanga, with the aid of external resources and manned by foreign mercenaries;

2. *Further deprecates* the armed action against United Nations forces and personnel in the pursuit of such activities;

3. *Insists* that such activities shall cease forthwith, and *calls upon* all concerned to desist therefrom;

4. *Authorizes* the Secretary-General to take vigorous action, including the use of a requisite measure of force, if necessary, for the immediate apprehension, detention pending legal action and/or deportation of all foreign military and paramilitary personnel and political advisers not under the United Nations Command, and mercenaries as laid down in part A, operative paragraph 2 of the Security Council resolution of 21 February 1961;

5. *Further requests* the Secretary-General to take all necessary measures to prevent the entry or return of such elements under whatever guise and also of arms, equipment or other material in support of such activities;

6. *Requests* all States to refrain from the supply of arms, equipment or other material which could be used for warlike purposes, and to take the necessary measures to prevent their nationals from doing the same, and also to deny trans-

portation and transit facilities for such supplies across their territories, except in accordance with the decisions, policies and purposes of the United Nations;

7. *Calls upon* all Member States to refrain from promoting, condoning, or giving support by acts of omission or commission, directly or indirectly, to activities against the United Nations often resulting in armed hostilities against the United Nations forces and personnel;

8. *Declares* that all secessionist activities against the Republic of the Congo are contrary to the 'Loi fondamentale' and Security Council decisions and specifically *demands* that such activities which are now taking place in Katanga shall cease forthwith;

9. *Declares* full and firm support for the Central Government of the Congo, and the determination to assist that Government, in accordance with the decisions of the United Nations, to maintain law and order and national integrity, to provide technical assistance and to implement those decisions;

10. *Urges* all Member States to lend their support, according to their national procedures, to the Central Government of the Republic of the Congo, in conformity with the Charter and the decisions of the United Nations;

11. *Requests* all Member States to refrain from any action which may, directly or indirectly, impede the policies and purposes of the United Nations in the Congo and is contrary to its decisions and the general purpose of the Charter.

19. Statement to the Security Council by the Acting Secretary-General, U Thant, 24 November 1961[1]

Mr. President, in this, my first intervention in the Security Council as Acting Secretary-General, I have no need to take up very much of your time. Indeed, I ask to speak even briefly only because I think the members of the Council and all interested parties are entitled to know without delay what they may expect from me with respect to those provisions of the resolution just adopted[2] which call for action by the Secretary-General. In this regard, I may refer particularly to paragraphs 4 and 5 of the resolution.

102. The subject of the activities of mercenaries in Katanga is one on which we are all entitled to have strong views. For it is intolerable that efforts to prevent civil war and to achieve reconciliation in the Congo should be persistently obstructed and thwarted by professional adventurers who fight and kill for money. I intend, therefore, to discharge the responsibilities entrusted to me in paragraphs 4 and 5 of the resolution with determination and vigour. It will be my purpose to employ toward that end, and to the best advantage, as much as possible of the total resources available to the United Nations Operation in the Congo.

103. I am sorry in this connexion, however, to have to utter a word of realistic caution. It would be highly desirable, in fact, to be in a position to focus all of our resources on the elimination of mercenaries and hostile elements in Katanga, for that objective is of major importance and I believe its realization could lead to decisive results. But the recent tragic events in Luluabourg, Albertville and

[1] S.C.O.R., Sixteenth Year, 982nd meeting, 24 November 1961, pp. 19-22.
[2] Above, pp. 763-5.

Kindu—or more important, the causes underlying those events—carry implications of the most serious nature for the United Nations Force. It is clear that the need for continuing United Nations assistance in the maintenance of law, order and security in many parts of the Congo is still critical. Moreover, recent performances by Congolese troops, as pointedly indicated in addendum 13 to document S/4940,[1] certainly are not encouraging as to the capability of the Central Government, at this stage, to assume an increased responsibility in the vital sphere of law and order. It may be necessary, therefore, from time to time to establish temporary, short-range priorities in the continuing efforts to achieve the various objectives.

104. All the United Nations responsibilities flowing from past resolutions on the Congo continue with new emphasis, since these resolutions have all been reaffirmed in the action just taken. Assistance must be given to the Central Government in the maintenance of law and order. Everything possible must be done to avert civil war, even by the employment of force, should this prove necessary as a last resort. This, I believe, necessarily implies a sympathetic attitude of a part of ONUC toward the efforts of the Government to suppress all armed activities against the Central Government and secessionist activities. Supporting the territorial integrity of the country, the United Nations position, it seems to me, is automatically against all armed activities against the Central Government and against secessionist forces. This, of course, is reinforced by our confidence in Mr. Adoula and his Government. More determined and effective steps must be taken with regard to the training and reorganization of the Congolese armed forces under the terms of the previous resolutions adopted by this Council. The United Nations programme of technical assistance should be steadily expanded, particularly as conditions in the country permit the military assistance to be reduced.

105. It is true that at the present critical stage in the Congo, there is actually an acute need for more troops and I must make a strong appeal to Member States, and particularly the African States, for added contingents or for increases in existing contingents. Nevertheless, once the current phase of disorder and secessionist threat is over, I feel that there will be a real possibility for undertaking a gradual reduction in the size of the Force, beginning, I hope, in early 1962.

106. Above all, I may assure you that the United Nations will continue and even redouble its attempts to achieve reconciliation, by peaceful means of course, of the sharp differences which now seriously endanger the unity of the country. Much skill and effort have already been employed by the United Nations in this direction. It might be a further useful step for me to designate a special representative of high standing to devote his energies exclusively to the purpose of national reconciliation for a limited time, if the Government of the Republic of the Congo so desires. I am pondering over this since, in my view, national reconciliation should figure in our attempts to restore law and order in the Republic of the Congo.

107. My duty now, as I see it, is to do all that can be done to give full effect

[1] S.C.O.R., Sixteenth Year, Supplement for October, November, and December 1961, pp. 19–28.

to the resolutions of the General Assembly and of this Council relating to the Congo, including the one just adopted. I shall devote myself steadfastly to that purpose.

108. Before concluding, I feel impelled to say a word or two about Kindu. There, on 11 November 1961, a horrifying crime was committed by Congolese troops against thirteen brave Italian men serving the United Nations. This was an act of bestiality, and I assure you that ONUC, on my orders, is taking all possible measures to see to it that all who are guilty of the crime will be severely punished. But I must point out that the Kindu tragedy is not a new experience for the United Nations in the Congo, nor is it necessarily an indication of any new condition. There has been a long and very painful series of such experiences at the hands of Congolese soldiers which ONUC personnel, both civilian and military, have suffered with patience and fortitude, beginning in August 1960. This includes the savage beatings of American, Canadian and Indian air-crew personnel at the Leopoldville and Stanleyville airports; the ambush of the Irish in Niemba, North Katanga, with eight casualties; the massacre of the forty-two Ghanaians and two Swedes at Port Francqui; the assault on the Sudanese at Matadi; and the besieging of the Irish at Jadotville. It will be noted from this recital, incidentally, that these attacks follow no pattern with regard to the race, colour or nationality of the victims. Undisciplined but heavily armed troops who do not respect their officers are a threat to the security of everyone, Congolese and non-Congolese alike.

109. I must also say, without opening up any new debates or entering into a defence of the United Nations Secretariat—for I think it needs none—that I welcome constructive criticism of the Secretariat and that I will be the first to admit its faults and errors and try to do all possible to correct them. Without specific reference to persons or events and without admitting any particular charge, I would grant that mistakes have undoubtedly been made in the Congo; no operation of that scope and complexity could be free of them. But to allege discrimination is quite a different matter, for it is a harsh and ugly charge. I am sorry that it has been made at all, and especially that it should be done publicly without any prior reference to me. I do not think that that charge is justified.

110. Finally, I need not stress that the task of guiding the Congo operation is a difficult and complex one, under any circumstances. It becomes possible of achievement only if I can count on the goodwill of Member Governments and especially on their readiness to provide the resources, and particularly the financial support, that is essential for its successful accomplishment.

111. There is, unfortunately, no reason to anticipate in the next few months an order of expenditure appreciably different from that being incurred at present. I am confident, however, that ONUC will fulfil all of its responsibilities if the necessary resources are made available.

20. Statement by U Thant, 10 December 1961[1]

My attention has been drawn to statements in the press alleging that the aim of the present United Nations operations in Katanga is to force a political

[1] United Nations press release, 11 December 1961. Fighting between United Nations and Katangan forces had broken out on 5 December.

solution of the Katanga problem by smashing the military strength of the present political leadership there, as also the political leadership itself, that instructions to this end have been given to officials of ONUC, and that I have given them carte blanche or a completely free hand in order to achieve the above-mentioned aim.

I wish to state categorically that the above description of the aim of the present Katanga operations is false. It is equally false to say that I have given the ONUC officials a free hand in the pursuit of such an objective. All member governments of the United Nations have been informed of the genesis and purpose of the present military operations in Katanga in two reports to the Security Council, S/4940/Add. 16 and 17.[1]

The military action was forced on the United Nations by a series of deliberate attacks on United Nations officials, soldiers and military officers in Katanga, and particularly Elisabethville, involving wanton and brutal assault, cold-blooded murder, and seizure of such personnel; the setting-up of road blocks impeding the freedom of movement in Elisabethville; and attacks in strength on positions held by the United Nations elsewhere in Katanga, all of which were clearly part of a plan. The UN military action was undertaken with the greatest reluctance, and only when it became obvious that there was no use in continued negotiations, which were marked by repeated instances of bad faith and failure to implement agreed measures on the part of the political leaders of Katanga, who indulged in a violent and inflammatory campaign against the United Nations over the press and radio even while they were engaged in negotiation with our representatives.

The purpose of the present military operation is to regain and to assure our freedom of movement, to restore law and order, and to ensure that for the future United Nations forces and officials in Katanga are not subjected to such attacks; and meanwhile to react vigorously in self-defence to every assault on our present positions, by all the means available to us.

These military operations will be pursued up to such time, and only up to such time, that these objectives are achieved, either by military or by other means, and we have satisfactory guarantees in this regard for the future, not only in Elisabethville but over the whole of Katanga. We shall also need to be satisfied that we shall be able to go ahead with the implementation of the Security Council and General Assembly resolutions, and especially the latest Security Council resolution of 24 November, 1961, without let or hindrance from any source.

We have endeavoured to make our objectives known to the people of Katanga, as also the rest of the Congo, by pamphlets, broadcasts and public announcements. I shall welcome any initiative which would enable us to achieve our aims as peacefully and as speedily as possible. In this connection I am fully aware of the need for reconciliation and pacification, and I recall that I stated in the Security Council on 24 November, 1961, that 'in my view national reconciliation should figure in our attempts to restore law and order in the Republic of the Congo'.[2] Our long term mandate is stated and restated in the various

---

[1] S.C.O.R., Sixteenth Year, Supplement for October, November, and December 1961, pp. 37–50.
[2] Above, p. 765.

resolutions of the Security Council and the General Assembly, which it is my responsibility to implement. I shall continue to strain every nerve, and to use all the resources available to me to execute this mandate in the spirit of the UN Charter.

21. Message from Sir Patrick Dean, British Permanent Representative at the United Nations, to U Thant, 13 December 1961[1]

Her Majesty's Government are deeply disturbed by the course of events of the past week in the Congo. As they have made clear on a number of occasions recently they fully support the efforts of the United Nations to bring about a restoration of law and order in the Congo and to encourage a peaceful reconciliation between the Central Government and the Provincial Government of the Katanga. They also recognise the undoubted right of the United Nations forces to act in self-defence when, as has happened in the last fortnight, they are attacked.

2. H.M.G. have already also made clear to the Acting Secretary-General that they cannot agree that it is the duty of the United Nations to impose a political solution on the Katanga whether by force or not. To do so would be directly contrary to the Resolution of the Security Council of 9th August, 1960.[2] For this reason they view with alarm the course of military events of the last few days, which they find difficult to understand in the light of the Acting Secretary General's assurance, that the objectives of the United Nations forces are to restore freedom of their communications and to defend themselves. The form of attacks which have been reported to have been made by U.N. aircraft including those on industrial installations and other civilian targets, do not in H.M.G.'s view appear to fall within this definition.

3. In the circumstances H.M.G. believe that the duty of the United Nations is to bring about at the earliest possible moment an end to hostilities and a return to the path of conciliation and negotiation. They therefore call upon the Acting Secretary-General to secure an immediate ceasefire in Katanga, in order to bring to an end the destruction of life and property resulting from the present fighting, and thus create conditions in which, in a united Congo, the peaceful and just basis for co-operation may be negotiated.

4. H.M.G. have noted with satisfaction the references to reconciliation and pacification in the Secretary-General's statement of December 10.[3] In this spirit, therefore, they approach him with confidence that he will set about the task forthwith. They assure him that they stand ready to be of every assistance in this connexion and if a ceasefire can be achieved they will exert all the influence they can bring to bear in any way or at any point to encourage a very early meeting between the General Government and Mr. Tshombe. Such a meeting they regard as an essential first step towards the reintegration of the Katanga within the Congo.

[1] Foreign Office press release, 13 December 1961.
[2] *Documents*, 1960, pp. 285–6.
[3] Above, p. 767.

22. Statement by the United States Under-Secretary of State, Mr. Ball, 13 December 1961[1]

I wanted to meet with you today to explain our attitude toward the current situation in the Katanga. I know you must find the picture somewhat confusing. There has been little which has happened in the Congo since its independence that has not been confusing.

We believe that every reasonable attempt must be made to bring Tshombe together with Prime Minister Adoula to seek agreement on the reintegration of the Katanga. As Secretary Rusk said at his press conference Friday:[2]

> Our aim is the consolidation of the country under a stable government which will be able to pursue freely the true national interests of the Congolese. . . . If Katanga is not peacefully reintegrated, the Congo will face civil war and anarchy and be open to Communist penetration. . . . We hope that the leaders of the Katanga will recognize that their present path leads nowhere and that the Katanga will soon be reconciled with the rest of the Congolese people.

The main problem facing us at the moment is whether or not there should be an immediate cease-fire. The answer to this question is not easy and is one on which there can be honest differences of opinion. The attitude of the United States is simply this: We want a cease-fire as soon as feasible. But we do not believe any cease-fire is feasible until the minimum objectives of the U.N. have been attained. There cannot be a repetition of the events of September, when the United Nations was widely regarded as having suffered a defeat at the hands of the Katanga authorities and the situation further deteriorated. The United Nations has not only the need but the right to protect itself, to maintain its freedom of movement and communications in order to discharge the mission given it by the Security Council and the General Assembly. We believe that force should be used only to the extent necessary to achieve this limited objective. The U.N. has made it clear again and again that its purpose is not to crush the Katanga forces militarily or to impose a political solution by force. U Thant denied categorically that the U.N. operations were designed 'to force a political solution of the Katanga problem by smashing the military strength of the present political leadership there.'[3] Charges to this effect were the result of a gross misunderstanding of what Mr. Linner said to a Swedish correspondent last Saturday, and the Swedish correspondent has since retracted his story.

Having said these things, I would say that once the U.N.'s limited objectives are achieved, the United States would urge an immediate cease-fire. We hope and believe these objectives will be attained quickly and with a minimum of loss of life and damage to property.

23. Declaration by M. Tshombe at Kitona, 21 December 1961[4]

The President of the Government of the Province of Katanga:

(1) Accepts the application of the *Loi fondamentale* of 19 May 1960:

[1] *D.S.B.*, 1 January 1962, pp. 12–13.   [2] ibid., 25 December 1961, pp. 1053–4.
[3] See above, p. 767.
[4] S.C.O.R., Sixteenth Year, Supplement for October, November, and December 1961,

(2) Recognizes the indissoluble unity of the Republic of the Congo:

(3) Recognizes President Kasa-Vubu as Head of State;

(4) Recognizes the authority of the Central Government over all parts of the Republic;

(5) Agrees to the participatian of representatives of the province of Katanga in the Governmental commission to be convened at Leopoldville on 3 January 1962 with a view to study and consideration of the draft constitution;

(6) Pledges himself to take all necessary steps to enable deputies and senators of the province of Katanga to discharge, from 27 December 1961, their national mandate within the Government of the Republic;

(7) Agrees to the placing of the Katanga *gendarmerie* under the authority of the President of the Republic;

(8) Pledges himself to ensure respect for the resolutions of the General Assembly and the Security Council and to facilitate their implementation.

B. THE KUWAIT INCIDENT

1. Exchange of Notes between the British Political Resident in the Persian Gulf and the Ruler of Kuwait, 19 June 1961[1]

(i) *The British Political Resident in the Persian Gulf, Mr. Luce, to the Ruler of Kuwait*

I have the honour to refer to the discussions which have recently taken place between Your Highness and my predecessor[2] on behalf of Her Majesty's Government in the United Kingdom about the desirability of adapting the relationship of the United Kingdom of Great Britain and Northern Ireland and the State of Kuwait to take account of the fact that Your Highness' Government has the sole responsibility for the conduct of Kuwait's internal and external affairs.

The following conclusions were reached in the course of these discussions:

(a) The Agreement of the 23rd of January, 1899,[3] shall be terminated as being inconsistent with the sovereignty and independence of Kuwait.

(b) The relations between the two countries shall continue to be governed by a spirit of close friendship.

(c) When appropriate the two Governments shall consult together on matters which concern them both.

---

pp. 215–16. The Tshombe Declaration together with a letter from him to Mr. Bunche (the United Nations Under-Secretary for Special Political Affairs), a letter of reply from Mr. Bunche, and a letter from Mr. Bunche to M. Adoula, comprise the 'Kitona Agreement'. Texts in ibid., pp. 216–17. It is important to note that in his letter to Mr. Bunche, M. Tshombe implied that the declaration would have to be ratified by the 'competent authorities' of Katanga; in the United Nation's view, however, the declaration had been made 'without reservation'. (ibid., p. 217.)

[1] Cmnd. 1409. Annexed to this exchange of notes was the Agreement made by the British with the Sheikh of Kuwait, 23 January 1899.

[2] Sir George Middleton.

[3] Not printed here. See J. C. Hurewitz, *Diplomacy in the Near and Middle East*, vol. I (Princeton, 1956), p. 218.

(*d*) Nothing in these conclusions shall affect the readiness of Her Majesty's Government to assist the Government of Kuwait if the latter request such assistance.

If the foregoing correctly represents the conclusions reached between Your Highness and Sir George Middleton I have the honour to suggest, on the instructions of Her Majesty's Principal Secretary of State for Foreign Affairs, that the present Note together with Your Highness' reply to that effect shall be regarded as constituting an Agreement between the United Kingdom and Kuwait in this matter which shall continue in force until either party gives the other at least three years' notice of their intention to terminate it, and that the Agreement of the 23rd of January, 1899, shall be regarded as terminated on this day's date.

(ii) *The Ruler of Kuwait to the British Political Resident in the Persian Gulf*

I have the honour to refer to Your Excellency's Note of today's date which reads as follows:

[As in *i*]

I confirm that Your Excellency's Note correctly represents the conclusions reached by myself and Sir George Middleton and I agree that Your Excellency's Note and my reply shall be regarded as constituting an Agreement between Kuwait and the United Kingdom in this matter.

2. Press conference given by the Prime Minister of Iraq, General Kassem, Baghdad, 25th June 1961[1] (extracts)

Kuwait is an integral part of Iraq. The Republic of Iraq has decided not to recognize the 1899 agreement[2] because it is a factitious document. No individual, in or outside Kuwait, whatever his position, has the right to dominate the Kuwaiti people who are among the people of Iraq. The Republic of Iraq, which has decided to protect the Iraqi people in Kuwait and to claim all territory falling within the borders of the Vilayet of Basrah, refuses to relinquish any part of this territory. We have the power to make our deeds match our words.

I do not believe that the Shaikh of Kuwait would wish to block the progress of the victorious Arab advance or the prosperity of the people Iraq whose borders extend from the north of Zakho to the south of Kuwait. He who impedes the progress of the Iraqi people as a whole—their sovereignty, freedom and independence—will be the loser; he will be a traitor who defies the consensus of the Arab people and the solidarity of his brothers in Iraq. The age of the anachronistic shaikhdoms is over and done with.

Tomorrow, we shall deliver memoranda to all the countries of the world, including the Arab states, affirming that Kuwait is an integral part of Iraq. If the imperialists oppose this move, we shall be ready for them. We shall not

---

[1] General Kassem's press conference, which took place in the Ministry of Defence at Baghdad, lasted for three hours. The text printed here, which is 'a full summary of the Prime Minister's statement as reported in the Arab press', is taken from the *Middle East Economic Survey*, 30 June 1961.

[2] See above, p. 771, n. 3.

deviate one iota from our position. The reactions of imperialists are sometimes feeble and sometimes strong; nevertheless they will be the losers.

A presidential decree will shortly be issued appointing the present, honorable Shaikh of Kuwait as the Qayim Maqam (Prefect) of the Kuwait District of the Basrah Liwa (Province). We shall warn the Shaikh not to disregard the rights of the Kuwaiti people who are among the people of Iraq. If he acts rashly, he will receive severe punishment and be considered a saboteur.

I wish to remind you, brothers, that sometime ago it was intended that Kuwait should apply for membership of the British Commonwealth of Nations. But our intelligence service, which protects Arab interests and keeps a careful eye on the imperialists, revealed this plan whereupon we took steps to frustrate it. The Shaikhs of Kuwait, who had become objects of reproach to their subjects, then decided to conclude this recent agreement with the treacherous object of strengthening the position of imperialism.

Prime Minister Kassem then declared the Kuwaiti army attached to the Basrah garrison.

Later, he went on to cite various historical precedents in support of the Iraqi claim to Kuwait. He said:

A former Shaikh of Kuwait, Mubarak al-Sabah, concluded an agreement with Britain in the year 1899 in return for the sum of Rs 15,000 which he received from the British Political Agent in al-Muhammarah (now the Iranian port of Khurramshahr). I want to explain the significance of the 1899 Agreement, and I intend to start by reading out the text of the agreement to acquaint you with what imperialism has in store for us. For our battle is with imperialism; we are not fighting a section of our own people, but the enemies who continue to plot against our country, exploiting our resources and profiting from our weakness and ignorance.

After reading out the text of the 'factitious Agreement of 1899', he said:

At that time the imperialists graced the agreement with the epithet 'legal'. The truth is that the brothers and companions of Shaikh Mubarak objected on the ground that his post of Qayim Maqam of Kuwait did not give him the authority to conclude agreements without reference to his seniors. How then could they find a way to make this fraudulent agreement legal? Faced with this crisis the imperialists began to search for witnesses and lackeys. Their choice fell on Agha Muhammad Rahim of Bahrain and an Indian officer whom they used as false witnesses. All the circumstances and consequences of the alleged Agreement of 1899 stink of treachery.

Rs 15,000 were paid to Shaikh Mubarak in return for the fraudulent agreement which was then concealed from the Ottoman authorities and the Wali of Basrah. When the Ottoman authorities got to know of this agreement, they asked the Shaikh of Kuwait to clarify his position, threatening that otherwise they would take stern measures. After an exchange of correspondence between the Wali of Basrah and the Shaikh of Kuwait, the latter called for a meeting in Kuwait in the year 1901, which was attended by Muhsin Pasha, the Wali of Basrah, and Qasim Pasha, a nephew of the Ottoman Sultan and the military governor of Iraq. After the meeting, the Shaikh of Kuwait accompanied the others to Basrah where he publicly declared that as Qayim Maqam of Kuwait he was attached to the Vilayet of Basrah, and reaffirmed his allegiance to the Ottoman Sultan.

Shortly before this date, a caravan belonging to the Shaikh of Bahrain was ambushed by members of the Al Murrah tribe at al-Qatif, 30 kms. from Kuwait. Thirty-three persons, including the son and nephew of the Shaikh of Bahrain, were killed. The Shaikh of Bahrain protested to the British Political Resident in the Gulf. But, on the basis of a report by Colonel Tanbell, the British Political Resident and the Indian Government replied that the incident had taken place on Ottoman territory, falling under the Qayim Maqam of the Kuwait District of the Vilayet of Basrah. The Shaikh of Bahrain therefore petitioned the Ottoman Sultan to punish the Al Murrah tribe. The Sultan replied that stern measures would be taken against the tribe and promised to pay Rs 30,000 compensation to the relatives of the deceased in Bahrain.

This incident proves that even after the conclusion of the factitious agreement, Britain recognized that Kuwait formed part of the Vilayet of Basrah. . . . Two years before the conclusion of the agreement, the British Ambassador at Constantinople wrote to the British Foreign Office enquiring about the scope of British relations with Kuwait and the Gulf territories. In its letter No. 307 dated 1 July 1897, the Foreign Office replied that the Ottoman Sultan's suzerainty over Kuwait was an undeniable fact since it was common knowledge that the Kuwait District was attached to the Vilayet of Basrah.

All the historical facts bear witness to the fraud involved in the 1899 Agreement which the imperialists have used as a weapon against those lacking in courage and conscience. Honest men who care for the people's welfare combat such agreements. Since its liberation, the Republic of Iraq has by various means helped to liberate the Kuwaiti people from British and other forms of imperialism. When the imperialists leave by one door, they try to re-enter by another. After the glorious July Revolution, the imperialists found themselves forced gradually to withdraw from the areas bordering on Iraq. I assure you that we did not embark on our revolution in order to achieve no more than a partial independence. So long as parts of the homeland continue to be exploited by foreigners and imperialists, the glorious revolution will not have reached its final goal.

We have the power to attain our rights, but as you know we always employ peaceful means. But I assure you that peaceful means are of no avail with the imperialists, the enemies of peace. Anyway, at present we are limiting ourselves to peaceful means to protect our rights and the rights of our brothers in an integral part of Iraq.

The British imperialists wished to confirm the fraudulent and unrecognized Agreement of 1899 by the conclusion of another agreement. I will now read out the text of the new agreement which has been concluded by irresponsible people under the control of the imperialists. Iraq and Kuwait remained an indivisible unit until the year 1913, when the British occupied Iraq as they had previously occupied Kuwait. From 1913 till now, the people have been struggling to rid themselves from the imperialists and their lackeys.

The rulers of the former regime sold their country to the British and the imperialists, and were therefore unable openly to demand the formation of a unified administration to govern the two countries—even if such an administration were under imperialist control.

This part of Iraq has now been liberated, but there remains the Kuwaiti people who still suffer under the imperialists, under a clique which juggles with their destiny and fortunes, and a pack of feudalists and shaikhs which has even denied them water supplies from the land of their brothers in Iraq.

We wanted to supply them with sweet water, but the shaikhs refused on the advice of the imperialists who are selling them thousands of sea water distillation plants. Kuwait remained barren though it is our land; it remained without plant life while the imperialists benefited from its oil and stored its wealth in British banks; meanwhile the Kuwaiti people are still suffering from poverty and privation.

Kuwait is an integral part of Iraq. There is no border separating us, and it is not within anyone's power to establish a frontier between Iraq and Kuwait.

Prime Minister Kassem, explained that by re-establishing their position in Kuwait, the imperialists were preparing for the formation of an eastern Arab federation by which they intend to surround Iraq and prevent it from liberating the other parts of the Arab world. By forming this federation, which would be similar to the South Arabian Federation which was threatening the independence of the Yemen, the imperialists wished to injure the Arabs in general and Iraq in particular.

The Arab states, know nothing about the new agreement which is being hailed by the imperialist circles, or about the way in which the imperialists are plotting against the Arabs and the independent states. The state particularly affected by the continued presence of imperialist spheres of influence in the area is the Republic of Iraq.

Asked whether he has discussed this matter with the Kuwaitis, he replied that Iraq had repeatedly explained that it recognized no frontiers between it and Kuwait, and added that the border would shortly be opened up. In conclusion, he said that the first projects which the Iraqi Republic would undertake in Kuwait would be the opening of new schools and hospitals and the provision of sweet water supplies.

3. Speech by Sir Patrick Dean, Permanent Representative of the United Kingdom at the United Nations, to the Security Council, 2 July 1961[1]

17. In order to complete the picture of the most recent events relating to the situation in Kuwait, I should now like to read to the Council the text of a statement which was issued early yesterday morning in London by Her Majesty's Government:

'In accordance with Her Majesty's Government's obligations to the Ruler of Kuwait, and at his urgent and formal request, a British force was today moved into the State of Kuwait and placed at the Ruler's disposal. It is to afford him such assistance as he may consider necessary for the preservation of the independence of Kuwait in the face of recent developments in Iraq.

'The Secretary-General of the United Nations is being informed.

'Her Majesty's Government earnestly hopes that the necessity to make use

[1] S.C.O.R., Sixteenth Year, 957th meeting, 2 July 1961, paras. 17–38.

of this force will not arise. It is intended that it should be withdrawn as soon as the Ruler considers that the threat to the independence of Kuwait is over.'

The Prime Minister of the United Kingdom, Mr. Macmillan, when speaking later yesterday in England,[1] reiterated this statement of the policy of Her Majesty's Government.

18. In order that the Council may be fully apprised of the developments which have led to the present situation in regard to Kuwait, I must now give a short account of the latter stages of the development of relations between the State of Kuwait and the outside world.

19. Fortunately, I can spare the Council many details. The point is that for some time past the State of Kuwait has possessed entire responsibility for the conduct of its own international relations and, with the full support of Her Majesty's government, Kuwait has in the past joined a number of international organizations as an independent sovereign State. This development rendered obsolete and inappropriate the terms of the Anglo-Kuwaiti agreement of 23 January 1899. Her Majesty's Government and the Ruler of Kuwait therefore agreed that the necessary formal step should be taken to cancel this agreement.

20. Accordingly, on 19 June last, notes were exchanged by the Ruler of Kuwait and the British Political Representative in the Persian Gulf, the effect of which was formally to establish and recognize a state of affairs which had in fact obtained for some time previously.[2] This step was in accordance with the wishes and aspirations of Kuwait. It was also a step fully in accordance with the long established policy of the United Kingdom. It was in accordance with the Charter of the United Nations and with the aims which have often found expression at this Council and in the General Assembly.

21. We had thought that, in the words of my Prime Minister, this represented an advance which all countries, and particularly all Arab countries, would have welcomed. This was indeed the reaction of practically all countries and it was evident that the prospect of a new member shortly to be added to the family of nations was very widely approved.

22. It was, therefore, with surprise and shock that the news was received that Iraq had reacted not with approval, but with a threat. It is—and I regret to have to say this—because of the hostility which Iraq has shown to the neighbouring country of Kuwait that the present situation has arisen and that the Council, at the request of the Ruler of Kuwait, has now met to consider his complaint.

23. I must at this point remind the Council of the form which this hostility has taken. On 25 June 1961 a statement was made by General Kassem, the Prime Minister of Iraq.[3] The tenor of that statement will be well known to members of the Council; at this juncture I merely wish to draw the Council's attention to General Kassem's assertions that Iraq had decided 'to protect the Iraqi people in Kuwait and to demand all the·territory belonging to the Qadha of Kuwait in the Liwa of Basrah'; that Iraq would issue a decree appointing the present Ruler of Kuwait as Qaimaqam of Kuwait—Qaimaqam means District Governor—and that if he, the Ruler, were to misbehave he would receive 'a

---

[1] H. C. Deb., vol. 642, 1 July 1961.
[3] Above, p. 771.
[2] Above, p. 772.

severe punishment and be considered a rebel'. General Kassem also said that it was in his power to realize what he claimed were Iraq's full rights.

24. These remarks were followed by a press and radio campaign from Baghdad, the object of which was to undermine the independence and integrity of the State of Kuwait and to publicize claims that Kuwait was part of Iraq.

25. That was serious enough. But there was something more. Reports were beginning to circulate early last week that Iraq was preparing to launch an attack against Kuwait in support of the claims made by General Kassem. These reports were based on the existence of considerable Iraqi military forces in the Basrah area. To convey to you, Mr. President, the extremely precarious situation in which the Ruler of Kuwait and his country felt themselves placed, I should like for a moment to remind the Council of the physical situation which is particularly relevant in present circumstances.

26. Kuwait, as you know, is a small country. Basra, in Iraq, is only about 30 miles from the Kuwaiti border and Kuwait town itself only another 60 miles or so further on. The country is flat and open desert and Iraqi military forces, which greatly outnumber the military forces of Kuwait, could invade Kuwait in a few hours after an order had been given to attack. There have also been indications during the past few days that reinforcements, particularly tanks, have been moved down southwards from Baghdad. This, of course, not only increased the already existing Iraqi potential to attack, but indicated its possible imminence.

27. I hope that I have said enough to suggest the considerations that must have weighed with the Ruler; in particular, he must have been conscious that if outside support for his small army were delayed until the attack had been launched, the reinforcements would have arrived too late and Kuwait would have been totally overrun.

28. I may add that the existence of a threat to Kuwait from the attitude and military dispositions of its neighbour was also recognized by, among others, the Government of the United Arab Republic. It can, therefore, be well understood why the Ruler of Kuwait should have issued his formal request for assistance by Her Majesty's Government when he did and also appealed to King Saud of Saudi Arabia. This formal request to Her Majesty's Government in the United Kingdom was made under paragraph (d) of the exchange of notes of 19 June last to which I have already referred. The Council will wish to know the terms of this paragraph which reads as follows:

'Nothing in these conclusions shall affect the readiness of Her Majesty's Government to assist the Government of Kuwait if the latter request such assistance.'

The Council will see that the obligation imposed on Her Majesty's Government by this provision is inescapable, and once a request for aid is addressed to it by the Ruler under this paragraph Her Majesty's Government has no alternative but to respond positively.

29. As evidence of the seriousness with which the Ruler regarded the threat confronting his country and people from Iraq, may I now quote from the translation of a statement which was issued in the early hours of yesterday

morning by the Kuwaiti State secretariat. It was addressed to the people of Kuwait. After referring to the statement made by General Kassem and the military preparations being made by Iraq, to which I have just referred, and also to the messages sent by the Ruler to the Heads of Arab States drawing their attention to the situation and asking for support, this statement continued as follows:

'After your Government received confirmation that Kassem had begun to mass his forces on the frontiers in preparation for invasion of your beloved homeland, your beloved Amir telegraphed his brother, H.M. King Saud, informing him of the Iraqi concentrations on Kuwaiti borders and of an expected invasion from Iraq. Following this telegram H. M. King Saud ordered the despatch of Saudi forces to aid us in these difficult circumstances. At the same time trusting in God and in response to your true wish for the defence of the homeland and in view of situation brought about by Kassem, which left us no alternative, His Highness has requested military assistance from the Government of the United Kingdom in accordance with the agreement concluded between your Government and British Government contained in the exchange of letters of 19 June 1961. Your Government announce that the United Kingdom has immediately responded and sent forces to assist our gallant army and support them in defending our precious homeland, and that as soon as the crisis is over these forces will be withdrawn immediately.

'We ask Almighty God to help and support us and guide our steps to success May He grant our prayer.'

30. Mr. President, I have described to the Council the events which have led up to the present situation and I have given an account of the threat with which the Ruler was faced and of the steps he has taken to deal with it.

31. I should say at once that Her Majesty's Government shares the anxiety of the Ruler for the continued independence of his country and were as impressed as he was at the threat which was developing to that independence. As soon as they became aware, therefore, of the gravity of the situation, Her Majesty's Government informed a number of friendly governments in the Middle East and elsewhere of their deep concern at this situation, and expressed to them the hope that they could use their moderating influence with the Iraqi Government so that Kuwait could continue her existence as an independent Arab State amongst the nations of the world.

32. When, however, it became clear that these counsels of moderation might not prevail and the threat to the independence of Kuwait still existed, Her Majesty's Government, as in duty bound, and in accordance with the obligation in the exchange of notes to which I have already referred, responded to the justified appeal of the Ruler of Kuwait for military aid.

33. In supporting the request to you, Mr. President, for an early meeting of the Security Council, my Government has thought it desirable to take this opportunity to report to the Council ·as early as possible on the steps which they have felt constrained to take. My delegation also informed the Secretary-General yesterday at the earliest possible moment about these steps.

34. I have nothing to add at present to the facts of the situation as I have tried briefly to describe them.

35. Before I conclude my statement, I should, however, like to emphasize two points. First, I should like to repeat, as was stated in the official statement of 1 July issued in London, that Her Majesty's Government earnestly hopes that the necessity to make use of this British force will not arise, and that it is intended that the force should be withdrawn as soon as the Ruler considers that the threat to the independence of his country is over.

36. Secondly, following on the point which I have just made, Her Majesty's Government continues to hope that counsels of moderation will prevail.

37. My Government has noted and welcomed the statesmanlike efforts of a number of Governments to this end. Under the Charter the responsibility of all Member States is to work as best they may for the peace and stability of the area. In this connexion, I should like to assure the representative of Iraq that our action is in no way hostile to Iraq. Our forces present no threat to Iraq: they have no aggressive intentions. Our forces could only be employed in a combat role if Kuwait were to be attacked from across the border. My Government sincerely wishes to remain on friendly terms with Iraq and its people, and we hope that the existing ties which we have with that country will be maintained and indeed strengthened.

38. Mr. President, finally, I regret that this Council has had to meet in circumstances which I am afraid must have been very inconvenient to many members. I am sure, however, that having heard the report, which I have just made, the Council will recognize that the issues were such that no delay could be permitted in bringing them to the notice of the Council, and will accept the reasons why my delegation accordingly felt bound to support the request made by the Ruler of Kuwait for an early meeting to be held.

4. Speech by Mr. Loutfi, Permanent Representative of the United Arab Republic, to the Security Council, 5 July 1961[1]

It is with great regret that I turn once again to the agenda item which we are discussing today.[2] This is a dispute between two sister countries: Iraq and Kuwait.

93. We have followed with deep anxiety the course of the latest events in this crisis between two sister countries. Kuwait has submitted a complaint against Iraq to our Council. Kuwait is complaining of the situation arising from threats by Iraq to the territorial independence of Kuwait which is likely to endanger the maintenance of international peace and security.

94. In considering this problem, the United Arab Republic is basing itself

---

[1] S.C.O.R., Sixteenth Year, 958th meeting, 5 July 1961, paras. 92–104.
[2] The agenda was as follows:
(a) Complaint by Kuwait in respect of the situation arising from the threat by Iraq to the territorial independence of Kuwait, which is likely to endanger the maintenance of international peace and security (S/4844/5).
(b) Complaint by the Government of the Republic of Iraq in respect of the situation arising out of the armed threat by the United Kingdom to the independence and security of Iraq, which is likely to endanger the maintenance of international peace and security (S/4847).

D.I.A.–CC

upon principles which have always guided its policy in the problems with which it was faced. In adopting a position between two Arab countries, we apply the principles of Arab nationalism and of the struggle of the Arab people. For these reasons, the United Arab Republic cannot support the idea of annexation. On the other hand, we are always ready to support the idea of total or partial unity. The United Arab Republic, which is the result of the total union of Egypt and Syria, cannot on this account, fail to support any movement towards unity. This unity can only be the manifestation of the freely expressed will of the Arab people.

95. The United Arab Republic supports the independence of Kuwait, on the basis of self-determination and of the right of peoples to decide their own fate.

96. In his statement to the Council on 2 July 1961, the representative of Iraq said:

'The Government of Iraq has repeatedly stated that it would employ only peaceful means to settle the difficulty, and has denied the reports of troop concentrations in southern Iraq.' [957th meeting, para. 52.]

97. Today the representative of Iraq has reiterated the substance of this statement. My delegation takes note of this statement and is confident that the actions of the Government of Iraq will be in conformity with it.

98. As I have already said, in our view all Arab territory belongs to the Arab nation, in accordance with historical logic. We cannot imagine that Arab soldiers could take up arms against each other when the Arab nation is in the throes of a struggle against imperialism.

99. For the solution of this problem, we must allow the interests of the future of the Arab nation to prevail, for those interests must override any personal considerations or ambitions.

100. We are sure that the noble people of Iraq will apply only the principles of the struggle of Arab nationalism, which were, moreover, the principles on which the Iraqi revolution of 14 July 1958 was based.

101. In the opinion of my delegation, this dispute between two Arab countries should be settled within the framework of the Arab League and in accordance with Arab principles and traditions. We are confident that this dispute can be settled by the Arabs among themselves.

102. The United Arab Republic has noted with regret the concentrations of the British fleet and the landing of British troops in Kuwait. In our opinion, the landing of foreign forces belonging to a great Power, in a part of the Arab world, cannot but have serious repercussions and increase the tension; far from helping to solve the problem, it can only aggravate it. It is for that reason that the United Arab Republic is asking for the withdrawal of these forces.

103. My delegation will not go into details of the dispute between Kuwait and Iraq, for, as I have already stated, we consider that it should be settled within the framework of the Arab League.

104. In conclusion, the position of my delegation may be summarized as follows: my delegation supports the independence of Kuwait on the basis of self-determination and the right of peoples to independence; it requests the withdrawal of the British forces in Kuwait and expresses its confidence that a

peaceful solution will be found to this problem. In addition, my delegation is certain that Iraq, as its representative has just stated, will not commit any act which might threaten the security and peace of the region.

5. Security Council resolutions regarding Kuwait, 7 July 1961

(i) *Resolution sponsored by the United Arab Republic*[1]

The Security Council,

Having considered the items on the agenda,

Noting the statements of the representatives of Iraq and Kuwait,

Noting the statement by the representative of Iraq to the effect that the Iraqi Government is pursuing peaceful means in the solution of the question,

Bearing in mind that peaceful conditions should prevail in the area,

1. *Urges* that the question be solved by peaceful means,

2. *Calls* upon the United Kingdom to withdraw immediately its forces from Kuwait.

(ii) *Resolution sponsored by Britain*[2]

The Security Council,

Having considered the question of Kuwait,

Noting the statements of the representatives of the parties concerned,

Noting that in response to the appeal of the Ruler of Kuwait, Saudi Arabian and British forces have been placed at the disposal of the Ruler,

Noting the statement by the representative of Iraq to the effect that the Iraq Government undertakes to employ only peaceful means in the pursuance of its policy,

Noting the statement by the representative of the United Kingdom that British forces will be withdrawn from Kuwait as soon as the Ruler considers that the threat to Kuwait is removed,

Recognizing the importance of re-establishing peaceful conditions in the area,

Welcoming any constructive steps which may be taken by the Arab League on the line of the present resolution,

1. *Calls upon* all States to respect the independence and territorial integrity of Kuwait;

2. *Urges* that all concerned should work for peace and tranquillity in the area;

3. *Agrees* to keep the situation under review.

---

[1] S.C.O.R., Sixteenth Year, Supplement for July–September, Document S/4856. *In favour:* Ceylon, U.A.R., U.S.S.R. *Against:* none. *Abstentions:* Chile, China, Ecuador, France, Liberia, Turkey, United Kingdom, United States.

[2] ibid., Document S/4855. *In favour:* Chile, China, France, Liberia, Turkey, United Kingdom, United States. *Against:* U.S.S.R. *Abstentions:* Ceylon, Ecuador, United Arab Republic.

C. FRANCE IN THE WESTERN MEDITERRANEAN

(a) Algeria

1. Decree of the President of the French Republic, 8 December 1960, containing the Bill submitted to public referendum in France, 8 January 1961[1]

*Décret no 60–1299 du 8 décembre 1960
décidant de soumettre un projet de loi au référendum*

Le Président de la République,
Sur proposition du Gouvernement,
Vu les articles 11, 19 et 60 de la Constitution;[2]
Le Conseil constitutionnel consulté dans les conditions prévues par l'article 46 de l'ordonnance portant loi organique du 7 novembre 1958,[3]
    Décrète:

Art. 1er. — Le projet de loi annexé au présent décret, délibéré en conseil des ministres après avis du conseil d'Etat, sera soumis au référendum le 8 janvier 1961 conformément aux dispositions de l'article 11 de la Constitution.

Art. 2. — Les électeurs auront à répondre par Oui ou par Non à la question suivante: Approuvez-vous le projet de loi soumis au peuple français par le Président de la République et « concernant l'autodétermination des populations algériennes et l'organisation des pouvoirs publics en Algérie avant l'auto-détermination » ?

Art. 3. — Le présent décret sera publié au *Journal officiel* de la République française.

Fait à Paris, le 8 décembre 1960.

C. DE GAULLE.

ANNEXE

Projet de loi

concernant l'autodétermination des populations algériennes et l'organisation des pouvoirs publics en Algérie avant l'autodétermination.

Art. 1er. — Dès que les conditions de la sécurité en Algérie permettront d'y rétablir le plein exercice des libertés publiques, les populations algériennes feront connaître, par la voie d'une consultation au suffrage direct et universel, le destin politique qu'elles choisiront par rapport à la République française.

Les conditions de cette consultation seront fixées par décret pris en conseil des ministres.

Les actes qui seraient éventuellement établis en conséquence de l'autodétermination seront soumis au peuple français conformément aux procédures constitutionnelles.

Art. 2. — Jusqu'à l'accomplissement de l'autodétermination, tel que prévu à l'article 1er, des décrets pris en conseil des ministres régleront l'organisation des

---

[1] *Journal Officiel, Lois et Decrets*, 9 December 1960, p. 11043. The Bill was approved by 17,447,669 votes to 5,817,775 and became law on 14 January.
[2] ibid., 5 October 1958, pp. 9153–4, 9155, 9163.
[3] ibid., 9 November 1958, p. 10131.

pouvoirs publics en Algérie suivant les dispositions de l'article 72 de la Constitution[1] et d'après les conditions suivantes:

a) Attribuer aux populations algériennes et à leurs représentants les responsabilités relatives aux affaires algériennes, tant par l'institution d'un organe exécutif et d'assemblées délibérantes ayant compétence pour l'ensemble des départements algériens, que par celle d'organes exécutifs et délibérants régionaux et départementaux appropriés.

b) Assurer la coopération des communautés ainsi que les garanties appropriées à chacune d'elles.

c) Instituer des organismes ayant compétence relativement aux domaines concernant en commun la métropole et l'Algérie et assurer, au sein de ces organismes, la coopération de représentants de la métropole et de représentants de l'Algérie.

2. Address given by President de Gaulle over French radio and television, 23 April 1961[2]

Un pouvoir insurrectionnel s'est établi en Algérie par un pronunciamiento militaire.

Les coupables de l'usurpation ont exploité la passion des cadres de certaines unités spécialisées, l'adhésion enflammée d'une partie de la population de souche européenne qu'égarent les craintes et les mythes, l'impuissance des responsables submergés par la conjuration militaire.

Ce pouvoir a une apparence: un quarteron de généraux en retraite. Il a une réalité: un groupe d'officiers, partisans, ambitieux et fanatiques. Ce groupe et ce quarteron possèdent un savoir-faire expéditif et limité. Mais ils ne voient et ne comprennent la nation et le monde que déformés à travers leur frénésie. Leur entreprise conduit tout droit à un désastre national.

Car l'immense effort de redressement de la France, entamé depuis le fond de l'abîme, le 18 juin 1940; mené ensuite jusqu'à ce qu'en dépit de tout la victoire fût remportée, l'indépendance assurée, la République restaurée; repris depuis trois ans, afin de refaire l'Etat, de maintenir l'unité nationale, de reconstituer notre puissance, de rétablir notre rang au dehors, de poursuivre notre œuvre outre-mer à travers une nécessaire décolonisation, tout cela risque d'être rendu vain, à la veille même de la réussite, par l'aventure odieuse et stupide des insurgés en Algérie. Voici l'Etat bafoué, la nation défiée, notre puissance ébranlée, notre prestige international abaissé, notre place et notre rôle en Afrique compromis. Et par qui? Hélas! hélas! hélas! par des hommes dont c'était le devoir, l'honneur, la raison d'être de servir et d'obéir.

Au nom de la France, j'ordonne que tous les moyens, je dis tous les moyens, soient employés pour barrer partout la route à ces hommes-là, en attendant de les réduire. J'interdis à tout Français et, d'abord, à tout soldat d'exécuter aucun de leurs ordres. L'argument suivant lequel, il pourrait être localement nécessaire d'accepter leur commandement, sous prétexte d'obligations opérationnelles ou administratives, ne saurait tromper personne. Les seuls chefs, civils et militaires, qui aient le droit d'assumer les responsabilités, sont ceux qui ont été régulièrement nommés pour cela et que, précisément, les insurgés empêchent de le faire.

[1] ibid., 5 October 1958, p. 9166.
[2] *La Documentation Française, Articles et Documents*, 16 May 1961, p. 1.

L'avenir des usurpateurs ne doit être que celui que leur destine la rigueur des lois.

Devant le malheur qui plane sur la patrie et la menace qui pèse sur la République, ayant pris l'avis officiel du Conseil Constitutionnel, du Premier Ministre, du Président du Sénat, du Président de l'Assemblée Nationale, j'ai décidé de mettre en cause l'Article 16 de notre Constitution.[1] A partir d'aujourd'hui, je prendrai, au besoin directement, les mesures qui me paraîtront exigées par les circonstances. Par là même, je m'affirme, pour aujourd'hui et pour demain, en la légitimité française et républicaine que la nation m'a conférée, que je maintiendrai, quoiqu'il arrive jusqu'au térme de mon mandat ou jusqu'à ce que me manquent, soit les forces, soit la vie, et dont je prendrai les moyens d'assurer qu'elle demeure après moi.

Françaises, Français! Voyez où risque d'aller la France par rapport à ce qu'elle était en train de redevenir.

Françaises, Français! Aidez-moi!

3. Declaration of the French Government before the National Assembly, 25 April 1961[2]

Le 18 avril je recevais une lettre du général Gambiez. Par cette lettre le général commandant en chef des forces en Algérie rendait compte de la situation militaire à la suite de l'exécution des ordres donnés quatre semaines auparavant. Il pouvait se féliciter d'un mois d'offensives continues dans plusieurs secteurs, notamment les Aurès, où des succès très importants venaient de couronner le combat de nos troupes, et d'heureuses résistances sur les barrages, notamment le barrage ouest, où trois fortes bandes rebelles venant du territoire marocain avaient été promptement annihilées.

En d'autres termes, le général Gambiez pouvait rendre compte au gouvernement d'une nouvelle amélioration de la situation militaire. La position de l'armée, c'est-à-dire de la France, était plus forte que jamais sur l'ensemble du territoire algérien.

Cet effort lui avait été demandé, et il l'avait entrepris parce que l'autorité indiscutée de l'armée était un élément indispensable pour le succès de la politique définie par le général de Gaulle et approuvée par la nation. Qu'il s'agisse de la venue éventuelle en France de représentants de la rébellion pour entreprendre les pourparlers annoncés ou qu'il s'agisse à la suite d'un refus ou d'une rupture, de l'application de la loi du 8 janvier, approuvée par la nation, il était en effet indispensable que notre autorité en Algérie fût incontestée. En fait, elle l'était plus que jamais.

Quelques heures après cette lettre du général Gambiez arrivaient à la connaissance du gouvernement les indices d'une opération encore indéterminée dont certains éléments de l'armée pouvaient être les auteurs. Des mesures d'enquête décidées dans la journée du 21 ent sans doute précipité le mouvément qui, dans la nuit de vendredient samedi dernier, a installé à Algérie une équipe de généraux rebelles. Comme l'a dit le général de Gaulle, derrière les chefs qui ont donné leur nom, voire leur renommée, l'appareil de l'insurrection est aux mains d'un

---

[1] *Journal Officiel, Lois et Decrets*, 5 October 1958, pp. 9154–5.
[2] *Le Monde*, 27 April 1961. The declaration was read by M. Debré, the Prime Minister.

petit groupe qui a moins d'ambitions militaires que d'appétits politiques et dont certains pensent moins à Alger et à la nation qu'à la prise du pouvoir au profit d'une junte militaire.

Vous avez suivi le déroulement des événements. Au jour où vous vous réunissez je peux vous dire d'abord que la situation en Algérie n'est en aucune façon la manifestation de prétendue unanimité que se plaisent à décrire les chefs de l'insurrection. Ils ont rencontré dès le début en n'ont cessé depuis lors de rencontrer les plus réelles difficultés. La loyauté, le sens du devoir, la juste appréciation de l'intérêt national animent le plus grand nombre des officiers et des fonctionnaires.

Qu'il s'agisse de l'Oranie, où les auteurs du coup d'Etat ne sont arrivés à réduire le général de Pouilly, commandant le corps d'armée, qu'en l'attirant dans un guet-apens et dont les subordonnés ont, pour la plupart, refusé tout allégeance à Alger; qu'il s'agisse du Constantinois, où plusieurs généraux exercent aujourd'hui encore leur commandement au nom du gouvernement de la République et du général de Gaulle; qu'il s'agisse de la Kabylie, où plusieurs officiers, suivis de quelques troupes fidèles, refusent tout contact avec Alger, de nombreux secteurs ont manifesté et manifestent encore leur loyalisme à l'égard du gouvernement de la République. Plusieurs généraux de l'armée de l'air ont affirmé leur refus de se soumettre, et l'amiral commandant la marine s'est officiellement désolidarisé. Je puis même dire qu'à côté des télégrammes quotidiens ou des messages téléphonés des préfets ou des fonctionnaires civils, nous recevons depuis quelques heures la preuve que de nombreuses unités dont le ralliement avait été pompeusement annoncé, demeurent non seulement réservées, mais notoirement hostiles au directoire qui s'est installé à Alger.

L'objectif du coup d'Etat n'était pas, n'est pas seulement l'Algérie: il était, il est toujours de s'étendre dans la métropole, en essayant d'imposer la révolte à certaines unités ou à certains corps stationnés en métropole ou près de la métropole, en fomentant ici ou là quelques troubles et en envoyant aussitôt après les premières manifestations d'insoumission ou d'insécurité des renforts aériens. Occuper le cœur de Paris était, et est encore sans doute un des objectifs recherchés.

Le général de Gaulle a parlé dimanche soir aux Français. Vous l'avez entendu. Ce message est la loi de la nation.

Le gouvernement de son côté a d'abord pris les mesures d'urgence qui s'imposaient en métropole même. La plupart de ces mesures ont été rendues publiques. Je ne dois pas dissimuler au Parlement que l'alerte n'est pas terminée. Les auteurs du coup d'Etat ne peuvent se contenter de ce qui a été fait. Ils le peuvent d'autant moins qu'une part de l'Algérie leur échappe et que leur préoccupation politique, en fait, ne leur permet plus de poursuivre les feilagas. Ils doivent chercher un succès politique. Le soutien de l'opinion nationale, la confiance du pays dans le générale de Gaulle, sont pour l'action gouvernementale un atout précieux, mais qui n'empêche pas, bien au contraire, une vigilance absolue. La discipline et la résolution des forces de l'ordre et de sûreté, la loyauté des unités de l'armée, tant d'active que de réserve, donnent chaque jour une plus grande valeur aux mesures édictées dès le premier jour.

En Algérie, après les troubles des premières heures, la situation s'éclaircit.

Le gouvernement, dès samedi, a nommé le général Olié général commandant en chef des forces en Algérie. Après une mission qu'il a accomplie sur le territoire même en compagnie de M. Joxe, ministre d'Etat, chargé de la plus large délégation gouvernementale, des mesures de réorganisation du commandement ont été et seront prises. Nous avons nommé de nouveaux commandants de corps d'armées qui sont sur place, ainsi qu'un nouveau commandant de l'air qui est sur place.

Les liaisons sont rétablies et des actions coordonnées pourront prochainement être entreprises.

Dominant les mesures prises en métropole et notre action en Algérie, une grande décision est intervenue. Vous la connaissez, et le message que vient de lire votre président vous en apporte la confirmation. Le général de Gaulle a décidé de recourir à l'application de l'article 16 de la Constitution.[1] Il peut ainsi prendre les mesures qu'exigent les circonstances. Elles sont et seront des mesures de rigueur. Comment en serait-il autrement?

Dans l'immense partie qui se joue l'Etat doit disposer d'une force particulière, et les libertés essentielles, si leur principe doit être sauvegardé, doivent s'incliner devant un impératif absolu de salut public. Déjà le gouvernement a reçu du chef de l'Etat la possibilité de prolonger la durée des arrestations préventives et de procéder à des internements par décision administrative. Des mesures de révocation ou de destitution peuvent atteindre instantanément fonctionnaires et militaires coupables de subversion.

Demain d'autres dispositions seront décidées qui renforceront les possibilités d'action de l'autorité en tous domaines, et sans tenir compte des exigences légales. La sauvegarde de la nation est à ce prix, et je ne veux pas cacher au Parlement la gravité de certaines mesures qui seront publiées, ni la fermeté avec laquelle nous agirons désormais en écartant les règles légales. Comment en pourrait-il être autrement? On ne peut répondre à l'illégalité, proclamée, agissante et révolutionnaire, par la seule légalité.

Les auteurs du coup d'Etat ont pris une grande responsabilité. Cette responsabilité les mène immanquablement à verser le sang. Cela n'a pas encore été le fait, mais cela peut l'être demain. On sait déjà à Alger que les armes qui étaient tournées hier contre les bandes armées de la rébellion, il va falloir les tourner contre les officiers, les soldats et les fonctionnaires qui ne veulent pas s'insurger, et que ceux-ci s'ils reçoivent des ordres qui n'émanent pas du gouvernement ont reçu instruction d'accomplir leur devoir, c'est à dire de résister par tous les moyens.

La marine a tiré pour ralentir l'entrée des troupes insurgées dans Mers-El-Kébir. Un peu partout il en sera de même, en Algérie comme en métropole, si les auteurs du coup d'Etat veulent poursuivre leurs ambitions. Je tiens à ce que le Parlement comprenne bien que dans les conditions où ils se sont placés les auteurs du coup d'Etat ne peuvent pas ne pas ouvrir un jour le jeu ou provoquer l'ouverture du feu. L'aventure commencée, si ces auteurs n'y renoncent pas très vite, est une aventure de guerre civile avec toutes ses conséquences.

Ce que le Parlement doit savoir également, c'est que cette aventure représente pour la France un choc très dur, un choc dont les conséquences ne sont pas pré-

[1] *Journal Officiel, Lois et Decrets*, 5 October 1958, pp. 9154–5.

visibles. Choc très dur pour l'armée: comments des chefs ont-ils pu penser qu'ils trouveraient une armée unanime pour se dresser contre le général de Gaulle? Choc très dur pour l'Algérie: il est éclatant aux yeux de tous que si la paix en Algérie et le libre choix des populations peuvent un jour être réussis, il faut à côté de l'effort militaire un effort politique.

Si la France est affaiblie, est affaiblie par là même la chance d'une heureuse solution. Choc enfin très dur pour la nation: son redressement intérieur et extérieur est, depuis deux ans, une des réalités mondiales; en un instant les résultats acquis sont plus que compromis, ses possibilités d'influence et d'audience profondément atteintes.

De cette nouvelle et terrible épreuve la France sortira, nul n'en doute, mais elle ne se retrouvera pas demain comme elle était hier! Pour demeurer ellemême — je dirai, hélas! pour redevenir elle-même — il lui faudra redoubler d'efforts. De moins en moins il s'agira de suivre telle ou telle idéologie ou de s'incliner devant tel ou tel intérêt.

Ce qui importera avant tout, c'est le travail, la discipline et le loyalisme au seul service de la nation.

Dans cette épreuve, comme pour la suite de cette épreuve, le général de Gaulle est assuré du soutien populaire. Le gouvernement ne doute pas qu'il aura le soutien du Parlement.

4. President de Gaulle's directive to the French armed forces, 25 April 1961[1]

1) La criminelle insurrection militaire d'Algérie compromet gravement la défense nationale dans son ensemble, et dans l'immédiat le succès de nos armes sur le territoire algérien. Elle risque de porter atteinte à l'attachement de la nation pour son armée, et par là à l'unité et à l'avenir de celle-ci.

Face à une pareille menace, la mission générale des forces armées consiste d'abord à arrêter l'insurrection, puis à la briser, enfin à la liquider par tous les moyens voulus, y compris l'emploi des armes. Rien n'est plus nécessaire et rien n'est plus urgent que de hâter une dislocation qui est d'ailleurs commencée.

2) Aussi longtemps que l'insurrection n'agit pas sur le sol de la métropole, l'effort principal doit évidemment se déployer en Algérie. Toutes les opérations, qu'elles aient trait à la destruction de l'insurrection militaire ou à la lutte contre la rébellion du F.L.N., sont du seul et unique ressort du commandement responsable, savoir:

— Le général Olié, chef d'état-major général de la défense nationale, commandant en chef en Algérie, en l'absence du général Gambiez;

— L'amiral Querville, commandant la marine en Algérie;

— Le général Fourquet, commandant les forces aériennes en Algérie;

— Le général Perrotat, commandant le corps d'armée d'Oran en l'absence du général de Pouilly; le général Arfouilloux, commandant le corps d'armée d'Alger, en l'absence du général Vezinet; le général Ailleret, commandant le corps d'armée de Constantine.

3) La conduite à tenir est la suivante: le commandement responsable donne ses ordres à toutes les unités et à tous les services.

[1] *Le Monde*, 27 April 1961.

S'il ne peut, pour certains d'entre eux, les faire parvenir ou les faire exécuter, ceux-ci agiront au mieux pour leur compte, mais à aucun moment, d'aucune façon, sous aucun prétexte, aucun militaire, marin ou aviateur ne doit tenir aucun compte des ordres que prétendrait donner l'insurrection ni s'associer à l'un quelconque de ces éléments.

Pour ce qui concerne notamment la pacification intérieure ou la défense des barrages aux frontières tunisiennes, ce que peut prescrire ou demander l'organisation insurgée est à tenir pour nul et pour non avenu.

Dans ce domaine, comme dans tous les autres, c'est au commandement légitime, et à lui seul, qu'il appartient de commander dans toute la mesure où le lui permet le trouble impardonnable jeté par l'insurrection dans le dispositif et dans l'action militaire.

Au cas où un élément insurgé tente de faire violence à un échelon du commandement ou à une force sous ses ordres, il y a lieu de le repousser par tous les moyens, y compris le feu.

Chaque fois que se présente l'occasion de contraindre à la soumission un élément insurgé, il est nécessaire de le faire en employant au besoin les armes.

Si ces dispositions ne suffisent pas à provoquer l'effondrement de l'insurrection, des instructions ultérieures prescriront les opérations à engager pour la réduire.

5. Communiqué of the French Government on 20 May 1961[1]

Le gouvernement a ordonné l'interruption des operations offensives sur l'ensemble du territoire algérien à partir du 20 mai à 18 heures. Les forces de l'ordre n'entreront désormais en action qu'en cas de légitime défense ou pour la poursuite des auteurs d'attentats. Cette interruption est prévue pour une période d'un mois. Elle sera suspendue ou au contraire prolongée suivant l'évolution de la situation.

Le délégué général a reçu instruction d'accélérer les mesures de libération que le gouvernement a déjà prises en faveur d'internés et de prisonniers. Il est prévu six mille libérations au cours des quatre semaines à venir.

En outre, dans un grand nombre d'arrondissements les autorités prendront les mesures nécessaires pour rétablir la situation normale des personnes et des biens.

Des crédits spéciaux permettront enfin l'exécution accélérée des travaux d'intérêt général ou local prévus par le plan de Constantine.

Ahmed Benbella, Hocine Aït Ahmed, Rabah Bitat, Mohammed Boudiaf et Mohammed Khider sont mis en résidence surveillée. Mostafa Lacheraf est mis en liberté.

6. Address given by the Minister of State in charge of Algerian affairs, M. Joxe, over French radio and television, 1 August 1961[2]

J'ai rendu compte à M. le président de la République et au gouvernement de la réunion qui s'est tenue à Lugrin entre les représentants de la France et ceux du F.L.N. Je me dois maintenant d'expliquer à mes concitoyens les conditions

[1] *Le Monde*, 21/22 May 1961.   [2] *Le Monde*, 3 August 1961.

dans lesquelles notre délégation a travaillé avec la volonté d'instaurer la paix et de préparer la construction d'une Algérie nouvelle. Je le ferai avec la conviction qu'à Lugrin nos objects auraient pu être atteints.

Depuis longtemps nous avons en effet défini un esprit et proposé une méthode. L'esprit, c'est celui qui nous dirige depuis que nous avons entrepris la grande œuvre de décolonisation de l'Afrique, dans le monde tel qu'il est et tel qu'il sera demain. Nous nous sommes donné pour but de remettre l'Afrique aux Africains et de rendre ceux-ci responsables de leur destiné.

La méthode, c'est celle de l'autodétermination telle que l'a définie le général de Gaulle le 16 septembre 1959.[1] Elle ouvre la voie au choix et à l'indépendance en faveur des populations des treize départements d'Algérie si elles en expriment le désir. Approuvée par la nation, elle est devenue sa loi. Nos interlocuteurs l'ont également adoptée.

L'œuvre est lourde et grande. A l'esprit, à la méthode, s'ajoute un souci constant, un double devoir: celui d'assurer un état de paix qui ne puisse être remis constamment en question parce que nous nous aurions mal assuré les fondements; celui de permettre à des hommes, qui de notoriété publique sont profondément différents les uns des autres, de vivre dans la concorde. Il va de soi que nous pensons à tous les hommes d'Algérie quels qu'ils soient. Toute autre attitude manquerait à la fois au réalisme, à la sagesse et à l'honnêteté.

Nous avons tout d'abord vécu la recontre d'Evian avec les representants du F.L.N. Nous leur réconnaissons la qualité de combattants. Nous voyons en eux les délégués d'une organisation politique qui se déclarent candidats au pouvoir. A Evian, il s'agissait d'une exploration sans préalable et sans ordre du jour de tous les sujets qui concernent le retour à la paix et la construction d'une Algérie nouvelle. Lentement, trop lentement, pendant une quarantaine d'heures réparties sur trois semaines, nous avons exposé nos vues les uns aux autres. Nous avons tout d'abord convié nos interlocuteurs à se joindre à nous pour adopter des mesures condamnant effectivement le terrorisme, menant au cessez-le-feu et à la paix. Nous les avons invités à participer avec toutes les tendances algériennes à la préparation du scrutin du référendum d'autodétermination afin que chaque habitant de l'Algérie puisse librement et sincèrement exprimer son opinion. Nous leurs avons exprimé notre souci de voir donner aux Européens d'Algérie, qui eux aussi sont nés et travaillent sur ce sol, les garanties indispensables pour qu'ils puissent participer à la construction du nouvel Etat, dans lequel ils doivent trouver leur place et envisager l'avenir de leurs enfants. Nous avons évoqué devant eux l'idée d'une association entre la France et l'Algérie dans le respect de la souveraineté de chacun, si toutefois le nouvel Etat algérien en avait quelque envie.

Sur aucun de ces points nous n'avons pu connaitre les positions du F.L.N., nous nous sommes même vu reprocher la suspension des opérations offensives que nous avions décidées, on y trouvait une sorte de machine de guerre. Paradoxe évident, mais tout est possible à la seule propagande. Dans les autres domaines, ou bien nos interlocuteurs se sont cantonnés dans l'abstraction, réfugiés dans le silence, ou bien ont fait état d'intentions pures qui toujours se dérobaient lorsque nous les voulions saisir.

[1] *Documents*, 1959, pp. 533–7.

Pour ces raisons, le 13 juin dernier, nous avons suspendu les travaux d'Evian en demandant au F.L.N. de mettre à profit le temps de réflexion que nous nous accordions.

C'est dans ces conditions et avec cet espoir que nous avons repris la conversation, le 20 juillet dernier à Lugrin. Nous estimions que le moment était venu — comme on dit — de « nouer » la négociation, car une négociation ne'est pas un échange de plaidoyers sur des thèmes qu'anime seule la passion de chaque partie en cause. La négociation, c'est la conduite d'un travail complet, c'est le dessin à grands traits d'un règlement d'ensemble. Encore faut-il, je le répète, que tous les aspects des problèmes en suspens soient simultanément envisagés et que toutes les préoccupations de l'un aient été prises en considération par l'autre.

Or qu'avons-nous constaté? Sur l'ensemble nous avons proposé une façon de faire qui consistait à travailler par tous les moyens les cinq sujets essentiels qui sont présents à nos esprits et dont nous avions formellement convenu, ensemble, que l'examen détaillé permettrait seul un règlement général.

Le retour à la paix, les garanties de l'autodétermination, la période transitoire qui s'étendra entre le cessez-le-feu et l'autodétermination, les garanties à donner aux personnes et notamment aux Européens et aux musulmans liés à la France.

Sur tous ces sujets les représentants du F.L.N. s'étaient déclarés prêts à discuter, à rechercher les formules d'entente, à essayer de réduire les difficultés. Or, dès la première séance de travail, ils se sont arrêtés au mot « Sahara », ils ont refusé d'aller plus loin avant que satisfaction leur soit donnée, c'est-à-dire que leur soit reconnue immédiatement la souveraineté sur le Sahara.

Eh bien! parlons du Sahara.

Que leur avons-nous déclaré sur ce point? Ils savent depuis longtemps que pour nous l'autodétermination s'applique aux treize départements de l'Algérie, mais que le problème algérien dépasse ce cadre géographique. Avons-nous écarté toute discussion sur le Sahara? Non, et précisément parce que le problème est complexe. Nous leur avons dit, redit et confirmé ce que voici:

1) Une ligne directrice inspire toute notre politique en Afrique, c'est aux populations qu'il appartient de choisir leur avenir, de déterminer elles-mêmes, en pleine connaissance de cause, leur allégéance politique, cela est vrai du Sahara;

2) Pour le reste, dans une region aussi peu peuplée, aussi immense, aussi stérile dans presque toute son étendue, il est évident qu'aux yeux de la France le problème de la souveraineté n'est pas l'essentiel. Par contre, les richesses mises en valeur par nous posent un problème d'une importance considérable non seulement parce qu'elles créent un lien économique constant entre le Sahara et la France, mais parce que nous entendons ne pas les garder pour nous seuls.

Dès la promulgation du code pétrolier, en 1958, nous marquions notre désintéressement à l'égard des ressources fiscales créées par l'exploitation du pétrole et du gaz. En agissant ainsi, nous assurions déjà à l'Algérie non suelement la fourniture d'énergie dans les meilleures conditions, mais également des moyens de financement pour faciliter son développement économique.

Dans le même esprit, à Lugrin, nous avons envisagé la création, par la France et l'Algérie, d'un organisme technique qui serait chargé de la mise en valeur des richesses du sous-sol du Sahara et auxquelles pourraient participer tous ceux de ses voisins qui auraient passé des accords avec nous et pourraient en passer.

Où trouverait-on dans cette politique, soit la volonté de défendre quelque intérêt privé, soit celle de tenir l'Algérie à notre merci.

Nous ne sommes donc pas restés dans le vague, le F.L.N. le sait bien. Nous avons proposé, l'autodétermination des treize départements étant chose faite, de régler en accord avec le jeune Etat, s'il doit naître, l'avenir des populations et les modalités d'exploitation des richesses, tout en sauvegardant le strict nécessaire des intérêts économiques de la nation française.

Il reste que, lorsque nous parlons de l'Algérie, nous pensons à l'Algérie tout entière et non pas aux bénéfices de la propagande F.L.N. Je suis bien contraint, en effet, de me demander ce que valent les déclarations d'intentions que nos interlocuteurs font miroiter tant sur l'avenir des Européens en Algérie que sur l'association avec la France, et sur les gestes d'apaisement qui sont si attendus et si désirés. Nous n'avons jamais pu connaître le contenu de telles propositions. Dès la première étape, le F.L.N. a coupé court. Ces révélations qu'ils devaient faire n'étaient-elles donc que du vent? Il faut même aller plus loin. S'agit-il pour le F.L.N. de créer un Etat solide et harmonieux? S'agit-il au contraire de remporter un succès de prestige? Pourquoi ce simulacre de pourparlers? Pourquoi avoir accepté de renouer la négociation pour, soudain, la dénouer? Pourquoi toujours « faire comme si » et « faire croire que » ?

De l'autre côté, on parle maintenant de reprise possible du dialogue, nous ne saurions être les adversaires d'une telle proposition: ce n'est pas nous, en effet, qui avons ajourné *sine die* les pourparlers. Il faudrait tout au moins que nos interlocuteurs acceptent de concevoir l'ensemble des problèmes et du problème. Pour nous, nous n'avons pas besoin d'un temps de réflexion.

Le harcèlement, la guérilla transposés sur le plan politique ne peuvent nous atteindre. Nos nerfs sont bons. Nous suivrons notre ligne: l'Algérie doit pouvoir suivre son destin, nous nous tenons au principe de l'autodétermination, nous en avons pris l'initiative, nous la gardons. Quoi qu'il arrive, nous mettrons tout en œuvre pour que les hommes et les femmes d'Algérie puissent s'exprimer sans craints et construire ensemble leur avenir.

7. Communiqué issued by the National Council of the Algerian Revolution, 28 August 1961[1]

Le Conseil national de la révolution algérienne s'est réuni à Tripoli du 9 au 27 août 1961.

Sur le plan de la lutte, le C.N.R.A. a consacré ses travaux aux moyens de lutte de la révolution algérienne. Les décisions du C.N.R.A. ont notamment porté sur le renforcement de l'action de l'A.L.N.[2] et la mobilisation des masses algériennes l'élévation du niveau de leur lutte et leur encadrement sur le plan politique et social.

Sur le plan extérieur des décisions ont été prises pour étendre l'action de la révolution qui s'inscrit dans une politique de non-engagement. Cette action tend a la mobilisation du maximum de soutien matériel, politique et diplomatique et à affaiblir la position internationale du colonialisme français.

Le C.R.N.A. a précisé le contenu démocratique et social de la lutte du peuple

[1] *Le Monde*, 29 August 1961   [2] Armée de Libération Nationale.

algérien dont les aspirations sont exprimées par le F.L.N. guide de la nation. Ces aspirations tendent à édifier une nation moderne, une économie au service du peuple et une renaissance culturelle.

Le C.N.R.A. a réaffirmé les positions de la révolution algérienne sur les plans maghrébin arabe, africain et afro-asien, positions qui rejoignent les mouvements de libération des peuples du joug colonialiste, de ses vestiges et des structures néo-colonialistes. La révolution algérienne inscrit également sa lutte dans les mouvements d'unification maghrébine, arabe et africaine.

Le C.N.R.A. a souligné l'importance du soutien matériel politique et diplomatique des pays socialistes, d'Afrique, d'Aisie et d'Amérique latine à la révolution algérienne.

Le C.N.R.A. a confirmé les positions de la révolution algérienne sur le problème d'une solution négociée sur la base du droit du peuple algérien à l'independance et à l'autodétermination. Il réaffirme qu'une telle solution est possible dans le cadre des principes fondamentaux sauvegardant l'intégrité de tout le territore algérien et la coopération, sur un pied d'égalité, basée sur le respect de la souveraineté du peuple algérien.

Le C.N.R.A. a souligné sa satisfaction de l'appui apporté au peuple algérien par la plupart des pays africains. Il a discuté des moyens de renforcer la lutte du peuple algérien pour la défense de l'intégrité et de l'unite de son territoire, Sahara compris, et la mise en échec des convoitises extérieures.

8. Statement by the Prime Minister of the Provisional Government of the Algerian Republic, M. Ben Khedda, 24 October 1961[1]

La répression policière et militaire qui s'abat sur le peuple algérien constitue un génocide caractérisé et s'aggrave chaque jour. Les lynchages se multiplient sous l'œil bienveillant de la police et de l'armée colonialiste, tandis que les tortures, les arrestations et les exécutions sommaires continuent comme auparavant.

Cette répression se déchaine maintenant avec une ampleur sans précédent en territoire français. Les patriotes algériens sont tués, arrêtés, expulsés pour avoir manifesté pacifiquement leur volonté de libérer leurs pays et de s'opposer aux mesures de discrimination raciale qu'on leur fait subir.

Les cinq ministres algériens emprisonnés en France font l'objet de mesures vexatoires et humiliantes. Mais tout le poids immense des difficultés et des épreuves ne saurait ne pas être supporté et surmonté quand on est habité par la certitude que l'on est dans la bonne voie et que l'idéal pour lequel on a tout donné est sur le point de triompher.

En cette période d'essor que connait la lutte anticolonialiste, la force irrésistible des mouvements nationaux de libération n'est plus à démontrer. L'indépendance est maintenant universellement admise comme une nécessité historique de notre temps. On ne s'oppose plus à l'indépendance. C'est d'emblée que les peuples colonisés y accèdent les uns après les autres.

Qu'en est-il de l'Algérie? Peut-elle rester pour longtemps encore en dehors de l'évolution générale de l'Afrique et du monde alors que le peuple algérien est l'un de ceux qui ont contribué le plus vaillamment à une telle évolution?

[1] *Le Monde,* 26 October 1961.

Va-t-on laisser se poursuivre indéfiniment une guerre qui entre dans sa huitiéme année et se résigner aux dangereux déferlements qu'elle engendre sans cesse, alors que les conditions d'une paix rapide sont à portée de la main?

Aujourd'hui c'est la France elle-même qui convient que notre cause est fondée et que notre indépendance est non seulement possible mais qu'elle constitue la solution nette et digne du conflit.

Il y a une évolution que nous ne saurions sous-estimer, persuadés que nous sommes qu'elle pourrait, en toute logique, précipiter la fin de la guerre et permettre à la paix de s'instaurer au plus vite.

Il y a deux ans la France proposait le recours à la procédure d'autodétermination, c'est-à-dire au verdict populaire. Le choix d'une telle formule consacrait l'abandon du vieux mythe de « l'Algérie française » et représentait un pas décisif vers une approche plus réaliste du problème algérien. Cette procédure avait essentiellement pour objectif de nous départager d'avec la France en laissant à la consultation populaire le soin de trancher le fond du débat. Pour nous le choix du peuple algérien était fait, et une consultation vraiment libre ne pouvait qu'aboutir à confirmer ce choix: l'indépendance.

La France en revanche, marquait ses préférences pour l'association et ne cachait pas son opposition formelle à l'indépendance conçue par elle-même comme une indépendance-sécession, radicalement incompatible avec toute coopération franco-algérienne.

Mais, depuis, les données du débat se sont profondément modifiées. D'abord, le gouvernement français admet désormais que l'Algérie sera nécessairement indépendante. C'est le chef de l'Etat français qui a souligné récemment que la France ne concevait aucun doute quant à l'issue de la consultation populaire: les Algériens se prononceront pour un Etat souverain et indépendant.

En second lieu, le gouvernement français ne pose plus l'indépendance de l'Algérie comme une solution qui exclut fatalement la coopération, mais une solution raisonnable sur laquelle peut être fondé l'espoir de relations nouvelles et fécondes entre l'Algérie et la France.

Ainsi sur la question fondamentale de l'avenir de l'Algérie, les points de vue français et algérien se sont rapprochés donnant à une eventuelle négociation des bases plus précises et plus sûres.

C'est dans ce contexte qu'on peut s'interroger si la procédure d'autodétermination n'est pas dépassée et s'il n'existe pas un chemin nouveau, plus court et plus aisé pour parvenir à la cessation des hostilités.

Nous pensons quant à nous qu'il est possible aujourd'hui de promouvoir une solution rapide du conflit, et qu'il existe pour y parvenir une méthode qui nous ferait aux uns et aux autres une économie de temps et de sacrifice, et permettrait d'instaurer immédiatement la paix. Cette méthode consisterait à engager des négociations en vue de rechercher un accord sur le principe, les modalités et la date de la proclamation de l'indépendance, ainsi que sur la conclusion d'un cessez-le-feu. Après quoi de nouvelles négociations pourraient s'ouvrir, qui auraient pour objet la définition de nouveaux rapports entre l'Algérie et la France et les garanties aux Français d'Algérie.

Il n'est certes pas dans notre esprit de revenir sur la procédure que nous avions acceptée il y a deux ans mais il s'agirait, et cela dans l'intérêt de la paix de tirer les conséquences de l'évolution récente dans laquelle est entré le problème algérien.   Celui-ci n'est pas une dispute juridique c'est un problème politique qui ne peut se résoudre que dans le cadre d'une négociation directe et efficace. Ce qui est en jeu à l'heure actuelle, ce n'est pas une procédure mais la vie et l'avenir de tout un peuple, mais la paix qui tarde à s'établir et à laquelle nos deux peuples aspirent avec la même force et la même ardeur.

Il est grand temps d'inscrire en termes clairs et urgents la décolonisation de l'Algérie à l'ordre du jour.   Nous savons que la liquidation des structures coloniales soulève des problèmes ardus et nombre de difficultés sérieuses, mais que sont-ils en comparaison des dangers profonds et imprévisibles développés par la continuation de la guerre ?

L'indépendance pour nous est avant tout l'intégrité territoriale de l'Algérie, Sahara compris.   C'est le peuple algérien exerçant sa souveraineté en dehors de toute entrave coloniale.   Pour nous, l'indépendance n'exclut pas la coopération. Elle l'appelle, et cela dans l'intérêt bien compris de nos deux pays.

Pour nous enfin l'indépendance n'est pas la négation du problème posé par les Français d'Algérie, mais bien le point de départ d'une ère nouvelle, où, tout en cessant d'être des super-citoyens d'une époque révolue, ils auront une place place conforme à leur rôle, à leurs dignités d'hommes et à leurs intérêts bien compris.

Les conditions d'une solution pacifique ont mûri.   La méthode que nous proposons peut en accélérer l'avènement.   Si toutefois le gouvernement français continue à estimer que l'autodétermination est encore la meilleure procédure pour parvenir à la paix, nous nous déclarons disposés aujourd'hui, comme hier, à œuvrer pour une solution pacifique sur cette base.

En tout état de cause le G.P.R.A. est prêt à reprendre contact avec le gouvernement français en vue de la reprise de la négociation sur des bases sérieuses.

9.   Press conference given by M. Joxe, 27 October 1961[1] (extracts)

Au début de la conférence de presse qu'il a tenue vendredi soir au Rocher-Noir, M. Louis Joxe, répondant à une première question, a commencé par reprendre les arguments présentés par M. Ben Khedda à l'appui de la nouvelle méthode de négociation en deux temps qu'il préconise, et qui tendent par ailleurs à remettre en question l'autodétermination.

C'est là, une façon de faire qui demande à être analysée de près, car elle spécule en grande partie sur l'impatience légitime des uns et des autres. . . .

. . . Nous sommes transportés sur un autre terrain que ceux que nous avons connus à Evian et à Lugrin.   Qu'attendait-on à Evian et à Lugrin, et qu'a-t-on répété ?   On nous avait dit qu'il y a un seul obstacle: l'intégrité du territoire algérien.   Si cet obstacle était levé, il n'y aurait plus d'objection à examiner, avant de conclure — et je dis bien: avant de conclure, — tous les problèmes qui sont relatifs à la protection des intérêts de la France, parmi lesquels il y a ceux qui concernent la population européenne et la coopération.

Cette déclaration comporte un autre aspect: le principe de l'autodétermination a été exprimé, mis en œuvre, adopté par le peuple français.   Il est devenu la

[1] *Le Monde*, 29/30 October 1961.

loi du peuple français, à la suite du référendum du 8 janvier.[1] Mais il a été, également, reconnu par le F.L.N. dans ses déclarations nombreuses. Il a servi de base à toutes les rencontres. Le voilà maintenant dépassé, selon l'expression même de M. Ben Khedda. Pourquoi? Il est vrai qu'après avoir exposé sa méthode en deux temps le chef du F.L.N. s'est déclaré, aujourd'hui comme hier, disposé à œuvrer pour une solution pacifique sur cette base.

Je me hâte de dire que nous avions nos raisons pour définir l'autodétermination, que nous avions nos raisons pour la préconiser, que nous avons nos raisons pour la maintenir.

Ce principe d'autodétermination est une application du principe des peuples à disposer librement d'eux-mêmes, qui peut nous permettre de régler les problèmes que nous avons devant nous, y compris celui du Sahara.

Je dis d'autre part que ce principe d'autodétermination est la seule méthode qui permette d'asseoir les fondements d'un Etat démocratique en permettant à tous de s'exprimer et en assurant un état de paix qui soit reconnu par les uns et par les autres. C'est le seul moyen qui permette à des hommes d'origines différentes de vivre dans la concorde. C'est le seul moyen de faire connaitre et admettre par une minorité une solution.

Si nous abandonnions ce principe, au lieu de gagner du temps nous en perdrions. Si nous acceptions de diviser la négociation en deux parts, nous abandonnerions à l'aventure l'une des familles qui constituent l'Algérie, je veux dire les Européens. Et comme on nous dit qu'ils sont des Algériens comme les autres, ils ont droit de savoir comment sera défini leur avenir.

S'il est vrai, comme l'a dit M. Ben Khedda, que les points de vue français et algériens se sont rapprochés depuis quelque temps et qu'ils mènent à une prochaine négociation sur des bases plus précises et plus sûres, l'ensemble des questions qui forment le problème algérien doit pouvoir être évoqué rapidement et réglé dans les plus brefs délais.

Unee caractère original du problème algérien ne permet pas d'utiliser les méthodes qui ont servi pour les autres pays d'Afrique.

Nous restons fidèles à deux idées:

1) Appliquer l'autodétermination, ce qui consiste à rechercher un règlement d'ensemble dans une Algérie unitaire, où les deux communautés puissent vivre en harmonie;

2) Fonder ainsi la paix par la fin des combats. Voilà ce que m'inspire la déclaration de M. Ben Khedda. Entre les deux méthodes soumises à l'examen, nous maintenons la nôtre.

Les options définies le 16 septembre 1959[2] par le général de Gaulle restent les mêmes. Il est certain que nous recherchons la constitution d'un Etat où la coopération des deux communautés soit possible et qui vive en association avec la France . . . Il est clair que la plupart des Européens, même ceux qui s'adonnent au monologue du plastic, veulent rester dans ce pays et que les musulmans dans leur grande majorité estiment que les Européens doivent rester. Ce que je dis là, je l'ai entendu dire en de nombreux points de l'Algérie.

Quant au partage, quant au regroupement, quant au départ, ce peuvent être les nécessités, les circonstances. Ce ne sont pas forcément des solutions durables

---

[1] For which, see above, p. 782.　　　　　[2] *Documents*, 1959, pp. 533–7.

ni acceptables. Créér deux Algéries opposées l'une à l'autre, nous ne cherchons pas à en arriver là. Nous avons proposé tous les moyens qui permettent d'éviter une solution dans la peur . . . Il est hélas! des fois où nécessité fait loi, mais nous ne voudrions pas en arriver là.

Puis le ministre est revenu sur les négociations d'Evian et de Lugrin.

A Evian et à Lugrin les difficultés essentielles ont porté sur trois points d'une importance capitale. Le premier portait sur la conception que nous avions sur le champ d'application de l'autodétermination. Cela signifiait la question du Sahara. Nous avons toujours déclaré que la question était complexe et qu'il fallait distinguer trois choses: le sol, les hommes et les ressources.

Le second point portait sur la question des Européens et des musulmans attachés à la France. Nous avons le devoir d'assurer à ces populations des garanties complètes.

Le troisième point était le rétablissement de la paix.

Je reprends ces trois points. En ce qui concerne le champ d'application de l'autodétermination, le général de Gaulle a répondu pour le Sahara qu'il fallait tenir compte des réalités et de nos intérêts, tels que le pétrole et nos liaisons avec l'Afrique noire.

Restent les deux autres points. Le rétablissement de la paix . . . On nous a dit que tout progrès vers un accord politique amènerait à la paix. Nous sommes prêts. Nous n'avons pas encore reçu de précision sur ce point.

Sur l'autre question, celle des Européens, on avait des précisions à apporter, a-t-on dit. Nous les attendons encore. Et là aussi nous sommes prêts.

Alors M. Joxe a parlé en ces termes des Européens d'Algérie:

On ne perd pas la nationalité française, sauf quand on le demande. Ce qui est vrai aussi, c'est que tout Français continue à participer à la communauté française quand il est sur le territoire national.

Mais on peut être un bon Français et avoir envie d'être un bon citoyen algérien. On peut en tant qu'Algérien vivre avec les mêmes garanties que les autres Algériens, sans qu'il soit question d'aucune discrimination. Il n'y a là rien qui ne soit conforme au bon sens et au droit.

Leur avenir doit être aussi assuré . . . Ils doivent pouvoir participer à la gestion du pays. Ils doivent être sûrs de garder leur originalité, leur langue, leurs croyances, leurs méthodes d'enseignement, avoir des garanties pour leurs biens et leurs intérêts privés. Ils doivent être assurés de pouvoir constituer une sorte d'association permanente qui leur donne la possibilité de conserver leurs droits.

Bien entendu, il s'agit là de propositions qui devraient être faites à l'Algérie, ratifiées par l'Algérie, garanties non seulement par une association entre la France et l'Algérie, mais par une série de précautions et de transitions indispensables avec une certaine prudence.

Je n'oublie ni les musulmans attachés à la France, ni le sort des travailleurs musulmans en France, qui doivent être traités naturellement dans le même esprit et selon le même droit.

Interrogé sur la création éventuelle d'un « exécutif provisoire ». M. Joxe a répondu:

Il se peut, si les choses se passent comme elles pourraient se passer, que dans les transitions nécessaires il soit bon et juste de faire apparaitre une sorte d'auto-rité provisoire. Ce serait seulement si nous étions arrivés à nous entendre sur le plan politique, donc au moment de passer à l'autodétermination. Nous n'en sommes pas.

Il y aurait intérêt, pour préparer à l'autodétermination, à grouper des hommes, représentant les différentes tendances aux côtés du délégué général, et l'autorité de la France restant intacte.

Il ne serait pas exclu que cette autorité provisoire s'accompagne de la créa-tion d'une force de l'ordre avec des missions bien déterminées et qui veillerait à ce que les suffrages soient exprimés dans des conditions normales. Le tout, naturellement, sous l'autorité de la France.

. . . On a confondu mon travail quotidien, mes consultations — aujourd'hui j'ai rencontré les présidents et vice-présidents des conseils généraux — avec la création de l'exécutif provisoire.

Plusieurs questions furent ensuite posées au ministre d'Etat. Ainsi:

Dans l'état des choses, voyez-vous une possibilité de prochaine reprise des négociations?

— Etant donné le discours de M. Ben Khedda et étant donné ce que nous-mêmes avions dit, après la séparation de Lugrin, que nous ne fermions pas la porte, la chose est possible.

— Le but d'une tendance de l'O.A.S. semble être d'accéder à la représentati-vité des Européens, qu'en pensez-vous?

— Il faut voir ce qu'il y a dans la tête de celui qui s'est révolté et qui cherche à se séparer de la France. Pensez-vous que l'O.A.S. veuille se séparer de la France?

A propos des « moyens d'expression » en Algérie et des éventuelles manifesta-tions du 1er novembre, le ministre a déclaré: Il y a mille moyens pacifiques de s'exprimer. C'est surtout la volonté d'expression qui manque . . . L'ordre sera, je crois, maintenu partout.

M. Joxe évoqua d'autre part les appels à la réconciliation lancés ces derniers jours. Ce qui s'est passé à Saïda, où des hommes de bonne volonté se sont groupés pour lancer des appels au calme, et dans le Constantinois, ainsi qu'à Mostaganem et à Orléansville, ce mouvement, simple dans ses données, on ne saurait trop l'encourager. Ces musulmans épris d'un besoin de justice, de dignité et d'indépendance répètent que les Européens peuvent vivre avec eux. Cela, on ne peut pas le négliger. Comme on ne peut pas négliger ce que disent les Européens, s'ils expriment leur fidélité à cette terre, à l'œuvre accompli par leurs pères.

(b) Tunisia and Bizerta

1. Joint communiqué issued by President de Gaulle and the Tunisian President, M. Bourguiba, 27 February 1961[1]

Le général de Gaulle, président de la République française, et M. Habib Bourguiba, président de la République tunisienne, se sont rencontrés le 27 février au château de Rambouillet. Ils ont eu des entretiens prolongés auxquels ont

---

[1] *La Documentation Française, Articles et Documents*, 2 March 1961.

été associés le premier ministre français, les ministres des affaires étrangères et le ministre de l'information tunisien.

Tous les problèmes qui intéressent les deux pays ont été passés en revue dans un esprit de franchise et de compréhension réciproques. Il s'est agi notamment des relations franco-tunisiennes. Les interlocuteurs ont pris note avec satisfaction de l'amélioration intervenue à cet égard et qui doit permettre d'envisager favorablement la solution des problèmes encore en suspens.

La question algérienne a été évoquée largement, à la lumière des récents développements et dans la perspective de l'avenir de l'Afrique du Nord. Le général de Gaulle et le président Bourguiba ont été d'accord pour constater les possibilités et l'espoir qui existent désormais d'une évolution positive et rapide.

Les deux présidents ont partagé la même émotion au sujet de la mort du roi du Maroc et ont souligné que leurs deux pays s'associaient au deuil de la nation marocaine.

Les questions internationales qui intéressent la France et la Tunisie dans les différentes régions du monde ont été examinées. Le général de Gaulle et le président Bourguiba ont constaté à quel point leurs conceptions générales étaient proches.

2. M. Bourguiba to President de Gaulle, 6 July 1961[1]

Monsieur le Président,

Une situation grave et qu'il nous faut rapidement redresser pour sauver les relations entre nos deux pays, m'impose de vous adresser, sans délai, un message de caractère exceptionnel. J'ai chargé mon plus proche collaborateur de vous le remettre.

J'ai consacré trente années de ma vie à lutter pour une coopération libre entre la Tunisie et la France. Cela m'autorise, je pense, à affirmer hautement chaque fois que les circonstances l'exigent, qu'il y a une choque que je place au-dessus de cette coopération et, en vérité, au-dessus de tout: la souveraineté complète de la Tunisie, sans limitation autre que librement consentie.

Or la Tunisie, qui a recouvré sa souveraineté interne et externe le 20 mars 1956[2] continue, plus de cinq ans après, à être dans l'impossibilité de l'exercer sur l'ensemble de son territorire et ce contre la volonté de son peuple et de son gouvernement, clairement et publiquement exprimée en toutes circonstances, dûment communiquée au gouvernement français par la voie diplomatique, et présentée par moi à vous même le 27 février dernier.

En dépit de ces demandes réitérées, la France, s'est refusée, jusqu'ici, à admettre le principe de l'évacuation et d'envisager sérieusement le retrait de ses forces de la base de Bizerte et de nos territoires du Sud.

Au cours de l'entretien que j'ai eu l'honneur d'avoir avec vous le 27 février dernier à Rambouillet, je vous ai moi-même exposé notre position sur ce point: l'objectif de la Tunisie est d'obtenir, dans les délais les plus rapides, l'évacuation

---

[1] *La Documentation Française, Articles et Documents*, 3 August 1961. An English text is printed in S.C.O.R., Sixteenth Year, Supplement for July, August, and September 1961, pp. 18–20.

[2] *Documents*, 1956, pp. 692–3.

complète par les troupes françaises de la base de Bizerte et de la zone frontalière du Sud Tunisien. Je vous ai proposé, pour atteindre cet objectif, l'ouverture de négociations pour fixer les modalités et le calendrier de cette évacuation. J'ai enfin exprimé, devant vous, la conviction que cette dernière séquelle de l'ère coloniale levée par voie amiable, les relations entre nos deux pays se renforceraient immédiatement puisque la base de Bizerte elle-même et l'arsenal voisin pourraient être reconvertis, en coopération avec la France, en un chantier naval disposant d'installations industrielles précieuses pour le développement du potentiel économique de la Tunisie.

Récemment encore, voyant qu'aucune suite n'était donnée à ces propositions j'ai été amené à prier le Représentant de la France à Tunis d'exprimer à votre Excellence mon inquiétude devant l'attitude du Gouvernement français.

Je me permets de vous rappeler que le 25 janvier 1960[1] devant le comportement toujours négatif de la France et l'ampleur des réactions de l'opinion tunisienne, j'ai annoncé la décision du Gouvernement d'engager la bataille de l'évacuation, bataille que je souhaitais toute pacifique à partir du 8 février suivant, deuxième anniversaire du bombardement de Sakiet. Vous savez dans quelles conditions et dans quel esprit, à la suite de l'affaire des barricades d'Alger, j'ai pris sur moi la grave responsabilité de stopper l'élan du peuple en attendant la solution de la crise française, dans l'espoir toujours vivace, qu'une fois cette épreuve surmontée, une solution amiable du problème qui nous divise serait plus facilement réalisée.

Or, aujourd'hui, au lieu de la solution espérée, nous constatons que le Gouvernement français ou tout au moins le commandant français de Bizerte fait procéder dans la zone en question à des travaux de génie sous forme d'allongement de la piste d'atterrissage en vue de permettre l'utilisation de nouveaux types d'avion ce qui revient à augmenter le potentiel militaire de la base.

Ce fait nouveau apparait grave dans la mesure ou il trahit sans conteste la volonté des autorités française de s'installer dans le statu-quo et même de l'aggrave. Le peuple tunisien et moi-même, ne pouvons le prendre que comme la preuve que le Gouvernement français semble faire fi de notre dignité nationale, ne prend pas au sérieux notre juste revendication et ne croit pas beaucoup à notre détermination à réaliser coûte que coûte la libération de notre territoire national.

Dans ces conditions, je suis obligé de porter à votre connaissance. Monsieur le Président, notre décision ferme et irrévocable de voir mettre un terme à cette situation contre laquelle le peuple tunisien est unanimement dressé.

Si comme je veux encore l'espérer le principe de l'évacuation est admis par le Gouvernement français, les contacts nécessairés pour en préciser les modalités pourront avoir lieu le plus tôt possible.

Je vous confirme enfin que nous voulons en ce qui nous concerne faire en sorte que ce qui est aujourd'hui cause de litige soit, demain, le point de départ d'une coopération libre et fructueuse entre nos deux pays.

La Tunisie a montré beaucoup de compréhension et de bonne volonté tout au long du processus qui conduit à substituer des rapports normaux à ceux de l'ère coloniale que vous avez vous-même, Monsieur le Président, et à maintes

[1] *Le Monde*, 27 January 1960.

reprises déclaré révolue. Elle a apporté, de diverses manières, sa contribution au mûrissement, puis à la solution, aujourd'hui en vue, du conflit algérien. Elle n'a jamais cédé à la « frénésie ».

Dans le vaste mouvement de décolonisation elle a pris la tête du peloton: elle ne peut, aujourd'hui, sans mettre en danger sa position, son autorité et ses intérêts vitaux continuer à supporter des empiètements sur sa souveraineté et des atteintes à son intégrité territoriale.

Vous-même, Monsieur le Président, avez suffisamment souligné combien « il est intolérable à un Etat que son destin soit laissé à l'action et à la décision d'un autre Etat quelque amical qu'il puisse être », pour que vous compreniez aisément notre sentiment et notre décision.

Nous savons, vous et moi, que les bases militaires dans des pays étrangers prolongent une ère dépassée, et que, partout, les grandes puissances et la France elle-même y renoncent. Nous savons aussi que l'entreprise de décolonisation entamée doit être achevée; qu'elle n'est pas pour affaiblir nos liens, mais pour les renforcer; que c'est en renonçant aux ultimes aspects de la domination qu'on obtient la vraie coopération.

L'homme qui, lui aussi, a donné le meilleur de lui-même pour restaurer l'indépendance de son pays et qui veut, de son côté, consacrer ses derniers efforts au redressement de sa patrie, à son progrès et à son rayonnement, vous adjure de faire en sorte que de nouvelles et inutiles épreuves soient épargnées à nos deux pays.

3. The French Embassy in Tunis to the Tunisian Government, 18 July 1961[1]

Au cours de la déclaration qu'il a faite le 17 juillet[2] à Tunis devant l'Assemblée nationale le président de la République tunisienne a indiqué qu'à partir du 19 juillet des dispositions seraient prises pour « reprendre la bataille au point où il l'avait laissée le 17 juin 1959 avec les moyens et les procédés mis en œuvre au lendemain de l'affaire de Sakiet ».

Le gouvernement français a déjà marqué dans les communications, faites par le chargé d'affaires de France le 13 et le 16 juillet qu'une solution au problème de Bizerte ne saurait être recherchée dans une atmosphère de passion ni sous la menace de manifestations populaires.

Si au contraire la situation devenait normale, sans menace ni mise en demeure, une réponse serait adressée au message que le président Bourguiba a fait remettre au général de Gaulle le 7 juillet.[3]

Le gouvernement français ne peut que constater que les mesures annoncées par le président de la République tunisienne visent non pas au rétablissement d'une situation normale, mais bien au contraire à une aggravation de la tension.

Il tient à mettre en garde de la manière la plus sérieuse le gouvernement tunisien contre les consequences possibles d'une telle tentative. Celle-ci, au surplus, ne peut avoir pour effet que de retarder toute discussion au sujet de la

---

[1] *La Documentation Française, Articles et Documents*, 3 August 1961.
[2] *Le Monde*, 19 July 1961. English text in *The Battle for Evacuation, Bizerta and the South* (Tunisian Secretariat for Information and Tourism), pp. 7–27.
[3] Above, p. 998. The message was actually sent on 6 July.

base de Bizerte, discussion qui a été prévue par l'échange de lettres du 17 juin 1959,[1] et dont le gouvernement français persiste à souhaiter l'ouverture.

Devant les menaces de plus en plus pressantes dont la base de Bizerte est l'objet, le gouvernement français est contraint de prendre toutes dispositions pour assurer l'inviolabilité des installations aussi bien que la liberté de communication entre celles-ci.

Le gouvernement français a relevé d'autre part que dans son discours précité le président de la République tunisienne avait annoncé que des éléments de l'armée tunisienne franchiraient la frontière du Sahara en direction de Garet-el-Hamel.

Il ne peut ici encore qu'attirer l'attention du gouvernement tunisien sur la gravité d'une telle incursion au-delà de la frontière tunisienne, à laquelle les forces françaises stationnées dans la région ne pourraient que s'opposer.

Le gouvernement français demeure profondément désireux d'éviter tout incident. Il est contraint de rejeter à l'avance sur les autorités tunisiennes la responsabilité de tout acte de violence. Il espère que le gouvernement tunisien voudra bien mesurer les dangers de la situation et éviter toute action de nature à l'aggraver.

Le gouvernement français est obligé également de déclarer que l'action annoncée par le gouvernement tunisien risque de compromettre gravement la coopération franco-tunisienne dans tous les domaines, coopération dont pourtant le président de la République tunisienne a tenu à dire dans son discours qu'il y demeurait attaché en même temps qu'à l'amitié entre les deux pays.

Le gouvernement français ne peut concevoir comment le maintien de cette coopération, à laquelle il est lui aussi attaché, pourrait se concilier avec les tentatives de force qui sont maintenant annoncées et qui font l'objet de la présente note.

4. Security Council resolution, adopted 22 July 1961[2]

The Security Council,
Considering the gravity of the situation prevailing in Tunisia,
Pending the conclusion of the debate of the item on its agenda,

1. *Calls for* an immediate cease-fire and a return of all armed forces to their original position;

2. *Decides* to continue the debate.

5. The French Government to the Tunisian Government, 28 July 1961[3]

Après l'accord du 20 mars 1956,[4] par lequel la France a mis un terme au traité du Bardo et reconnu l'indépendance de la Tunisie, et avant l'ordre d'evacuation

---

[1] *Documents*, 1958, pp. 400–1.
[2] S.C.O.R., Sixteenth Year, Supplement for July, August, and September 1961, p. 25. S/4882, sponsored by Liberia. Two other draft resolutions, one sponsored by Liberia and the United Arab Republic, one by Britain and the United States, were both defeated. Texts in ibid., pp. 22–23.
[3] *La Documentation Française, Articles et Documents*, 26 August 1961, pp. 1–2. The treaty of Bardo, signed in 1881, established the French presence in Tunisia. Text in *British and Foreign State Papers 1880–1881*, vol. 72, pp. 247–9 (London, William Ridgway, 1888).
[4] *Documents*, 1956, pp. 692–3.

donné par le général de Gaulle aux troupes françaises présentes en Tunisie, exception faite de la base de Bizerte, il fut convenu, le 17 juin 1958,[1] entre les gouvernements de Tunis et de Paris, que le régime de la base serait réglé d'un commun accord.

En ce qui concerne la France, la base n'a d'intérêt qu'au point de vue de sa sécurité dans l'actuelle et dangereuse conjoncture internationale. Mais, à cet égard, Bizerte peut du jour au lendemain prendre une grande importance en raison de sa situation géographique exceptionnelle à l'entrée de la Méditerranée occidentale.

L'occupation par des forces hostiles, ou simplement menaçantes, de ce point stratégique majeur pourrait avoir de graves conséquences quant à la défense de la France et de l'Occident. C'est pour parer à une telle éventualité que la France, dans toutes les discussions survenues avec la Tunisie, et faute qu'aucun accord de défense ait pu être conclu entre les deux pays, a toujours réservé la possibilité d'utiliser la base aussi longtemps que le danger mondial est ce qu'il est. Toutefois, la France était et demeure disposée à régler avec la Tunisie les conditions dans lesquelles la base serait utilisée pendant cette période dangereuse. Au cours des entretiens que le Président de la République tunisienne a eus à Paris le 27 février 1961 avec le Président de la République française,[2] celui-ci a nettement précisé la position de la France sans qu'il en soit alors résulté aucune tension dans les rapports. Bien au contraire, tout donnait à penser au gouvernement de Paris que du côté tunisien ces rapports étaient désormais engagés dans la voie d'une amicale coopération.

C'est alors que le gouvernement de Tunis, changeant brusquement d'attitude, a prétendu obtenir par la menace, puis par l'agression, que la France accepte d'évacuer la base et que la date du départ de ses forces soit fixée. En même temps le gouvernement de Tunis faisait envahir le territoire et attaquer les postes français au Sahara. Mais l'action de force qu'il entreprenait sur les deux théâtres aboutissait pour lui à un double échec.

A présent le gouvernement tunisien tente d'obtenir par une intervention de l'Organisation des Nations Unies ce qu'il n'a pu réussir par les armes.

Il est nécessaire de faire connaître que la France n'a aucunement l'intention de régler l'affaire suivant une telle procédure. Quelles que puissent être éventuellement la tournure et la conclusion des débats qui s'engagent sur un pareil forum, la France, devant les grands périls que comporte pour elle la menace du conflit mondial, compte tenu des responsabilités qui sont les siennes dans ce domaine, étant donnés les engagements conclus naguère entre elle et la Tunisie, eu égard enfin à la nécessité d'interdire toute invasion de son territoire au Sahara, entend rester juge de sa propre sécurité.

En fait comme en droit, la voie qui peut conduire à la solution de cette déplorable affaire est celle des négociations directes que la France continue de proposer à la Tunisie.

---

[1] ibid., 1958, pp. 400–1.   [2] Above, p. 797.

6. The French Government to the Tunisian Government, 17 August 1961[1]

Un communiqué du 28 juillet[2] a précisé la position du gouvernement français au sujet de la base de Bizerte. Il a été indiqué que la seule voie susceptible de conduire à une solution était celle de négociations directes entre la France et la Tunisie.

Il est indispensable, dans une première étape, de discuter des arrangements nécessaires pour revenir à Bizerte à une situation plus normale. Acceptée le 23 juillet, en principe, par les autorités tunisiennes, cette discussion n'a pu cependant être engagée par suite du refus opposé par Tunis aux offres faites du côté français.

Ces offres ont été renouvelées le 11 août. A cette date la représentation suisse à Tunis qui est chargée des intérêts français en Tunisie a, sur la demande du gouvernement français, fait savoir au secrétaire d'Etat aux affaires étrangères tunisien que Paris était disposé à engager des pourparlers en vue d'aboutir aux arrangements visés.

Ces arrangements pourraient porter aussi sur les problèmes concernant la libération éventuelle des Tunisiens faits prisonniers par les forces françaises et des ressortissants français détenus dans l'enemble du territoire tunisien.

Si le gouvernement tunisien acceptait le principe de telles discussions, le gouvernement français était prêt en ce qui concerne la procédure à considérer les propositions qui pourraient lui être faites.

En même temps, le gouvernement français décidait de rappeler l'un des régiments qui avaient été envoyés en renforts à Bizerte le 20 juillet.

Le gouvernement tunisien a décliné les offres ainsi faites. Il a fait savoir à Paris, par l'intermédiaire de l'ambassade de Suède, qui assume la représentation de ses intérêts en France, qu'il n'estimait pas opportun d'engager des pourparlers à seule fin de faciliter un retour à une situation plus normale à Bizerte. La communication du gouvernement tunisien précise qu'une reprise de contact avec le gouvernement français n'est utile que dans la mesure où l'accord est déjà réalisé sur le principe d'une solution définitive du problème fondamental, objet du conflit.

Le gouvernement tunisien ajoute qu'il est prêt à discuter sur les modalités et le calendrier de l'évacuation des forces françaises de l'ensemble du territoire tunisien. Autrement dit, le gouvernement tunisien refuse de discuter des moyens de rétablir une situation pacifique à Bizerte tant que le résultat de la négociation générale n'est pas acquis d'avance. Il revient à sa position primitive lorsqu'il exigeait que satisfaction lui soit donnée sans délai sous la menace, par la suite mise à effet, d'une agression armée à Bizerte et au Sahara.

Le gouvernement français ne peut que prendre acte de cette attitude en rappelant que, dans le même temps, le gouvernement tunisien maintient, malgré des protestations répétées, la plupart des mesures arbitraires et contraires au droit des gens qu'il a prises depuis le 19 juillet et qui affectent gravement la liberté et les intérêts des ressortissants français résidant en Tunisie.

[1] *La Documentation Française*, *Articles et Documents*, 26 August 1961.
[2] Above, p. 801.

7. The Tunisian Government to the French Government, 17 August 1961[1]

Le communiqué français publié cette nuit au sujet des derniers développements du conflit franco-tunisien appelle la mise au point suivante:

L'allégation que le gouvernement tunisien a refusé da prendre en considération une offre du gouvernement français tendant au « retour » à des conditions plus normales à Bizerte est absolument sans fondement.

En effet, le gouvernement tunisien a fait connaître au gouvernement français, par l'entremise de l'ambassade de Suède à Paris, que s'il n'estime pas « opportun » d'engager avec le gouvernement français des pourparlers à seule fin de faciliter un retour à une situation plus normale à Bizerte, il préfère laisser au gouvernement français sa complète initiative en la matière. Il est toutefois précisé que si le gouvernement français est disposé à retirer ses forces armées sur leurs bases initiales, le gouvernement tunisien n'y fera pas obstacle. A cet égard des instructions ont été données aux autorités locales qualifiées pour que « les mouvements ayant trait à cette opération ne soient pas entravés ». Contrairement aux affirmations du communiqué français, les autorités tunisiennes ne se sont jamais refusées à considérer des offres qui, au surplus, ne leur ont pas été présentées.

Par contre, le gouvernement tunisien estime toujours qu'il ne peut suivre le gouvernement français dans la voie que ce dernier semble rechercher, à savoir la discussion d'arrangements destinés à garantir le *statu quo ante*. Le gouvernement tunisien ne peut consentir à une procédure qu'il juge sans issue. Il est souligné enfin que les pourparlers envisagés dans la communication française du 11 août 1961 ne sauraient nullement constituer, ainsi que le laisse entendre le gouvernement français, une ouverture, encore moins une première étape vers la discussion d'un règlement définitif du problème de fond. Le dernier communiqué du gouvernement français ne laisse pas le moindre doute: il se refuse systématiquement à toute discussion loyale et constructive.

Le gouvernement tunisien ne peut quant à lui que réitérer sa proposition d'engager avec le gouvernement français des pourparlers en vue de mettre au point les modalités et le calendrier de l'évacuation des forces françaises de l'ensemble du territoire tunisien.

8. Resolution adopted by the General Assembly of the United Nations, 25 August 1961[2]

The General Assembly,

Having examined the grave situation prevailing in Tunisia since 19 July 1961 which was the subject matter of Security Council consideration in its meetings of 21, 22, 28 and 29 July 1961,[3]

Noting with concern and regret that France has not fully complied with the provisions of the interim resolution adopted by the Security Council on 22 July 1961,[4]

---

[1] *La Documentation Française, Articles et Documents,* 26 August 1961.
[2] G.A.O.R., Third Special Session, Supplement No. 1, p. 2.
[3] S.C.O.R., Sixteenth Year, 961st to 966th meetings.
[4] Above, p. 801.

Noting that the Security Council has failed to take further appropriate action,
Convinced that the presence of French armed forces in Tunisian territory against the express will of the Tunisian Government and people constitutes a violation of Tunisia's sovereignty, is a permanent source of international friction and endangers international peace and security,

1. *Reaffirms* the Security Council's interim resolution and urges the Government of France to implement fully the provisions of operative paragraph 1 thereof;

2. *Recognizes* the sovereign right of Tunisia to call for the withdrawal of all French armed forces present on its territory without its consent;

3. *Calls upon* the Governments of France and Tunisia to enter into immediate negotiations to devise peaceful and agreed measures in accordance with the principles of the Charter of the United Nations for the withdrawal of all French armed forces from Tunisian territory.

9. President Bourguiba's press conference, 8 September 1961[1] (extract)

. . . Je laisse les questions du passé à l'Histoire et je dis qu'il ressort de la conférence du Général de Gaulle,[2] de ce qu'il a dit sur Bizerte, que la situation peut évoluer vers une solution raisonnable du conflit. L'impression que j'ai indiquée à Belgrade[3] a été confirmée quand j'ai lu le texte intégral de la conférence de presse. Evidemment, il n'est pas possible au Général de Gaulle de se déjuger complètement et nous n'avons jamais cherché à lui faire perdre la face. Ce n'est pas dans nos habitudes et ce n'est pas l'intérêt de la Tunisie. Le moyen, pour lui, de s'en sortir, c'est de dire: je ne quitterai pas la base dans les circonstances actuelles, dans l'état de tension actuel, dans la période dangereuse actuelle. Cette précision, je constate qu'il l'a apportée textuellement plusieurs fois dans sa conférence de presse. Il y revient à plusieurs reprises sous toutes sortes de formes. Sous la réserve que l'on peut se tromper et qu'il peut vouloir dire tant qu'il y a la guerre froide, tant qu'il y a possibilités de conflit entre l'Est et l'Ouest; auquel cas, je me serais trompé sur les intentions du Général de Gaulle. Avec lui, on n'est jamais sûr. Mais je crois que cette façon d'insister sur le caractère précaire de la présence militaire française à Bizerte, c'est une façon de préparer le retrait des troupes dès que cette situation dangereuse, cet état de crise actuel, surtout à propos de Berlin, serait dépassé.

Voilà ce que je comprends, comment je veux interpreter cette insistance de la part du Général de Gaulle. Je veux lui accorder le préjugé favourable d'une telle interprétation et agir en conséquence, quitte, si je m'aperçois que je me suis trompé — et je ne serais pas très long à m'en apercevoir — à reprendre le lutte. Le Général de Gaulle sait très bien, de même que le peuple français et le monde entier, que pour ce qui concerne le retrait des troupes françaises, je n'en démordrai pas, que la lutte continuera sous toutes sortes de formes et que la paix ne se fera entre la France et nous qu'une fois que nous serons débarrassés de cette dernière séquelle de l'ère coloniale en Tunisie.

[1] *Conference de Presse de Monsieur le Président de la République Tunisienne* (Tunisian Secretariat for Information and Tourism), pp. 11–16.
[2] For the de Gaulle press conference of 5 September, see above, pp. 110–8.
[3] In a radio and television interview recorded in Belgrade; see *N. Y. Times*, 7 September 1961.

C'est pour cela que nous acceptons le processus qu'il a indiqué en ce qui concerne la solution du problème de Bizerte: la discussion d'un modus-vivendi pour éviter tous ces incidents, ces accrochages, cette situation précaire qui peut à chaque instant déboucher sur une catastrophe; entamer ensuite des négociations sur « les conditions d'utilisation de la base dans la période dangereuse que traverse le monde actuellement.» Cela ne peut pas dépasser la crise de Berlin. Nous pouvons la fixer dans le temps; il est exclu qu'elle soit laissée à l'appréciation du Général de Gaulle, des seules autorités françaises. Je fais un pari et j'accepte ce processus comme étant le prélude, le commencement d'une discussion qui, une fois dépassée la période dangereuse que traverse le monde actuellement — et elle le sera certainement dans quelques semaines — pourra aborder le vrai problème, le problème du retrait des troupes françaises.

Or ce problème, pour la première fois dans cette même conférence de presse, le Général de Gaulle le pose formellement. Dans une phase incidente, selon sa manière, mais il est posé. En parlant de la souveraineté sur Bizerte, il dit: « Du côté du Tunis, nous pouvons penser que tout en proclamant la souveraineté de la Tunisie sur Bizerte, souveraineté qui n'a jamais été contestée en principe du côté français et qui ne l'est pas, et tout en déclarant qu'il faudrait qu'un jour soit négocié le retrait des troupes françaises, on comprenait que la situation générale ne comportait pas actuellement cette issue. »

Devant cet ensemble d'affirmations réunies, je vous dis et je dis au peuple tunisien: j'accepte de faire ce pari. Je ne pose pas de préalables qui pourraient comporter des concessions d'amour-propre. Du moment qu'on envisage le retrait des troupes françaises, qu'on parle d'une situation dangereuse mais provisoire, j'accepte le pari d'engager la discussion pour normaliser la situation à Bizerte, envisager un modus-vivendi pour l'utilisation de la base dans cette période dangereuse que les négociations fixeront d'une façon précise, pour ensuite aborder la négociation qu'il faudra un jour ouvrir en vue du retrait des troupes françaises de la totalité du territoire tunisien. D'abord de Bizerte où la souveraineté tunisienne n'a jamais été contestée jusqu'à maintenant et de la borne 233 en vertu des accords de frontières qui ont été signés par les autorités françaises représentant la Tunisie.[1]

Je crois qu'on ne peut montrer plus de bonne volonté pour faciliter les choses et éviter de prolonger des situation pénibles qui ne peuvent que faire du tort aussi bien à la France qu'à la Tunisie. Dans cet esprit des contacts seront pris entre les Affaires Etrangères tunisiennes et le Consulat de France.

Je ne vois pas d'inconvénient à un échange de prisonniers qui pourrait se faire à partir de demain par l'intermédiaire de la Croix Rouge et du Croissant Rouge. Evidemment, les déserteurs de la Légion Etrangère, il n'est pas de tradition qu'on les réclame. Ils appartiennent à cinq ou six nationalités et seront rendus comme c'est la coutume à leurs représentants diplomatiques. Pour ceux qui ont été fait prisonniers ou qui sont détenus dans les camps d'internement, ils seront libérés après accord sur les modalités, la date, etc., de façon

---

[1] Boundary marked 233 was claimed by Tunisia as the extreme limit of its frontier with Libya. The frontier agreement referred to was signed in 1910 between France and the Ottoman Empire. For further details, see Bourguiba's speech of 17 July 1961 in *The Battle for Evacuation, Bizerta and the South* (Tunisian Secretariat for Information and Tourism), pp. 18–19.

que les choses se passent sans aucune difficulté. En ce qui concerne les français condamnés de droit commun pour port d'armes prohibées, par exemple, ils n'entrent pas dans le cadre de l'échange de prisonniers. Lorsque les négociations auront réussi, pour créer le climat d'apaisement, nous envisagerons volontiers des mesures de grâce ou de libération conditionnelle en faveur de ceux qui seront encore en prison.

Voici une autre manifestation de bonne volonté qui, je l'espère, sera appréciée à sa juste valeur par les autorités françaises: nous autorisons nos étudiants en France à aller passer leurs examens devant leurs professeurs des Universités françaises. Vous savez que j'ai toujours souhaité tenir en dehors des vicissitudes politiques nos relations culturelles, notre coopération culturelle avec la France. C'est parce que la Mission culturelle fait partie de l'Ambassade que nous avons été contraints de la fermer à partir du moment où nous avons rompu les relations diplomatiques avec la France. Mais j'ai toujours souhaité que ces questions là restent au-dessus et en dehors.

Les problèmes de Bizerte, du Sahara, les difficultés, les heurts, laisseront évidemment des traces qu'il ne sera pas facile d'effacer. Les blessures laisseront des cicatrices. Mais c'est tout de même une page que nous essayerons de tourner. Nous ferons de notre mieux non pas seulement pour la tourner nous-mêmes — nous avons suffisamment de volonté pour dominer nos colères — mais pour la faire tourner par le peuple tunisien. C'est pour cela qu'en pleine bataille, dans la réunion de Médenine, j'ai eu le courage — et il est réel, je vous assure — de parler de coopération nécessaire avec la France et avec les Français une fois qu'on aura tourné cette page douloureuse de notre histoire.

Je souhaite que je n'aurai plus à faire de conférence de presse sur ce sujet. L'Histoire dira comment les choses se sont passées. Je souhaite que d'ici lundi on aura mis le problème sur les rails qui doivent mener à une solution véritable dans le respect de la souveraineté tunisienne, du prestige de la France, une solution qui, par dessus les secousses et les remous, laisse la voie toujours ouverte à une coopération sur le pied d'égalité aussi bien dans le domaine économique que dans le domaine culturel avec le peuple français.

D. LATIN AMERICA

1. Statement by the Government of Venezuela, 3 June 1961[1]

The Government of Venezuela, in view of the situation created by the physical elimination of the Dominican despot, Rafael Leonidas Trujillo, declares:

The despotic and nepotist government which existed in Santo Domingo when the Sixth Conference of Foreign Ministers imposed diplomatic and economic sanctions on that regime, for having organized and directed the attempted assassination of the President of Venezuela, has not changed its structure or character with the death of Trujillo. The rulers, the methods they use and their challenging disdain for the pattern of the inter-American juridical system are

---

[1] *Venezuela Up-to-date*, May–June 1961, vol. X, no. 8, p. 2.

today the selfsame methods and ways that prevailed during the thirty years duration of that regime, which continues to be responsible for the criminal action for which it was accused and sanctioned in San José, Costa Rica.

The Government of Venezuela believes, therefore, that the sanctions applied to that regime, during the life of its founder, in virtue of the accords taken by the Sixth Conference of Foreign Ministers, must be continued, because his death has left intact the framework of the usurped power of the Dominican regime, and latent the danger it implies to the peace of America.

The Government of Venezuela has decided to request, through its Representative before the Organization of American States, an urgent meeting of the proper Organization body.

At that meeting, Venezuela shall present concrete proposals to put in motion a process that will lead to the establishment in Santo Domingo of a government observant of the Charter of Bogotá. Venezuela shall request the Dominican government to free political prisoners, allow the exiled to return, guarantee political freedom, and give way to a fitting electoral process, which might be supervised, at the request of the Dominicans, by representatives of the OAS.[1]

The Government of Venezuela categorically rejects and repudiates, in the name and by the application of explicit rulings of the regional system, any unilateral intervention in the Dominican Republic, by a government of the Americas. Should such an action take place, the Government of Venezuela shall request the application of the Pact of Rio de Janeiro, to prevent an armed intervention by a government of the Americas in the affairs of a member country of the regional community.

2. Declaration to the peoples of America, adopted by the Inter-American Economic and Social Council at the Special Meeting at Ministerial Level, Punta del Este, Uruguay, 17 August 1961[2]

Assembled in Punta del Este, inspired by the principles consecrated in the Charter of the Organization of American States, in Operation Pan America and in the Act of Bogotá,[3] the representatives of the American Republics hereby agree to establish an Alliance for Progress: a vast effort to bring a better life to all the peoples of the Continent.

This Alliance is established on the basic principle that free men working through the institution of representative democracy can best satisfy man's aspirations, including those for work, home and land, health and schools. No system can guarantee true progress unless it affirms the dignity of the individual which is the foundation of our civilization.

Therefore the countries signing this declaration in the exercise of their sovereignty have agreed to work towards the following goals during the coming years:

[1] On 5 June the Organization of American States decided to send an investigating committee to the Dominican Republic; its membership was composed of delegates from Colombia, Panama, the United States and Uruguay.

[2] *Organization of American States*, Series H/XII.1 (English). Pan-American Union, Washington, 1961.

[3] *Documents*, 1960, pp. 607–12.

To improve and strengthen democratic institutions through application of the principle of self-determination by the people.

To accelerate economic and social development, thus rapidly bringing about a substantial and steady increase in the average income in order to narrow the gap between the standard of living in Latin American countries and that enjoyed in the industrialized countries.

To carry out urban and rural housing programs to provide decent homes for all our people.

To encourage, in accordance with the characteristics of each country, programs of comprehensive agrarian reform, leading to the effective transformation, where required, of unjust structures and systems of land tenure and use; with a view to replacing latifundia and dwarf holdings by an equitable system of property so that, supplemented by timely and adequate credit, technical assistance and improved marketing arrangements, the land will become for the man who works it the basis of his economic stability, the foundation of his increasing welfare, and the guarantee of his freedom and dignity.

To assure fair wages and satisfactory working conditions to all our workers; to establish effective systems of labor-management relations and procedures for consultation and cooperation among government authorities, employers' associations, and trade unions in the interests of social and economic development.

To wipe out illiteracy; to extend, as quickly as possible, the benefits of primary education to all Latin Americans; and to provide broader facilities, on a vast scale, for secondary and technical training and for higher education.

To press forward with programs of health and sanitation in order to prevent sickness, combat contagious disease, and strengthen our human potential.

To reform tax laws, demanding more from those who have most, to punish tax evasion severely, and to redistribute the national income in order to benefit those who are most in need, while, at the same time, promoting savings and investment and reinvestment of capital.

To maintain monetary and fiscal policies which, while avoiding the disastrous effects of inflation or deflation, will protect the purchasing power of the many, guarantee the greatest possible price stability, and form an adequate basis for economic development.

To stimulate private enterprise in order to encourage the development of Latin American countries at a rate which will help them to provide jobs for their growing populations, to eliminate unemployment, and to take their place among the modern industrialized nations of the world.

To find a quick and lasting solution to the grave problem created by excessive price fluctuations in the basic exports of Latin American countries on which their prosperity so heavily depends.

To accelerate the integration of Latin America so as to stimulate the economic and social development of the Continent. This process has already begun through the General Treaty of Economic Integration of Central America and, in other countries, through the Latin American Free Trade Association.[1]

This declaration expresses the conviction of the nations of Latin America that these profound economic, social, and cultural changes can come about only

[1] Set up by the Treaty of Montevideo; *Documents*, 1960, pp. 535–53.

through the self-help efforts of each country. Nonetheless, in order to achieve the goals which have been established with the necessary speed, domestic efforts must be reinforced by essential contributions of external assistance.

The United States, for its part, pledges its efforts to supply financial and technical cooperation in order to achieve the aims of the Alliance for Progress. To this end, the United States will provide a major part of the minimum of twenty billion dollars, principally in public funds, which Latin America will require over the next ten years from all external sources in order to supplement its own efforts.

The United States will provide from public funds, as an immediate contribution to the economic and social progress of Latin America, more than one billion dollars during the twelve months which began on March 13, 1961, when the Alliance for Progress was announced.[1]

The United States intends to furnish development loans on a long-term basis, where appropriate running up to fifty years and in general at very low or zero rates of interest.

For their part, the countries of Latin America agree to devote a steadily increasing share of their own resources to economic and social development, and to make the reforms necessary to assure that all share fully in the fruits of the Alliance for Progress.

Further, as a contribution to the Alliance for Progress, each of the countries of Latin America will formulate a comprehensive and well-conceived national program for the development of its own economy.

Independent and highly qualified experts will be made available to Latin American countries in order to assist in formulating and examining national development plans.

Conscious of the overriding importance of this declaration, the signatory countries declare that the inter-American community is now beginning a new era when it will supplement its institutional, legal, cultural and social accomplishments with immediate and concrete actions to secure a better life, under freedom and democracy, for the present and future generations.

3. **The Charter of the Alliance for Progress, adopted by the Inter-American Economic and Social Council of the Organization of American States, at the Special Meeting at Ministerial Level, Punta del Este, Uruguay, 5–17 August, 1961**[2]

PREAMBLE

We, the American Republics, hereby proclaim our decision to unite in a common effort to bring our people accelerated economic progress and broader social justice within the framework of personal dignity and political liberty.

Almost two hundred years ago we began in this Hemisphere the long struggle for freedom which now inspires people in all parts of the world. Today, in ancient lands, men moved to hope by the revolutions of our young nations search for liberty. Now we must give a new meaning to the revolutionary heri-

[1] *Public Papers*, 1961, pp. 170–5.
[2] *Organization of American States*, Series H/XII.1 (English). Pan-American Union, Washington, 1961.

tage. For America stands at a turning point in history. The men and women of our Hemisphere are reaching for the better life which today's skills have placed within their grasp. They are determined for themselves and their children to have decent and ever more abundant lives, to gain access to knowledge and equal opportunity for all, to end those conditions which benefit the few at the expense of the needs and dignity of the many. It is our inescapable task to fulfil these just desires—to demonstrate to the poor and forsaken of our countries, and of all lands, that the creative powers of free men hold the key to their progress and to the progress of future generations. And our certainty of ultimate success rests not alone on our faith in ourselves and in our nations but on the indomitable spirit of free man which has been the heritage of American civilization.

Inspired by these principles, and by the principles of Operation Pan America and the Act of Bogotá,[1] the American Republics hereby resolve to adopt the following program of action to establish and carry forward an Alliance for Progress.

Title I. Objectives of the Alliance for Progress

It is the purpose of the Alliance for Progress to enlist the full energies of the peoples and governments of the American republics in a great cooperative effort to accelerate the economic and social development of the participating countries of Latin America, so that they may achieve maximum levels of well-being, with equal opportunities for all, in democratic societies adapted to their own needs and desires.

The American republics hereby agree to work toward the achievement of the following fundamental goals in the present decade:

1. To achieve in the participating Latin American countries a substantial and sustained growth of per capita income at a rate designed to attain, at the earliest possible date, levels of income capable of assuring self-sustaining development, and sufficient to make Latin American income levels constantly larger in relation to the levels of the more industrialized nations. In this way the gap between the living standards of Latin America and those of the more developed countries can be narrowed. Similarly, presently existing differences in income levels among the Latin American countries will be reduced by accelerating the development of the relatively less developed countries and granting them maximum priority in the distribution of resources and in international cooperation in general. In evaluating the degree of relative development, account will be taken not only of average levels of real income and gross product per capita, but also of indices of infant mortality, illiteracy, and per capita daily caloric intake.

It is recognized that, in order to reach these objectives within a reasonable time, the rate of economic growth in any country of Latin America should be not less than 2.5 per cent per capita per year, and that each participating country should determine its own growth target in the light of its stage of social and economic evolution, resource endowment, and ability to mobilize national efforts for development.

2. To make the benefits of economic progress available to all citizens of all economic and social groups through a more equitable distribution of national

[1] *Documents*, 1960, pp. 607–12.

income, raising more rapidly the income and standard of living of the needier sectors of the population, at the same time that a higher proportion of the national product is devoted to investment.

3. To achieve balanced diversification in national economic structures, both regional and functional, making them increasingly free from dependence on the export of a limited number of primary products and the importation of capital goods while attaining stability in the prices of exports or in income derived from exports.

4. To accelerate the process of rational industrialization so as to increase the productivity of the economy as a whole, taking full advantage of the talents and energies of both the private and public sectors, utilizing the natural resources of the country and providing productive and remunerative employment for unemployed or part-time workers. Within this process of industrialization, special attention should be given to the establishment and development of capital-goods industries.

5. To raise greatly the level of agricultural productivity and output and to improve related storage, transportation, and marketing services.

6. To encourage, in accordance with the characteristics of each country, programs of comprehensive agrarian reform leading to the effective transformation, where required, of unjust structures and systems of land tenure and use, with a view to replacing latifundia and dwarf holdings by an equitable system of land tenure so that, with the help of timely and adequate credit, technical assistance and facilities for the marketing and distribution of products, the land will become for the man who works it the basis of his economic stability, the foundation of his increasing welfare, and the guarantee of his freedom and dignity.

7. To eliminate adult illiteracy and by 1970 to assure, as a minimum, access to six years of primary education for each school-age child in Latin America; to modernize and expand vocational, technical, secondary and higher educational and training facilities; to strengthen the capacity for basic and applied research; and to provide the competent personnel required in rapidly-growing societies.

8. To increase life expectancy at birth by a minimum of five years, and to increase the ability to learn and produce, by improving individual and public health. To attain this goal it will be necessary, among other measures, to provide adequate potable water supply and sewage disposal to not less than 70 per cent of the urban and 50 per cent of the rural population; to reduce the present mortality rate of children less than five years of age by at least one-half; to control the more serious communicable diseases, according to their importance as a cause of sickness, disability, and death; to eradicate those illnesses, especially malaria, for which effective techniques are known; to improve nutrition; to train medical and health personnel to meet at least minimum requirements; to improve basic health services at national and local levels; and to intensify scientific research and apply its results more fully and effectively to the prevention and cure of illness.

9. To increase the construction of low-cost houses for low-income families in order to replace inadequate and deficient housing and to reduce housing shortages; and to provide necessary public services to both urban and rural centers of population.

10. To maintain stable price levels, avoiding inflation or deflation and the consequent social hardships and maldistribution of resources, always bearing in mind the necessity of maintaining an adequate rate of economic growth.

11. To strengthen existing agreements on economic integration, with a view to the ultimate fulfillment of aspirations for a Latin American common market that will expand and diversify trade among the Latin American countries and thus contribute to the economic growth of the region.

12. To develop cooperative programs designed to prevent the harmful effects of excessive fluctuations in the foreign exchange earnings derived from exports of primary products, which are of vital importance to economic and social development; and to adopt the measures necessary to facilitate the access of Latin American exports to international markets.

TITLE II. ECONOMIC AND SOCIAL DEVELOPMENT

Chapter 1. Basic Requirements for Economic and Social Development

The American republics recognize that to achieve the foregoing goals it will be necessary:

1. That comprehensive and well-conceived national programs of economic and social development, aimed at the achievement of self-sustaining growth, be carried out in accordance with democratic principles.

2. That national programs of economic and social development be based on the principle of self-help—as established in the Act of Bogotá—and on the maximum use of domestic resources, taking into account the special conditions of each country.

3. That in the preparation and execution of plans for economic and social development, women should be placed on an equal footing with men.

4. That the Latin American countries obtain sufficient external financial assistance, a substantial portion of which should be extended on flexible conditions with respect to periods and terms of repayment and forms of utilization, in order to supplement domestic capital formation and reinforce their import capacity; and that, in support of well-conceived programs, which include the necessary structural reforms and measures for the mobilization of internal resources, a supply of capital from all external sources during the coming ten years of at least 20 billion dollars be made available to the Latin American countries, with priority to the relatively less developed countries. The greater part of this sum should be in public funds.

5. That institutions in both the public and private sectors, including labor organizations, cooperatives, and commercial, industrial, and financial institutions, be strengthened and improved for the increasing and effective use of domestic resources, and that the social reforms necessary to permit a fair distribution of the fruits of economic and social progress be carried out.

Chapter II. National Development Programs

1. Participating Latin American countries agree to introduce or strengthen systems for the preparation, execution, and periodic revision of national programs for economic and social development consistent with the principles, objectives, and requirements contained in this document. Participating Latin

American countries should formulate, if possible within the next eighteen months, long-term development programs. Such programs should embrace, according to the characteristics of each country, the elements outlined in the Appendix.

2. National development programs should incorporate self-help efforts directed toward:

a. Improvement of human resources and widening of opportunities by raising general standards of education and health; improving and extending technical education and professional training with emphasis on science and technology; providing adequate remuneration for work performed, encouraging the talents of managers, entrepreneurs, and wage earners; providing more productive employment for underemployed manpower; establishing effective systems of labor relations, and procedures for consultation and collaboration among public authorities, employer associations, and labor organizations; promoting the establishment and expansion of local institutions for basic and applied research; and improving the standards of public administration.

b. Wider development and more efficient use of natural resources, especially those which are now idle or under-utilized, including measures for the processing of raw materials.

c. The strengthening of the agricultural base, progressively extending the benefits of the land to those who work it, and ensuring in countries with Indian populations the integration of these populations into the economic, social, and cultural processes of modern life. To carry out these aims, measures should be adopted, among others, to establish or improve, as the case may be, the following services: extension, credit, technical assistance, agricultural research and mechanization; health and education; storage and distribution; cooperatives and farmers' associations; and community development.

d. More effective, rational and equitable mobilization and use of financial resources through the reform of tax structures, including fair and adequate taxation of large incomes and real estate, and the strict application of measures to improve fiscal administration. Development programs should include the adaptation of budget expenditures to development needs, measures for the maintenance of price stability, the creation of essential credit facilities at reasonable rates of interest, and the encouragement of private savings.

e. Promotion through appropriate measures, including the signing of agreements for the purpose of reducing or eliminating double taxation, of conditions that will encourage the flow of foreign investments and help to increase the capital resources of participating countries in need of capital.

f. Improvement of systems of distribution and sales in order to make markets more competitive and prevent monopolistic practices.

Chapter III. Immediate and Short-Term Action Measures

1. Recognizing that a number of Latin American countries, despite their best efforts, may require emergency financial assistance, the United States will provide assistance from the funds which are or may be established for such purposes. The United States stands ready to take prompt action on applications for such assistance. Applications relating to existing situations should be submitted within the next 60 days.

2. Participating Latin American countries should, in addition to creating or strengthening machinery for long-term development programming, immediately increase their efforts to accelerate their development by giving special emphasis to the following objectives:

a. The completion of projects already under way and the initiation of projects for which the basic studies have been made, in order to accelerate their financing and execution.

b. The implementation of new projects which are designed:

(1) To meet the most pressing economic and social needs and benefit directly the greatest number of people;

(2) To concentrate efforts within each country in the less developed or more depressed areas in which particularly serious problems exist;

(3) To utilize idle capacity or resources, particularly under-employed manpower; and

(4) To survey and assess natural resources.

c. The facilitation of the preparation and execution of long-term programs through measures designed:

(1) To train teachers, technicians, and specialists;

(2) To provide accelerated training to workers and farmers;

(3) To improve basic statistics;

(4) To establish needed credit and marketing facilities; and

(5) To improve services and administration.

3. The United States will assist in carrying out these short-term measures with a view to achieving concrete results from the Alliance for Progress at the earliest possible moment. In connection with the measures set forth above, and in accordance with the statement of President Kennedy,[1] the United States will provide assistance under the Alliance, including assistance for the financing of short-term measures, totalling more than one billion dollars in the year ending March 1962.

Chapter IV. External Assistance in Support of National Development Programs

1. The economic and social development of Latin America will require a large amount of additional public and private financial assistance on the part of capital-exporting countries, including the members of the Development Assistance Group and international lending agencies. The measures provided for in the Act of Bogotá[2] and the new measures provided for in this Charter, are designed to create a framework within which such additional assistance can be provided and effectively utilized.

2. The United States will assist those participating countries whose development and social policies and programs establish self-help measures and economic and social policies and programs consistent with the goals and principles of this Charter. To supplement the domestic efforts of such countries, the United States is prepared to allocate resources which, along with those anticipated from other external sources, will be of a scope and magnitude adequate to realize the goals envisaged in this Charter. Such assistance will be allocated to both social

[1] *Public Papers*, 1961, pp. 170–5.   [2] *Documents*, 1960, pp. 607–12.

and economic development and, where appropriate, will take the form of grants or loans on flexible terms and conditions. The participating countries will request the support of other capital-exporting countries and appropriate institutions so that they may provide assistance for the attainment of these objectives.

3. The United States will help in the financing of technical assistance projects proposed by a participating country or by the General Secretariat of the Organization of American States for the purpose of:

a. Providing experts contracted in agreement with the governments to work under their direction and to assist them in the preparation of specific investment projects and the strengthening of national mechanisms for preparing projects, using specialized engineering firms where appropriate;

b. Carrying out, pursuant to existing agreements for cooperation among the General Secretariat of the Organization of American States, the Economic Commission for Latin America, and the Inter-American Development Bank, field investigations and studies, including those relating to development problems, the organization of national agencies for the preparation of development programs, agrarian reform and rural development, health, cooperatives, housing, education and professional training, and taxation and tax administration; and

c. Convening meetings of experts and officials on development and related problems.

The governments or above mentioned organizations should, when appropriate, seek the cooperation of the United Nations and its specialized agencies in the execution of these activities.

4. The participating Latin American countries recognize that each has in varying degree a capacity to assist fellow republics by providing technical and financial assistance. They recognize that this capacity will increase as their economies grow. They therefore affirm their intention to assist fellow republics increasingly as their individual circumstances permit.

Chapter V. Organization and Procedures

1. In order to provide technical assistance for the formulation of development programs, as may be requested by participating nations, the Organization of American States, the Economic Commission for Latin America, and the Inter-American Development Bank will continue and strengthen their agreements for coordination in this field, in order to have available a group of programming experts whose services can be used to facilitate the implementation of this Charter. The participating countries will also seek an intensification of technical assistance from the specialized agencies of the United Nations for the same purpose.

2. The Inter-American Economic and Social Council, on the joint nomination of the Secretary General of the Organization of American States, the President of the Inter-American Development Bank, and the Executive Secretary of the United Nations Economic Commission for Latin America, will appoint a panel of nine high-level experts, exclusively on the basis of their experience, technical ability, and competence in the various aspects of economic and social development. The experts may be of any nationality, though if of Latin American origin an appropriate geographical distribution will be sought. They will be

attached to the Inter-American Economic and Social Council, but will nevertheless enjoy complete autonomy in the performance of their duties. They may not hold any other remunerative position. The appointment of these experts will be for a period of three years, and may be renewed.

3. Each government, if it so wishes, may present its program for economic and social development for consideration by an ad hoc committee, composed of no more than three members drawn from the panel of experts referred to in the preceeding paragraph together with an equal number of experts not on the panel. The experts who compose the ad hoc committee will be appointed by the Secretary General of the Organization of American States at the request of the interested government and with its consent.

4. The committee will study the development program, exchange opinions with the interested government as to possible modifications and, with the consent of the government, report its conclusions to the Inter-American Development Bank and to other governments and institutions that may be prepared to extend external financial and technical assistance in connection with the execution of the program.

5. In considering a development program presented to it, the ad hoc committee will examine the consistency of the program with the principles of the Act of Bogotá and of this Charter, taking into account the elements in the Appendix.

6. The General Secretariat of the Organization of American States will provide the personnel needed by the experts referred to in paragraphs 2 and 3 of this Chapter in order to fulfill their tasks. Such personnel may be employed specifically for this purpose or may be made available from the permanent staffs of the Organization of American States, the Economic Commission for Latin America, and the Inter-American Development Bank, in accordance with the present liaison arrangements between the three organizations. The General Secretariat of the Organization of American States may seek arrangements with the United Nations Secretariat, its specialized agencies and the Inter-American Specialized Organizations, for the temporary assignment of necessary personnel.

7. A government whose development program has been the object of recommendations made by the ad hoc committee with respect to external financing requirements may submit the program to the Inter-American Development Bank so that the Bank may undertake the negotiations required to obtain such financing, including the organization of a consortium of credit institutions and governments disposed to contribute to the continuing and systematic financing on appropriate terms, of the development program. However, the government will have full freedom to resort through any other channels to all sources of financing, for the purpose of obtaining, in full or in part, the required resources.

The ad hoc committee shall not interfere with the right of each government to formulate its own goals, priorities, and reforms in its national development programs.

The recommendations of the ad hoc committee will be of great importance in determining the distribution of public funds under the Alliance for Progress which contribute to the external financing of such programs. These recommendations shall give special consideration to Title I. 1.

The participating governments will also use their good offices to the end that these recommendations may be accepted as a factor of great importance in the decisions taken, for the same purpose, by inter-American credit institutions, other international credit agencies, and other friendly governments which may be potential sources of capital.

8. The Inter-American Economic and Social Council will review annually the progress achieved in the formulation, national implementation, and international financing of development programs; and will submit to the Council of the Organization of American States such recommendations as it deems pertinent.

Appendix Elements of National Development Programs

1. The establishment of mutually consistent targets to be aimed at over the program period in expanding productive capacity in industry, agriculture, mining, transport, power and communications, and in improving conditions of urban and rural life, including better housing, education, and health.

2. The assignment of priorities and the description of methods to achieve the targets, including specific measures and major projects. Specific development projects should be justified in terms of their relative costs and benefits, including their contribution to social productivity.

3. The measures which will be adopted to direct the operations of the public sector and to encourage private action in support of the development program.

4. The estimated cost, in national and foreign currency, of major projects and of the development program as a whole, year by year over the program period.

5. The internal resources, public and private, estimated to become available for the execution of the programs.

6. The direct and indirect effects of the program on the balance of payments, and the external financing, public and private, estimated to be required for the execution of the program.

7. The basic fiscal and monetary policies to be followed in order to permit implementation of the program within a framework of price stability.

8. The machinery of public administration—including relationships with local governments, decentralized agencies and nongovernmental organizations, such as labor organizations, cooperatives, business and industrial organizations —to be used in carrying out the program, adapting it to changing circumstances and evaluating the progress made.

TITLE III. ECONOMIC INTEGRATION OF LATIN AMERICA

The American republics consider that the broadening of present national markets in Latin America is essential to accelerate the process of economic development in the Hemisphere. It is also an appropriate means for obtaining greater productivity through specialized and complementary industrial production which will, in turn, facilitate the attainment of greater social benefits for the inhabitants of the various regions of Latin America. The broadening of markets will also make possible the better use of resources under the Alliance for Progress. Consequently, the American republics recognize that:

1. The Montevideo Treaty[1] (because of its flexibility and because it is open to the adherence of all of the Latin American nations) and the Central American Treaty on Economic Integration[2] are appropriate instruments for the attainment of these objectives, as was recognized in Resolution No. 11 (III) of the Ninth Session of the Economic Commission for Latin America.

2. The integration process can be intensified and accelerated not only by the specialization resulting from the broadening of markets through the liberalization of trade but also through the use of such instruments as the agreements for complementary production within economic sectors provided for in the Montevideo Treaty.

3. In order to insure the balanced and complementary economic expansion of all of the countries involved, the integration process should take into account, on a flexible basis, the condition of countries at a relatively less advanced stage of economic development, permitting them to be granted special, fair, and equitable treatment.

4. In order to facilitate economic integration in Latin America, it is advisable to establish effective relationships between the Latin American Free Trade Association and the group of countries adhering to the Central American Economic Integration Treaty,[3] as well as between either of these groups and other Latin American countries. These arrangements should be established within the limits determined by these instruments.

5. The Latin American countries should coordinate their actions to meet the unfavourable treatment accorded to their foreign trade in world markets, particularly that resulting from certain restrictive and discriminatory policies of extra-continental countries and economic groups.

6. In the application of resources under the Alliance for Progress, special attention should be given not only to investments for multinational projects that will contribute to strengthening the integration process in all its aspects, but also to the necessary financing of industrial production, and to the growing expansion of trade in industrial products within Latin America.

7. In order to facilitate the participation of countries at a relatively low stage of economic development in multinational Latin American economic cooperation programs, and in order to promote the balanced and harmonious development of the Latin American integration process, special attention should be given to the needs of these countries in the administration of financial resources provided under the Alliance for Progress, particularly in connection with infrastructure programs and the promotion of new lines of production.

8. The economic integration process implies a need for additional investment in various fields of economic activity and funds provided under the Alliance for Progress should cover these needs as well as those required for the financing of national development programs.

9. When groups of Latin American countries have their own institutions for financing economic integration, the financing referred to in the preceding

[1] *Documents*, 1960, pp. 535–53.
[2] Text in Joseph Pincos, *The Central American Common Market* (Agency for International Development, Regional Office for Central America and Panama Affairs, September 1962), pp. 196–208.
[3] Pincos, loc cit.

paragraph should preferably be channeled through these institutions. With respect to regional financing designed to further the purposes of existing regional integration instruments, the cooperation of the Inter-American Development Bank should be sought in channeling extra-regional contributions which may be granted for these purposes.

10. One of the possible means for making effective a policy for the financing of Latin American integration would be to approach the International Monetary Fund and other financial sources with a view to providing a means for solving temporary balance-of-payments problems that may occur in countries participating in economic integration arrangements.

11. The promotion and coordination of transportation and communications systems is an effective way to accelerate the integration process. In order to counteract abusive practices in relation to freight rates and tariffs, it is advisable to encourage the establishment of multinational transport and communication enterprises in the Latin American countries, or to find other appropriate solutions.

12. In working toward economic integration and complementary economies, efforts should be made to achieve an appropriate coordination of national plans, or to engage in joint planning for various economies through the existing regional integration organizations. Efforts should also be made to promote an investment policy directed to the progressive elimination of unequal growth rates in the different geographic areas, particularly in the case of countries which are relatively less developed.

13. It is necessary to promote the development of national Latin American enterprises, in order that they may compete on an equal footing with foreign enterprises.

14. The active participation of the private sector is essential to economic integration and development, and except in those countries in which free enterprise does not exist, development planning by the pertinent national public agencies, far from hindering such participation, can facilitate and guide it, thus opening new perspectives for the benefit of the community.

15. As the countries of the Hemisphere still under colonial domination achieve their independence, they should be invited to participate in Latin American economic integration programs.

TITLE IV. BASIC EXPORT COMMODITIES

The American republics recognize that the economic development of Latin America requires expansion of its trade, a simultaneous and corresponding increase in foreign exchange incomes received from exports, a lessening of cyclical or seasonal fluctuations in the incomes of those countries that still depend heavily on the export of raw materials, and the correction of the secular deterioration in their terms of trade.

They therefore agree that the following measures should be taken:

Chapter I. National Measures

National measures affecting commerce in primary products should be directed and applied in order to:

1. Avoid undue obstacles to the expansion of trade in these products;
2. Avoid market instability;
3. Improve the efficiency of international plans and mechanisms for stabilization; and
4. Increase their present markets and expand their area of trade at a rate compatible with rapid development.

Therefore:

A. Importing member countries should reduce and if possible eliminate, as soon as feasible, all restrictions and discriminatory practices affecting the consumption and importation of primary products, including those with the highest possible degree of processing in the country of origin, except when these restrictions are imposed temporarily for purposes of economic diversification, to hasten the economic development of less developed nations, or to establish basic national reserves. Importing countries should also be ready to support, by adequate regulations, stabilization programs for primary products that may be agreed upon with producing countries.

B. Industrialized countries should give special attention to the need for hastening economic development of less developed countries. Therefore, they should make maximum efforts to create conditions, compatible with their international obligations, through which they may extend advantages to less developed countries so as to permit the rapid expansion of their markets. In view of the great need for this rapid development, industrialized countries should also study ways in which to modify, wherever possible, international commitments which prevent the achievement of this objective.

C. Producing member countries should formulate their plans for production and export, taking account of their effect on world markets and of the necessity of supporting and improving the effectiveness of international stabilization programs and mechanisms. Similarly they should try to avoid increasing the uneconomic production of goods which can be obtained under better conditions in the less developed countries of the Continent, in which the production of these goods is an important source of employment.

D. Member countries should adopt all necessary measures to direct technological studies towards finding new uses and by-products of those primary commodities that are most important to their economies.

E. Member countries should try to reduce, and, if possible, eliminate within a reasonable time export subsidies and other measures which cause instability in the markets for basic commodities and excessive fluctuations in prices and income.

Chapter II. International Cooperation Measures

1. Member countries should make coordinated, and if possible, joint efforts designed:

a. To eliminate as soon as possible undue protection of the production of basic products;

b. To eliminate taxes and reduce excessive domestic prices which discourage the consumption of imported basic products;

c. To seek to end preferential agreements and other measures which limit world consumption of Latin American basic products and their access to international markets, especially the markets of Western European countries in process of economic integration, and of countries with centrally planned economies; and

d. To adopt the necessary consultation mechanisms so that their marketing policies will not have damaging effects on the stability of the markets for basic commodities.

2. Industrialized countries should give maximum cooperation to less developed countries so that their raw material exports will have undergone the greatest degree of processing that is economic.

3. Through their representation in international financial organizations, member countries should suggest that these organizations, when considering loans for the promotion of production for export, take into account the effect of such loans on products which are in surplus in world markets.

4. Member countries should support the efforts being made by international commodity study groups and by the Commission on International Commodity Trade of the United Nations. In this connection, it should be considered that producing and consuming nations bear a joint responsibility for taking national and international steps to reduce market instability.

5. The Secretary General of the Organization of American States shall convene a group of experts appointed by their respective governments to meet before November 30, 1961 and to report, not later than March 31, 1962 on measures to provide an adequate and effective means of offsetting the effects of fluctuations in the volume and prices of exports of basic products. The experts shall:

a. Consider the questions regarding compensatory financing raised during the present meeting;

b. Analyze the proposal for establishing an international fund for the stabilization of export receipts contained in the Report of the Group of Experts to the Special Meeting of the Inter-American Economic and Social Council, as well as any other alternative proposals;

c. Prepare a draft plan for the creation of mechanisms for compensatory financing. This draft plan should be circulated among the member Governments and their opinions obtained well in advance of the next meeting of the Commission on International Commodity Trade.

6. Member countries should support the efforts under way to improve and strengthen international commodity agreements and should be prepared to cooperate in the solution of specific commodity problems. Furthermore, they should endeavor to adopt adequate solutions for the short- and long-term problems affecting markets for such commodities so that the economic interests of producers and consumers are equally safeguarded.

7. Member countries should request other producer and consumer countries to cooperate in stabilization programs, bearing in mind that the raw materials of the Western Hemisphere are also produced and consumed in other parts of the world.

8. Member countries recognize that the disposal of accumulated reserves and surpluses can be a means of achieving the goals outlined in the first chapter of

this Title, provided that, along with the generation of local resources, the consumption of essential products in the receiving countries is immediately increased. The disposal of surpluses and reserves should be carried out in an orderly manner, in order to:

a. Avoid disturbing existing commercial markets in member countries, and

b. Encourage expansion of the sale of their products to other markets.

However, it is recognized that:

a. The disposal of surpluses should not displace commercial sales of identical products traditionally carried out by other countries; and

b. Such disposal cannot substitute for large scale financial and technical assistance programs.

IN WITNESS WHEREOF this Charter is signed, in Punta del Este, Uruguay, on the seventeenth day of August, nineteen hundred sixty-one.

The original texts shall be deposited in the archives of the Pan American Union, through the Secretary General of the Special Meeting, in order that certified copies may be sent to the Governments of the Member States of the Organization of American States.

CHRONOLOGICAL LIST OF DOCUMENTS
1961

October 1960

January 1961

February

April

PRINTED IN GREAT BRITAIN BY
W. & J. MACKAY & CO LTD, CHATHAM, KENT